# 2013

## the best campsites
# in France

alan rogers

alan rogers publishing

**expert in camping for 45 years**

Compiled by: Alan Rogers Guides Ltd

Designed by: Vine Design Ltd

Additional photography: T Lambelin, www.lambelin.com
Maps created by Customised Mapping (01769 540044)
contain background data provided by GisDATA Ltd

Maps are © Alan Rogers Guides and GisDATA Ltd 2013


© Alan Rogers Guides Ltd 2013

Published by: Alan Rogers Guides Ltd,
Spelmonden Old Oast, Goudhurst, Kent TN17 1HE
www.alanrogers.com  Tel: 01580 214000

British Library Cataloguing-in-Publication Data:
A catalogue record for this book is available
from the British Library.

ISBN 978-1-909057-16-6


Printed in Great Britain by Stephens & George Print Group

# Contents

# Alan Rogers - in search of 'the best'

Alan Rogers Guides were first published over 40 years ago. Since Alan Rogers published the first campsite guide that bore his name, the range has expanded and now covers 27 countries in six separate guides. No fewer than 20 of the campsites selected by Alan for the first guide are still featured in our 2013 editions.

There are over 11,000 campsites in France of varying quality: this guide contains impartially written reports on almost 1,100, including many of the very finest, each being individually inspected and selected. We aim to provide you with a selection of the best, rather than information on all – in short, a more selective, qualitative approach. New, improved maps and indexes are also included, designed to help you find the choice of campsite that's right for you.

Finally, for 2013 we have launched the new Alan Rogers Travel Card. Free to readers, it offers exclusive online extras, money saving deals and offers on many campsites. Find out more on page 10.

We hope you enjoy some happy and safe travels – and some pleasurable 'armchair touring' in the meantime!

" ...the campsites included in this book have been chosen entirely on merit, and no payment of any sort is made by them for their inclusion."

**Alan Rogers, 1968**

## How do we find the best?

The criteria we use when inspecting and selecting campsites are numerous, but the most important by far is the question of good quality. People want different things from their choice of site so we try to include a range of campsite 'styles' to cater for a wide variety of preferences: from those seeking a small peaceful campsite in the heart of the countryside, to visitors looking for an 'all singing, all dancing' site in a popular seaside resort. Those with more specific interests, such as sporting facilities, cultural events or historical attractions, are also catered for.

The size of the site, whether it's part of a chain or privately owned, makes no difference in terms of it being required to meet our exacting standards in respect of its quality and it being 'fit for purpose'. In other words, irrespective of the size of the site, or the number of facilities it offers, we consider and evaluate the welcome, the pitches, the sanitary facilities, the cleanliness, the general maintenance and even the location.

## Expert opinions

We rely on our dedicated team of Site Assessors, all of whom are experienced campers, caravanners or motorcaravanners, to visit and recommend campsites. Each year they travel some 100,000 miles around Europe inspecting new campsites for the guide and re-inspecting the existing ones. Our thanks are due to them for their enthusiastic efforts, their diligence and integrity.

We also appreciate the feedback we receive from many of our readers and we always make a point of following up complaints, suggestions or recommendations for possible new campsites. Of course we get a few grumbles too – but it really is a few, and those we do receive usually relate to overcrowding or to poor maintenance during the peak school holiday period. Please bear in mind that, although we are interested to hear about any complaints, we have no contractual relationship with the campsites featured in our guides and are therefore not in a position to intervene in any dispute between a reader and a campsite.

## Independent and honest

Whilst the content and scope of the Alan Rogers guides have expanded considerably since the early editions, our selection of campsites still employs exactly the same philosophy and criteria as defined by Alan Rogers in 1968.

## 'telling it how it is'

Firstly, and most importantly, our selection is based entirely on our own rigorous and independent inspection and selection process. Campsites cannot buy their way into our guides – indeed the extensive Site Report which is written by us, not by the site owner, is provided free of charge so we are free to say what we think and to provide an honest, 'warts and all' description. This is written in plain English and without the use of confusing icons or symbols.

## Looking for the best

Highly respected by site owners and readers alike, there is no better guide when it comes to forming an independent view of a campsite's quality. When you need to be confident in your choice of campsite, you need the Alan Rogers Guide.

- Sites only included on merit
- Sites cannot pay to be included
- Independently inspected, rigorously assessed
- Impartial reviews
- Over 40 years of expertise

Written in plain English, our guides are exceptionally easy to use, but a few words of explanation regarding the layout and content may be helpful. Regular readers will see that our site reports are grouped into 23 official regions (plus the Vendée) and then by the various départements in each of these regions in numerical order.

### Index town
#### Site name
Postal address (including département) T: telephone number. E: email address
**alanrogers.com web address** (including Alan Rogers reference number)

A description of the site in which we try to give an idea of its general features – its size, its situation, its strengths and its weaknesses. This section should provide a picture of the site itself with reference to the facilities that are provided and if they impact on its appearance or character. We include details on pitch numbers, electricity (with amperage), hardstandings etc. in this section as pitch design, planning and terracing affects the site's overall appearance. Similarly we include reference to pitches used for caravan holiday homes, chalets, and the like. Importantly at the end of this column we indicate if there are any restrictions, e.g. no tents, no children, naturist sites.

| Facilities | Directions |
|---|---|
| Lists more specific information on the site's facilities and amenities and, where available, the dates when these facilities are open (if not for the whole season). Off site: here we give distances to various local amenities, for example, local shops, the nearest beach, plus our featured activities (bicycle hire, fishing, horse riding, boat launching). Where we have space we list suggestions for activities and local tourist attractions. | Separated from the main text in order that they may be read and assimilated more easily by a navigator en-route. Bear in mind that road improvement schemes can result in road numbers being altered. |
| | GPS: references are provided in decimal format. All latitudes are North. Longitudes are East unless preceeded by a minus sign e.g. 48.71695 is North, 0.31254 is East and -0.31254 is West. |
| **Open:** Site opening dates. | **Charges 2013** (or a general guide) |

### Maps, campsite listings and indexes

For this 2013 guide we have changed the way in which we list our featured campsites and also the way in which we help you locate the sites within each region.

We now include a map immediately after our Introduction to that region. These maps show the towns near which one or more of our featured campsites are located.

Within each regional section of the guide, we list these towns and the site(s) in that vicinity in alphabetical order.

You will certainly need more detailed maps for navigation, for example the Michelin atlas. We provide G.P.S. coordinates for each site to assist you. Our three indexes will also help you to find a site by its reference number and name, by region and site name, or by the town where the site is situated.

# Understanding the entries

## Regions and départements

For administrative purposes France is divided into 23 official regions covering the 95 départements (similar to our counties). The départements included in each region are stated in our introductions, together with their official number (eg. the département of Manche is number 50). We use these département numbers as the first two digits of our campsite reference numbers, so any campsite in the Manche département will start with the number 50, prefixed with FR.

## Facilities

### Toilet blocks

Unless we comment otherwise, toilet blocks will be equipped with WCs, washbasins with hot and cold water and hot showers with dividers or curtains, and will have all necessary shelves, hooks, plugs and mirrors. We also assume that there will be an identified chemical toilet disposal point, and that the campsite will provide water and waste water drainage points and bin areas. If not the case, we comment. We do mention certain features that some readers find important: washbasins in cubicles, facilities for babies, facilities for those with disabilities and motorcaravan service points. Readers with disabilities are advised to contact the site of their choice to ensure that facilitiesare appropriate to their needs.

### Shop

Basic or fully supplied, and opening dates.

### Bars, restaurants, takeaway facilities and entertainment

We try hard to supply opening and closing dates (if other than the campsite opening dates) and to identify if there are discos or other entertainment.

### Children's play areas

Fenced and with safety surface (e.g. sand, bark or pea-gravel).

### Swimming pools

If particularly special, we cover in detail in our main campsite description but reference is always included under our Facilities listings. We will also indicate the existence of water slides, sunbathing areas and other features. Opening dates, charges and levels of supervision are provided where we have been notified. There is a regulation whereby Bermuda shorts may not be worn in swimming pools (for health and hygiene reasons). It is worth ensuring that you do take 'proper' swimming trunks with you.

### Leisure facilities

For example, playing fields, bicycle hire, organised activities and entertainment.

### Dogs

If dogs are not accepted or restrictions apply, we state it here. Check the quick reference list at the back of the guide.

### Off site

This briefly covers leisure facilities, tourist attractions, restaurants etc. nearby.

## Charges

These are the latest provided to us by the sites. In those cases where 2013 prices have not been provided to us by the sites, we try to give a general guide.

## Reservations

Necessary for high season (roughly mid-July to mid-August) in popular holiday areas (i.e. beach resorts). You can reserve many sites via our own Alan Rogers Travel Service or through other tour operators. Or be wholly independent and contact the campsite(s) of your choice direct, using the phone or e-mail numbers shown in the site reports, but please bear in mind that many sites are closed all winter.

### Telephone Numbers

All numbers assume that you are phoning from within France.

To phone France from outside that country, prefix the number shown with the relevant International Code (00 33) and drop the first 0, shown as (0) in the numbers indicated.

## Opening dates

These are advised to us during the early autumn of the previous year – sites can, and sometimes do, alter these dates before the start of the following season, often for good reasons. If you intend to visit shortly after a published opening date, or shortly before the closing date, it is wise to check that it will actually be open at the time required. Similarly some sites operate a restricted service during the low season, only opening some of their facilities (e.g. swimming pools) during the main season; where we know about this, and have the relevant dates, we indicate it – again if you are at all doubtful it is wise to check.

Sometimes, campsite amenities may be dependent on there being enough customers on site to justify their opening and, for this reason, actual opening dates may vary from those indicated.

Some French site owners are very relaxed when it comes to opening and closing dates. They may not be fully ready by their stated opening dates – grass and hedges may not all be cut or perhaps only limited sanitary facilities open. At the end of the season they also tend to close down some facilities and generally wind down prior to the closing date. Bear this in mind if you are travelling early or late in the season – it is worth phoning ahead.

The Camping Cheque low season touring system goes some way to addressing this in that many participating campsites will have all key facilities open and running by the opening date and these will remain fully operational until the closing date.

## Taking a tent?

In recent years, sales of tents have increased dramatically. With very few exceptions, the campsites listed in this guide have pitches suitable for tents, caravans and motorcaravans. Tents, of course, come in a dazzling range of shapes and sizes. Modern family tents with separate sleeping pods are increasingly popular and these invariably require large pitches with electrical connections. Smaller lightweight tents, ideal for cyclists and hikers, are also visible on many sites and naturally require correspondingly smaller pitches. Many (but not all) sites have special tent areas with prices adjusted accordingly. If in any doubt, we recommend contacting the site of your choice beforehand.

500

### Our Accommodation section

Over recent years, more and more campsites have added high quality mobile home and chalet accommodation. In response to feedback from many of our readers, and to reflect this evolution in campsites, we have now decided to include a separate section on mobile homes and chalets. If a site offers this accommodation, it is indicated above the site report with a page reference where full details are given. We have chosen a number of sites offering some of the best accommodation available and have included full details of one or two accommodation types at these sites.

Please note however that many other campsites listed in this guide may also have a selection of accommodation for rent.

# You're on your way!

Whether you're an 'old hand' in terms of camping and caravanning or are contemplating your first trip, a regular reader of our Guides or a new 'convert', we wish you well in your travels and hope we have been able to help in some way.

We are, of course, also out and about ourselves, visiting sites, talking to owners and readers, and generally checking on standards and new developments.

**We wish all our readers thoroughly enjoyable Camping and Caravanning in 2013 – favoured by good weather of course!** The Alan Rogers Team

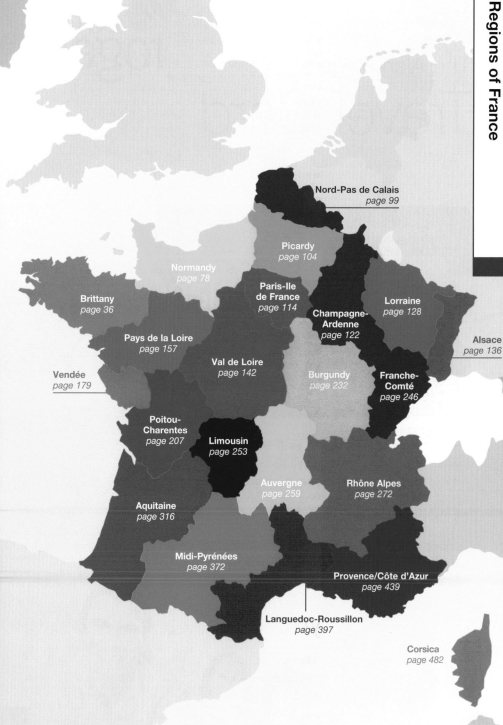

Nord-Pas de Calais
*page 99*

Picardy
*page 104*

Normandy
*page 78*

Brittany
*page 36*

Paris-Ile
de France
*page 114*

Lorraine
*page 128*

Champagne-
Ardenne
*page 122*

Alsace
*page 136*

Pays de la Loire
*page 157*

Val de Loire
*page 142*

Burgundy
*page 232*

Franche-
Comté
*page 246*

Vendée
*page 179*

Poitou-
Charentes
*page 207*

Limousin
*page 253*

Auvergne
*page 259*

Rhône Alpes
*page 272*

Aquitaine
*page 316*

Midi-Pyrénées
*page 372*

Provence/Côte d'Azur
*page 439*

Languedoc-Roussillon
*page 397*

Corsica
*page 482*

9

# FREE

The Alan Rogers

# Travel Card

Across the Alan Rogers guides you'll find a network of thousands of quality inspected and selected campsites. We also work with numerous organisations, including ferry operators and tourist attractions, all of whom can bring you benefits and save you money.

Our brand **NEW** Travel Card binds all this together, along with exclusive extra content in our cardholders' area at **alanrogers.com/travelcard**

# Advantage all the way

Carry the Alan Rogers Travel Card on your travels and save money all the way. Enjoy exclusive offers on many partner sites - as well as hotels, apartments and campsite accommodation. We've even teamed up with Camping Cheque, the low season discount scheme, so you can load your card with Cheques before you travel. So register today - hundreds of campsites already have special offers just for you.

Holiday **discounts**, **free** kids' meals, **free** cycle hire, **discounted** meals, **free** sports activities, **free** gifts on arrival, **free** wine with meals, **free** wifi, **free** tennis, **free** spa day, **free** access to local attractions.

Check out all the offers at **alanrogers.com/travelcard** and present your card on arrival.

## Benefits that add up

- Offers and benefits on many Alan Rogers campsites across Europe

---

- Save up to 60% in low season on over 600 campsites

---

- Savings on rented accommodation and hotels at over 400 locations

---

- Free cardholders' magazine

---

- Exclusive cardholders' area on our website – exchange opinions with other members

---

- Discounted ferries

---

- Savings on Alan Rogers guides

---

- Travel insurance deals

## Register today - and start saving

**Step 1**
Register at www.**alanrogers.com/travelcard** (you can now access exclusive content on the website).

---

**Step 2**
You'll receive your activated card, along with a Welcome email containing useful links and information.

---

**Step 3**
Start using your card to save money or to redeem benefits during your holiday.

Register now at
**alanrogers.com/travelcard**

# The Alan Rogers Awards

The Alan Rogers Campsite Awards were launched in 2004 and have proved a great success.

Our awards have a broad scope and before committing to our winners, we carefully consider more than 2,000 campsites featured in our guides, taking into account comments from our site assessors, our head office team and, of course, our readers.

Our award winners come from the four corners of Europe, from southern Portugal to Croatia, and this year we are making awards to campsites in 10 different countries.

Needless to say, it's an extremely difficult task to choose our eventual winners, but we believe that we have identified a number of campsites with truly outstanding characteristics. In each case, we have selected an outright winner, along with two highly commended runners-up. Listed below are full details of each of our award categories and our winners for 2012.

## Alan Rogers Progress Award 2012

This award reflects the hard work and commitment undertaken by particular site owners to improve and upgrade their site.

**Winner**

| UK0970 | Cofton Country Holidays *England* |
|---|---|

**Runners-up**

| FR86010 | Castel Camping Le Petit Trianon *France* |
|---|---|
| CR6765 | Camping Kovacine *Croatia* |

## Alan Rogers Welcome Award 2012

This award takes account of sites offering a particularly friendly welcome and maintaining a friendly ambience throughout readers' holidays.

**Winner**

| ES80330 | Camping Las Palmeras *Spain* |
|---|---|

**Runners-up**

| FR29180 | Camping Les Embruns *France* |
|---|---|
| IT60280 | Camping Vela Blu *Italy* |

**Our warmest congratulations to all our award winners and our commiserations to all those not having won an award on this occasion.**

The Alan Rogers Team

## Alan Rogers Active Holiday Award 2012

This award reflects sites in outstanding locations which are ideally suited for active holidays, notably walking or cycling, but which could extend to include such activities as winter sports or watersports.

**Winner**

| DE3003 | Camping Wulfener Hals *Germany* |
|---|---|

**Runners-up**

| IT62030 | Caravan Park Sexten *Italy* |
|---|---|
| AU0065 | Camping Seehof *Austria* |

## Alan Rogers Innovation Award 2012

Our Innovation Award acknowledges campsites with creative and original concepts, possibly with features which are unique, and cannot therefore be found elsewhere. We have identified innovation both in campsite amenities and also in rentable accommodation.

**Winner**

| NL6470 | Camping de Papillon *Netherlands* |
|---|---|

**Runners-up**

| FR85625 | Camping Les Moulins *France* |
|---|---|
| ES92120 | Camping Monte Holiday *Spain* |

## Alan Rogers Small Campsite Award 2012

This award acknowledges excellent small campsites (less than 75 pitches) which offer a friendly welcome and top quality amenities throughout the season to their guests.

**Winner**

| FR58040 | Camping l'Etang de la Fougeraie *France* |
|---|---|

**Runners-up**

| UK0115 | Tehidy Holiday Park *England* |
|---|---|
| CZ4896 | Camping Country *Czech Republic* |

## Alan Rogers Seaside Award 2012

This award is made for sites which we feel are outstandingly suitable for a really excellent seaside holiday.

**Winner**

| IT60450 | Camping Marina di Venezia *Italy* |
|---|---|

**Runners-up**

| FR64060 | Camping le Pavillon Royal *France* |
|---|---|
| PO8202 | Turiscampo *Portugal* |

## Alan Rogers Country Award 2012

This award contrasts with our former award and acknowledges sites which are attractively located in delightful, rural locations.

**Winner**

| FR74140 | Camping Les Dômes de Miage *France* |
|---|---|

**Runners-up**

| UK0710 | Hidden Valley Touring Park *England* |
|---|---|
| NL5823 | Camping Waalstrand *Netherlands* |

## Alan Rogers Family Site Award 2012

Many sites claim to be child friendly but this award acknowledges the sites we feel to be the very best in this respect.

**Winner**

| IT60200 | Camping Union Lido Vacanze *Italy* |
|---|---|

**Runners-up**

| NL6710 | Recreatiepark de Achterste Hoef *Netherlands* |
|---|---|
| ES85400 | Camping La Torre del Sol *Spain* |

## Alan Rogers Readers' Award 2012

We believe our Readers' Award to be the most important. We simply invite our readers (by means of an on-line poll at www.alanrogers.com) to nominate the site they enjoyed most.

The outright winner for 2012 is:

**Winner**

| FR85150 | Camping La Yole *France* |
|---|---|

## Alan Rogers Special Award 2012

A Special Award is made to campsites which have suffered a very significant setback and have not only returned to their former condition, but can fairly be considered to be even better than before. In 2012 we acknowledge a Spanish campsite which suffered a devastating forest fire and we feel is a worthy recipient of this award.

| ES80240 | Camping Les Pedres *Spain* |
|---|---|

The Alan Rogers Travel Service

14

# The aims of the
## Travel Service are simple

- **To provide convenience - a one-stop shop to make life easier.**

- **To provide peace of mind - when you need it most.**

- **To provide a friendly, knowledgeable, efficient service
  – when this can be hard to find.**

- **To provide a low cost means of organising your holiday
  – when prices can be so complicated.**

When you book with us, you will be allocated an experienced Personal Travel Consultant to provide you with personal advice and manage every stage of your booking. Our Personal Travel Consultants have first-hand experience of many of our campsites and access to a wealth of information. They can check availability, provide a competitive price and tailor your holiday arrangements to your specific needs.

- Discuss your holiday plans with a friendly person with first-hand experience

- Let us reassure you that your holiday arrangements really are taken care of

- Tell us about your special requests and allow us to pass these on

- Benefit from advice which will save you money – the latest ferry deals and more

- Remember, our offices are in Kent not overseas and we do NOT operate a queuing system!

## Call us for advice or
## an instant quote

**01580 214000** or visit
**www.alanrogers.com/travel**

**Look for a campsite entry like this to indicate which campsites we can book for you.**

**The list is growing so please call for up to the minute information.**

alan rogers 🌀 travel

# Value, Value, Value

### Great Savings AND Complete Service

We work hard to offer quality and choice at remarkably low prices. And we pride ourselves on providing a friendly, personal service coupled with the in-depth knowledge of a specialist tour operator.

Our prices are based on the campsite's 'at-the-gate' prices. The campsite's own booking fees are not charged but are replaced by a standard Travel Service fee of just £45 per booking (up to 3 sites). Please bear in mind campsites typically charge a booking fee of around 30€ (perhaps £25) to customers booking direct - you will avoid this by booking with our Travel Service.

What's more, a campsite's own booking fee is charged at each campsite you visit. Our booking fee applies only **once**.

Our in-house travel team handles all aspects of your booking, for your peace of mind.

- Payment in sterling with **no risk** of exchange rate fluctuations

- **Secure bookings** – all campsite fees and deposits are paid in advance*
  with all ferry-inclusive holidays fully protected by our **ABTA bond**

- We have long-standing relationships with all campsites and **Special Requests**
  are passed on – details that can make a real difference

- Low cost ferries – **special fares** only available when booking a ferry-inclusive holiday

- A one-stop-shop for all your travel plans – campsite booking, overnight stops,
  low cost ferries and travel insurance – all in one place

*excluding any nominal local tourist taxes, payable locally

# Pitch only bookings

**We're confident that our ferry inclusive booking service offers unbeatable value.**

**However, if you have already booked your ferry then we can still make a pitch-only**

**reservation for you (minimum 5 nights). Since our prices are based on our ferry**

**inclusive service, you need to be aware that a non-ferry booking may result in**

**slightly higher prices than if you were to book direct with the site.**

# Want independent campsite reviews at your fingertips?

You'll find them here...

Over 3,000 in-depth campsite reviews at
**www.alanrogers.com**

# Getting the most from
# off peak touring

## £13.95/night
## single tariff
## 2 people

There are many reasons to avoid high season, if you can. Queues are shorter, there's less traffic, a calmer atmosphere and prices are cheaper. And it's usually still nice and sunny!

And when you use Camping Cheques you'll find great quality facilities that are actually open and a welcoming conviviality.

### Did you know?

Camping Cheques can be used right into mid-July and from late August on many sites. Over 90 campsites in France alone accept Camping Cheques from 20th August.

## Save up to 60% with Camping Cheques

Camping Cheque is a fixed price scheme allowing you to go as you please, staying on over 600 campsites across Europe, always paying the same rate and saving you up to 60% on regular pitch fees. One Cheque gives you one night for 2 people + unit on a standard pitch, with electricity. It's as simple as that.

Special offers mean you can stay extra nights free (eg 7 nights for 6 Cheques) or even a month free for a month paid! Especially popular in Spain during the winter, these longer-term offers can effectively halve the nightly rate. See Site Directory for details.

## Check out our amazing Ferry Deals!

## Why should I use Camping Cheques?

- It's a proven system, recognised by all 600+ participating campsites - so no nasty surprises.

- It's flexible, allowing you to travel between campsites, and also countries, on a whim - so no need to pre-book. (It's low season, so campsites are rarely full, though advance bookings can be made).

- Stay as long as you like, where you like - so you travel in complete freedom.

- Camping Cheques are valid 2 years - so no pressure to use them up. (If you have a couple left over after your trip, simply keep them for the following year, or use them up in the UK).

## Tell me more... (but keep it brief!)

Camping Cheques was started in 1999 and has since grown in popularity each year (nearly 2 million were used last year). That should speak for itself. There are 'copycat' schemes, but none has the same range of quality campsites that save you up to 60%.

Ask for your **FREE** continental road map, which explains how Camping Cheque works

## 01580 214002

**FREE**

downloadable Site Directory
**alanrogers.com/directory**

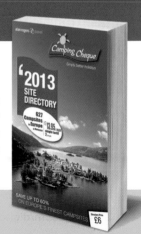

# campingcheque.co.uk

# Digital iPad
# editions

**FREE** Alan Rogers bookstore app
- digital editions of all 2013 guides

**alanrogers.com/digital**

## What's In A Name?
## Differentiating between the groups

At Alan Rogers we have been inspecting and reviewing campsites since 1968. There's

no question things are very different today: facilities, standards, professionalism, technology

have all evolved beyond all recognition. But we find there is still room for individuality,

style and personality.

Campsites may still be small and uncommercial with modest facilities and the charm

of a family-run establishment. Others may be larger and offer the impressive amenities

of a modern resort. Some may favour highlighting their historic pedigree and ambience,

others prefer to stress their rural location.

To achieve these various aims, many have joined forces with other like-minded campsites

to raise their profile via glossy brochures and the like. Of course it's not black and white

but over the following pages we try to clarify the distinctions between some of these

groups of campsites, each of which claim to be unique in their own way.

## LES ★★★★★
## CASTELS
*Hôtellerie de Plein Air*

Les Castels is a well-established and highly regarded group of campsites set in the grounds of stunning châteaux, beautiful manors and charming country houses. This ensures unique natural settings for some of France's finest touring sites. You will be assured of a warm and courteous welcome, tranquil surroundings, great service and a taste of authentic French 'art de vivre'.

**Campsites**

Le Château de Galinée

Domaine de Keravel

Le Domaine des Ormes

La Grande Métairie

Manoir de Ker An Poul

L'Orangerie de Lanniron

Le Ty Nadan

Château de la Grenouillère

Le Parc de Fierbois

L'Anse du Brick

Le Brévedent

Le Château de Iez Eaux

Le Château de Martragny

Le Château de Chanteloup

L'Étang de la Brèche

Camping L'Océan

La Garangeoire

La Forge de Sainte Marie

Le château de l'Epervière

Le Val de Bonnal

La Pergola

La Bien-Assise

Le Domaine de Drancourt

Le Moulin du Roch

Le Ruisseau des Pyrénées

Saint-Avit Loisirs

Le Château de Leychoisier

Le Château de Poinsouze

Le Caussanel

Le Domaine de la Paille Basse

Les Gorges du Chambon

Le Petit Trianon de Saint Ustre

Séquoia Parc

Le Château de Boisson

Les Criques de Porteils

Le Domaine de Massereau

Domaine du Verdon

Douce Quiétude

Le Château de Rochetaillée

Camping l'Ardéchois

Le Domaine de Sévenier

# Les Castels

**In Their Own Words...**

### Quality Assured

All campsites subscribe to the Les Castels Quality Charter and it was the first group to join the respected Camping Qualité label - a guarantee of excellence in facilities and services.

### Whether you're on the move or just lazing

Many Les Castels campsites offer supervised activities for children: organised games, fun workshops, outings and picnics, singing, dancing and real shows. You can go off and leave your children behind with your mind at rest because you know they'll have fun and make new friends. There is a wide range of activities for the whole family: football, tennis, mountain biking, aqua aerobics, tree climbing, pedal boats, canoeing, archery, boules and more.

### Preserving our environmental heritage

Choosing to holiday on a Les Castels campsite means you already share our values. Each property contributes largely to the historical, environmental and architectural heritage of its region.

### Benefit with our loyalty programme, the Castellissime Card

Enjoy Castellissime Card advantages, all year round. Earn points during your stay in any of Les Castels campsites, the points you earn are converted in Euros at the rate of 1 point = 1 euro and automatically credited to your account 7 days after the end of your stay. Then, use your Castellissime Card as a real method of payment to pay for part or all your holiday!

The Castellissime Program General Terms and Conditions in its entirely is available on our website.

### Premium offer: the freedom of the outdoor life plus the very best in contemporary comfort

All our sites can now offer the Les Castels essential art-of-living package:

- Prestigious, secluded, large pitches in magnificent settings.
- Stylishly furnished and decorated spacious accommodation (bungalows, mobile homes or chalets) offering their own private terraces.
- All you need to enjoy a heavenly holiday: barbecue, garden furniture, lounge chairs and a sunshade.
- VIP services: bed linen and towels included, cleaning supply kit, television or hi-fi sound system, free internet access, etc.

www.camping-castels.co.uk

# Campéole

**CAMPSITES AND RENTED ACCOMMODATION**

Most Campéole campsites enjoy a great location close to water, first-class infrastructures and are designed where possible to sit harmoniously within their environments. They are popular with families with children of all ages, as well as couples and small groups.

## Campsites

1. Saint Grégoire
2. Les Monts Colleux
3. Penn Mar
4. La Grande Côte
5. Les Sirènes
6. Dornier
7. La Redoute
8. Le Platin
9. Les Amis de la Plage
10. Clairefontaine
11. Médoc Plage
12. Le Lac de Sanguinet
13. Le Vivier
14. Plage Sud
15. Navarrosse
16. Les Tourterelles
17. Ondres
18. Le Coiroux
19. Les Reflets du Quercy
20. La Boissière
21. Le Domaine de Combelles
22. Millau
23. La Côte des Roses
24. Île des Papes
25. Les Mûriers
26. Les Arbousiers
27. Eurosurf
28. Le Dramont
29. La Croix du Sud
30. Le Belgodère
31. L'Avena
32. Le Clos du Lac
33. Camping du Lac
34. Le Courounba
35. Les Vaudois
36. La Nublière
37. La Pinède
38. Le Lac des Sapins
39. Le Brabois
40. Le Giessen
41. Le Val de Coise
42. Castell Mar
43. Castell Montgri
44. Neptuno
45. Interpals
46. Valldaro
47. Montblanc park
48. Torre del Sol
59. La Masia
50. Ca' Savio
51. Club del Sole Spina
52. Adriano
53. Il capannino
54. Free Time
55. Orbetello

# Campéole

**In Their Own Words...**

### We will listen to you and advise you

Our helpful booking office is there to listen to you and to advise you accordingly. We can recommend a campsite suited to your needs and making a reservation is only a simple phone call away.

### We will offer you a variety of holiday options

With over 50 destinations in France and elsewhere, around ten different types of accommodation, several possible lengths of stay and two arrival days per week, Campéole aims to provide maximum choice and flexibility.

### We will ensure that our holidays are affordable for everyone

A range of services is available to make life easier for you during your holiday. We also guarantee the quality and comfort of our accommodation and therefore offer several solutions at different price levels.

### We will all be committed to making a success of your holiday

The Campéole teams are professionals set on providing a holiday to remember. Each team member has your holiday at heart and will take it on themselves to make your stay as pleasant as possible.

### We will cater for young children and teenagers

Campéole welcomes children and has created special amenities for them in its campsite villages: like Campitoo, popular with the little ones, or activity clubs for each age bracket and a dedicated Teen Space for teenagers.

### We will create a friendly and festive atmosphere

On Campéole campsites you can take your pick from a range of sporting activities and join in the evening entertainments. Each site has a specific entertainment programme for all ages.

### We will respect nature

Do your bit for the environment by opting for the unique Campéole holiday experience in unspoilt natural surroundings. Come and join us – we look forward to welcoming you!

www.campeole.co.uk

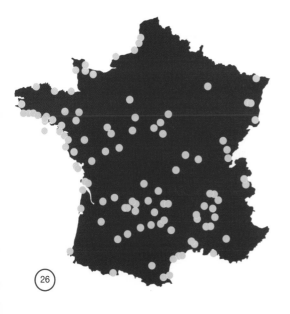

## Campsites on a human scale

The Flower philosophy is to avoid the style
of so-called 'factory campsites'; to ignore
anonymous standardisation but celebrate
individuality and personality. Campsites
in this group are all modestly sized: high
quality facilities, for sure, but all on a very
personable level and with a distinct
personal touch.

### Campsites

**By the sea**
Les Vertes Feuilles
Les Aubépines
Le Domaine du Rompval
La Chênaie
Utah Beach
Le Haut Dick
Camping du Golf
Camping Longchamp
Camping des Vallées
Le Domaine de Mesqueau
Camping de la Baie de Douarnenez
Les Genêts
Aux Deux Chênes
Le Cabellou-Plage
Le Kergariou
Camping de l'Océan
Le Bois d'Amour
Le Kernest
Camping Le Lac
Le Conleau
Le Domaine de Pont-Mahé
Les Paludiers
Camping du Bord de Mer
Les Brillas
Plein Sud
La Bretonnière
Les Ilates
Les Maraises
Le Bel Air
Les Côtes de Saintonge
Le Walmone
Camping Des Pins
La Canadienne
Camping Harrobia
La Garenne
Le Soleil Bleu
Le Soleil d'Oc
Le Neptune
Le Robinson
Le Mas de Mourgues
Le Marius

**In the mountains**
La Sténiole
Verte Vallée
Le Belvédère
La Pène Blanche
L'Eden de la Vanoise
Les Lanchettes

**In the countryside**
L'Escapade
Camping du Lac
Le Domaine de Kervallon

# Flower Campings

### In Their Own Words...

### Campsites on a human scale

On a Flower campsite you are not a number; you are not lost in the crowd. It's a sociable place, and camping is all about enjoying the company of others so the staff like to say hello and chat. We often remark on the warm and friendly 'micro climate' among residents on our campsites.

### Quality campsites

On all our campsites, neither too big nor too small, quality is uppermost. We like small scale but we insist on high quality. We run campsites, we often live on campsites and we enjoy campsite life – we want you to enjoy it too. We have developed our ideal: camping on a human scale where you get to become part of the 'family', great facilities, wonderful locations. We hope this is your ideal too.

### Discover the locality

The best advice we can give you is to get out of the campsite to explore our various regions. Each adds a real flavour to life: meet the local people, attend the local festivals and markets, and enjoy the local produce and the local traditions.

www.flowercampings.com

The Indigo group comprises 13 campsites in attractive locations throughout France.

These are categorised as either 'green', with appealing rural situations, 'blue', some excellent sites at the seaside, or 'red', ideal bases for city breaks.

These are 'proper' campsites, all quite small and with the emphasis on touring pitches, and a limited selection of high quality rentable accommodation.

**Green Indigo Campsites:**

Indigo Le Moulin

Indigo Forcalquier

Indigo Royat

Indigo Vallouise

Indigo Les Molières

Indigo Les Châteaux

Indigo Parc des Oiseaux

**Blue Indigo Campsites:**

Indigo Oléron Les Pins

Indigo Oléron Les Chênes Verts

Indigo Noirmoutier

Indigo Douarnenez

**Red Indigo Campsites:**

Indigo Paris

Indigo Lyon

# Indigo

### In Their Own Words...

Camping is, by its nature, one of life's simple pleasures, to be shared with family or friends. A holiday on an Indigo Campsite provides an opportunity to be outdoors all day long, in touch with nature, in a protected area of natural beauty at the heart of one of France's many beautiful regions - just waiting to be explored.

It's a great way of appreciating the simplicity of camping and sharing some of life's good experiences. At our Indigo campsites, you won't find too many mobile homes spoiling your views, but simply families with their own tents and caravans as well as fully equipped tents which are available as rental accommodation.

### Discover our Indigo campsites...

- Green Indigo campsites are those situated in the unspoiled French countryside.
- Blue Indigo campsites are beautiful seaside sites, with no mobile homes but with the beach close at hand.
- Red Indigo campsites are all near big cities, in attractive parks. These sites are ideal for those simply passing by, or for those wanting to explore some of France's most exciting cities.

### At our campsites you'll find...

- Plenty of well maintained camping pitches where you can put up your tent or site your caravan.
- High quality rental accommodation including chalets, cosy Romany style caravans, mobile homes and fully equipped modern tents.
- A warm welcome from our staff who will help you discover the local area and provide fun activities for all the family. A cosy area to relax and meet new friends, a restaurant during the summer months, a fresh daily bread delivery for a proper breakfast, a swimming pool or other swimming area, and free wifi in the communal area...

Everything is here to ensure that your holidays are both fun and simple!

www.camping-indigo.com

## kawan
VILLAGES

Kawan Villages is a group of 41 high quality, family campsites, mostly located in France but with a number of locations in Spain and Italy. Invariably equipped to a high standard, often with excellent swimming pools, these sites offer a selection of large touring pitches and recently manufactured rental accommodation.

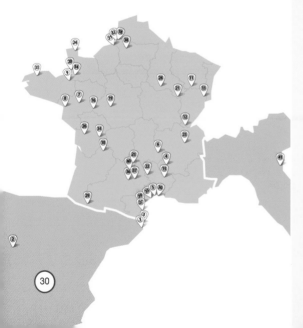

### Campsites

| | |
|---|---|
| 1. | Kawan Village Camping l'Amfora |
| 2. | Kawan Village El Astral |
| 3. | Kawan Village Mas Nou |
| 4. | Kawan Village Ardèche Camping |
| 5. | Kawan Village Beau Rivage |
| 6. | Kawan Village Camping de Vaubarlet |
| 7. | Kawan Village Camping du Port Caroline |
| 8. | Kawan Village Château du Deffay |
| 9. | Kawan Village Château du Gandspette |
| 10. | Kawan Village Château le Verdoyer |
| 11. | Kawan Village Club Lac de Bouzey |
| 12. | Kawan Village Domaine de l'Epinette |
| 13. | Kawan Village Domaine Les Ballastières |
| 14. | Kawan Village Haliotis |
| 15. | Kawan Village L'Apamée |
| 16. | Kawan Village L'Isle Verte |
| 17. | Kawan Village La Belle Etoile |
| 18. | Kawan Village La Ferme des Aulnes |
| 19. | Kawan Village La Grande Tortue |
| 20. | Kawan Village La Route Blanche |
| 21. | Kawan Village Lac de la Liez |
| 22. | Kawan Village Le Capelan |
| 23. | Kawan Village Le Coin Tranquille |
| 24. | Kawan Village Le Cormoran |
| 25. | Kawan Village Le Domaine du Surgié |
| 26. | Kawan Village Le Futuriste |
| 27. | Kawan Village Le Haras |
| 28. | Kawan Village Le Lac d'Orient |
| 29. | Kawan Village Le Lavedan |
| 30. | Kawan Village Le Mas de Reilhe |
| 31. | Kawan Village Le Ridin |
| 32. | Kawan Village Le Val d'Authie |
| 33. | Kawan Village Les Alizés |
| 34. | Kawan Village Les Bois du Bardelet |
| 35. | Kawan Village Les Champs Blancs |
| 36. | Kawan Village Les Genêts |
| 37. | Kawan Village Les Peupliers Rivière sur Tarn |
| 38. | Kawan Village Les Puits Tournants |
| 39. | Kawan Village Ma Prairie |
| 40. | Kawan Village Marmotel |
| 41. | Kawan Village Florenz |

# Kawan Villages

### In Their Own Words...

Seaside, mountains or countryside? In 2013 Kawan Villages welcome you to 41 of the most beautiful 3, 4 or 5 star campsites in Europe. Fresh air and a natural setting, well shaded pitches, top quality amenities and a friendly atmosphere – these will all contribute to your holiday's success.

Many readers will already know the best things about our group – the best quality campsites, always well equipped and welcoming, with great pitches and comfortable accommodation, and also an important focus on protecting the environment and ensuring that your children have a great time!

**For us, every little detail is important!**

## Our rented accommodation

Whether for a weekend break, or a longer holiday, Kawan Villages offer a wide range of accommodation, varying in size and levels of equipment. Our accommodation always has a stylish living area and fully equipped kitchen, a well designed shower room and comfortable bedrooms for parents and children. There's also a great terraced area outside for soaking up the sun!

Everything has been designed to make you feel at home, whilst benefiting from a convivial campsite environment and closeness to nature.

Choose the holiday accommodation of your dreams, and benefit from all the advantages of a Kawan Village!

## Pitches (Camping /Caravanning)

What better way to escape life's hustle and bustle than to put up a tent or site your caravan or motor home on one of our pitches. Make the most of the surrounding countryside, and clear, fresh air, with all the comforts and attractions of a Kawan Village campsite. All our campsites, no matter what their size may be, will be delighted to welcome you and offer one of their large, fully equipped pitches (average size 100 sq.m) – a great way to rediscover the joy of a camping holiday with family or friends.

www.kawan-villages.com

The Revea Group offer more than 100 destinations throughout many of France's most alluring regions. Holiday options include chalets, mobile homes and other types of high quality accommodation.

Revea campsites operate on a human scale and invariably offer great service and a friendly, convivial environment for holidays, whether 'en famille' or between friends.

**Campsites**

1. Chatelus Malvaleix, La Roussille
2. Donzenac, la Rivière
3. Saint Martin Valmeroux, le Moulin du Teinturier
4. Baudreix, les O'Kiri
5. La Chapelle Hermier, le Pin Parasol
6. Pont de Vaux, Champ d'été
7. Saint-Valérien, les Rulières
8. Saint Pierre de Trivisy, la Forêt
9. Ribes, les Cruses
10. Bégard, le Donant
11. Touquin, les Etangs Fleuris
12. Signy le Petit, le domaine de la Motte
13. Montpezat de Quercy, le Faillal
14. Tonnerre, la Cascade
15. Saint Rémy sur Durolle, les Chanterelles
16. Bagnols les Bains, le Tivoli
17. Ruynes en Margeride, le Petit Bois
18. Lapeyrouse, les Marins

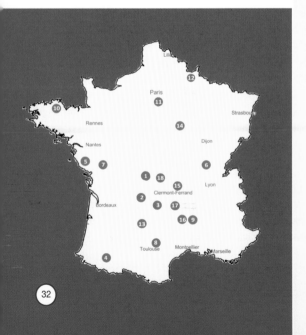

# Revea

## In Their Own Words...

Revea offers various accommodation options throughout France, in the countryside, by the seaside or in the mountains. A wide range of destinations for every kind of holiday: hiking in the Pyrenees or in the Auvergne, beach holidays and relaxing in the Vendée, culture and gastronomy in France's south west or in Burgundy.

## Holidays for everyone

Our aim is to offer great value, nature holidays for everyone. We have special offers throughout the year: week-end breaks, one week or two week holidays, and always attractive prices whether you holiday with your partner, your family or your friends.

## Revea – environment and heritage

Revea welcome you to a natural and authentic holiday environment. A great way to discover wonderful places, amazing landscapes and unspoiled villages.

www.revea-holidays.com

Your holiday **"in nature's colours"**
*SUNELIA, WITH THE SUN!*

Sunêlia
CAMPSITES - LEISURE RESORTS

Emerging in 2006, this is a group of 34 professionally run campsites sharing a common view towards quality and investment. With campsites located on the coast, countryside and mountains, there is 'something for everyone'.
What's more, campsites are rated as either Sunêlia Club (livelier, plenty going on) or Sunêlia Zen (calmer, relaxed).

### Campsites

| |
|---|
| La Ribeyre |
| Domaine les Ranchisses |
| Aluna Vacances |
| Le Ranc Davaine |
| L'Hippocampe |
| Le Soleil Fruité |
| Lac de Panthier |
| Village de la Guyonnière |
| Port'Land |
| L'Escale Saint-Gilles |
| L'Atlantique |
| Le Fief |
| La Loubine |
| Interlude |
| La Pointe du Médoc |
| Le Col Vert |
| Framissima Nature |
| Berrua |
| Le Col d'Ibardin |
| Rubina Resort |
| Les Pins |
| Les Tropiques |
| Le California |
| Domaine de la Dragonnière |
| Le Clos du Rhône |
| Holiday Green |
| Perla di Mare |
| Résidence Lisa Maria |
| Villaggio dei Fiori |
| Limone Piemonte |
| Les Chalets du Logis d'Orres |
| Domaine de Champé |
| Les Trois Vallées |
| Le Malazéou |

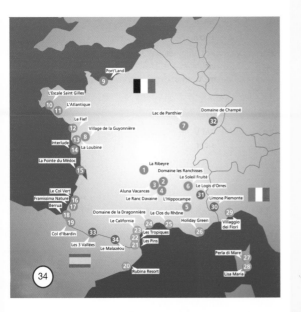

# Sunêlia

## In Their Own Words...

All Sunêlia campsites are 3- or 4-star rated and guarantee facilities of the highest standards.

On each campsite you will receive a warm, personal welcome from Sunêlia-trained staff keen to ensure your stay is pleasant and comfortable.

Rather like a village, each Sunêlia campsite offers a range of services: restaurant, grocery store, barbecue, etc.

On Sunêlia sites, everything is laid on for children so that you can make the most of your free time with full peace of mind.

## What is your Sunêlia style?

At the seaside, in the countryside, in the mountains, by the ocean: Sunêlia offers holidays tailored to your every whim...

**Mountains:** at the heart of the Alps or the Pyrenees, you can make the most of the pure air and exceptional environment to let off steam or recharge your batteries, as a family or with friends!

**Countryside:** An Auvergne campsite, or perhaps an Ardèche or Provence one... whatever your favourite destination, beautiful surroundings are guaranteed.

**Seaside:** From the glorious beaches of the Med (choose from many between the Côte d'Azur and the Pyrenees) to the charming little bays and rockpools of Brittany, via the sweeping Atlantic beaches. The choice is yours.

## Sunêlia quality

Sunêlia is committed to sustainable tourism standards and the Clef Verte accreditation and Camping Qualité standards testify to this (Camping Qualité alone conforms to over 500 quality criteria).

www.sunelia.com

Rolling sandy beaches, hidden coves, pretty villages and a picturesque coastline all combine to make Brittany a very popular holiday destination. Full of Celtic culture steeped in myths and legends, Brittany is one of the most distinctive regions of France.

**DÉPARTEMENTS: 22 CÔTES D'ARMOR, 29 FINISTÈRE, 35 ILLE-ET-VILAINE, 56 MORBIHAN**

**MAJOR CITIES: RENNES AND BREST**

Secluded bays, busy little fishing villages and broad sandy beaches dotted with charming seaside resorts are all to be found along the 2,700 km. of Brittany's coastline. The rugged north shore is a maze of rocky coves, while to the south, there are miles of golden sandy beaches. Inland, tiny country roads weave their way through farmland dotted with stone cottages, alternating with the mysterious forests of Arthurian legend.

Brittany's rich Celtic heritage is evident today in its festivals, folklore and customs, and the area is famous for its standing stones, notably the granite megaliths at Carnac. Castles and manor houses, ornate churches and cathedrals are waiting to be explored, as are the bustling weekly markets displaying the freshest regional produce.

The abbey fortress of Mont Saint-Michel on the north coast (in Normandy) should not be missed and Concarneau in the south is a lovely walled town enclosed by granite rocks.

### Places of interest

*Cancale*: small fishing port and the 'oyster capital' of Brittany.

*Carnac*: 3,000 standing stones (menhirs).

*Concarneau*: fishing port, old walled town.

*Dinan*: historic walled town.

*Perros-Guirec*: leading resort of the Pink Granite Coast.

*Quiberon*: boat service to three islands: Belle Ile (largest of the Breton islands), Houat, Hoëdic.

*Rennes*: capital of Brittany, medieval streets, half-timbered houses; Brittany Museum.

*St Malo*: historic walled city, fishing port.

### Cuisine of the region

Fish and shellfish are commonplace; traditional *crêperies* abound and welcome visitors with a cup of local cider.

*Agneau de pré-salé*: leg of lamb from animals pastured in the salt marshes and meadows.

*Beurre blanc*: sauce for fish dishes made with shallots, wine vinegar and butter.

*Cotriade*: fish soup with potatoes, onions, garlic and butter.

*Crêpes Bretonnes*: the thinnest of pancakes with a variety of sweet fillings.

*Galette*: can be a biscuit, cake or pancake; with sweet or savoury fillings.

*Gâteau Breton*: rich cake.

*Poulet blanc Breton*: free-range, quality, white Breton chicken.

www.brittanytourism.com
tourism-crtb@tourismebretagne.com
(0)2 99 28 44 30

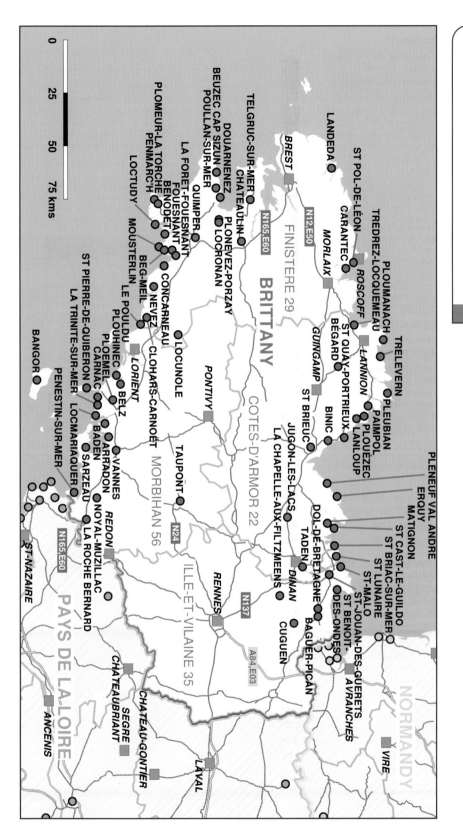

**FREE** Alan Rogers Travel Card
Extra benefits and savings - see page 10

## Arradon
### Camping de Penboch

9 chemin de Penboch, F-56610 Arradon (Morbihan) T: 02 97 44 71 29. E: camping.penboch@wanadoo.fr

**alanrogers.com/FR56040**

Penboch is 200 metres by footpath from the shores of the Golfe du Morbihan with its many islands, and plenty to do including watersports, fishing and boat trips. The site, in a peaceful, rural area, is divided into two – the main part, on open ground, with hedges and young trees, the other across a minor road in woodland with lots of shade. Penboch offers 192 pitches on flat grass, 112 are for touring and they are mostly divided into groups. Electricity (10A) is available on all pitches and most also have water and drainage. A Sites et Paysages member.

**Facilities**

Three toilet blocks, two on the main part (one heated) and one in the annex, include washbasins in cabins. There are new washing facilities including private family cabins (extra charge). Laundry facilities. Motorcaravan service point. Bar with snacks and takeaway. Shop (all 15/5-10/9). Heated pool with slide and paddling pool (15/5-15/9). Indoor pool with relaxation area, jacuzzi and massage tables. Good playground. WiFi in bar. Off site: Beach and fishing 200 m.

**Open:** 5 April - 29 September.

**Directions**

From N165 at Auray or Vannes, take D101 along northern shores of Golfe du Morbihan; or leave N165 at D127 signed Ploeren and Arradon. Take turn to Arradon and site is signed. GPS: 47.62206, -2.8007

**Charges guide**

| | |
|---|---|
| Per unit incl. 2 persons and electricity (10A) | € 20.40 - € 39.30 |
| extra person | € 4.20 - € 6.20 |

## Baden
### Camping Mané Guernehué

52 rue Mané er Groez, F-56870 Baden (Morbihan) T: 02 97 57 02 06. E: info@camping-baden.com

**alanrogers.com/FR56130**

Located close to the Morbihan gulf, Mané Guernehué is a smart, modern site with excellent amenities and a variety of pitches. Some are terraced beneath pine trees, others in a former orchard with delightful views of the surrounding countryside. The 377 pitches are generally large, 210 being occupied by mobile homes and chalets. Most pitches have 10A electricity and a few also have water and drainage. Many are level but a few, particularly in the centre of the site, slope to varying degrees. A new indoor pool complex has been added to the existing outdoor pools and there is a new spa and wellness facility.

**Facilities**

Three modern toilet blocks include washbasins in cabins. Facilities for disabled visitors. Laundry facilities. Small shop, bar and takeaway (13/4-30/9). Heated outdoor swimming pool (1/5-20/9). Heated indoor pool, water slide, jacuzzi, gym and spa. Fishing. Minigolf. Pony trekking. Fitness room. Teenagers' room. Play area. Tree top adventure area. Entertainment in high season. WiFi (charged). Off site: Beach and golf 3 km.

**Open:** 9 April - 1 November.

**Directions**

From Auray or Vannes use the D101 to Baden and watch for signs to site. GPS: 47.61419, -2.92596

**Charges guide**

| | |
|---|---|
| Per unit incl. 2 persons and electricity | € 19.90 - € 42.90 |
| Camping Cheques accepted. | |

## Baguer-Pican
### Camping le Vieux Chêne

Baguer-Pican, F-35120 Dol-de-Bretagne (Ille-et-Vilaine) T: 02 99 48 09 55. E: vieux.chene@wanadoo.fr

**alanrogers.com/FR35000**

This attractive, family owned site is situated between Saint-Malo and le Mont Saint-Michel. Developed in the grounds of a country farmhouse dating from 1638, its young and enthusiastic owner has created a really pleasant, traditional atmosphere. In spacious, rural surroundings it offers 199 good sized pitches on gently sloping grass, most with 10A electricity, water tap and a light. They are separated by bushes and flowers, with mature trees for shade. A very attractive tenting area (without electricity) is in the orchard. The site is used by a Dutch tour operator (20 pitches). A Sites et Paysages member.

**Facilities**

Three very good, unisex toilet blocks include washbasins in cabins, a baby room and facilities for disabled visitors. Small laundry. Motorcaravan services. Shop, bar, takeaway and restaurant (1/6-4/9). Heated swimming pool, paddling pool, slides (17/5-11/9; lifeguard July/Aug). TV room. Games room. Tennis. Minigolf. Giant chess. Play area. Riding (July/Aug). Fishing. WiFi (charged). Off site: Supermarket 3 km. Riding 2 km. Beach 20 km.

**Open:** 17 May - 25 September.

**Directions**

Site is by the D576 Dol-de-Bretagne-Pontorson road, just east of Baguer-Pican. It can be reached from the new N176 taking exit for Dol-Est and Baguer-Pican. GPS: 48.54924, -1.684

**Charges guide**

| | |
|---|---|
| Per unit incl. 2 persons and electricity | € 19.00 - € 33.00 |
| extra person | € 4.50 - € 6.00 |

For latest campsite news, availability and prices visit

# alanrogers.com

**Parc d'attractions et Camping** * * * *

# DE LA RÉCRÉ DES 3 CURÉS

29290 MILIZAC - www.larecredes3cures.fr
Tel: (+33) 02 98 07 95 59

*By renting a mobile home on Campsite La Récré des 3 Curés for 1 week,
you'll have access to attraction parc La Récré des 3 Curés during the entire week.*

## Bangor
### Flower Camping le Kernest

Bangor, F-56360 Belle Ile-en-Mer (Morbihan) T: 02 97 31 56 26. E: info@camping-kernest.com
**alanrogers.com/FR56460**

Belle Ile is a large island lying around 14 km. off the Quiberon peninsula. Access to the island can be made by ferry from either Quiberon, Vannes or Lorient (reservation is recommended in high season). Le Kernest is a family site and a member of the Flower group. It is located around 800 m. from a sandy beach with direct access via a footpath. There are 100 pitches here, most of which are occupied by wooden chalets and mobile homes. The 16 touring pitches are grassy and well shaded, and all have electrical connections. There is a wooded area for a wilder style of camping. Numerous cycle tracks cross the island, including one around the perimeter. If the idea of spending your holiday on a small island off the coast of Brittany appeals, then Belle Ile en Mer will not disappoint.

| Facilities | Directions |
|---|---|
| One large, clean toilet block has preset showers and washbasins in cabins. Family room with baby bath and shower. Facilities for disabled visitors are some distance away. Washing machines and dryers. Basic shop in reception. Bar/restaurant/snack bar (July/Aug). Boules. Tennis. Multisports terrain. Play area. TV room. Activity and entertainment programme. Chalets for rent. Off site: Nearest beach 800 m. (direct path). Riding. Fishing. Cycle tracks. | Upon arrival at Le Palais, follow signs to Bangor on D90 and then to Kernest. Site is well signed from here. GPS: 47.31479, -3.18912 |

**Open:** 31 March - 27 October.

**Charges guide**

| Per unit incl. 2 persons | |
|---|---|
| and electricity | € 15.10 - € 24.90 |
| extra person | € 3.50 - € 5.00 |
| child (2-7 yrs) | € 2.20 - € 4.00 |
| dog | € 2.50 - € 3.00 |

## Bégard
### Camping du Donant

Gwénézhan, F-22140 Bégard (Côtes d'Armor) T: 02 96 45 46 46. E: camping.begard@wanadoo.fr
**alanrogers.com/FR22220**

Camping du Donant is a purpose-built municipal site conveniently situated for visiting the Trégor countryside, the pink granite coast, the beaches at Trégastel and the sculptured rocks of Ploumanach. The well maintained site has 91 pitches of which 71 are for touring units; 41 have 10A electricity with the remainder being more suitable for tents. The pitches are separated by young trees and bushes providing shade in some places. This is a very pleasant, spacious and reasonably priced campsite. Although there is no shop, bar, restaurant or takeaway, these are available in the town, a short walk away.

| Facilities | Directions |
|---|---|
| Toilet facilities are modern and clean. The main block has controllable showers and some washbasins in cubicles, facilities for disabled visitors and laundry with washing machine and dryer. A small block near the more distant pitches has two wet rooms and WCs. TV room. Play area. Boules. Entertainment programme (July/Aug). Bicycle hire. WiFi over site (charged). Chalets and tents for rent. Off site: Bar 50 m. Armoripark 100 m. Town amenities within 2 km. Golf 4 km. Fishing 5 km. Lannion 20 km. Beach and sailing 25 km. | Site is on southern edge of Bégard mid-way between Guingamp and Lannion, just off the D767. Leave at Saint Laurent exit onto D32 and site is across the Amoripark roundabout. GPS: 48.617477, -3.28311 |

**Open:** 1 April - 30 October, (accommodation all year).

**Charges guide**

| Per unit incl. 2 persons | |
|---|---|
| and electricity | € 13.30 - € 15.00 |
| extra person | € 3.15 |
| child | € 1.60 |
| dog | € 1.35 |

**FREE** Alan Rogers Travel Card
Extra benefits and savings - see page 10

## Beg-Meil
### Camping de la Piscine

B.P. 12 Kerleya, Beg-Meil, F-29170 Fouesnant (Finistère) T: 02 98 56 56 06.
E: contact@campingdelapiscine.com **alanrogers.com/FR29170**

There are many campsites in this area but la Piscine is notable for the care and attention to detail that contribute to the well-being of its visitors. Created by the Caradec family from an apple orchard, the 199 level, grass pitches are of a generous size and are separated by an interesting variety of hedges and trees. Water, drainage and electricity points (10A) are provided, normally one stand between two pitches. The small bar and takeaway with terrace overlooking the pool complex provides a relaxing focal point. A quiet site, set back from the sea, la Piscine will appeal to families looking for good quality without many on-site activities. A new covered, heated pool with a wellness centre was added in 2011.

| Facilities | Directions |
|---|---|
| Two refurbished toilet units include washbasins in cabins and showers. Facilities for disabled visitors. Laundry facilities. Motorcaravan service point. Shop (1/6-14/9). Bar and takeaway (3/7-31/8). Pool complex with three slides, waterfall and jacuzzi. Covered, heated pool. Wellness centre with jacuzzi, massage, sauna and Turkish bath. Play area. BMX track. Bicycle hire. Half-court tennis. TV room. Entertainment organised in high season. WiFi (charged July/Aug). Off site: Fouesnant 3 km. Beach 1 km. **Open:** 11 May - 14 September. | Site is 5 km. south of Fouesnant. Turn off N165 expressway at Coat Conq signed Concarneau and Fouesnant. At Fouesnant join D45 (Beg-Meil) and shortly turn right on D145 (Mousterlin). In 1 km. turn left. Follow signs to site. GPS: 47.86568, -4.01553 |

**Charges guide**

| Per unit incl. 2 persons and electricity | € 22.60 - € 35.60 |
|---|---|
| extra person | € 4.50 - € 7.20 |

## Belz
### Camping le Moulin des Oies

21 rue de la Côte, F-56550 Belz (Morbihan) T: 02 97 55 53 26. E: lemoulindesoies@orange.fr
**alanrogers.com/FR56500**

This delightful rural site is lovingly cared for by the owners M. and Mme. Guillois. The 68 generously sized pitches (with electricity 6A) are grassy, level and marked by trees and shrubs. Separated from the sea by the width of a small road, the campsite has its own salt water inlet, controlled by a sluice, not being affected by the tide and with a small sandy beach, there is safe bathing at all times. To the side of this, there is a shady, grassed picnic area.

| Facilities | Directions |
|---|---|
| Sanitary block with showers. Facilities for disabled visitors. Washing machine, games room, TV. Multisports court. Bar, restaurant and take away (Jul/Aug). Saltwater swimming pool with beach. Kitchen with dining area for campers. Only certain breeds of dog accepted. WiFi (free). Off site: Boat launching 50 m. Bicycle hire 500 m. Belz town 1 km. for shops and restaurants and transport services. Golf and riding 6 km. **Open:** 6 April - 28 September. | Leave the N165 at Auray and take the D22 signed Lorient. At Belz the site is signed on the right after entering the town and the site is 1 km. further. GPS: 47.680403, -3.175821 |

**Charges guide**

| Per unit incl. 2 persons and electricity | € 16.75 - € 18.75 |
|---|---|
| extra person | € 4.85 |
| No credit cards. | |

## Bénodet
### Sunêlia l'Escale Saint-Gilles

Corniche de la Mer, F-29950 Bénodet (Finistère) T: 02 98 57 05 37. E: sunelia@stgilles.fr
**alanrogers.com/FR29430**

This is a large and busy holiday style campsite with 467 pitches but only around 70 for tourers. It is facing the Glénan Islands, 50 m. from the beach and close to the River Odet, and offers various types of accommodation. Families with young children, rather than teenagers, could find that the wide range of activities and entertainment offered, as well as a large sports and fitness complex (100 metres away off site) makes l'Escale St-Gilles a good choice. The touring pitches are small to medium in size, nicely hedged but in close proximity to the tour operator tents and mobile homes.

| Facilities | Directions |
|---|---|
| Two toilet blocks with showers and washbasins in cubicles. Baby room. Facilities for disabled visitors. Laundry room. Large shop. Bar and takeaway (8/5-15/9), restaurant (26/5-1/9). Indoor heated swimming pool complex. Spa and massage. Games room. Entertainment. Multisports court. Bicycle hire. WiFi (charged). No dogs in July/Aug. **Open:** 20 April - 23 September. | From Quimper take D34 south to Bénodet. Before town take D44 east (Fouesnant). Site signed on right as you leave Bénodet. GPS: 47.862888, -4.095776 |

**Charges guide**

| Per unit incl. 2 persons and electricity | € 20.00 - € 42.00 |
|---|---|
| extra person | € 4.00 - € 8.00 |

For latest campsite news, availability and prices visit
# alanrogers.com

## Bénodet
### Camping du Letty

Chemin de Creisanguer, F-29950 Bénodet (Finistère) T: 02 98 57 04 69. E: reception@campingduletty.com

**alanrogers.com/FR29030**

The Guyader family have ensured that this excellent and attractive site has plenty to offer for all the family. With a charming ambience, the site on the outskirts of the popular resort of Bénodet spreads over 22 acres with 542 pitches, all for touring units. Groups of four to eight pitches are set in cul-de-sacs with mature hedging and trees to divide each group. All pitches have electricity (10A), water and drainage. As well as direct access to a small sandy beach, with a floating pontoon (safe bathing depends on the tides), the site has recently built a grand aquatic parc, with heated open-air and indoor pools including children's pools, jacuzzi, and slides. At the attractive floral entrance, former farm buildings provide a host of facilities including an extensively equipped fitness room and new wellness rooms for massage and jacuzzis. There is also a modern, purpose built nightclub and bar providing high quality live entertainment most evenings (situated well away from most pitches to avoid disturbance).

### Facilities

Six well placed toilet blocks are of good quality and include mixed style WCs, washbasins in large cabins and controllable hot showers (charged). One block includes a separate laundry and dog washing enclosures. Baby rooms. Separate facility for disabled visitors. Launderette. Hairdressing room. Motorcaravan service points. Well stocked shop. Extensive snack bar and takeaway. Bar with games room and night club. Library/reading room with four computer stations. Entertainment room with satellite TV. New pool complex with indoor and outdoor pools, children's pool, jacuzzi and slide. Fitness centre (no charge). Sauna and solarium (both charged). Tennis and squash (charged). Boules. Archery. Well equipped play area. Entertainment and activities (July/Aug). WiFi in reception. Off site: Sailing, fishing, riding and golf all nearby. Bénodet and Quimper.

**Open:** 12 June - 6 September.

### Directions

From N165 take D70 Concarneau exit. At first roundabout take D44 to Fouesnant. Turn right at T-junction. After 2 km. turn left to Fouesnant (still D44). Continue through La Forêt Fouesnant and Fouesnant, picking up signs for Bénodet. Shortly before Bénodet at roundabout turn left (Le Letty). Turn right at next mini-roundabout and site is 500 m. on left. GPS: 47.86700, -4.08783

### Charges guide

| | |
|---|---|
| Per unit incl. 2 persons and electricity | € 20.50 - € 36.00 |
| extra person | € 4.06 - € 8.20 |
| child (2-6 yrs) | € 2.03 - € 4.11 |
| dog | € 2.30 |

Direct access to the beach

Camping

*Le Letty*

Bénodet - South Brittany

Tel. + 33 (0)2 98 57 04 69

Waterpark

www.campingduletty.com

Campsite without any mobile home

## Beuzec-Cap-Sizun

### Camping Pors Peron

F-29790 Beuzec-Cap-Sizun (Finistère) T: 02 98 70 40 24. E: info@campingporsperon.com

**alanrogers.com/FR29540**

This small site situated on the Cap Sizun peninsula is lovingly cared for by English owners Graham and Nikki Hatch. The site is hilly but the terrain has been terraced to provide 98 fairly level pitches. Many mature trees and shrubs provide some shade and areas of privacy. Long leads are required for the 60 electric hook-ups (10A). The owners have recently purchased new, wooden mobile homes to blend in with the rural ambiance of their campsite. These are all equipped with televisions which receive English and French channels. A 200 m. walk takes you to a delightful sandy bay and you can also access a coastal path. Pors Peron is very popular with English visitors looking for a quiet and relaxing holiday.

**Facilities**

One central toilet block has open style washbasins and preset showers. Facilities for disabled visitors and babies (kept locked). Laundry facilities. Small shop in reception, bread delivered daily. Small, unfenced but safe play area with trampoline. Bicycle hire. Boules. Library and board games. WiFi. Off site: Pont Croix 5 km. Douarnenez 12 km.

**Open:** 1 April - 31 October.

**Directions**

West from Douarnenez on D7 for 12 km. Site signed on right towards Pors Peron. GPS: 48.08435, -4.48191

**Charges guide**

| Per unit incl. 2 persons and electricity | € 15.10 - € 17.50 |
| extra person | € 3.30 - € 4.00 |

## Binic

### Camping le Panoramic

Rue Gasselin, F-22520 Binic (Côtes d'Armor) T: 02 96 73 60 43. E: camping.le.panoramic@wanadoo.fr

**alanrogers.com/FR22310**

You will receive a warm welcome from the owners of this site on the Goëlo coast. It is in a woodland setting, yet only 800 m. from the beaches and the popular resort of Binic. It is ideally situated for visiting the many charming little resorts along this coast. There are 176 pitches in total, 69 are available for touring of which 50 have 10A electricity. All are divided by neat hedging and are easily accessible. A feature of this campsite is the vast range of activities for all ages. These are arranged during July and August and include themed soirées, night markets and Breton games.

**Facilities**

Two well appointed toilet blocks with all necessary facilities, including those for disabled visitors. Bar with basic shop and takeaway. Restaurant (Tues/Thurs in low season, daily in high season). Bread to order. Covered and heated pool. Fenced play area. Boules. Games/TV room. Extensive range of entertainment (July/Aug). WiFi over site. Off site: Casino. Zoo. Bicycle hire 800 m.

**Open:** 1 April - 30 September.

**Directions**

From the N12 Saint Brieuc bypass head north on D786 towards Paimpol. On approaching Binic look for campsite sign to the right. GPS: 48.591895, -2.824237

**Charges guide**

| Per unit incl. 2 persons and electricity | € 16.40 - € 27.10 |
| extra person | € 4.40 - € 6.10 |

## Carantec

### Yelloh! Village les Mouettes

50 route de la Grande Grève, F-29660 Carantec (Finistère) T: 02 98 67 02 46. E: camping@les-mouettes.com

**alanrogers.com/FR29000**

Les Mouettes is a sheltered site on the edge of an attractive bay with access to the sea at the front of the site. In a wooded setting with many attractive trees and shrubs, the 474 pitches include 125 for touring units, all with electricity, water and drainage. The remainder are taken by tour operators and by 207 mobile homes and chalets for rent. At the centre of the 'village' are shops, a bar, a restaurant, an entertainment stage, sports facilities and an impressive heated pool complex with swimming, paddling and water slide pools, a tropical river, jacuzzi and sauna. An indoor swimming pool was recently added.

**Facilities**

Two clean sanitary blocks include controllable showers, washbasins in cabins and mainly British toilets. In the main block there are showers with washbasins and delightful rooms for children and babies. Facilities for disabled visitors. Laundry. Motorcaravan services. Shop (limited hours outside main season). Takeaway. Bar with TV. Restaurant/pizzeria/grill. Pool complex. Beauty salon. Games rooms. Play area. Half-court tennis. Minigolf. Bicycle hire (July/Aug). Entertainment (July/Aug). WiFi in central area (charged). Off site: Beach and golf 2 km.

**Open:** 12 April - 8 September.

**Directions**

Carantec is 15 km. northwest of Morlaix. From D58 Roscoff-Morlaix road, turn east to Carantec on D173. In 4 km. site is signed to the left at the roundabout immediately after passing supermarket on right. GPS: 48.65807, -3.92833

**Charges guide**

| Per unit incl. 2 persons, electricity and water | € 18.00 - € 47.00 |
| extra person | € 6.00 - € 9.00 |
| child (0-7 yrs) | free - € 7.00 |

For latest campsite news, availability and prices visit

# alanrogers.com

## Carnac
### Castel Camping la Grande Métairie

Route des Alignements de Kermario, B.P. 85, F-56342 Carnac (Morbihan) T: 02 97 52 24 01.
E: info@lagrandemetairie.com **alanrogers.com/FR56010**

La Grande Métairie is a good quality site situated a little back from the sea, close to the impressive rows of the famous Carnac menhirs (giant prehistoric standing stones). The site has 575 individual pitches (108 for touring units), surrounded by hedges and trees. All have electricity (some need long leads). The site is well known and popular and has many British visitors with 314 pitches taken by tour operators. It is ideal for families with children of all ages and is lively and busy over a long season. Musical evenings, barbecues and other organised events including occasional dances are held in an outdoor amphitheatre (pitches near these facilities may be noisy late at night – the bar closes at midnight). Paddocks with ponds are home for ducks, goats and ponies to watch and feed. There are also pony rides around the site. A super pool complex comprises heated indoor and outdoor pools, water slides and toboggans and a jacuzzi. A local market takes place at Carnac on Wednesdays and Sundays.

### Facilities

Three large well maintained toilet blocks with washbasins in cabins. Facilities for babies and disabled visitors. Laundry facilities. Motorcaravan service points. Shops (from 19/5). Bar lounge and terrace, restaurant and takeaway (all from 19/5). TV and games rooms. Swimming pool complex with bar. Playgrounds and playing field. Tennis. Minigolf. BMX track. Bicycle hire. Fishing. Zip-wire. Paintball. Helicopter rides (July/Aug). Amphitheatre. Organised events and entertainment. American-style motorhomes accepted up to 27 ft. Off site: Riding 1 km. Nearest beach 3 km. Golf 12 km.

**Open:** 2 April - 10 September (all services from 19/5).

### Directions

From N165 take Quiberon/Carnac exit onto the D768. After 5 km. turn south onto D119 towards Carnac. At roundabout and after 4 km. turn left (northeast) onto D196 to the site.
GPS: 47.5973, -3.0607

### Charges guide

| | |
|---|---:|
| Per unit incl. 2 persons and electricity | € 18.00 - € 43.80 |
| extra person | € 4.00 - € 7.90 |
| child (4-7 yrs) | free - € 5.40 |
| dog | € 4.00 |

Less 20% 22/5-29/6 and after 1/9.

**BRETAGNE SUD**

Route des Alignements de Kermario
B.P. 85 - 56342 Carnac Cedex
Tél. 33(0)2 97 52 24 01
Fax 33(0)2 97 52 83 58
**www.lagrandemetairie.com**

Camping Qualité

## Carnac
### Camping les Druides

55 chemin de Beaumer, F-56340 Carnac (Morbihan) T: 02 97 52 08 18. E: contact@camping-les-druides.com

**alanrogers.com/FR56370**

Situated in a small village just 2 km. from the town of Carnac, this very pleasant site has 110 pitches on level grass, most having high mature hedges giving a good feel of privacy. Eighty have good access to electricity (6-10A) and water. We had a very warm welcome from Mme. Simon and her daughter, who have built this site up over many years. The new reception building is impressive and registration is dealt with efficiently. This is a lovely base from which to explore the region; the famous megaliths are close by and the beaches are only 500 m. away.

### Facilities

Two modern sanitary blocks, some basins in cubicles, preset showers and British style WCs. Baby changing room. Laundry room with washer/dryer and sinks (all kept very clean). Excellent facilities for disabled visitors. Bread and snacks available from reception. Superb fenced swimming pool (heated 16/6-3/9) with jacuzzi and tropical plants. Games room with TV, table football, pool, table tennis and electronic games. Play areas. Multisport court. Pétanque. WiFi (charged). Off site: Beaches 500 m. Fishing and bicycle hire 1 km. Sailing 3 km. Riding 4 km. Golf 15 km.

**Open:** 13 April - 7 September.

### Directions

From N165 Vannes-Lorient dual carriageway south of Auray, take Carnac/Ploemel exit. Head southwest on D768 for 7 km. Turn south on D119 (Carnac). On entering Carnac centre, head east on D781 towards St Philibert. Turn right and follow signs to site – on the right just before the Carnac-Plage area. GPS: 47.58033, -3.05685

### Charges guide

| Per unit incl. 2 persons | |
|---|---|
| and electricity | € 23.40 - € 38.10 |
| extra person | € 4.20 - € 6.30 |
| child (under 7 yrs) | € 2.50 - € 4.30 |
| dog | € 2.50 |

Open from 13 April till 7 September

3 star family campsite with 110 pitches. No animation. Well located at Carnac-Plage, close to facilities (supermarket, beaches, city centre). Sanitary bloc renewed in 2011!

Camping les Druides***    55, Chemin de Beaumer    56340 Carnac
E-mail : contact@camping-les-druides.com    Web : www.camping-les-druides.com

## Carnac
### Camping Moulin de Kermaux

F-56340 Carnac (Morbihan) T: 02 97 52 15 90. E: moulin-de-kermaux@wanadoo.fr

**alanrogers.com/FR56090**

Only 100 m. from the famous Carnac megaliths, Moulin de Kermaux is an excellent base from which to see these ancient stones as they portray their ever changing mood, colour and profile. Family run, the site has 150 pitches, all with 6/10A electricity. There are 75 pitches for touring units and 75 mobile homes, mostly separated by hedges and with many mature trees offering welcome shade. The compact nature of the site offers a safe environment for parents and children. Ideal for children of all ages, there is an aquatic complex with a heated pool and a slide with an indoor pool planned. This is a well run, quiet and comfortable site.

### Facilities

The fully equipped heated toilet block has washbasins in cabins. Facilities for disabled visitors. Baby bath. Laundry facilities. Motorcaravan service point. Shop (26/6-31/8). Bar with satellite TV. Takeaway (26/6-31/8). Swimming and paddling pools. Sauna and jacuzzi. Adventure playground. Minigolf. Organised activities (July/Aug). WiFi (charged). Off site: Bus service 100 m. Fishing, bicycle hire and riding 2 km. Beaches 3 km.

**Open:** 7 April - 29 September.

### Directions

From N165 take Quiberon/Carnac exit onto D768. After 5 km. turn south on D119 towards Carnac. After 4 km. at roundabout turn left (northeast) on D196 to site. GPS: 47.59675, -3.06162

### Charges guide

| Per unit incl. 2 persons | |
|---|---|
| and electricity | € 21.70 - € 30.90 |
| extra person | € 2.60 - € 3.50 |
| child (under 7 yrs) | € 2.60 - € 3.50 |
| dog | € 1.50 - € 2.50 |

For latest campsite news, availability and prices visit
## alanrogers.com

# Carnac
## Camping le Moustoir

Route du Moustoir, F-56340 Carnac (Morbihan) T: 02 97 52 16 18. E: info@lemoustoir.com

**alanrogers.com/FR56110**

Camping le Moustoir is a friendly, family run site situated about three kilometres inland from the many beaches of the area and close to the famous alignments of standing stones. Pitches are grassy and separated by shrubs and hedges, with several shaded by tall pine trees. There is a popular pool area with slides, swimming pool and a paddling pool with mushroom fountain and a second covered pool complex. The bar and terrace become the social centre of the site in the evenings. A high season entertainment programme includes a daily Kids' Club attracting children of several nationalities.

### Facilities

The traditional style toilet block is well maintained. Motorcaravan service point. Shop, bar, restaurant and takeaway. Heated swimming pool (21x8 m), water slides, and paddling pool (1/5-15/9). Heated indoor swimming pool (all season). Wellness area. Adventure playground. Tennis. Boules. Volleyball, football and basketball. Table tennis and pool. 'Kids' Club'. Barrier deposit € 20. WiFi (free). Off site: Watersports at Carnac-Plage. Fishing, bicycle hire, riding 2 km. Beach 3 km. Golf 10 km.

**Open:** 13 April - 15 September.

### Directions

From N165, take exit to D768 (Carnac and Quiberon). At second crossroads after 5 km. turn left (D119) towards Carnac. After 3 km. turn left (oblique turning) after a hotel. Site is 500 m. on left. GPS: 47.60825, -3.06587

### Charges guide

| | |
|---|---|
| Per unit incl. 2 persons and electricity | € 21.50 - € 36.50 |
| extra person (over 2 yrs) | € 5.50 |

Camping Cheques accepted.

# Carnac
## Flower Camping du Lac

F-56340 Carnac (Morbihan) T: 02 97 55 78 78. E: info@lelac-carnac.com

**alanrogers.com/FR56390**

Overlooking the lake and situated between the Morbihan Gulf and the Quiberon peninsula, this site is only 3 km. from the port of La Trinité-sur-Mer while the famous megaliths are even closer. The site is well maintained with flowering landscaped gardens and mature trees and shrubs, giving plenty of shade and some privacy. The 120 pitches are of various sizes, many giving superb views of the lake; there is good access for larger units. The owner is aiming to appeal to young families and couples looking for a quiet holiday in an idyllic setting.

### Facilities

Two sanitary blocks, kept clean and well maintained, have British style WCs, baby bath and laundry units. Facilities for disabled visitors. Small shop (all season) with limited takeaway food (1/7-30/8). Heated swimming pool (15/5-30/9). Play area. Games room. TV room. Fishing. Bicycle hire. Cycling and canoe activities arranged regularly. Kayaks, surfboards and cars for hire. WiFi (free). Off site: Riding 3 km. Sailing 4 km. Coastal beaches 5 km.

**Open:** 1 April - 30 October.

### Directions

From N165 Vannes-Lorient dual carriageway, south of Auray, take exit for Carnac/Ploemel. Head southwest on D768 for 4 km. then south on D186 La Trinité-sur-Mer road. Site signed from here. 1.5 km access road. GPS: 47.61135, -3.0288

### Charges guide

| | |
|---|---|
| Per unit incl. 2 persons and electricity | € 20.40 - € 27.40 |
| extra person (over 2 yrs) | € 5.20 |

# Châteaulin
## Camping de Rodaven

Rocade de Prat Bihan, F-29150 Châteaulin (Finistère) T: 02 98 86 32 93. E: contact@campingderodaven.fr

**alanrogers.com/FR29640**

This former municipal campsite has been transformed by its enthusiastic owner M. Gerente into a most delightful place to stay. There are 94 reasonably sized, level, grassy pitches (40 with 10A electricity). They are divided by various flowering shrubs, small trees and, in the more open area of the site, by white lines on the grass. The site is alongside the Nantes Brest canal, which offers good fishing (permit required). The town of Châteaulin is only ten minutes walk away. The nearest sandy beach is at Pentrez.

### Facilities

Toilet and shower block with facilities for disabled campers. Washing machine and dryer. Small bar with covered terrace. Snack bar/takeaway. Play area. Bicycle and canoe hire. Archery. Boules. Fishing on canal (permit required). Free WiFi over part of site. Off site: Swimming pool and tennis courts 200 m. Town centre 350 m. Locronan and Quimper. Sandy beach at Pentrez 15 km.

**Open:** 7 April - 30 September.

### Directions

From the direction of Brest on N165 leave at first sign for Châteaulin and follow D770 to the town. Within the town follow signs for Piscine. Opposite Piscine you will see sign for the campsite. GPS: 48.189855, -4.090122

### Charges guide

| | |
|---|---|
| Per unit incl. 2 persons and electricity | € 12.20 - € 14.20 |
| extra person | € 3.40 |

**FREE** Alan Rogers Travel Card
Extra benefits and savings - see page 10

## Châteaulin

### Camping la Pointe

Route de Saint Coulitz, F-29150 Châteaulin (Finistère) T: 02 98 86 51 53. E: lapointecamping@aol.com

alanrogers.com/FR29280

This small rural campsite situated by the River Aulne on the outskirts of Châteaulin, was taken over by new English owners, Julie and Marcus Gregory, in 2008. They have developed the site to provide a friendly and relaxed atmosphere. The 60 pitches vary in size and quality, all have 10A electricity and a few provide hardstanding for heavier units. There is a small kitchen garden complete with chickens, where campers can purchase free range eggs and other produce and are also welcome to just sit and relax. A family/games room can be found above the well maintained toilet block. A new pathway, just opposite the site entrance, gives direct access to the river Aulne where fishing is popular (permit required) and the towpath into the town for shops, bars, restaurants and a weekly market can either be walked or cycled. The twice hourly train service provides easy access into the cathedral city of Quimper.

| Facilities | Directions |
|---|---|
| The toilet and shower block also provides facilities for disabled visitors. Baby changing area. Laundry facilities. Motorcaravan service point. Family/games room. Small shop for basics and bread. Fresh eggs and produce available from the kitchen garden. Free WiFi over site. Bicycle hire. Off site: Fishing in the Aulne 200 m (permit needed). Châteaulin 1.5 km. with shops, bars and restaurants. Medieval village of Locronan 15 km. Nearest beach 20 km with windsurfing and yachting. | From Quimper or Brest on N165, exit at 'Châteaulin Centre'. From Châteaulin follow signs for St Coulitz. After 1.5 km. turn left and continue 100 m. Site well signed. GPS: 48.18746, -4.0848 |

**Open:** 15 March - 15 October.

**Charges guide**

| | |
|---|---|
| Per unit incl. 2 persons and electricity | € 17.50 - € 20.00 |
| extra person | € 4.00 |
| child (under 10 yrs) | € 2.50 |

No credit cards.
Camping Cheques accepted.

## Clohars-Carnoët

### Flower Camping le Kergariou

Kervec, F-29360 Clohars-Carnoët (Finistère) T: 02 98 71 54 65. E: camping.lekergariou@wanadoo.fr

alanrogers.com/FR29950

Le Kergariou is a pleasant family site close to the pretty village of Clohars-Carnoët, and is located around a mile from the beach. There are 100 grassy pitches here and most have electrical connections. The site boasts an attractive swimming pool with an adjoining paddling pool, and also has a football pitch and well equipped children's play area. A number of mobile homes and chalets are available for rent. The pretty, and typically Breton, port of Doëlan is around 1.5 km. away and has proved a popular film location. The larger resort of Le Pouldu is also close at hand.

| Facilities | Directions |
|---|---|
| One modern toilet block has a baby room and facilities for disabled campers. Family shower room. Washing machines and dryers. No shop, but bread can be ordered. Swimming pool (15/6-30/8). Paddling pool. Games room. Play area. Sports field. Tourist information. Mobile homes and caravans for rent. Bicycle hire. Off site: Shops and restaurants in Doëlan and Clohars-Carnoët. Cycling and coastal walking trails. Sailing. Fishing 1.5 km. Riding 3 km. Golf 15 km. | Approaching from the north (N165) leave at the Quimperlé exit (D28) and head south on D16 to Clohars-Carnoët. Continue on D16 towards Doëlan and you will see the site before reaching Doëlan. GPS: 47.782737, -3.588833 |

**Open:** 1 April - 7 September.

**Charges guide**

| | |
|---|---|
| Per unit incl. 2 persons and electricity | € 10.00 - € 14.20 |
| extra person | € 3.60 |

## Concarneau
### Flower Camping le Cabellou Plage

Avenue du Cabellou, F-29185 Concarneau (Finistère) T: 02 98 97 37 41. E: info@le-cabellou-plage.com
**alanrogers.com/FR29520**

Le Cabellou Plage is a very pleasant, well maintained site located close to Concarneau. The large, grassy pitches are divided by young hedges, all have 10A electricity and some also have water and drainage. Many have fine views to the nearby beach and the old walled town beyond. The enthusiastic owner has tastefully landscaped many areas of the site with a profusion of shrubs and flowers. A large swimming pool on site is overlooked by a terrace and bar and the beach is just 25 m. away. The wide and attractive bay is ideal for canoeing and canoes are available for hire from the site. The area for mobile homes is most attractive and cars are parked in an adjacent parking area. La Cabellou is ideally situated for those wishing to visit Concarneau with shops, restaurants and bars and its twice weekly market. A regular bus service is available from outside the campsite. Pont Aven and the cathedral city of Quimper are also within easy reach.

**Facilities**

One bright, modern toilet block provides mainly open style washbasins and preset showers. Baby room. Facilities for disabled visitors. Laundry room. Shop. Bar with TV and Internet access (June-Aug). Outdoor heated swimming pool (all season). Scuba lessons and water gymnastics. Bicycle hire. Off site: Bus stop outside site. Supermarkets, shops and restaurants in Concarneau 4 km. Tennis 3 km. Riding 7 km. Golf 10 km.

**Open:** 7 April - 15 September.

**Directions**

Site is just south of Concarneau. Take the D783 towards Tregunc. Turn right onto Avenue Cabellou. Site is well signed from here.
GPS: 47.85616, -3.90005

**Charges guide**

| Per unit incl. 2 persons | |
|---|---|
| and electricity | € 15.00 - € 30.00 |
| extra person | € 3.00 - € 5.50 |
| child (2-7 yrs) | free - € 4.50 |

Camping
**le Cabellou Plage**
❋ ❋ Bretagne Sud

A peninsula facing
*Concarneau*

Tél : 00 (33) 2 98 97 37 41
www.le-cabellou-plage.com

## Concarneau
### Camping les Sables Blancs

Avenue Le Dorlett, F-29900 Concarneau (Finistère) T: 02 98 97 16 44.
E: contact@camping-lessablesblancs.com **alanrogers.com/FR29150**

This is an attractive, terraced site overlooking the sea on the outskirts of Concarneau. Most of the 105 touring pitches are shaded by large mature trees and shrubs. All with 10A electricity, they are level and well shaded though access to some could prove a little difficult for large units. A traditionally styled bar, restaurant and conservatory opens out onto a terrace with a swimming pool overlooking the Baie de la Forêt. Although the site is terraced with steep steps in places, the main touring pitches are on the top part of the site close to the main facilities.

**Facilities**

One new modern toilet block provides very good facilities including washbasins (both open and in cubicles) and showers. Facilities for babies and disabled visitors. New laundry facilities. Bar and restaurant (3/4-30/9). Heated outdoor swimming pool (23/4-15/9). Play area. Evening entertainment (July/Aug). Billiards room. Free WiFi in bar. Off site: Concarneau with shops and restaurants. Beach 150 m. Riding 1 km. Bicycle hire 1.5 km. Golf 6 km.

**Open:** 2 April - 31 October.

**Directions**

Leave the N165 for Concarneau on D70. Site is situated on the northern edge of town on the coast road. Well signed. GPS: 47.88195, -3.92915

**Charges guide**

| Per unit incl. 2 persons | |
|---|---|
| and electricity (10A) | € 17.00 - € 27.00 |
| extra person | € 2.00 - € 7.00 |
| child (under 7 yrs) | € 1.00 - € 2.50 |
| dog | € 2.00 |

**FREE** Alan Rogers Travel Card
**Extra benefits and savings** - see page 10

## Concarneau
### Camping les Prés Verts

B.P. 612, Kernous-Plage, F-29186 Concarneau (Finistère) T: 02 98 97 09 74. E: info@presverts.com

**alanrogers.com/FR29190**

What sets this family site apart from the many others in this region are its more unusual features – its stylish pool complex with Romanesque style columns and statue, and its plants and flower tubs. The 150 pitches are mostly arranged on long, open, grassy areas either side of main access roads. Specimen trees, shrubs and hedges divide the site into smaller areas. There is an area towards the rear of the site where the pitches have sea views. There is direct access to the sandy beach with no roads to cross (300 m). Concarneau is just 2.5 km. A Sites et Paysages member.

**Facilities**

Two toilet blocks provide unisex WCs, but separate washing facilities for ladies and men. Preset hot showers and washbasins in cabins for ladies (closed 21.00-08.00). Some child size toilets. Laundry facilities. Shop (1/7-25/8). Pizza service twice weekly. Heated swimming pool (1/6-31/8) and paddling pool. Playground (0-5 yrs). Minigolf (charged). Off site: Path to sandy/rocky beach 300 m. Coastal path. Riding 1 km. Supermarket 2 km.

**Open:** 1 May - 22 September.

**Directions**

Turn off C7 road, 2.5 km. north of Concarneau, where site is signed. Take third left after Hotel de l'Océan. GPS: 47.89616, -3.95433

**Charges guide**

| | |
|---|---|
| Per unit incl. 2 persons and electricity (6A) | € 24.75 - € 28.20 |
| extra person | € 5.95 - € 7.00 |
| child (2-7 yrs) | € 4.25 - € 5.00 |

## Cuguen
### Camping le Bois Coudrais

F-35270 Cuguen (Ille-et-Vilaine) T: 02 99 73 27 45. E: info@vacancebretagne.com

**alanrogers.com/FR35010**

This gem of a campsite, owned and run by Claire and Philippe Ybert, a delightful couple from Jersey, is the kind of small, rural site that is becoming a rarity in France. It has 25 well kept, grassy pitches (19 with electrical connections nearby), some separated by young shrubs, others with mature trees. They are spread over three small fields, one for tents with an area set aside for ball games. The owners are intent on keeping their site a peaceful and natural retreat.

**Facilities**

The toilet block beside the house provides washbasins in cubicles, showers, plus facilities for disabled visitors. Bar (all season) with takeaway (June-Sept). Small heated swimming pool (15/5-15/9). Animal enclosure. Bicycle hire. WiFi in bar area. Gîtes for hire. Off site: Bar with small épicerie in village 1 km. Shops and restaurants in Combourg 10 km. Fishing 13 km. Golf, riding, lake with beach, sailing and boat launching 15 km. Dinan, Dinard, Saint Malo and Rennes all within 50 km.

**Open:** 28 April - 30 September.

**Directions**

Cuguen is 40 km. southeast of Saint Malo From N137 Saint Malo-Rennes road turn east on D794 to Combourg and on towards Fougères. Turn north on D83 for Mont St-Michel. Site is 1 km. past Cuguen on the left, well signed. GPS: 48.45395, -1.651333

**Charges guide**

| | |
|---|---|
| Per unit incl. 2 persons and electricity | € 21.00 |
| extra person | € 3.50 |
| child (0-14 yrs) | € 3.00 |
| No credit cards. | |

## Dol-de-Bretagne
### Castel Camping le Domaine des Ormes

Epiniac, F-35120 Dol-de-Bretagne (Ille-et-Vilaine) T: 02 99 73 53 00. E: info@lesormes.com

**alanrogers.com/FR35020**

This impressive site in the grounds of the Château des Ormes is in the north east part of Brittany, about 30 km. from the old town and ferry port of Saint Malo. In an estate of wooded parkland and lakes, it has a pleasant atmosphere, busy in high season but peaceful at other times, with an impressive range of facilities. Of the 700 pitches, only 160 are for tourers (155 with 6/16A electricity, 12 also with their own water and waste water). They are of varying sizes (80-120 sq.m) and there is a choice of terrain – flat or gently sloping, wooded or open. The rest are occupied by tour operators (550) and by mobile homes.

**Facilities**

The toilet blocks are of fair standard, one recently refurbished but still rather cramped, with washbasins in cabins and facilities for disabled visitors. A new, more spacious block has family cubicles. Motorcaravan services. Supermarket, bar, restaurant, pizzeria and takeaway. Games room, bar and disco. Indoor and outdoor pool complex. Play area. Golf. Bicycle hire. Fishing. Equestrian centre. Minigolf. Tennis. Paintball. Archery. Cricket club. WiFi in bar (free). Off site: Beaches 25 km.

**Open:** 20 April - 22 September (with all services).

**Directions**

Site is off D795 8 km. south of Dol-de-Bretagne, 11 km. north of Combourg. GPS: 48.49030, -1.72787

**Charges guide**

| | |
|---|---|
| Per unit incl. 2 persons and electricity | € 29.00 - € 60.00 |
| extra person | € 4.50 - € 7.50 |
| child (3-13 yrs) | € 3.00 - € 5.00 |
| dog | € 2.00 |

For latest campsite news, availability and prices visit

# alanrogers.com

## Douarnenez
### Camping Indigo Douarnenez

Avenue du Bois d'Isis, F-29100 Douarnenez (Finistère) T: 02 98 74 05 67.
E: douarnenez@camping-indigo.com  **alanrogers.com/FR29940**

This is a recent addition to the Indigo group, renowned for its 'natural' campsites. Indigo Douarnenez has an attractive forest setting, just 400 m. from the superb Plage des Sables Blancs. There are 120 pitches here, of which 105 are reserved for touring, some with excellent views across the vast sweep of the Bay of Douarnenez. They are well shaded and grassy, and all have 13A electricity. There are also 15 fully equipped safari-style tents (some with woodburning stoves) for hire. An impressive range of new amenities added for 2012 includes a swimming pool and bar/restaurant, and a large safari tent with wood fire, for communal entertainment. Douarnenez lies at the mouth of the Pouldavid estuary and maintains a fishing fleet, although nowadays the town is more important as a tourist centre, renowned for its fine beaches, marinas and interesting maritime museum.

**Facilities**

Two modern toilet blocks have hot showers and washbasins in cubicles. Facilities for disabled visitors were under construction when we visited. Washing machines and dryers. Motorcaravan service point. Bar. Snack bar. Takeaway. Swimming pool. Play area. Multisports court. Boules. Activity programme. Tourist information. Fully equipped safari-style tents for rent. Off site: Beach and fishing 250 m. Bicycle hire 1.3 km. Riding 2.4 km. Shops and restaurants in Douarnenez.

**Open:** 29 March - 30 September.

**Directions**

The site is located west of the centre of Douarnenez. From Quimper head north on D765 to Douarnenez and then follow D207 passing to the western side of the Pouldavid. The site is on Avenue du Bois d'Isis and is well signed. GPS: 48.103056, -4.358889

**Charges 2013**

| Per unit incl. 2 persons | |
|---|---|
| and electricity | € 16.80 - € 25.10 |
| extra person | € 3.70 - € 4.70 |
| child (2-7 yrs) | free - € 2.80 |
| dog | € 2.00 - € 4.00 |

DOUARNENEZ ★★
Tel : +33 (0)2 98 74 05 67
Looking over the Douarnenez bay, 400m from the beach...
www.camping-indigo.com

## Erquy
### Camping le Vieux Moulin

14 rue des Moulins, F-22430 Erquy (Côtes d'Armor) T: 02 96 72 34 23. E: camp.vieux.moulin@wanadoo.fr
**alanrogers.com/FR22050**

Le Vieux Moulin is a family run site, just 2 km. from the little fishing port of Erquy on Brittany's Emerald Coast on the edge of a pine forest and nature reserve. It is about 900 m. from a beach of sand and shingle. Taking its name from the old mill opposite, the site has 173 pitches all with electricity (6/9A) and some with electricity, water and drainage. One section of 39 pitches is arranged around a pond. Most pitches are of a fair size, arranged in square boxes, with trees giving shade. Evening entertainment is organised and there is a friendly pizzeria. The site becomes quite lively in high season.

**Facilities**

Two good quality toilet blocks have mostly British style toilets, individual washbasins, facilities for disabled visitors and babies. A further small block provides toilets and dishwashing only. Laundry facilities. Motorcaravan services. Shop. Pizzeria and takeaway. Bar and terrace. Heated, covered pool complex with jacuzzi and paddling pool. Play areas. Tennis. Fitness gym. TV room. Games room. Bicycle hire. No electric barbecues. WiFi. Off site: Beach 900 m.

**Open:** 9 April - 17 September.

**Directions**

Site is 2 km. east of Erquy. Take minor road towards Les Hôpitaux and site is signed from junction of D786 and D34 roads. GPS: 48.63858, -2.44189

**Charges guide**

| Per unit incl. 2 persons | |
|---|---|
| and electricity | € 24.80 - € 39.00 |
| extra person | € 4.90 - € 6.80 |
| child (under 7 yrs) | € 3.80 - € 4.90 |

# Erquy

## Camping Bellevue

Route de la libération, F-22430 Erquy (Côtes d'Armor) T: 02 96 72 33 04. E: campingbellevue@yahoo.fr

**alanrogers.com/FR22210**

Situated a mile from the beaches between Erquy and Pléneuf Val-André, Camping Bellevue offers a quiet country retreat with easy access to the cliffs of Cap Fréhel, Sables d'Or and St Cast. There are 160 pitches of which 120 are available for touring units, most with electricity (10A) and 50 extra large ones with water and drainage. The site also has 20 mobile homes and tents to rent. Children are well catered for at this campsite – there are heated swimming and paddling pools, three play areas with minigolf, pétanque and volleyball. Indoor entertainment for all includes themed evenings, Breton dancing and visits to a local cider house. There are numerous walks in the area and a vast range of aquatic sports at nearby Erquy. For the gardener and plant lover this site is a delight. At reception, hundreds of flowers, shrubs and trees found on the site are identified in a photo album where they are named and located by pitch number. A Sites et Paysages member.

### Facilities

Two modern, unisex toilet blocks are of a high standard. Some washbasins in cubicles. Facilities for disabled visitors. Laundry facilities. Shop and bar (15/6-10/9). Restaurant and takeaway (12/6-30/9). Swimming and paddling pools (April-Sept). Play areas. Games room and library. Minigolf. Pétanque. Entertainment and organised activities in high season. There is also a multi-sport area with basketball, football etc. Max. 2 dogs. WiFi. Off site: Beach and fishing 2 km. Golf 4 km. Bicycle hire and boat launching 5 km. Riding 6 km.

**Open:** 6 April - 16 September.

### Directions

From St Brieuc road take D786 towards Erquy. Site is adjacent to the D786 at St Pabu and is well signed. GPS: 48.59426, -2.48475

### Charges guide

| Per unit incl. 2 persons | |
|---|---|
| and electricity | € 21.40 - € 27.40 |
| child (0-12 yrs) | free - € 4.50 |
| extra person | € 4.40 - € 5.40 |
| dog | € 1.50 - € 2.00 |

# Erquy

## Camping la Plage de Saint Pabu

Saint Pabu, F-22430 Erquy (Côtes d'Armor) T: 02 96 72 24 65. E: camping@saintpabu.com

**alanrogers.com/FR22500**

Saint Pabu is a pretty site beside a broad, sandy beach close to Erquy. There is a fine panoramic view of the sea from the site. Pitches here are mostly divided by mature hedges and are of a good size. All 375 touring pitches have 10A electrical connections. A number of large, family pitches (130 sq.m) and 'grand confort' pitches are available (with electricity, water and drainage). Mobile homes are available for rent (one, two or three-bedroom models). On-site amenities include a bar and well stocked shop.

### Facilities

Four toilet blocks (one large and three smaller) provide hot showers and washbasins in cubicles. Facilities for babies and disabled visitors. Laundry facilities. Motorcaravan service point. Dog shower. Shop (1/5-30/9). Bar/snack bar (1/5-30/9). Takeaway (high season). Play area. Games room. Tourist information. Mobile homes for rent. Direct beach access. WiFi. Off site: Watersports. Fishing. Boat trips. Cliff-top walks. Shops and restaurants in Erquy 4 km.

**Open:** 1 April - 11 October.

### Directions

St Pabu can be found just south of Erquy. Approaching from Erquy, head south on D34 and follow signs to St Pabu and then to site. GPS: 48.6067, -2.49674

### Charges guide

| Per unit incl. 2 persons | |
|---|---|
| and electricity | € 21.05 - € 29.15 |
| extra person | € 4.25 - € 5.35 |
| child (under 7 yrs) | € 2.30 - € 2.80 |

For latest campsite news, availability and prices visit

## alanrogers.com

## Fouesnant
### Camping de PenHoat

Pointe de Mousterlin, 5 chemin de Kost ar Moor, F-29170 Fouesnant (Finistère) T: 02 98 56 51 89.
E: caradec2@wanadoo.fr **alanrogers.com/FR29630**

This small rural campsite is set in two acres of trees, shrubs and well tended flowerbeds. The 87 touring pitches are level, grassy, generous in size and separated by hedges and/or small trees. The 58 pitches with electricity (5A and 10A) may need long leads. The 32 mobile homes are mostly separated from the touring pitches. There are also six traditional gîtes for hire. The pleasant wooden chalet-style bar and takeaway has a covered terrace. Kayaks can be hired at the campsite. The long sandy beach is 300 m. away. And for lovers of wildlife, the protected Mousterlin nature reserve is next to the campsite.

| Facilities | Directions |
|---|---|
| Two toilet and shower blocks with facilities for campers with disabilities. Laundry. Nursery. Bar, takeaway and restaurant. Games room. Playground. Trampoline. Bicycle and kayak hire. Gîtes for hire. Off site: Beach 300 m. Riding 1 km. Shops in Fouesnant 6 km. Golf 6 km. | Site is 5 km. south of Fouesnant. Turn off N165 at Coat Cong signed Concarneau and Fouesnant. Join D45 signed Beg-Meil and shortly turn right on D145 signed Mousterlin. Site signed in 5 km. GPS: 47.851024, -4.035341 |

**Open:** 3 April - 30 September.

**Charges guide**

| | |
|---|---|
| Per unit incl. 2 persons and electricity | € 16.00 - € 18.40 |
| extra person | € 4.40 - € 5.30 |
| child (under 7 yrs) | € 2.40 - € 2.80 |
| dog | € 1.80 - € 1.90 |

## Fouesnant
### Camping le Kervastard

Chemin Kervastard, Beg Meil, F-29170 Fouesnant (Finistère) T: 02 98 94 91 52.
E: camping.le.kervastard@wanadoo.fr **alanrogers.com/FR29690**

Camping Kervastard has a pleasant situation at the heart of the pretty Breton resort of Beg-Meil. The owner, M. Beaurin, is always keen to practise his English. It is 300 m. from the pleasure port and 600 m. from a magnificent sandy beach (other good beaches are nearby). The 122 pitches are of a good size and grassy. Most have electrical connections (6/10A). On-site amenities include a swimming pool (and separate paddling pool). The centre of Beg-Meil is easily reached on foot and there are plenty of shops, cafés, restaurants and crêperies there. The atmosphere on site is relaxed, particularly in low season.

| Facilities | Directions |
|---|---|
| Two modern toilet blocks with facilities for babies and disabled visitors. Washing machines and dryers. Swimming pool. Paddling pool. Play area. TV/Games room. Tourist information. Occasional activities (high season). Accommodation to rent. Off site: Nearest beach 400 m. Beg-Meil centre (shops and restaurants). Riding 5 km. Bicycle hire 1 km. | Approachng from N165 (Vannes-Quimper), leave at the Concarneau exit and follow D44 to Fouesnant (passing through La Forêt-Fouesnant). Follow signs to Beg-Meil and continue to the village, where the site is well signed. GPS: 47.86652, -4.01481 |

**Open:** 20 May - 8 September.

**Charges guide**

| | |
|---|---|
| Per unit incl. 2 persons and electricity | € 19.40 - € 28.20 |
| extra person | € 3.80 - € 5.90 |
| child (under 7 yrs) | € 1.90 - € 3.10 |
| dog | € 1.50 - € 2.20 |

**FREE** Alan Rogers Travel Card
Extra benefits and savings - see page 10

## Jugon-les-Lacs

### Camping Au Bocage du Lac

Rue du Bocage, F-22270 Jugon-les-Lacs (Côtes d'Armor) T: 02 96 31 60 16.

E: contact@campinglacbretagne.com  **alanrogers.com/FR22200**

This well kept former municipal site has been updated over the past few years by the current owners, M. and Mme. Rivière. It is on the edge of a small village beside a lake, a short drive from the sea. It offers 138 large touring pitches, all with electrical connections, set on gently sloping grass and divided by shrubs and bushes, with mature trees providing shade. Some 45 wooden chalets and mobile homes are intermingled with the touring pitches. On-site facilities include an excellent pool with children's section and sunbathing patio. There is also an extensive play area and a small animal park. A full programme of activities and entertainment for the whole family is organised in July and August, when the site becomes lively. At other times it is quiet and peaceful. The whole site is securely fenced and access to the lake with its beach, fishing and sailing is through coded gates. The village is an easy walk along the lakeside.

**Facilities**

Two sanitary blocks, one updated with controllable showers, the other (open high season) is more traditional. Facilities for disabled visitors. British and Turkish style WCs and some washbasins in cabins. Washing machines and dryers. Small shop sells basics. Bar/restaurant with takeaway. Swimming pool (1/5-9/9). Tennis. Boules. Play area. Small animal park. Activity programmes July/Aug. Fishing. WiFi in bar area (charged). Off site: Bicycle hire, and boat launching 200 m. Supermarket in village 1 km.

**Open:** 12 April - 15 September.

**Directions**

Jugon is 40 km. southeast of Saint Brieuc. From N12 (St Brieuc/Rennes) turn east after Lamballe on N176 towards Dinan. In 7 km. take exit for Jugon-les-Lacs. In village turn south and follow signs to lake and site. GPS: 48.40120, -2.31736

**Charges guide**

| | |
|---|---|
| Per unit incl. 2 persons and electricity (10A) | € 17.35 - € 27.60 |
| extra person | € 3.90 - € 5.95 |

## La Forêt-Fouesnant

### Camping du Manoir de Penn ar Ster

2 chemin de Penn Ar Ster, F-29940 La Forêt-Fouesnant (Finistère) T: 02 98 56 97 75.

E: info@camping-pennarster.com  **alanrogers.com/FR29100**

This site will appeal to those who prefer a quiet place to stay away from the noise and bustle of busier sites. In the grounds of an old Breton house and arranged on terraces up the steep sides of a valley, the site has a picturesque, garden-like quality. There are 105 pitches, of which about half are for touring units (the remainder used for mobile homes). Pitches vary in size (80-100 sq.m) and some are accessed by steep slopes, but all are on flat, grassy terraces, with low hedging and all have electricity (6/10A), water and drainage. The campsite is open for a long season and its location in La Forêt-Fouesnant makes it popular with those camping by bicycle, motorbike or in a motorcaravan.

**Facilities**

Two sanitary blocks include mixed British and Turkish style toilets, cabins with washbasins and showers, baby areas and children's toilets. One block is heated in low season and contains facilities for disabled campers. At the rear of the old house is a laundry room with washing machines and dryers. Play area. Tennis. Bicycle hire. Barrier with card. Off site: Baker 50 m. Village with all amenities 150 m. Golf 800 m. Riding 2 km.

**Open:** 2 April - 31 October.

**Directions**

From N165 take D70 Concarneau exit. At first roundabout take D44 (Forêt-Fouesnant). Follow to T-junction and turn right on D783. After 2 km. turn left back onto D44 to Forêt-Fouesnant. In village take first exit right at roundabout to site 150 m. on left. GPS: 47.911316, -3.979679

**Charges guide**

| | |
|---|---|
| Per unit incl. 2 persons and electricity | € 21.00 - € 27.00 |

No credit cards.

For latest campsite news, availability and prices visit

**alanrogers.com**

## La Chapelle-aux-Filtzmeens
### Domaine du Logis

Le Logis, F-35190 La Chapelle-aux-Filtzmeens (Ille-et-Vilaine) T: 02 99 45 25 45.
E: domainedulogis@wanadoo.fr **alanrogers.com/FR35080**

This is an attractive rural site under new, young and enthusiastic ownership, set in the grounds of an old château. The site's upgraded modern facilities are housed in traditional converted barns and farm buildings, which are well maintained and equipped. There are a total of 188 pitches, 70 of which are for touring. The grass pitches are level, of a generous size and divided by mature hedges and trees. All have 10A electricity connections. This site would appeal to most age groups with plenty to offer the active, including a new fitness room with a good range of modern equipment and a sauna for those who prefer to relax, or perhaps a quiet day's fishing beside the lake. Although set in a peaceful, rural part of the Brittany countryside, the nearby village of La Chapelle-aux-Filtzmeens has a bar, restaurant and shops. A 20 minute car ride will bring you to the large town of Rennes. Thirty minutes north are Mont Saint-Michel, Dinan, Dinard and the old fishing port of Saint Malo, renowned for its seafood.

| Facilities | Directions |
|---|---|
| One comfortable toilet block with washbasins and showers. Toilet and shower for disabled visitors. Laundry facilities. Bar with Sky TV (1/4-7/11). Restaurant and takeaway (1/7-29/8). Outdoor swimming pool (from 1/5). Fitness and games rooms. Sauna. BMX circuit. Bicycle hire. Unfenced play areas. Children's club (high season). Free WiFi. Lake fishing. Off site: Boating on the canal. Riding 10 km. Golf 15 km. | Turn south off N176 onto D795 (Dol-de-Bretagne). Continue to Combourg and then take D13 to La Chapelle-aux-Filtsmeens. Continue for 2 km. to site on right. GPS: 48.37716, -1.83705 |

**Open:** 1 April - 7 November.

**Charges guide**

| | |
|---|---|
| Per unit incl. 2 persons and electricity | € 23.00 - € 30.00 |
| extra person | € 5.00 - € 5.50 |

Camping Cheques accepted.

35190 LA CHAPELLE AUX FILTZMEENS (Ille et Vilaine)
Tél.: 02 99 45 25 45 - Fax: 02 99 45 30 40
E-mail: domainedulogis@wanadoo.fr
www.domainedulogis.com

## La Forêt-Fouesnant
### Camping de Kéranterec

Route de Port la Forêt, F-29940 La Forêt-Fouesnant (Finistère) T: 02 98 56 98 11.
E: info@camping-keranterec.com **alanrogers.com/FR29240**

A well established family run site with a very French ambience, Kéranterec has 265 grassy pitches in two distinct areas. The upper part of the site is more open and has little shade, and is also largely taken up by private mobile homes. The lower and more mature area is predominantly for tourers, with terraced pitches set in a former orchard. Spacious and divided by mature hedging, all pitches have electrical connections (25 m. cable advised) and most also offer water and drainage. Some pitches have shade from the many trees on the lower part of the site, and some also overlook the little cove at the rear of the site. The trees still provide fruit for the cider produced on site (which we can highly recommend!).

| Facilities | Directions |
|---|---|
| Two modern, fully equipped toilet blocks kept very clean include washbasins in cubicles, baby baths and facilities for disabled visitors. Laundry facilities. Small shop and bar (15/6-10/9) and takeaway (1/7-31/8). TV room with satellite. Heated outdoor swimming pool (1/6-10/9) with paddling pool, jacuzzi and three slides, and a covered, heated pool. Tennis. Boules. Play area. Events and family activities and free children's club (July/Aug). Free WiFi. Off site: Attractive sandy beach 10 mins. walk. | From N165 take D70 Concarneau exit. At the first roundabout take D44 (Fouesnant). After 2.5 km. turn right at T-junction, and follow for 2.5 km. and turn left (Port La Forêt). Go over roundabout, (Port La Forêt). After 1 km. turn left (site signed), then in 400 m. turn left to site. GPS: 47.8991, -3.95198 |

**Open:** 5 April - 21 September.

**Charges guide**

| | |
|---|---|
| Per unit incl. 2 persons and electricity | € 15.00 - € 34.00 |
| extra person | € 7.00 - € 8.50 |

**FREE** Alan Rogers Travel Card
Extra benefits and savings - see page 10

## La Roche Bernard
### Camping Municipal le Pâtis

3 chemin du Pâtis, port de plaisance, F-56130 La Roche Bernard (Morbihan) T: 02 99 90 60 13.
E: camping.lrb56@gmail.com **alanrogers.com/FR56080**

This is another of those excellent municipal sites one comes across in France. Situated beside the River Vilaine, a five minute walk from the centre of the very attractive old town of La Roche Bernard and beside the port and marina, it provides 69 level grass, part-hedged pitches in bays of four, with 6A electricity and water. Eighteen special pitches for motorcaravans have been created at the entrance, along with two wooden chalets to hire. Next door is a sailing school, boats to hire, fishing, tennis, archery, etc. A restaurant and bar are on the quayside, with others uphill in the town.

**Facilities**

There are two fully equipped sanitary blocks, one new and very modern, the other fully refurbished. Facilities for disabled visitors. Motorcaravan service point. Laundry room behind reception with washing machine and dryer. Bicycle hire. WiFi. Off site: Fishing 500 m. Riding 5 km. Golf 15 km.

**Open:** April - mid October.

**Directions**

Go into town centre and follow signs for the port around a one-way system and then a sharp turn downhill. GPS: 47.51817, -2.30317

**Charges guide**

| | |
|---|---|
| Per unit incl. 2 persons and electricity | € 13.15 - € 20.65 |
| extra person | € 3.50 - € 4.00 |

---

## La Trinité-sur-Mer
### Camping de la Plage

Plage de Kervillen, F-56470 La Trinité-sur-Mer (Morbihan) T: 02 97 55 73 28.
E: camping@camping-plage.com **alanrogers.com/FR56020**

The Carnac and La Trinité area of Brittany is popular with British holidaymakers. Camping de la Plage is one of two sites, close to each other and owned by members of the same family, with direct access to the safe, sandy beach of Kervillen Plage. There are 195 grass pitches of which 122 are for touring (34 are used by tour operators). All are hedged and have electricity (6/10A), water and drainage. The site has a slight slope and a few pitches reflect this. With narrow roads and sharp bends, it is not suitable for large units. The shop, restaurant and bar are 200 m. along the coast opposite Camping de la Baie.

**Facilities**

Toilet blocks (one heated) have free hot water, washbasins in cubicles, baby baths and facilities for children and disabled visitors. Laundry facilities. Small swimming pool with water slides. Play areas including ball pool. Tennis. TV. Entertainment in high season. Bicycle hire. Beach. Guided tours. Internet access and WiFi (charged). Gas or electric barbecues only on pitches. Off site: Fishing 50 m. Shop with bakery. Bar, restaurant, crêperie, takeaway all 200 m. Sailing 1.5 km. Riding 3.5 km. Golf 13 km.

**Open:** 27 April - 15 September.

**Directions**

From N165 at Auray take D28 (La Trinité-sur-Mer). On through town following signs to Carnac-Plage on D186. Site signed off this road to the south. Take care to take road signed to Kervillen Plage where it forks. At seafront turn right. Site is 300 m. on right. Site is well signed. GPS: 47.57563, -3.02890

**Charges guide**

| | |
|---|---|
| Per unit incl. 2 persons and electricity (10A) | € 22.60 - € 43.30 |
| extra person | € 5.20 |

---

## Landéda
### Camping des Abers

Dunes de Sainte Marguerite, F-29870 Landéda (Finistère) T: 02 98 04 93 35.
E: camping-des-abers@wanadoo.fr **alanrogers.com/FR29130**

This delightful 12-acre site is in a beautiful location almost at the tip of the Presqu'île Sainte Marguerite on the northwestern shores of Brittany. The peninsula lies between the mouths (abers) of two rivers, Aber Wrac'h and Aber Benoît. Camping des Abers is set just back from a wonderful sandy beach with rocky outcrops and islands you can walk to at low tide. There are 180 pitches, landscaped and terraced, some with amazing views, others sheltered by mature hedges, trees and flowering shrubs. Hubert le Cuff and his team make you very welcome and speak excellent English.

**Facilities**

Three toilet blocks, all recently refurbished are kept very clean and provide washbasins in cubicles and roomy showers (charged). Good facilities for disabled visitors and babies. Laundry. Motorcaravan service point. Shop stocks essentials (25/5-22/9). Simple takeaway dishes (1/7-31/8). Play area. Games room. Hairdresser. The site is famous for its Breton music and dancing, cooking classes and guided walks. Splendid beach with good bathing (best at high tide) and watersports. Torch useful. Free Internet and WiFi. Off site: Pizzeria next door. Tennis nearby.

**Open:** 28 April - 30 September.

**Directions**

Landéda is 55 km. west of Roscoff via D10 to Plouguerneau then D13 crossing river bridge (Aber Wrac'h) and turning west to Lannilis. From the N12 Morlaix-Brest road turn north on D59 to Lannilis. Continue through town taking road to Landéda and from there follow signs for Dunes de Ste Marguerite, Camping and des Abers. GPS: 48.59306, -4.60305

**Charges guide**

| | |
|---|---|
| Per unit incl. 2 persons and electricity | € 16.20 - € 18.00 |
| extra person | € 3.24 - € 3.60 |

## La Trinité-sur-Mer
### Camping de la Baie

Plage de Kervillen, F-56470 La Trinité-sur-Mer (Morbihan) T: 02 97 55 73 42.
E: contact@campingdelabaie.com  **alanrogers.com/FR56030**

This site is one of two owned by members of the same family. It is situated on the coast overlooking the safe, sandy beach of Kervillen Plage, with its little rocky outcrops providing a naturally enclosed swimming area. This is a very friendly site, which is ideal for quiet or family holidays in an area with lots of local interest. There are 170 pitches, of which around 50 are used by tour operators. The 92 touring pitches are all of good size, hedged and all have electricity (6/10A) water and drainage. Some shade is provided by mature and maturing trees. In the bar and restaurant complex, just outside the entrance, one can sit and watch the sun set over the bay. The restaurant has an extensive menu, from excellent seafood to snacks, as does the takeaway. American-style motorhomes should book ahead.

**Facilities**

Two very clean toilet blocks include well equipped baby rooms and full en-suite facilities for disabled visitors. Laundry facilities. Bar, restaurant and takeaway (open to the public all season). Well stocked shop (all season). Small (12 m.) swimming pool with slide. Play areas. Multi-sport pitches. TV room. Indoor games room. Bicycle hire. Off site: Beach, fishing and boat ramp 50 m. Tennis and minigolf 200 m. (shared with Camping de la Plage). Sailing school 1.5 km. Riding and golf 5 km.

**Open:** 12 May - 16 September.

**Directions**

From N165 at Auray take D28 (La Trinité-sur-Mer). Keep on through the town following signs to Carnac Plage on D186. Site is well signed off this road to the south. Be careful to take the road signed to Kervillen Plage where it forks. GPS: 47.57364, -3.02758

**Charges guide**

| Per unit incl. 2 persons | |
| --- | --- |
| and electricity (10A) | € 17.20 - € 47.90 |
| extra person | € 2.90 - € 8.00 |
| child (under 2 yrs) | free |

## Lanloup
### Camping le Neptune

Ker Guistin, F-22580 Lanloup (Côtes d'Armor) T: 02 96 22 33 35. E: contact@leneptune.com
**alanrogers.com/FR22160**

Situated on the Côte de Goëlo at Lanloup, le Neptune offers a peaceful, rural retreat for families. The friendly owners, François and Marie Jo Camard, keep the site neat and tidy and there is a regular programme of renovation. There are 84 level, grass pitches (56 for touring units) separated by trimmed hedges providing privacy and all with electricity (10A). There are also 22 mobile homes to rent. Within walking distance is the local village, with a restaurant and shop, and sandy beaches are only a short drive away. The area is good for cycling and walking.

**Facilities**

The modern, heated, toilet block is of a good standard, clean and well maintained and provides washbasins in cubicles and pushbutton showers. Facilities for disabled visitors. Laundry room. Motorcaravan services. No restaurant but good takeaway (all season). Small shop well stocked for basic needs. Bar with indoor and outdoor seating. Heated swimming pool with retractable roof. Pétanque. Play area. Entertainment and children's activities in high season. WiFi throughout. Off site: Tennis 300 m. Fishing and beach 2 km. Golf 4 km. Riding 8 km. Restaurant and shop within walking distance.

**Open:** 29 March - 14 October.

**Directions**

Lanloup is 30 km. northwest of Saint Brieuc and 100 km. from both Roscoff and Saint-Malo. From N12 Saint Brieuc bypass take D786 Paimpol (par la côte). After 28 km. on approaching Lanloup, site is well signed, turning right at crossroads by café. GPS: 48.71372, -2.96704

**Charges guide**

| Per unit incl. 2 persons | |
| --- | --- |
| and electricity | € 19.00 - € 25.00 |
| extra person | € 4.00 - € 5.50 |
| Camping Cheques accepted. | |

**FREE** Alan Rogers Travel Card
Extra benefits and savings - see page 10

## Le Pouldu
### Camping les Embruns

2 rue du Philosophe Alain, le Pouldu Plages, F-29360 Clohars-Carnoët (Finistère)
T: 02 98 39 91 07. E: camping-les-embruns@orange.fr  **alanrogers.com/FR29180**

This site is unusual in that it is located in the heart of a village, yet is only 250 metres from a sandy cove. The entrance with its code operated barrier and wonderful floral displays, is the first indication that this is a well tended and well organised site, and the owners have won numerous regional and national awards for its superb presentation. The 176 pitches (100 occupied by mobile homes) are separated by trees, shrubs and bushes, and most have electricity (16A Europlug), water and drainage. There is a covered, heated swimming pool, a circular paddling pool and a water play pool and slide. It is only a short walk to the village centre with all its attractions and services. It is also close to beautiful countryside and the Carnoët Forest which are good for walking and cycling.

### Facilities

Two modern sanitary blocks, recently renovated and heated in winter, include mainly British style toilets, some washbasins in cubicles, baby baths and good facilities for disabled visitors. Family bathrooms. Laundry facilities. Motorcaravan service point (€ 4). Shop. Restaurant, bar and takeaway (13/4-15/9). Covered, heated swimming and paddling pools. Games hall. Play area. Football field. Minigolf. Communal barbecue area. Activities for children and adults (July/Aug). Bicycle hire. Internet access and WiFi in reception area (charged). Off site: Beach 250 m.

**Open:** 13 April - 23 September.

### Directions

From N165 take either exit for Kervidanou, Quimperlé Ouest or Kergostiou, Quimperlé Centre, Clohars Carnoët exit and follow D16 to Clohars Carnoët. Then take D24 for Le Pouldu and follow site signs in village. GPS: 47.76867, -3.54508

### Charges guide

| Per unit incl. 2 persons and electricity | € 10.50 - € 31.50 |
|---|---|
| extra person | € 3.95 - € 5.90 |
| child (under 7 yrs) | € 2.80 - € 3.80 |
| dog | € 2.70 |

## Locronan
### Camping Locronan

Rue de la Troménie, F-29180 Locronan (Finistère) T: 02 98 91 87 76. E: contact@camping-locronan.fr
**alanrogers.com/FR29650**

Camping Locronan is a well cared for, friendly site on the edge of the village of Locronan (400 m). The site has a heated covered pool and a children's play area. The 100 pitches are level, grassy and divided by low hedges. These are arranged on four different levels as the site is on the side of a steep hill. Vehicle access between the levels is steep and pedestrian access is by wooden steps which would not be suitable for the disabled visitor. Many of the pitches offer panoramic views across the countryside to the distant bay of Douarnenez. The nearest beach is 5 km. away and is ideal for windsurfing.

### Facilities

Two modern toilet blocks have facilities for campers with disabilities. Laundry facilities. Shop. Covered swimming pool. Play area. WiFi. Mobile homes and equipped tents to hire. Off site: Shops and restaurants in Locronan 300 m. Riding, tennis 300 m. Nearest beach 5 km. Walking and cycling tracks. Quimper 13 km.

**Open:** 9 April - 3 November.

### Directions

Locronan is northwest of Quimper. From there, head north on D39 and D63 (towards Douarnenez) until you reach the village. The site is clearly signed in the village. GPS: 48.095824, -4.199181

### Charges guide

| Per unit incl. 2 persons and electricity (10A) | € 17.90 - € 19.80 |
|---|---|
| extra person | € 4.00 - € 4.60 |
| child (0-7 yrs) | € 2.60 - € 2.90 |

For latest campsite news, availability and prices visit
## alanrogers.com

# Locmariaquer
## Camping Lann Brick

Lann Brick, F-56740 Locmariaquer (Morbihan) T: 02 97 57 32 79. E: camping.lannbrick@wanadoo.fr
**alanrogers.com/FR56690**

Lann Brick can be found close to Carnac and La Trinité-sur-Mer, on the western side of the Morbihan gulf. The site can be found just 200 m. from the sea. Pitches here are generally sized between 70 and 90 sq.m, and are grassy with reasonable shade and high hedges. Most have electricity (6/10A). This small family site is lovingly cared for with manicured trees, shrubs and flowers. It has a very small, convivial bar with an outdoor terrace, alongside a modest pool complex and these are the focal point of the site. Various games and activities are organised in peak season, including themed evenings and dances. There is much of interest around the Morbihan gulf, including pretty villages such as Locmariaquer and Arzon, prehistoric sites and some excellent opportunities for watersports. Carnac is, of course, renowned for its 9,000 standing stones (alignments) and is certainly worth a visit. La Trinité is one of Brittany's premier sailing centres and is a pleasant spot for an evening stroll.

### Facilities
One traditional, clean toilet block has preset showers and washbasins in cabins. Facilities for babies and disabled visitors, although gravel paths could challenge wheelchair users. Washing machines and dryers. Small shop for essentials. Takeaway food. Swimming pool. Paddling pool. Bicycle hire. Small play area. Programme of activities and entertainment. Mobile homes and caravans for rent. Off site: Shops and restaurants in Locmariaquer. Cycling and walking trails around the gulf. Sailing and watersports. Prehistoric sites.

**Open:** 1 April - 14 October.

### Directions
Approaching from north (N165) leave at second Auray exit (D28) and head south on D28 to Le Chat Noir. Here, join the southbound D781 and at Kercadoret follow local signs to site, on right. GPS: 47.578567, -2.97443

### Charges guide
| | |
|---|---|
| Per unit incl. 2 persons and electricity | € 18.70 - € 24.40 |
| extra person | € 3.90 - € 4.90 |
| child (under 7 yrs) | € 2.60 - € 3.20 |
| dog | € 1.50 - € 2.50 |

# Loctudy
## Camping les Hortensias

38 rue des Tulipes, F-29750 Loctudy (Finistère) T: 02 98 87 46 64. E: hortensias@camping-loctudy.com
**alanrogers.com/FR29930**

Les Hortensias is a friendly, family site located close to Loctudy, 300 m. from the broad, sandy beach at Lodonnec which is overlooked by a small bar and restaurant. There are 105 grassy, hedged pitches here. These are of a good size and most have electrical connections (3/6A). On-site amenities include an attractive swimming pool with a wide sunbathing terrace, and a well designed children's pool area. A number of caravans and mobile homes are available for rent. There is a limited takeaway food service that offers pizzas, crêpes and paella all season. Bread and croissants are also available.

### Facilities
One toilet block with showers, baby room and facilities for disabled visitors. Washing machine and dryer. Motorcaravan service point. Shop. Bar. Takeaway. Heated swimming pool (15/5-15/9). Minigolf. Play area. TV room. Mobile homes for rent. WiFi. Off site: Beach 300 m. Shops and restaurants in Loctudy. Fishing. Sailing.

**Open:** 1 April - 30 September.

### Directions
From Quimper take southbound D785 to Pont l'Abbé. Continue south on D2 to Loctudy and follow signs to site. GPS: 47.812632, -4.18166

### Charges guide
| | |
|---|---|
| Per unit incl. 2 persons and electricity (6A) | € 17.00 - € 22.60 |
| extra person | € 4.40 |

**FREE** Alan Rogers Travel Card
Extra benefits and savings - see page 10

## Matignon

### Camping Vert le Vallon aux Merlettes

Route de Lamballe, F-22550 Matignon (Côtes d'Armor) T: 02 96 41 11 61. E: giblanchet@wanadoo.fr

**alanrogers.com/FR22260**

Le Vallon aux Merlettes is situated on the edge of the town and has a quiet, simple and rural ambience. The friendly owners are very welcoming and take care to maintain the site well. There are almost 100 grass touring pitches which are level and numbered and all have electricity (10A). Many shrubs and trees provide shade to some areas. Although there are limited leisure facilities on site, there are several sporting opportunities adjacent. The magnificent beaches of Saint Cast and a swimming pool with sea water are within 5 km. This site is ideally situated for excursions to Cap Fréhel, Erquy, Dinard, Saint Malo and Mont Saint-Michel.

**Facilities**

One modern and centrally located toilet block includes washbasins both open style and in cabins and preset showers. Facilities for disabled visitors. Laundry facilities. Motorcaravan service point. Small shop in reception for basics. Bar and basic snack bar. TV. Small unfenced play area. Internet access. WiFi (charged). Off site: Leisure facilities adjacent. Beach and swimming pool 5 km.

**Open:** 1 May - 30 September.

**Directions**

From the N12 take the D786 northeast to Erquy. Matignon is 16 km. east of Erquy still on the D786. Site is well signed in the town.
GPS: 48.59111, -2.29578

**Charges guide**

| | |
|---|---|
| Per unit incl. 2 persons and electricity | € 13.00 - € 16.60 |
| extra person | € 2.70 - € 3.80 |

## Mousterlin

### Sunêlia l'Atlantique

Kerbader, B.P 11, F-29170 Fouesnant (Finistère) T: 02 98 56 14 44. E: sunelia@latlantique.fr

**alanrogers.com/FR29350**

L'Atlantique is quietly situated just outside Beg-Meil. The 432 pitches are predominantly used by tour operators with about 90 for independent visitors. Pitches are level and grassy, all with electricity, separated by low shrubs. Apple orchards used for cider production are also on the site. All the facilities are grouped together in the centre including an innovative play area and pool complex with both indoor and outdoor pools, water slides and a paddling pool. The sandy beach faces the Glénan Islands and is a pleasant 400 m. walk away through a nature reserve. Coastal paths await exploration and Concarneau, Pont-Aven and La Pointe du Raz are nearby. Eight pitches have their own sanitary facilities.

**Facilities**

Fully equipped toilet blocks (cleaned three times a day) include facilities for disabled visitors. Restaurant (July/August). Shop, bar, snack bar with takeaway meals and pizza (all season). Heated outdoor and indoor pools, water complex with slides (all season). Tennis. TV room. Billiards. Minigolf. Sports ground. Play area. Children's club (4-12 yrs) and evening entertainment in July/Aug. Play room for children 0-4 yrs. Bicycle hire. WiFi throughout (charged). Off site: Fishing 400 m. Windsurf hire 1 km. Boat hire 3 and 5 km. Riding 3 km. Golf 8 km.

**Open:** 20 April - 8 September.

**Directions**

From Fouesnant follow directions for Mousterlin for 2 km, then follow Chapelle de Kerbader. Site is signed. GPS: 47.856564, -4.020658

**Charges guide**

| | |
|---|---|
| Per unit incl. 2 persons and electricity (6A) | € 22.00 - € 41.00 |
| with own sanitary facility | € 33.00 - € 62.00 |
| extra person | € 3.00 - € 8.00 |
| child (0-10 yrs) | € 2.00 - € 4.00 |
| Low season reductions. | |
| Camping Cheques accepted. | |

For latest campsite news, availability and prices visit

**alanrogers.com**

## Locunolé
## Castel Camping le Ty-Nadan

Route d'Arzano, F-29310 Locunolé (Finistère) T: 02 98 71 75 47. E: info@camping-ty-nadan.fr
**alanrogers.com/FR29010**

Camping le Ty-Nadan is a well organised site set amongst wooded countryside along the bank of the River Elle. There are 183 grassy pitches for touring units, many with shade and 99 fully serviced. The pool complex with slides and paddling pool is very popular as are the large indoor pool complex and indoor games area. There is also an adventure play park and a play park for 5-8 year olds, not to mention tennis courts, table tennis, pool tables, archery and trampolines. New 'floating' accommodation on the lake was opened in 2012. This is a wonderful site for families with children. Several tour operators use the site. An exciting and varied programme of activities is offered throughout the season – canoeing and sea kayaking expeditions, mountain biking, Segway and electric quad bikes for children, aquagym, paintball, riding and walking – all supervised by qualified staff. A full programme of entertainment for all ages is provided in high season, including concerts, Breton evenings with hog roasts, dancing, etc. (be warned, you will be actively encouraged to join in!).

### Facilities

One new, split-level toilet block is of good quality and includes washbasins in cabins and baby rooms. Two other blocks provide easier access for disabled campers. Washing machines and dryers. Restaurant, takeaway, bar and well stocked shop. Heated outdoor pool (17x8 m). Indoor pool. Small river beach (unfenced). Indoor badminton. Activity and entertainment programmes (all season). Riding centre. Bicycle hire. Boat hire. Canoe trips. Fishing. Segway and electric quad bikes for children. Internet access and WiFi (charged). Off site: Beaches 20 minutes by car. Golf 12 km.

**Open:** 20 April - 2 September.

### Directions

Make for Arzano which is northeast of Quimperlé on the Pontivy road and turn off D22 just west of village at site sign. Site is 3 km. GPS: 47.90468, -3.47477

### Charges guide

| | |
|---|---|
| Per unit incl. 2 persons and electricity | € 19.80 - € 50.40 |
| extra person | € 4.30 - € 8.80 |
| child (2-6 yrs) | € 2.00 - € 5.40 |
| dog | € 2.10 - € 5.80 |

Camping Cheques accepted.

## Mousterlin

### Camping le Grand Large

48 route du Grand Large, Mousterlin, F-29170 Fouesnant (Finistère) T: 02 98 56 04 06.
E: grandlarge@franceloc.fr **alanrogers.com/FR29290**

Le Grand Large is a beach-side site situated on the Pointe de Mousterlin in natural surroundings. The site is separated from the beach by the road that follows the coast around the point. It is also protected from the wind by an earth bank with trees and a fence. There are 260 pitches with just 51 places for tourers. Electricity is available throughout (long leads useful) and some pitches have drainage. The focal point of the site is an imaginative pool complex with slides, flumes and water features. A small river runs through the site but it is fenced.

### Facilities

Two neat toilet blocks, the largest only opened in high season, have washbasins in cabins. Facilities for children in the larger block, for disabled visitors in both. Laundry facilities. Shop. Bar overlooking the sea with attractive terrace. Grill restaurant including takeaway. New covered pool complex and outdoor, heated swimming pool with paddling pool and water slides in a separate pool. Tennis. Multisports court. Small play area. TV and games rooms. Bicycle hire. Off site: Beach 100 m. Golf and riding 5 km.

**Open:** 6 April - 9 September.

### Directions

Site is 7 km. south of Fouesnant. Turn off N165 expressway at Coat Conq, signed Concarneau and Fouesnant. At Fouesnant take A45 signed Beg-Meil, then follow signs to Mousterlin. In Mousterlin turn left and follow camping signs. GPS: 47.84826, -4.03702

### Charges guide

| | |
|---|---|
| Per unit incl. 2 persons and electricity | € 24.00 - € 37.00 |
| extra person | € 4.70 - € 7.00 |

## Névez

### Camping le Raguénès-Plage

503

19 rue des Iles, F-29920 Névez (Finistère) T: 02 98 06 80 69. E: info@camping-le-raguenes-plage.com
**alanrogers.com/FR29090**

Mme. Guyader and her family will ensure you receive a warm welcome on arrival at this well kept and pleasant site. Le Raguénès-Plage is an attractive and well laid out campsite with many shrubs and trees. The 287 pitches are a good size, flat and grassy, separated by trees and hedges. All have electricity, water and drainage. The site is used by two tour operators (51 pitches), and has 61 mobile homes of its own. A pool complex complete with heated indoor pool and water toboggan is a key feature and is close to the friendly bar, restaurant, shop and takeaway. From the far end of the campsite a delightful five minute walk along a path and through a cornfield takes you down to a pleasant, sandy beach looking out towards the Ile Verte and the Presqu'île de Raguénès.

### Facilities

Two clean, well maintained sanitary blocks include mixed style toilets, washbasins in cabins, baby baths and facilities for disabled visitors. Laundry room. Motorcaravan service point. Small shop (from 15/5). Bar and restaurant (from 1/6) with outside terrace and takeaway. Reading and TV room. Heated indoor and outdoor pools with sun terrace and paddling pool. Sauna (charged). Play areas. Games room. Various activities are organised in July/Aug. Internet access. WiFi (charged). Off site: Beach, fishing and watersports 300 m. Supermarket 3 km. Riding 4 km.

**Open:** 1 April - 30 September.

### Directions

From N165 take D24 Kerampaou exit. After 3 km. turn right towards Nizon and bear right at church in village following signs to Névez (D77). Continue through Névez, following signs to Raguénès. Continue for 3 km. to site entrance on left (entrance is quite small and easy to miss). GPS: 47.79337, -3.80049

### Charges guide

| | |
|---|---|
| Per unit incl. 2 persons and electricity | € 20.30 - € 39.70 |
| extra person | € 4.40 - € 6.00 |
| child (under 7 yrs) | free - € 3.90 |

## Névez

### Camping les Deux Fontaines

Feunteun Vilian, Raguenèz, F-29920 Névez (Finistère) T: 02 98 06 81 91. E: info@les2fontaines.fr
**alanrogers.com/FR29470**

Les Deux Fontaines is a large site with 288 pitches. Of these 115 are for touring, 118 are used by tour operators, and the remainder for mobile homes. The well cared for pitches are on grass, level and attractively laid out amongst mature trees and shrubs. All have 10A electricity connections (Europlug). Trees have been carefully planted creating one area with silver birch, one with apple trees and another with palms and tropical plants. The pool complex is an excellent feature complete with chutes, flumes and waterfalls, and a covered pool with adjacent gym and massage room.

**Facilities**

Two toilet blocks are of good quality and provide washbasins in cabins and preset showers. Separate facilities for disabled visitors. Laundry facilities. Shop, bar, takeaway. Basic motorcaravan services. Large indoor and outdoor swimming pool complex. Fitness and pamper room. Play area. Skateboard park. 6-hole golf course. Driving range. Rollerblade hire. Archery. Scuba diving. Daytime activities and evening entertainment. WiFi in bar (free). Bicycle hire. Off site: Fishing 1 km. Riding 5 km.

**Open:** 5 May - 9 September.

**Directions**

Travel south from Névèz on the D1. The site is on the left after 3 km. and is well signed.
GPS: 47.79937, -3.79017

**Charges guide**

| Per unit incl. 2 persons | |
| --- | --- |
| and electricity | € 20.90 - € 37.80 |
| extra person | € 3.70 - € 6.70 |
| child (2-7 yrs) | € 1.50 - € 4.30 |
| No credit cards. | |

## Noyal-Muzillac

### Camping Moulin de Cadillac

Route de Berric, F-56190 Noyal-Muzillac (Morbihan) T: 02 97 67 03 47. E: infos@moulin-cadillac.com
**alanrogers.com/FR56430**

Le Moulin de Cadillac is a riverside site located 15 minutes by car from the beaches of the Morbihan. Set in the heart of rural Brittany, this attractive site has 192 pitches, 123 of which are for touring (10A electricity). Pitches are generous (100-150 sq.m) although access to some is tight and may not be suitable for larger units. They are well laid out on grass and a profusion of trees and shrubs provide both shade and privacy. There is an impressive indoor pool complex and the fishing lake ensures that there is plenty to keep the family entertained. Boat trips around the Gulf of Morbihan are popular.

**Facilities**

Three well appointed toilet blocks include facilities for children and disabled visitors. Covered laundry area. Shop. Bar (July/Aug). Indoor aquatic park with slides flumes and fountains. Outdoor pool (1/6-2/9; heated July/Aug) and paddling pool. Games room. TV room. Sports pitch. Tennis. Minigolf. Play areas. Fishing lakes. Children's zoo. Some entertainment in high season. No electric barbecues. Mobile homes, chalets and tents for rent. Off site: Muzillac 8 km. Beaches, bicycle hire 10 km.

**Open:** 13 April - 15 September.

**Directions**

From Vannes travel southeast on the N165. Exit on D140 towards Berric. After 3 km. at Lauzach, site is well signed on the right. Continue for a further 4 km.
GPS: 47.61310, -2.50140

**Charges guide**

| Per unit incl. 2 persons | |
| --- | --- |
| and electricity | € 16.80 - € 28.70 |
| extra person | € 4.00 - € 6.20 |
| child (under 7 yrs) | € 2.00 - € 3.00 |

## Paimpol

### Camping Municipal de Cruckin

Rue de Cruckin, Kérity, F-22500 Paimpol (Côtes d'Armor) T: 02 96 20 78 47.
E: contact@camping-paimpol.com **alanrogers.com/FR22250**

A neat and well managed municipal site situated close to the historical fishing port of Cité des Islandais and within easy reach of the Ile de Bréhat. This is an ideal location for many interesting walks. The site has 130 well maintained, mostly level pitches set in both wooded and open areas and all have electricity connections (5-12A). A very large area has been provided for sports, a play area and picnic tables. Although the site does not have its own swimming pool, the beach is just a short walk away. There are Bengali static tents for hire. A communal barbecue is available.

**Facilities**

One modern and heated toilet block. Washbasins in cabins and showers. Facilities for babies and disabled visitors. Laundry facilities. Bread and milk (high season). Snack bar/takeaway (July/Aug). Motorcaravan service point. Large field for football. Pétanque. Fenced play area. Internet access on request. Bicycle hire. Fishing. Off site: Beach. Kérity village with shops, restaurants and cafés. Riding 2 km. Golf 10 km.

**Open:** 1 April - 10 October.

**Directions**

From N12 St Brieuc bypass, take D786 north towards Paimpol. Village of Kérity is 3 km. south of Paimpol. Site is signed. GPS: 48.76966, -3.02209

**Charges guide**

| Per unit incl. 2 persons | |
| --- | --- |
| and electricity | € 15.40 - € 17.50 |
| child (under 7 yrs) | € 1.70 - € 2.20 |
| dog | € 1.30 - € 1.60 |

**FREE** Alan Rogers Travel Card
Extra benefits and savings - see page 10

## Pénestin-sur-Mer
### Camping le Cénic

F-56760 Pénestin-sur-Mer (Morbihan) T: 02 99 90 45 65. E: info@lecenic.com

**alanrogers.com/FR56180**

Le Cénic is beautifully set amidst trees and flowers, providing activities for all tastes. An attractive covered aquatic complex has water slides, bridges, rivers and a jacuzzi, whilst the outdoor pool comes complete with water slide, mushroom fountain and sunbathing areas. You may fish in the lake or use inflatables, watched by the peacock, the geese and turkeys. There is a hall for table tennis and a range of indoor games. There are 310 pitches, 160 of which are for touring. Of these, 90 have electricity (6A), but long leads will be required. The area has much to offer from the beaches of La Mine d'Or, the harbour at Trébiguier-Pénestin, the Golfe du Morbihan with its numerous islands, La Baule with its magnificent beach and the medieval city of Guérande to the unique Brière nature reserve.

**Facilities**

Good new toilet block includes washbasins in cabins. Facilities for disabled visitors. Baby room. Separate laundry. Bar and shop (1/7-31/8). TV and games rooms (1/7-31/8). Indoor (15/4-15/9) and outdoor (1/7-31/8) swimming pools. Play area. Fishing. Off site: Riding 500 m. Bicycle hire 1 km. Sailing 2 km. Pénestin town 2 km. Sandy beaches 2.5 km. Golf 30 km.

**Open:** 1 May - 30 September.

**Directions**

From D34 (La Roche-Bernard), at roundabout just after entering Pénestin take D201 south (Assérac). After 100 m. take first turning on left. After 800 m. turn left and campsite is 300 m. on right down a narrow winding lane. GPS: 47.47910, -2.45643

**Charges 2013**

| Per unit incl. 2 persons and electricity | € 19.00 - € 32.00 |
|---|---|

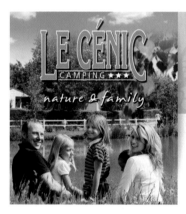

Covered Aquatic Centre (heated swimming-pool, balneotherapy area, children's pool), outdoor pool, water chute, games room, bar, fishing in the lake.

Le Cénic offers a range of accommodation : static caravans, chalets to rent.

BP 12 - 56760 PÉNESTIN
**Tél. +33 (0)2 99 90 45 65** • Fax +33 (0)2 99 90 45 05
info@lecenic.com • www.lecenic.com

## Pénestin-sur-Mer
### Camping les Iles Pénestin

La Pointe du Bile, B.P. 4, F-56760 Pénestin-sur-Mer (Morbihan) T: 02 99 90 30 24.
E: contact@camping-des-iles.fr **alanrogers.com/FR56120**

You will receive a warm, friendly welcome at this family run campsite. The owner, Madame Communal, encourages everyone to make the most of this beautiful region. Of the 184 pitches, 109 are for touring. Most are flat, hedged and of a reasonable size (larger caravans and American style motorhomes are advised to book) and all have electricity (10A). Some pitches have sea views and overlook the beach. There is direct access to cliff-top walks and local beaches (you can even walk to small off-shore islands at low tide). The attractive heated swimming pool complex provides a focal point for all ages.

**Facilities**

The new large central toilet block is spotlessly clean with washbasins in cabins and showers. Laundry facilities. Facilities for disabled visitors and baby room. Shop (all season). Bar and restaurant with takeaway (15/6-22/9). Pool complex. Bicycle hire. Riding. Entertainment and activities (July/Aug). Across the road in mobile home section of site: Motorcaravan service point. TV room. Multisports pitch. Tennis court. No electric barbecues. WiFi over site (charged). Off site: Windsurfing 500 m.

**Open:** 6 April - 30 September.

**Directions**

From D34 (La Roche-Bernard), at roundabout just after entering Pénestin take D201 south (Assérac). Take right fork to Pointe-du-Bile after 2 km. Turn right at crossroads just before beach. Site is on left. GPS: 47.44543, -2.48396

**Charges guide**

| Per unit incl. 2 persons and electricity | € 20.50 - € 39.50 |
|---|---|

Camping Cheques accepted.

For latest campsite news, availability and prices visit

# alanrogers.com

## Pénestin-sur-Mer

### Yelloh! Village Domaine d'Inly

Route de Couarne, B.P. 24, F-56760 Pénestin-sur-Mer (Morbihan) T: 02 99 90 35 09. E: inly-info@wanadoo.fr
**alanrogers.com/FR56240**

This very large site is mainly taken up with mobile homes and cottages, some belonging to the site owner, some private and some belonging to tour operators. Most of these pitches are arranged in groups of 10 to 14 around a central stone circle with a water point in the middle. Of the 500 pitches, 100 are for touring units and all are large (150-200 sq.m) with a 10A electrical connection (Europlug). Most are level and are situated by the attractive lake at the bottom of the site where one can fish or canoe. Pony rides are possible around the lake.

**Facilities**

One toilet block (an additional block is planned) with facilities for disabled visitors, and a baby room. Laundry. Shop. Small, comfortable bar with large screen satellite TV, attractive restaurant and takeaway. Heated swimming pool complex with slide (outdoor 15/5-15/9, indoor all season). Games room. Play areas. Football pitch (weekly games organised in July/Aug). Wellness. Lake for fishing and canoeing. Pony rides. Bicycle hire. Activities and sports. WiFi. Off site: Supermarket 1 km. Town centre 2 km.

**Open:** 6 April - 22 September.

**Directions**

From D34 from La Roche-Bernard, at roundabout just after entering Pénestin take D201 south, signed Assérac. After 100 m. take first turning on left (site signed) opposite Carrefour supermarket. After 650 m. turn right, again signed, and campsite is 400 m. on left. GPS: 47.471483, -2.467267

**Charges guide**

| Per unit incl. 2 persons | |
|---|---|
| and electricity | € 17.00 - € 42.00 |
| extra person | € 6.00 - € 7.00 |

## Pléneuf-Val-André

### Campéole les Monts Colleux

26 rue Jean Lebrun, F-22370 Pléneuf-Val-André (Côtes d'Armor) T: 02 96 72 95 10.
E: monts-colleux@campeole.com **alanrogers.com/FR22380**

Les Monts Colleux is a member of the Campéole group with an unusual town centre location in Le Val André. The site, however, has a hilltop setting and some pitches have fine views of the sea. This was formerly a municipal site and is well managed with well kept hedges and pitches. The reception area and shop are modern, although the wash blocks are older. Pitches are generally flat, although, given its hillside location, there are a number of sloping pitches. The 104 pitches all have electrical connections (10A). Although there is no swimming pool on site, there is a large covered municipal pool adjacent with limited free access for campers. Around 66 pitches are occupied by mobile homes, chalets and fully equipped bungalow tents (available for rent). The nearest beach is close – just 300 m, and boats can be launched nearby. An attractive golf course is 1 km. distant. Val André is an attractive resort and the town centre is just 300 m. from the site via a steep hill. There are many activities here during the high season, including weekly free jazz concerts.

**Facilities**

Two toilet blocks, one with special facilities for children, the other also includes facilities for disabled visitors. Motorcaravan service point. Shop, snack bar and takeaway meals (all high season). Games/TV room. Play area. Bouncy castle. Activity and entertainment programme. Tourist information. Mobile homes and chalets for rent. WiFi (charged). Off site: Municipal covered swimming pool adjacent. Val André and beach 300 m.

**Open:** 1 April - 30 September.

**Directions**

Approaching from the east (St Malo and Dinard) on the D786, bypass Erquy and continue to Pléneuf-Val-André and then to Le Val-André. Follow signs to Piscine Municipale – the site is adjacent. GPS: 48.5894, -2.5508

**Charges guide**

| Per unit incl. 2 persons | |
|---|---|
| and electricity | € 15.10 - € 23.10 |
| extra person | € 4.00 - € 6.70 |

## Penmarc'h
### Flower Camping les Genêts

Rue de Gouesnac'h Nevez, F-29760 Penmarc'h (Finistère) T: 02 98 58 66 93. E: nohartp@wanadoo.fr
**alanrogers.com/FR29260**

Les Genêts' owners, Bridgette and Pascal Rohart, bought this rural campsite a few years ago and have enthusiastically transformed it beyond recognition. The modern reception is in front of a modestly sized swimming pool that has a section for small children. A covered pool should now be open. There are two new heated toilet blocks. The 100 pitches are divided by trees and hedges and vary in both size and quality. The clever design of the flower beds and shrubs around the site is particularly attractive. There are 52 pitches for mobile homes which are placed to one side of the campsite.

| Facilities | Directions |
|---|---|
| Two new heated toilet blocks with showers and wash cubicles. Laundry room. Bar and snack bar (July/Aug). Bread available (July/Aug). Outdoor swimming pool. Play area and trampoline. Free WiFi by pool and office. Off site: Shops and restaurants 1.5 km. Riding, beach, fishing and boat launching 1.5 km. Golf 3 km. | From Pont l'Abbé, take the D785 southwest towards Penmarc'h. Before the town turn left eastwards on the D53 (Loctudy) and site is on left in 2 km. GPS: 47.81838, -4.309452 |

**Open:** 1 April - 30 September.

**Charges guide**

| Per unit incl. 2 persons and electricity | € 15.00 - € 20.40 |
|---|---|
| extra person | € 3.20 - € 4.50 |

## Pleubian
### Camping de Port la Chaine

F-22610 Pleubian (Côtes d'Armor) T: 02 96 22 92 38. E: info@portlachaine.com
**alanrogers.com/FR22140**

Michelle and Thierry Suquet offer a warm welcome to this comfortable, quiet, family site with stunning views. In a beautiful location on the Presqu'île Sauvage between Paimpol and Perros-Guirec, attractive trees and shrubs provide a balance of sun and shade for the 200 pitches. Of these, 140 are for touring, all with electricity (long leads may be needed in places) and some also have water and drainage. Pitches are on grassy terraces on the gradual descent towards the bay and the sea (a sandy bay with rocks). Most terraces have a slight slope, so those with motorcaravans will need to choose their pitch carefully.

| Facilities | Directions |
|---|---|
| Two traditional style toilet blocks are comfortable and fully equipped. Washbasins in cabins, British and Turkish style toilets. Cabins for families and disabled visitors. Washing machines and dryer. Bar/snacks with takeaway (30/6-24/8). Bread and croissants. New covered, heated swimming pool, and outdoor heated pool (1/7-3/9). Play area. Games room. Pétanque. Children's entertainer (July/Aug). Beach, fishing and sailing. WiFi in reception area. Off site: Bus 1 km. Boat launching 1 km. Good fishing and diving. Village 2 km. Riding 6 km. Golf 18 km. | Pleubian is 37 km. north of Guingamp and 87 km. by road east of Roscoff. From D786 Lannion-Paimpol road, east of Tréguier turn north on D20 to Pleubian and on for 2 km. towards l'Armor Pleubian. Site signed to left. GPS: 48.8555, -3.1327 |

**Open:** 7 April - 22 September.

**Charges guide**

| Per unit incl. 2 persons and electricity | € 18.00 - € 26.60 |
|---|---|
| extra person | € 4.10 - € 6.40 |
| child (2-7 yrs) | € 3.50 - € 4.20 |

## Ploemel
### Camping Saint Laurent

Kergonvo, F-56400 Ploemel (Morbihan) T: 02 97 56 85 90. E: saintlaurent@camp-in-ouest.com
**alanrogers.com/FR56330**

This is an attractive, peaceful and rural site ten minutes from the beaches and 10 km. from Carnac. There are 70 touring pitches out of a total of 90 which are set among pine trees and wiry hedges giving some shade. Long leads are required. There is a more casual camping area being developed further away amongst some trees. The welcoming bar and patio area also has a communal barbecue. Basic provisions are available from reception where good English is spoken. This pleasant, wooded site is now part of a group of seven sites called Camp'in Ouest. Some activities are organised in July and August.

| Facilities | Directions |
|---|---|
| One bright modern sanitary block provides adequate facilities with excellent en suite facilities for disabled visitors and is centrally located. Small bar/restaurant (July/Aug). New covered, heated swimming pool with sun loungers. Paddling pool. Volleyball. Table tennis. Basketball. Small play area. Bicycle hire. Off site: Golf 1 km. Riding 5 km. Fishing and beaches 10 km. | From the N165 Vannes-Lorient dual carriageway, take the exit signed D768 Ploemel/Carnac. After 4 km. turn right heading northwest towards Ploemel. Once in the village centre follow signs to St Laurent Camping. GPS: 47.66406, -3.09985 |

**Open:** April - October.

**Charges guide**

| Per unit incl. 2 persons and electricity | € 17.80 - € 23.70 |
|---|---|
| extra person | € 3.90 - € 5.00 |

For latest campsite news, availability and prices visit
**alanrogers.com**

## Plomeur-la Torche
### Camping de la Torche

Pointe de la Roche, F-29120 Plomeur-la Torche (Finistère) T: 02 98 58 62 82. E: info@campingdelatorche.fr
**alanrogers.com/FR29370**

Probably a 'must stay' site for surfers, this rural, family owned, wooded campsite, like so many in this part of Brittany, comes to life in July and August. The natural beauty of the wide sandy beaches of La Torche can be accessed direct from the site via a footpath (1.5 km). La Torche is internationally renowned as a paradise for all boardsports, particularly windsurfing. The site has 155 pitches (115 for tourers), divided by trees and hedges and quite generous in size. Around 40 chalets and mobile homes are discreetly positioned amongst the trees. Provisions are available at a supermarket in Plomeur (3 km).

**Facilities**

The main (heated) toilet block provides British style toilets, showers, washing cubicles and good facilities for disabled visitors. A second block opens in high season. Washing machine and dryers. Shop, bar and terrace, with snacks (all 1/7-31/8). Covered swimming pool (15/6-15/9). Play area. Games/TV room. Entertainment in July/Aug. Free WiFi in bar. Off site: Riding 500 m. Beach 1.5 km.

**Open:** 1 April - 23 September.

**Directions**

From Pont l'Abbé the D785 south to Plomeur, then follow signs for Pointe de La Torche. After 3 km. site is signed to left. GPS: 47.832859, -4.326355

**Charges guide**

| | |
|---|---|
| Per unit incl. 2 persons and electricity | € 17.10 - € 23.40 |
| extra person | € 3.50 - € 4.90 |
| child (0-7 yrs) | € 2.20 - € 3.00 |

---

## Plonévez-Porzay
### Kawan Village La Plage de Tréguer

Plage de Sainte Anne-la-Palud, F-29550 Plonévez-Porzay (Finistère) T: 02 98 92 53 52.
E: camping-treguer-plage@wanadoo.fr **alanrogers.com/FR29590**

Set right on the dunes adjacent to a large, sandy beach on the huge sweep of Douarnenez Bay, this is apparently one of only seven campsites in Brittany with direct access to a beach, with no paths or roads to cross. It certainly is an impressive location, not manicured but on the 'wild' side, being a protected area. Tall hedges provide wind shelter, tamarisk grows in profusion and there are uninterrupted views out to sea. Some pitches nestle in the shelter of the dunes (sandier ground), others are in groups of four or eight, bordered by hedging. There are mobiles homes available for rent.

**Facilities**

One central toilet block has showers, washbasins in cabins, and facilities for babies and disabled visitors. Bar, takeaway and shop (July/Aug). Heated outdoor swimming pool with jacuzzi, waterfall for children and paddling pool (1/6-30/9). Play area. Bouncy castle. Multisports court. Games/TV room. Entertainment (July/Aug). Direct beach access. Off site: Restaurant 2 km. Shops 3 km. Boat launching 3 km. Sailing 5 km. Bicycle hire 10 km. Riding 15 km. Golf 18 km. Fishing. Medieval Locronan.

**Open:** 6 April - 29 September.

**Directions**

Situated on the north side of the village, it is well signed from Plonevez-Porzay.
GPS: 48.14485, -4.26882

**Charges guide**

| | |
|---|---|
| Per unit incl. 2 persons and electricity | € 17.40 - € 25.50 |
| extra person | € 3.60 - € 5.50 |
| child (2-7 yrs) | € 2.60 - € 3.60 |
| Camping Cheques accepted. | |

---

## Plouézec
### Camping le Cap Horn

Port Lazo, F-22470 Plouézec (Côtes d'Armor) T: 02 96 20 64 28. E: lecaphorn@hotmail.com
**alanrogers.com/FR22320**

Le Cap Horn is in a magnificent setting with exceptional views of the Bay of Paimpol and the Ile de Bréhat. The enthusiastic owners are keen to make visitors welcome at their site which is well positioned for exploring the Goëlo Coast, Paimpol and the Pink Granite Coast. The campsite is in two sections and slopes down to the beach. The upper section is mostly devoted to mobile homes and is reached by a road or a series of steep steps, the lower section is for tourers. There are 149 pitches with 115 good sized grass pitches for touring (90 with 10A electricity).

**Facilities**

Two toilet blocks include facilities for disabled visitors but the site is not ideal for those with walking difficulties. Small shop. Bar and restaurant with terrace and views over the bay (July/Aug). Takeaway. Covered swimming pool and paddling pool. Play area. Boules. Fishing. Sports area. Bicycle hire. Organised activities (July/Aug). WiFi (charged). Off site: Beach 100 m. Riding 6 km. Golf 12 km. Shops, bars and restaurants at Plouézec and Paimpol.

**Open:** 31 March - 30 September.

**Directions**

From Saint Brieuc take D786 north towards Paimpol. Site is at Plouézec, south of Paimpol, well signed from D786. GPS: 48.759792, -2.962795

**Charges guide**

| | |
|---|---|
| Per unit incl. 2 persons and electricity | € 18.50 - € 27.90 |
| extra person | € 3.50 - € 5.50 |
| child (under 12 yrs) | free - € 4.50 |

---

**FREE** Alan Rogers Travel Card
Extra benefits and savings - see page 10

## Plouhinec

### Camping Moténo

Route du Magouër, F-56680 Plouhinec (Morbihan) T: 02 97 36 76 63. E: camping-moteno@wanadoo.fr
alanrogers.com/FR56440

This site is situated on the east side of the river d'Etel, just before it enters the sea. The grass pitches are of average size, hedged and shaded by large trees. Of the 256 pitches, 181 are occupied by mobile homes, mostly for rent. The new aqua park complex with covered and open areas is superb and includes slides, flumes and various pools. The beach is easily accessible, just 800 m. as is the little port facing Etel which can be reached by a regular ferry service. Plouhinec, the nearest town, is 5 km. by road where you will find shops and restaurants.

**Facilities**

New modern and heated toilet block. Facilities for disabled visitors. Washing machines and dryer. Shop, bar and takeaway (July/Aug). New aqua complex including spa pool. Multisports court. Gym. Bicycle hire. Riding. Play area. Entertainment (July/Aug). WiFi. Off site: Beach 800 m. Ferry to Etel for bars and shopping. Golf 15 km. Lorient, Auray and the Quiberon peninsular.

**Open:** 5 April - 13 September.

**Directions**

From Plouhinec, southeast of Lorient, take the D781 towards Carnac. Site is signed on right in 4 km. Follow signs for Plage. GPS: 47.66457, -3.22098

**Charges guide**

| | |
|---|---|
| Per unit incl. 2 persons and electricity | € 18.40 - € 34.00 |
| extra person (over 7 yrs) | € 3.60 - € 6.60 |

## Ploumanach

### Yelloh! Village le Ranolien

Ploumanach, F-22700 Perros-Guirec (Côtes d'Armor) T: 02 96 91 65 65. E: info@yellohvillage-ranolien.com
alanrogers.com/FR22080

Le Ranolien has been attractively developed around a former Breton farm – everything here is either made from, or placed on or around the often massive pink rocks. Of the 520 pitches 110 are for touring, mostly large and flat, but some quite small, all with electricity (10A) and some with water and drainage. The rest of the site is taken up with mobile homes and chalets for hire and several tour operators. The site is on the coast, with beaches and coves within walking distance and there are spectacular views from some pitches.

**Facilities**

The main toilet block is heated in cool weather and has washbasins in cabins, mostly British style WCs and good showers. Facilities for disabled visitors. Laundry. Motorcaravan service point. Supermarket and gift shop. Restaurant, crêperie and bar (all open all season). Indoor and outdoor (from end May) swimming pool complex. Wellness centre. Gym and steam room. Disco in high season. Minigolf. Games room. Play area. Cinema. Mobile homes for hire, including Romany-style caravans and luxury chalets. Internet and WiFi (on payment).

**Open:** 6 April - 23 September.

**Directions**

From Lannion take D788 to Perros-Guirec. Follow signs to Centre Ville past harbour area, then turn right along coast road (Centre Ville par la Corniche and Trégastel). Continue through north of town and on to La Clarté. After a sharp left hand bend site is immediately on the right. GPS: 48.82798, -3.47623

**Charges guide**

| | |
|---|---|
| Per unit incl. 2 persons and electricity | € 17.00 - € 43.00 |
| extra person | € 6.00 - € 9.00 |

## Poullan-sur-Mer

### Flower Camping de la Baie de Douarnenez

30 rue Luc Robert, F-29100 Poullan-sur-Mer (Finistère) T: 02 98 74 26 39. E: info@camping-douarnenez.com
alanrogers.com/FR29060

This is an attractive, family run site just back from the sea near Douarnenez. It has 190 pitches on fairly flat ground, marked out by separating hedges and of quite good quality, though varying in size and shape. With 88 pitches used for touring units, the site also has a number of mobile homes and chalets. These are sympathetically positioned amongst the trees and shrubs, away from the touring pitches. All pitches have electrical connections and the original trees provide shade in some areas. A large room, the Woodpecker Bar, is used for entertainment with discos and cabaret in July/August.

**Facilities**

Two main toilet blocks in modern style include washbasins mostly in cabins and facilities for disabled visitors. Laundry facilities. Motorcaravan service point. Gas supplies. Small shop for basics. Bar, restaurant and takeaway (all 1/6-31/8). Heated, indoor and outdoor swimming and paddling pools (no Bermuda-style shorts). Tennis. Minigolf. Fishing. Bicycle hire. Playground. Weekly outings and clubs for children (30/6-30/8). Off site: Restaurants in village 500 m. Riding 4 km. Sandy beach 5 km.

**Open:** 7 April - 16 September.

**Directions**

Site is 500 m. east from the centre of Poullan on D7 road towards Douarnenez. From Douarnenez take circular bypass route towards Audierne. Turn onto D7, signed for Poullan. Site is well signed. GPS: 48.0824, -4.40805

**Charges guide**

| | |
|---|---|
| Per unit incl. 2 persons and electricity | € 17.00 - € 32.00 |
| extra person | € 3.30 - € 5.30 |

For latest campsite news, availability and prices visit
**alanrogers.com**

# Quimper
## Castel Camping l'Orangerie de Lanniron

 504

Château de Lanniron, F-29000 Quimper (Finistère) T: 02 98 90 62 02. E: camping@lanniron.com
**alanrogers.com/FR29050**

L'Orangerie is a beautiful and peaceful family site set in ten acres of a 17th-century, 38-hectare country estate on the banks of the Odet river, formerly the home of the Bishops of Quimper. The site has 199 grassy pitches (156 for touring units) of three types varying in size, services and price. They are on flat ground, laid out in rows alongside access roads with shrubs and bushes providing separation. All have electricity and 88 have three services. The original outbuildings have been attractively converted around a walled courtyard. Used by tour operators (30 pitches). There are lovely walks within the grounds and in spring the rhododendrons and azaleas are magnificent – the gardens and the restaurant are both open to the public. The site is just to the south of Quimper and about 15 km. from the sea and beaches at Bénodet. The restoration of the park, including the original canal, fountains, ornamental 'bassin de Neptune', the boathouse and gardens, is now complete. In addition to the golf course and driving range, a training bunker and pitching area have been created along with a second putting green. The Aquapark has a waterfall and exotic plants; it provides in excess of 600 sq.m. of heated water and includes balnéotherapy, spa, jacuzzi, fountains, slides and games (free of charge to campers).

### Facilities

Excellent heated block in the courtyard and second modern block serving the top areas of the site. Facilities for disabled visitors and babies. Washing machines and dryers. Motorcaravan services. Shop (15/5-10/9). Gas supplies. Bar (23/5-7/9). Restaurant and takeaway (open daily). Swimming and paddling pool. Aquapark. Small play area. Tennis. Minigolf. Golf course (9 holes), driving range, two putting greens, training bunker and pitching area (weekly green fee package available). Fishing. Archery. Bicycle hire. Games and billiards rooms. TV/video room. Karaoke. Outdoor activities. Pony rides and tree climbing (high season). Internet access and WiFi over site (charged). Off site: Two hypermarkets 1 km. Quimper within 3 km.

**Open:** 28 March - 15 November.

### Directions

From Quimper follow Quimper Sud signs, then Toutes Directions and general camping signs, finally signs for Lanniron. GPS: 47.97685, -4.11102

### Charges guide

| | |
|---|---|
| Per unit incl. 2 persons and electricity | € 23.60 - € 40.00 |
| extra person | € 4.60 - € 8.00 |
| child (2-9 yrs) | € 3.00 - € 5.20 |
| dog | € 3.30 - € 4.80 |

94 acres of park, gardens and nature reserve.
Gites, cottages, mobile homes and studios for rent. Aqua park with paddling pool, spa, balnéo and 4 waterslides. 9-holes golf, golf practice, restaurant, bar, tennis, kayak, fishing, ponies, children's farm.

**FREE** Alan Rogers Travel Card
Extra benefits and savings - see page 10

## Saint Brieuc
### Flower Camping des Vallées

Chemin des Vallées, Parc de Brézillet, F-22000 Saint Brieuc (Côtes d'Armor) T: 02 96 94 05 05.

E: campingdesvallees@wanadoo.fr  alanrogers.com/FR22000

Previously run by the municipality, this site is now privately managed. Neat and tidy, it has 106 good size pitches, 70 with electrical connections (10A), set mainly on flat terraced grass and separated by shrubs and bushes. There are 14 pitches with hardstanding and electricity, water and sewage connections. Mature trees are plentiful, providing shade if required, and a small stream winds through the middle of the site creating a quiet, peaceful atmosphere. A key system operates the access gate (closed 22.30-07.00 hrs). Saint Brieuc's pedestrianised centre is filled with small shops and boutiques and several speciality food emporia. The old quarter of the town and the excellent street markets on Wednesday and Saturday mornings are worth a visit.

**Facilities**

The two main toilet blocks include some washbasins in cabins, facilities for disabled visitors and baby room. Laundry facilities. Motorcaravan services. Two further smaller blocks are at the bottom of the site. Shop with basic provisions. Compact bar with snacks. Play area. Arcade games. Bicycle hire. Animation organised in peak season, also weekly pony days for children. Off site: Aquatic centre, gym and fitness centre (part of a holiday village). Saint Brieuc 800 m. Beach 10 km.

**Open:** Easter - 15 October.

**Directions**

From the east, on entering St Brieuc, look for the sign to the railway station and from there, signs for Brézillet or site. GPS: 48.5004, -2.76001

**Charges guide**

| | |
|---|---|
| Per unit incl. 2 persons and electricity | € 17.80 - € 19.20 |
| extra person | € 3.00 - € 4.70 |
| child (under 7 yrs) | € 2.50 - € 3.10 |
| dog | € 2.00 - € 2.60 |

No credit cards.

flower Camping des Vallées***
Boulevard Paul Doumer
22000 Saint Brieuc
Tél/fax 02 96 94 05 05

Two steps from the center of Saint Brieuc and near the beach, the flower campsite of Valleys welcomes you in a family atmosphere and a green setting.

www.camping-desvallees.com • GPS: long 48.501172 - lat 2.76135

## Saint Benoit-des-Ondes
### Camping de l'Ile Verte

42 rue de l'Ile Verte, F-35114 Saint Benoit-des-Ondes (Ille-et-Vilaine) T: 02 99 58 62 55.

E: camping-ile-verte@sfr.fr  alanrogers.com/FR35180

L'Ile Verte is located at the heart of the bay of Le Mont Saint-Michel, close to Cancale and St Malo, and is a good base for discovering the culture, gastronomy and coast of this beautiful area. The campsite is just 400 m. from the sea and has 28 mobile homes for rent, as well as 40 generously sized touring pitches, all with 6A electricity. On-site amenities include a covered, heated swimming pool and a good children's play area. Special kitchen facilities have been provided for visitors with tents. In peak season, a variety of activities and events are organised including evening swimming and local folk groups.

**Facilities**

One older style toilet block has new shower fittings and provides washbasins in cubicles. Facilities for disabled visitors (key access). Laundry area. Motorcaravan service point. Bar/takeaway in high season. Pizza van once a week. Seafood platters delivered in July/Aug. Covered and heated swimming pool. Play area. Boules. Tourist information. Activity and entertainment programme. Mobile homes for rent. WiFi (charged). Off site: Shops and restaurants in the village and Cancale. Cycling and walking. Fishing. Kite surfing. Sand yachting. Le Mont St-Michel.

**Open:** 1 April - 4 November.

**Directions**

The site can be found on the edge of the village of St Benoit-des-Ondes. Approaching from St Malo, follow D155 and D6, passing through At St Meloir-des-Ondes until reaching St Benoit-des-Ondes. Follow signs to the site. GPS: 48.615779, -1.851835

**Charges guide**

| | |
|---|---|
| Per unit incl. 2 persons and electricity | € 19.10 - € 23.20 |
| extra person | € 3.00 - € 4.00 |
| child (3-12 yrs) | € 2.10 - € 3.00 |

For latest campsite news, availability and prices visit
# alanrogers.com

## Saint Briac-sur-Mer
### Camping Emeraude

7 chemin de la Souris, F-35800 Saint Briac-sur-Mer (Ille-et-Vilaine) T: 02 99 88 34 55.
E: camping.emeraude@wanadoo.fr **alanrogers.com/FR35100**

M. and Mme Giroux have, over the past ten years, created a pleasant site with a French feel and some surprising features for such a compact site. Notably these include an attractive heated leisure pool with water slides, whirlpool and a paddling pool, safely separated from the main pool and with its own little slide. There are 71 level pitches for touring, separated by hedges or shrubs and all with electricity connection adjacent (6A). Beyond these are 121 mobile homes and chalets (77 for rent). Although in an urban setting, the sandy beaches of the attractive Côte Eméraude are only a short drive away. Saint Briac has a choice of shops, bars and restaurants and the resort of Dinard is only seven kilometres to the east. A bus service will take you there and you could then hop on the sea bus across to Saint Malo.

| Facilities | Directions |
|---|---|
| Large toilet block with washbasins in cubicles and controllable showers. Facilities for disabled visitors. Baby room. Washing machine and dryer. Motorcaravan service points. Swimming pool (8/5-10/9). Shop and takeaway (all season). Bar (July/Aug). Games room. Excellent play area. Minigolf. Bicycle hire. Children's activities and evening entertainment for families (July/Aug). Gas barbecues only (for hire). No twin-axle caravans or motorcaravans. Only dogs under 15 kg. accepted in rental accommodation. Off site: Beach, fishing, sailing and boat launching 900 m. Golf 3 km. Shops, bars and restaurants nearby. | Saint Briac is 7 km. west of Dinard. From ferry terminal follow signs for Dinard. Turn west onto D168. Keep west onto D603 and follow signs for 'Camping Emeraude par la côte' (avoids town centre); site is well signed from there. From other directions take D976/N176 following signs for Dinard. GPS: 48.62776, -2.130865 |

**Open:** 13 April - 22 September.

**Charges guide**

| Per unit incl. 2 persons | |
|---|---|
| and electricity | € 22.80 - € 32.00 |
| extra person | € 5.50 - € 6.50 |
| child (under 7 yrs) | € 3.00 - € 4.50 |

CAMPING
*Emeraude*
Saint-Briac sur mer / Bretagne

7, Chemin de la Souris - 35800 Saint Briac sur Mer - France
Tel. 0033 299 88 34 55 - camping.emeraude@wanadoo.fr - www.campingemeraude.com

## Saint Cast-le-Guildo
### Castel Camping le Château de Galinée

La Galinée, F-22380 Saint Cast-le-Guildo (Côtes d'Armor) T: 02 96 41 10 56. E: chateaugalinee@wanadoo.fr
**alanrogers.com/FR22090**

Situated a few kilometres back from Saint Cast and owned and managed by the Vervel family, Galinée is in a parkland setting on level grass with numerous and varied mature trees. It has 273 pitches, all with electricity, water and drainage and separated by many mature shrubs and bushes. The top section is mostly for mobile homes. An attractive outdoor pool complex has swimming and paddling pools and two pools with a water slide and a stream. A new indoor complex has now also been added and includes a swimming pool, bar, restaurant and large entertainment hall.

| Facilities | Directions |
|---|---|
| The large modern sanitary block includes washbasins in private cabins, facilities for babies and a good unit for disabled visitors. Laundry room. Shop for basics, bar and excellent takeaway menu (all 25/5-4/9). Attractive outdoor heated pool complex with swimming and paddling pools. Covered heated swimming pool complex. Bar, restaurant, entertainment hall and outside terrace with large play area. Tennis. WiFi over site (charged). Off site: Beach 3.5 km. | From D168 Ploubalay-Plancoët road turn onto D786 towards Matignon and St Cast. Site is very well signed 1 km. after leaving Notre Dame de Guildo. GPS: 48.58475, -2.25656 |

**Open:** 14 May - 10 September.

**Charges guide**

| Per unit incl. 2 persons | |
|---|---|
| and electricity | € 22.00 - € 41.90 |

Camping Cheques accepted.

**FREE** Alan Rogers Travel Card
Extra benefits and savings - see page 10

## Saint Cast-le-Guildo
### Camping le Châtelet

Rue des Nouettes, F-22380 Saint Cast-le-Guildo (Côtes d'Armor) T: 02 96 41 96 33. E: chateletcp@aol.com

**alanrogers.com/FR22040**

Carefully developed over the years from a former quarry, le Châtelet is pleasantly and quietly situated with lovely views over the estuary from many pitches. It is well laid out, mainly in terraces with fairly narrow access roads. There are 216 good sized pitches separated by hedges, all with electricity and 112 with water and drainage. Some pitches are around a little lake (unfenced) which can be used for fishing. Used by three different tour operators (73 pitches). A 'green' walking area is a nice feature around the lower edge of the site and a path leads from the site directly down to a beach (about 200 m. but including steps). Saint Cast, 1 km. away to the centre, has a very long beach with many opportunities for sail-boarding and other watersports. The nearby towns of Dinan, Dinard and the old walled town of St. Malo are all within a comfortable distance for a day's excursion. The campsite has added a few well equipped Safari-style tents for hire.

### Facilities

Four toilet blocks with access at different levels include washbasins in cabins and facilities for children. Three small toilet blocks on the lower terraces. Some facilities are closed outside July/Aug. Motorcaravan services. Heated swimming and paddling pools. Shop for basics, takeaway, bar lounge and general room with satellite TV and pool table. 'Zen' room for rest, meditation and massage sessions (high season). Games room. Play area. Organised games and activities in season. Dancing (June, July and Aug). Off site: Beach 200 m. Bicycle hire, riding and golf within 1.5 km.

**Open:** 15 April - 13 September.

### Directions

Best approach is to turn off D786 road at Matignon towards St Cast; just inside St Cast limits turn left at sign for 'campings' and follow camp signs on the C90. GPS: 48.63723, -2.26934

### Charges guide

| Per unit incl. 2 persons | |
|---|---|
| and electricity | € 22.00 - € 42.00 |
| extra person | € 4.00 - € 7.00 |
| child (2-7 yrs) | € 3.00 - € 5.00 |
| dog | € 4.00 |

# CAMPING LE CHATELET ★★★★★

Campsite is situated on terraces, overlooking the sea. Direct access to hiking paths and to two beaches. Covered and heated swimming pool (telescopic roof). Fishing lake. Childrens playground, Wifi.

Openingdates : from the 15th of April until the 13th of September 2013

**CAMPING LE CHATELET ★★★★★ • Rue des Nouettes • 22380 Saint Cast le Guido**
Tél : +33 (0)2.96.41.96.33 • Mail : info@lechatelet.com • Web : www.lechatelet.com

## Saint Jouan-des-Guerets
### Camping le P'tit Bois

Saint Malo, F-35430 Saint Jouan-des-Guerets (Ille-et-Vilaine) T: 02 99 21 14 30.
E: camping.ptitbois@wanadoo.fr **alanrogers.com/FR35040**

On the outskirts of Saint Malo, this neat, family oriented site is very popular with British visitors, being ideal for one night stops or for longer stays in this interesting area. Le P'tit Bois provides 274 large level pitches with 114 for touring units. In two main areas, either side of the entrance lane, these are divided into groups by mature hedges and trees, separated by shrubs and flowers and with access from tarmac roads. Most have electrical hook-ups and over half have water taps. The site-owned mobile homes and chalets ensure that the facilities are open over a long season (if only for limited hours).

### Facilities

Two toilet blocks include washbasins in cabins. Baby baths. Laundry facilities. Simple facilities for disabled visitors. Motorcaravan services. Small shop, bar, snack bar with takeaway. TV and games rooms. Heated swimming pool, paddling pool and water slides (from 15/5). Heated indoor pool. Turkish baths and jacuzzi. Playground. Multisports court. Tennis. Minigolf. WiFi (free).

**Open:** 2 April - 11 September.

### Directions

St Jouan is west off St Malo-Rennes road (N137) outside St Malo. Site is signed from N137 (take 2nd exit for St Jouan on D4). GPS: 48.60993, -1.98665

### Charges guide

| Per unit incl. 2 persons | |
|---|---|
| and electricity | € 23.00 - € 41.00 |
| extra person | € 5.00 - € 8.00 |

For latest campsite news, availability and prices visit

# alanrogers.com

## Saint Lunaire
### Camping la Touesse

171 rue de la Ville Gehan, F-35800 Saint Lunaire (Ille-et-Vilaine) T: 02 99 46 61 13.
E: camping.la.touesse@wanadoo.fr **alanrogers.com/FR35060**

This family campsite was purpose built and has been developed since 1987 by Alain Clément who is keen to welcome more British visitors. Set just back from the coast road, 300 metres from a sandy beach, it is in a semi-residential area. It is, nevertheless, a pleasant, sheltered site with a range of trees and shrubs. Of the 141 level, grass pitches in bays, 90 are for touring units, all with electricity (5/10A). The plus factor of this site, besides its proximity to Dinard, is the fine sandy beach which is sheltered – so useful in early season – and safe for children. The owners speak English. There is a good choice of sandy beaches along the delightful Côte Eméraude. Buses run into Dinard with its wide range of shops, bars and restaurants. From here it is possible to take a sea bus across to Saint Malo.

**Facilities**

The central toilet block is well maintained, heated in low season with all modern facilities. Part of it may not be open outside July/Aug. Baby bath. Toilet for disabled campers. Laundry facilities. Motorcaravan service point. Shop for basics, pleasant bar/restaurant with TV and takeaway (all 1/4-20/9). Video games for children. Sauna. Bouncy castle. Bicycle hire. Internet access in reception. WiFi over site (charged). Off site: Buses 100 m. Sandy beach, fishing 300 m. Sailing 400 m. Riding 500 m. Golf 3 km. Shops, bars and restaurants nearby.

**Open:** 1 April - 30 September.

**Directions**

Saint Lunaire is 5 km. west of Dinard. From ferry terminal follow signs for Dinard. From other directions take D976/N176 and follow signs for Dinard. Turn west onto D168, then northwest onto D64 towards St Lunaire. Follow signs to campsite at La Fourberie east of town. GPS: 48.63084, -2.08418

**Charges guide**

| | |
|---|---|
| Per unit incl. 2 persons and electricity (10A) | € 19.80 - € 26.10 |
| extra person | € 3.90 - € 5.70 |
| child (under 7 yrs) | € 2.70 - € 3.00 |
| dog | € 1.50 |

Camping La Touesse

171 Rue de la ville Géhan • F-35800 SAINT LUNAIRE • campinglatouesse.com
camping.la.touesse@wanadoo.fr • Tel : 00 33 (0)299 46 61 13

At 300m from the beaches, in a quiet, friendly and greep environment, near Dinard and Saint Malo, campsite La Touesse at Saint Lunaire offers you mobile home rental, pitches, bar, restaurant, grocery's, take-away, evening entertainment and children's playground. Numerous marked bicycle routes and hiking trails GR34 allow you to discover our beautiful Brittany region.

## Saint Pierre-de-Quiberon
### Flower Camping l'Océan

16 avenue de Groix, B.P. 18 Kerhostin, F-56510 Saint Pierre-de-Quiberon (Morbihan) T: 02 97 30 91 29.
E: info@relaisdelocean.com **alanrogers.com/FR56470**

L'Océan is a member of the Flower group and can be found just 100 m. from the nearest beach, along the Quiberon peninsula. The site forms a part of a holiday complex that was established in 1925 and which also includes a large hostel. There are 275 pitches which are generally well shaded, although some sunnier pitches are also available. A selection of mobile homes and fully equipped tents are for rent. In peak season, a varied entertainment programme is on offer, including traditional Celtic folk evenings and magic shows, as well as discos and concerts. The site's bar/restaurant Ty Mouss is the focal point and specialises in pizzas and crêpes, as well as other light meals in high season.

**Facilities**

Sanitary facilities provide hot showers, but are a little dated. Facilities for disabled visitors. Laundry facilities. Motorcaravan services. Shop, bar/restaurant and takeaway (July/Aug). Multisports terrain. Fishing. Bicycle hire. Tennis. Bicycle hire. Canoe hire. Play area. TV/games room. Activities and entertainment. Mobile homes and equipped tents for rent. WiFi (charged). Off site: Beach 100 m. Riding 3 km. Golf 15 km. Cycle tracks.

**Open:** April - November.

**Directions**

Leave the N165 at the Quiberon exit and head south on the D768. Continue towards St Pierre-de-Quiberon, passing through Plouharnel. Site is located at Kerhostin and is signed to the right, before St Pierre. GPS: 47.534327, -3.139558

**Charges guide**

| | |
|---|---|
| Per unit incl. 2 persons and electricity | € 15.50 - € 24.50 |
| extra person | € 3.50 - € 5.00 |

**FREE** Alan Rogers Travel Card
Extra benefits and savings - see page 10

## Saint Malo
### Domaine de la Ville Huchet

Route de la Passagère, Quelmer, F-35400 Saint Malo (Ille-et-Vilaine) T: 02 99 81 11 83.
E: info@villehuchet.com  alanrogers.com/FR35050

Domaine de la Ville Huchet was taken over a few years ago by the owners of Camping Les Ormes (FR35020). It has been transformed into a superb site with modern facilities and lots of character. The pitches are well laid out and of generous size, most with 6A electricity and some with shade. They are set around an old manor house (disused) at the centre of the site. A splendid pool complex with its slides and pirate theme is particularly exciting for children, and alongside is a large, new, covered pool. A range of entertainment for young and old takes place in the spacious bar area and a new crêperie provides a range of food. This is a useful site, positioned on the edge of St Malo with easy access to the ferry terminal, old town and beaches. A bus service to take you into the town is 400 m. away.

### Facilities

The sanitary blocks are modern and clean. Facilities for disabled visitors. Shop. Bar, crêperie and snack bar. Aqua park with water slides (June-Aug). Covered pool (all season). Bicycle hire. Play area. Entertainment programme in peak season (including live bands). WiFi. Off site: Aquarium 700 m. Fishing 1.5 km. Riding 6 km. Golf 12 km. St Malo (beaches, ferry terminal and old town) 4 km.

**Open:** 10 April - 12 September.

### Directions

From St Malo take D137 towards Rennes. Take exit for St Jouan (D4) heading south. The site is well signed (2 km). GPS: 48.61507, -1.98782

### Charges guide

| Per unit incl. 2 persons | |
|---|---|
| and electricity | € 21.45 - € 33.50 |
| extra person | € 3.90 - € 6.40 |
| child (2-13 yrs) | € 2.55 - € 3.85 |
| dog | € 3.20 |

## Saint Pol-de-Léon
### Camping Ar Kleguer

Avenue de la Mer, F-29250 Saint Pol-de-Léon (Finistère) T: 02 98 69 18 81. E: info@camping-ar-kleguer.com
alanrogers.com/FR29040

Ar Kleguer is less than 20 minutes from the Roscoff ferry terminal in the heart of the Pays du Léon in north Finistère. One section of the site (used in high season) has a country feel and incorporates a small domestic animal park. The main section is divided into several areas, some on terraces at the edge of the sea with spectacular views overlooking the Bay of Morlaix. There are 182 large and well kept pitches, 122 for touring units, all with 10A electricity connections. This neat site is decorated with attractive flowers, shrubs and trees.

### Facilities

Three modern, tiled toilet blocks are well maintained and kept clean. Facilities for babies, children and disabled visitors. Laundry room. Shop, bar and takeaway (July/Aug). Good heated pool complex with paddling pools and slide (20/6-5/9). Pool table. Tennis. Bicycle hire. Animal park. Play area. Activities for children and some entertainment in high season. Beach adjacent with fishing and sailing. Free WiFi over part of site. Off site: Restaurant at site entrance. Sailing and boat launching 1 km. Riding 4 km. Golf 7 km.

**Open:** 8 April - 30 September.

### Directions

Saint-Pol is 18 km. northwest of Morlaix just off the D58 Morlaix-Roscoff road. Site is best approached from south, leaving D58 on the D769 signed Saint-Pol Littoral. Turn right at cemetery following signs for Plages et Port and campsites. Turn left along seafront to site at end. GPS: 48.69151, -3.96717

### Charges guide

| Per unit incl. 2 persons | |
|---|---|
| and electricity | € 20.20 - € 26.00 |
| extra person | € 4.20 - € 5.60 |
| child (2-7 yrs) | € 2.50 - € 3.80 |
| dog | € 2.20 - € 2.90 |

## Saint Quay-Portrieux

### Camping Bellevue

68 boulevard du Littoral, F-22410 Saint Quay-Portrieux (Côtes d'Armor) T: 02 96 70 41 84.
E: campingbellevue22@orange.fr  alanrogers.com/FR22230

With magnificent coastal views, this attractive and well cared for site lives up to its name. Family owned for many years, it is situated on the outskirts of the popular seaside resort of St Quay-Portrieux and you will be made to feel most welcome by the owners. The 173 numbered touring pitches vary in size and 140 have 6A electricity. Some are separated by hedges, whilst others are in groups of four. Entertainment on site is limited but there is plenty to do and see in the area and opportunities for exploring the Goëlo coast. Lazy hours could be spent gazing at the superb views of this spectacular part of the Brittany coast which can be seen from many of the Bellevue pitches. Further afield, a day's excursion could take you to Dinan, Dinard or the old walled town of St Malo. Some of the finest seafood can be found in this area of France.

#### Facilities

Two clean sanitary blocks provide both open and cubicled washbasins and controllable showers. Facilities for disabled visitors and babies. Laundry facilities. Motorcaravan service point. Shop for basics. Simple snack bar (1/7-31/8). Outdoor pool (1/6-18/9; no Bermuda shorts). Paddling pool. Volleyball. Boules. Play area. WiFi (free). Off site: Within walking distance of St Quay-Portrieux with shops, bars, restaurants and casino. Bicycle hire 1 km. Riding 8 km. Golf 10 km.

**Open:** 27 April - 15 September.

#### Directions

From N12 St Brieuc by-pass, take D786 north towards Paimpol. Site is well signed northwest of St Quay-Portrieux, 13 km. from the bypass. GPS: 48.66277, -2.84443

#### Charges guide

| | |
|---|---|
| Per unit incl. 2 persons and electricity | € 17.00 - € 22.10 |
| extra person | € 4.00 - € 5.40 |
| child (under 7 yrs) | € 3.00 - € 3.40 |
| dog | free |

# Camping Bellevue★★★

Exceptional view on the bay, lovely situated at the seaside. Direct access to small creek. Situated 800m from the village and the beaches through a nice hiking path (GR34)

Opening dates:
27 April till 15 September 2013

68 Boulevard du Littoral - 22410 Saint Quay Portrieux - tel: +33 296 704 184
fax: +33 296 705 546 - campingbellevue22@orange.fr - www.campingbellevue.net

## Sarzeau

### Lodge Club Presqu'île de Rhuys

Route d'Arzon, F-56370 Sarzeau (Morbihan) T: 02 97 41 29 93. E: info@lodgeclub.fr
alanrogers.com/FR56250

Lodge Club Presqu'île de Rhuys is a 13-hectare site close to the Gulf of Morbihan and the medieval towns of Vannes and Auray. It is divided into three main areas by trees. The larger area by the entrance was an orchard and some mature apple trees have been left to mark the touring pitches and provide some shade. The second area has a mixture of mobile homes and touring pitches divided into small groups by hedges. All the pitches are flat and of good size, and have electricity (10A). The third area is being developed for privately owned mobile homes. The converted farm building houses reception and a pleasant bar overlooking the swimming pool.

#### Facilities

Three toilet blocks, one fairly new, with some washbasins in cabins, baby rooms and facilities for disabled visitors. Washing machines and dryer. Motorcaravan service point. Shop (28/4-13/9). Bar and takeaway (23/5-31/8). Heated swimming and paddling pools (28/4-13/9). Games tent. TV room. Three play areas. Children's club (1/7-31/8). Bicycle hire. WiFi (charged). Off site: Supermarket and town centre 2 km. Bicycle hire and riding 2 km. Fishing and sailing 3 km. Beach and golf 6 km. Local markets daily.

**Open:** 28 April - 21 September.

#### Directions

East of Vannes on the N165, join the D780 towards Sarzeau. Bypass Sarzeau, keeping on D780, following signs to Arzon. Take third exit at new roundabout (Le Bohat) after 2 km. and site is 300 m. on right. GPS: 47.5225, -2.797067

#### Charges guide

| | |
|---|---|
| Per unit incl. 2 persons and electricity | € 21.50 - € 34.30 |
| extra person | € 3.50 |
| child (3-13 yrs) | € 5.20 |

**FREE** Alan Rogers Travel Card
Extra benefits and savings - see page 10

## Sarzeau

### Camping la Ferme de Lann-Hoëdic

Rue Jean de la Fontaine, F-56370 Sarzeau (Morbihan) T: 02 97 48 01 73. E: contact@camping-lannhoedic.fr
**alanrogers.com/FR56200**

Camping la Ferme de Lanne-Hoëdic is an attractively landscaped site with many flowering shrubs and trees. The 108 touring pitches, all with electricity (10A) are large and mostly level, with maturing trees which offer some shade. The 20 pitches with mobile homes are in a separate area. The working farm produces cereal crops and the summer months are an interesting time for children to see the harvest in progress. Mireille and Tim, the owners, go out of their way to make this a welcoming and happy place to stay. Located in the countryside on the Rhuys Peninsula, Golfe du Morbihan, it is an ideal base for cycling, walking and water-based activities. Since Camping la Ferme de Lann-Hoëdic opened in 2002, it has developed into one of the prettiest campsites in the Morbihan region of France. A visitor remarked that it is like 'camping in a garden'. Ecology is taken very seriously with solar panels for water heating and a composting system that you are encouraged to use for any waste food.

**Facilities**

Two high quality toilet blocks with facilities for disabled visitors and babies. Washing machines and dryers. Bread delivery. Ice creams and soft drinks available at reception. Takeaway and traditional Breton 'soirées' (high season). Bicycle hire. Playground with modern well designed equipment. Pétanque. Internet access and free WiFi. Off site: Beach, fishing and boating 800 m. Sarzeau 2 km. Riding 4 km. Golf 6 km.

**Open:** 1 April - 31 October.

**Directions**

East of Vannes on the N165, join the D780 towards Sarzeau. Exit D780 at the Super U roundabout south of Sarzeau, following signs for Le Roaliguen. Campsite is signed. GPS: 47.50745, -2.76092

**Charges guide**

| | |
|---|---|
| Per unit incl. 2 persons and electricity | € 16.10 - € 21.00 |
| extra person | € 3.60 - € 4.80 |

No credit cards.
Camping Cheques accepted.

★★★
The comfort of a 3-star campsite, the charm of a country setting.

Rue Jean de la Fontaine - 56370 Sarzeau   Tél : +33 297 48 01 73   www.camping-lannhoedic.fr

---

## Taden

### Camping International la Hallerais

4 rue de la Robardais, F-22100 Taden (Côtes d'Armor) T: 02 96 39 15 93. E: camping.la.hallerais@wanadoo.fr
**alanrogers.com/FR22060**

La Hallerais has a lot more to offer than most municipal sites. It is ideally located for exploring this fascinating area and is a short run from Saint Malo and from the resorts of the Côte d'Armor. It is just outside the attractive old medieval town of Dinan, beyond and below the little harbour on the River Rance. There is a pleasant riverside walk to the port and up into the town. Of the 226 pitches, 107 are for touring, all with electricity (6A), water and drainage, and are mainly on level, shallow terraces, with trees and hedges giving a park-like atmosphere. The friendly and helpful staff speak excellent English.

**Facilities**

Two good quality toilet blocks (one refurbished) are heated in cool weather. Pushbutton showers and washbasins in cubicles and some spacious cabins with shower and washbasin. Unit for disabled visitors. Launderette. Shop. Bar/restaurant with terrace and takeaway. Swimming and paddling pools (1/6-30/9). Tennis. Minigolf. Games room with TV room above. Play area. Fishing. Mobile homes for rent. Free Internet and WiFi. Off site: Riding 2 km. Restaurants and bars at port 3 km. Dinan 4 km.

**Open:** 10 March - 11 November.

**Directions**

Dinan is due south of Saint Malo (32 km. by road). From N176 (Avranches/Saint Brieuc) take Taden exit north of Dinan, turn towards Taden and follow blue signs to site. Do not attempt Dinan centre. GPS: 48.47148, -2.02284

**Charges guide**

| | |
|---|---|
| Per unit incl. 2 persons and electricity | € 16.10 - € 20.30 |
| extra person | € 3.30 - € 3.90 |

For latest campsite news, availability and prices visit
# alanrogers.com

## Taupont
### Camping la Vallée du Ninian

Le Rocher, F-56800 Taupont (Morbihan) T: 02 97 93 53 01. E: infos@camping-ninian.fr
**alanrogers.com/FR56160**

Murielle and Stéphane Veaux have recently acquired this peaceful family run site in central Brittany from a former farm and they continue to make improvements to ensure that their visitors have an enjoyable holiday. The level site falls into three areas – the orchard with 85 large, hedged touring pitches with electricity (3-10A), the wood with about 13 pitches more suited to tents, and the meadow by the river providing a further 35 pitches delineated by small trees and shrubs, with electricity. The bar has as its centrepiece: a working cider press with which Stéphane makes his own 'potion magique'.

#### Facilities

A central building houses unisex toilet facilities including washbasins in cubicles, large cubicle with facilities for disabled visitors and laundry area with washing machines, dryer and ironing board. Shop (1/4-30/9) selling bread. Bar and takeaway (1/7-31/8). Small (7x12 m) heated swimming pool and children's pool with slide and fountain (1/5-15/9). Swings, slides and large trampoline. Boules. Trout fishing (permits from office). Free WiFi over site. Off site: Riding 2 km. Golf 5 km. Bicycle hire 7 km.

**Open:** 30 March - 30 September.

#### Directions

From Ploërmel follow signs to Taupont north on N8. Continue through Taupont and turn left (east) signed Vallée du Ninian. Follow road for 3 km. to site on left. From Josselin follow signs for Hellean. Through village, sharp right after river Ninian bridge. Site is 400 m. on right. GPS: 47.96931, -2.47014

#### Charges guide

| Per unit incl. 2 persons | |
| --- | --- |
| and electricity | € 14.15 - € 20.10 |
| extra person | € 3.40 - € 4.50 |

Credit cards accepted in July/Aug. only.

## Telgruc-sur-Mer
### Camping le Panoramic

Route de la Plage-Penker, F-29560 Telgruc-sur-Mer (Finistère) T: 02 98 27 78 41.
E: info@camping-panoramic.com **alanrogers.com/FR29080**

This medium sized, traditional site is situated on quite a steep, ten-acre hillside with fine views. It is personally run by M. Jacq and his family who all speak good English. The 200 pitches are arranged on flat, shady terraces, in small groups with hedges and flowering shrubs, and 20 pitches have services for motorcaravans. Divided into two parts, the main upper site is where most of the facilities are located, with the swimming pool, its terrace and a playground located with the lower pitches across the road. Some up-and-down walking is therefore necessary, but this is a small price to pay for such pleasant and comfortable surroundings. This area provides lovely coastal footpaths. The sandy beach and a sailing school at Trez-Bellec-Plage are a 700 m. walk. A Sites et Paysages member.

#### Facilities

The main site has two well kept toilet blocks with another very good block opened for main season across the road. All three include showers, washbasins in cubicles, facilities for disabled visitors, baby baths, plus laundry facilities. Motorcaravan services. Small shop (1/7-31/8). Refurbished bar/restaurant with takeaway (1/7-31/8). Barbecue area. Heated pool, paddling pool and jacuzzi (1/6-15/9). Playground. Games and TV rooms. Tennis. Bicycle hire. WiFi. Off site: Beach and fishing 700 m. Riding 6 km. Golf 14 km. Sailing school nearby.

**Open:** 1 May - 15 September.

#### Directions

Site is just south of Telgruc-sur-Mer. On D887 pass through Ste Marie du Ménez Horn. Turn left on D208 signed Telgruc-sur-Mer. Continue straight on through town and site is on right within 1 km. GPS: 48.22409, -4.37186

#### Charges guide

| Per unit incl. 2 persons | |
| --- | --- |
| and electricity (10A) | € 26.50 |
| extra person | € 5.00 |
| child (under 7 yrs) | € 3.00 |
| dog | € 3.00 |

## Tredrez-Locquémeau
### Camping les Capucines

Kervourdon, F-22300 Tredrez-Locquémeau (Côtes d'Armor) T: 02 96 35 72 28. E: les.capucines@wanadoo.fr
**alanrogers.com/FR22010**

A warm welcome awaits at this beautifully kept, family-run site, quietly situated about a kilometre from the village of Saint-Michel-en-Grève with its good, sandy beach and close to Locquémeau, a pretty fishing village. There are 106 pitches on terraces or on slightly sloping ground, separated by hedges, with mature trees providing shade in places; 69 have electricity, water and drainage, 20 are more suitable for tents and there are 16 chalets and mobile homes for hire including a luxury model with its own hot tub. A pleasant bar overlooks the modern swimming pool. A good value restaurant/crêperie can be found at Trédrez and other bars and restaurants at Saint-Michel, while Locquémeau has a delightful Café du Port and an up-market restaurant There are numerous towns and villages along this stretch of coastline, so there is a good choice of markets, shops and supermarkets. The nearest big towns are Lannion, just ten kilometres northeast, and Morlaix, 28 km. southwest.

### Facilities
Two traditional toilet blocks, clean and very well kept, include controllable showers, washbasins mainly in cabins and facilities for babies and disabled campers. Laundry. Small shop for essentials (bread to order). Takeaway, bar with TV and games room. New covered and heated swimming pool. Paddling pool. Playground. Bouncy giraffe. Minigolf. Multisports court. Aviaries. Electric barbecues are not permitted. Chalets and mobile homes to rent. WiFi over site (charged). Off site: Restaurants, bicycle hire, beach and fishing within 2 km. Riding 3 km.

**Open:** 23 March - 21 September.

### Directions
Site is just off D786 Lannion/Morlaix road. From Morlaix turn left on bend on hill 1 km. after Saint-Michel then sharp right to site.
GPS: 48.69274, -3.55663

### Charges guide

| | |
|---|---|
| Per unit incl. 2 persons and electricity | € 18.00 - € 27.00 |
| extra person | € 4.00 - € 5.50 |
| child (under 7 yrs) | € 2.90 - € 3.60 |
| dog | € 2.00 |

## Vannes
### Camping du Haras

5 rue de Kersimon, Vannes-Meucon, F-56250 Monterblanc (Morbihan) T: 02 97 44 66 06.
E: contact@campingvannes.com **alanrogers.com/FR56150**

Close to Vannes and the Golfe du Morbihan in southern Brittany, le Haras is a small, family run, rural site that is open all year. There are 140 pitches, in a variety of settings, both open and wooded, the pitches are well kept and of a good size, all with electricity (4-16A) and most with water and drainage. Whilst M. Danard intends keeping the site quiet and in keeping with its rural setting, he provides plenty of activities for lively youngsters, including some organised games and evening parties. Adults will enjoy the new wellness area with indoor pool, spa, sauna and hammam. The beaches are 25 km. away.

### Facilities
The two modern toilet blocks (heated in winter) provide a few washbasins in cabins and controllable showers. Facilities for babies and disabled visitors. Laundry facilities. No shop but basics are kept in the bar. Bar with snacks (May-Oct). Takeaway (July/Aug). Swimming pool with waves and slide (1/5-31/10). Play area. Animal park. Trampoline. Minigolf. Bicycle hire. Organised activities (high season). Free WiFi in reception and bar (charged over site). Off site: Riding 400 m. Beach 15 km. Golf 25 km.

**Open:** All year.

### Directions
From Vannes on N165 take exit signed Pontivy and airport on the D767. Follow signs for airport and Meucon. Turn right on the D778, follow airport and yellow campsite signs. GPS: 47.730477, -2.72801

### Charges guide

| | |
|---|---|
| Per unit incl. 2 persons and electricity (10A) | € 14.00 - € 31.00 |
| extra person | € 4.00 - € 5.00 |
| child (0-7 yrs) | € 2.00 - € 3.00 |

For latest campsite news, availability and prices visit
**alanrogers.com**

## Trélévern
### RCN Camping de Port l'Epine

Venelle de Pors Garo, F-22660 Trélévern (Côtes d'Armor) T: 02 96 23 71 94. E: portlepine@rcn.fr
**alanrogers.com/FR22130**

Port l'Epine is a very pretty site in a unique situation on a promontory with direct access to the sea, and with superb views across the bay to Perros Guirec. The site is now part of the Dutch RCN group and is managed by a very enthusiastic young couple who are keen to ensure that all visitors enjoy their stay. There are 101 pitches for touring units, all on closely mown, level grass with electricity (16A). They are well defined and separated by attractive hedging and trees. There are 47 mobile homes for rent. This site is ideal for families with young children, though not necessarily for teenagers looking for lots to do! On the north side of the promontory is a little port facing an archipelago of seven small islands. It is a charming spot – you can sail or swim from both sides. The site's own beach has rock pools, a jetty and a slipway for small boats or fishing. As an added attraction, the site has its own small heated pool. The area is ideal for walking and cycling, and from Perros-Guirec you can take boat trips out to the islands.

### Facilities

The original toilet block is well equipped and a second block has been refurbished in modern style with thermostatically controllable showers and washbasins in cubicles. Baby room. Facilities for disabled visitors. Modern launderette. Shop, bar, restaurant with takeaway, small heated swimming pool and paddling pool (all open all season). Fenced play area near the bar/restaurant. Activity programme. Fishing and boat launching. Free WiFi in bar (charged over site). Off site: Bicycle hire 2 km. Sailing 5 km. Golf 15 km. Useful small supermarket up hill from site. Many coastal paths. Perros-Guirec 10 km.

**Open:** 22 April - 28 September.

### Directions

Trélévern is 14 km. northeast of Lannion. From D778 turn east at roundabout south of Perros-Guirec, take D6 towards Tréguier. After Louannec, turn left on D38 for Trélévern. Go through village following camping signs – Port l'Epine is clearly marked and opposite municipal site. GPS: 48.81311, -3.38598

### Charges guide

| Per unit incl. 2 persons | |
|---|---|
| and electricity | € 20.70 - € 48.65 |
| extra person | € 2.60 - € 5.10 |
| child (2-11 yrs) | € 3.00 - € 5.00 |
| dog | € 3.50 - € 5.00 |

**RCN Port l'Epine**
**Camping - Mobile homes - Chalets**
2013

Perfectly located in Bretagne on the Côte de Granit Rose; gorgeous view of the sea from your own spot at RCN Port L'Epine.

www.rcn.fr - 0033 296 237 194 - portlepine@rcn.fr

## Vannes
### Flower Camping de Conleau

188 avenue Maréchal Juin, F-56000 Vannes (Morbihan) T: 02 97 63 13 88.
E: camping.conleau@flowercampings.com **alanrogers.com/FR56410**

This well maintained site on the edge of the Gulf of Morbihan in southern Brittany has been recently acquired by the Flower group and is being upgraded to a high standard. It is divided into three areas: one for new mobile homes, one for ready erected tents, and the third for tourers with hardstandings available for larger motorcaravans. The 216 pitches are grassy, some slightly sloping, and many have views over the Morbihan. The new bar and restaurant has a patio that overlooks the covered swimming pool. A bus that stops outside the site entrance will take you to Vannes town centre.

### Facilities

Three well positioned sanitary blocks provide very good modern facilities and are kept very clean. Separate laundry room. Bar/restaurant (July/Aug). New covered pool. TV/games room with pool tables and electronic games. Bicycle hire. Bouncy castle. Children's club and evening entertainment. Off site: Bus stop nearby. Small seawater swimming pool and beach 500 m. Boat trips 500 m. Town centre 3 km. Cinema 4 km.

**Open:** 1 April - 30 September.

### Directions

From N165 Vannes-Lorient dual carriageway, take any of the four exits south towards Vannes town centre. Site well signed, as is the Port of Conleau, where site is located. GPS: 47.63365, -2.78008

### Charges guide

| Per unit incl. 2 persons | |
|---|---|
| and electricity | € 16.00 - € 24.00 |
| extra person | € 3.50 - € 4.50 |

**FREE** Alan Rogers Travel Card
Extra benefits and savings - see page 10

A striking area whose beauty lies not only in the landscape. Famed for its seafood and Celtic tradition, certain areas of Normandy remain untouched and wonderfully old fashioned.

**DÉPARTEMENTS: 14 CALVADOS, 27 EURE, 50 MANCHE, 61 ORNE, 76 SEINE MARITIME**

**MAJOR CITIES: CAEN AND ROUEN**

Normandy has a rich landscape full of variety. From the wild, craggy granite coastline of the northern Cotentin to the long sandy beaches and chalk cliffs of the south. It also boasts a superb coastline including the Cotentin Peninsula, cliffs of the Côte d'Albâtre and the fine beaches and fashionable resorts of the Côte Fleurie. Plus a wealth of quiet villages and unspoilt countryside for leisurely exploration.

The history of Normandy is closely linked with our own. The famous Bayeux Tapestry chronicles the exploits of the Battle of Hastings and there are many museums, exhibitions, sites and monuments, including the Caen Memorial Museum, which commemorate operations that took place during the D-Day Landings of 1944.

Normandy is known as the dairy of France and its dishes often feature cream, butter, and fine cheeses such as Camembert and Pont l'Evêque. The cider route takes in the countryside and pretty villages of the Pays d'Auge, where Calvados, the distinctive apple brandy, and cider are produced.

### Places of interest

*Bayeux*: home to the famous tapestry; 15th-18th-century houses, cathedral, museums.

*Cherbourg*: La Cité de la Mer; Château des Ravalet; Thomas Henry Museum.

*Omaha Beach*: D-Day beaches, Landing site monuments, American Cemetery.

*Deauville*: seaside resort, horse racing centre.

*Giverny*: home of impressionist painter Claude Monet, Monet Museum.

*Honfleur*: picturesque port city with old town.

*Lisieux*: pilgrimage site, shrine of Ste Thérèse.

*Mont St-Michel*: world famous abbey on island.

*Rouen*: Joan of Arc Museum; Gothic churches, cathedrals, abbey, clock tower.

### Cuisine of the region

*Andouillette de Vire*: small chitterling (tripe) sausage.

*Barbue au cidre*: brill cooked in cider and Calvados.

*Douillon aux pommes à la Normande*: baked apples in pastry.

*Escalope (Vallée d'Auge)*: veal sautéed and flamed in Calvados with cream and apples.

*Teurgoule*: rice pudding with cinnamon.

*Tripes à la Mode de Caen*: stewed beef tripe with onions, carrots, leeks, garlic, cider and Calvados.

www.normandy-tourism.co.uk
info@normandie-tourisme.org
(0)2 32 33 79 00

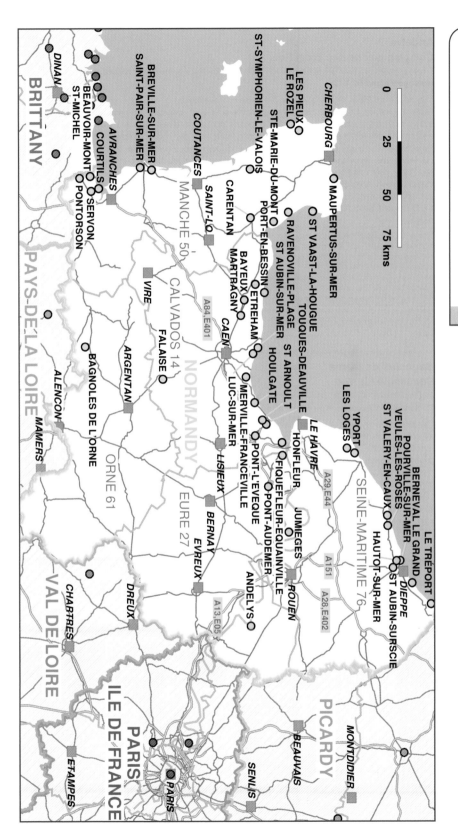

**FREE** Alan Rogers Travel Card
Extra benefits and savings - see page 10

## Andelys
### Camping de l'Ile des Trois Rois

1 rue Gilles Nicolle, F-27700 Andelys (Eure) T: 02 32 54 23 79. E: campingtroisrois@aol.com

**alanrogers.com/FR27070**

One hour from Paris, on the banks of the Seine and overlooked by the impressive remains of Château Gaillard (Richard Coeur de Lion), this attractive and very spacious ten-hectare site will appeal to everyone. There is easy access to the 108 touring pitches on level grass, in a well landscaped setting and all with electricity (6A), although some long leads may be required. Many of these back onto the River Seine where you can watch the barges, and most have views of the château. Of the 80 mobile homes on site, there are five to let, leaving lots of space to enjoy the surroundings, including the large lake full of perch and bream for those eager fishermen. Others can try their luck in the Seine. A nearby station will whisk you to Paris for the day, or a short drive will bring the delights of Monet's house and garden. A Medieval Festival is held in Les Andelys in the last weekend of June. Walk along the banks of the Seine and watch the passenger boats, or stroll into the main town for shopping and restaurants.

| Facilities | Directions |
|---|---|
| Four small, unheated toilet blocks have British style toilets (no seats), showers and washbasins, all in cubicles; One has facilities for disabled visitors, another has a laundry facility. Motorcaravan service point. Heated swimming and paddling pools (15/5-30/9). Bar and restaurant (1/4-30/9). Fenced play area. Evening entertainment (4/7-30/8). Bicycles and barbecues for hire. Satellite TV. Internet access and WiFi (charged). Adult open-air exercise area. Off site: Riding 5 km. Golf 9 km. Giverny 20 km. | Les Andelys is 40 km. southeast of Rouen. From the town centre, continue on D125 and follow signs until roundabout by bridge where second exit leads directly into site. GPS: 49.23564, 1.40005 |

**Open:** 15 March - 15 November.

**Charges guide**

| | |
|---|---|
| Per unit incl. 2 persons and electricity | € 21.00 |
| extra person | € 5.50 |
| child (under 3 yrs) | free |
| dog | € 2.00 |

## Bagnoles de l'Orne
### Camping de la Vée

5 rue du Président Coty, F-61140 Bagnoles-de-l'Orne (Orne) T: 02 33 37 87 45.
E: info@campingbagnolesdelorne.com  **alanrogers.com/FR61030**

Camping de la Vée is a pleasant municipal site in the town of Bagnoles de l'Orne, and is open for a long season (March to November). Pitches are large and grassy and are grouped around the two well maintained toilet blocks. Some 40 hardstandings are available for motorcaravan users. On-site amenities include a snack bar with special meal offers in peak season, a play area and free WiFi. A number of fully equipped mobile homes are for rent. Bagnoles is an important thermal spa centre and can be reached on the shuttle bus. The town's Bell Epoque quarter is deservedly famous, lined with fine villas with extravagant polychrome façades, influenced by the Art Deco style. Bagnoles is surrounded by the vast Andaines forest, which forms a part of the Parc Naturel Régional de Normandie Maine.

| Facilities | Directions |
|---|---|
| Snack bar. Play area. Free WiFi. Tourist information. Mobile homes for rent. Shuttle bus to spa. Off site: Shops, restaurants and spa in Bagnoles de l'Orne. Alençon. Walking and cycling tracks. | Approaching from the north (La Ferté Macé), head south on D916 to Bagnoles de l'Orne. The site is on the rue Auguste Gautier, to the south of the town centre and is well signed. GPS: 48.54778, -0.41983 |

**Open:** 9 March - 16 November.

**Charges guide**

| | |
|---|---|
| Per unit incl. 2 persons and electricity | € 14.35 - € 16.00 |
| extra person | € 7.20 - € 8.30 |

For latest campsite news, availability and prices visit
**alanrogers.com**

# L'Ile des Trois Rois

The park Ile des Trois Rois is situated in the most beautiful bend of the Seine nearby Castle Gaillard in Normandy and is a haven of peace. Paris is situated of less than an hour and Rouen is half an hour driving from the campsite.

Facilities:
- Two heated swimming pools
- Ping pong
- Camper service
- Bar eand restaurant (high season)
- Play Area

1, Rue Gilles Nicole - F-27700 Les Andelys - France
Tel. 0033 (0) 2 32 54 23 79 - Fax 0033 (0) 2 32 51 14 54
Email campingtroisrois@aol.com - www.camping-troisrois.com

## Bayeux
### Camping des Bords de l'Aure

Boulevard Eindhoven, F-14400 Bayeux (Calvados) T: 02 31 92 08 43. E: campingmunicipal@mairie-bayeux.fr
alanrogers.com/FR14020

Only a few kilometres from the coast and the landing beaches, this excellent site makes a very useful night stop on the way to or from Cherbourg, whether or not you want to see the tapestry at Bayeux. The 140 pitches are in two areas (many on hardstanding), well marked and generally of good size with electricity. The site is busy over a long season – early arrival is advised as reservations are not taken. Reception is open 08.00 to 12.30 and 14.00 to 19.00 (all day in July/August). There is no parking outside for tourers. There may be some road noise on one side of the site.

**Facilities**

The two good quality toilet blocks have British style WCs, washbasins in cabins in main block, and units for disabled visitors. Baby changing. Motorcaravan service point. Laundry room. Van calls with takeaway food (Mon-Fri eves). Bread to order. Two playgrounds. Reading room with TV. Games room. Five mobile homes to rent. Off site: Free admission to public indoor swimming pool adjacent to site. Supermarket nearby. Bayeux Tapestry, town centre 1 km. Riding 5 km. D-Day beaches 8 km.

**Open:** 16 April - 29 October.

**Directions**

On the northernmost point of the inner ring road (D613), just west of the junction to Arromanches (D516), the site is well signed in this area. GPS: 49.2839, -0.6976

**Charges guide**

| | |
|---|---|
| Per unit incl. 2 persons and electricity | € 16.20 |
| extra person | € 4.10 |
| child (under 7 yrs) | € 2.40 |
| dog | free |

## Beauvoir-Mont Saint-Michel
### Camping Caravaning Aux Pommiers

28 route du Mont Saint-Michel, F-50170 Beauvoir-Mont Saint-Michel (Manche) T: 02 33 60 11 36.
E: pommiers@aol.com  alanrogers.com/FR50120

This site changed hands in 2011 and, although little English is spoken, the resident owners offer a warm, friendly welcome at their quiet site in the small village of Beauvoir, just 4 km. from Mont St-Michel. The 70 well defined grass touring pitches, 50 with 10A electricity, are of a reasonable size, well maintained and level, although access to some of them may be difficult in very wet weather, particularly for larger units. Some are separated by hedges and there are trees providing some shade. The large fenced, heated swimming pool has a paved terrace and the bar serves takeaway food during July and August.

**Facilities**

Two clean, well equipped toilet blocks with free showers and British style WCs. Facilities for disabled visitors. Laundry facilities. Motorcaravan service point. Shop. Bar with TV and pool table. Takeaway food (July/Aug). Outdoor heated pool (15/6-15/9). Bicycle hire. Small play area. WiFi over site (charged). Chalet and mobile homes for hire. Off site: Fishing 500 m. Riding 2 km. Shops, bars and restaurants all within 4 km. Beach 5 km.

**Open:** 20 March - 11 November.

**Directions**

Beauvoir is 50 km. east of Saint Malo and 5 km. north of Pontorson. From the N175/N176 (E401), following signs for Mont St-Michel on the D976. Site is on right in the village of Beauvoir. GPS: 48.596344, -1.511725

**Charges guide**

| | |
|---|---|
| Per unit incl. 2 persons and electricity | € 18.90 - € 24.40 |
| extra person | € 4.40 - € 6.40 |

## Berneval-le-Grand
### Camping Municipal le Val Boise

Avenue du Capitaine Portheous, F-76370 Berneval-le-Grand (Seine-Maritime) T: 02 35 85 29 18.
E: camping-berneval@wanadoo.fr  alanrogers.com/FR76020

This pleasant, well run municipal site is located in a wooded valley running down from the village to the sea. The reception and a group of 14 larger pitches, a few occupied by seasonal caravans, are situated next to the road leading down to the sand and shingle beaches. There are also six attractive wooden chalets for hire. The remaining 16 touring pitches are on wooded terraces accessed via a steep slope. All pitches have 16A electricity but only a few have shade. Val Boisé is ideal for those seeking a simple, inexpensive site close to Dieppe, from which to explore this stretch of coast.

**Facilities**

Two well maintained toilet blocks provide free hot showers (pushbutton) and some washbasins in cubicles. Facilities for disabled visitors. Washing machine. Motorcaravan service point. Activities room. Small play area. Large field for kite flying and ball games. Children's activities and tournaments (July/Aug). Free WiFi over part of site. Bicycle hire. Off site: Beach and sea fishing 800 m. Boat launching 3 km. Riding 10 km. Golf 12 km. Fishing 15 km.

**Open:** 1 April - 1 November.

**Directions**

Berneval is 10 km. east of Dieppe. From A29 take N27 to Dieppe, turn east on ring road to join D925 towards Le Tréport. From ferry: after 2 km. turn east (D925). In 5 km. turn north (D54, Berneval le Grand). In village follow site signs. GPS: 49.96203, 1.19362

**Charges guide**

| | |
|---|---|
| Per unit incl. 2 persons and electricity | € 12.20 - € 13.45 |
| extra person | € 1.75 - € 2.25 |

For latest campsite news, availability and prices visit

# alanrogers.com

## Breville-sur-Mer
### Kawan Village la Route Blanche

6 la route Blanche, F-50290 Breville-sur-Mer (Manche) T: 02 33 50 23 31.
E: larouteblanche@camping-breville.com  **alanrogers.com/FR50150**

La Route Blanche has a bright and cheerful atmosphere and Philippe and Corinne, the owners, are working continually to make an excellent site even better. The 140 pitches for touring are average in size, numbered, on well cut grass and divided by young conifers. There are many shrubs and flowers and mature trees give shade to some areas. One hundred and eighteen pitches have 6/10A electricity and long leads may be necessary for some. Although the site does not have its own restaurant, there are five to choose from within a short distance. Three hundred and twenty square metres of swimming pool complex, with exceptional facilities for visitors with disabilities, will be enjoyed by all. If golf is your game, then you will not be disappointed. There is an 18-hole course and a nine-hole course only 400 m. away. The area has the highest tides in Europe and each visitor to the site is given a current tide timetable. The sandy beach is only 800 m. away and there are several walking routes waymarked through the dunes. Corinne cooks moules and frites a couple of times in the high season for site visitors and on-site entertainment is arranged during July and August. After 21.00 hours late arrivals are not accepted. WiFi is available all round the site.

### Facilities

Well maintained sanitary facilities with British style toilets, washbasins in cabins and showers. Good provision for disabled visitors. Laundry facilities. Bread available all season. Bar and takeaway (July/Aug). Large swimming pool complex. Play area. Multisports court. Entertainment in high season. WiFi (charged). Off site: Golf (opposite). Fishing 500 m. Riding 1 km. Shops, restaurants and supermarket at Donville-les-Bains 3 km. Boat trips to the Channel Islands and the Isles de Chausey from Granville. Mont St-Michel. Cruises on board old tall ships.

**Open:** 1 April - 30 September.

### Directions

Take D971 that runs between Granville and Coutance. Then one of the roads west to Breville-sur-Mer. Site is well signed.
GPS: 48.869658, -1.563873

### Charges guide

| Per unit incl. 2 persons | |
|---|---|
| and electricity | € 23.00 - € 34.00 |
| extra person | € 5.00 - € 7.00 |
| child (2-7 yrs) | free - € 4.80 |
| dog | € 2.50 - € 3.00 |

Camping Cheques accepted.

**FREE** Alan Rogers Travel Card
Extra benefits and savings - see page 10

## Carentan

### Flower Camping le Haut Dick

30 chemin du Grand Bas Pays, F-50500 Carentan (Manche) T: 02 33 42 16 89.
E: contact@camping-lehautdick.com **alanrogers.com/FR50240**

Le Haut Dick is located at the heart of the south Cotentin peninsula. On the banks of the Haut Dick canal, this is a simple campsite but offers all comforts required. It comprises 120 good sized pitches which are flat, grassy and well divided by hedges. The village of Carentan is a 10 minute walk away and features a brand new pool complex. Le Haut Dick is an ideal departure point for visiting the Landing Beaches, such as Omaha Beach, and Arromanches. The famous Mont Saint-Michel is also a short drive.

**Facilities**

Sanitary buildings include showers, baby rooms and facilities for disabled visitors. Washing machine. Snack bar. Minigolf. Play area. Boules courts. Accommodation to rent. Fishing.

**Open:** 28 March - 6 October.

**Directions**

Leave the A13 and follow the RN13 and then the E46 to Carentan. GPS: 49.309859, -1.238869

**Charges guide**

| Per unit incl. 2 persons | |
|---|---|
| and electricity | € 18.00 - € 25.00 |
| extra person | € 3.50 - € 4.50 |
| child (under 7 yrs) | € 3.00 - € 4.00 |
| dog | € 1.50 |

## Courtils

### Camping Saint Michel

35 route du Mont Saint-Michel, F-50220 Courtils (Manche) T: 02 33 70 96 90.
E: infos@campingsaintmichel.com **alanrogers.com/FR50110**

This delightful, quiet site is located in a peaceful, rural setting, yet is only 8 km. from the busy tourist attraction of Mont St-Michel. The site has 100 pitches which include 45 for touring units and 42 for mobile homes to rent. Electricity connections (6/10A) are available to all pitches and many trees and shrubs provide a good amount of shade. An excellent restaurant is adjacent to the welcoming reception and has a terrace overlooking the pool. The site slopes gently down to a small enclosure of farm animals kept to entertain children and adults alike. Here you can meet Nestor and Napoléon, the donkeys, and Linotte the mare, as well as miniature goats, sheep, chickens and ducks. The owners intend to maintain a quiet and peaceful site, hence there are no discos or organised clubs.

**Facilities**

Two small, well maintained toilet blocks have washbasins in cubicles and pushbutton showers. Separate laundry. Baby room. En-suite facilities for disabled visitors. Motorcaravan service point. Shop (all season) and bar (15/3-15/10). Restaurant and takeaway (7/6-7/9). Heated swimming pool (1/5-20/9). Animal farm. Play area. Games room. Bicycle hire. Internet access and WiFi (free) in reception area. Off site: Fishing (sea) 2 km, (river) 6 km. Beaches 2 km. and (for swimming) 30 km. Riding 9 km. Sailing 25 km. Golf 30 km.

**Open:** 22 February - 11 November.

**Directions**

Courtils is 8 km. east of Mont Saint-Michel. From south on A84 and from north on A84/N175 leave at exit 33/34 and follow signs for Mont Saint-Michel (N175/D43) and Courtils. From St Malo take D137 south and join N176 east to Pontorson where it becomes N175. In 12 km. turn northwest on D43 signed Courtils. Site is through village on left. GPS: 48.627616, -1.416

**Charges guide**

| Per unit incl. 2 persons | |
|---|---|
| and electricity | € 19.00 - € 25.00 |
| extra person | € 5.00 - € 7.00 |
| child (7-12 yrs) | € 2.00 - € 3.50 |
| dog | € 1.50 - € 2.50 |

For latest campsite news, availability and prices visit
**alanrogers.com**

## THE MERVILLE BATTERY

The Merville Battery, a German army strongpoint in the Atlantic Wall, was situated at the eastern flank of the allied invasion of 6 June 1944. Bombed ineffectively many times, it was neutralised by the British 9th Parachute Battalion after an incredible attack.

On this totally preserved historic site, an educational trail winds between the different bunkers and invites you to learn the story of the Merville Battery. Every 20 minutes, you can experience "total immersion". Sound, light smoke and odours will convey you for a few short minutes into the hell that was the bombardment and the attack on the Battery.

The 9th Battalion
The Parachute Regiment

MUSÉE DE LA BATTERIE DE MERVILLE
Place du 9è Bataillon
14810 MERVILLE-FRANCEVILLE
Tél : 02 31 91 47 53
E-mail : museebatterie@wanadoo.fr
Web : www.batterie-merville.com

## Etreham/Bayeux
### Camping la Reine Mathilde

Route de Sainte Honorine, F-14400 Etreham/Bayeux (Calvados) T: 02 31 21 76 55.
E: campingreinemathilde@gmail.com  **alanrogers.com/FR14300**

Camping la Reine Mathilde can be found at Etreham, close to the fine city of Bayeux, the D-Day beaches and the interesting fishing port of Port-en-Bessin. The site is in the grounds of a large stone farmhouse. The 76 touring pitches are grassy and of variable sizes. Most are equipped with electrical connections (6A). Fifty pitches are occupied by mobile homes, chalets and fully equipped bungalow-style tents, with 14 available for rent. The excellent Omaha Beach Golf Course (36 holes) is close at hand and Port-en-Bessin is an important centre for watersports. The cider and Calvados tastings are a must. Besides the Bayeux Tapestry and the invasion beaches, there is a great deal to see in the area.

**Facilities**

All main facilities are housed in a beautifully converted stone outbuilding fronted by a piazza with tables and chairs. These include separate male and female toilets, showers, washbasins in cabins, baby changing and facilities for disabled visitors. Laundry room. Motorcaravan services. Shop. Bar, snack bar and takeaway (all season). Heated swimming and paddling pool (1/6-15/9). Play area. Entertainment and activity programme (high season). Mobile homes and tents for rent. WiFi. Off site: Shops, bars, restaurants and watersports in Port-en-Bessin 4 km. Riding 3 km. Golf 4 km. Beaches 6 km. Bayeux 12 km.

**Open:** 1 April - 30 September.

**Directions**

Etreham can be found northwest of Bayeux. From there take the westbound N13 and leave shortly after Tour-en-Bessin, following signs to Etreham (D206). The site is well signed in the village. Continue through village to boundary sign, take first right and follow signs to campsite.
GPS: 49.331316, -0.802447

**Charges guide**

| Per unit incl. 2 persons | |
|---|---|
| and electricity | € 21.70 - € 23.80 |
| extra person | € 5.80 - € 6.50 |
| child (0-13 yrs) | € 2.60 - € 4.50 |

## Falaise
### Camping Municipal du Château

3 rue du Val d'Ante, F-14700 Falaise (Calvados) T: 02 31 90 16 55. E: camping@falaise.fr
**alanrogers.com/FR14100**

The location of this site is really quite spectacular, lying in the shadow of the Château of William the Conqueror, within walking distance of the historic town of Falaise in the Coeur de Normandie. The site itself is small, with only 66 pitches (most with electricity) either beside the little river, on a terrace above or on gently sloping ground. With trees and hedges providing some shade as well as open grassed areas, this site has a rather intimate, up-market feel about it, different from the average municipal site. Charges are reasonable and the reception friendly.

**Facilities**

Although the sanitary facilities are dated, they are of good quality and kept clean. Free hot water to showers, washbasins in cubicles for the ladies and laundry and dishwashing sinks (all closed overnight). Unit for disabled visitors (shower room and separate WC). Motorcaravan service point. Excellent play area for younger children. Tennis courts and boules pitch. TV room. Fishing. Free WiFi access. Off site: Bicycle hire 300 m. Riding 500 m. Tree-top adventure park 17 km. Kayak club with canoe hire and river descent 19 km.

**Open:** 1 May - 30 September.

**Directions**

Falaise is 35 km. southeast of Caen. Site on western side of town, well signed from ring road. From N158 heading south take first roundabout into Falaise and follow signs through residential suburb to site. These roads become one way and 0.6 km. from where you turn into the suburb, there is a 180° left-hand turn downwards. GPS: 48.89556, -0.20468

**Charges guide**

| Per unit incl. 2 persons and electricity | € 16.60 |
|---|---|
| extra person | € 3.80 |
| child (3-12 yrs) | € 2.70 |

**FREE** Alan Rogers Travel Card
Extra benefits and savings - see page 10

## Fiquefleur-Equainville
### Camping du Domaine Catinière

Route de Honfleur, F-27210 Fiquefleur-Equainville (Eure) T: 02 32 57 63 51. E: info@camping-catiniere.com
**alanrogers.com/FR27020**

This is a peaceful, rural site, close to the Normandy coast and the pretty harbour town of Honfleur, where you are assured of a friendly welcome from the resident owners. There are 130 pitches, 90 for tourers, all with 4-13A electricity. Some have shade, while others are more open. There are 20 mobile homes and a thatched cottage (sleeps 4) for rent. A large, open field houses the tents and other units not requiring electricity. Well fenced streams run through the site. Improvements are being steadily made, and this is an ideal base for exploring this part of Normandy. A Sites et Paysages member.

**Facilities**

A simple, modern toilet block contains mostly British style WCs, hot showers, some washbasins in cubicles, and facilities for disabled visitors and babies. Laundry facilities. Reception with small shop. Bar/restaurant. Heated swimming pool with slides and flume (1/6-15/9). Two playgrounds. Trampoline. Children's farm. Boules. Barrier (card deposit). WiFi throughout (charged). Off site: Large supermarket nearby, smaller one in Beuzeville 7 km. Riding 4 km. Bicycle hire 6 km. Beach 7 km. Golf 15 km.

**Open:** 6 April - 18 September.

**Directions**

From Pont de Normandie (toll bridge) take first exit on leaving bridge (exit 3, A29) signed Honfleur. At roundabout turn left under motorway in direction of Le Mans and Alencon on D180. Take second exit on right after 2.5 km, onto D22 towards Beuzeville. Site is on right after 1 km. GPS: 49.40090, 0.30608

**Charges guide**

| | |
|---|---|
| Per unit incl. 2 persons and electricity | € 20.00 - € 28.50 |
| Credit cards accepted (minimum of € 70). | |

## Hautot-sur-Mer
### Camping la Source

Petit Appeville, F-76550 Hautot-sur-Mer (Seine-Maritime) T: 02 35 84 27 04. E: info@camping-la-source.fr
**alanrogers.com/FR76040**

This friendly, attractive site with a new heated pool is just four kilometres from Dieppe and is useful for those using the Newhaven-Dieppe ferry crossing, either as a one night stopover or for a few days' break before heading on. The 120 pitches (54 with electricity 10A) are flat and there is some shade. There are good hardstandings for motorcaravans. The site is quietly located in a valley with the only disturbance from the occasional passing train. A fast-flowing small river runs along one border (not protected for young children). There are opportunities for fishing, rowing and canoeing.

**Facilities**

A good, clean single toilet block (men left, ladies right) includes washbasins in cubicles and mainly British style WCs. Unit for disabled visitors (unmade gravel roads may cause problems). Laundry facilities. Motorcaravan service point. Small bar and terrace. Swimming pool. Playing field. TV and games rooms. Fishing. Bicycle hire. Mobile homes (3) for rent. WiFi throughout (charged). Off site: Baker in the village. Riding 2 km. Beach 3 km. Golf 4 km.

**Open:** 15 March - 15 October.

**Directions**

From Dieppe follow D925 west to Fécamp. At foot of descent at traffic lights in Petit Appeville turn left. From west, turn right (D153 St Aubin). Just after railway, left under bridge and ahead on narrow road. Site is shortly on left. GPS: 49.89846, 1.05694

**Charges guide**

| | |
|---|---|
| Per unit incl. 2 persons and electricity | € 20.70 - € 23.70 |
| Camping Cheques accepted. | |

## Honfleur
### Camping la Briquerie

Equemauville, F-14600 Honfleur (Calvados) T: 02 31 89 28 32. E: info@campinglabriquerie.com
**alanrogers.com/FR14180**

La Briquerie is a large, neat municipal site on the outskirts of the attractive and popular harbour town of Honfleur. Very well cared for and efficiently run by a family team, the site has 420 pitches, many of which are let on a seasonal basis. There are also 130 medium to large, hedged touring pitches. All have electricity (5/10A), water and drainage. Among the main attractions here are the splendid swimming complex with indoor and outdoor pools, and the close proximity to Honfleur where one can watch the fishing boats from the quay. The D-Day landing beaches are within reach.

**Facilities**

The sanitary facilities were completely renovated in 2011. Good facilities for disabled visitors. Laundry facilities. Restaurant (July/Aug). Takeaway (1/6-15/9). Bar (1/6-30/9). Small shop (July/Aug). Large pool complex (7/4-30/9). Sauna. Jacuzzi. Fitness room. Boules. Minigolf. Astroturf multisports pitch. TV. WiFi throughout. Off site: Supermarket 100 m. Town 2 km. Beach 2.5 km.

**Open:** 31 March - 30 September.

**Directions**

Site is well signed from Honfleur on the D579, beside the Intermarché on the D62. GPS: 49.39735, 0.20849

**Charges guide**

| | |
|---|---|
| Per unit incl. 2 persons, electricity, water and drainage | € 21.00 - € 31.00 |
| No credit cards. | |

For latest campsite news, availability and prices visit
# alanrogers.com

## Houlgate
### Yelloh! Village la Vallee

88 route de la Vallée, F-14510 Houlgate (Calvados) T: 02 31 24 40 69. E: camping.lavallee@wanadoo.fr
**alanrogers.com/FR14070**

Camping de la Vallée is an attractive site with good, well maintained facilities, situated on the rolling hillside above the seaside resort of Houlgate. The original farmhouse building has been converted to house a bar/brasserie and a TV lounge and billiards room overlooking the pool. The site has 372 pitches with 170 for touring units. Large, open and separated by hedges, all the pitches have 6A electricity and some also have water and drainage. Part of the site is sloping, the rest level, with gravel or tarmac roads. Shade is provided by a variety of well kept trees and shrubs. (No arrivals 12.00-14.00 in low season).

**Facilities**

Three good toilet blocks include washbasins in cabins, mainly British style toilets, facilities for disabled visitors and baby bathrooms. Laundry facilities (no washing lines allowed). Motorcaravan services. Shop (from 1/5). Bar. Snack bar with takeaway in season (from 1/5). Heated swimming pool (1/4-31/10; no Bermuda shorts). Games room. Playground. Bicycle hire. Volleyball, football, tennis, pétanque. Entertainment in Jul/Aug. WiFi (charged). Only one dog per pitch. Off site: Riding 500 m. Town, golf, beach and fishing, all 1 km.

**Open:** 1 April - 4 November.

**Directions**

From A13 take exit for Cabourg and follow D400 to Dives-sur-Mer, then D513 (Hougate/Deauville) as far as seafront. After 1 km. at lights go straight on direction 'centre ville'. Just before street in main centre turn right, folllow site sign to town hall's roundabout then straight, past tourist office on left, then first right. Site in 1 km. GPS: 49.2940, -0.0683

**Charges guide**

| | |
|---|---|
| Per unit incl. 2 persons and electricity | € 21.00 - € 34.00 |
| Credit card minimum € 50. | |

## Jumièges
### Camping de la Forêt

Rue Mainberthe, F-76480 Jumièges (Seine-Maritime) T: 02 35 37 93 43. E: info@campinglaforet.com
**alanrogers.com/FR76130**

This is a pretty family site with a friendly, relaxed atmosphere. It is located just 10 km. from the A13 Paris-Caen autoroute. Cars and smaller motorcaravans can approach by ferry across the River Seine (not caravans). Formerly a municipal site, it has recently been taken over by the Hoste family. The 111 grassy pitches (84 for tourers) are attractively located in woodland. Many pitches have some shade and all have 10A electrical connections. There is a separate area for tents. The site organises some activities in high season including treasure hunts and guided walks. Chalets and mobile homes to let.

**Facilities**

Two modern toilet blocks maintained to a good standard with some basins in cubicles and preset showers. Baby room. Facilities for disabled visitors. Laundry facilities. Motorcaravan service point. Shop. Pizzas (Fri/Sat evenings). Small swimming pool and paddling pool (heated 1/6-15/9). Playground. Boules. Games room with TV. Bicycle hire. Off site: Bar/restaurant 600 m. Rouen 20 km. Riding and golf 8 km.

**Open:** 11 April - 25 October.

**Directions**

From A29, exit 8, follow Yvetot-Pont de Brotonne. Before bridge, turn left and follow Le Trait and Jumièges. Site signed. GPS: 49.43487, 0.82897

**Charges guide**

| | |
|---|---|
| Per unit incl. 2 persons and electricity | € 21.00 - € 23.50 |
| extra person | € 4.50 |
| Camping Cheques accepted. | |

## Le Rozel
### Camping le Ranch

La Mielle, F-50340 Le Rozel (Manche) T: 02 33 10 07 10. E: contact@camping-leranch.com
**alanrogers.com/FR50230**

Le Ranch is a pleasantly situated, family run site with direct access to a long and wide sandy beach that extends to some 3 km. The reception area is well presented and has a small shop that stocks all the basic provisions. An outdoor pool complex has a large heated pool, paddling pool and a small separate pool with water slides. Access to site is controlled by a magnetic key, which is also used to activate the showers in the splendid sanitary block. The 72 touring pitches are large and well defined by small hedges; some are on raised terraces but are easily accessed. All have 10A electricity.

**Facilities**

One modern, clean and heated toilet block. Sinks in closed cabins and showers operated by barrier entry key. Baby changing area. Facilities for disabled visitors. Laundry facilities. Shop for basics. Bar with TV. Pizzeria. Covered games area. Outdoor pool complex. Indoor pool. Play area. Exercise machines. Boules. TV in bar. Barbecue areas. WiFi (charged). Off site: Restaurant by entrance.

**Open:** 1 April - 30 September.

**Directions**

Heading to or from Cherbourg on D650, 3 km. south of Les Pieux take D62 signed Le Rozel. D62 leads directly to the site which is well signed. GPS: 49.480199, -1.842055

**Charges guide**

| | |
|---|---|
| Per unit incl. 2 persons and electricity | € 22.00 - € 35.00 |

**FREE** Alan Rogers Travel Card
Extra benefits and savings - see page 10

## Le Tréport

### Camping Municipal les Boucaniers

Rue Pierre Mendès France, F-76470 Le Tréport (Seine-Maritime) T: 02 35 86 35 47.
E: camping@ville-le-treport.fr **alanrogers.com/FR76110**

This is a large, good quality, modern municipal site. It has an attractive floral entrance, tarmac roads and easy access to pitches. The 193 touring pitches (176 with electricity 6A: some long leads necessary) are on level grass, some with dividing hedges, and trees to provide a little shade. There are 50 good quality wooden chalets for rent, and some privately owned mobile homes. A small unit acts as shop, bar and takeaway all season. The baker calls daily in high season, and every day except Wednesday in low season. The town centre is within walking distance with a choice of many good seafood restaurants. The resort is popular with the French, and has been so for more than a century.

**Facilities**

Three well equipped sanitary blocks (the larger one can be heated) provide mainly British style WCs, washbasins in cubicles, preset hot showers, with facilities for small children and disabled visitors in one block. Multisport court. Minigolf. Boules. Max. 2 dogs. Motorcaravan parking and services adjacent (€ 5.00) Off site: Tennis, football and gymnasium nearby. Fishing, golf and beach 2 km. Riding 3 km. Markets at Le Tréport (Mon and Sat) and at Eu (Fri).

**Open:** 1 April - 30 September.

**Directions**

From D925 Abbeville-Dieppe road take D1915 towards Le Tréport centre. At new roundabout take first exit to right and site entrance is 150 m. on the right in rue Pierre Mendès-France.
GPS: 50.05772, 1.38870

**Charges guide**

| | |
|---|---|
| Per unit incl. 2 persons and electricity | € 20.80 - € 22.20 |
| extra person | € 4.20 - € 4.80 |

## Les Loges

### Camping l'Aiguille Creuse

F-76790 Les Loges (Seine-Maritime) T: 02 35 29 52 10. E: camping@aiguillecreuse.com
**alanrogers.com/FR76160**

L'Aiguille Creuse, not far from Le Havre and Dieppe, is named after a rock, alleged to be hollow, near Etretat. The site is set back from the Côte d'Albâtre in the village of Les Loges, only 10 km. from Fécamp. There are 89 good sized grassy pitches, slightly sloping in parts, of which 80 are for touring, all with 10A electricity. They are divided by neat hedges and some trees while the remaining nine are chalets for rent. The site, being three hectares, is left with lots of space for playing or just quiet enjoyment. The local shops and bar are within easy walking distance. The fishing port of Fécamp has many festivities connected with the sea as well as the Bénédictine distillery. The picturesque villages of Etretat and Yport were an attraction for the Impressionist painters of the late 19th century and have largely remained intact.

**Facilities**

Modern toilet block (2012) with unisex toilets (no seats), showers, washbasins in cubicles, baby changing and facilities for disabled visitors. Laundry. Motorcaravan services. Bar and snack bar (all season). Takeaway (July/Aug). Heated covered pool (15/4-15/9). WiFi (charged). Card-operated barrier. Off site: Local shops and bicycle hire 1 km. Beach, golf, riding, sailing, Etretat 5 km. Supermarket 7 km. Fécamp with banks, bars, restaurants and shops 10 km.

**Open:** 1 April - 30 September.

**Directions**

From Fécamp, take the D940 towards Etretat. Passing through Les Loges, site is well signed to the left. GPS: 49.698782, 0.275602

**Charges guide**

| | |
|---|---|
| Per unit incl. 2 persons and electricity | € 19.30 - € 23.30 |
| extra person | € 4.00 - € 5.50 |
| child (2-6 yrs) | € 2.30 - € 3.20 |
| dog | € 2.50 - € 3.00 |

Camping Cheques accepted.

## Les Pieux
### Kawan Village Le Grand Large

F-50340 Les Pieux (Manche) T: 02 33 52 40 75. E: info@legrandlarge.com

**alanrogers.com/FR50060**

Le Grand Large is a well established, quality family site with direct access to a long sandy beach and within a 20 km. drive of Cherbourg. It is a neat and tidy site with 126 touring pitches divided and separated by hedging giving an orderly, well laid out and attractive appearance. A separate area has 51 mobile homes for rent. The reception area is at the entrance (with a security barrier) and the forecourt is decorated with flower beds. To the rear of the site and laid out in the sandhills is an excellent play area. Not surprisingly the sandy beach is the big attraction. The length of units is restricted to eight metres to prevent any problems accessing pitches. Roads around the site are tarmac and many of the plants and shrubs that you see bordering these carry name tags in four languages. The views from the site stretch across the bay to the tip of the Cherbourg peninsula. Every effort is made at le Grand Large to attract and cater for families with young children, so noisy entertainment is not an option. Most of the pitches have electricity (10A Europlug), water and drainage and the site owner hopes that this will extend to all pitches in the near future. Plans are in place to replace the showers in all the cubicles.

### Facilities

Two well maintained toilet blocks include washbasins in cubicles and some family rooms. WCs are mostly to the outside of the building. Provision for disabled visitors. Baby bathroom. Laundry area. Motorcaravan services. Shop for basics. Bar. Restaurant and takeaway (6/7-30/8). WiFi throughout (charged). Heated swimming and paddling pools (indoor all season, outdoor 15/6-1/9). Play area. Tennis. Boules. Fishing. TV room. Some entertainment (July/Aug). Off site: Bicycle hire and riding 5 km. Golf 15 km. Two supermarkets in Les Pieux. Day trips by ferry to the Channel Islands (May-Sept) from nearby Diellette.

**Open:** 13 April - 22 September.

### Directions

From Cherbourg port take N13 south for 2 km. Branch right on D650 (previously D904) signed Carteret. Continue for 18 km. to Les Pieux. Take the D4 in town and turn left just after 'Super U' supermarket. Follow site signs via D117/517. GPS: 49.49452, -1.84246

### Charges 2013

| Per unit incl. 2 persons | |
| --- | --- |
| and electricity | € 21.00 - € 37.00 |
| extra person | € 4.50 - € 8.00 |
| child (3-10 yrs) | € 3.00 - € 4.00 |

Camping Cheques accepted.

Le Grand Large ★★★★
Camping 50340 Les Pieux
www.legrandlarge.com
info@legrandlarge.com
Tél : 00.33.(0)2.33.52.40.75

## Luc-sur-Mer
### Camping la Capricieuse

2 rue Brummel, F-14530 Luc-sur-Mer (Calvados) T: 02 31 97 34 43. E: info@campinglacapricieuse.com

**alanrogers.com/FR14170**

La Capricieuse is situated on the edge of the delightful, small, seaside town of Luc-sur-Mer. It is an ideal location for visiting the D-Day landing beaches, which are just a few minutes drive from the Ouistreham car ferry. This immaculate site has 192 touring pitches of varying sizes, most are on level grass with hedges and a variety of trees giving some shade. One hundred and five have electricity (6/10A) and 52 also have water and drainage. Shop, bars and restaurants are within walking distance in Luc-sur-Mer.

### Facilities

Three modern and clean toilet blocks with washbasins in cubicles and showers. Facilities for disabled visitors. Laundry facilities. Motorcaravan service point. Large TV room. Games room. Adventure playground (unfenced). Tennis. Boules. Free WiFi over site. Off site: Fishing and bicycle hire nearby. Beach and watersports 200 m.

**Open:** 1 April - 30 September.

### Directions

Take the D514 from Ouistreham car ferry and head west to Luc-sur-Mer. Campsite is signed from the western end of St Luc. GPS: 49.31797, -0.35780

### Charges guide

| | |
| --- | --- |
| Per unit incl. 2 persons and electricity | € 21.25 |

**FREE** Alan Rogers Travel Card
Extra benefits and savings - see page 10

# Martragny

## Castel Camping le Château de Martragny

52 Hameau Saint Leger, F-14740 Martragny (Calvados) T: 02 31 80 21 40. E: chateau.martragny@wanadoo.fr
**alanrogers.com/FR14030**

Martragny is an attractive site in the parkland of a château. Close to D-Day beaches and Bayeux, it is also convenient for the ports of Caen and Cherbourg, and has the facilities and charm to encourage both long stays and stopovers. The lawns surrounding and approaching the château take 160 units, with electricity connections (10A). Most pitches are divided by either a small hedge or a few trees. Bed and breakfast accommodation is available in the château all year (reservation essential). The de Chassey family will make you very welcome within the peace and calm of their home.

| Facilities | Directions |
|---|---|
| Three sanitary blocks include washbasins in cabins, showers, sinks for dishwashing and laundry, and two baby baths. Disabled visitors are well catered for. Good laundry. Shop (all season). Bar, brasserie and takeaway (20/5-29/8). Swimming pool (20x6 m) and paddling pool heated in poor weather. Play areas. Tennis. Minigolf. Games and TV room. Fishing pond. WiFi. Off site: Riding 1 km. Bayeux Tapestry 8 km. D-Day Beaches 15 km. **Open:** 6 May - 6 September. | From Caen on N13 take exit for Martragny, ignore turning to village, continue for 100 m, site signed on right. From Bayeux (8 km) on N13, follow exit signs for Martragny, at D82B turn left (ignore village sign), on for 100 m. as above. GPS: 49.24941, -0.60237 |

**Charges 2013**

| | |
|---|---|
| Per unit incl. 2 persons and electricity | € 30.40 - € 35.40 |

Camping Cheques accepted.

---

# Maupertus-sur-Mer

## Castel Camping Caravaning l'Anse du Brick

Route du Val de Saire, F-50330 Maupertus-sur-Mer (Manche) T: 02 33 54 33 57.
E: welcome@anse-du-brick.com  **alanrogers.com/FR50070**

A friendly, family site, l'Anse du Brick overlooks a picturesque bay on the northern tip of the Cotentin peninsula, eight kilometres east of Cherbourg port. This quality site makes a pleasant night halt or an ideal longer stay destination for those not wishing to travel too far. Its pleasing location offers direct access to a small sandy beach and a woodland walk. This is a mature, terraced site with magnificent views from certain pitches. Tarmac roads lead to the 117 touring pitches (all with 10A electricity) which are level, separated and mostly well shaded by many trees, bushes and shrubs.

| Facilities | Directions |
|---|---|
| New sanitary facilities are kept spotlessly clean and are well maintained. Washbasins mainly in cubicles and push button showers. Provision for disabled visitors. Laundry area. Motorcaravan service point. Shop (1/4-30/9). Restaurant and bar/pizzeria (1/5-10/9). Heated swimming pool (all season). Tennis. Play area. Organised entertainment in season. Miniclub (6-12 yrs). Bicycle and kayak hire. WiFi throughout (charged). Off site: Fishing 100 m. Riding 4 km. Golf 10 km. **Open:** 1 April - 30 September. | From Cherbourg port follow signs for Caen and Rennes. After third roundabout, take slip road to right (Bretteville-en-Saire, D116). From southeast on N13 at first (Auchan) roundabout, take slip road to right (Tourlaville, N13 car ferry), ahead at next roundabout, right at third lights on D116 (Bretteville). On for 7 km. Site signed. GPS: 49.66715, -1.48704 |

**Charges guide**

| | |
|---|---|
| Per unit incl. 2 persons and electricity | € 21.90 - € 39.60 |

---

# Merville-Franceville

## Camping les Peupliers

Allée des Pins, F-14810 Merville-Franceville (Calvados) T: 02 31 24 05 07.
E: contact@camping-peupliers.com  **alanrogers.com/FR14190**

Les Peupliers is run by friendly, family managers who keep this site attractive and tidy. It is just 300 metres from a long, wide, sandy beach. The touring pitches, of which there are 85, are on level open ground, all with 10A electricity. Those in the newest part are hedged but, with just a few trees on the edge of the site, there is little shade. The campsite amenities are housed in neat, modern buildings. An animation programme for children and various activities are organised in high season. This site is ideally located for visiting Caen, Bayeux and the traditional seaside towns of Deauville and Trouville.

| Facilities | Directions |
|---|---|
| Two excellent heated toilet blocks with washbasins in cabins and showers. Good facilities for disabled visitors and for babies. Laundry room. Small shop, bar with terrace and takeaway (all July/Aug). Heated outdoor swimming pool and paddling pool (May-Sept). Play area. Games room. Entertainment in high season. WiFi (free). Bicycle hire. Off site: Fishing, riding and golf within 1 km. **Open:** 1 April - 31 October. | From Ouistreham take D514 to Merville-Franceville. Site signed off Allée des Pins. From Rouen on A13 (exit 29B), take D400 to Cabourg then the D514 to Merville-Franceville. GPS: 49.28326, -0.17053 |

**Charges guide**

| | |
|---|---|
| Per unit incl. 2 persons and electricity | € 22.50 - € 29.60 |

---

For latest campsite news, availability and prices visit
# alanrogers.com

## Pont-Audemer
### Camping Caravaning des Etangs Risle-Seine

19 route des Etangs, Toutainville, F-27500 Pont-Audemer (Eure) T: 02 32 42 46 65.
E: camping@ville-pont-audemer.fr **alanrogers.com/FR27010**

This attractive and well maintained site is owned by the Pont-Audemer Council and run by an enthusiastic manager. It is well laid out with 61 hedged pitches on level grass and electricity connections for 28 of them. Fishing and watersports are possible as the site is positioned next to some large lakes, but swimming is not allowed. In high season a shuttle bus goes to Pont-Audemer where you will find shops, restaurants and a good swimming complex.

| Facilities | Directions |
|---|---|
| Two well maintained toilet blocks with facilities for disabled visitors. They include washbasins in cabins and preset showers. Laundry facilities. Bar area with terrace (no alcohol licence, visitors may bring their own). Bread and milk available. Playing field. TV. Bicycle hire. Fishing. Takeaway (high season). Accommodation available all year. Off site: Pont-Audemer swimming complex. | Approaching from north or south on D810, at the bridge over the River Risle, turn to the west on south side of river and travel 1.5 km. on rue des Etangs. Site is well signed. GPS: 49.3666, 0.48739 |

**Charges guide**

| | |
|---|---|
| Per unit incl. 2 persons and electricity (10A) | € 16.70 - € 18.10 |
| extra person | € 3.15 |

**Open:** 15 March - 15 November.

## Pontorson
### Kawan Village Haliotis

Chemin des Soupirs, F-50170 Pontorson (Manche) T: 02 33 68 11 59. E: camping.haliotis@wanadoo.fr
**alanrogers.com/FR50080**

The staff at this beautiful campsite offer a warm welcome to visitors. Situated on the edge of the little town of Pontorson, the site has 152 pitches, including 118 for touring units. Most have 16A electricity and 24 really large ones also have water and drainage. Excellent private sanitary facilities are also available on 12 'luxury' pitches. The comfortable reception area incorporates a pleasant bar where breakfast is served. This opens onto the swimming pool terrace. The site is attractively laid out and includes a Japanese garden. Haliotis (which takes its name from a large shell) is next to the River Couesnon and it is possible to walk, cycle and canoe along the river to Mont Saint-Michel, 9 km. away. A good bus service is available from close to the site entrance to all major towns in the area. Welcoming families and couples, the site amenities include good sports facilities, a new playgound and a mini-farm.

| Facilities | Directions |
|---|---|
| Well equipped, heated toilet block with controllable showers and washbasins in cubicles. Good facilities for disabled visitors. Baby room. Laundry facilities. Bar serving breakfast. Bread to order. Outdoor heated swimming pool (1/5-30/9) with jacuzzi and paddling pool. Sauna and solarium. Good fenced play areas. Pétanque. Archery. Games room. Tennis. Golf practice range. Multisports court. Outdoor fitness equipment. Bicycle hire. Fishing. Japanese garden and animal park. Miniclub. Free WiFi over site. Off site: Local services including supermarket, bars, restaurants and takeaways in Pontorson within easy walking distance. Riding 3 km. Bay 10 km. Golf 20 km. Beach and sailing 30 km. | Pontorson is 22 km. southwest of Avranches and bypassed by the N176 which links with D137 from Saint Malo to the west and (via N175) with A84 (Caen-Rennes) to the east. Site is 300 m. north of town centre. Note: Entrance is on rue du Général Patton. Sat nav users should follow signs! GPS: 48.55836, -1.51429 |

**Charges guide**

| | |
|---|---|
| Per unit incl. 2 persons and electricity | € 19.50 - € 25.50 |
| with individual sanitary facility | € 25.00 - € 31.00 |
| extra person | € 5.00 - € 6.00 |
| Camping Cheques accepted. | |

**Open:** 15 March - 11 November.

**FREE** Alan Rogers Travel Card
Extra benefits and savings - see page 10

## Pont-l'Evêque

### Castel Camping du Brévedent

Le Brévedent, F-14130 Pont-l'Evêque (Calvados) T: 02 31 64 72 88. E: contact@campinglebrevedent.com

**alanrogers.com/FR14090**

Le Brévedent is a well established, traditional site with 144 pitches (109 for tourists, 31 used by tour operators) set in the grounds of an elegant 18th-century hunting pavilion. Pitches are either around the fishing lake, in the lower gardens (level), or in the old orchard (gently sloping). Most have electricity. It is an excellent holiday destination within easy reach of the Channel ports and its peaceful, friendly environment makes it ideal for mature campers or families with younger children (note: the lake is unfenced). Reception provides vast tourist information and English is spoken. Dogs are not accepted.

**Facilities**

Three toilet blocks include washbasins in cubicles and facilities for disabled visitors. One has been refurbished with spacious en-suite cubicles (shower, washbasin and baby bath). Laundry facilities. Motorcaravan service point. Shop. Bar (evenings). Restaurant (15/5-19/9). Takeaway (1/5-25/9). Clubroom. TV and library. Heated swimming and paddling pools (unsupervised) (1/5-25/9). Playground. Minigolf. Boules. Games room. Fishing. Rowing. Bicycle and buggy hire. Entertainment and children's club (high season). WiFi. No dogs. Off site: Riding 1 km. Tennis. Golf and boat launching 12 km. Beach 25 km.

**Open:** 28 April - 23 September.

**Directions**

Pont-l'Evêque is due south of Le Havre. Le Brévedent is 13 km. southeast from Pont-l'Evêque: take D579 toward Lisieux for 4 km. then D51 towards Moyaux. At Blangy-le-Château continue ahead on D51 to Le Brévedent. GPS: 49.22525, 0.30438

**Charges guide**

| | |
|---|---|
| Per unit incl. 2 persons and electricity | € 21.00 - € 31.10 |
| extra person | € 5.00 - € 8.00 |
| child (1-12 yrs) | € 3.20 - € 5.80 |

## Port-en-Bessin

### Sunêlia Port'land

Chemin du Castel, F-14520 Port-en-Bessin (Calvados) T: 02 31 51 07 06. E: campingportland@wanadoo.fr

**alanrogers.com/FR14150**

The Gerardin family will make you most welcome at Port'land, now a mature site lying 700 m. to the east of the little resort of Port-en-Bessin, one of Normandy's busiest fishing ports. The 300 pitches are large and grassy with 202 available for touring units, including 128 with 15A electricity. There is a separate area for tents without electricity. The camping area has been imaginatively divided into zones, some overlooking small fishing ponds and another radiating out from a central barbecue area. A modern building houses reception and the amenities which include a shop and a bar/restaurant with fine views over the Normandy coastline. In peak season a range of entertainment is organised including disco and karaoke evenings, and activities for children. A coastal path leads to the little town, and Omaha Beach is 4 km away. There are ten site-owned mobile homes for rent. A member of the Sunelia Group.

**Facilities**

The two sanitary blocks are modern and well maintained. Special facilities for disabled campers. Heated swimming pool (covered in low season) and paddling pool. Bar, restaurant, takeaway. Large TV and games room. Multisports pitch. Fishing. Play area. WiFi. Off site: 27-hole Omaha Beach International Golf Course adjacent. Fishing 600 m. Beach 4 km. Bicycle hire and riding 10 km. D-Day beaches. Colleville American war Cemetery. Bayeux.

**Open:** 1 April - 3 November.

**Directions**

Site is clearly signed off the D514, 4 km. west of Port-en-Bessin. GPS: 49.3463, -0.7732

**Charges guide**

| | |
|---|---|
| Per unit incl. 2 persons and electricity | € 20.50 - € 35.00 |
| extra person | € 5.00 - € 8.40 |
| child (2-10 yrs) | € 3.00 - € 5.30 |
| dog | € 3.00 |

For latest campsite news, availability and prices visit

## alanrogers.com

## Pourville-sur-Mer
### Camping le Marqueval

1210 rue de la Mer, F-76550 Pourville-sur-Mer (Seine-Maritime) T: 02 35 82 66 46.
E: contact@campinglemarqueval.com **alanrogers.com/FR76010**

Le Marqueval is a well established, family site of 290 pitches, located close to the seaside town of Hautot-sur-Mer, just west of Dieppe. The site has been developed around three small lakes (one unfenced, suitable for fishing). There are 60 grass pitches for touring units, all of a good size, separated by hedges and 40 with electrical connections (6A). The majority of the pitches here are used for privately owned mobile homes. Leisure amenities include a swimming pool and smaller children's pools. The site's bar also functions as a snack bar and during the high season evening entertainment is occasionally organised here. The site's owners will be happy to recommend places of interest in the area and these include Dieppe, with its old town, and the stylish resort of Le Tréport. This stretch of the Normandy coastline is well known for its towering white cliffs and fine sandy beaches. There are some superb coastal walks along the cliff tops and quiet lanes, ideal for exploration by cycle.

**Facilities**

The single toilet block is at the entrance to the site. Motorcaravan service point (charged). Shop. Bar, snack bar, takeaway (July/Aug and w/ends). Outdoor, heated swimming pool (15/6-15/9). Fishing (charged). Playground. Entertainment and activities. Mobile homes for rent. WiFi (charged). Off site: Nearest beach 1.2 km. Riding 1.5 km. Tennis. Cycle and walking tracks. Dieppe 5 km. St Valery-en-Caux (fishing port). Supermarket in Dieppe.

**Open:** 18 March - 15 October.

**Directions**

Head west from Dieppe on the D925 as far as Hautot-sur-Mer. Then turn right onto the D153 towards Pourville. Site is well signed from here. GPS: 49.9088, 1.0406

**Charges guide**

| Per unit incl. 2 persons | |
| --- | --- |
| and electricity | € 18.00 - € 24.00 |
| extra person | € 4.00 - € 7.50 |
| child (under 7 yrs) | € 3.00 - € 4.00 |

**CAMPING LE MARQUEVAL***

**CAMPING LE MARQUEVAL*** - 1210 RUE DE LA MER - 76550 POURVILLE SUR MER TEL: 0033 235 82 66 46 - FAX: 09 744 434 16 CONTACT@CAMPINGLEMARQUEVAL.COM - WWW.CAMPINGLEMARQUEVAL.COM**

## Ravenoville-Plage
### Kawan Village le Cormoran

2 le Cormoran, F-50480 Ravenoville Plage (Manche) T: 02 33 41 33 94. E: lecormoran@wanadoo.fr
**alanrogers.com/FR50050**

This welcoming, environmentally friendly, family run site, close to Cherbourg and Caen, is situated just across the road from a long sandy beach. It is also close to Utah beach and is ideally located for those wishing to visit the many museums, landing beaches and remembrance gardens of WW2. On flat, quite open ground, the site has 110 good sized pitches on level grass, all with 6/10A electricity (Europlug). Some extra large pitches are available. The well kept pitches are separated by hedges and the site is decorated with flowering shrubs. A covered pool, a sauna and a gym are among recent improvements.

**Facilities**

Four toilet blocks (three heated) are maintained to a good standard. Laundry facilities. Shop. Bar and terrace. Snacks and takeaway. Outdoor pool (1/6-1/9, unsupervised). New covered pool, sauna and gym. Play areas. Tennis. Boules. Entertainment, TV and games room. Billiard golf (one of only three in Europe). Playing field with archery (July/Aug). Hairdresser and masseuse. Bicycle and shrimp net hire. Riding (July/Aug). Communal barbecues. BMX park. WiFi (charged). Off site: Beach 20 m. Sand yachting. Golf (18 holes) 3 km.

**Open:** 6 April - 28 September.

**Directions**

From N13 take Ste-Mère-Eglise exit and in centre of town take road to Ravenoville (6 km), then Ravenoville-Plage (3 km). Just before beach turn right and site is 500 m. GPS: 49.46643, -1.23533

**Charges guide**

| Per unit incl. 2 persons | |
| --- | --- |
| and electricity | € 22.00 - € 34.00 |
| extra person | € 4.00 - € 8.00 |

Advanced booking advised in peak season.
Camping Cheques accepted.

We can book this site for you! Call 01580 214000 alan rogers travel

**FREE** Alan Rogers Travel Card
**Extra benefits and savings** - see page 10

## Saint Arnoult
### Camping la Vallée de Deauville

Avenue de la Vallée, F-14800 Saint Arnoult (Calvados) T: 02 31 88 58 17. E: contact@camping-deauville.com
**alanrogers.com/FR14200**

Close to the traditional seaside resorts of Deauville and Trouville, this large, modern site is owned and run by a delightful Belgian couple. With a total of 450 pitches, there are many mobile homes, both for rent and privately owned, and 150 used for touring units. These pitches are level, of a reasonable size and mostly hedged, and 60 have 10A electricity connections. A brand new pool complex complete with flumes, lazy river, jacuzzi and fun pool makes an attractive focal point near the entrance and there is a large fishing lake. The bar and restaurant are comfortable and there is a very good shop on the site.

**Facilities**

Two heated toilet blocks with showers and washbasins in cubicles. Good facilities for babies and disabled visitors. Laundry facilities. Small shop, bar and restaurant (high season). Takeaway (all season). New swimming pool complex. Good play area and play room. Entertainment in high season. WiFi (charged). Off site: Golf and riding 2 km. Bicycle hire and beach 3 km.

**Open:** 1 April - 31 October.

**Directions**

From the north, take the A29, then the A13 at Pont l'Eveque. Join the N177 (Deauville/Trouville) and after 9 km. take the D27 signed St Arnoult. Site is well signed on edge of village. GPS: 49.32864, 0.086

**Charges guide**

| | |
|---|---|
| Per unit incl. 2 persons and electricity | € 20.40 - € 34.00 |
| extra person | € 5.40 - € 9.00 |

## Saint Aubin-sur-Mer
### Yelloh! Village la Côte de Nacre

Rue du Général Moulton, F-14750 Saint Aubin-sur-Mer (Calvados) T: 02 31 97 14 45.
E: info@yellohvillage-cote-de-nacre.com **alanrogers.com/FR14010**

La Côte de Nacre is a large, popular, commercial site with many facilities, all of a high standard. It is an ideal holiday location for families. Two thirds is given over to mobile homes and there are four tour operators on the site. The 149 touring pitches are reasonable, both in size and condition, all having 10A electricity. With pleasant, well cared for flowerbeds, there is some hedging and a few trees. A state of the art, heated pool complex includes both open and covered (sliding roof) areas, slides, whirlpools and water jets, and on a hot day becomes the focal point of the campsite.

**Facilities**

The toilet block provides toilets and showers, washbasins in cubicles, and a room for toddlers and babies. Facilities for disabled visitors. Laundry room. Grocery with fresh bread. Motorcaravan services. Bar, restaurant and takeaway. Pool complex. Hammam, sauna, dry and humid heat, body treatments. Play area. Multisports pitch. Synthetic skating rink. Library. Games room. Bicycle hire. Children's clubs and mini-discos. Entertainment. WiFi. Mobile homes for rent. Off site: Town 1 km. Ferry 11 km.

**Open:** 30 March - 23 September.

**Directions**

Travel west from Ouistreham on D514 to St Aubin-sur-Mer. Site is well signed, to the left, just off the main road in a residential area. Take care as signage is small and you are in an urban area with no turning back. GPS: 49.322333, -0.387333

**Charges guide**

| | |
|---|---|
| Per unit incl. 2 persons and electricity | € 23.00 - € 44.00 |
| extra person | € 5.00 - € 8.00 |

## Saint Aubin-Surscie
### Camping Vitamin

865 chemin de Vertus, F-76550 Saint Aubin-Sur-Scie (Seine-Maritime) T: 02 35 82 11 11.
E: camping.vitamin@wanadoo.fr **alanrogers.com/FR76030**

Although the address is St Aubin, this compact site is actually on the outskirts of Dieppe and is only a couple of kilometres from the seafront. Those arriving or leaving by ferry could find it useful for a stopover as it is just off the main N27 to Rouen. It has a very French atmosphere, with large numbers of privately owned mobile homes and seasonal caravans. The 44 touring pitches (all with 10A electricity) are attractively laid out on level grass, and some are positioned between the mobile homes. The Morelle family work hard to ensure that everything is as it should be, but they speak very little English.

**Facilities**

Two excellent and well maintained unisex toilet blocks provide free showers and washbasins in cubicles. Facilities for disabled visitors. Baby bath. Laundry facilities. Motorcaravan service point. Bar serving snacks (1/6-30/9) and entertainment (July/Aug). Heated swimming pool (16/5-15/9). Adventure playground and field for games. Multisports court. Games barn. Pétanque pitch. Sports tournaments in high season. WiFi over site (charged). Off site: Supermarket 200 m. Golf and riding 1 km.

**Open:** 1 April - 15 October.

**Directions**

From Dieppe ferry terminal head out southeast to turn west onto ring road and follow this, keeping right at large roundabout (Leclerc) and left at next (Intermarché) onto N27 (Rouen). At roundabout (Auchan), turn south on N27. Take sliproad and turn right to site. GPS: 49.90063, 1.0747

**Charges guide**

| | |
|---|---|
| Per unit incl. 2 persons and electricity | € 16.90 - € 22.90 |
| extra person | € 4.50 - € 5.30 |

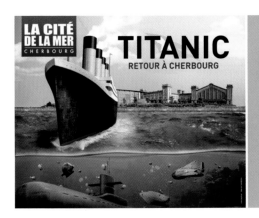
## Saint Pair-sur-Mer
### Castel Camping le Château de Lez Eaux

Saint Aubin des Préaux, F-50380 Saint Pair-sur-Mer (Manche) T: 02 33 51 66 09. E: bonjour@lez-eaux.com
**alanrogers.com/FR50030**

Set in the spacious grounds of a château, Lez Eaux lies in a rural situation just off the main route south, under two hours from Cherbourg (90 km. from Saint Malo). There are 229 pitches of which 113 are for touring units, all with electricity (either 10 or 16A Europlug) and 84 fully serviced. Most of the pitches are of a very good size, partly separated by trees and shrubs on either flat or very slightly sloping, grassy ground overlooking Normandy farmland or beside a small lake (with carp and other fish). The large indoor pool complex also has a fun pool for very small children and an outdoor pool which is heated.

### Facilities

Three modern clean toilet blocks (one heated in low season) include hot showers and washbasins in cabins, facilities for children and babies, and for disabled visitors. Shop, bar, snacks and takeaway (all from 1/5). Small heated swimming pool and indoor tropical-style fun pool (all season, no T-shirts or Bermuda-style shorts). Play area. Tennis. Games and TV rooms. Bouncy castle. Bicycle hire. Lake fishing. Cash machine. Torches useful. Internet access and WiFi (charged). Only one dog per pitch. Off site: Beach 4 km. Riding 5 km. Golf 7 km. Markets in Granville and Avranches (Sat), St Pair (Thu).

**Open:** 30 March - 30 September.

### Directions

Lez Eaux is just to the west of the D973 17 km. northwest of Avranches and 7 km. southeast of Granville. Site is between the two turnings east to St Aubin-des-Préaux and is well signed. GPS: 48.79778, -1.52498

### Charges guide

| | |
|---|---|
| Per unit incl. 2 persons and electricity | € 20.00 - € 49.00 |
| extra person | € 8.00 |
| child (under 7 yrs) | € 6.00 |
| dog | free |

## Saint Symphorien-le-Valois
### Camping l'Etang des Haizes

43 rue Cauticotte, F-50250 Saint Symphorien-le-Valois (Manche) T: 02 33 46 01 16.
E: info@campingetangdeshaizes.com **alanrogers.com/FR50000**

This is an attractive and very friendly site with a swimming pool complex that has a four-lane slide, a jacuzzi and a paddling pool. L'Etang des Haizes has 160 good sized pitches, of which 100 are for touring units, on fairly level ground and all with electricity (10A). They are set in a mixture of conifers, orchard and shrubbery, with some very attractive, slightly smaller pitches overlooking the lake and 60 mobile homes inconspicuously sited. The fenced lake has a small beach (swimming is permitted), with ducks and pedaloes, and offers good coarse fishing for huge carp (we are told!).

### Facilities

Two well kept and modern unisex toilet blocks include washbasins in cabins, units for disabled visitors, and two family cabins. Small laundry. Motorcaravan services. Milk, bread and takeaway snacks available (no gas). Snack bar/bar with TV and terrace (1/6-1/9). Swimming pool complex (18/5-1/9). Play areas. Bicycle hire. Pétanque. Organised activities including treasure hunts, archery, water polo and food tasting (5/7-25/8). Tourist information. WiFi (charged). Off site: Riding 1 km. Beach, kayaking and Forest Adventure 10 km. Walking. Cycling. Normandy landing beaches 30 km.

**Open:** 1 April - 15 October.

### Directions

Site is just north of La Haye-du-Puits on the primary route from Cherbourg to Mont St-Michel, St Malo and Rennes. It is 24 km. south of N13 at Valognes and 29 km. north of Coutances: leave D900 at roundabout at northern end of bypass (towards town). Signed on right. GPS: 49.300413, -1.544775

### Charges guide

| | |
|---|---|
| Per unit incl. 2 persons and electricity | € 16.00 - € 37.00 |
| extra person (over 4 yrs) | € 5.00 - € 7.00 |
| Camping Cheques accepted. | |

**FREE** Alan Rogers Travel Card
Extra benefits and savings - see page 10

## Saint Vaast-la-Hougue
### Camping la Gallouette

10 bis rue de la Gallouette, F-50550 Saint Vaast-la-Hougue (Manche) T: 02 33 54 20 57.
E: contact@camping-lagallouette.fr  alanrogers.com/FR50010

Claudine and Jean Luc Boblin will give you a warm welcome at their seaside campsite which is ideally placed for visiting Barfleur, Ste-Mère-Eglise and the Normandy landing beaches. There are 176 level pitches in total, 111 of which are for touring and all have 6/10A electricity. Some are separated by hedges and there are many colourful flower beds, shrubs and trees but little shade. A light and airy bar faces onto a terrace and swimming pool and there is also a state-of-the-art multisport court. The site is close to the cross-channel ferry terminal at Cherbourg. Saint Vaast-la-Hougue is a busy fishing port with freshly caught fish on sale and a good choice of fish restaurants. Just a couple of hundred yards from the site, on a Saturday morning, you will find a bustling, traditional French market. A regular bus service from near the site entrance will take you to most of the surrounding areas including Barfleur and Cherbourg. For those wanting to take a leisurely stroll there is a pleasant walk along the raised sea wall to Fort de la Hougue which can be seen from the site.

### Facilities

Three modern sanitary blocks, one open and two enclosed, have British style toilets, showers and washbasins (some in cabins). Area for disabled visitors and for babies. Laundry facilities. Small shop. Snack bar. Bar with terrace. Swimming pool. Multisports court. Play area. Pétanque. WiFi throughout (charged). Entertainment in high season. Off site: Beach 300 m. Shops and restaurant in St Vaast. Riding 5 km. Golf 12 km. Fishing. Sailing. Boat trips to Ile de Tatihou.

**Open:** 1 April - 30 September.

### Directions

The D902 runs between Barfleur and Valognes on the eastern side of the Cherbourg peninsula. About half way along at Quettehou take the D1 to St Vaast. Site signed on right on entering town.
GPS: 49.58400, -1.26783

### Charges guide

| | |
|---|---|
| Per unit incl. 2 persons and electricity (6A) | € 20.10 - € 29.35 |
| extra person | € 4.70 - € 6.60 |
| child (2-10 yrs) | € 2.95 - € 3.75 |

## Saint Valery-en-Caux
### Camping Municipal d'Etennemare

Hameau d'Etennemare, F-76460 Saint Valery-en-Caux (Seine-Maritime) T: 02 35 97 15 79
alanrogers.com/FR76090

This comfortable, neat site is two kilometres from the picturesque harbour and town, 30 km. west of Dieppe. Quietly located, it has 116 pitches of which 49 are available for touring units. The grassy pitches are all on a slight slope, with electricity (6/10A), but there is very little shade. Reception is open all day in July and August, but in low season is closed 12.00-15.00 daily and all day Wednesday: there is a card-operated security barrier. Not far from Fécamp, with its Benedictine Distillery – indeed, the chalky cliffs along this coast were made famous by the many artists and sculptors who visited here in the late 1800s.

### Facilities

Two modern, clean and well maintained sanitary buildings are side by side, one containing showers and the other toilets, with open and cubicle washbasins and facilities for disabled visitors. Both blocks are heated in winter. Washing machines. Small shop (July/Aug). Playground. Off site: Hypermarket 1.5 km. Harbour and beach 2 km.

**Open:** All year.

### Directions

From Dieppe keep to D925 Fécamp road (not through town). At third roundabout turn right on D925E towards hypermarket. From Fécamp turn left on D925E as before. Take first right (site signed) to site on left in 1 km. GPS: 49.8585, 0.7046

### Charges guide

| | |
|---|---|
| Per unit incl. 2 persons and electricity | € 14.90 |
| extra person | € 3.05 |

For latest campsite news, availability and prices visit
# alanrogers.com

## Sainte Marie-du-Mont
### Flower Camping Utah Beach

F-50480 Sainte Marie-du-Mont (Manche) T: 02 33 71 53 69. E: utah.beach@wanadoo.fr
**alanrogers.com/FR50140**

Situated in an area rich in modern history, this family run campsite has a very French atmosphere. It is very well cared for, with landscaped areas, flower beds and shrubs. The 32 spacious pitches reserved for touring units are on level grass, separated by hedges and all have 6A electricity. A feature of the site is the heated swimming pool with adjacent sauna and jaccuzi. A well stocked aviary and BMX facility are also on the site. The site is only 50 m. from Utah Beach (one of the D-Day landing beaches) and within 500 m. there is a museum dedicated to it. A short drive will take you to many other places of interest, and plenty of information is available at the site reception.

#### Facilities
One well equipped and clean sanitary block provides British style toilets, washbasins in cabins and showers. Baby bath. Facilities for disabled visitors. Laundry facilities. Motorcaravan service point. Shop. Bar, restaurant and takeaway. Swimming pool (15/5-30/9). Multisports court. BMX area. Play area (unfenced). Volleyball. Tennis. Games room. Aviary. Free WiFi over site. Entertainment in high season. Mobiles homes for rent. Off site: Riding 10 km. Bicycle hire and golf 15 km.

**Open:** 1 April - 17 September.

#### Directions
From the N13 south of Sainte-Mère-Église take D70 west to Sainte-Marie du-Mont, then D913 to the coast. Turn left on D421 coast road and site is 500 m. on left. GPS: 49.41931, -1.18058

#### Charges guide
| Per unit incl. 2 persons | |
|---|---|
| and electricity | € 21.00 - € 27.40 |
| extra prson | € 5.10 - € 5.60 |
| child (3-7 yrs) | € 2.60 - € 4.00 |
| dog | € 2.80 |

---

## Servon
### Campéole Saint Grégoire

Campéole

47 rue Saint Grégoire, F-50170 Servon (Manche) T: 02 33 60 26 03. E: saint-gregoire@campeole.com
**alanrogers.com/FR50190**

This small rural site is simple and well cared for. Modestly sized pitches are in groups of three or four with very little indication of pitch boundaries. Shrubs and well trimmed hedges are planted throughout. Twenty-nine of the 72 pitches are occupied by chalets and mobile homes. One building houses all of the facilities which are modern, bright and of a high standard. The site is now managed by a young couple who work hard to ensure the comfort of their visitors. It would particularly suit families with very young children. Le Mont St-Michel is a 20 minute drive and well worth a visit. Do remember that this is one of the tourist Meccas of France and a visit outside of July/August is recommended. A little further away, the old port of St Malo is splended, with many restaurants where you can enjoy the local seafood. Dinan and Dinard are also popular destinations.

#### Facilities
One modern sanitary block has washbasins in cabins and controllable showers. Baby room. Very good facilities for disabled visitors. Washing machine. Takeaway (July/Aug). Small swimming pool (7/4-15/9). Boules. Play area (3-8 yrs). WiFi. Torches required. Off site: Several beaches can be reached by car. Le Mont St-Michel. St Malo. Avranches.

**Open:** 1 April - 22 September.

#### Directions
On the RN175 from Avranches towards St Malo, take exit for Servon on the right. Site is on the right in 200 m. GPS: 48.59703, -1.41316

#### Charges guide
| Per unit incl. 2 persons | |
|---|---|
| and electricity | € 15.10 - € 20.40 |
| extra person | € 4.00 - € 6.90 |
| child (2-6 yrs) | free - € 3.90 |

**FREE** Alan Rogers Travel Card
Extra benefits and savings - see page 10

## Touques-Deauville
### Camping des Haras

Chemin du Calvaire, F-14800 Touques-Deauville (Calvados) T: 02 31 88 44 84.
E: campingdesharas@orange.fr **alanrogers.com/FR14270**

Les Haras is located in Touques, just outside the stylish resort of Deauville. This is a mature site with grassy and well shaded pitches. A number of mobile homes are available for rent. Leisure amenities include a heated pool (July and August) with a separate children's pool and spa bath. There is a bar and snack bar, with many other restaurants in nearby Deauville. The sandy beaches of Deauville and its neighbour, Trouville, are deservedly renowned and are likely to be the main appeal here. The site is open for a long season and may appeal as a short break destination.

**Facilities**

Bar and snack bar. Swimming pool and children's pool. Playground. Games room. Mobile homes for rent. Off site: Shops and restaurants in Deauville and Trouville. Golf. Riding.

**Open:** 1 March - 30 October.

**Directions**

Site is south of Trouville. Approaching from A132 motorway, continue on D677 towards Trouville and Deauville. On reaching Touques, take eastbound D62 (Route d'Honfleur) and the site is well signed. GPS: 49.349567, 0.111711

**Charges guide**

| | |
|---|---|
| Per unit incl. 2 persons and electricity | € 20.00 - € 35.00 |
| extra person | € 5.50 - € 9.00 |

## Veules-les-Roses
### Camping les Mouettes

Avenue Jean Moulin, F-76980 Veules-les-Roses (Seine-Maritime) T: 02 35 97 61 98.
E: contact@camping-lesmouettes-normandie.com **alanrogers.com/FR76060**

Les Mouettes is set back from the cliffs, with the pretty seaside resort of Veules-les-Roses below. It is a busy site, attracting many visitors en route from Dieppe. There are 152 pitches in total but many are occupied by mobile homes and seasonal caravans, leaving only 82 for touring, all with 6A electricity, and 21 for tents without electricity. They are level, grassy and divided by hedges, but have no shade. The narrow roads may cause difficulty for larger units. A special area for 16 motorcaravans is by the entrance. The site is open for a longer season and may be useful for those travelling south for winter.

**Facilities**

Toilet facilities are in a central group of buildings and provide separate male and female facilities, and those for disabled visitors. Washbasins in cubicles, showers, toilets (no seats) and baby changing. Motorcaravan services. Covered heated swimming pool (15/4-15/10). Play area. Games room. Bicycle hire. WiFi (charged). Off site: Village centre and beach 300 m. Tennis. Walking and cycle trails. Cinema, shops and restaurants.

**Open:** 1 April - 4 November.

**Directions**

Veules-les-Roses is west of Dieppe. From there, head west on the D925 towards St Valéry-en-Caux. On arrival at town sign for Veules-les-Roses, site is immediately on left. GPS: 49.876239, 0.802935

**Charges guide**

| | |
|---|---|
| Per unit incl. 2 persons and electricity | € 18.80 - € 25.50 |
| extra person | € 3.70 - € 5.40 |
| child (5-10 yrs) | € 2.60 - € 3.60 |

## Yport
### Flower Camping la Chênaie

Rue Henry Simon, F-76111 Yport (Seine-Maritime) T: 02 35 27 33 56. E: camping.yport@flowercampings.com
**alanrogers.com/FR76170**

La Chênaie, part of the Flower Camping group, is set in a wooded valley, just 1 km. from the traditional fishing village of Yport, renowned for its fishermen's houses and beautiful 19th-century villas. Of the 114 pitches, 50 are for touring and the rest are wooden chalets and FreeFlower tents, all for rent. The touring pitches are on open level grass with no shade, so may not offer the privacy some may require. All have 6A electricity. The nearby village of Etretat, with its famous chalk cliffs, inspired the paintings of Claude Monet and Gustave Courbet.

**Facilities**

Modern toilet block with toilets, washbasins in cubicles and showers. Facilities for babies and disabled visitors. Laundry. Heated covered pool (all season). Games room and play area. Communal barbecue. WiFi (charged). Off site: Local shops, bars, restaurants in village. Fishing 1 km. Riding 4 km. Bicycle hire, sailing and boat launching 5 km. Golf 10 km.

**Open:** 1 April - 15 October.

**Directions**

Yport is between Etretat and Fécamp. From Fécamp (42 km. NE of Le Havre), take D940 southwest for 5 km, turn right on D104 towards Yport and site is on the left in 1 km. GPS: 49.732805, 0.320682

**Charges guide**

| | |
|---|---|
| Per unit incl. 2 persons and electricity | € 13.90 - € 23.90 |
| extra person | € 3.00 - € 5.00 |
| child (2-7 yrs) | € 2.00 - € 3.00 |

Nord/Pas-de-Calais, with its lush countryside and market towns, is much more than just a stop off en-route to or from the ports. The peaceful rural unspoilt charms of the region provide a real breath of fresh air.

**DÉPARTEMENTS: 59 NORD, 62 PAS-DE-CALAIS**

**MAJOR CITY: LILLE**

Whether travelling by ferry or through the tunnel, this is one of the most accessible regions of France and has much to offer – the elegant resorts and sandy beaches of the opal coast, beautiful Flemish architecture in Arras, and all the attractions of the region's bustling capital, Lille. The landscape around Flanders is most closely associated with the battles of the First World War, and is the site of numerous military cemeteries and monuments to those who fell.

The area however is predominately rural. Inland and south are long vistas of rolling farmland broken by little rivers and well scattered with pockets of forest woodland. The coastline is characterised by sandy beaches, shifting dunes and ports. It is a quiet and sparsely populated area with peaceful villages and churches that provide evidence of the glorious achievements of French Gothic architecture. Boulogne is home to Nausicaa, the world's largest sea-life centre and from Cap Griz-Nez you may be able to see the White Cliffs of Dover. There are also many huge hypermarkets where you may stock up on wine, beer and cheese.

### Places of interest

*Arras:* on the river Scarpe, has beautiful 13th- and 14th-century houses and the lovely Abbey of Saint Waast.

*Boulogne:* best entered by way of the lower town with the 13th-century ramparts of the upper town in the background. The castle next to the Basilica of Notre Dame is impressive.

*Lille:* Palais des Beaux-Arts; Cathedral; Sunday market; Euralille shopping complex.

*Le Touquet:* pleasant, all year round, coastal resort town with six miles of sandy beaches.

### Cuisine of the region

Hearty stews and game from the forests of the Ardennes feature strongly, and in the north beer is commonly used in dishes such as carbonnade flamande.

*Caudière (Chaudière, Caudrée):* versions of fish and potato soup.

*Croquelots or Bouffis:* lightly salted and smoked herring.

*Gris de Lille:* a really salty square of cheese with a strong smell.

*Hochepot:* a thick Flemish soup with virtually everything in it but the kitchen sink.

*Waterzooï:* a cross between soup and stew, usually of fish or chicken.

www.northernfrance-tourism.com
contact@crt-nordpasdecalais.fr
(0)3 20 14 57 57

## Boiry-Notre-Dame

### Camping la Paille Haute

145 rue de Sailly, F-62156 Boiry-Notre-Dame (Pas-de-Calais) T: 03 21 48 15 40.
E: la-paillehaute@wanadoo.fr **alanrogers.com/FR62080**

La Paille Haut is quietly situated in a small village overlooking beautiful countryside yet easily accessed from the A1, A2 and A26 autoroutes. This is an ideal overnight stop on your holiday route whilst also a great base for exploring the Flemish city of Arras with its underground tunnels, begun in the tenth century and used in both world wars; the battlefields of the Somme and the Thiépval Memorial. Of the 149 pitches, 65 are for touring on level grass and all with 6/10A electricity. The friendly owner has worked hard over the years, expanding and developing this site to what it is today. Northern France is often overlooked by holidaymakers but is full of folklore and traditions.

**Facilities**

One modern, basic unisex toilet block. Extra toilets by pool. One toilet/shower room for disabled visitors. Washing machine and dryer under canopy. Motorcaravan service point. Swimming pool (1/6-15/9). Poolside bar, snacks and pizza oven (15/6-15/9). TV in bar. Fishing pond. Playground. Boules. WiFi throughout. Entertainment (in season). Off site: Supermarket 500 m. Riding 10 km. Golf 15 km. WW1 Canadian memorial at Vimy Ridge.

**Open:** 1 April - 31 October.

**Directions**

From A1 take exit 15 and D939 southeast. After 3 km. turn left for Boiry-Notre-Dame and follow camping signs to site. GPS: 50.273533, 2.948667

**Charges guide**

| Per unit incl. 2 persons | |
|---|---|
| and electricity (6A) | € 21.00 - € 24.50 |
| extra person | € 3.50 - € 4.00 |
| child (under 7 yrs) | € 2.50 - € 3.00 |

## Buysscheure
### Camping Caravaning la Chaumière

529 Langhemast Straete, F-59285 Buysscheure (Nord) T: 03 28 43 03 57.
E: camping.LaChaumiere@wanadoo.fr **alanrogers.com/FR59010**

This is a very friendly, pleasant site, in the départment du Nord with a strong Flanders influence. There is a real welcome here. Set just behind the village of Buysscheure, the site has 29 touring pitches separated by trees and bushes. Each pair shares a light, electricity connections, water points and rubbish container. Access from narrow site roads can be difficult, although once on site there are several pitches available for extra large units. A small, fenced fishing lake contains some large carp. A bonus is that Bernadette works for the local vet and can arrange all the documentation for British visitors' pets.

**Facilities**

Modern unisex toilet facilities are simple and small in number, with two WCs, one shower and one washbasin cabin. Facilities for disabled visitors may also be used (a toilet and separate washbasin/shower room). Laundry facilities. Motorcaravan services. Basic chemical disposal. Bar (daily) and restaurant (weekends only, all day, in season). Dog exercise area. Heated outdoor pools (July/Aug). Play area. Minigolf. Archery. Fishing. WiFi (free). Off site: St Omer. Beach 30 km. Lille 60 km.

**Open:** 1 April - 30 September.

**Directions**

From Calais take N43 (St Omer) for 25 km. Just beyond Nordausques take D221 left (Watten). In Watten turn left for centre, then right (D26, Cassel). After Lederzeele site signed to right. On reaching Buysscheure turn left, then right, site signed. Single track road with bend. GPS: 50.80152, 2.33924

**Charges guide**

| | |
|---|---|
| Per unit incl. 2 persons and electricity | € 19.00 - € 20.00 |

No credit cards.

## Condette
### Caravaning du Château d'Hardelot

21 rue Nouvelle, F-62360 Condette (Pas-de-Calais) T: 03 21 87 59 59. E: campingduchateau@libertysurf.fr
**alanrogers.com/FR62040**

Within about 15 minutes drive of Boulogne and only five minutes by car from the long sandy beach at Hardelot, this modern site has 70 pitches with around 50 for touring units, the rest occupied by long stay or units to rent. Pitches are of varying size on level grass, all with access to electricity (10A). Hedging plants between pitches are maturing well and there is shade from mature trees. With friendly and accommodating owners, this site provides a useful overnight stop, but is also a good base for longer.

**Facilities**

Modern sanitary facilities in two small units (one heated) include large hot showers and baby bath (all spotless). Laundry facilities (washing machine and dryer). Motorcaravan services. Excellent playground and entertainment for children in season. Small fitness room. WiFi (charged). Off site: English-run pub/restaurant within walking distance. Fishing 800 m. Riding 1 km. Bicycle hire, golf and boat launching 3 km.

**Open:** 1 April - 31 October.

**Directions**

South of Boulogne, take N1 Amiens (Paris) road, then on outskirts take right fork for Le Touquet-Paris Plage (D940). Continue for 5 km. passing a garage and signs for Condette, right at new roundabout. Turn right again at next roundabout. Site entrance (narrow) is ahead on site. GPS: 50.6466, 1.6256

**Charges guide**

| | |
|---|---|
| Per unit incl. 2 persons and electricity | € 20.20 - € 26.00 |

No credit cards.

## Eperlecques
### Kawan Village Château du Gandspette

133 rue de Gandspette, F-62910 Eperlecques (Pas-de-Calais) T: 03 21 93 43 93.
E: contact@chateau-gandspette.com **alanrogers.com/FR62030**

This spacious family run site, in the grounds of a 19th-century château, conveniently situated for the Channel ports and tunnel, provides overnight accommodation together with a range of facilities for longer stays. There are 110 touring pitches, all with electric hook-ups, intermingled with 20 privately owned mobile homes and caravans, with a further 18 for hire. Pitches are delineated by trees and hedging. Mature trees form the perimeter of the site, through which there is access to woodland walks.

**Facilities**

Two sanitary blocks with a mixture of open and cubicled washbasins. Good facilities for disabled visitors and babies. Laundry facilities. Motorcaravan service point. Bar, grill restaurant and takeaway (all 1/5-15/9). Swimming pools (15/5-15/9). Playground. Multisport court. Tennis. Pétanque. Children's room. Entertainment in season. WiFi in bar area (charged). Off site: Supermarket 1 km. Fishing 3 km. Riding and golf 5 km. Beach 30 km.

**Open:** 1 April - 30 September.

**Directions**

From Calais follow D943 (Saint Omer) for 25 km. southeast of Nordausques take D221 (east). Follow site signs for 5-6 km. From Dunkirk ferry follow signs for Saint Omer D300. At Watten roundabout exit right (Gandspette). GPS: 50.81924, 2.17753

**Charges guide**

| | |
|---|---|
| Per unit incl. 2 persons and electricity (6A) | € 18.00 - € 28.00 |

Camping Cheques accepted.

**FREE** Alan Rogers Travel Card
Extra benefits and savings - see page 10

## Escalles

### Camping les Erables

17, rue du Château d'Eau, F-62179 Escalles (Pas-de-Calais) T: 03 21 85 25 36.
E: boutroy-les.erables@wanadoo.fr **alanrogers.com/FR62200**

This small site on the Cote d'Opale is very convenient for the Calais ferries and Eurotunnel as well as being just a few minutes from the A16. The 41 pitches are terraced and set on open ground separated by low privet hedging. There is some shade around the perimeter and all pitches have electricity (6A Europlug). Just two kilometres from the beach, the pitches have spectacular views over the coast towards the Channel, Cap Blanc-Nez and the English coastline. Some pitches have a hardstanding area for motorcaravans. With few facilities or activities for children, this site is perhaps better suited to those who appreciate peace and quiet. The gate is closed 22.00-08.00 and no vehicle can enter the site during lunch break 12.00-14.00.

**Facilities**

One small toilet block, heated in low season, has British style toilets, washbasins and pushbutton showers in cubicles. Facilities for disabled visitors. Washing machine and dryer. Motorcaravan service point. No shop, but bread available to order. Caravan storage. Ice packs frozen. Off site: Shops, bar and restaurant in village. Beach 1.5 km. Golf 3 km. Boat launching and sailing 4 km. Fishing and bicycle hire 5 km. Riding 8 km. Coastal walks. Cité de l'Europe 15 km.

**Open:** 1 April - 11 November.

**Directions**

Leave A16/E402 at exit 40. Join D243 west bound. After passing the village sign, take the second turning on the left. Watch out for small site sign at road junction. The site entrance is 300 yds. on the left. N.B. Turn left when leaving the site. GPS: 50.91229, 1.72047

**Charges guide**

| | |
|---|---|
| Per unit incl. 2 persons and electricity | € 16.00 |
| extra person | € 3.50 |

No credit cards.

## Guînes

### Castel Camping Caravaning la Bien-Assise

D231, F-62340 Guînes (Pas-de-Calais) T: 03 21 35 20 77. E: castels@bien-assise.com
**alanrogers.com/FR62010**

A mature and well developed site, the history of la Bien-Assise goes back to the 1500s. There are 198 grass pitches, mainly set among mature trees with others on a newer field. Connected by gravel roads and of a good size (up to 300 sq.m), shrubs and bushes divide most of the pitches. Being close to Calais, the Channel Tunnel exit and Boulogne, makes it a good stopping point en-route, but it is well worth a longer stay. The site can have heavy usage at times (when maintenance can be variable). Used by tour operators (40 pitches). The château, farm and mill now form the focal point for this popular site.

**Facilities**

Three well equipped toilet blocks provide many washbasins in cabins, mostly British style WCs and provision for babies. Laundry facilities. The main block is in four sections, two unisex. Motorcaravan service point. Shop. Restaurant. Bar/grill and takeaway (all 1/5). TV room. Pool complex (1/5-20/9) with toboggan, covered paddling pool and outdoor pool. Play areas. Minigolf. Tennis. Bicycle hire. Only gas and charcoal barbecues are allowed. WiFi (charged). Off site: Riding 3 km. Fishing 8 km. Beach 12 km.

**Open:** 30 March - 26 September.

**Directions**

From ferry or tunnel follow signs for A16 Boulogne. Take exit 40 (Frethun, Gare TGV) and RD215 (Frethun). At first roundabout take third exit (Guines). In Frethun take RD246 towards Guines and St Tricat and at roundabout take exit for Guines. Pass through St Tricat and Hames Boucres, and in Guines follow site signs. GPS: 50.86632, 1.85698

**Charges guide**

| | |
|---|---|
| Per unit incl. 2 persons and electricity | € 24.50 - € 33.00 |
| extra person | € 4.50 - € 6.50 |

For latest campsite news, availability and prices visit
**alanrogers.com**

## Licques

### Camping les Pommiers des 3 Pays

273 rue du Breuil, F-62850 Licques (Pas-de-Calais) T: 03 21 35 02 02. E: contact@pommiers-3pays.com

**alanrogers.com/FR62190**

This delightful site, close to the Channel ports and A26 and A16 autoroutes, on the outskirts of Licques, is in the beautiful Boulonnais countryside. Of the 58 level, grassy pitches, 20 are for touring, all with 16A electricity and some fully serviced. Motorcaravans are especially welcome. The pretty brasserie caters for dining and takeaway in pleasant surroundings near the pool. There is a small, fenced play area for children. A longer stay enables visits to the beaches of the Opal Coast, and many sites of both World Wars; Dunkirk and Ypres for example.

#### Facilities

One toilet block with British style toilets, showers, washbasins, baby changing and a separate facility for disabled visitors. Second block with toilets only. Laundry facilities. Bar/restaurant/snack bar (1/4-15/10). Small heated swimming pool (25/4-15/9). Play area. Children's activities and entertainment (July/Aug). TV/games room. Field for groups/rallies. Chalets and mobile homes to rent. WiFi. Off site: Small supermarket 1 km. Larger shops and vet at Ardres 10 km. Golf 22 km. Nausicaa Sealife Centre at Boulogne 27 km.

**Open:** 15 March - 15 November.

#### Directions

From Calais to Ardres on D943, turn left at traffic lights then, after 200 m, right on D224 and follow to Licques. Take D191 and site is on left in 1 km. GPS: 50.779825, 1.947707

#### Charges guide

| Per unit incl. 2 persons | |
|---|---|
| and electricity | € 19.30 - € 23.30 |
| extra person | € 4.20 - € 5.50 |
| child (2-10 yrs) | € 3.20 - € 3.50 |

## Wimereux

### Camping l'Eté Indien

Hameau Honvault, F-62930 Wimereux (Pas-de-Calais) T: 03 21 30 23 50. E: ete.indien@wanadoo.fr

**alanrogers.com/FR62120**

L'Eté Indien is located near the resort of Wimereux, a little to the north of Boulogne. It offers a quiet and tranquil environment in which to enjoy your holiday – despite some occasional (every 30 mins) train noise during the day. Of the 176 pitches, 40 for tourers vary in size, are well marked and are on a terraced incline furthest from the site entrance and pool complex. All have electrical connections (10/16A) and 25 have hardstanding. In keeping with its Wild West theme, there is a small village of eight Indian teepees for rent, as well as 30 conventional mobile homes and chalets.

#### Facilities

Two toilet blocks include facilities for babies and disabled visitors. Laundry. Small shop. Bar. Snack bar and takeaway. Motorcaravan services. Swimming pool. Children's pool. Play area with trampoline. Boules. Games room. Internet access and WiFi. Fishing pond. Off site: Wimereux, Le Touquet, Boulogne and the Nausicaa museum. Cité de l'Europe shopping complex at Calais. Beach 1 km. Riding adjacent. Golf 1.5 km.

**Open:** All year.

#### Directions

From the A16 take exit 32 (Wimereux) and follow signs to Wimereux (D96 and D940). After 1.5 km. turn right. Site is well signed from here and is located on the left, close to a riding centre. Approach is rather narrow, with speed ramps and is poorly surfaced. GPS: 50.75142, 1.60728

#### Charges guide

| Per unit incl. 2 persons | |
|---|---|
| and electricity | € 16.50 - € 24.00 |
| extra person | € 4.00 - € 6.00 |
| child (2-7 yrs) | € 3.00 - € 5.00 |
| dog | € 2.00 - € 3.00 |

The birthplace of Gothic architecture in France with no less than six cathedrals, the region is still predominately rural with deep river valleys, forests of mature beech and oak, peaceful lakes and sandy beaches, providing plenty of contrast.

**DÉPARTEMENTS: 02 AISNE, 60 OISE, 80 SOMME**

**MAJOR CITY: AMIENS**

Picardy lies between the Marne and Somme rivers. It has a rich history, being the settlement site of the Franks around 600 AD, undergoing periods of rule by the English and the Spanish, and as the site of some of Europe's most famous battles, notably Crécy and the Somme. More recently, two world wars have left their indelible marks on the area, with preserved World War One tranches, pristine military cemeteries and poignant memorials, from small village crosses to the towering edifices of Thiepval and Vimy.

Picardy's unspoilt coastline with its wild beauty and changing light has inspired generations of artists, Degas and Seurat among them. Today's visitors can enjoy a wide range of activities – cycling, windsurfing, kayaking, sand-yachting, horse riding and hot-air ballooning. The region also has some of the best golf courses in France. Do not miss the spectacular 'Baie de Somme' with its dunes and saltwater meadows, and the magnificent Gothic cathedral at Amiens.

### Places of interest

*Abbeville:* church of St Vulfran, Bagatelle Château, Baie de Somme nature reserve.

*Amiens:* Notre Dame cathedral, impressive for its size and richly sculpted façade and the stone carvings of the choir; monument to the 1918 Battle of the Somme; remarkable 'hortillonnages' (water gardens) and interlocking canals.

*Aisne:* surrounded by 60 fortified churches.

*Chantilly:* Château of Chantilly with a 17th-century stable with a 'live' Horse Museum.

*Compiègne:* Seven miles east of the town is Clairière de l'Armistice. The railway coach here is a replica of the one in which the 1918 Armistice was signed and in which Hitler received the French surrender in 1942.

*Laon:* 12th-century cathedral, WW1 trenches, Vauclair Abbey.

*Marquenterre:* one of Europe's most important bird sanctuaries.

### Cuisine of the region

Fresh fish and seafood is popular, as is chicory flavoured coffee.

*Carbonnade de Boeuf à la Flamande:* braised beef with beer, onions and bacon.

*Caudière (Chaudière, Caudrée):* versions of fish and potato soup.

*Ficelles Picardes:* ham pancakes with mushroom sauce.

*Flamiche aux poireaux:* puff pastry tart with cream and leeks.

*Soupe courquignoise:* soup with white wine, fish, moules, leeks and Gruyère cheese.

**www.picardietourisme.com/en**
**documentation@picardietourisme.com**
**(0)3 22 22 33 63**

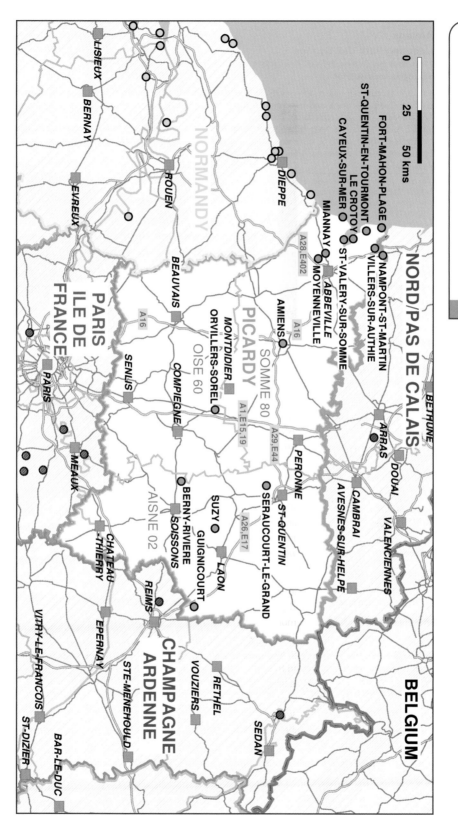

NORD/PAS DE CALAIS

BELGIUM

NORMANDY

PICARDY

SOMME 80

OISE 60

AISNE 02

PARIS
ILE DE
FRANCE

CHAMPAGNE
ARDENNE

0    25    50 kms

FORT-MAHON-PLAGE
ST-QUENTIN-EN-TOURMONT
LE CROTOY
CAYEUX-SUR-MER
ST-VALERY-SUR-SOMME
NAMPONT-ST-MARTIN
VILLERS-SUR-AUTHIE
MIANNAY
MOYENNEVILLE
ABBEVILLE
AMIENS
MONTDIDIER
ORVILLERS-SOREL
COMPIEGNE
BEAUVAIS
SENLIS
MEAUX
PARIS
SOISSONS
BERNY-RIVIERE
GUIGNICOURT
SUZY
LAON
SERAUCOURT-LE-GRAND
ST-QUENTIN
PERONNE
AVESNES-SUR-HELPE
CAMBRAI
ARRAS
DOUAI
VALENCIENNES
BETHUNE
REIMS
CHATEAU
-THIERRY
EPERNAY
STE-MENEHOULD
VOUZIERS
RETHEL
SEDAN
VITRY-LE-FRANCOIS
ST-DIZIER
BAR-LE-DUC
EVREUX
BERNAY
LISIEUX
ROUEN
DIEPPE

A28,E402
A16
A16
A1,E15,19
A29,E44
A26,E17

**FREE** Alan Rogers Travel Card
Extra benefits and savings - see page 10

## Amiens

### Camping Parc des Cygnes

111 avenue des Cygnes, F-80080 Amiens (Somme) T: 03 22 43 29 28. E: alban@parcdescygnes.com

**alanrogers.com/FR80100**

This 3.2 hectare site has been completely levelled and attractively landscaped. Bushes and shrubs divide the site into areas and trees around the perimeter provide some shade. Of the 145 pitches, 136 are for touring, with nine mobile homes for rent. All pitches are grassed with plenty of space on the tarmac roads in front of them for motorcaravans to park in wet conditions. There are 81 pitches with electricity (10A), of which 37 also have water and drainage and further water points can be accessed throughout the rest of the site. A Sites et Paysages member.

**Facilities**

Two toilet blocks (both open when site is busy) with separate toilet facilities but unisex shower and washbasin area. Baby bath. Facilities for disabled visitors. Reception building also has toilets, showers and washbasins. Laundry facilities. Shop (open on request all season), bar and takeaway (4/5-8/9; weekends only in low season). Games and TV room. Bicycle hire. Fishing. WiFi over part of site (charged). Off site: Golf and riding 12 km.

**Open:** 1 April - 14 October.

**Directions**

From A16, leave at exit 20. Take the Rocade Nord (northern bypass) to exit 40, follow signs for Amiens Longpré. At roundabout take second exit to Parc de Loisirs, then right to site (signed). For sat nav use Rue du Grand Marais. GPS: 49.920916, 2.258833

**Charges 2013**

| | |
|---|---|
| Per unit incl. 2 persons and electricity | € 20.50 - € 26.50 |
| extra person | € 6.40 |

---

## Berny-Rivière

### Caravaning la Croix du Vieux Pont

F-02290 Berny-Rivière (Aisne) T: 03 23 55 50 02. E: info@la-croix-du-vieux-pont.com

**alanrogers.com/FR02030**

Located on the banks of the River Aisne, la Croix du Vieux Pont is a very smart, modern 34 hectare site offering a high standard of facilities. Many pitches are occupied by mobile homes and tour operator tents, but there are 100 large and pleasant touring pitches, some on the banks of the Aisne. Maintained to a high standard, the excellent amenities include three heated swimming pools, two indoors with a waterslide and jacuzzi. At the heart of the site are two well stocked fishing lakes which are also used for pedaloes and canoes. There are two tennis courts, an amusement arcade and multisport court.

**Facilities**

Nine toilet blocks are modern and kept very clean, with washbasins in cabins and free hot showers. Laundry facilities. Facilities for disabled visitors and babies. Motorcaravan services. Supermarket. Bar, takeaway and good value restaurant (most amenities 1/4-30/9). Swimming pool complex. Play area. Fishing. Bicycle hire. Trampoline. Minigolf. Archery. Climbing tower. Multisports area. Apartments, chalets and mobile homes to let. WiFi (charged). Off site: Pony club adjacent. Riding 100 m.

**Open:** 2 weeks before Easter - 31 October.

**Directions**

From Compiègne take N31 towards Soissons. At site sign, turn left onto D13. At Vic-sur-Aisne turn right, towards Berny-Riviere and follow site signs. GPS: 49.40487, 3.12840

**Charges guide**

| | |
|---|---|
| Per unit incl. 2 persons and electricity | € 25.50 - € 30.50 |
| incl. 4 persons | € 36.00 - € 41.00 |
| Camping Cheques accepted. | |

---

## Cayeux-sur-Mer

### Camping les Galets de la Mollière

Rue Faidherbe, la Mollière, F-80410 Cayeux-sur-Mer (Somme) T: 03 22 26 61 85.
E: info@campinglesgaletsdelamolliere.com **alanrogers.com/FR80190**

Cayeux-sur-Mer is a traditional seaside resort close to the Somme estuary, and les Galets de la Mollière is located just to the north of the town. Formerly a municipal site, it has undergone a recent renovation programme and now provides the opportunity to experience a typical French family holiday. The site extends over six hectares and has 195 pitches on level grass, of which 125 are reserved for touring units. All have 10A electrical connections (most French style two pin). Site amenities include a swimming pool complex, bar, shop and a games room. A fine sandy beach is adjacent to the site.

**Facilities**

Toilet blocks include hot showers, washbasins in cabins and facilities for babies and disabled visitors. Laundry facilities. Small shop. Bar, snack bar and takeaway (all 1/7-31/8). Games room. Play area. A heated outdoor swimming pool (1/5-16/9). Boules. WiFi (charged). Mobile homes for rent. Off site: Motorcaravan services across the road. Beach 300 m. Riding and fishing 1 km. Bicycle hire 2 km. Cayeux-sur-Mer 3 km. Tennis 3 km. Golf 20 km.

**Open:** 1 April - 1 November.

**Directions**

From A16 take exit 24 (Le Crotoy) and join the D32 to Rue, and then D940 to St Valéry. Bypass St Valéry on the D940 and then the D3 signed Cayeux-sur-Mer. After a further 4 km. you will arrive at La Mollière. Site signed. GPS: 50.2026, 1.5251

**Charges guide**

| | |
|---|---|
| Per unit incl. 3 persons and electricity | € 18.00 - € 31.00 |
| extra person (over 1 yr) | € 7.00 |

For latest campsite news, availability and prices visit
# alanrogers.com

# Fort-Mahon-Plage

## Camping le Royon

1271 route de Quend, F-80120 Fort-Mahon-Plage (Somme) T: 03 22 23 40 30. E: info@campingleroyon.com

**alanrogers.com/FR80040**

This busy site, some two kilometres from the sea, has 376 pitches of which just 30 are used for touring units. Fourteen are near the entrance, the remainder are set amongst the mobile homes. They are of either 95 or 120 sq.m, level, marked, numbered and divided by hedges. There is also an additional space for 50 tents. Electricity (6A) and water points are available to all. The remaining 296 pitches are used for mobile homes. The site is well lit, fenced and guarded at night (€ 30 deposit for barrier card). Entertainment is organised for adults and children in July/Aug when it will be very full. Nearby there are opportunities for windsurfing, sailing, sand yachting, canoeing, swimming, climbing and shooting. The site is close to the Baie de l'Authie which is an area noted for migrating birds.

### Facilities

Four toilet blocks provide unisex facilities with British and Turkish style WCs and washbasins in cubicles. Units for disabled visitors. Baby baths. Laundry facilities. Shop (15/3-1/11). Gas supplies. Mobile takeaway calls evenings in July/Aug. Clubroom and bar (15/3-1/11). Heated, open-air and covered pools, children's pool and sun terrace (15/6-15/9). Play area. Games room with TV. Multisport court. Tennis. Boules. Bicycle hire. WiFi over site (charged). Off site: Fishing, riding, golf and watersports centre within 1 km. Train station 15 km.

**Open:** 15 March - 1 November.

### Directions

From A16 exit 24, take the D32 around Rue (road becomes D940 for a while then continues as D32 Fort-Mahon-Plage). Site is on right after 19 km. GPS: 50.33229, 1.5796

### Charges guide

| Per unit incl. up to 3 persons | |
|---|---|
| and electricity | € 19.00 - € 33.00 |
| extra person (over 1 yr) | € 7.00 |
| dog | € 3.00 |

Open from 9th of March until the 1st of November 2012.

Campsite at 2.5 km of the beach.
Mobil Homes for rent per night or per week.

Covered and heated swimmingpool (Easter until September).
Animations, Kidsclub, Sportsterrain, Fitnessarea, playground.

**Camping le Royon****

1271 route de quend - 80120 fort mahon plage
téléphone 03.22.23.40.30
info@campingleroyon.com - www.campingleroyon.com

VOTRE CAMPING FORT-MAHON PLAGE

# Fort-Mahon-Plage

## Camping le Vert Gazon

741 route de Quend, F-80120 Fort-Mahon-Plage (Somme) T: 03 22 23 37 69.

E: camping@camping-levertgazon.com **alanrogers.com/FR80140**

Discover the French seaside resort of Fort-Mahon-Plage by staying at this small, family run site with its 123 pitches on level grass. There are 40 places for touring units and two dedicated sections for tents. The enthusiastic owner organises entertainment in high season which will be very French in style. The whole area gets very busy in high season with all the aquatic activities you could wish for; the local council even provides free hand-drawn tri-cars to enable disabled visitors to be taken across the wide sandy beaches. There are flat cycle routes through the pine forest and down to the coast. The Marquenterre bird reserve is nearby, as is the steam train around the Somme Bay.

### Facilities

The single large toilet block is old but renovated, giving a clean, bright feel, with unisex showers, washbasins in cubicles and British style WCs. Ramped facilities for disabled visitors. Bar with snacks and disco (July/Aug). Small heated swimming pool and children's pool. Pétanque. Play area. Organised entertainment (July/Aug). Bicycle hire. Free WiFi over part of site. Off site: Supermarket with fuel 1 km. Golf and beach 2 km. Riding 5 km. Local markets.

**Open:** 1 April - 7 October.

### Directions

From A16 exit 24, take D32 around Rue, when the road becomes the D940 for a while, then continues again as D32 towards Fort-Mahon-Plage. Site is on right 18 km. from the A16. GPS: 50.334395, 1.57403

### Charges guide

| Per unit incl. 2 persons | |
|---|---|
| and electricity | € 23.90 - € 25.90 |
| extra person | € 5.00 - € 7.00 |

**FREE** Alan Rogers Travel Card
Extra benefits and savings - see page 10

## Guignicourt
### Camping Municipal Guignicourt

14 bis rue des Godins, F-02190 Guignicourt (Aisne) T: 03 23 79 74 58. E: mairie-guignicourt@wanadoo.fr
**alanrogers.com/FR02060**

This very pleasant, little municipal site has 100 pitches, 20 for long stay units and 80 for touring units. These two sections are separated by the main facilities on a higher terrace. Pitches are generally large and level, although you might need an extra long electricity lead for some, but there are few dividing hedges. Pitches along the river bank have most shade, with a few specimen trees providing a little shade to some of the more open pitches. On a quiet evening you are likely to hear the site's nightingales. The town is quite attractive and is worthy of an evening stroll.

| Facilities | Directions |
|---|---|
| The modern sanitary unit has British and Turkish style toilets, washbasins (cold only except for the one in a cubicle), pushbutton hot showers. Play area. Boules. Fishing. Off site: The town has all services including a supermarket and bank. Golf 3 km. Beach 15 km. Good train service into Reims with its spectacular cathedral. | Guignicourt is 20 km. north of Reims, just east of the A26, exit 14. The site is well signed from D925 in the village. GPS: 49.4320, 3.9704 |

**Open:** 1 April - 30 September.

**Charges guide**

| | |
|---|---|
| Per person | € 2.20 |
| pitch incl. electricity | € 11.10 - € 13.20 |

---

## Le Crotoy
### Kawan Village le Ridin

Lieu-dit Mayocq, F-80550 Le Crotoy (Somme) T: 03 22 27 03 22. E: leridin@baiedesommepleinair.com
**alanrogers.com/FR80110**

Le Ridin is a popular family site in the countryside just 2 km. from Le Crotoy with its beaches and marina, and 6 km. from the famous bird reserve of Le Marquenterre. The site has 162 pitches, including 40 for touring, the remainder occupied by mobile homes and chalets (for rent). There is some shade. The pitches and roads are unsuitable for large units. The site amenities are housed in beautifully converted barns across the road and these include a heated pool, fitness centre, bar/restaurant and bicycles for hire. Reception staff are helpful and will advise on local excursions.

| Facilities | Directions |
|---|---|
| Toilet blocks are heated in cool weather and provide good showers and special facilities for children. Laundry facilities. Motorcaravan service point. Restaurant/bar. Small shop. Swimming and paddling pools (15/5-15/9). Fitness centre. Games room. Play area. TV room. Bicycle hire. Entertainment and activity programme in high season. WiFi over site (charged). Off site: Golf 2 km. Fishing and riding 3 km. Birdwatching 6 km. | From A16 (Calais-Abbéville) take exit 24 and follow signs to Le Crotoy. At roundabout on arrival at Le Crotoy turn towards St Férmin, then second road on right. GPS: 50.23905, 1.63182 |

**Open:** 29 March - 3 November.

**Charges 2013**

| | |
|---|---|
| Per person incl. 2 persons and electricity | € 19.50 - € 31.00 |
| extra person | € 5.30 - € 5.80 |

Camping Cheques accepted.

---

## Miannay
### Camping le Clos Cacheleux

12, route de Bouillancourt, F-80132 Miannay (Somme) T: 03 22 19 17 47.
E: raphael@camping-lecloscacheleux.fr **alanrogers.com/FR80210**

Le Clos Cacheleux is a well situated campsite of eight hectares bordering woodland in the park of the Château Bouillancourt, which dates from the 18th century. It is 11 km. from the Bay of the Somme, regarded as being amongst the most beautiful bays in France. There are 90 very large, grassy pitches (230-250 sq.m) and all have electricity (10A Europlug), five also with water and waste water. The aim of the owners is to make your stay as enjoyable as possible and improvements are being made each year. There is no shop or bar, but all visitors have access to the swimming pool, shop, bar and children's club of the sister site – le Val de Trie, less than five minutes' walk away. A Sites et Paysages member.

| Facilities | Directions |
|---|---|
| Two modern sanitary blocks are clean and well maintained with a baby room and facilities for disabled visitors. Laundry facilities. Fridge hire. Adult fitness area. Fishing pond. Free WiFi. At the sister site: shop, bar with terrace (21/4-15/9). Restaurant and takeaway (27/4-1/9). Covered pool (13/4-30/9). Library and TV room. Play area. Boules. Picnic tables. Off site: Village 1 km. Hypermarket in Abbeville. Riding 4 km. Golf 9 km. Beaches 15 km. | From the A28 at Abbeville take the D925 towards Eu and Le Tréport; do not go towards Moyenville. Turn left in Miannay village onto the D86 towards Toeufles. After 2 km. site is on right opposite road into Bouillantcourt village. GPS: 50.08352, 1.71343 |

**Open:** 15 March - 15 October.

**Charges 2013**

| | |
|---|---|
| Per unit incl. 2 persons and electricity | € 18.50 - € 27.00 |
| extra person | € 3.30 - € 5.60 |

---

For latest campsite news, availability and prices visit

# alanrogers.com

## Moyenneville
### Camping le Val de Trie

Rue des Sources, Bouillancourt-sous-Miannay, F-80870 Moyenneville (Somme) T: 03 22 31 48 88.
E: raphael@camping-levaldetrie.fr **alanrogers.com/FR80060**

Le Val de Trie is a natural countryside site in woodland, near a small village. The 80 numbered, grassy touring pitches are of a good size, divided by hedges and shrubs with mature trees providing good shade in most areas, and all have electricity (10A), 11 also with water and waste water. It can be very quiet in April, June, September and October. If there is no-one on site, just choose a pitch or call at the farm to book in. This is maturing into a well managed site with modern facilities and a friendly, relaxed atmosphere. It is well situated for the coast and also the cities of Amiens and Abbeville. There are five new wooden chalets (including one for disabled visitors). There are good walks around the area and a notice board keeps campers up to date with local market, shopping and activity news. English is spoken. The owners of le Val de Trie have recently opened a new campsite nearby, le Clos Cacheleux (FR80210), where larger units can be accommodated.

### Facilities

Two clean, recently renovated sanitary buildings include washbasins in cubicles, units for disabled visitors, babies and children. Laundry facilities. Microwave. Shop, bar with TV (all season), bread to order and butcher visits in season. Snack bar with takeaway (27/4-1/9). Room above bar for children. Covered heated swimming pool with jacuzzi (13/4-29/9). Outdoor pool for children (27/4-8/9). WiFi in bar area (free). Electric barbecues are not permitted. Off site: Riding 4 km. Golf 10 km. Beach 12 km.

**Open:** 29 March - 15 October.

### Directions

From A28 take exit 2 near Abbeville and D925 to Miannay. Turn left on D86 to Bouillancourt-sous-Miannay: site is signed in village. GPS: 50.08539, 1.71499

### Charges 2013

| Per unit incl. 2 persons | |
| --- | --- |
| and electricity | € 18.90 - € 27.10 |
| extra person | € 3.30 - € 5.60 |
| child (under 7 yrs) | € 2.10 - € 3.60 |
| dog | € 1.80 - € 2.10 |

Camping Cheques accepted.

## Nampont-Saint Martin
### Kawan Village la Ferme des Aulnes

505

1 rue du Marais, Fresne-sur-Authie, F-80120 Nampont-Saint Martin (Somme) T: 03 22 29 22 69.
E: contact@fermedesaulnes.com **alanrogers.com/FR80070**

This peaceful site, with 134 pitches, has been developed on the meadows of a small, 17th-century farm on the edge of Fresne and is lovingly cared for by its new enthusiastic owners, Marie and Denis Lefort and their hard working team. Restored outbuildings house reception and the facilities, around a central courtyard that boasts a fine heated swimming pool. A new development includes a bar and entertainment room. Outside, facing the main gate, are 20 large, level grass pitches for touring. There is also an area for tents. The remaining 22 touring pitches are in the main complex, hedged and fairly level. Activities are organised for children and there are indoor facilities for poor weather. From here you can visit Crécy, Agincourt, St Valéry and Montreuil (where Victor Hugo wrote Les Misérables). The nearby Bay of the Somme has wonderful sandy beaches and many watersports.

### Facilities

Both sanitary areas are heated and include washbasins in cubicles with a large cubicle for disabled visitors. Shop. Piano bar and restaurant. Motorcaravan service point. TV room. Swimming pool (16x9 m; heated and with cover for cooler weather). Jacuzzi and sauna. Fitness room. Aquagym and balnéotherapy. Playground. Boules. Archery. Free WiFi over part of site. Shuttle service to stations and airports. Off site: Private lake fishing 2 minutes away. River fishing 100 m. Golf 1 km. Riding 8 km.

**Open:** 30 March - 3 November.

### Directions

From Calais, take A16 to exit 25 and turn for Arras for 2 km. and then towards Abbeville on N1. At Nampont-St Martin turn west on D485 and site will be found in 2 km. GPS: 50.33645, 1.71285

### Charges guide

| | |
|---|---|
| Per unit incl. 2 persons and electricity | € 27.00 - € 35.00 |
| extra person | € 7.00 |
| child (under 7 yrs) | € 4.00 |
| dog | € 4.00 |

Camping Cheques accepted.

La Ferme des Aulnes
★★★★
www.fermedesaulnes.com

For latest campsite news, availability and prices visit
**alanrogers.com**

## Orvillers-Sorel
### Aestiva Camping de Sorel

Rue Saint-Claude, F-60490 Orvillers-Sorel (Oise) T: 03 44 85 02 74. E: contact@aestiva.fr
**alanrogers.com/FR60020**

Aestiva Camping de Sorel is located north of Compiègne, close to the A1 motorway and is ideal as an overnight stop. The site has 94 large grassy pitches, of which 50 are available for touring, all with electrical connections (three with water and waste water). The original farm buildings have been carefully converted to house the site's main amenities including a bar, restaurant and the toilet facilities. The site is open for a long season but most amenities are only open from April to September. The site is, however, close to the village of Sorel with its shops and restaurants. There are five mobile homes for rent. Compiègne lies 15 km. to the south and its château and several museums are well worth a visit.

**Facilities**

Toilet block with facilities for children and disabled visitors. Laundry facilities. Motorcaravan service point. Bar, restaurant, snack bar and takeaway 15/5-15/10). Play area. Boules. Hairdressing service. Multigym and sauna. WiFi throughout (charged). Off site: Tennis. Fishing 5 km. Riding and golf 8 km. Compiègne 15 km.

**Open:** 1 February - 14 December.

**Directions**

Take exit 11 from the A1 motorway (Lille-Paris) and join the northbound N17. Site is signed to the right on reaching village of Sorel after 8 km.
GPS: 49.56688, 2.70841

**Charges guide**

| Per unit incl. 2 persons | |
| --- | --- |
| and electricity | € 17.00 - € 18.50 |
| extra person | € 6.00 |

Camping Cheques accepted.

## Saint Quentin-en-Tourmont
### Camping Caravaning le Champ Neuf

Rue du Champ Neuf, F-80120 Saint Quentin-en-Tourmont (Somme) T: 03 22 25 07 94.
E: contact@camping-lechampneuf.com **alanrogers.com/FR80020**

Le Champ Neuf is located in Saint Quentin-en-Tourmont, on the Bay of the Somme. It is a quiet site, 900 m. from the ornithological reserve of Marquenterre, the favourite stop for thousands of migratory birds; birdwatchers will appreciate the dawn chorus and varied species. This eight-hectare site has 157 pitches with 34 for touring, on level grass with 6/10A electricity. The site is only 75 minutes from Calais, 18 km. from the motorway. An excellent covered pool complex has been added, including a flume, jacuzzi and pool for toddlers, and a fitness room and sauna. This area is particularly good for cycling with several level, traffic-free routes nearby. The Bay of the Somme, Saint Valéry, watersports and the cathedral city of Amiens are all close.

**Facilities**

Four unisex toilet blocks have showers, washbasins in cubicles, family cubicles and facilities for disabled visitors. Laundry facilities. Motorcaravan service point. Bar, entertainment area and snack bar. Play area. TV. Games room. Covered, heated pool complex including slides, jacuzzi and children's pool. Fitness room. Sauna. Multisport court. WiFi in bar area (free). Off site: Shops, restaurants and bars in Rue 7 km.

**Open:** 1 April - 1 November.

**Directions**

From A16 exit 24, take D32 towards and around Rue. At second roundabout take second exit on D940, then left on D4 for 1.5 km. before turning right on D204 to Le Bout des Crocs. Site is signed to the left. GPS: 50.26895, 1.60263

**Charges guide**

| Per unit incl. 2 persons | |
| --- | --- |
| and electricity | € 20.00 - € 30.00 |
| extra person | € 5.00 - € 6.50 |
| child (2-7 yrs) | € 3.00 - € 4.00 |
| dog | € 1.50 |

**FREE** Alan Rogers Travel Card
Extra benefits and savings - see page 10

## Saint Valery-sur-Somme
### Castel Camping le Château de Drancourt
B.P. 80022, F-80230 Saint Valery-sur-Somme (Somme) T: 03 22 26 93 45. E: chateau.drancourt@wanadoo.fr

**alanrogers.com/FR80010**

This is a popular, busy and lively site within easy distance of the Channel ports, between Boulogne and Dieppe. There are 356 pitches in total, of which 130 are occupied by several tour operators; 30 units for rent, and 26 privately owned. The 170 touring pitches are on level grass, of good size, some in shade and others in the open, all with electricity (10A). The site is well landscaped and, in spite of the numbers in high season, does not feel overcrowded. It can be dusty around the reception buildings and the château in dry weather. Day trips to Paris are organised in high season.

**Facilities**

Three toilet blocks include washbasins in cubicles, family bathrooms and facilities for disabled visitors. Laundry facilities. Drainage difficulties can cause occasional problems. Shop, restaurant and takeaway, several bars (all Easter-mid Sept). TV rooms. Games room. Heated pools, one indoor, one outside (1/6-15/9) and paddling pool. Tennis. Golf practice range. Minigolf. Bicycle hire. Fishing. WiFi in bar area (charged). Off site: Beach 14 km.

**Open:** Easter - 1 November.

**Directions**

Site is 2.5 km. south of St Valery and signed from the D940 Berck-Le Tréport road. Turn south on the D48 Estreboeuf road. Turn immediately left to Drancourt and site. GPS: 50.15281, 1.63614

**Charges guide**

| | |
|---|---|
| Per unit incl. 2 persons and electricity | € 17.00 - € 35.00 |
| extra person | € 4.50 - € 7.50 |
| child (under 5 yrs) | € 3.50 - € 5.20 |

---

## Saint Valery-sur-Somme
### Camping Airotel Le Walric

**505**

Route d'Eu, F-80230 Saint Valery-sur-Somme (Somme) T: 03 22 26 81 97. E: info@campinglewalric.com

**alanrogers.com/FR80150**

A clean, well kept and well managed site, Le Walric is about 75 minutes from Calais. A former municipal site, it has been completely updated with a new bar and snack bar, a pool complex, two play areas and entertainment in high season. There are 263 well laid out, large and level grass pitches. Of these, 47 with electricity connections are for touring, with the remainder used for a mix of new mobile homes and semi-residential caravans. The site's situation on the outskirts of the town make it an ideal holiday location. Medieval Saint Valéry is renowned for its association with William the Conqueror.

**Facilities**

Two heated toilet blocks include washbasins in cubicles and showers. Facilities for disabled visitors. Laundry room with baby changing. Motorcaravan service point. Shop. Bar with snacks and TV (1/4-1/11). Heated outdoor pool (15/4-16/9). Play areas. Tennis. Volleyball. Boules. Children's club and entertainment (July/Aug). WiFi (charged). Off site: Shops, restaurants, bars in Saint Valery. Fishing 1 km. Bicycle hire 2 km. Beach 7 km.

**Open:** 1 April - 1 November.

**Directions**

From A16 exit 24, follow D32 across N1. At the roundabout take D235 to Morlay; turn left on D940 and continue around Saint Valery until second roundabout where take first exit on D3 to site on right. GPS: 50.1838, 1.61791

**Charges guide**

| | |
|---|---|
| Per unit incl. 3 persons and electricity | € 19.00 - € 33.00 |
| extra person | € 7.00 |

---

## Seraucourt-le-Grand
### Camping du Vivier aux Carpes
10 rue Charles Voyeux, F-02790 Seraucourt-le-Grand (Aisne) T: 03 23 60 50 10.
E: contact@camping-picardie.com  **alanrogers.com/FR02000**

Vivier aux Carpes is a small quiet site, close to the A26, two hours from Calais, so is an ideal overnight stop but is also worthy of a longer stay. The 65 well spaced pitches, are at least 100 sq.m. on flat grass with dividing hedges. The 40 for touring units all have electricity (6A), some also with water points, and there are special pitches for motorcaravans. This is a neat, purpose designed site imaginatively set out with a comfortable feel. The enthusiastic owners and manager speak excellent English and are keen to welcome British visitors. This site is good for couples or fishing enthusiasts.

**Facilities**

The spacious, clean toilet block has separate, heated facilities for disabled visitors. Laundry facilities. Motorcaravan service point. Bar, snack bar and takeaway (July/August). Large TV/games room. Small play area. Bicycle hire. Pétanque. Fishing (about € 5.50 p/day). Gates open 07.00-22.00. Rallies welcome. WiFi (free). Cycling and walking tours from site. Off site: Village has a small shop, brasserie, café, nurse. Supermarket 8 km.

**Open:** 1 March - 31 October.

**Directions**

Leave A26 (Calais-Reims) at exit 11. Take D1 left (Soissons) for 4 km. Take D8, on entering Essigny-le-Grand (4 km), sharp right on D72 (Seraucourt-le-Grand, 5 km). Site signed. GPS: 49.78217, 3.21403

**Charges guide**

| | |
|---|---|
| Per unit incl. 2 persons and electricity | € 20.50 |
| extra person | € 4.00 |
| No credit cards. | |

---

For latest campsite news, availability and prices visit
# alanrogers.com

## Suzy

### Camping les Etangs du Moulin

F-02320 Suzy (Aisne) T: 03 23 80 92 86. E: contact@etangsdumoulin.fr
**alanrogers.com/FR02020**

Camping les Etangs du Moulin is a unique, small and friendly site to the south of Saint Quentin, which over the last few years has been transformed into a Wild West-themed holiday village. As well as the 61 touring pitches (with 6A electricity), an assortment of teepees, wagons and cabins are also available to rent. There are no fewer than eight lakes here, two stocked with trout and two with carp, making this site a good choice for anglers (fishing materials available for rent). The reception, restaurant and bar also follow the Wild West theme. Mountain bikes are available for hire.

#### Facilities

Two well maintained and modern unisex toilet blocks include hot showers and washbasins in cubicles. Family shower room with baby bath. Laundry facilities. Restaurant, bar/snack bar. Play area. Trampolines. Volleyball. Fishing. Mountain bike and go-kart hire. Tourist information. Teepees, wagons and cabins for rent. Free WiFi over part of site. Off site: Walking and cycle routes. Riding 10 km. Chateau de Coucy 10 km.

**Open:** 6 April - 30 September.

#### Directions

The site is close to the village of Suzy, to the west of Laon. From Laon, head west on D7 to Cessieres and then follow signs to Suzy and the site.
GPS: 49.548957, 3.470092

#### Charges guide

Contact the site for details.

---

## Villers-sur-Authie

### Kawan Village Caravaning le Val d'Authie

20 route de Vercourt, F-80120 Villers-sur-Authie (Somme) T: 03 22 29 92 47. E: camping@valdauthie.fr
**alanrogers.com/FR80090**

In a village location, this well organised site is fairly close to several beaches, but also has its own excellent pool complex, small restaurant and bar. The owner has carefully controlled the size of the site, leaving space for a leisure area with an indoor pool complex. There are 170 pitches in total, but with many holiday homes and chalets, there are only 60 for touring units. These are on grass, some are divided by small hedges, with 6/10A electric hook-ups, and ten have full services. The site has a fitness trail and running track, mountain bike circuit, and plenty of good paths for evening strolls. Ideas for excursions include the 15/16th century chapel and hospice and the Aviation Museum at Rue, Valloire Abbey and gardens, and the steam railway which runs from Le Crotoy to Cayeux-sur-Mer around the Baie de Somme. Another enjoyable day out would be to cycle the traffic-free route around the bay.

#### Facilities

Good toilet facilities, some unisex, include shower and washbasin units, washbasins in cubicles, and limited facilities for disabled campers and babies. Shop (not October). Bar/restaurant (5/4-12/10; hours vary). Swimming and paddling pools (lifeguards in July/Aug). Playground, club room with TV. Weekend entertainment in season. Multisport court, beach volleyball, football, boules and tennis court. Trampoline. Internet room. Fitness room including sauna (charged). WiFi throughout (charged). Off site: Shops, banks and restaurants in Rue 6 km.

**Open:** 30 March - 10 October.

#### Directions

Villers-sur-Authie is 25 km. NNW of Abbeville. From A16 exit 24 take N1 to Vron, then left on D175 to Villers-sur-Authie. Or use D85 from Rue, or D485 from Nampont St Martin. Site is at southern end of village at road junction. GPS: 50.31357, 1.69488

#### Charges guide

| Per unit incl. 2 persons | |
| --- | --- |
| and electricity | € 25.00 - € 33.00 |
| extra person | € 6.00 |
| child (2-6 yrs) | € 3.50 |

Camping Cheques accepted.

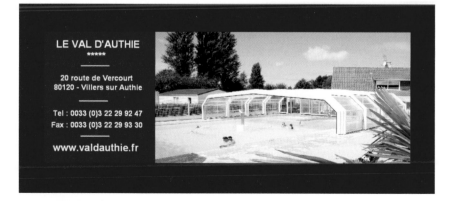

LE VAL D'AUTHIE
★★★★★

20 route de Vercourt
80120 - Villers sur Authie

Tel : 0033 (0)3 22 29 92 47
Fax : 0033 (0)3 22 29 93 30

www.valdauthie.fr

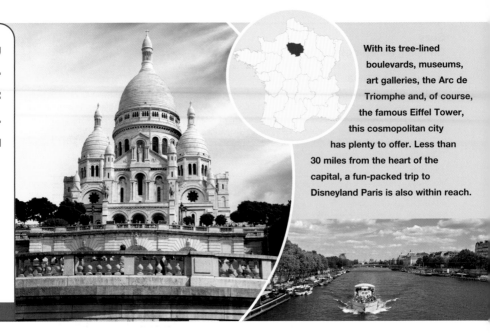

With its tree-lined boulevards, museums, art galleries, the Arc de Triomphe and, of course, the famous Eiffel Tower, this cosmopolitan city has plenty to offer. Less than 30 miles from the heart of the capital, a fun-packed trip to Disneyland Paris is also within reach.

**DÉPARTEMENTS: 75 PARIS, 77 SEINE-ET-MARNE, 78 YVELINES, 91 ESSONE, 92 HAUTS-DE-SEINE, 93 SEINE-ST-DENIS, 94 VAL DE MARNE, 95 VAL D'OISE**

**MAJOR CITIES: PARIS, VERSAILLES, IVRY, MELUN, NANTERRE, BOBIGNY, CRETEIL AND PONTOISE**

It is almost impossible to capture the magic and sophistication of Paris, an elegant city that enchants every visitor, whether they are scaling the heights of the Eiffel Tower, gliding along the Seine on a 'bateau mouche', or just watching the world go by from a romantic pavement café.

Away from the famous sights and luxurious shops, a verdant oasis awaits in the hills and secret woodlands of the Ile de France. Square bell towers in gentle valleys, white silos on endless plains of wheat; soft and harmonious landscapes painted and praised by La Fontaine, Corot and all the landscape painters. Paris is surrounded by forests, Fontainebleau, Compiègne, Saint-Germain-en-Laye and majestic châteaux such as Fontainbleau and Vaux-le-Vicomte.

Disneyland Resort Paris provides a great day out for all the family with two fantastic theme parks with over 70 attractions and shows to choose from. On the outskirts of Paris is Parc Astérix, with one of Europe's most impressive roller-coasters.

### Places of interest

*Fontainebleau:* château and national museum, history of Napoléon from 1804-1815.

*Malmaison:* château and national museum.

*Meaux:* agricultural centre, Gothic cathedral, chapter house and palace.

*Paris:* obviously! The list of places is too extensive to include here.

*St Germain-en-Laye:* château, Gallo-roman and Merovingian archaeological museum.

*Sèvres:* ceramics museum.

*Thoiry:* château and Parc Zoologique, 450-hectare park with gardens and African reserve containing 800 animals.

*Versailles:* Royal Castle, Royal Apartments, Hall of Mirrors, Royal Opera and French History Museum.

### Cuisine of the region

Although it has no specific regional cuisine, Paris and the Ile de France offer a wide selection of dishes from all the regions of France. Paris also has a wide choice of restaurants serving dishes from around the world.

**www.new-paris-idf.com**
**info@nouveau-paris-idf.com**
**(0)1 44 50 19 98**

---

## Crèvecoeur-en-Brie

### Caravaning des 4 Vents

Rue de Beauregard, F-77610 Crèvecoeur-en-Brie (Seine-et-Marne) T: 01 64 07 41 11. E: f.george@free.fr
**alanrogers.com/FR77040**

This peaceful, pleasant site has been owned and run by the same family for over 35 years. There are around 200 pitches, with many permanent and seasonal units, however, there are 140 spacious grassy pitches for tourists, well separated by good hedges, all with 6A electricity and a water tap shared between two pitches. The whole site is well landscaped with flowers and trees everywhere. This is a great family site with pool and games facilities located at the top end of the site so that campers are not disturbed. Crèvecoeur-en-Brie celebrates the 'feast of small villages' on 21/22 June each year. Central Paris is just a 40 minute train ride from the nearest railway station (8 km). Disneyland is just 15 minutes by road.

### Facilities

Three modern sanitary units (heated in cooler weather) provide British style WCs, washbasins (mainly in cubicles) and pushbutton showers. Facilities for disabled visitors. Laundry facilities. Motorcaravan service point. In high season (July/Aug) a mobile snack bar and pizzeria (open 16.00-23.00), and a baker (07.30-11.00). Well fenced, circular swimming pool (16 m. diameter; May to Sept). Playground, games room, volleyball and boules court. Riding (high season). Free WiFi. Off site: La Houssaye 1 km. Fontenay Tresigny 5 km.

**Open:** 15 March - 1 November.

### Directions

Crèvecoeur is just off the D231 between A4 exit 13 and Provins. From north, pass obelisk and turn right onto the C3 in 3 km. From south 19 km. after junction with N4, turn left at signs to village. Follow site signs. GPS: 48.75060, 2.89714

### Charges guide

| | |
|---|---|
| Per unit incl. 2 persons and electricity | € 27.00 |
| extra person (over 5 yrs) | € 6.00 |
| dog | € 3.00 |

**FREE** Alan Rogers Travel Card
Extra benefits and savings - see page 10

## Jablines
### International de Jablines

Base de Loisirs, F-77450 Jablines (Seine-et-Marne) T: 01 60 26 09 37. E: welcome@camping-jablines.com

alanrogers.com/FR77030

Jablines is a modern site which, with the leisure facilities of the adjacent Espace Loisirs, offers an interesting, if a little impersonal, alternative to other sites in the region. Man-made lakes provide opportunities for many water-based activities. The Grand Lac is said to have the largest beach on the Ile-de-France. The site itself has 150 pitches, of which 141 are for touring units. Most are of a good size (100-120 sq.m), often slightly sloping, with gravel hardstanding and grass, accessed by tarmac roads and marked by young trees. All have electrical connections, 60 with water and waste connections also. The whole complex close to the Marne has been developed around old gravel workings. Whilst staying on the campsite admission to the Base de Loisirs is free. Water activities include catamaran sailing, windsurfing, water boarding, canoeing, fishing and supervised bathing. There is a large equestrian centre, an orienteering course, a multisports court and mountain-bike trails.

**Facilities**

Two toilet blocks, heated in cool weather, include pushbutton showers, some washbasins in cubicles. Laundry facilities. Motorcaravan service point (charged). Shop (all season). Play area. Internet point in reception. Ticket sales for Disneyland and Parc Astérix. Mobile homes for rent. Off site: Bar/restaurant adjacent (500 m) at Base de Loisirs with watersports, riding, tennis and minigolf. Fishing, riding, bicycle hire, beach, boat launching all 500 m. Golf 15 km.

**Open:** 30 March - 29 September.

**Directions**

From A4 Paris-Rouen turn north on A104. Take exit 8 on D404 Meaux. From A1 south, follow signs for Marne-la-Vallée on A104. Take exit 6A Clay-Souilly on N3 (Meaux). After 6 km. turn south on D404 and follow signs. GPS: 48.91378, 2.73451

**Charges 2013**

| | |
|---|---|
| Per unit incl. 2 persons and electricity (10A) | € 26.00 - € 29.00 |
| extra person | € 6.50 - € 7.50 |

Camping Cheques accepted.

L'international de Jablines - www.camping-jablines.com - Tel: 0160260937

Base de loisirs de Jablines-Annet (77450)

## Louan
### Yelloh! Village Paris/Ile-de-France

Route de Montaiguillon, F-77560 Louan (Seine-et-Marne) T: 04 66 73 97 39.
E: info@yellohvillage-paris-iledefrance.com  alanrogers.com/FR77140

Formerly known as La Cerclière, this Yelloh! Village site 80 km. east of Paris lies at the heart of the Montaiguillon forest. This 11 hectare site contains 220 pitches, of which 40 are for touring units; the rest are occupied by chalets including 40, which are privately owned. The touring pitches occupy a small corner of the site, they are on sandy soil, are generally small and access to some is difficult; most are well shaded. The site boasts some impressive amenities including a swimming pool with water slides, as well as a balnéotherapy pool.

**Facilities**

The toilet block by the touring area was being refurbished when we visited, and will provide family rooms with shower and washbasin. Facilities for disabled visitors, and motorcaravan services appear to be in older, distant blocks and are very limited. Shop. Bar. Restaurant. Takeaway. Swimming pool complex with slides. Covered balnéotherapy pool. Multisports pitch. Bicycle hire (chalets only). Tennis. Fishing. Overhead cable runway (over 8s, charged). Pony rides (charged). Activity programme. Play area. WiFi (charged). Off site: Riding 2 km. Golf 10 km.

**Open:** All year.

**Directions**

Louan is 17 km. northeast of Provins. From the N4 Paris-Nancy road at Montceaux (west of Esterhay) turn south on D403 to Villiers St Georges, then east on D60 to Louan Villegruis Fontaine. The site is signed to the left. GPS: 48.63095, 3.49193

**Charges guide**

| | |
|---|---|
| Per unit incl. 2 persons and electricity | € 15.00 - € 36.00 |
| extra person | € 5.00 - € 7.00 |
| child (under 7 yrs) | free - € 7.00 |

For latest campsite news, availability and prices visit
# alanrogers.com

## Maisons-Laffitte
### Camping Caravaning International

1 rue Johnson, F-78600 Maisons-Laffitte (Yvelines) T: 01 39 12 21 91. E: ci.mlaffitte@wanadoo.fr

alanrogers.com/FR78010

This site on the banks of the Seine is consistently busy, has multilingual, friendly reception staff and occupies a grassy, tree covered area bordering the river. There are 317 pitches, 107 occupied by mobile homes and tour operators, plus two areas dedicated to tents. Most pitches are separated by hedges, are of a good size with some overlooking the Seine (unfenced access), and all 210 touring pitches have electricity hook-ups (6A). The roads leading to the site are a little narrow so large vehicles need to take care. Train noise can be expected.

### Facilities

Three sanitary blocks, two insulated for winter use and one more open (only used in July/Aug). Facilities are clean with constant supervision necessary, due to volume of visitors. Provision for disabled visitors. Motorcaravan service point. Self-service shop. Restaurant/bar. Takeaway food and pizzeria (all open all season). TV in restaurant, table tennis, football area. Fishing possible with licence. Internet point and WiFi (charged). Off site: Sports complex adjoining. Riding 500 m. Bicycle hire 5 km.

**Open:** 1 week before Easter - 3 November.

### Directions

From A13 take exit 7 (Poissy) and follow D153 (Poissy), D308 (Maisons-Laffitte), then site signs on right before town centre. From A15 exit 7 take D184 towards St Germain, after 11 km. turn left on D308 (Maisons-Laffitte). Follow site signs. GPS: 48.9399, 2.14589

### Charges guide

| Per unit incl. 2 persons and electricity | € 26.70 - € 32.20 |
|---|---|
| extra person | € 5.70 - € 6.40 |
| child (4-8 yrs) | € 2.60 - € 3.50 |

## Melun
### Kawan Village la Belle Etoile

Quai Joffre, la Rochette, F-77000 Melun (Seine-et-Marne) T: 01 64 39 48 12.
E: info@campinglabelleetoile.com  alanrogers.com/FR77070

Alongside the River Seine, this site has an overall mature and neat appearance, although the approach road is somewhat off-putting with several industrial plants. However, you will discover that la Belle Etoile enjoys a pleasant position with pitches to the fore of the site within view of the barges which continually pass up and down. The 165 touring pitches, 130 with 6A electricity connections, are on grass and laid out between the many shrubs and trees. There are ten units for hire. A friendly, family run site with pleasant and helpful English-speaking owners, it is ideally situated for visiting Fontainebleau and Paris.

### Facilities

The toilet blocks are not new but they are kept very clean and the water is very hot. Laundry room. Baby bath. Facilities for disabled visitors (shower, washbasin and WC). Motorcaravan service point. Shop, small bar, snacks and takeaway (all 1/7-29/8). Heated outdoor swimming pool (1/5-1/9). Play area. Bicycle hire. WiFi over site (charged). Only gas and charcoal barbecues are allowed. Tickets for Disney and Vaux le Vicomte are sold by the site. Off site: Bus to connect with trains 100 m. Fishing 100 m. Golf and riding 15 km. Fontainebleau and Paris.

**Open:** 30 March - 12 October.

### Directions

Travelling north on RD606 Fontainebleau-Melun road, on entering La Rochette, pass petrol station on left. Turn immediately right into Ave de la Seine. At end of road turn left at river, site on left in 500 m. GPS: 48.52502, 2.66940

### Charges guide

| Per unit incl. 2 persons and electricity | € 21.00 - € 25.00 |
|---|---|
| extra person | € 5.75 - € 6.90 |
| child (3-11 yrs) | € 3.80 - € 4.80 |
| dog | € 1.50 |

Camping Cheques accepted.

**Got yours yet?**
Extra benefits and savings - see page 10

**FREE** Alan Rogers Travel Card
Extra benefits and savings - see page 10

# Paris
## Camping Indigo Paris

2 allée du Bord de l'Eau, F-75016 Paris (Paris) T: 01 45 24 30 00. E: paris@camping-indigo.com
**alanrogers.com/FR75020**

A busy site and the nearest to the city, set in a wooded area between the Seine and the Bois de Boulogne. The site is quite extensive but nevertheless becomes very full with many international visitors, with noise well into the night, despite the rules. There are 510 pitches of varying size (including mobile homes) of which 280 are marked, with electricity (10A), water, drainage and TV aerial connections. The site is under new management and as a result an improvement and development programme is in progress including the refurbishment of some toilet blocks. Reservations are made for pitches – if not booked, arrive early in season (mornings). At the entrance is a functional, modern reception building (07.00-22.00) with a code operated barrier system. One can reach the Champs Elysees in 10-15 minutes by car or, from April to October, a shuttle bus runs every half hour from the site to the Metro station. Excursions are organised in July and August and there are ticket sales for Disneyland, Asterix Parc, etc. Note: you are in a major city environment – take care of valuables.

### Facilities

New sanitary blocks have British style WCs, washbasins in cubicles and showers with divider and seat (warm water throughout). All these facilities suffer from heavy use in season. Laundry room. Two motorcaravan service points. Shop, bar, restaurant and takeaway. Bar open 07.00-24.00 most times and until 02.00 in peak season. Pizza bar and takeaway. Small Playground. Bicycle hire. WiFi (free). Off site: Fishing 1 km. Bicycle hire 2 km.
**Open:** All year.

### Directions

Site is on east side of Seine between the river and the Bois de Boulogne, just north of the Pont de Suresnes. Easiest approach is from Port Maillot. Traffic lights at site entrance. Follow signs closely and use a good map. GPS: 48.86833, 2.234753

### Charges guide

| | |
|---|---|
| Per unit incl. 2 persons and electricity | € 28.90 - € 39.10 |
| extra person | € 5.25 - € 7.45 |

# Pommeuse
## Camping le Chêne Gris

24 place de la Gare de Faremoutiers, F-77515 Pommeuse (Seine-et-Marne) T: 01 64 04 21 80.
E: info@lechenegris.com **alanrogers.com/FR77020**

This site is being progressively developed by a Dutch holiday company. Of the 350 pitches, 53 are for touring, many of which are on aggregate stone, the remainder (higher up the hill on which the site is built) being occupied by over 217 mobile homes and 80 tents belonging to a Dutch tour operator. The pitches are not suitable for larger units (over 7 m). Terraces look out onto the heated leisure pool complex and an outdoor adventure-style play area for over-fives, whilst the indoor soft play area is in a large tent at the side of the bar. The site is next to a railway station with trains to Paris (45 minutes).

### Facilities

One toilet block with pushbutton showers and washbasins in cubicles. At busy times these facilities may be under pressure. Facilities for disabled visitors and children. Laundry area. Bar, restaurant, takeaway and swimming pool complex (from Easter weekend). Indoor and outdoor play areas. WiFi (charged). Off site: Shops, bars and restaurants within walking distance. Fishing and riding 2 km.
**Open:** 20 April - 8 November.

### Directions

Pommeuse is 55 km. east of Paris. From A4 at exit 16 take N34 towards Coulommiers. In 10 km. turn south for 2 km. on D25 to Pommeuse; site is on right after level-crossing. GPS: 48.808213, 2.993935

### Charges guide

| | |
|---|---|
| Per unit incl. 2 persons and electricity | € 25.00 - € 44.00 |
| extra person | € 2.50 - € 5.00 |

Camping Cheques accepted.

For latest campsite news, availability and prices visit
# alanrogers.com

# Rambouillet

## Huttopia Rambouillet

Route du Château d'Eau, F-78120 Rambouillet (Yvelines) T: 01 30 41 07 34. E: rambouillet@huttopia.com

**alanrogers.com/FR78040**

HUTTOPIA

This pleasant site is now part of the Huttopia group whose philosophy is to rediscover the camping spirit. It is in a peaceful forest location beside a lake, with good tarmac access roads and site lighting. The 136 touring pitches, 100 with electrical connections (10A), are set among the trees and in clearings. As a result, shade is plentiful and grass sparse. The main area is kept traffic-free but there is a section for motorcaravans and those who need or prefer to have their car with them. The result is a safe, child-friendly site. There is an Espace Nature with 40 huge pitches for campers. As part of their efforts to be environmentally friendly, Huttopia have built a natural swimming pool. The water is filtered by reeds and was used for the first time in 2008, passing the stringent tests of France's Ministry of Health. The opening date each year depends on how quickly the reeds do their work, but it will certainly be open from June to September. From your pitch, you can stroll out into the forest and there are many good cycle routes and footpaths in the area.

### Facilities

The brand new sanitary block has controllable showers, some washbasins in cubicles and a number of more spacious family cubicles. Facilities for disabled visitors. Laundry facilities. Three outlying 'rondavels' each with two family rooms. Motorcaravan service point. Small shop (all season) selling basics plus bar/restaurant with terrace (weekends in low season and daily in July and August). Games room with TV. Play area. Natural swimming pool (June-Sept, earlier if possible). Bicycle hire. Fishing. Children's and family activities with a nature theme (July/Aug). Off site: Golf 2 km. Riding 3 km. Lake beach 15 km. Sailing 20 km. Shops, bars and restaurants in town plus large supermarket nearby.

**Open:** 28 March - 4 November.

### Directions

Rambouillet is 52 km. southwest of Paris. Site is southeast of town: from N10 southbound take Rambouillet/Les Eveuses exit, northbound take Rambouillet centre exit, loop round (site signed) and rejoin N10 southbound, taking next exit. Pass under N10, following signs to site in 1.7 km. GPS: 48.62638, 1.84375

### Charges 2013

| | |
|---|---|
| Per unit incl. 2 persons and electricity | € 23.30 - € 38.50 |
| extra person | € 5.60 - € 7.70 |
| child (2-7 yrs) | € 4.00 - € 4.90 |

**FREE** Alan Rogers Travel Card
Extra benefits and savings - see page 10

## Touquin

### Camping les Etangs Fleuris

Route Couture, F-77131 Touquin (Seine-et-Marne) T: 01 64 04 16 36. E: contact@etangs-fleuris.com

**alanrogers.com/FR77090**

This is a pleasant, peaceful site which has a very French feel. Of the 190 pitches, the 90 for touring are grouped on the level ground around the three attractive lakes, all with electricity (10A) and water, separated by hedges and with shade from mature trees. The life of the site centres round a smart bar/function room which doubles as reception and a shop, as well as the lakes and an attractive, irregularly shaped pool. The lakes are home to some sizeable carp as well as being restocked daily with trout (fishing € 5 for half a day). Ideal base to go to Paris (50 km) and Disneyland (23 km) and to provide a practical alternative to the busier sites nearer the centre.

**Facilities**

A fairly simple, heated toilet block has pushbutton showers and open washbasins (with dividers and hooks) for men but mainly in cubicles for ladies. No facilities for disabled visitors. Another heated block is only opened when site is very busy. Laundry facilities. Motorcaravan service area. Shop for basics in bar (1/4-15/9). Heated pool with paddling section (15/5-15/9). Takeaway and snacks (weekends and B.Hs in low season, every night high season). Internet access and WiFi (free). Multisports pitch. Minigolf. Trampoline. Off site: Riding 5 km. Zoo 7 km. Golf 15 km.

**Open:** 4 April - 15 September.

**Directions**

Touquin is off the D231, 21 km. from exit 13 of the A4 motorway and 30 km. northeast of Provins. From D231 follow signs for Touquin, then Etangs Fleuris. Site is 2.5 km. west of village. Well signed from D231. GPS: 48.733054, 3.046978

**Charges 2013**

| | |
|---|---|
| Per unit incl. 2 persons and electricity | € 22.00 |
| extra person | € 11.00 |
| child (3-11 yrs) | € 4.50 |
| dog | € 1.50 |

CAMPING Les Etangs Fleuris★★★

*Only 25 minutes from Disneyland Resort Paris!*

CAMPING Les Etangs Fleuris★★★ • Route de la Couture • 77131 Touquin
Tél.: +33 164 04 16 36 • Fax: +33 164 04 12 28
E-mail: contact@etangs-fleuris.com • www.etangs-fleuris.com

GPS location:
48.733054 / 3.046978

## Varreddes

### Le Village Parisien

Route de Congis (D121), F-77910 Varreddes (Seine-et-Marne) T: 01 64 34 80 80.
E: contact@villageparisien.com **alanrogers.com/FR77050**

If you are intending to visit Disneyland, this site is ideally situated 12 km. away. Tickets can be purchased at the site and taxi travel can be arranged. The site has 224 pitches and is reasonably well cared for with mature hedges dividing the pitches. There are 50 used for touring units and these vary both in size and quality. Access on some could be difficult for larger units. Unfortunately, Le Village Parisien is rather dominated by a large number of seasonal pitches (80%). The three toilet blocks are old and only just adequate. There is a reasonably large swimming pool (unheated).

**Facilities**

Three toilet blocks (old and in need of refurbishment, one closed in low season). Facilities for disabled visitors. Motorcaravan service point. Laundry facilities. Small shop and takeaway, bar with entertainment and TV (1/5-15/9). Swimming and paddling pools (1/5-15/9, unheated). Tennis. Play area. Fishing. Minigolf. Tickets and taxis for Disneyland. WiFi (charged). Off site: Golf 10 km.

**Open:** 15 March - 1 November.

**Directions**

Heading south on the A1 towards Paris, turn southeast on N330 at Senlis. Head towards Meaux, then turn left on D405 for Varreddes. Site is well signed from here (about 2 km). GPS: 49.002938, 2.941412

**Charges guide**

| | |
|---|---|
| Per unit incl. 2 persons and electricity | € 19.00 - € 27.00 |
| extra person (over 4 yrs) | € 4.00 |
| dog | free |

For latest campsite news, availability and prices visit
# alanrogers.com

## Veneux-les-Sablons
### Camping les Courtilles du Lido

Les Courtilles du Lido, chemin du Passeur, F-77250 Veneux-les-Sablons (Seine-et-Marne)
T: 01 60 70 46 05. E: lescourtilles-dulido@wanadoo.fr  **alanrogers.com/FR77130**

Les Courtilles du Lido is a well established, family run site located just outside the 14th-century village of Moret-sur-Loing on the edge of the Forêt de Fontainebleau. There are 180 well shaded grassy pitches with 10A electricity, dispersed throughout the five-hectare terrain, although access to some may be difficult due to low branches on overhanging trees. A good range of amenities includes a pool and an 18-hole minigolf course, as well as a pizzeria and bar. There are 19 mobile homes for rent. Some train noise can be heard from the site.

**Facilities**

A single toilet block provides adequate facilities including those for children. Shop, pizzeria, bar and takeaway (all season). Outdoor swimming pool (15/5-22/9). Play area. Games room. Motorcaravan services. Minigolf. Short tennis. Boules. Internet access and free WiFi. Off site: Fishing 500 m. Canoeing. Moret-sur-Loing (Gallo-Roman village) 2 km. Fontainebleau 5 km.

**Open:** 1 April - 30 September.

**Directions**

From Fontainebleau take southbound D606 (towards Sens). Upon arrival at Veneux-les-Sablons follow signs for Moret-sur-Loing and then St Mammès. Final approach is through a tunnel. Site is well signed. GPS: 48.38321, 2.80303

**Charges guide**

| | |
|---|---|
| Per unit incl. 2 persons and electricity | € 19.50 |
| extra person | € 4.00 |

---

## Versailles
### Huttopia Versailles

**HUTTOPIA**

31 rue Berthelot, F-78000 Versailles (Yvelines) T: 01 39 51 23 61. E: versailles@huttopia.com
**alanrogers.com/FR78060**

This Huttopia site is rather different. When the French owners visited Canada and experienced 'back to nature' camping, they were so impressed that they decided to introduce the idea to France. This is probably a little like camping as it used to be, but with some big differences. Gone are the formal pitches with neatly trimmed hedges, and instead there are 141 of ample size arranged informally amongst the trees, 93 with electricity (10A) and 14 with water and drainage as well. The terrain is as nature intended with very little grass and much of it steep and rugged. Long electricity leads are required and be prepared to use blocks and corner steadies on many pitches. Most pitches have good shade.

**Facilities**

Three well designed toilet blocks provide basic facilities, including those for children and disabled visitors. Laundry. Motorcaravan services. Bivouacs for cooking. Restaurant with takeaway (July/Aug and weekends). Bar. No shop but supermarket nearby. Games room. Simple swimming and paddling pools (11/4-23/9). Playground. Bicycle hire. Boules. No charcoal barbecues. Off site: Versailles and its château (tickets can be purchased at the site). Hiking.

**Open:** 21 March - 4 November.

**Directions**

From the front of the château of Versailles take the Avenue de Paris and the site is signed after 2 km. GPS: 48.79396, 2.16075

**Charges 2013**

| | |
|---|---|
| Per unit incl. 2 persons and electricity | € 34.20 - € 47.50 |
| extra person | € 7.20 - € 9.70 |
| child (2-7 yrs) | € 3.20 - € 5.30 |

Call 01580 214000 We can book this site for you! alan rogers ◉ travel

---

## Villiers-sur-Orge
### Camping le Beau Village de Paris

1 voie des Prés, F-91700 Villiers-sur-Orge (Essonne) T: 01 60 16 17 86. E: le-beau-village@wanadoo.fr
**alanrogers.com/FR91010**

This is a pleasant, typically French campsite just 25 km. south of Paris and conveniently located at the centre of a triangle formed by the A6 motorway, the N20/A10 to Orleans and the N104 east/west link road, La Francilienne. Half of its 124 pitches are occupied on a seasonal basis by Parisians or by mobile homes to rent; the remainder are touring pitches, all hedged and with 10A electricity. Trees provide some shade. Reception, in a traditionally-styled building, also has a pleasant little bar, a games room and an attractive terrace with wooden tables, benches, thatched canopies and a stone-built barbecue.

**Facilities**

Three toilet blocks, can be heated, have controllable showers and some washbasins in cabins. The main block has a baby changing room and laundry facilities. A second (older) block has facilities for disabled visitors. Small bar (high season and on demand). Games room. WiFi in reception area. Adventure play area. Free loan of canoes. Boules. Off site: Station with trains to Paris (20 mins) 700 m. Shops and restaurants nearby. Golf 2 km.

**Open:** All year.

**Directions**

From A6 leave at exit 6 (Savigny-sur-Orge). Turn southwest, follow signs for Quartier Latin on D25 then right at roundabout on D35 to Villiers-sur-Orge. Turn left just after river on Voie des Prés along river bank to site on left. GPS: 48.65527, 2.30409

**Charges guide**

| | |
|---|---|
| Per unit incl. 2 persons and electricity | € 18.00 - € 20.00 |
| extra person | € 4.50 - € 5.00 |

**FREE** Alan Rogers Travel Card
Extra benefits and savings - see page 10

The varied landscapes of Champagne-Ardenne include dense forests, vineyards and winding rivers. The whole area is dotted with fascinating ancient churches and castles, towns and villages.

**DÉPARTEMENTS: 08 ARDENNES, 51 MARNE, 10 AUBE, 52 HAUTE-MARNE**

**MAJOR CITY: REIMS**

Situated on the flatlands of Champagne are the most northerly vineyards in France where special processing turns the light, dry wine into 'le Champagne'. Nowhere else in the world are you allowed to make sparkling wine and call it Champagne. Reims and Epernay are the centres for the wine trade. It is not the names of the vineyards that have become famous but those of the shippers, such as Veuve Clicquot and Moët & Chandon.

This is essentially a place of rural peace, with chalky rolling fields, although there is some heavy industry in the north. This north-eastern slice of France has seen many European battles and the hilly terrain and deep forests of the Ardennes gave some advantage to the Resistance fighters of the last war when Ardennes was annexed to Germany. Its main city of Charleville-Mezieres was two distinct towns lying on either side of the Meuse river until their amalgamation in 1966 and each retains its individuality.

### Places of interest

*Charleville-Mezieres:* arcaded Palace Ducale, similar in style to the Place des Vosges in Paris. Birthplace of the poet Arthur Rimbaud.

*Chalons-sur-Marne:* perfect Gothic-style cathedral with 12th-century tower.

*Épernay:* home of Champagne production. Guided tours and tastings are available at some of the larger Champagne houses.

*Reims:* 13th-century Gothic cathedral. In 406, Clovis the first king of France was baptised here and the kings of France from Louis V11 to Charles X were crowned here.

*Troyes:* ancient capital of the Champagne region with a beautifully preserved city centre with a Gothic cathedral, dozens of churches and 15th-century houses. A system of boulevards shaped like a Champagne cork. Musée d'Art Moderne including works by Degas and Gaugin.

### Cuisine of the region

*Andouillettes de Troyes:* chitterlings sausage made from pork and onions and season with herbs.

*Madeleine de Commercy:* small, shell-shaped, buttery pastries with orange flavouring.

*Flamiche aux Maroilles/Goyere:* a hot creamy tart based on local cheese.

*Biscuits roses:* traditional pink biscuits made with eggs, flour and sugar, originally baked to accompany Champagne.

www.tourisme-champagne-ardenne.com
contact@tourisme-champagne-ardenne.com
(0)3 26 21 85 80

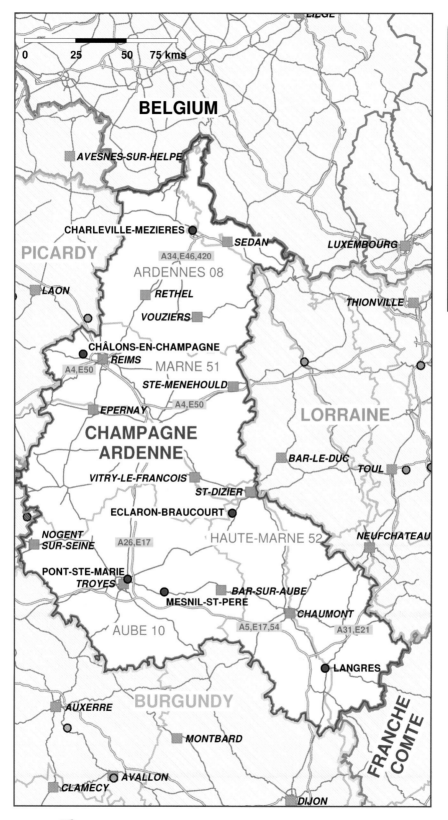

**FREE** Alan Rogers Travel Card
Extra benefits and savings - see page 10

## Châlons-en-Champagne

### Camping de Châlons-en-Champagne

Rue de Plaisance, F-51000 Châlons-en-Champagne (Marne) T: 03 26 68 38 00.
E: camping.chalons@orange.fr **alanrogers.com/FR51020**

The location of Châlons, south of Reims and near the A4 and A26 autoroutes, about 300 km. from Calais and Boulogne, makes this an ideal stopover. This site on the southern edge of town bears all the hallmarks of the good municipal site it was formerly: the wide entrance with its neatly mown grass and flowerbeds leads to tidy rows of large pitches separated by hedges, many with taps and drains adjacent. Of the 148 pitches, 89 are on gravel, the rest on grass; 96 have electricity (10A). Some overlook a small lake. Boat trips are available on the various rivers and canals.

**Facilities**

Two fairly basic toilet blocks include washbasins in cabins, baby room and hairdressing station. Good en-suite unit for disabled visitors. Laundry facilities. Bread to order. Open-air bar, snack bar and takeaway (1/5-30/9). Games (pool and babyfoot) and TV rooms. Fishing lake. Playground. Minigolf, tennis, volleyball, boules, mini-football. Motorcaravan service point. WiFi. Four mobile homes to rent. Off site: Bus stop 800 m. Fishing. Riding 1 km. Bicycle hire 3 km. Golf 15 km.

**Open:** 15 March - 15 November.

**Directions**

Châlons-en-Champagne is 50 km. southeast of Reims. From north on A4, take La Veuve exit (27) onto N44 Reims-Vitry road which bypasses town. Leave at St Memmie exit and follow camping signs. GPS: 48.9359, 4.3832

**Charges guide**

| | |
|---|---|
| Per unit incl. 2 persons and electricity | € 27.50 |
| extra person | € 5.15 |
| child (under 16 yrs) | € 2.50 - € 5.15 |

Camping Cheques accepted.

## Charleville-Mezieres

### Camping Municipal du Mont Olympe

Rue des Paquis, F-08000 Charleville-Mezieres (Ardennes) T: 03 24 33 23 60.
E: camping-charlevillemezieres@wanadoo.fr **alanrogers.com/FR08010**

Attractively situated alongside the Meuse River, within easy walking distance across a footbridge to the centre of the pleasant large town, this site was completely rebuilt in 2002. It now offers excellent facilities, with 121 grass pitches, 112 with electricity (10A), water and waste water connections. There are 66 from 108 to 219 sq.m. in size, 49 up to 106 sq.m. and seven hardstandings for motorcaravans. Many pitches are shaded by mature trees and all are separated by well kept hedges.

**Facilities**

Two heated buildings provide first class showers, private cabins, baby room and facilities for disabled visitors. Well equipped laundry room. Motorcaravan service point. Shop (July/Aug). Play area. TV and games room. Barbecues allowed at communal area only. WiFi. Off site: Municipal pool next door. Boat trips on the river. Attractive town centre close by. Bicycle hire 1 km. Golf 20 km.

**Open:** 1 April - 1 October.

**Directions**

Site north of Charleville on island of Montcy-Saint Pierre. From north D988/D1 follow river, over bridge, then immediately left. Site is 150 m. on from old site. GPS: 49.7790, 4.7207

**Charges guide**

| | |
|---|---|
| Per unit incl. 2 persons and electricity | € 16.25 |
| extra person | € 3.50 |
| child (2-10 yrs) | € 1.75 |
| dog | € 1.50 |

## Eclaron-Braucourt

### Camping la Presqu'ile de Champaubert

F-52290 Eclaron-Braucourt (Haute-Marne) T: 03 25 04 13 20. E: ilechampaubert@free.fr
**alanrogers.com/FR52010**

This site is situated beside what is said to be the largest man-made inland lake in Europe, the Lac du Der Chantecoq. This provides superb facilities for windsurfing, sailing, etc. and even for swimming from a 100 m. beach alongside the site (lifeguard in main season). The site itself is situated on the shores of the lake, with 195 fairly level grassy pitches of a good size, 70 for tourers, all with electrical connections (7A) and many with hardstanding. They are separated by hedges and trees that also provide a fair amount of shade. The general appearance and the views across the lake are very attractive.

**Facilities**

The current toilet block, although old, is fully equipped and clean. There are plans to replace it with a brand new block. Laundry facilities. Motorcaravan service point. Small shop for essentials in reception area. Bar/restaurant. New heated swimming pool is planned. Playground. Bicycle hire. Fishing. Mobile homes for rent. Off site: Beach for swimming. Miles of walking and cycle tracks. Birdwatching. Sailing and windsurfing on Lac du Der. Montier-en-Der with shops, restaurants and ATM 10 km.

**Open:** 3 April - 11 September.

**Directions**

From St Dizier, take D384 past Eclaron to Braucourt and follow signs to the site (3 km). GPS: 48.55425, 4.79235

**Charges guide**

| | |
|---|---|
| Per unit incl. 2 persons and electricity | € 15.00 - € 31.00 |
| extra person | € 4.00 - € 5.00 |
| child (3-7 yrs) | free - € 5.00 |
| dog | € 4.00 |

For latest campsite news, availability and prices visit
# alanrogers.com

## Eclaron-Braucourt

### Yelloh! Village en Champagne

F-52290 Eclaron-Braucourt (Haute-Marne) T: 03 25 06 34 24. E: info@yellohvillage-en-champagne.com
**alanrogers.com/FR52050**

Also known as Les Sources du Lac, this Yelloh! Village site is located close to the village of Eclaron and has direct access to the Lac du Der. This is a very large lake with 77 km. of shoreline and home to over 270 species of birds. Part of the lake is an ornithological reserve but a wide range of water based activities are on offer in other areas. These include fishing, windsurfing and sailing, and a separate area is reserved for motorboats. There are just 30 touring pitches here and around 120 mobile homes and chalets for rent. The town of St. Dizier and the city of Troyes are both an easy drive away.

#### Facilities

Two toilet blocks include facilities for babies. The facilities may be under pressure at busy times. Shop for basics. Bar. Restaurant. Takeaway. Swimming pool. Paddling pool. Direct access to the lake and beach. Play area. Bicycle hire. Fishing. Ornithological activities. Activity and entertainment programme. Off site: Sailing 6 km. Riding 10 km. Golf 30 km. Walking and cycle trails. Fishing. The Champagne route.

**Open:** 1 May - 30 November.

#### Directions

Eclaron is 7 km. southwest of St Dizier. From N4 (Paris-Nancy) on the St Dizier southern by-pass take D384 (Montier-en-Der). After passing Eclaron look for signs to the site on right. GPS: 48.57213, 4.84891

#### Charges guide

| | |
|---|---|
| Per unit incl. 2 persons and electricity | € 18.00 - € 35.00 |
| extra person (over 7 yrs) | € 5.00 - € 7.00 |

## Langres

### Kawan Village Lac de la Liez

Peigney, F-52200 Langres (Haute-Marne) T: 03 25 90 27 79. E: campingliez@free.fr
**alanrogers.com/FR52030**

Managed by the enthusiastic Baude family, this excellent lakeside site is near the city of Langres. Only twenty minutes from the A5/A31 junction, Camping Lac de la Liez provides an ideal spot for an overnight stop en route to the south of France. However, there is also a lot on offer for a longer stay. The site provides 131 fully serviced pitches, some with panoramic views of the 250 hectare lake with its sandy beach and small harbour where boats and pedaloes may be hired. Ideal for swimming and watersports, access to the lake is down steps and across quite a fast road. It is possible to cycle, or even walk, the 18 km. circuit around the lake. As well as all the activities on the lake, sporting provision on site includes a tennis court, volleyball, boules, archery and bicycle hire. The city of Langres with its old ramparts and ancient city centre is within easy reach (it was elected one of the fifty most beautiful towns in France). There are markets in Langres and many of the surrounding towns and villages.

#### Facilities

Two heated toilet blocks (one closed in low season) have all facilities including washbasins in cabins, controllable showers, and facilities for disabled campers and babies. A new block for 2013 has 8 en-suite units, along with new, large pitches with private sanitary facilities. Laundry facilities. Motorcaravan services. Shop, bar and restaurant (with takeaway food). Indoor pool complex with spa and sauna. Heated outdoor pool (1/6-15/9). Games room. Playground. Extensive games area. Tennis (free in low season). Bicycle hire. WiFi. Off site: Lake with beach.

**Open:** 1 April - 15 October.

#### Directions

From A5/A31 motorways follow signs for Langres. From Langres via N19 towards Vesoul. After 3 km. turn right, straight after large river bridge, then follow site signs. GPS: 47.87317, 5.38069

#### Charges guide

| | |
|---|---|
| Per unit incl. 2 persons and electricity | € 22.00 - € 33.50 |
| extra person | € 6.00 - € 8.00 |
| Camping Cheques accepted. | |

**FREE** Alan Rogers Travel Card
Extra benefits and savings - see page 10

## Langres

### Camping Navarre

9 boulevard Maréchal de Lattre de Tassigny, F-52200 Langres (Haute-Marne) T: 03 25 87 37 92.
E: campingnavarre@free.fr **alanrogers.com/FR52060**

Camping Navarre is a small municipal site of 66 pitches located in a unique position within the walls of the historic town of Langres. The pitches are grassy, well shaded and of a good size, 48 with electrical connections (10A). Although there are few amenities on site, the town centre is just a short walk away with a wide selection of shops, cafés and restaurants. Langres, with its 3.5 km. of ancient ramparts and imposing towers – including two within the grounds of the campsite – is classified as one of the 50 most beautiful towns in France. This site is ideal for a short stay, especially for those who like to be able to leave their vehicle on-site and walk. For those choosing to spend longer in the Haute-Marne, the surrounding countryside is well worth exploring, The Lac de la Liez (created in the 1880s to feed the Marne - Saône canal) has opportunities for water-based activities including windsurfing, sailing, and canoe and pedalo hire, and there is an 18 km. track around the lake for walking or cycling. For the less energetic, a drive along the Marne valley could be an attractive option.

**Facilities**

Modern, heated toilet block is clean and well maintained, with washbasins in cabins, good showers and basic facilities for disabled visitors. Dishwashing and laundry rooms. Fridge hire. Play area. Free WiFi in reception area. Off site: Langres centre. Fishing and watersports at Lac de la Liez 6 km. Cycle and walking tracks. Riding 10 km. Golf 20 km.

**Open:** 9 March - 2 November.

**Directions**

Langres is close to the intersection of the A5 and A31 motorways. Leave either motorway and head for the town centre. Site is just inside southern gate to city and is well signed. GPS: 47.86085, 5.33029

**Charges guide**

| | |
|---|---|
| Per unit incl. 2 persons and electricity | € 13.90 - € 16.80 |
| extra person | € 2.70 - € 3.65 |

**Camping Navarre**

*For a one-night stop or a longer stay in the historical city of Langres the campsite Navarre is ready to welcome you with a brand new toilet block*

Camping Navarre • 9, Boulevard Marechal de Lattre de Tassigny • 52200 Langres
Tél.: 0033 (0)325 87 37 92 • E-mail: campingnavarre@free.fr • www.camping-navarre-langres.fr

## Mesnil-Saint Père

### Kawan Resort Lac d'Orient

Rue du Lac, F-10140 Mesnil-Saint Père (Aube) T: 03 25 40 61 85. E: info@camping-lacdorient.com
**alanrogers.com/FR10020**

Le Lac d'Orient opened in 2009 and is one of the first Kawan Resorts, a new group of campsites in attractive rural locations and equipped with a good range of leisure amenities. The site can be found at the centre of the large Forêt d'Orient natural park and is just 100 m. from the Lac d'Orient which is ideal for all manner of watersports. Previously, a small municipal site, Kawan Resort Lac d'Orient has been rebuilt and offers a new restaurant, bar and takeaway, as well as a heated indoor pool and outdoor swimming pools with slides, all in one complex with the reception and the shop. The pitches are large and are semi-shaded with mature trees.

**Facilities**

One new, purpose built toilet block and one totally refurbished, both of a high standard. Facilities for disabled visitors. Laundry facilities. Motorcaravan services (outside site). Restaurant, bar and takeaway (31/3-16/9). Shop (as site). Heated indoor pool (as site) and outdoor swimming pools with slides (28/4-16/9). Paddling pool. Spa bath. TV room. Play area. Multisport court. Only one dog per pitch accepted. WiFi (free). Off site: Lac d'Orient 100 m. Windsurfing and sailing. Canoe and pedalo hire. Fishing.

**Open:** 31 March - 30 September.

**Directions**

Mesnil Saint-Père is 20 km. east of Troyes. From the north, leave A26 at exit 23 and join eastbound D619 (Lac d'Orient). Turn left on D43 following signs to Mesnil Saint-Père and then site.
GPS: 48.254856, 4.341359

**Charges guide**

| | |
|---|---|
| Per unit incl. 2 persons and electricity | € 25.00 - € 34.00 |
| extra person | € 6.00 - € 8.00 |
| Camping Cheques accepted. | |

For latest campsite news, availability and prices visit
# alanrogers.com

## Pont-Sainte-Marie
### Camping Municipal de Troyes

7 rue Roger Salengro, F-10150 Pont-Sainte-Marie (Aube) T: 03 25 81 02 64. E: info@troyescamping.net

**alanrogers.com/FR10010**

This municipal campsite, within the Troyes city boundary and about 2 km. from the centre, has been developed by two young enthusiastic managers who are turning it into an attractive place to stay. There are 150 level, grassy pitches (six with hardstanding), 140 for tourers, about equally shaded and open, and with electricity (10A Europlug). Being on one of the main routes from Luxembourg to the southwest of France, and on the main route from Calais to the Mediterranean, Troyes makes a good night stop or a base for discovering the lively city. As the old capital of the Champagne region, it is also a delightful city, with a marvellous mediaeval centre and interesting museums, and is well worth a longer stay.

### Facilities

Two modern toilet blocks contain British style WCs, washbasins and preset showers. Facilities for disabled visitors. Motorcaravan services. Washing machines and dryer. Shop for basics. Gas supplies. Restaurant, snack bar and takeaway (15/5-15/9), bar (20/6-10/9). Heated outdoor swimming pool (15/5-15/9). WiFi throughout (free). TV room. Games room. Play area. Minigolf. Boules. Bicycle hire. Off site: Bus to Troyes centre 100 m. Supermarket 100 m. Other shops, restaurants, bars, ATM 300 m. Riding 8 km.

**Open:** 1 April - 15 October.

### Directions

From all routes follow signs for Troyes and Pont-Sainte-Marie (just north of the old city centre), then signs for Camping Municipal. Site is on the Chalons road no. 77. GPS: 48.31124, 4.09683

### Charges guide

| Per unit incl. 2 persons | |
|---|---|
| and electricity | € 20.50 - € 24.80 |
| extra person | € 5.20 - € 6.20 |
| child (2-11 yrs) | € 3.35 - € 4.40 |
| dog | € 1.00 |

**FREE** Alan Rogers Travel Card
**Extra benefits and savings** - see page 10

For centuries, Lorraine has been a major European crossroads, resulting in a rich mixture of cultural influences. Today, it is an idyllic setting for holidays with a diverse historical and cultural heritage, plus endless forests, lakes, rivers and mountains to explore.

**DÉPARTEMENTS: 54 MEURTHE-ET-MOSELLE, 55 MEUSE, 57 MOSELLE, 88 VOSGES**

**MAJOR CITIES: NANCY, METZ**

Lorraine's position on the French border has made it vulnerable to war, and the history of those conflicts can be seen in many of the region's museums. It underwent periods of German rule, most recently from 1872-1918, and this is evident in its architecture, cuisine and language.

With a strong industrial tradition, Lorraine is a treasure trove of arts and crafts, in particular crystalware, earthenware and enamelwork, with many historical examples on display in specialist museums.

There are no less than three outstanding country parks, home to deer and wild boar, while mountain goats scale the high pastures of the Vosges mountains. The Vosges crests formed part of the battle front in World War One and military requirements led to the building of the road now known as the Route des Cretes which runs near to the highest peaks. It goes past more WWI sites than vineyards, and more 'ballons' (the highest peaks are so-called because they are round and bald) than villages but the view from the top is utterly breathtaking.

### Places of interest

*Epinal:* picturesque town and capital of the Vosges.

*Fermont:* underground fort at Longuyon, 50 km. north of Verdun.

*Metz:* 13th-century cathedral of St Etienne; Centre Pompidou Metz museum of modern art; Place St. Louis; Old City with Renaissance and Medieval architecture.

*Nancy:* Place Stanislas, a UNESCO World Heritage Site; 14th-century Porte de la Craffe; Arc de Triomphe.

*Verdun:* hill forts such as Fort de Vaux and Fort de Douaumont, large military cemetery at Douaumont.

Amnéville: 40-acre zoological park, one of the three largest in France, has 2,000 animals and a primate facility.

### Cuisine of the region

The cooking is peppery and hearty and quite unlike any other region.

*Bar-le-Duc ('Lorraine caviar'):* redcurrant jam de-seeded with a goose quill.

*Quiche Lorraine:* made only in the classical manner with cream, eggs and bacon.

*Potée Lorraine:* smoked meats combined with carrots, leeks and sometimes beans.

*Eau-de-vie:* a strong, white alcohol liqueur distilled from fermented fruit juices, including mirabelles (small yellow plums), cherries and pears.

**www.tourism-lorraine.com**
**contact@tourisme-lorraine.fr**
**(0)3 83 80 01 80**

## Burtoncourt

### Camping la Croix du Bois Sacker

F-57220 Burtoncourt (Moselle) T: 03 87 35 74 08. E: camping.croixsacker@wanadoo.fr

**alanrogers.com/FR57080**

This very attractive site is quiet and child friendly and has been run for the last few years by a young and enthusiastic couple who have made many improvements to this former municipal site. For example, the terrace has been enlarged, a small shop added and the facilities for disabled visitors improved. There are 60 small to medium, uneven and open pitches, some with shade and all with electricity and water taps. The site is not far from Metz and is well suited for travellers going south to Germany, Switzerland or Italy. Forming part of the site, a lake is good for fishing (carp).

**Facilities**

The seasonal and touring parts of the site have separate facilities. Showers are on payment (token). Turkish style toilets outnumber British style. Washbasins, some in cabins. Facilities for disabled visitors. Facilities may be stretched at peak times. Washing machine. Shop. Bar. Sports field. Tennis court. Play area. Lake swimming (July/Aug). Fishing. WiFi. Off site: Woodland walks.

**Open:** 1 April - 20 October.

**Directions**

From the A4 take exit 37 (Argancy) and follow signs for Malroy, Chieulles and Vany on RD3 towards Bouzonville. Then take D53 to Burtoncourt and site. GPS: 49.22499, 6.39943

**Charges guide**

| | |
|---|---|
| Per unit incl. 2 persons and electricity | € 18.00 |
| extra person | € 5.00 |
| child (2-12 yrs) | € 3.00 |
| dog | € 2.00 |
| No credit cards. | |

## Celles-sur-Plaine

### Camping des Lacs

F-88110 Celles-sur-Plaine (Vosges) T: 03 29 41 28 00. E: camping@paysdeslacs.com

**alanrogers.com/FR88140**

This is a well organised site with its own pool, close to the village centre, with many water-based and sporting activities available at the nearby lakes. There are 127 level touring pitches, 109 with electricity (16A) and 16 chalets and tents for hire. Some shady pitches border the tiny Plaine river, 35 pitches have gravel hardstanding, others are on grass, but all are surrounded by well trimmed mature hedges. The site is owned by a collaboration of regional and local organisations, with a very active and enthusiastic resident manager.

**Facilities**

Three good sanitary units equally spaced along the length of the site, have been completely refurbished to a very high standard. Each has controllable showers and washbasins in cabins, baby room with bath, children's unit, en-suite units for disabled visitors and laundry facilities. Small shop for basics. Bar, snack bar and takeaway (July/Aug plus weekends and on demand). Swimming and paddling pools. Play area. Entertainment in high season. Eco-friendly chalets for hire. WiFi in bar area. Off site: Beach with supervised lake swimming (July/Aug). Many activities at Base Nautique, adjacent to site, including fishing, bicycle hire and boat launching, and at nearby Lake Pierre-Percée including sailing 8 km. Tennis, minigolf etc. in the adjacent parkland. Riding 22 km.

**Open:** 1 April - 30 September.

**Directions**

Celles is 80 km. south east of Nancy. From N59 Nancy/St Dié, take exit for Raon l'Etape, from north turn right at T-junction in town, then take D392a north east for 10 km. to Celles-sur-Plaine, and follow camping signs. GPS: 48.454933, 6.94725

**Charges guide**

| | |
|---|---|
| Per unit incl. 2 persons and electricity | € 16.50 - € 25.50 |
| extra person | € 5.20 - € 6.20 |
| child (4-7 yrs) | € 3.70 - € 4.70 |
| dog | € 1.50 - € 2.00 |

For latest campsite news, availability and prices visit

**alanrogers.com**

# Corcieux

## Camping Au Clos de la Chaume

21 rue d'Alsace, F-88430 Corcieux (Vosges) T: 03 29 50 76 76. E: info@camping-closdelachaume.com
**alanrogers.com/FR88120**

This pleasant site is within walking distance of the town, on level ground with a small stream adjacent. The friendly family owners, who are British and French, live on site and do their best to ensure campers have an enjoyable relaxing stay. There are 94 level grassy pitches of varying sizes and with varying amounts of sun and shade. All 64 touring pitches have electricity hook-ups (6/10A) and some are divided by shrubs and trees. There are some chalets and caravan holiday homes on the site. The site boasts an attractive, well fenced, new swimming pool and an excellent small adventure-style playground.

### Facilities

Two units (one newly refurbished) provide well maintained facilities including a dual-purpose room for families and disabled visitors. Laundry with washing machines and dryers. Motorcaravan service point. Reception keeps basic supplies (July/Aug). New swimming pool (July-Sept). Play area. Games room. Boules. Volleyball. WiFi throughout (charged). Off site: Bicycle hire 800 m. Riding 2 km. Fishing 3 km. Golf 30 km. Corcieux market (Mon).

**Open:** 5 April - 18 September.

### Directions

Corcieux is 17 km. southwest of St Dié-des-Vosges. Site is on the D60, east of town centre, by the town boundary sign. GPS: 48.16826, 6.89025

### Charges guide

| | |
|---|---|
| Per unit incl. 2 persons and electricity | € 16.00 - € 22.50 |
| extra person | € 5.50 |
| child (2-7 yrs) | € 3.10 |

---

# Granges-sur-Vologne

## Flower Camping la Sténiole

1 le Haut Rain, F-88640 Granges-sur-Vologne (Vosges) T: 03 29 51 43 75. E: steniole@wanadoo.fr
**alanrogers.com/FR88110**

Set in a lovely rural area in the heart of the Vosges massif, this attractive site is run by a dedicated young couple who are constantly improving the site and its facilities. There are 125 pitches, either separated by hedges or beside the water. A small river has been used to form a small lake for fishing and swimming and a series of separate ponds (water quality is checked regularly). An atmosphere of relaxation is encouraged and the whole family can have a good time here. At an altitude of 720 m. there is easy access to 160 km. of paths and tracks for walking and cycling.

### Facilities

A new toilet block now supplements the original with further facilities in the main building provide all necessities including 4 private cabins. Washing machines and dryers. Bar. Restaurant (July/Aug). Takeaway (1/6-30/8). WiFi throughout (charged). Lake swimming. Fishing. Games room with TV and library. Play area. Tennis. Apartments and mobile homes to rent. Off site: Woods and hills for walking and cycling. Riding 5 km. Bicycle hire 4.5 km.

**Open:** 1 May - 30 September.

### Directions

Take the N420 from Epinal to Gérardmer then the D423 to Granges. There are two sites not far away from each other. GPS: 48.1217, 6.8284

### Charges guide

| | |
|---|---|
| Per unit incl. 2 persons and electricity | € 17.00 |
| extra person | € 3.50 |
| child (under 8 yrs) | € 2.50 |
| dog | € 1.00 |

---

# Granges-sur-Vologne

## Camping Gadémont Plage

2 Gadémont, F-88640 Granges-sur-Vologne (Vosges) T: 03 29 51 44 60. E: deleeuw697@aol.com
**alanrogers.com/FR88400**

Camping Gadémont Plage is open all year and can be found within the Parc Naturel Régional des Ballons des Vosges, close to the town of Granges-sur-Vologne. Pitches here are terraced and are generally well shaded. A number of pitches can be found on the banks of the little river which runs through the site. There is also direct access to a small lake (canoeing is possible – courses available) with fishing (free to campers). This is a good base for exploring the Vosges, which is, of course, a very popular region for adventure sports. Various activities are organised on site in peak season including occasional discos and sports competitions.

### Facilities

Two modern, clean toilet blocks, one by reception is heated. Showers by token in July/Aug. Facilities for disabled visitors in one block. Restaurant/snack bar. Takeaway. Activity and entertainment programme. Canoeing. Fishing. Play area. Fully equipped chalets and mobile homes for rent. WiFi. English and Dutch spoken. Off site: Shops, restaurants and cafés in Granges-sur-Vologne 2 km. Bicycle hire 3 km. Riding 4 km.

**Open:** All year.

### Directions

Approaching from Gérardmer, head north on D423 to Granges-sur-Vologne. You will see the site signed to the left 100 m. before reaching the village. GPS: 48.123783, 6.818449

### Charges guide

| | |
|---|---|
| Per unit incl. 2 persons and electricity | € 10.20 - € 17.00 |
| dog | € 1.50 |

---

**FREE** Alan Rogers Travel Card
Extra benefits and savings - see page 10

## Herpelmont

### Camping Caravaning Domaine des Messires

1 rue des Messires, F-88600 Herpelmont (Vosges) T: 03 29 58 56 29. E: mail@domainedesmessires.com

**alanrogers.com/FR88070**

Nestling in woods beside a lake, des Messires is a haven of peace and is perfect for nature lovers – not just birds and flowers but beavers, too. The Vosges is famous for its mountains and you can easily cross the Col de Schlucht to the Moselle vineyards and the medieval villages like Riquewihr with their old walls and storks on chimneys. The 114 good sized and fully serviced pitches are on grass over stone, with some directly by the lakeside, excellent for fishing. When the day is over, enjoy a leisurely meal at the restaurant overlooking the lake or just relax over a glass of wine. There are 22 mobile homes for rent.

#### Facilities

The fully equipped, airy toilet block has all washbasins in cabins, provision for disabled visitors (key from reception), baby room and laundry. Bar (all season) and restaurant (15/5-10/9) overlooking the lake. Takeaway (15/5-10/9). Two small play areas. Games and TV room. Canoeing and lake swimming. Programme of activities for children and adults in high season. WiFi (charged). Off site: Weekly markets in nearby Bruyères, Corcieux and St Dié.

**Open:** 19 April - 29 September.

#### Directions

From Épinal, exit N57 on N420 for St Dié and follow signs until you pick up signs for Bruyères. Lac du Messires is signed as you leave Bruyères on D423, at Laveline go south to Herpelmont and site. GPS: 48.1787, 6.74309

#### Charges 2013

| Per unit incl. 2 persons | |
|---|---|
| and electricity | € 19.00 - € 27.00 |
| extra person | € 4.00 - € 5.70 |

## La Bresse

### Domaine du Haut des Bluches

5 route des Planches, F-88250 La Bresse (Vosges) T: 03 29 25 64 80. E: hautdesbluches@labresse.fr

**alanrogers.com/FR88210**

Le Haut des Bluches is attractively located in the rolling hills of the Vosges and is close to the ski resorts of Gérardmer and La Bresse. The site is open most of the year with skiing possible in winter and it is a good base for nature lovers in summer. There are 140 slightly uneven and sloping grass/gravel pitches informally laid out in groups on terraces. These include 105 for touring, all with electricity (4/8/13A Europlug), long leads and rock pegs advised. Special areas of hardstanding for motorcaravans include some electricity hook-ups. Although there is little organised on the site, La Bresse (4 km) has a wide range of activities on offer.

#### Facilities

Two well appointed, modern, heated toilet blocks include cabins with WC, basin and shower. Facilities for babies and campers with disabilities. Motorcaravan services. Small shop (bread to order) and bar (all year). Restaurant and takeaway (high season and weekends in low season). Games/TV room. Play area. Multisport court. Boules. Internet. Off site: Several ski resorts, 5-8 km. La Bresse with shops, bars, restaurants, museums and market 4 km.

**Open:** All year excluding November to mid December.

#### Directions

La Bresse is 25 km. south of Gérardmer on the D486. At the eastern end of the town turn south on Route des Planches. Site is signed, entrance in 350 m. GPS: 47.998986, 6.918324

#### Charges guide

| Per unit incl. 2 persons | |
|---|---|
| and electricity | € 13.90 - € 23.20 |
| extra person | € 3.10 |
| child (4-12 yrs) | € 2.00 |

## Le Tholy

### JP Vacances - Camping de Noirrupt

15 chemin de l'Etang, F-88530 Le Tholy (Vosges) T: 03 29 61 81 27. E: info@jpvacances.com

**alanrogers.com/FR88030**

An attractive, modern, family run site, Camping de Noirrupt has a commanding mountainside position with some magnificent views, especially from the upper terraces. This is a very comfortable and high quality site and one that is sure to please. The tarmac site road winds up through the site with pitches being terraced and cars parked in separate small car parks close by. The 77 lawn-like tourist pitches are generally spacious, and the whole site is beautifully landscaped and divided up with many attractive shrubs, flower beds, decking and trees. Paved paths and steps take more direct routes between levels.

#### Facilities

Two very modern buildings at different levels, plus a small unit behind reception, all immaculate offer washbasins in cubicles, facilities for children and disabled campers. Washing machines and dryer. Shop. Bar, snack bar and takeaway (6/7-22/8). Swimming pool (15x10 m. 1/6-15/9). TV room (1/6-15/9). Tennis. Organised activities in high season. WiFi (charged). Heated chalets for rent. No double-axle caravans or American RVs.

**Open:** 1 May - 15 October.

#### Directions

From Gérardmer take D417 west towards Remiremont. In Le Tholy turn right on D11, continue up hill for 2 km, and site is signed to your left. GPS: 48.0889, 6.728483

#### Charges guide

| Per unit incl. 2 persons | |
|---|---|
| and electricity | € 19.10 - € 28.00 |
| extra person | € 4.13 - € 5.90 |
| child (under 7 yrs) | € 2.45 - € 3.50 |

## Metz

### Camping Municipal de Metz-Plage

Allée de Metz-Plage, F-57000 Metz (Moselle) T: 03 87 68 26 48. E: campingmetz@mairie-metz.fr

**alanrogers.com/FR57050**

As this site is just a short way from the autoroute exit and within easy walking distance for the city centre, it could make a useful night stop if travelling from Luxembourg to Nancy or for a longer stay if exploring the area. By the Moselle river, the 151 pitches are on fairly level grass and most are under shade from tall trees. Sixty-five pitches are fully serviced and 84 have electricity (10A). Tent pitches have a separate place beside the river.

**Facilities**

The two sanitary blocks, one newer than the other, are acceptable if not luxurious. Facilities for disabled visitors. Baby room. Laundry facilities. Motorcaravan service point. Shop. Bar, restaurant and takeaway. Hardstanding pitches for overnight stops for motorcaravans without electricity. WiFi (free). Bicycle hire. Fishing (permits for sale). Off site: Indoor pool adjacent (free entry). Riding 5 km. Golf 8 km.

**Open:** 24 April - 5 October.

**Directions**

From autoroute take Metz-Nord-Pontiffray exit (no. 33) and follow site signs. GPS: 49.12402, 6.16917

**Charges guide**

| | |
|---|---|
| Per unit incl. 2 persons and electricity | € 18.00 |
| extra person | € 3.00 |
| child (4-10 yrs) | € 1.50 |
| dog | € 0.50 |

## Saint Maurice-sur-Moselle

### Camping les Deux Ballons

17 rue du Stade, F-88560 Saint Maurice-sur-Moselle (Vosges) T: 03 29 25 17 14. E: stan0268@orange.fr

**alanrogers.com/FR88010**

Les Deux Ballons is in a narrow valley near the source of the River Moselle in the Vosges. The 150 pitches (all fully serviced, 4-10A electricity) are on stony ground or grass, some under trees and others in the open by a stream that runs through the site. Wild birds are abundant, including kingfishers. Try an exhilarating walk to the top of the nearby Ballon d'Alsace, 1,250 m. (or drive and walk the last half a mile). Theatre lovers should visit Bussang (6 km) and see the large wooden People's Theatre, built in 1895 and still performing in July and August every year; you will marvel at the raked stage and the enormous backstage areas which may be visited at any time.

**Facilities**

Two new up-to-date toilet blocks (open all season) and two older ones (high season only). Facilities for disabled campers and babies. Laundry. Motorcaravan service point. Gas supplies. Bar and takeaway (July/Aug). Large heated swimming pool with slide and children's pool (15/6-31/8). Fishing. Boules. TV. Internet point and WiFi (charged). Tennis. Bicycle hire. Off site: Shops and restaurant nearby. Riding 3 km. Paragliding 6 km. Mulhouse and car museum 30 minutes.

**Open:** 10 April - 15 September.

**Directions**

Site is on main N66 Le Thillot-Bussang road on western edge of St Maurice behind Avia filling station (entrance partly obscured so keep a look out). GPS: 47.85517, 6.81108

**Charges guide**

| | |
|---|---|
| Per unit incl. 2 persons and electricity | € 28.00 - € 34.00 |
| extra person | € 5.50 - € 5.80 |
| child (2-7 yrs) | € 4.10 - € 4.20 |
| dog | € 3.00 - € 3.50 |

No credit cards (except for online bookings).

**FREE** Alan Rogers Travel Card
Extra benefits and savings - see page 10

## Sanchey

### Kawan Village Lac de Bouzey

19 rue du Lac, F-88390 Sanchey (Vosges) T: 03 29 82 49 41. E: lacdebouzey@orange.fr

**alanrogers.com/FR88040**

Open all year, Camping Lac de Bouzey is 8 km. west of Épinal, at the start of the Vosges Massif. The 147 reasonably level grass pitches are separated by very tall trees and some hedging giving varying amounts of shade. There are 107 for touring, all with electricity (6-10A) and 100 fully serviced. They are on a gently sloping hillside above the lake and there are views over the lake and its sandy beaches. In high season there is entertainment for all ages, especially teenagers, and the site will be very lively.

**Facilities**

The refurbished toilet block includes a baby room and one for disabled visitors (there are some gradients). Small, heated section in the main building with toilet, washbasin and shower is used in winter. Laundry facilities. Motorcaravan service point. Shop and bar (all year), restaurant and takeaway (1/3-1/11). Heated pool (1/5-30/9). Fishing. Riding. Games room. Archery. Bicycle hire. Internet access. Soundproofed room for cinema shows and discos (high season). Lake beach, bathing and boating. WiFi. Off site: Golf 8 km.

**Open:** All year.

**Directions**

Site is 8 km. west of Épinal on the D460. From Épinal follow signs for Lac de Bouzey and Sanchey. At western end of Sanchey turn south, site signed. GPS: 48.16692, 6.35990

**Charges guide**

| Per unit incl. 2 persons | |
|---|---|
| and electricity | € 23.00 - € 34.00 |
| extra person | € 7.00 - € 10.00 |
| child (4-9 yrs) | free - € 7.00 |

Camping Cheques accepted.

---

## Saulxures-sur-Moselotte

### Base de Loisirs du Lac de la Moselotte

Les Amias B.P. 34, F-88290 Saulxures-sur-Moselotte (Vosges) T: 03 29 24 56 56. E: contact@lac-moselotte.fr

**alanrogers.com/FR88090**

This well run, spacious lakeside site, part of a leisure village complex, has 105 grassy pitches with 63 for touring. All have electricity (10A) and 30 of these also have water and a drain. They are individually hedged and a variety of young trees give only a little shade. The site is fully fenced with a security barrier with a key used for the gates to the lakeside. The adjacent Base de Loisirs offers a wide variety of activities and the area is very good for walking and cycling. Other attractions in the region include the Route des Vins in summer, and skiing in winter.

**Facilities**

The heated toilet block has key entry, controllable hot showers, some washbasins in cubicles and good facilities for babies and disabled campers. Laundry facilities. Shop (July/Aug). Bread to order. Bar/snack bar and terrace (all year). Bicycle hire. Play area. Outdoor skittle alley. Entertainment programme (July/Aug). Base de Loisirs adjacent with lake (swimming supervised July/Aug), sandy beach, play area, climbing wall, fishing, archery and hire of pedaloes, canoes and kayaks. 30 chalets for rent.

**Open:** All year.

**Directions**

From Remiremont take D417 east (St Amé), then right on D43 towards La Bresse for 10.5 km. Turn left into Saulxures (site signed), entrance on right by lake after 700 m. GPS: 47.95273, 6.75212

**Charges guide**

| Per unit incl. 2 persons | |
|---|---|
| and electricity | € 18.00 - € 21.00 |
| extra person | € 4.00 - € 5.00 |
| child (4-10 yrs) | € 2.40 - € 3.00 |

---

## Verdun

### Camping les Breuils

Allée des Breuils, F-55100 Verdun (Meuse) T: 03 29 86 15 31. E: contact@camping-lesbreuils.com

**alanrogers.com/FR55010**

Thousands of soldiers of many nations are buried in the cemeteries around this famous town and the city is justly proud of its determined First World War resistance. Les Breuils is a neat, attractive site beside a small fishing lake and close to the town and Citadel. It provides 162 flat pitches of varying sizes on two levels (144 for touring units), many with shade. Separated by trees or hedges, they are beside the lake and 120 offer 6A electricity connection (long leads will be necessary for some). The Citadelle Souterraine is well worth a visit and is within walking distance of the site.

**Facilities**

Two sanitary blocks are a mixture of old and new, including washbasins in cabins for ladies. Facilities for babies and disabled visitors. Laundry facilities. Cleaning variable. Motorcaravan services. Shop (1/5-30/9). Guide books sold at reception (1/5-31/8). Restaurant (1/6-20/8), bar (evenings 1/5-30/9). Swimming pool (200 sq.m) and children's pool (15/5-31/8). Play area. Multisports complex. Bicycle hire. WiFi. Off site: Town and boat launching 1 km.

**Open:** 1 April - 30 September.

**Directions**

The RN3 forms a sort of ring road round the north of the town. Site is signed from this on the west side of the town (500 m. to site). GPS: 49.15404, 5.36573

**Charges guide**

| Per unit incl. 2 persons | |
|---|---|
| and electricity | € 17.10 - € 20.80 |
| extra person | € 4.20 - € 5.80 |

Credit cards accepted for minimum of € 15.

For latest campsite news, availability and prices visit

# alanrogers.com

## Villers-les-Nancy

Campé●le

### Campéole le Brabois

Avenue Paul Muller, F-54600 Villers-les-Nancy (Meurthe-et-Moselle) T: 03 83 27 18 28.
E: brabois@campeole.com **alanrogers.com/FR54000**

This former municipal site is within the Nancy city boundary and 5 km. from the centre. Situated within a forest area, there is shade in most parts and, although the site is on a slight slope, the 185 good sized, numbered and separated pitches are level. Of these, 160 pitches have electrical connections (5/15A) and 30 also have water and drainage. Being on one of the main routes from Luxembourg to the south of France, le Brabois makes a good night stop. However, Nancy is a delightful city in the heart of Lorraine and worth a longer stay. There are many attractions in the area including the interesting 18th-century Place Stanislas (pedestrianised) and 11th-century city centre. The British manager has a wide range of tourist literature, publishes a monthly English newsletter and is pleased to help plan day trips. Horse racing takes place fortnightly at the race track next to the campsite, and good wine is produced nearby.

**Facilities**

Four sanitary blocks have been completely updated. Facilities for babies and disabled visitors. Laundry facilities. Motorcaravan service point. Shop (incl. eggs and other produce grown on site). Bread to order. Restaurant with bar, takeaway and small shop (15/6-15/9). Library. Two playgrounds. WiFi (1st night charged). Off site: Shops and restaurants 1 km. Walking and cycling. Regular buses to Nancy.

**Open:** 1 April - 15 October.

**Directions**

From autoroute A33 take exit 2b for Brabois and continue for 500 m. to 'Quick' restaurant on left. Turn left, pass racetrack to T-junction, turn right and after 400 m. turn right on to site entrance road. GPS: 48.66440, 6.14330

**Charges guide**

| Per unit incl. 2 persons | |
|---|---|
| and electricity | € 13.60 - € 18.70 |
| extra person | € 4.00 - € 5.60 |
| child (2-6 yrs) | free - € 3.60 |
| dog | € 2.50 - € 2.60 |

Credit cards minimum € 15. Barrier card deposit € 20.

LORRAINE

Campé●le

CAMPSITES AND RENTALS

**Le Brabois**★★★

Peaceful, ideal to visit Nancy
(Stanilas square).
Amenities, pitches and
accommodations of high quality.

54600 Villers Les Nancy - Tel.: +33-383-2718-28 - www.campeole.co.uk / brabois@campeole.com

## Villey-le-Sec

### Camping de Villey-le-Sec

34 rue de la Gare, F-54840 Villey-le-Sec (Meurthe-et-Moselle) T: 03 83 63 64 28.
E: info@campingvilleylesec.com **alanrogers.com/FR54010**

This neat campsite is a popular overnight stop, but the area is worth a longer stay. Villey-le-Sec has its own fortifications, part of the defensive system built along France's frontiers after the 1870 war, and a long cycle track passes near the site. On a bank of the Moselle river, there are 96 level grassy marked touring pitches, with electricity (6/10A) and plenty of water taps. There are also individual water taps and waste water drainage for eight of these pitches. Another area without electricity accommodates 11 tents. Just outside the site is an overnight stopping place for motorcaravans.

**Facilities**

Two modern toilet blocks (one heated) contain British style WCs, washbasins in cabins and controllable showers. Facilities for disabled visitors and babies. Motorcaravan services. Washing machine and dryer. Bar/restaurant. Snack bar and takeaway. Shop (all 15/4-20/9). Playground. Playing field. Boules. Fishing. Off site: Riding 2 km. Rock climbing 4 km. Golf 15 km.

**Open:** 1 April - 30 September.

**Directions**

Villey-le-Sec is 7 km. east of Toul. Leave A31 west of Nancy at exit 15 and after 1 km. at roundabout (Leclerc supermarket) take D909 to Villey-le-Sec. In village follow Camping signs to right. At bottom of hill turn left to site (300 m). GPS: 48.65281, 5.99151

**Charges guide**

| Per unit incl. 2 persons | |
|---|---|
| and electricity (6A) | € 17.50 - € 20.30 |
| extra person | € 3.50 |

**FREE** Alan Rogers Travel Card
Extra benefits and savings - see page 10

Lying between the Rhine and the Vosges mountains, to the north and east, Alsace shares a border with Germany, to the south with German-speaking Switzerland and to the west with Lorraine and Franche Comté.

**DÉPARTEMENTS: 67 BAS-RHIN, 68 HAUT-RHIN**

**MAJOR CITY: STRASBOURG**

Alsace lies between the River Rhine and the Vosges mountains. It is largely regarded as the Germanic region of France, bordering Germany in the north and east, and German-speaking Switzerland in the south. Indeed, a significant number of its inhabitants speak the Alsacian dialect, a form of German similar to that spoken in Switzerland. Having been under both German and French rule during the development of modern day Europe, it shows the influence of both countries.

Alsace has two départements, both geographically similar, with the Vosges mountains in the west sweeping down to the Rhine Valley and the fertile plains of the east. The capital of the Lower Rhine is Strasbourg, home of the European Parliament, and a vibrant city with an attractive medieval centre and an outlying industrial belt. The capital of the Upper Rhine is Colmar, with its beautifully preserved medieval houses; however, the largest city is Mulhouse, a major manufacturing centre with a wealth of museums and attractions.

**Places of interest**

*Colmar:* interesting for its 16th-century timber houses. Musée d'Unterlinden.

*Kayserberg:* small town, birthplace of Albert Schweitzer. Special Christmas market.

*Haut-Koenigsberg:* legendary hilltop castle in the Vosges mountains, close to Strasbourg.

*Mulhouse:* famous for the Musée National de l'Automobile and the Musée Français de Chemin de Fer.

*Riquewihr:* almost untouched since the 18th century (whilst almost every other village was decimated by war) with 13/14th-century fortifications and medieval houses.

**Cuisine of the region**

*Beckenoffe (Baeckeoffe):* a hotpot of potatoes, lamb, beef, pork and onions, cooked in local wine.

*Choucroute:* sauerkraut with peppercorns, boiled ham, pork, Strasbourg sausages and boiled potatoes.

*Flammekuche:* bread dough topped with cream, onions and bacon.

*Munster:* a soft, strong tasting cheese with orange rind, believed to have been invented by the monks of the Benedictine Abbey.

*Tarte à l'oignon Alsacienne:* onion and cream tart.

**www.tourisme-alsace.com
crt@tourisme-alsace.com
(0)3 89 24 73 50**

GERMANY

SAARBRUCKEN

KARLSRUHE

SARREGUEMINES

WISSEMBOURG

A35

HAGUENAU

A4,E25

BAS-RHIN 67

SARREBOURG

WASSELONNE

LORRAINE

STRASBOURG

MOLSHEIM

A35

ALSACE

A35,E25

RHINAU

BASSEMBERG

SELESTAT

SAINT-DIE

GERMANY

RIBEAUVILLE

COLMAR

FREIBURG

STE-CROIX-EN-PLAINE

HAUT-RHIN 68

GUEBWILLER

RANSPACH

THANN

MASEVAUX

MULHOUSE

BURNHAUPT-LE-HAUT

A36
E54/60

A35
E25/60

LURE

ALTKIRCH

BASEL

SEPPOIS-LE-BAS

MONTBELIARD

SWITZERLAND

FRANCHE
-COMTE

0  10  20  30  40 kms

## Bassemberg

### Campéole le Giessen

Route de Villé, F-67220 Bassemberg (Bas-Rhin) T: 03 88 58 98 14. E: giessen@campeole.com

**alanrogers.com/FR67070**

Le Giessen is a member of the Campéole group and can be found at the foot of the Vosges mountains, with easy access to many of the best loved sights in Alsace. Although there is no pool on site, a large complex, comprising indoor and outdoor pools with a water slide, can be found adjacent to the site, with free admission for all campers. The 80 touring pitches here are grassy and of a good size, mostly with 6A electrical connections and some shaded by mature trees. A number of mobile homes and fully equipped tents are available for rent. Various activities are organised in high season including a children's club and disco evenings. Nearby places of interest include the magnificent fortified castle of Haut-Koenigsbourg, as well as the great cities of Strasbourg and Colmar. This is a good base for exploring the Vosges and the Route du Vin (bicycle hire in the village). The site's friendly managers will be pleased to recommend possible itineraries.

**Facilities**

Three toilet blocks with all facilities including controllable hot showers and facilities for disabled visitors. Laundry. Bar. Snack bar/takeaway (July/Aug). Play area. Multisports court. Activities and entertainment. Bicycle hire. Mobile homes and equipped tents for rent. WiFi (charged). Off site: Swimming pool complex adjacent. Tennis. Rollerblading rink. Hiking and mountain biking. Fishing 1.5 km. Riding 5 km. Strasbourg 50 km.

**Open:** 1 April - 18 September.

**Directions**

Leave the A35 autoroute at exit 17 (Villé) and follow the D697 to Villé. Continue south on D39 to Bassemberg from where the site is well indicated. GPS: 48.33722, 7.28862

**Charges guide**

| Per unit incl. 2 persons | |
| --- | --- |
| and electricity | € 15.10 - € 24.50 |
| extra person | € 4.00 - € 6.10 |
| child (2-6 yrs) | free - € 4.00 |
| dog | € 2.00 - € 2.60 |

## Rhinau

### Camping la Ferme des Tuileries

1 rue des Tuileries, F-67860 Rhinau (Bas-Rhin) T: 03 88 74 60 45. E: camping.fermetuileries@neuf.fr

**alanrogers.com/FR67040**

Close to the German border, this ten-hectare, family run site has 150 large open pitches, hardstanding for 15 motorcaravans and room for 50 seasonal caravans. The site buildings have a traditional external appearance but all have modern interiors. Welcoming reception staff will provide information about the site and the local area. A small lake with two water slides is used for swimming, fishing and boating (divided into two areas) and there is also a small unsupervised swimming pool (hats compulsory). A newly built restaurant and bar are at the lakeside. A ferry (1 km) crosses the Rhine river into Germany.

**Facilities**

Three modern, bright and cheerful blocks with the usual facilities. Two washing machines and two dryers. Controllable showers. Family bathroom at no extra charge. Fully equipped facilities for disabled visitors (no key, no coins). Motorcaravan services. Bar, restaurant and takeaway (July/Aug). Small lake for swimming, fishing, boating, two water slides. Swimming pool (unguarded) open July/Aug. Tennis. Pétanque. Minigolf. Bicycle hire. Dogs are not accepted. Off site: Supermarket 500 m.

**Open:** 1 April - 30 September.

**Directions**

Coming from Colmar (A35) take exit 14 (Kogenheim-Benfeld-Erstein) then the N83 to exit for Benfeld-Rhinau, following site signs. From Strasbourg on A35 take exit 7 (Erstein-Fegersheim) then the N83. GPS: 48.321, 7.698

**Charges guide**

| Per unit incl. 2 persons and electricity | € 14.60 |
| --- | --- |
| extra person | € 3.80 |
| child (under 7 yrs) | € 1.80 |

No credit cards or cheques.

# Wasselonne

## Camping Municipal Wasselonne

Route de Romanswiller, F-67310 Wasselonne (Bas-Rhin) T: 03 88 87 00 08.
E: camping-wasselonne@wanadoo.fr **alanrogers.com/FR67050**

A good quality municipal site with a resident warden. Facilities include a well stocked small shop, a crêperie in season and the added bonus of free admission to the superb indoor heated swimming pool adjacent to the site. There are 80 tourist pitches and around 20 seasonal units, on grass with a slight slope, all with electricity hook-ups (16A). Six new rental chalets are in a separate fenced area and there are six new private chalets. This could be an excellent base from which to visit Strasbourg. A full programme of events is offered in the town by the Tourist Office, including welcome evenings, guided tours, concerts, musical festivals and food tasting evenings.

### Facilities

The single, large and well maintained sanitary unit has unisex facilities with ample sized showers and washbasins in cubicles. Laundry facilities. No specific facilities for disabled visitors but the rooms are spacious and should be accessible to many. Excellent drive-over motorcaravan service point. Off site: Heated pool, hotel with restaurant, tennis courts and athletics stadium, all adjacent. Supermarket 500 m. Fishing and fitness trail 1 km. Riding 1.5 km.

**Open:** 15 April - 15 October.

### Directions

Wasselonne is 25 km. west of Strasbourg. Site is southwest of town centre on D224 towards Romanswiller, and is well signed.
GPS: 48.6377, 7.4318

### Charges guide

| Per unit incl. 2 persons | |
|---|---|
| and electricity | € 14.20 - € 14.80 |
| extra person | € 3.60 - € 3.80 |
| child (0-10 yrs) | € 2.00 - € 2.10 |
| dog | € 0.50 - € 0.60 |

**FREE** Alan Rogers Travel Card
Extra benefits and savings - see page 10

## Burnhaupt le Haut

### Camping les Castors

4 route de Guewenheim, F-68520 Burnhaupt le Haut (Haut-Rhin) T: 03 89 48 78 58.
E: camping.les.castors@wanadoo.fr  alanrogers.com/FR68300

Camping les Castors provides a convenient starting point from which to explore the Alsace region. It is close to the Vosges mountains which are dominated by the Ballon d'Alsace (1427 m). This well cared for site with its stream and small lake offers 135 pitches with electricity 5/10A. Most are of a reasonable size and some have some shade. Fishing is possible in the lake and the site is on the banks of the river. Bicycle hire is available and there are walks in the adjacent forest and the surrounding countryside. The small village of Burnhaupt-le-Haut is within 1.5 km and has a supermarket, ATM and pharmacy.

**Facilities**

A new sanitary block offers modern facilities with showers and wash cubicles. Facilities for babies and disabled visitors. Laundry facilities. Attractive restaurant and bar with terrace serving traditional local food. Takeaway. Bread can be ordered from reception. Small play area. Fishing. Bicycle hire. WiFi on the terrace (charged). Off site: Excursions. Hiking. Supermarket 1.5 km.

**Open:** 1 April - 31 October.

**Directions**

Exit the D38 signed to Masevaux and Burnhapt-le-Haut. Take the D466 towards Masevaux. The site is signed to the right after 1 km.
GPS: 47.746877, 7.124494

**Charges guide**

| | |
|---|---|
| Per unit incl. 2 persons and electricity | € 16.00 - € 16.80 |
| extra person | € 4.00 |
| child (under 10 yrs) | € 2.00 |
| Camping Cheques accepted. | |

## Masevaux

### Camping de Masevaux

3 rue du Stade, F-68290 Masevaux (Haut-Rhin) T: 03 89 82 42 29. E: camping-masevaux@tv-com.net
alanrogers.com/FR68030

Masevaux is a pleasant little town in the Haut-Rhin department of Alsace, just north of the A36 Belfort-Mulhouse motorway. The neatly mown 110 pitches for tourers are on level grass, of reasonable size, marked by trees and hedges, and all have electricity (3/6A). Most are well shaded with good views of the surrounding hills. The pleasant and helpful Scottish managers, who take pride in the site, would like to welcome more British visitors. A good choice for one night or a longer stay to explore this interesting region, and an ideal destination for serious walkers.

**Facilities**

A modern, well designed and well equipped sanitary block has most washbasins in private cabins. Baby room. Laundry. Café/bar serving snacks. Baker calls in high season. Ice creams and soft drinks from reception. TV room, small library. Boules. Play area. Tennis (extra charge). Fishing. WiFi. Off site: Supermarket, restaurants and indoor pool. Wednesday market in Masevaux.

**Open:** 10 January - 10 December.

**Directions**

From D466 in Masevaux follow signs for Belfort and then Camping Complexe Sportif.
GPS: 47.7782, 6.9909

**Charges guide**

| | |
|---|---|
| Per unit incl. 2 persons and electricity | € 17.30 |
| extra person | € 4.40 |
| child (2-16 yrs) | € 2.00 - € 3.20 |

## Ranspach

### Flower Camping les Bouleaux

8 rue des Bouleaux, F-68470 Ranspach (Haut-Rhin) T: 03 89 82 64 70. E: contact@alsace-camping.com
alanrogers.com/FR68140

Les Bouleaux is a well maintained site with 100 touring pitches of a rather small size (80 sq.m), although they are flat and grassy. The site is open all year round, although the outdoor swimming pools and the shop are only opened during the high season. The site is ideally situated if you are coming by motorbike or are planning to go paragliding or skiing. Les Bouleaux is set in the heart of the Thur valley, at the foot of the Vosges mountains. It offers many possibilities for outdoor activities such as climbing, playing golf, hiking and fishing, to name just a few. Also recommended is a visit to the Wesserling park and its beautiful gardens, which were established in 1699!

**Facilities**

Two traditional, clean sanitary blocks with showers. Good baby room. Facilities for disabled visitors. Shop (July/Aug). Bar, restaurant, snack bar/takeaway (all year except Nov). Outdoor swimming and paddling pools (hats compulsory, no Bermuda shorts). Boules. Volleyball. Minigolf. Play area. WiFi (charged). Accommodation to rent. Off site: Fishing 1 km. Bicycle hire, beach and sailing 3 km.

**Open:** All year.

**Directions**

Leave A31 and follow signs for Epinal on E23. Approaching Epinal follow the E512 towards Mulhouse. Continue on E512 until Ranspach. Drive on 700 m. on the Route National, then right on rue des Bouleaux to site. GPS: 47.880743, 7.010334

**Charges guide**

| | |
|---|---|
| Per unit incl. 2 persons and electricity | € 16.50 - € 22.90 |
| extra person | € 3.80 - € 5.00 |

For latest campsite news, availability and prices visit

# alanrogers.com

## Ribeauvillé

### Camping Municipal Pierre de Coubertin

23 rue de Landau, F-68150 Ribeauvillé (Haut-Rhin) T: 03 89 73 66 71. E: camping.ribeauville@wanadoo.fr

**alanrogers.com/FR68050**

The fascinating medieval town of Ribeauvillé on the Alsace Wine Route is within walking distance of this attractive, quietly located site. Popular and well run, it has 208 touring pitches, all with 16A electricity and some separated by shrubs or railings. There are tarmac and gravel access roads. This is a site solely for touring units – there are no mobile homes or seasonal units here. The small shop is open daily for most of the season (hours vary) providing bread, basic supplies and some wines. Only breathable groundsheets are permitted.

| Facilities | Directions |
|---|---|
| Large, heated block provides modern facilities with washbasins in cubicles. Baby facilities. Large laundry room. A smaller unit at the far end of the site is opened for July/Aug. Very good facilities for disabled campers at both units. Shop (Easter-Oct). Excellent adventure style play area with rubber base. Tennis. Boules. TV room. Free WiFi over site. Off site: Outdoor pool (June-Aug). Bicycle hire 200 m. Fishing and riding 500 m. Golf 12 km. | Ribeauvillé is 13 km. southwest of Sélestat and site is well signed. Turn north off the D106 at traffic lights by large car park, east of the town centre. GPS: 48.19482, 7.33654 |

**Open:** 15 March - 15 November.

**Charges 2013**

| Per unit incl. 2 persons and electricity | € 15.50 - € 16.50 |
|---|---|
| extra person | € 4.00 |

## Saint Croix-en-Plaine

### Camping ClairVacances

Route de Herrlisheim, F-68127 Saint Croix-en-Plaine (Haut-Rhin) T: 03 89 49 27 28.
E: clairvacances@orange.fr  **alanrogers.com/FR68080**

ClairVacances is a very neat, tidy and pretty site with 135 level pitches (120 for touring) of generous size, numbered and mostly separated by trees and shrubs. All have 16A electricity connections and 12 are fully serviced with water and drainage. The site has been imaginatively laid out with the pitches reached from hard access roads. This is a quiet family site. The friendly couple who own and run it will be pleased to advise on the attractions of the area. The site is 1 km. from the A35 exit, not far from Colmar in the region of Alsace, a popular and picturesque area.

| Facilities | Directions |
|---|---|
| Two excellent, modern toilet blocks include washbasins in cabins, baby rooms and facilities for disabled visitors. Laundry facilities. Swimming and paddling pools (heated) with large sunbathing area (1/5-15/9). Playground. Community room. Archery in high season. Camping Gaz. Dogs are not accepted. No football. Gas and electric barbecues only. American-style motorhomes and twin axle caravans are not accepted. Free WiFi over part of site. | Site is signed from exit 27 of the A35 on D1, halfway between St Croix-en-Plaine and Herrlisheim. GPS: 48.01606, 7.35016 |

**Open:** Week before Easter - 15 October.

**Charges guide**

| Per unit incl. 2 persons and electricity | € 17.00 - € 29.00 |
|---|---|
| extra person | € 4.00 - € 7.50 |
| child (2-12 yrs) | € 1.50 - € 5.50 |

## Seppois-le-Bas

### Village Center les Lupins

1 rue de la Gare, F-68580 Seppois-le-Bas (Haut-Rhin) T: 04 99 57 21 21. E: contact@village-center.fr

**alanrogers.com/FR68120**

Only ten kilometres from the Swiss border and within walking distance of a small village, this is a pleasant, traditional site. It has 138 level grass touring pitches, all with electrical connections (6A), a few seasonal units and 13 chalets (10 available to rent). Shade is provided in places by mature trees. The main site building (formerly a railway station) houses reception which has a few basic supplies, tourist information, a pool table and electronic games. Snacks and drinks are served on the terrace overlooking the small, fenced swimming pool. The site is a member of the Village Center group.

| Facilities | Directions |
|---|---|
| The central toilet block provides plenty of facilities in a traditional style. A second block (open in high season) is older but with similar facilities. En suite units for disabled visitors. Washing machines and dryer. Bread to order and basic supplies from reception. Drinks and simple snacks served on the terrace. Swimming pool (15/5-15/9). Play area. Bicycle hire. Internet access and WiFi (charged). Gas barbecues only. Off site: Restaurant across the road. Village 400 m. Fishing 2 km. Golf 4 km. Riding 8 km. | Seppois is 30 km. south west of Mulhouse. On A36 from Besançon at exit 11, take N1019 to Grandvillars, then D463 east to Seppois. From Mulhouse on A36 at exit 15, take D466 to Altkirch, D432 towards Ferrette, then D17 to Seppois. Site is signed in village. GPS: 47.53913, 7.17998 |

**Open:** 4 April -17 September.

**Charges guide**

| Per unit incl. 2 persons and electricity | € 15.00 - € 17.00 |
|---|---|
| extra person | € 3.00 - € 4.00 |

**FREE** Alan Rogers Travel Card
Extra benefits and savings - see page 10

With over one hundred of France's finest châteaux, this is a region to inspire the imagination. The Loire valley is a charming region of lush countryside, fields of sunflowers, rolling vineyards and of course the great river itself.

**DÉPARTEMENTS: 18 CHER, 28 EURE-ET-LOIR, 36 INDRE, 37 INDRE-ET-LOIRE, 41 LOIR-ET-CHER, 45 LOIRET**

**MAJOR CITIES: ORLÉANS, TOURS**

For centuries the Loire valley was frequented by French royalty, and the great river winds its way past some of France's most magnificent châteaux: Amboise, Azay-le-Rideau, Chenonceau with its famous arches that span the river and appear to 'float' on the water, and the fairytale Ussé with myriad magical turrets, are just some of the highlights.

Known as the Garden of France, the Loire Valley is a patchwork of lush fields, cool forests and meandering rivers. Following the course of the Loire are the vineyards that produce some of France's most renowned wines, notably Sancerre and the sparking Vouvray. Its stunning architecture, troglodyte caves, tiny Romanesque churches and magical son-et-lumière productions are just an hour from Paris by TGV. The Loire à Vélo long-distance cycle path offers visitors the chance to disover the region's charming villages and historic cities while enjoying all that nature has to offer.

### Places of interest

*Amboise*: château, Leonardo da Vinci museum.

*Beauregard*: château with Delft tiled floors.

*Blois*: château with architecture from Middle Ages to Neo-Classical periods.

*Chambord*: Renaissance château.

*Chartres*: cathedral with stained glass windows.

*Chinon*: old town, Joan of Arc museum

*Loches*: old town, château and its fortifications.

*Orléans*: Holy Cross cathedral, house of Joan of Arc.

*Tours*: Renaissance and Neo-Classical mansions, cathedral of St Gatien.

*Vendôme*: Tour St Martin, La Trinité.

*Villandry*: famous Renaissance gardens.

### Cuisine of the region

Wild duck, pheasant, hare, deer, and quail are classics, and fresh water fish such as salmon, perch and trout are favourites. Specialities include rillettes, andouillettes, tripe, mushrooms, and regional cheeses such as Pouligny St. Pierre and Ste. Maure de Touraine, and Petit Sable and Ardoises d'Angers cookies.

*Bourdaines*: baked apples stuffed with jam.

*Tarte à la citrouille*: pumpkin tart.

*Tarte Tatin*: upside-down tart of caramelised apples and pastry.

www.visaloire.com
crtcentre@visaloire.com
(0)2 38 79 95 28

MONTDIDIER

LE HAVRE

ROUEN

COMPIEGNE
BEAUVAIS

SOISSONS

PICARDY

SENLIS

LISIEUX

BERNAY
EVREUX

MEAUX

NORMANDY

PARIS

ALENCON

DREUX

PARIS
ILE DE FRANCE

PROVINS

SENONCHES

CHARTRES

ETAMPES

EURE-ET-LOIR 28

PITHIVIERS

SENS

MAMERS

A11,E50

CHATEAUDUN

VAL DE LOIRE

MONTARGIS

LE MANS

LOIR-ET-CHER 41

ORLEANS

A77

PAYS DE
LA LOIRE

A10,E05,60

LOIRET 45

VENDOME

POILLY-LEZ-GIEN

GIEN

MUIDES-SUR-LOIRE

SUEVRES

NOUAN-LE-FUZELIER

BLOIS

BRACIEUX

PIERREFITTE-SUR-SAULDRE

SONZAY

CHEVERNY

AUBIGNY-SUR-NERE

RILLE
TOURS

MESLAND

CANDE-SUR-BEUVRON

NEUNG-SUR-BEUVRON

BALLAN-MIRE

FAVEROLLES-SUR-CHER

FRANCUEIL-CHENONCEAU

VIERZON

A71,E11

INDRE-ET-LOIRE 37

CHINON

CHEMILLE-SUR-INDROIS

BOURGES

TROGUES

LOCHES-EN-TOURAINE

STE CATHERINE-DE-FIERBOIS

CHER 18

INDRE 36

CHATEAUROUX

CHATELLERAULT

A20,E09

AUVERGNE

POITIERS

MONTMORILLON

MONTLUCON

POITOU
CHARENTES

BELLAC

GUERET

LIMOUSIN

AUBUSSON

0   25   50   75 kms

LIMOGES

## Aubigny-sur-Nère

### Flower Camping les Etangs

Route de Sancerre, F-18700 Aubigny-sur-Nère (Cher) T: 02 48 58 02 37. E: camping.aubigny@orange.fr
**alanrogers.com/FR18010**

Les Etangs is a site of 100 pitches, close to the Sancerre vineyards and the lakes of the Sologne. A member of the Flower group, this site extends over two hectares and borders a small lake (suitable for fishing). Pitches are large and grassy (most have electrical connections). There are chalets available for rent. The town of Aubigny-sur-Nère is nearby (1 km) and has a close attachment with Scotland, thanks to the 'Auld Alliance'. The town is the only one in France to celebrate French-Scottish friendship on Bastille Day. Bring your bicycle as there are many tracks running through the surrounding forests.

| Facilities | Directions |
|---|---|
| Two heated toilet blocks are a good provision and are well located. Bar (high season). Play area. Fishing (permit required). Activity and entertainment programme. WiFi (free). Chalets and tents for rent. Off site: Swimming pool 50 m. (with aqua-gym). Aubigny-sur-Nère 1 km. Riding 20 km. Sancerre vineyards. Walking and cycle tracks. | Aubigny is southeast of Orléans. Approaching from the north (Orléans) on the A71 autoroute take exit 4 for Salbris and head east on D724 and D924 until Aubigny. Take the D923 towards Sancerre and site is 1 km. GPS: 47.48435, 2.45703 |

**Open:** 1 April - 30 September.

**Charges guide**

| | |
|---|---|
| Per unit incl. 2 persons | € 11.50 - € 18.90 |
| extra person | € 3.00 - € 4.00 |

## Bracieux

### Camping Indigo les Châteaux

11 rue Roger Brun, F-41250 Bracieux (Loir-et-Cher) T: 02 54 46 41 84.
E: chateaux@camping-indigo.com **alanrogers.com/FR41120**

Camping Indigo des Châteaux has recently joined the Indigo group, and there have been developments and modernisation. This is a well located site on the outskirts of Bracieux, convenient for many of the best known châteaux of the Loire valley. There are 350 flat, grassy pitches here, most of which are reserved for touring. Some pitches are grouped in blocks of four between hedges, with electricity (10A), water and drainage provided for each group. The majority, however, are more open with scattered water points and electrical connection boxes. Mature trees provide shade to most pitches. Accommodation is available to rent in mobile homes or safari style tents. There is a good municipal swimming pool next door. The church is immediately opposite the site and the bustling village centre is an easy 300 m. walk away. A new central building was completed in 2012, and includes a café/restaurant, tourist information and reception area. Bicycle hire is on offer and the site managers will be pleased to recommend possible routes. There are many châteaux close at hand, most notably Chambord (8 km) and Cheverny (9 km).

| Facilities | Directions |
|---|---|
| The four toilet blocks were renovated in 2012 and are well spaced among the pitches, with modern, clean facilities. Facilities for disabled visitors. Motorcaravan service point. Small shop, snack bar/bar/pizzeria (all 1/7-31/8). Play area. Games/TV room and small library. Activity and entertainment programme. Internet access. Mobile homes and tents for rent. WiFi at café (free). Off site: Bicycle hire (300 meters). Municipal swimming pool (15/6-31/8) 50 m. Shops and restaurants 300 m. Golf and riding 10 km. | From Blois take D765 south towards Cheverny. At roundabout (junction with D956) turn east on D923, signed Bracieux. Turn south on D112 at roundabout and the site is 300 m. on right, just over the river. GPS: 47.550883, 1.537867 |

**Open:** 28 March - 4 November.

**Charges 2013**

| | |
|---|---|
| Per unit incl. 2 persons and electricity | € 20.90 - € 32.30 |
| extra person | € 5.10 - € 6.00 |
| child (2-13 yrs) | free - € 3.90 |

For latest campsite news, availability and prices visit
**alanrogers.com**

## Candé-sur-Beuvron
### Kawan Village la Grande Tortue

3 route de Pontlevoy, F-41120 Candé-sur-Beuvron (Loir-et-Cher) T: 02 54 44 15 20.
E: grandetortue@wanadoo.fr **alanrogers.com/FR41070**

505

In the region that the Kings of France chose to build their most beautiful residences, this pleasant, shady site has been developed in the surroundings of an old 800-hectare forest, just 1 km. from the banks of the Loire river. For those seeking a relaxing holiday, it provides 169 pitches, including 116 for touring units (most over 100 sq.m), all with 10A electricity and 58 with full services. The friendly family owners continue to develop the site with a multisport court and an attractive swimming pool complex. During July and August, they organise a programme of trips including canoeing and riding excursions, as well as twice weekly concerts and shows. La Grande Tortue is very well placed for visiting the châteaux of the Loire or the cities of Orléans and Tours. It is located on the long distance 'Loire à Vélo' cycle track and this leads from the site to Chaumont, Blois and Chambord, with over 300 km. of marked cycle tracks in the surrounding area. There are several good restaurants close at hand, although the site restaurant is also recommended with a range of good value meals in a pleasant environment.

### Facilities

Three sanitary blocks offer British style WCs, washbasins in cabins and pushbutton showers. Facilities for disabled visitors in one block. Laundry facilities. Motorcaravan service point. Shop, terraced bar and restaurant with takeaway service (all 13/4-15/9). Heated swimming pool covered in poor weather, shallow outdoor pools for children (1/5-15/9). Trampolines, ball crawl with slide and climbing wall, two bouncy inflatables. Club for children (July/Aug). Multisport court. Bicycle hire (13/4-22/9). WiFi (charged). Barbecues not permitted. Off site: Walking and cycling. Fishing 1 km. Riding 3 km. Golf 10 km. Châteaux at Blois 10 km. Chambord 20 km. Chenonceau 20 km.

**Open:** 13 April - 22 September.

### Directions

Site is just outside Candé-sur-Beuvron on the D751, between Amboise and Blois. From Amboise, turn right just before Candé, then left into site. GPS: 47.4900069, 1.2583208

### Charges guide

| | |
|---|---|
| Per unit incl. 2 persons and electricity | € 24.00 - € 35.00 |
| extra person | € 7.00 - € 10.00 |
| child (3-9 yrs) | € 4.25 - € 6.75 |
| dog | € 4.00 |

Camping Cheques accepted.

## Ballan-Miré

### Camping de la Mignardière

22 avenue des Aubépines, F-37510 Ballan-Miré (Indre-et-Loire) T: 02 47 73 31 00. E: info@mignardiere.com
**alanrogers.com/FR37010**

Southwest of the city of Tours, this site is within easy reach of several of the Loire châteaux, notably Azay-le-Rideau. There are also many varied sports amenities on the site or very close by. The site has 177 numbered pitches of which 139 are for touring units, all with electricity (6/10A) and 37 with drainage and water. Pitches are of a good size (60-130 sq.m) on rather uneven grass, accessed by tarmac roads. The barrier gates (coded access) are closed 22.30-07.30 hrs. Reservation is essential for July/August.

**Facilities**

Three very clean toilet blocks (one recently upgraded) include washbasins in private cabins, good facilities for disabled campers, baby room and laundry facilities. Motorcaravan service point. Well stocked shop sells snacks (all season). Takeaway. Indoor heated swimming pools (1/4-25/9) and outdoor heated pool (15/5-15/9). Paddling pool. Tennis. Bicycle hire. WiFi over site (charged). Torch useful. Off site: Attractive lake 300 m. Family fitness run. Fishing and sailing 500 m. Riding 1 km. Boat launching 1.5 km. Golf and riding 4 km.

**Open:** 1 April - 25 September.

**Directions**

From A10 autoroute take exit 24 and D751 towards Chinon. Turn right after 5 km. at Campanile Hotel following signs to site. From Tours take D751 towards Chinon. GPS: 47.35509, 0.63408

**Charges guide**

| | |
|---|---|
| Per unit incl. 2 persons | € 16.00 - € 24.00 |
| incl. electricity, water and drainage | € 21.00 - € 34.00 |
| extra person | € 4.20 - € 5.80 |
| child (2-12 yrs) | € 2.80 - € 3.70 |

## Chemillé-sur-Indrois

### Flower Camping les Coteaux du Lac

Base de Loisirs, F-37460 Chemillé-sur-Indrois (Indre-et-Loire) T: 02 47 92 77 83.
E: lescoteauxdulac@wanadoo.fr **alanrogers.com/FR37150**

This former municipal site has been completely refurbished to a high standard and is being operated efficiently by a private company owned by the present enthusiastic manager, Emmanuel Dugas. There are 47 touring pitches, all with electricity (10A) and individual water tap; four have hardstanding for motorcaravans. At present there is little shade apart from that offered by a few mature trees, but new trees and bushes have been planted and flower beds are to be added. In a few years this promises to be a delightful site; meanwhile it is smart and very well tended. The site is in pleasant countryside above a lake and next to a rapidly developing Base de Loisirs with watersports provision and a bar/restaurant. There is a good, well equipped little swimming pool with paddling area securely separated from the main pool (open and heated 1/6-30/9). The site is near the town of Loches with its attractive château, and is an easy drive from Tours and the many châteaux along the Loire and the Indre, including Chenonceaux.

**Facilities**

Excellent sanitary block with controllable showers, some washbasins in cabins and en-suite facilities for disabled visitors. Laundry facilities. Reception sells a few basic supplies and bread can be ordered. Swimming and paddling pools (1/5-15/9). Playing field. Play equipment for different ages. Fishing. Bicycle hire. WiFi over site (charged). Chalets to rent (15) are grouped at far end of site. Off site: Fishing 100 m. Lakeside beach, sailing and other watersports 200 m. Riding 4 km. Golf 15 km.

**Open:** 1 April - 15 October.

**Directions**

Chemillé-sur-Indrois is 55 km. southeast of Tours and 14 km. east of Loches, just off the D760 from Loches to Montrésor. Site is to the north of this road and is signed just west of Montrésor. GPS: 47.15786, 1.15986

**Charges guide**

| | |
|---|---|
| Per unit incl. 2 persons | € 13.90 - € 19.00 |
| extra person | € 3.90 - € 5.70 |
| child (2-9 yrs) | € 2.30 - € 3.60 |
| electricity | € 3.90 |

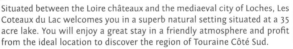

For latest campsite news, availability and prices visit
# alanrogers.com

# Cheverny
## Camping les Saules

Les Saules, F-41700 Cheverny (Loir-et-Cher) T: 02 54 79 90 01. E: contact@camping-cheverny.com

**alanrogers.com/FR41100**

Set in the heart of the château region, les Saules has developed into a popular, friendly campsite run by a local family. The well renovated, traditional reception buildings in their lakeside setting give a very pleasant welcome. There are 164 good sized, level pitches with 149 available for touring units. All have shade from the many trees on the site, and electrical connections (a few will require leads longer than 25 m), and there are ample water taps. A large, grassy field provides room for youngsters to play safely. There are many designated cycle paths and walking circuits in the area, often linking châteaux through attractive, sleepy countryside. Cheverny, just a five minute cycle ride away, is considered to have the best interior and furnishings of all the châteaux in the Loire region, and many others are within easy reach (Chambord, Chenonceau, Chaumont and more). A Sites et Paysages member.

### Facilities

Two sanitary blocks with toilets, showers, washbasins in cubicles and facilities for disabled visitors. Laundry facilities. Motorcaravan service point. Gas supplies. Shop. Restaurant (July/Aug). Bar. Snack bar and takeaway. Swimming and paddling pools. TV/social room with toys, board games, books. Two play areas. Large grass area for ball games. Minigolf (free). Fishing. Bicycle hire. Internet and WiFi. Off site: Golf and riding 3 km.

**Open:** 30 March - 21 September.

### Directions

From Cheverny take D102 south towards Contres. Site is on the right after 2 km. GPS: 47.478003, 1.450842

### Charges guide

| | |
|---|---|
| Per unit incl. 2 persons and electricity | € 20.00 - € 31.50 |
| extra person | € 4.50 |
| child (4-10 yrs) | € 2.00 |
| dog | € 2.00 |

In the heart of the Kings Valley, next to the Château of Cheverny and its 18-hole golf course, just near the forest, welcome to the quiet atmosphere of the Camping Les Saules and its green and shady setting of 8 hectares.

Excellent starting point for walking and cycling.

Rental of chalets.

CAMPING LES SAULES F. 41700 CHEVERNY

**Tel. : 33 (0) 254 799 001**

**Fax : 33 (0) 254 792 834**

www.camping-cheverny.com - contact@camping-cheverny.com

# Chinon
## Camping de l'Ile Auger

Quai Danton, F-37500 Chinon (Indre-et-Loire) T: 02 47 93 08 35. E: camping-ile-auger@hotmail.fr

**alanrogers.com/FR37070**

This traditional, good value site is well placed for exploring the old medieval town of Chinon. It lies alongside the River Vienne with views of the impressive château, which has a museum to Joan of Arc and was once the home of England's Henry II. A five minute walk over the bridge takes you to the château and town centre. The 277 level pitches are numbered but not separated and trees provide some shade. All have 8/12A electricity (long leads may be needed). Nearby are châteaux at Ussé, Azay-le-Rideau and Villandry and the abbey at Fontevraud.

### Facilities

The main toilet block by the entrance, with all the usual facilities, is undergoing refurbishment. Three small blocks around the rest of the site, have WCs and basins with cold water. Motorcaravan service point. Laundry facilities. Playground. Boules court. Fishing. Canoes. Barrier locked 22.00-07.00. A warden lives on site. WiFi (charged). Off site: Indoor and outdoor swimming pools nearby. Bicycle hire and boat launching 100 m. Town with shops, bars and restaurants 400 m. Tennis. River beach (no swimming) 1 km. Boat trips. Riding 10 km.

**Open:** 1 April - 31 October.

### Directions

Chinon is 45 km. southwest of Tours. West of Chinon, at roundabout, leave Chinon bypass (D751) and take D8 east to town centre (3 km). Turn south, cross river and immediately turn west to site in 300 m. GPS: 47.16433, 0.23327

### Charges guide

| | |
|---|---|
| Per unit incl. 2 persons and electricity (12A) | € 13.10 |
| extra person | € 2.20 |
| child (under 7 yrs) | € 1.50 |

**FREE** Alan Rogers Travel Card

Extra benefits and savings - see page 10

## Faverolles-sur-Cher

### Camping Couleurs du Monde

1 Rond point de Montparnasse, F-41400 Faverolles-sur-Cher (Loir-et-Cher) T: 02 54 32 06 08.
E: contact@camping-couleurs-du-monde.com **alanrogers.com/FR41150**

Les Couleurs du Monde is a welcoming site in the heart of the Loire Valley. It is close to the River Cher and the small, medieval town of Montrichard, and well placed for exploring some of the region's best known sights. The 96 touring pitches are of a very good size, grassy and well shaded, most with electrical connections. On-site amenities include a swimming pool, paddling pool and a snack bar/takeaway. A supermarket with ATM is nearby (50 m). The barrier gates are closed 22.00-07.00. Reservation is essential for July/August. The site has a good play area with a bouncy castle, go-karts and trampolines, with a small animal petting area.

### Facilities

One very clean, newly refurbished toilet block has vanity style washbasins and hot water. Baby room. Facilities for disabled visitors (key access). Washing machine and dryer. Shop for basics. Snack bar/takeaway (July/Aug). Swimming pool (no Bermuda shorts). Paddling pool. Games room. Play areas. Minigolf. Boules pitch. Volleyball. Go-carts. Canoe trips. Bicycle hire. Entertainment (July/Aug). Mobile homes and chalets to rent. WiFi (charged). Off site: Supermarket with ATM 50 m. Shops, cafés and restaurants in Montrichard. Walking and cycle trails. Chenonceau. Chaumont.

**Open:** 31 March - 25 October.

### Directions

The site is situated on south side of River Cher. From A85/E604 leave at junction 11. Follow signs for Montrichard on D976. Site is next to Carrefour market on the Montrichard roundabout.
GPS: 47.33399, 1.18768

### Charges guide

| Per unit incl. 2 persons and electricity | € 20.00 - € 25.00 |
|---|---|
| extra person | € 3.50 - € 5.00 |
| child (0-7 yrs) | € 2.50 - € 4.00 |
| dog | € 2.00 |

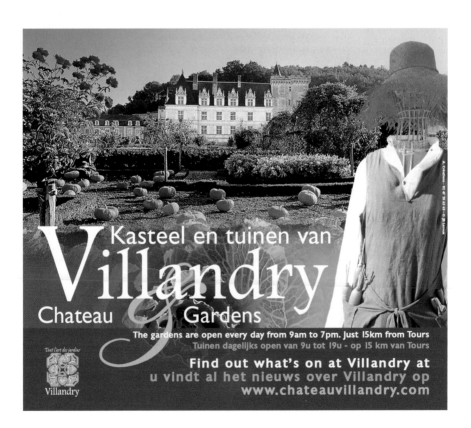
For latest campsite news, availability and prices visit
**alanrogers.com**

# Francueil-Chenonceau
## Camping le Moulin Fort

F-37150 Francueil-Chenonceau (Indre-et-Loire) T: 02 47 23 86 22. E: lemoulinfort@wanadoo.fr

**alanrogers.com/FR37030**

Camping le Moulin Fort is a tranquil, riverside site with British owners, John and Sarah Scarratt. The 130 pitches are enhanced by trees and shrubs offering plenty of shade and 110 pitches have electricity (6A). From the snack bar terrace adjacent to the restored mill building, a timber walkway over the mill race leads to the unheated swimming pool and paddling pools. The site is ideal for couples and families with young children, although the river is unfenced. There is occasional noise from trains passing on the opposite bank of the river. All over the campsite, visitors will find little information boards about local nature (birds, fish, trees and shrubs), and the history of the mill. The owners are keen to encourage recycling on the site. The picturesque Château of Chenonceau is little more than 1 km. along the Cher riverbank and many of the Loire châteaux are within easy reach, particularly Amboise and its famous Leonardo de Vinci museum. Twin-axle caravans and large motorcaravans accepted.

### Facilities

Two toilet blocks with all the usual amenities of a good standard, include washbasins in cubicles, baby baths and facilities for disabled visitors. Washing machine. Motorcaravan service point. Shop, bar (24/5-27/9), restaurant and takeaway (all 24/5-16/9). Swimming pool (24/5-27/9). Excellent play area. Minigolf. Pétanque. Games room and TV. Library. Fishing. Bicycle and canoe hire. In high season regular family entertainment including wine tasting, quiz evenings, activities for children, light hearted games tournaments and live music events. WiFi (charged). Off site: Trains to Tours 1.5 km. Shops, bars and restaurants within 2 km. Boat launching 2 km. River beach 4 km. Riding 12 km. Golf 20 km.

**Open:** 24 May - 27 September.

### Directions

Site is 35 km. east of Tours off D976 Vierzon road. From A85 at exit 11 take D31 towards Bléré and turn east on D976 (Vierzon) for 7 km. then north on D80 (Chenonceau) to site. GPS: 47.32735, 1.08936

### Charges guide

| | |
|---|---|
| Per unit incl. 2 persons and electricity | € 19.00 - € 27.00 |
| extra person | € 4.00 - € 5.00 |
| child (4-12 yrs) | € 3.00 - € 4.00 |
| dog | € 2.00 - € 3.00 |

**FREE** Alan Rogers Travel Card
Extra benefits and savings - see page 10

# Gien
## Kawan Village les Bois du Bardelet

Route de Bourges, le Petit Bardelet, F-45500 Gien (Loiret) T: 02 38 67 47 39. E: contact@bardelet.com
**alanrogers.com/FR45010**

This attractive, high quality site, ideal for families with young children, is in a rural setting and well situated for exploring the less well known eastern part of the Loire Valley. Two lakes (one for boating, one for fishing) and a pool complex have been attractively landscaped in 18 hectares of former farmland, blending old and new with natural wooded areas and more open grassland with rural views. There are 245 large, level grass pitches with 120 for touring units. All have at least 10A electricity, 15 have water, waste water and 16A electricity, and some 30 have hardstanding. Eight have individual en-suite sanitary units beside the pitch.

### Facilities

Two heated toilet blocks have some washbasins in cubicles, controllable showers, an en-suite unit for disabled visitors and a baby room. Washing machines and dryers. Minimart, bar, takeaway and restaurant (1/5-15/9). Heated outdoor pool (1/5-31/8), indoor pool and children's pool. Wellness centre. Fitness and jacuzzi rooms. Beach on lake. Games area. Canoeing and fishing. Tennis. Minigolf. Volleyball. Pétanque. Playground. Kids' club, sports tournaments, excursions, aquagym, archery (July/Aug). Bicycle hire. Free WiFi in bar area.

**Open:** 19 April - 30 September.

### Directions

Gien is 60 km. southeast of Orléans. Site is 7 km. south of Gien. Leave A77 autoroute at exit 19 and take D940 (Bourges) to bypass Gien. Continue on D940 for 5 km. At junction with D53 (no left turn) turn right and right again to cross D940. Follow signs for 1.5 km. to site. GPS: 47.64152, 2.61528

### Charges guide

| | |
|---|---|
| Per unit incl. 2 persons and electricity | € 20.10 - € 33.50 |

Camping Cheques accepted.

---

# Loches-en-Touraine
## Camping la Citadelle

Avenue Aristide Briand, F-37600 Loches-en-Touraine (Indre-et-Loire) T: 02 47 59 05 91.
E: camping@lacitadelle.com **alanrogers.com/FR37050**

A pleasant, well maintained site, la Citadelle's best feature is probably that it is within walking distance of Loches, noted for its perfect architecture and its glorious history, yet at the same time the site has a rural atmosphere. The 102 standard touring pitches are all level, of a good size and with 10A electricity. Numerous trees offer varying degrees of shade. The 27 larger serviced pitches have 16A electricity but little shade, a further six luxury pitches have all facilities including furniture, fridge and barbecue. Mobile homes (28 for hire) occupy the other 48 pitches. Loches with its château is a 500 m. walk along the river.

### Facilities

Three sanitary blocks provide mainly British style WCs, washbasins and controllable showers. Laundry facilities. Motorcaravan service point. Two baby units and provision for disabled visitors. Heated swimming pool (May-Sept). Paddling pool. Play area. Small bar and snack bar (1/7-31/8). Boules. Games room. Miniclub (July/Aug). TV. WiFi over site (charged). Off site: Supermarket within 1 km.

**Open:** 19 March - 30 September.

### Directions

Loches is 45 km. southeast of Tours. Do not enter town centre. Approach from roundabout by supermarket at southern end of bypass (D943). Site signed towards town centre and is on right in 800 m. GPS: 47.12303, 1.00223

### Charges guide

| | |
|---|---|
| Per unit incl. 2 persons and electricity | € 20.50 - € 38.50 |

---

# Mesland
## Yelloh! Village Parc du Val de Loire

155 route de Fleuray, F-41150 Mesland (Loir-et-Cher) T: 02 54 70 27 18. E: parcduvaldeloire@wanadoo.fr
**alanrogers.com/FR41010**

Between Blois and Amboise, quietly situated among vineyards away from the main roads and towns, this site is nevertheless centrally placed for visits to the châteaux; Chaumont, Amboise and Blois (21 km) are the nearest in that order. There are 150 touring pitches of reasonable size (80-120 sq.m), either in light woodland marked by trees or on open meadow with separators. All the pitches have electricity (10A) and 50 also have water and drainage. Sports and competitions are organised in July/August with a weekly disco and dance for adults and opportunities for wine tasting are arranged weekly.

### Facilities

Three original toilet blocks are barely acceptable. One unit is very old and only open in July/Aug. Units for disabled visitors and babies. Laundry facilities. Motorcaravan services. Shop with bakery, bar, restaurant, snack service, pizzeria and takeaway. TV room. Three swimming pools, one heated and covered (outdoor 25/4-11/9). Balnéo. Tennis. Three playgrounds. Bicycle hire. Minigolf.

**Open:** 6 April - 23 September.

### Directions

From A10 exit 18 (Amboise) take D31 south to Autrèche. Turn left on D55 for 3.5 km. In Darne-Marie Les Bois turn left and then right onto D43 to Mesland. Follow site signs. GPS: 47.51002, 1.10481

### Charges guide

| | |
|---|---|
| Per unit incl. 2 persons | € 17.00 - € 35.00 |
| extra person | € 6.00 - € 8.00 |

---

For latest campsite news, availability and prices visit
**alanrogers.com**

## Muides-sur-Loire
### Camping Château des Marais
27 rue de Chambord, F-41500 Muides-sur-Loire (Loir-et-Cher) T: 02 54 87 05 42.
E: chateau.des.marais@wanadoo.fr **alanrogers.com/FR41040**

The Château des Marais campsite is well situated for visiting the château at Chambord (its park is impressive) and the other châteaux in the Vallée des Rois. The site, providing 115 large touring pitches, all with electricity (10A), water and drainage and ample shade, is situated in the oak and hornbeam woods of its own small château. An excellent swimming complex offers pools with two slides, two flumes and a lazy river. A new wellness centre is a recent addition. English is spoken and the reception from the enthusiastic owners and the staff is very welcoming. Used by tour operators (90 pitches).

### Facilities

Four sanitary blocks have good facilities including some large showers and washbasins en-suite which would also be suitable for visitors with disabilities. Washing machines and dryers. Motorcaravan service point. Shop. Bar/restaurant with large terrace. Takeaway (11/4-13/9). Breakfast service. Swimming complex with heated and unheated pools, slide and cover for cooler weather. New wellness spa centre with massage. Bicycle and go-kart hire. Games room. Music/TV room and library in the Manor House. Children's club (high season). Fishing pond. Excursions to Paris, an entertainment programme and canoe trips organised in high season. Free WiFi in bar area. Off site: Riding and golf 10 km. Muides-sur-Loire.

**Open:** 8 May - 14 September.

### Directions

From A10 autoroute take exit 16 to Mer-Chambord. Follow signs for Chambord, cross the River Loire, then go straight on for 1 km. before turning right and following signs to site. GPS: 47.66580, 1.52877

### Charges 2013

| | |
|---|---|
| Per unit incl. 2 persons and electricity | € 31.00 - € 47.00 |
| extra person | € 8.00 |
| child | free - € 7.00 |
| dog | € 8.00 |

Credit cards accepted for amounts over € 80.

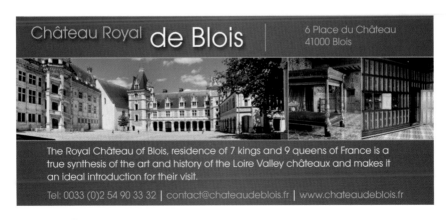

**FREE** Alan Rogers Travel Card
Extra benefits and savings - see page 10

## Neung-sur-Beuvron

### Camping Municipal de la Varenne

34 rue de Veillas, F-41210 Neung-sur-Beuvron (Loir-et-Cher) T: 02 54 83 68 52.
E: camping.lavarenne@wanadoo.fr **alanrogers.com/FR41090**

This is a particularly well organised site in a peaceful location, just 16 km. from the A71 autoroute. The site has a slight slope but most of the 69 grass touring pitches are fairly level, all with electricity hook-ups (10A). Some pitches are individual, others in bays of four, and some for tents amongst trees. There is good shade in most areas. To the rear is a large open field which slopes down to the small river. Each evening the manager visits every pitch to take bread orders, which are available from reception at 08.00 the following morning. Four mobile homes are for rent.

**Facilities**

An excellent, clean and well equipped modern building includes spacious showers, baby changing facilities and a suite for disabled visitors. A second unit at the rear of the reception building has additional older facilities. Washing machine and dryer. Freezer for ice blocks. A third unit is planned. Motorcaravan service point. Playground. Two tennis courts. Bicycle hire. River fishing adjacent to site. Communal barbecue.

**Open:** Easter - 30 September.

**Directions**

Neung-sur-Beuvron is 40 km. east of Blois, and 2 km. west of the D922, 22 km. north of Romarantin-Lanthenay. From the east, in the town centre, turn right at church and follow signs for camping. From the west turn left in the town centre, then as above. GPS: 47.53822, 1.81508

**Charges guide**

| Per unit incl. 2 persons | |
|---|---|
| and electricity | € 10.00 - € 11.00 |

## Pierrefitte-sur-Sauldre

### Leading Camping les Alicourts

Domaine des Alicourts, F-41300 Pierrefitte-sur-Sauldre (Loir-et-Cher) T: 02 54 88 63 34.
E: info@lesalicourts.com **alanrogers.com/FR41030**

A secluded holiday village set in the heart of the forest, with many sporting facilities and a super spa centre, Camping les Alicourts is midway between Orléans and Bourges, to the east of the A71. There are 490 pitches, 150 for touring and the remainder occupied by mobile homes and chalets. All pitches have electricity connections (6A) and good provision for water, and most are 150 sq.m. (min. 100 sq.m). Locations vary, from wooded to more open areas, thus giving a choice of amount of shade. All facilities are open all season and the leisure amenities are exceptional. The Senseo Balnéo centre offers indoor pools, hydrotherapy, massage and spa treatments for over 18s only (some special family sessions are provided). An inviting outdoor water complex (all season) includes two swimming pools, a pool with wave machine and a beach area, not forgetting three water slides. Competitions and activities are organised for adults and children, including a high season club for children with an entertainer twice a day, a disco once a week and a dance for adults. A member of Leading Campings group.

**Facilities**

Three modern sanitary blocks include some washbasins in cabins and baby bathrooms. Laundry facilities. Facilities for disabled visitors. Motorcaravan services. Shop. Restaurant. Takeaway in bar with terrace. Pool complex. Spa centre. Lake (fishing, bathing, canoes, pedaloes, cable-ski). 9-hole golf course. Adventure play area. Tennis. Minigolf. Boules. Rollerskating and skateboarding (bring own equipment). Bicycle hire. Internet access and WiFi (charged).

**Open:** 27 April - 7 September.

**Directions**

From A71, take Lamotte-Beuvron exit (no 3) or from N20 Orléans to Vierzon turn left on to D923 towards Aubigny. After 14 km. turn right at camping sign on to D24E. GPS: 47.54398, 2.19193

**Charges guide**

| Per unit incl. 2 persons | |
|---|---|
| and electricity | € 20.00 - € 46.00 |
| extra person | € 7.00 - € 10.00 |
| child (1-17 yrs acc. to age) | free - € 9.00 |
| dog | € 5.00 - € 7.00 |

For latest campsite news, availability and prices visit
# alanrogers.com

## Nouan-le-Fuzelier
### Camping la Grande Sologne

Rue des Peupliers, F-41600 Nouan-le-Fuzelier (Loir-et-Cher) T: 02 54 88 70 22.
E: info@campinggrandesologne.com **alanrogers.com/FR41180**

The enthusiastic new managers, who speak many languages, are working hard to raise this site to a high standard. It is in a parkland setting on the southern edge of Nouan-le-Fuzelier close to the A71 autoroute, making this an ideal spot to spend some time relaxing whilst en route north or south. It has 165 spacious, level, grass pitches with a variety of mature trees giving some shade, with 150 for touring. All have 10A electricity, but long leads may be necessary. They are marked but not delineated. Access is easy for large outfits.

**Facilities**

Three modern toilet blocks with all necessary facilities including those for campers with disabilities. Washing machine, dryer. Snack bar (July/Aug). Small shop (all season). Games/TV room. Motorcaravan services. Fishing. Bicycle hire. Play area. WiFi. Off site: Adjacent Municipal swimming pool (free), tennis courts (reduced price).

**Open:** 1 April - 15 October.

**Directions**

Nouan-le-Fuzelier is between exits 3 and 4 on A71 autoroute, south of Orléans. Take D2020 to site at southern edge of Nouan-le-Fuzelier, opposite railway station. Well signed. GPS: 47.533863, 2.037674

**Charges guide**

| | |
|---|---|
| Per unit incl. 2 persons and electricity | € 18.10 - € 22.50 |

## Poilly-lez-Gien
### Camping Touristique de Gien

Rue des Iris, F-45500 Poilly-lez-Gien (Loiret) T: 02 38 67 12 50. E: camping-gien@wanadoo.fr
**alanrogers.com/FR45030**

This open, attractive, well cared for site lies on a bank of the Loire with views of the town of Gien and its château. It has a long river frontage, which includes a good expanse of sandy beach. There are 200 good sized, level, grassy pitches with 165 for touring. All have 10A electricity. Some are shaded by mature trees and many have good views over the river. The bar and restaurant, with a pleasant outdoor area, are open to the public and meals are reasonably priced. Soirées with different themes are held weekly in July and August. The town of Gien, with its shops, bars, restaurants and château, is within a kilometre just across the bridge. A long distance cycle path passes the entrance. This is an excellent base for exploring the eastern end of the Loire valley, and Gien has a festival celebrating the heritage of this part of the Loire at Ascensiontide. The tourist office organises a wide range of activities both sporting and cultural. There is a regular bus service to the ancient city of Orléans.

**Facilities**

Two unisex toilet blocks, one heated, are fairly basic but clean and have washbasins in cabins, controllable showers and facilities for disabled visitors. Laundry. Bar and restaurant (8/5-30/9), both open to the public. Shop 50 m. outside gates (all year; closed Sun. outside July/Aug). Inflatable swimming pool (with removable roof) and paddling pools (15/5-15/9). Play area and grassed games area. Outdoor exercise equipment. Minigolf. Bicycle and pedal cart hire. Canoe hire. Fishing. Large sandy beach. Some organised activities (July/Aug). WiFi over site (charged). Off site: Children's club on beach. Town centre less than 1 km. Hypermarket 1.5 km.

**Open:** First weekend in March - All Saints' in November.

**Directions**

Gien is 70 km. southeast of Orléans. Leave the A77 autoroute at exit 19 and take D940 (Bourges) to bypass Gien to east; cross Loire and turn north at roundabout towards town centre. At traffic lights before bridge, turn west to Poilly-lez-Gien and site is on right in 800 m. GPS: 47.68229, 2.62315

**Charges guide**

| | |
|---|---|
| Per unit incl. 2 persons and electricity | € 20.00 |
| extra person | € 6.00 |
| child (under 12 yrs) | € 4.00 |
| dog | € 2.00 |

CAMPING TOURISTIQUE DE GIEN ★★★
Rue des Iris - 45500 Poilly-Lez-Gien
Tel 0033-(0)2 38 67 12 50
Fax 0033-(0)2 38 67 12 18
GPS N47°40'56"E2°37'23"
camping-gien@wanadoo.fr
www.camping-gien.com

# Rillé

## Huttopia Rillé

Lac de Rillé, F-37340 Rillé (Indre-et-Loire) T: 02 47 24 62 97. E: rille@huttopia.com

alanrogers.com/FR37140

Huttopia Rillé is a rural site ideal for tent campers seeking a more natural, environmentally friendly, peaceful campsite close to a lake. Cars are parked outside the barrier but allowed on site to unload and load. The 133 slightly uneven and sloping pitches, 80 for touring, are scattered between the pine trees. All have 10A electricity (very long leads needed) and 24 are fully serviced. They vary in size and are numbered but not marked. This site is designed for those with tents, though small caravans and motorcaravans (special area) are accepted. It is not ideal for those with walking difficulties. Communal barbecues only. The site is situated in an area ideal for exploring and there are numerous marked footpaths and cycle tracks close by. The area north of the lake, in easy reach of the site, is designated a nature reserve offering excellent opportunities for birdwatching. After a long day exploring the region, you can unwind with a refreshing drink or a light meal on the terrace overlooking the lake and small swimming pool. In July and August activities include a goat farm, jam making and star gazing.

### Facilities

Modern central toilet block with family rooms and facilities for disabled visitors (no ramps and difficult access for wheelchairs). A smaller block has separate showers, washbasins and facilities for disabled visitors. Motorcaravan service point. Small heated swimming pool with paddling area (20/4-30/9). Play area. Fishing. Canoes on lake. Communal barbecue areas (no charcoal barbecues). Max. 1 dog. Off site: Small steam train passes site. Several châteaux to visit. Riding 10 km.

**Open:** 20 April - 9 November.

### Directions

Rillé is 40 km. west of Tours. Leave D766 Angers-Blois road at Château la Vallière take D749 southwest. In Rillé turn west on D49. Site is on right in 2 km. GPS: 47.44600, 0.33291

### Charges guide

| | |
|---|---|
| Per unit incl. 2 persons and electricity | € 15.70 - € 33.70 |
| extra person | € 5.50 - € 7.60 |
| child (2-7 yrs) | € 3.30 - € 5.00 |

# Sainte Catherine-de-Fierbois

## Castel Camping Parc de Fierbois

F-37800 Sainte Catherine-de-Fierbois (Indre-et-Loire) T: 02 47 65 43 35. E: contact@fierbois.com

alanrogers.com/FR37120

Parc de Fierbois has an impressive entrance and a tree-lined driveway and is set among 250 acres of lakes and forest in the heart of the Loire Valley. In all, there are 320 pitches including 133 for touring, the remainder being used by tour operators and for chalets and mobile homes. The touring pitches (all with 10A electricity) are mostly level and separated by low hedging or small trees. The other pitches are small or medium in size, many unmarked and some sloping and in the shade. A lively family holiday site.

### Facilities

Two toilet blocks include preset hot showers and washbasins in cubicles. Baby room. Good facilities for disabled visitors. Laundry facilities. Supermarket. Motorcaravan service point. Restaurant, pizzas and takeaway food (June-Aug). Bar. Water park complex. Indoor heated pool. Children's club. Tennis. Pétanque. Minigolf. Bicycle hire. Multisports area. Skateboard park. Go-karts and electric cars. TV/video room. Gym. Fishing. WiFi over site (charged; free on premium pitches).

**Open:** 22 April - 6 September.

### Directions

Travelling south on N10 from Tours, go through Montbazon and on towards St Maure and Chatellerault. Site signed 16 km. outside Montbazon near Ste Catherine. Turn off main road. Follow site signs. From A10 autoroute use St Maure exit and turn north up N10. GPS: 47.1487, 0.6548

### Charges guide

| | |
|---|---|
| Per unit incl. 2 persons and electricity | € 21.00 - € 49.00 |
| extra person | € 7.00 - € 9.00 |

For latest campsite news, availability and prices visit

**alanrogers.com**

## Senonches

### Huttopia Senonches

Etang de Badouleau, avenue de Badouleau, F-28250 Senonches (Eure-et-Loir) T: 02 37 37 81 40.
E: senonches@huttopia.com  alanrogers.com/FR28140

Huttopia Senonches is hidden away in the huge Forêt Dominiale de Senonches and in keeping with other Huttopia sites, combines a high standard of comfort with a real sense of back woods camping. There are 91 touring pitches here, some with 10A electricity. The pitches are very large ranging from 100 sq.m. to no less than 300 sq.m. There are also 30 Canadian style log cabins and tents available for rent. A good range of on-site amenities includes a shop and a bar/restaurant. The chlorine free natural pool, with terrace, overlooks a lake and is open from early July until September.

#### Facilities

The toilet blocks are modern and heated in low season, with special facilities for disabled visitors. Shop (all season). Bar, snack bar and takeaway (limited in low season). Swimming pool. Fishing. Play area. Bicycle hire and riding. Entertainment and activity programme. Tents, Cahuttes and chalets for rent. Gas barbecues only. Max. 1 dog. Off site: Riding 4 km. Senonches (good selection of shops, bars and restaurants). Cycle and walking tracks. Chartres.

**Open:** 4 April - 7 November.

#### Directions

Approaching from Chartres, use the ring road (N154) and then take the D24 in a northwesterly direction. Drive through Digny and continue to Senonches. Site well signed from here. GPS: 48.5533, 1.04146

#### Charges guide

| | |
|---|---|
| Per unit incl. 2 persons and electricity | € 20.50 - € 38.10 |
| extra person | € 4.35 - € 6.40 |
| child (2-7 yrs) | € 2.75 - € 4.55 |
| dog | € 4.00 |

---

## Sonzay

### Camping l'Arada Parc

Rue de la Baratière, F-37360 Sonzay (Indre-et-Loire) T: 02 47 24 72 69. E: info@laradaparc.com
alanrogers.com/FR37060

A good, well maintained site in a quiet location, easy to find from the motorway and popular as an overnight stop, Camping l'Arada Parc is an attractive family site nestling in the heart of the Tourangelle countryside between the Loire and Loir valleys. The 61 grass touring pitches have electricity (10A) and 18 have water and drainage. The clearly marked pitches, some slightly sloping, are separated by trees and shrubs, some of which now provide a degree of shade. An attractive, heated pool is on a pleasant terrace beside the restaurant. Entertainment, themed evenings and activities for children in July/August. This is a new site with modern facilities which include a superb new covered pool and fitness room.

#### Facilities

Two modern toilet blocks provide unisex toilets, showers and washbasins in cubicles. Baby room. Facilities for disabled visitors recently improved. Laundry facilities. Shop, bar, restaurant and takeaway (all season). Motorcaravan service point. Outdoor swimming pool with slide and new terrace surround (no Bermuda-style shorts; 1/5-15/9). Heated, covered pool (all season). Fitness room. Small play area. Games area. Boules. TV room. Bicycle hire (high season). Internet access. WiFi over site (charged). Footpath to village. Off site: Tennis 200 m. Fishing 9 km. Golf 12 km. Riding 14 km.

**Open:** 29 March - 18 October.

#### Directions

Sonzay is northwest of Tours. From the new A28 north of Tours take the exit to Neuillé-Pont-Pierre which is on the N138 Le Mans-Tours road. Then take D766 towards Château la Vallière and turn southwest to Sonzay. Follow campsite signs. GPS: 47.526208, 0.450879

#### Charges 2013

| | |
|---|---|
| Per unit incl. 2 persons and electricity (10A) | € 19.30 - € 28.80 |
| extra person | € 4.00 - € 5.50 |
| child (3-12 yrs acc. to age) | free - € 4.00 |
| Camping Cheques accepted. | |

**FREE** Alan Rogers Travel Card
Extra benefits and savings - see page 10

## Suèvres

### Castel Camping de la Grenouillère

RN152, F-41500 Suèvres (Loir-et-Cher) T: 02 54 87 80 37. E: la.grenouillere@wanadoo.fr

**alanrogers.com/FR41020**

Château de la Grenouillère is an attractive site set in a 28-acre park midway between Orléans and Tours, well situated for visiting many of the Loire châteaux. The 280 pitches, with 130 for touring, are in three distinct areas. The majority are in a wooded area, with about 60 in the old orchard and the remainder in open meadows. There are varying amounts of shade from the trees. There is one water point for every four pitches and all have electric hook-up (10A). Additionally, there are 14 fully serviced pitches with a separate sanitary block in the outbuildings of the château.

**Facilities**

Three excellent sanitary blocks are well appointed. Laundry facilities. Shop. Bar. Pizzeria and pizza takeaway. Restaurant and grill takeaway (20/5-31/8). Swimming complex of four pools (one covered) and slide. Spa with whirlpool, jacuzzi, sauna, massage. Tennis. Games room. Bicycle and canoe hire (July/Aug). Fishing. WiFi (charged). Off site: Suèvres 3 km. Riding 5 km. Golf 10 km.

**Open:** 13 April - 14 September.

**Directions**

Site is on the D2155 between Suèvres and Mer, 3 km. from Mer and is well signed.
GPS: 47.68557, 1.48686

**Charges guide**

| Per unit incl. 2 persons | |
|---|---|
| and electricity | € 26.00 - € 39.00 |
| incl. full services | € 30.00 - € 45.00 |
| extra person | € 6.00 - € 8.00 |

---

## Trogues

### Camping du Château de la Rolandière

F-37220 Trogues (Indre-et-Loire) T: 02 47 58 53 71. E: contact@larolandiere.com

**alanrogers.com/FR37090**

This is a charming site set in the grounds of a château and you are assured of a very warm welcome here. There are 50 medium sized, level or gently sloping pitches, separated by hedges with a variety of trees giving some shade. Most have 6A electricity (long leads advised) with water taps nearby. There is a large chalet and mobile homes for hire, and bed and breakfast is also available. The site has a pleasant swimming pool, paddling pool, fitness room and games/TV room. The bar and restaurant have a sunny terrace overlooking the château. Minigolf, swings, slides and an area for ball games are adjacent. The site is a delightfully peaceful spot from which to visit the châteaux at Chinon, Loches, Villandry or Azay-le-Rideau and the villages of Richelieu and Crissay-sur-Manse. There are many interesting excursions to beautiful gardens and grottos and you should find time to enjoy the local gastronomy and wines. In July and August, there is an interesting programme of activities aimed at families with younger children. A Sites et Paysages member.

**Facilities**

The older style toilet block has been refurbished to provide good facilities with modern showers, washbasin and laundry areas. Provision for disabled visitors. Small shop for basics. Bar with terrace. Snacks and takeaway (July/Aug). Swimming pool (15/5-30/9). Minigolf. Play area. Fitness room. TV lounge. WiFi. Off site: Fishing 1 km. on River Vienne. River beach and boat launching 4 km. Restaurant 4 km. Bicycle hire and shops 6 km. St Maure 7 km. Golf 15 km.

**Open:** 23 April - 24 September.

**Directions**

Trogues is 40 km. southwest of Tours on the D760 Loches-Chinon road. Site is on D760, midway between Trogues and A10 (exit 25). Entrance is signed and marked by a model of the château.
GPS: 47.10767, 0.51052

**Charges guide**

| Per unit incl. 2 persons | |
|---|---|
| and electricity | € 20.90 - € 28.90 |
| extra person | € 4.50 - € 6.00 |
| No credit cards. | |

For latest campsite news, availability and prices visit

**alanrogers.com**

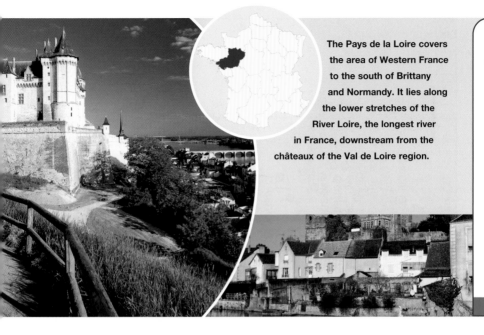

The Pays de la Loire covers the area of Western France to the south of Brittany and Normandy. It lies along the lower stretches of the River Loire, the longest river in France, downstream from the châteaux of the Val de Loire region.

**DÉPARTEMENTS: 44 LOIRE-ATLANTIQUE, 49 MAINE-ET-LOIRE, 53 MAYENNE, 72 SARTHE**

*Strictly speaking, the département of 85 Vendée is also part of this region. Because of its importance as a holiday destination for British people, we have featured it separately in this guide.*

**MAJOR CITIES: ANGERS, NANTES**

Created in the late 20th century, the Pays de la Loire is a relatively new region embracing parts of the old provinces of Anjou, Brittany, Maine and Poitou. Two of its five departments are coastal, with over 450 km. of Atlantic shoreline and some of France's most popular seaside resorts – La Baule, Le Croisic, Saint Jean-de-Monts – and includes the islands of Yeu and Noirmoutier.

Further inland, Anjou is dominated by the historic city of Angers with its medieval castle, once home to the Plantagenet kings of England. Much of this area is rural, with a strong agricultural heritage, but every year visitors flock to Le Mans, capital of Sarthe, for its 24-hour motor race.

Other attractions include the small town of La Flèche on the River Loir, home to France's oldest zoo, while Laval has some fine 16th- and 18th-century houses and two châteaux. It lies on the River Mayenne, a navigable waterway with 85 km. of towpaths, popular with walkers and cyclists.

**Places of interest**

*Angers:* art town, medieval castle and tapestries, cathedral.

*Brissac:* 15th-century castle.

*Le Croisic:* small fishing port, Naval Museum.

*Fontevraud:* 11th-century Royal abbey.

*Guérande:* walled city with historic centre.

*La Baule:* holiday resort with lovely sandy bay.

*Le Mans:* the annual 24-hour car race attracting visitors from all over the world; car museum, old town, cathedral.

*Le Puy de Fou:* 15-16th-century castle, son-et-lumière production; popular theme park.

*Les Sables d'Olonne:* fishing port and seaside resort.

*Nantes:* major city with sightseeing and shopping opportunities; boat trips along the River Erdre.

*Saumer:* 13th-century castle, Cadre Noir National School of Horse Riding, wine cellars and Mushroom Museum.

**Cuisine of the region**

*Beurre blanc:* a buttery sauce that goes well with fish.

*Rillauds d'Anjou:* muscadet sausages.

*Curé Nantais and Port-Salut:* local cheeses.

*Pâté aux prunes:* A speciality of the Angers region and found in all good local bakers in July and August, this sugary pastry is filled with plums.

www.paysdelaloire.co.uk
infotourisme@sem-paysdelaloire.fr
(0)2 40 48 24 20

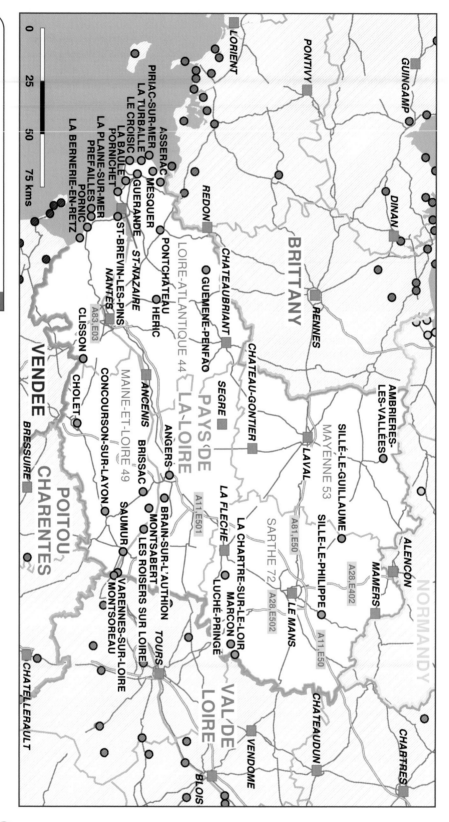

0
25
50
75 kms

LORIENT
PONTIVY
GUINGAMP
DINAN
PIRIAC-SUR-MER
LA TURBALLE
LE CROISIC
LA BAULE
PORNICHET
LA PLAINE-SUR-MER
PREFAILLES
PORNIC
LA BERNERIE-EN-RETZ
ASSERAC
MESQUER
GUERANDE
ST-BREVIN-LES-PINS
ST-NAZAIRE
NANTES
CLISSON
PONTCHATEAU
HERIC
REDON
CHATEAUBRIANT
GUEMENE-PENFAO
CHATEAU-GONTIER
BRITTANY
RENNES
AMBRIERES-
LES-VALLEES
LOIRE-ATLANTIQUE 44
PAYS DE
LA-LOIRE
SEGRE
LAVAL
MAYENNE 53
SILLÉ-LE-GUILLAUME
ALENÇON
MAMERS
VENDEE
CHOLET
MAINE-ET-LOIRE 49
ANCENIS
BRISSAC
ANGERS
CONCOURSON-SUR-LAYON
SAUMUR
MONTSABERT
LES ROISERS SUR LOIRE
VARENNES-SUR-LOIRE
MONTSOREAU
BRAIN-SUR-L'AUTHION
LA FLECHE
LA CHARTRE-SUR-LE-LOIR
MARCON
LUCHÉ-PRINGÉ
SILLE-LE-PHILIPPE
LE MANS
SARTHE 72
A81.E50
A28.E402
A28.E502
A11.E50
A11.E501
TOURS
BRESSUIRE
POITOU
CHARENTES
CHATELLERAULT
A83.E03
VAL DE
LOIRE
VENDOME
CHATEAUDUN
CHARTRES
BLOIS
NORMANDY

For latest campsite news, availability and prices visit
**alanrogers.com**

## Ambrières-les-Vallées

### Camping Parc de Vaux

35 rue des Colverts, F-53300 Ambrières-les-Vallées (Mayenne) T: 02 43 04 90 25.
E: parcdevaux@camp-in-ouest.com  **alanrogers.com/FR53010**

Parc de Vaux is an ex-municipal site which was acquired in 2010 by the owners of FR72080. This 3.5 hectare site has 90 pitches, 18 occupied by mobile homes, chalets and bungalow tents, available to rent. The 59 touring pitches are generally grassy and well sized (mostly with 10A electricity and water). The site is located close to the pretty village of Ambrières-les-Vallées, and there is direct access to the village from the site by a footbridge over the river. The village is around 12 km. north of Mayenne, and may prove a convenient en-route stop. There is a swimming pool adjacent (with water slide) and the site also has access to a lake and a good range of amenities.

**Facilities**

Three small toilet blocks, one with facilities for disabled visitors. No children's facilities. Laundry. Motorcaravan service point. Bar and snack bar/takeaway in high season. Heated outdoor swimming pool. Sports field. Fishing. Football. Basketball. Minigolf. Boules. Canoes. Pedaloes. Bicycle hire. Archery and tennis adjacent. Games room with TV and library. Play area. Accommodation for rent. Off site: Ambrières-les-Vallées (shops and restaurants).

**Open:** 1 April - 1 November.

**Directions**

From Mayenne head north on D23 to Ambrières-les-Vallées. The site is clearly signed on your right-hand side from here. GPS: 48.391908, -0.61709

**Charges guide**

| | |
|---|---|
| Per unit incl. 2 persons | € 10.40 - € 12.90 |
| extra person | € 3.20 - € 4.20 |
| child (under 13 yrs) | € 1.70 - € 2.30 |
| electricity | € 3.10 |

## Angers

### Camping du Lac de Maine

Avenue du Lac de Maine, F-49000 Angers (Maine-et-Loire) T: 02 41 73 05 03. E: camping@lacdemaine.fr
**alanrogers.com/FR49000**

The Lac de Maine campsite is situated in the heart of the Anjou region. Most of the 143 level touring pitches are part grass and part gravel hardstanding, with the remainder all gravel. All have water, a drain and electricity. Some pitches are unsuitable for awnings. The main entrance has a height restriction of 3.2 m, although there is an alternative gate for higher vehicles. This is a useful site, open for a long season and only five minutes from the centre of Angers. With wide access roads, it is also suitable for American RVs. This site has the advantage of being at the southern end of the Parc de Loisirs du Lac de Maine. The adjacent 220 acre lake has a sandy beach for swimmers, windsurfing, sailing and pedaloes available, while the parkland provides tennis courts and a nature reserve.

**Facilities**

Two sanitary blocks, one which can be heated and includes some washbasins in cubicles. British style WCs. Facilities for babies and disabled visitors. Laundry facilities. Motorcaravan service point. Restaurant/bar (both 20/6-10/9). Heated L-shaped swimming pool (1/5-30/9). Spa. Pétanque. Bicycle hire. Play area. Internet point and WiFi (free). Barrier card deposit (€ 20). Off site: Supermarket within walking distance. Lake beach 500 m. Fishing 1 km. Riding 3 km. Golf 5 km.

**Open:** 25 March - 10 October.

**Directions**

Site is just west of Angers near the N23 (Angers-Nantes road). Turn south at signs for Quartier de Maine and Lac de Maine. Follow signs for Pruniers and Bouchemaine. Site on D111 and signed. GPS: 47.45434, -0.59619

**Charges 2013**

| | |
|---|---|
| Per unit incl. 2 persons and electricity (10A) | € 18,90 - € 26,30 |
| extra person | € 3.40 |
| child (under 13 yrs) | € 2.30 |
| dog | € 2.30 |

Camping Cheques accepted.

**Camping du Lac de Maine**
★★★★
Discover this pretty campsite nestling in the heart of the Anjou wine region, close to the historic town of Angers and a beautiful vast 100 ha lake.

Openingdates:
25/03 to 10/10/2011

Mobile homes and bungalows for rent

Heated Swimming Pool, Paddling pool, SPA, Restaurant, Bar, Takeaway, Bike hire, Internet Facilities (WiFi)...

Avenue du Lac de Maine - F-49000 Angers - Tel: 0033 (0)2.41.73.05.03
camping@lacdemaine.fr - www.camping-angers.fr

**FREE** Alan Rogers Travel Card
Extra benefits and savings - see page 10

## Assérac

### Camping le Moulin de l'Eclis

Pont Mahé, F-44410 Assérac (Loire-Atlantique) T: 02 40 01 76 69. E: info@camping-moulin-de-leclis.fr
**alanrogers.com/FR44330**

Le Moulin de L'Eclis is an attractive, rural site with direct access to a safe sandy beach. There are 180 pitches of which around half are available for tourers, most with 10A electricity. Most pitches are of a generous size on grass and are divided by small trees and shrubs. There are many tall pine trees which provide good shade. A newer area has somewhat sloping pitches and here there is no shade. A solar heated, covered pool is ideal for when the tide goes out from the wide shallow bay, and there is direct access to the beach. Watersports are popular and some are organised. This site will appeal to windsurfers. This is a very friendly and typically French site. A mixture of wooden chalets and traditional brick buildings house the facilities, which are of a good standard. In high season as well as watersports, the site organises walks and bicycle rides.

**Facilities**

Three modern and bright, heated toilet blocks include some washbasins in cabins and large preset showers with dividers. A new block has family cabins and facilities for children. Good facilities provided for disabled visitors. Laundry facilities. Small shop sells freshly baked bread (July/Aug). A butcher's van calls in high season. Bar with snacks and takeaway (July/Aug). Covered, solar heated pool and paddling pool. Play area. Watersports. Free WiFi over part of site. Off site: Kayak and windsurf hire. Riding 2 km. Bicycle hire 5 km. Supermarket 10 km.

**Open:** 29 March - 11 November.

**Directions**

Take the D82 from Asserac in a northwest direction for 5 km. Site is on left and well signed.
GPS: 47.44548, -2.45161

**Charges guide**

| Per unit incl. 2 persons | |
| --- | --- |
| and electricity | € 18.40 - € 31.60 |
| incl. services | € 21.50 - € 32.20 |
| child | € 2.50 - € 3.60 |
| dog | € 4.10 |

Pont-Mahé - 44 410 Assérac | Tél: 0033 2.40.01.76.69
E-mail: info@camping-leclis.com | www.camping-leclis.com

## Brain-sur-l'Authion

### Kawan Village  Camping du Port Caroline

rue du Port, F-49800 Brain-sur-l'Authion (Maine-et-Loire) T: 02 41 80 42 18.
E: info@campingduportcaroline.fr  **alanrogers.com/FR49030**

Camping du Port Caroline is an attractive site, lying alongside a small river and close to the little village of Brain-sur-l'Authion, which is at the heart of the Anjou region. This is a quiet, relaxing site with little in the way of organised activities. There are 121 large, level, grassy pitches, 103 for touring, all with 10A electricity, though very long leads may be needed. They are separated by a variety of hedging and tall grees give most pitches ample shade. This is a useful base for visiting the vineyards of the Anjou which are all around. The very small River Authion, just 200 metres from the site, is popular with anglers.

**Facilities**

The two sanitary blocks of very different designs are clean and well maintained. Facilities for disabled visitors. Swimming pool and paddling pool. Shop. Snack bar. Takeaway (Tues. and Thurs). Play area. Bicycle hire. Mobile homes and chalets (one for disabled visitors) for rent. Off site: Tennis. Fishing (charge applies). Boating. Multisports pitch. Walking and cycle trails. Boat trips on the Loire.

**Open:** 15 March - 15 November.

**Directions**

From Angers take D347 east towards Saumur for 7 km. At roundabout turn south onto D113 for 2 km. to Brain-sur-l'Authion. Site is signed just south of village. GPS: 47.44278, -0.40832

**Charges guide**

| Per unit incl. 2 persons | |
| --- | --- |
| and electricity | € 15.00 - € 20.00 |
| child (0-9 yrs) | free - € 3.50 |
| extra person | € 3.00 - € 4.00 |
| Camping Cheques accepted. | |

For latest campsite news, availability and prices visit
# alanrogers.com

## Brissac

### Camping de l'Etang

Route de Saint Mathurin, F-49320 Brissac-Quincé (Maine-et-Loire) T: 02 41 91 70 61.
E: info@campingetang.com  **alanrogers.com/FR49040**

At Camping de l'Etang many of the 124 level touring pitches have lovely views across the countryside. Separated and numbered, some have a little shade and all have electricity (10A) with water and drainage nearby; 21 are fully serviced. A small bridge crosses the River Aubance which runs through the site (well fenced) and there are two lakes where fisherman can enjoy free fishing. The site has its own vineyard and the wine produced can be purchased on the campsite. The adjacent Parc de Loisirs is a paradise for young children with many activities (free for campers). A Sites et Paysages member.

| Facilities | Directions |
|---|---|
| Three well maintained toilet blocks. Laundry facilities. Baby room. Disabled visitors are well catered for. Motorcaravan services. The farmhouse houses reception, a small shop and takeaway snacks (July/Aug) when bar is closed. A bar/restaurant (crêpes, salads, etc, evenings July/Aug). Covered swimming pool and paddling pool. Fishing. Play area. Bicycle hire. WiFi over site (charged). **Open:** 27 April - 15 September. | Brissac-Quincé is 17 km. southeast of Angers on D748 towards Poitiers. Do not enter the town but turn north on D55 (site signed) in direction of St Mathurin. GPS: 47.3611, -0.4353 |

**Charges guide**

| | |
|---|---|
| Per unit incl. 2 persons and electricity | € 19.00 |
| extra person | € 4.00 - € 5.00 |

## Cholet

### Centre Touristique Lac de Ribou

Allée Léon Mandin, F-49300 Cholet (Maine-et-Loire) T: 02 41 49 74 30. E: info@lacderibou.com
**alanrogers.com/FR49120**

Situated just 58 km. southeast of Nantes and a similar distance from the River Loire at Angers and Saumur, this could be a useful place to break a journey or to spend a few days relaxing. Camping Lac de Ribou, with the adjacent 'Village Vacances', forms a holiday complex in pleasant parkland next to an extensive lake on the outskirts of the busy market town of Cholet. One hundred and sixty-two touring pitches are on undulating land (some are sloping), divided by hedges and with mature trees providing shade on many; most have electricity (10A) and 115 also have individual water tap and drainage.

| Facilities | Directions |
|---|---|
| One sanitary block has preset showers and washbasins in cabins. Facilities for disabled visitors. Motorcaravan service points. Small shop (July/Aug). Bar and snack bar with takeaway (July/Aug). Large heated swimming pool and smaller pool with slide and paddling pool (1/6-30/9). Play area. Multisports pitch. Volleyball. Boules. Activities for all ages (July/Aug). Professional standard cabaret evenings. Night club (high season). WiFi (with deposit). Off site: Small beach (no swimming) 500 m. **Open:** 28 April - 16 September. | From Cholet ring road east of town, turn east on D20 towards Maulévrier and Mauléon. At roundabout by Leclerc supermarket, take first exit to site, which is signed 'Parc de Loisirs de Ribou' all around town. GPS: 47.036367, -0.843733 |

**Charges guide**

| | |
|---|---|
| Per unit incl. 1 or 2 persons and electricity | € 10.20 - € 23.00 |
| extra person | € 3.05 - € 5.10 |
| No credit cards. | |

## Clisson

### Camping Municipal du Moulin

Route de Nantes, F-44190 Clisson (Loire-Atlantique) T: 02 40 54 44 48
**alanrogers.com/FR44020**

This good value, small site is conveniently located on one of the main north – south routes on the edge of the interesting old town of Clisson and in the middle of the wine growing region. A typical municipal site, it is useful for short stays. There are 45 good sized, marked and level pitches with electricity, which are divided by hedges and trees giving a good degree of privacy and some shade. There is also an unmarked, wooded area for small tents. A barbecue and campfire area is to the rear of the site above the river where one can fish or canoe (via a steep path).

| Facilities | Directions |
|---|---|
| The fully equipped toilet block, cleaned each afternoon, includes some washbasins in cabins and others in a separate large room, with hot and cold water. Unit for disabled visitors. Laundry facilities. Bread delivered daily. Small playground. Fishing. No double axle or commercial vehicles accepted. Off site: Supermarket with fuel just across the road. Bicycle hire, riding 5 km. Sailing 15 km. **Open:** Mid April - mid October. | From N249 Nantes-Cholet road, take exit for Vallet/Clisson and D763 south for 7 km. then fork right towards Clisson town centre. At roundabout after passing Leclerc supermarket on your right take second exit (into site). GPS: 47.09594, -1.28271 |

**Charges guide**

| | |
|---|---|
| Per unit incl. 1 person and electricity | € 12.91 - € 13.62 |
| No credit cards. | |

**FREE** Alan Rogers Travel Card
Extra benefits and savings - see page 10

## Concourson-sur-Layon

### Camping Caravaning la Vallée des Vignes

La Croix Patron, F-49700 Concourson-sur-Layon (Maine-et-Loire) T: 02 41 59 86 35.
E: info@campingvdv.com **alanrogers.com/FR49070**

The enthusiasm of the English owners here comes across instantly in the warm welcome received by their guests. Bordering the Layon river, the 79 good sized grass pitches (50 for tourers) are reasonably level and fully serviced (10A electricity, water tap and drain) but have little shade. Five pitches have a hardstanding for cars. Attractions include an enclosed bar and restaurant overlooking a generously sized sun terrace surrounding the pool. In high season there are activities for children and adults. This is an ideal base for visiting the châteaux of the Loire and the many local caves and vineyards.

**Facilities**

The toilet block includes washbasins in cabins, and dishwashing facilities. Baby room. Facilities for disabled visitors. Washing machine. Bar meals/takeaway (15/5-15/9). Swimming and paddling pools (15/5-15/9). Playground, games area and football pitch. Minigolf. Volleyball. Basketball. Table tennis. Internet access and free WiFi over part of site. Fishing. Caravan storage. Pets' corner. Off site: Riding and bicycle hire 5 km. Golf 10 km.

**Open:** 15 April - 30 September.

**Directions**

Site is 20 km. southwest of Saumur. Take D347 then D960, bypass Doué-la-Fontaine. Site entrance is on right 500 m. beyond Concourson-sur-Layon.
GPS: 47.17431, -0.34730

**Charges guide**

| | |
|---|---|
| Per unit incl. 2 persons and electricity | € 21.00 - € 29.00 |
| extra person | € 4.00 - € 6.00 |

## Guemene-Penfao

### Flower Camping l'Hermitage

36 aveenue du Paradis, F-44290 Guemene-Penfao (Loire-Atlantique) T: 02 40 79 23 48.
E: camping.hermitage@wanadoo.fr **alanrogers.com/FR44130**

L'Hermitage is a pretty wooded site set in the Vallée du Don and would be useful for en-route stops or for longer stays. The enthusiastic staff, even though their English is a little limited, provide a warm welcome and maintain this reasonably priced site to a good standard. There are 110 pitches of which 80 are a good size for touring and camping. Some are formally arranged on open, level grass pitches, whereas others are informal amongst light woodland. Electricity (6A) is available to all (a long lead may be useful). A further 18 pitches are taken by mobile homes, most of which are for rent.

**Facilities**

A clean and well serviced toilet block includes some washbasins in cabins with warm water. Laundry and dishwashing sinks under cover (cold water but a hot tap is provided). Smallish pool, paddling pool and slide, nicely maintained and carefully fenced. Small play area. Pétanque. Bicycle hire. Games room with video games. WiFi (free). Off site: Leisure complex with indoor pool opposite. Fishing 500 m. Village 1 km. for all facilities.

**Open:** 1 April - 31 October.

**Directions**

Exit N137 at Derval (signed Châteaubriant) but take D775 for Redon. Guémené-Penfao is 13 km. Watch for site signs before village centre. Site is on the outskirts in a semi-residential area to the northeast.
GPS: 47.62595, -1.8181

**Charges guide**

| | |
|---|---|
| Per unit incl. 2 persons and electricity | € 16.00 - € 21.50 |
| extra person | € 3.50 - € 5.00 |

## Guérande

### Le Domaine de Léveno

506

Route de Sandun, F-44350 Guérande (Loire-Atlantique) T: 02 40 24 79 30. E: domaine.leveno@wanadoo.fr
**alanrogers.com/FR44220**

There have been many changes to this extensive site over the past years and considerable investment has been made to provide some excellent new facilities. The number of mobile homes and chalets has increased considerably, leaving just 83 of the 600 pitches for touring. However, these are in a new area with generous pitches and a new sanitary block. Pitches are divided by hedges and trees which offer a good deal of shade and all have 6A electricity. Access is tricky to some and the site is not recommended for larger units. Twin-axle caravans and American-style motorhomes are not accepted.

**Facilities**

Main refurbished toilet block has preset showers, washbasins in cubicles and facilities for disabled visitors. Laundry facilities. Small shop sells basics and takeaway snacks. Restaurant. Bar with TV and games (all April-Sept). Indoor pool. Heated outdoor pool complex (15/5-15/9). Fitness room. Excellent, safe play area. Multisports court and crazy golf. Activities and events (high season). No electric barbecues. WiFi in bar (free). Off site: Hypermarket 1 km. Fishing 2 km. Beach, golf and riding all 5 km.

**Open:** 6 April - 29 September.

**Directions**

Site is less than 3 km. from the centre of Guérande. From D774 and from D99/N171 take D99E Guérande bypass. Turn east following signs for Villejames and Leclerc hypermarket and continue on D247 to site on right. GPS: 47.33352, -2.3906

**Charges 2013**

| | |
|---|---|
| Per unit incl. 2 persons, electricity and water | € 22.00 - € 38.00 |
| extra person | € 3.00 - € 7.00 |

For latest campsite news, availability and prices visit

**alanrogers.com**

## Heric
### Camping la Pindière

La Denais, La Denais, F-44810 Heric (Loire-Atlantique) T: 02 40 57 65 41.
E: contact@camping-la-pindiere.com **alanrogers.com/FR44430**

Camping la Pindière can be found between Nantes and Rennes, close to the Nantes-Brest canal. The site is open all year and may appeal as an en-route stop, although there is much to see in the area. Pitches here are of a good size and generally well shaded (48 for touring). Most have electrical connections. A number of mobile homes and roulottes are available for rent. The adjacent Auberge des Pyrénées is a pleasant restaurant, open throughout the year. Cycling is popular in the area, with a number of excellent cycle tracks, including routes alongside the canal. The great city of Nantes, the largest in Brittany, is within easy reach.

**Facilities**

New, heated toilet block. Facilities for disabled visitors. Laundry facilities. Motorcaravan service point. Restaurant and takeaway. Children's pool (July/Aug). Play area. Volleyball. Mobile homes for rent. WiFi (part site, free). Off site: Shops, bars and restaurants in Heric. Cycle trails along the banks of the Nantes-Brest canal. Nantes. Riding 1 km. Fishing 5 km. Golf 25 km.

**Open:** All year.

**Directions**

Heric is north of Nantes. If approaching from the north, use the N137 Rennes-Nantes road and leave at Fay-de-Bretagne exit. The site is well signed from here. GPS: 47.41329, -1.6705

**Charges guide**

| | |
|---|---|
| Per unit incl. 2 persons and electricity | € 17.60 - € 20.10 |
| extra person | € 3.80 - € 4.30 |

No credit cards.

---

## La Baule
### Camping les Ajoncs d'Or

Chemin du Rocher, F-44500 La Baule (Loire-Atlantique) T: 02 40 60 33 29. E: contact@ajoncs.com
**alanrogers.com/FR44170**

This site is situated in pinewoods, 1.5 km. inland of La Baule and its beautiful bay. A well maintained, natural woodland setting provides a wide variety of pitch types (just over 200), some level and bordered with hedges and tall trees to provide shade and many others that maintain the natural characteristics of the woodland. Most pitches have electricity and water nearby and are usually of a larger size. A central building provides a shop and an open friendly bar that serves snacks and takeaways. The new, English-speaking owner has extensive plans for this campsite. Large areas of woodland have been retained for quiet and recreational purposes and are safe for children to roam. It can be difficult to find an informal campsite close to an exciting seaside resort that retains its touring and camping identity, but les Ajoncs d'Or does this. Enjoy the gentle breezes off the sea that constantly rustle the trees. The family are justifiably proud of their site.

**Facilities**

Two good quality sanitary blocks are clean and well maintained providing plenty of facilities including a baby room. Washing machines and dryers. Shop and bar (July/Aug). Snack bar (July/Aug). Good sized swimming pool and paddling pool (1/6-15/9). Sports and playground areas. Bicycle hire. Reception with security barrier (closed 22.30-07.30). Off site: Everything for an enjoyable holiday can be found in nearby La Baule. Beach, fishing and riding 1.5 km. Golf 3 km.

**Open:** 1 March - 30 November.

**Directions**

From N171 take exit for La Baule-les-Pins. Follow signs for La Baule Centre, then left at roundabout in front of Carrefour supermarket and follow site signs. GPS: 47.28950, -2.37367

**Charges guide**

| | |
|---|---|
| Per unit incl. 2 persons and electricity | € 18.00 - € 30.00 |
| extra person | € 4.00 - € 9.00 |
| child (2-7 yrs) | € 3.50 - € 8.00 |
| dog | € 2.00 |

CAMPING ☆ ☆ ☆
Les Ajoncs d'Or

• 800m from store
• 1km from center of LA BAULE
• 2km from the sea
• Les Ajoncs d'Or a naturel parc of 6ha

www.ajoncs.com - contact@ajoncs.com

Tel: (+33)2 40 60 33 29

Chemin du Rocher - 44 500 - La Baule

**FREE** Alan Rogers Travel Card
Extra benefits and savings - see page 10

## La Baule
### Airotel la Roseraie

20 avenue Jean Sohier, route du Golf, F-44500 La Baule (Loire-Atlantique) T: 02 40 60 46 66.
E: camping@laroseraie.com **alanrogers.com/FR44280**

This is a lively site with plenty of potential and some good features. There is a warm welcome from the Burban family and their reception staff in very pleasant and smart surroundings. An excellent pool complex by the entrance is open all season and includes a heated pool with a roof that is opened when the sun shines, a separate flume and a paddling pool. There are 230 level pitches of which 100 are for touring, all with electricity (6/10A) and 50 with water and drainage. In places we felt a little more care could have been taken with maintenance. There is a lively programme of activities for children and families in high season. The site is just 2 km. from the sophisticated seaside resort of La Baule and within easy reach of other attractive beaches, the historic town of Guérande with its salt marshes and the Natural Reserve of La Brière which can be explored by horse and cart or by boat. The one disadvantage is that a very busy dual carriageway passes alongside and some of the pitches actually back onto it.

### Facilities

Two traditional sanitary blocks have controllable showers, some washbasins in cubicles, facilities for disabled visitors, washing machines and dryers. A modern extension to one block has en-suite showers and washbasins and an attractively decorated children's section. Small shop. Bar with snacks and restaurant facility and separate takeaway (all July/Aug). Play area. Games/TV and fitness rooms. Multisports court. Boules. Off site: Riding 1 km. Beach, fishing and golf 2 km. Boat launching 6 km. Fishing 10 km.

**Open:** 1 April - 30 September.

### Directions

Site is beside the N171/D99 Nantes and St Nazaire-Guérande road (Route Bleue). Leave at exit for La Baule, Les Pins and Escoublac and go towards La Baule (still N171). At church in Escoublac turn right and site is 500 m. on right, just after bridge over Route Bleue. GPS: 47.29884, -2.3566

### Charges guide

| | |
|---|---|
| Per person | € 4.50 - € 7.50 |
| child (1-5 yrs) | € 2.50 - € 4.50 |
| pitch | € 8.00 - € 13.00 |
| electricity (6A) | € 5.00 |

Camping Cheques accepted.

## La Bernerie-en-Retz
### Camping les Ecureuils
24 avenue Gilbert Burlot, F-44760 La Bernerie-en-Retz (Loire-Atlantique) T: 02 40 82 76 95.
E: camping.les-ecureuils@wanadoo.fr **alanrogers.com/FR44050**

Just 350 metres from both the sea and the centre of the little town of La Bernerie, les Ecureuils is a family run site. The sandy beach here is great for children; swimming is restricted to high tide, since the sea goes out a long way, although at low tide a shallow lagoon remains which is perfect for young children. The site has 163 touring pitches, all with 10A electricity close by and 19 with their own water tap and drain. There are also 86 mobile homes and chalets for rent and a further 62 privately owned. The site prides itself on its pool complex with heated leisure, swimming and paddling pools.

| Facilities | Directions |
|---|---|
| Two toilet blocks have been renovated to a good standard with controllable showers and washbasins in cubicles. Facilities for disabled visitors are not all easily accessible. Baby room. Bar with terrace, also selling bread (1/7-31/8). Snack bar and takeaway (July/Aug). Swimming pools (15/5-15/9). Playground. Only gas barbecues are permitted. WiFi in bar area. Off site: Shops, restaurants and bars 350 m. Also beach, fishing, sailing and boat launching. Golf, riding and bicycle hire 6 km. | La Bernerie-en-Retz is 5 km. south of Pornic and 26 km. south of the Saint Nazaire bridge. From the D213/D13 (St Nazaire-Noirmoutier) turn west on D66 to La Bernerie. Site is signed to right by railway station before reaching town. GPS: 47.0845, -2.036667 |

**Open:** 1 May - 16 September.

**Charges guide**

| Per unit incl. 2 persons | |
|---|---|
| and electricity | € 21.00 - € 36.00 |
| extra person | € 4.00 - € 7.00 |

## La Plaine-sur-Mer
### Camping la Tabardière
2 route de la tabardière, F-44770 La Plaine-sur-Mer (Loire-Atlantique) T: 02 40 21 58 83.
E: info@camping-la-tabardiere.com **alanrogers.com/FR44150**

Owned and managed by the Barré family, this campsite is pleasant, peaceful and immaculate. It will suit those who want to enjoy the local coast and towns but return to an oasis of relaxation. However, it still provides activities and fun for those with energy remaining. The pitches are mostly terraced and care needs to be taken in manoeuvring caravans into position – although the effort is well worth it. The pitches have access to electricity and water taps are conveniently situated nearby. The site is probably not suitable for people using wheelchairs. Whilst this is a rural site, its amenities are excellent with covered swimming pool, paddling pool and water slides, volleyball, tennis, boules and a very challenging 18-hole minigolf to keep you occupied, plus a friendly bar. The beautiful beaches are 3 km. away, with the fishing harbour town, Pornic, some 5 km, ideal for cafés, restaurants and evening strolls.

| Facilities | Directions |
|---|---|
| Two good, clean toilet blocks are well equipped and include laundry facilities. Motorcaravan service point. Shop, bar, snacks and takeaway (high season). Good sized covered swimming pool, paddling pool and slides (supervised). Playground. Minigolf. Volleyball. Basketball. Half size tennis courts. Boules. Fitness programme. Bicycle hire (July/Aug). Overnight area for motorcaravans (€ 14 per night). Off site: Beach and sea fishing 3 km. Golf, riding and bicycle hire all 5 km. | Site is well signed, situated inland off the D13 Pornic - La Plaine-sur-Mer road. GPS: 47.140767, -2.15052 |

**Open:** 16 April - 25 September.

**Charges guide**

| Per unit incl. 2 persons | |
|---|---|
| and electricity (3/10A) | € 19.00 - € 34.60 |
| extra person | € 3.00 - € 6.90 |
| child (2-9 yrs) | € 3.00 - € 4.75 |
| dog | € 3.40 |

Camping Cheques accepted.

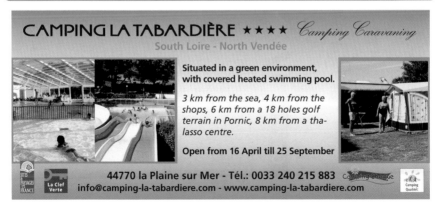

**FREE** Alan Rogers Travel Card
Extra benefits and savings - see page 10

## La Chartre-sur-le-Loir

### Camping du Vieux Moulin

Chemin des Bergivaux, F-72340 La Chartre-sur-le-Loir (Sarthe) T: 02 43 44 41 18. E: camping@lachartre.com

**alanrogers.com/FR72070**

Le Vieux Moulin is a pleasant family site, located on the banks of the Loir, close to the pretty town of La Chartre-sur-le-Loir, to the south east of Le Mans. Pitches here are grassy and of a good size. There are also a number of mobile homes and fully equipped tents available for rent. On-site amenities include a heated swimming pool, a paddling pool and a sports field. Canoeing is popular here and canoes can be rented on site. The site becomes livelier in peak season with a limited entertainment and activity programme, including a children's club and occasional karaoke evenings.

**Facilities**

Traditional sanitary block provides pushbutton showers and some washbasins in cubicles. Facilities for disabled visitors. Washing machine and dryer. Motorcaravan service point. Small shop selling basics, restaurant and takeaway with licence (weekends and July/Aug). Swimming and paddling pools (1/6-20/9). Fishing. Canoeing. Bicycle hire. Large sports field. Play area. Mobile homes and equipped tents for rent. Internet access and free WiFi. Off site: Village with shops, bars and restaurants 1 km. Lake with swimming 4 km.

**Open:** 1 May - 20 September.

**Directions**

La Chartre-sur-le-Loir is 47 km. southeast of Le Mans. From A28 exit 26, head east to Château du Loir, turn south on D938/D338 (Caen-Tours road) and cross the Loir. Then northeast on D305 to La Chartre-sur-le-Loir. After one-way system follow signs to the site, turning left immediately after crossing river. GPS: 47.7324, 0.57095

**Charges guide**

| | |
|---|---|
| Per unit incl. 2 persons and electricity | € 13.10 - € 18.20 |

## La Plaine-sur-Mer

### Camping le Ranch

Les Hautes Raillères, F-44770 La Plaine-sur-Mer (Loire-Atlantique) T: 02 40 21 52 62.
E: info@camping-le-ranch.com **alanrogers.com/FR44240**

This is a pleasant, family run campsite with a friendly atmosphere, close to the beaches of the Jade Coast between Pornic and St Brévin-les-Pins, yet not right on the seashore. The 88 touring pitches all have access to electricity (10A) although on some a long cable may be required; these occupy the central part of the site, with the fringe areas taken up by mobile homes and chalets, 28 for rent and 74 privately owned (although 30 of these are also available for rent in high season). The rows of pitches are separated by well kept hedges, and small trees mark the corners of most plots. In high season there is a very lively atmosphere and at less busy times it is almost certainly a very peaceful site. A pleasant bar and terrace overlook the attractive pool complex with a swimming pool and paddling pool, together with water slides and a flume. Linked to the bar is a large barn with a stage and a dance floor, which at other times is a games room and an indoor volleyball court.

**Facilities**

The central sanitary block has preset showers and washbasins in cubicles. Facilities for disabled visitors. Baby room. Further small toilet block. Motorcaravan service point. Bar has small shop selling bread, basics and camping gaz. Good takeaway (6/7-31/8). Heated swimming pool complex with slides and flume (1/5-15/9). Activities for children and entertainment and sports events for families in high season. Electric barbecues are not permitted. WiFi. Off site: Beach and fishing 800 m.

**Open:** 29 March - 30 September.

**Directions**

La Plaine-sur-Mer is 16 km. south of the St Nazaire bridge. Site is on D96 5 km. northeast of the town. From D213 (Route Bleue) just south of St Michel-Chef-Chef turn southwest on D96 towards La Plaine. Site on left in 2 km. GPS: 47.155216, -2.1649

**Charges guide**

| | |
|---|---|
| Per unit incl. 2 persons and electricity | € 17.40 - € 30.90 |
| extra person | € 3.20 - € 5.90 |

For latest campsite news, availability and prices visit
**alanrogers.com**

## La Turballe
### Camping le Parc Sainte Brigitte

Domaine de Bréhet, chemin des Routes, F-44420 La Turballe (Loire-Atlantique) T: 02 40 24 88 91.
E: saintebrigitte@wanadoo.fr **alanrogers.com/FR44040**

Le Parc Sainte Brigitte is a well established site in the attractive grounds of a manor house, three kilometres from the beaches. It is a spacious site with 150 good pitches, 110 with electricity, water and drainage. Some are arranged in a circular, park-like setting near the entrance, others are in wooded areas under tall trees and the remainder are on more open grass in an unmarked area near the pool. This is a quiet place to stay outside the main season, whilst in high season, it can become very busy. One can walk around many of the areas of the estate that are not used for camping; there are farm animals to see and a carp fishing lake will be popular with anglers.

### Facilities

The main toilet block, supplemented by a second block, is of good quality. They include washbasins in cabins and two bathrooms. Laundry facilities and lines provided. Motorcaravan services. Small shop. Pleasant restaurant/bar with takeaway (both 15/5-15/9). Heated swimming pool with retractable roof and paddling pool. Playground. Bicycle hire. Boules. TV room and traditional 'salle de réunion'. Fishing. WiFi (free). Charcoal barbecues are not permitted. Off site: Riding 2 km. Nearest beach 2.5 km. Golf 15 km.

**Open:** 1 April - 1 October.

### Directions

Entrance is off the busy La Turballe-Guérande D99 road, 3 km. east of La Turballe. A one-way system operates – in one lane, out via another. GPS: 47.34253, -2.47168

### Charges guide

| | |
|---|---|
| Per unit incl. 2 persons, water, waste water and electricity | € 30.60 |
| extra person | € 6.60 |
| child (under 7 yrs) | € 5.20 |
| dog | € 1.65 |

No credit cards.

---

## Le Croisic
### Camping la Pierre Longue

B.P. 13, rue Henri Dunant, F-44490 Le Croisic (Loire-Atlantique) T: 02 40 23 13 44.
E: lapierrelongue@orange.fr **alanrogers.com/FR44320**

Le Croisic can be found on a peninsula which stretches over 5 km. into the ocean. The friendly owners have a great sense of humour at this delightful site. There are a total of 56 grass touring pitches of ample size which are well tended and divided by small trees and young shrubs. There is some shade, but not a great deal. A comfortable bar and a restaurant with a comprehensive menu serving speciality seafood dishes open out onto a terrace and a small swimming pool. This site is open for a long season and has a very pleasant ambience.

### Facilities

The main modern toilet block is heated with washbasins both open and in cubicles. Large shower area. Facilities for disabled visitors. Laundry facilities. Shop (June-Sept). Bar, restaurant and takeaway (May-Sept). Outdoor heated swimming pool and paddling pool (May-Sept). WiFi. Off site: Riding, golf, boat launching within 1.5 km. Medieval town of Guérande. Beaches of La Baule. Salt beds of the Salines.

**Open:** 1 March - 30 November.

### Directions

Take D774 from Guérande south to Pouliguen. Follow northwest to Le Croisic. Site is well signed and on left after 1.5 km. GPS: 47.29244, -2.52923

### Charges guide

| | |
|---|---|
| Per unit incl. 2 persons and electricity | € 16.50 - € 25.80 |
| extra person | € 4.80 - € 6.80 |
| child (7-13 yrs) | € 3.20 - € 4.80 |
| dog | free |

**FREE** Alan Rogers Travel Card
Extra benefits and savings - see page 10

## Le Croisic
### Castel Camping de l'Océan

15 route de la Maison Rouge, F-44490 Le Croisic (Loire-Atlantique) T: 02 40 23 07 69.
E: camping-ocean@wanadoo.fr **alanrogers.com/FR44210**

Camping de l'Océan is situated on the Le Croisic peninsula, an attractive part of the Brittany coastline. Out of a total of 400 pitches, some 50 are available for touring units with the remainder being taken by mobile homes either privately owned or for rent. The pitches are level and 80-100 sq.m. in size (they were rather worn when we visited). The leisure facilities, which include a restaurant, bar and pool complex, are of an excellent standard. This site, probably more suitable for families with young teenagers, can be very lively in high season with a wealth of activities and entertainment for all ages. Sports are well catered for and there are tournaments in high season. After an excellent meal in the restaurant you can enjoy a range of entertainment on most evenings in July and August. The site is within walking distance of the Atlantic Ocean and white sandy beaches, just 150 m. away.

### Facilities

Three adequate toilet blocks with facilities for disabled visitors. Washing machines and dryers. Restaurant and bar. Takeaway. Shop. Motorcaravan service point. Swimming pool complex comprising an indoor pool, outdoor pool and paddling pool. A spa/wellness centre is under construction for 2013. Volleyball. Football. Basketball. Tennis. Bicycle hire. Charcoal barbecues are permitted. WiFi over site (charged; free in bar area). Mobile homes and maisonettes for rent. Off site: Riding, fishing and beach 150 m. Golf 400 m. Sailing 2 km. Market (most days). Shops, bars and restaurants in Le Croisic.

**Open:** 5 April - 30 September.

### Directions

From Le Pouliguen, travel west on the N171 to Le Croisic. Site is well signed from here and found in 1.5 km. GPS: 47.29752, -2.53593

### Charges guide

| Per unit incl. 2 persons and electricity | € 25.00 - € 54.00 |
|---|---|
| extra person | € 6.00 - € 9.00 |
| child (2-7 yrs) | € 4.00 - € 7.00 |
| dog | € 5.00 - € 7.00 |

For latest campsite news, availability and prices visit
## alanrogers.com

## Les Rosiers-sur-Loire
### Flower Camping Val de Loire

6 rue Sainte-Baudruehe, F-49350 Les Rosiers-sur-Loire (Maine-et-Loire) T: 02 41 51 94 33.
E: contact@camping-valdeloire.com **alanrogers.com/FR49180**

This small, attractive site is on the outskirts of the village close to the River Loire between Saumur and Angers. There are 84 touring pitches, all with electricity (10A), individual water taps and waste water drainage. A further 28 pitches are used for mobile homes, mostly for hire. Beech hedging provides good privacy. Recent additions include a pleasant little bar with a terrace and an adjacent marquee used for games and entertainment. There are two new heated swimming pools, one covered, the other surrounded by sunbathing terraces and with a large (linked) paddling pool.

| Facilities | Directions |
|---|---|
| The main toilet block is modern and offers all the necessary facilities, including those for babies and disabled campers. Two older blocks and a new Portacabin unit provide additional facilities. Bar with TV serves snacks (fresh bread to order; June-Aug). Covered pool (1/4-30/9). Outdoor pool (1/6-15/9). Children's activities, events and outings. Evening entertainment (high season). Play area. Minigolf. Tennis. Bicycle hire. Free WiFi over site. **Open:** 1 April - 30 September. | Les Rosiers is 17 km. northwest of Saumur. From the A85 motorway at exit 1 take the D144 south to Beaufort-en-Vallée. Continue south on the D59. Site is signed to right on approach to village. GPS: 47.35877, -0.22604 |

**Charges guide**

| Per unit incl. 2 persons and electricity | € 17.00 - € 27.50 |
|---|---|
| extra person | € 4.00 - € 5.50 |

## Luché-Pringé
### Camping la Chabotière

Place des Tilleuls, F-72800 Luché-Pringé (Sarthe) T: 02 43 45 10 00. E: contact@lachabotiere.com
**alanrogers.com/FR72100**

This is a delightful little municipal site on the River Loir, just a few steps from the main square of an interesting village classed as a Petite Cité de Caractère. There are 85 pitches, 65 for touring and all with access to electricity and the remainder used for wooden chalets and canvas bungalows for rent. The main part of the site down by the river is kept vehicle free in July and August, ensuring a safer and quieter environment. A child-proof gate leads out onto the river bank and footpath. There are many opportunities for walking, cycling and sightseeing in the area.

| Facilities | Directions |
|---|---|
| The traditional toilet block is clean and well maintained with pushbutton showers and some washbasins in cubicles. Baby room. Facilities for disabled visitors. Washing machines and dryer. Motorcaravan service point. Quiet room with free Internet access (adults only). Adventure play area. Bicycle hire. Fishing. Evening activities for children. Free WiFi over site. Off site: Espace de Loisirs (July/Aug) at entrance with free access from site: supervised swimming and paddling pools. **Open:** 1 April - 15 October. | Luché-Pringé is 40 km. south of Le Mans. From A11 between Le Mans and Angers, leave at exits 10 or 11 and head eastwards to La Flèche, then north on D323 towards Le Mans. At Clermont-Créans turn east on D13 to Luché-Pringé. In main square (ignore earlier campsite sign) turn sharp right then left, signed 'Minigolf' then site. GPS: 47.70252, 0.07364 |

**Charges guide**

| Per unit incl. 2 persons and electricity | € 11.90 - € 14.50 |
|---|---|

## Marçon
### Camping Lac des Varennes

Saint Lezin, route de Port-Gauthier, F-72340 Marçon (Sarthe) T: 02 43 44 13 72.
E: lacdesvarennes@camp-in-ouest.com **alanrogers.com/FR72080**

This extensive site is located near the massive forest of Bercé in the Vallée du Loir and is on the shore of the lake from which it takes its name. There are 250 pitches here, with 175 for tourers, all grassy and with electrical connections (10A). Many also have lake views. The site has its own sandy beach (with a beach volleyball court) and canoes are available for rent. In high season, various activities are organised including a club for children and riding. Mobile homes are available for rent.

| Facilities | Directions |
|---|---|
| Three clean, traditional sanitary blocks provide pushbutton showers, some washbasins in cubicles and a mixture of British and Turkish style toilets. Washing machines and dryer. Basic facilities for disabled visitors. Motorcaravan service point. Shop, snack bar and takeaway (July/Aug). Simple bar with games and TV. Play area. Motorcaravan services. Organised entertainment (July/Aug). Direct access to lake with fishing and swimming. Off site: Base de Loisirs. Riding 5 km. Walking and cycling in the forest. **Open:** 27 March - 12 November. | Marçon is 50 km. southeast of Le Mans. From the A28 exit 26, head east to Château du Loir, turn south on D938/D338 (Caen-Tours) and cross the Loir. Then head northeast on D305 to Marçon, and turn west in village centre to Base de Loisirs and site on right in 1 km. GPS: 47.7125, 0.4993 |

**Charges guide**

| Per unit incl. 2 persons and electricity | € 15.10 - € 18.60 |
|---|---|

**FREE** Alan Rogers Travel Card
Extra benefits and savings - see page 10

## Mesquer
### Camping le Château du Petit Bois

1820 route de kerlagadec, F-44420 Mesquer (Loire-Atlantique) T: 02 40 42 68 77.
E: info@campingdupetitbois.com  alanrogers.com/FR44270

This pleasant campsite is located in the wooded grounds of a small château. The 125 good sized touring pitches, all with electricity (3/6A) have varying degrees of shade and a few are in the open for those who like a sunny plot. Reception is housed in a wooden chalet and is welcoming and informative. The Marin family and their staff are friendly and helpful and the site is very well run. On site there is an attractive swimming pool complex: a heated main pool and paddling pool, and a separate pool with two good water slides which is only open when the pool is supervised. The sea is just over a kilometre away, as is the village of Mesquer and nearby are the salt marshes which produce the famous Sel de Guérande.

**Facilities**

The main sanitary block has preset showers and open style washbasins together with some cubicles with controllable shower and a washbasin. Laundry facilities. Facilities for disabled visitors. Combined bar, snack bar and takeaway. Small shop selling bread and basics (July/Aug). Pool complex with heated pool, paddling pool and a pool with water slides (only open when supervised). Programme of activities (all July/Aug). WiFi in bar (free). Off site: Fishing, bicycle hire, riding and sailing all nearby. Golf 12 km.

**Open:** 1 April - 15 October.

**Directions**

From N165 Nantes-Vannes road, leave at exit 15 towards La Roche Bernard, turn left to join D774 towards La Baule. 8 km. after Herbignac, turn right on D52 to St Molt and Mesquer. Site is on D52 just west of village. GPS: 47.399016, -2.471316

**Charges guide**

| | |
|---|---|
| Per unit incl. 2 persons and electricity | € 13.00 - € 27.60 |
| extra person | € 4.90 - € 6.40 |
| child (3-7 yrs) | € 3.40 - € 4.40 |

Camping & Rental accommodations

the Celtic spirit in Southern Brittany !

★★★
LE CHÂTEAU
DU PETIT BOIS

1820, route de Kerlagadec
44420 MESQUER - France
tél. : (+33) (0)2 40 42 68 77
fax : (+33) (0)2 40 42 65 58
www.campingdupetitbois.com

## Montsabert
### Yelloh! Village Parc de Montsabert

Montsabert, F-49320 Coutures (Maine-et-Loire) T: 02 41 57 91 63.
E: info@yellohvillage-parcdemontsabert.com  alanrogers.com/FR49060

This extensive site has recently been taken over by a friendly French couple who already have plans for improvements. It has a rural atmosphere in the shadow of Montsabert château, from where visiting peacocks happily roam in the spacious surroundings. The main features are the heated swimming pool (with cover) and the adjoining refurbished, rustic style restaurant. There are 160 pitches with 89 large, well marked touring pitches, divided by hedges and all with water tap, drain and 10A electricity. Picnic tables are provided. The site is used by several small tour operators (12 pitches). This partially wooded site offers the peace of the countryside and a wealth of activities in high season.

**Facilities**

The main toilet block can be heated and has all necessary facilities including a baby room and facilities for disabled visitors. Laundry facilities. A second block serves the pool and another provides more WCs. Shop, bar and takeaway. Restaurant. Heated pool (can be covered) and paddling pool. Sports hall. Minigolf. Tennis. Play area. Archery. Riding. Bicycle hire. Entertainment (high season). Max. 2 dogs. WiFi over part of site (charged). Off site: Canoeing nearby. Fishing 5 km. Riding 7 km. Golf 8 km. Wine tasting.

**Open:** 12 April - 8 September.

**Directions**

Coutures lies on D751, 25 km. southeast of Angers. In village, turn north to site (well signed). GPS: 47.3744, -0.3469

**Charges guide**

| | |
|---|---|
| Per unit incl. 2 persons and electricity | € 17.00 - € 39.00 |
| extra person | € 5.00 - € 7.00 |
| child (3-7 yrs) | free - € 6.00 |
| dog | € 4.00 |

For latest campsite news, availability and prices visit

**alanrogers.com**

# Montsoreau
## Kawan Village l'Isle Verte

Avenue de la Loire, F-49730 Montsoreau (Maine-et-Loire) T: 02 41 51 76 60. E: isleverte@cvtloisirs.fr

**alanrogers.com/FR49090**

This friendly, natural site, with pitches overlooking the Loire, is just 200 m. from the nearest shop, bar and restaurant in Montsoreau, and is an ideal base from which to explore the western Loire area. Most of the 90 shaded, level and good sized tourist pitches are separated by low hedges but grass tends to be rather sparse during dry spells. All have electricity (16A). Excellent English is spoken in the reception and bar/restaurant. Attractions within walking distance include the château, troglodyte caves (used for traditional mushroom production) and restaurant, wine tasting in the cellars nearby, and a Sunday market in the village. Fishermen are particularly well catered for at Isle Verte, with an area to store equipment and live bait (permits are available in Saumur). Cyclists and walkers could also well be in their element here. For the less energetic, there is a bus service into Saumur with its château and other historic buildings, and all its shops, bars and restaurants. Trains or buses are available in Saumur to take you on to other towns along the Vallée de la Loire. Just 5 km. south of Montsoreau is the fascinating 12th-century Abbaye Royale de Fontévraud.

## Facilities

A modern, well maintained building provides all necessary facilities, including those for disabled campers. Baby room. Laundry facilities. Motorcaravan service point. Bar and restaurant (15/5-30/9). Heated swimming and paddling pools (15/4-30/9). Small play area. Table tennis. Bouncy castle. Trampoline. Tennis. Boules. Fishing. Organised family activities. Boat launching. WiFi (charged). Off site: Boat launching and river beach 300 m. Bicycle hire and sailing 1 km. Golf and riding 7 km. Montsoreau Château.

**Open:** 30 March - 12 October.

## Directions

Montsoreau lies on the south bank of the River Loire, on D947 Saumur-Chinon road, 12 km. from Saumur. Site is clearly signed on western side of village. GPS: 47.21820, 0.05265

## Charges 2013

| Per unit incl. 2 persons | |
|---|---|
| and electricity | € 19.50 - € 26.50 |
| extra person | € 4.00 - € 6.00 |
| child (5-10 yrs) | € 3.00 - € 4.00 |
| dog | € 2.00 |

Camping Cheques accepted.

Camping l'Isle Verte — Montsoreau — kawan — •Paris •Montsoreau — *Classé parmis les plus beaux villages de France*

**FREE** Alan Rogers Travel Card
Extra benefits and savings - see page 10

## Piriac-sur-Mer
### Camping Parc du Guibel

Route de Kerdrien, F-44420 Piriac-sur-Mer (Loire-Atlantique) T: 02 40 23 52 67.
E: camping@parcduguibel.com **alanrogers.com/FR44070**

This is a very large site situated in extensive woodland and just back from the coast. A keen birdwatcher once told the owner that he had seen 50 different species of birds. There are 450 pitches of which 300 are for touring, mainly shaded but some in small clearings. One section at the top of the site, across a minor road, is always quiet and peaceful. One hundred and sixty pitches have electricity (10A), of which 60 also have a water tap and drainage. There are also 134 mobile homes and chalets for rent.

**Facilities**

Five sanitary blocks: the newest is smart and well equipped, with controllable showers and washbasins. Two others have been partially refurbished to the same standards. The others are rather old-fashioned, with preset showers and washbasins in cubicles. Facilities for disabled visitors. Baby room. Laundry. Motorcaravan service point. Swimming pool complex (1/4-30/9). Bar, snack bar, takeaway and restaurant (July/Aug only). WiFi. Off site: Riding 400 m. Fishing 1 km. Beach 1.2 km.

**Open:** 1 April - 30 September.

**Directions**

On N165 from Vannes, leave at exit 15 towards La Roche Bernard, turn left to join D774 towards La Baule. 8 km. after Herbignac, turn right on D52 to St Molt and Mesquer towards Piriac. Do not take coast road but turn left on D52. Site signed on right in 3 km. GPS: 47.38616, -2.51029

**Charges guide**

| | |
|---|---|
| Per unit incl. 2 persons and electricity (10A) | € 13.80 - € 22.20 |
| extra person | € 3.10 - € 5.90 |

## Pontchâteau
### Kawan Village du Deffay

506

B.P. 18 Le Deffay, Sainte Reine-de-Bretagne, F-44160 Pontchâteau (Loire-Atlantique) T: 02 40 88 00 57.
E: campingdudeffay@wanadoo.fr **alanrogers.com/FR44090**

A family managed site, Château du Deffay is a refreshing departure from the usual formula in that it is not over organised or supervised and has no tour operator units. The 170 good sized, fairly level pitches have pleasant views and are either on open grass, on shallow terraces divided by hedges, or informally arranged in a central, slightly sloping wooded area. Most have electricity (6/10A). The bar, restaurant and covered pool are located within the old courtyard area of the smaller château that dates from before 1400. A significant attraction is the large, unfenced lake which is well stocked for fishermen and has free pedaloes for children. The landscape is wonderfully natural and the site blends well with the rural environment of the estate, lake and farmland which surround it. Alpine type chalets overlook the lake and fit in well with the larger château (built 1880 and now offering B&B), which stands slightly away from the camping area but provides a wonderful backdrop for an evening stroll. The site is close to the Brière Regional Park, the Guérande Peninsula, and La Baule and is just 20 minutes drive from the beach.

**Facilities**

The main toilet block is well maintained, if a little dated, and is well equipped including washbasins in cabins, provision for disabled visitors, and a baby bathroom. Laundry facilities. Shop. Bar and small restaurant with takeaway (1/5-15/9). Covered and heated swimming pool and paddling pool (all season). Play area. Entertainment in season. Fishing and pedalos on the lake. WiFi (charged). Off site: Golf 7 km. Riding 10 km. Beach 25 km.

**Open:** 1 May - 30 September.

**Directions**

Site is signed from D33 Pontchâteau-Herbignac road near Ste Reine. Also signed from the D773 and N165-E60 (exit 13). GPS: 47.44106, -2.15981

**Charges guide**

| | |
|---|---|
| Per unit incl. 2 persons and electricity | € 19.55 - € 29.69 |
| extra person | € 3.43 - € 5.74 |
| child (2-12 yrs) | € 2.35 - € 4.00 |
| Camping Cheques accepted. | |

For latest campsite news, availability and prices visit
# alanrogers.com

## Pontchâteau
### Camping du Bois de Beaumard

1 rue de l'Ile de Beaumard, F-44160 Pontchâteau (Loire-Atlantique) T: 02 40 88 03 36.
E: camping.boisbeaumard@orange.fr **alanrogers.com/FR44490**

Le Bois de Beaumard is a small site with just 25 pitches, located close to the interesting town of Pontchâteau, and the new owners are an enthusiastic, young couple. This is a very rural site with a variety of well shaded, level and grassy pitches divided by hedges and surrounded by a profusion of different trees and shrubs. A small lake adjoins the site and is well stocked with carp and other fish. There is a small bar here in high season and a children's playing area. Basic provisions can be bought on site, including some regional produce and fresh bread and croissants.

| Facilities | Directions |
|---|---|
| Two toilet blocks (part heated). Facilities for disabled visitors. Washing machine and dryer. Small shop. Bar with TV and new terrace for 2012 (July/Aug). Fishing lake. Play area. Boules. Trampoline. Bicycle hire. Tourist information. Free WiFi in reception area. Mobile homes and caravans for rent. Off site: Canoeing. Grand Brière National Park. **Open:** All year. | Approaching from Nantes, head north on N165. Leave at Pontchâteau and follow signs to the town centre, and then to site. GPS: 47.45162, -2.10356 |

**Charges guide**

| | |
|---|---|
| Per unit incl. 2 persons and electricity | € 15.00 |
| extra person | € 3.50 |
| child (under 10 yrs) | € 2.00 |

## Pornic
### Yelloh! Village La Chênaie

36 rue du Patisseau, F-44210 Pornic (Loire-Atlantique) T: 02 40 82 07 31. E: accueil@campinglachenaie.com
**alanrogers.com/FR44080**

La Chênaie is a pleasant, family run campsite in countryside close to the fishing port of Pornic and less than three kilometres from the nearest beach. There are 94 touring pitches in two areas on gently sloping ground, with the pool and other leisure facilities in the dip between. All the pitches are well tended with electricity available (10A; longer leads may be needed in places) and there is some shade in places from maturing trees and bushes. Some of the 50 mobile homes (35 for rent) are scattered among the touring pitches, others are at the top of the site.

| Facilities | Directions |
|---|---|
| Two good sanitary blocks, one central to each area. Some washbasins in cubicles. Baby room. Facilities for disabled visitors. Large washing machines and dryer. Motorcaravan service point. Heated indoor swimming pool and paddling pool (6/4-16/9). Outdoor pool (1/7-31/8). Bar and shop selling bread and a few basics. Restaurant and snack bar with takeaway. Play area. Some activities for children and adults. Off site: Fishing 300 m. Sailing and boat launching 3 km. Golf 4 km. Riding 5 km. **Open:** 6 April - 16 September. | Pornic is 19 km. south of the St Nazaire bridge. Road to site is at junction of D751 (Nantes-Pornic) with D213 (St Nazaire-Noirmoutier) Route Bleue. From north take exit for D751 Nantes. At roundabout on D751 north of D213 take exit for la Chênaie and follow signs to site. Avoid Pornic town centre. GPS: 47.118483, -2.070817 |

**Charges guide**

| | |
|---|---|
| Per unit incl. 2 persons and electricity | € 19.00 - € 35.00 |
| extra person | € 5.00 - € 8.00 |

## Pornic
### Camping le Patisseau

29 rue du Patisseau, F-44210 Pornic (Loire-Atlantique) T: 02 40 82 10 39. E: contact@lepatisseau.com
**alanrogers.com/FR44100**

Le Patisseau is situated in the countryside just a short drive from the fishing village of Pornic. It is a relaxed site with a large number of mobile homes and chalets, and is popular with young families and teenagers. The 102 touring pitches, all with electrical connections (6A), are divided between the attractive forest area with plenty of shade from mature trees and the more open 'prairie' area. Some are on a slight slope and access to others might be tricky for larger units. A railway runs along the bottom half of the site with trains several times a day, (but none overnight) and the noise is minimal.

| Facilities | Directions |
|---|---|
| The modern heated toilet block is very spacious and well fitted; most washbasins are open style, but the controllable showers are all in large cubicles which have washbasins. Also good facilities for disabled visitors and babies. Laundry rooms. Shop (1/7-30/8). Bar, restaurant and takeaway (all season). Indoor heated pool with sauna, jacuzzi and spa (all season). Small heated outdoor pools and water slides (1/6-30/9). Play area. Multisport court. Bicycle hire. WiFi in bar area. Off site: Beach 2.5 km. **Open:** 3 April - 11 November. | Pornic is 19 km. south of the St Nazaire bridge. From north take exit for D751 Nantes. From south follow D751 Clion-sur-Mer. At roundabout north of D213 take exit for le Patisseau and follow signs to site. Avoid town centre. GPS: 47.118833, -2.072833 |

**Charges guide**

| | |
|---|---|
| Per unit incl. 2 persons and electricity (6A) | € 25.00 - € 41.00 |
| extra person | € 4.00 - € 8.00 |
| child (under 7 yrs) | € 3.00 - € 5.00 |

**FREE** Alan Rogers Travel Card
Extra benefits and savings - see page 10

## Pornic

### Camping de la Boutinardière

Rue de la Plage de la Boutinardière 23, F-44210 Pornic (Loire-Atlantique) T: 02 40 82 05 68.
E: info@laboutinardiere.com **alanrogers.com/FR44180**

This is truly a holiday site to suit all the family, whatever their ages, just 200 m. from the beach. It has 150 individual, good sized pitches, 90-120 sq.m. in size, many bordered by three metre high, well maintained hedges for shade and privacy. All pitches have electricity available (6/10A). It is a family owned site and part of the Airotel group. English is spoken by the helpful, obliging reception staff. There is an excellent site shop and, across the road, a water complex comprising indoor and outdoor pools, a paddling pool and a twin toboggan water slide, in addition to sports and entertainment areas.

**Facilities**

Toilet facilities are in three good blocks, one large and centrally situated and two supporting blocks. Washbasins are in cabins. Laundry facilities. Shop. New complex of bar, restaurant, terraces. Three heated swimming pools, one indoor (April-Sept), a paddling pool and water slides (15/5-22/9). Games room. Sports and activity area. Playground. Minigolf. Fitness equipment and wellness suite. Maisonette accommodation for rent. WiFi throughout. Off site: Sandy cove and fishing 200 m. Riding 2 km. Golf and sailing 4 km. Restaurants, cafés, fishing harbour, boat trips, windsurfing, all within 5 km.

**Open:** 1 April - 30 September.

**Directions**

From north or south on D213, take Nantes D751 exit. At roundabout (with McDonalds) take D13 signed La Bernarie-en-Retz. After 4 km. site is signed to right. Note: do NOT exit from D213 at Pornic Ouest or Centre. GPS: 47.09805, -2.05176

**Charges guide**

| Per unit incl. 2 persons | |
|---|---|
| and electricity | € 23.50 - € 49.30 |
| extra person | € 4.50 - € 8.00 |
| child (under 8 yrs) | € 3.50 - € 6.00 |
| dog | € 4.10 - € 5.60 |

## Pornichet

### Camping Bel Air

150 avenue de Bonne Source, F-44380 Pornichet (Loire-Atlantique) T: 02 40 61 10 78.
E: reception@belairpornichet.com **alanrogers.com/FR44410**

Camping Bel Air is located in a quiet suburb of Pornichet, just 50 metres from a sandy beach. There are 132 touring pitches (with a further 180 pitches used by long stay occupants or mobile homes to rent). The site extends over 12 hectares and the many trees and shrubs ensure some tranquil areas in what is a busy campsite in high season. The pitches are generally of a good size, sandy and well shaded. Some have an attractive sea view, others are located on a lower section of the site, which, although bordered by a road, is quite peaceful. Access to this part of the site is quite steep.

**Facilities**

Three toilet/shower blocks with facilities for disabled campers. Bar. Restaurant/snack bar (open daily Jul/Aug, weekends in low season). Morning bread delivery. Swimming pool. Playground. Sports field. Activity and entertainment programme. Children's club. WiFi in reception. Mobile homes for rent. Off site: Nearest beach 50 m. Fishing. Pornichet centre 500 m. La Baule 2 km.

**Open:** 2 April - 26 September.

**Directions**

Approaching from the east (St Nazaire) on the D213 (towards La Baule), take D392 to Pornichet and then follow signs to Sainte Marguerite and the campsite. GPS: 47.249722, -2.321389

**Charges guide**

| Per unit incl. 2 persons | € 32.00 - € 38.00 |
|---|---|
| child (8-14 yrs) | € 2.00 - € 4.00 |
| electricity (10A) | € 5.00 - € 6.00 |

## Saint Brévin-les-Pins

### Camping le Fief

57 chemin du Fief, F-44250 Saint Brévin-les-Pins (Loire-Atlantique) T: 02 40 27 23 86.
E: camping@lefief.com **alanrogers.com/FR44190**

If you are a family with young children or lively teenagers, this could be the campsite for you. Le Fief is a well established site only 800 m. from sandy beaches on the southern Brittany coast. It has a great aquapark with outdoor and covered swimming pools, paddling pools, slides, river rapids, fountains, jets and more. The site has 125 pitches for touring units. These all have 8A electricity and vary slightly in size. There are also 205 mobile homes and chalets to rent and 43 privately owned units. An impressive Taos mobile home village includes a new Sunny Club for children. This is a lively site in high season. There is a variety of entertainment and organised activity for all ages which ranges from a miniclub for 5-12 year olds, to Tonic Days in a state-of-the-art wellness centre with aquagym, jogging and sports competitions, and to evening events which include karaoke, themed dinners and cabaret. There are plenty of sporting facilities for active youngsters.

### Facilities

One excellent new toilet block and three others of a lower standard. Laundry facilities. Shop (1/6-31/8). Bar, restaurant and takeaway (3/4-26/9) with terrace overlooking the pool complex. Outdoor pools, etc. (1/5-15/9). Covered pool (all season). Wellness centre. Play area. Tennis. Pétanque. Archery. Games room. Internet access. Organised entertainment and activities (weekends April/June, daily July/Aug). Bicycle hire. WiFi over site (charged). Off site: Beach 800 m. Bus stop 1 km. Riding 1 km. Golf 15 km. Planète Sauvage safari park.

**Open:** 3 April - 3 October.

### Directions

From the St Nazaire bridge take the fourth exit from the D213 signed St Brévin-l'Océan. Continue over first roundabout and bear right at the second to join Chemin du Fief. The site is on the right, well signed. GPS: 47.23486, -2.16757

### Charges 2013

| Per unit incl. 2 persons | |
|---|---|
| and electricity | € 23.00 - € 47.00 |
| extra person | € 6.00 - € 11.00 |
| child (0-7 yrs) | € 3.00 - € 6.00 |
| dog | € 3.00 - € 10.00 |

No credit cards.

CAMPING, RENTAL & SPA

GROCERY
BAR - RESTAURANT - TAKE AWAY
CHILDREN'S PLAYGROUND
TENNIS - MULTISPORTS TERRAIN
INDOOR, HEATED SWIMMING POOL
9 ENTERTAINERS IN SEASON

**FULL AND HALF PENSION**

**ADRIANA KAREMBEU SPA**
Aqua relaxation area, jets, waterfalls, pebble walk river, body treatments and facials, sauna, steam room, gym, Sillicium+® treatments, Power Plate® and LPG®

57, chemin du Fief 44250 SAINT BREVIN LES PINS
tel. : 0033 2 40 27 23 86
fax : 0033 2 40 64 46 19 www.lefief.com

SAINT BREVIN LES PINS — CÔTE DE JADE — SUD BRETAGNE — FRANCE

## Préfailles

### Camping EléoVic

Route de la Pointe Saint Gildas, F-44770 Préfailles (Loire-Atlantique) T: 02 40 21 61 60.
E: contact@camping-eleovic.com  **alanrogers.com/FR44230**

This is a well situated site overlooking the sea on the attractive Jade Coast west of Pornic. There are 70 touring pitches which are rather worn, some with wonderful views of the sea, and a similar number of mobile homes, many of which are available for rent. All pitches have access to electricity (10A), though on some you may need a long cable. Much of the ground is sloping, so a really level pitch may not be available and access for larger units to some pitches may be tricky. The site has so much to offer, however, that any extra effort that may be needed to get installed is likely soon to be forgotten. There is an excellent covered, heated pool (with paddling pool) which has a canopy that can be opened up in good weather. A path from the site leads directly to a small rocky cove where you can gather oysters and mussels freely at low tide. Other wider, sandy beaches are a short distance away.

### Facilities

Central sanitary block has spacious preset showers and washbasins in cabins. Facilities for children and disabled visitors. Family room. Room for dishwashing and laundry. Motorcaravan service point. Good restaurant (July/Aug; not Wed) with small bar and terrace. Indoor, heated swimming pool with paddling pool (4/4-27/9). Fitness room. Playground. Boules. Children's activities and entertainment and sporting events for families (high season). Bicycle hire. Direct access to small rocky cove. Free WiFi over part of site. Off site: Beach 800 m.

**Open:** 3 April - 26 October.

### Directions

Préfailles is 9 km. west of Pornic. From Pornic take D13 to La Plaine but do not enter town. Follow signs for Préfailles. Continue on D313 towards La Pointe Saint-Gildas and at 50 km. sign turn left, then left again to site. GPS: 47.132616, -2.2315

### Charges guide

| Per unit incl. 2 persons | |
|---|---|
| and electricity | € 18.40 - € 34.00 |
| extra person | € 3.60 - € 6.60 |
| child (under 7 yrs) | € 2.50 - € 4.50 |
| dog | € 2.50 - € 4.00 |

Route de la Pointe St. Gildas - 44770 Préfailles
Loire Atlantique - Bretagne sud
Tel: 0033 240 21 61 60 - E-mail: contact@camping-eleovic.com
www.camping-eleovic.com

★★★★ camping-caravaning

Eleovic is situated in a green envrionment with direct access to the beach with exceptional view on Ile de Noirmoutier. You will enjoy our fine beaches, shellfish picking, walking. To relax, the campsite offers a magnificent covered heated pool. Various activities are organised during the day for young and old (high season).

## Saumur

### Flower Camping de Ile d'Offard

Boulevard de Verden, Ile d'Offard, F-49400 Saumur (Maine-et-Loire) T: 02 41 40 30 00.
E: iledoffard@cvtloisirs.fr  **alanrogers.com/FR49080**

This site occupies a prime position on an island in the River Loire within walking distance of the centre of the historic town of Saumur. The 207 touring pitches are mainly on grass with plenty of shade provided by mature trees. Twelve hardstandings nearer the entrance can be rather dusty in dry weather. One hundred and fifty pitches have access to electricity (10A) and some also have water and drainage. Ile d'Offard is useful as an overnight stop on the journey south (or north) but it is also an excellent base from which to visit the numerous châteaux in the region.

### Facilities

Three unisex sanitary blocks, one heated in winter, include provision for disabled visitors. Block one has a laundry. These facilities are generally kept reasonably clean, but are fairly basic and lack finesse. Motorcaravan services. Restaurant and bar (1/5-30/9) with takeaway. Heated swimming, paddling and spa pools (15/4-30/9). Internet access and WiFi (charged). Play area. Some activities and a children's club, wine tastings, etc. in high season. Off site: River beach, sailing and bicycle hire all 1 km.

**Open:** 1 March - 15 November.

### Directions

From north and A85 exit 3, take D347 south (Saumur). After 2.5 km. go left at roundabout signed 'Saumur touristique'. Follow old road towards river and town. Cross bridge onto island and immediately go left at roundabout. Site is ahead in 1 km. GPS: 47.25762, -0.06100

### Charges guide

| Per unit incl. 2 persons | |
|---|---|
| and electricity | € 20.00 - € 33.00 |
| extra person | € 5.00 - € 6.00 |

For latest campsite news, availability and prices visit
**alanrogers.com**

## Saumur
### Camping de Chantepie

La Croix, Saint Hilaire-Saint Florent, F-49400 Saumur (Maine-et-Loire) T: 02 41 67 95 34.
E: info@campingchantepie.com **alanrogers.com/FR49020**

On arriving at Camping de Chantepie with its colourful, floral entrance, a friendly greeting awaits at reception, set beside a restored farmhouse. The site is owned by a charitable organisation which provides employment for local people with disabilities. Linked by gravel roads (which can be dusty), the 150 grass touring pitches are level and spacious, with some new larger ones (200 sq.m. at extra cost – state preference when booking). All pitches have electricity (16A) and are separated by low hedges of flowers and trees which offer some shade. This is a good site for families. The panoramic views over the Loire from the pitches on the terraced perimeter of the meadow are stunning and from here a footpath leads to the river valley. Leisure activities for all ages are catered for in July/August by the Chantepie Club, including wine tastings, excursions and canoeing. A Sites et Paysages member.

**Facilities**

The toilet block is clean and facilities are good with washbasins in cubicles, new showers (men and women separately) and facilities for disabled visitors. Baby area. Laundry facilities. Shop, bar, terraced café and takeaway (all 21/6-31/8). Covered and heated pool, outdoor pool and paddling pool. Play area with apparatus. Terraced minigolf, TV. Video games. Pony rides. Bicycle hire. WiFi (charged). Off site: Fishing 500 m. Golf, riding 2 km. Sailing 7 km.

**Open:** 29 April - 14 September.

**Directions**

St Hilaire-St Florent is 2 km. west of Saumur. Take D751 (Gennes). Right at roundabout in St Hilaire-St Florent and on until Le Poitrineau and campsite sign, then turn left. Continue for 3 km. then turn right into site road. GPS: 47.29381, -0.14264

**Charges guide**

| Per unit incl. 2 persons | |
|---|---|
| and electricity | € 20.00 - € 39.00 |
| extra person | € 4.00 - € 6.00 |

Camping Cheques accepted.

**Panoramic view of the *Loire*.**
**Quiet Holidays with family.**

Camping Qualité

Route de Chantepie - Saint Hilaire Saint Florent - 49400 SAUMUR (FR.)
**Tél. +33(0)2 41 67 95 34 - Fax. +33(0)2 41 67 95 85**
**info@campingchantepie.com - www.campingchantepie.com**

## Sillé-le-Philippe
### Castel Camping le Château de Chanteloup

Chanteloup, F-72460 Sillé-le-Philippe (Sarthe) T: 02 43 27 51 07. E: chanteloup.souffront@wanadoo.fr
**alanrogers.com/FR72030**

This attractive and peaceful site, close to Le Mans, is situated in the park of a 19th-century château in the heart of the Sarthe countryside. There are 90 very large pitches all with 8A electricity although long leads may be required in some places. Some pitches adjoin woodland, many are around the edges of the lawns and completely open, and a few overlook a small fishing lake. The pitches are unobtrusively marked out and the resident owners, the Souffront family, who are very keen to welcome you, consider that this lack of regimentation enhances the feeling of spaciousness around the old château.

**Facilities**

All sanitary facilities are in the château outbuildings and are well maintained and kept very clean. Washbasins are in cabins. Baby facilities and good en-suite unit for disabled visitors. Laundry facilities. Small shop, takeaway and restaurant with covered outdoor seating (all 5/7-30/8). Bar. Swimming pool. Play area ( supervision essential). Games room. Volleyball. Activities (high season). Rowing boat and fishing rods free to use on site lake. Bicycle hire. WiFi over site (charged). Off site: Riding 3 km.

**Open:** 1 June - 1 September.

**Directions**

Sillé-le-Philippe is 18 km. northeast of Le Mans on the D301 to Bonnétable. From autoroute take exit 23, follow signs for Le Mans and Tours, then Le Mans and Savigné l'Evèque. Site is to the east just off main road. GPS: 48.10586, 0.34108

**Charges guide**

| Per unit incl. 2 persons | |
|---|---|
| and electricity | € 28.60 - € 35.80 |

Charges are higher during Le Mans race week.

**FREE** Alan Rogers Travel Card
**Extra benefits and savings** - see page 10

## Sillé-le-Guillaume
### Camping Indigo les Molières

Sillé Plage, F-72140 Sillé-le-Guillaume (Sarthe) T: 02 43 20 16 12. E: molieres@camping-indigo.com

**alanrogers.com/FR72040**

Les Molières is an attractive recent addition to the Indigo group. It can be found close to Sillé-le-Guillaume, around 30 km. north of Le Mans. There are 120 large shady pitches here, 83 for tourers. Most are equipped with electrical connections (10A). A large lake of 32 hectares is ideal for sailing and windsurfing, and the forested surrounds of the Parc Naturel Régional provide an excellent environment for cycling or walking. Swimming is also popular from the large sandy beach. The Maison du Lac et de la Forêt is an interesting centre with a wealth of information about the area. In high season, a little tourist train trundles around the lake. Sillé-le-Guillaume is a pleasant town with a fine château dating back to the 15th century. Le Mans, to the south, needs little introduction. Best known for its famous 24 Heures du Mans sports car race, the city has a great deal more to offer. The old town (Cité Plantagenet) is well worth exploration with its half timbered houses and cathedral of St Julien.

| Facilities | Directions |
|---|---|
| Direct access to lake. Sailing. Fishing. Bicycle hire. Play area. Tourist information. Max. 1 dog. Only electric barbecues are permitted. Shop (all season). Bar and restaurant/takeaway (1/7-31/8). Heated outdoor pool (all season). WiFi (free). Off site: Walking and cycling tracks. Le Mans 30 km. | From Le Mans head north on D338 and then D304 to Sillé-le-Guillaume. Then follow signs to the Parc Naturel Régional and the site. GPS: 48.204216, -0.128577 |

**Open:** 25 April - 23 September.

**Charges 2013**

| Per unit incl. 2 persons and electricity | € 19.00 - € 28.50 |
|---|---|
| extra person | € 3.40 - € 5.10 |
| child (under 7 yrs) | free - € 3.50 |

## Varennes-sur-Loire
### Castel Camping Domaine de la Brèche

L'Etang de la Brèche, 5 impasse de la Brèche (RN152), F-49730 Varennes-sur-Loire (Maine-et-Loire)
T: 02 41 51 22 92. E: contact@domainedelabreche.com **alanrogers.com/FR49010**

The Saint Cast family have developed Domaine de la Brèche with care and attention. The attractive site occupies a 24-hectare estate on the edge of the Loire behind the dykes. There are 235 spacious, level, grass pitches, with 135 for touring. Trees and bushes give some shade. All have electricity (some require long cables). Eighty have a water supply and drainage. The restaurant, bar and terrace, also open to the public, provide a social base and are popular with British visitors. The pool complex includes one with a removable cover, one outdoor, and one for toddlers.

| Facilities | Directions |
|---|---|
| Three modern toilet blocks include facilities for babies and disabled campers. Laundry facilities. Shop and épicerie. Restaurant, pizzeria and takeaway. Outdoor swimming pool (22/5-27/8) and heated indoor swimming pool (28/4-3/9). Tennis. Multisports pitch. Go-karts. Minigolf. Bicycle hire. Games and TV rooms. Varied sporting and entertainment programme (10/7-25/8). Pony riding. Torch useful. WiFi over site (charged; free in reception area). Off site: Boat launching 5 km. Golf 7 km. | Site is well signed on the north bank of the River Loire, 100 m. north of the main D952, Saumur-Tours road, 5 km. northeast of Saumur. GPS: 47.24731, -0.00048 |

**Open:** 27 April - 15 September.

**Charges 2013**

| Per unit incl. 2 persons and electricity | € 17.50 - € 38.00 |
|---|---|
| with water and drainage | € 19.00 - € 40.50 |
| extra person | € 6.50 - € 8.50 |

For latest campsite news, availability and prices visit
**alanrogers.com**

It's not only the fine beaches that make this holiday region so appealing – sleepy fishing harbours, historic ports and charming towns all create a great holiday atmosphere.

**DÉPARTEMENT: VENDÉE**

**MAJOR CITY: LA ROCHE-SUR-YON**

Because of its importance as a holiday destination for British visitors to France we have decided in this guide to list the Vendée département as a region in its own right. Administratively the department lies in the region of Pays de la Loire.

With a sunshine record to rival the south of France, the Vendée is among the most popular areas in France. Visitors flock to the region to enjoy the exceptionally mild climate and 160 km. stretch of gently shelving, mostly sandy beaches. Popular resorts in the Vendée include Les Sables-d'Olonne, La Tranche-sur-Mer, and St Jean-de-Monts. Explore the coasts for traditional fishing villages or head inland for fields of sunflowers and unspoilt rural villages.

The Vendée was the centre of the counter-revolutionary movement between 1793 and 1799 and a 'son et lumière' held at Le Puy-du-Fou tells the whole story. Les Sables-d'Olonne is its main resort renowned for its excellent sandy beach. The area between the Vendée and Charente, the Marais Poitevin, is one of the most unusual in France – a vast tract of marshland with a thousand or more tree-lined canals and slow moving streams.

**Places of interest**

*L'Aiguillon-sur-Mer:* famous for its mussels and other shellfish; site of migrating birds between August and November.

*Apremont:* pretty village with a Renaissance castle; Vendée's largest lake with a sandy beach, watersports and boat hire.

*Île-d''Yeu:* one hour by boat from the coast, a major tourist destination with colourful shops, cafés and restaurants. Art galleries and exhibitions. Bicycles and cars for hire.

*Jard-sur-Mer:* Abbey of Lieu-Dieu (financed by Richard the Lionheart), seaside with attractive, colourful houses.

*Le Puy-du-Fou:* 15/16th-century castle, son et lumière production and historical theme park.

*Les Sables-d'Olonne:* the start and finish line of the grand Vendée Globe yacht race; arts and crafts shops.

**Cuisine of the region**

Locally produced meat and poultry include Charolais beef, salt-marsh lamb, duck from Challans and foie gras. Seafood includes sole sablaise, cooked with lemon, barbecued sardines from Saint Gilles Croix-de-Vie, baked white tuna and mussels from the Baie de l'Aiguillon cooked in white wine.

*Samphire:* a herb that grows on the edges of the salt marshes.

*Mogette:* slow-cooked baby haricot beans, traditionally served with gammon.

*Jambon de Vendee:* local raw-cured ham.

www.vendee-tourisme.com/en
info@vendee-tourisme.com
(0)2 51 47 88 20

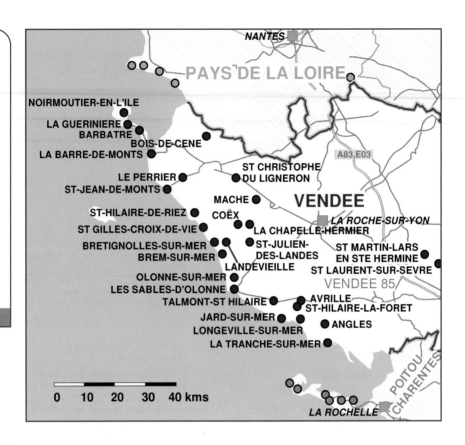

NANTES

PAYS DE LA LOIRE

NOIRMOUTIER-EN-L'ILE

LA GUERINIERE
BARBATRE
BOIS-DE-CENE
LA BARRE-DE-MONTS

A83,E03

ST CHRISTOPHE
LE PERRIER
DU LIGNERON
ST-JEAN-DE-MONTS

MACHE

VENDEE

ST-HILAIRE-DE-RIEZ
COËX
ST GILLES-CROIX-DE-VIE
LA CHAPELLE-HERMIER
LA ROCHE-SUR-YON

BRETIGNOLLES-SUR-MER
ST-JULIEN-
ST MARTIN-LARS
BREM-SUR-MER
DES-LANDES
EN STE HERMINE
LANDEVIEILLE
ST LAURENT-SUR-SEVRE

OLONNE-SUR-MER
LES SABLES-D'OLONNE
VENDEE 85

TALMONT-ST HILAIRE
AVRILLE
ST-HILAIRE-LA-FORET

JARD-SUR-MER
LONGEVILLE-SUR-MER
ANGLES

LA TRANCHE-SUR-MER

0   10   20   30   40 kms

POITOU CHARENTES

LA ROCHELLE

---

## Angles
### Camping le Clos Cottet

Route de la Tranche-sur-Mer, F-85750 Angles (Vendée) T: 02 51 28 90 72.
E: contact@camping-clos-cottet.com  **alanrogers.com/FR85950**

Le Clos Cottet is an attractive family site, based around an old Vendéen farm. This is a lively site in high season with activities for children and the whole family, including regular discos and karaoke evenings, as well as many sports tournaments. There are 196 pitches here, all of which have reasonable shade. Many of them are occupied by mobile homes and chalets, but 70 are available for touring, all with electricity (10A). In high season (July and August) a free shuttle bus service runs to the nearest beach (6 km). On site, a fine swimming pool complex provides a large outdoor pool with water slides and a heated indoor pool, plus a sauna and Turkish bath.

### Facilities

Two traditional toilet blocks provide pre-set showers and washbasins in cubicles. Baby room. En suite unit for disabled visitors. Hot water to washing machine and dryer. Motorcaravan service point. Shop, plus bar with snack bar and takeaway (July/Aug). Pool complex (all season). Sauna. Fitness room. Play area. Multisports court. Sports field. Minigolf. Fishing lake. Activity and entertainment programme (July/Aug plus holiday weekends). Free WiFi in bar area. Mobile homes and chalets for rent. Off site: Cycle and walking tracks. Angles village centre 1.5 km. Riding 5 km. Nearest beach, sailing 6 km. Golf 30 km. Les Sables d'Olonne 37 km. Marais Poitevin 70 km. Puy du Fou 75 km.

**Open:** 5 April - 20 September.

### Directions

Angles is 34 km south of La Roche-sur-Yon. From A87 Cholet/La Roche-sur-Yon leave at exit 32 for La Tranche-sur-Mer and follow D747 towards La Tranche. Site is south of Angles and is well signed to the right. GPS: 46.39239, -1.40365

### Charges guide

| Per unit incl. 2 persons | |
|---|---|
| and electricity | € 18.00 - € 29.00 |
| extra person | € 4.00 - € 6.00 |
| child (under 4 yrs) | € 2.50 - € 4.00 |
| dog | € 3.00 |

For latest campsite news, availability and prices visit
**alanrogers.com**

## Avrillé
### Camping Domaine des Forges

Rue des Forges, F-85440 Avrillé (Vendée) T: 02 51 22 38 85. E: contact@campingdomainedesforges.com
**alanrogers.com/FR85930**

Le Domaine des Forges was acquired by Cathy and Thierry Pacteau a few years ago, and since then they have undertaken a vast improvement programme with huge investments made to improve the site's infrastructure. Arranged in the beautiful grounds of a 16th-century manor house, the 295 touring pitches are very generous in size (170-300 sq.m) and fully serviced, including 32A electricity, Internet access and cable TV. The owners' aim is to develop a prestige campsite with the highest quality of services and they have made a very good start.

**Facilities**

Four brand new toilet blocks including facilities for disabled visitors and babies. Laundry facilities. Shop (1/7-31/8). Restaurant (15/6-31/8). Bar and takeaway (15/6-early Sept). Outdoor pool (15/5-15/9). Indoor pool (March-Nov). Tennis. Minigolf. Fishing lake. Multisports area. Boules. Fitness room. Internet access (charged). One dog per pitch. Off site: Village 400 m. Vendée beaches 7 km. Golf Port Bourgenay (with discount) 10 km.

**Open:** 11 February - 15 November.

**Directions**

Travel south from La Roche-sur-Yon on the D747 for 21 km. At the D19, turn right for Avrillé (about 6 km). At junction with the D949 turn right and first right again into rue des Forges. Site at the end of the road. GPS: 46.47609, -1.49454

**Charges guide**

| | |
|---|---|
| Per unit incl. 2 persons, electricity, water and waste water | € 16.50 - € 32.50 |
| extra person | € 2.00 - € 6.00 |

---

## Barbâtre
### Camping du Midi

Rue du camping, F-85630 Barbâtre (Vendée) T: 02 51 39 63 74. E: contact@campingdumidi.com
**alanrogers.com/FR85014**

This family site is a member of the Original Camping group and is located close to the village of Barbâtre, on the west coast of the island of Noirmoutier. The site has direct access to a fine sandy beach. There are 539 pitches, of which around 335 are available for touring units (the remainder are occupied by an imaginative range of chalets, mobile homes and fully equipped tents, including teepees, many of which are for rent). Touring pitches are mostly equipped with 6/10A electricity. On-site amenities include two swimming pools and a paddling pool, surrounded by a wide sunbathing area.

**Facilities**

Shop (July/Aug). Swimming pool complex (1/6-15/9). Sailing school. Games room. Play area. Activity and entertainment programme. Mobile homes, tents and chalets for rent. Direct beach access. Off site: Shops and restaurants in Barbâtre 5 minutes walk. Tennis. Riding. Watersports. Fishing. Riding 10 km. Golf 15 km.

**Open:** 1 April - 30 September.

**Directions**

Noirmoutier can be accessed either by the Gois causeway (at low tide only) or by the bridge from Fromentine, to the south of the island. From the bridge head north to Barbâtre on D944 and the site is well signed. GPS: 46.94508, -2.1853

**Charges guide**

| | |
|---|---|
| Per unit incl. 2 persons and electricity | € 17.00 - € 32.90 |
| extra person | € 3.90 - € 6.90 |

---

## Bois-de-Céné
### Camping le Bois Joli

2 rue de Châteauneuf, F-85710 Bois-de-Céné (Vendée) T: 02 51 68 20 05.
E: contact@camping-leboisjoli.com  **alanrogers.com/FR85510**

A warm welcome is given by the English-speaking owners, Martine and Eric Malard, who make every effort to ensure that your stay is enjoyable. On site is a small, attractive lake with fishing and a large sports field. Next to the small swimming pool and paddling pool are a pleasant bar with terrace and a dancing area. There are 152 pitches of which 91 are for touring units, all with electricity; water taps may be less close. The site has 24 mobile homes for rent, including one equipped for disabled visitors, and there are 37 which are privately owned.

**Facilities**

Three unisex toilet blocks offer washbasins in cubicles, some controllable showers, two family shower cubicles, washing machines and a dryer. Facilities for disabled visitors. Motorcaravan services. Bar serving simple meals, with evening entertainment and takeaway (July/Aug and busy weekends). Play area. Tennis. Volleyball. Pétanque. Bicycle hire. WiFi (charged) over most of site. Activities and entertainment (July/Aug). Off site: Small supermarket.

**Open:** 1 April - 15 October.

**Directions**

Bois-de-Céné is 47 km. southwest of Nantes and 10 km. north of Challans, at junction of D21 Bouin-La Garnache and D28 Châteauneuf-Machecoul. Site is south of village where D58 from Challans meets D21 and D28 (signed). GPS: 46.93382, -1.88791

**Charges guide**

| | |
|---|---|
| Per unit incl. 2 persons and electricity | € 15.80 - € 20.80 |
| Camping Cheques accepted. | |

**FREE** Alan Rogers Travel Card
Extra benefits and savings - see page 10

## Brem-sur-Mer

### Camping Caravaning le Chaponnet

Rue du Chaponnet (N16), F-85470 Brem-sur-Mer (Vendée) T: 02 51 90 55 56.

E: campingchaponnet@wanadoo.fr **alanrogers.com/FR85480**

This well established, family run site is within five minutes' walk of Brem village and 1.5 km. from a sandy beach. The 81 touring pitches are level with varying amounts of grass, some with shade from mature trees. Pitches are separated by tall hedges and serviced by tarmac or gravel roads and have frequent water and electricity points (long leads may be required). Tour operators have mobile homes and tents on 100 pitches and there are 146 other mobile homes and chalets, over half available for rent. The swimming pool complex features heated indoor and outdoor pools with a jacuzzi, slides and a children's pool, together with a sauna and fitness centre. It is overlooked by the spacious bar and restaurant/snack bar. Entertainment and activities for all ages are organised in high season with a children's club and daytime family activities (Sun-Fri) and entertainment every evening. Brem has shops and restaurants, two supermarkets and a weekly market; neighbouring Brétignolles has two thriving markets each week.

#### Facilities

The five sanitary blocks are well maintained with washbasins in cubicles, and some showers and basins with controllable water temperature. Facilities for babies and disabled visitors. Laundry facilities. Bar, restaurant, snack bar and pizzeria (early June-late Aug). Indoor and outdoor heated pools. Waterslide, jacuzzi and sauna. Play area with space for ball games. Tennis. Bicycle hire. Indoor games room. WiFi in bar/pool area (charged). Children's club (4-14 yrs) and family activities and entertainment (July/Aug). Free bus to beach and back (July/Aug). Off site: Shops and bus stops 200 m.

**Open:** 2 April - 30 September.

#### Directions

Brem is 35 km. west of La Roche-sur-Yon, on the D38. From A87 at La Roche continue on the D160 towards Les Sables d'Olonne. Take exit for La Mothe-Achard and Brétignolles-sur-Mer. Follow D54 to Brem-sur-Mer. Site is signed just off one-way system in village. GPS: 46.60433, -1.83244

#### Charges guide

| | |
|---|---|
| Per unit incl. 2 persons and electricity | € 21.60 - € 30.80 |
| extra person | € 4.90 - € 6.90 |

## Brem-sur-Mer

### Camping l'Océan

Rue des Gabelous, F-85470 Brem-sur-Mer (Vendée) T: 02 51 90 59 16. E: contact@campingdelocean.fr

**alanrogers.com/FR85110**

Set amongst grapevines and fir trees, Camping l'Océan is only 600 metres from a beautiful sandy beach while the village centre is also within walking distance. A warm welcome awaits you at the modern reception area which is well stocked with local information. The 90 touring pitches, all with electricity connections reasonably close, are of a good size, separated by bushes (and in some cases vines) and with some mature trees providing shade. They are centrally located close to the entrance and you are largely unaware of the 260 mobile homes (120 available to rent) on either side.

#### Facilities

Two toilet blocks include preset showers and washbasins in cubicles. Separate toilet and shower for disabled visitors. Laundry facilities. Shop (July/Aug). Bar, snack bar and takeaway service (July/Aug and busy weekends). Heated swimming pool (15/6-15/9) with slide. Heated indoor pool. Fitness room. Bicycle hire. Two playgrounds. WiFi over site (charged). Off site: Beach 600 m.

**Open:** 1 April - 31 October.

#### Directions

From A87 at La Roche continue on D160 towards Les Sables-d'Olonne. Take exit for La Mothe-Achard and Brétignolles-sur-Mer. Follow D54 to Brem-sur-Mer. Site is to north of village on D38 to Brétignolles and is signed to west. GPS: 46.601654, -1.84404

#### Charges guide

| | |
|---|---|
| Per unit incl. 2 persons and electricity | € 17.00 - € 27.00 |

## Brétignolles-sur-Mer
### Chadotel Camping la Trévillière

1 rue de Bellevue, F-85470 Brétignolles-sur-Mer (Vendée) T: 02 51 90 09 65. E: info@chadotel.com
**alanrogers.com/FR85310**

In a pleasant rural setting, la Trévillière is on the edge of the little resort town of Brétignolles. There are 200 pitches, 110 for tourers, all with access to water and electricity (long leads required in places). Some are level, some sloping; all are separated by hedges or low bushes either with shade or more open. Although just 2 km. from the nearest beach and less than 5 km. from the Plage des Dunes (one of the southern Vendée's best beaches), la Trévillière has a more laid back feel than many other sites in the area, particularly in low season.

**Facilities**

Three traditional toilet blocks, a little tired in parts, include washbasins in cubicles, pushbutton showers, a unit for disabled visitors and a baby room with bath, shower and toilet. Warm water for washing machines and dryers. Bar, small shop and snack bar with takeaway (10/6-15/9). Heated pool with slide and paddling pool. Play area. Minigolf. Max. 1 dog. Off site: Shops, restaurants and bars 1 km. Beach 2 km. Fishing, sailing and riding 3 km.

**Open:** April - September.

**Directions**

Brétignolles is 40 km. west of La Roche-sur-Yon on D38 coast road. From north, after St Gilles go through Brétignolles-La Sauzaie (left fork) and before Brétignolles turn left on sharp right hand bend, heading for water tower. Site on right in 800 m. GPS: 46.63632, -1.85844

**Charges guide**

| | |
|---|---|
| Per unit incl. 2 persons and electricity | € 15.50 - € 30.50 |

## Coëx
### RCN Camping la Ferme du Latois

Le Latoi, F-85220 Coëx (Vendée) T: 02 51 54 67 30. E: ferme@rcn.fr
**alanrogers.com/FR85770**

Originally a simple 'camping à la ferme', this site has been developed by a Dutch organisation into an extensive, very well equipped and well maintained campsite. Located round two attractive fishing lakes, the 215 pitches, most available for touring, are spacious and attractively laid out with plenty of grass, hedges and trees, some young, some mature. All have electricity and a few are very large. There are 30 mobile homes for rent. An old barn has been converted into a large restaurant offering an extensive French menu, including a 'menu du jour'. Also here are a small bar, a shop selling basic provisions and the reception area. Nearby is a smaller, open-ended barn that has been fitted out for activities and has a large television to screen key events and football matches. There is a good heated pool with a paddling pool, water slides and a long flume. This stretch of coast offers a good choice of other sandy beaches and there are plenty of well documented places to go and things to do in the area.

**Facilities**

Two large, modern sanitary blocks have excellent toilets, showers and washbasins in cubicles. Good facilities for disabled visitors. Attractively tiled areas for babies and children, with special toilets, basins and showers. Two smaller blocks provide additional facilities. Laundry room. Small shop. Bar counter with terrace. Restaurant. Heated outdoor swimming pool with slides. Play area. Bicycle hire. Fishing lakes. WiFi over site (charged). Internet point. Max. 1 dog. Accommodation for rent. Off site: Shops, bars and restaurants in Coëx 2 km. Golf and riding 3 km.

**Open:** 20 April - 21 September.

**Directions**

Coëx is 29 km. west of La Roche-sur-Yon via the D938 to Aizenay, then the D6 St Gilles Croix-de-Vie road. Site is south of the village just off the D40 to La Chaize-Giraud and is clearly signed. GPS: 46.677033, -1.76885

**Charges guide**

| | |
|---|---|
| Per unit incl. 2 persons and electricity | € 14.00 - € 35.50 |
| extra person | € 2.50 - € 4.95 |
| dog | € 7.00 |

**RCN la Ferme du Latois**
**Camping - Mobile homes**

2013

This lovely campsite with spacious pitches is located just 15 minutes from the Atlantic Ocean with its fabulous beaches.

www.rcn.fr - 0033 251 546 730 - ferme@rcn.fr

**FREE** Alan Rogers Travel Card
Extra benefits and savings - see page 10

## Jard-sur-Mer
### Chadotel Camping l'Océano d'Or

84 Rue Georges Clémenceau, F-85520 Jard-sur-Mer (Vendée) T: 02 51 33 05 05. E: info@chadotel.com

**alanrogers.com/FR85270**

This eight-hectare site should appeal to families with children of all ages. It is very lively in high season but appears to be well managed, with a full programme of activities (it can therefore be noisy, sometimes late at night). The site is only 1 km. from the excellent beach. There are 450 flat, grass and sand pitches occupied by tour operators and mobile homes. The 121 for touring units, all with 10A electricity (French sockets, long leads may be required), are quite large (about 100 sq.m). Some are separated by high hedges, others are more open with low bushes between them. There is a good aquatic area – the flume takes you past rocks before plunging into the pool. There are shops, bars and restaurants, and a weekly market in the pleasant little town of Jard-sur-Mer.

### Facilities

Four recently refurbished unisex toilet blocks include washbasins all in cabins. Facilities for disabled visitors and children. Laundry facilities. Shop (1/6-10/9). Bar, snack bar and takeaway (1/6-10/9, limited hours outside high season). Swimming pool (heated 20/5-20/9) with slides, waterfalls and children's pool. Fitness suite. Walled (three sides) boat-themed play area. Tennis. Bicycle hire. Pétanque. Minigolf. Multisports pitch. Electric barbecues are not allowed. Max. 1 dog. Internet and WiFi (charged). Off site: Cycle paths adjacent. Excellent beach within walking distance. Shops and restaurant 400 m. Château de Talmont 6 km. Golf, riding, karting and other activities within 15 km.

**Open:** April - September.

### Directions

Site is on the D21 Talmont-St Hilaire-Longeville-sur-Mer, just east of the turning to the town centre. GPS: 46.42075, -1.5694

### Charges guide

| Per unit incl. 2 persons | |
|---|---|
| and electricity | € 15.90 - € 31.50 |
| extra person | € 6.00 |
| child (2-13 yrs) | € 4.00 |
| dog | € 3.50 |

---

## Jard-sur-Mer
### Camping les Ecureuils

Route des Goffineaux, F-85520 Jard-sur-Mer (Vendée) T: 02 51 33 42 74. E: ecureuils@franceloc.fr

**alanrogers.com/FR85210**

Les Ecureuils is a wooded site in a quieter part of the southern Vendée. It is undoubtedly one of the prettiest sites on this stretch of coast, with an elegant reception area, attractive vegetation and large pitches separated by low hedges with plenty of shade. Of the 278 pitches, 77 are for touring units, each with water and drainage, as well as easy access to 10A electricity. This site is popular with tour operators (54 pitches). Jard is rated among the most pleasant and least hectic of Vendée towns. The harbour is home to some fishing boats and rather more pleasure craft. There is a public slipway for those bringing their own boats.

### Facilities

Two toilet blocks, well equipped and kept very clean, include baby baths, and laundry rooms. Small shop (bread baked on site). Snack bar and takeaway (1/6-30/8). Bar with snacks and ice creams. Good sized L-shaped swimming pool and separate paddling pool (30/5-15/9). New large flume into separate pool. Indoor pool and fitness centre (all season). New, imaginative play area for ages 3-10. Minigolf. Boules. Multisports pitch. Bouncy castle. Club for children (5-10 yrs, July/Aug). Games room. Bicycle hire. Internet access and WiFi (free). Only gas barbecues are allowed. Dogs are not accepted. Off site: Beach, fishing 400 m. Marina and town.

**Open:** 9 April - 25 September.

### Directions

From Les Sables-d'Olonne take N949 towards Talmont-St Hilaire. Keep right in centre (D21 towards Jard). From La Roche-sur-Yon follow D474 and D49 towards Jard-sur-Mer. Do not use sat nav for final approach. From village follow signs for Autres Campings or Camping les Ecureuils. Site is on the left. GPS: 46.4113, -1.5896

### Charges guide

| Per unit incl. 2 persons, | |
|---|---|
| and electricity | € 16.00 - € 32.00 |
| extra person | € 4.70 - € 7.00 |
| child (0-7 yrs) | € 3.50 - € 4.50 |

For latest campsite news, availability and prices visit
## alanrogers.com

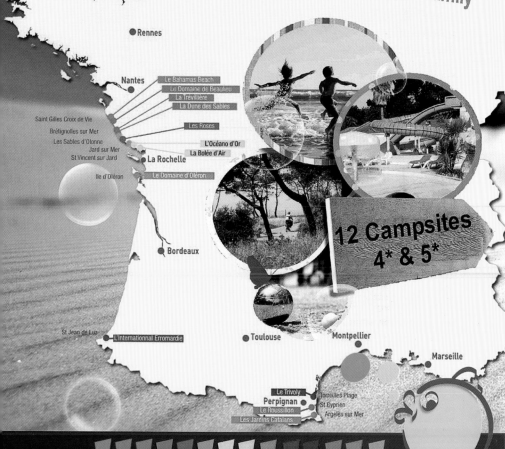

## La Barre-de-Monts

**Campéole la Grande Côte**

Route de la Grande Côte, F-85550 La Barre-de-Monts (Vendée) T: 02 51 68 51 89.

E: grande-cote@campeole.com **alanrogers.com/FR85840**

Campé●le

A site that lives up to its name, this one is very large, with 727 pitches. However, 245 are occupied by Bengali tents to rent, 60 by private caravans and 29 by tour operators. There are still 394 numbered touring pitches in rows, all with 10A electricity and spread over undulating sand dunes with sparse grass under pine trees. The site is served by eight fairly modern and fairly well maintained toilet blocks around the site. Some of the terraced pitches at the rear of the site have views of the impressive bridge onto the Ile de Noirmoutier, and there is direct access to a sandy beach via a gate. In July and August, the site offers clubs for children whilst adults can enjoy themed tapas, karaoke, cabaret, and aquagym. Whilst in high season this site is very busy, in low season it is rather quiet with only the pool and the playground open. Footpaths lead to the village of Fromentine where there are shops and services plus the historic 19th-century Estacade and an old lighthouse. You can also buy oysters and other seafood.

### Facilities

Eight toilet blocks include some washbasins in cubicles, seatless toilets, baby bath, and a good unit for disabled campers. One laundry room. Outdoor heated swimming pool (15/5-19/9). Shop for bread and basics. Bar and takeaway (1/7- 31/8). Playgrounds, trampoline and bouncy castle. Entertainment for children (1/7-31/8). Multi-sports court. Boules. Bicycle hire. No charcoal barbecues. Supplement for double axle caravans. WiFi (charged). Off site: Fishing, sailing 50 m. Riding 2 km. Golf 15 km. Boat launching 25 km. Eco-museum du Daviaud.

**Open:** 1 April - 19 September.

### Directions

Site is on mainland approach to Ile de Noirmoutier. From north via Bourgneuf-en-Retz take D758 to Beauvoir-sur-Mer, then D22 to La Barre-de-Monts. Continue through town ignoring road to Fromentine. At town boundary turn right on D38b. In 500 m, straight on at roundabout for 1 km. then right (Grand Côte). Take next left to site. GPS: 46.8858, -2.1477

### Charges guide

| Per unit incl. 2 persons and electricity | € 17.10 - € 26.60 |
|---|---|
| extra person | € 7.20 - € 12.30 |

Campé●le

CAMPSITES AND RENTALS

## La Grande Côte***

Close to Ile de Noirmoutier,
swimming pool, direct access to the beach
and the village. Amenities, pitches and
accommodations of high quality.

PAYS DE LA LOIRE

85550 La Barre de Monts - Tel.: +33 251-6851-89 - www.campeole.co.uk / grande-cote@campeole.com

## La Chapelle-Hermier

**Camping le Pin Parasol**

Lac du Jaunay, F-85220 La Chapelle-Hermier (Vendée) T: 02 51 34 64 72. E: contact@campingpinparasol.fr

**alanrogers.com/FR85680**

Tucked away in the Vendée countryside, yet just 15 minutes' drive from the beach, this attractive friendly campsite enjoys a pleasant rural setting above the Lac du Jaunay, well away from the bustle of the coast. There are 229 good sized touring pitches, all with 10A electricity and 32 with water tap and drainage. Some have shade, others are in the open with maturing hedges and trees. The enthusiastic family owners are very hands-on and the facilities are of a high standard, most notably the elegant entrance and reception building, and the pool area with its excellent indoor pool and fitness suite.

### Facilities

Four fully equipped toilet blocks include hot showers, washbasins in cabins and facilities for babies and disabled visitors. Washing machines and dryers. Shop and bar with terrace (19/4-25/9). Takeaway (July/Aug). Heated outdoor pool with paddling pool (15/6-15/9). Indoor pool. Play areas. Multisports pitch. Boules. Fishing. Tennis. Bicycle hire. Entertainment in high season. WiFi over site (charged). Internet boxes for hire. Off site: Golf 5 km. Riding 10 km.

**Open:** 19 April - 25 September.

### Directions

La Chapelle-Hermier is 26 km. west of La Roche-sur-Yon. Site is south of D42 La Chapelle-Hermier-l'Aiguillon-sur-Vie road, 2 km. east of junction with D40 Coëx-La Chaize-Giraud road and is well signed. GPS: 46.66622, -1.75528

### Charges guide

| Per unit incl. 2 persons and electricity | € 16.50 - € 33.50 |
|---|---|
| extra person | € 4.50 - € 6.50 |

For latest campsite news, availability and prices visit

**alanrogers.com**

## La Guérinière

### Domaine les Moulins

54 rue des Moulins, F-85680 La Guérinière (Vendée) T: 02 51 39 51 38.
E: contact@camping-les-moulins.com **alanrogers.com/FR85625**

New owners have completely transformed this site on the Ile de Noirmoutier, making it an ideal choice for a seaside holiday. It is on the edge of a forest with direct access across dunes to a pleasant sandy beach. One area has 113 touring pitches on generally level ground and separated by hedges; most have electricity and a few also have water and drainage. Two other areas have an impressive range of tented accommodation, fully in keeping with the forest setting. The heated pool has two paddling pools and a jacuzzi, whilst the bar also serves a full range of meals and snacks. Other facilities are of an equally high standard, with attention to detail in evidence everywhere.

| Facilities | Directions |
|---|---|
| Two modern, very well equipped sanitary blocks provide unisex, preset showers and washbasins, segregated WCs with hand washing, good facilities for babies and disabled visitors. Washing machines and dryers. Motorcaravan service point. Bar/restaurant and takeaway service (Jul/Aug; weekends May-Sept). Heated pool complex with paddling pools and jacuzzi (15/4-15/9). Wellness suite. Small gym. WiFi (charged). Multisports court. Pétanque. Bicycle hire. Off site: Small supermarket outside entrance. | The Ile de Noirmoutier is 70 km. southwest of Nantes. At la Barre-de-Monts take D38 across bridge to island and continue to fifth roundabout. Take exit for La Guérinière and immediately turn left to site. GPS: 46.966233, -2.217173 |

**Open:** 1 April - 30 September.

**Charges guide**

| Per unit incl. 2 persons | |
|---|---|
| and electricity | € 22.00 - € 42.00 |
| extra person | € 4.00 - € 7.00 |

## La Tranche-sur-Mer

### Camping Baie d'Aunis

10 rue du Pertuis Breton, F-85360 La Tranche-sur-Mer (Vendée) T: 02 51 27 47 36.
E: info@camping-baiedaunis.com **alanrogers.com/FR85870**

This very popular 2.5-hectare site has direct access to a sandy beach through a pedestrian gate (with key code) and across a car park. The town centre is also only 500 m. away. Shady and level, there are 130 touring pitches, all with 10A electricity. A good number of pitches are on a gravel base and a few are suitable only for smaller units. There are chalets and mobile homes (19) to rent. On-site amenities include a heated swimming pool and a good restaurant and bar. This is a popular seaside resort with 13 km. of good quality sandy beaches. All have first aid posts, lifeguards in season and dogs are forbidden on the sands. From the pier by the Centre Nautique, just 50 m. from the site's rear pedestrian gate, you can catch ferries to the islands of Aix and Ré and to the larger resort of La Rochelle across the bay. You can also learn to fly or take pleasure flights from the aerodrome behind the town.

| Facilities | Directions |
|---|---|
| The main centrally located sanitary unit is large, good quality and very well appointed with British style WCs, washbasins in cubicles, provision for children and disabled campers. Laundry rooms. Motorcaravan service point. Bar/restaurant and takeaway (30/4-13/9, Thu & Sun in low season). Outdoor swimming pool (10x20 m; heated May-Sept). Playground. Games room. TV room. Dogs not accepted July/Aug or in rental accommodation. Free WiFi over site. Off site: Bicycle hire adjacent. Beach, bicycle hire, sea fishing all within 50 m. Boat launching 100 m. | La Tranche-sur-Mer is 35 km. south of La Roche-sur-Yon. From La Roche-sur-Yon take D747 to La Tranche. At roundabout (D747 and D1046) straight on to next roundabout, turn right towards town centre. At next (new) roundabout continue straight on to site on left (signed). GPS: 46.34638, -1.43184 |

**Open:** 30 April - 19 September.

**Charges guide**

| Per unit incl. 2 persons | |
|---|---|
| and electricity | € 25.10 - € 33.40 |
| extra person | € 5.80 - € 7.00 |

**CAMPING BAIE D'AUNIS★★★★**

Camping Baie d'Aunis | 10, Rue du Pertuis Breton | 85360 La Tranche sur Mer
Tel: 0033 (0) 251 27 47 36 | Fax: 0033 (0) 251 27 44 54
info@camping-baiedaunis.com | www.camping-baiedaunis.com

## La Tranche-sur-Mer

### Camping du Jard

123 boulevard Maréchal de Lattre de Tassigny, F-85360 La Tranche-sur-Mer (Vendée) T: 02 51 27 43 79.
E: info@campingdujard.fr **alanrogers.com/FR85020**

Camping du Jard is a well maintained site between La Rochelle and Les Sables-d'Olonne. With a friendly welcome from M. Marton and his staff, first impressions are good. The 160 touring pitches, all with electricity and 60 also with water and drainage, are level and grassy; many are hedged by bushes and a large variety of trees provide shade in places. An impressive pool complex has a heated outdoor pool with toboggan and paddling pool, plus an indoor pool with jacuzzi. The site is 700 m. from a sandy beach with many shops and restaurants nearby.

**Facilities**

Three toilet blocks (one open in low season) provide basic facilities for babies and disabled visitors. Controllable showers in one block; some washbasins in cabins. Laundry facilities. Shop, restaurant and bar (all July/Aug). Heated outdoor pool (from 18/5); heated indoor pool. Sauna, solarium and fitness room. Tennis. Minigolf. Bicycle hire. Play area, games and TV rooms. Internet point; free WiFi around bar. No American style motorhomes. No pets.

**Open:** 20 April - 14 September.

**Directions**

From A87 Cholet/La Roche-sur-Yon leave at exit 32 for La Tranche-sur-Mer and take D747 to La Tranche. Turn east following signs for La Faute-sur-Mer along bypass. Take exit for La Grière and then turn east to site. GPS: 46.34836, -1.38738

**Charges guide**

| | |
|---|---|
| Per unit incl. 2 persons and electricity | € 23.50 - € 32.00 |
| extra person | € 5.00 - € 6.00 |

---

## Landevieille

### Camping Pong

Rue du Stade, F-85220 Landevieille (Vendée) T: 02 51 22 92 63. E: info@lepong.com
**alanrogers.com/FR85130**

A comfortable family run site, in a rural situation close to St Gilles Croix-de-Vie, and just 5 km. from the coast at Brétignolles, Camping Pong has 237 pitches of which 177 are for tourers. All are of a good size and have electricity; most also have a water tap and drainage. The bar, snack bar, function room, games room, gym and shop are in a neat group of buildings next to the reception. The original area around the small, lightly fenced fishing lake has mature trees, whilst in the newer section, trees and shrubs are developing well. Les Sables d'Olonne with a wide range of shops, bars and restaurants is 20 km. away.

**Facilities**

A modern, well equipped sanitary block serves the main touring area and has controllable showers, washbasins in cabins, facilities for disabled visitors, baby room. The older blocks are of a more traditional style. Shop (July/Aug), Bar plus snack bar and takeaway (15/6-15/9). Heated pool (from 15/5). Small gym, TV lounge and games room. Bicycle hire. Fishing. Fenced play area. Children's club and family activities (July/Aug). WiFi in bar area (charged). Off site: Small supermarket, restaurant and bakery nearby. Tennis 200 m. Lac du Jaunay 2.5 km. Beach 5 km.

**Open:** 1 April - 15 September.

**Directions**

Landevieille is 32 km. west of La Roche-sur-Yon via the A87/D160 Les Sables road; take exit for La Motte-Achard and follow D12 for St Gilles Croix-de-Vie. Site is on the edge of Landevieille and is signed from the D12 and from the D32 (Challans-les Sables-d'Olonne). GPS: 46.64231, -1.79935

**Charges guide**

| | |
|---|---|
| Per unit incl. 2 persons and electricity | € 15.00 - € 24.00 |
| extra person | € 3.20 - € 4.90 |

---

## Landevielle

### Camping l'Evasion

Route des Sables, F-85220 Landevielle (Vendée) T: 02 51 22 90 14. E: contact@camping-levasion.fr
**alanrogers.com/FR85885**

L'Evasion is located close to the Lac de Jaunay, well known for its water-based activities. This modern, well equipped site boasts a natural swimming pool bordered by white sand. There is also a second, traditional outdoor swimming pool in addition to a large, covered pool with water slides. There are 72 good sized touring pitches here, all equipped with electrical connections. There are also mobile homes available for rent. Other amenities include a bar/restaurant (with takeaway food service).

**Facilities**

Shop. Bar/restaurant. Takeaway. Outdoor swimming and paddling pools. Covered pool. Aqua gym. Multisports pitch. Bicycle hire. Play area. Activity and entertainment programme. Mobile homes for rent. Off site: Watersports on Lac de Jaunay. Shops and restaurants at Landevielle. Nearest beach 5 km. Les Sables d'Olonne 18 km.

**Open:** 1 April - 30 September.

**Directions**

Approaching from the north (Challans), head south on D32 towards Les Sables d'Olonne. Pass through Landevielle and continue on D32 (rue des Sables). The site is well signed. GPS: 46.635, -1.79747

**Charges guide**

| | |
|---|---|
| Per unit incl. 2 persons and electricity | € 18.80 - € 31.50 |

---

For latest campsite news, availability and prices visit
# alanrogers.com

## Le Perrier

### Domaine le Jardin du Marais

208 route de Saint-Gilles, F-85300 Le Perrier (Vendée) T: 02 51 68 09 17. E: info@lejardindumarais.eu

**alanrogers.com/FR85635**

A delightful, family campsite situated, as its name suggests, in a country setting on the edge of the marshes. It is beautifully kept and has excellent facilities including a well stocked shop, a pleasant bar/restaurant and a good pool complex. The enthusiastic and hardworking owners are keen to welcome more British visitors who will be sure of a warm reception. Of the 120 pitches, 50 are available for touring: the established pitches offer some shade and have electricity and water nearby; a new area offers large pitches with electricity, water and drainage. The beaches are just seven kilometres away. For shops, bars and restaurants you can use the nearby village of Le Perrier or head for the resorts of Saint Jean-de-Monts or Saint Hilaire-de-Riez where there are also large supermarkets and frequent markets. Just south of Saint Hilaire is the busy fishing port and resort of Saint Gilles Croix-de-Vie.

**Facilities**

Two bright, modern sanitary blocks provide hot showers and washbasins in cubicles. Baby bath and changing. En-suite facility for disabled visitors. Hot water to washing machine and dryer. Chemical disposal and motorcaravan services arranged. Shop. Bar/restaurant and takeaway. Outdoor pool with paddling pool (15/6-15/9). Indoor pool (15/4-15/9). Solarium. Fitness room. Play area. Free fishing on small lake (fenced and gated). Children's club, daytime activities and evening entertainment (July/Aug). Games area (with TV projected onto large screen for major events). TV in side room. Bicycle hire. Internet. WiFi (charged) in bar area. Off site: Riding 4 km. Beach 7 km.

**Open:** 15 March - 15 November.

**Directions**

Le Perrier is 51 km. northwest of La Roche-sur-Yon and 11 km. southwest of Challans. Site is 2 km. to south on D59 to Le Pissot and St Gilles; from the new route of the D205 Challans-St Jean-de-Monts road turn south on D59 and site is on right in 300 m. GPS: 46.80133, -1.980656

**Charges guide**

| Per unit incl. 2 persons | |
|---|---|
| and electricity | € 19.00 - € 33.00 |
| extra person | € 5.00 - € 7.50 |
| child (2-11 yrs) | € 3.00 - € 6.00 |
| dog (max. 2) | € 3.50 |

## Les Sables-d'Olonne

### Chadotel Camping les Roses

Rue des Roses, F-85100 Les Sables-d'Olonne (Vendée) T: 02 51 33 05 05. E: info@chadotel.com

**alanrogers.com/FR85450**

Les Roses has an urban location, with the fashionable town centre and lovely beach of Les Sables just a short walk away. It has an informal air with 210 pitches arranged interestingly on a knoll. Mature trees give good shade to some areas. There are 90 touring pitches of varying sizes, all with access to water and electricity (long cables may be needed). The site has 120 mobile homes and chalets, some for rent and some owned by a tour operator. Roads around the site can get crowded in high season.

**Facilities**

Three fairly basic toilet blocks have push-button showers, washbasins in cubicles, a unit for disabled visitors, a baby room, washing machines and dryers. Simple bar and takeaway and small shop (10/6-15/9). Small, attractively laid out, heated, outdoor pool with water slide and paddling pool (15/5-15/9). Play area. Volleyball, basketball, pétanque and table tennis. Bicycle hire. Gas barbecues only (for hire). WiFi in bar area (charged). Max. 1 dog. Off site: Beach 500 m. Golf, riding, karting, watersports, zoo, sea and river fishing all within 5 km.

**Open:** April - November.

**Directions**

From end of A87 (Cholet/La Roche-sur-Yon) at exit 33, continue on D160 to Les Sables ring road. In Château d'Olonne (Géant Casino roundabout), turn west on Ave d'Aquitaine towards centre. Site is signed to left at small roundabout. GPS: 46.49167, -1.76517

**Charges guide**

| Per unit incl. 2 persons | |
|---|---|
| and electricity | € 20.50 - € 33.50 |
| extra person | € 6.00 |

**FREE** Alan Rogers Travel Card
**Extra benefits and savings** - see page 10

## Longeville-sur-Mer
### Camping le Petit Rocher

1250 avenue de Docteur Mathevet, F-85560 Longeville-sur-Mer (Vendée) T: 02 51 90 31 57.
E: contact@camp-atlantique.com **alanrogers.com/FR85000**

Le Petit Rocher has a seaside location (150 m. from the beach) set in a pine forest, with an air of peace and tranquillity. Although the area is undulating, the 150 good sized touring pitches are flat and arranged in terraces throughout the wooded area. Electricity hook-ups are available (10A Euro plugs) and there are adequate water points. A grassy play area for children is thoughtfully situated in a hollow, but has limited equipment. There is a heated outdoor pool and an indoor entertainment area was added in 2012.

**Facilities**

Three spacious sanitary blocks are clean and well maintained with showers, British style WCs. Facilities for visitors with disabilities. Washing machine and dryer. Bar, restaurant and takeaway 50 m. from the site (July/Aug). Tennis court. Heated outdoor pool (6/5-22/9). Max. 1 dog. WiFi throughout (charged). Only gas barbecues permitted. Off site: Beach 150 m. Bars, restaurant, and shops nearby. Riding and bicycle hire 2 km. Boat launching 11 km-.

**Open:** 13 April - 22 September.

**Directions**

From Longeville-sur-Mer follow signs for le Rocher towards La Tranche-sur-Mer. Turn right at first roundabout, following campsite signs to site on right. GPS: 46.403767, -1.507183

**Charges guide**

| Per unit incl. 2 persons and electricity | € 16.00 - € 27.00 |
| extra person | € 4.00 - € 7.00 |

## Longeville-sur-Mer
### Camping les Brunelles

Le Bouil, F-85560 Longeville-sur-Mer (Vendée) T: 02 51 33 50 75. E: camping@les-brunelles.com
**alanrogers.com/FR85440**

This is a well managed site with a wide range of facilities and a varied programme of high season entertainment for all the family. A busy site in high season, there are plenty of activities to keep children happy and occupied. In 2007, les Brunelles was combined with an adjacent campsite to provide 600 pitches of which 200 are for touring units; all have electricity (10A) and 20 of the new touring pitches also have water and a drain. All are in excess of 100 sq.m. to allow easier access for larger units. On the original les Brunelles site, the touring pitches are all level on sandy grass and separated by hedges.

**Facilities**

Four well maintained and modernised toilet blocks have British and Turkish style toilets and washbasins, both open style and in cabins. Laundry facilities. Shop, takeaway and large modern, airy bar. Covered pool with jacuzzi (all season). Outdoor pool with slides and paddling pools (15/5-22/9). Tennis. Bicycle hire. Max. 1 dog. WiFi over site (charged). Only gas barbecues only. Off site: Riding 3 km. Good, supervised, sandy beach 900 m. St Vincent-sur-Jard 2 km. Golf 20 km.

**Open:** 13 April - 22 September.

**Directions**

From D21 (Talmont-Longeville), between St Vincent and Longeville, site signed south from main road towards coast. Turn left in Le Bouil (site is signed). Site is 800 m. on left. GPS: 46.41330, -1.52313

**Charges guide**

| Per unit incl. 2 persons and electricity | € 21.00 - € 39.00 |
| extra person | € 5.00 - € 9.00 |

Camping Cheques accepted.

## Longeville-sur-Mer
### Camping le Zagarella

Route de la Tranche, F-85560 Longeville-sur-Mer (Vendée) T: 02 51 33 30 60. E: zagarella@franceloc.com
**alanrogers.com/FR85010**

This pleasant campsite is set in a wooded, six-hectare area, a 1,300-metre walk from the beach (or 1.5 km. by road). Scattered among the 130 mobile homes (110 to rent) are 70 touring pitches, which are of a reasonable size, though the site is probably unsuitable for larger units. On well drained grass and shaded, the pitches are hedged and all have water and electricity. An impressive landscaped pool complex with indoor and outdoor pools, includes water slides paddling pool and a pirate-themed adventure area. Nearby is a large adventure playground with a huge bouncy castle.

**Facilities**

Three well maintained toilet blocks of traditional design include washbasins in cubicles and free preset showers. Separate baby room and facilities for disabled visitors. Laundry facilities. Shop (from 25/5). Bar (from 20/5). Restaurant and takeaway. Outdoor heated pool (from 1/6) and indoor pool (all season). Adventure playground. Multisports court. Tennis. Bicycle hire. Free WiFi in bar area. Only gas barbecues permitted (available for rent).

**Open:** 1 May - 30 September.

**Directions**

Longeville-sur-Mer is 32 km. south of La Roche-sur-Yon. Site is 3 km. south of town on D105 to La Tranche-sur-Mer. From A87 Cholet/La Roche leave at exit 32 (La Tranche) and take D747 to La Tranche. Turn northwest on D105 for 8.5 km. to site on right. GPS: 46.40390, -1.48810

**Charges guide**

| Per unit incl. 2 persons | € 16.00 - € 33.00 |
| extra person | € 4.70 - € 8.00 |

For latest campsite news, availability and prices visit
## alanrogers.com

## Maché

### Camping Caravaning Val de Vie

Rue du Stade, F-85190 Maché (Vendée) T: 02 51 60 21 02. E: campingvaldevie@orange.fr

**alanrogers.com/FR85320**

Opened in 1999, Val de Vie is a good quality, three-hectare site run with enthusiasm and dedication by its new owners, Florence and Pascal Faudrit, on the outskirts of a rural village set back from the coast. There are 92 pitches in total, 71 for touring units, with electricity (6/10A), that vary in size from 70-130 sq.m. on mostly level grass with hedging. There are nine extra large super pitches (booking essential for high season). The ground can become very hard so steel pegs are advised. The pitches are arranged in circular fashion around the toilet block which, with reception, is built in local style with attractive, red tiled roofs. If you are looking for a beach, the Vendée coast is 20 km.

**Facilities**

The two toilet blocks provide excellent facilities including some washbasins and showers in cubicles. Baby bath. Facilities for disabled visitors. Laundry facilities. Basic motorcaravan services. Drinks and ice cream in reception. Bread to order (high season). Play area. Bouncy castle. Trampoline. Heated pool (from mid May). Bicycle hire.

**Open:** 1 April - 30 September.

**Directions**

From La Roche-sur-Yon take D948 northwest. At end of Aizenay bypass continue for 2 km; cross River Vie and take next right, following signs for Maché into village centre. GPS: 46.75268, -1.68633

**Charges guide**

| Per unit incl. 2 persons and electricity | € 16.10 - € 23.10 |
|---|---|

## Noirmoutier-en-l'Ile

### Camping Indigo Noirmoutier

23 allée des Sableaux, Bois de la Chaize, F-85330 Noirmoutier-en-l'Ile (Vendée) T: 02 51 39 06 24. E: noirmoutier@camping-indigo.com  **alanrogers.com/FR85720**

Located in woodland and on dunes along a two kilometre stretch of sandy beach, just east of the attractive little town of Noirmoutier on the island of the same name, this could be paradise for those who enjoy a simple campsite in a natural setting. On land belonging to France's forestry commission, this site is operated by Huttopia whose aim is to adapt to the environment rather than take it over. The 398 touring pitches, all with electricity (10A), are situated among the pine trees and accessed along tracks. Those on the sand dunes have fantastic views across the Baie de Bourgneuf. They cost a few euros extra – if you are lucky enough to get one. Cars are only allowed in these areas on arrival and departure. There are no mobile homes, but Indigo have installed 100 large, well equipped canvas tents on wooden bases for rent. Nearby are salt marshes, an aquarium and a water theme park and there are opportunities to walk, cycle, sail and windsurf. The little town of Noirmoutier-en-l'Ile is just two kilometres away, so it is possible to walk if you are feeling energetic.

**Facilities**

Five sanitary blocks currently provide basic facilities including preset showers and some washbasins (with warm water) in cubicles. The central one is larger and more modern, and another has been refurbished with controllable showers and hot and cold water to washbasins. Bar, restaurant (July-Aug). Takeaway (all season).Play area. Bicycle hire. Only electric barbecues allowed. WiFi (free). Off site: Shops, bars and restaurants in Noirmoutier-en-l'Ile 2 km. Riding 4 km. Sailing 5 km.

**Open:** 11 April - 7 October.

**Directions**

The Ile de Noirmoutier is 70 km. southwest of Nantes. At La Barre-de-Monts, take D38 across bridge to island and continue to Noirmoutier-en-l'Ile. Go through town past three sets of lights and at roundabout turn right following blue signs to Campings. Site is in 2 km. GPS: 46.9969, -2.2201

**Charges 2013**

| Per unit incl. 2 persons and electricity | € 19.80 - € 33.00 |
|---|---|
| extra person | € 3.60 - € 5.40 |

**FREE** Alan Rogers Travel Card
Extra benefits and savings - see page 10

## Olonne-sur-Mer

### Domaine de l'Orée

13 route des Amis de la Nature, F-85340 Olonne-sur-Mer (Vendée) T: 02 51 33 10 59. E: loree@free.fr

**alanrogers.com/FR85180**

On the edge of a national forest, close to marshes and a bird sanctuary, and just 1,800 m. from a fine sandy beach, Domaine de l'Orée will provide ample opportunities for an active holiday whether in the impressive pool complex, using the many sports facilities, venturing out onto the network of footpaths and cycle tracks or just going to the beach. The 53 touring pitches are level and separated by bushes; all have electricity (16A) and 40 also have a water tap and drainage. The remaining 243 pitches are occupied by chalets and mobile homes, many available for rent.

**Facilities**

Two blocks providing adequate sanitary facilities are of traditional design with British style WCs, good, hot showers (preset) and washbasins in cabins; many of the fittings are a little tired and in need of attention. Baby bath. Basic facilities for disabled visitors. Washing machines, dryers and ironing facilities. Small, well stocked shop, bar with TV, snack bar and takeaway (all from 1/5). Heated outdoor swimming pool and fun pool with slides (from 1/5) plus heated indoor swimming pool with jacuzzi (all season). Play areas. Trampolines. Tennis (free). Bicycle hire. Free WiFi in bar and pool area. Off site: Restaurant nearby. Riding 50 m. Canoeing 500 m. Beach 1.8 km. Olonne-sur-Mer 5 km. Golf and sailing 6).

**Open:** 11 April - 13 September.

**Directions**

Olonne-sur-Mer is 5 km. north of Les Sables-d'Olonne. Site is on D80 coast road between Olonne-sur-Mer and Brem-sur-Mer. From La Roche-sur-Yon via A87/D160, turn west on D949 Les Sables ring road then north on D32 to Olonne-sur-Mer. Site is signed to left in town centre. GPS: 46.54979, -1.80159

**Charges guide**

| Per unit incl. 2 persons | |
|---|---|
| and electricity | € 18.30 - € 33.50 |
| extra person | € 3.00 - € 6.00 |
| child (2-6 yrs) | € 2.00 - € 4.00 |
| dog | free - € 3.50 |

## Olonne-sur-Mer

### Airotel le Trianon

95 rue du Maréchal Joffre, F-85340 Olonne-sur-Mer (Vendée) T: 02 51 23 61 61.
E: campingletrianon@wanadoo.fr  **alanrogers.com/FR85005**

Le Trianon can be found at the edge of the bustling village of Olonne-sur-Mer, close to the Vendée's most important resort, Les Sables d'Olonne. Pitches are of a good size - around 120 sq.m. - and are equipped with electricity (6/10/16A). They all have reasonable shade. A good selection of mobile homes, chalets and fully equipped, bungalow-style tents are also available, including some which have been specially adapted for disabled visitors. There is an impressive aquapark, which has a covered pool and water slides. Bracelets must be worn in the complex and these are issued on arrival. The site has a good restaurant/pizzeria and a takeaway meal service. On-site, there is a lively activity and entertainment programme in high season, including children's activities, and evening entertainment twice weekly.

**Facilities**

Shop. Bar/restaurant/snack bar. Takeaway. Swimming pool complex with covered pool and water slides. TV room. Playground. Tennis. Basketball. Volleyball. Fishing. Activity and entertainment programme. Tourist information. Mobile homes, tents and chalets for rent. Off site: Shops, restaurants and bars in Olonne-sur-Mer and Les Sables. Zoo. Watersports. Le Puy du Fou. La Rochelle.

**Open:** 13 April - 28 September.

**Directions**

Approaching from La Roche-sur-Yon, head west on D160 towards Les Sables d'Olonne and leave at exit for Olonne-sur-Mer (D80). Continue on this road, crossing D760 and you will see the site (well signed) on the right. GPS: 46.53172, -1.758279

**Charges guide**

| Per unit incl. 2 persons | |
|---|---|
| and electricity | € 21.72 - € 42.57 |

For latest campsite news, availability and prices visit

# alanrogers.com

# Discover wonderful outdoor holidays in France!

With Vacances Krusoë, discover a new way of enjoying your holidays in comfort, and come stay in a fantastic place with family or friends.

- 27 campsites in France
- The same quality standards in each location
- Our fully equipped mobile homes are all less than 5 years old, with decks and sleeping accommodations for 2 to 6 people
- A wide choice of free activities and entertainment at select campgrounds
- 3 environments to choose from: garden, active or village

Book online at **www.alanrogers.com/travel**
or call us on **01580 214000**
Find all our promotions on **www.vacances-krusoe.com**

vacances
**Krusoë**
L'art de vivre au grand air

PROJET ATLANTIQUE - N1305 - ATOUT France - iM085100026 - Groupe BENETEAU - S.A.S. au capital de 100 000 € Siret 449 625 920 000 11 - R.C.S. La Roche sur Yon - TVA intracommunautaire FR 40449625920.

## Olonne-sur-Mer
### Camping Sunêlia la Loubine

1 route de la Mer, F-85340 Olonne-sur-Mer (Vendée) T: 02 51 33 12 92. E: info@la-loubine.fr

**alanrogers.com/FR85030**

On the edge of a forest and just 1.8 kilometres from a sandy beach, la Loubine is a busy campsite close to Les Sables d'Olonne. Under new ownership from 2011, the site has 80 grass touring pitches which are mostly shaded, all with electricity and with water points nearby. Mobile homes and chalets, many for rent, and tour operator tents occupy the remaining 300 pitches. The focal point is an excellent restaurant with an attractive covered terrace, and a bar with an entertainment area for karaoke and discos, plus a patio overlooking the splendid pool complex with its water slides and heated indoor pool. The camping areas have many mature trees and hedges, some quite high, providing plenty of shade.

**Facilities**

Four toilet blocks have British style WCs, washbasins in cubicles and controllable showers. Facilities for disabled visitors. Hot water to washing machines and dryers. Shop (1/7-15/9). Bar, restaurant and takeaway (15/5-15/9). Outdoor pools and heated indoor pool. Tennis. Fitness room. Minigolf. New play area. Bicycle hire. Internet and WiFi over site (charged). Shuttle bus to beach (July/Aug). Dogs are not allowed in high season. Off site: Restaurant nearby. Riding 200 m. Canoeing 1 km. Beach 1.8 km. Golf 4 km. Olonne-sur-Mer 4 km. Hypermarket 6 km.

**Open:** 6 April - 15 September.

**Directions**

Olonne-sur-Mer is 5 km. north of Les Sables d'Olonne. From La Roche-sur-Yon via A87/D160, turn west on D949 Les Sables ring road then north on D32 to Olonne-sur-Mer. Site is signed to left in town centre. GPS: 46.54626, -1.80556

**Charges guide**

| | |
|---|---|
| Per unit incl. 2 persons and electricity | € 19.80 - € 31.80 |
| extra person | € 3.30 - € 5.20 |
| child (under 6 yrs) | free - € 3.00 |

## Saint Christophe du Ligneron
### Camping du Domaine de Bellevue

Bellevue de Ligneron, F-85670 Saint Christophe du Ligneron (Vendée) T: 02 51 93 30 66.
E: campingdebellevue85@orange.fr **alanrogers.com/FR85385**

Domaine de Bellevue is a family site located in the northern Vendée, close to the town of Challans (famous for its market), and around 20 minutes from the broad, sandy beaches at St Gilles-Croix-de-Vie. There are 126 large (minimum 110 sq.m) pitches here, all with 16A electricity, dispersed around a large park, which has two generous fishing ponds stocked with carp and other species. An entertainment programme runs during July and August and includes special activities for children. There is a range of mobile homes, chalets and bungalow-style tents for rent. The nearest shops are around 1 km. away and there is a restaurant some 500 m. distant. The Vendée is renowned for its excellent cycle trails and several of these run close to the site. Other places of interest include the fine 16th-century château at Apremont and the island of Noirmoutier to the north. Further inland, the world class Puy du Fou theme park and evening spectacular is some 70 km. away.

**Facilities**

New sanitary blocks with facilities for children and disabled visitors. Snack bar. Covered swimming pool. Play area. Games room. Volleyball. Pétanque pitch. Activity and entertainment programme. WiFi. Tourist information. Mobile homes and chalets for rent. Off site: Restaurant 500 m. Shops 1 km. Apremont 12 km. Beaches 25 km. Noirmoutier 40 km. Puy du Fou 70 km.

**Open:** All year.

**Directions**

From Challans, head south on D2948 towards Aizenay. On reaching St Christophe du Ligneron, follow signs to site. GPS: 46.81511, -1.77472

**Charges guide**

| | |
|---|---|
| Per unit incl. 2 persons and electricity | € 13.00 - € 19.00 |
| extra person | € 3.10 - € 4.50 |
| child (under 7 yrs) | € 2.80 - € 3.50 |

## Saint Gilles-Croix-de-Vie
### Camping les Cyprès
41 rue du Pont Jaunay, F-85806 Saint Gilles-Croix-de-Vie (Vendée) T: 02 51 55 38 98.
E: camping-lescypres85@voila.fr **alanrogers.com/FR85495**

On the edge of a pine forest and just a short walk across the dunes from a fine sandy beach, this could be an ideal spot for a seaside holiday. Les Cyprès is a very French campsite with good basic facilities and a pleasant modern pool complex. The 278 pitches are in an arc curving out towards the sea in both directions from reception; the 146 touring pitches of varying shapes and sizes occupy the southern end of the arc. All have access to electricity (10A) and water, though long leads are required in places and some are more suitable for tents because of the trees. Seasonal units occupy a number of these pitches except in high season. Other sections are for mobile homes and chalets for rent or privately owned. A walking and cycle route passes the site linking to an extensive network of tracks. The site is a short drive from the busy fishing port and resort of Saint Gilles Croix-de-Vie with a good range of shops, bars and restaurants along its pedestrianised streets and on the quayside. An impressive new hypermarket has been built on the edge of town and there are lively weekly markets here and in neighbouring towns.

### Facilities
Two traditional toilet blocks serving the touring areas have preset showers and washbasins in cubicles. Baby bath in ladies' section of main block. Ramped unit for disabled visitors opposite reception plus washing machines, dryers and ironing facilities. Small shop (July/Aug). Bar, snack bar and takeaway with shared terrace (July/Aug and weekends). Outdoor pool (from 1/6) and heated indoor pool with jacuzzi (from 4/4) with paddling pools (no Bermuda shorts). Games room. Play area. Multisports court. Bicycle hire and children's go-karts. Free WiFi in bar area. Off site: Fishing 100 m. Beach 500 m. Buses 1 km. Sailing 3 km. Saint Gilles-Croix-de-Vie 3 km. Riding 10 km. Golf 15 km.

**Open:** 7 April - 30 September.

### Directions
St Gilles-Croix-de-Vie is 45 km. west of La Roche-sur-Yon on the D38 coast road. From roundabout at southern end of Saint Gilles bypass, head towards town and take first left in 400 m. Site is signed and is in 1 km. GPS: 46.67089, -1.909132

### Charges guide
| | |
|---|---|
| Per unit incl. 2 persons and electricity | € 20.40 - € 27.90 |
| extra person | € 6.60 - € 6.70 |
| child (2-5 yrs) | € 4.40 - € 4.60 |
| dog (max. 1) | € 3.30 |

**FREE** Alan Rogers Travel Card
Extra benefits and savings - see page 10

## Saint Hilaire-de-Riez
### Camping les Ecureuils

100 avenue de la Pège, F-85270 Saint Hilaire-de-Riez (Vendée) T: 02 51 54 33 71.
E: info@camping-aux-ecureuils.com **alanrogers.com/FR85230**

Of the seaside sites on the Vendée, les Ecureuils has to be one of the best, run by a friendly and most helpful family. Just 300 m. from a superb beach, the site is ideally situated for exploring from Les Sables-d'Olonne to Noirmoutier. Developed on what was originally a farm, there are 215 pitches (39 for touring units). On sandy grass, all have electricity (6A, Euro adaptors available free of charge), water and drainage. Well kept hedges and mature trees give shade and privacy, although some more open pitches are also available for sun lovers. The site is popular with British tour operators (60%).

**Facilities**

The two main sanitary blocks are spacious, and include some washbasins in cubicles, and facilities for babies and disabled visitors. Laundry facilities. Motorcaravan service point. Dog shower. Small shop. Restaurant. Large, airy bar with screened terrace. Pool complex including pool for small children with its own mini aqua park, large heated pool, and water slide with separate splash pool. Lazy river. Indoor pool, paddling pool and jacuzzi. Gym. Tennis court. Games room. Play area. Wellness area, sauna, steam room, relaxing area and chromotherapy shower.

**Open:** 27 April - 7 September.

**Directions**

South on D38 (St Jean-de-Monts-St Gilles), turn right at L'Oasis hotel/restaurant in Orouet (6 km. outside St Jean-de-Monts), signed Les Mouettes. After 1.5 km. at roundabout turn left (St Hilaire-de-Riez). Site is in 500 m. GPS: 46.74473, -2.00869

**Charges 2013**

Per unit incl. 2 persons
and electricity                € 27.95 - € 38.55

## Saint Hilaire-de-Riez
### Camping Caravaning la Ningle

Chemin des Roselières 66, F-85270 Saint Hilaire-de-Riez (Vendée) T: 02 51 54 07 11.
E: campingdelaningle@wanadoo.fr **alanrogers.com/FR85350**

At Camping la Ningle you are guaranteed to receive a warm welcome from M. et Mme. Guibert-Guilbald, who have established a very pleasant campsite with a friendly, family atmosphere. There are 148 pitches, 48 available for touring units. All are fully serviced (electricity 6/10A, water and drainage). Pitches are spacious with dividing hedges and all have some shade. The nearest beach is a 500 m. walk through a pine forest, but there are also three small heated swimming pools on site, one with a flume.

**Facilities**

Two very clean toilet blocks include washbasins and showers in cubicles. Toilet/shower room for disabled visitors and a large family shower room. Laundry facilities. Bread available and takeaway three evenings per week (July/Aug). Bar (July/Aug). Main swimming pool, larger children's pool, paddling pool and slide (all season). Fitness suite. Tennis court. Games field. Games room. Fishing lake. Children's activities (July/Aug), and regular pétanque competitions. Free WiFi in bar area..

**Open:** 1 May - 15 September.

**Directions**

Driving south on D38 (St Jean-de-Monts-St Gilles), turn right at L'Oasis hotel in Orouet, (Les Mouettes). After 1.5 km. at roundabout, turn left (St Hilaire-de-Riez). Pass two campsites, then next left, signed la Ningle. GPS: 46.74476, -2.0044

**Charges guide**

Per unit incl. 2 persons
and electricity                € 18.60 - € 30.90
extra person                  € 3.10 - € 4.80
child (under 7 yrs)           € 1.65 - € 2.90

## Saint Hilaire-la-Forêt
### Camping des Batardières

2 rue des Batardières, F-85440 Saint Hilaire-la-Forêt (Vendée) T: 02 51 33 33 85
**alanrogers.com/FR85390**

Camping des Batardières is a haven of tranquillity on the edge of an unspoilt village, yet just 5 km. from the sea. It is an attractive, unsophisticated little site, lovingly maintained by its owners for more than 25 years. Many visitors return year after year. There are 75 good sized, manicured, grassy pitches (a few up to 130 sq.m) and all are available for touring units (there are no mobile homes and no tour operators!). All have easy access to water and electricity (6A). Otherwise there are few facilities on site.

**Facilities**

The sanitary block is kept very clean and visitors are encouraged to keep it that way (no shoes in the shower cubicles, for instance). Some washbasin and shower combination cubicles. Laundry facilities. Tennis court. Play area and field for games, kite-flying etc. Not suitable for American motorhomes or twin-axle caravans. Off site: Village shop and bar 200 m. Jard-sur-Mer 5 km.

**Open:** 1 July - 1 September.

**Directions**

From Les Sables-d'Olonne take D949 towards Talmont-St Hilaire and Luçon. 7 km. after Talmont turn right on D70 to St Hilaire-la-Forêt. Site signed to the right approaching village. GPS: 46.4486, -1.5286

**Charges guide**

Per unit incl. 2 persons and electricity    € 23.50
extra person                                € 4.00
No credit cards.

For latest campsite news, availability and prices visit
**alanrogers.com**

# Saint Jean-de-Monts

## Camping la Yole

13 chemin des Bosses, Orouet, F-85160 Saint Jean-de-Monts (Vendée) T: 02 51 58 67 17.
E: contact@la-yole.com **alanrogers.com/FR85150**

La Yole is an attractive and well run site, two kilometres from a sandy beach. It offers 369 pitches, some of which are occupied by tour operators and mobile homes to rent. There are 180 touring pitches, most with shade and separated by bushes and trees. A newer area at the rear of the site is a little more open. All the pitches are of at least 100 sq.m. and have electricity (10A), water and drainage. The pool complex includes an attractive outdoor pool, a paddling pool, slide and an indoor heated pool with jacuzzi. There are also new gym facilities. Entertainment is organised in high season. This is a clean and tidy site, ideal for families with children and you will receive a helpful and friendly welcome.

### Facilities

Two toilet blocks include washbasins in cabins and facilities for disabled visitors and babies. A third block has a baby room. Laundry facilities. Shop (15/5-5/9). Bar, restaurant and takeaway (1/5-10/9). Outdoor pool and paddling pool. Indoor heated pool with jacuzzi (all season, no shorts). Gym centre. Play area. Tennis. Games room. Entertainment in high season. WiFi (charged). Gas barbecues only. Max. 1 dog. Off site: Beach, bus service, bicycle hire 2 km. Riding 3 km. Fishing, golf and watersports 6 km.

**Open:** 2 April - 26 September.

### Directions

Site is signed off the D38, 6 km. south of St Jean-de-Monts in the village of Orouet. Coming from St Jean-de-Monts turn right at l'Oasis restaurant towards Mouette and follow signs to site.
GPS: 46.75659, -2.00792

### Charges guide

| | |
|---|---|
| Per unit incl. 2 persons, electricity and water | € 18.00 - € 31.00 |
| extra person | € 4.00 - € 7.00 |
| child (under 9 yrs) | free - € 6.50 |
| dog | € 5.00 - € 7.00 |

Camping Cheques accepted.

Hot Spot WiFi

**Camping La Yole** ★★★★ Camping Cheque

Wake up to the sound of birdsong in a wooded park of 17 acres with four star comfort. Space, security, informal atmosphere:
la yole, tucked away between fields and pine trees, only 2 km from the beach.

– Chemin des Bosses - Orouet - F 85160 Saint Jean de Monts –
– Tel: 0033 251 58 67 17 - Fax: 0033 251 59 05 35 –
– contact@la-yole.com / www.la-yole.com –

**FREE** Alan Rogers Travel Card
Extra benefits and savings - see page 10

## Saint Jean-de-Monts
### Camping l'Abri des Pins

Route de Notre-Dame-de-Monts, F-85160 Saint Jean-de-Monts (Vendée) T: 02 51 58 83 86.
E: contact@abridespins.com **alanrogers.com/FR85090**

L'Abri des Pins is situated on the outskirts of St Jean-de-Monts and is separated from the sea and a long sandy beach by a strip of pine forest. The site has 218 pitches, 30 of which are for touring units, most with electricity and water; they are separated by hedges and most have shade. Seventy pitches have mobile homes and chalets for rent, the rest being occupied by privately-owned mobiles. It has an impressive entrance, good leisure facilities which include a recently added indoor pool and the sanitary blocks are modern and clean. From the site, it is a pleasant 15 minute walk to the beach.

**Facilities**

The two traditional sanitary blocks are modern and clean. Washbasins in cabins, preset showers, basic facilities for babies and disabled visitors. Laundry facilities. Bar and restaurant (July/Aug) with takeaway. Heated indoor and outdoor pools and decked sunbathing area. Sauna and steam room. Gym equipment. Daily children's club, activities and entertainment for the family (July/Aug). Play area. Games rooms. Tennis court. Pétanque. Bicycle hire arranged. WiFi in bar (charged). Off site: Beach 700 m.

**Open:** 15 June - 16 September.

**Directions**

St Jean-de-Monts is 55 km. northwest of La Roche-sur-Yon. Site is 4 km. north of town on western side of D38 Notre Dame-de-Monts road, almost opposite Les Places Dorées. GPS: 46.8093, -2.109

**Charges guide**

| | |
|---|---|
| Per unit incl. 3 persons and electricity | € 24.20 - € 36.20 |
| extra person | € 3.90 - € 6.70 |

## Saint Jean-de-Monts
### Camping les Places Dorées

Route de Notre-Dame-de-Monts, F-85160 Saint Jean-de-Monts (Vendée) T: 02 51 59 02 93.
E: contact@placesdorees.com **alanrogers.com/FR85280**

Les Places Dorées is, in high season, a busy, popular site with a lively programme of activities and entertainment. At other times it is quieter, but still has plenty to offer. There are 288 grassy pitches, of which just 60 are available for touring units, the quietest being towards the back of the site. Those nearer the leisure complex can be noisy in high season with the bar and disco closing late. Pitches are separated by hedges and there is some shade from maturing trees. A 20 minute walk will take you to a long sandy beach. Nearby Saint Jean is a busy resort with plenty of shops, bars and restaurants.

**Facilities**

Three traditional toilet blocks are tired but clean. Preset showers and washbasins in cubicles. Facilities for disabled visitors. Laundry facilities. Bread to order. Bar/restaurant (July/Aug and busy weekends); themed evenings in high season. Snack bar and takeaway. Outdoor pool complex. Covered, heated pool, spa facilities, gym. Multisports pitch. Entertainment. (July/Aug). Bicycle hire arranged. WiFi in bar (charged). Facilities at L'Abri des Pins (opposite) may be used.

**Open:** 11 June - 11 September.

**Directions**

Saint Jean-de-Monts is 55 km. northwest of La Roche-sur-Yon. Site is 4 km. north of St Jean-de-Monts on the D38 St Jean-de-Monts-Notre Dames-de-Monts road on the eastern side, almost opposite L'Abri des Pins. GPS: 46.80993, -2.10992

**Charges guide**

| | |
|---|---|
| Per unit incl. 3 persons and electricity | € 24.20 - € 36.20 |
| No credit cards. | |

## Saint Jean-de-Monts
### Camping la Forêt

190 chemin de la Rive, F-85160 Saint Jean-de-Monts (Vendée) T: 02 51 58 84 63.
E: camping-la-foret@wanadoo.fr **alanrogers.com/FR85360**

Camping la Forêt is an attractive, well run site with a friendly family atmosphere, thanks to the hard working owners, M and Mme Jolivet. It provides just 61 pitches with 46 for touring units. They are of a reasonable size and surrounded by mature hedges; all have water and electricity, and some also have drainage. A variety of trees provides shade to every pitch. There are 15 mobile homes for rent and one tour operator on site, but their presence is not intrusive and the site has a quiet and relaxed atmosphere.

**Facilities**

The central toilet block includes hot showers and washbasins in cubicles. Laundry facilities. Baby bath. Facilities for disabled visitors. Motorcaravan tanks emptied on request. Basic provisions sold in reception. Takeaway (15/5-15/9). Small heated swimming pool (8/5-15/9). TV/games room. WiFi over site (charged). Play area. Bicycle hire. Gas and electric barbecues only. Unsuitable for American-style motorhomes. Off site: Beach 400 m.

**Open:** 1 May - 28 September.

**Directions**

The site is 6 km. north of St Jean-de-Monts just off D38 towards Notre Dame-de-Monts. At southern end of Notre Dame, turn west at sign for site and Plage de Pont d'Yeu. Bear left and site is on left in 200 m. GPS: 46.80807, -2.11384

**Charges guide**

| | |
|---|---|
| Per unit incl. 2 persons and electricity | € 17.00 - € 32.90 |
| extra person | € 3.50 - € 5.00 |

For latest campsite news, availability and prices visit
**alanrogers.com**

## Saint Jean-de-Monts
### Camping Acapulco

63 avenue des Epines, F-85160 Saint Jean-de-Monts (Vendée) T: 02 51 54 33 87. E: info@sunmarina.com
**alanrogers.com/FR85220**

Ideal for family beach holidays, this large, friendly site is just 700 m. from the beach. Most of the 450 pitches here are taken by mobile homes; at present there are 40 available for touring, although some of these are destined for more mobiles. The few existing touring pitches, which have electricity and water nearby, are of average size on grass and divided by hedges. There is an excellent pool complex with water slides, a children's pool, an imaginative new balnéo area and a sunbathing terrace. Adjacent to this is a spacious bar/restaurant. Acapulco is midway between the resort of Saint Jean-de-Monts and the more laid back Saint Hilaire-de-Riez, so opportunities for shopping and eating out are numerous. The site has opened its own exciting leisure complex nearby that incorporates bowling, laser games and a bar/restaurant. The busy fishing port of Saint Gilles-Croix-de-Vie, a little further south, has quayside bars and restaurants, pedestrianised streets and a thriving marina.

**Facilities**

Three sanitary blocks are clean and include washbasins in cabins and preset showers. Facilities for disabled visitors. Hot water to washing machines and dryers. Shop, takeaway and bar/restaurant. Heated outdoor pool complex. Play area. Tennis. Bicycle hire. WiFi (charged). Children's club, full programme of activities, entertainment plus excursions (July/Aug). Off site: Shopping centre and supermarket 400 m. Sandy beach 600 m. Riding 2 km. Fishing, sailing and golf 6 km. St Jean-de-Monts 6 km.

**Open:** 1 May - 11 September.

**Directions**

The site is off the D38 St Jean-de-Monts-Saint Gilles road at Orouët. At mini roundabout by l'Oasis hotel turn southwest signed Les Mouettes and campsite. Site is on left in 2 km. GPS: 46.7637, -2.009

**Charges guide**

| | |
|---|---|
| Per unit incl. 2 persons and electricity | € 25.00 - € 41.00 |
| extra person | € 3.00 - € 4.00 |
| child (under 5 yrs) | € 1.00 - € 2.00 |

## Saint Jean-de-Monts
### Flower Camping Plein Sud

246 route de Notre-Dame-de-Monts, F-85160 Saint Jean-de-Monts (Vendée) T: 02 51 59 10 40.
E: info@campingpleinsud.com **alanrogers.com/FR85590**

Plein Sud is a small, friendly site, immaculately kept and with a very French ambience. Of the 110 grassy pitches separated by hedges, 40 are available for touring. They are of a reasonable size and all have electricity and water; most also have drainage. Twenty pitches have site-owned mobile homes, cabins or tents for rent, the rest have privately-owned mobiles. The touring pitches at the far end of this long, narrow site are particularly peaceful. Only 800 m. away, via another campsite across the road and through a strip of forest, is a long stretch of safe, sandy beach.

**Facilities**

Two well maintained and immaculate sanitary blocks have pushbutton showers and washbasins in cabins. Good facilities for disabled visitors. Baby room. Laundry facilities. Small bar with TV and terrace (July/Aug). Heated pool with paddling pool (15/5-15/9). Play areas. Multisports court. Bread and milk can be ordered daily at reception (high season) and a variety of outside caterers provide takeaways (Tue-Sun). Bicycle hire. Pony and trap rides for young children. Children's club, activities for teenagers and family entertainment (July/Aug). WiFi planned.

**Open:** 1 May - 15 September.

**Directions**

Saint Jean-de-Monts is 55 km. northwest of La Roche-sur-Yon. Site is 4 km. north of the town on the D38 towards Notre Dame-de-Monts, on the right almost opposite Camping L'Abri des Pins. GPS: 46.809805, -2.109557

**Charges guide**

| | |
|---|---|
| Per unit incl. 2 persons and electricity | € 14.00 - € 29.00 |
| extra person | € 2.00 - € 5.00 |

**FREE** Alan Rogers Travel Card
Extra benefits and savings - see page 10

## Saint Jean-de-Monts
### Camping Caravaning le Bois Joly

46 route de Notre-Dame-de-Monts, B.P. 507, F-85165 Saint Jean-de-Monts (Vendée) T: 02 51 59 11 63.
E: campingboisjoly@wanadoo.fr **alanrogers.com/FR85780**

This is an attractive, family run holiday site with indoor and outdoor pool complexes and 385 pitches, most of which are fully serviced. Of these 202 are taken by mobile homes and chalets, leaving 183 good sized, hedged pitches with 10A electric hook-ups for tourists. Grassy and level, these are served by tarmac roads and four fresh, clean, modern, toilet blocks. A good family holiday location, there are lots of activities and entertainment in July and August. The indoor pool is open all season, the L-shaped outdoor pool complex has a 'menhirs' theme and attractive flower beds. There are four toboggans, a paddling pool and a raised solarium deck. On site there are several small playgrounds for younger children, plus a very large and comprehensive adventure playground. The river behind the site offers opportunities for fishing and canoeing.

#### Facilities

Four modern toilet blocks with controllable showers and washbasins in cubicles. Facilities for babies and disabled visitors. Laundry facilities. Drive-over motorcaravan service point. Bar/snack bar (15/6-15/9). Takeaway (July/Aug). Indoor pool. Outdoor pools (15/6-15/9). Sauna, solarium and gym (July/Aug, charged). Playgrounds. Multisports court. Pétanque. TV room. Games room. Bicycle hire. Events, entertainment and canoeing on site in July/Aug. River fishing. No charcoal barbecues allowed. No double axle caravans accepted. WiFi (charged). Off site: Riding and tennis 500 m. Beach and boat launching 1.5 km.

**Open:** 13 April - 39 September.

#### Directions

Site is at the northern end of St Jean-de-Monts, on eastern side of D38, 300 m. north of junction (roundabout) with D51. GPS: 46.79963, -2.07442

#### Charges guide

| | |
|---|---|
| Per unit incl. 2 persons and electricity | € 19.00 - € 34.00 |
| extra person | € 2.00 - € 6.00 |
| child (1-7 yrs) | € 1.00 - € 3.00 |
| dog | € 1.50 - € 3.00 |

## Saint Jean-de-Monts
### Camping les Amiaux

223 rue de Notre Dame de Monts, F-85169 Saint Jean-de-Monts (Vendée) T: 02 51 58 22 22.
E: accueil@amiaux.fr **alanrogers.com/FR85760**

This is a busy, family run campsite that is very popular with British holidaymakers and is used by a number of tour operators, who occupy 150 of the 544 pitches. However, there are still 300 touring pitches, all with electricity (10A), water tap and drain; there are also 32 mobile homes for hire. The site is on both sides of the main road, linked by a tunnel. Most of the larger pitches are on the far side, so owners of high units would need to ask for a pitch on the main part of the site. There are outstanding leisure facilities.

#### Facilities

Seven sanitary blocks provide washbasins in cubicles, controllable showers, and facilities for children and disabled visitors. Washing machines and dryers. No motorcaravan service point. Indoor pool all season, outdoor pools July/Aug. Shop, bar, restaurant and takeaway (8/5-31/8). Play areas. Multisports court. Tennis. Volleyball. Minigolf. Bicycle hire. Children's club, daytime sporting activities and evening entertainment. WiFi over part of site (charged). Off site: Beach 700 m. Riding 2 km.

**Open:** 8 May - 15 September.

#### Directions

Site is on D38 3 km. north of St Jean-de-Monts, midway between St Jean-de-Monts and Notre-Dame-de-Monts, with the entrance on the western side of the road. GPS: 46.808533, -2.104467

#### Charges guide

| | |
|---|---|
| Per unit incl. 2 persons with full services | € 19.00 - € 35.20 |
| extra person | € 4.50 |
| child (1-6 yrs) | € 3.00 |
| dog | € 1.00 - € 3.00 |

# Saint Jean-de-Monts

## Campéole Dornier

18 route de la Tonnelle, BP 10115, F-85161 Saint Jean-de-Monts (Vendée) T: 02 51 58 81 16.
E: dornier@campeole.com **alanrogers.com/FR85960**

Le Dornier is an extensive site (25 ha), located on land belonging to the French forestry commission and close to the popular resort of St Jean-de-Monts. The site has direct access to a superb sandy beach and also has a good sized heated swimming pool. The 232 touring pitches, all with electricity (6A) available, are mostly sandy and of a reasonable size. A range of chalets, fully equipped bungalow tents and mobile homes are available for rent including some models specially adapted for campers with disabilities. The site has a small bar and snack bar (July/Aug) just along the road. There is also a small supermarket and a large bar and restaurant close by. The site can become quite lively in high season with a daily children's club and a wide range of daytime activities and evening entertainment, including concerts and discos. However, touring pitches are well scattered on this vast site, so it should be possible to ask to be located well away from these events if desired. A number of cycle tracks pass through the woods close to the site (cycle hire available). Saint Jean is a well equipped resort with dozens of restaurants, cafés and other attractions.

## Facilities

Three sanitary blocks, serving each section of the site, have recently been attractively refurbished to a very high standard with modern preset showers, washbasins in cubicles, and excellent facilities for babies, children and disabled visitors. Hot water for washing machines and dryers. Motorcaravan service point. Heated swimming pool and paddling pool (15/5-15/9, supervised July/Aug). Bicycle hire. Archery (July/Aug). Multisports court. Bouncy castle. Snack bar adjacent (July/Aug). Play area. Activities and entertainment programme (July/Aug). WiFi (charged) around reception. Mobile homes, equipped tents and chalets for rent. Gas or electric barbecues only. Direct beach access. Off site: Golf and riding 3 km. Shops, bars, restaurants, daily markets in St Jean-de-Monts 6 km.

**Open:** 5 April - 15 September.

## Directions

Saint Jean-de-Monts is 55 km. northwest of La Roche-sur-Yon. The site is 6 km. north of St Jean-de-Monts on the D38 towards Notre Dame-de-Monts. Turn west at the roundabout at Les Tonnelles where site is signed and is on right in 300 m.
GPS: 46.8094, -2.1208

## Charges guide

| | |
|---|---|
| Per unit incl. 2 persons | |
| and electricity | € 17.10 - € 27.90 |
| extra person | € 4.50 - € 7.10 |
| child (2-6 yrs) | free - € 4.40 |
| dog | € 2.50 - € 3.20 |

## Saint Jean-de-Monts

### Campéole les Sirènes

Campé●le

Avenue des Demoiselles - BP 427, F-85164 Saint Jean-de-Monts (Vendée) T: 02 51 58 01 31.
E: sirenes@campeole.com  alanrogers.com/FR85970

Les Sirènes is a large campsite located in the forest behind the popular resort of St Jean-de-Monts. The nearest beach, just 700 m. away, is long and sandy, shelving very gradually into the sea. The 338 touring pitches vary considerably; some, ideal for tents, are among the tall pine trees, whilst others are on flat ground but still with shade provided by a variety of younger trees (190 have 6-10A electrical connections and water taps nearby). A number of equipped tents and mobile homes (including specially adapted models for disabled visitors) are available for rent. On-site amenities include a swimming pool and separate children's pool, a multisports pitch and archery. This is a lively site in high season with plenty going on, including a daily children's club and regular sporting competitions. Evenings, however, are generally quiet, with just a weekly 'soirée dansante'.

### Facilities

Several small sanitary blocks are fairly basic, although a programme of refurbishment has begun. Some modern preset showers and mainly open-style washbasins (a few are in cabins) with only cold water. Washing machines and dryers. Shop, bar and takeaway (July/Aug). Heated swimming pools with paddling pool (1/6-11/9, supervised July/Aug). Multisports pitch. Bicycle hire. Bouncy castle. Archery. Play area. Children's club and activities (July/Aug). WiFi in reception (charged). Gas and electric barbecues only. Mobile homes and equipped tents for rent.
Off site: Restaurant at site entrance. Beach 700 m.

**Open:** 6 April - 16 September.

### Directions

From southern end of D38/D38bis St Jean bypass turn north on D38 Route des Sables towards town. At next roundabout go left on D123 Avenue Valentin, (La Plage). Right at 2nd roundabout, after 1.2 km. right at roundabout along ave des Mimosas into ave des Demoiselles. GPS: 46.780083, -2.055881

### Charges guide

| Per unit incl. 2 persons | |
|---|---|
| and electricity | € 17.10 - € 26.60 |
| extra person | € 4.50 - € 7.60 |
| child (2-6 yrs) | free - € 4.60 |

## Saint Julien-des-Landes

### Castel Camping La Garangeoire

Route de la Chapelle-Hermier, F-85150 Saint Julien-des-Landes (Vendée) T: 02 51 46 65 39.
E: info@garangeoire.com  alanrogers.com/FR85040

La Garangeoire is a stunning campsite, some 15 km. inland near the village of St Julien-des-Landes. Set in 200 hectares of parkland surrounding the small château of la Garangeoire, of which there is a superb view as you approach through the gates. With a spacious, relaxed atmosphere, the main camping areas are on either side of the old road which is edged with mature trees. The 356 pitches (150 for touring), all named rather than numbered, are individually hedged, some with shade. They are well spaced and are especially large (most 150-200 sq.m), 100 have electricity (16A) and 45 have water and drainage also.

### Facilities

Ample, first class sanitary blocks have washbasins in cabins. Facilities for babies and disabled visitors. Laundry facilities. Motorcaravan services. Shop, restaurant and takeaway (8/5-20/9) with bars and terrace. Pool complex with a new covered pool, water slides and a children's pool. Play field. Football pitch. Games room. Tennis. Multisports court. Bicycle hire. Minigolf. Archery. Riding (July/Aug). Fishing and boating. Trampolines. Quadricycles (charged). Gas and electric barbecues only. WiFi (charged).

**Open:** 20 April - 21 September.

### Directions

Site is signed from St Julien; entrance is to the east off the D21 road, 2.5 km. north of St Julien-des-Landes. GPS: 46.663648, -1.713395

### Charges 2013

| Per unit incl. 2 persons | |
|---|---|
| and electricity | € 17.80 - € 38.00 |
| extra person | € 4.60 - € 8.00 |
| child (under 10 yrs) | € 2.60 - € 4.50 |

Camping Cheques accepted.

# Saint Julien-des-Landes

## Village de la Guyonnière

La Guyonnière, F-85150 Saint Julien-des-Landes (Vendée) T: 02 51 46 62 59. E: info@laguyonniere.com
**alanrogers.com/FR85260**

La Guyonnière is a spacious (30 hectare), rural site. It is Dutch owned but English is spoken and all visitors are made very welcome. The pitches are arranged on eight different fields, each being reasonably level and seven having a toilet block. There are 270 mostly large pitches (225 sq.m) with a mix of sun and shade and large units are welcome. Some are open, others are separated by a tree and a few bushes. All have access to electricity connections and 115 are occupied by mobile homes and chalets. A new pool complex includes an outdoor pool with a wild water river and a heated indoor pool with a waterfall. Bar and restaurant facilities are housed in original farm buildings, attractively converted. Entertainment is provided in the bar on high season evenings. This is a perfect place for families, with large play areas on sand and grass, and a paddling pond with shower. Visitors with disabilities are made especially welcome with a range of facilities (for example, a lift in the pool and special scooters to rent). Being in the country, it is ideal for cyclists and walkers with many signed routes from the site. A pleasant 500 m. walk takes you to the Jaunay Lake where fishing is possible (permits from the village), canoeing (life jackets from reception) and pedaloes to hire. There are no tour operators and, needless to say, no road noise. This site is popular for many reasons, the main one being the relaxed atmosphere.

### Facilities

Modern toilet blocks. Most cubicles are quite small. Washbasins are in cubicles. Provision for disabled visitors (including lift in the pool, scooters to rent). Laundry facilities. Shop, bar with TV and pool table (all season). Restaurant (15/6-31/8). Pizzeria with takeaway (all season). Pool complex with outdoor pool (heated 1/5-16/9) and wild water river and covered pool with waterfall. Paddling pool. New spa centre. Play areas, sand pit. Tennis. Bicycle hire. WiFi (free). Off site: Riding 3 km. Golf 8 km. Beaches 10 km.

**Open:** 1 April - 27 September.

### Directions

Site is signed off the D12 road (La Mothe Achard-St Gilles-Croix-de-Vie), 4 km. west of St Julien-des-Landes. The site is 1 km. from the main road. GPS: 46.65273, -1.74987

### Charges 2013

| | |
|---|---|
| Per unit incl. 2 persons and electricity | € 19.90 - € 39.90 |
| extra person | € 5.00 - € 7.50 |
| child (3-9 yrs) | € 3.00 - € 4.30 |
| dog | € 4.00 |

Less 10-20% outside high season.

## Saint Julien-des-Landes
### Flower Camping la Bretonnière

F-85150 Saint Julien-des-Landes (Vendée) T: 02 51 46 62 44. E: camp.la-bretonniere@wanadoo.fr

**alanrogers.com/FR85850**

An attractive, modern site on a family farm surrounded by beautiful, peaceful countryside, this site is sure to please. With 165 pitches in an area of six hectares, there is plenty of space for everyone. There are 101 touring pitches, eight tents, eight mobile homes and 17 Alpine-style chalets, spread around several fields, some quite open, others with some shade from perimeter hedges. The grassy pitches are all of a really generous size with 12A electricity. Two swimming pools, one covered, the other outdoor, are surrounded by a pleasant terrace, with the bar and reception close by. Also on site is a lovely large fishing lake (unfenced) with a pleasant walk all around. A club for children runs in July and August. The village of Saint Julien-des-Landes is 2.5 km. and the larger town of La Mothe-Achard is 7 km. away.

**Facilities**

Four modern, clean and well appointed toilet blocks. Baby rooms and facilities for disabled visitors at two blocks (may not be open April/May). Motorcaravan service point. Bar, snack bar and takeaway (July/Aug). Covered swimming pool (15.5x7 m). Outdoor pool (11x5 m) and wellness centre (June-Sept). WiFi (free) around bar and reception. Playgrounds. Games/TV room. Tennis. Boules. Basketball. Volleyball. Indoor and outdoor football pitches. Fishing lake. Caravan storage. Off site: Paintball and tree climbing adventure trail 2 km. Village 2.5 km. Riding 3 km. Boat launching 4 km. La Mothe-Achard 7 km. Golf 12 km.

**Open:** 1 April - 30 September.

**Directions**

Saint Julien-des-Landes is 18 km. northeast of Les Sables-d'Olonne and 5 km. northwest of La Mothe-Achard. From La Mothe-Achard take the D12 west towards Bretignolles-sur-Mer, pass through St Julien and after 2 km. take first right (site signed). Site is 500 m. GPS: 46.64463, -1.73328

**Charges guide**

| Per unit incl. 2 persons | |
|---|---|
| and electricity | € 14.00 - € 28.90 |
| extra person | € 3.50 - € 5.50 |
| child (2-7 yrs) | free - € 4.50 |

www.la-bretonniere.com

## Saint Julien-des-Landes
### Yelloh! Village Château La Forêt

Route de Martinet, La Forêt, F-85150 Saint Julien-des-Landes (Vendée) T: 02 51 46 62 11.
E: camping@domainelaforet.com **alanrogers.com/FR85820**

Set in the tranquil and beautiful natural parkland surrounding an 19th-century château, this lovely site has 209 large pitches, of which 110 are for touring units. There are also 30 units for rent and 60 pitches are occupied by tour operators. All are on grass and fully serviced including 10A electricity; some are in shady woodland and others, for sun worshippers, are more open. The camping area is only a small part of the 50-hectare estate, with a mix of woodland, open meadows and fishing lakes, all accessible to campers. The beaches of the Côte de Lumière are just 12 km. away.

**Facilities**

Three sanitary blocks are newly refurbished and include washbasins in cubicles, with good provision for babies and disabled campers. No motorcaravan service point. Laundry facilities. Shop, bar, small restaurant and takeaway. Two swimming pools (one outdoor, one heated and covered). Play area. Evening entertainment, children's clubs and disco (July/Aug). Large adventure playground (charged). Trampoline. Games room. Tennis. Boules. Fishing lakes. 6-hole swing golf course (pitch and putt with soft balls) and minigolf. Canoeing trips. Bicycle hire. Free WiFi. Bubble room for hire (includes breakfast).

**Open:** 4 May - 15 September.

**Directions**

St Julien-des-Landes is 25 km. west of La Roche-sur-Yon, northwest of La Mothe-Achard. From La Mothe-Achard take D12 to St Julien, turn northeast on D55 at crossroads towards Martinet. Site is on left almost immediately. GPS: 46.6432, -1.71198

**Charges 2013**

| Per unit incl. 2 persons | |
|---|---|
| and electricity | € 18.00 - € 38.00 |
| extra person | € 5.00 - € 7.00 |
| child (3-6 yrs) | free - € 6.00 |

For latest campsite news, availability and prices visit
## alanrogers.com

## Talmont-Saint Hilaire

### Camping Loyada

Avenue de l'Atlantique, F-85440 Talmont-Saint-Hilaire (Vendée) T: 02 51 21 28 10.

E: contact@camping-loyada.fr **alanrogers.com/FR85920**

Camping Loyada is a family campsite which takes its name from a beach in Djibouti. It is spacious, covering five hectares with 224 grassy pitches, most of which are used for accommodation to rent (144). The pitches are comfortable, modern and hedged, although these are not yet tall enough to provide shade or privacy. The enthusiastic and friendly owners are working hard to build the site and to create a family holiday atmosphere. A club runs for small children, with regular games and entertainment. A large pool complex (300 sq.m) will delight all age groups with its outdoor and indoor heated swimming pools, water slide, jacuzzi and paddling pool. There are beaches within 3.5 km. There is much to do in the area including the pleasant beach of Le Veillon which is situated between dunes and forest.

### Facilities

Two very modern toilet blocks with all the necessary facilities, including those for disabled visitors, a baby room and a shower and WC for children. Washing machines. Shop (July/Aug). Bar with WiFi. Snack bar. Indoor, heated swimming pool, jacuzzi, outdoor swimming pool with water slide, paddling pool. Playground. Animation in high season (karaoke, dancing). Off site: Diving, golf, riding, karting, sailing and fishing nearby. Automobile museum.

**Open:** 1 April - 30 September.

### Directions

From the A10 take exit for Niort and follow signs for Niort then Talmont-St Hilaire via Fontenay Le Comte and Luçon. Or in Niort take A83 towards Nantes, then exit 7 (Ste Hermine) towards Luçon and Talmont-Saint Hilaire. Once in Talmont-Saint-Hilaire, follow signs for Port Bourgenay and site.
GPS: 46.465838, -1.652852

### Charges guide

| | |
|---|---|
| Per unit incl. 2 persons and electricity | € 16.50 - € 25.00 |
| extra person | € 3.50 - € 4.50 |
| child (1-7 yrs) | € 1.00 - € 3.00 |
| dog | € 1.50 - € 2.50 |

**Camping Loyada**\*\*\*\*\*
Avenue de l'Atlantique 111
rue de la Source - BP 5
85440 Talmont Saint Hilaire
Tél : +33 2 51 21 28 10
contact@camping-loyada.fr
*www.camping-loyada.fr*

**FREE** Alan Rogers Travel Card
Extra benefits and savings - see page 10

## Saint Laurent-sur-Sèvre
### Camping le Rouge Gorge

Route de la Verrie, F-85290 Saint Laurent-sur-Sèvre (Vendée) T: 02 51 67 86 39.
E: campinglerougegorge@wanadoo.fr  **alanrogers.com/FR85890**

A family run site, le Rouge Gorge has 72 touring pitches, plus some units for rent and privately-owned caravans and chalets. The site does accept a small number of workers' units. Slightly sloping and undulating pitches are on grass in a garden-like setting and a small wildlife pond (fenced) is in the centre of the site. It would make a suitable base from which to visit the spectacles of Puy de Fou and the steam railway which runs from Mortagne-sur-Sèvre to Les Herbiers. This is also an excellent stopover for those heading to and from southern France and Spain, or the ski-resorts.

**Facilities**

Two toilet blocks, one can be heated, with washbasins in cubicles and facilities for disabled campers and babies. Laundry with washing machine and dryer. Bar and shop (bread and basic provisions) (1/7-31/8). Snack bar/takeaway (15/6-15/9). Heated swimming pool (8/5-23/9). Children's club (July/Aug). Boules. Bouncy castle. Playground. TV room. WiFi. No charcoal barbecues. Off site: Mortagne-Les Herbiers steam railway.

**Open:** 1 March - 25 October.

**Directions**

St Laurent-sur-Sèvre is 10 km. due south of Cholet, just south of the N149. Site is on D111 west of town towards la Verrie, entrance at top of hill on right. GPS: 46.95781, -0.90309

**Charges guide**

| Per unit incl. 2 persons | |
|---|---|
| and electricity | € 18.80 - € 23.40 |
| extra person | € 3.90 |

## Talmont-Saint Hilaire
### Yelloh! Village le Littoral

Le Porteau, F-85440 Talmont-Saint-Hilaire (Vendée) T: 02 51 22 04 64. E: info@campinglelittoral.com
**alanrogers.com/FR85250**

One hundred metres from the sea, five minutes from Les Sables-d'Olonne, le Littoral is situated on the south Vendée coast. It has been fully modernised over recent years by the Boursin family. The site's 484 pitches are mainly used for mobile homes and chalets, but there are 90 touring pitches, hedged, of a good size and all with water, electricity (10A) and drainage. The site has a heated pool complex with outdoor and indoor pools. The minimarket, bar and restaurant are open all season with frequent themed evenings and lots of entertainment and activities in high season.

**Facilities**

Three sanitary blocks have British and Turkish style WCs, showers and washbasins in cubicles. Baby rooms. Facilities for disabled visitors. Laundry facilities. Fridge hire. Shop, bar, restaurant and takeaway. Outdoor and indoor pools. Bicycle hire. Multisports court. Tennis. Excellent play areas. Games room with TV. Club for younger children (all season), teens club (July/Aug). Activities, entertainment, excursions, July/Aug and holiday weekends. WiFi (charged). Free shuttle bus to beach and town (July/Aug). Mobile homes and chalets for hire.

**Open:** 12 April - 15 September.

**Directions**

From Les Sables or Talmont, follow direction 'Aquarium 7ième continent'. The site is situated at the next roundabout after the aquarium. GPS: 46.451633, -1.702017

**Charges 2013**

| Per unit incl. 2 persons | |
|---|---|
| and electricity | € 18.00 - € 44.00 |
| extra person | € 6.00 - € 7.00 |
| child (3-6 yrs) | free - € 6.00 |

## Talmont-Saint Hilaire
### Camping le Paradis

Route de Port Bourgenay, rue de la Source, F-85440 Talmont-Saint-Hilaire (Vendée) T: 02 51 22 22 36.
E: info@camping-leparadis85.com  **alanrogers.com/FR85915**

Camping le Paradis can be found close to the popular seaside resort of Talmont-Saint Hilaire, between Jard-sur-Mer and the larger resort of Les Sables-d'Olonne. Talmont makes up part of the Côte de Lumière, and its 3.5 km. sandy beach (Le Veillon) has longstanding Blue Flag accreditation. There is a free shuttle bus from the campsite to the beach. Pitches here are of average size with limited shade. A number of mobile homes are available for rent. On-site amenities include a covered, heated pool and an all-weather sports pitch (basketball, volleyball, football).

**Facilities**

The single toilet block provides washbasins and showers in cubicles. Laundry. Shop. Bar/snack bar and takeaway (July/Aug). Covered swimming pool. Play area. All weather sports pitch. Activity and entertainment programme (July/Aug). No charcoal barbecues. WiFi over part of site (charged). Max. 1 dog. Mobile homes and caravans for rent. Off site: Beach 1 km. Shops in Talmont, 3 km.

**Open:** 1 May - 30 September.

**Directions**

Approaching from the north (Les Sables-d'Olonne) take the southbound D9494 towards Talmont-Saint-Hilaire. Before reaching Talmont turn right on D4 and follow signs to the site. GPS: 46.46486, -1.65484

**Charges guide**

| Per unit incl. 2 persons | |
|---|---|
| and electricity | € 17.00 - € 26.00 |
| extra person | € 3.00 - € 4.50 |

For latest campsite news, availability and prices visit
**alanrogers.com**

On the Atlantic coast, between the châteaux of the Loire Valley and the Bordeaux vineyards, lies Poitou-Charentes, one of the sunniest parts of the French western coast. Its mild climate, with 2,250 hours of sunshine per year, makes it popular with visitors from early spring to late autumn.

**DÉPARTEMENTS: 16 CHARENTE, 17 CHARENTE-MARITIME, 79 DEUX SÈVRES, 86 VIENNE**

**MAJOR CITIES: POITIERS, LA ROCHELLE, COGNAC**

The Poitou-Charentes region was formed as recently as 1956 and comprises the central section of the Atlantic coast, with undulating inland regions extending to the foothills of the Massif Central. It is the sunniest area of France outside the Mediterranean, and with miles of beautiful, sandy beaches and bustling resorts such as Royan and La Rochelle, it is a magnet for holidaymakers and sailing enthusiasts.

In the south, the area around Cognac is home to extensive vineyards that produce the grapes for the famous brandy, and for the local apéritif, Pineau des Charantes. The familiar names of Rémy Martin, Hennessy and Martell can be seen above the distilleries that line the river Charante.

The region's capital, Poitiers, is one of France's oldest cities and sits on a hilltop overlooking the River Clain. Its historic centre has a wealth of Romanesque art and ancient buildings, including St. John's Baptistry, believed to be the oldest place of Christian workship in the country. In complete contrast, the technological theme park, Futuroscope, is just 8 km. away, and with some 3 million visitors annually is among the top 20 visitor attractions in France.

### Places of interest

*Angoulême:* hilltop town surrounded by ramparts, cathedral, Renaissance château.

*Cognac:* the most celebrated 'eau de vie' in the world, cellars, Valois castle.

*Marais Poitevin:* marshes also known as the 'Green Venice'.

*Poitiers:* Palais de Justice, Notre Dame la Grande Romanesque church, old city.

*La Rochelle:* port, Porte de la Grosse Horloge (clock gate), Museum of the New World.

*Saint Savin:* 17th-century abbey, mural painting.

### Cuisine of the region

Fish predominates, both fresh water (eel, trout, pike) and sea water (shrimps, mussels, oysters).

*Bouilliture (bouilleture):* eel stew with shallots and prunes in Sauvignon white wine.

*Boulaigou:* thick sweet or savoury pancake.

*Bréjaude:* cabbage, leek and bacon soup.

*Cagouilles:* snails from Charente.

*Casserons en matelote:* squid in red wine sauce with garlic and shallots.

*Farcidure:* a dumpling (poached or sautéed).

*Farci Poitevin:* paté of cabbage, spinach and sorrel, encased in cabbage leaves.

*Tourteau Fromage:* cake baked with sugar, eggs, flour and goat's cheese and having a unique caramelised top.

**www.visit-poitou-charentes.com**
**crt@poitou-charentes-vacances.com**
**(0)5 49 50 10 50**

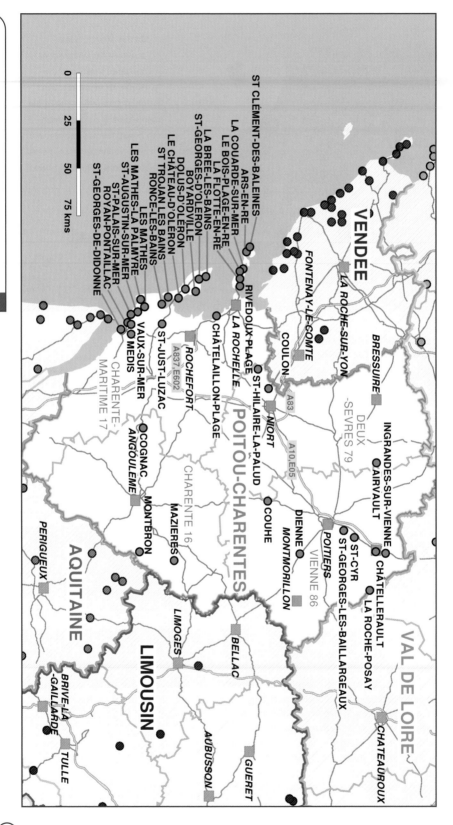

For latest campsite news, availability and prices visit

**alanrogers.com**

## Ars-en-Ré

### Camping le Cormoran

Route de Radia, F-17590 Ars-en-Ré (Charente-Maritime) T: 05 46 29 46 04. E: info@cormoran.com

**alanrogers.com/FR17260**

On the outskirts of Ars-en-Ré, le Cormoran offers a quiet rural holiday. Touring pitches vary in size and are a mixture of sand and grass. Large units may be advised to call ahead. There are 33 pitches for touring units (all with 10A electricity) and the clean sanitary facilities are a mix of modern and traditional. A small comfortable bar and restaurant are located next to the pleasant pool. Being close to the local oyster beds and with numerous cycle paths which include routes through a nature reserve, this campsite is popular with families of all ages. Although rural, the campsite is only 500 m. from the sea. During July and August children's clubs and evening entertainment are organised. The village of Ars-en-Ré is only 800 m. away and a local market is held regularly during the season.

### Facilities

One traditional toilet block and one modern unit provide good facilities. Washbasins are mainly in cabins. Provision for disabled visitors. Laundry. Motorcaravan services. Bar, restaurant and takeaway meals (4/4-15/9). Swimming pool (unheated). Fitness centre. Tennis. Games room. Play area. Entertainment programme in high season. Bicycle hire. WiFi. Off site: Nearest beach and fishing 500 m. Ars-en-Ré 800 m. Boat launching 1 km. Riding 3 km. Golf 10 km.

**Open:** 4 April - 26 September.

### Directions

Cross the toll bridge from La Rochelle onto the Ile de Ré and continue on D735 to Ars-en-Ré from where site is well signed. GPS: 46.21121, -1.5298

### Charges guide

| Per unit incl. 2 persons | |
| --- | --- |
| (3 in high season) and electricity | € 23.65 - € 51.60 |
| extra person | € 5.60 - € 13.00 |
| child (0-10 yrs) | € 3.60 - € 13.00 |
| dog | € 2.80 - € 5.80 |

## Airvault

### Camping de Courte Vallée

8 rue de Courte Vallée, F-79600 Airvault (Deux-Sèvres) T: 05 49 64 70 65.
E: camping@caravanningfrance.com **alanrogers.com/FR79020**

This small, landscaped site, run by a very friendly family, is set in ten acres of parkland close to the small River Thouet. In the heart of rural France and off the main tourist tracks, the site offers tranquillity in surroundings maintained to the highest standards. It is only 15 minutes walking distance from the small, medieval market town of Airvault (the birthplace of Voltaire). There are 64 level or slightly sloping grass pitches, all with electricity (13A) and 11 have water and drainage. They are separated by a variety of shrubs and tall trees offering some shade.

**Facilities**

A clean, modern and well maintained unisex block has spacious cubicles for showers and washbasins, and shower and WC cubicles for disabled visitors. Dishwashing. Washing machine and dryers. Bar/coffee shop selling snacks and ice cream (bread to order). Heated swimming pool (20/5-30/9). Boules. Play area. Bicycle hire. WiFi over site (charged). Caravan storage.

**Open:** 24 March - 27 October.

**Directions**

From D938 (Parthenay-Thouars) take D725 Airvault. Site is well signed, follow blue and white signs. Note: caravans are not allowed in village. GPS: 46.833056, -0.148333

**Charges guide**

| | |
|---|---|
| Per unit incl. 2 persons and electricity | € 29.00 - € 33.00 |

No credit cards.

## Boyardville

### Camping Signol

121 avenue des Albatros, F-17190 Boyardville (Charente-Maritime) T: 05 46 47 01 22.
E: contact@camp-atlantique.com **alanrogers.com/FR17600**

Occupying an eight-hectare site, just 800 metres from the sandy beaches, this campsite has plenty to offer. Of the 300 pitches, 107 are for touring and are set amongst high pine trees and one metre high hedges give plenty of shade and privacy; some have sea views. The pitches are generous (80-120 sq.m) although access to some is tight and may not be suitable for larger units. Levelling blocks are required on some. Electricity (6A) is available to all, although long leads are required occasionally as hook-ups can be shared between three or four pitches. There may be a short walk to the water supply.

**Facilities**

Three modern, fully equipped toilet blocks provide washbasins and showers in cubicles and facilities for children and disabled campers. Laundry. Motorcaravan services. Shop, bar/snack bar, takeaway. Two heated swimming pools (outdoor from 6/5). Enclosed play area. Children's club (from 1/7). Boules. Evening entertainment (from 1/7). WiFi over site (charged). Dogs are not accepted in July/Aug. Only gas barbecues allowed (communal area provided). Mobile homes and chalets available to hire. Off site: Nearest beach 800 m.

**Open:** 13 April - 22 September.

**Directions**

Cross the viaduct and continue on the D26 to Dolus and turn right on D126 signed Boyardville. Continue on this road for 6 km. until the canal bridge at the edge of the town. Cross bridge and turn immediately sharp right along the quayside. Site signed from here. GPS: 45.96807, -1.24456

**Charges guide**

| | |
|---|---|
| Per unit incl. 2 persons and electricity | € 21.00 - € 36.00 |

Camping Cheques accepted.

## Châtellerault

### Camping le Relais du Miel

Route d'Antran, F-86100 Châtellerault (Vienne) T: 06 07 52 04 74. E: camping@lerelaisdumiel.com
**alanrogers.com/FR86030**

This is a good site situated halfway between Poiters and Tours and with very easy access to the A10 and N10 roads. The site is set in the ten-acre grounds of a grand house dating from Napoleonic times, beside the River Vienne. Divided by trees and bushes that provide plenty of shade, there are 80 level pitches with 10A electricity and 13 also with water and drainage. One of the two old barns which form the sides of the courtyard behind the house has been converted to provide 19 apartments and these provide additional accommodation to rent.

**Facilities**

Excellent toilet facilities include washbasins in cabins. Facilities for disabled visitors. Laundry facilities. Shop for basics (July/Aug). Bar. Restaurant (July/Aug). Pizzas (from local pizzeria). Takeaway. Snack bar (evenings July/Aug). Swimming and paddling pools. Playground. Tennis. Bicycle hire. Boules. Games room. Fishing. Internet. Torch useful. Off site: Supermarket 400 m. Riding 5 km.

**Open:** 15 May - 2 September.

**Directions**

Site is north of town close to A10 autoroute. Take exit 26 (Châtellerault-Nord) and site is signed just off roundabout. From N10 follow signs for motorway (Tours-Péage) and at roundabout take exit for Antran. GPS: 46.83858, 0.53441

**Charges guide**

| | |
|---|---|
| Per unit incl. 2 persons and electricity | € 20.00 - € 25.00 |

For latest campsite news, availability and prices visit
# alanrogers.com

## Châtelaillon-Plage
### Camping Au Port-Punay

Allée Bernard Moreau, les Boucholeurs, F-17340 Châtelaillon-Plage (Charente-Maritime) T: 05 46 56 01 53.
E: contact@camping-port-punay.com **alanrogers.com/FR17340**

Au Port-Punay is a friendly, well run site just 200 metres from the beach and 3 km. from the centre of the resort of Châtelaillon-Plage. There are 115 touring pitches laid out on well trimmed grass, with many mature poplars and low shrubs. The site has a well stocked shop, open all season, and a small bar and restaurant open mid June-mid September. A heated swimming pool has a separate gated area for paddling. A good range of activities is available and in high season some entertainment is arranged. This is a family run site (Famille Moreau) and the son of the family speaks excellent English, as does his wife, Angelique. Rochefort to the south and La Rochelle to the north are well worth a visit (buses from outside the site), as is the nearby town of Châtelaillon-Plage, which has an all-year covered market.

**Facilities**

One large toilet block with good facilities including washbasins in cubicles and large shower cubicles. Facilities for disabled visitors and babies. Washing machines. Motorcaravan services. Shop. Bar, restaurant and takeaway (15/6-15/9). Swimming pool (heated May-Sept). Indoor pool and wellness facility planned. Games area. Play area. Bicycle hire. WiFi over site (charged). Off site: Buses to Rochefort and La Rochelle from outside site. Beach 200 m. Châtelaillon-Plage 1.5 km. along the seafront on foot or bike, 3 km. by road. Riding 2 km.

**Open:** 27 April - 29 September.

**Directions**

From N137 (La Rochelle-Rochefort) take Châtelaillon-Plage exit. At first roundabout follow sign for town centre. At second roundabout turn left. Follow signs to site at seaside hamlet of Les Boucholeurs. Drive to the sea wall then turn left through village to site. GPS: 46.05480, -1.08340

**Charges guide**

| | |
|---|---|
| Per unit incl. 2 persons and electricity | € 26.50 - € 36.00 |
| extra person | € 5.30 - € 6.30 |
| child (2-7 yrs) | € 3.90 - € 4.90 |

# Camping Au Port-Punay

Cosy campsite, partly under large trees at 200m from the sea. Luxurious sanitary block maintained to a high standard. An ideal choice for families with small children. Charming fisherman's village, good starting point to visit the islands of Ré and Aix and located in between the historical and tourist cities of La Rochelle and Rochefort. Châtelaillon and its surroundings can be easily discovered by bicycle. Wireless internet available. French, English, Dutch and German spoken.

Camping Au Port-Punay • Les Boucholeurs • 17340 CHATELAILLON-PLAGE
FRANCE • Tel. +33 (0)5 46 56 01 53 • Fax +33 (0)5 46 56 86 44
www.camping-port-punay.com • Email contact@camping-port-punay.com

## Cognac
### Camping de Cognac

Boulevard de Châtenay, route de Sainte Sévère, F-16100 Cognac (Charente) T: 05 45 32 13 32.
E: info@campingdecognac.com **alanrogers.com/FR16050**

Situated close to the historic town of Cognac, this municipal site is set in parkland beside the river Charente. It has 168 pitches, 160 for touring, all have 6A electricity (long leads required), ten have hardstanding and a water tap but no drainage. The pitches are separated by shrubs and some hedging, with a variety of trees giving varying amounts of shade. Access for large units is good, though twin-axle caravans are not accepted. There is some noise from the adjacent road. Public transport is available to the town centre (daily July/Aug; Saturdays at other times).

**Facilities**

Two well equipped, fairly modern toilet blocks (access by steps) include children's toilets and washing machines. Separate ground level facilities for disabled visitors. Motorcaravan services. Small swimming pool on site (June-Sept, municipal pool nearby). Shop, snack bar and takeaway (mid June-mid Sept). Fishing. Play area on grass. Minigolf. WiFi by reception. Off site: Bicycle hire 1 km. Riverside walks. Restaurants, bars and shops in the town (2.3 km). Golf 5 km. Riding 6 km.

**Open:** 29 April - 25 September.

**Directions**

Site is 2.4 km. north west of the town on the D24 to St Sévère just after crossing the river.
GPS: 45.70916, -0.31289

**Charges guide**

| | |
|---|---|
| Per unit incl. 2 persons and electricity | € 13.00 - € 20.00 |
| extra person | € 4.50 - € 5.50 |
| child (2-13 yrs) | € 3.50 - € 4.00 |
| dog | € 2.00 |

**FREE** Alan Rogers Travel Card
Extra benefits and savings - see page 10

## Couhé

### Camping Caravaning les Peupliers

F-86700 Couhé (Vienne) T: 05 49 59 21 16. E: info@lespeupliers.fr

**alanrogers.com/FR86080**

Les Peupliers is situated in a valley just 25 km. south of Poitiers and close to the N10 motorway. The site has been family owned and run since 1968, and continually updated to provide good facilities. The camping area is divided in the middle by a small river (unfenced) with crossing points at various intervals. There are 170 pitches, 43 of which are for mobile homes available to rent. The 136 level touring pitches are on grass and separated by trees and shrubs. All have 16A electricity and 50 are fully serviced. The site enjoys a rural position within this region and tends to benefit from long hours of sunshine.

**Facilities**

Three sanitary blocks also provide facilities for babies and disabled visitors. Laundry facilities. Motorcaravan service point. TV and fridge rental. Shop. Restaurant, bar and snack bar (July/Aug). Pool complex. Playgrounds. Fishing lake. Minigolf. Multisport court. Entertainment in high season. WiFi throughout (charged). Off site: Tennis 800 m. Bicycle hire 1 km. Riding 5 km. Golf 40 km.

**Open:** 1 May - 30 September.

**Directions**

Couhé is 30 km. south of Poitiers on N10. From north, follow signs to Couhé town centre and campsite (a short distance from slip road on right). GPS: 46.31177, 0.17783

**Charges guide**

| Per unit incl. 2 persons | |
|---|---|
| and electricity | € 22.70 - € 32.50 |
| extra person | € 5.20 - € 7.50 |

Camping Cheques accepted.

---

## Coulon

### Camping de la Venise Verte

178 route des Bords de Sèvre, F-79510 Coulon (Deux-Sèvres) T: 05 49 35 90 36.
E: accueil@camping-laveniseverte.fr **alanrogers.com/FR79040**

This family run site on the edge of the Sèvre Nortaise and the Marais Poitevin is ideal for short or long stays. With canoe and bicycle hire on site you have no excuse for not exploring the local area. In the Deux-Sèvres, the department of discovery, so named because it has two rivers named Sèvre, the Noirtaise and Nantaise, the Venise Verte provides an excellent site. There are 120 flat pitches here with 88 used for touring units, the remainder occupied by mobile homes. The pitches are of a good size, all with 10A electricity, water and drainage and with some shade. A Sites et Paysages member.

**Facilities**

Modern toilet facilities are of a high standard with free showers. Washing machine and dryer. Motorcaravan services. Bar (July/Aug). Restaurant. Takeaway on request. Swimming pool (1/6-31/8). Play area. Bicycle and canoe hire. Boules area. Fishing. WiFi throughout (free). Electric barbecues are not permitted. Off site: Fishing 200 m. Coulon 1 km. Boat trips in the Marais. Ideal for walking, fishing, cycling or canoeing. Golf and riding 15 km.

**Open:** 1 April - 30 October.

**Directions**

From Niort take N11 towards La Rochelle. Turn on the D3 towards Sansais and then north on D1 (Coulon). At traffic lights head towards Centre Ville (Coulon) at mini-roundabout turn slightly right. Follow Sèvre Noirtaise for 1.5 km. to site on the right. GPS: 46.31492, -0.60835

**Charges guide**

| Per unit incl. 2 persons | |
|---|---|
| and electricity | € 18.50 - € 30.00 |
| extra person | € 4.00 - € 6.00 |

---

## Dienné

### Camping Domaine de Dienné

F-86410 Dienné (Vienne) T: 05 49 45 87 63. E: info@domaine-de-dienne.fr

**alanrogers.com/FR86120**

This is without doubt a wonderful site and unique in what it offers. It concentrates on your well being and provides all the facilities you could wish for in achieving that aim. The site extends over 47 hectares but there are just 16 pitches for touring units and these are on generous plots of 250 sq.m. All have their own water supply, drainage and 10A electricity and access for even the largest of units will not cause a problem. The accommodation to rent includes Romany-style caravans, tree houses, yurts, a gîte and cottages, which are all of superb quality and again on large plots.

**Facilities**

Shop, bar, restaurant and takeaway food (Feb-Dec). Heated swimming pools. Health and fitness centre. Hairdressing salon. Riding centre. Mountain biking. Adventure park. Climbing tower. Children's games. Walking trails. Fishing. Cooking lessons. Free WiFi over site. Off site: Poitiers airport 25 km. Futuroscope. Crocodile Planet. Monkey Park. Historical sites.

**Open:** February - December.

**Directions**

From Poitiers take N147 towards Limoges. After the village of Fleure the site is well signed. GPS: 46.445028, 0.559294

**Charges guide**

| Per unit incl. 2 persons | |
|---|---|
| and electricity | € 21.00 - € 39.00 |
| extra person | € 4.00 - € 7.50 |

---

For latest campsite news, availability and prices visit

# alanrogers.com

## Dolus-d'Oléron
### Camping Indigo les Chênes Verts
20 passe de l'Ecuissière, F-17550 Dolus-d'Oléron (Charente-Maritime) T: 05 46 75 32 88.
E: chenes-verts@camping-indigo.com **alanrogers.com/FR17985**

This site is a recent addition to the Indigo group of campsites and is located just 50 m. from the beach at Dolus-d'Oléron, on the eastern side of the Ile d'Oléron. Pitches here are of a good size and most have electrical connections. Several are occupied by fully equipped safari-style tents. Recent improvements include a small shop (with bread and croissants) and snack bar. Various activities are organised, including workshops for children and opportunities to discover more about the island and its inhabitants. Dolus is one of the larger towns on the Ile d'Oléron and is still reliant on fishing and oyster cultivation, as well as tourism. It is best known now for its broad sandy beach, and is also home to a cluster of excellent seafood restaurants. Cycling is popular across the island, with miles of dedicated cycle tracks. Back on the mainland, a popular excursion is the large zoo at La Palmyre, by some distance the most popular in France.

| Facilities | Directions |
|---|---|
| Bar, snack bar takeaway (July-Aug). Play area. Tourist information. Fully equipped tents for hire. WiFi (free). Electric barbecues only. Bicycle hire. Off site: Nearest beach 50 m. Riding 3.5 km. Shops and restaurants in Dolus-d'Oléron. Fishing. Boat trips. Cycle tracks across the island. | Dolus-d'Oléron can be found north of Le Château d'Oléron. Approaching from the mainland, cross the (toll-free) bridge at Marennes and head north on D26 to Dolus-d'Oléron. The site is well signed from here. GPS: 45.886995, -1.275433 |
| **Open:** 6 June - 30 September. | **Charges guide** |
| | Per unit incl. 2 persons and electricity   € 20.00 |

OléRON
LES CHÊNES VERTS
★★★★
Tel : +33 (0)5 46 75 32 88

**50 metres from the beach,**
in the heart of nature

www.camping-indigo.com

## Ingrandes-sur-Vienne
### Castel Camping le Petit Trianon

Saint Ustre, 1 rue du Moulin de Saint-Ustre, F-86220 Ingrandes-sur-Vienne (Vienne)
T: 05 49 02 61 47. E: chateau@petit-trianon.fr **alanrogers.com/FR86010**

A family owned site for many years, le Petit Trianon is situated halfway between Tours and Poitiers. It enjoys a countryside position within the lovely grounds of an 18th-century château. Visitors to the site often return several times after their first visit for the calm and tranquil atmosphere here. There are 99 pitches all with electricity (10A), set in seven hectares which gives a real sense of spaciousness. Plants are well tended and shade is provided in parts by the many attractive trees. Access around the site is good and large units are accepted by prior arrangement.

| Facilities | Directions |
|---|---|
| The sanitary facilities include washbasins in cabins, some washbasin and shower units, baby baths, washing machines and dryer. Facilities for disabled visitors. Motorcaravan service point. Shop. Snack bar. Takeaway. Heated swimming pool and paddling pool. Playground. Minigolf. Badminton, croquet, volleyball and boules. Satellite TV. Reading room. Bicycle hire. Bread making. Internet access. WiFi (charged). Caravan storage. Off site: Restaurant 50 m. Tennis 2 km. Fishing 3 km. | Take the N10 to Ingrandes-sur-Vienne and take the D75 towards Oyre. Follow D121 to St Ustre (1.5 km) and site is then well signed. GPS: 46.885533, 0.586133 |
| **Open:** 12 April - 27 September. | **Charges guide** |

| | |
|---|---|
| Per unit incl. 2 persons and electricity | € 23.10 - € 35.30 |
| extra person | € 6.00 - € 8.00 |
| child (under 13 yrs) | € 2.00 - € 3.50 |

**FREE** Alan Rogers Travel Card
Extra benefits and savings - see page 10

## La Brée-les-Bains

### Antioche d'Oléron

16 Route de Proires, F-17840 La Brée-les-Bains (Charente-Maritime) T: 05 46 47 92 00.
E: info@camping-antiochedoleron.com **alanrogers.com/FR17570**

Situated to the northeast of the island, Camping Antioche is quietly located within a five minute walk of the beach. There are 129 pitches, of which 86 are occupied by mobile homes and 43 are for touring units. The pitches are set amongst attractive shrubs and palm trees and all have electricity (16A), water and a drain. A nice pool area which comprises two swimming pools (heated), two jacuzzis, two paddling pools and a raised sunbathing deck, is beautifully landscaped with palms and flowers. A small bar, restaurant and takeaway offer reasonably priced food and drinks. The site becomes livelier in season with regular evening entertainment and activities for all the family. With specially prepared trails for cycling, and oyster farms and salt flats to visit, the Ile d'Oléron offers something for everyone. Bresnais market, selling local produce and products, is within easy reach on foot and is held daily in high season.

**Facilities**

The single sanitary block is of a good standard and is kept clean and fresh. Facilities for disabled visitors. Laundry. Bar, restaurant and snack bar. Swimming and paddling pools. Play area. WiFi. Bicycle hire. Off site: Beach and fishing 150 m. Riding 1.5 km. Golf 7 km.

**Open:** 6 April - 28 September.

**Directions**

Cross the bridge on the D26 and join the D734. After St Georges turn right onto the D273E1 towards La Brée-les-Baines. At T-junction turn left from where the campsite is signed. GPS: 46.02007, -1.35764

**Charges guide**

| Per unit incl. 2 persons | |
|---|---|
| and electricity | € 22.40 - € 38.25 |
| extra person | € 7.60 - € 8.90 |
| child (1-14 yrs) | € 4.30 - € 5.50 |
| dog | € 4.25 |

Camping 150 m from the sea

la Brée-les-Bains          Île d'Oléron - France

**camping Antioche d'Oléron**
Route de Proires
17840 La Brée-les-Bains - France
tel. : 0033 5 46 47 92 00

**www.camping-antiochedoleron.com**

## La Couarde-sur-Mer

### Camping l'Océan

50 route d'Ars, F-17670 La Couarde-sur-Mer (Charente-Maritime) T: 05 46 29 87 70.
E: info@campingocean.com **alanrogers.com/FR17230**

L'Océan lies close to the centre of the Ile de Ré, just 50 m. from a sandy beach. There are 338 pitches here with 161 for touring units, the remainder occupied by mobile homes and chalets. The camping area is well shaded and pitches are of a reasonable size, all with electricity (10A). A pleasant bar/restaurant overlooks the large heated swimming pool which is surrounded by an attractive sunbathing terrace. Bicycle hire is popular here as the island offers over 100 km. of interesting cycle routes. A bus goes to La Rochelle from 300 metres outside the site.

**Facilities**

The two toilet blocks are modern and well maintained with facilities for children and disabled visitors. Laundry. Dog shower. Motorcaravan services. Shop. Bar, restaurant and takeaway. Swimming pool (27/4-29/9). Games room. Riding. Tennis. Fishing pond adjacent. Play area. Minigolf (free). Trampolines and bouncy castle. Boules. Multisports area. Entertainment in high season. Bicycle hire. No charcoal barbecues. Internet and WiFi (free). Mobile homes for rent. Off site: Jet ski hire adjacent. Beach 50 m. La Couarde 2.5 km. Golf 5 km.

**Open:** 27 April - 28 September.

**Directions**

After toll bridge, join D735 which runs along the north side of island until you pass La Couarde. The site is 2.5 km. beyond village (in direction of Ars-en-Ré). GPS: 46.20433, -1.46767

**Charges guide**

| Per unit incl. 1 or 2 persons | |
|---|---|
| and electricity | € 25.00 - € 49.00 |
| extra person | € 5.00 - € 11.00 |
| dog | € 3.00 - € 5.00 |

Camping Cheques accepted.

For latest campsite news, availability and prices visit
**alanrogers.com**

## La Flotte-en-Ré

### Camping la Grainetière

Route de Saint Martin, Chemin des Essarts, F-17630 La Flotte-en-Ré (Charente-Maritime) T: 05 46 09 68 86.
E: la-grainetiere@orange.fr **alanrogers.com/FR17280**

A truly friendly welcome awaits you from Isabelle, Eric and Fanny at la Grainetière. It is a peaceful campsite set in almost three hectares of pine trees which provide some shade for the 53 touring pitches of various shapes and sizes. There are also 70 well spaced chalets for rent. Some pitches are suitable for units up to seven metres (these should be booked in advance). There are no hedges for privacy and the pitches are sandy with some grass. Ample new water points and electricity (10A) hook-ups (Euro plugs) serve the camping area. The site is well lit. At the site entrance there is a very attractive swimming pool surrounded by tropical plants and with plenty of space to sunbathe. There are no toboggans here and the atmosphere is convivial and relaxed. The site is situated just two kilometres from the beach and La Flotte-en-Ré with its harbour-side restaurants is even closer.

| Facilities | Directions |
|---|---|
| The unisex, heated sanitary block is first class, with washbasins in cubicles, showers, British style WCs, facilities for children and disabled campers. Shop. Takeaway. Covered swimming pool (heated all season) and jacuzzi. Bicycle hire. Fridge hire. TV room. Charcoal barbecues are not permitted. Free WiFi over site. Off site: Beach, fishing, boat launching and sailing 2 km. Bar and restaurant 2 km. Riding 3 km. Golf 10 km.<br><br>**Open:** 1 April - 30 September. | Follow the signs for St Martin. The site is on the main road between La Flotte and St Martin. GPS: 46.18755, -1.344933 |

**Charges 2013**

| Per unit incl. 2 persons | |
|---|---|
| and electricity | € 21.50 - € 37.50 |
| extra person | € 5.50 - € 9.00 |
| child (0-7 yrs) | € 4.00 - € 5.00 |
| dog | € 2.50 - € 4.00 |

**LA GRAINETIERE** ★★★★

Open from April to September - Mobilhomes rentals and camping pitches
Reservation advised

Route de St Martin - Chemin des Essarts - 17630 La Flotte en Ré
Tél : (0033)5.46.09.68.86 - Fax : (0033)5.46.09.53.13
www.la-grainetiere.com / la-grainetiere@orange.fr

## La Roche-Posay

### Airotel la Roche Posay Vacances

Route de Lesigny, F-86270 La Roche-Posay (Vienne) T: 05 49 86 21 23. E: info@larocheposay-vacances.com
**alanrogers.com/FR86050**

Camping la Roche Posay is set in eight hectares and has direct access to the Creuse river on which fishing and canoes are popular. There are 200 pitches, of which 80 are used for mobile homes to rent. Access around the site is good for larger units. The pitches are all large and 16A electricity is available. This is a good, well run site in very natural surroundings. There is a sense of spaciousness where you can relax in a convivial atmosphere. Many different types of trees offer a mix of shade and the site is pleasantly landscaped.

| Facilities | Directions |
|---|---|
| Two fully equipped, heated toilet blocks, one in each section. Excellent facilities for disabled visitors and children. Bar, snack bar and takeaway. Heated, covered swimming and paddling pools. Play area. Games room. Fishing. Canoes. Boules. Riding. Barbecues are not permitted. Entertainment in high season. Bicycle hire. Off site: Shops, restaurants etc. 1 km. Golf 3 km.<br><br>**Open:** 13 April - 22 September. | Site is signed from the D725 town bypass, turning north at roundabout onto D5 towards Lesigny. Site is 50 m. on right. GPS: 46.799646, 0.80945 |

**Charges guide**

| Per unit incl. 2 persons | |
|---|---|
| and electricity | € 16.00 - € 28.00 |
| extra person | € 6.00 - € 8.00 |
| child | € 4.00 - € 6.00 |
| dog | € 1.00 - € 1.50 |

**FREE** Alan Rogers Travel Card
Extra benefits and savings - see page 10

## Le Bois-Plage-en-Ré

**Campéole les Amis de la Plage**

Campé**o**le

68 avenue du Pas des Boeufs, F-17580 Le Bois Plage en Ré (Charente-Maritime) T: 05 46 09 24 01.

E: les-amis-de-la-plage@campeole.com **alanrogers.com/FR17610**

Les Amis de la Plage, a former municipal site, is now a member of the Campéole group and located on the southern side of the Ile de Ré, at Le Bois-Plage-en-Ré. The site has direct access to a superb sandy beach (across sand dunes). This is a large site with 219 pitches, some of which are occupied by mobile homes, chalets and fully equipped tents. The 136 touring pitches are sandy with varying degrees of shade (some are rather small). Most have electrical connections (10A). There is a small shop on site for essentials, as well as a snack bar/pizzeria, and the island's largest market is held daily, just 500 m. from the site. The Ile de Ré is well known for its cycle tracks and a number of these pass close to the site. It has to be the best way to explore the island (rental service close to site). We also recommend the Maison du Platin, an interesting eco-museum, dedicated to the Ile de Ré's heritage and traditions.

**Facilities**

Three toilet blocks (one closed low season) provide some washbasins in cubicles and facilities for disabled visitors and children. Laundry. Motorcaravan service point. No shop, but bread to order daily. Play area with bouncy castle. Boules. Activity and entertainment programme (high season). Direct access to beach. Communal barbecue area. No charcoal barbecues on pitch. Mobile homes, chalets and tents for rent. WiFi (charged). Off site: Swimming pool and bar/restaurant near site entrance (charged). Market 500 m. Bicycle hire 1 km.

**Open:** 6 April - 30 September.

**Directions**

From La Rochelle, cross the toll bridge and take D201 along the southern coast of the island until you reach Le Bois-Plage-en-Ré, and then follow signs to the campsite. GPS: 46.177401, -1.386514

**Charges guide**

| | |
|---|---|
| Per unit incl. 2 persons and electricity | € 18.10 - € 24.00 |
| extra person | € 4.10 - € 6.30 |
| child (2-6 yrs) | free - € 4.00 |
| dog | € 2.50 - € 2.60 |

## Le Château-d'Oléron

**Airotel Oléron**

Domaine de Montravail, F-17480 Le Château-d'Oléron (Charente-Maritime) T: 05 46 47 61 82.

E: info@camping-airotel-oleron.com **alanrogers.com/FR17060**

This family run site on the outskirts of Le Château-d'Oléron has very good facilities, including a superb equestrian centre, a full range of sporting activities and an attractive heated pool complex. This is a mature site with 272 pitches of a good size, with varying degrees of shade provided by trees and attractive shrubs. It is well laid out and most of the 133 touring pitches have electricity (10A), four with individual water and drainage. The remaining pitches are used for mobile homes of which 50 are for rent. A full entertainment programme is provided in high season. Visitors can enjoy exploring the island with its fine sandy beaches on the Atlantic coast. There are miles of flat tracks on the island for walking.

**Facilities**

Two modern toilet blocks with facilities for disabled visitors and babies. Washing machine and dryer. Motorcaravan service point. Shop. Bar, restaurant and takeaway (15/6-15/9). Heated swimming and paddling pools. Equestrian centre. Playground. Multisport court. Tennis. Minigolf. Fishing. Bicycle hire. TV and games room. Internet access. WiFi (charged). Off site: Supermarket. Local markets. Zoo. Aquarium.

**Open:** Easter - 30 September.

**Directions**

Cross the bridge onto the island and continue on D26. At second roundabout turn right, marked Dolus and Le Château. Proceed 500 m. and take first right, marked Campings. Site is 1 km. on the right. GPS: 45.88207, -1.20648

**Charges guide**

| | |
|---|---|
| Per unit incl. 2 persons and electricity | € 19.70 - € 28.70 |
| extra person | € 4.50 - € 7.00 |

For latest campsite news, availability and prices visit
**alanrogers.com**

## Le Château-d'Oléron
### Camping la Brande

Route des Huitres, F-17480 Le Château-d'Oléron (Charente-Maritime) T: 05 46 47 62 37.
E: info@camping-labrande.com **alanrogers.com/FR17220**

An environmentally friendly site, run and maintained to a high standard, la Brande offers an ideal holiday environment on the delightful Ile d'Oléron. La Brande is situated on the oyster route and close to a sandy beach. Pitches here are generous and mostly separated by hedges and trees, the greater number for touring outfits. All are on level grassy terrain and have electricity hook-ups, some are fully serviced. Some of the most attractive pitches are in a newer section towards the back of the site. The many activities during the high season, plus the natural surroundings, make this an ideal choice for families. A feature of this site is the heated indoor pool (28°C) open all season. The Barcat family ensures that their visitors not only enjoy quality facilities, but Gerard Barcat offers guided bicycle tours and canoe trips. This way you discover the nature, oyster farming, vineyards and history of Oléron, which is joined to the mainland by a 3 km. bridge.

### Facilities

Three clean sanitary blocks have spacious, well equipped showers and washbasins (mainly in cabins). Baby facilities. Excellent facilities for visitors with disabilities (separate large shower, washbasin and WC). Private facilities (shower, basin and toilet) to rent. Laundry rooms. Motorcaravan service point. Superb restaurant/takeaway and bar (July/Aug). Shop (July/Aug). Heated indoor swimming pool (all season). Jacuzzi. Sauna. Well equipped playground. Games room. Football field. Tennis. Minigolf. Fishing. Archery. Bicycle hire. Canoe hire. Free WiFi. New building for children. Off site: Beach 300 m. Sailing 2 km. Riding 6 km. Golf 7 km.

**Open:** 20 March - 14 November.

### Directions

After crossing bridge to l'Ile d'Oléron turn right towards Château d'Oléron. Continue through village and follow sign for Route des Huitres. Site is on left after 2.5 km. GPS: 45.90415, -1.21525

### Charges guide

| | |
|---|---|
| Per unit incl. 2 persons and electricity | € 21.20 - € 44.00 |
| extra person | € 5.10 - € 8.10 |
| dog | € 3.00 |

## Les Mathes
### Camping l'Orée du Bois

225 route de la Bouverie, la Fouasse, F-17570 Les Mathes (Charente-Maritime) T: 05 46 22 42 43.
E: info@camping-oree-du-bois.fr **alanrogers.com/FR17050**

L'Orée du Bois has 341 pitches of about 100 sq.m. in a very spacious, pinewood setting. There are 88 for touring units, mainly scattered amongst the permanent chalets and tents. They include 40 large pitches with hardstanding and individual sanitary facilities (in blocks of four with shower, toilet, washbasin and dishwashing sink). Pitches are on flat, fairly sandy ground, separated by trees, shrubs and hedges and all have electrical connections (6A). The forest pines offer some shade. This is a family site with a good aqua park amongst the amenities as well as a splendid new children's playground.

**Facilities**

Four main toilet blocks include some washbasins in cabins. Facilities for disabled visitors. Laundry. Shop. Bar, restaurant, crêperie and takeaway service (1/5-13/9). Heated swimming pools (1/5-13/9), water slide and paddling pool (trunks, not shorts). Play areas. Tennis, boules, football and basketball. Games room and TV lounge. Adventure park. Bicycle hire. Entertainment in July/Aug. Discos. Barbecues provided in special areas only. WiFi (charged). Off site: Riding 300 m. Fishing 4 km.

**Open:** 1 May - 13 September.

**Directions**

From north follow D14 La Tremblade. At roundabout before Arvert turn on D268 (Les Mathes, La Palmyre). Site is on right in Fouasse. GPS: 45.7326, -1.1785

**Charges guide**

| | |
|---|---|
| Per unit incl. 2 persons and electricity | € 18.00 - € 41.50 |
| incl. private sanitary facility | € 27.00 - € 51.50 |
| extra person | € 8.00 |

Camping Cheques accepted.

## Les Mathes-La Palmyre
### Camping Caravaning Monplaisir

26 avenue de la Palmyre, F-17570 Les Mathes-La Palmyre (Charente-Maritime) T: 05 46 22 50 31.
E: camping-monplaisir@orange.fr **alanrogers.com/FR17110**

Monplaisir provides a small, quiet haven in an area with some very hectic campsites. It is ideal for couples or families with young children. Quite close to the town and set back from the road, the entrance leads through an avenue of trees, past the owner's home to a well kept, garden-like site with many trees and shrubs. There are 114 level, marked pitches and all but a few have 6A electrical connections. On 14 there are caravans for hire and a modern building provides flats and studios for rent. There is no shop, bar or restaurant but it is a happy, friendly site. Visitors return year after year.

**Facilities**

The toilet block has some washbasins in cabins and facilities for disabled visitors. Ice pack service in reception. Bread delivered daily. TV, games room and library. Heated swimming and paddling pools (early May-30/9). Small play area. Winter caravan storage. Off site: Bicycle hire opposite. Supermarket short walk. Minigolf adjacent (owned by site). Riding 500 m. Beach 4 km. Golf 5 km.

**Open:** Easter - 1 October.

**Directions**

From north on D14 (La Tremblade) turn onto D268 (Les Mathes and La Palmyre) at roundabout just before Arvert. Keep straight on to Les Mathes, road becomes D141. Turn left (north) at roundabout. Site is 600 m. on left. GPS: 45.71530, -1.15533

**Charges guide**

| | |
|---|---|
| Per unit incl. 2 persons and electricity | € 19.00 - € 22.50 |
| extra person | € 6.00 |

## Mazières
### Camping le Paradis

Mareuil, F-16270 Mazières (Charente) T: 05 45 84 92 06. E: info@le-paradis-camping.com
**alanrogers.com/FR16130**

Camping le Paradis is a small, immaculate, family run site open all year. You are assured of a very warm welcome here. There are 29 large, well spaced pitches with 24 for touring, separated by hedging and a variety of maturing trees give some shade. Nine are on grass and 15 have hardstanding. All have 10/16A electricity and many have a water tap. Five very large pitches are fully serviced with satellite TV point and drainage; ideal for very large units. The excellent facilities include large, spotlessly clean bathrooms with shower, washbasin and toilet.

**Facilities**

Superb toilet facilities with rooms having toilet, washbasin and shower, part heated in winter. Washing machine and dryer. Motorcaravan service point. Small shop for basics, bread to order (July/Aug). Internet point near reception. Caravan storage. Off site: Bakers and fishing 3 km. Riding, beach and bicycle hire 5 km. Supermarket 7 km. Many châteaux, chocolate factory, old towns and villages.

**Open:** All year.

**Directions**

Midway between Angoulême and Limoges leave N141 at La Péruse. Take D16 south, continue through Mazières. About 1 km. after Mazières turn right to site (signed). GPS: 45.832836, 0.558114

**Charges guide**

| | |
|---|---|
| Per unit incl. 2 persons and electricity | € 19.50 - € 22.50 |

Credit cards not accepted.

For latest campsite news, availability and prices visit
**alanrogers.com**

## Les Mathes-La Palmyre
### Camping la Clé des Champs

1188 route de la Fouasse, F-17570 Les Mathes-La Palmyre (Charente-Maritime) T: 05 46 22 40 53.
E: contact@cledeschamps.com **alanrogers.com/FR17540**

Situated on the edge of the large Forêt de la Coubre and around 1.5 km. from the village of Les Mathes, la Clé des Champs is a large site (7.6 hectares) and has 129 grass touring pitches (90 sq.m). Set amongst avenues of small trees, 80 have electricity (6/10A). This quiet campsite is flat, with 170 mobile homes (51 available to rent, the others privately owned) well positioned at the top end of the site. A new toilet block has been added which can be heated in cool weather. The swimming pool can be covered by a polythene structure in low season and a bar and shop are open from mid-June to September. Various cycle tracks lead through the forest to the beaches of the Côte Sauvage (bicycle hire is available on site). These stretch for 70 km. and sandy beaches alternate with rocky coves.

### Facilities

New toilet block, heated in cool weather. Washing machine. Shop. Bar. Snack bar/takeaway (mid June-Sept). Swimming pool. Paddling pool. Games room. Play area. Bicycle hire. Activity and entertainment programme (July/Aug). WiFi (charged). New wellness (jacuzzi, sauna) and fitness rooms. Mobile homes for rent. Charcoal barbecues are not permitted. Off site: Riding centre nearby. Minigolf 800 m. Les Mathes village 1.5 km. (good range of shops and restaurants). Nearest beach 4 km.

**Open:** 31 March - 15 November.

### Directions

From Saujon take the D14 heading northwest towards La Tremblade. At Arvert head south on the D141 to Les Mathes. Beyond the village, head right on the Route de la Fouasse and the site is on the right after a further 500 m.
GPS: 45.72098, -1.17149

### Charges guide

| Per unit incl. 2 persons | |
|---|---|
| and electricity | € 16.95 - € 29.95 |
| extra person | € 3.65 - € 5.10 |
| child (2-6 yrs) | € 3.05 - € 4.05 |
| dog | € 3.05 - € 3.25 |

**La Clé des Champs**
Hôtellerie de plein air ★★★★

**TEL. 05 46 22 40 53**
**www.la-cledeschamps.com**

Covered and heated swimming pool
Spa • Sauna • Animation • Gym
Mobil home rental
Multisport • Minigolf

1188, RTE DE LA FOUASSE • 17 570 LES MATHES-LA PALMYRE • FAX 05 46 22 56 96 • CONTACT@LA-CLEDESCHAMPS.COM

## Médis
### Camping le Clos Fleuri

8 impasse du Clos Fleuri, F-17600 Médis (Charente-Maritime) T: 05 46 05 62 17. E: clos-fleuri@wanadoo.fr
**alanrogers.com/FR17160**

Camping le Clos Fleuri really does live up to its name. The profusion of different trees and the lawns and flower beds give this small site a very rural atmosphere. There is always a warm welcome from the Devais family who created this site in 1974. The 123 touring pitches are mostly of generous size (a little uneven in places). They vary from being in full sun to well shaded and 100 have electrical connections. The bar/restaurant is a converted barn providing a cool haven on hot days and a venue for evening entertainment. The season here is short and services are only fully open in the height of the summer.

### Facilities

Toilet facilities are kept clean. One block is segregated male and female, the other is unisex with each unit in its own cubicle. Facility for disabled visitors. Baby baths. Laundry facilities. Small pool and paddling pool. Sauna. Shop (9/7-15/9). Restaurant (11/7-31/8) and bar (9/7-15/9). In high season there are twice weekly soirées and boules and archery competitions. Minigolf. WiFi. Large units should call in high season to check there is space. Off site: Médis 2 km.

**Open:** 1 June - 18 September.

### Directions

Médis is on the N150 from Saintes, halfway between Saujon and Royan. Drive into village. Site signed to south at various points in Médis and is 2 km. outside village. GPS: 45.63011, -0.9458

### Charges guide

| Per unit incl. 2 persons | |
|---|---|
| and electricity | € 22.90 - € 35.50 |
| extra person | € 6.50 - € 9.00 |
| child | € 5.00 - € 7.00 |

**FREE** Alan Rogers Travel Card
Extra benefits and savings - see page 10

## Montbron
### Castel Camping les Gorges du Chambon

Eymouthiers, F-16220 Montbron (Charente) T: 05 45 70 71 70. E: info@gorgesduchambon.fr

**alanrogers.com/FR16020**

This is a wonderful Castel site with 28 hectares of protected natural environment to be enjoyed in the rolling Perigord Vert countryside. Of 132 pitches, the 94 for touring are extremely generous in size (150 sq.m), slightly sloping and enjoy a mixture of sunshine and shade. There are 85 with water and 10A electricity, the remaining five are fully serviced. The spaciousness is immense, with fine walks through the woodlands and around the grounds. Flora and fauna are as nature intended. Here you can feel at peace and enjoy precious moments of quiet. There has been much work done with the ecology association. The songs of the birds can be heard against the backdrop of water flowing gently down a small river on one side of the campsite. The different types of birds that can be found here are numerous. Guided walks are a feature. Les Gorges du Chambon is arranged around a restored Charentaise farmhouse and its outbuildings. A converted barn provides space for the restaurant and bar and the food is excellent, at a reasonable price. There is a pleasant swimming pool together with a paddling pool. There is also a sand beach area along the river and canoes can be hired on the site. The site owners are friendly and very helpful and want you to enjoy your time at their site.

### Facilities

Traditional style blocks include facilities for disabled visitors. Washing machine, dryer. Shop. Bar, restaurant (all season). Takeaway (all season). Swimming pool (all season), children's pool (high season). Large play area. Games room, TV and library with English books. Tennis. Archery. Minigolf. Bicycle hire. Beach and canoe hire. Organised activities July/Aug, children's club, youth disco, teenagers' corner. WiFi (charged). Dogs are not accepted. Off site: Private fishing (free) 6 km, with licence 200 m. Golf and riding 6 km. Sailing 20 km. Visits are organised to local producers and day trips (low season).

**Open:** 20 April - 13 September.

### Directions

Leave N141 Angoulême-Limoges road at Rochefoucauld take D6 to Montbron (14 km). Continue on D6 for 4 km, turn north on D163, site is signed. After 2 km. turn right and follow lane up to site. GPS: 45.6598, 0.557667

### Charges guide

| Per unit incl. 2 persons | |
|---|---|
| and electricity | € 19.27 - € 33.26 |
| extra person | € 4.51 - € 9.13 |
| child (1-7 yrs) | € 1.83 - € 6.54 |

## Rivedoux-Plage

Campé**o**le

### Campéole le Platin

125 avenue Gustave Perreau, F-17940 Rivedoux-Plage (Charente-Maritime) T: 05 46 09 84 10.
E: platin@campeole.com **alanrogers.com/FR17560**

Located at the gateway to the Ile de Ré, le Platin is just a short walk from the pleasant village of Rivedoux Plage where there are several good restaurants and shops. In high season a small market is held every morning in the village square. A long, narrow site, the beach is on one side and the main road on the other. It is divided into small avenues with around 20 pitches in each. All have 8/10A electricity and most are shaded, although the pitches nearest the beach have little shade (but the best views). Of the 200 pitches, 50 are used for canvas bungalows for hire, the rest are seasonal and for touring. Popular with motorcaravanners, le Platin has a short stay area outside the barrier, and a bus stop 100 m. away makes it easy to explore the island and also to visit La Rochelle on the mainland.

### Facilities

The toilet facilities here are a little below standard, although one block has good showers and an en-suite bathroom for disabled visitors. Children's room. Motorcaravan service point. Small bar. Swimming pool complex is due for completion in June 2013. Play area. Trampoline. Entertainment in high season. WiFi (charged). Off site: Baker opposite. Bus to La Rochelle 100 m. Shops and restaurants in Rivedoux Plage 200 m. Bicycle hire 200 m. Cycle routes. Chaveau lighthouse.

**Open:** 6 April - 20 September.

### Directions

After crossing the toll bridge from La Rochelle, continue on the D735 into Rivedoux Plage. Site is well signed on the right. GPS: 46.1588, -1.2708

### Charges guide

| | |
|---|---|
| Per unit incl. 2 persons and electricity | € 19.10 - € 24.40 |
| extra person | € 7.80 - € 13.00 |
| child (over 6 yrs) | € 4.10 - € 6.20 |
| dog | € 2.50 - € 2.70 |

Campé**o**le
CAMPSITES AND RENTALS
Le Platin***
Three stars site facing the Ocean with direct access to the beach; quality facilities, touring pitches, and accommodations.
17940 Rivedoux-Plage · Tél.: +33-546-0984-10 · www.campeole.co.uk / platin@campeole.com

## Rivedoux-Plage

Campé**o**le

### Campéole la Redoute

504 avenue Gustave Perreau, F-17940 Rivedoux-Plage (Charente-Maritime) T: 05 46 09 84 10.
E: redoute@campeole.com **alanrogers.com/FR17565**

La Redoute is a member of the Campéole group and is located on the Ile de Ré, just 100 m. from one of the island's fine sandy beaches. This site has a range of mobile homes for rent but no touring pitches (although these are available on the adjacent Camping du Platin). Rental accommodation includes the new, top quality three bedroom Fisherman's Huts. All accommodation is provided with a fully equipped kitchen, including fridge freezer, and a terrace. On-site amenities include a children's play area with bouncy castle, entertainment room and a communal barbecue area. The site is attractively located close to the 100 km. of cycle tracks for which the island is renowned. There is a market, a bakery, a supermarket, a crêperie and a restaurant less than 200 m. away, and a bus stop with a direct service to La Rochelle. The nearby beach, accessed directly from the site via the back gate and a tunnel, is ideal for swimming, windsurfing or family beach games.

### Facilities

Laundry. Bar on sister site. Play area. Terraced sunbathing area. Entertainment room. Bouncy castle. WiFi (charged). Off site: Bus to La Rochelle 100 m. Shops and restaurants in Rivedoux Plage 200 m. Chaveau Lighthouse. Bicycle hire.

**Open:** 6 April - 30 September.

### Directions

From La Rochelle take N237 and continue over the bridge to the Ile de Ré. Continue towards Rivedoux and at the island turn immediately left into rue de Garenne. Site on right in 100 m.
GPS: 46.158956, -1.267545

### Charges guide

Contact site.

## Ronce-les-Bains

### Camping la Clairière

Rue des Roseaux, F-17390 Ronce-les-Bains (Charente-Maritime) T: 05 46 36 36 63.
E: info@camping-la-clairiere.com  **alanrogers.com/FR17480**

This site is attractively laid out with flowers, shrubs and trees. It is set away from the other campsites in the area and only 2.5 km. from the sea. Tranquil and peaceful, there is a feeling of spaciousness due to its setting within 12 hectares. The 147 pitches are level, shady and have easy access for large units. There are 32 mobile homes and chalets for rent. On-site facilities are impressive and include a covered pool, as well as a large outdoor aquapark with water slides. The gym here is well equipped with a good range of muscular training equipment for the energetically minded. Massages are also on offer.

**Facilities**

Two modern sanitary blocks. Baby room. No facilities for disabled visitors. Washing machines. Shop, bar, restaurant and takeaway (from June). Indoor and outdoor heated swimming pools, children's pool and 55 metre toboggan (all season). Games room with electronic games. Gym with exercise equipment. Massage. Children's club. Entertainment in July/Aug. Tennis. Pétanque. Minigolf. Basketball. Charcoal barbecues are not permitted. WiFi in some areas (charged). Dog shower. Off site: Riding 100 m. Fishing 2 km. Beach 2.5 km. Bicycle hire 3 km. Golf 9 km.

**Open:** 2 April - 24 September.

**Directions**

From roundabout at Les Mathes, take D25 to La Palmyre. Take first right and follow the signs for the site. GPS: 45.772933, -1.166734

**Charges guide**

| Per unit incl. 2 persons | |
|---|---|
| and electricity | € 20.00 - € 31.50 |
| extra person | € 5.00 - € 8.00 |
| child (2-10 yrs) | free - € 5.00 |
| dog | € 3.50 |

## Royan-Pontaillac

### Campéole Clairefontaine

Campé●le

6 rue du Colonel Lachaud, F-17200 Royan-Pontaillac (Charente-Maritime) T: 05 46 39 08 11.
E: clairefontaine@campeole.com  **alanrogers.com/FR17100**

Campéole Clairefontaine is situated on the outskirts of Royan, 300 m. from a golden sandy beach and a casino. This is a busy site which has benefited from much recent investment, and many of the facilities, especially the sanitary facilities, are of a high standard. There are 300 pitches, of which 115 are available for touring units. Electricity is available to all pitches, but some may require long leads. The site is mostly shaded with easy access to pitches. American motorhomes are accepted but care is needed on the entrance road to the site as it is not wide enough for two vehicles to pass. The reception area is large and welcoming and English is spoken. A programme of entertainment is provided in July and August and includes karaoke, singers and folk groups. There are many places of interest to visit: the nature reserves, the lighthouse at Cordouan, forests and the oyster beds of Marennes.

**Facilities**

Two very modern sanitary blocks. Good facilities for disabled visitors. Washing machines. Ironing room. Motorcaravan services. Bar and restaurant with takeaway (June-mid Sept). Large swimming and paddling pools (from June). Four play areas. Games room with TV. Tennis. Basketball. Entertainment in high season. Internet access. WiFi in some areas (charged). Accommodation to rent (123 units). Off site: Beach and sailing 300 m. Bicycle hire 350 m. Fishing 200 m. Riding and golf 10 km.

**Open:** 6 April - 30 September.

**Directions**

Exit Royan on Avenue de Pontaillac towards La Palmyre. Turn right at the casino on the front, up Avenue Louise. Site is on left after 200 m. and is signed. GPS: 45.631388, -1.050122

**Charges guide**

| Per unit incl. 2 persons | |
|---|---|
| and electricity | € 20.00 - € 31.70 |
| extra person | € 4.60 - € 9.60 |
| child (2-10 yrs) | free - € 5.60 |
| dog | € 2.50 - € 3.50 |

For latest campsite news, availability and prices visit
## alanrogers.com

## Saint Augustin-sur-Mer

### Le Logis du Breuil

F-17570 Saint Augustin-sur-Mer (Charente-Maritime) T: 05 46 23 23 45. E: info@logis-du-breuil.com
**alanrogers.com/FR17190**

The first impression on arrival at this impressive campsite is one of space. The site covers a 30-hectare expanse of farm pasture where (on different areas) cattle graze and children play. The 9 hectare camping areas are set among rows of mature and shady trees giving a dappled effect to the 314 grassy pitches. There are 250 with 3-10A electricity and all are very large with direct access to wide, unpaved alleys which lead on to the few tarmac roads around the site. The amenities are centred around the reception area and pool complex. The area around the site is very pleasant agricultural land and the beaches of the Atlantic coast are nearby, as are the oyster and mussel beds of Marennes and La Tremblade.

**Facilities**

Four well maintained toilet blocks are spaced around the camping area. Laundry facilities. Excellent shop, bar, restaurant and takeaway. Swimming pools (20/5-15/9). No evening entertainment. Play area. Indoor games area. Bicycle hire. Tennis. Excursions organised. WiFi (charged). Gites, mobile homes and chalets to rent. Off site: Beach 10 minute drive to St Palais-sur-Mer and La Grande-Côte. Sailing 5 km.

**Open:** 12 May - 30 September.

**Directions**

From A10 exit 35, take the N150 to Saujon and continue on the N150 to Royan. Take the D25 towards La Palmyre (Zoo), then turn right onto the D145 towards Saint Augustin. Site is signed and is 2 km. on the left. GPS: 45.67448, -1.096232

**Charges guide**

| Per unit incl. 2 persons | |
|---|---|
| and electricity | € 19.35 - € 28.10 |
| extra person | € 4.15 - € 7.20 |

## Saint Clément-des-Baleines

### Camping les Baleines

Le Gillieux, F-17590 Saint Clément-des-Baleines (Charente-Maritime) T: 05 46 29 40 76.
E: camping.lesbaleines@wanadoo.fr  **alanrogers.com/FR17400**

This campsite is situated at the far end of the island near the Balaines lighthouse and Le Conche beach, considered to be one of the most beautiful beaches on the island. This is an attractive well maintained, spacious site on different levels, occupying a good position next to the long golden sandy beach. It has 206 pitches of which 150 are for touring (most with 10A electricity) and the remaining 56 are for chalets and mobile homes. They are level, mostly open and easily accessible with some of a generous size. Large American-style motorhomes are accepted. The campsite has a large attractive 18-hole minigolf course together with a well equipped adventure-style playground. A children's miniclub is arranged in July and August. This is a good base to explore the islands many sites and monuments of interest, such as the ornithological park, the salt marshes and the charming little ports of local character. Saint Martin has an array of shops, restaurants and bars which surround the marina.

**Facilities**

Three modern sanitary blocks with good facilities for disabled visitors and babies. Washing machine, dryer and ironing room. Snack bar (July/Aug). Small shop. Boules. Play area. Organised activities for children in July/Aug. Minigolf. TV room. WiFi. Bicycle hire. No barbecues. Off site: Fishing and riding 500 m. Golf 4 km. Sailing 10 km. Cycle trails.

**Open:** 14 April - 22 September.

**Directions**

Take D735 to Phare des Baleines. When you approach the lighthouse, go through the car park and turn left just before the shops and the campsite is 300 m. further on. (3 km. after Ars-en-Ré, the site is signed). GPS: 46.23991, -0.55994

**Charges guide**

| Per unit incl. 2 persons | |
|---|---|
| and electricity | € 20.50 - € 35.00 |
| extra person (over 2 yrs) | € 4.10 - € 5.10 |
| dog | € 2.00 - € 4.00 |

Camping *Les Baleines* ★★★
Le Gillieux | 17590 ST-CLEMENT DES BALEINES
Ile de Ré | Charente maritime | Poitou-Charentes

Tel: +33 (0)5 46 29 40 76 | www.camping-lesbaleines.com | camping.lesbaleines@wanadoo.fr

**FREE** Alan Rogers Travel Card
Extra benefits and savings - see page 10

## Saint Clément-des-Baleines
### Village Center la Côte Sauvage

336 rue de la Forêt, F-17590 Saint Clément-des-Baleines (Charente-Maritime) T: 08 25 00 20 30.
E: contact@village-center.com **alanrogers.com/FR17965**

Camping la Côte Sauvage is a member of the Village Center Group, located on the Ile de Ré, close to the pretty village of Saint Clement-des-Baleines. There are 274 pitches here (80-100 sq.m), as well as a number of fully equipped tents which are available for rent. Unusually, the site also offers ten traditional yurts which have been attractively prepared in traditional style. Activities here are designed to take advantage of the site's natural setting and include ornithology and twilight nature trails. In high season, there is a mobile snack bar which also serves ice creams. Shops, bars and restaurants can be found within walking distance.

**Facilities**

Three (unheated) toilet blocks with British style WCs, mainly open washbasins and preset showers in cubicles. Facilities for children and disabled visitors. Laundry. Motorcaravan service point. Mobile snack bar. Play area. Children's activity programme. Small library. Volleyball. Boules. Bicycle hire. WiFi over part of site (charged). Fully equipped tents for rent. Off site: Shops and restaurants at St Clement-des-Baleines. Daily market in all villages (July/Aug). Cycle tracks. Riding. Ornithology and nature trails. Nature reserve at Lilleau des Niges 10 km.

**Open:** 2 April - 1 October.

**Directions**

Approaching from the toll bridge, follow D735 past La Couarde-sur-Mer and Ars-en-Ré as far as St Clement-des-Baleines. The site is well signed from here. GPS: 46.225423, -1.54462

**Charges guide**

| Per unit incl. 2 persons | |
|---|---|
| and electricity | € 17.00 - € 25.00 |
| extra person | € 5.00 |
| dog | € 3.00 |

## Saint Cyr
### Flower Camping du Lac de Saint Cyr

F-86130 Saint Cyr (Vienne) T: 05 49 62 57 22. E: contact@campinglacdesaintcyr.com
**alanrogers.com/FR86090**

This well organised, five-hectare campsite is part of a 300-hectare leisure park, based around a large lake with sailing and associated sports, and an area for swimming (supervised July/Aug). Land-based activities include tennis, two half courts, table tennis, fishing, badminton, pétanque, beach volleyball, TV room, and a well equipped fitness suite, all of which are free of charge. The campsite has around 185 touring pitches, ten mobile homes and three yurts (canvas and wooden tents) for rent. The marked and generally separated pitches are all fully serviced with electricity (10A), water and drainage. Spacious and very natural, this is a tranquil setting. This site will appeal to a wide range of people of all ages.

**Facilities**

The main toilet block is modern and supplemented for peak season by a second unit, although they do attract some use by day trippers to the leisure facilities. They include washbasins in cubicles, laundry facilities, and facilities for babies and disabled visitors. Shop, restaurant and takeaway (April-Sept). Playground on beach. Bicycle hire. Barrier locked 22.00-07.00 (€ 10 deposit for card). WiFi (free). New heated swimming pool (2011). Off site: Riding 200 m. Golf 800 m. Watersports and numerous other leisure activities around the lake.

**Open:** 1 April - 30 September.

**Directions**

Saint Cyr is midway between Châtellerault and Poitiers. Site signed to east of N10 at Beaumont along D82 towards Bonneuil-Matours, and is part of the Parc de Loisirs de Saint Cyr. GPS: 46.71972, 0.46018

**Charges guide**

| Per unit incl. 2 persons | |
|---|---|
| and electricity | € 15.00 - € 27.00 |
| extra person | € 3.00 - € 5.00 |
| child (2-7 yrs) | € 2.00 - € 3.00 |
| dog | € 1.50 |

Advantage all the way

alan rogers

Travel Card

Got yours yet?
**Extra benefits and savings** - see page 10

For latest campsite news, availability and prices visit
# alanrogers.com

## Saint Georges-d'Oléron
### Camping les Gros Joncs

850 route de Ponthezieres, les Sables Vignier B.P. 17, F-17190 Saint Georges-d'Oléron (Charente-Maritime)
T: 05 46 76 52 29. E: info@les-gros-joncs.fr **alanrogers.com/FR17070**

Situated on the west coast of the island of Ile d'Oléron, les Gros Joncs is owned and run by the Cavel family who work hard to keep the site up to date and of high quality. There are 50 or so touring pitches of a good size (some extra large) with tall pine trees providing a choice between full sun and varying degrees of shade. All have water and 10A electricity to hand. The main building not only houses a light and airy reception, but also a modern, beautifully presented bar and restaurant, a fully stocked and competitively priced shop, an attractive indoor swimming pool and a magnificent spa. The indoor pool, with water jets and jacuzzi, has glass sides which in good weather are opened out onto an outdoor pool area where there are also water slides, a paddling area and plenty of sunbathing terraces. Both pools are heated. The spa offers hydrotherapy and beauty treatments, sauna, and a comprehensive fitness room. Much attention has been given to the needs of disabled visitors here, including chalets where space and equipment are specially adapted. All the amenities are of a standard unusual on a campsite.

### Facilities

Traditional style toilet facilities are kept to a high standard. Laundry facilities. Motorcaravan services. Well stocked shop with bakery and restaurant (1/4-15/9). Indoor pool with first class spa and wellness centre (all year, with professional staff). Outdoor pool (heated, 1/4-15/9). Bicycle hire. Children's clubs (July-Aug). Internet access and WiFi (charged). ATM. No charcoal barbecues.
Off site: Beach 200 m and 400 m. via a sandy path. Bus service from Chéray. Fishing 2 km. Riding 2 km. Golf 12 km.

**Open:** April - October.

### Directions

Cross the viaduct onto the Ile d'Oléron. Take D734 (St Georges-d'Oléron). At traffic lights in Chéray turn left. Follow signs for camping and Sable Vignier. Soon signs indicate directions to les Gros Joncs. GPS: 45.95356, -1.37979

### Charges guide

| | |
|---|---|
| Per unit incl. 2 persons and electricity | € 19.30 - € 48.10 |
| extra person | € 3.00 - € 12.60 |
| child (0-7 yrs) | € 3.00 - € 7.70 |
| dog | free - € 3.00 |

Les Sables Vignier - Route Côtière entre Domino et La Cotinière - 17190 Saint-Georges d'Oléron
Tél. : 05 46 76 52 29 - www.camping-les-gros-joncs.com

**FREE** Alan Rogers Travel Card
**Extra benefits and savings** - see page 10

## Saint Georges-d'Oléron
### Camping l'Anse des Pins

Chemin du Râteau-Domino, F-17190 Saint Georges-d'Oléron (Charente-Maritime) T: 02 51 56 08 78.
E: contacts@camping-apv.com **alanrogers.com/FR17270**

Rock pools, sand dunes and spectacular sunsets, with sea views from many of the pitches, help to make this site attractive to those seeking an 'away from it all' holiday in a quiet part of the island of the Ile d'Oléron. The campsite, which has direct access to a beautiful sandy beach, is arranged in three areas, some with good shade, others in full sun. There are 350 pitches including 137 for touring units, the remainder used for mobile homes. All pitches have electricity (3-10A) and 22 also have water and drainage. Across the road are the leisure facilities which include a complex of outdoor pools (unheated) with a toboggan and a flume, and an indoor pool with a sauna.

**Facilities**

Two main toilet blocks (plus two small blocks for high season use) with mainly British style toilets. Showers and washbasins in cabins. Laundry facilities. Gas supplies. Bar. Shop with limited takeaway and snack bar. Indoor pool (all season) and outdoor swimming and paddling pools with slides (April-Sept). Play area. Activities in high season (1/7-31/8). Tennis. Boules. Bicycle hire. Internet point and WiFi. Entertainment and business complex. Barbecues only permitted in a communal area.

**Open:** 7 April - 23 September.

**Directions**

Cross bridge onto Ile d'Oléron and follow the D734 (St Dennis). In Chéray, turn left at lights (signed Camping). Continue to Domino (avoid side roads). Follow green signs to Rex and l'Anse des Pins Camping. Narrow roads. GPS: 45.97059, -1.3864

**Charges guide**

| | |
|---|---|
| Per unit incl. 2 persons and electricity | € 22.50 - € 37.30 |
| extra person | € 7.80 - € 8.30 |

## Saint Georges-d'Oléron
### Camping la Campière

Chemin de l'Achnau, Chaucre, F-17190 Saint Georges-d'Oléron (Charente-Maritime) T: 05 46 76 72 25.
E: contact@la-campiere.com **alanrogers.com/FR17275**

Close to the Côte Sauvage and the Plage de Chaucre, this friendly, family run site is probably best suited to couples looking for a quiet, relaxing break. It is in a protected area of the state forest, 400 m. from one of the most beautiful beaches on the island. There are 66 good sized, grassy pitches, some open, others among tall pine trees. Most have electricity (10A), water and drainage. The surrounding area is well worth exploring and has numerous cycling and walking routes. The focal point of the site is a small wine bar. Owners of large outfits should phone ahead to reserve the larger pitches.

**Facilities**

One unheated toilet block has washbasins (some in cubicles) and controllable showers. Family room. Facilities for disabled visitors. Laundry facilities. Motorcaravan service point. Small wine bar with terrace, and takeaway (7/4-30/9). Bread can be ordered. Small heated swimming pool. Library. Play area. Basketball. Bicycle hire. Communal barbecue. Free WiFi over part of site. Accommodation to rent. Off site: Beach 300 m. Fishing 2 km. Riding 6 km. Golf 8 km. Amenities in Cheray 6 km.

**Open:** 7 April - 30 September.

**Directions**

Take exit 35 from A10 (Saintes), then west on D728 to Marennes. Cross viaduct to Ile d'Oléron and follow D26 and D734 to Saint Pierre d'Oléron. Continue on D734 to Cheray. At end of village take second left turn to Chaucre then follow campsite signs. GPS: 45.992475, -1.38001

**Charges guide**

| | |
|---|---|
| Per unit incl. 2 persons and electricity | € 21.80 - € 34.80 |
| extra person | € 4.50 - € 8.00 |

## Saint Georges-d'Oléron
### Chadotel le Domaine d'Oléron

La Jousselinière, F-17190 Saint Georges-d'Oléron (Charente-Maritime) T: 05 46 76 54 97.
E: domainedoleron@orange.com **alanrogers.com/FR17470**

This is a neat, well presented and well managed site where you will receive a warm and friendly welcome from Anneke and Freddy who speak excellent English. The site is set in a peaceful rural location between St Pierre and St Georges and is part of the Chadotel group. At present there are 172 pitches of which 60 are for touring units. The pitches are generously sized (100-150 sq.m) and are mostly sunny, level and easily accessible, all with 10A electricity. The site is just 3 km. from the beach.

**Facilities**

Two modern sanitary blocks include facilities for disabled visitors and babies. Washing machines and dryers. Ironing room. Restaurant, snack bar and takeaway, bar with TV (all 15/5-10/9). Bread delivered daily. Swimming pool with slides (1/5-14/9). Adventure style play area. Six pétanque lanes. Bicycle hire. Organised entertainment two or three times a week in July/Aug. Gas barbecues only on pitches, communal areas for charcoal. WiFi over site (charged).

**Open:** 6 April - 21 September.

**Directions**

Take D734 to St Pierre. Turn right after Leclerc supermarket. At next roundabout turn left towards Le Bois Fleury. After airfield, turn right, then left and site is on the left. GPS: 45.9674685, -1.3192605

**Charges guide**

| | |
|---|---|
| Per unit incl. 2 persons and electricity | € 15.50 - € 31.00 |
| extra person | € 5.90 |

For latest campsite news, availability and prices visit
# alanrogers.com

## Saint Georges-les-Baillargeaux
### Kawan Village le Futuriste

RD 20, F-86130 Saint Georges-les-Baillargeaux (Vienne) T: 05 49 52 47 52.
E: camping-le-futuriste@wanadoo.fr **alanrogers.com/FR86040**

Le Futuriste is a neat, modern site, open all year and close to Futuroscope. Its location is convenient for the A10 and N10 motorway network. There are 123 individual, level, grassy pitches of a generous size and divided by flowering hedges. Seventy-six have electricity (6A) and 64 also have water and waste water connections. Pitches are mostly open although some do have the benefit of shade from trees. All are accessed via tarmac roads. There are lovely panoramic views from this site and the popular attraction of Futuroscope can be clearly seen. Large units are accepted by prior arrangement. There is a pleasant restaurant on site offering good food at reasonable prices. Entertainment takes place in the daytime rather than in the evenings. This site is ideal for a short stay to visit Futuroscope which is only 2 km. away but it is equally good for longer stays to see the region.

### Facilities

Excellent, clean sanitary facilities in two heated blocks. Good facilities for disabled visitors and babies. Laundry facilities. Shop (1/5-30/9, bread to order). Bar/restaurant snack bar and takeaway (1/7-31/8). Heated outdoor pool with slide and paddling pool (1/7-31/8). Covered pool. Games room. TV. Boules. Multisports area. Lake fishing. Daily activities in season. Youth groups not accepted. Only gas and electric barbecues allowed. Off site: Bicycle hire 500 m. Hypermarket 600 m. Futuroscope 2 km. Golf 5 km. Riding 10 km.

**Open:** All year.

### Directions

From either A10 autoroute or N10, take Futuroscope exit. Site is east of both roads, off D20 (St Georges-les-Baillargeaux). Follow signs to St Georges. Site on hill; turn by water tower and site is on left. GPS: 46.66447, 0.394564

### Charges guide

| | |
|---|---|
| Per unit incl. 3 persons and electricity | € 21.60 - € 29.10 |
| extra person | € 2.60 - € 3.50 |
| dog | € 2.50 |

Camping Cheques accepted.

Open all year. Panoramic view over the Futuroscope situated at 2 kms. Heated swimming pool, pond, snack, bar, restaurant. Chalets for hire.

86130 St-Georges les Baillargeaux
Tel.: 0033 549 52 47 52
Fax: 0033 549 37 23 33
www.camping-le-futuriste.fr

## Saint Georges-de-Didonne

### Camping Bois Soleil

2 avenue de Suzac, F-17110 Saint Georges-de-Didonne (Charente-Maritime) T: 05 46 05 05 94.
E: camping.bois.soleil@wanadoo.fr **alanrogers.com/FR17010**

Close to the sea, Bois Soleil is a large site in three parts, with 165 serviced pitches for touring units and a few for tents. All the touring pitches are hedged and have electricity (6/10A), with water and drainage between two. The main part, Les Pins, is attractive with trees and shrubs providing shade. Opposite is La Mer with direct access to the beach, some areas with less shade and an area for tents. The third part, La Forêt, is for caravan holiday homes. It is best to book your preferred area as it can be full mid June to late August. Excellent private sanitary facilities are available to rent, either on your pitch or at a block (subject to availability). There are a few pitches with lockable gates. The areas are all well tended and are cleared and raked between visitors. This lively site offers something for everyone, whether it be a beach-side spot or a traditional pitch, plenty of activities or the quiet life. Recent additions include a new toilet block and some accommodation to rent with sea views. The wide sandy beach is popular with children and provides a pleasant walk to the pretty town of Saint Georges-de-Didonne.

**Facilities**

Each area has one large and one small sanitary block. Heated block near reception. Cleaned twice daily, they include facilities for disabled visitors and babies. Launderette. Supermarket, bakery and beach shop (15/4-15/9). Restaurant, bar and takeaway (15/4-15/9). Swimming pool (heated 15/6-15/9). Steam room. Tennis. Bicycle hire. Play area. TV room and library. Internet terminal and WiFi. Charcoal barbecues are not permitted. Dogs are not accepted 26/6-5/9. Off site: Fishing 200 m. Riding 500 m. Golf 20 km.

**Open:** 2 April - 9 October.

**Directions**

From Royan centre take coast road (D25) along the seafront of St Georges-de-Didonne towards Meschers. Site is signed at roundabout at end of the main beach. GPS: 45.583583, -0.986533

**Charges guide**

| | |
|---|---|
| Per unit incl. 3 persons and electricity | € 26.00 - € 45.00 |
| extra person | € 3.00 - € 8.50 |
| child (3-7 yrs) | free - € 6.50 |
| dog (not 26/6-5/9) | € 3.00 - € 4.00 |

Less 20% outside July/Aug.
Camping Cheques accepted.

## Saint Hilaire-la-Palud

### Flower Camping le Lidon

F-79210 Saint Hilaire-la-Palud (Deux-Sèvres) T: 05 49 35 33 64. E: info@le-lidon.com
**alanrogers.com/FR79060**

Le Lidon is located within the Marais Poitevin, an enchanting region of over 400 km. of rivers, canals and fens lying to the west of Niort. This site has 132 grassy pitches scattered across three hectares, 116 for touring. The site's selection of rented accommodation includes fully equipped, Canadian-style tents and chalets. The Marais Poitevin is undeniably best explored by canoe or punt and it is possible to rent these on site. During high season, an activity and entertainment programme is organised including a children's club and family activities. The site bar/restaurant is open all season and specialises in local cuisine.

**Facilities**

Two toilet blocks (one closed in low season) with facilities for disabled visitors and children. Shop, bar, snack bar (all season). Bread available to order from the restaurant. Laundry. Heated swimming pool (15/6-31/8). Games room. Play area. Motorcaravan service point. Direct access to river. Fishing. Bicycle and canoe hire. Entertainment and activity programme (July/Aug). Tents and chalets for rent. Off site: St Hilaire-la-Palud with a good selection of shops and cafés, as well as an open-air cinema. Fishing (river). La Maison des Oiseaux (ornithological centre). Riding 2 km. Tennis 3 km. Golf 25 km. Vendée beaches 50 km. Cycle and walking tracks.

**Open:** 9 April - 17 September.

**Directions**

St Hilaire-la-Palud is midway between Niort and La Rochelle. From the north (Niort) leave A10 at exit 33 and head west on N248 as far as Epannes. Head north here on D1 to Sansais, then west on D3 to St Hilaire-la-Palud. Site is signed to right just after village. Long access road. GPS: 46.2838, -0.74345

**Charges guide**

| | |
|---|---|
| Per unit incl. 2 persons and electricity | € 20.10 - € 26.00 |
| extra person | € 5.20 - € 6.00 |
| child (2-7 yrs) | € 2.00 - € 2.60 |
| dog | € 2.00 - € 2.50 |

Camping Cheques accepted.

For latest campsite news, availability and prices visit
**alanrogers.com**

# ★★★★★ BOIS - SOLEIL

Half-way between Great Britain and Spain in the middle of the Romanesque Saintonge area, Bois Soleil will seduce you with its wooded parks and its direct access to a 4 km long sand beach.

Bar, restaurant, panoramic terraces, heated swimming pool 240 m² with balneo and paddling pool, hammam, fitness, internet, library.
Entertainment in July and August.

2, avenue de Suzac, 17110 Saint-Georges de Didonne
Tél. +33 (0)5.46.05.05.94
http://www.bois-soleil.com
camping.bois.soleil@wanadoo.fr

## Saint Just-Luzac

### Castel Camping Séquoia Parc

La Josephtrie, F-17320 Saint Just-Luzac (Charente-Maritime) T: 05 46 85 55 55. E: info@sequoiaparc.com

alanrogers.com/FR17140

This is definitely a site not to be missed. Approached by an avenue of flowers, shrubs and trees, Séquoia Parc is a Castel site set in the grounds of La Josephtrie, a striking château with beautifully restored outbuildings and courtyard area with a bar and restaurant. Most of the 640 pitches are 140 sq.m. with 6/10A electricity connections and separated by mature shrubs providing plenty of privacy. The site has 350 mobile homes and chalets, with a further 65 used by tour operators. This is a popular site with a children's club and entertainment throughout the season and reservation is necessary in high season. The site itself is designed to a high specification with reception in a large, light and airy room retaining its original beams and leading to the courtyard area where you find the bar and restaurant. The pool complex with water slides, large paddling pool and sunbathing area is impressive. A new terraced area adjacent to the snack bar allows you to enjoy your food in a very pleasant garden setting with sunshades. A member of Leading Campings group.

**Facilities**

Three spotlessly clean luxurious toilet blocks (one heated) include units with washbasin and shower and facilities for disabled visitors and children. Large laundry. Motorcaravan service point. Gas supplies. Large supermarket. Boutique. Restaurant/bar and takeaway. Impressive swimming pool complex with water slides and large paddling pool. Massage (July/Aug). Multisports pitch. Tennis. Games and TV rooms. Bicycle hire. Play areas. Pony trekking. Entertainment all season. Children's farm. WiFi (charged). Off site: Bank and supermarket 5 km.

**Open:** 8 May - 8 September (with all services).

**Directions**

Site is 5 km. southeast of Marennes. From Rochefort take D733 south for 12 km. Turn west on D123 to Ile d'Oléron. Continue for 12 km. Turn southeast on D728 (Saintes). Site signed, in 1 km. on left. From A10 at Saintes take D728 and turn right shortly after St Just. Site signed. GPS: 45.81095, -1.06109

**Charges guide**

| | |
|---|---|
| Per unit incl. 2 persons and electricity | € 18.00 - € 48.00 |
| extra person | € 7.00 - € 9.00 |

### Castel Camping Séquoia Parc
★★★★★

www.sequoiaparc.com

NEAR OLÉRON ISLAND AND ITS BEACHES
AQUAPARK OF 2000 M²!
KIDS CLUB DURING WHOLE SEASON
ANIMATIONS AND HORSERIDING
BAR RESTAURANT LE CARROUSEL
LARGE PITCHES
LUXURIOUS COTTAGES, MOBILEHOMES

Open from 08/05 - 08/09/2013
Online bookings: www.sequoiaparc.com
17320 Saint Just-Luzac, France,
tel.: +33 5 46 85 55 55

## Saint Palais-sur-Mer

### Camping Le Logis

22 rue des Palombes, F-17420 Saint Palais-sur-Mer (Charente-Maritime) T: 05 46 23 20 23.
E: reservations@yukadivillages.com  alanrogers.com/FR17530

Le Logis is a member of the Yukadi Villages group and is a popular site close to the attractive resort of St-Palais-sur-Mer on the edge of the forest of St Augustin. The site was established back in 1936 and there are now 647 pitches here. The majority of these are occupied by mobile homes and chalets (many for rent) but there are 208 touring pitches also available. These are grassy and of a reasonable size, and all have 5A electrical connections. This is a lively site in high season with a varied programme of entertainment and activities, including concerts and discovery excursions into the forest.

**Facilities**

Four heated sanitary blocks are well situated around the site. Facilities for disabled visitors. Laundry. Shop, bar and snack bar. Excellent water park with heated pools, children's pool and water slides. Games room. Tennis. Play area. TV room. New multisports area. Bicycle hire. Activity and entertainment programme. Free WiFi over part of site. Mobile homes and chalets for rent. Off site: Fishing and golf 600 m. Nearest beach 600 m. Riding 800 m.

**Open:** 27 April - 9 September.

**Directions**

From Royan, head west on D25 towards La Palmyre. Pass the golf course (on the right), and then turn left immediately towards St Palais-sur-Mer. Turn left at the next crossroads and site is 200 m. further on the right. GPS: 45.65208, -1.1159

**Charges guide**

| | |
|---|---|
| Per unit incl. 2 persons | € 21.00 - € 40.80 |
| extra person | € 4.20 - € 8.40 |

For latest campsite news, availability and prices visit
## alanrogers.com

## Saint Trojan-les-Bains
### Camping Indigo Oléron les Pins
11 avenue des Bris, F-17370 Saint Trojan les Bains (Charente-Maritime) T: 05 46 76 02 39.
E: oleron@camping-indigo.com **alanrogers.com/FR17580**

This attractive five hectare site is a member of the Indigo group. It can be found close to the popular seaside resort of St-Trojan-les-Bains on the south side of the island. There are 225 pitches, which vary in size, most of which have electrical connections (10A French type). Indigo Oléron is situated in a lightly wooded setting on undulating, sandy terrain, just 1 km. from the nearest sandy beach. Building materials must be sympathetic with the natural environment, for example, the use of wooden decking around the pool and you won't find mobile homes for rent here, only specially designed wood and canvas safari-style tents. The island is popular with cyclists and a track leads from the site to the village centre. In high season, a snack bar service is available. There is a Spar shop in the village. Oléron is the second largest French island (after Corsica) and is easily accessed thanks to the toll-free bridge. The island's beaches are deservedly famous, backed by the large pine forest, and surfing is also very popular here.

### Facilities
Two very modern toilet blocks provide washbasins in cabins, showers and British style toilets. Ramped facilities for disabled visitors. Laundry. Motorcaravan service point. Heated swimming pool (June-Sept). Small bar, snack bar and takeaway (July/Aug). Bicycle hire. Sandy play area. Activity and entertainment programme. Only gas or electric barbecues allowed. Max. 1 dog. Off site: Beach and fishing 500 m. Tourist train at St Trojan. Walking and cycling tracks. Riding 1 km. Supermarket 3 km.

**Open:** End April - end September.

### Directions
From Marennes, cross bridge to Ile d'Oléron (D26) then follow signs to St Trojan on D126. Drive through shopping area to second roundabout. Turn right and continue ahead. Follow the railway track and where the road bends left, follow the road and the site is on your left. GPS: 45.831247, -1.213591

### Charges guide
Per unit incl. 2 persons
and electricity € 19.60 - € 31.00
extra person € 3.60 - € 5.20

## Vaux-sur-Mer
### Camping le Nauzan Plage
39 avenue de Nauzan Plage, F-17640 Vaux-sur-Mer (Charente-Maritime) T: 05 46 38 29 13.
E: info@campinglenauzanplage.com **alanrogers.com/FR17825**

Le Nauzan Plage is a well equipped family site close to the popular resort of Royan. This is a lively site in peak season with a wide range of amenities and activities. These include swimming pools for adults and children, a children's playground and bouncy castle, as well as a snack bar with takeaway food, and a well stocked shop. The nearest beach (Nauzan Plage) is just 450 m. away. Pitches are grassy and generally well shaded; most have electricity (10A). The site is divided into two parts by a small stream.

### Facilities
Four (unheated) toilet blocks have washbasins and showers in cubicles. Separate facilities for children and disabled visitors. Laundry facilities. Motorcaravan service point. Shop, bar, snack bar and takeaway (all July/Aug). Swimming pool. Games and TV room. Sports field. Play area. Children's farm. Activity and entertainment programme. Bicycle hire. WiFi over part of site (charged). Mobile homes for rent. Off site: Nearest beach 450 m. Golf 5 km. Cycle and walking tracks. Royan.

**Open:** 2 April - 30 September.

### Directions
From Royan head west towards La Palmyre and Saint Palais. Upon reaching Vaux, head inland on Avenue de Anuran Plage and the site is well signed. GPS: 45.642683, -1.071905

### Charges guide
Per unit incl. 2 persons
and electricity € 22.40 - € 38.60
extra person € 3.75 - € 8.50
child (2-10 yrs) € 2.05 - € 6.40

 **FREE** Alan Rogers Travel Card
Extra benefits and savings - see page 10

We can book this site for you! alan rogers travel  Call 01580 214000

Burgundy is a wonderfully evocative region offering breathtaking châteaux and cathedrals, rolling hills and heady mountain views, vineyards and superlative cuisine, not to mention of course, a wide variety of world-renowned wines.

**DÉPARTEMENTS: 21 CÔTE D'OR, 58 NIÈVRE, 71 SAÔNE-ET-LOIRE, 89 YONNE**

**MAJOR CITY: DIJON**

In the rich heartland of France, Burgundy was once a powerful independent state and important religious centre. Its golden age is reflected in the area's magnificent art and architecture: the grand palaces and art collections of Dijon, the great pilgrimage church of Vézelay, the Cistercian Abbaye de Fontenay and the evocative abbey remains at Cluny, once the most powerful monastery in Europe.

However, Burgundy is best known for its wine, including some of the world's finest, notably from the great vineyards of the Côte d'Or and Chablis, and also for its sublime cuisine. You'll also notice how driving through the country villages is like reading a wine merchant's list with plenty of opportunities for tasting and choosing your wine.

The area is criss-crossed by navigable waterways and includes the Parc Régional du Morvan; good walking country amidst lush, rolling wooded landscape.

**Places of interest**

*Autun*: 12th-century St Lazare cathedral.

*Beaune*: medieval town; Museum of Burgundy Wine.

*Cluny*: Europe's largest Benedictine abbey.

*Dijon*: Palace of the Dukes, Fine Arts Museum, Burgundian Folklore Museum.

*Fontenay*: Fontenay Abbey and Cloister.

*Joigny*: medieval town.

*Mâcon*: Maison des Vins (wine centre).

*Paray-le-Monial*: Romanesque basilica, pilgrimage centre.

*Sens*: historic buildings, museum with fine Gallo-Roman collections.

*Vézelay*: fortified medieval hillside.

**Cuisine of the region**

Many dishes are wine based, and use fine ingredients such as Charolais beef, Bresse poultry, snails, truffles and mushrooms.

*Boeuf Bourguignon*: braised beef simmered in a red wine-based sauce.

*Garbure*: heavy soup, a mixture of pork, cabbage, beans and sausages.

*Gougère*: cheese pastry based on Gruyère.

*Jambon persillé*: parsley-flavoured ham, served cold in jelly.

*Matelote*: freshwater fish soup, usually based on a red wine sauce.

*Meurette*: red wine-based sauce with small onions, used with fish or poached egg dishes.

**www.burgundy-tourism.com**
**documentation@crt-bourgogne.fr**
**(0)3 80 28 02 80**

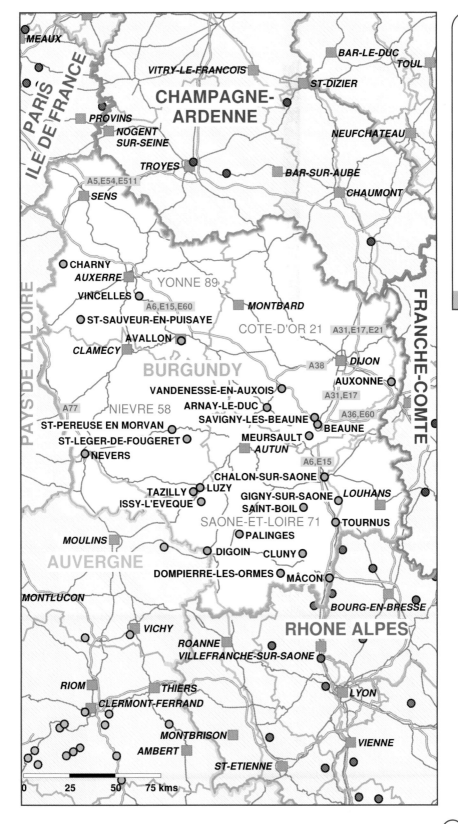

## Arnay-le-Duc

### Camping de l'Etang de Fouché

Rue du 8 mai 1945, F-21230 Arnay-le-Duc (Côte d'Or) T: 03 80 90 02 23. E: info@campingfouche.com

alanrogers.com/FR21040

Useful as a stop en route to or from the Mediterranean or indeed for longer stays, this quite large but peaceful, lakeside site with its new bar/restaurant and swimming pool complex, can be very busy during the school holidays, and is probably better visited outside the main season. There are over 200 good sized pitches, on fairly level grass and all with 10A electricity (some with water). Many are hedged and offer a choice of shade or more open aspect. In July/August there are regular activities for children and adults. A 2 km. stroll around the lake is very pleasant.

**Facilities**

Two new toilet blocks and third (totally refurbished) provide all the necessary modern facilities (male and female are separate). Facilities for disabled visitors. Baby room. Washing machines. Shop, bar, restaurant, takeaway (all 15/5-15/9). New small heated outdoor swimming pool (15/5-10/9). Boules. TV/games room. Playground. Fishing. Bicycle hire. WiFi. Off site: Town centre 800 m. Lakeside beach with playground, water slides, pedaloes, canoes.

**Open:** 15 April - 15 October.

**Directions**

From A6 (exit 24) take D981, 16 km. to the town. Turn left on D906 for 400 m. and site is signed to left. GPS: 47.13411, 4.49840

**Charges guide**

| Per unit incl. 2 persons | |
|---|---|
| and electricity | € 19.90 - € 25.90 |
| extra person | € 4.70 - € 6.50 |
| child (2-10 yrs) | € 2.40 - € 3.60 |
| dog | € 2.00 |

## Auxonne

### Camping de l'Arquebuse

Route d'Athée, F-21130 Auxonne (Côte d'Or) T: 03 80 31 06 89. E: camping.arquebuse@wanadoo.fr

alanrogers.com/FR21090

This is an all-year-round site located in the Northern Jura with a riverside setting on the Saône. L'Arquebuse has 100 level, unmarked pitches on grass, of which 17 are occupied by mobile homes and chalets. Most have 10A electricity and a variety of trees give shade to some pitches. Auxonne is close to both the A36 and A39 motorways and this site may prove a useful overnight stop. The site has bar/restaurant, Le Pinocchio, and the adjacent Base Nautique offers a good range of leisure activities, including canoeing, windsurfing, mountain biking as well as a large swimming pool. Auxonne is an attractive town, fortified by Vauban, and is renowned as the capital of the Saône valley. The town's most famous former occupant is Napoleon and he spent two years at the Auxonne military academy. Not surprisingly there are several monuments celebrating his time here!

**Facilities**

Basic toilet block, heated in winter, provides mostly Turkish-style toilets and open washbasins (cleaning can be variable). Washing machine. Small shop (1/5-31/10). Restaurant/bar (15/1-15/12). Pizzeria. Takeaway. Play area. TV room. WiFi. Chalets for rent. Off site: Swimming pool, windsurfing, canoeing, boat trips and fishing. Motorcaravan services. Fortified town of Auxonne with shops, bars and restaurants 1 km. Dijon 34 km.

**Open:** All year.

**Directions**

From the A39 autoroute take exit 5 and the N5 for 6 km. to Auxonne. Site is signed to the left just before crossing the bridge over the Saône. Site is a few hundred metres. GPS: 47.19941, 5.38365

**Charges guide**

| Per unit incl. 2 persons | |
|---|---|
| and electricity | € 18.00 - € 20.50 |
| extra person | € 3.00 - € 3.80 |
| child (2-6 yrs) | € 1.50 - € 2.00 |
| dog | € 1.00 - € 1.40 |

## Avallon

### Camping Municipal Sous Roche

Rue Sous Roche, F-89200 Avallon (Yonne) T: 03 86 34 10 39. E: campingsousroche@ville-avallon.fr

**alanrogers.com/FR89180**

This attractive and tranquil site is one of those municipal gems one finds from time to time. Tucked away next to the pretty River Cousin, at the bottom of the hill on which Avallon stands, there are 97 medium to large pitches, of which 80 have access to electricity (10A). Long leads may be necessary on some smaller pitches. All are on grass except for three hardstandings, and are divided by shrubs and small trees. A separate eating room, with a tea and coffee machine and a microwave oven, is a welcome consideration for those under canvas. This is an excellent place to relax and break your journey when travelling south on the A6 motorway. Avallon centre and medieval town is some 2 km. along a road that climbs gently to the town.

**Facilities**

A modern, clean and well maintained toilet block with washbasins in cabins and controllable showers. Baby changing and excellent facilities for disabled visitors. Washing machine and dryer. Small well stocked shop (all season). Separate eating and coffee room. Bread to order. Childrens play area. Free WiFi over site. Off site: Shops, restaurants and museums in Avallon. Markets on Thursday and Saturday mornings.

**Open:** 1 April - 15 October.

**Directions**

From A6 take J22 and follow D606 signed Avallon. At central crossroads (with traffic lights) turn left onto D944, signed Municipal Camping. Follow road for 2 km. and turn left immediately before the bridge over the River Cousin. Site is approximately 100 m. on left. GPS: 47.48007, 3.91364

**Charges guide**

| | |
|---|---|
| Per unit incl. 2 persons and electricity | € 15.30 |
| dog | free |

## Beaune

### Camping Municipal les Cent Vignes

10 rue Auguste Dubois, F-21200 Beaune (Côte d'Or) T: 03 80 22 03 91.
E: campinglescentvignes@mairie-beaune.fr **alanrogers.com/FR21020**

Les Cent Vignes is a very well kept site offering 116 individual pitches of good size, separated by neat beech hedges high enough to maintain a fair amount of privacy. Over half of the pitches are on grass, ostensibly for tents, the remainder on hardstandings with electricity for caravans. A popular site, within walking distance of the town centre, les Cent Vignes becomes full mid-June to early September but with many short-stay campers there are departures each day and reservations can be made. The Côte de Beaune, situated southeast of the Côte d'Or, produces some of the very best French wines.

**Facilities**

Two modern, fully equipped and well constructed sanitary blocks, one of which can be heated, should be large enough. Nearly all washbasins are in cabins. Laundry facilities. Shop, bar, restaurant with takeaway (1/4-15/10). Playground. Sports area with tennis, basketball, volleyball and boules. TV room. Barbecue area. WiFi. Off site: Centre of Beaune 1 km. Bicycle hire 1 km. Riding 2 km. Fishing and windsurfing 3 km. Golf 4 km.

**Open:** 15 March - 31 October.

**Directions**

From autoroute exit 24 follow signs for Beaune centre on D2 road, camping signs to site in 1 km. Well signed from other routes. GPS: 47.03304, 4.83911

**Charges guide**

| | |
|---|---|
| Per unit incl. 2 persons and electricity | € 14.90 - € 16.30 |
| extra person | € 3.40 - € 3.90 |
| child (under 7 yrs) | € 1.70 - € 1.90 |

**FREE** Alan Rogers Travel Card
Extra benefits and savings - see page 10

## Châlon-sur-Saône
### Camping du Pont de Bourgogne

Rue Julien Leneveu, SaintMarcel, F-71380 Châlon-sur-Saône (Saône-et-Loire) T: 03 85 48 26 86.
E: campingchalon71@wanadoo.fr **alanrogers.com/FR71140**

This is a well presented and cared for site, useful for an overnight stop or for a longer stay to explore the local area. It is close to the A6 Autoroute, and the interesting market town of Châlon-sur-Saône is only 2 km. There are 100 slightly sloping pitches (90 sq.m) all with 10A electricity, most on grass, but 30 have a gravel surface. They are separated by beech hedging, and a variety of mature trees give varying amounts of shade. Many pitches overlook the river, a good spot to watch the passing boats. Access is easy for large outfits.

**Facilities**

Three toilet blocks, two traditional in style and fittings. The third is a superb modern building, including a children's bathroom, disabled bathroom and family shower. Motorcaravan services. Laundry facilities. No shop but essentials kept in the bar (bread to order). Modern bar/restaurant (July/Aug). Simple play area. Bicycle hire arranged. WiFi. Off site: Fishing and boat ramp 200 m. Municipal swimming pool 300 m. Golf, sailing 1 km. Riding 10 km. Châlon-sur-Saône with many shops, bars, banks etc.

**Open:** 1 April - 30 September.

**Directions**

From A6 exit 26 (Châlon-Sud), take N80 (signed Dôle) to second roundabout. Take fourth exit (signed Roseraie) and fork right (les Chavannes). At traffic lights turn right (signed Roseraie) under bridge to site entrance 500 m. GPS: 46.78448, 4.87295

**Charges guide**

| | |
|---|---|
| Per unit incl. 2 persons and electricity | € 19.40 - € 26.10 |
| extra person | € 4.70 - € 6.30 |

Camping Cheques accepted.

## Charny
### Flower Camping des Platanes

41 route de la Mothe, F-89120 Charny (Yonne) T: 03 86 91 83 60. E: campingdesplatanes@wanadoo.fr
**alanrogers.com/FR89070**

Peacefully situated in the village of Charny, this is a tranquil, quiet site, yet within easy reach of the A6 autoroute. The Loire Valley is easily accessed, as is Paris (1.5 hours). The important archaeological site of Guédelon castle is nearby, the Chablis wines of the Yonne are ready for discovery and there are delightful walks around two local lakes. There are currently 82 level, grass pitches, all with 16A electricity. With 27 used for touring units (some now with water and waste water), the remainder are used for rented holiday homes and seasonal units.

**Facilities**

A modern, purpose-built, heated toilet block provides separate areas for men and women. Washbasins in cabins. Facilities for disabled visitors. Laundry. Motorcaravan service point. Takeaway (June-Sept). Heated swimming pool (1/5-30/9). Bicycle and barbecue hire. Play area for under fives. WiFi. Off site: Fishing 500 m. Riding 7 km. Walking.

**Open:** 1 April - 30 October.

**Directions**

Leave A6 at exit 18 and follow D943 towards Montargis for 14 km. Turn left on D950 and site is on right at start of village. GPS: 47.891, 3.092

**Charges guide**

| | |
|---|---|
| Per unit incl. 2 persons and electricity | € 15.50 - € 19.50 |
| extra person | € 3.00 - € 4.50 |

## Cluny
### Camping Municipal Saint Vital

Rue des Griottons, F-71250 Cluny (Saône-et-Loire) T: 03 85 59 08 34. E: cluny-camping@wanadoo.fr
**alanrogers.com/FR71030**

Close to this attractive small town (300 m. walk) with its magnificent abbey (the largest in Christendom) and next to the municipal swimming pool (free for campers), this site has 174 pitches. On gently sloping grass, with some small hedges and shade in parts, 6A electricity is available (long leads may be needed). Some rail noise is noticeable during the day but we are assured that trains do not run 23.30-07.00. On Monday and Thursday evenings during high season, there is a presentation of local produce in the 'salle de réunion'. Ask for a free copy of 'Cluny, Town of Art and History', at reception or the tourist office.

**Facilities**

Two sanitary buildings provide British and Turkish style WCs, some washbasins in cubicles and controllable showers. Facilities for disabled visitors. Washing machine, dryer and ironing board. Chemical disposal. Shop (July/Aug). Outdoor swimming pool (June-Sept). Play area. WiFi (charged). Off site: Fishing and bicycle hire 100 m. Riding 1 km. Wine routes, châteaux, churches.

**Open:** 26 April - 30 September.

**Directions**

Site is east of town, by the D15 road towards Azé and Blanot. GPS: 46.43196, 4.66755

**Charges guide**

| | |
|---|---|
| Per unit incl. 2 persons and electricity | € 16.85 |
| extra person | € 3.80 |
| child (under 7 yrs) | € 2.30 |

For latest campsite news, availability and prices visit
**alanrogers.com**

# Digoin
## Flower Camping la Chevrette

Rue de la Chevrette, F-71160 Digoin (Saône-et-Loire) T: 03 85 53 11 49. E: info@lachevrette.com
**alanrogers.com/FR71180**

This pretty town site has been leased from the municipality for some years by an enthusiastic, friendly couple. There are 81 neat and tidy pitches which are separated by hedges and flowers decorate the site. The level pitches include 71 with electricity (10A) for touring units and ten for tents. There are four chalets for rent. At the far end of the site there is a slipway onto the River Loire and it is this aspect that attracts campers with canoes. The site also has its own canoes for hire and include free transfers.

| Facilities | Directions |
| --- | --- |
| Four small toilet blocks, one with cold water only, each provide separate facilities for men and women and some washbasins in cabins. Facilities for disabled visitors. Washing machine and dryer. Restaurant/snack bar and takeaway (all 1/7-31/8). Bread to order. Heated outdoor pool (1/6-7/9). Club room/library with TV for bad weather. Canoe hire and transfers. Fishing and boat launching. Free WiFi over part of site. Off site: Municipal pool (free to campers 15/6-7/9). Supermarket 500 m. Restaurants and bars in the town. Riding 3 km. Bicycle hire 15 km. | Digoin is off the N79 and site is well signed from all directions. Look for signs showing Piscine Camping. The site is located beside the bridge over the River Loire and the D979 and behind the municipal pool. GPS: 46.47973, 3.96755 |

**Open:** 15 March - 15 October.

**Charges guide**

| | |
| --- | --- |
| Per unit incl. 2 persons and electricity | € 16.90 - € 19.50 |
| extra person | € 3.70 - € 4.50 |

Twin-axle units are charged much more.

---

# Dompierre-les-Ormes
## Camping le Village des Meuniers

344 rue du Stade, F-71520 Dompierre-les-Ormes (Saône-et-Loire) T: 03 85 50 36 60.
E: contact@villagedesmeuniers.com **alanrogers.com/FR71020**

In a tranquil setting with panoramic views, the neat appearance of the reception building sets the tone for the rest of this attractive site. It is an excellent example of current trends in French tourism development. This is a super site, on the gentle slopes of a hilltop, tastefully landscaped, with a high standard of cleanliness in all areas. The main part has 90 terraced, grassy touring pitches, some with hardstanding. They are fairly level and 86 have electricity (15A) and ample water points. Of these, 25 also have waste water outlets. A second section, used only in high season contains 16 standard pitches.

| Facilities | Directions |
| --- | --- |
| Sanitary facilities with modern fittings are of high standard. Excellent facilities for disabled visitors. Smaller unit in the lower area of the site, plus further toilets in the main reception building. Motorcaravan service point in car park. Shop (all season). Bar, café and takeaway (all 15/3-1/11). Swimming pool complex with three heated pools and toboggan run (1/5-31/9). Activities for children (high season). Minigolf. WiFi. Off site: Village 500 m. for all services (banks and some shops, closed Sun/Mon). | Town is 35 km. west of Mâcon. Leave the A6 at exit 29 and follow N79/E62 (Charolles, Paray, Digoin) road and turn south onto D41 to Dompierre-les-Ormes (3 km). Site is clearly signed through village. GPS: 46.36369, 4.47460 |

**Open:** 15 March - 1 November.

**Charges 2013**

| | |
| --- | --- |
| Per unit incl. 2 persons and electricity | € 23.00 - € 30.50 |
| extra person | € 6.00 - € 7.50 |

---

# Issy-l'Évêque
## Camping de l'Etang Neuf

L'Etang Neuf, F-71760 Issy-l'Évêque (Saône-et-Loire) T: 03 85 24 96 05. E: info@issy-camping.com
**alanrogers.com/FR71080**

This well tended, tranquil campsite overlooking a lake, with views of a forest and the 19th-century Château de Montrifaut, is a real countryside haven for relaxation. The birdsong includes nightingales and golden orioles. The 61 marked, grass pitches have 6A electricity, a small hardstanding area for a car and are separated by a variety of maturing trees giving some shade. There is a separate area nearer the lake for tents. There is no organised entertainment but a play area and a fenced area of the lake, with beach for swimming and paddling plus plenty of space, will keep children happily amused.

| Facilities | Directions |
| --- | --- |
| Two very clean sanitary blocks include washbasins in cabins. Washing machine, ironing board and baby room. Separate shower and toilet rooms for disabled visitors are in the lower block. Motorcaravan services. Bar (1/7-31/8). Bread and croissants to order. Boules. TV/games room. Internet access (WiFi). Off site: Minigolf by site entrance. Riding and tennis 500 m. Nearest shops 1.2 km. in Issy-l'Évêque. 120 km. of marked footpaths in the area. | From N81 (Autun-Bourbon-Lancy) turn left onto D27/D25 just west of Luzy and continue for 11 km. Turn right, D42 in centre of Issy-l'Évêque, signed to campsite. GPS: 46.70773, 3.96018 |

**Open:** 13 May - 15 September.

**Charges guide**

| | |
| --- | --- |
| Per unit incl. 2 persons and electricity | € 17.00 - € 19.40 |
| extra person | € 3.00 - € 5.00 |

---

**FREE** Alan Rogers Travel Card
Extra benefits and savings - see page 10

## Gigny-sur-Saône

### Castel Camping Château de l'Epervière

Rue du Château, F-71240 Gigny-sur-Saône (Saône-et-Loire) T: 03 85 94 16 90.
E: domaine-de-leperviere@wanadoo.fr **alanrogers.com/FR71070**

This popular and high quality site is peacefully situated in the wooded grounds of a 16th-century château, close to the A6 and near the village of Gigny-sur-Saône. It is within walking distance of the river where you can watch the cruise boats on their way to and from Châlon-sur-Saône. There are 160 pitches in two separate areas, of which 100 are used for touring, all with 6A electricity. Some are on hardstanding and 30 are fully serviced. Some pitches, close to the château and fishing lake, are hedged and have shade from mature trees; another area has a more open aspect. Red squirrels, ducks and the occasional heron can be found on the campsite and the pitches around the periphery are good for birdwatchers. The château's main restaurant serves regional dishes and there is a good range of takeaway meals. Gert-Jan, François and their team enthusiastically organise many activities, mainly for children, but including wine tasting in the cellars of the château. Don't forget, here you are in the Maconnais and Châlonnaise wine regions, so arrange some visits to the local caves.

**Facilities**

Two well equipped, very clean toilet blocks with all necessary facilities including those for babies and campers with disabilities. Washing machine/dryer. Basic shop (1/5-30/9). Restaurant with good menu and takeaway (1/4-30/9). Cellar with wine tasting. Converted barn with bar, large TV. Unheated outdoor swimming pool (1/5-30/9) partly enclosed by old stone walls. Smaller indoor heated pool, jacuzzi, sauna (1/4-30/9). Play areas with paddling pool. Fishing. Bicycle hire. Motorcaravan services. WiFi (free) in bar area. Off site: Boat launching 500 m. Riding 15 km. Golf 20 km. Historic towns of Châlon and Tournus, both 20 km. The Monday market of Louhans, to see the famous Bresse chickens 26 km.

**Open:** 30 March - 30 September.

**Directions**

From A6 heading south, take exit 26 Châlon-Sud, or from A6 heading north take exit 27 Tournus. Then N6 to Sennecey-le-Grand, turn east D18, signed Gigny. Follow site signs to site (6.5 km). GPS: 46.65485, 4.94463

**Charges guide**

| | |
|---|---|
| Per unit incl. 2 persons and electricity | € 24.30 - € 35.10 |
| extra person | € 5.90 - € 8.50 |
| child (under 7 yrs) | € 3.60 - € 5.80 |
| dog | € 2.40 - € 3.00 |

## Mâcon

### Camping Municipal Mâcon

RN 6, F-71000 Mâcon (Saône-et-Loire) T: 03 85 38 16 22. E: camping@ville-macon.fr
**alanrogers.com/FR71010**

A well cared for site worth considering as a stopover or for longer stays, as it is close to the main route south. The 266 good sized, level, grassy pitches, 190 with 5/10A electricity and 60 with fresh and waste water points, are easily accessed by tarmac roads. This is a pleasant site, remarkably quiet considering its location, and with a generally bright and cheerful ambience. Extra charge for outfits over 3,5 tonnes and with twin axles. Only gas and electric barbecues. Reservations are not accepted so, in July and August, arrive by late afternoon to avoid disappointment. Some road and rail noise.

**Facilities**

Four well maintained toilet blocks, one new, others being refurbished. All necessary facilities including those for campers with disabilities. Washing machine and dryer. Motorcaravan service point (with Fiamma sewage couplings). Shop/tabac, bar, takeaway and restaurant (le Tipi) open midday and evenings. Heated swimming and paddling pools (campers only, 15/5-15/9). TV lounge. Playground. Free WiFi. Off site: Sports centre on banks of river close by. Supermarket 400 m. Fishing 500 m. Golf, riding 10 km. Centre of Mâcon 3 km. Bus passes site.

**Open:** 15 March - 31 October.

**Directions**

Site is on northern outskirts of Mâcon on main N6, 3 km. from the town centre, well signed (just south of A40 autoroute exit). GPS: 46.3021, 4.8325

**Charges guide**

| | |
|---|---|
| Per unit incl. 2 persons | € 15.30 - € 16.90 |
| with electricity (10A) | € 19.20 - € 21.40 |
| extra person | € 4.10 - € 4.60 |
| child (under 7 yrs) | € 2.30 - € 2.40 |
| dog | € 1.20 - € 1.40 |

For latest campsite news, availability and prices visit
**alanrogers.com**

# 3 campsites in the heart of southern burgundy

## www.campings-bourgogne.com

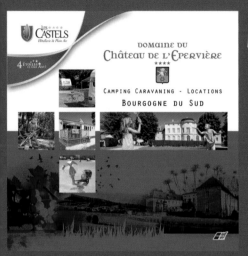

Holiday
in château park

www.domaine-eperviere.com

Discover Tournus

www.camping-tournus.com

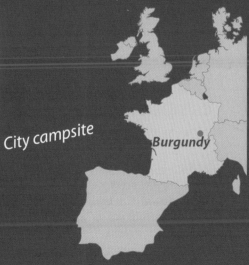

City campsite

Burgundy

www.camping-chalon.com

## Meursault

### Camping la Grappe d'Or

2 route de Volnay, F-21190 Meursault (Côte d'Or) T: 03 80 21 22 48. E: info@camping-meursault.com

alanrogers.com/FR21050

Meursault, the capital of the great white wines of Burgundy, is southwest of Beaune and Camping la Grappe d'Or offers terraced pitches overlooking acres of vineyards. Most of the 130 touring pitches are flat, of varying sizes, and some have shade from mature trees. Almost all have electrical connections (15A). There is an outdoor pool and flume and, during July and August, aqua gym and other water activities are organised. There is a fenced play area for youngsters and, just across the road from the entrance, there are two tennis courts for campers.

### Facilities

Sanitary facilities are in three blocks with some washbasins in cabins. Child/baby room. Facilities for visitors with disabilities. Laundry facilities. Shop. Bar, restaurant, takeaway (1/5-30/9). Swimming pool (15/6-15/9). Play area. Tennis. Bicycle hire. Off site: Golf and riding 7 km. Indoor pool 7 km. Fishing 8 km. Beaune 9 km.

**Open:** 1 April - 15 October.

### Directions

Site is north of Meursault. Take N74 from Beaune and follow the sign for Meursault. Site is signed from town but not very clearly (tents with three arrows). GPS: 46.98574, 4.76858

### Charges guide

| Per unit incl. 2 persons | |
|---|---|
| and electricity | € 18.00 - € 22.00 |
| extra person | € 3.00 - € 3.80 |
| child (under 7 yrs) | € 1.50 - € 2.00 |

Camping Cheques accepted.

---

## Nevers

### Camping de Nevers

Rue de la Jonction, F-58000 Nevers (Nièvre) T: 06 84 98 69 79. E: info@campingnevers.com

alanrogers.com/FR58100

On the banks of the Loire in Nevers, facing the cathedral and the Palais des Ducs across the river, this site has just 73 pitches. The area nearest the river is for tents and the terraces above for touring pitches, mainly grass but five hardstandings; there are 60 pitches with electricity (6/10A). The pitches are quite tight but larger units can be accommodated and the site is ideal for those who enjoy being able to wander into town or as a base to explore the region with its famous Burgundy wines of Sancerre and Pouilly Fumé. The shops, bars and restaurants of Nevers are within easy reach on foot or by bus.

### Facilities

One modern unisex toilet block with washbasins in cabins and controllable showers. Bright and clean, they may be under pressure in high season. Baby area. En-suite unit for disabled visitors. Laundry with washing machine, dryer and ironing facilities. Motorcaravan service point. Simple bar with basic snacks (all season). Bicycle hire. Play area (3-12 yrs). Pétanque. Internet (charged). Two mobile homes for rent. Off site: All the amenities of Nevers, including shops, restaurants, bars, large stores and supermarkets within easy reach. Bus stop at entrance. Boat launching 500 m. Golf and riding 15 km.

**Open:** 13 April - 14 October.

### Directions

Nevers is 150 km. north of Clermont-Ferrand. Do not approach through the town. From A77/N7 (Paris-Lyon) take exit 37 onto D976 (Bourges). Turn north at first roundabout towards 'Centre Ville'. Site is signed to right immediately before bridge across the Loire. Site is closed 12.00-15.00 – there is no waiting place outside. GPS: 46.98209, 3.16098

### Charges guide

| Per unit incl. 2 persons | |
|---|---|
| and electricity | € 17.70 - € 21.45 |
| extra person | € 2.10 - € 3.10 |
| child (7+ yrs) | € 1.30 - € 2.80 |
| dog | € 0.50 |

Camping Cheques accepted.

---

## Palinges

### Camping du Lac

Le Fourneau, F-71430 Palinges (Saône-et-Loire) T: 03 85 88 14 49. E: camping.palinges@hotmail.fr

**alanrogers.com/FR71110**

Camping du Lac is a very special campsite and it is all due to M. Labille and his wife, the owners, who think of the campsite as their home and every visitor as their guest. The campsite has 40 pitches in total, 16 of which have 10A electricity and 16 are fully serviced. There are seven chalets to rent. The site is adjacent to a lake with a beach and safe bathing. Set in the countryside yet within easy reach of many tourist attractions, especially Cluny, the local Château Digoin and Mont St Vincent with distant views of Mont Blanc on a clear day. If you want to visit a specific place, then Monsieur Labille knows where you should go – he never recommends anything that he hasn't personally tried out. Tables and chairs are provided for tent campers and bottles of water can be frozen for cyclists to take away (free of charge).

**Facilities**

The central sanitary block provides all necessary facilities including those for campers with disabilities. This site is well adapted for disabled visitors. Motorcaravan services. Washing machine and fridge. Bread and croissants to order. Boules. Play area. TV room. Sports field, lake beach and swimming adjacent. WiFi. Off site: Bar/snack bar outside entrance (1/7-31/8). Palinges is within walking distance, cycle and walking routes, museums, cruises on canals, châteaux. Riding 8 km.

**Open:** 1 April - 30 October.

**Directions**

Palinges is midway between Montceau-les-Mines and Paray-le-Monial. From Montceau take N70, then turn left onto D92 to Palinges. Follow campsite signs. Site is also well signed from D985 Toulon-sur-Arroux to Charolles road. GPS: 46.56095, 4.22492

**Charges guide**

| | |
|---|---|
| Per unit incl. 2 persons and electricity | € 21.00 |
| extra person | € 3.70 |
| dog | € 1.70 |

No credit cards.

Open 1st April to 30th October

**Palinges**
South Burgundy

CAMPING DU LAC ***

33(0)3 85 88 14 49
Silence, nature, peace
40 pitches
7 chalets

## Saint Boil

### Camping le Moulin de Collonge

Moulin de Collonge, F-71390 Saint Boil (Saône-et-Loire) T: 03 85 44 00 32. E: millofcollonge@wanadoo.fr

**alanrogers.com/FR71050**

This small campsite is situated on the wine route between Baume and Cluny and close to the long cycle route through the Burgundy vineyards. This well run, family site offers an 'away from it all' situation and it will appeal to those seeking a quiet, relaxing environment in a garden-like setting. There are 61 small to average sized, level, grassy pitches, with 50 for touring (6A electricity although long leads may be required). Most pitches are well shaded by a wide variety of mature trees making access for tall outfits quite difficult. No twin-axle caravans or large outfits accepted.

**Facilities**

Well kept toilet facilities housed in a converted barn. Washing machine and dryer. Freezer for campers' use. Bread each morning. Basic shop (1/5-30/9). Restaurant/pizzeria, snack bar (all season). Swimming pool, covered but some walls can be opened in good weather (all season). Playgrounds. Bouncy castle. Bicycle hire. Fishing. Pony trekking. WiFi. Off site: La Voie Verte, a 117 km. track for cycling or walking near the site. Riding 4 km. Châteaux, wine route, churches.

**Open:** 1 April - 30 September.

**Directions**

From Chalon-sur-Saône, take N80 west 9 km. Turn south on D981 through Buxy (6 km). Continue south to Saint Boil 7 km. and site is signed at south end of the village. GPS: 46.64621, 4.69479

**Charges guide**

| | |
|---|---|
| Per unit incl. 2 persons and electricity | € 19.00 - € 23.60 |
| extra person | € 4.75 - € 5.80 |
| child (under 7 yrs) | € 2.50 - € 3.50 |

Less 20% outside July/Aug.

**FREE** Alan Rogers Travel Card
Extra benefits and savings - see page 10

# Saint Léger-de-Fougeret

## Camping l'Etang de la Fougeraie

Hameau de Champs, F-58120 Saint Léger-de-Fougeret (Nièvre) T: 03 86 85 11 85.
E: campingfougeraie@orange.fr  **alanrogers.com/FR58040**

This is a quiet and peaceful, spacious campsite laid out on a hillside deep in the Parc Naturel Régional du Morvan, with views over the lake, meadows and surrounding hills. The spring water lake is ideal for fishing and swimming. There is a small bar and restaurant serving good quality regional meals and a well stocked shop with local produce. There are 73 terraced pitches, with 67 for touring, 45 with electricity (10/16A). The site is not suitable for double-axle or large outfits, or people with walking difficulties, as the site roads are steep and narrow. Large RVs are not accepted. Here is a place where you can sit back and relax after a day exploring the surrounding peaceful countryside lying within the Parc du Morvan. For those seeking the really quiet life there are 'Introduction to Fishing' courses when it may be possible to catch one of the summer trout or large 12 kg. carp. Fishing parties are welcome. For the more adventurous, a day hiking with donkeys is recommended. These excursions leave directly from the site. There are also several marked walks within the forest and information on routes and local fauna are available at reception.

**Facilities**

Traditional and modern buildings with all necessary facilities and a heated family/disabled room lie at the top of the site, a fair distance uphill from some pitches. Washing machine and dryer. Shop. Bar and restaurant. Free WiFi over part of site. Lake swimming. Fishing. Playgrounds. Go-karts and all-terrain scooters for hire. Caravan storage. American RVs not accepted, site not really suitable for large units. Chalets for rent with TV and DVD player. Off site: Riding 2 km. Shops, bank with ATM and services 7 km.

**Open:** 1 April - 30 September.

**Directions**

St Léger-de-Fougeret is 10 km. south of Château-Chinon. From Château-Chinon take D27 south for 3 km, then fork right on D157 for 5.5 km. to St Léger. Continue through village, follow signs to site 1 km. GPS: 47.00587, 3.90548

**Charges guide**

| Per unit incl. 2 persons | |
|---|---|
| and electricity | € 17.50 - € 19.00 |
| extra person | € 5.30 |
| child (0-16 yrs) | € 2.80 - € 3.10 |
| dog | € 1.90 |

---

---

For latest campsite news, availability and prices visit
**alanrogers.com**

## Saint Pereuse-en-Morvan
### Camping le Manoir de Bezolle

F-58110 Saint Pereuse-en-Morvan (Nièvre) T: 03 86 84 42 55. E: info@camping-bezolle.com

**alanrogers.com/FR58030**

Manoir de Bezolle is in the heart of Burgundy, well situated to explore the Morvan Nature Park and the Nivernais area and is open all year round. It has been attractively landscaped to provide a number of different areas, some giving pleasant views over the surrounding countryside. There are 100 spacious pitches with 76 for touring, all with 10A electricity (long leads advised). One area is set out on terraces and some pitches are slightly sloping. Many have good shade from a variety of magnificent trees. There is a good children's play area and three well stocked, small lakes for anglers. There is a bar, restaurant and takeaway with an attractive terrace overlooking the large, heated swimming pools. The lower, level area is more suitable for those with walking difficulties. There are many small towns and villages to visit in an area renowned for its gastronomy and history.

**Facilities**

Two main toilet blocks provide washbasins in cabins, mostly British style WCs, baths, provision for disabled visitors and a baby bath. A small unit contains two tiny family WC/basin/shower suites for rent. Facilities by the pools can be heated in winter. Laundry. Motorcaravan services. Shop (1/6-31/8). Bar (1/6-31/8) and restaurant (1/5-30/9). Pizza and takeaway (all year). Free WiFi over site. Two heated pools (1/5-15/9). Large play area. Minigolf. Boules. Fishing. Off site: Châtillon-en-Bazois with shops, bars and restaurants 14 km. Interesting old towns and villages with their châteaux, museums and markets.

**Open:** All year.

**Directions**

Site is between Nevers and Autun. Leave D978, 13 km. east of Châtillon-en-Bazois (site signed) onto D11. Site is a few hundred metres on the right. GPS: 47.0327, 3.4857

**Charges 2013**

| | |
|---|---|
| Per unit incl. 2 persons and electricity | € 20.00 - € 31.00 |
| extra person | € 5.00 - € 5.50 |
| child (0-6 yrs) | € 4.00 - € 4.50 |
| dog | € 3.00 |

Camping Cheques accepted.

## Saint Sauveur-en-Puisaye
### Camping Parc des Joumiers

F-89520 Saint Sauveur-en-Puisaye (Yonne) T: 03 86 45 66 28. E: camping-motel-joumiers@wanadoo.fr

**alanrogers.com/FR89040**

This is an attractive, spacious, family run site in the north of Burgundy and east of the Loire. It is set beside a lake and a forest which offers many opportunities for walks and bike rides. There are 200 large, slightly sloping, grass pitches separated by hedges with a variety of trees giving varying amounts of shade. All 174 for touring have 16A electricity, water, drainage and TV point. There are no organised on-site activities but within 10 km. there are many interesting old towns, a medieval-style castle being built using traditional methods, and Château de Saint Fargeau with its pageants and 'son-et-lumière'.

**Facilities**

Two well appointed toilet blocks with all necessary facilities, including those for children and campers with disabilities. Washing machine. Motorcaravan services. Small swimming and paddling pools (June-mid-Sept). Play area with bouncy castle. Bar, restaurant and takeaway (all season) overlooking lake (fishing only). WiFi near bar. Fishing. Off site: Large village of St Sauveur with small shops, bar, restaurant 1 km. Riding 5 km. Bicycle hire 8 km. Children's pedal cars. Château de Saint Fargeau.

**Open:** 28 March - 5 November.

**Directions**

Leave A77 at exit 21 and take D965 east for 17 km. to St Fargeau. Turn right on D85 southeast to St Sauveur-en-Puisaye in 11 km. In village turn hard left on D7. In 800 m. turn right (site well signed) to site in 800 m. GPS: 47.63083, 3.19405

**Charges guide**

| | |
|---|---|
| Per unit incl. 2 persons and electricity | € 17.80 - € 20.10 |
| extra person | € 3.80 |
| child (under 7 yrs) | € 1.80 |

## Savigny-les-Beaune
### Camping les Premier Pres

Route de Bouilland, F-21420 Savigny-les-Beaune (Côte d'Or) T: 03 80 26 15 06.
E: contact.camping@x-treme-bar.fr  **alanrogers.com/FR21030**

This popular site is ideally located for visiting the Burgundy vineyards, for use as a transit site or for spending time in the town of Beaune. During the high season it is full every evening, so it is best to arrive by 4 pm. The 90 level pitches are marked and numbered, with 6A electric hook-ups and room for an awning. A former municipal site, now privately owned. Whilst the famed wine region alone attracts many visitors, Beaune, its capital, is unrivalled in its richness of art from times gone by. Narrow streets and squares are garlanded with flowers, pavement cafés are crammed with tourists and overlooking the scene is the glistening Hôtel Dieu.

**Facilities**

Well kept sanitary facilities are housed in a modern building behind reception. Additional WCs and water points are conveniently placed towards the middle of the site. Motorcaravan service point. Ice available to purchase. Torch useful. Fishing. Bicycle hire. WiFi. Off site: Village with Sunday market 1 km. Beaune 7 km.

**Open:** 15 March - 15 October.

**Directions**

From A6 autoroute take exit 24 signed Beaune and Savigny-les-Beaune onto D2. Turn right towards Savigny-les-Beaune (3 km) and follow signs to site. GPS: 47.069, 4.803

**Charges guide**

| | |
|---|---|
| Per unit incl. 2 persons and electricity | € 11.40 - € 12.70 |

No credit cards.

## Tazilly
### Airotel Château de Chigy

Chigy, F-58170 Tazilly (Nièvre) T: 03 86 30 10 80. E: reception@chateaudechigy.com.fr
**alanrogers.com/FR58050**

This very spacious site (20 hectares for pitches and another 50 hectares of fields, lakes and woods) lies at the southern tip of the Morvan Nature Park. The château houses the reception and apartments. Most of the facilities are nearby, and behind are 54 good sized, shaded and slightly sloping pitches, many uneven, all with 6A electricity. There is a large woodland area with paths, beyond which are 100 or so less shaded pitches, some of up to 150 sq.m. Most are slightly sloping and some are on low terraces, nearly all with electricity. Most have very good views.

**Facilities**

Two toilet blocks provide British style WCs, washbasins in cubicles, and showers but are a good distance from many pitches. A portacabin-style unit has private facilities for hire in July/Aug. Facilities for disabled visitors and babies. Laundry facilities. Gas supplies. Shop. Bar, restaurant and takeaway (July/Aug). Two outdoor pools, one with paddling pool (15/5-30/9). Covered pool. Games and TV rooms. Playground. Minigolf. Boules. All weather sports terrain. Playing field. Fishing. Off site: Luzy 4 km.

**Open:** 26 April - 30 September.

**Directions**

Leave Autun on the N81 southwest (signed Bourbon-Lancy) through Luzy (D973, Bourbon-Lancy). Site is signed to the left after 4 km. GPS: 46.75746, 3.94478

**Charges guide**

| | |
|---|---|
| Per unit incl. 2 persons and electricity | € 21.00 - € 28.00 |
| extra person | € 5.00 - € 7.00 |
| child (6-17 yrs) | € 4.00 - € 6.00 |

## Tournus
### Camping de Tournus

14 rue des Canes, F-71700 Tournus (Saône-et-Loire) T: 03 85 51 16 58. E: info@camping-tournus.com
**alanrogers.com/FR71190**

This very well maintained, pleasant site is just a few minutes from the A6 autoroute, 200 metres from the River Saône and close to the interesting old market town of Tournus. It is ideal for a night halt but deserving of a longer stay. The new owners have made some hardstanding pitches to complement the fairly level grassy pitches. All 90 pitches are for touring and 70 have 6A electricity. A few trees give some pitches varying amounts of shade. A municipal outdoor swimming pool is adjacent to the site.

**Facilities**

Two clean toilet blocks near the entrance provide all necessary facilities, including those for disabled visitors. Motorcaravan services. Small bar and shop in the reception area where bread can be ordered daily and light snacks purchased. Small play area. Internet terminal. Bicycle hire. WiFi. Off site: Municipal pool next door. Fishing 100 m. Tournus, Saturday market, shops, bars, cafés, banks etc. short walk/cycle ride along river.

**Open:** 1 April - 30 September.

**Directions**

From the A6 take exit 12 for Tournus and the N6 south for just over 1 km. In Tournus (opposite railway station), turn left signed camping and follow signs to site, 1 km. GPS: 46.57372, 4.909349

**Charges guide**

| | |
|---|---|
| Per unit incl. 2 persons and electricity | € 19.10 - € 24.50 |
| extra person | € 4.20 - € 5.60 |

Camping Cheques accepted.

For latest campsite news, availability and prices visit
**alanrogers.com**

## Vandenesse-en-Auxois
### Sunêlia Lac de Panthier

1 chemin du lac, F-21320 Vandenesse-en-Auxois (Côte d'Or) T: 03 80 49 21 94. E: info@lac-de-panthier.com

**alanrogers.com/FR21000**

Camping Lac de Panthier is an attractively situated lakeside site in the Burgundy countryside. It is divided into two areas, one housing the reception, shop, restaurant, indoor pool and sauna. The other, larger area is 200 m. along the lakeside road and is where the other site activities take place and the outdoor pools can be found. Many of the pitches here have views across the countryside. The 207 pitches (143 for touring) all have 6A electricity and are mostly on gently sloping grass, although in parts there are shallow terraces. The restaurant and some pitches have views over the lake.

**Facilities**

Each area has two adequate unisex toilet blocks including provision for babies and disabled visitors. Shop, bar and restaurant. Games and TV rooms. Swimming pool, children's pool and slide (15/5-15/9). Indoor pool, sauna and gym. Fishing. Bicycle hire and canoe hire. Watersports. Entertainment and activities organised in high season and clubs for children and teenagers. Internet access and WiFi (charged). Trampoline. Electric barbecues are not permitted. Max. 1 dog. Off site: Boat excursions from Pouilly-en-Auxois (8 km). Riding and golf 10 km.

**Open:** 12 April - 13 October.

**Directions**

From A6 join the A38 and exit at exit 24. Take the N81 south towards Arnay Le Duc, over A6, shortly turn left on D977 for 5 km. Fork left for Vandenesse-en-Auxois. Through village on D977 for 2.5 km, turn left and site is on left. GPS: 47.23661, 4.62810

**Charges guide**

| Per unit incl. 2 persons | |
|---|---|
| and electricity | € 19.00 - € 28.00 |
| extra person | € 5.00 - € 7.00 |

Camping Cheques accepted.

---

## Vincelles
### Camping les Ceriselles

Route de Vincelottes, F-89290 Vincelles (Yonne) T: 03 86 42 50 47. E: camping@cc-payscoulangeois.fr

**alanrogers.com/FR89060**

A distinctive, modern site, les Ceriselles was created in 1998 on land adjacent to the Canal du Nivernais and is owned by a group of communities. A very level site, it has 84 pitches on grass (67 for touring), all with electricity and 38 with full services. There are also 17 mobile homes. Staff live on site and the gates are locked 22.00-07.00 hrs. Cars are now parked on pitches which can make the site seem more crowded in high season. Double-axle caravans are not accepted. A covered terrace houses a restaurant with a good range of meals, takeaway and drinks. This good value site is just off the D606 and ideal for exploring the Yonne valley and Auxerre region.

**Facilities**

Four small heated toilet blocks each provide a toilet, two washbasins in cubicles and two showers per sex, with a unit for disabled visitors in block one (nearest reception). A further block has a baby room, WCs and laundry. Restaurant (all season, hours vary acc. to demand). Clubroom with TV. Playground. Bicycle hire. Fishing. Boules. Volleyball. Basketball. Archery, canoeing and kayaking on certain days in high season. Off site: Supermarket and restaurant within walking distance. Cycle path along canal for 8 km.

**Open:** 1 April - 30 September.

**Directions**

Vincelles is 10 km. south of Auxerre. From A6 take Auxerre Sud exit and follow N65 towards Auxerre. After 4 km. turn south on D606 towards Avallon and after 10 km. turn left on D38. Site entrance is on left just before canal. GPS: 47.706644, 3.635678

**Charges guide**

| Per unit incl. 2 persons | |
|---|---|
| and electricity | € 15.00 - € 19.00 |
| extra person | € 3.10 - € 4.10 |
| child (3-10 yrs) | € 1.25 - € 2.00 |

Camping Cheques accepted.

# Camping Les Ceriselles ★★★★

tél : 03 86 42 50 47  camping@cc-payscoulangeois.fr
fax : 03 86 42 39 39  www.campingceriselles.com

*Les Ceriselles*

*Small and comfortable campsite situated along the Nivernais Canal with a cycle path to the heart of the vineyards and cherry trees. Good starting point for sightseeing.*

**For nature holidays**

Camping les Ceriselles ★★★★ - Route de Vincelottes - 89290 VINCELLES

**FREE** Alan Rogers Travel Card
Extra benefits and savings - see page 10

Located to the south of Alsace, the historic province of Franche-Comté boasts a varied landscape ranging from flat plains to dense woodlands, rugged dramatic mountains and limestone valleys.

# Franche-Comté

**DÉPARTEMENTS: 25 DOUBS, 39 JURA, 70 HAUTE-SAÔNE, 90 TRE. DE BELFORT**

**MAJOR CITY: BESANÇON**

Franche-Comté is a beautiful rural area bordered by Burgundy, Alsace, Champagne and Switzerland. It is an immensely varied landscape – the rolling farmland and small towns of the Haute-Saône contrasting with the dense forests, soaring cliffs and thundering waterfalls of the Jura. A paradise for nature lovers, there are endless opportunities for hiking, cycling and caving, with some skiing in winter. The streams and lakes provide world-class fishing, while more therapeutic waters can be found in spa towns such as Luxeuil-les-Bains, Salins-les-Bains and Lons-le-Saunier.

The historic capital, Besançon, with its walled citadel, lies on a loop of the river Doubs and is listed as a UNESCO World Heritage Site. The city remains unspoilt by development and has some charming old buildings. Visitors should not miss the impressive Musée des Beaux Arts, which houses works by Titian, Rembrandt, Rubens and other old masters.

## Places of interest

*Arbois*: Pasteur Family Home and Museum, Museum of Wine and Wine Growing.

*Belfort*: sandstone lion sculpted by Bartholdi; Memorial and Museum of the French Resistance.

*Besançon*: citadel with good views over the city.

*Champlitte*: Museum of Folk Art.

*Dole*: lovely old town, Louis Pasteur's birthplace.

*Gray*: Baron Martin Museum.

*Luxeuil-les-Bains*: Tour des Echevins Museum.

*Ornans*: Gustave Courbet birthplace, museum.

*Ronchamp*: Chapel of Notre-Dame du Haut de Ronchamp designed by Le Corbusier.

*Salins-les-Bains*: Salt mines and tunnels.

*Sochaux*: Peugeot Museum.

## Cuisine of the region

Freshwater fish such as trout, grayling, pike and perch are local specialities. The region has a rare wine known as *vin de paille* as well as *vin jaune* (deep yellow and very dry) and *vin du jura*, Jura wine.

*Brési*: water-thin slices of dried beef; many local hams.

*Gougère*: hot cheese pastry based on the local *Comté* cheese.

*Jésus de Morteau*: fat pork sausage smoked over pine and juniper.

*Papet jurassien*: orange blossom tart.

**www.franche-comte.org**
**info@franche-comte.org**
**00800 2006 2010** (free from the UK)

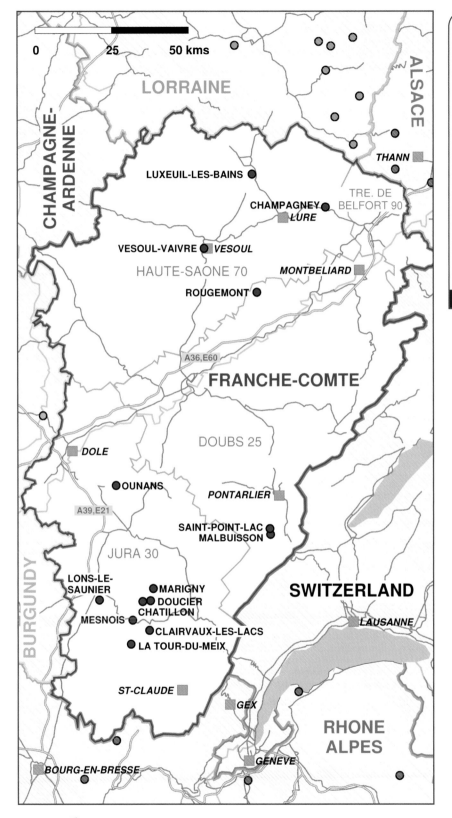

LORRAINE

CHAMPAGNE-ARDENNE

ALSACE

0    25    50 kms

THANN

LUXEUIL-LES-BAINS

CHAMPAGNEY
LURE

TRE. DE
BELFORT 90

VESOUL-VAIVRE VESOUL

HAUTE-SAONE 70

MONTBELIARD

ROUGEMONT

A36,E60

FRANCHE-COMTE

DOUBS 25

DOLE

OUNANS

PONTARLIER

A39,E21

SAINT-POINT-LAC
MALBUISSON

JURA 30

LONS-LE-SAUNIER

MARIGNY
DOUCIER
CHATILLON

MESNOIS

CLAIRVAUX-LES-LACS

LA TOUR-DU-MEIX

SWITZERLAND

LAUSANNE

ST-CLAUDE

GEX

RHONE
ALPES

GENEVE

BOURG-EN-BRESSE

**FREE** Alan Rogers Travel Card
Extra benefits and savings - see page 10

## Champagney
### Kawan Village Domaine les Ballastières
F-70290 Champagney (Haute-Saône) T: 03 84 23 11 22. E: contact@campinglesballastieres.com
alanrogers.com/FR70030

Within easy reach of the historic town of Belfort, les Ballastières opened in 2008. The landscaping is becoming established and the 100 touring pitches are very large, level and easily accessible. Reception building also houses the bar and snack bar, while outside a patio with tables and chairs overlooks the pool and adjacent lake. The site has been designed with disabled campers in mind; there is a sloping path to the pool, a hoist has been installed, and one of the ten mobile homes is ramped for easy access.

### Facilities
Two toilet blocks each with good facilities including those for disabled visitors, but may become stretched in high season. Washbasins in cabins. Laundry. Swimming and paddling pools (July/Aug). Shop (Jul/Aug), bar with TV and snack bar (all season). Special climbing facilities for children (3-11) with supervisor all season. Kayaks and canoes all season. Play area for under 5s. Motorcaravan services. Off site: ATM 300 m. Chapelle de Notre Dame du Haut, supermarket and amenities in Ronchamp 4 km.
**Open:** 1 April - 31 October.

### Directions
Site is 20 km. northwest of Belfort; from roundabout on east side of Ronchamp on D19, take D4 eastwards for 2 km. Site is signed on left. GPS: 47.706841, 6.671437

### Charges guide
| | |
|---|---|
| Per unit incl. 2 persons and electricity | € 18.00 - € 20.60 |
| extra person | € 3.70 |

Camping Cheques accepted.

## Chatillon
### Kawan Village Domaine de l'Epinette
15 rue de l'Epinette, F-39130 Chatillon (Jura) T: 03 84 25 71 44. E: info@domaine-epinette.com
alanrogers.com/FR39080

This site is set in charming wooded countryside on land sloping down to the River Ain, which is shallow and slow moving. There are 150 grassy pitches, 110 are available for touring units, some slightly sloping. These are arranged on terraces and separated by hedges, bushes and trees, about half being shaded. Nearly all have electricity hook-ups, although some long leads are needed. Ten pitches have hardstanding. There is an attractive swimming pool (heated 1/7-31/8) with a paddling pool. An activity club for children runs in July/August. Guided canoe trips on the river start and finish at the campsite.

### Facilities
Two modern toilet blocks. Unit for disabled visitors. Baby bath. Washing machine and dryer. Small shop for basics. Snack bar and takeaway (evenings). New reception, bar, TV room and shop. Swimming pool with toboggan. Playground. Boules. Direct access to river for swimming and canoeing. WiFi (free). Gas and charcoal barbecues permitted. Off site: Riding 6 km. Shops, etc. in Doucier 6 km. Golf 25 km.
**Open:** 9 June - 15 September.

### Directions
From Lons-le-Saunier take D471 eastwards towards Pontarlier-Genève. After 8 km. fork right onto D39 towards Vevy. After 11 km. at Chatillon turn right onto D151 south towards Blye. Site is less than 2 km. on the left. GPS: 46.65887, 5.72978

### Charges guide
| | |
|---|---|
| Per unit incl. 2 persons and electricity | € 17.00 - € 27.00 |
| extra person | € 3.50 - € 4.50 |

Camping Cheques accepted.

## Clairvaux-les-Lacs
### Yelloh! Village Fayolan
B.P. 52, F-39130 Clairvaux-les-Lacs (Jura) T: 03 84 25 88 52. E: lefayolan@oclesia.eu
alanrogers.com/FR39050

This large, spacious site is modern and well equipped. Backed by wooded hills, it is situated on the shores of Le Petit Lac amid the lakes and forests of the Jure, about a mile from the town of Clairvaux-les-Lacs. It is in two parts, with 516 pitches either on terraces overlooking the lake or on the flatter area near the shore. With 456 for touring units, all have electricity (10A) and 200 are fully serviced. The pitches are separated by hedges and mature trees giving most some shade. Many activities are organised on site, some in low season. Used by tour operators (130 pitches).

### Facilities
Four modern well equipped toilet units. Baby room. Washing and drying machines. Shop. Restaurant. Bar. Snack bar/pizzeria and takeaway. Swimming pool complex with indoor pool, outdoor pool (7/5-14/9; heated 5/6-31/8). Fitness centre with sauna, steam bath, massage (16/5-2/9). Entertainment area. Playground. Organised activities, children's club. Internet access. Fishing. Beach sports area and lake swimming. Boules.
**Open:** 28 April - 9 September.

### Directions
Clairvaux-les-Lacs is on the D678 23 km. southeast of Lons-le-Saunier. In Clairvaux follow signs for 'Lacs Campings' and Fayolan (1.5 km. southeast of town). GPS: 46.56438, 5.75621

### Charges guide
| | |
|---|---|
| Per unit incl. 2 persons and electricity | € 17.00 - € 45.00 |
| extra person | € 6.00 - € 8.00 |

For latest campsite news, availability and prices visit
## alanrogers.com

# Doucier

## Camping les Mérilles

Rue des 3 Lacs, F-39130 Doucier (Jura) T: 03 84 25 73 06. E: camping.lesmerilles@wanadoo.fr
**alanrogers.com/FR39170**

Camping les Mérilles is a small, good quality, family run campsite 500 m. from the small town of Doucier and only 2 km. from the beautiful Lac de Chalain. It has 96 good sized, level, grass pitches separated by hedging. A variety of trees give some shade. There are 76 pitches for touring with 16 having a private bathroom. All have electricity (10A). This site is a quieter alternative to the much busier sites near the lake. The surrounding area is well worth exploring and is well known for its lakes, waterfalls and caves. Owners of large outfits should phone ahead to reserve the larger pitches.

### Facilities

One modern, well appointed and heated toilet block near reception, one older and very small block plus 16 private cabins to rent with certain pitches. Motorcaravan services. Shop and bar with TV (1/6-30/9). Takeaway (1/7-30/9). Outdoor heated pool and paddling pool (1/5-30/9). Playground. Bicycle hire. WiFi (charged). Organised family activities (July/Aug). Off site: Riding 50 m. Fishing 100 m. Doucier with small shops, bar and restaurant 500 m. Lac de Chalain, indoor pool, beach and watersports 2 km.

**Open:** 1 April - 30 September.

### Directions

Doucier is 25 km. east of Lons-le-Saunier. The site is 500 m. east of Doucier on the D39 with the entrance on the right. GPS: 46.65178, 5.77491

### Charges guide

| | |
|---|---|
| Per unit incl. 2 persons and electricity | € 16.00 - € 20.40 |
| incl. private bathroom | € 20.00 - € 27.45 |
| extra person | € 3.80 - € 4.10 |
| child (2-7 yrs) | € 2.50 |

# La Tour-du-Meix

## Camping de Surchauffant

Le Pont de la Pyle, F-39270 La Tour-du-Meix (Jura) T: 03 84 25 41 08. E: info@camping-surchauffant.fr
**alanrogers.com/FR39020**

With only 200 pitches, this site may appeal to those who prefer a more informal atmosphere, however it can be lively in high season. It is pleasantly situated above the beaches bordering the Lac de Vouglans, which can be reached quickly on foot directly from the site. The 157 touring pitches are of a reasonable size and are informally arranged, some are fully serviced and most have electricity (10A). They are divided by hedges and there is some shade. The lake offers a variety of watersports activities, boat trips, etc. and is used for fishing and swimming (guarded in high season as it shelves steeply). Two signposted walks start from within 100 m. of the site entrance. English is spoken.

### Facilities

The sanitary facilities are older in style and adequate rather than luxurious, but reasonably well maintained and clean when we visited. They include some washbasins in private cabins. Laundry. Heated swimming pool (200 sq.m), paddling pool and surround (15/6-15/9). Three playgrounds. Entertainment (July/Aug). Safety deposit boxes. Off site: Bicycle hire and riding 5 km. Restaurant, takeaway and shops adjacent.

**Open:** 26 April - 16 September.

### Directions

From A39 take exit 7 and N1082 to Lons-le-Saunier. Continue south on D52 for 20 km. to Orgelet. Site is by the D470, at La Tour-du-Meix, 4 km. east of Orgelet. GPS: 46.5231, 5.67401

### Charges guide

| | |
|---|---|
| Per unit incl. 2 persons and electricity | € 15.00 - € 23.50 |
| extra person (over 4 yrs) | € 2.50 - € 4.70 |
| dog | € 1.00 - € 1.60 |

SURCHAUFFANT
Camping ★ ★ ★ Jura
www.camping-surchauffant.fr

Le Pont de la Pyle • F - 39270 LA TOUR DU MEIX
Tél. 0033 384 25 41 08 • Fax 0033 384 35 56 88 • info@camping-surchauffant.fr

**FREE** Alan Rogers Travel Card
Extra benefits and savings - see page 10

## Lons-le-Saunier
### Camping la Marjorie

640 boulevard de l'Europe, F-39000 Lons-le-Saunier (Jura) T: 03 84 24 26 94. E: info@camping-marjorie.com
**alanrogers.com/FR39060**

La Marjorie is a spacious site set on the outskirts of the spa town of Lons-le-Saunier with a long season. Bordering one area of the site are open fields and woodlands. It has 200 level pitches, 180 for touring units and 127 with electricity (6/10A). Some are on hardstanding and 37 are fully serviced. They are separated by well trimmed hedges interspersed with tall trees which gives privacy plus some shade. There is a cycle path from the site into town (2.5 km) and a mountain bike track behind the site. This is a good site for a long or short stay.

**Facilities**

Three well maintained toilet blocks, two modern and heated, baby baths, facilities for disabled visitors. Small shop (15/6-31/8). Small bar with takeaway meals (all 15/6-31/8). TV room. Small play area. Boules. Football field. Archery, canoeing and riding. Motorcaravan service point (charged). Bicycle hire. Free WiFi throughout. Off site: Swimming pool 200 m. (free for min. 5 day stay). Bus stop 400 m. Restaurants 500 m. Fishing 3 km.

**Open:** 1 April - 15 October.

**Directions**

Site is off the N1083 Lons-le-Saunier-Besançon road, just north of Lons. Follow signs for camping and piscine. GPS: 46.68437, 5.56843

**Charges guide**

| Per unit incl. 2 persons | |
|---|---|
| and electricity | € 15.95 - € 21.90 |
| extra person | € 3.50 - € 5.15 |
| child (under 10 yrs) | € 2.30 - € 3.40 |

## Luxeuil-les-Bains
### Domaine du Chatigny

14 rue du Gramont, F-70300 Luxeuil-les-Bains (Haute-Saône) T: 03 84 93 97 97.
E: camping.ot-luxeuil@wanadoo.fr **alanrogers.com/FR70010**

An excellent example of a well cared for municipal site, du Chatigny is located on a hillside backing onto woods, yet is only a five minute walk from the centre of the interesting old spa town of Luxeuil-les-Bains. As the site has only recently been opened, all facilities are of a high quality and were very clean when we visited. There are 98 good sized, level or slightly sloping, grass pitches separated by young shrubs and trees with not much shade. Of the 78 touring pitches 52 have electricity (16A) and 26 are fully serviced. Some activities are on site, but a wide programme of events is offered within walking distance.

**Facilities**

One modern, heated toilet block is excellent and provides all necessary facilities. Motorcaravan services. Snack bar, swimming and paddling pool (open weekends June, Sept and daily July/Aug). Games/TV room. Tennis. Internet, WiFi. Off site: Spa town of Luxeuil-les-Bains with good range of shops, bars, restaurants, Casino, Saturday market and many organised events, 5 minutes walk. Fishing and riding 2 km. Golf 10 km.

**Open:** 1 April - 31 October.

**Directions**

The site is 45 km. south of Epinal. Bypass Luxeuil-les-Bains (no vehicle access in centre) on N57 and at supermarket (site signed) turn west into rue Ste Anne. Bear right three times to site (900 m). GPS: 47.8236, 6.381667

**Charges guide**

| Per unit incl. 2 persons | |
|---|---|
| and electricity | € 16.00 - € 20.00 |
| extra person | € 2.00 - € 4.00 |

## Malbuisson
### Camping les Fuvettes

24 route de la Plage et des Perrières, F-25160 Malbuisson (Doubs) T: 03 81 69 31 50.
E: les-fuvettes@wanadoo.fr **alanrogers.com/FR25080**

High in the Jura and close to the Swiss border, les Fuvettes is a well established family site beside Lac Saint Point. The 320 reasonably sized grass pitches are separated by hedges and small trees with varying degrees of shade and many are slightly sloping. There are 250 for touring with 200 having electricity (6A). Only a few have views over the lake. The swimming pool complex is impressive with water slides and a separate children's pool. The site's bar/snack bar is housed in an attractive, steep roofed building and offers panoramic views across the lake.

**Facilities**

Three toilet blocks include facilities for babies and disabled visitors. Shop. Bar and snack bar. Swimming pool with water slides, jacuzzi and paddling pool (from June). Play area. Minigolf. Archery. Bicycle hire. Sports pitch. Fishing (permit needed). Boat and pedalo hire. Games room. TV room. Children's club in peak season. Entertainment and excursion programme (July/Aug). Mobile homes and chalets for rent. WiFi (charged). Off site: Lake beach. Sailing school. Tennis. Riding 1 km.

**Open:** 1 April - 30 September.

**Directions**

From Besançon, head south on the N57 to just beyond Pontarlier. Take the D437 signed Lac Saint Point and Mouthe. The road skirts the lake and through Malbuisson. Site is on right at end of village. GPS: 46.79197, 6.29334

**Charges guide**

| Per unit incl. 2 persons | |
|---|---|
| and electricity | € 18.90 - € 24.90 |
| extra person | € 3.80 - € 5.00 |

For latest campsite news, availability and prices visit
**alanrogers.com**

## Marigny
### Castel Camping la Pergola

1 rue des Vernois, F-39130 Marigny (Jura) T: 03 84 25 70 03. E: contact@lapergola.com
**alanrogers.com/FR39040**

Close to the Swiss border and overlooking the sparkling waters of Lac de Chalain, la Pergola is a good quality terraced site set amongst the rolling hills of the Jura. Neat and tidy, it is very well appointed, with 350 pitches, 100 for touring, mainly on grass and gravel and separated by small hedges. All have electricity (6A), water and drainage and some have shade from a variety of mature trees. The well appointed bar/restaurant and terrace are next to the three swimming pools and the entertainment area, with good views over the lake. This is a good holiday base in high season for families. English is spoken.

| Facilities | Directions |
|---|---|
| Three good quality and well appointed toilet blocks provide all the necessary facilities. Motorcaravan services. Shop (15/6-9/9). Self service restaurant (15/5-9/9). Bar, takeaway (all season). Pool complex (all season), two pools heated. Good play areas and children's club. Archery. Boules. Lake swimming. Fishing. Organised programme in high season. Internet access and WiFi (charged). Off site: Riding 3 km. Golf 25 km.  **Open:** 1 April - 15 October. | Doucier is 25 km. east of Lons-le-Saunier. On outskirts of Doucier turn north onto D27, site signed. Site in 3 km. beside Lac de Chalain. GPS: 46.6771, 5.78094 |

**Charges guide**

| | |
|---|---|
| Per unit incl. 2 persons and electricity | € 19.00 - € 38.00 |
| extra person | € 5.50 - € 7.00 |
| Camping Cheques accepted. | |

## Mesnois
### Camping Beauregard

2 Grande rue, F-39130 Mesnois (Jura) T: 03 84 48 32 51. E: reception@juracampingbeauregard.com
**alanrogers.com/FR39120**

A hillside site on the edge of a small village with views of the rolling countryside, Beauregard has 192 pitches. A fenced area encloses indoor and outdoor pools and sun terrace. The indoor area includes a jacuzzi, sauna and hot tub. Mobile homes and tents for rent leave around 155 for touring units, all with 6A electricity (long leads may be necessary). The tarmac roads are narrow in places, and many pitches are compact and could be more level. Larger outfits may have difficulty fitting everything on the pitch and with levelling, although the newer pitches on the lower level could be more suitable (but no shade).

| Facilities | Directions |
|---|---|
| Three very clean toilet blocks evenly distributed around the site make a good provision, although the newest on the lower section is only opened in peak season. Baby room and facilities for disabled visitors. Indoor and outdoor pools (15/6-31/8) with toilet and shower facilities. Play areas. WiFi (charged). Off site: Restaurant, bar and takeaway (1/4-30/9) adjacent to site. Fishing 500 m. Boat launching 2 km. Pont de Poitte 2 km. Riding 5 km.  **Open:** 1 April - 30 September. | From Lons-le-Saunier (easily accessed from A39) take N78 southeast towards Clairvaux-les-Lacs. After 17 km. in Thuron (before Pont-de-Poitte) turn left on D151 to Mesnois. Site is 1 km. on left by road junction. GPS: 46.59976, 5.68824 |

**Charges guide**

| | |
|---|---|
| Per unit incl. 2 persons and electricity | € 22.80 - € 27.50 |
| extra person | € 3.80 - € 4.80 |

## Ounans
### Camping la Plage Blanche

3 rue de la Plage, F-39380 Ounans (Jura) T: 03 84 37 69 63. E: reservation@la-plage-blanche.com
**alanrogers.com/FR39010**

In the Jura, by the rippling waters of the River Loue, this spacious eight-hectare site has 220 pitches (193 for touring, 70 on the riverbank). All are large, grassy and level with 10A electricity (Europlugs). In low season, this is a perfect site for couples; in high season it is ideal for family holidays with its children's club (5-11 yrs), two evening events per week in the bar/restaurant (DJ or live music), swimming pool, kayaking, canoeing, fishing, fly fishing and woodland walks in the site's own wood. La Plage Blanche is an excellent base for exploring Dole, Arbois and its vineyards.

| Facilities | Directions |
|---|---|
| Three modern, clean sanitary blocks, recently renovated, include showers, washbasins in cabins and facilities for babies and campers with disabilities. Launderette. Motorcaravan service area. Shop for basics, bar/restaurant with terrace, takeaway (1/5-15/9). Swimming and paddling pools (15/5-15/9). New (2012) adults only spa. Play area. Activities and children's club (1/7-30/8). Volleyball. Boules. River fishing and fishing lake. Free WiFi.  **Open:** 1 April - 30 September. | Ounans is 20 km. southeast of Dole. From autoroute A39 exit 6 (Dole Choisey) follow signs for Pontarlier. In Ounans turn left just before the pizzeria (campsite signed). GPS: 47.00284, 5.663 |

**Charges 2013**

| | |
|---|---|
| Per unit incl. 2 persons and electricity | € 28.00 |
| extra person | € 5.50 |
| No credit cards. | |

**FREE** Alan Rogers Travel Card
Extra benefits and savings - see page 10

## Rougemont
### Castel Camping le Val de Bonnal

1 Chemin du Moulin, F-25680 Bonnal (Doubs) T: 03 81 86 90 87. E: val-de-bonnal@wanadoo.fr
alanrogers.com/FR25000

This is an impressive, generally peaceful, well managed site in a large country estate, designed to blend harmoniously with the surrounding countryside, well away from main roads and other intrusions. The site itself is very busy, with a wide range of activities and amenities. The 280 good sized, landscaped pitches (160 for touring) with electricity (6-10A) are separated by a mixture of trees and bushes. The main attraction must be the variety of watersports on the three large lakes and nearby river. The range of activities available in high season is almost inexhaustible, not to say exhausting!

**Facilities**

Four toilet blocks include washbasins in cabins, suites for disabled visitors. Facilities for children and babies. Laundry facilities. Riverside restaurant, snack bar, takeaway, bar and terrace, shop (all 7/5-6/9). Swimming pool complex with water slides. Well equipped play areas. Sport and fitness facilities. Boules. Watersports. Fishing on the river and lake. Bicycle hire. Fitness suite. WiFi (charged). Off site: Rougemont 3.5 km. Golf 6 km. Riding 7 km. Day trips to Switzerland.

**Open:** 4 May - 7 September.

**Directions**

From Vesoul take D9 towards Villersexel. After 20 km. turn right in Esprels signed Val-de-Bonnal. Continue for 3.5 km. to site on left. From autoroute A36, exit Baume-les-Dames; go north on D50, then D486 to Rougemont and follow site signs. GPS: 47.50698, 6.35487

**Charges 2013**

| Per unit incl. 2 persons | |
|---|---|
| and electricity | € 27.00 - € 47.70 |
| extra person | € 7.30 - € 13.50 |

## Saint Point-Lac
### Camping Municipal de Saint-Point-Lac

8 rue du Port, F-25160 Saint Point-Lac (Doubs) T: 03 81 69 61 64. E: camping-saintpointlac@wanadoo.fr
alanrogers.com/FR25050

This pleasant, well run municipal site occupies a fine position on the shore of the third largest natural lake in France, with views across to the distant hills. The 84 level, numbered pitches are on grass and 61 have electricity (16A). It could be used for an overnight stop if passing Pontarlier but above all it is an ideal base for those who enjoy fishing, walking, cycling, or watersports. You can fish or swim in the lake, and just outside the entrance, you can have a drink at the open-air bar, hire canoes and rowing-boats or play boules and volleyball.

**Facilities**

Well maintained, traditional style central sanitary block is fully enclosed and heated. Modern preset showers, warm water to washbasins (open-style except two for ladies). Hot water to dishwashing and laundry sinks. Basic en-suite unit for disabled visitors. Washing machine and dryer. Play area (2-6 yrs). Table tennis. Shop with terrace. Fishing and swimming in the lake. Bicycle hire. WiFi over most of site (charged). Off site: Lakeside walk. Motorcaravan services opposite. Beach and swimming area (supervised in high season). Various leisure activities. Village 200 m.

**Open:** 15 April - 15 October.

**Directions**

The site is 70 km. southeast of Besançon. From Pontarlier take N57 south (Lausanne). After station, take exit for D437 towards Malbuison and in 5 km. turn right along west side of lake (D129) to Saint-Point Lac; from south exit N57 at Les Hôpitaux-Neufs and turn west via D9 to lake then north on D129. GPS: 46.8118, 6.3031

**Charges guide**

| Per unit incl. 2 persons | |
|---|---|
| and electricity | € 15.00 - € 16.00 |
| extra person | € 3.00 |

## Vesoul-Vaivre
### Camping International du Lac

Avenue des Rives du Lac, F-70000 Vesoul-Vaivre (Haute-Saône) T: 03 84 76 22 86.
E: camping_dulac@yahoo.fr  alanrogers.com/FR70020

Part of a leisure park around a large lake, this campsite has 160 good sized, level pitches, mostly on grass, but with 29 hardstandings; they are separated by shrubs and bushes and 133 have electricty (6A). There is a large area in the centre of the site with a play area, a volleyball court and boules. Just outside the gate is a bar/restaurant and a pleasant beach for swimming and fishing. A five kilometre path runs around the lake for jogging, walking and cycling and there are zones for boating and windsurfing.

**Facilities**

Three traditional, clean toilet blocks, one heated, provide British (seatless) and Turkish style WCs, some washbasins in cabins, and preset showers. Baby room. Three superb suites for disabled visitors. Washing machines and dryer. Motorcaravan service point outside site. Baker calls daily (July/Aug); bread ordered from reception at other times. Entertainment (July/Aug). Bicycle hire. TV and games rooms. Volleyball. Boules. Internet access. WiFi (charged).

**Open:** 4 January - 19 December.

**Directions**

Vesoul is 50 km. north of Besançon. Site is 2 km. west of town. From D457 Epinal/Besançon turn west at roundabout following signs for Vaivre-et-Montoille and campsite. GPS: 47.63054, 6.12946

**Charges guide**

| Per unit incl. 2 persons and electricity | € 17.45 |
|---|---|
| extra person | € 3.90 |
| child (under 7 yrs) | € 1.85 |

This quiet and deeply rural province is right in the centre of France to the south of the tourist region of the Loire Valley. Unspoilt and thinly populated, it is unknown to many but by others is considered close to paradise.

**DÉPARTEMENTS: 19 CORRÈZE, 23 CREUSE, 87 HAUTE-VIENNE**

**MAJOR CITIES: LIMOGES, BRIVE-LA-GAILLARDE**

On the western side of the Massif Central, this stunningly beautiful region of still lakes, fast flowing streams, gentle rolling valleys and forested mountains has been one of the best kept secrets in France. Lush green meadows are grazed by the Limousin breed of cattle, numerous ancient villages and churches dot the landscape, as well as more imposing abbey churches and fortresses. The region's moorland has made it popular with horse breeders and the Anglo-Arab horse originated from the famous studs of Pompadour.

The city of Limoges, synonymous with porcelain production, produced the finest painted enamelware of Europe in the 16th and 17th centuries and today remains the porcelain capital of France. Aubusson is renowned for its beautiful and intricate tapestries.

But Limousin's appeal is more than anything the freedom of the countryside and it has not yet been discovered except by the discerning traveller. It is said that in Limousin a discovery awaits you at the end of every path and we consider this to be a fairly accurate description.

### Places of interest

*Aubusson:* long tradition of tapestry making, Hotel de Ville tapestry collections.

*Grimel-les-Cascades:* a pretty hamlet set in a deep gorge.

*Gueret:* built around a monastery founded in the 8th century, the municipal museum houses a fine collection of porcelain.

*Limoges:* porcelain, enamel and faience work, château, church of St Michel-de-Lions, cathedral of St Etienne.

*Oradour sur Glane:* war-damaged village preserved from 1944.

*Segur-le-Château:* picturesque village dominated by its fortified château, Henry IV's house.

*Treignac:* Rocher des Folles with a view of the Vézères gorges.

*Tulle:* 12th-century cathedral and cloister, City museum, Maison de Loyac.

### Cuisine of the region

Traditional dishes include a variety of stews such as pote, cassoulet, beans and pork and sauced dishes accompanied by chestnuts or rye pancakes. Limousin beef is tender and full of flavour.

*Bréjaude:* a soup eaten with rye bread and so thick with cabbage and other vegetables that a spoon will stand up in it.

*Clafoutis:* a pancake batter poured, for example, over fruit.

*Galette Corrzienne:* almond cake.

*Pâté aux pommes de terre:* potatoes and crème fraîche in a puff pastry crust.

www.tourismelimousin.com or
www.massifcentral-tourisme.com
documentation@crt-limousin.fr
(0)5 55 11 05 90

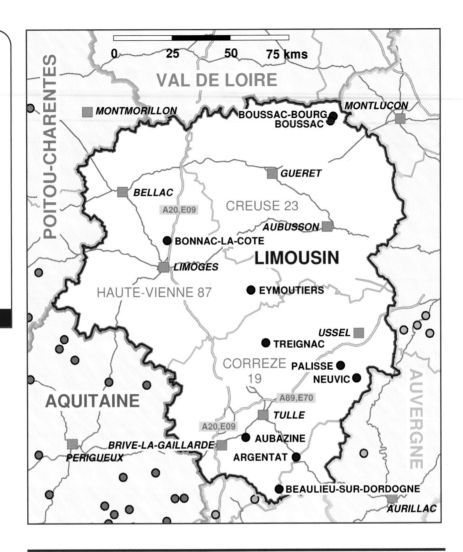

## Argentat
### Camping le Vaurette

Monceaux-sur-Dordogne, F-19400 Argentat (Corrèze) T: 05 55 28 09 67. E: info@vaurette.com

**alanrogers.com/FR19090**

You are assured of a warm welcome at this immaculate site, beautifully situated beside the shallow River Dordogne and just a few kilometres from Argentat. There are 120 large, gently sloping grass pitches, 118 for touring. Separated by a large variety of beautiful trees and shrubs offering varying amounts of shade, all have 6A electricity and many have good views over the River Dordogne as the pitches nearest the river are slightly terraced. The owners run an active campsite for all the family whilst maintaining an air of tranquillity (no radios). Excellent English and Dutch are spoken.

### Facilities

Two very clean traditional toilet blocks offer all the expected facilities, including facilities for disabled visitors. Further facilities are near the bar and heated pool. Motorcaravan service point. Shop and takeaway (July/Aug). Football. Gym. Badminton. Boules. Tennis. Fishing. River bathing. Accompanied canoe trips, walks and mountain bike rides. Organised activities for all the family (July/Aug) but no late night discos etc. WiFi. Off site: Argentat with shops and watersports centre 9 km. Riding 15 km.

**Open:** 1 May - 21 September.

### Directions

From the A20 or A89 take the exit for Tulle then the N120 to Argentat, onto the D12 towards Beaulieu. The site is on the left. GPS: 45.0464, 1.8821

### Charges 2013

| | |
|---|---|
| Per unit incl. 2 persons and electricity | € 19.80 - € 30.70 |
| extra person (over 2 yrs) | € 4.15 - € 6.20 |
| dog | € 2.00 - € 3.50 |

## Argentat
### Sunêlia Au Soleil d'Oc

Monceaux-sur-Dordogne, F-19400 Argentat (Corrèze) T: 05 55 28 84 84. E: info@dordogne-soleil.com
**alanrogers.com/FR19100**

You will be assured of a very warm welcome, throughout the long season, at this attractive family run site set amongst a variety of tall trees on the banks of the River Dordogne. The 120 large, level, grass pitches, 80 for tourists, all with 6A electricity, are mostly separated by neatly trimmed shrubs and hedges. They are set out on two levels; the lower level nearer the river, with fewer static pitches, being some distance from the toilet facilities and sports area. This site should appeal to lovers of watersports and other activities, particularly in July and August when there is plenty to do for all the family.

**Facilities**

Two unisex toilet blocks offer all the facilities one would expect. Baby facilities. Shop (1/7-31/8). Bar (1/5-31/10). Restaurant and takeaway (1/6-30/9). Outdoor pool (1/5-15/10). New indoor pool planned. Motorcaravan service point. Bathing in the River Dordogne. Canoe hire and organised trips. Volleyball, football, pool table and electronic games. Archery. Minigolf. Fishing. Bicycle hire. Guided walks and bike rides. Entertainment programme (July/Aug). WiFi. Torches useful. Off site: River Dordogne. Argentat 4 km. Riding 15 km. Rocamadour is well worth a visit. Waterfall at Murel. Prehistoric caves at Gouffre de Padirac and Lacave.

**Open:** 4 April - 15 November.

**Directions**

Leave Argentat on D12 heading southwest (Beaulieu). In 3.5 km. (village of Laygue) turn left across a single track bridge spanning the River Dordogne. Immediately turn left and site is a few hundred metres on left. GPS: 45.0753, 1.91699

**Charges guide**

| | |
|---|---|
| Per unit incl. 2 persons and electricity (6A) | € 17.90 - € 27.90 |
| extra person | € 3.90 - € 6.90 |
| child (2-13 yrs) | free - € 4.30 |
| dog | free - € 3.20 |

Camping Cheques accepted.

---

## Aubazine
### Campéole le Coiroux

Campé●le

Centre Touristique du Coiroux, F-19190 Aubazine (Corrèze) T: 05 55 27 21 96. E: coiroux@campeole.com
**alanrogers.com/FR19140**

Le Coiroux, part of the Campéole group, is set in a picturesque location in the heart of a forest on the edge of a large leisure park and lake. There are 174 large pitches, 62 for touring all with 10A electricity. They are flat and grassy with small dividing hedges and trees giving shade. The large number of mobile homes and chalets on site are separate from the camping area and not intrusive. There is everything one needs for a family holiday at this site which caters for adults and children of all ages.

**Facilities**

One large modern very well equipped sanitary block with all necessary facilities including those for disabled campers. Baby room. Washing machines and tumble dryers. Second smaller sanitary block. Motorcaravan service point. Large heated swimming pool (1/5-30/9). Poolside bar, snack bar and large shop selling groceries, fruit and vegetables (1/7-31/8). Boules. Tennis. Organised daytime activities for children, teenagers and adults (July/Aug). Accommodation for hire. Free WiFi. Off site: Leisure park (reduced fees charged). Lake fishing 300 m. Excellent 27-hole golf complex 800 m. Tree walking adventure course. Paintball. Rocamadour.

**Open:** 1 April - 30 September.

**Directions**

Leave A20 exit 50 Brive centre, take N28 towards Tulle. At Gare d'Aubazine turn right to Aubazine. Continue for 6 km. through village, take road to Chastang and follow signs to Parc Touristique du Coiroux 4 km. GPS: 45.18633, 1.70775

**Charges guide**

| | |
|---|---|
| Per unit incl. 2 persons and electricity | € 15.10 - € 24.50 |
| extra person | € 4.00 - € 5.90 |
| child (2-6 yrs) | free - € 3.90 |
| dog | € 2.00 - € 2.60 |

**FREE** Alan Rogers Travel Card
Extra benefits and savings - see page 10

## Beaulieu-sur-Dordogne
### Flower Camping des Iles

Boulevard Rodolphe de Turenne, F-19120 Beaulieu-sur-Dordogne (Corrèze) T: 05 55 91 02 65.
E: info@campingdesiles.fr **alanrogers.com/FR19130**

This is a very pleasant and well equipped site in a beautiful location on a small island in the River Dordogne. Camping les Iles is a very attractive family run site only five minutes walk away from the centre of the medieval town of Beaulieu-sur-Dordogne with its ancient streets, old churches, many shops and restaurants. This five-hectare site has 120 shady, grass pitches, 80 of which are available for touring, all with 10A electricity. The added bonus of its close proximity to the centre of the village makes this an ideal site for tourers.

**Facilities**

Three modern, clean toilet blocks. Baby room. Facilities for campers with disabilities. Laundry room. Motorcaravan service point. Heated pool (June-Sept), poolside bar, snacks. No shop or bread on site but town nearby. Children's entertainment (3-12 yrs) 4 days per week. Soirées 2 evenings per week. Boules. Canoe hire. Fishing. WiFi. Off site: Pizzeria and takeaway 200 m. Tennis 600 m. Bicycle hire 8 km. Golf and riding 18 km. Gouffre de Padirac, Rocamadour, Collonges-la-Rouge (less than 1 hour). Caves, museums and ancient villages.

**Open:** 23 April - 24 September.

**Directions**

The site is in the centre of Beaulieu-sur-Dordogne on the D940. From Tulle turn right or from Montal turn left. Approach site with care through the narrow streets. Enter the site through a narrow archway (3 m. high). GPS: 44.979705, 1.840146

**Charges guide**

| | |
|---|---|
| Per unit incl. 2 persons and electricity | € 13.90 - € 26.90 |
| extra person | € 3.90 - € 6.90 |
| child (2-7 yrs) | free - € 3.30 |
| dog | free - € 1.70 |

---

## Bonnac-la-Côte
### Castel Camping le Château de Leychoisier

Domaine de Leychoisier, 1 route de Leychoisier, F-87270 Bonnac-la-Côte (Haute-Vienne)
T: 05 55 39 93 43. E: contact@leychoisier.com **alanrogers.com/FR87020**

You will receive a warm welcome at this beautiful, family run 15th-century château site. It offers peace and quiet in superb surroundings. It is ideally situated for short or long stays being only 2 km. from the A20/N20 and 10 km. north of Limoges. The large, slightly sloping and grassy pitches are in a parkland setting with many magnificent mature trees offering a fair amount of shade. The 80 touring pitches have 10A electricity (reversed polarity) and many have a tap, although long leads and hoses may be necessary. Explore the grounds and walk down to the four-hectare lake. The lake provides free fishing, boating, canoeing and a marked off area for swimming.

**Facilities**

The toilet block is very clean, but perhaps cramped at busy times. Some washbasins in cabins with good provision for disabled visitors. Washing machine and dryer. Basic food provisions (bread can be ordered). Restaurant (from 10/5). Bar, TV room and snack bar. Small swimming pool with sunbathing area (no Bermuda shorts). Lake. Play area. Tennis and boules courts (requiring repair when we visited). Torch useful. WiFi (charged). Off site: Shop 2 km. Supermarket 5 km. Riding 7 km. Golf 20 km.

**Open:** 15 April - 20 September.

**Directions**

From A20, north of Limoges, take exit 27 (west) signed Bonnac-La-Côte. In village turn left and follow signs to site. GPS: 45.93299, 1.29006

**Charges guide**

| | |
|---|---|
| Per unit incl. 2 persons and electricity | € 23.00 - € 30.00 |
| extra person | € 5.00 - € 8.00 |
| child (under 7 yrs) | € 4.00 - € 5.00 |
| dog | € 2.00 - € 3.00 |

No credit cards.

For latest campsite news, availability and prices visit
# alanrogers.com

## Boussac-Bourg

### Castel Camping le Château de Poinsouze

Route de la Châtre, B.P. 12, F-23600 Boussac-Bourg (Creuse) T: 05 55 65 02 21.
E: info.camping-de.poinsouze@orange.fr **alanrogers.com/FR23010**

Le Château de Poinsouze is a well established site arranged on an open, gently sloping, grassy park with views over a small lake and château. It is an attractive, well maintained, high quality site situated in the unspoilt Limousin region. The 118 touring pitches, some with lake frontage, all have electricity (6-20A Europlug), water and drainage, and 68 have sewerage connections. The site has a friendly family atmosphere with many organised activities in main season including dances, children's games and crafts. All facilities are open all season. There are marked walks around the park and woods. This great site should ensure an enjoyable, stress-free holiday for all the family. Exceptionally well restored outbuildings on the opposite side of the drive house a shop, bar and a new restaurant serving excellent cuisine. The pool complex has a new superb water play area for children with many fun fountains. The château is not open to the public.

### Facilities

High quality, sanitary unit, washing machines, dryer, ironing, suites for disabled visitors. Motorcaravan services. Well stocked shop. Takeaway. Bar, Internet and WiFi, two satellite TVs, library. Restaurant with new mini-bar for low season. Heated swimming pool, slide, children's pool and new water play area with fountains. Fenced playground. Pétanque. Bicycle hire. Free fishing in the lake, boats and lifejackets can be hired. Sports facilities. No dogs in high season (14/7-18/8). Off site: Boussac (2.5 km) has a market every Thursday morning. The 12th/15th-century Château de Boussac is open daily all year.

**Open:** 1 June - 1 September.

### Directions

Boussac is 35 km. west of Montluçon, between the A20 and A71 autoroutes. Site is 2.5 km. north of Boussac on D917 (towards La Châtre). GPS: 46.37243, 2.20268

### Charges guide

| | |
|---|---|
| Per unit incl. 2 persons and full services | € 19.00 - € 35.00 |
| extra person | € 3.00 - € 6.00 |
| child (2-7 yrs) | € 2.00 - € 5.00 |
| dog | € 3.00 |

### Centre of France
# Château de Poinsouze
★★★★

**WiFi**

Family Campsite. Calm & Nature. Exceptional fully enclosed sanitary facilities.
Heated swimming pool. Animation 4-12 years. Chalets, gîtes & mobile homes for hire.

Route de la Châtre, 23600 Boussac-Bourg | Tel: 0033 555 65 02 21 | Fax: 0033 555 65 86 49
info.camping-de.poinsouze@orange.fr | www.camping-de-poinsouze.com

**FREE** Alan Rogers Travel Card
Extra benefits and savings - see page 10

## Neuvic
### Camping Domaine le Mialaret
Route d'Egletons, F-19160 Neuvic (Corrèze) T: 05 55 46 02 50. E: info@lemialaret.com
alanrogers.com/FR19060

Mialaret is 4 km. from the village of Neuvic and only 6 km. from the Gorges of the Dordogne. It is set in a 44-hectare estate with a 19th-century château, now a hotel and restaurant offering gastronomic dishes. More simple meals are served at the brasserie/pizzeria. Most pitches are set in a gently sloping parkland situation with numerous trees and shrubs. Some are level and separated by small bushes, most have some shade and 10A electricity. A feature of the site is the 340 sq.m. pool designed by the Art Deco architect, Hector Guimard. Entertainment and activities are organised in high season.

**Facilities**

Refurbished sanitary blocks, one heated, give an adequate provision, with facilities for disabled visitors and washing machines. Motorcaravan services. Shop with bread. Bar. Brasserie/pizzeria. Takeaway. Dinner at hotel. Large swimming pool with shallow area (15/6-15/9). Pool. Play areas. Tennis. Football. Volleyball. Pétanque. 2 fishing ponds. WiFi. Safari lodge tents, chalets and teepees for rent. Off site: Village with shops 4 km. Golf 4 km.

**Open:** 1 April - 31 October.

**Directions**

From Clermont-Ferrand or Brives on the A89, take exit 23 and follow signs for Neuvic (20 km). In Neuvic follow signs for la Mialaret (take first right after Ecomarché). Site is 4 km. GPS: 45.38242, 2.22910

**Charges guide**

| Per unit incl. 2 persons | |
|---|---|
| and electricity | € 22.00 - € 33.00 |
| extra person | € 5.00 - € 9.00 |

Camping Cheques accepted.

## Palisse
### Camping le Vianon
F-19160 Palisse (Corrèze) T: 05 55 95 87 22. E: info@levianon.com
alanrogers.com/FR19080

You will receive a very warm welcome from the Dutch owners of this spacious and peaceful site and they speak excellent English. The site is tucked away in the lesser known, very beautiful Corrèze region yet it is only a few kilometres from the River Dordogne. This region is reputed to have the purest air in France. The grassy, slightly sloping pitches are of a good size in a natural woodland setting with tall trees offering shade and all have 16A electricity. The bar, restaurant and terrace overlook the swimming pool and sunbathing area and are open all season.

**Facilities**

Modern toilet blocks with all the necessary facilities. Unit for disabled visitors. Bar. Restaurant, takeaway. Shop. Boules. Spacious play area. Bicycle hire. Lake fishing. Off site: Small town Neuvic with shops, restaurants 9 km. Large lake with water sports, swimming. Canoeing in the Dordogne (30 minutes). Riding and golf course at Neuvic. Marked walks and cycle rides.

**Open:** 1 April - 15 October.

**Directions**

Leave A89 southwest of Ussel and take N89 towards Egletons. In 7 km. just before Combressol, turn left on D47 signed Palisse and Camping le Vianon. Site entrance is on the left in 7 km. GPS: 45.42678, 2.20583

**Charges guide**

| Per unit incl. 2 persons | |
|---|---|
| and electricity | € 20.30 - € 29.65 |
| extra person (over 2 yrs) | € 4.00 - € 5.50 |

## Treignac
### Flower Camping la Plage
Lac des Bariousses, F-19260 Treignac (Corrèze) T: 05 55 98 08 54. E: camping.laplage@flowercampings.com
alanrogers.com/FR19030

La Plage is situated 3 km. from Treignac across the road from Lac des Bariousses. There are 130 large grassy pitches, 100 for touring all with 6A electricity. The site is well shaded and the flat pitches are terraced down the slope, all have easy access and many have views across the lake. Swimming and fishing are possible from the sandy beach. In high season there is a lifeguard on duty and all of the site's activities are centred on the beach and lake. There is a tunnel under the road from the site to the beach. This former municipal site is now run by M and Mme Montegut for Flower Camping and makes a good base from which to explore the many old villages and towns.

**Facilities**

Two clean, spacious, basic toilet blocks with all necessary facilities including those for campers with disabilities. Washing machine. Small basic shop in high season selling wine and some local specialities. Motorcaravan service point. Snack bar on the beach (July/Aug). Fishing, canoes and pedaloes. Small children's games room. Library with English books. Organised activities on the beach (high season). WiFi over site. Torches recommended.

**Open:** 1 April - 30 September.

**Directions**

Leave Treignac on D940, direction Guéret, site is 3 km. on the left opposite Lac des Barriousses. GPS: 45.5596, 1.8134

**Charges guide**

| Per unit incl. 2 persons | |
|---|---|
| and electricity (6A) | € 13.90 - € 21.90 |
| extra person | € 3.00 - € 4.00 |
| child (2-7 yrs) | € 2.00 - € 2.50 |

For latest campsite news, availability and prices visit
**alanrogers.com**

Set in the heart of the Massif-Central, the Auvergne was formed by a series of volcanic eruptions and is a dramatic region of awe-inspiring, non-active volcanoes, lakes, sparkling rivers, green valleys and forests.

**DÉPARTEMENTS: 03 ALLIER, 15 CANTAL, 43 HAUTE-LOIRE, 63 PUY-DE-DÔME**

**MAJOR CITY: CLERMONT-FERRAND**

The ancient province of Auvergne is a largely mountainous and sparsely populated region reputed for its natural environment and the thermal spa resorts of Vichy, Chatel Guyon and Le Mont Dore.

The 'Parc Naturel Régional des Volcans d'Auvergne' – the Auvergne Volcano Park – is the largest national park in France and is a protected environment for exceptional flora and fauna. The mountains provide three classified downhill ski resorts and excellent cross-country skiing. The area around Clermont-Ferrand is characterised by mineral-rich volcanic rock and the source of prominent mineral waters including Vichy and Volvic.

Popular destinations for visitors include the Vulcania theme park, where adults and children can learn about the fascinating science of volcanoes, and the vibrant city of Clermont-Ferrand with its black rock buildings and views of the Dôme mountains.

**Places of interest**

*Aurillac:* old town, wax museum, archaeology museum.

*Clermont-Ferrand:* old city centre, 11th-12th-century Notre Dame du Port Basilica, 13th-century cathedral; known as 'ville noire' for its houses built in local black volcanic rock.

*Le Mont-Dore:* spa, winter sports, panoramic view.

*Le Puy en Velay:* old city with cathedral and chapel in a dramatic volcanic landscape.

*Puy-de-Dôme:* Gallo-Roman site, television tower and observatory.

*Vichy:* spa buildings, opera house, riverside gardens.

*Vulcania:* 15 km. from Clermont-Ferrand. A scientific exploration park, designed for children and adults who want to discover and understand the fascinating world of volcanoes and the earth sciences.

**Cuisine of the region**

Local specialities include ham and andouille sausages, stuffed cabbage and bacon with lentil and cèpes (mushrooms). Le Puy is famed for its lentils and Vereine du Velay – yellow and green liqueurs made from over 30 mountain plants.

*Aligot:* purée of potatoes with Tomme de Cantal cheese, cream, garlic and butter.

*Perdrix à l'Auvergnate:* partridge stewed in white wine.

*Potée Auvergnate:* a stew of vegetables, cabbage, pork and sausage.

www.auvergne-tourisme.info.uk or
www.massifcentral-tourisme.com
documentation@crt-auvergne.fr
(0)4 73 29 49 99

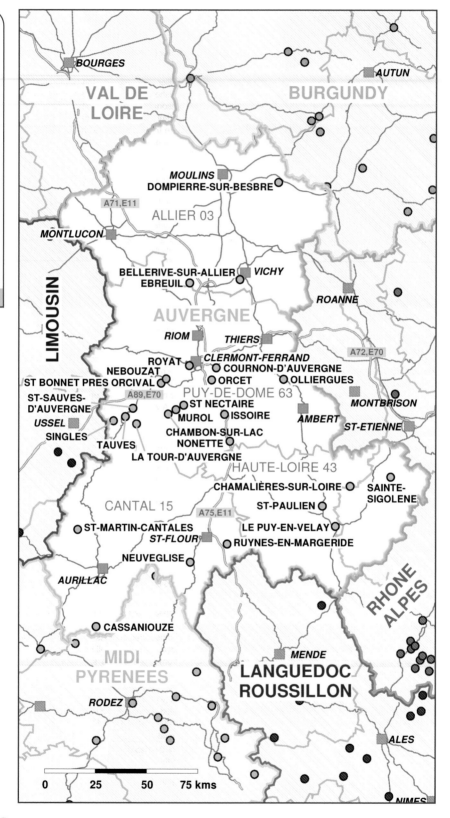

For latest campsite news, availability and prices visit

**alanrogers.com**

## Bellerive-sur-Allier
### Camping Beau Rivage
Rue Claude Decloître, les Berges de l'Allier, F-03700 Bellerive-sur-Allier (Allier) T: 04 70 32 26 85.
E: camping-beaurivage@wanadoo.fr **alanrogers.com/FR03030**

This well maintained, compact, urban site is beside the River Allier and just over the water from the famous spa town of Vichy. It has recently been completely refurbished by the enthusiastic new owners (good English and Dutch spoken). There are 80 medium sized, reasonably level grass pitches with 47 for touring. Some have delightful views across the river to the beautiful Parc Napoléon beyond. They are separated by flowering shrubs and some tall hedging, and mature trees offer some shade. All pitches have 10A electricity and 12 are fully serviced. On-site access is not easy for large outfits.

**Facilities**

Very clean, modern airy sanitary facilities in individual cubicles in pleasantly decorated buildings. Fully equipped, including a baby room and facilities for campers with disabilities. Laundry facilities. Motorcaravan service point. Small bar with snacks (Mar-Oct). River fishing. Play area. Bicycles and pedaloes. Minigolf. Archery. Internet. WiFi (first hour free). Off site: Riding, canoeing and tennis nearby. Several bars and restaurants nearby. Hypermarket complex within 1 km. Vichy 2 km.

**Open:** 1 April - 15 October.

**Directions**

From A71 exit 12 (Vichy), head east, A719 then D2209 to Bellerive-sur-Allier. Turn right at roundabout with fountains, follow signs to Berges des Allier, Campings and then Beau Rivage. Site is in 3 km. GPS: 46.11567, 3.43012

**Charges guide**

| | |
|---|---|
| Per unit incl. 2 persons and electricity (6A) | € 16.00 - € 20.30 |
| extra person | € 4.10 - € 5.30 |

Camping Cheques accepted.

---

## Cassaniouze
### Camping de Coursavy
D141, F-15340 Cassaniouze (Cantal) T: 04 71 49 97 70. E: camping.coursavy@wanadoo.fr
**alanrogers.com/FR15110**

This is a tranquil, rural site located on the banks of the Lot river. There are just 50 pitches, of which four are used for chalets. All the pitches have electricity, although some require long leads. Many have shade and some are separated by hedges. Very large units may have difficulties reaching a few pitches. Fishing from the river bank on the site is possible, as is swimming. The site also has a small, unheated swimming pool. Many interesting walks are possible in the surrounding hills. A well equipped basic site for a taste of the real countryside.

**Facilities**

One central, very clean toilet block includes facilities for disabled visitors and family and baby rooms. Washing machine, mangle and washing line. Fresh bread daily, fresh vegetables twice weekly. Small swimming pool. Sports field. Fishing. Chalets for rent. Free WiFi over site. Torches required. Off site: Walking and mountain biking. Riding. Golf. River sports.

**Open:** 20 April - 20 September.

**Directions**

Site is northwest of Rodez. From Entraygues-sur-Truyère take the D107 west for 8.5 km. where road number changes to D141. Continue 10 km. to site on the left. Go beyond the site for 500 m. to turn and enter site. GPS: 44.642551, 2.366282

**Charges guide**

| | |
|---|---|
| Per unit incl. 2 persons and electricity | € 23.90 |
| extra person | € 4.20 |

---

## Chambon-sur-Lac
### Camping les Bombes
Chemin de Pétary, F-63790 Chambon-sur-Lac (Puy-de-Dôme) T: 04 73 88 64 03. E: lesbombes@orange.fr
**alanrogers.com/FR63250**

Les Bombes is a former municipal campsite, and has been refurbished over the past few years. Recently added amenities include a heated swimming pool, a snack bar and a number of chalets for rent (single night bookings accepted in low season). The site extends over 12.5 hectares and has 150 pitches. These are large (minimum 100 sq.m), flat, grassy and generally well shaded. The site is well located for walking and mountain biking with a number of routes leading direct from the site. The site owners will be delighted to recommend possible routes.

**Facilities**

Three toilet blocks are a mix of traditional and modern and can be a long way from pitches. They have washbasins in cabins and preset showers. Baby changing. Facilities for disabled visitors (key access). Shop. Bar/snack bar (15/6-30/8). Swimming and paddling pools. Games room. Play area. Giant chess. Fishing. Bicycle hire. Weekly entertainment (high season). WiFi. Chalets for rent. Off site: Lac de Chambon 10 minutes on foot. Murol with medieval château and supermarket 3 km. Fishing.

**Open:** 1 May - 15 September.

**Directions**

Site is west of Lac de Chambon. From Murol, head west on D996 skirting the lake to Chambon-sur-Lac and follow signs to site. GPS: 45.56979, 2.90185

**Charges guide**

| | |
|---|---|
| Per unit incl. 2 persons and electricity | € 18.50 - € 23.20 |
| extra person | € 4.30 - € 4.90 |
| child (1-7 yrs) | € 3.00 - € 4.00 |
| dog | € 2.00 - € 2.50 |

---

## Chamalières-sur-Loire

### Le CosyCamp

Les Ribes, F-43800 Chamalières-sur-Loire (Haute-Loire) T: 04 71 75 91 56. E: cosycamp@sfr.fr

alanrogers.com/FR43070

Le CosyCamp is a very natural site located close to Le Puy en Velay on the banks of the River Loire. It enjoys views towards basalt columns typical of the region and the ruins of the Château d'Artias. The site is run along strict environmental lines and operates on a car-free basis. Pitches are very large (200-300 sq.m) and have electrical connections. Additonally, there is an innovative range of rental accommodation including tree houses, safari-style tents and Romany-style caravans. Other amenities include an imaginative play area and a breakfast service. The nearby town of Chamalières-sur-Loire is an attractive spot with origins dating back to Gallo Roman times. There is a good range of shops and restaurants here. A little further afield, Le Puy needs little introduction. One of France's major medieval bishoprics and traditional starting point for the pilgrimage to Santiago de Compostela, its cathedral has featured on UNESCO's World Heritage list since 1998.

**Facilities**

New sanitary facilities. Heated outdoor pool. Play area. Tourist information. Tree houses, chalets and equipped tents for rent. Off site: Shops and restaurants in Chamalières-sur-Loire. Le Puy en Velay. Golf. Walking and cycling tracks.

**Open:** 1 April - 4 October.

**Directions**

Approaching from the north (N88), head towards Le Puy as far as Monistrol-sur-Loire. Join the southbound D46, D9 and then D102 as far as Chamalières-sur-Loire, from where the site is well signed. GPS: 45.207915, 3.995343

**Charges 2013**

| | |
|---|---|
| Per unit incl. 2 persons | € 15.00 - € 23.00 |

Le CosyCamp'
Comfortably Natural

CAMPING **** • SUSPENDED TREEHOUSES • SAFARI LODGES • GIPSY CARAVANS • COTTAGES

South of Auvergne
On the banks of the Loire

Le CosyCamp'
Les Ribes
43800 Chamalières-sur-Loire
Tel 0033 (0)6 28 06 83 04
cosycamp@sfr.fr
www.cosycamp.fr

Botanical gardens
Heated swimming pools
Wellness center
Bar
Restaurant
Children's play area
Spacious tent pitches
Camper service
Pedestrian campsite

## Cournon-d'Auvergne

### Camping le Pré des Laveuses

Rue des Laveuses, F-63800 Cournon-d'Auvergne (Puy-de-Dôme) T: 04 73 84 81 30. E: camping@cournon-auvergne.fr alanrogers.com/FR63230

A well equipped municipal site, le Pré des Laveuses is adjacent to a boating and fishing lake and its beach, alongside the River Allier, close to Cournon-d'Auvergne and the A75 autoroute. This site will be busy in the high season due to its public bar/restaurant, new heated swimming pool complex, nearby activities and its proximity to Clermont-Ferrand. There are 150 large, grassy, mostly level pitches with 120 for touring (all with 10A electricity, long leads advised). They are in small groups separated from other groups by neat low hedges. Mature trees give some shade to some pitches and many have pleasant views over the surrounding hills and the town, although hedging obscures views of the lake.

**Facilities**

Two modern toilet blocks with all necessary facilities, including those for disabled campers, may be stretched when site busy. Washing machine and dryer. Public bar/restaurant with TV (June-Sept). Swimming pool complex by entrance. Children's room (TV). Play area. Boules. Overnight parking and motorcaravan services outside gate. WiFi (charged). Many high season sporting and family activities, children's club. Off site: Lake, bathing, boating and free fishing (adjacent). Canoeing (high season) and free fishing in River Allier.

**Open:** 1 April - 31 October.

**Directions**

Site is 12 km. southeast of Clermont-Ferrand. Leave autoroute A75 at exit 1, taking D212 to Cournon-d'Auvergne. Site is well signed to east of town, beside River Allier. Follow Zone de Loisirs. GPS: 45.74019, 3.22266

**Charges guide**

| | |
|---|---|
| Per unit incl. 2 persons and electricity | € 18.60 - € 22.50 |
| extra person | € 4.70 - € 5.20 |

For latest campsite news, availability and prices visit

## alanrogers.com

## Dompierre-sur-Besbre

### Camping les bords de Besbre

F-03290 Dompierre-sur-Besbre (Allier) T: 04 70 34 55 57. E: camping.dompierre@free.fr

**alanrogers.com/FR03170**

This immaculate, attractive and excellent value-for-money site has 67 level, partly shaded, individually hedged, grassy pitches, all with easy access. There are a few long stay units, leaving about 65 for tourists, all with electricity (10A) and most being fully serviced. It is located next to the municipal sports fields and is ideal for motorcaravans being within easy walking distance of the town centre and supermarket (700 m). The warden is very proud of his efficiently run site and its award-winning floral displays. Twin-axle caravans are not accepted.

#### Facilities

Modernised, heated toilet blocks, very clean with all necessary facilities including provision for disabled visitors. Some washbasins in curtained cubicles for ladies. Washing machine. Excellent motorcaravan services. Heated indoor swimming pool. Charcoal barbecues are not permitted. Off site: Small town has shops, restaurants and Saturday market. Vallée de la Besbre. Le Pal theme park and zoo 8 km.

**Open:** 15 May - 15 September.

#### Directions

Dompierre is 35 km. east of Moulins. Leave N79 at eastern end of Dompierre bypass, turn southwest on N2079 towards town. Entrance to sports complex and campsite is on left beyond D55 before the river bridge and town centre. GPS: 46.51564, 3.68434

#### Charges guide

| | |
|---|---|
| Per unit incl. 2 persons and electricity | € 9.40 |
| extra person | € 2.40 |

---

## Ebreuil

### Camping de la Filature

Route de Chouvigny, F-03450 Ebreuil (Allier) T: 04 70 90 72 01. E: camping.filature@gmail.com

**alanrogers.com/FR03010**

Beside a fine fly fishing river, not far from the spa town of Vichy, this spacious family campsite makes a good base for exploring the Auvergne, the nearby river gorges, châteaux, mountains and lakes. There are 80 spacious, grassy pitches, 74 for touring, in a parkland setting. Most have 6A electricity and some shade from mature trees. Many are directly by the river, which is clean, shallow and pleasant to play in. There is a deeper area for swimming 500 m. away. You will receive a warm welcome from the English owners, who also provide good value and very popular takeaway food. In May and June, the fields abound with wild flowers, some quite rare. Bird songs are many and varied. Listen for the songs of the nightingale and golden oriole, often heard but seldom seen. The quiet country roads are ideal for walking and cycling, especially mountain biking and for touring by car. The interesting village of Ébreuil with its Thursday market, is just a 15 minute level stroll. Just west of the site are the gorges of the River Sioule, and the extinct volcanoes of the Puy-de-Dôme with the Vulcania Exhibition are well worth a visit.

#### Facilities

Clean, fully equipped sanitary facilities, bathroom and facilities for campers with disabilities. Laundry facilities. Small shop for essentials (1/5-30/9). Baker calls. Bar (15/5-30/9). Excellent takeaway (1/6-15/9). Barbecues and pizza nights organised in high season. River bathing and fishing. Large play areas. Minigolf. WiFi. Only electric barbecues are permitted. Off site: Riding, canoeing, tennis, bicycle hire, motorcaravan services 500 m. Ébreuil with shops, bar, restaurants 1 km. Vichy 30 km.

**Open:** 31 March - 1 October.

#### Directions

Site is well signed from exit 12 of A71 autoroute to Clermont-Ferrand towards Ebreuil. It is 6 km. from the A71 and 1 km. west of Ebreuil beside the river on the D915 towards the Chouvigny gorges. GPS: 46.10877, 3.07338

#### Charges guide

| | |
|---|---|
| Per unit incl. 2 persons and electricity | € 21.50 |
| extra person | € 6.00 |
| child (under 16 yrs) | € 3.50 |

---

## Issoire

### Château Camping la Grange Fort

Les Pradeaux, F-63500 Issoire (Puy-de-Dôme) T: 04 73 71 02 43. E: chateau@lagrangefort.com
alanrogers.com/FR63040

This tranquil campsite of seven hectares is within the 25 hectare estate of the picturesque 15th-century Chateau of Grange Fort. There are 120 pitches (90 for touring units) some with panoramic views over the River Allier, others with views of the historic château. There is a mix of well drained grass and hardstanding pitches with varying degrees of shade. A short steep path leads down to the river. Guided tours of the château are available and high quality evening meals are provided in its vaulted restaurant. The campsite is just ten minutes from the A75.

**Facilities**

Three good sanitary blocks have facilities for disabled visitors and a hydra-shower. Laundry room. Bread. Restaurant and takeaway (1/5-15/9). Bar (15/6-15/9). Indoor pool, sauna, massage table (15/4-15/10). Outdoor pools (15/6-1/10). Large outdoor swimming pool with jacuzzi. Play area, games room. Internet. WiFi (charged). Tennis, minigolf, football, boules. Organised activities in season. Torches useful. Off site: Fishing 250 m. Riding 8 km. Good touring area with magnificent scenery.

**Open:** 10 April - 15 October.

**Directions**

From A75 autoroute take exit 13 onto D996 east towards Parentignat. At first roundabout take first exit on D999 new road (St Remy, La Vernet). At next roundabout take first exit (D34) and follow campsite signs. GPS: 45.50875, 3.28488

**Charges guide**

| Per unit incl. 2 persons | |
|---|---|
| and electricity | € 19.50 - € 30.25 |
| extra person | € 3.50 - € 6.00 |

## La Tour-d'Auvergne

### Camping la Chauderie

Route de Besse, F-63680 La Tour-d'Auvergne (Puy-de-Dôme) T: 06 33 78 53 45. E: info@la-chauderie.com
alanrogers.com/FR63350

La Chauderie has recently been taken over by an enthusiastic young Dutch couple. It boasts its own beautiful and totally natural waterfall on the small La Burande river. There are 70 terraced pitches arranged in small groups radiating from the winding central site road. All have 6A electricity and some are separated by hedging. There are two well specified sanitary blocks, one with facilities for disabled campers and a baby room. A new bar serving light meals adds to the relaxed, family atmosphere at this happy, well run site. Views from the site include the Mont de Sancy and village of La Tour-d'Auvergne.

**Facilities**

Two very clean sanitary blocks with good separate facilities for ladies and men include provision for disabled visitors. Laundry facilities in lower block. New bar and snack bar. Takeaway (June-Aug). TV room. Games room. Playground for small children has recently been renewed. Minigolf. Boules. WiFi (free). Off site: Shops, bars, restaurants and bank in town. Lake for swimming and fishing 900 m.

**Open:** 28 April - 30 September.

**Directions**

Leave A89 at exit 25 (St Julien Puy Laveze) and head south on D98. Join D922 Westbound for 8 km. then take D203 south to site 9 km. on left. GPS: 45.527824, 2.700008

**Charges guide**

| Per unit incl. 2 persons | |
|---|---|
| and electricity | € 14.50 - € 16.50 |
| extra person | € 3.50 |

## Le Puy-en-Velay

### Camping de Bouthezard

Avenue d'Aiguilhe, Aiguilhe, F-43000 Le Puy-en-Velay (Haute-Loire) T: 04 71 09 55 09.
E: adamluc@wanadoo.fr alanrogers.com/FR43020

This city site is located at the foot of a towering needle of volcanic rock with a church on top, which is spectacularly lit at night. This is one of three major attractions in Puy-en-Velay, a World Heritage site. The excellent location, in a wooded area within walking distance of the medieval city, is protected by a good security barrier and the manager, who speaks good English, lives on site. Tarmac roads lead to 80 marked, grassy pitches with 6A electricity, including some with water and drainage. Access is good and as the site may be popular in high season, early arrival is advised.

**Facilities**

Refurbished toilet block, facilities for disabled campers. Older and more basic unit at rear of site is used in peak season. The facilities may be stretched in high season. Motorcaravan services. Boules, volleyball and badminton. Restaurant (1/4-31/10). WiFi (free). Twin-axle caravans not accepted. Off site: Indoor pool and tennis adjacent. Fishing. Baker and small supermarket 5 minutes walk. Several other shops, bar and restaurants close by. Golf 4 km. Riding 5 km.

**Open:** 15 March - 31 October.

**Directions**

Site is northwest of town, close to where N102 crosses River Borne, and Rocher St Michel d'Aiguilhe (a church on a rocky pinnacle). Site is well signed from around town. GPS: 45.05042, 3.88094

**Charges guide**

| Per unit incl. 2 persons and electricity | € 13.60 |
|---|---|
| extra person | € 3.05 |
| child (2-10 yrs) | € 0.75 - € 1.75 |
| dog | € 0.95 |

No credit cards.

For latest campsite news, availability and prices visit
**alanrogers.com**

## Murol
### Camping du Pré Bas

Lac Chambon, F-63790 Chambon-sur-Lac (Puy-de-Dôme) T: 04 73 88 63 04.
E: prebas@campingauvergne.com **alanrogers.com/FR63070**

Le Pré Bas is suitable for families and those seeking the watersports opportunities that the lake provides. Level, grassy pitches are divided up by mature hedging and trees, with 108 mobile homes for rent, including one for visitors with mobility problems, and around 72 pitches available for tourers, all with electricity (6A). A gate leads to the lakeside, where in high season there is windsurfing, pedaloes, canoes and fishing, and 50 m. away is a beach with supervised bathing and a snack bar. There is a pool complex with heated swimming pools (one covered), a large slide and a paddling pool, plus a new wellness centre and supervised club for children. The site is in the heart of the Parc des Volcans d'Auvergne, beside the beautiful Lac de Chambon with its clear, clean water. The cable car ride up to the Puy-de-Sancy, the highest peak in the area, provides superb views. The area has opportunities for trekking and mountain bike rides (suggested routes available in reception). Superb scenery abounds; wooded mountains rising to over 6,000 feet, flower filled valleys and deep blue lakes.

**Facilities**

Refurbished toilet building with facilities for disabled guests, plus four smaller units. Washing machines, dryers, ironing, baby room. Motorcaravan services. Bar and snack bar (1/5-5/9 and some weekends in low season). Three pools of different depths (20/5-10/9, lifeguard in July/Aug). Watersports, fishing in lake. Games room, table tennis, table football, pool, TV, library. Adventure style playground. Football. Basketball. Bicycle hire. Organised activities. WiFi. Max. 1 dog. Off site: Lakeside bars, restaurants, shops. Murol 3 km. St Nectaire famous for cheese.

**Open:** 1 May - 20 September.

**Directions**

Leave A75 autoroute at exit 6 and take D978 signed St Nectaire and Murol, then D996. Site is located on left, 3 km, west of Murol towards Le Mont Dore, at the far end of Lac de Chambon. GPS: 45.57516, 2.91428

**Charges guide**

| | |
|---|---|
| Per unit incl. 2 persons and electricity | € 17.70 - € 29.90 |
| extra person | € 4.00 - € 6.70 |

No credit cards.

**Le Pré Bas**
Camping Couleur Nature ★★★★

**New : The Splashpad® : a water garden for a family adventure!!**

Discover the Splashpad®, a water playground of more than 350m², completely secure with around 15 games (geysers, water cannons, magic bucket...) - the Family Center : this area of more than 300sqm, called "Family Center", is entirely covered. It includes spa, hammam, sauna, rest area and massage (on demand) – for the adults and a play area for children. This one is made of 4 levels (pool with balls, slides, trampoline and a mini-football pitches) for the greatest joy of children from 3 to 12. Mobile homes for rent (1 special for persons in reduced mobility)
Situated at the Lac Chambon.

Lac Chambon – 63790 Murol – www.leprebas.com – prebas@campingauvergne.com

## Murol
### Sunêlia la Ribeyre

Jassat, F-63790 Murol (Puy-de-Dôme) T: 04 73 88 64 29. E: info@laribeyre.com
**alanrogers.com/FR63050**

The friendly Pommier family have put much personal care into the construction of this site. There are 460 level, grassy pitches, of which 290 are for tourers and 250 of these have electricity (6A/10A). Electricity, water and drainage is available for 71 pitches. A superb large indoor/outdoor water park includes slides, toboggan and lazy river. A small man-made lake at one end of the campsite provides facilities for water sports. It is a great base for touring being only 1 km. from Murol, dominated by its ancient château, 6 km. from St Nectaire and about 20 km. from Le Mont Dore and Puy-de-Sancy.

**Facilities**

Six excellent, very clean modern toilet blocks with facilities for disabled campers. Washing machines, dryers. Snack bar in peak season (15/6-31/8). Large indoor/outdoor water park (heated July/Aug). TV. Games room. Tennis. Fishing. Lake swimming and canoeing. Many organised activities in high season. WiFi (charged). Off site: Riding 300 m. Bicycle hire 1 km. Shops, restaurants and Wed. market (high season) in Murol 1.5 km. Lac Chambon 3 km.

**Open:** 1 May - 15 September.

**Directions**

From A75 autoroute, exit 6 (St Nectaire), continue to Murol, D978 then D996, several sites signed in town. Turn left up hill, D5, turn right opp. car park, D618. Site is second on left. GPS: 45.56251, 2.93852

**Charges guide**

| | |
|---|---|
| Per unit incl. 2 persons and electricity | € 25.05 - € 33.55 |
| extra person | € 5.75 - € 7.40 |

**FREE** Alan Rogers Travel Card
Extra benefits and savings - see page 10

## Murol

### Camping le Repos du Baladin

Groire, F-63790 Murol (Puy-de-Dôme) T: 04 73 88 61 93. E: reposbaladin@free.fr

**alanrogers.com/FR63130**

A lovely, small and friendly campsite that offers an alternative to the larger sites in this area. The owners are aiming for a quiet, relaxing site, attracting nature lovers who want to spend time walking, cycling or touring in this beautiful region. Attractively and well laid out, there are 91 good sized pitches, some with superb views of the château, 70 for touring (all with 5A electricity, 19 with water, waste water and 10A electricity), and many with good privacy. They are separated by neat conifer hedges with mature trees offering varying amounts of shade. Murol and its ancient château are half an hour's walk away.

**Facilities**

One excellent, very clean and central, heated toilet block provides all the necessary facilities including those for babies and disabled visitors. Small shop, bar with TV, restaurant with snacks and takeaway (all 15/6-30/8). Heated swimming pool and sunbathing area (1/5-10/9). Large play area. Boules. WiFi. Off site: Murol 1.5 km. Bicycle hire and boat launching at Lac Chambon 2 km.

**Open:** 27 April - 10 September.

**Directions**

Leave A75 at exit 6 (St Nectaire) and take D978 beyond St Nectaire to Murol (34 km). At far end of village turn left up hill on D5. In 800 m. turn right on D146, signed Groire and site. Entrance on right in 900 m. GPS: 45.57373, 2.95708

**Charges guide**

| | |
|---|---|
| Per unit incl. 2 persons and electricity | € 17.90 - € 22.70 |
| extra person | € 3.90 - € 4.80 |

## Nébouzat

### Camping les Domes

Les Quatre Routes de Nébouzat, F-63210 Nébouzat (Puy-de-Dôme) T: 04 73 87 14 06. E: camping.les-domes@orange.fr  **alanrogers.com/FR63090**

A popular site, it is ideally situated for exploring the beautiful region around the Puy-de-Dôme. The site has 65 small to medium sized pitches, most for touring, 50 with 10A electricity, separated by trees and hedges. Rock pegs are advised. The attractive reception area comprising the office, a small shop for essentials (high season only) and a meeting room has lots of local information and interesting artefacts. A small heated, covered swimming pool, which can be opened in good weather, is provided. There is some low key entertainment in high season.

**Facilities**

Well appointed, clean toilet block with limited facilities for disabled visitors. Basic shop (baker calls). Breakfast, snacks. Boules, pool table, table football, table tennis, giant chess, drafts. Small play area. TV and games room. WiFi. Off site: Fishing 100 m. Restaurant 200 m. Nebouzat 1.3 km. (shops etc). Riding 6 km. Hang-gliding and parascending in Puy-de-Dôme 8 km. New Vulcania exhibition 15 minutes drive. Watersports 9 km. Golf 10 km.

**Open:** 1 May - 15 September.

**Directions**

Site is 18 km. southwest of Clermont-Ferrand and signed from roundabout at junction of D2089 and D941A. It is along the D216 towards Orcival. GPS: 45.72562, 2.89005

**Charges guide**

| | |
|---|---|
| Per unit incl. 2 persons and electricity (10A) | € 17.70 - € 22.20 |
| extra person | € 5.50 - € 6.90 |

No credit cards.

## Neuvéglise

### Flower Camping le Belvédère du Pont de Lanau

F-15260 Neuvéglise (Cantal) T: 04 71 23 50 50. E: contact@campinglebelvedere.com

**alanrogers.com/FR15010**

This is a very steeply terraced, family run site in the picturesque southern Auvergne. Of the 120 pitches around 80 are for touring. The highest pitches, affording wonderful views, have no electricity and are only suitable for tents. The lower pitches have 6A electricity and some pitches have a sink, draining board and barbecue. The pitches are of a good size and separated by tall conifers and pines, offering good shade and privacy. The site roads are very steep and have sharp bends, so access may be difficult for large units. Many pitches are some distance from the toilet blocks and access may involve climbing a large number of steep steps.

**Facilities**

Two basic toilet blocks include some basins in cabins. Baby room. Facilities for disabled visitors. Sauna. Washing machine and dryer. Motorcaravan service point. Small shop (mid June-mid Oct). Spacious bar/restaurant and TV room provides meals and takeaways (July/Aug). Exercise room. Organised activities for all the family (July/Aug). WiFi (charged). Off site: Fishing and boat launching 500 m.

**Open:** 20 April - 15 October.

**Directions**

Site is 5 km. north of Chaudes-Aigues on the D921 St Flour-Rodez road. Turn west at site sign, entrance is just beyond the Belvédère Centre de Vacances. GPS: 44.89518, 3.00130

**Charges guide**

| | |
|---|---|
| Per unit incl. 2 persons and electricity | € 18.00 - € 25.00 |
| extra person | € 3.00 - € 6.00 |

For latest campsite news, availability and prices visit
**alanrogers.com**

## Nonette
### Camping les Loges

F-63340 Nonette (Puy-de-Dôme) T: 04 73 71 65 82. E: les.loges.nonette@wanadoo.fr

**alanrogers.com/FR63140**

Les Loges is a pleasant, spacious, rural site bordering the River Allier and close to the A75 autoroute. The 126 good sized, level, grassy pitches offer plenty of shade, 100 are for touring, all with 6A electricity. This site would suit those seeking a quieter holiday without too many organised activities. The river is good for bathing and canoeing and there are many walks and bike rides in the area. It is well placed to explore the beautiful Auvergne countryside, the extinct volcanoes and the many old towns and villages.

**Facilities**

Modern toilet blocks contain all the usual facilities. Small shop (July/Aug). Bar, restaurant, takeaway (mid June-mid Sept). TV room. Heated swimming pool with toboggan, paddling pool (June-Sept). Sauna, spa room (July/Aug). Volleyball. Play areas, play room. River fishing, bathing. Sunday evening dances in high season. Canoe trips. Off site: Walking and cycling routes. Small village of Nonette 3 km. Riding 5 km. Small range of shops at Saint Germain 5 km. Larger range of shops in Issoire 13 km.

**Open:** 1 April - 13 October.

**Directions**

From A75 exit 17 (south of Issoire), turn left (D214) signed Le Breuil. Bypass Le Breuil, turn left (D123, Nonette). Cross river, turn left then immediately very sharp left just after roundabout – take care (site signed). Entrance is 1 km. GPS: 45.47310, 3.27223

**Charges guide**

| Per unit incl. 2 persons | € 13.10 - € 16.80 |
| extra person | € 3.90 - € 4.70 |
| child (2-7 yrs) | € 2.50 - € 3.30 |

---

## Olliergues
### Camping les Chelles

lieu dit les Chelles, F-63880 Olliergues (Puy-de-Dôme) T: 04 73 95 54 34. E: info@camping-les-chelles.com

**alanrogers.com/FR63220**

A very rural, rustic site, les Chelles is run by enthusiastic Dutch owners. It is situated in the Parc Naturel Livradois, 25 km. south of Thiers, and is ideal for nature lovers and those seeking a quiet retreat. There are many marked walks and challenging cycle routes close by. There are 65 pitches with 55 slightly sloping, grassy pitches for touring, some with views over the surrounding wooded hills (10A electricity, long leads advised). The pitches are naturally laid out on woodland terraces but not ideal for those with walking difficulties or for large or underpowered units due to the hilly terrain.

**Facilities**

Centrally placed basic toilet block. Facilities for disabled campers. Washing machine and dryer. Motorcaravan service point (charge). Bar/restaurant (all season) with TV. Bread to order. Small swimming and paddling pools (1/6-15/9). Small play area. Tennis. Boules. Bicycle hire (high season). Small fishing lake. Activities for younger children, bike rides (high season). Free WiFi near bar. Off site: Bank, shops and restaurants in Olliergues 5 km. Wider range of shops and cutlery museum in Thiers 25 km.

**Open:** 1 April - 30 October.

**Directions**

Olliergues is on D906 25 km. south of Thiers. On entering Olliergues bear left up hill, D37. Shortly turn sharp left on D87. In 1.5 km. at church turn right and shortly left to site. Well signed from Olliergues. GPS: 45.68987, 3.63336

**Charges guide**

| Per unit incl. 2 persons and electricity | € 20.80 - € 22.80 |
| extra person | € 3.00 |

---

## Orcet
### Camping le Clos Auroy

15 Rue de la Narse, F-63670 Orcet (Puy-de-Dôme) T: 04 73 84 26 97. E: orcet@wanadoo.fr

**alanrogers.com/FR63060**

Le Clos Auroy is a very well maintained and popular site, 300 metres from Orcet, a typical Auvergne village just south of Clermont-Ferrand. Being close (3 km) to the A75, and open all year, it makes an excellent stopping off point on the journey north and south, but you may be tempted to stay longer. The 85 good sized pitches are on level grass, separated by very high, neatly trimmed conifer hedges, offering lots of privacy but not much shade. All have 10A electricity and eight are fully serviced. In winter only 20 pitches are available. Access is possible for a limited number of large units.

**Facilities**

Three very clean high quality toilet blocks. Washing machine, dryer. Motorcaravan services. Small shop, bar and takeaway (1/7-31/8). Heated pool, jacuzzi, pool for children (15/5-15/9), terrace near bar (1/6-31/8). Playground. Coffee evenings. Children's activities. Off site: Large playground and tennis court nearby and riverside walk just outside gate. Village with shops and three wine 'caves' 300 m. Fishing and canoeing 500 m.

**Open:** 1 January - 31 December.

**Directions**

From A75 take exit 4 or 5 towards Orcet and follow campsite signs. It is just before the village. GPS: 45.70018, 3.16902

**Charges guide**

| Per unit incl. 2 persons and electricity | € 30.00 |
| extra person | € 6.00 |
| child (4-14 yrs) | € 3.95 - € 6.00 |
| dog | € 2.25 |

**FREE** Alan Rogers Travel Card
Extra benefits and savings - see page 10

## Royat

### Camping Indigo Royat

Route de Gravenoire, Quartier l'Oclède, F-63130 Royat (Puy-de-Dôme) T: 04 73 35 97 05.
E: royat@camping-indigo.com **alanrogers.com/FR63120**

This is a spacious and attractive site sitting high on a hillside on the outskirts of Clermont-Ferrand, but close to the beautiful Auvergne countryside. It has 197 terraced pitches on part hardstanding. There are 137 available for touring units, all with 10A electricity (long leads may be needed) and in addition five pitches offer water and drainage. The pitches are informally arranged in groups, with each group widely separated by attractive trees and shrubs. The bar and terrace overlooks the irregularly shaped swimming pool, paddling pool, sunbathing area, tennis courts and play areas. Although very peaceful off season, the site could be busy and lively in July and August. This site would be ideal for those who would like a taste of both the town and the countryside. Royat is a 20 minute walk, but a bus runs every 30 minutes in the mornings. Dotted with lakes and forests, the Auvergne has the greatest gathering of volcanoes in Europe. The unique European Volcano theme park, Vulcania, is less than ten minutes away.

**Facilities**

Five well appointed toilet blocks, some heated. They have all the usual amenities but it could be a long walk from some pitches. Small shop (all season). Bar, restaurant and takeaway (July/Aug). Attractive heated swimming and paddling pools (26/4-16/9), sunbathing area. Tennis. Boules. Two grassy play areas. Organised entertainment in high season. Internet. Torches advised. Max. 1 dog. Off site: Royat 20 minutes walk. Bus service every 30 mins. in the mornings. Golf 7 km. Clermont-Ferrand, Puy-de-Dôme, Parc des Volcans and Vulcania Exhibition.

**Open:** 28 March - 4 November.

**Directions**

From A75 exit 2 (Clermont-Ferrand) follow signs for Bordeaux (D799). At third roundabout exit left. Shortly take exit right then turn right (Ceyrat). Leaving Ceyrat, at lights take D941C signed Royat and Puy-de-Dôme. At top of hill turn left (D5) site signed. Entrance 800 m. GPS: 45.7587, 3.05509

**Charges 2013**

| | |
|---|---|
| Per unit incl. 2 persons and electricity | € 20.70 - € 29.80 |
| extra person | € 5.40 - € 6.10 |

Camping Cheques accepted.

**ROyat**
★★★★
Tel : +33 (0)4 73 35 97 05

In a unique natural setting, at the foot of the Auvergne Volcanoes

www.camping-indigo.com

## Ruynes-en-Margeride

### Camping le Petit Bois

F-15320 Ruynes-en-Margeride (Cantal) T: 04 71 23 42 26. E: lepetitbois0639@orange.fr
alanrogers.com/FR15190

With spectacular views of the Auvergne countryside, this pleasant site on the edge of an interesting village could be no more than a convenient overnight stop when using the A75 Clermont-Ferrand/Béziers motorway. Yet it has a great deal more to offer, and we met some British visitors who came for a night and stayed a week. There are 90 touring pitches, all with electricity (10A); 16 also have water and drainage. Some are level with views across to the village, some on the hilltop among trees, others on sloping, grassy land with panoramic views of the Monts du Cantal and the distant mountains.

**Facilities**

The main central toilet block has preset showers, washbasins in cabins, children's WCs and en-suite units for disabled visitors (building is on a hill, so access may be difficult). Washing machines. Motorcaravan services. Play areas. Children's club. Weekly entertainment evening (July/Aug). TV/games room. Pétanque. Mobile homes and wooden huts for rent. WiFi (charged). Off site: Municipal swimming pool adjacent (July/Aug). Village 500 m.

**Open:** 30 April - 17 September.

**Directions**

Ruynes-en-Margeride is 110 km. due south of Clermont-Ferrand and 6 km. east from exit 30 of the A75 motorway. Village and site signed. Site is 500 m. southwest of village. GPS: 44.99904, 3.21908

**Charges guide**

| | |
|---|---|
| Per unit incl. 2 persons and electricity | € 16.50 - € 20.00 |

Camping Cheques accepted.

For latest campsite news, availability and prices visit
# alanrogers.com

## Saint Bonnet-près-Orcival
### Camping de la Haute Sioule
Route du Camping, F-63210 Saint Bonnet-près-Orcival (Puy-de-Dôme) T: 04 73 65 83 32.
E: info@chalets-auvergne.info  **alanrogers.com/FR63210**

This simple, small site is family run in a quiet, rural location in the heart of the beautiful Parc des Volcans. With good views over the surrounding hills, it is close to the Puy-de-Dôme and several winter and summer resorts. Developed from a farm with sheep and geese roaming freely until mid June, the site has 70 sloping, slightly uneven, grassy pitches with about 45 for touring (4-13A electricity, long leads needed). Access is not easy for motorcaravans and large outfits. It would be a good base for touring the region but may be noisy in the high season due to the seasonal caravans.

**Facilities**

Central basic toilet block with mainly Turkish toilets. New heated sanitary block with baby changing and facilities for campers with disabilities. Washing machine and dryer. Shop. Bar with TV. Restaurant (July/Aug). Play area for younger children. Minigolf. Boules. Fishing. WiFi. Off site: St Bonnet 200 m. with small shops, restaurant and bar. Orcival 4 km. with wider range of shops. Puy-de-Dôme and other extinct volcanoes. Vulcania exhibition.

**Open:** All year.

**Directions**

A75 just south of Clermont-Ferrand at exit 2, signed Bordeaux and La Bourboule. Continue on D2089 until Les Quatre Routes. Turn left at roundabout, D216. Bear left to site entrance in just over 500 m. GPS: 45.7084, 2.86087

**Charges guide**

| | |
|---|---|
| Per unit incl. 2 persons and electricity | € 18.70 - € 23.90 |
| extra person | € 4.40 |

---

## Saint Martin Cantalès
### Camping Pont du Rouffet
Pont du Rouffet, F-15140 Saint Martin Cantalès (Cantal) T: 04 71 69 42 76. E: pontdurouffet@live.nl
**alanrogers.com/FR15060**

A very tranquil and rural site located on the banks of the lac d'Enchanet. There are just 34 pitches, four of which have mobile homes for hire. All pitches have electricity (4/6/10A) and some require long leads. Many have shade and some are separated by young hedges. Fishing from the banks by the site is possible, as is swimming. Large units are advised to telephone in advance for suitable pitches. The showers and washing areas have recently been refurbished. There are many interesting walks in the surrounding hills and along the disused railway track. This is a well equipped but basic site aimed at those wishing to get away from the fast pace of city life, in a good walking and fishing area.

**Facilities**

Refurbished shower block. Washing machine and tumble dryer. Fishing. Indoor games. Tourist information. Mobile homes for rent. Torches required. WiFi. Off site: Nearest supermarket 9 km. Walking on marked routes and along disused railway viaducts and through tunnels. Fishing. Mountain trails for bikes. Bicycle hire 12 km. Riding 18 km. Golf 38 km. Lake sports.

**Open:** 27 April - 8 September.

**Directions**

The site is 80 km. southeast of Clermont-Ferrand. From Mauriac take D681 south for 9 km, bear right onto D680 (1 km) then left onto D37 (7 km). Turn right onto D27 then immediately left onto D6 (8.5 km) then right onto D42 (4.6 km). Site is on right. GPS: 45.072187, 2.258865

**Charges guide**

| | |
|---|---|
| Per unit incl. 2 persons and electricity | € 15.65 - € 17.65 |
| extra person | € 2.50 - € 3.25 |

---

## Saint Nectaire
### Camping la Vallée Verte
Route des Granges, F-63710 Saint Nectaire (Puy-de-Dôme) T: 04 73 88 52 68. E: lavalleeverte@libertysurf.fr
**alanrogers.com/FR63180**

Vallée Verte is a very well tended, peaceful, good value campsite. Set in the heart of the beautiful Parc des Volcans d'Auvergne, it is only a short walk from the small spa town of Saint Nectaire and close to Lac Chambon with its sandy beach and some water sports. There are many other interesting towns and villages waiting to be explored. The site has 88 level grass pitches with 70 for touring units (most with 5/8A electricity). Separated by wooden rails or a variety of hedging, a mixture of trees gives shade to some of the pitches. Twin-axle caravans are not accepted.

**Facilities**

Excellent new toilet block with all necessary facilities including a superb room for families and campers with disabilities. Motorcaravan services. Shop, bar, restaurant with takeaway. Play areas. Boules. Organised meals and walks in high season. WiFi. Off site: Fishing 100 m. St Nectaire with shops, bars, restaurants. Casino. Caves. Petrified fountains 500 m. Lac Chambon with beach 6 km.

**Open:** 15 April - 15 September.

**Directions**

Leave autoroute A75 at exit 6 south of Clermont-Ferrand. Take D978 then D996 to St Nectaire. On entering St Nectaire turn left, D642 (site signed). GPS: 45.57523, 2.99981

**Charges guide**

| | |
|---|---|
| Per unit incl. 2 persons and electricity | € 9.50 - € 15.00 |
| extra person | € 3.50 - € 5.00 |

---

## Saint Paulien
### Camping de la Rochelambert
Route de Lanthenas, F-43350 Saint Paulien (Haute-Loire) T: 04 71 00 54 02.
E: infos@camping-rochelambert.com **alanrogers.com/FR43060**

Rochelambert can be found at the beautiful heart of Auvergne, north of Le Puy-en-Velay. The site extends over four hectares and is located at the foot of the Château de la Rochelambert. It is bordered by a river and a wooded nature trail. There are 80 large pitches here (120 sq.m), mostly well shaded and equipped with 10A electricity. Some riverside pitches for 'back to nature' camping have no electricity. A number of good quality timber chalets are for rent. The emphasis here is on peace and tranquillity in an idyllic natural setting, and for this reason the site is run along very environmentally friendly lines. Several imaginative activities are organised in high season. These include workshops for children, treasure hunts, themed meals and outdoor cinema. On-site amenities include a snack bar and small shop. The nearby village of Saint Paulien has a good range of shops and other amenities.

**Facilities**

Two well positioned toilet blocks (one heated) are well maintained and kept clean. Baby room. Excellent room for disabled visitors. Good motorcaravan services. Small shop for basic needs. Snack bar serving pizza and regional specialities. Pleasant bar and terrace. Swimming and paddling pools. Fishing with chalet for preparation and freezing. Bicycle hire. Tennis. Archery. Boules. Play area. Entertainment and activity programme. Wooden chalets to rent and two caravans. WiFi (free). Off site: St Paulien 2.5 km. Walking and cycle trails. Riding 10 km. Golf 15 km.

**Open:** 1 April - 30 September.

**Directions**

Site is north of Le Puy-en-Velay. From there, head north on N102 and turn north to St Paulien from where the château and the site are well signed. GPS: 45.120173, 3.793674

**Charges guide**

| | |
|---|---|
| Per unit incl. 2 persons and electricity | € 15.20 - € 19.70 |
| extra person | € 1.70 - € 4.60 |
| child (3-7 yrs) | € 2.75 - € 3.70 |
| dog | € 1.20 - € 1.50 |

## Saint Sauves-d'Auvergne
### Camping du Pont de la Dordogne
F-63950 Saint Sauves-d'Auvergne (Puy-de-Dôme) T: 04 73 81 01 92. E: camping.pont.dordogne@gmail.com
**alanrogers.com/FR63240**

Camping du Pont de la Dordogne is attractively situated at the heart of the Auvergne, 4 km. from the important resort of La Bourboule. Given its proximity to the A89 autoroute (5 km), this site may also appeal as a stopover. There are 56 pitches here (on a 3.5 hectare site), some of which have fine views towards the chain of extinct volcanoes of the Auvergne. The site borders the River Dordogne, and therefore may appeal to anglers. There is also a small fishing lake. On-site amenities include a bar, minigolf, bowling, archery, spa and a fitness trail.

**Facilities**

Refurbished sanitary block with hot showers. Facilities for disabled visitors are good and include a fully adapted chalet. Laundry facilities. Motorcaravan service point. Bar. Takeaway. Play area. TV room. Fitness trail. Club house. Spa. Jacuzzi. Sauna. Direct access to river. Fishing. Bicycle hire. Tourist information. WiFi over site. Chalets and Romany caravans for rent. Off site: Shops and restaurants in St Sauves-d'Auvergne. Walking and mountain biking. Rock climbing. Canoeing. Rafting.

**Open:** 15 June - 15 September.

**Directions**

Leave A89 autoroute at exit 25 (St Julien Puy Laveze) and head south on D98 to Le Trador. Then join the westbound D922 to St Sauves-d'Auvergne The site is well signed in the town. GPS: 45.60249, 2.689861

**Charges guide**

| | |
|---|---|
| Per unit incl. 2 persons and electricity | € 19.00 - € 23.50 |
| extra person | € 6.00 |
| Camping Cheques accepted. | |

## Sainte Sigolène

### Kawan Village Camping de Vaubarlet

Vaubarlet, F-43600 Sainte Sigolène (Haute-Loire) T: 04 71 66 64 95. E: camping@vaubarlet.com
**alanrogers.com/FR43030**

Expect a warm welcome at this peacefully and beautifully located, spacious riverside family site. It has 131 marked, level, grassy, open pitches, with those around the perimeter having shade. The family has made great efforts to offer equal opportunity to all guests throughout its rental and touring facilities. There are 102 pitches all with 6A electricity for touring units. Excellent facilities for disabled guests include smooth paths, electric buggy, hoist to assist entry into the pool, well equipped sanitary facilities and two specially adapted mobile homes for rent.

**Facilities**

Very good, clean toilet blocks include a baby room. Two family bathrooms are also suitable for disabled visitors. Washing machine, dryer. Small shop, bread. Takeaway, bar (all season). Attractive swimming pool, children's pool. Separate solarium. Boules. Extensive riverside grass games area. Playground. Activities in season include camp fire, music evenings, children's canoe lessons. Trout fishing. Birdwatching. WiFi (free). Off site: Shops and supermarkets in Ste Sigolène 6 km. Riding 15 km.

**Open:** 1 May - 30 September.

**Directions**

Site is 6 km. southwest of Ste Sigolène on the D43 signed Grazac. Keep left by river bridge, site signed. Site is shortly on right. GPS: 45.2163, 4.2124

**Charges guide**

| Per unit incl. 2 persons | |
|---|---|
| and electricity | € 15.00 - € 24.00 |
| extra person | € 3.00 - € 4.00 |
| Camping Cheques accepted. | |

## Singles

### Camping le Moulin de Serre

Vallée de la Burande (D73), F-63690 Singles (Puy-de-Dôme) T: 04 73 21 16 06. E: moulindeserre@orange.fr
**alanrogers.com/FR63080**

Off the beaten track, this spacious and well maintained site is set in a wooded valley beside a lively river where one can join the locals panning for gold. It offers a good base for those seeking quiet relaxation in this lesser known area of the Auvergne. The 99 large pitches (63 for touring) are separated by a variety of trees and hedges giving good shade. Some pitches have hardstanding and all have electricity (5/10A), long leads may be necessary. This tranquil site is an ideal base for walkers and cyclists.

**Facilities**

Two clean and well equipped central toilet blocks, one heated, have excellent facilities for disabled visitors and babies. Washing machine, dryer. Motorcaravan services. Takeaway, bar/snack bar. Restaurant (July/Aug). Bread to order. Heated swimming pool, terrace (18/5-15/9). Large play area. Tennis. Canoe hire in high season. Organised activities (July/Aug). Bicycle hire. New communal barbecue. Free WiFi over part of site. Off site: Lake for fishing 2 km. Riding 9 km. Château de Val 20 km.

**Open:** 12 April - 15 September.

**Directions**

Site is 25 km. southwest of La Bourboule. Turn west off the D922 just south of Tauves at site sign. Follow site signs along the D29 and then the D73 for 10 km. GPS: 45.54317, 2.54275

**Charges guide**

| Per unit incl. 2 persons | |
|---|---|
| and electricity | € 13.95 - € 23.00 |
| extra person | € 2.40 - € 4.35 |

## Tauves

### Camping les Aurandeix

F-63690 Tauves (Puy-de-Dôme) T: 04 73 21 14 06. E: contact@camping-les-aurandeix.fr
**alanrogers.com/FR63200**

This municipal site is under a long term management contract by a friendly family with plans for refurbishment. It is only a few minutes walk from the centre of the village which is in the beautiful Parc des Volcans with its many extinct volcanoes and is ideal for touring on foot, bike or in the car. There are 80 small sized, grass pitches on terraces. There are 55 for touring, separated by hedges and trees offering good shade and some privacy (6/10A electricity).

**Facilities**

Two adequate toilet blocks with facilities for campers with disabilities. Motorcaravan services. Shop (July/Aug). Bread to order. Heated swimming and paddling pools (mid June-end Sept). Play area. Volleyball, basketball, football. Communal barbecue (charcoal barbecues are not permitted). WiFi. Off site: Small shops, bank, restaurant/takeaway in village 500 m. Fishing, riding and bicycle hire 1 km. Lakeside beach 8 km. Chain of extinct volcanoes.

**Open:** 4 April - 30 September.

**Directions**

Site is well signed in Tauves, 9 km. southwest of La Bourboule, just off the D922. GPS: 45.56089, 2.62446

**Charges guide**

| Per unit incl. 2 persons | |
|---|---|
| and electricity | € 15.55 - € 20.20 |
| extra person | € 3.45 - € 4.40 |
| child (2-10 yrs) | free - € 3.85 |
| dog | € 1.75 |

**FREE** Alan Rogers Travel Card
Extra benefits and savings - see page 10

With a rich and varied landscape, the Rhône Alpes offers a spectacular region that includes the craggy gorges and scented hills of the Rhône Valley, the deep valleys and mountain slopes of the Savoy Alps and the forbidding Dauphiné Alps, all offering spectacular scenery.

**DÉPARTEMENTS: 01 AIN, 07 ARDÈCHE, 26 DRÔME, 38 ISÈRE, 42 LOIRE, 69 RHÔNE, 73 SAVOIE, 74 HAUTE-SAVOIE**

**MAJOR CITIES; LYON, GRENOBLE**

The Rhône valley holds areas of great interest and natural beauty. From the sun-baked Drôme, with its ever changing landscapes and the isolated mountains of the Vercors, to the deep gorges and high plateaux of the Ardèche, studded with prehistoric caves and lush valleys filled with orchards; and encompassing the vineyards of the Beaujolais and the Rhône Valley. For the energetic there are cycling, horse riding and even white-water rafting opportunities, while for the more leisurely inclined, the remote areas are a haven for birdwatching and walking.

Lying between the Rhône Valley and the Alpine borders with Switzerland and Italy are the old provinces of Savoie and Dauphiné. This is an area of enormous granite outcrops, deeply riven by spectacular glacier hewn valleys. One of the world's leading winter playgrounds, there is also a range of outdoor activities in the summer. Despite development, great care has been taken to blend the old with the new and many traditional villages still retain their charm and historical interest. For many, it is an opportunity to escape the crowds and enjoy some clean air, unusual wildlife, stunning views and hidden lakes.

### Places of interest

*Aix-les-Bains:* spa resort on the Lac du Bourget, boat excursions to the Royal Abbey of Hautecombe.

*Annecy:* canal-filled lakeside town, 12th-century château, old quarter.

*Bourg en Bresse:* late Gothic Eglise de Brou; wetlands centre rich in birdlife.

*Bourg-Saint-Maurice:* centre of Savoie café society.

*Chambéry:* old quarter, Dukes of Savoie château, Savoie museum.

*Chamonix:* site of first Winter Olympics in 1924, world capital of mountain climbing.

*Grenoble:* Fort de la Bastille by cable car; museum with 19th- and 20th-century art.

*Lyon:* Gallo-Roman artifacts, Renaissance quarter, historical Fabric Museum, silk museum.

*Vallon-Pont d'Arc:* base from which to visit Gorges de l'Ardèche.

### Cuisine of the region

*Bresse (Poulet, Poularde, Volaille de):* the best French poultry, fed on corn and when killed bathed in milk.

*Farcement (Farçon Savoyard):* potatoes baked with cream, eggs, bacon, dried pears and prunes.

*Gratin Dauphinois:* potato dish with cream, cheese and garlic.

*Gratin Savoyard:* another potato dish with cheese and butter.

*Tartiflette:* potato, bacon, onions and Reblochon cheese.

www.rhonealpes-tourism.co.uk
info@rhonealpes-tourisme.com
(0)4 72 59 21 59

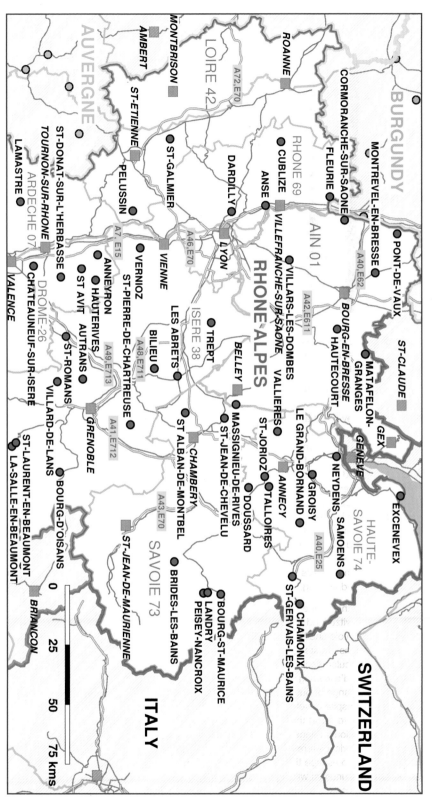

Rhône Alpes – north

**FREE** Alan Rogers Travel Card
Extra benefits and savings - see page 10

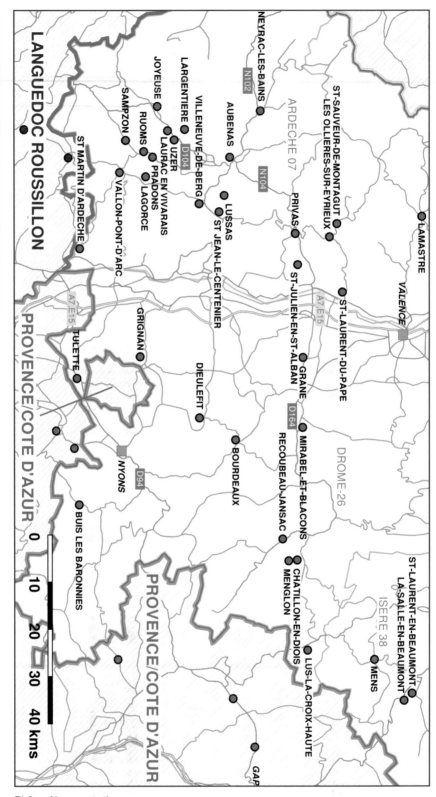

Rhône Alpes – south

For latest campsite news, availability and prices visit
alanrogers.com

## Anneyron

### Flower Camping la Châtaigneraie

Route de Mantaille, F-26140 Anneyron (Drôme) T: 04 75 31 43 33. E: contact@chataigneraie.com
**alanrogers.com/FR26140**

La Châtaigneraie is a small, neat, terraced site run by a very friendly family (English spoken). It is tucked away in the countryside high above the village of Anneyron with magnificent far reaching views over the valley of the Rhone. There are 71 medium sized, slightly sloping, grassy pitches, 28 for touring away from the static units. They are separated by a variety of hedges and young trees provide varying degrees of shade and all have 6/10A electricity. Twin-axle caravans and large outfits are not admitted and only gas barbecues are allowed on site. The Drôme is a beautiful area to explore on foot, by bike or by car.

**Facilities**

A well appointed and very clean toilet block has all the necessary facilities including those for campers with disabilities. Bar and small shop (all season). Good restaurant/takeaway with full menu at weekends and high season, otherwise a 'menu du jour'. Swimming and paddling pools (15/5-15/9). Short tennis. Two small play areas. Bicycle hire. Entertainment (July/Aug). WiFi over site (charged). Off site: Fishing, riding and golf 3 km.

**Open:** 1 April - 30 September.

**Directions**

Leave A7 autoroute, exit 12, then N7 south for 7 km. Turn east, D1, to Anneyron (7 km). In the village turn right D161, signed Mantaille. In 3 km. turn right D301, signed Albon, to site immediately on right (well signed). GPS: 45.2547, 4.9039

**Charges guide**

| Per unit incl. 2 persons | |
|---|---|
| and electricity | € 17.50 - € 29.00 |
| extra person | € 4.00 - € 5.50 |

## Anse

### Camping les Portes du Beaujolais

Avenue Jean Vacher, F-69480 Anse (Rhône) T: 04 74 67 12 87. E: campingbeaujolais@wanadoo.fr
**alanrogers.com/FR69030**

Situated just off the A6 at Anse, a warm welcome awaits you from Valerie and her enthusiastic team. This well run site has much to offer, both on site and locally. The reception area is comfortable and welcoming, and has a selection of local wines for tasting offered by the knowledgable staff. There are 133 touring pitches, some open and some with shade, and with neatly trimmed grass and hedges. All have 16A electrical connections, and many have own water. There are 65 chalets for rent which include two eco-lodges (with plants growing on the roof). Friendly staff will offer advice on cycle routes and interesting villages to visit. To one side of the site, the Azergues river passes on its last 200 m. to the Saône, where there are fishing and other water activities. On the other side of the site is a delightful, narrow-gauge tourist railway, which operates at weekends and runs into the town and to a nearby artificial lake. In July/August activities are organised by trained staff. Valerie and her staff have a wealth of knowledge about the area, which they are happy to share to enhance your visit.

**Facilities**

Modern toilet blocks include facilities for disabled visitors and baby rooms. Motorcaravan services. Washing machines. Shop. Gas supplies. Bar, restaurant, takeaway (1/6-15/9). Swimming and paddling pools (1/5-30/9). Playground. Playing field. Tennis. Minigolf. Boules. Games room. WiFi over site (charged). Free loan of barbecues. Chalets, mobile homes and 3 teepees (up to 5 persons) to rent. Off site: Fishing 200 m (permits sold on site). Anse 1 km. Riding 1.5 km. Golf 2 km.

**Open:** 1 March - 31 October.

**Directions**

Leave the A6 at exit 32 and join the D306 (N6) to Anse. Site is signed from northern and southern ends of village. There are height limits on all approaches (3 m. from the south or 2.8 m from the north). GPS: 45.9405, 4.7268

**Charges 2013**

| Per unit incl. 2 persons | |
|---|---|
| and electricity | € 22.90 - € 27.50 |
| extra person | € 4.50 - € 4.80 |

Camping Cheques accepted.

495 Avenue Jean Vacher - 69480 ANSE - Tel: 0033(0)4.74.67.12.87
E-mail: campingbeaujolais@wanadoo.fr - Internet: www.camping-beaujolais.com
Exit A6: 31.2 from North (Paris) and 32 from South (Lyon) - GPS: Longitude : 4° 43' 35,8'' - Latitude : 45° 56' 25,1''

**FREE** Alan Rogers Travel Card
Extra benefits and savings - see page 10

## Aubenas

### Camping Domaine de Gil

Route de Vals-les-Bains, Ucel, F-07200 Aubenas (Ardèche) T: 04 75 94 63 63. E: info@domaine-de-gil.com
alanrogers.com/FR07150

This very attractive and well organised site is set in a less busy part of the Ardèche and should appeal to couples and families with younger children. The 80, good sized, level pitches, 34 for touring, are surrounded by a variety of trees offering plenty of shade. All have 10A electricity. The focal point of the site is formed by the very attractive swimming pool and paddling pool which are heated all season and their large sunbathing area. The bar, restaurant and well appointed play areas for children are all adjacent. A spacious sports area and shady picnic and play area are alongside the River Ardèche.

**Facilities**

Modern well appointed toilet block, washing machine and iron. Motorcaravan services. Basic shop. Bar/restaurant, takeaway (26/5-2/9). Heated swimming pool, paddling pool. Two play areas. Boules, minigolf, football and tennis. Canoeing, boating and fishing. Organised activities in high season. Only gas and electric barbecues. WiFi over site (charged). Max. 1 dog per pitch. Off site: Shops at Vals-les-Bain 1.5 km. Interesting old town of Aubenas 3 km. Bicycle hire and riding 4 km.

**Open:** 21 April - 23 September.

**Directions**

Site is north of Aubenas. From southeast (N102), after tunnel, turn right, roundabout (signed Ucel), cross river into Pont d'Ucel (3.5 tonne limit). Bear right and at roundabout, last exit (Ucel). Shortly turn left (signed Ucel D218), then right (Ucel D578B). Site is 2 km. beyond Ucel. GPS: 44.64263, 4.37958

**Charges guide**

| | |
|---|---|
| Per unit incl. 2 persons and electricity | € 22.00 - € 38.00 |
| extra person | € 4.00 - € 6.00 |

## Autrans

### Yelloh! Village Au Joyeux Reveil

Le Château, F-38880 Autrans (Isère) T: 04 76 95 33 44. E: camping-au-joyeux-reveil@wanadoo.fr
alanrogers.com/FR38080

This superb site is run by a very friendly family (English is spoken). It is on the outskirts of Autrans, high on a plateau (1,050 m) in the Vercors region close to a ski jump and short lift. There are 101 pitches with 70 for touring, all with electricity (6A). They are mainly on gently sloping grass, in a sunny location with fantastic views over the surrounding wooded mountains with small trees giving just a little shade. There is a new pool area with two pools, one covered, a river and slide plus a separate paddling pool.

**Facilities**

The spotless toilet block is very well appointed, with underfloor heating and all the expected facilities. Another chalet-style building houses a bar with terrace, snack bar/takeaway. Two pools, one covered, toboggan for children, sunbathing area and a separate paddling pool. Wellness facilities including sauna and jacuzzi (1/5-30/8). Small play area. TV room. Internet point and WiFi (free). Family entertainment (July/Aug). Off site: Fishing 200 m. Riding 300 m. Autrans 500 m. Bicycle hire 500 m.

**Open:** 1 May - 30 September.

**Directions**

Leave A48, northwest of Grenoble, exit 13 (going south) or 3A (north). Follow N532 to Sassenage, turn west at roundabout, D531 to Lans-en-Vercors. At roundabout turn right, D106 Autrans. At roundabout in Autrans turn right and very shortly right again. Site is on left. GPS: 45.17517, 5.54762

**Charges guide**

| | |
|---|---|
| Per unit incl. 2 persons and electricity | € 25.00 - € 40.00 |
| extra person | € 5.00 |

## Bilieu

### Camping le Bord du Lac

687, route du Bord du Lac, F-38850 Bilieu (Isère) T: 04 76 06 67 00. E: camping.bilieu@live.fr
alanrogers.com/FR38470

Le Bord du Lac is located on the banks of the large Lac du Paladru, close to the village of Bilieu. It is a pleasant, terraced site with 76 grassy pitches, all with 6/10A electricity and some shade from mature birch trees. There is direct access to the lake where swimming is possible as well as various watersports, including sailing and windsurfing, and launching of your own boat can be arranged. There are many excellent walking and cycling opportunities in the area, and the campsite managers will be pleased to recommend routes. The steep access roads may be difficult for large units.

**Facilities**

Two traditional toilet blocks include preset showers. Facilities for disabled visitors (key access). Laundry facilities. Motorcaravan service point. Small shop. Bar and takeaway. Direct lake access for swimming and watersports. Small play area. Covered recreation space. Tourist information. WiFi throughout (free). Off site: Shops, cafés and restaurants in Bilieu. Bicycle hire 2 km. Walking and cycle trails. Riding. Watersports.

**Open:** 1 April - 30 September.

**Directions**

From the north on the N75 3 km. after Abrets, take the D50 to the right, signed for Paladru. After 3 km. turn left onto the D90 and follow the lake for 5 km. Site is signed to the right. GPS: 45.446127, 5.53132

**Charges guide**

| | |
|---|---|
| Per unit incl. 2 persons and electricity (10A) | € 16.40 - € 17.50 |
| extra person | € 4.50 - € 4.60 |
| child (2-10 yrs) | € 2.50 - € 2.60 |

For latest campsite news, availability and prices visit
# alanrogers.com

## Bourdeaux
### Yelloh! Village les Bois du Chatelas
Route de Dieulefit, F-26460 Bourdeaux (Drôme) T: 04 75 00 60 80. E: contact@chatelas.com
**alanrogers.com/FR26210**

Located at the heart of the Drôme Provençale, les Bois du Chatelas is a quality, family run site just 1.5 km. from the delightful village of Bourdeaux which offers some shops, cafés, etc. There are 138 level, good sized, terraced pitches, 70 for touring. They all have electricity, water and drainage. There is a superb swimming pool complex with indoor and outdoor pools, toboggan, paddling pool, fitness room, jacuzzi and sauna. Overlooking the pool area is a restaurant with superb views over the valley and hills beyond. Les Bois du Chatelas is a good choice for those seeking an active holiday.

**Facilities**

Two excellent toilet blocks (one heated), on upper and lower levels, with facilities for babies and visitors with disabilities (though not ideal for those with mobility problems). Shop. Bar. Restaurant/takeaway/pizzeria. Indoor and outdoor pools. Outdoor pool with water slide, waterfall, sauna, aquagym and jacuzzi. Sports pitch. Archery. Play area. Bicycle hire. Entertainment and excursion programme (July/Aug). WiFi everywhere. Off site: Fishing 1 km. Bourdeaux 1.5 km. Riding 5 km.

**Open:** 6 April - 16 September.

**Directions**

Leave A7 autoroute, exit 16 (Loriol). Take D104 east to Crest. Leave Crest bypass at traffic lights, take D538 south to Bourdeaux and continue towards Dieulefit for 1.5 km. Site is on the left (well signed). GPS: 44.57825, 5.12795

**Charges guide**

| | |
|---|---|
| Per unit incl. 2 persons and electricity | € 21.70 - € 38.50 |
| extra person | € 4.90 - € 8.30 |
| child (2-7 yrs) | € 3.90 - € 5.20 |

## Bourg-d'Oisans
### Camping la Cascade
Route de l'Alpe d'Huez, F-38520 Bourg-d'Oisans (Isère) T: 04 76 80 02 42. E: lacascade@wanadoo.fr
**alanrogers.com/FR38030**

La Cascade has a long season as it is at the heart of a popular skiing and cycling area. It is within sight and sound of the waterfall from which it takes its name. It is only 2 km. from Bourg-d'Oisans which lies in the Romanche valley 725 m. above sea level surrounded by high mountains. The area is a sun trap and gets very hot in summer. The site has 133 individual grassy pitches, 106 for touring units, all with 16A electricity, on mainly flat ground and of varying size. Although most are quite adequate, larger units are best near the entrance as the pitches and roads do become narrow.

**Facilities**

Two heated sanitary blocks are of good quality with mainly British style toilets, washbasins in cabins and showers. Laundry facilities. Bar and snack bar (25/6-30/8). Fresh bread daily (July/Aug). Good sized, heated swimming pool and paddling pool (1/6-30/9). WiFi. Chalets for hire (all year). Off site: Fishing 100 m. Riding and supermarket 500 m. Bicycle hire 1 km. Bourg-d'Oisans 1 km.

**Open:** 20 December - 30 September.

**Directions**

From Grenoble take D1091 (previously N91) to Bourg d'Oisans, cross river bridge, after 730 m. turn left on to D211, signed Alpe d'Huez. Site is on right in 600 m. GPS: 45.06408, 6.03903

**Charges guide**

| | |
|---|---|
| Per unit incl. 2 persons and electricity | € 24.50 - € 31.00 |
| extra person (over 5 yrs) | € 5.50 - € 7.00 |

## Bourg-d'Oisans
### Camping à la Rencontre du Soleil
Route de l'Alpe d'Huez, F-38520 Bourg-d'Oisans (Isère) T: 04 76 79 12 22. E: rencontre.soleil@wanadoo.fr
**alanrogers.com/FR38040**

The Isère is an attractive and popular region with exceptional scenery. Bourg-d'Oisans lies in the Romanche valley 725 m. above sea level surrounded by high mountains. This compact site, pleasant, friendly and family run, nestles between two impressive mountain ranges, at the base of France's largest National Park, Le Parc des Ecrins. It is a real sun trap and gets very hot in summer. It is only 2 km. from the busy town of Bourg-d'Oisans. It has 77 level, hedged pitches of small to average size with mature trees offering good shade (52 touring). Rock pegs are advised. A Sites et Paysages member.

**Facilities**

Heated toilet block provides all the usual amenities, but no facilities for disabled visitors. Washing machine and dryer. Motorcaravan services. Bread to order. Restaurant and takeaway (all season). Room with TV, play room. Small, sheltered swimming pool (all season). Play area. Children's club. WiFi throughout (charged). Off site: Supermarket 1 km. Bicycle hire and riding 2 km. Fishing 5 km. Cable car at Alpe d'Huez.

**Open:** 1 May - 30 September.

**Directions**

From Grenoble bypass Bourg-d'Oisans on N1091 towards Briançon. At end of bypass turn left at roundabout on D211 signed Alpe-d'Huez. Site is on left beyond Camping la Piscine, just before a sharp left-hand bend – take care. GPS: 45.06547, 6.0394

**Charges guide**

| | |
|---|---|
| Per unit incl. 2 persons and electricity | € 25.00 - € 36.00 |
| extra person | € 5.50 - € 7.50 |

**FREE** Alan Rogers Travel Card
Extra benefits and savings - see page 10

## Bourg-d'Oisans
### Camping le Colporteur

Le Mas du Plan, F-38520 Bourg-d'Oisans (Isère) T: 04 76 79 11 44. E: info@camping-colporteur.com
**alanrogers.com/FR38140**

This site is within a few minutes level walk of an attractive market town and ski resort, making this an ideal spot for motorcaravanners. There are 150 level grassy pitches, 120 for touring. All pitches have 15A electricity and rock pegs are advised. They are mostly separated by hedging and a variety of mature trees that offer some shade. There is no pool on site but campers have free entry to the adjacent municipal pool. In July and August the attractive bar/restaurant is the focal point for evening activities. Bourg-d'Oisans is in the largest national park in France. It is at an altitude of 700 m. and is surrounded by high mountains making it a real suntrap. The days can be very hot, especially in summer. The area is revered by serious cyclists as several mountain roads close by are regularly used by the Tour de France. This is an ideal base for exploring this scenic region with its abundance of wild flowers, old villages and rushing waterfalls; by car, on foot or by bike.

**Facilities**

Two large, clean toilet blocks are well equipped, modern and airy with all the necessary facilities including washbasins in cabins, baby room and en-suite room for disabled campers. Shop with fresh bread to order (July/Aug). Restaurant, bar and takeaway (mid June-end Aug). Games room. Boules. Small play area. Organised family activities (July/Aug). Fishing. WiFi over site (charged). Off site: Open-air swimming pool adjacent. Shops, bars, restaurants in town and supermarket 500 m.

**Open:** 1 May - 30 September.

**Directions**

Site is in Bourg-d'Oisans. From Grenoble follow the N91. Take the town bypass to the first roundabout. Site is signed from the first exit. Follow signs to site, a few hundred metres. GPS: 45.0526, 6.0355

**Charges guide**

| | |
|---|---|
| Per unit incl. 2 persons and electricity | € 25.50 - € 31.50 |
| extra person | € 5.00 - € 8.00 |
| child (0-10 yrs) | free - € 5.00 |

Pedestrian village on 5 minutes distance. Large pitches. Chalets for rent overlooking l'Alpe d'Huez
36 Chalets & 2 Gipsy Wagons for rent
info@camping-colporteur.com - www.camping-colporteur.com

## Bourg-d'Oisans
### RCN Camping Belledonne

Rochetaillée, F-38520 Bourg-d'Oisans (Isère) T: 04 76 80 07 18. E: info@rcn-belledonne.fr
**alanrogers.com/FR38100**

This spacious site is now owned by the RCN group and many improvements are planned. It has 180 well drained, level, generous, grassy pitches, most for touring, and all with electricity (10A). Beech hedges and abundant mature trees provide ample privacy and shade. A bar/restaurant with terrace is open all season and next to an attractive pool complex, comprising two pools (one covered and heated) and a large sunbathing space surrounded by gardens. In July and August the site becomes quite lively with many organised activities. Twin-axle caravans are not accepted and large outfits should phone ahead.

**Facilities**

Two well appointed sanitary blocks (one new) include baby rooms and facilities for disabled visitors. Shop. Bar/restaurant and takeaway (all open all season). TV/games room. Swimming and paddling pools (one covered and heated). Sauna. Tennis. Good play area, large meadow with fitness course. Bicycle hire (July/Aug). WiFi throughout (charged). Max. 1 dog. Off site: Riding 500 m. Allemont with shops 2 km. Fishing 4 km. Bourg-d'Oisans 8 km.

**Open:** 23 April - 21 September.

**Directions**

Site is 8 km. west of Bourg-d'Oisans. From Grenoble take N85 to Vizille and then N91/D1091 towards Bourg-d'Oisans. In Rochetaillée branch left (site signed) onto D526, signed Allemont. Site is 250 m. on right. GPS: 45.11423, 6.00765

**Charges guide**

| | |
|---|---|
| Per unit incl. 2 persons and electricity | € 20.70 - € 45.65 |
| extra person (3 yrs and older) | € 2.60 - € 5.10 |
| Camping Cheques accepted. | |

For latest campsite news, availability and prices visit
**alanrogers.com**

## Bourg-d'Oisans
### Castel Camping le Château de Rochetaillée

Chemin de Bouthean, Rochetaillée, F-38520 Bourg-d'Oisans (Isère) T: 04 76 11 04 40.
E: jcp@camping-le-chateau.com  **alanrogers.com/FR38180**

Set in the grounds of a small château with spectacular views, this site's ratings have recently been upgraded and it provides high quality amenities. The grounds are shared with chalets and tents to rent, with these in a separate area. There are 88 touring pitches, all with 6/10A electricity hook-ups on level areas (some large) separated by hedges and trees. The site has an excellent heated swimming pool, a fitness room, sauna, bar/restaurant and takeaway food together with a small shop selling bread and basic groceries. The site is in the centre of an area ideal for walkers, cyclists and climbers.

**Facilities**

Three very good toilet blocks (two very large) are colourful and very clean. Family room with facilities for babies. Excellent, spacious facilities for disabled visitors. Small launderette with ironing. Freezer space. Shop. Bar, snacks, takeaway and separate restaurant (all 18/5-15/9). Heated swimming pool (13/5-13/9). Sauna, fitness room and jacuzzi (13/5-15/9). Climbing wall. Daily activities for children (July/Aug). Guided mountain walks and other activities. Fishing. Safe hire. Barbecue area. WiFi over site (charged). Off site: Bicycle hire and riding 7 km.

**Open:** 13 May - 15 September.

**Directions**

South of Grenoble take exit 8 from A480 signed Stations de L'Oisans and follow the D1091 to Briançon. The site is signed just north of Rochetaillée at the junction with the D526. Turn here and site is immediately on the left. GPS: 45.11530, 6.00548

**Charges guide**

| Per unit incl. 2 persons | |
|---|---|
| and electricity | € 23.20 - € 38.60 |
| extra person | € 5.60 - € 8.70 |
| child (0-10 yrs) | € 3.60 - € 5.50 |

## Bourg-Saint-Maurice
### Camping Caravaneige le Versoyen

Route des Arcs, F-73700 Bourg-Saint-Maurice (Savoie) T: 04 79 07 03 45. E: leversoyen@wanadoo.fr
**alanrogers.com/FR73020**

Bourg-St-Maurice is on a small, level plain at an altitude of 830 m. on the River Isère, surrounded by mountains. Le Versoyen attracts visitors all year round (except for a short time when they close). The site's 160 unseparated, flat pitches (140 for touring) are marked by numbers on the tarmac roads and all have electrical connections (4/6/10A). Most are on grass but some are on tarmac hardstanding making them ideal for use by motorcaravans or in winter. Trees give shade in most parts, although some pitches have almost none. Duckboards are provided for snow and wet weather.

**Facilities**

Two well maintained toilet blocks can be heated and have British and Turkish style WCs. No facilities for disabled visitors. Laundry. Motorcaravan service facilities. No shop but bread to order. Small bar with takeaway in summer. Play area. Free shuttle in high season to funicular railway. WiFi on part of municipal pool adjacent (discounted entry). Fishing and bicycle hire 200 m. Riding 1 km. Golf 15 km.

**Open:** All year excl. 7/11-14/12 and 2/5-25/5.

**Directions**

Site is 1.5 km. east of Bourg-St-Maurice on CD119 Les Arcs road. GPS: 45.62248, 6.78475

**Charges guide**

| Per unit incl. 2 persons | |
|---|---|
| and electricity (10A) | € 18.00 - € 23.30 |
| extra person | € 4.40 - € 5.30 |
| child (4-13 yrs) | € 2.00 - € 4.90 |

## Brides-les-Bains
### Camping la Piat

Avenue du Comte Greyffie de Bellecombe, F-73570 Brides-les-Bains (Savoie) T: 04 79 55 22 74.
E: contact@camping-brideslesbains.com  **alanrogers.com/FR73160**

La Piat enjoys a fine setting with the mountains of the Vanoise as a backdrop, close to the important resorts of Courchevel and Méribel. This is a family site close to the pretty spa resort of Brides-les-Bains. This is a typical Savoyard village with its own sports and entertainment club. It is located at 600 m. altitude and is just 30 minutes from many magnificent hiking and mountain bike trails in the Vanoise National park. There are 80 pitches here extending over the site's 2.5 hectares. Pitches are of a good size and laid out on grassy terraces. Most have 10A electrical connections. There are also five mobile homes available for rent and two caravans.

**Facilities**

Two modern toilet blocks with baby room and facilities for disabled visitors. Washing machine and dryer. Bread and newspapers for sale (July/Aug). Play area. Children's entertainment (July/Aug). Bouncy castle. Babyfoot. Pétanque. Volleyball. Mobile homes for rent. WiFi (charged). Off site: Swimming pool. Tennis. Walking and cycle tracks. Shops and restaurants in Brides-les-Bains.

**Open:** 9 April - 15 October.

**Directions**

Site is to the south of Moûtiers. From Albertville, head south on N90 as far as Moûtiers and join the D915 as far as Brides-les-Bains. From here, follow signs to the site. GPS: 45.45294, 6.56232

**Charges guide**

| Per unit incl. 2 persons | |
|---|---|
| and electricity | € 12.95 - € 14.50 |
| extra person | € 2.90 - € 3.30 |

## Buis-les-Baronnies
### Camping Domaine de l'Ecluse

Bénivay, F-26170 Buis-les-Baronnies (Drôme) T: 04 75 28 07 32. E: camp.ecluse@wanadoo.fr
**alanrogers.com/FR26200**

Tucked away in the beautiful Drôme Provençale region, this quiet, rural site is situated high in the hills northeast of the Roman city of Vaison-la-Romaine and surrounded by vineyards. There are 75 level, stony pitches of average size, with 53 for touring (6A electricity, long leads needed). They are separated by hedges and mature poplar trees giving varying amounts of shade. Some 15 of these are on an upper level, larger and more open, and separate from the rest of the site, with views of the surrounding hills. Rock pegs are advised. The attractive, L-shaped swimming pool has a toboggan and sunbathing area.

**Facilities**

Two toilet blocks with all the necessary modern facilities include rooms for babies and campers with disabilities. Small shop. Bar/restaurant and takeaway (all July/Aug). Swimming pool (April-Sept). Games field. Simple programme of events and some excursions (July/Aug). Gas barbecues only. Internet link via a cable. Max. 1 dog. Off site: Restaurant nearby. Bicycle hire, fishing, lake bathing and riding 8 km. Historic villages of Buis-les-Baronnies 8 km. Mollans 8 km. Vaison la Romaine 14 km. Nyons 20 km. Mont Ventoux.

**Open:** 5 April - 15 November.

**Directions**

Site is northeast of Vaison la Romaine. Advised access is via Buis-le-Baronnies. Just south of village turn northwest on D147 for 7 km. over the pass to Propiac. Turn right on D347 and climb to site in 2 km. At entry use turning area to take sharp left-hand bend down to site. GPS: 44.28995, 5.1917

**Charges guide**

| | |
|---|---|
| Per unit incl. 2 persons and electricity | € 19.50 - € 25.50 |
| extra person | € 4.00 - € 5.00 |
| child (2-6 yrs) | € 2.50 - € 3.00 |

## Chamonix
### Camping de la Mer de Glace

200 chemin de la Bagna, les Praz, F-74400 Chamonix (Haute-Savoie) T: 04 50 53 44 03. E: info@chamonix-camping.com **alanrogers.com/FR74150**

This attractive site is convenient for Chamonix but is in a tranquil setting away from its hustle and bustle. The buildings are of typical regional timber construction, decorated with traditional painted flower designs. The English-speaking owners (since 2004) make every effort to keep it as natural as possible, therefore it is without a pool, restaurant, bar or disco and is well suited to those looking for quiet and relaxation. There are 150 pitches of varying sizes, most with shade and 75 have electricity (10A). Visitors are provided with a free bus pass in order to visit Chamonix town, as well as the surrounding area.

**Facilities**

Three sanitary blocks with facilities for disabled visitors. Washing machine, dryer. Motorcaravan services. Bread. Pizza van twice weekly in July/Aug. Meeting room, snack preparation and meeting room. Small playground for young children. Free WiFi over part of site. Free charging point for mobile phones etc. Off site: Fishing and golf 500 m. Shops etc. in les Praz 700 m. Bicycle hire 1 km. Chamonix 1.5 km. Riding 5 km.

**Open:** 26 April - 29 September.

**Directions**

From Chamonix take D1506 (previously N506) northeast towards les Praz. After 1 km. site signed to right. NOTE: the first two signs direct you under a 2.4 m. high bridge. Continue to a small roundabout at entrance to les Praz, turn right and follow signs. GPS: 45.93805, 6.89267

**Charges 2013**

| | |
|---|---|
| Per unit incl. 2 persons and electricity | € 22.80 - € 27.20 |

## Chamonix
### Camping l'Ile des Barrats

185 chemin de l'Ile des Barrats, F-74400 Chamonix (Haute-Savoie) T: 04 50 53 51 44. E: campingiledesbarrats74@orange.fr **alanrogers.com/FR74160**

l'Ile des Barrats is a delightful neat, tidy, small and tranquil site. It is within easy walking distance of the beautiful town of Chamonix, although there are bus and train services close by if needed. There are 48 slightly sloping, grassy pitches, all for touring, mostly separated by small hedges and a variety of trees that offer some shade. All have electricity (10A) and 32 have water and drainage. This is an ideal site for those wishing to roam the mountain trails and for those seeking a peaceful and relaxing holiday in a most superb setting. There are four quality chalets available to rent. No twin-axle caravans.

**Facilities**

A modern, clean toilet block offers all facilities, including those for disabled visitors. Covered picnic area with table and benches, ideal for those with small tents. Store room for mountaineers. Mobile shop in July/Aug. No organised activities. WiFi (charged). Off site: Baker 500 m. Chamonix 800 m. level walk.

**Open:** 15 May - 1 October.

**Directions**

On entering Chamonix from Geneva, turn left at first roundabout after turn for the Mont Blanc Tunnel (follow signs for hospital). At next roundabout, turn left and site is on right. GPS: 45.9143, 6.8615

**Charges guide**

| | |
|---|---|
| Per unit incl. 2 persons and electricity | € 24.20 - € 28.20 |
| No credit cards. | |

For latest campsite news, availability and prices visit
**alanrogers.com**

## Châteauneuf-sur-Isère

### Camping le Soleil Fruité

Les Peches, F-26300 Châteauneuf-sur-Isère (Drôme) T: 04 75 84 19 70. E: contact@lesoleilfruite.com
**alanrogers.com/FR26220**

Le Soleil Fruité is a new site conveniently located a little to the north of Valence, only 6 km. from the autoroute. The site lies amidst a large fruit farm growing peaches, apricots and olives with views over the Ardèche mountains. Campers are invited to pick fruit and there is a twice weekly market featuring the farm's produce. There are 137 large, level, grassy pitches with 100 for touring (electricity 6A). They are separated by small shrubs and young trees giving little shade. Twin-axle caravans are not allowed on site. Only gas and electric barbecues. Dogs are not accepted in July and August.

**Facilities**

Excellent, clean toilet block with facilities for babies and disabled visitors. Bar, TV/snack bar, small shop (all season). Twice weekly market in high season. Swimming pool with jacuzzi. Paddling pool. Play area. Bicycle hire. WiFi (free). Motorcaravan services. Entertainment for under 10s and excursion programme (July/Aug). Off site: Canoeing on the River Drôme. Covered pool.

**Open:** 28 April - 15 September.

**Directions**

Leave A7 autoroute exit 14 (Valence Nord) take the N7 north for 2 km. Turn right, D877, site signed. After 2 km. turn left, then left at roundabout then left again to site. GPS: 45.002716, 4.895514

**Charges guide**

| | |
|---|---|
| Per unit incl. 2 persons and electricity | € 20.10 - € 27.90 |

## Cormoranche-sur-Saône

### Camping du Lac

Base de Loisirs, les Luizants, F-01290 Cormoranche-sur-Saône (Ain) T: 03 85 23 97 10.
E: contact@lac-cormoranche.com **alanrogers.com/FR01090**

This attractive, family orientated site forms part of a landscaped recreation park that surrounds a tree lined lake. The 117 generous pitches, with a modern sanitary block in the centre, are level, grassed and enclosed by hedges. All have electricity (10A) and drainage. An area has been set aside for three teepees, and a further area for chalets. The whole site has been well thought out. A small dam divides the lake into two areas, one for swimming, with a beach, the other larger section for fishing, kayaks and pedaloes. Children will love the adventure playground in front of the beach area. There is some train noise from the nearby TVR, but only during daytime, and only a moderate rumble. Situated in a region famous for its wines, gastronomy and picturesque villages, there is much to explore locally. The town of Mâcon is ony 5 km. distant. There are some 220 km. of cycle paths, on and off road, which are all marked and newly signed. Maps are available at reception. During the summer there are monthly events organised around and on the lake. There is something here for everyone.

**Facilities**

A recently built sanitary building provides clean, well maintained facilities with showers and washbasins in cabins. Facilities for babies and disabled visitors. Laundry room with washing machine. Motorcaravan service point. Small shop (order bread for following morning). A mobile shop selling fresh produce calls each morning. Bar and restaurant with takeaway, overlooking lake. Lake swimming. Adventure playground. Lifeguards and first aid during high season. Bicycle hire. WiFi (charged). Off site: Riding 8 km. Golf 10 km.

**Open:** 1 April - 30 September.

**Directions**

Site is 5 km. south-southwest of Mâcon on the eastern side of the Saône. It is signed Base de Loisirs Cormoranche. From A6 exit 28 or A40 exit 1 follow N6 to Mâcon centre. At roundabout by Pont Urban Sud take third exit signed Bourge-en-Bresse over bridge. Then D51 signed Cormoranche. On entering village go right on D51B and follow signs for site. GPS: 46.25167, 4.8261

**Charges guide**

| | |
|---|---|
| Per unit incl. 2 persons and electricity | € 15.40 - € 20.20 |

BASE DE LOISIRS DU LAC
CAMPING ★★★★
To rent - Chalets - Mobile Homes - Tipis
SNACK - BAR - ANIMATION
01290 Cormoranche-sur-Saône
00 33-( 0 )3-85-23-97-10
www.lac-cormoranche.com

**FREE** Alan Rogers Travel Card
Extra benefits and savings - see page 10

## Châtillon-en-Diois

### Camping Lac Bleu

Quarter la Touche, F-26410 Châtillon-en-Diois (Drôme) T: 04 75 21 85 30. E: info@lacbleu-diois.com

alanrogers.com/FR26150

This spacious and peaceful site is run by a very friendly family who have made many improvements to the site with many more in the pipeline. It lies in a beautiful valley surrounded by mountains, south of the Vercors National Park. The 199 pitches (76 for touring) are level with rough grass, slightly uneven and separated by a variety of trees offering some shade (rock pegs advised). All have 10A electricity. At the centre of the site is a lake of 2.5 hectares with warm clean water fed by springs, making it ideal for swimming and fishing. A good bar, restaurant and terrace overlook the lake and there is plenty of space for children to play.

#### Facilities

Two clean toilet blocks, one new, the other refurbished, with all the necessary facilities. Baby room. Facilities for disabled campers. Bar/restaurant, takeaway. TV/games room (all season). Covered heated swimming pool and paddling pool (all season). Motorcaravan service point. Play area bordering the lake, which has footpaths around it, bathing and fishing. Pedaloes. Large sports/play area. Bicycle hire. WiFi in bar/terrace area (charged). Charcoal barbecues not permitted. Visitors with dogs should contact site first. Off site: Riding 7 km.

**Open:** 1 April - 30 September.

#### Directions

Take D93 southeast from Die, signed Gap. After 5 km. turn left on D539 signed Châtillon-en-Diois. After 4.5 km. bear right onto D140, site signed. Site shortly on left. GPS: 44.6824, 5.44795

#### Charges guide

| Per unit incl. 2 persons | |
|---|---|
| and electricity | € 15.30 - € 25.20 |
| extra person | € 3.60 - € 5.80 |
| child (2-7 yrs) | € 2.50 - € 4.10 |
| dog | € 1.30 - € 2.50 |

---

## Cublize

### Campéole le Lac des Sapins

Campé●le

F-69550 Cublize (Rhône) T: 04 74 89 52 83. E: lacdessapins@campeole.com

alanrogers.com/FR69060

Lac des Sapins can be found deep within the Beaujolais countryside. This site is a member of the Campéole group and is located very close to the large Lac des Sapins and the pretty village of Cublize. There are 174 grassy pitches here, mostly well shaded, many with electrical connections. A further 94 pitches are occupied by mobile homes and chalets (many available for rent). Various watersports are possible on the lake, with a well equipped base nearby. On-site amenities include a multisports pitch and a tennis court. There is also a small shop and a snack bar. Generally not too challenging, and with a gentle climate, southern Burgundy is wonderful walking and cycling country. The great city of Lyon is just an hour away and is, of course, renowned as France's gastronomic capital. Le Vieux Lyon is made up of dozens of inviting, narrow streets with seemingly hundreds of tempting bistros and brasseries. The city features on UNESCO's World Heritage list and there is much of interest for visitors.

#### Facilities

Small shop. Snack bar. Takeaway. Swimming lake. TV room. Play area. Multisports terrain. Tennis. Fishing. Tourist information. Mobile homes and chalets for rent. Off site: Shops and restaurants in Cublize. Golf. Walking and cycling routes. Lyon.

**Open:** 1 May - 30 September.

#### Directions

Approaching from the east (Meaux la Montagne), head west on D504 to Cublize and the site is well signed in the village. GPS: 46.013093, 4.381496

#### Charges 2013

| Per unit incl. 2 persons | |
|---|---|
| and electricity | € 18.00 - € 22.00 |

For latest campsite news, availability and prices visit

# alanrogers.com

# Dardilly

## Camping Indigo Lyon

Porte de Lyon, allée Camping International, F-69570 Dardilly (Rhône) T: 04 78 35 64 55.
E: lyon@camping-indigo.com **alanrogers.com/FR69010**

This is a short stay, city site just off the A6 autoroute and within easy reach of Lyon centre. Kept busy with overnight trade, the reception and the café (in main season) are open until quite late. There are 180 separate numbered plots all with 6/10A electricity and 140 of these also provide water and waste water drainage. Those for caravans and motorcaravans are mostly on hardstandings on a slight slope, while those for tents are on a flatter area of grass. All have shade. A large commercial centre is just outside the site, with hotels, restaurants, a supermarket, petrol station, etc. There is some road noise from the adjacent motorway. Lyon is a very attractive city, especially noted for the excellence of its food, and well worth a visit. A bus stop for the centre (8 km) is nearby. Bus routes, metro map and town map are given to all visitors on arrival.

**Facilities**

One large, modern (heated) sanitary block is in the central lodge, with two further blocks (solar heated) open in high season. Baby changing facilities and washing machines. Motorcaravan service point. Bar (daily July/Aug; weekends in low season). Restaurant (July/Aug). Takeaway (Fri. and Sat). Swimming and paddling pools (27/4-16/9). TV room. Games room. Reading room (books and local information). Playground. Boules. Picnic and barbecue area. Only electric barbecues allowed. Free Internet in reception. Off site: Bicycle hire 1 km. Golf 4 km. Riding 6 km.

**Open:** All year.

**Directions**

Travelling south, do not take A46 motorway around Lyon, continue on A6, take exit Limonest, Dardilly, Porte de Lyon. 8 km. north of Lyon tunnel; turn left for Porte de Lyon (well signed). GPS: 45.819739, 4.761196

**Charges 2013**

| | |
|---|---|
| Per unit incl. 2 persons and electricity | € 22.20 - € 27.75 |

Camping Cheques accepted.

**Lyon**
★★★★
Tel : +33 (0)4 78 35 64 55

At the gateway of Lyon,
an ideal base to visit Lyon
& the Beaujolais region

www.camping-indigo.com

# Doussard

## Camp de la Ravoire

Bout-du-Lac, route de la Ravoire, F-74210 Doussard (Haute-Savoie) T: 04 50 44 37 80.
E: info@camping-la-ravoire.fr **alanrogers.com/FR74040**

La Ravoire is a high quality site, 800 m. from Lake Annecy, noted for its neat and tidy appearance and the quietness of its location in this popular tourist region. The 112 level pitches are on well mown grass with some shade and separated by small shrubs and some hedging. The 90 pitches for touring (21 with water and drainage) have electricity (5-15A). Those looking for a campsite in this attractive region, without the 'animation' programmes that many French sites consider necessary, will find this a peaceful base. Access to the banks of the lake is a walk away (albeit across a busy road).

**Facilities**

Very good toilet block with facilities for disabled visitors. Laundry room has washing machines, dryers and irons. Shop. Bar, snack bar and takeaway. Outdoor pool, water slide and paddling pool (all open all season). Good play area. Sports areas. Off site: Lake with restaurants 800 m. Cycle track (30 km) almost to Annecy passes close by. Fishing, boat launching, bicycle hire 1 km. Riding 6 km. Golf 8 km. Shops in Doussard and Annecy (18 km). Canyoning and hang-gliding. Boat trips.

**Open:** 15 May - 7 September.

**Directions**

Site signed from D1508 (previously N508) Annecy-Albertville road. 13 km. south of Annecy, at traffic lights in Brédannaz, turn right (site signed) and then immediately left. Site on left in 1 km. Large outfits should use alternative access at the next right turn after the traffic lights. GPS: 45.80256, 6.20977

**Charges guide**

| | |
|---|---|
| Per unit incl. 2 persons and electricity | € 24.50 - € 35.20 |

Camping Cheques accepted.

## Dieulefit

### Huttopia Dieulefit

Quartier d'Espeluche, F-26220 Dieulefit (Drôme) T: 04 75 54 63 94. E: dieulefit@huttopia.com

**alanrogers.com/FR26580**

The site is located just north of the town of Dieulefit. The name originates from Dieu l'a fait, meaning 'God made it', so it is not surprising to find this latest addition to the Huttopia group set in a managed forest, by a small lake, with stunning views over the town and the valley. It follows Huttopia's philosophy of high standards combined with a sense of real camping, therefore no cars are generally allowed on pitches. Of 120 pitches, 54 are rental accommodation in the form of Cahuttes, Cabanes or Canadiennes, all varying types of wood and canvas structures. The remaining pitches are for camping amongst the trees, although there are some closer to the central lodge which are more open. There is an activity programme for families and children who are looking to discover more about the region of Drôme Provençale. A range of nature discovery activities is organised in July/August.

### Facilities

Modern well equipped heated sanitary facilities in the central lodge, plus outlying 'rondavels' containing family rooms, toilets and water points. Heated outdoor pool (Apr-Sep). Bar/restaurant, pizzeria (July/Aug and weekends). Small shop (all season). Large central lodge with wood-burning fire and communal area. Bicycle hire. Off site: Dieulefit town 2 km. Acro Pole Adventure (tree walk and other activities) 2 km. Riding 7 km.

**Open:** 11 April - 4 November.

### Directions

From A7 take exit 18 on N7 to Montélimar. Go right on ring road and follow D540 towards La Batise Rolland. Continue to Dieulefit. On entering town go left at roundabout on D538 (north). Continue, passing the Pompiers on the right and picking up campsite signs. GPS: 44.53505, 5.059274

### Charges 2013

| | |
|---|---|
| Per unit incl. 2 persons and electricity | € 20.50 - € 44.00 |

HUTTOPIA

DiEULEfit★★★

Tel : +33 (0)4 75 54 63 94

In the heart of
Drôme provençale
on a shady 20 hectare site...

www.huttopia.com

## Doussard

Campéole

### Campéole la Nublière

30 allée de la Nublière, F-74210 Doussard (Haute-Savoie) T: 04 50 44 33 44. E: nubliere@wanadoo.fr

**alanrogers.com/FR74190**

If you are looking for large pitches, shady trees, mountain views and direct access to a lakeside beach, this site is for you. There are 271 touring pitches, of which 243 have electrical hook-ups (6A). This area is very popular and the site is very likely to be busy in high season. There may be some noise from the road and the public beach. La Nublière is 16 km. from old Annecy and you are spoilt for choice in how to get there. Take a ferry trip, hire a sailing boat or pedalo, or walk or cycle along the traffic free track towards the town. The local beach and sailing club are close and there is a good restaurant on the site perimeter. Across the road from the site are courts for tennis and boules. The site is perfect for walking, cycling or sailing and in low season provides a tranquil base for those just wishing to relax in natural surroundings on the edge of a nature reserve.

### Facilities

Large clean sanitary blocks include free hot showers and good facilities for disabled visitors. Laundry. Shop (1/5-15/9). Restaurant on site perimeter (closed Mon). Children's club (3/7-26/8) for 4-8 yrs. Safe deposit. WiFi (charged). Off site: Small supermarket adjacent to site. Good watersports area within 70 m. Access to town and beach from site. Fishing 100 m. Golf and riding 4 km.

**Open:** 30 May - 23 September.

### Directions

Site is 16 km. south of Annecy on Route d'Albertville, well signed. GPS: 45.7908, 6.2197

### Charges guide

| | |
|---|---|
| Per unit incl. 2 persons and electricity | € 17.50 - € 26.60 |
| extra person | € 4.50 - € 6.80 |
| child (2-6 yrs) | free - € 4.30 |

For latest campsite news, availability and prices visit
**alanrogers.com**

## Doussard
### Camping International le Lac Bleu

Route de la Plage, F-74210 Doussard (Haute-Savoie) T: 04 50 44 30 18. E: contact@camping-lac-bleu.com
**alanrogers.com/FR74180**

This lakeside site has its own beach and jetty and a short walk brings you to the lake ferry. The site has breathtaking views, a swimming pool (a 'fun pool' was added in 2010) and 220 pitches divided by privet and beech hedges. This site is perfect for walking, cycling or sailing and in low season provides a tranquil base for those just wishing to relax. In high season it will be busy and popular. The proximity of the public lakeside area, which is often used as a festival venue, could be either a source of noise or an exciting place to be, depending on your point of view. When we visited the music stopped at 23.00. A nearby cycle track on a disused railway to Annecy gives a level 16 km. ride with mountains on the left and the lake to the right. In high season there is a children's club for the under eights. The bar has a thriving takeaway (roast whole chickens and pizza) and an 'al fresco' eating area.

| Facilities | Directions |
|---|---|
| Three toilet blocks are of a high standard with free showers. Good provision for babies and disabled visitors. Bar (15/5-15/9) and integral small shop. Takeaway. Swimming pool (15/5-15/9). Bicycle hire. Boat launching (sailing lessons and boat hire nearby). Multisports pitch. Private beach. Off site: Small supermarket 100 m. Village nearby with bars and restaurants. Fishing 100 m. Hypermarket 4 km. Riding and golf 7 km. | Site is 16 km. south of Annecy on Route d'Albertville, well signed. GPS: 46.317367, 6.362967 |

**Directions**

Site is 16 km. south of Annecy on Route d'Albertville, well signed. GPS: 46.317367, 6.362967

**Charges guide**

| Per unit incl. 2 persons and electricity | € 20.70 - € 37.00 |
|---|---|
| extra person (over 3 yrs) | € 4.00 - € 6.30 |
| dog | € 2.90 - € 4.50 |

**Open:** 1 April - 25 September.

## Excenevex

### Campéole la Pinède

10 avenue de la plage, F-74140 Excenevex-Plage (Haute-Savoie) T: 04 50 72 85 05.
E: pinede@campeole.com **alanrogers.com/FR74280**

La Pinède is a member of the Campéole group and has direct access to Excenevex beach, the only naturally sandy beach on Lake Geneva. The site has a pleasant woodland setting and the 300 touring pitches are of a good size, all with 16A electricity. Mobile homes, chalets and fully equipped tents are available for rent (including specially adapted units for wheelchair users). There is a supervised bathing area on the beach, which shelves gradually, and a small harbour (suitable only for boats with a shallow draught). Other amenities include a shop and takeaway food service, as well as an entertainment marquee and children's play area. There is plenty of activity here in high season with a children's club and regular discos and karaoke evenings. Geneva is just 25 km. and other possible excursions include Thonon-les-Bains and, of course, boat trips on Lake Geneva. Dramatic mountain scenery is close at hand, notably the spectacular Dent d'Oche (2,222 m) and the Gorges du Pont du Diable.

**Facilities**

Heated toilet blocks include some private cabins, family shower room and facilities for children and disabled visitors. Washing machine. Motorcaravan service point. Lake beach. Fresh bread (July/Aug). Takeaway. Small swimming pool (15/6-10/9). Play area. Bouncy castle. Activities and entertainment programme. Bicycle hire. Tourist information. WiFi over part of site (charged). Mobile homes, chalets and equipped tents for rent. Off site: Hiking and cycle tracks. Riding 5 km. Golf 20 km. Thonon-les-Bains 15 km. Geneva 25 km.

**Open:** 12 April - 15 September.

**Directions**

From Geneva head along the south side of the lake on the D1005 as far as Massongy and shortly beyond here take the northbound D324 to Escenevex. The site is well indicated from here. GPS: 46.34492, 6.35808

**Charges guide**

| Per unit incl. 2 persons and electricity | € 17.10 - € 26.60 |
|---|---|

**Campéole**

CAMPSITES AND RENTALS

**La Pinède** ★★★

**New : swimming pool**
Opposite Switzerland, direct access to the beach of Lake Geneva. Pitches and accommodations of high quality.

74140 Excenevex - Tel.: +33-450-7285-05 - www.campeole.co.uk / accueil.pinede@campeole.com

RHÔNE-ALPES

## Fleurie

### Camping Municipal la Grappe Fleurie

La Lie, F-69820 Fleurie (Rhône) T: 04 74 69 80 07. E: camping@fleurie.org
**alanrogers.com/FR69020**

With easy access from both the A6 autoroute and the N6, this site is ideally situated for night stops or indeed for longer stays to explore the vineyards and historic attractions of the Beaujolais region. Virtually surrounded by vineyards, but within walking distance (less than 1 km) of the pretty village of Fleurie, this is an immaculate small site, with 85 separated touring pitches. All are generous, grassy and fairly level with the benefit of individual access to water, drainage and electrical connections (10A). A baker calls 07.30-08.30. Wine tasting is arranged twice weekly in high season. Restaurant and shopping facilities are available in the village.

**Facilities**

Sanitary facilities in two blocks have British and Turkish style toilets and very satisfactory shower and washing facilities (showers closed 22.00-07.00). Facilities for disabled visitors. Two cold showers are provided. Washing machine and dryer. Outdoor swimming pool (15x7 m). Small playground. Only gas or electric barbecues are allowed. WiFi (code). Off site: Fleurie 600 m. Bicycle hire 5 km. Fishing 10 km.

**Open:** Late March - end October.

**Directions**

From N6 at Le Maison Blanche/Romanech-Thorins, take D32 to village of Fleurie from where site is signed. GPS: 46.1879, 4.69916

**Charges guide**

| Per unit incl. 2 persons | |
|---|---|
| and electricity | € 18.50 - € 20.00 |
| extra person | € 6.00 - € 7.00 |
| child (3-10 yrs) | € 4.50 - € 5.00 |

For latest campsite news, availability and prices visit

# alanrogers.com

## Grâne

### Flower Camping les Quatre Saisons

Route de Roche-sur-Grâne, F-26400 Grâne (Drôme) T: 04 75 62 64 17. E: contact@camping-4-saisons.com

**alanrogers.com/FR26110**

This small, terraced site, open all year, nestles in the hillsides of the lower Drôme valley close to the Vercors Mountains. With its 80 pitches (69 touring), it provides mainly overnight accommodation but it is worth a longer stay. The pitches are level and stony, of variable size, cut out of the hillside and reached by a one-way system on tarmac roads. All pitches have 6A electricity, some with water and drainage. The modern main building houses reception on the upper level as you enter the site, with the pool, bar and other facilities to the side and below. The clever terracing provides commanding views across the valley towards Crest and the Vercors.

| Facilities | Directions |
|---|---|
| Good sanitary facilities include baby room, en-suite facilities for disabled visitors (but site is very sloping and not suitable for wheelchairs). Washing machine. Bar (1/5-30/9). Small swimming pool (1/5-15/9). Play area. Children's club (high season). Only electric and gas barbecues. Chalets to rent. Off site: Fishing 1 km. Bicycle hire 2/3 km. Riding 3 km. Canoeing in Crest 3 km. | From A7 exit 17, or the N7 at Loriol, take the D104 towards Crest. After 8 km. in Grâne take the D113 south. Site is on left 600 m. beyond the village. GPS: 44.7277, 4.9265 |

**Open:** 1 April - 30 September.

**Charges guide**

| | |
|---|---|
| Per unit incl. 2 persons | € 18.00 - € 29.00 |

Camping Cheques accepted.

## Grignan

### Camping les Truffières

1100 chemin de Bellevue d'Air, F-26230 Grignan (Drôme) T: 04 75 46 93 62. E: info@lestruffieres.com

**alanrogers.com/FR26090**

This small, pleasant site in a rural setting next to a lavender field and within walking distance of the picturesque ancient village of Grignan provides a haven of tranquillity. The 85 good sized pitches are level and fairly stony with 79 for touring units, all with 10A electricity. They are shaded by oak trees and separated by rosemary or laurel hedging. The Croze family is most welcoming and achieves high standards while maintaining a friendly and relaxed atmosphere. The Drôme is one of the most beautiful regions of France; vineyards, olive orchards, lavender, sunflowers, wild flowers and orchards abound.

| Facilities | Directions |
|---|---|
| Good toilet block provides all necessary facilities. Bar (all season), snack bar, takeaway (May-Aug). Heated swimming pool, smaller pool for children (all season). Boules. Little in the way of on site entertainment but many off site activities can be booked. No dogs. Gas and electric barbecues only. Free WiFi in bar area. Off site: Riding 100 m. Fishing 2 km. Bicycle hire 5 km. Golf 6 km. Grignan with its château. Nyons with excellent market (Thurs) 26 km. Vaison la Romaine 33 km. | From N7 (or A7 autoroute exit 18) south of Montélimar, take D133 (changes to D541) signed Grignan. After 9 km, just before entering Grignan, take D71 towards Charamet and site is shortly on the left. GPS: 44.41131, 4.8911 |

**Open:** 20 April - 20 September.

**Charges guide**

| | |
|---|---|
| Per unit incl. 2 persons and electricity | € 19.20 - € 23.40 |

No credit cards.

## Groisy

### Camping Moulin Dollay

206 rue du Moulin Dollay, F-74570 Groisy (Haute-Savoie) T: 04 50 68 00 31. E: moulin.dollay@orange.fr

**alanrogers.com/FR74170**

Nestling between Annecy (15 km) and Geneva (35 km), this spacious site is a gem with only 45 pitches, 30 for touring. The friendly and enthusiastic owner has worked hard to develop this site to a high quality. The large to very large, level, grass pitches are partially separated by hedging and a variety of trees provide some shade. All pitches have 6A electricity and rock pegs are recommended. As there are only a few activities organised for youngsters on site it is perhaps better suited to those who would appreciate a peaceful site in a parkland setting alongside a rushing stream.

| Facilities | Directions |
|---|---|
| Spacious, well appointed, heated toilet block, including facilities for disabled visitors and a baby room. Washing machine, dryer. Motorcaravan services. Bar, TV corner. Large open play and sports area. Fishing and bathing in shallow river. Off site: Some shops, restaurants, bank and supermarkets at Groisy 1 km. Riding 4 km. Interesting little town of Thorens-Glières with its 11th-century château 5 km. Golf 6 km. Annecy 12 km. Lake Annecy 15 km. | Site is north of Annecy. Heading north on N1203 Annecy-Bonneville road, turn right on D2 signed Thorens-Glières and site, then immediately right again. Site is 300 m. GPS: 46.00238, 6.19079 |

**Open:** 1 May - 30 September.

**Charges guide**

| | |
|---|---|
| Per unit incl. 2 persons and electricity | € 18.00 - € 22.00 |
| extra person | € 5.00 |

No credit cards.

**FREE** Alan Rogers Travel Card

**Extra benefits and savings - see page 10**

## Hautecourt
### Camping de l'Ile Chambod
3232 route du Port, F-01250 Hautecourt (Ain) T: 04 74 37 25 41. E: camping.chambod@sholnet.fr

**alanrogers.com/FR01020**

This small, attractive rural site is situated in a valley close to the Gorges de l'Ain. Many improvements have been made by its current owners; it has two modern toilet blocks, a swimming pool and small café. The 110 medium sized, slightly sloping, grassy pitches (many with views of the surrounding wooded hills) are separated by low hedges and most have some shade. All have access to water points and electricity (5/10A) although some may need extremely long leads. Some pitches are close to the pool and bar area, which may be noisy in July and August.

**Facilities**

Two modern toilet blocks include some washbasins in cabins. Washing machines and dryer. Both blocks have facilities for disabled visitors and one has a baby room. Bread available to order. Small shop (June-Aug). Bar/restaurant and takeaway (May-Aug). Swimming pool (May-Aug). Small play area. Activities organised in high season for all the family. Off site: Fishing 100 m. Riding 5 km. Golf 20 km.

**Open:** 29 April - 1 October.

**Directions**

Site is 23 km. southeast of Bourg-en-Bresse via the D979. It is well signed from the crossroads in Hautecourt, and is a further 4 km. southeast down a long lane. GPS: 46.12777, 5.42818

**Charges guide**

| | |
|---|---|
| Per unit incl. 2 persons and electricity | € 17.00 - € 21.00 |
| extra person | € 4.90 |

---

## Hauterives
### Flower Camping le Château
5 route de Romans, F-26390 Hauterives (Drôme) T: 04 75 68 80 19. E: camping-hauterives@orange.fr

**alanrogers.com/FR26360**

Le Château is a former municipal campsite which is now run by the friendly and very helpful Valérie and Franck. It is a family oriented site set an hour south from Lyon near the motorway. In high season activities are organised for the whole family. This site comprises 137 neat, good sized touring pitches with 13 used for rental accommodation, well spread over an area of four hectares. There is also a dedicated area for tent campers near the entrance of the site. The old château buildings and courtyard are used for entertainment, bar and snacks, with the pools adjacent.

**Facilities**

Sanitary buildings include controllable showers. Facilities for disabled visitors. Bar/snack bar (June-Aug). Heated outdoor pools (salt water) and children's pool (15/6-31/8). TV room. Playground. Library. Boules. Bicycle hire. WiFi (charged). Off site: Supermarket by entrance. Shops, restaurants and weekly market in village. Fishing 1 km. Riding 5 km. Golf 15 km.

**Open:** 1 April - 30 September.

**Directions**

Leave the A7 at exit 12 (Chanas) and take third exit from roundabout (D519 for Grenoble-Beaurepaire). At Beaurepaire take D538 and through Lens Lestang, then Hauterives. At roundabout by the church, turn left for Romans. Site is 200 m. on the left. GPS: 45.252796, 5.026717

**Charges guide**

| | |
|---|---|
| Per unit incl. 2 persons and electricity | € 14.50 - € 25.50 |

---

## Joyeuse
### Camping Caravaning les Cruses
Ribes, F-07260 Joyeuse (Ardèche) T: 04 75 39 54 69. E: les-cruses@wanadoo.fr

**alanrogers.com/FR07260**

High in the quiet hills of the southern Ardèche, among the sweet chestnut trees, this small site is carefully terraced. A warm welcome awaits you on arrival. M. and Mme. Rouvier are very keen to promote a quiet family atmosphere, personal contact with their guests is important and weekly entertainment is tailored to guests' needs. For instance he will lead walks, arrange boules competitions against other campsites, canyoning and canoe trips on the river. There are 45 pitches and 22 mobile homes and chalets for hire. Pitches are of varying sizes, some on grass and some gravel, and some are only accessible for tents.

**Facilities**

The toilet block is up to date and clean with pre-set showers and a few en-suite shower, toilet and basin cabins. Baby room. Facilities for disabled visitors. Laundry room. Bar, restaurant and pizzeria (weekends only in low season). Swimming pool (1/5-20/9). Play area. Chalets, mobile homes and Romany type caravans for rent. Gas barbecues only. WiFi (charged). Off site: Fishing and river beach 1 km. Riding 3 km. Bicycle hire 5 km.

**Open:** 4 April - 26 September.

**Directions**

From Joyeuse take the D203 towards Ribes. Turn left at D450 signed Ribes and continue for 1 km. The site is signed on the left some 1 km. before the village. GPS: 44.492417, 4.207267

**Charges guide**

| | |
|---|---|
| Per unit incl. 2 persons and electricity | € 15.50 - € 27.10 |

For latest campsite news, availability and prices visit
# alanrogers.com

## La Salle-en-Beaumont

### Camping le Champ Long

Le Champ Long, F-38350 La Salle-en-Beaumont (Isère) T: 04 76 30 41 81. E: champlong38@orange.fr
**alanrogers.com/FR38190**

Set at the entrance to the Ecrins National Park and overlooked by the great Obiou massif, this site has been carved from a hilly forest. It provides 67 touring pitches (8/10A electricity) arranged in glades between mature trees. The setting is such that it is hard to see the other units around you, yet the mountain views through the trees are wonderful. The site is terraced and hilly and the winding access tracks need adequate power in reserve for towing, so it is not really suitable for large outfits. There are some steep paths to the sanitary blocks.

**Facilities**

Two sanitary blocks, one at reception, the other high on the steep terraces provide British and Turkish style WCs, washbasins in cabins and unexceptional showers. Laundry facilities. Motorcaravan services. Milk, bread and a few essentials kept (May-Sept). Bar, good restaurant and takeaway (all April-Oct). Heated outdoor pool (1/5-31/8). Play area. Barbecues to rent. WiFi (charged). Off site: Riding school. Fishing 700 m. Golf 18 km.

**Open:** 1 April - 15 October.

**Directions**

From the D1085 turn off at sign for La Roche which is close to La Salle en Beaumont. Site is signed through long country roads. GPS: 44.85554, 5.84503

**Charges guide**

| | |
|---|---|
| Per unit incl. 2 persons and electricity | € 17.50 - € 19.50 |
| extra person | € 3.50 - € 3.80 |

## Lagorce

### Castel Domaine de Sévenier

508

Sévenier, F-07150 Lagorce (Ardèche) T: 04 75 88 29 44. E: domainedesevenier@orange.fr
**alanrogers.com/FR07660**

Le Domaine de Sévenier is a modern, high quality chalet complex enjoying a hilltop location with fine panoramic views over the surrounding garrigue, a unique mix of oak trees, juniper, rosemary and thyme. Located 4 km. from Vallon-Pont-d'Arc and 800 m. from the pretty village of Lagorce, the domaine is an old winery which has been sensitively converted and offers accommodation in well appointed wooden chalets. Rest and relaxation is the theme here and the restaurant has a good reputation. On-site amenities include a pool. The site has links to Nature Parc Camping de l'Ardèche and guests are welcome to use the camping site's evening entertainment but there are no touring pitches at Sévenier.

**Facilities**

The sanitary block includes hot showers and provision has been made for disabled visitors. Washing machine. Restaurant. Bar. Shop. Outdoor, heated swimming pool. Children's pool. Activity programme. Bicycle hire. Play area. Minigolf. Tourist information. Fully equipped chalets for rent. No touring pitches. Off site: Lagorce 800 m. (shops and cafés). Fishing 4 km. Riding 15 km.

**Open:** 30 March - 4 November.

**Directions**

Head north from Vallon-Pont-d'Arc (at western end of the Ardèche gorges) on D1 and upon reaching Lagorce, follow signs to the site. GPS: 44.434151, 4.410989

**Charges 2013**

Contact the site for details.
*See advertisement on page 313.*

## Lamastre

### Camping de Retourtour

1 rue de Retourtour, F-07270 Lamastre (Ardèche) T: 04 75 06 40 71. E: campingderetourtour@wanadoo.fr
**alanrogers.com/FR07460**

This family run site is situated in the lesser-known, but beautiful, northern Ardèche and, you can be sure of a good welcome here. Delightfully situated near a tiny village below the ruins of a chateau, there are 130 good sized, level, grass pitches with 70 for touring, all with electricity. They are separated by hedges and mature trees which offer varying amounts of shade. Entertainment for all the family is organised in July and August making this a good site for those seeking a more relaxing holiday. The site is situated in the valley of the Doux river, and a beautiful natural river swimming area is within 150 m.

**Facilities**

Three very clean, refurbished toilet blocks with all the necessary facilities including those for babies and campers with disabilities. Small shop. Bar (all season). Restaurant/takeaway (July/Aug otherwise weekends). Good play area. Multisports area. Fitness room. Boules. Minigolf. Climbing. WiFi (charged). Only gas and electric barbecues are allowed. Mobile homes to rent. Off site: Fishing and small riverside beach 150 m. Restaurant. Lamastre 1.5 km. Riding 5 km. Golf 12 km.

**Open:** Easter - 30 September.

**Directions**

Leave A7 at exit 13 (Tournon) or 15 (Valence). Go west to Lamastre following signs to Le Puy (35 km). Continue through Lamastre. After 1.5 km. turn right down lane to site. GPS: 44.99165, 4.56477

**Charges guide**

| | |
|---|---|
| Per unit incl. 2 persons and electricity (4-13A) | € 16.16 - € 20.66 |
| extra person | € 3.78 - € 4.58 |
| No credit cards. | |

## Landry

### Flower Camping l'Eden

F-73210 Landry (Savoie) T: 04 79 07 61 81. E: campingleden@gmail.com

**alanrogers.com/FR73060**

L'Eden is open to touring units in summer and winter. It is beside the Isere river and set in beautiful woodland glades, and is perfect for winter skiing and walking and cycling in summer. The site is set in a valley with the Alpine peaks as a backdrop. The 133 good, spacious pitches all have 10A electrical hook-ups and individual water supplies (available when no frost is likely). The clean, modern sanitary blocks are heated in colder weather and include a large drying room. There is a pool for summer lounging, a bar and a welcoming communal area with bar, TV and Internet access.

| Facilities | Directions |
|---|---|
| Two heated toilet blocks include drying rooms, good facilities for disabled visitors and for babies. Small launderette. Communal area with bar, TV and Internet. Snack bar and takeaway (July/Aug). Swimming pool (13.5x5 m; June-Sept). Games room. Play area. Fishing. Ski passes for sale on-site. Off site: Rafting and canoeing opposite entrance. Shops and restaurants in village. | From the RN90 take D87 towards Landry. Site is on left after 250 m. and is well signed from the RN90. GPS: 45.57652, 6.73457 |

**Open:** 25 May - 15 September, 15 December - 5 May.

**Charges guide**

| | |
|---|---|
| Per unit incl. 2 persons and electricity | € 27.40 |
| extra person | € 5.30 |
| child (under 12 yrs) | € 2.80 - € 4.00 |

## Largentière

### Domaine les Ranchisses

Route de Rocher, F-07110 Largentière (Ardèche) T: 04 75 88 31 97. E: reception@lesranchisses.fr

**alanrogers.com/FR07070**

This is a very well equipped, modern campsite in a lesser known area of the Ardèche. There are 96 good sized, level pitches, all for touring with electricity (10A) including 78 which are fully serviced, both shaded and part shaded. Good quality mobile homes and chalets are available to rent. A small river pool provides opportunities for bathing, fishing or canoeing (free life jackets), with one part of the area quite safe for youngsters. A high quality pool area, close to a wellness centre provides good free exercise and relaxation. Well run and with the emphasis on personal attention, this is a highly recommended site.

| Facilities | Directions |
|---|---|
| Comprehensive toilet buildings include facilities for babies and disabled visitors. Laundry facilities. Motorcaravan services. Shop. Bar. Restaurant (regional specialities), takeaway/pizzeria and terrace. Two large pools, paddling pool (heated). Separate water slides. Wellness centre with semi-covered pool. Adventure playground. Organised amusements (from 1/7). Very good miniclub. Skate park. Tennis. Minigolf. Boules. Canoeing. Internet access. WiFi over site (charged). Only one dog per pitch. Off site: Canoe, kayaking arranged (mid June-end Aug). Largentière 1.5 km. Riding 8 km. Bicycle hire 20 km. | Largentière is southwest of Aubenas and best approached using D104. Just beyond Uzer, 16 km. from Aubenas, turn northwest on D5. After 5 km. at far end of Largentière, fork left downhill signed Rocher and Valgorge. Site on left in 1.8 km. just beyond rocky gorge. The approach from Valgorge is not recommended. GPS: 44.56071, 4.28463 |

**Open:** 13 April - 29 September.

**Charges guide**

| | |
|---|---|
| Per unit incl. 2 persons and electricity | € 19.00 - € 47.00 |
| extra person (over 1 yr) | € 5.00 - € 10.00 |
| Camping Cheques accepted. | |

## Laurac-en-Vivarais

### Flower Camping Saint-Amand

Route des Défilés de Ruoms, quartier St Amand, F-07110 Laurac-en-Vivarais (Ardèche) T: 04 75 36 84 45. E: st-amand@wanadoo.fr **alanrogers.com/FR07640**

Saint-Amand is a member of the Flower group and can be found around 15 km. west of Vallon Pont d'Arc, close to the appropriately named village of Bellevue. There are 68 touring pitches, most with electrical connections (6A) and good shade. A further 42 pitches are occupied by mobile homes and fully equipped tents available for rent. From the site's pool, there are some fine views across the surrounding scrubland and vineyards. Other amenities include a small restaurant, specialising in homemade pizzas and a new playing area for children. The closest shops are in the village of Laurac (2.5 km).

| Facilities | Directions |
|---|---|
| Sanitary building with family shower and laundry facilities. Facilities for disabled visitors. Small shop. Pizzeria and snack bar. Swimming pool. Children's pool. Play area. Activity and entertainment programme. Mobile homes for rent. Free WiFi. Off site: Laurac 2.5 km. Vallon-Pont-d'Arc 15 km. Cycle and walking tracks. | From the north (Privas), head southwest using the D104 towards Aubenas, continuing via Uzer and on for 3 km. to Bellevue. Turn left and site is signed from here to a right turn down a track which may be difficult for larger units. GPS: 44.49964, 4.30619 |

**Open:** 2 April - 17 September.

**Charges guide**

| | |
|---|---|
| Per unit incl. 2 persons and electricity | € 15.50 - € 23.90 |

For latest campsite news, availability and prices visit

# alanrogers.com

## Le Grand-Bornand
### Camping Caravaning l'Escale

Route de la Patinoire, F-74450 Le Grand-Bornand (Haute-Savoie) T: 04 50 02 20 69.
E: contact@campinglescale.com **alanrogers.com/FR74070**

You are assured a good welcome in English from the Baur family at this beautifully maintained and picturesque site, situated at the foot of the Aravis mountain range. There are 149 pitches with 122 for touring. Of average size, part grass, part gravel they are separated by trees and shrubs that give a little shade. All pitches have electricity (2-10A) and 86 are fully serviced. Rock pegs are essential. A 200-year-old building houses a bar/restaurant decorated in traditional style and offering regional dishes in a delightful, warm ambience. The village is 200 metres away and has all the facilities of a resort with activities for both summer and winter holidays. In summer, a variety of well signed footpaths and cycle tracks provide forest and mountain excursions. In winter the area provides superb facilities for downhill and cross-country skiing. This very popular campsite, set beside the picture postcard ski resort of Le Grand-Bornand, has wonderful views and is surrounded by fields of flowers in summer.

**Facilities**

Good toilet blocks (heated in winter) have all the necessary facilities. Drying room. Superb pool complex with interconnected indoor (all season) and outdoor pools and paddling pools (30/6-30/8), jacuzzi and water jets. Cosy bar/restaurant and takeaway (all season). Play area. Tennis. WiFi (free). Activities. Discounts on organised walks and visits to Chamonix-Mont Blanc. Off site: Village (5 minutes walk). Bicycle hire 200 m. Riding and golf 3 km. Free bus to cable car (500 m).

**Open:** 14 December - 14 April, 17 May - 22 September.

**Directions**

From Annecy follow D16 and D909 towards La Clusaz. At St Jean-de-Sixt, turn left at roundabout D4 signed Grand-Bornand. Just before village fork right signed Vallée de Bouchet and camping. Site entrance is on right at roundabout in 1.2 km. GPS: 45.94036, 6.42842

**Charges guide**

| | |
|---|---|
| Per unit incl. 2 persons and electricity | € 19.80 - € 35.80 |
| extra person (over 2 yrs) | € 5.20 - € 5.90 |

Camping Caravaneige L'Escale

74450 Le Grand Bornand - France - Tel: +33 (0)4 50 02 20 69 - Fax: +33 (0)4 50 02 36 04
Email: contact@campinglescale.com - www.rentlescale.com

## Les Abrets
### Kawan Village le Coin Tranquille

6 chemin des Vignes, F-38490 Les Abrets (Isère) T: 04 76 32 13 48. E: contact@coin-tranquille.com
**alanrogers.com/FR38010**

Les Abrets is well placed for visits to the Savoie regions and the Alps. It is an attractive, well maintained site of 192 grass pitches (178 for tourers), all with 6A electricity. They are separated by neat hedges of hydrangea, flowering shrubs and a range of trees to make a lovely environment doubly enhanced by the rural aspect and marvellous views across to the mountains. This is a popular, family run site with friendly staff, making it a wonderful base for exploring the area. Set in the Dauphiny countryside north of Grenoble, le Coin Tranquille is truly a quiet corner, especially outside school holiday times, although it is still popular with families in high season.

**Facilities**

The central well appointed sanitary block is well kept, heated in low season. Facilities for children and disabled visitors. Two smaller blocks provide facilities in high season. Busy shop. Excellent restaurant. Heated swimming pool and paddling pool (1/5-30/9; no Bermuda style shorts). Play area. Weekly entertainment (July/Aug) including live music (not discos). Bicycle hire (limited). WiFi. Off site: Les Abrets 2 km. Riding 6 km.

**Open:** 1 April - 31 October.

**Directions**

Les Abrets is 70 km. southeast of Lyon at junction of D1006 (previously N6) and D1075 (previously N75). From roundabout in town take N6 towards Chambéry, turning left in just under 2 km. Follow signs along lane for 1 km. GPS: 45.54115, 5.60778

**Charges 2013**

| | |
|---|---|
| Per unit incl. 2 persons and electricity | € 19.00 - € 34.50 |

Camping Cheques accepted.

## Les Ollières-sur-Eyrieux
### Camping le Domaine des Plantas

F-07360 Les Ollières-sur-Eyrieux (Ardèche) T: 04 75 66 21 53. E: plantas.ardeche@wanadoo.fr

**alanrogers.com/FR07090**

This is a good quality site in the beautiful, steep sided Eyrieux valley. There is a sandy beach beside the fairly fast-flowing river but the attractive swimming pool complex tempts you back for either sedate bathing or exciting slides. There are 76 steeply terraced and shaded touring pitches with 10A electricity. The walk up from some pitches to the original old farm buildings housing the reception, restaurant and bar is rewarded by a terrace with a spectacular viewpoint. The touring pitches occupy the heart of the campsite, with a further 100 chalets and mobile homes in their own section of the site.

**Facilities**

Two excellent well equipped toilet blocks (one heated) Facilities for children. Washing machines. Motorcaravan services. Small shop, bar and restaurant. Heated, covered and outdoor swimming pools. Paddling pool. Adventure play area. Games area. Pétanque. Entertainment. High season children's activities, discos (14-18 yrs, no alcohol). Activities and excursions. WiFi. Chalets and mobile homes to rent. Only gas and electric barbecues. Off site: Riding 15 km. Mountain biking, canoeing, riding and walking.

**Open:** 21 April - 19 September.

**Directions**

Leave A7 exit 15 (Valence Sud). Follow signs to Montélimar via N7 for 7 km. At Beauchastel, take D120 to Ollières-sur-Eyrieux. Cross river, turn left and campsite signs give reassurance along the (3 km) narrow road with wider passing places (possible problem for larger outfits). GPS: 44.80917, 4.63581

**Charges guide**

| Per unit incl. 2 persons | |
|---|---|
| and electricity | € 24.00 - € 40.00 |
| extra person | € 4.70 - € 7.00 |

## Les Ollières-sur-Eyrieux
### Flower Camping le Chambourlas

F-07360 Les Ollières-sur-Eyrieux (Ardèche) T: 04 75 66 24 31. E: info@chambourlas.com

**alanrogers.com/FR07190**

Tucked away in a beautiful setting, in the hills above Privas, this is a small, neat and tidy, family owned site. The 78 large, grassy, some slightly sloping pitches (72 for touring, electricity 10A) are set on low terraces, separated by an interesting variety of trees with excellent views over the wooded hills. The attractive reception, restaurant and shop are in one building close to all the facilities. There is a private lake with a beach making it a tranquil place for fishing or canoeing. The site is not ideal for very large units due to the steep and narrow local roads.

**Facilities**

One modern, very clean toilet block includes facilities for disabled visitors. Bar (1/7-31/8). Restaurant and takeaway (15/5-28/8). Small shop (mid May-Oct). Swimming pool, paddling pool and sunbathing area (1/5-30/9). Play area. Boules. Activities, no discos. River fishing. Only gas or electric barbecues. WiFi. Chalets and tents for rent. Off site: Walks and bike rides. Bicycle hire 6 km. Excursions. Village of les Ollières-sur-Eyrieux 6 km.

**Open:** 1 May - 1 October.

**Directions**

At traffic lights in Privas take D2 north, signed Les Ollieres/Le Cheylard. Follow road over two river bridges through the hills before descending to site entrance after 14 km. Site access is not as steep and narrow as it appears. GPS: 44.78155, 4.61806

**Charges guide**

| Per unit incl. 2 persons | |
|---|---|
| and electricity | € 17.50 - € 31.50 |
| extra person | € 6.00 - € 6.50 |

## Les Ollières-sur-Eyrieux
### Camping Mas de Champel

Quartier Champel, F-07360 Les Ollières-sur-Eyrieux (Ardèche) T: 04 75 66 23 23. E: masdechampel@wanadoo.fr **alanrogers.com/FR07440**

At Mas de Champel you will be invited to relax in a region of natural beauty. Once a farm with orchards located at the heart of the valley of the Eyrieux, rounded river worn boulders are featured in the buildings that house the site's restaurant, bar, wellness centre and reception. With 51 generously sized touring pitches with 6A electricity and varying degrees of shade and 44 chalets and mobile homes to rent, the campsite is able to provide a programme of entertainment for all family members. There is a variety of pools and a riverside beach offers fishing, bathing and canoeing.

**Facilities**

Two clean toilet blocks (a third opened in high season). Motorcaravan services. Bar, good restaurant with terrace and takeaway. Swimming pool, heated paddling pool, fun pool, jacuzzi and sunbathing area. Wellness centre. Games/TV room. Play area. Pétanque. Bicycle hire. Fishing. Canoe hire. Organised family activities (July/Aug). Gas barbecues only. WiFi. Off site: Aquarock Centre canoeing and aerial adventure park 1 km.

**Open:** 14 April - 23 September.

**Directions**

Leave N86 south of Valence at Beauchastel. Turn west, D120, to Ollières-sur-Eyrieux (about 20 km). Site is on right at entrance to village and is signed. GPS: 44.80721, 4.61489

**Charges guide**

| Per unit incl. 2 persons | |
|---|---|
| and electricity | € 19.00 - € 28.80 |
| extra person | € 4.40 - € 6.90 |

For latest campsite news, availability and prices visit
**alanrogers.com**

## Lus-la-Croix-Haute

### Camping Champ la Chèvre

F-26220 Lus-la-Croix-Haute (Drôme) T: 04 92 58 50 14. E: info@campingchamplachevre.com
**alanrogers.com/FR26270**

This is a pleasant, unpretentious site with some really magnificent views across towards the western Alps. Formerly a farm (hence its name!) and now under new management, Champ la Chèvre is undergoing a steady process of refurbishment and is attractively located just 200 m. from the village and 500 m. from the D1075. There are 100 pitches, for the most part sunny and quite spacious, and many with fine mountain views. Some pitches are sloping and most pitches have 6A electrical connections.

| Facilities | Directions |
|---|---|
| Centrally located toilet block with facilities for disabled visitors, and a second block by the entrance. Motorcaravan services. Bar, restaurant and takeaway (all season). New heated and covered swimming pool (15/6-31/8). Play area. Children's club (July/Aug). Minigolf. Mobile homes and chalets for rent. WiFi. Off site: Riding 100 m. Village of Lus-La-Croix Haute 200 m. Railway station 300 m. Bicycle hire 500 m. Fishing 3 km. Tennis.<br><br>**Open:** 23 April - 17 September. | From the north, head south from Grenoble initially on the A480 and then the A51 towards Sisteron. Then join the southbound N75 for 35 km. to Lus-la-Croix Haute. Drive through the village and site is well signed. GPS: 44.66440, 5.70742 |

**Charges guide**

| Per unit incl. 2 persons and electricity | € 19.00 - € 23.30 |
|---|---|
| extra person | € 4.30 - € 5.50 |

Camping Cheques accepted.

---

## Lussas

### Ludocamping

Route de Lavilledieu, F-07170 Lussas (Ardèche) T: 04 75 94 21 22. E: info@ludocamping.com
**alanrogers.com/FR07170**

Ludocamping is set amongst the magnificent scenery of the Auzon valley. This is a quiet family campsite run by a very friendly French family with access to a wide range of activities. The 160 grassy pitches, all for touring, with 5/10A electricity, are in two areas. The upper terrace has large pitches with wonderful views but little shade. The lower area, closer to the small river, has pitches set naturally amongst the trees and they have good shade. There is a large swimming pool (heated all season) and a good sized paddling pool, both with attractively terraced sunbathing areas with views of the forested slopes.

| Facilities | Directions |
|---|---|
| Clean, good quality toilet blocks. Bar, restaurant and takeaway (15/5-15/9) with terrace. Play area. Recreational area next to river. Fishing. Bicycle hire. Club (over 6/7 yrs). Off season club for older children. Seniors coach excursions. Only gas and electric barbecues. WiFi around the bar (free). Chalets, mobile homes and tents for rent. Off site: Lussas (few shops, restaurant, bar) 600 m. Riding 6 km. Gliding, hang-gliding, canoeing, speed boating.<br><br>**Open:** 15 April - 15 October. | From Montélimar take N102 west towards Aubenas, pass around Villeneuve, at traffic lights in Lavilledieu turn right onto D224 towards Lussas. Site entrance is on right just before village (about 4 km. from N102). GPS: 44.60495, 4.4712 |

**Charges guide**

| Per unit incl. 2 persons and electricity | € 18.00 - € 31.00 |
|---|---|
| extra person | € 3.00 - € 6.50 |

---

## Massignieu-de-Rives

### Camping du Lac du Lit du Roi

La Tuillière, F-01300 Massignieu-de-Rives (Ain) T: 04 79 42 12 03. E: info@camping-savoie.com
**alanrogers.com/FR01040**

This attractive and well cared for family run site is ideal for those seeking an active holiday in a peaceful lakeside setting. This picturesque area offers wonderful opportunities for exploration by foot, bicycle, car and boat. Sample the wines and other local produce on offer. Of 120 pitches (electricity 10A), 90 are available for touring. All are close to the lake and many have wonderful views. The slightly sloping, grassy pitches are set on low terraces and are partly separated by hedging and trees giving some shade. Two raised teepees, set on the lakeside, are a recent addition to the rental accommodation available.

| Facilities | Directions |
|---|---|
| Two modern toilet blocks offer all necessary facilities, with provision for disabled visitors. Washing machines. Small shop, bar, restaurant and terrace (May-Sept). Swimming pool, play area with water features. Tennis. Play area beside lake. Grassy beach, pedaloes, canoes, surf bikes for hire. Bicycle hire. Lake fishing. Free WiFi over part of site. Barbecue rental. Off site: Shops at Belley 8 km. Lac du Bourget (watersports, boat hire). Cycle tracks and walks. Marina, boat ramp nearby. Golf 8 km.<br><br>**Open:** 11 April - 4 October. | Travelling south on N504 (Aix-les-Bains) bypass Belley and at roundabout (Champion supermarket) turn east D992 (Culoz and Seyssel). After 4 km. turn right over bridge, D37 signed Massignieu. Follow signs to site (2 km). GPS: 45.76883, 5.76942 |

**Charges guide**

| Per unit incl. 2 persons and electricity | € 18.00 - € 28.00 |
|---|---|
| extra person | € 4.50 - € 6.50 |

Camping Cheques accepted.

---

**FREE** Alan Rogers Travel Card
**Extra benefits and savings** - see page 10

## Matafelon-Granges

### Camping des Gorges de l'Oignin

Rue du Lac, F-01580 Matafelon-Granges (Ain) T: 04 74 76 80 97. E: camping.lesgorgesdeloignin@wanadoo.fr
alanrogers.com/FR01050

This attractively landscaped, terraced site (English spoken) offers stunning views across the lake to the hills beyond. There are 130 good sized pitches, 120 for touring, which are thoughtfully laid out and separated by young trees and flowering shrubs. Most have grass and hardstanding. Forty-five have their own water point and most have 10A electricity. The reception, bar/restaurant and the pool complex are at the top of the site with a gently sloping road down to the lower terraces and lake. At the lowest part of the site is a large grassy area next to the lake for sunbathing and activities. Twin-axle caravans are not accepted.

**Facilities**

Two modern, well equipped and clean toilet blocks with all the usual facilities. There are no facilities for disabled visitors. Washing machine and dryer (tokens). Bar/restaurant, takeaway and TV room (July/Aug). Swimming pool, paddling pool and new lazy river (1/6-22/9). Play and sports areas. Pétanque. Swimming, fishing and boating on the lake (no motorboats). Free WiFi over part of site. Off site: Matafelon 800 m. Golf 2 km. Riding 6 km. Thoirette 6 km. Oyonnax with range of shops, market, bar/restaurants 10 km.

**Open:** 15 April - 22 September.

**Directions**

Matafelon is 40 km. east of Bourg-en-Bresse. Leave autoroute A404 at Nantua, exit 9 and turn right towards D18 road and continue to Matafelon (10 km). On entering village and opposite the Mairie turn left, signed camping, and descend to site (800 m). GPS: 46.25535, 5.55717

**Charges 2013**

| | |
|---|---|
| Per unit incl. 2 persons and electricity | € 17.00 - € 28.00 |
| extra person | € 3.60 - € 6.20 |

## Menglon

### Camping l'Hirondelle

Bois Saint Ferreol, F-26410 Menglon (Drôme) T: 04 75 21 82 08. E: contact@campinghirondelle.com
alanrogers.com/FR26130

This is a natural, spacious and popular, family run site; you are assured of a good welcome. It lies in a beautiful valley, south of the Vercors mountains and the Vercors National Park, beside the River Bez. The 170 large to very large pitches, 118 for touring, are stony and slightly uneven (rock pegs advised). They lie in natural openings in woodland and some have views over the fields and hills beyond. In 2012, 53 new large pitches were added, some with good views and 16 have a private bathroom. All have electricity (3/6A) and long leads are advised.

**Facilities**

Six large toilet blocks offer all the necessary facilities (16 private bathrooms). Good bar/restaurant/takeaway (all season). Small shop, including bread. Excellent pool complex with toboggans, paddling pool, water games and beach area (1/5-15/9). Ample play room. River bathing. Club/TV room. Fishing. Football, boules, volleyball, archery. Multisports court. Bicycle hire. Organised events (high season). WiFi (charged). No charcoal barbecues, communal available. Off site: Riding 3 km. Canoeing, kayaking, climbing, rambling, mountain biking and cycling over the steep local passes.

**Open:** 28 April - 15 September.

**Directions**

From Die follow D93 southwards and after 6 km. at Pont de Quart, turn left on D539 signed Châtillon. After 4 km. turn right on D140, signed Menglon. Site entrance is shortly on right just after crossing a small river. GPS: 44.68142, 5.44743

**Charges guide**

| | |
|---|---|
| Per unit incl. 2 persons and electricity | € 21.20 - € 38.70 |
| extra person | € 5.30 - € 9.45 |
| child (2-10 yrs) | free - € 7.50 |
| dog | free - € 3.35 |

Camping Cheques accepted.

For latest campsite news, availability and prices visit
**alanrogers.com**

## Mens

### Camping le Pré Rolland

Rue de la Piscine, F-38710 Mens (Isère) T: 04 76 34 65 80. E: contact@camping-prerolland.fr

**alanrogers.com/FR38230**

Camping le Pré Rolland is a small, well maintained family run site on the outskirts of the little town of Mens. It is surrounded by beautiful mountain scenery making it an ideal base for nature lovers touring this little known region of the Trièves. There are 98 mainly level, good sized grass pitches, 90 for touring and all having electricity (10A). Some are delineated by flowering shrubs and mature trees and are quite shady, others are more open and sunny. There is no on-site entertainment.

#### Facilities

Two well maintained and clean toilet blocks include facilities for babies and campers with disabilities. Covered area with tables, small kitchen and bunk room. Bar/snack bar. Adjacent municipal swimming pool, free (1/6-31/8). Day room/TV. Playground. Bicycle hire. WiFi (free). Electric barbecues only on pitches, communal barbecue areas provided. Off site: Small town of Mens with range of small shops, bar and restaurant 500 m. Fishing 1.5 km. Riding 2 km. Many marked walks and cycle rides.

**Open:** 1 May - 30 September.

#### Directions

From the A51 going south from Grenoble take the N75 towards Sisteron. After 50 km, at Clelles, turn east on D521 to Mens. On entering town turn right, signed site and 'piscine'. GPS: 44.814807, 5.7485

#### Charges guide

| | |
|---|---|
| Per unit incl. 2 persons and electricity | € 19.50 - € 22.00 |
| extra person | € 6.50 - € 8.50 |
| child (3-12 yrs) | € 4.00 - € 7.50 |

---

## Mirabel-et-Blacons

### Gervanne Camping

Bellevue, F-26400 Mirabel-et-Blacons (Drôme) T: 04 75 40 00 20. E: info@gervanne-camping.com

**alanrogers.com/FR26120**

This spacious, riverside site, run by a friendly family, has 174 pitches, with 150 for touring (with 6A electricity). It is in two sections either side of a road, connected by an underpass. The upper section is adjacent to the bar, restaurant and good swimming pool with mountain views. The pitches are of average size with some shade and are separated by a few small shrubs and trees. The lower section, closer to the river, is less formally laid out with mature trees offering plenty of shade. Access to and on site is easy here. This site would make a good base to explore the interesting historic area.

#### Facilities

Four well appointed, very clean toilet blocks including good facilities for babies and disabled visitors. Laundry. Bar/restaurant (1/5-20/9), takeaway service and free WiFi. Heated swimming pool (28/4-30/9). Play area. Football. Boules. Bicycle hire. Electric and gas barbecues only. Motorcaravan services. WiFi. Off site: Supermarket next door. Canoeing and bathing in adjacent Drôme river. Old village of Mirabelle 1.5 km. Riding 5 km. Golf 13 km.

**Open:** 29 March - 30 September.

#### Directions

Leave A7 autoroute at exit 16 for Loriol. Take D104 then D164 bypassing Crest. After 6 km, at roundabout, turn left on to D164A. Cross river into Mirabel-et-Blacons, left at roundabout, site in 200 m. GPS: 44.71110, 5.09015

#### Charges guide

| | |
|---|---|
| Per unit incl. 2 persons and electricity | € 18.00 - € 27.00 |
| extra person | € 4.00 - € 6.70 |

---

## Montrevel-en-Bresse

### Camping la Plaine Tonique

Base de Plein Air, F-01340 Montrevel-en-Bresse (Ain) T: 04 74 30 80 52. E: plaine.tonique@wanadoo.fr

**alanrogers.com/FR01010**

This excellent site, ideal for active families, belongs to a syndicate of several local villages. It is a very well maintained, large site with 560 marked and numbered pitches, 345 with 10A electricity. The majority are of a good size, hedged and on flat grass, with shade in most parts. The site is spacious and broken up into sections by trees and hedges. One area has been allocated for eight teepees to rent, with cooking facilities. It is on the edge of an attractive, 320-acre lake with its own beach and adjacent public beach. A separate area is used by Dutch tour operators (100 pitches).

#### Facilities

Very clean sanitary facilities are in twelve blocks and include some washbasins in cabins, baby rooms and washing machines. Motorcaravan services. Restaurant and bar. Takeaway and shop (July/Aug) next to site. Aquatonic centre with five pools (no Bermuda shorts). Indoor pool. Outdoor pool (17/6-2/9). Watersports and fishing. Minigolf. Tennis. Adventure play area. Games and TV rooms. Archery. Bicycle hire. Roller skating. Fitness trail. WiFi in reception area (charged). Chalets and teepees for rent. Off site: Montrevel 300 m. walk. Riding 4 km.

**Open:** 14 April - 21 September.

#### Directions

Montrevel is 20 km. north of Bourg-en-Bresse and 25 km. east of Mâcon. The site is on the D28 500 m. east of town towards Etrez and is well signed. GPS: 46.33972, 5.13592

#### Charges guide

| | |
|---|---|
| Per unit incl. 2 persons and electricity | € 15.70 - € 24.10 |
| extra person | € 3.80 - € 6.00 |
| child (3-7 yrs) | € 2.40 - € 3.50 |
| dog | € 1.80 - € 2.40 |

---

**FREE** Alan Rogers Travel Card

Extra benefits and savings - see page 10

## Neydens

### Camping la Colombière

Saint Julien-en-Genevois, F-74160 Neydens (Haute-Savoie) T: 04 50 35 13 14. E: la.colombiere@wanadoo.fr

alanrogers.com/FR74060

La Colombière, a family owned site, is on the edge of the small village of Neydens, a few minutes from the A40 autoroute and only a short drive from Geneva. It is an attractive site with 156 pitches (134 for touring with electricity 5-15A), all reasonably level and separated by fruit trees, flowering shrubs and hedges. Forty-one new pitches and a toilet block have recently been added in an attractive, landscaped field. It is a very pleasant, friendly site where you may drop in for a night stop – and stay for several days! The site is open all year for motorcaravans and suitable caravans. There are views to the east and west of the mountain ridges. M. Bussat owns a small vineyard close to the site and has the wine made in Switzerland and sold in his restaurant. One of France's long-distance footpaths (GR65) passes close to the site. Neydens is the first stage for pilgrims from Northern Europe on the pilgrim route to Santiago de Compostella on their way to cross the Pyrénées at St Pied-de-Port. The site has a dormitory with eight beds for pilgrims or for anyone else who may need a bed. A Sites et Paysages member.

### Facilities

Good sanitary blocks (one heated) include facilities for disabled visitors. Motorcaravan services. Fridge hire. Gas supplies. Good bar/restaurant and terrace. Pool (1/5-15/9). New heated, indoor pool, spa pool and jacuzzi (21/3-11/11). Games room. Organised visits and activities. Bicycle hire. Archery. Boules. Playground. WiFi throughout (charged). Max. 1 dog. Off site: Fishing and riding 1 km. Switzerland 3 km. St Julien-en-Genevois 5 km. Golf 7 km. Lake beach and windsurfing 12 km. Bus to Geneva. Lake Geneva and surrounding area with walks and cycle rides.

**Open:** 28 March - 11 November.

### Directions

From A40 south of Geneva take exit 13 and then N201 towards Annecy. After 2 km. turn left into village of Neydens and follow campsite signs to site in just over 1 km. GPS: 46.1201, 6.10552

### Charges guide

| | |
|---|---|
| Per unit incl. 2 persons and electricity (6A) | € 22.00 - € 34.00 |
| extra person | € 4.00 - € 6.00 |
| child (2-12 yrs) | € 3.50 - € 4.50 |
| dog | € 2.00 |

# Camping La Colombière★★★★

Open from 28 March till 11 November 2013

Pool complex enlargement planned for 2013

Camping La Colombière★★★★ • Famille Bussat • 166 Chemin Neuf • F-74160 Neydens
Tel. : 00.33.(0)4.50.35.13.14 • Fax : 00.33.(0)4.50.35.13.40
www.camping-la-colombiere.com • la.colombiere@wanadoo.fr

## Neyrac-les-Bains

### Domaine de la Plage

Neyrac-les-Bains, F-07380 Aubenas (Ardèche) T: 04 75 36 40 59. E: contact@lecampingdelaplage.com

alanrogers.com/FR07570

A great deal of care and attention to detail has gone into developing this compact site and its superb facilities. Of its 45 pitches, only 12 are available for camping and advance booking is essential. The site is beautifully landscaped and the facilities are sympathetically incorporated into a former textile factory. It has a very attractive solar heated pool and sunbathing terrace, with bar and snack service, on-site shop, games room and library. The river is directly accessed from the site with a delightful bridge walkway crossing a waterfall and leading to a sports and picnic area. A Sites et Paysages member.

### Facilities

Modern sanitary facilities include superb facilities for disabled visitors although access around the site is quite steep. Laundry room. Gas. Bar. Snack service. Shop. Solar heated swimming pool and poolside bar. Games room, library and TV room. Pétanque. Play area. Multisports area. Entertainment and children's animation. Fishing. Canoeing excursions. WiFi (free). Off site: Thermal baths 700 m. Bicycle hire 2 km. Tennis 3 km. Golf 8 km.

**Open:** 29 March - 23 October.

### Directions

From A7 exit 17 take N7 (Montélimar) for 20 km. Turn west on N102 to Aubenas. Continue on N102 for 30 km. towards Neyrac-les-Bains. Cross river at Pont-de-Labeaume and site is 2 km, on left just before entering village. GPS: 44.6733, 4.2594

### Charges guide

| | |
|---|---|
| Per unit incl. 2 persons and electricity | € 19.00 - € 31.00 |
| extra person | € 4.00 - € 5.00 |

For latest campsite news, availability and prices visit

**alanrogers.com**

## Peisey-Nancroix
### Flower Camping les Lanchettes

Route de Boverêche (D87), Nancroix, F-73210 Peisey-Nancroix (Savoie) T: 04 79 07 93 07.
E: lanchettes@free.fr  **alanrogers.com/FR73030**

This site is close to the beautiful Vanoise National Park and at 1,470 m. is one of the highest campsites in this guide. There is a climb to the site but the spectacular scenery is well worth the effort. It is a natural, terraced site with 90 good sized, reasonably level and well drained, grassy pitches, with 70 used for touring units, all having electricity (3-10A). Outside taps are only available in summer because of the altitude and cold winters. For those who love walking and mountain biking, wonderful scenery, flora and fauna, this is the site for you.

**Facilities**

Well appointed heated toilet block. Motorcaravan services. Restaurant, takeaway (July/Aug. and winter). Playground. Club/TV room. Large tent/marquee used in bad weather. Free bus to ski lifts in winter. Free WiFi. Off site: Riding next to site. Peisey-Nancroix, restaurants, bars and shops 3 km. Les Arcs winter sports centre, outdoor swimming pool and bicycle hire 6 km. Golf and indoor pool 8 km. Lakeside beach 10 km. Walks in National Park.

**Open:** 15 December - 30 April, 1 June - 15 October.

**Directions**

From Albertville take N90 (Bourg-St-Maurice), through Aime. In 9 km, right on D87 (Peisey-Nancroix). Follow a winding hilly road (hairpin bends) for 10 km. Pass through Peisey-Nancroix; site in 1 km. beyond Nancroix. GPS: 45.53137, 6.77560

**Charges guide**

| Per unit incl. 2 persons | |
|---|---|
| and electricity | € 12.50 - € 14.10 |
| extra person | € 4.20 - € 4.70 |

## Pélussin
### Camping Bel'Epoque du Pilat

Route de Malleval, F-42410 Pélussin (Loire) T: 04 74 87 66 60. E: camping-belepoque@orange.fr
**alanrogers.com/FR42030**

This is a peaceful, family run site located within the relatively little known Pilat Regional Park overlooking the attractive town of Pélussin. There are 70 good sized, slightly uneven and sloping, grassy pitches, of which 50 are for touring (electricity 6A). They are separated by trees and some hedging with most having some shade and some having good views over the valley below. The site is well maintained with an attractive pool and a new, large bar with terrace and views. Large outfits accepted but care needed on narrow winding roads, please use recommended route. A Sites et Paysages member.

**Facilities**

Well appointed toilet block with facilities for children and disabled visitors. Laundry facilities. Motorcaravan services. Bar (1/5-30/8), snack bar, takeaway meals (1/7-31/8). Outdoor, heated swimming pool (May-Sept). Tennis. Play area. WiFi. Bicycle hire. Entertainment for young children in peak season. WiFi on terrace (free). Off site: Fishing, riding 500 m. Water sports 7 km. Golf 25 km. Vienne (Roman town). Safari park at Peaugres.

**Open:** 1 April - 30 September.

**Directions**

Leave A7 autoroute, exit 10 Vienne 34 km. south of Lyon, take N86 south to Chavanay. Turn west on D7, climb to Pélussin. On entering the village bear left, site signed. Site on right in 1.5 km. Only recommended route. GPS: 45.4139, 4.69139

**Charges guide**

| Per unit incl. 2 persons | |
|---|---|
| and electricity (6A) | € 19.80 - € 23.80 |
| extra person | € 5.00 |

## Pont-de-Vaux
### Camping les Ripettes

Chavannes-sur-Reyssouze, F-01190 Pont-de-Vaux (Ain) T: 03 85 30 66 58. E: info@camping-les-ripettes.com
**alanrogers.com/FR01030**

A friendly welcome is assured from the owners of this spacious site situated in quiet, flat countryside near the pleasant small town of Pont-de-Vaux. The six-acre site has 54 large (100-400 sq.m) level grassy pitches, all of which are available to tourers. Almost all are separated by hedges and most are shaded by trees. All but three have electrical connections (10A) and water. Because of its friendly and tranquil atmosphere, the site is popular with English and Dutch visitors alike.

**Facilities**

Two well appointed, small sanitary blocks contain a suite for disabled visitors. Washing machine and dryer. Limited range of food stocked and wine, ice cream, meat for barbecues at reception. Two swimming pools. Play area. Areas for ball games. Board games, books. Free WiFi over part of site. Communal Sunday barbecues are popular. Off site: Supermarket within 1 km. Restaurant 1 km. Riding 2 km. Fishing 4 km. Golf 15 km.

**Open:** 1 April - 30 September.

**Directions**

Leave N6 at Fleurville (14 km. south of Tournus). Go east on D933A to Pont-de-Vaux (5 km). In town turn left briefly onto D933 then take D2 east towards St Trivier-de-Courtes. After 3 km. turn left after water tower, then almost immediately left again (100 m). Site is 300 m. GPS: 46.44455, 4.98067

**Charges guide**

| Per unit incl. 2 persons | |
|---|---|
| and electricity | € 17.50 - € 21.00 |
| extra person | € 3.60 - € 4.00 |

**FREE** Alan Rogers Travel Card
Extra benefits and savings - see page 10

## Pradons
### Camping les Coudoulets

Pradons, F-07120 Ruoms (Ardèche) T: 04 75 93 94 95. E: camping@coudoulets.com

**alanrogers.com/FR07130**

Situated beside the River Ardèche between Ruoms and the pretty village of Balazuc, Camping les Coudoulets is well cared for and would suit those who prefer a more intimate and peaceful campsite. It is run by a very friendly family who also own a small vineyard and their highly recommended wine is on sale in the bar. There are 123 good sized, grassy and well shaded pitches, separated by trees and shrubs. There are 102 for touring, all with 10/16A electricity. There is an area for bathing in the river and it is an ideal spot for canoeists. Organised family activities take place in July/August.

**Facilities**

New sanitary block has facilities for families and children, excellent facilities for disabled visitors, and a dog shower. Motorcaravan services. Bar, TV, terrace (May-Sept). Bread and newspapers to order, ices, drinks. Snacks and takeaway (May-Sept). Small heated swimming pool, paddling pool. New aquatic play area and pool (May-Sept). Play areas. Bouncy castles. Fishing. Bicycle hire. WiFi (charged). Off site: Shop 300 m. Riding 2 km.

**Open:** 20 April - 21 September.

**Directions**

Leave Montélimar westwards on N102 towards Aubenas. After passing Villeneuve-de-Berg turn left on D103 towards Vogüé for 5 km. Turn left on D579 towards Ruoms, site on right on entering Pradons (10 km). GPS: 44.47663, 4.35857

**Charges 2013**

| Per unit incl. 2 persons and electricity | € 18.20 - € 33.70 |
| extra person | € 4.00 - € 7.00 |

## Pradons
### Camping du Pont

Route de Chauzon, F-07120 Pradons (Ardèche) T: 04 75 93 93 98. E: campingdupont07@wanadoo.fr

**alanrogers.com/FR07420**

This is a delightful campsite, which has been run by a friendly outgoing family for several years. Beside the Ardèche river, the site has a small sandy beach and a deep river pool for swimming. There are 80 average sized, grassy pitches with 61 for touring (10A electricity), all separated by hedges and trees giving good shade. The bar, restaurant, takeaway and pool are all located close to reception and open all season. The site is ideal for those seeking a less commercialised site close to the Ardèche Gorges.

**Facilities**

The good toilet block provides separate facilities for men and ladies, room for children and facilities for disabled visitors. Small shop. Bar, restaurant, snacks and takeaway. Heated swimming and paddling pools (1/4-30/9). Games/TV room. Play areas. Small sandy river beach, deep pool for swimming. Fishing. Canoe trips. Organised walks from site. WiFi. No charcoal barbecues. Off site: Supermarket 200 m. Bicycle hire 3 km. Riding 4 km. Vallon-Pont-d'Arc 12 km. Canyoning, rafting etc.

**Open:** Easter - 30 September.

**Directions**

Leave Montélimar westwards on N102 (Aubenas). Passing Villeneuve-de-Berg, turn left on D103 (Vogüé) for 5 km. Turn left on D579 (Ruoms). In Pradons turn right D308 (Chauzon). Site shortly on left before river bridge. GPS: 44.40716, 4.35333

**Charges guide**

| Per unit incl. 2 persons and electricity | € 18.50 - € 33.00 |
| extra person | € 4.00 - € 6.50 |

## Privas
### Kawan Village Ardèche

Boulevard de Paste, F-07000 Privas (Ardèche) T: 04 75 64 05 80. E: jcray@wanadoo.fr

**alanrogers.com/FR07180**

This spacious, family run site is on the southern outskirts of Privas and aims to provide a warm friendly atmosphere. The site has 166 large, grass, mostly level pitches, of which 131 are for touring units with 10A electricity and trees offering varying degrees of shade. It is a good base for exploring the lesser known parts of the Ardèche with bus and coach trips available. On site amenities include a bar, restaurant, heated swimming pool complex, and a mulisports area with outdoor gym equipment.

**Facilities**

Two toilet blocks, only one open in low season. Facilities for disabled visitors. Motorcaravan service point. Bar and restaurant (1/5-30/9). Swimming pool planned. Boules. Play area. Trampoline. Multisports court. Miniclub (1/5-11/9). Entertainment (high season). WiFi at the bar (free). Only gas barbecues are permitted. Chalets, mobile homes and tents for rent. Off site: Supermarket 100 m. Bicycle hire 2 km. Riding 5 km.

**Open:** 15 April - 30 September.

**Directions**

From the A7 motorway (Loriol) take exit 16 towards Privas. At Le Pouzin use heavy goods route, D86, D22 then D2. In Privas at roundabout (near Intermarché) look for signs Espace Ouvèze exit left and take second left, signed campsite and Espace Ouvéze. GPS: 44.72611, 4.59845

**Charges guide**

| Per unit incl. 2 persons and electricity | € 19.50 - € 26.80 |
| extra person | € 4.50 - € 6.00 |

Camping Cheques accepted.

For latest campsite news, availability and prices visit
# alanrogers.com

## Recoubeau-Jansac
### Camping le Couriou

F-26310 Recoubeau-Jansac (Drôme) T: 04 75 21 33 23. E: camping.lecouriou@wanadoo.fr
**alanrogers.com/FR26340**

Le Couriou is a family run site in the beautiful Drôme countryside just south of Die. There are 131 stony/grassy, level pitches of varying sizes with 102 for touring (6A electricity). They are laid out on high terraces with views over the surrounding wooded hills; not ideal for those with walking difficulties. The pitches are separated by some shrubs and a variety of trees giving some shade. Though the site roads are quite steep, access is not difficult for large outfits. It has a large swimming pool complex, bar and restaurant, all open to the public. Only electric barbecues allowed on site.

| Facilities | Directions |
|---|---|
| Three adequate toilet blocks with facilities for babies and campers with disabilities. Washing machines/dryer. Shop, bar, restaurant/takeaway (1/6-30/8). Four heated swimming pools, toboggans, paddling pool, sauna, massage (all season, open to public). Multisport area. Boules. Off site: Fishing 500 m. Recoubeau 1 km. Luc-en-Diois 5 km. Riding 5 km. Bicycle hire 10 km. | From Die take D93 south for 14 km. Just before Recoubeau turn right, site signed, to site. GPS: 44.658534, 5.407172 |

**Open:** 1 May - 30 August.

**Charges guide**

| | |
|---|---|
| Per unit incl. 2 persons and electricity | € 16.60 - € 28.90 |
| extra person | € 4.00 - € 7.30 |

## Ruoms
### Yelloh! Village la Plaine

F-07120 Ruoms (Ardèche) T: 04 75 39 65 83. E: info@yellohvillage-la-plaine.com
**alanrogers.com/FR07250**

This is a high quality campsite with full provision for families of all ages with a beautiful riverside location. La Plaine is quiet in low season, but in high season with all day and evening activities for both teenagers and adults, and a miniclub each day, there should be something for everyone! There are 212 pitches of moderate size, of which 160 have electricity. They are protected from the sun and marked by many trees. This is a young family site for people with lots of energy, perhaps not for a quiet holiday in high season! There are 77 pitches used for their own air-conditioned mobile homes.

| Facilities | Directions |
|---|---|
| Three sanitary blocks, clean and modern provide all facilities under cover. Young children's toilet facilities. Good facilities for disabled visitors. Excellent laundry room. Fridge hire. Shop, restaurant, bar and takeaway. Heated swimming pool complex with good slides (all season). Gym. Games area and TV. Boules. Small football field. Play area. Fitness room. Activity and entertainment programme day and evening. Miniclub (5-12 yrs). Fishing. River beach. Multisport area. Bicycle hire. WiFi throughout (charged). Off site: Riding 2 km. Town facilities 3 km. | Exit Ruoms south on the D579 and at junction 2 km, south, take D111 signed St Ambroix. Site is on the left. GPS: 44.427067, 4.335617 |

**Open:** 16 April - 17 September.

**Charges guide**

| | |
|---|---|
| Per unit incl. 2 persons and electricity (6A) | € 15.00 - € 42.00 |
| extra person | € 5.00 - € 8.00 |
| child (3-7 yrs) | free - € 7.00 |
| dog | € 4.00 |

## Ruoms
### Camping la Digue

Chauzon, F-07120 Ruoms (Ardèche) T: 04 75 39 63 57. E: info@camping-la-digue.fr
**alanrogers.com/FR07330**

The circuitous route to la Digue is worth the effort as you will be greeted with a warm welcome from its resident owners who provide their visitors with a great, yet calm, family atmosphere. M. Elne and his busy small team organise many activities, including canoeing and fishing on the River Ardèche which flows past the site, mountain biking, hill walking and caving. It is less than 200 metres to the river and a wide beach that can be a mixture of sand and rounded pebbles. The 74 touring pitches are on grass and of a good size, with 6-10A electricity available to all. La Digue is open for an unusually long season.

| Facilities | Directions |
|---|---|
| The first rate sanitary unit is kept in excellent condition. Cubicles for young children and babies and good facilities for disabled visitors. Good laundry room. Well stocked shop. Restaurant, bar and takeaway (1/4-21/10). Swimming pool (heated in season). Play area. Pony riding. Bicycle hire. Canoe hire. Tennis. Fishing. WiFi near bar and reception (free). Tourist information. Mobile homes to rent. Off site: River beach 200 m. Riding 5 km. | From the D579 Vallon-Pont-d'Arc-Ruoms road, turn left immediately on entering village of Pradon, signed Chauzon. Immediately after crossing river bridge, bear right 400 m. taking ring road on left around the village. Follow signs. GPS: 44.48485, 4.372983 |

**Open:** 15 March - 3 November.

**Charges guide**

| | |
|---|---|
| Per unit incl. 2 persons and electricity | € 17.90 - € 31.30 |
| extra person | € 4.20 - € 6.20 |

**FREE** Alan Rogers Travel Card
Extra benefits and savings - see page 10

## Ruoms
### Camping le Petit Bois

87 rue du Petit Bois, F-07120 Ruoms (Ardèche) T: 04 75 39 60 72. E: vacances@campinglepetitbois.fr
**alanrogers.com/FR07360**

Situated only 800 metres from the ancient town centre of Ruoms, and yet within an area of trees and rocky outcrops, this site offers a centre for those wishing to explore this part of the Ardèche valley. The 110 pitches are of irregular shape and size and a mix of stone and grass, with 76 spaces for touring units. There is some shade and access to the river for swimming and fishing. The site is now thirty years old and is needing some restoration, which is now underway. Some standpipes have coils of tubing attached. Perhaps these should not be used for domestic water purposes. A Sites et Paysages member.

| Facilities | Directions |
|---|---|
| Refurbished toilet block, older second block open in high season. Motorcaravan service point. Bar. Restaurant, pizzeria and takeaway (1/7-31/8). Heated swimming pool, covered in early season (1/4-30/6) and solarium. Slides and child splash pool. Sauna and massage. Pétanque. Play area. Games and TV rooms in season. Entertainment in high season. Mobile homes and tents for rent. WiFi in the bar. Off site: Town with shops 800 m. Riding 1 km. | Approaching Ruoms on the D579 from Vallon-Pont-d'Arc go straight on at first (Super U) and second roundabouts. At third roundabout turn left (southwest) signed Largentier (site is signed). GPS: 44.46063, 4.3373 |

**Charges guide**

| | |
|---|---|
| Per unit incl. 2 persons and electricity | € 21.00 - € 33.00 |
| extra person | € 5.90 - € 6.90 |

**Open:** 1 April - 30 September.

## Ruoms
### Aluna Vacances

Route de Lagorce, F-07120 Ruoms (Ardèche) T: 04 75 93 93 15. E: alunavacances@wanadoo.fr
**alanrogers.com/FR07630**

Aluna is a high quality, large holiday park close to the market town of Ruoms in the southern Ardèche, famous for its gorges and the large range of watersports and other tourist activities. This will be a very lively site in July and August with a wide range of activities organised for all age groups, all day and into the night. There are 200 pitches mainly occupied by mobile homes and tour operators with 61 slightly uneven and sloping pitches for touring (electricity 6A, rock pegs advised). All the main activities take place in a single area, including a magnificent aqua park. Only one dog per pitch permitted.

| Facilities | Directions |
|---|---|
| Well appointed and very clean modern toilet blocks including facilities for disabled visitors. Motorcaravan services. Shop, bar, restaurant, takeaway (15/4-18/9). Aqua park complex. Fitness room. Play area. Miniclubs (over 5 yrs). Tennis. Multisport court. Boules. Mini football stadium (artificial surface). Underground disco (until 02.00), outdoor stage, activities (all July/Aug). Gas and electric barbecues only. WiFi throughout. Off site: Bicycle hire and river bathing 2 km. Riding 5 km. | Site is in the southern Ardèche south of Aubenas. Leave Aubenas on D104 signed Alès. Shortly turn left on D579 signed Vallon-Pont-d'Arc. Bypass Vogüé, cross river and keep right. At Ruoms turn left at roundabout on D559 signed Lagorce. In 1 km. turn right to site on right. GPS: 44.44407, 4.36704 |

**Charges guide**

| | |
|---|---|
| Per unit incl. 2 persons and electricity | € 20.00 - € 43.00 |
| extra person | € 6.50 - € 10.30 |

**Open:** 1 April - 18 September.

## Saint Avit
### Domaine la Garenne

156 chemin de Chablezin, F-26330 Saint Avit (Drôme) T: 04 75 68 62 26. E: garenne.drome@wanadoo.fr
**alanrogers.com/FR26160**

This very spacious, and cleverly terraced rural site lies in pleasant countryside, quite hidden from the roads by its own wood, and situated to the east of the Rhône valley. Most of the very large pitches are spread out and appear to form natural clearings under pine trees. A grassy lower area is more open and young trees give little shade. All pitches have electricity (3/6A) but very long leads are necessary. Of the 74 touring pitches, 25 are taken up by long stay units. The facilities are old but very clean and could entail a long walk. A new pool complex was added in 2011. Torches and rock pegs essential.

| Facilities | Directions |
|---|---|
| Four basic toilet blocks with washbasins in cabins. Some facilities for disabled visitors but site is unsuitable for those with walking difficulties. Washing machine. Motorcaravan services. Baker calls July/Aug. Small bar plus takeaway (July/Aug). Kitchen area. Swimming pool, shallow pool and fun pool. Sports area. Play area. Family activities (July/Aug). Communal barbecue only. WiFi at reception. Off site: Fishing 1 km. Riding 2 km. Châteauneuf 3 km. | Leave the N7 16 km. north of Tournon. Turn east on D51, signed Châteauneuf. After 15 km. at Mureils, turn right on D363, signed St Avit. After 2 km. turn left on D53 (site signed) and site entrance is shortly on the right. GPS: 45.20205, 4.95719 |

**Charges guide**

| | |
|---|---|
| Per unit incl. 2 persons and electricity | € 19.50 - € 25.00 |
| extra person | € 5.50 |

**Open:** 16 April - 15 September.

For latest campsite news, availability and prices visit
**alanrogers.com**

## Saint Alban-de-Montbel
### Camping le Sougey

Lac Rive Ouest, F-73610 SaintAlban-de-Montbel (Savoie) T: 04 79 36 01 44. E: info@camping-sougey.com
**alanrogers.com/FR73120**

In scenic surroundings, this site is only 200 m. from Lake Aiguebelette, the third largest natural lake in France. The 165 pitches (140 for touring units) all have 6/10A electricity and are set amongst many mature trees and well manicured hedges, giving plenty of shade and privacy. Most pitches are flat, but some are on a steep hillside and therefore sloping. There are adequate water points around the site and there are 30 serviced pitches available. This is a very peaceful, quality site with good views of the surrounding countryside and mountains. The owner, Philippe Kremer, is very friendly and speaks excellent English. The restaurant and shop, open during the high season, are in a converted barn just outside the main entrance. The patio has terrific views across the lake. A traditional wood oven is used for pancakes and pizzas or there is a good choice of speciality Savoyard dishes. The lake offers many types of water sports, but to keep the purity of the water, motorboats are not allowed. The beach is free for campsite users, and lifeguards are present in July and August (dogs are not permitted). Walks with llamas and paragliding are organised from reception.

**Facilities**

Two identical sanitary blocks provide excellent facilities, washbasins in cabins, controllable showers, baby bath, 2 shower units with en-suite washbasin. Good facilities for disabled visitors. Separate laundry. Freezer. Shop (1/7-21/8). Bar and restaurant (open to public, just outside main gate). Small play area. Miniclub. TV room. Chalets to rent. Off site: Fishing, boating, swimming, rafting at lake 200 m. Bicycle hire 3 km. Walks with llamas.

**Open:** 1 May - 16 September.

**Directions**

From A43 Chambéry-Lyon motorway, take exit 12 and D921 south towards Lac d'Aiguebelette. Follow signs to Plage du Sougey. Site is on the left just before the beach. GPS: 45.55582, 5.79081

**Charges guide**

| Per unit incl. 2 persons | |
|---|---|
| and electricity | € 18.70 - € 22.70 |
| with full services | € 18.90 - € 26.70 |
| extra person (over 5 yrs) | € 4.00 |

# CAMPING LE SOUGEY****

Campsite du Sougey is nestled in the heart of a site naturally rich in exceptional panoramas, located at a height of 380 meters at the foot of the 'Massif de l'Epine'. You are looking for quality services and service, for a complete and diversified atmosphere of tourism then do not hesitate: **you found your place for holidays!**

**Lac Rive Ouest - 73610 Saint Alban de Montbel**
**Tel : 0033 479 36 01 44 - Fax : 0033 479 44 19 01**
**E-mail : info@camping-sougey.com - Internet : www.camping-sougey.com**

## Saint Donat-sur-Herbasse
### Camping des Ulèzes

Route de Romans, F-26260 Saint Donat-sur-Herbasse (Drôme) T: 04 75 47 83 20.
E: contact@domaine-des-ulezes.com **alanrogers.com/FR26330**

A neat and tidy family run site with a long season only five minutes' walk from St Donat and only 16 km. from the A7 and A49 autoroutes. There are 85 level, grassy pitches with 77 for touring; all are fully serviced with 10A electricity and close to one of the nine toilet blocks. Those in the older section are separated by hedging and a variety of mature trees giving good shade to most pitches. The hedges and trees in the newer section offer little shade at the moment. No twin-axle caravans and only gas and electric barbecues. A good site for the quieter family to unwind and to explore this lesser known region.

**Facilities**

Nine small toilet blocks with all the necessary facilities, some new and others to be refurbished soon. Facilities for children and disabled campers. Washing machines. Basic shop, bar, restaurant and takeaway (15/4-15/9). Small swimming pool (8/5-15/9). Play area. Minigolf. Boules. Games/TV room. Free WiFi over part of site. Gas and electric barbecues only. Off site: St Donat five minutes walk. River bathing. Riding 3 km. Fishing 10 km.

**Open:** 1 April - 31 October.

**Directions**

Leave A7 autoroute (exit 13), take D532 east for 5 km. to Curson. Take D67 north 10 km. through St Donat. At a roundabout turn south, D53 and follow signs to site (1 km). GPS: 45.1192, 4.9927

**Charges guide**

| Per unit incl. 2 persons | |
|---|---|
| and electricity | € 19.20 - € 23.70 |
| extra person | € 4.50 |
| child (over 2 yrs) | € 3.50 |

**FREE** Alan Rogers Travel Card
Extra benefits and savings - see page 10

## Saint Galmier

### Campéole Val de Coise

Route de la Thiéry, F-42330 Saint Galmier (Loire) T: 04 77 54 14 82. E: val-de-coise@campeole.com
alanrogers.com/FR42040

Val de Coise is a member of the Campéole group and is situated in the undulating landscape of the Massif Central, north of St Etienne. It is an attractive site located between the River Coise and a dense forest. The 92 pitches are grassy and of a good size, and 28 of the 30 touring pitches have 16A electricity. Mobile homes, chalets and fully equipped tents are available for rent. There is plenty of activity here in high season with a children's club and regular discos and karaoke evenings. This is rugged, dramatic country – ideal for walking and mountain biking. The nearby spa town of St Galmier is home to the Badoit water plant, a casino, restaurants and a number of art galleries.

#### Facilities

The single toilet block is central. It is kept clean and is neatly tiled and painted. Small baby room. Facilities for disabled visitors. Good motorcaravan services. Fridge hire. Small shop in reception. No bar or snacks. Swimming pool (July/Aug). Multisports terrain. TV room. Play area. Minigolf. Boules. Bouncy castle. Fishing. Activities and entertainment programme. WiFi (first hour free). Mobile homes, chalets and equipped tents for rent. Off site: St Galmier and tennis 2 km. River fishing. Hiking and cycling tracks. Riding. Golf. St Etienne 22 km.

**Open:** 15 April - 15 October.

#### Directions

From St Etienne, head north on the A72 and leave at the Andrezieux Bouthéon St Galmier exit. Take the D100, then the D12 to St Galmier. Site is well signed from here. GPS: 45.59272, 4.33542

#### Charges guide

| Per unit incl. 2 persons | |
|---|---|
| and electricity | € 15.10 - € 19.50 |
| extra person | € 4.00 - € 5.40 |
| child (2-6 yrs) | € 3.00 - € 3.50 |
| dog | € 2.00 - € 2.50 |

**Campéole**
CAMPSITES AND RENTALS

RHÔNE-ALPES

## Val de Coise ★★★★

Pitches and accommodations
of high quality,
with swimming pool.

42330 St Galmier· Tel.: +33-477-5414-82 · www.campeole.co.uk / val-de-coise@campeole.com

## Saint Jean-de-Chevelu

### Camping Lacs de Chevelu

F-73170 Saint Jean-de-Chevelu (Savoie) T: 06 62 48 37 38. E: camping-des-lacs@wanadoo.fr
alanrogers.com/FR73080

This is a beautifully kept, small, family orientated campsite which is run by a friendly family and surrounded by delightful scenery, not far from Lac du Bourget. Beside the site is a small lake which is fed by springs and has a small sandy beach ideal for swimming and playing around in small boats. The site has 120 average to large sized, grass pitches with 110 for touring. There are 50 with 10A electricity (long leads advised). They are numbered and marked by very small trees with a few having some shade. This site is ideal for families who are happy to make their own entertainment.

#### Facilities

Excellent newly refurbished toilet block with all necessary facilities including those for babies and campers with disabilities. Motorcaravan services. Shop. Bar (1/6-30/8). Takeaway snacks (1/6-30/8). Fishing. Lake bathing. Organised walks and bike rides. Covered games area. Boules. TV room. Play area. Some family entertainment in high season. WiFi. Off site: Riding, bicycle hire, canoeing, hang-gliding 5 km. Yenne with shops, bars and restaurants 5 km. Boat launching and tennis 7 km. Golf 10 km. Chambéry (much larger) 13 km.

**Open:** 15 May - 15 September.

#### Directions

Leave A43 at exit 13 (Chambéry) and take D1504 (previously N504) north towards Belley. After Tunnel du Chat, continue into St Jean-de-Chevelu, turn right at roundabout (site signed). Site is just over 1 km. GPS: 45.69378, 5.82491

#### Charges guide

| Per unit incl. 2 persons | |
|---|---|
| and electricity | € 20.30 - € 31.90 |
| dog | € 3.00 - € 4.80 |
| extra person | € 3.90 - € 5.90 |
| child (2-7 yrs) | € 2.90 - € 5.90 |

For latest campsite news, availability and prices visit
# alanrogers.com

## Saint Gervais-les-Bains
### Camping les Dômes de Miage

197 route des Contamines, F-74170 Saint Gervais-les-Bains (Haute-Savoie) T: 04 50 93 45 96.
E: info@www.natureandlodge.fr/ **alanrogers.com/FR74140**

Saint Gervais is a pretty spa town in the picturesque Val-Monjoie valley and this site is 2 km. from its centre. It is 22 km. west of Chamonix and centrally located for discovering this marvellous mountain region. Nestled among the mountains, this sheltered, well equipped site provides 150 flat, grassy pitches. Of a good size, about half have shade and there are 100 with electricity points (10A). The remainder on terraced ground are used for tents. Third generation hosts, Stéphane and Sophie, will welcome you to the site and their passion for this area at the foot of Mont Blanc is infectious. A number of Savoyard style chalets to let are planned for the future. This is a good site for large motorcaravans. There is no on-site entertainment programme, but a wealth of information about the area and activities available nearby is provided at reception, where they will help you plan your itinerary. The region is good for walking and there is a bus service into Saint Gervais, from where there is a frequent shuttle bus to its spa, and a tramway to the Mont Blanc range. There is also good public transport between the town and Chamonix.

### Facilities

Two sanitary blocks, one heated, with a suite for disabled visitors and baby room. Washing machines, dryer and ironing board. Motorcaravan services. Small basic shop. Bar/restaurant. TV room. Library. Excellent playground. Playing field. WiFi (free). Off site: Fishing 100 m. Bicycle hire 1 km. Riding 7 km. Shops, etc. and outdoor swimming pool in St Gervais.

**Open:** 6 May - 15 September.

### Directions

From St Gervais take D902 towards Les Contamines and site is on left after 2 km.
GPS: 45.87389, 6.7199

### Charges guide

| Per unit incl. 2 persons | |
|---|---|
| and electricity | € 22.90 - € 28.50 |
| extra person | € 3.00 - € 5.50 |
| child (2-9 yrs) | € 2.50 - € 4.50 |
| dog | free - € 2.00 |

## Saint Jean-le-Centenier
### Camping les Arches

Route de Mirabel, F-07580 Saint Jean-le-Centenier (Ardèche) T: 04 75 36 75 19.
E: info@camping-les-arches.com **alanrogers.com/FR07280**

Situated behind the arches of a 19th-century viaduct, not presently in use, this ten-hectare site is a real delight, being divided by a small river, which is dammed for swimming, and with a short causeway crossing. The owners have developed a site which shuns the razzmatazz of many holiday sites, yet is welcoming and relaxing, making the most of its natural setting. There are 137 touring pitches, ranging from small to very large, all with 10A electricity. Although one side of the site is on a gentle hill, all pitches are flat and almost all are shaded. A few have wooden terraces overlooking the river.

**Facilities**

Two refurbished toilet blocks and a newly built block are kept very clean and tidy. Baby room. Facilities for disabled visitors. Laundry facilities. Bread is available in high season. Outdoor heated pool (15/5-31/8). Bar (15/6-31/8). Small restaurant (1/7-31/8). Well constructed play areas. Boules. Fishing. River swimming. Bicycle hire. Chalets for rent (plus 2 gites at the farm). Off site: Village with shop, restaurant and bar 2 km. Riding 8 km.

**Open:** 27 April - 14 September.

**Directions**

From Aubenas take N102 (Montélimar, 18 km) and exit for St Jean-le-Centenier. Go under main road and turn left on D458 (Mirabel). Site is 500 m. on right. From Montélimar (20 km) take exit for Mirabel and right onto D458. Site is signed. Do not drive enter village while towing. GPS: 44.58756, 4.525766

**Charges guide**

| | |
|---|---|
| Per unit incl. 2 persons and electricity | € 18.20 - € 26.20 |
| extra person | € 4.00 - € 5.00 |

## Saint Jorioz
### Village Camping Europa

1444 route Albertville, F-74410 Saint Jorioz (Haute-Savoie) T: 04 50 68 51 01. E: info@camping-europa.com
**alanrogers.com/FR74100**

You will receive a friendly welcome at this quality, family run site. The flowers, shrubs and trees are lovely and everything is kept neat and tidy. There are 210 medium to large sized pitches (110 for touring) on level stony grass. Rock pegs are advised. All pitches have electricity (6A) close by and 18 have 10A electricity, water and drainage. The static units are to one side of the site giving the impression that you are on a small site. There may be some noise from the adjacent main road. This is a good base from which to tour the Lake Annecy area and there is direct access to a 30 km. cycle path.

**Facilities**

Two very good toilet blocks, modernised to a high standard, including some large cubicles with both showers and washbasins. Bar and restaurant (26/5-10/9). Boulangerie with fresh bread daily (1/6-15/9). Swimming pool complex (entry bracelet € 2 each 1/5-17/9). Bicycle hire. WiFi (charged). Miniclub. Some musical evenings. Off site: Fishing 300 m. Boat launching 500 m. Lakeside beach 2 km. Riding 3 km. Golf 8 km. St Jorioz.

**Open:** 30 April - 17 September.

**Directions**

From Annecy take D1508 (previously N508) signed Albertville. Site is well signed on the right on leaving Saint Jorioz. GPS: 45.8246, 6.1758

**Charges guide**

| | |
|---|---|
| Per unit incl. 2 persons and electricity | € 19.00 - € 35.50 |
| serviced pitch | € 23.50 - € 40.00 |
| extra person | € 4.20 - € 6.80 |
| dog | € 4.00 |

## Saint Julien-en-Saint Alban
### Camping l'Albanou

Quartier Pampelonne, F-07000 Saint Julien-en-Saint Alban (Ardèche) T: 04 75 66 00 97.
E: campingalbanou@orange.fr **alanrogers.com/FR07210**

Guests are warmly welcomed at this small, very clean and neat site. It is situated in the beautiful northern Ardèche region with its many old villages, markets and museums – well worth exploring. The site's 87 large, level and easily accessible pitches (84 for touring) are in groups separated by tall hedges, all with electricity (6A). An attractive modern building houses the reception and a small bar with a terrace. Snacks and bread are available to order. In high season a few games are organised for younger children but the emphasis here is on a quiet and peaceful site.

**Facilities**

Refurbished toilet block includes facilities for disabled visitors. Motorcaravan services. Small shop, bar, takeaway, good heated swimming pool, paddling pool and small slide (all 1/5-30/9). Spa/jacuzzi. Play area. Area for ball games. Information and maps for walking and driving. WiFi (free). Only gas or electric barbecues. Off site: Fishing 1 km. St Julien 2 km. Le Pouzin 4 km. Supermarket 5 km. Bicycle hire 10 km. Riding 15 km.

**Open:** 20 April - 30 September.

**Directions**

From A7 autoroute take exit 16 for Loriol, head west across the Rhône to Le Pouzin. At roundabout take N104, signed Aubenas, follow road up hill. Turn left in 4 km. just before St Julien. Site is signed. GPS: 44.75716, 4.71286

**Charges guide**

| | |
|---|---|
| Per unit incl. 2 persons and electricity | € 21.00 - € 24.50 |
| extra person | € 4.00 - € 5.00 |

For latest campsite news, availability and prices visit
# alanrogers.com

## Saint Laurent-du-Pape
### Camping la Garenne

Montée de la Garenne, F-07800 Saint Laurent-du-Pape (Ardèche) T: 04 75 62 24 62. E: info@lagarenne.org
**alanrogers.com/FR07100**

This spacious, split level site has a long season and is within easy reach of the A7/N7 south of Valence. The 120 pitches are on open flat land or on terraced sloping land, all have 6A electricity and varying degrees of shade. Some pitches are separated by hedges, and some need longer leads or rock pegs. It is only a short walk from the village which has a few shops. Guests are predominantly Dutch but all are made welcome and English is widely spoken. Visitors' pursuits have been carefully considered resulting in a varied programme of activities from mid May to mid September.

**Facilities**

Excellent and very clean, modern toilet blocks include facilities for children and disabled visitors. Small shop for basics. Bar, restaurant and takeaway (all 15/5-15/9). Swimming pool and sunbathing terrace (20/5-30/9). Paddling pool. Boules. Games room. Barbecues are not permitted. WiFi (charged). Two mobile homes and four tents for rent. Off site: Village. Fishing 1 km. Riding 2 km. Walking, biking, canoeing and canyoning.

**Open:** 1 March - 1 November.

**Directions**

Leave the N86 at Beauchastel, 20 km. south of Valence and follow the D21 to Saint Laurent-du-Pape. In the village, turn right just before the post office and the site is at the end of this road, beyond the tennis court. GPS: 44.82616, 4.76184

**Charges guide**

| | |
|---|---|
| Per unit incl. 2 persons and electricity | € 18.50 - € 31.50 |
| extra person | € 5.50 |

## Saint Martin-d'Ardèche
### Camping Indigo le Moulin

F-07700 Saint Martin-d'Ardèche (Ardèche) T: 04 75 04 66 20. E: moulin@camping-indigo.com
**alanrogers.com/FR07650**

Le Moulin is a member of the Indigo group and is situated just 300 m. from the centre of St Martin-d'Ardèche. The site has its own river beach and is very well placed for canoe trips on the Ardèche. There are 134 touring pitches here, extending over the site's seven hectares. The pitches are well shaded and most have 10A electrical connections. Rental accommodation includes innovative wood and canvas tents (47) and Romany style caravans (16). Amenities include a pleasant snack bar and a café. A children's club (recré-enfants) operates in peak season, focusing on craft activities and games. Canoeing is almost unavoidable here. The classic trip is by bus to Vallon Pont d'Arc and then back to the campsite (30 km) by canoe – all organised by the site. The Ardèche is, however, renowned for all manner of activities – mountain biking, trekking, riding, caving and rock climbing are all popular. St Martin is a pretty village, once the home of the surrealist painter Max Ernst, standing between the Ardèche and Gard départements.

**Facilities**

Three modern, well appointed sanitary units placed over the site. Snack bar/café. Pizza. Bread to order and local produce at reception. Play area with climbing frame. Children's activity programme. Heated outdoor swimming pool (all season). Direct river access. Canoeing. Football. Bicycle hire. WiFi throughout (free). Tents and caravans for rent. Max. 1 dog per pitch. Off site: St Martin 300 m. (shops, cafés and restaurants). Cycle and walking tracks.

**Open:** 11 April - 30 September.

**Directions**

From Pont St Esprit, take northbound D6086, becoming D86 after crossing the river, and then D290 to St Martin-d'Ardèche. The site is clearly signed. GPS: 44.300272, 4.571171

**Charges 2013**

| | |
|---|---|
| Per unit incl. 2 persons and electricity | € 20.50 - € 31.90 |
| extra person | € 4.20 - € 6.60 |
| child (2-7 yrs) | € 3.00 - € 4.50 |

**FREE** Alan Rogers Travel Card
Extra benefits and savings - see page 10

## Saint Laurent-en-Beaumont

### Camping Belvédère de l'Obiou

Les Egats, F-38350 Saint Laurent-en-Beaumont (Isère) T: 04 76 30 40 80. E: info@camping-obiou.com
alanrogers.com/FR38130

This extremely good and well maintained small Alpine site with just 45 pitches is close to the Ecrins National Park, with great mountain views. It is therefore ideal for walkers and cyclists looking to take advantage of the well marked trails. It has most things a good site should have, with its restaurant, heated pool and sitting room with TV and library. The welcoming owners will even supply you with breakfast. The views from the 45 terraced pitches are spectacular and there is a wealth of activities in the area, from bungee jumping and high walkways across the lake to a more sedate trip by boat to take in the stunning views. Mobile homes are available to rent as well as two comfortable rooms (B&B).

**Facilities**

Two modern toilet blocks, one part of the main building, the other Portacabin style, are immaculate and can be heated. Good facilities for disabled visitors. Laundry. Motorcaravan services. Small shop for ice cream and soft drinks. Restaurant (May-Sept), good takeaway and breakfast. Heated swimming pool (May-Sept). Play area. WiFi on pitches (free). Off site: Fishing 5 km. Walking, cycling and mountain activities.

**Open:** 15 April - 15 October.

**Directions**

The site is just off the N85 (Route Napoleon) between Grenoble and Gap, 7 km. south of La Mure and is clearly signed on the left.
GPS: 44.876067, 5.837833

**Charges guide**

| | |
|---|---|
| Per unit incl. 2 persons and electricity | € 14.00 - € 20.50 |
| extra person | € 3.70 - € 5.70 |

Camping Cheques accepted.

## Saint Pierre-de-Chartreuse

### Camping de Martinière

Route du Col de Porte, F-38380 Saint Pierre-de-Chartreuse (Isère) T: 04 76 88 60 36.
E: camping-de-martiniere@orange.fr  alanrogers.com/FR38160

Chamechaude, the 2,082 m. Eiger-like peak, presides benevolently over the 90 touring pitches at this beautiful, high alpine site open from May to September for the summer season. The large touring pitches, all with electricity (2-10A), have some shade and are slightly sloping. The site has a heated pool in the open air so that not a moment of the views is lost. This well run, family owned enterprise, set around a traditional Savoyard farmhouse, is a peaceful centre for walking, climbing and cycling. It is in the centre of the Chartreuse National Forest. A Sites et Paysages member.

**Facilities**

Two heated toilet blocks, one at each end of the site provide excellent, clean facilities. Facilities for babies and disabled visitors. Laundry facilities. Shop (1/6-11/9). Bar (10/6-5/9) with snacks (1/7-31/8). Swimming and paddling pools (1/6-5/9; heated July/Aug). Play area. Indoor sitting area for poor weather. Paperback library (NL, IT, Fr, UK). Off site: Restaurant 50 m. from site. Fishing 500 m. Bicycle hire 3 km. Skiing 6 km. Walking, cycling and mountain activities. Riding 15 km.

**Open:** 30 April - 11 September.

**Directions**

From St Laurent-du-Pont (north from Voiron or south from Chambery), take D512 signed St Pierre-de-Chartreuse. Site is well signed in the village (the road south from St Pierre-d'Entremont is not recommended for towing). GPS: 45.3258, 5.7972

**Charges guide**

| | |
|---|---|
| Per unit incl. 2 persons and electricity | € 17.00 - € 26.20 |
| extra person | € 4.90 - € 5.60 |

## Saint Romans

### Flower Camping Lac du Marandan

F-38160 Saint Romans (Isère) T: 04 76 64 41 77. E: contact@camping-lac-marandan.com
alanrogers.com/FR38250

Lac du Marandan is ideally situated at the foot of the regional park of the Vercors. It has direct access to an inviting lake which has a temperature of 28 degrees at its shallowest point and is surrounded by a fine sandy beach. Christelle and Yannick will make sure you enjoy your stay. The site has 100 pitches (88 for touring, all with 6A electricity) from 100-200 sq.m. in size and located in a wooded area where old oaks will provide shade. Many activities are possible around the lake and the area itself also offers a rich variety of sporting activities and sightseeing.

**Facilities**

Sanitary buildings with showers. Facilities for disabled visitors. Washing machine. Shop. Bar/restaurant (weekends only in low season). Boules court. Playground. Canoe hire. Fishing. Accommodation to rent. WiFi. Off site: Lakeside restaurant. St Roman 2 km. Mountain bike hire and riding 5 km. Hiking. Stunning gorges.

**Open:** 7 April - 30 September.

**Directions**

South of Grenoble, leave the A49 at exit 9 and follow the D518 towards Saint Romans. Then take the D1532, to Base de Loisirs du Marandan (signed). GPS: 45.103198, 5.292631

**Charges guide**

| | |
|---|---|
| Per unit incl. 2 persons and electricity | € 15.00 - € 24.00 |
| extra person | € 3.50 - € 5.00 |

For latest campsite news, availability and prices visit
# alanrogers.com

## Saint Sauveur-de-Montagut
### Camping Caravaning l'Ardéchois

Le Chambon, Gluiras, F-07190 Saint Sauveur-de-Montagut (Ardèche) T: 04 75 66 61 87.
E: ardechois.camping@wanadoo.fr **alanrogers.com/FR07020**

This attractive site is quite a way off the beaten track but it is worth the effort to find it in such a peaceful and spectacular setting. This site has 106 spacious pitches (83 for touring with 10A electricity) laid out on steep terraces and many separated by trees and plants. Some are alongside the Glueyre river that tumbles between pools, while the rest are on higher, terraced ground nearer the restaurant, bar and pool. The main site access roads are quite steep but are made of good tarmac. A convivial family atmosphere is encouraged by the owners and entertainment is tailored to the guests' needs. There is weekly live music and a comprehensive entertainment package for children.

**Facilities**

Two very good sanitary blocks include facilities for families and visitors with disabilities. Laundry facilities. Motorcaravan services. Shop. Cosy restaurant. Swimming and paddling pools (heated), adjacent bar, snack bar, terrace. TV. Bicycle hire, archery, fishing. Large sports field with football, various courts for volleyball/badminton and a second adventure play area. Comprehensive entertainment programme. Only gas/electric barbecues. WiFi (charged). Off site: Aquarock Adventure Park. Canyoning, climbing, river walking and canoeing trips.

**Open:** 11 May - 20 September.

**Directions**

From Valence take N86 south for 12 km. At La Voulte-sur-Rhône turn right onto D120 to St Sauveur-de-Montagut (site well signed), in centre turn left onto D102 towards Mézilhac for 8 km. to site. The road narrows in places. GPS: 44.82842, 4.52332

**Charges guide**

| | |
|---|---|
| Per unit incl. 2 persons and electricity | € 19.00 - € 28.75 |
| extra person | € 4.20 - € 6.50 |

Camping Cheques accepted.

---

## Samoëns
### Camping Caravaneige le Giffre

La Glière, F-74340 Samoëns (Haute-Savoie) T: 04 50 34 41 92. E: camping.samoens@wanadoo.fr
**alanrogers.com/FR74230**

Surrounded by magnificent mountains in this lesser known Alpine area, yet accessible to major ski resorts, le Giffre could be the perfect spot for those seeking an active, yet relaxing holiday. There are 212 firm, level pitches on stony grass (rock pegs advised) with 154 for touring units. Most have electricity (6/10A) but long leads may be needed. They are spaced out amongst mature trees which give varying amounts of shade and some overlook the attractive lake and leisure park. The small winter/summer resort of Samoëns is only a 15 minute, level stroll away. There is little in the way of on-site entertainment but there are many activities available in Samoëns and the surrounding area.

**Facilities**

Three adequate toilet blocks, heated in winter with facilities for disabled visitors. Games room. Play area. Boules. Fishing. Lake swimming. Accommodation for hire. WiFi throughout. Off site: Leisure park next to site with pool (entry free summer), ice skating (entry free winter), tennis (summer), archery, adventure park. Paragliding. Rafting, walks and bike rides (summer). Ski runs (winter). Snack bar and baker (high season) 100 m. Samoëns with shops, bars, restaurants 1 km. Grand Massif Express cable car 150 m. Bicycle hire 200 m. Riding 2 km.

**Open:** All year.

**Directions**

Leave A40 autoroute at Cluses (exit 18 or 19). Go north on D902 towards Taninges. In Taninges turn east on D907 to Samoëns (avoiding weight and width restriction on D4). Site signed from village. Park outside the entrance. GPS: 46.07731, 6.71851

**Charges guide**

| | |
|---|---|
| Per unit incl. 2 persons and electricity | € 16.75 - € 28.05 |
| extra person | € 4.10 |
| child (4-12 yrs) | € 2.80 |
| dog | € 2.20 |

*Camping Caravaneige Le Giffre ★★★*

Open all year, located on the edge of the Giffre and the 'Lacs aux Dames', 700m from the town and its shops and at the heart of the leisure park, our campsite has 312 level grass pitches on a well shaded site of 6.9h.

In winter, departures for cross-country skiing from the campsite and ski lifts 150m away. Access within 8 min to 265 km of downhill slopes.

Camping Caravaneige Le Giffre • La Glière • F-74340 Samoens
www.camping-samoens.com

## Sampzon
### Yelloh! Village Soleil Vivarais

F-07120 Sampzon (Ardèche) T: 04 75 39 67 56. E: info@yellohvillage-soleil-vivarais.com
alanrogers.com/FR07030

A large, lively, high quality site bordering the River Ardèche, complete with beach, Soleil Vivarais offers much to visitors, particularly families with children. Of the 350 pitches, 104 generously sized, shady and level pitches are for touring units, all with 10A electricity. During the day the proximity of the swimming pools to the terraces of the bar and restaurant make it a pleasantly social area. In the evening the purpose built stage provides regular family entertainment, six evenings a week. An additional attractive pool complex can be used by guests located in a separate mobile home section beyond the beach.

**Facilities**

Modern, clean, well equipped toilet blocks. Facilities for babies and children and for disabled visitors. Laundry facilities. Motorcaravan services. Small supermarket. Bar/restaurant, takeaways and pizzas. Heated pool complexes and paddling pool. Water polo. Aquarobics. Fishing. Boules. Archery. Bicycle and canoe hire. River bathing. Animation in June, July and Aug. Massage and beauty parlour. WiFi near bars. Off site: Riding 800 m. Mountain biking, walking, canoeing, rafting and climbing.

**Open:** 1 April - 12 September.

**Directions**

On D579, 2 km. south of Ruoms, turn left at roundabout, signed Vallon-Pont-d'Arc. Shortly turn right over river bridge, site on right. GPS: 44.42917, 4.35531

**Charges guide**

| | |
|---|---|
| Per unit incl. 2 persons and electricity | € 15.00 - € 44.00 |
| extra person | € 5.00 - € 8.00 |
| child (3-7 yrs) | free - € 7.00 |

## Sampzon
### RCN la Bastide en Ardèche

Route d'Alès (D111), Sampzon, F-07120 Ruoms (Ardèche) T: 04 75 39 64 72. E: bastide@rcn.fr
alanrogers.com/FR07080

You are assured of a good welcome at this site and much recent attention has been paid to the layout of the park with floral areas around the buildings and the separation of rented accommodation and touring pitches. There are 300 good sized, level, grassy pitches marked out by trees giving plenty of shade. There are 260 for touring units, all with 6A electricity, and 86 with full services. Canoe trips are arranged down the Gorge d'Ardèche and annually a large section of the river bank next to the site is cleared of boulders and sand put down. Security patrols ensure quiet nights. There is an emphasis on families and there is good entertainment and activity available on site.

**Facilities**

Two well equipped toilet blocks, one new and one refurbished, with baby room and facilities for disabled visitors. Shop, attractive restaurant and bar (all season). Heated swimming pool (1/4-1/10) and sunbathing area. Play area. Tennis. Fishing. Organised activities. Recreation room in restored medieval building. Bicycle hire. WiFi (charged). Only gas barbecues are permitted. Max. 1 dog.

**Open:** 23 March - 28 September.

**Directions**

Going south from Ruoms on the D579, after 2.5 km. at roundabout, turn right on D111 signed Alès. After 1 km. cross river bridge and site is 200 m. on the left. GPS: 44.42292, 4.32162

**Charges 2013**

| | |
|---|---|
| Per unit incl. 2 persons, electricity and water | € 16.50 - € 55.50 |
| extra person | € 2.60 - € 5.65 |

## Sampzon
### Flower Camping le Riviera

3319, route du rocher, F-07120 Sampzon (Ardèche) T: 04 75 39 67 57. E: leriviera@wanadoo.fr
alanrogers.com/FR07400

This well organised, family run and orientated site is situated beside the River Ardèche not far from Vallon-Pont-d'Arc. There are 176 pitches in total with 114 of varying size for touring units, although access to certain pitches may prove difficult for larger units. Separated by hedges and trees, pitches have varying degrees of shade and 10A electricity connections. The site's facilities are of a high standard and disabled visitors are well provided for. In July and August, daily and evening activities are organised. The site maintains a sandy beach by the river with good opportunities for fishing and canoeing.

**Facilities**

Two modern toilet blocks provide cubicles with washbasins, showers, baby room and facilities for disabled visitors. Laundry facilities. Bar, restaurant with terrace, takeaway (1/5-10/9). Shop (July/Aug). Swimming and paddling pools (heated). New play and multisports areas. Bicycle and canoe hire (July/Aug). Fishing. Riding. River beach. Activities for children. Entertainment for adults. WiFi throughout. Off site: Shop close to entrance.

**Open:** 13 April - 22 September.

**Directions**

On D579 2 km. south of Ruoms, turn left at roundabout (Vallon-Pont-d'Arc). Shortly right over river bridge. Site on left. GPS: 44.42838, 4.35527

**Charges guide**

| | |
|---|---|
| Per unit incl. 2 persons and electricity (10A) | € 19.50 - € 46.50 |
| extra person | € 5.50 - € 8.50 |
| child (under 7 yrs) | € 4.50 - € 7.50 |
| dog | free - € 4.00 |

For latest campsite news, availability and prices visit
# alanrogers.com

## Talloires
### Camping la Chapelle Saint Claude

125 rue du Ponton, Angon, F-74290 Talloires (Haute-Savoie) T: 04 50 60 36 97.
E: contact@chapellesaintclaude.com **alanrogers.com/FR74310**

La Chapelle Saint Claude is an attractively located site with direct access to Lake Annecy. The site can be found on the eastern shore of the lake, close to the pretty town of Talloires. There are 125 pitches here, many of which have fine views across the lake. All have electrical connections (6A). A number of chalets are available for rent. A private beach is available and a larger, gently shelving public beach is around 200 m. distant. Boats can be moored on site but these must be booked beforehand (charged).

| Facilities | Directions |
|---|---|
| The toilet facilities, in a modern block, are adequate and well maintained. Excellent facilities for children and disabled visitors. Takeaway (July/Aug). Morning bread delivery. Direct access to lake. Beach volleyball. Playground. Activity and entertainment programme (July and August). Children's club. Tourist information. Chalets for rent. Limited WiFi (charged). Fishing. Off site: Public beach and several restaurants 200 m. Supermarket 1 km. Bicycle hire 1 km. Golf and riding 5 km. Annecy 15 km. | Approaching from the north (Annecy), take the D909 along the eastern shores of the lake and continue to Talloires. Drive through Talloires towards Faverges and continue as far as Angon. Site is well indicated from here. GPS: 45.825869, 6.220526 |

**Open:** 7 April - 30 September.

**Charges guide**

| Per unit incl. 2 persons and electricity | € 19.00 - € 28.00 |
|---|---|
| extra person | € 4.00 - € 7.00 |

No credit cards.

## Trept
### Domaine les Trois Lacs du Soleil

La Plaine, F-38460 Trept (Isère) T: 04 74 92 92 06. E: les3lacsdusoleil@hotmail.fr
**alanrogers.com/FR38060**

Les Trois Lacs is situated on the edge of three lakes in flat, open country in the north of Dauphine. The camping area is on one side of the largest lake with tall trees on one edge and views of distant mountains. The 200 good sized pitches, with 150 for tourists, are well spaced and separated by trees and hedges. All have 6A electricity. There is plenty of activity on offer for the whole family including fishing in one lake, swimming in the other two and, for the more energetic, roller blading. There is plenty of space around the lake for children to play.

| Facilities | Directions |
|---|---|
| Two modern toilet blocks are in the centre of the camping area. Toilets for children. Baby room. Laundry facilities. Small shop (May-Aug). Bar/snack bar and restaurant (June-Aug). New outdoor pool and paddling pool. (May-Aug). Lakeside beach and water slide. Discos and entertainment in high season. TV and sports hall. Roller blade hire. Fitness. Walking. Fishing. Gas barbecues only. WiFi. Off site: Riding 500 m. Mountain bike hire 10 km. | From A43 take exit 7 on to D522 north. Turn left after 7 km. on to D65 then after 5 km. turn right on the D517. Site is 2 km. east of Trept with signs in village. GPS: 45.68699, 5.35191 |

**Open:** 1 May - 17 September.

**Charges guide**

| Per unit incl. 2 persons and electricity | € 19.00 - € 32.50 |
|---|---|
| extra person | € 3.50 - € 7.00 |

## Tulette
### Camping les Rives de l'Aygues

Route de Cairanne, F-26790 Tulette (Drôme) T: 04 75 98 37 50. E: camping.aygues@wanadoo.fr
**alanrogers.com/FR26240**

As the name implies, this spacious, family run site is situated by the bank of the river. Set in beautiful countryside and surrounded by vineyards for the famous Côtes du Rhône wines, this is a delightful site to unwind and explore this picturesque region. There are 100 very large, stony pitches with some grass laid out in the natural landscape and separated by attractive shrubs and trees giving good shade and privacy. There are 92 for touring units (electricity 6A, long leads advised). A number of pitches back onto the bank separating the site from the river, which is accessible for paddling.

| Facilities | Directions |
|---|---|
| A single, large building provides adequate facilities including some washbasins in cabins. It is quite a walk from some pitches. Bread to order. Bar, restaurant and takeaway (July/Aug). Games/TV room. Swimming and paddling pools (May-Sept). Play areas. Boules. Playing field. Only gas barbecues are permitted. WiFi (charged). Off site: Fishing 200 m. Bicycle hire 2 km. Riding 3 km. Shops and restaurants in Tulette 3 km. and Sainte Cecile-les-Vignes 3.5 km. Golf 15 km. Vaison la Romaine 16 km. | Leave A7 at exit 19 (Bollène) and take D94 towards Nyons. On entering Tulette (about 16 km) turn hard right onto D193 (site signed) and follow signs to site (2 km). GPS: 44.26518, 4.93149 |

**Open:** 1 May - 25 September.

**Charges guide**

| Per unit incl. 2 persons and electricity | € 20.20 - € 24.20 |
|---|---|
| extra person | € 5.10 |

No credit cards.

## Uzer
### Camping la Turelure

Quartier Fontane, F-07110 Uzer (Ardèche) T: 04 75 89 29 21. E: camping-la-turelure@orange.fr
**alanrogers.com/FR07920**

Set on the banks of the rivers La Lande and La Ligne, the site is in the heart of the Southern Ardèche with easy access to the many nearby tourist sights and activities. This friendly, family site has a secluded atmosphere being set in natural surroundings and away from the road. Of 65 pitches, 44 are for tourers and are large, grassy and well drained. Some are open, though many have shade, and all have 10A electricity. In high season you can swim in a private stretch of the river. Canoes and fishing are also allowed. The approach track is a little narrow, so care is needed. Good English is spoken.

**Facilities**

Two modern sanitary blocks (one very new, which is covered rather than inside) with nursery area and a family cabin, and facilities for disabled visitors. Washing machine (tokens). Fridge rental. Bar. Snack bar and takeaway (July/Aug). Swimming and paddling pools (15/5-30/9). Play area. Pétanque. River swimming (unsupervised; July-Aug). Fishing. WiFi (first 30 mins. free). Off site: Boat launching 10 km. Canoeing. Canyoning. Fishing. Marked hiking. Bike trails. Bicycle hire 3 km. Riding 8 km.

**Open:** 1 April - 31 October.

**Directions**

From north on A7, take J16 (D104 Privas and Aubenas). Continue through Aubenas on D104 (now signed Uzer and Ales). Shortly after Uzer, 3rd exit on roundabout, still on D104, and after 100 m. turn left onto track through farm and vineyards. Follow signs to site and river (500 m). GPS: 44.50833, 4.32045

**Charges guide**

| | |
|---|---|
| Per unit incl. 2 persons and electricity | € 17.00 - € 23.00 |
| extra person | € 4.00 - € 5.00 |

## Vallières
### Camping les Charmilles

D14, 625 route du val de fier, F-74150 Vallières (Haute-Savoie) T: 04 50 62 10 60.
E: les.charmilles.camping@wanadoo.fr **alanrogers.com/FR74290**

Les Charmilles is a friendly site in the village of Vallières, to the west of Annecy. There are 76 pitches, 18 with electricity (8A). A number of pitches are occupied by chalets and caravans (for rent). The site restaurant, Le Marilyn, is open to the general public and specialises in Savoyard cuisine. Takeaway meals are also possible. On-site leisure amenities include a new, large swimming pool, paddling pool and volleyball. During peak season, various activities are organised including theme evenings, as well as a children's club specialising in craft activities and games. The village centre is around 500 m. distant and has a number of shops including a post office and a specialist cheese shop. Rumilly is a larger village, around 5 km. to the south, and has two supermarkets and a wider selection of shops, cafés and restaurants. It also has a popular market every Thursday. Annecy is, of course, a delightful town and its old quarters and lakeside promenades are highly recommended.

**Facilities**

New sanitary blocks. Facilities for disabled visitors. Washing machine. Bar, restaurant, takeaway service and swimming pool (all 1/4-31/10). Paddling pool. Play area. Entertainment and activity programme. Chalets and caravans for rent. Washing machine and motorcaravan service point. Trampolines. WiFi (free). Off site: Village centre 500 m. Rumilly 5 km. Vineyards. Mountain biking. Fishing and riding 5 km. Bicycle hire 6 km. Golf 20 km.

**Open:** 1 April - 31 October.

**Directions**

Approaching from the north, leave A40 autoroute at exit 11 and head south on D1508 and D1504 to Frangy. Then continue south on D910 to Vallières and then follow signs to the site.
GPS: 45.90194, 5.92766

**Charges guide**

| | |
|---|---|
| Per unit incl. 2 persons and electricity | € 17.50 - € 20.00 |
| extra person | € 3.00 - € 4.00 |
| child (2-7 yrs) | € 1.50 - € 2.00 |

## Vallon-Pont-d'Arc
### Mondial Camping

Route des Gorges de l'Ardèche, F-07150 Vallon-Pont-d'Arc (Ardèche) T: 04 75 88 00 44.
E: reserv-info@mondial-camping.com **alanrogers.com/FR07370**

Located at the head of the spectacular Ardèche Gorge, Mondial Camping is one of many campsites along the banks of the river and offers the experience of canoe trips downstream with minibuses provided for the return. There are 211 pitches with 6/10A electricity and 33 of these also provide water and drainage. The grass pitches are an acceptable size, with good shade and separated by some topiary styled hedges. There are 24 mobile homes and five tents available for rent. The site has a good sports provision and a pool complex with one pool for swimming, one for children and another with water slides. Mondial is located at the head of the Gorge d'Ardèche close to Vallon-Pont-d'Arc. It is some nine hours by river down to the end of the canoe trip. A number of canoe hire agencies exist but Mondial has one on site. Shorter trips are available and the trip can be made with an overnight stop. The Gorges d'Ardèche has a route for those who prefer tarmac. A good wide road, the D290, takes you along the sides of the valley with numerous stunning viewpoints conveniently sited on your side of the road.

| Facilities | Directions |
|---|---|
| Three modern sanitary units are tiled, very clean and heated in low season. Good facilities for disabled visitors. A fourth smaller block services the multisport court and outdoor heated pools (open all season) and has facilities for babies. Full motorcaravan service point. Restaurant and takeaway, bar. good mini-supermarket (all open all season). Games room. Play area, organised entertainment for children and sports in high season. Archery. Canoe hire and launching. Fishing (licence required). WiFi (free). | From Vallon Pont d'Arc take the Route Gorges d'Ardèche.(D290). Site is 1 km. on the right and well signed. GPS: 44.397313, 4.40107 |

**Open:** 23 March - 29 September.

**Charges 2013**

| | |
|---|---|
| Per unit incl. 2 persons and electricity | € 21.00 - € 45.00 |
| extra person | € 5.50 - € 9.20 |
| child (under 13 yrs) | free - € 6.50 |
| dog | € 3.00 - € 5.00 |

**On the banks of the Ardèche**
**Heated swimming pool**

**In a beautiful green environment**
**Open 23.03 - 29.09.2013**

Off-season heated sanitation • Illuminated tennis courts • Comfortable sanitation Rental of canoes • Rental of mobil-homes • Camper service station • Bar with air conditioning • Ice cubes for sale • Accessible places for cars with water and drainage • Restaurant • Small supermarket • Activity program • Archery • Discounts outside the season • We speak english

Route des Gorges - 07150 Vallon-Pont-d'Arc
Tél. : 33 4 75 88 00 44 • Fax : 33 4 75 37 13 73
www.mondial-camping.com
reserv-info@mondial-camping.com

**Duo + 60 years**
**- 15%**
**off season on stay camping site**

---

## Vallon-Pont-d'Arc
### Camping la Roubine

Route de Ruoms, F-07150 Vallon-Pont-d'Arc (Ardèche) T: 04 75 88 04 56. E: roubine.ardeche@wanadoo.fr
**alanrogers.com/FR07310**

This site on the bank of the Ardèche has been in the same family ownership for some 30 years. During this time there has been constant upgrading. There are 114 touring pitches, all with electricity (10A) and quite spacious. Well tended grass, trimmed hedging and mature trees and smart tarmac roads create a calm and well kept atmosphere. The proprietors, M. Moulin and Mme. Van Eck, like to welcome their guests and are available to help during the day – they are rightly proud of their well run campsite.

| Facilities | Directions |
|---|---|
| Several small sanitary blocks include washbasins in cubicles. The main toilet block has showers, washbasins in vanity units, a baby bathroom and facilities for disabled visitors. Laundry. Swimming pools, paddling pool and separate children's pool. Tennis. Boules. Fishing. Barbecues only permitted on communal sites. River beach. Off site: Footpath to town 700 m. Supermarket in town. Bicycle hire and riding 1 km. | From Vallon take D579 (Ruoms). Site signed on left 400 m. from town. From west (Ruoms) signed on right. If missed proceed to roundabout at entrance to Vallon, go around and return some 400 m. (as above). GPS: 44.40547, 4.37916 |

**Open:** 26 April - 18 September.

**Charges guide**

| | |
|---|---|
| Per unit incl. 2 persons and electricity | € 22.50 - € 45.00 |
| extra person | € 3.40 - € 9.20 |

## Vallon-Pont-d'Arc

### Castel Camping Nature Parc l'Ardéchois

Route touristique des Gorges, F-07150 Vallon-Pont-d'Arc (Ardèche) T: 04 75 88 06 63.
E: ardecamp@bigfoot.com **alanrogers.com/FR07120**

This very high quality, family run site is within walking distance of Vallon-Pont-d'Arc. It borders the River Ardèche and canoe trips are run, professionally, direct from the site. This campsite is ideal for families with younger children seeking an active holiday. The facilities are comprehensive and the central toilet unit is of an extremely high standard. Of the 244 pitches, there are 225 for touring units, separated by trees and individual shrubs. All have electrical connections (6/10A) and 125 have full services. Forming a focal point are the bar and restaurant (good menus), with a terrace and stage overlooking the attractive heated pool. There is also a large paddling pool and sunbathing terrace. For children, there is a well thought out play area plus plenty of other space for youngsters to play, both on the site and along the river. Activities are organised throughout the season; these are family based – no discos. Patrols at night ensure a good night's sleep. Access to the site is easy and suitable for large outfits. The campsite is ideally situated near the Pont-d'Arc, a huge arch of limestone in the Ardèche Gorge. The local tourist centre of Vallon-Pont-d'Arc is within comfortable walking distance. A worthwhile trip down the gorge by car passes a number of spectacular viewpoints with good parking. Member of Leading Campings group.

**Facilities**

Two well equipped toilet blocks, one superb with everything working automatically. Facilities are of the highest standard, very clean and include good facilities for babies, those with disabilities, washing up and laundry. Four private bathrooms to hire. Washing machines. Well stocked shop. Swimming pool and paddling pool (no Bermuda shorts). Massage. Gym. Tennis. Very good play area. Internet access. Organised activities, canoe trips. Only gas barbecues are permitted. Communal barbecue area. WiFi (charged). Off site: Canoeing, rafting, walking, riding, mountain biking, golf, rock climbing, bowling, wine tasting and dining. Vallon-Pont-d'Arc 800 m. Explore the real Ardèche on the minor roads and visit Labaume, Balazuc and Largentière (market Tuesday).

**Open:** 1 April - 30 September.

**Directions**

From Vallon-Pont-d'Arc (western end of the Ardèche Gorge) at a roundabout go east on the D290. Site entrance is shortly on the right.
GPS: 44.39804, 4.39878

**Charges guide**

| Per unit incl. 2 persons and electricity | € 26.00 - € 58.00 |
|---|---|
| extra person | € 6.00 - € 10.00 |
| child (0-13 yrs) | € 4.30 - € 7.90 |
| dog | € 3.60 - € 7.70 |

## Vernioz

### Camping le Bontemps

5 impasse du Bontemps, F-38150 Vernioz (Isère) T: 04 74 57 83 52. E: info@campinglebontemps.com
**alanrogers.com/FR38120**

This spacious, attractive and extremely well cared for site between Lyon and Valence in the Rhone Alpes is enhanced by a variety of trees planted by the original owner nearly 30 years ago. The 192 large, level and grassy pitches are arranged in groups, partly separated by neat hedges, all with water and 10A electricity. Fifteen pitches are used for mobile homes and chalets and a group at the back is used by weekenders. The shop, bar/restaurant and leisure facilities are conveniently positioned near the entrance. This is an excellent site for both short and long stays and the Dutch director and his wife, who speak excellent English, have spared no efforts in making this a most attractive and comfortable site.

**Facilities**

Two toilet blocks, one recently refurbished to a high standard. Motorcaravan service points. Shop (4/5-15/9). Bar, restaurant and takeaway (all 6/4-15/9). Heated swimming pool, children's fun pool and slide pool (all season). Several play areas. Minigolf. Tennis. Badminton. Electronic games. Fitness equipment. Bicycle hire. Extensive list of activities for all the family (high season). Small fishing lake. WiFi (charged). Off site: Small river for fishing. Vernioz 2 km. Pilat Regional Park 15 km. Golf 20 km. Vienne 20 km.

**Open:** 6 April - 29 September.

**Directions**

Exit A7 south of Lyons at exit 9. Continue south for 7 km. on N7. Just north of Auberives turn left on D37. Follow campsite signs for 7 km. Entrance is on right 4 km. beyond Vernioz. GPS: 45.2531, 4.5542

**Charges 2013**

| Per unit incl. 2 persons and electricity | € 23.00 - € 31.00 |
|---|---|
| extra person | € 6.00 - € 7.00 |
| child (under 7 yrs) | € 3.00 - € 4.00 |
| dog (max. 1) | € 3.00 |

Camping Cheques accepted.

For latest campsite news, availability and prices visit
# alanrogers.com

# IN SOUTH ARDECHE, 1 FAMILY, 2 CASTELS, 10 STARS!

## Villard-de-Lans

### Camping Caravaneige l'Oursière

F-38250 Villard-de-Lans (Isère) T: 04 76 95 14 77. E: oursiere@franceloc.fr

**alanrogers.com/FR38070**

This friendly, family run site is within easy walking distance of the attractive resort of Villard-de-Lans. The town provides a wide range of summer and winter activities and therefore little is organised on site. It is ideal for those who prefer a peaceful site in a more natural setting. The 189 good sized grass and stone pitches are slightly uneven but with magnificent views over the surrounding mountains. There are 146 for touring, most have electricity (10A). A variety of trees offer some shade. Rock pegs are essential. A fast flowing, unfenced stream runs through the site, so children should be supervised.

**Facilities**

Clean, heated toilet blocks with all necessary facilities including those for disabled visitors. Ski store and drying room. Motorcaravan services. Single building houses reception, bar and snack bar (both July/Aug), cosy lounge with open fireplace, TV room, games rooms. New outdoor swimming pool. Play area. Boules. Trout fishing. Internet access and WiFi. Off site: Bus to Autrans and Grenoble. Free bus to ski resorts (winter). Supermarket and bicycle hire 1 km. Skiing 2 km. Riding 4 km. Golf 8 km.

**Open:** All year excl. 23 September - 10 December.

**Directions**

Northwest of Grenoble, leave autoroute A48 exit 13 or 3A. Follow N532 to Sassenage, at roundabout take D531. In 25 km. on entering Villard-de-Lans, fork left signed Villard Centre, site is shortly on left. Only route for caravans and motorcaravans. GPS: 45.077583, 5.55616

**Charges guide**

| | |
|---|---|
| Per unit incl. 2 persons and electricity | € 22.00 - € 27.00 |
| extra person | € 4.70 - € 7.00 |

## Villars-les-Dombes

### Camping Indigo Parc des Oiseaux

Avenue des Nations, F-01330 Villars-les-Dombes (Ain) T: 04 74 98 00 21.

E: camping@parcdesoiseaux.com **alanrogers.com/FR01110**

The Parc des Oiseaux is one of Europe's largest and most popular ornithological parks and can be found at Villars-les-Dombes, northeast of Lyon. This campsite is a new member of the Indigo group and reopened in 2011 (it was formerly a municipal site). The 190 pitches here are large and grassy, and are mostly supplied with electricity (6A). A range of wooden chalets and specially made tents are available for rent. On-site amenities include a swimming pool and a small bar/restaurant. The River Chalaronne runs alongside the site and fishing is popular. A children's activity programme is run in high season, focusing on nature and the countryside. A great diversity of birds from around the world is on display at the nearby parc, and the emphasis is firmly on replicating the birds' natural habitat and conservation. The park has won several major awards for this reason. Villars-les-Dombes lies at the heart of the Dombes, a region notable for its hundreds of lakes which are ideal for fish rearing and water fowl.

**Facilities**

Hot showers, private cabins and family shower room. Facilities for children and disabled visitors. Washing machine. Motorcaravan services. Fridge hire. Shop. Bar/restaurant (June-Aug). Takeaway (July/Aug). Swimming pool. Fishing. Play area. Activities for children. Bicycle hire. Tourist information. Free WiFi over part of site. Max. 1 dog per pitch. Chalets and tents for rent. Off site: Parc des Oiseaux. Golf 1 km. Riding 10 km.

**Open:** 29 March - 3 November.

**Directions**

From A46, northeast of Lyons take exit 3 signed Bourg-en-Bresse. Take N83 northeast to Villars-les-Dombes, 20 km. On entering town turn right to site (D904) which is well signed. GPS: 45.99723, 5.03047

**Charges guide**

Contact site.
Camping Cheques accepted.

For latest campsite news, availability and prices visit

**alanrogers.com**

## Villeneuve-de-Berg
### Domaine le Pommier

RN 102, F-07170 Villeneuve-de-Berg (Ardèche) T: 04 75 94 82 81. E: info@campinglepommier.com
**alanrogers.com/FR07110**

Domaine le Pommier is an extremely spacious, Dutch owned site of 10 hectares in 32 hectares of wooded grounds centred around a spectacular pirate themed water park. The site is steeply terraced and has wonderful views over the Ardèche mountains and beyond. There are 611 pitches, with 275 for touring units, the rest used for mobile homes and chalets for rent. They are on sandy grass, of a good size and well spaced. Separated by trees and hedges, some have less shade. All have access to electricity and water is close by. The site is not recommended for very large units. The site has first class facilities, including the most up-to-date toilet blocks, a very good bar/restaurant and a pirate themed swimming and paddling pool complex with amazing water slides.

**Facilities**

Four excellent toilet blocks, one with underfloor heating, provide all the necessary facilities. Comprehensive shop. Bar/restaurant. Swimming pool complex with exciting slides, paddling pools, etc. Everything opens all season. Boules. Minigolf. Large multisports area. Activities including games in the woods, archery, water polo and tug-of-war. Watercolour classes. Tennis. Soundproofed disco. Very extensive programme of events on and off site. Low season excursions. Entertainment programme exclusively in Dutch. WiFi (charged). Off site: Town 1.5 km. River Ardèche 12 km. Potholing, rock climbing, canoeing, canyoning, mountain biking, walking and riding.

**Open:** 21 April - 15 September.

**Directions**

Site is west of Montélimar on the N102. The entrance is adjacent to the roundabout at the eastern end of the Villeneuve-de-Berg bypass. GPS: 44.57250, 4.51115

**Charges guide**

| | |
|---|---|
| Per unit incl. 2 persons and electricity | € 23.50 - € 43.50 |
| extra person | € 5.50 - € 9.50 |
| child (4-12 yrs) | € 3.50 - € 6.50 |
| dog | free - € 4.50 |

Max. 6 persons (one family) per pitch.
Special offers for longer stays in low season.

**FREE** Alan Rogers Travel Card
Extra benefits and savings - see page 10

From the endless shimmering beaches and dunes, and the fragrant pine forests of the Atlantic coast to the historical and beautiful Dordogne with its gastronomic delights, it's easy to see the attraction of this popular holiday region.

**DÉPARTEMENTS: 24 DORDOGNE, 33 GIRONDE, 40 LANDES, 47 LOT-ET-GARONNE, 64 PYRÉNÉES-ATLANTIQUES**

**MAJOR CITY: BORDEAUX**

The history of Aquitaine goes back many thousands of years to when man lived in the caves of the Périgord and left cave paintings at sites such as Les Eyzies and Lascaux. The ancient dukedom of Aquitaine was ruled by the English for 300 years following the marriage of Eleanor of Aquitaine to Henry Plantagenet, the future king, in 1154. The fortified villages and castles of the area bear evidence of the resulting conflict between the French and the English for control of Aquitaine, and today add character to the countryside.

This is a diverse region of mountains and vineyards, vast beaches, fertile river valleys, rolling grasslands and dense forests. The beaches of the Atlantic are renowned for their surfing, which was first introduced to Biarritz during the 1950s, and France's most complete long distance cycle route runs from La Baule to Biarritz.

Some of the world's most famous vineyards are around Bordeaux, the capital of the region. These are especially famous for their Médoc, Sauternes and St Emilion wines and most châteaux allow visits to their cellars and wine tastings.

### Places of interest

*Biarritz:* a cosmopolitan seaside resort with surfing beaches and sea museum.

*Bordeaux:* riverside, streets and markets; art gallery; Grand Theatre.

*Les Eyzies:* pre-history museum and troglodyte houses.

*Sarlat:* attractive small town with preserved historic centre and medieval houses.

*St Emilion:* visit the castle ramparts or drink 'premier cru' St Emilion at pavement cafés.

*St Jean-de-Luz:* seaside resort and fishing village.

*St Jean-Pied-de-Port:* ancient city with citadel, bright Basque houses in steep streets.

### Cuisine of the region

*Local specialities include fish dishes:* carp stuffed with foie gras, mullet in red wine and besugo (sea bream), plus cagouilles (snails from Charentes).

*Canelé:* a small fluted cake flavoured with rum and vanilla.

*Cassoulet:* a hearty stew of duck, sausages and beans.

*Cèpes:* fine, delicate mushrooms; sometimes dried.

*Chou farci:* stuffed cabbage, sometimes aux marrons (with chestnuts).

*Confit of duck:* duck legs preserved with spices and herbs.

*Magret de canard:* duck breast fillets.

*Lamproie:* eel-like fish with leeks, onions and red Bordeaux wine.

**www.tourisme-aquitaine.fr/en
tourisme@tourisme-aquitaine.fr
(0)5 56 01 70 00**

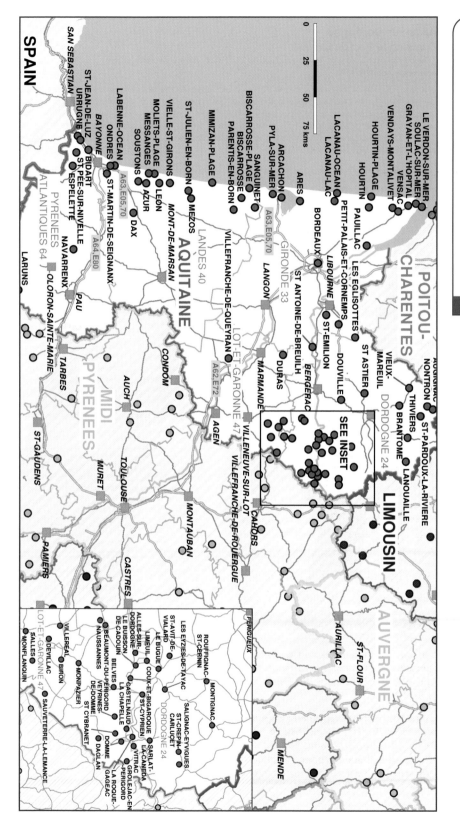

SPAIN

SAN SEBASTIAN

POITOU-
CHARENTES

LIMOUSIN

AUVERGNE

MIDI
PYRENEES

AQUITAINE

PYRENEES
ATLANTIQUES 64

LANDES 40

GIRONDE 33

LOT-ET-GARONNE 47

DORDOGNE 24

SEE INSET

**FREE** Alan Rogers Travel Card
Extra benefits and savings - see page 10

## Allés-sur-Dordogne

### Camping le Port de Limeuil

F-24480 Allés-sur-Dordogne (Dordogne) T: 05 53 63 29 76. E: didierbonvallet@aol.com

**alanrogers.com/FR24170**

At the confluence of the Dordogne and Vézère rivers, opposite the picturesque village of Limeuil, this delightful family site exudes a peaceful and relaxed ambience. There are 75 marked touring pitches on grass, some spacious and all with electricity (6/10A). The buildings are in traditional Périgourdine style and surrounded by flowers and shrubs. A sports area on a large, open, grassy space between the river bank and the main camping area adds to the feeling of space and provides an additional recreation and picnic area (there are additional unmarked pitches for tents and camper vans along the bank here).

**Facilities**

Two clean, modern toilet blocks provide excellent facilities. Bar. Restaurant with snacks and takeaway (20/5-5/9). Small shop. Swimming pool with jacuzzi, paddling pool and children's slide (1/5-30/9). Badminton. Tennis. Volleyball. Football. Boules. Trampoline. Mountain bike hire. Canoe hire, launched from the site's own pebble beach. Free WiFi in bar area. Off site: The pretty medieval village of Limeuil 200 m. Riding 1 km. Golf 10 km.

**Open:** 1 May - 30 September.

**Directions**

Site is 7 km. south of Le Bugue. From D51/D31E Le Buisson to Le Bugue road turn west towards Limeuil. Just before bridge into Limeuil, turn left (site signed), across another bridge. Site shortly on the right. GPS: 44.87977, 0.88587

**Charges guide**

| | |
|---|---|
| Per unit incl. 2 persons and electricity | € 17.00 - € 31.80 |
| extra person | € 4.50 - € 6.50 |

## Arcachon

### Camping Club Arcachon

5 allée Galaxie, B.P. 46, F-33312 Arcachon Cedex (Gironde) T: 05 56 83 24 15. E: info@camping-arcachon.com **alanrogers.com/FR33030**

This campsite enjoys a position well back from the hustle and bustle, where nights are quiet and facilities are of a high standard. The 176 touring pitches are divided into areas for caravans, motorcaravans and tents and are on neatly formed terraces beneath tall pine trees. Most have electricity (6/10A). The site is quite hilly and the narrow roads that wind around it could possibly make it difficult for larger motorcaravans to manoeuvre and find suitable pitches. At night, wardens ensure that security and noise levels are controlled. A 1 km. walk takes you to the town of Arcachon where there are plenty of shops, bars and restaurants.

**Facilities**

Three sanitary blocks with the usual facilities. Motorcaravan services. Washing machine, dryers. Fridge hire. Shop (15/6-15/9). Bar, restaurant, snack bar, takeaway (April-Sept). Swimming pool (1/5-30/9). Bicycle hire. Play area. Games room. Children's club and entertainment for all age groups (1/7-31/8). Barbecues are only permitted in communal areas. Internet access and WiFi. Off site: Beach 1 km. on foot. Riding 1 km. Golf 2 km. Arcachon 2-3 km.

**Open:** All year (excl. 12 November - 12 December).

**Directions**

Approaching Arcachon from Bordeaux on N250 take exit for Hôpital Jean Hameau (D217). Cross over bypass following signs for hospital, then for Abatilles. At next roundabout follow signs for Camping. Follow site signs, not sat nav. GPS: 44.6513, -1.174083

**Charges guide**

| | |
|---|---|
| Per unit incl. 2 persons and electricity | € 17.00 - € 36.00 |

Camping Cheques accepted.

## Arès

### Camping la Cigale

53 rue du Général de Gaulle, F-33740 Arès (Gironde) T: 05 56 60 22 59. E: contact.lacigale@gmail.com

**alanrogers.com/FR33120**

La Cigale is an attractive little site with charm and ambience where the owners extend a very warm welcome. Small and beautifully maintained, it is set amid a variety of trees that give some dappled shade. M. Pallet's floral displays add colour to the 44 neatly hedged, grassy touring pitches (100 sq.m. all with 6A electricity, 26 also with water and a drain). There is a small unheated swimming pool and a paddling pool. The bar has a shady terrace where drinks, meals and snacks are served.

**Facilities**

Well equipped toilet block includes a family room with two showers and facilities for disabled visitors. Washing machine and dryer. Motorcaravan services. Simple shop, bar, terrace, meals, snacks, pizza takeaway (24/6-10/9). Swimming and paddling pools (25/5-12/9). Small play area. Entertainers for children and adults in July/Aug. Free donkey cart rides every Sunday in season. Charcoal barbecues are not permitted. WiFi (free).

**Open:** 27 April - 26 September.

**Directions**

Leave Bordeaux ring road at exit 10 (D213) or exit 11 (D106) and continue direct to Arès. Turn into Arès following road to church square. Turn right following signs for Lège-Cap Ferret. Site is 800 m. on left. GPS: 44.77287, -1.14147

**Charges guide**

| | |
|---|---|
| Per unit incl. 2 persons and electricity | € 25.50 - € 35.50 |
| extra person | € 6.00 |

For latest campsite news, availability and prices visit

# alanrogers.com

## Augignac

### Manzac Ferme

Manzac, F-24300 Augignac (Dordogne) T: 05 53 56 31 34. E: info@manzac-ferme.com

**alanrogers.com/FR24645**

A gem of a small but spacious, family run, adults only campsite nestling in the beautiful Périgord Regional Park; you are sure of a very warm welcome here. At the entrance to the site is the old farmhouse, which houses the reception and the toilet facilities. There are only ten pitches, all for touring and all with electricity (6A). There are six large hardstanding pitches close to the farmhouse, with varying amounts of shade. Lower down, close to a small fishing river, are four very spacious, grassy tent pitches of irregular shape, laid out in a woodland glade.

**Facilities**

One excellent, small toilet block with modern facilities is kept spotlessly clean. Washing machine. Emergency supplies only. Off site: Restaurant, bar and boulangerie in Abjat-sur-Bandiat 5 km. Lake swimming, canoeing, restaurant at St Estephe 5 km. Wider range of shops and bars in Nontron 7 km. St Jean de Cole, the village reputed to have the best rooftops in France 18 km. Many walking and cycling routes.

**Open:** 1 March - 31 October.

**Directions**

Leave A20 autoroute north of Limoges, exit 28. Take N520 west then D2000 bypassing Limoges. Take N21 southwest for 11 km. Turn west, D699, to St Mathieu (27 km). Turn south, D675 to Augignac (16 km). At crossroads turn left (Abjat) then right to Manzac, follow signs to site, 4 km. GPS: 45.562088, 0.71956

**Charges guide**

| | |
|---|---|
| Per unit incl. 2 persons and electricity | € 22.00 |
| extra person | € 4.00 |

## Beaumont-du-Périgord

### Le Moulin de Surier

Le Surier, F-24440 Beaumont-du-Périgord (Dordogne) T: 05 53 24 91 98. E: contact@lemoulindesurier.com

**alanrogers.com/FR24950**

Le Moulin de Surier is a very spacious site midway between Bergerac and Sarlat, and is close to Beaumont-du-Périgord and Cadouin. Please note that this is a Parc Résidentiel de Loisirs and accommodation is in attractive wooden chalets and mobile homes. There are no touring pitches here. The chalets and mobile homes are all fully equipped and occupy large shady pitches. Some are on high terraces and others are on a level area adjacent to the two lakes. One lake is used for swimming, the other is well stocked for fishing. Leisure amenities include a swimming pool, a children's play area and a small animal park. The bar, takeaway and shop all function throughout the high season. The attractive village of Beaumont-du-Périgord has a small selection of shops. To the west, Monbazillac has a fine château and is renowned for its sweet white wines.

**Facilities**

Shop, snack bar and takeaway (July/Aug), bar (15/6-15/9). Heated swimming pool (1/5-2/11). Swimming lake. Fishing lake. Play area. Bicycle hire. Activity and entertainment programme. Tourist information. WiFi. Off site: Walking and cycle trails. Canoeing. Riding 10 km. Golf 15 km.

**Open:** 30 March - 2 November.

**Directions**

From Bergerac head east, D660 to Couze, then head south (still on D660) towards Beaumont-du-Périgord for 6 km. Turn right, C3 and follow signs to the site. GPS: 44.78596, 0.7554

**Charges guide**

Contact the site for details.

**FREE** Alan Rogers Travel Card
Extra benefits and savings - see page 10

## Azur

### Camping Village la Paillotte

66 route des Campings, F-40140 Azur (Landes) T: 05 58 48 12 12. E: info@paillotte.com

**alanrogers.com/FR40040**

La Paillotte, in the Landes area of southwest France, is a site with a character of its own. It lies beside the Soustons Lake only 1.5 km. from Azur village, with its own sandy beach. This is suitable for young children because the lake is shallow and slopes gradually. All 310 pitches at la Paillotte are mostly shady with shrubs and trees. The 75 pitches for touring vary in price according to size, position and whether they are serviced. La Paillotte is an unusual site with its own atmosphere which appeals to many regular clients. The buildings (reception, shop, restaurant, even sanitary blocks) are all Tahitian in style.

**Facilities**

Well equipped toilet blocks. Washing machines, dryers. Shop (1/6-1/9). Good restaurant with terrace overlooking lake, bar, takeaway (all 22/4-24/9). Swimming pool complex (22/4-24/9). Sports, games and organised activities. Miniclub. TV room, library. Fishing. Bicycle hire. Sailing, rowing boats and pedaloes for hire. Torches useful. Free WiFi. Dogs are not accepted. Off site: Riding 5 km. Golf and Atlantic beaches 10 km.

**Open:** 27 April - 22 September.

**Directions**

Coming from the north along N10, turn west on D150 at Magescq. From south go via Soustons. In Azur turn left before church (site signed). GPS: 43.78696, -1.3093

**Charges guide**

| | |
|---|---|
| Per unit incl. 2 persons and electricity | € 16.00 - € 43.00 |
| extra person (over 4 yrs) | € 3.00 - € 7.50 |

## Belvès

### RCN le Moulin de la Pique

Le Moulin de la Pique, F-24170 Belvès (Dordogne) T: 05 53 29 01 15. E: moulin@rcn.fr

**alanrogers.com/FR24350**

This high quality campsite set in the heart of the Dordogne has fine views looking up to the fortified town of Belvès. It is a splendid rural estate where there is plenty of space and a good mixture of trees and shrubs. Set in the grounds of a former mill, the superb traditional buildings date back to the 18th century. There are 200 level pitches with 154 for touring units, all with 6A electricity, a water point and drainage. The remainder are used for mobile homes to rent. The site is ideally suited for families with young and teenage children as there is so much to do, both on site and in the surrounding area. Moulin de Pique boasts four swimming pools (all season), two heated, and with three water slides – a water paradise. There is also a lake which can be used for boating and fishing. Large motorcaravans are catered for and access is good. Activities are organised daily and are a feature of this campsite. A recreation team is on hand from May to September. There is something for nearly everybody. You can have fun and pleasure in relaxing surroundings. Off site there are many fine châteaux to visit together with prehistoric caves and, of course, all the vineyards that produce such a superb array of regional wines.

**Facilities**

Three modern sanitary blocks include facilities for disabled visitors. Launderette. Shop, bar, restaurant, snack bar and takeaway (all open all season). Swimming pools (two heated). Recreational lake. Playgrounds. Library. Fossil field. Sports field. Tennis. Minigolf. Boules. Satellite TV. Games room. Bicycle hire. Internet. WiFi (charged). Off site: Bars, restaurants and shops in the village of Belvès 2 km. Canoeing 2 km. Riding 5 km. Golf 7 km.

**Open:** 9 April - 1 October.

**Directions**

Site is 35 km. southwest of Sarlat on D710, 7 km. south of Siorac-en-Périgord. GPS: 44.76228, 1.01412

**Charges guide**

| | |
|---|---|
| Per unit incl. 2 persons, electricity and water | € 19.90 - € 43.90 |
| extra person (over 3 yrs) | € 2.50 - € 4.90 |
| dog (max. 1) | € 6.00 |
| Camping Cheques accepted. | |

## Belvès
### Flower Camping les Nauves

Le Bos Rouge, F-24170 Belvès (Dordogne) T: 05 53 29 12 64. E: campinglesnauves@hotmail.com

**alanrogers.com/FR24470**

Les Nauves is a pretty and well maintained site, 4 km. from the beautiful medieval village of Belvès in the Périgord Noir region of the Dordogne. The site consists of 100 pitches, 60 for touring (on a slight slope, long leads necessary) and 40 dedicated to mobile homes, chalets and bungalow tents. There are some pitches that are separated and shaded by mature trees, while others are open with good views of the surrounding countryside. The ground on most of the pitches is soft, sandy soil and may cause some difficulty for large vehicles in wet weather. The owners are very dedicated to providing a quality site.

**Facilities**

The single sanitary block is clean and well maintained. Facilities for disabled visitors. Baby room (with adult shower). Laundry area with one washing machine. Good shop. Bar/restaurant with patio, and takeaway on request. Swimming pool and paddling pool. Good play area. Boules. Library (FR, NL). Games room. Riding. WiFi and Internet access. Off site: Fishing 2 km. Small supermarket in Belvès 4 km. Bicycle and mountain bike hire 4 km. Golf 10 km.

**Open:** 23 April - 24 September.

**Directions**

From Belvès take D53 southwest towards Monpazier. Site is 4 km. from Belvès on the left hand side. Follow signs and site is 800 m. off the main road. GPS: 44.75275, 0.98445

**Charges guide**

| | |
|---|---|
| Per unit incl. 2 persons and electricity | € 13.95 - € 24.50 |
| extra person | € 2.50 - € 4.90 |
| child (2-7 yrs) | € 2.00 - € 3.20 |
| dog | free - € 3.00 |

## Bidart
### Camping le Pavillon Royal

Avenue du Prince de Galles, F-64210 Bidart (Pyrénées-Atlantiques) T: 05 59 23 00 54. E: info@pavillon-royal.com **alanrogers.com/FR64060**

*alan rogers* Runner up 2012 Awards

Le Pavillon Royal has an excellent situation on raised ground overlooking the sea, with good views along the coast to the south and to the north coast of Spain beyond. There is a large heated swimming pool and sunbathing area in the centre of the site. The camping area is divided up into 303 marked, level pitches, many of a good size. About 50 are reserved for tents and are only accessible on foot. The remainder are connected by asphalt roads. All have electricity and most are fully serviced. Much of the campsite is in full sun, although the area for tents is shaded. Beneath the site – and only a very short walk down – stretches a wide sandy beach where the Atlantic rollers provide ideal conditions for surfing. A central, marked-out section of the beach is supervised by lifeguards (from mid June). There is also a section with rocks and pools. Reservation in high season is advisable.

**Facilities**

Good quality toilet blocks with baby baths and two units for disabled visitors. Washing facilities (only two open at night). Washing machines, dryers. Motorcaravan services. Shop (including gas). Restaurant and takeaway (from 1/6). Bar (all season). Heated swimming and paddling pools. Playground. General room, TV room, games room, films. Fishing. Surf school. Fitness room. Wellness (1/6-25/9). Dogs are not accepted. WiFi (charged). Off site: Golf 500 m. Bicycle hire 2 km. Riding 3 km. Sailing 5 km. New oceanographic centre at Biarritz.

**Open:** 14 May - 30 September.

**Directions**

From A63 exit 4, take the N10 south towards Bidart. At roundabout after the Intermarché supermarket turn right (signed for Biarritz). After 600 m. turn left at site sign. GPS: 43.45458, -1.57649

**Charges guide**

| | |
|---|---|
| Per unit incl. 2 persons, electricity and water | € 32.00 - € 55.00 |
| tent pitch | € 26.00 - € 45.00 |
| extra person (over 4 yrs) | € 8.00 - € 12.00 |

### Le Pavillon Royal
camping caravaning *****NN

64210 BIDART
Tél: 05.59.23.00.54
Website: www.pavillon-royal.com
E-mail: info@pavillon-royal.com

❚ Right by a sandy beach with direct access

❚ On the outskirts of Biarritz

❚ Very peaceful situation

❚ Sanitary installations of really exceptional quality

❚ Heated swimming pool

❚ New fitness room

**FREE** Alan Rogers Travel Card
Extra benefits and savings - see page 10

## Bidart

### Castel Camping le Ruisseau des Pyrénées

Route d'Arbonne, F-64210 Bidart (Pyrénées-Atlantiques) T: 05 59 41 94 50.
E: francoise.dumont3@wanadoo.fr **alanrogers.com/FR64070**

This busy site, with a large play area filled with equipment, is ideal for young families. It is about 2 km. from Bidart and 2.5 km. from a sandy beach. There are two swimming pools with slides on the main site and, across the road, there is an indoor heated pool and new spa complex (charged in July/August) with outdoor fitness equipment. Pitches on the main campsite are individual, marked and of a good size, either on flat terraces or around the lake. The terrain is wooded so the great majority of them have some shade. Electrical connections are available throughout. There are a number of steep slopes to negotiate.

**Facilities**

Two main blocks and some extra smaller units. Washing machines. Motorcaravan service point. Shop, self-service restaurant with takeaway and bar with terraces, and TV (all 22/5-4/9). Outdoor swimming pools, indoor heated pool and spa complex (all season). Sauna. Large play area. Two tennis courts (free outside July/Aug). Fitness track. TV and games rooms. Minigolf. Bicycle hire. Fishing. Small animal sanctuary. WiFi over site (charged).

**Open:** 7 April - 18 September.

**Directions**

Site is east of Bidart on a minor road towards Arbonne. From A63 autoroute take Biarritz exit (4), turn towards St Jean-de-Luz and Bidart on N10. After Intermarché turn left at roundabout and follow signs to site. GPS: 43.4367, -1.5677

**Charges guide**

| | |
|---|---|
| Per unit incl. 2 persons and electricity | € 19.00 - € 44.00 |

## Bidart

### Sunêlia Berrua

Rue Berrua, F-64210 Bidart (Pyrénées-Atlantiques) T: 05 59 54 96 66. E: contact@berrua.com
**alanrogers.com/FR64140**

Berrua is in a useful situation on the Basque coast, 10 km. from the Pyrenees, 20 km. from Spain and a five minute drive from Biarritz. Just 1 km. from the sea, it is an ideal location for visiting the beaches in southwest France. A neat and tidy site, it has 270 level pitches (140 for touring units) set amongst trees. Most have electricity (6A) and some are fully serviced. The focal point of the site is an excellent swimming pool complex with several pools, slides and paddling pools which is surrounded by sunbeds for sunbathing. Organised activities and entertainment for both adults and children in high season, guided walks, dances, sporting competitions, bingo and karaoke. A member of the Sunêlia group.

**Facilities**

Toilet facilities are good (unisex) consisting of two blocks with washbasins in cabins. Baby rooms. Facilities for disabled visitors. Washing machines. Motorcaravan services. Shop, bar/restaurant and takeaway. New pool complex. Games room. Play area (3-10 yrs only). Archery. Boules. WiFi throughout (charged). Off site: Fishing and beach 1 km. Golf and riding 3 km.

**Open:** 1 April - 30 September.

**Directions**

From A63 exit 4, take N10 south towards Bidart. At roundabout after the Intermarché supermarket, turn left. Bear right then take next right (site signed). GPS: 43.43822, -1.58237

**Charges guide**

| | |
|---|---|
| Per unit incl. 2 persons and electricity | € 19.00 - € 41.00 |

Camping Cheques accepted.

## Bidart

### Yelloh! Village Ilbarritz

Avenue de Biarritz, F-64210 Bidart (Pyrénées-Atlantiques) T: 04 66 73 97 39.
E: info@yellohvillage-ilbarritz.com **alanrogers.com/FR64150**

This is a very pleasant Yelloh! Village group site (formerly Résidence des Pins), which will appeal greatly to couples, young families and surfers. Set on a slightly gentle hillside, the top level has reception, shops and a bar. Slightly lower are the impressive paddling and swimming pools in a sunny location with sunbeds. Next comes the tennis courts and camping pitches. Some slightly sloping pitches, are under trees and separated by hydrangea hedges, others are more open and level. Some have electricity (10A, long leads required) and water. Large outfits should telephone to check availability.

**Facilities**

The single toilet block has some washbasins and showers together. Washing machines, dryers, ironing boards and facilities for disabled campers. Shop and bar open all season, restaurant (1/6-10/9) and takeaway (1/7-31/8). Two swimming pools (one open all season). Games room. Tennis (charged in July/Aug). Play area (3-8 yrs). Bicycle hire. WiFi (30 hours free). Off site: Beach with lifeguard, fishing (no licence required) and surfing 800 m. Golf 1 km.

**Open:** 31 March - 10 November.

**Directions**

Heading south on the A63 towards Spain, take exit J4 onto the N10 towards Bidart. At the roundabout straight after Intermarché turn right towards Biarritz. The site is on the right after 1 km. GPS: 43.4531, -1.5737

**Charges guide**

| | |
|---|---|
| Per unit incl. 2 persons and electricity | € 20.00 - € 46.00 |
| extra person | € 6.00 - € 9.00 |

For latest campsite news, availability and prices visit
# alanrogers.com

## Bidart

### Camping Ur-Onea

Rue de la Chapelle, F-64210 Bidart (Pyrénées-Atlantiques) T: 05 59 26 53 61. E: contact@uronea.com

**alanrogers.com/FR64280**

Situated on the outskirts of Bidart and 600 m. away from a fine sandy beach, this large, attractively terraced site has 280 grass pitches with little shade, 169 are for touring, 124 have electricity (10A) and ten have water and drainage also. There are some hardstandings for motorcaravans. A separate area is reserved for washing surf boards and barbecues, and there is even a shower for washing dogs. With local transport available all year (600 m) this campsite is ideal for exploring the surrounding areas. During the summer months, aquarobics, dancing and discos are arranged together with organised sports events and children's clubs.

#### Facilities

Three well maintained and clean sanitary blocks are of good size with large showers (all also have washbasins) and wall mounted hairdryers. Facilities for babies and disabled visitors. Laundry. Shop (all season). Bar, restaurant and takeaway (12/5-18/9). Heated swimming pool (3/4-18/9). Two excellent play areas for younger children. Organised activities in high season. WiFi. Off site: Beach, bars, restaurants and shops 600 m. Golf 1.5 km. Riding 2 km. Bicycle hire 3 km.

**Open:** 3 April - 19 September.

#### Directions

Take N10 north from St Jean-de-Luz. Continue through Guethary and site sign is on the right. Turn right and site is on the left in 800 m. GPS: 43.43397, -1.59074

#### Charges guide

| Per unit incl. 2 persons | |
|---|---|
| and electricity | € 19.00 - € 33.50 |
| extra person | € 3.80 - € 7.00 |
| child (under 10 yrs) | € 2.50 - € 5.00 |
| dog | € 2.60 |

## Biron

### Camping le Moulinal

F-24540 Biron (Dordogne) T: 05 53 40 84 60. E: lemoulinal@franceloc.fr

**alanrogers.com/FR24100**

A rural, lakeside site in woodland, now owned and run by the FranceLoc company, le Moulinal offers activities for campers of all ages. Of the 300 grassy pitches, only around 72 are available for touring units and these are spread amongst the site's own mobile homes, chalets and a small number of Dutch tour operator tents. All pitches are flat, grassy and have 6A electricity, but vary considerably in size (75-100 sq.m). The five acre lake has a sandy beach and is suitable for boating (canoe hire available), swimming and fishing. Ambitious, well organised animation is run throughout the season including craft activities and a children's club. A well stocked shop sells English newspapers.

#### Facilities

Toilet facilities include facilities for disabled campers and babies. Washing machines, dryers. Motorcaravan services. Excellent restaurant. Bar. Snack bar/takeaway. Large, heated swimming pool with jacuzzi and paddling pool. Rustic play area. Children's club. Multisport court. Boules. Tennis. Archery. Roller skating. Mountain bike hire. Canoeing. Fishing and swimming in lake. WiFi. Evening entertainment (July/Aug). All facilities are open all season. Max. 1 dog. Off site: Riding and climbing 5 km. Potholing 10 km. Shops and supermarket in Villeréal 12 km. Bastide towns of Monpazier and Monflanquin 15 km.

**Open:** 1 April - 16 September.

#### Directions

Site is 53 km. southeast of Bergerac. From D104 Villeréal-Monpazier road take the D53/D150 south. Just before Lacapelle Biron turn right onto D255 towards Dévillac, (site signed). Site is 1.5 km. on the left. GPS: 44.5998, 0.8708

#### Charges guide

| Per unit incl. 2 persons | |
|---|---|
| and electricity | € 19.00 - € 37.00 |
| extra person | € 5.00 - € 7.00 |

**FREE** Alan Rogers Travel Card
Extra benefits and savings - see page 10

## Biscarrosse

### Camping Resort la Rive

**509**

Route de Bordeaux, F-40600 Biscarrosse (Landes) T: 05 58 78 12 33. E: info@larive.fr
**alanrogers.com/FR40100**

Surrounded by pine woods, la Rive has a superb beach-side location on Lac de Sanguinet. With a total of 800 pitches, it provides 250 mostly level, numbered and clearly defined touring pitches of 100 sq.m. all with electricity connections (10A). The swimming pool complex is wonderful with pools linked by water channels and bridges. There is also a jacuzzi, paddling pool and two large swimming pools all surrounded by sunbathing areas and decorated with palm trees. An indoor pool is heated and open all season. This is a friendly site with a good mix of nationalities. The latest additions are a super children's aquapark with games, and a top quality bar/restaurant complex with regular entertainment.

**Facilities**

Three good clean toilet blocks have washbasins in cabins and mainly British style toilets. Facilities for disabled visitors. Baby baths. Motorcaravan services. Shop with gas. New bar/restaurant complex with entertainment. Swimming pool complex (supervised July/Aug). Games room. Play area. Tennis. Bicycle hire. Boules. Archery. Fishing. Water skiing. Watersports equipment hire. Tournaments (June-Aug). Skateboard park. Trampolines. Miniclub. No charcoal barbecues on pitches (communal area). WiFi (charged). Off site: Riding 2 km. Golf 12 km.

**Open:** 6 April - 8 September.

**Directions**

Take D652 from Sanguinet to Biscarrosse and site is signed on the right in 6 km. Turn right and follow tarmac road for 2 km. GPS: 44.46052, -1.13065

**Charges 2013**

| Per unit incl. 2 persons | |
|---|---|
| and electricity | € 26.50 - € 54.00 |
| extra person | € 3.60 - € 10.00 |
| child (3-7 yrs) | € 3.60 - € 8.20 |
| dog | € 6.20 - € 8.20 |

Camping Cheques accepted.

## Biscarrosse-Plage

Campé●le

### Campéole Navarrosse

712 chemin de Navarrosse, F-40600 Biscarrosse (Landes) T: 05 58 09 84 32. E: navarrosse@campeole.com
**alanrogers.com/FR40230**

Navarrosse is a member of the Campéole group and is located on the very large Lac de Sanguinet, just 7 km. from the Atlantic beaches. The location of this traditional campsite is attractive, with a long sandy beach (no dogs) and a small harbour (ideal for mooring small boats) on one side, and to the other, a small canal. Pitches are of a good size, mostly on fairly level, sandy soil with good shade. Most have 10A electricity. Many water-based activities take place on the lake, including sailing, jet skiing and windsurfing. For cyclists, there are many tracks to various places. Mobile homes, chalets and fully equipped tents are available for rent. Some units are specially adapted for disabled visitors.

**Facilities**

Two sanitary units are made up of separate blocks of toilets and showers. One modern block has all facilities under one roof including for disabled visitors. Laundry facilities. Motorcaravan services. Bar, snack bar and takeaway (1/7-31/8). Tennis. Multisports pitch. Archery. Play area. Bouncy castle. Activity and entertainment programme (1/7-31/8). WiFi (charged). Charcoal barbecues are not permitted. Mobile homes, equipped tents and chalets for rent. Off site: Bicycle hire 100 m. Sailing 300 m. Biscarrosse 3 km. Riding and fishing 5 km.

**Open:** 27 April - 16 September.

**Directions**

From the north on the D652 turn right onto the D305. After 1.5 km. turn right at campsite sign and towards lake. GPS: 44.43192, -1.16885

**Charges guide**

| Per unit incl. 2 persons | |
|---|---|
| and electricity | € 17.90 - € 31.60 |
| extra person | € 4.60 - € 9.40 |
| child (2-6 yrs) | € 4.80 - € 5.70 |
| dog | € 2.50 - € 3.50 |

For latest campsite news, availability and prices visit
**alanrogers.com**

## Biscarrosse
### Camping Bimbo

176 chemin du Bimbo, Navarrosse, F-40600 Biscarrosse (Landes) T: 05 58 09 82 33.
E: info@campingbimbo.fr **alanrogers.com/FR40460**

Camping Bimbo is a well maintained site in the popular resort of Biscarrosse. An excellent new aquapark was opened in 2010. This features a spa pool and an excellent children's pool with many water games. The complex is surrounded by a large 700 sq.m. sun terrace. The 70 touring pitches are of a good size and are well shaded. Most have 6/8A electrical connections. A good range of mobile homes and chalets are available for rent. Bimbo is a lively site in peak season with a varied activity and entertainment programme, including special activities for children. The site is located on the south side of the massive Etang de Cazaux, where a wide range of water sports are possible. Alternatively, the magnificent Atlantic beach is a short drive away, at Biscarrosse-Plage. Biscarrosse itself is a pleasant resort, and home to an interesting seaplane museum. The surrounding forest is ideal cycling and walking country.

**Facilities**

Toilet blocks have hot showers, washbasins in cabins and facilities for disabled visitors. Shop. Restaurant, bar/snack bar and takeaway (15/6-15/9, weekends in low season). Swimming pool complex. Sports area. Games room. Fitness room. Sauna and spa. Entertainment and activity programme (high season). Bicycle hire. Mobile homes and chalets for rent. WiFi (charged). Off site: Sailing and boat launching 600 m. Shops and restaurants in Biscarrosse centre. Riding and golf 2 km. Biscarrosse-Plage (Atlantic beach) 9 km.

**Open:** 1 April - 30 September.

**Directions**

Approaching Biscarrosse on D652 from Sanguinet, follow signs to Navarrosse. Pass through the hamlet of En Belliard, and the site is soon signed, and can be found on the right. GPS: 44.426828, -1.161091

**Charges guide**

| Per unit incl. 2 persons | |
|---|---|
| and electricity | € 18.30 - € 42.20 |
| extra person | € 5.00 - € 8.00 |
| child (2-7 yrs) | free - € 4.00 |
| dog | € 3.00 - € 5.00 |

## Biscarrosse
### Camping les Petits Ecureuils

254 chemin Crastail, F-40600 Biscarrosse (Landes) T: 05 58 78 01 97. E: bisca.petits.ecureuils@wanadoo.fr
**alanrogers.com/FR40780**

Les Petits Ecureuils is a small, family run campsite located 3 km. from the vast Etang de Cazaux and 8 km. from the region's celebrated Atlantic beaches. The 70 level touring pitches are of a good size, some are shaded and most have electrical connections (6A). A number of mobile homes are available for rent. On-site amenities include a swimming pool and paddling pool, and a bar/restaurant serving freshly cooked pizzas. Cycling is popular in this area and there are miles of excellent cycle routes leading through the forest. To the north, the Bassin d'Arcachon is famous for its oyster beds and bird life.

**Facilities**

One toilet block has a mixture of British and Turkish style WCs, some controllable showers and good facilities for disabled campers. Washing machine. Bar/restaurant. Swimming pool. Paddling pool. Games room. Small play area. Pétanque. Tourist information. Torches useful. Free WiFi over site. Mobile homes for rent. Off site: Restaurants and shops in Biscarrosse. Walking and cycling routes. Bicycle hire 2 km. Riding 4 km. Beach 8 km. Fishing 10 km. Sailing. Windsurfing.

**Open:** 31 March - 31 September.

**Directions**

From Sanguinet head south on D652 as far as Biscarrosse, and then follow signs to the site. GPS: 44.404536, -1.149064

**Charges guide**

| Per unit incl. 2 persons | |
|---|---|
| and electricity | € 14.00 - € 24.00 |
| extra person | € 5.00 - € 9.00 |
| child (3-7 yrs) | € 4.00 |
| dog | € 3.00 - € 5.00 |

# Biscarrosse

## Camping Mayotte Vacances

368 chemin des Roseaux, F-40600 Biscarrosse (Landes) T: 05 58 78 00 00.
E: camping@mayottevacances.com **alanrogers.com/FR40240**

This appealing site is set amongst pine trees on the edge of Lac de Biscarrosse. Drive down a tree- and flower-lined avenue and proceed toward the lake to shady, good sized pitches which blend well with the many tidy mobile homes that share the area. Divided by hedges, all 208 touring pitches have electricity (16A) and water taps. There may be some aircraft noise at times from a nearby army base. The pool complex is impressive, with various pools, slides, chutes, jacuzzi and sauna, all surrounded by paved sunbathing areas. The excellent lakeside beach provides safe bathing for all ages with plenty of watersports available. A comfortable restaurant and bar overlook the pool. A new, fully equipped gym is available free of charge. Children of all ages are catered for with organised clubs, play and sports areas and a games room. This well managed, clean and friendly site with helpful multi-lingual staff in reception should appeal to all and the facilities are open all season.

### Facilities

Four good quality, clean toilet blocks (one open early season). Good facilities for visitors with disabilities. Unusual baby/toddler bathroom. Motorcaravan services. Laundry. Supermarket. Boutique. Comprehensive rental shop (July/Aug). Restaurant. Swimming pools (one heated; supervised July/Aug. and weekends). Play area. Further children's area (extra cost) with trampolines, inflatables and a small train. Bicycle hire. Fishing. Watersports. Organised activities and entertainment (July/Aug). Clubs for toddlers and teenagers (July/Aug). Charcoal barbecues are not permitted. Hairdressers (seasonal). ATM. Internet access. Off site: Riding 100 m. Golf 4 km. Town 2 km. with restaurants, shops and bars. Beach 8 km.

**Open:** 1 April - 1 October.

### Directions

From the north on D652 turn right on D333 (Chemin de Goubern). Pass through Goubern and Mayotte village. Take next right (signed to site) into Chemin des Roseaux. GPS: 44.43495, -1.15505

### Charges guide

| | |
|---|---|
| Per unit incl. 2 persons | € 18.00 - € 45.00 |
| extra person | € 4.00 - € 7.00 |
| child (3-7 yrs) | free - € 4.00 |
| dog | € 3.00 - € 5.00 |

Aquitaine

Hôtel République - 2012 - © Lionel Puitalis.

★★★★★ CAMPING VILLAGE

**Mayotte Vacances**
BISCARROSSE - FRANCE

## Like an island's breeze

Camping Mayotte, a taste of paradise in the heart of the Landes... Come relax on the shores of Lake Biscarrosse where comfortable accommodation is waiting for you. A heavenly place to relax, but also for fun: with high quality performances, a water park with water slides and whirlpool, or a 250 m² spa... And for even more away-from-it-all atmosphere, discover our brand new Maori cottages.

368, chemin des Roseaux - 40600 Biscarrosse
Tél : 00 33(0)5 58 78 00 00 ~ Fax 00 33(0)5 58 78 83 91 · camping@mayottevacances.com · www.mayottevacances.com

## Biscarrosse-Plage

### Campéole Plage Sud

230 rue des Bécasses, F-40600 Biscarrosse-Plage (Landes) T: 05 58 78 21 24. E: plage-sud@campeole.com

**alanrogers.com/FR40420**

Biscarrosse-Plage is a lively holiday resort with a fabulous beach. La Plage Sud is a member of the Campéole group and is located around 800 m. from the beach. This is a massive site with 905 touring pitches and a further 479 pitches occupied by mobile homes, chalets and fully equipped tents (available for rent). The site is lively in peak season with a varied programme of activities and entertainment (N.B. numbers are limited for some activities). On-site amenities include a swimming pool and paddling pool. Pitches are sandy and generally well shaded. Most are equipped with electricity. Surfing is very popular here with a surf school nearby. There are many miles of good sandy beaches. Other sports away from the beach are also catered for. There are miles of cycle tracks through the forest (bicycle hire available on site). There is an adventure park in the tree tops and a theme park for younger children. Alternatively, there is a multisports pitch on site. The Marquèze eco-museum is fascinating, tracing life in this heavily forested region over many years. To the north, the Dune du Pyla, the highest in Europe, is recommended with fantastic views over the Arcachon basin and Landes forest.

### Facilities

Five modern toilet blocks were clean, with some washbasins in cabins, warm water and preset showers. Facilities for children and babies. Motorcaravan service point. Bar/snack bar. Shop. Swimming pool (4/6-18/9). Paddling pool. Multisport terrain. Play area. Activity and entertainment programme. Mobile homes, chalets and tents for rent. WiFi (charged). Charcoal barbecues are not allowed. Off site: Nearest beach 800 m. Surfing. Cycle and walking tracks. Dune de Pyla. Minigolf. Canoeing in the Leyre river. Wine tasting at many of the Bordeaux vineyards.

**Open:** 29 April - 18 September.

### Directions

From A63 motorway, take A66 towards Bassin d'Arcachon and Biscarrosse. Take Biscarrosse exit, then D216 towards Sanguinet and Biscarrosse. In Biscarrosse, take right turning off second roundabout, towards la Plage. The campsite is before Biscarrosse-Plage. Narrow entrance – large units ask at reception for access via side gate. GPS: 44.4419, -1.2455

### Charges guide

| | |
|---|---|
| Per unit incl. 2 persons and electricity | € 17.90 - € 31.70 |

## Biscarrosse-Plage

**Campéole le Vivier**

Campé●le

681 rue du Tit, F-40600 Biscarrosse-Plage (Landes) T: 05 58 78 25 76. E: vivier@campeole.com
**alanrogers.com/FR40430**

Le Vivier is a member of the Campéole group and can be found 2 km. from the seaside resort of Biscarrosse-Plage. The nearest beach is 800 m. away and the crashing Atlantic breakers can be heard on site. Pitches are located amongst the towering pine trees and mostly have electrical connections. Mobile homes, chalets are available for rent (including specially adapted units for wheelchair users). Although close to the beach, there is a large swimming pool on site, and other sports amenities include volleyball, basketball and tennis. This large, lively site in high season has plenty going on, including discos and karaoke evenings, as well as sports tournaments. The Arcachon Basin is easily accessible to the north, as well as the Dune de Pyla, Europe's highest sand dune and the Aqualand water theme park. Another popular day trip could be the great city of Bordeaux, accessible within an hour's drive. Closer to the site, there are miles of cycle trails through the forest and bikes can be hired on site. Riding is also popular – there are stables close to Biscarrosse.

### Facilities

Bar/snack bar and takeaway food (25/6-31/8). Swimming pool (12/6-18/9). Tennis. Bicycle hire. Bouncy castle. Play area. Activities and entertainment programme. Mobile homes, chalets and equipped tents for rent. Only communal barbecues are permitted. WiFi (charged). Off site: Nearest beach 800 m. Treetop adventure park 2 km. Lake beach 5 km. Hiking and cycle tracks. Riding 8 km. Golf 10 km.

**Open:** 26 April - 21 September.

### Directions

Head south from Arcachon on D218 passing the Dune de Pyla and continue to Biscarrosse-Plage. The site is well signed from here.
GPS: 44.45804, -1.23968

### Charges guide

| Per unit incl. 2 persons | |
|---|---|
| and electricity | € 17.90 - € 31.70 |
| extra person | € 4.60 - € 9.50 |
| child (2-6 yrs) | free - € 5.60 |
| dog | € 2.50 - € 3.50 |

AQUITAINE

Campé●le

CAMPSITES AND RENTALS

**Le Vivier** ★★★

Three stars site with swimming pool at 800 meters of a sandy beach. Quality facilities, touring pitches and accomodations for rent.

40600 Biscarrosse-Plage - Tel.: +33-558-7825-76 - www.campeole.co.uk / vivier@campeole.com

## Bordeaux

**Village du Lac, Camping de Bordeaux**

Boulevard Jacques Chaban Delmas, F-33520 Bruges (Gironde) T: 05 57 87 70 60.
E: contact@village-du-lac.com **alanrogers.com/FR33410**

Bordeaux is undeniably one of France's 'must see' cities and now it has a superior campsite. Adjacent to the exhibition centre and beside Bordeaux Lac, the site opened in 2009 and is open all year. The facilities and accommodation are of top quality. There are 119 touring pitches, some on well kept grass, others, primarily for motorcaravans, have hardstanding. All have electricity, 40 have water and drainage and 70 also have sewerage disposal. Within the 14-hectare campsite there are also 93 well equipped chalets and mobile homes (3 specifically for disabled visitors) for rent. The site is arranged around five attractive, man-made lakes and set amongst tall trees.

### Facilities

Modern, heated sanitary block. Laundry. Restaurant, bar and supermarket. Swimming pool. Play area. Table tennis, handball and basketball court. Mobile homes and chalets for rent. WiFi (charged). Off site: Golf and fishing (Bordeaux Lac complex). Large shopping centre. Cycle and walking tracks. Bordeaux centre 5 km. with public transport daily from site.

**Open:** All year.

### Directions

At Bordeaux, take the A630 ring road and exit 4A. Follow signs for Parc des Expositions and signs for campsite. At roundabout take second exit (right) and site is 700 m. on the right. GPS: 44.89805, -0.58194

### Charges guide

| Per unit incl. 2 persons | |
|---|---|
| and electricity | € 16.00 - € 31.00 |
| extra person | € 4.00 - € 9.00 |

**FREE** Alan Rogers Travel Card
Extra benefits and savings - see page 10

## Brantôme

### Camping Brantôme Peyrelevade

Avenue André Maurois, F-24310 Brantôme (Dordogne) T: 05 53 05 75 24. E: info@camping-dordogne.net
**alanrogers.com/FR24540**

Le Peyrelevade is a quiet and peaceful site in the Périgord Vert region. Of a very good standard, it comprises 170 spacious and well kept touring pitches and 17 mobile homes for rent. Most pitches have 6A electricity and 12 are fully serviced. The site is set in an area that is part open, part wooded and most pitches have partial shade from well sited trees and hedges. The beautiful village of Brantôme on an island surrounded by a river, is close by and there you will find small bars, restaurants and other amenities. There is a 3.5 tonne weight restriction on the main road through the village.

| Facilities | Directions |
|---|---|
| Two heated sanitary blocks are well maintained, clean and adequate for the number of pitches. One is new and includes good facilities for disabled visitors. Baby area with bath. Laundry with washing machine. Shop (1/6-15/9). Bar. Takeaway (1/7-31/8). Games room with TV. Open air swimming pool. Play area. River beach suitable for paddling. Fishing. WiFi (charge). Max. 2 dogs accepted. Off site: Boat trips. Riding 3 km. Golf 25 km. **Open:** 1 May - 30 September. | Take D939 south from Angoulême, or north from Périgueux. Brantôme is 20 km. north of Périgueux. Drive through Brantôme and look for site sign 1.5 km. to north. Note weight restriction of 3.5 tonnes on main road through village. GPS: 45.361, 0.661 |

**Charges guide**

| | |
|---|---|
| Per unit incl. 2 persons and electricity | € 14.50 - € 22.50 |
| extra person | € 3.00 - € 4.50 |

## Castelnaud-la-Chapelle

### Camping Maisonneuve

Vallée du Céou, F-24250 Castelnaud-la-Chapelle (Dordogne) T: 05 53 29 51 29.
E: contact@campingmaisonneuve.com **alanrogers.com/FR24450**

This family run site is beautifully situated in the Céou Valley, in the Périgord. There are 130 spacious touring pitches, all with 6/10A electricity. Some are well separated, whilst others are on two open, grassy areas. Most pitches have some shade. The site's facilities are grouped around the old farmhouse. Swimming, diving, fishing and canoeing are all possible in the Céou river bordering the site and can be accessed directly. There are swimming and paddling pools on site and in high season entertainment is organised several evenings each week. This is an excellent location from which to explore the beautiful region of the Périgord.

| Facilities | Directions |
|---|---|
| Three sanitary blocks, one has been totally refurbished, are kept clean and tidy. Facilities for babies and disabled visitors. Laundry. Bar (all season). Shop with bread, snack bar, takeaway (all July/Aug). Swimming and paddling pools (1/5-15/10). Minigolf. Play areas. TV room. Games room. Dance evenings. Karaoke. Sports tournaments. Canoe trips. Climbing. WiFi in reception and courtyard (free). Off site: Fishing and bicycle hire 1 km. Riding 3 km. Golf 5 km. Canoeing. Walking and cycle routes. **Open:** 1 April - 31 October. | From A20 exit 55 take D703 towards Sarlat and Beynac. Follow signs for D57 (Castelnaud la Chappelle). Site is well signed on edge of village. Caravans and large units over 5 m. continue on D57 for 2 km. then turn left. Site is signed here at junction with D50. GPS: 44.80367, 1.15533 |

**Charges guide**

| | |
|---|---|
| Per unit incl. 2 persons and electricity (6A) | € 17.70 - € 26.30 |
| extra person | € 4.50 - € 6.50 |

## Castelnaud-la-Chapelle

### Flower Camping Lou Castel

F-24250 Castelnaud-la-Chapelle (Dordogne) T: 05 53 29 89 24. E: contact@loucastel.com
**alanrogers.com/FR24465**

Lou Castel is attractively located close to Castelnaud-la-Chapelle, at the heart of the Périgord Noir, and close to many of the region's major attractions. There are 115 stony pitches here with just a little grass, 40 are available for touring under oak trees which provide good shade. All have electricity (10A). A range of mobile homes, chalets and bungalow style tents are available for hire. The impressive pool complex has three water slides and two swimming pools, and a separate children's paddling pool. There is a bar/restaurant with a large terrace which is used for entertainment in peak season.

| Facilities | Directions |
|---|---|
| The modern toilet block includes facilities for babies and disabled visitors. Basic shop. Restaurant/snack bar, takeaway and terrace (July/Aug). Heated swimming pool complex. Games room. Activity and entertainment (July/Aug). Play area. WiFi in bar. Off site: River beach and fishing 3.5 km. Bicycle hire 3.5 km. Riding 5 km. Castelnaud. Canoe trips. Cycling and walking. **Open:** 30 April - 1 October. | From the west (Bergerac) take D660, D29, D25, D703 passing through Bezenac and Beynac. After Beynac, take D57 south to Castelnaud-la-Chapelle, then follow signs to site. GPS: 44.79768, 1.13121 |

**Charges guide**

| | |
|---|---|
| Per unit incl. 2 persons and electricity | € 17.00 - € 31.00 |
| extra person | € 4.00 - € 6.50 |

For latest campsite news, availability and prices visit
# alanrogers.com

## Coux-et-Bigaroque
### Camping les Valades

D703, F-24220 Coux-et-Bigaroque (Dordogne) T: 05 53 29 14 27. E: info@lesvalades.com
**alanrogers.com/FR24420**

Sometimes we come across small but beautifully kept campsites which seem to have been a well kept secret, and les Valades certainly fits the bill. Set on a hillside overlooking lovely countryside between the Dordogne and Vézère rivers, each pitch is surrounded by a variety of flowers, shrubs and trees. The 85 pitches are flat and grassy, mostly on terraces, all with 10A electricity and most with individual water and drainage as well. Ten very large pitches (over 300 sq.m) are available for weekly hire, each having a private sanitary unit, dishwashing, fridge and barbecue. At the bottom of the hill, away from the main area, is a swimming pool and a good sized lake for carp fishing, swimming and canoeing (free canoes). Rustic chalets for rent occupy 19, and mobile homes six, of the largest pitches. From the moment you arrive you can see that the owners, M. and Mme. Berger, take enormous pride in the appearance of their campsite and there is an abundance of well tended flowers and shrubs everywhere you look. A convivial and family atmosphere is very much in evidence and the site is therefore ideal for families with young children. Couples both young and mature will also enjoy this site.

**Facilities**

Two clean modern toilet blocks, one with family shower rooms. Facilities for disabled visitors. Washing machine. Shop, bar and restaurant (all July/Aug) and a terrace overlooking the valley. Heated swimming pool with sun terrace and paddling pool (July/Aug). Play area near the lake and pool. Fishing. Canoeing. WiFi (free). Off site: Small shop, bar, restaurant in Coux-et-Bigaroque 5 km. Supermarket at Le Bugue 10 km. Riding and bicycle hire 5 km. Golf 6 km.

**Open:** 1 April - 15 October.

**Directions**

Site is signed down a turning on west side of D703 Le Bugue-Siorac-en-Perigord road, 3.5 km. north of village of Coux-et-Bigaroque. Turn off D703 and site is 1.5 km. along on right. GPS: 44.86056, 0.96385

**Charges guide**

| | |
|---|---|
| Per unit incl. 2 persons and electricity | € 26.00 |
| extra person | € 6.30 |
| child (under 7 yrs) | € 4.40 |
| No credit cards. | |

★★★★ A quiet piece of nature in the Périgord Noir

Pitches and wooden chalets • Heated swimming pool • Fishing & Canoeing • Perfect for children
24220 - Coux et Bigaroque • www.lesvalades.com • +33 (0) 5.53.29.14.27

## Daglan
### Camping le Moulin de Paulhiac

F-24520 Daglan (Dordogne) T: 05 53 28 20 88. E: Francis.Armagnac@wanadoo.fr
**alanrogers.com/FR24230**

You will be guaranteed a friendly welcome from the Armagnac family, who are justifiably proud of their attractive, well kept site, built in the grounds surrounding an old mill. The facilities have been continually updated and improved over the years. The 150 shady pitches (93 for touring) are separated by hedges and shrubs, all fully serviced. Many pitches are next to a small river that runs through the site and joins the River Ceou along the far edge. A tent field slopes gently down to the river, which is quite shallow and used for swimming. This site will appeal especially to families with younger children.

**Facilities**

Two clean toilet blocks provide modern facilities including those for disabled visitors. Good shop, restaurant, takeaway. Main pool, heated and covered by a sliding roof in low season, children's pool, a further small pool and a toboggan and slide. Boules. Bicycle hire. Small river with beach. Fishing. Canoe trips organised on the Dordogne. Organised evening activities. Children's club in high season. Off site: Riding 5 km. Golf 10 km.

**Open:** 15 May - 15 September.

**Directions**

Site is 17 km. south of Sarlat and is on the east side of the D57, 5 km. north of the village of Daglan. GPS: 44.76762, 1.17635

**Charges guide**

| | |
|---|---|
| Per unit incl. 2 persons and electricity | € 17.95 - € 29.85 |
| extra person | € 5.00 - € 7.50 |
| child (0-10 yrs) | € 2.70 - € 5.20 |

**FREE** Alan Rogers Travel Card
Extra benefits and savings - see page 10

## Dax
### Camping les Chênes

Bois de Boulogne, F-40100 Dax (Landes) T: 05 58 90 05 53. E: camping-chenes@wanadoo.fr
**alanrogers.com/FR40020**

Les Chênes is a well established site, popular with the French themselves and situated on the edge of town amongst parkland (also near the river) and close to the spa for thermal treatments. The 176 touring pitches are of two types, some large and traditional with hedges, 109 with electricity (5A), water and drainage, and others more informal, set amongst tall pines with electricity if required. This is a reliable, well run site, with a little of something for everyone, but probably most popular for adults taking the spa treatments or wanting a quiet holiday close to many small shops. Dax is not a place that springs to mind as a holiday town but, as well as being a spa, it promotes a comprehensive programme of events and shows during the summer season. The campsite lies on the route of the little tourist road train, so access to the centre of Dax and the cathedral of Sainte Marie is very easy. It is also possible to walk into the town along the river bank. A short drive takes you to the Atlantic coast and Biarritz.

**Facilities**

Two main toilet blocks, one with heating, washbasins in cubicles, facilities for disabled visitors, babies and young children. The older block has been refurbished. Laundry facilities. Shop also providing takeaway food (27/3-10/11). Swimming pool with paddling area (5/5-15/9). Play area. Field for ball games. Boules. Bicycle hire. Miniclub for children (July/Aug). Occasional special evenings for adults. Charcoal barbecues are not permitted. Free WiFi over site. Mobile homes and bungalows for rent. Off site: Restaurant opposite. Riding and golf within 200 m. Beaches 28 km.

**Open:** 16 March - 10 November.

**Directions**

Site is west of town on south side of river, signed after main river bridge and at many junctions in town – Bois de Boulogne (1.5 km). In very wet weather the access road to the site may be flooded (but not the site). GPS: 43.71182, -1.07329

**Charges guide**

| | |
|---|---|
| Per unit incl. 2 persons and electricity | € 15.20 - € 18.30 |
| extra person | € 6.00 |
| child (2-10 yrs) | € 4.00 |
| dog | € 1.50 |

Camping Les Chênes ★★★★

Hôtel de plein air
du Bois de Boulogne
4 0 1 0 0   D A X
Tel. 0033 558 90 05 53
Fax 0033 558 90 42 43

## Devillac
### Camping Fontaine du Roc

Dévillac, F-47210 Villeréal (Lot-et-Garonne) T: 05 53 36 08 16. E: fontaine.du.roc@wanadoo.fr
**alanrogers.com/FR47070**

Situated on the border between the lovely region of Périgord (Dordogne) and the Lot-et-Garonne, in the heart of the Pays des Bastides, is Camping Fontaine du Roc. It is a natural environment on a wooded hillside and quite isolated. The three hectare site has panoramic views of the nearby Château Biron. Each of the 70 pitches has access to electricity (5/10A Europlug); some are in the sun and others in the shade to suit your needs. A long established site now run by Dutch owners, the site blends well with the natural surroundings. The narrow, single-track approach road may cause problems for large units.

**Facilities**

One centally located sanitary block is kept spotlessly clean and includes good facilities for babies, children and disabled visitors. Washing machine. Small shop with daily deliveries of bread and milk. Bar and snack bar serving pizzas. Large swimming pool, children's pool, whirlpool. New wooden chalet with sauna, massage, whirlpool and bunkhouse. Two small play areas. Library with TV. Boules. Two purpose built stone barbecues. Activities for children (high season). Internet access. WiFi (free).

**Open:** 28 March - 1 October.

**Directions**

From Monflanquin, take D272 heading north towards Monpazier. Fontaine du Roc is 10 km. along the road on the left hand side. GPS: 44.61405, 0.81885

**Charges guide**

| | |
|---|---|
| Per unit incl. 2 persons and electricity | € 18.50 - € 23.50 |
| extra adult | € 4.50 - € 5.50 |
| child (under 6 yrs) | € 3.00 - € 3.50 |

No credit cards.

For latest campsite news, availability and prices visit
**alanrogers.com**

## Domme
### Camping le Perpetuum

La Ruiére, F-24250 Domme (Dordogne) T: 05 53 28 35 18. E: luc.parsy@wanadoo.fr

**alanrogers.com/FR24520**

Located alongside the Dordogne river, this is a small and friendly, family run site. Attractive and mature, the site is in an ideal location where you can make the most of the river and the Périgord region. The French owners are dedicated to providing a comfortable site and are warm and welcoming, particularly to families with young children. There are 180 pitches including 128 for touring units with 10A electricity. There are 40 mobile homes to rent. The pitches are level and most offer some shade. Access round the site is easy thus allowing large motorcaravans and twin-axle caravans. The river has two bathing areas, pebble and sand, and there are canoes to hire. The site is close to the beautiful towns of Sarlat and Domme, and the valley of the Dordogne with its châteaux and villages.

### Facilities

Three well maintained sanitary blocks. En-suite toilet for disabled visitors. Newly renovated toilet block. Toilet, shower, washbasins for children. Baby room. Laundry room. Motorcaravan service point. Well stocked shop with fresh bread and milk (July/Aug). Bar and snack bar with TV (high season). Swimming pool and paddling pool. Two play areas. Covered games area. Canoeing on the river. WiFi Internet access (reasonable cost). Activities and entertainment most days (high season). Off site: Sarlat less than 3 km. Golf 2 km. Tennis 2 km. Riding 3 km.

**Open:** 1 May - 10 October.

### Directions

Take D703 to Vitrac. At Vitrac, head south for several hundred metres and take the bridge over the river, onto the D46e. Follow for 1.5 km. until crossroads at the end. Turn right following signs to site. It is less than 1 km. from the crossroads on the right hand side. GPS: 44.81579, 1.22052

### Charges guide

| Per unit incl. 2 persons | |
|---|---|
| and electricity | € 16.60 - € 23.50 |
| extra person | € 4.80 - € 6.60 |
| child (under 7 yrs) | € 2.00 - € 4.00 |

No credit cards.

---

*Camping le Perpetuum* ★★★  
**La Rivière 24250 Domme**

Welcome to Le Perpetuum with Fabienne and David

Located on the riverbank, only 8 kilometres from Sarlat and near to the fascinating sites of Domme, La Roque-Gageac, Beynac, les Milandes, etcetera.

You will be seduced by the green and quiet surroundings. Familial and convivial reception. Campsite of 4 hectares offering 120 level touring pitches on grass. Motorcaravan service point.

Organized entertainment during the summer period (dance evenings, karaoke, canoe trips, boules competitions, morning activities for children...). On site snack bar, grocery and daily fresh bread. Heated swimming pool.

Mobile homes and caravans for rent, very attractive low season rates (off -30% up to -40%).

**For more information, please call 00 33 5 53 28 35 18 or send us an email. www.campingleperpetuum.com. So see you soon!**

---

## Domme
### Camping le Bosquet

La Riviere, F-24250 Domme (Dordogne) T: 05 53 28 37 39. E: info@lebosquet.com

**alanrogers.com/FR24760**

Located between Sarlat and Bergerac, this great little campsite is set in lovely countryside close to the River Dordogne. It is beautifully landscaped with flowers, shrubs and trees, maintained to a good standard and kept very clean. There are 57 level grass pitches of average size, 36 of which are for touring units. All have 10A electricity and are separated by shrubs and mature trees providing shade. The remainder are used for mobile homes to rent. The river is only 300 metres away and a canoeing centre can be found near the site entrance.

### Facilities

The modern, high quality toilet block includes facilities for babies and disabled visitors. Washing machine and iron. Small shop. Takeaway (1/5-20/9). Heated swimming pool. Library. Entertainment (July/Aug). Play area. Boules. TV. Free WiFi in reception area. Twin axle caravans are not accepted. Off site: River beach and fishing 300 m. Bicycle hire and canoeing 1 km. Golf and tennis 2 km. Riding 3 km.

**Open:** 1 April - 30 September.

### Directions

Take the D46 from Sarlat to Vitrac. Cross the river bridge in Vitrac and the site is on the right hand side 1 km. further on. GPS: 44.82241, 1.225319

### Charges guide

| Per unit incl. 2 persons | |
|---|---|
| and electricity | € 13.60 - € 16.80 |
| extra person | € 3.50 - € 4.50 |
| child (2-7 yrs) | € 2.00 - € 2.70 |
| dog | € 1.00 - € 2.00 |

**FREE** Alan Rogers Travel Card
Extra benefits and savings - see page 10

## Douville
### Camping d'Orpheo Negro

Les Trois Frères, (RN 21), F-24140 Douville (Dordogne) T: 05 53 82 96 58. E: camping@orpheonegro.com
**alanrogers.com/FR24880**

Camping d'Orpheo Negro can be found midway between Périgueux and Bergerac. There are 100 grassy pitches in a park which extends over 16 hectares. Pitches are large and generally well shaded. Most have electrical connections (6A). A few chalets and mobile homes are available for rent. The site has been developed on the banks of a three hectare lake which is well stocked with carp, so this is a popular site with anglers. Rowing boats and pedaloes are provided free of charge. Other leisure amenities include a swimming pool (with water slide), tennis, an open-air bowling alley and minigolf.

**Facilities**

The single toilet block was quite old when we visited but there are plans to renew it. Shop. Bar/snack bar. Swimming pool. Water slide. Fishing. Rowing boats and pedaloes. Tennis. Minigolf. Open-air bowling alley. Games room. Playground. Activity programme. WiFi (free). Off site: Cycle and walking tracks. Riding 1 km. Vergt 8 km. Périgueux and Bergerac 25 km.

**Open:** 1 April - 31 October.

**Directions**

Site is at Douville, north of Bergerac. From Bergerac, take northbound N21 towards Périgueux and follow signs to Douville (D36). Then, follow signs to site. GPS: 45.024654, 0.615967

**Charges guide**

| | |
|---|---|
| Per unit incl. 2 persons and electricity | € 17.70 - € 20.70 |
| extra person | € 4.50 - € 5.50 |

## Duras
### Le Cabri Holiday Village

Route de Savignac, F-47120 Duras (Lot-et-Garonne) T: 05 53 83 81 03. E: holidays@lecabri.eu.com
**alanrogers.com/FR47110**

This countryside site of 5.5 hectares is divided into three areas: camping, chalets and open fields. It is on the border of the Dordogne and the Lot-et-Garonne departments. Le Cabri Holiday Village is an English owned and run, small holiday complex. The owners, Peter and Eileen Marston who are keen caravanners themselves, have developed 24 new spacious pitches (generally 150 sq.m), all with electricity (4/16A) and water. The open, level pitches are all on hardstandings surrounded by grass and separated by young trees, so with limited shade. Access for large motorcaravans using the rear entrance is possible as this was considered when the site was planned. Open all year round, the site has a swimming pool, a small fishing pond and other leisure facilities. Wildlife watching is another pastime here with red deer and wild boar populating the area. Le Cabri also benefits from its own high quality restaurant which specialises in local cuisine. It draws clientele from the local area as well as those staying on the site. The historic village of Duras is only a ten minute walk, with a good selection of shops, restaurants, bars and the famous fortified château standing guard at the head of the village square.

**Facilities**

A recently refurbished sanitary block is heated in low season and includes three new private cabins. Separate cabin for disabled visitors. Washing machines, dryers and ironing board. Shop (all year) for basics including bread. Restaurant (all year) with occasional entertainment and Internet access. Swimming pool (June-Sept). Large play area. Boules. Well stocked fishing pond. WiFi (charged). Off site: Riding and tennis 1 km. Golf (international course) 10 km. Watersports 7 km. Canoeing 8 km.

**Open:** All year.

**Directions**

In Duras, look for the D203 and follow signs for site. It is less than 1 km. away. GPS: 44.68296, 0.18615

**Charges guide**

| | |
|---|---|
| Per unit incl. 2 persons and 10A electricity | € 18.00 - € 23.00 |
| extra person | € 4.00 - € 5.00 |
| child (under 12 yrs) | € 2.00 - € 3.00 |
| dog | € 2.00 |

**Le Cabri Holiday Village**
**Route de Savignac - 47120 Duras**
Tel-fax: 0033 (0) 553 838 103
Mobile: 0033 (0) 685 449 711
E-mail: holidays@lecabri.eu.com - www.lecabri.eu.com

For latest campsite news, availability and prices visit
**alanrogers.com**

## Espelette
### Camping Biper Gorri

Chemin de Lapitxague, F-64250 Espelette (Pyrénées-Atlantiques) T: 05 59 93 96 88.
E: info@camping-biper-gorri.com  **alanrogers.com/FR64390**

Camping Biper Gorri has recently joined the Airotel group and can be found at the heart of Basque country, south of Cambo-les-Bains. This is a small site of 70 touring pitches, all of which are grassy and mostly shaded. There are a number of mobile homes and fully equipped bungalow-style tents available for rent. The site boasts an attractive pool complex with a large main pool and separate children's pool. The site is livelier in peak season with a children's club, regular entertainment and activities for all the family. A number of excursions are on offer, including accompanied rafting and canoe trips.

**Facilities**

One toilet block is partly heated and includes some washbasins in cabins and preset showers. Facilities for disabled visitors. Motorcaravan services. Basic shop (15/6-15/9). Bar, restaurant, snack bar and takeaway (all season). Heated swimming pool. Spa. Play area. Entertainment and activity programme. Woodland walks. Mobile homes and tents for rent. WiFi over site (charged). Torches useful. Off site: Amenities in Espelette.

**Open:** 1 April - 6 November.

**Directions**

Take the exit for Bayonne Sud from A64 motorway (Maignon) and take D932 to Ustaritz. Continue to Cambo-les-Bains, then take D10 to Espelette and follow signs in village. GPS: 43.353374, -1.449635

**Charges guide**

| Per unit incl. 2 persons | |
|---|---|
| and electricity | € 17.60 - € 33.00 |
| extra person | € 3.00 - € 6.60 |

## Groléjac-en-Perigord
### Camping Caravaning les Granges

F-24250 Groléjac-en-Perigord (Dordogne) T: 05 53 28 11 15. E: contact@lesgranges-fr.com
**alanrogers.com/FR24020**

Situated only 500 metres from the village of Groléjac, les Granges is a lively and well maintained campsite set on sloping ground in woodland. There are 188 pitches, of which 100 are available for touring units. The pitches are marked and numbered on level terraces, some shaded by mature trees and shrubs whilst others are sunny. You can choose your preference when checking in at reception. All pitches have electricity (6A) and water either on the pitch or close by. The site has a good sized pool and a large shallow pool for children. A bridge connects these to a fun pool with water slides.

**Facilities**

The toilet blocks are of a very high standard with good facilities for disabled visitors. Bar (July/Aug). Restaurant and snack bar with takeaway food. No shop, but bread and milk can be ordered. Heated swimming pool. Play area. Minigolf. Canoe and bicycle hire. New outdoor gym equipment. Paintball. Quad bikes. Climbing wall (2-12 yrs). Canoe trips. Entertainment, sporting tournaments and children's club (all high season). Free WiFi in bar area. Off site: Shops in the nearby village of Groléjac 550 m. Hypermarkets in Sarlat or Gourdon. Sat. market in Sarlat.

**Open:** 27 April - 14 September.

**Directions**

In centre of village of Groléjac on main D704 road. Site signed through gravel parking area on west side of road. Drive through parking and follow road around to T-junction. Turn right, under railway bridge, and immediately left (site signed). Site is just along this road on left. GPS: 44.81593, 1.29086

**Charges guide**

| Per unit incl. 2 persons | |
|---|---|
| and electricity | € 18.20 - € 28.70 |
| extra person (over 2 yrs) | € 5.60 - € 7.50 |

## Hourtin
### Camping les Ourmes

90 avenue du Lac, F-33990 Hourtin (Gironde) T: 05 56 09 12 76. E: info@lesourmes.com
**alanrogers.com/FR33050**

Located only 500 metres from the largest fresh water lake in France, this flat, well maintained campsite is only ten minutes drive from the beach and, with its own pool, this is an attractive holiday site for those who enjoy watersports. Of the 300 pitches, 232 are for touring units. These are marked but not actually separated, and arranged amongst tall pines and other trees which give good shade. All have electricity (10A). The site's amenities are arranged around a pleasant entrance courtyard with a programme of evening entertainment in season. In low season, this is a quiet site with the added bonus of the bar and restaurant being open all season.

**Facilities**

Four refurbished toilet blocks. Washing machine, dryer. Small shop (1/7-31/8). Bar/restaurant with outdoor tables, takeaway food and reasonably priced meals (15/5-20/9). Medium sized swimming pool, paddling pool (15/5-20/9). Large leisure area, play area, volleyball. TV, games rooms. Boules. Internet and WiFi. 37 mobile homes to rent.

**Open:** 1 May - 20 September.

**Directions**

It is essential to follow Hourtin Port (Ave du Lac) from the town centre and site is signed on left. GPS: 45.182067, -1.0756

**Charges guide**

| Per unit incl. 2 persons | |
|---|---|
| and electricity | € 18.00 - € 31.50 |
| extra person | € 3.00 - € 6.00 |

**FREE** Alan Rogers Travel Card
Extra benefits and savings - see page 10

## Hourtin-Plage

### Airotel Camping de la Côte d'Argent

F-33990 Hourtin-Plage (Gironde) T: 05 56 09 10 25. E: info@cca33.com

alanrogers.com/FR33110

Côte d'Argent is a large, well equipped site for leisurely family holidays. It makes an ideal base for walkers and cyclists with over 100 km. of cycle lanes in the area. Hourtin-Plage is a pleasant invigorating resort on the Atlantic coast and a popular location for watersports enthusiasts. The site's top attraction is its pool complex, where wooden bridges connect the pools and islands, and there are sunbathing and play areas plus an indoor heated pool. The site has 600 touring pitches (all with 10A electricity), not always clearly defined, arranged under trees with some on sand. High quality entertainment takes place at the impressive bar/restaurant near the entrance. Spread over 20 hectares of sand-based terrain in the midst of a pine forest, the site is well organised and ideal for children.

**Facilities**

Very clean sanitary blocks include provision for disabled visitors. Washing machines. Motorcaravan service points. Large supermarket, restaurant, takeaway, pizzeria, bar (all open 1/6-15/9). Four outdoor pools with slides and flumes (1/6-19/9). Indoor pool (all season). Fitness room. Massage (Institut de Beauté). Tennis. Play areas. Miniclub, organised entertainment in season. Bicycle hire. WiFi (charged). ATM. Charcoal barbecues are not permitted. Hotel (12 rooms). Off site: Path to the beach 300 m. Fishing and riding. Golf 30 km.

**Open:** 14 May - 18 September.

**Directions**

Turn off D101 Hourtin-Soulac road 3 km. north of Hourtin. Then join D101E signed Hourtin-Plage. Site is 300 m. from the beach. GPS: 45.22297, -1.16465

**Charges guide**

| Per unit incl. 2 persons | |
|---|---|
| and electricity | € 28.00 - € 53.00 |
| extra person | € 4.00 - € 8.50 |
| child (3-9 yrs) | € 3.00 - € 7.50 |
| dog | € 2.00 - € 6.50 |

Camping Cheques accepted.

## La Roque Gageac

### Camping Beau Rivage

Gaillardou, F-24250 La Roque Gageac (Dordogne) T: 05 53 28 32 05. E: camping.beau.rivage@wanadoo.fr

alanrogers.com/FR24800

Beau Rivage has a fine location, just 7 km. from Sarlat, close to La Roque Gageac, with its ancient, honey-coloured houses, sheer rock face and Dordogne river frontage. There are 199 level or slightly sloping grass pitches of which 151 are for touring units with 6A electricity available to all. The pitches are of a good size, separated by shrubs and tall trees provide shade. Large units should phone ahead to check availability. The site has a good range of amenities including a swimming pool, a restaurant, a well stocked shop and a bar. Canoeing is popular on the River Dordogne and there is direct access to the river and a small beach. Beau Rivage is popular with families and couples as it has something for everyone. In high season, a programme of entertainment is provided including sporting competitions.

**Facilities**

Two toilet blocks include facilities for babies and disabled visitors. Washing machines. Shop, bar, restaurant and takeaway (all July/Aug). Heated swimming and paddling pools. Play area. Pétanque. Tennis. Canoeing. Fishing. WiFi in bar area. Electric barbecues are not permitted. Max. 2 dogs. Off site: Bicycle hire 2 km. Golf 3 km. Riding 5 km. Historic towns and villages with châteaux and museums.

**Open:** 21 April - 8 September.

**Directions**

From Sarlat, take the D46 to Vitrac and then D703 towards La Roque Gageac. Site is on the left, well signed. GPS: 44.81621, 1.21488

**Charges guide**

| Per unit incl. 2 persons | € 12.75 - € 22.95 |
|---|---|
| extra person | € 3.20 - € 5.50 |
| electricity | € 3.70 |

For latest campsite news, availability and prices visit

## alanrogers.com

**A 3500 m² aquatic complex with slides and jacuzzis, covered and heated swimming pool !**

Club Airotel - **Hourtin Plage**

★★★★★ Camping Caravaning

# de la côte d'argent

**Camping Special offer (except July and August)  14 = 11 and 7 = 6**

WIFI - hotel - shops - restaurant - bar - food - sportive animations - tennis - archery - mini-club - games room - sailing (4 km) - surf (300m)

## www.cca33.com

*Campsite La Cote d'Argent is a very attractive 20 acre park, situated in the heart of the pine forest and on only 300m distance from the Atlantic Ocean Beach.*
*This characteristic park is protected for the ocean wind by the dunes and the forest. The Village Club Cote d'Argent is the perfect destination for your calm holiday in nature.*

**33990 Hourtin Plage**
Tél : +33 (0)5.56.09.10.25     Fax : +33 (0)5.56.09.24.96
www.campingcotedargent.com   www.campingcoteouest.com
www.campingaquitaine.com

## Labenne-Océan
### Yelloh! Village le Sylvamar

Avenue de l'Océan, F-40530 Labenne-Océan (Landes) T: 05 59 45 75 16. E: camping@sylvamar.fr

**alanrogers.com/FR40200**

Less than a kilometre from a long sandy beach, this campsite has a good mix of tidy, well maintained chalets, mobile homes, a tree house and touring pitches. The 280 touring pitches (566 in total) are level, numbered and mostly separated by low hedges. A number of new, less shaded pitches have recently been added. Following development, all now have electricity (10A), water and drainage. They are set around a superb pool complex with pools of various sizes (one heated, one not) with a large one for paddling, a wild water river, toboggans and slides. In a sunny setting, all are surrounded by ample sunbathing terraces and overlooked by the excellent bar/restaurant. In the evenings, entertainment is organised for all ages. Every year new amenities are offered and new sporting facilities include a tennis court, multisports pitch and a 50x25 m. football pitch, all on all-weather surfaces. A member of Leading Campings group.

**Facilities**

Four modern toilet blocks have washbasins in cabins. Excellent facilities for babies and disabled visitors. Laundry. Fridge hire. Shop, bar/restaurant and takeaway (27/3-29/9). Play area. Games room. Cinema, TV and video room. Fitness centre. Wellness amenities. Tennis. Football pitch. Bicycle hire. Library. Entertainment for all ages. WiFi over site (charged). No charcoal barbecues. Off site: Beach 900 m. Fishing and riding 1 km. Golf 7 km.

**Open:** 31 March - 31 October.

**Directions**

Labenne is on the N10. In Labenne, head west on D126 signed Labenne-Océan and site is on right in 4 km. GPS: 43.59570, -1.45638

**Charges 2013**

| Per unit incl. 2 persons | |
| --- | --- |
| and electricity | € 18.00 - € 50.00 |
| extra person | € 6.00 - € 9.00 |
| child (3-6 yrs) | free |
| dog | € 5.00 |

Between the forest, the dunes and the océan

Yelloh! village SYLVAMAR ***** - Avenue de l'Océan - 40530 Labenne Océan
Tél. : +33 (0)5 59 45 75 16 - Fax : +33 (0)5 59 45 46 39 - E mail : camping@sylvamar.fr - Site Web : www.sylvamar.fr

## Lacanau-Océan
### Yelloh! Village les Grands Pins

Plage Nord, F-33680 Lacanau-Océan (Gironde) T: 05 56 03 20 77. E: reception@lesgrandspins.com

**alanrogers.com/FR33130**

This Atlantic coast holiday site with direct access to a fine sandy beach, is on undulating terrain amongst tall pine trees. A large site with 576 pitches, there are 370 hardstanding pitches of varying sizes for touring units all with electricity (12A). One half of the site is a traffic free zone (except for arrival or departure day, caravans are placed on the pitch, with separate areas outside for parking). There are a good number of tent pitches, those in the centre of the site having some of the best views. This popular site has an excellent range of facilities available for the whole season.

**Facilities**

Four well equipped toilet blocks, one heated, include baby room and facilities for disabled campers. Launderette. Motorcaravan services. Dog showers. Supermarket. Bar with TV. Restaurant and takeaway. Part-covered, heated swimming pool complex (800 sq.m; lifeguard July/Aug) with sunbathing surround and jacuzzi (all season). Fitness activities (charged) and wellness suite. Games room. Pool tables. Multisports pitch. Tennis. Boules. Two play areas. Adventure playground. BMX course. Bicycle hire. Organised activities. WiFi in bar (charged). Communal barbecue areas. Off site: Golf, riding and bicycle hire 5 km.

**Open:** 14 April - 22 September.

**Directions**

From Bordeaux take N125/D6 west to Lacanau-Océan. At second roundabout, take second exit: Plage Nord, follow signs to 'campings'. Les Grand Pins signed to right at the far end of road. GPS: 45.01107, -1.19337

**Charges guide**

| Per unit incl. 2 persons | |
| --- | --- |
| and electricity | € 20.00 - € 49.00 |
| extra person | € 6.00 - € 9.00 |
| child (3-12 yrs) | free - € 7.00 |
| dog | € 4.00 |

For latest campsite news, availability and prices visit
# alanrogers.com

## Lacanau-Lac
### Camping le Tedey

Par le Moutchic, route de Longarisse, F-33680 Lacanau-Lac (Gironde) T: 05 56 03 00 15.
E: camping@le-tedey.com **alanrogers.com/FR33290**

With direct access to a large lake and beach, this site enjoys a beautiful tranquil position set in an area of 14 hectares amidst mature pine trees. There are 680 pitches of which 620 are for touring units, with just 38 mobile homes and chalets available for rent. The pitches are generally level and grassy although parts of the site are on a slope. The pitches are shady with dappled sunlight breaking through the trees. Electricity is available to all pitches and 213 also have water and waste water drainage. The bar is close to the lake with a large indoor and outdoor seating area. The owners and staff are friendly and helpful and English is spoken. There is an open-air cinema on Saturdays and Wednesdays as well as other entertainment in July and August. A children's club is also organised. The takeaway sells a variety of food and the shop next door is well stocked. This is an attractive, well maintained site where you get a feeling of space and calm. There are many places of interest nearby and it is a short drive to Bordeaux.

**Facilities**

Four modern sanitary blocks with facilities for disabled visitors and babies. Laundry facilities. Shop (8/5-15/9). Bar with terrace (1/6-15/9). Crêperie (16/6-11/9). Takeaway (25/6-3/9). Bicycle hire. Boating on the lake. Fishing. Pétanque. Playground. Gas barbecues only on pitches. Dogs are not accepted in July/Aug. WiFi throughout (charged). Off site: Riding and golf 3 km. Beach 5 km. Surfing. Cycling.

**Open:** 27 April - 21 September.

**Directions**

From Lacanau take the D6 to Lacanau-Océan. Take Route de Longarisse and the site is well signed. GPS: 44.98620, -1.13410

**Charges guide**

Per unit incl. 2 persons
and electricity                                € 21.00 - € 30.00

## Lanouaille
### Moulin de la Jarousse

Moulin de la jarousse, F-24270 Lanouaille (Dordogne) T: 05 53 52 37 91.
E: contact@location-en-dordogne.com **alanrogers.com/FR24960**

Le Moulin de la Jarousse is in the Périgord Vert Regional Park covering 15 hectares of hilly forest, ponds and meadows. The accommodation includes the Gîtes de Clément, a restored farmhouse with its own private swimming pool and meadow, attractive log cabins located in the forest, overlooking the lake and yurts in an open meadow. Scattered around the site are some tree houses accessed via scramble nets or rope bridges. Most of these have few facilities and are a long way from the toilet blocks. Please note that there are no touring pitches here. The site is unsuitable for campers with walking difficulties, and torches are essential. On-site amenities include a covered swimming pool (with waterslide), a children's playground and free fishing in the large fishing lake.

**Facilities**

Two small, heated toilet blocks, one near the yurts, the other by the tree houses. Facilities for disabled visitors. Table d'hôte. Covered swimming pool. Waterslide. Canoe hire. Large children's playground. 2 fishing lakes. Football. Volleyball. Badminton. Organised children's activities. Wellness centre. Scandinavian treatments and a beauty salon. Free WiFi in reception area. Off site: Rouffiac recreational centre at Payzac. Tree climbing. Many ancient market towns and villages, caves, castles and museums.

**Open:** 1 March - 31 December.

**Directions**

Leave A20 autoroute south of Limoges, exit 36. Take D704 south through St Yrieix-la-Perche. After a further 12 km. at l'Hépital, turn east at site sign. Follow narrow lanes to site in 4 km. GPS: 45.437, 1.18421

**Charges guide**

Contact the site for details.

**FREE** Alan Rogers Travel Card
Extra benefits and savings - see page 10

## Laruns

### Camping des Gaves

Quartier Pon, F-64440 Laruns (Pyrénées-Atlantiques) T: 05 59 05 32 37. E: campingdesgaves@wanadoo.fr
alanrogers.com/FR64040

Set in a secluded valley, Camping des Gaves is a clean, small and well managed site, open all year, with very friendly owners and staff. It is set high in Pyrennean walking country on one of the routes to Spain and is only 30 km. from the Spanish border. There are 99 pitches including 43 level grassed touring pitches of which 38 are fully serviced, numbered and separated (the remainder are used for seasonal units). Mature trees provide plenty of shade. The river runs alongside the site (well fenced) and fishing is possible. The busy little tourist town of Laruns is only a short walk.

**Facilities**

The very clean toilet block can be heated in cool weather and has modern fittings. Washbasins for ladies in curtained cubicles and one shower in ladies' suitable for showering children. Basic facilities for disabled visitors. Laundry room. Motorcaravan service point. No shop but baker calls daily (July/Aug). Small bar with large screen TV, pool and video games (July/Aug). Larger bar with table tennis. Small play area. Boules. Volleyball. Fishing. Free WiFi. 16 mobile homes/chalets to rent. Off site: Bicycle hire 500 m. Shops, restaurant and bars 1 km.

**Open:** All year.

**Directions**

Take N134 from Pau towards Olorons and branch left on D934 at Gan. Follow to Laruns and just after town, turn left following signs to site. Note: the D918 to the east of Laruns is not recommended for large units. GPS: 42.98241, -0.41591

**Charges guide**

| Per unit incl. 2 persons and electricity | € 16.90 - € 24.40 |
| extra person | € 3.20 - € 4.80 |

## Le Bugue

### Camping le Rocher de la Granelle

Route de Buisson, la Borie, F-24260 Le Bugue (Dordogne) T: 05 53 07 24 32. E: info@lagranelle.com
alanrogers.com/FR24225

Le Rocher de la Granelle is a friendly site, attractively located on the banks of the River Vézère, and close to the lively market town of Le Bugue. There are 150 good sized, level grass pitches, 120 of which are for touring, all with 10A electricity. Most are well shaded and some have pleasant views across the Vézère. On-site amenities include a swimming pool, water slide and a bar/snack bar which is the base for activities and entertainment during the peak season. Many of the facilities here are being upgraded.

**Facilities**

Two toilet blocks are being refurbished and provide all the necessary facilities. Shop. Snack bar/bar (May-mid Sept). Swimming pool, children's pool, water slide (May-mid Sept). Sports field. Play area. Activity and entertainment programme. Direct river access. Fishing. Tennis. Pétanque. Bicycle hire. Free WiFi near reception. Off site: Shops and restaurants in Le Bugue 1 km. Beach and riding 5 km. Golf 10 km. Walking and cycle trails.

**Open:** 1 April - 1 October.

**Directions**

From Bergerac, head east on D660, D703 then D29 to le Buisson-de-Cadouin. Take D51 then D31e north towards Le Bugue. Follow signs to site on left, just south of Le Bugue. GPS: 44.911738, 0.916666

**Charges guide**

| Per unit incl. 2 persons and electricity | € 15.00 - € 29.00 |
| extra person | € 5.20 |

## Le Bugue

### Camping Caravaning la Linotte

F-24260 Le Bugue (Dordogne) T: 05 53 07 17 61. E: lalinotte@vagues-oceanes.com
alanrogers.com/FR24260

This is a pleasant, good quality site with plenty of space and fantastic views from the bar, restaurant and pool complex. It is located in the heart of the Périgord Noir and is conveniently placed to visit many of the attractions in the area. The amenities are very good and include a heated swimming pool, a children's pool, a jacuzzi and two toboggans. Of the 120 level pitches, 90 are for mobile homes and chalets, leaving just 30 pitches for touring units. These are of a good size, all with electricity (5A), separated by hedges for privacy and tall trees provide good shade.

**Facilities**

A modern toilet block includes facilities for babies and disabled visitors. Bar/restaurant also provide takeaway (1/7-30/8). Small shop with bread to order. Pool complex (1/6-mid Sept). Swimming pool and water slides. Splash pool and paddling pool (both heated). Jacuzzi. Small playground with trampolines. Bicycle hire. Boules. WiFi near reception (charged). Off site: Riding 8 km. Canoes. Ancient market towns and villages, châteaux and caves.

**Open:** 4 April - 27 September.

**Directions**

From Le Bugue follow signs for Périgueux north, D710. On outskirts of Le Bugue turn right onto D32E (site signed). After 1.5 km. turn right along narrow lane to site (900 m). GPS: 44.934117, 0.9371

**Charges guide**

| Per unit incl. 2 persons and electricity | € 21.00 - € 33.00 |
| extra person | € 4.50 - € 6.70 |
| child (under 5 yrs) | free - € 4.10 |

For latest campsite news, availability and prices visit
**alanrogers.com**

## Le Bugue
### Camping les Trois Caupain
Le Port, F-24260 Le Bugue (Dordogne) T: 05 53 07 24 60. E: info@camping-bugue.com
**alanrogers.com/FR24510**

A superb, mature, ex-municipal site, les Trois Caupain is less than 1 km. from Le Bugue, which has a range of supermarkets and tourist attractions. The site carefully blends mobile homes and camping pitches, and fruiting plum trees abound on the site. The well marked pitches are neat, level and mostly shaded, with water and electricity hook ups close by. The current owners, the three Caupain family members, will do all they can to make your stay a pleasant one. The campsite is less than fifty metres away from the river in an area that is popular with tourists.

**Facilities**

Two clean and well maintained sanitary blocks include toilet and shower for disabled visitors. Excellent laundry room. Baby room with bath. Motorcaravan service point. Small shop selling local produce all season. Bar with pool table and TV. Restaurant with terrace (high season). Takeaway. Heated swimming pool and paddling pool. Play area. Boules. Fishing. Twice weekly entertainment in high season. WiFi in bar area. Off site: Riding 3 km. Golf 8 km.

**Open:** 1 April - 30 October.

**Directions**

From Le Bugue, take D703 heading southeast and site is less than 1 km. from the town centre, well signed. Turn right off the main road and site is less than 800 m. along this road on the left.
GPS: 44.90932, 0.93144

**Charges guide**

| Per unit incl. 2 persons and electricity (6A) | € 15.20 - € 20.80 |
|---|---|

---

## Le Buisson-de-Cadouin
### Camping Domaine de Fromengal
F-24480 Le Buisson-de-Cadouin (Dordogne) T: 05 53 63 11 55. E: fromengal@domaine-fromengal.com
**alanrogers.com/FR24810**

Fromengal is a good quality site in the Périgord Noir. Set in over 22 acres, it was formerly an ancient farm and now offers a relaxed family atmosphere amid a calm, tranquil and natural setting. There is abundant vegetation. The pitches are of a good size, separated by shrubs and hedging with a mixture of sunshine and shade. There are 93 pitches, 37 for touring units, most with 6A electricity (ten also with water and drainage). The remaining pitches are used for chalets and mobile homes to rent. There is a good range of new amenities, notably a fine heated swimming pool and a restaurant built in the local style and serving food from the area. In high season there is an entertainment and activity programme.

**Facilities**

The single sanitary block includes facilities for disabled visitors. Washing machine and dryer. Bar, restaurant, takeaway and shop (July/Aug). Swimming pools (one heated) and slides. Pétanque. BMX circuit. Play area. Entertainment programme. Children's club. Library. Skate park. Bicycle hire. Tennis, archery and quad bikes for children (charged). WiFi (charged). Only charcoal barbecues are permitted. Off site: River beach 5 km.

**Open:** 13 April - 15 October.

**Directions**

Take the D703 Bergerac-Sarlat road turning off at Lalinde towards Le Buisson-de-Cadouin. Site is probably the best signed in the Dordogne.
GPS: 44.82298, 0.8604

**Charges guide**

| Per unit incl. 1 or 2 persons and electricity | € 22.00 - € 38.00 |
|---|---|

---

## Le Verdon-sur-Mer
### Sunêlia la Pointe du Medoc
Route de la Pointe de Grave, F-33123 Le Verdon-sur-Mer (Gironde) T: 05 56 73 39 99.
E: info@camping-lapointedumedoc.com **alanrogers.com/FR33210**

Situated roughly equidistant between a sandy Atlantic beach (accessed by a pleasant walk through the forest opposite the site) and the Gironde estuary, this site has 260 pitches. There are 112 for touring units with 10A electricity, 70 with water and drainage. Heavier units will need to use those pitches with plastic runners to ensure easy access on and off the sandy ground. The pitches are generally large and most are in full sun but some smaller ones towards the rear of the site offer much more shade. This is a quiet campsite, but in July and August it becomes busy with families enjoying the excellent facilities.

**Facilities**

Good clean sanitary facilities. Shop (July/Aug). Bar, restaurant and takeaway. Outdoor swimming pool (heated) with water jets, jacuzzi and paddling pool. Indoor pool. Massage. Minigolf. Multisports terrain. Bicycle hire. Communal barbecues. Organised entertainment and children's club (4-11 yrs) all season. Small farm and children's garden. Activities for teenagers in July/Aug. Internet and WiFi. Max. 1 dog. Off site: Sea fishing 1 km.

**Open:** 26 April - 12 September.

**Directions**

Site is on N215 (D1215) south of Le Verdon. Follow signs for Royan and Point de Medoc on approach to Le Verdon. Site is on right. The ferry from Royan is a more expensive option. GPS: 45.54540, -1.07950

**Charges guide**

| Per unit incl. 2 persons and electricity | € 18.00 - € 26.00 |
|---|---|
| extra person (over 4 yrs) | € 3.00 - € 6.00 |

**FREE** Alan Rogers Travel Card
Extra benefits and savings - see page 10

## Léon
### Yelloh! Village Punta Lago

Avenue du Lac, F-40550 Léon (Landes) T: 05 58 49 24 40. E: info@yellohvillage-punta-lago.com
alanrogers.com/FR40290

Eight hundred metres from the charming village of Léon, this site offers 90 above average size, level, grass touring pitches (some sandy). All have electricity (10A), water and drainage and they are separated by hedges. Shade on most pitches is provided by the tall oak trees. The toilets, showers, basins and laundry are housed in one central block adjacent to the heated indoor swimming pool, sauna, spa and gym room. All are in good order with facilities for disabled visitors, babies and children. The outdoor swimming pool and paddling pool are surrounded by plenty of sunbeds.

**Facilities**

The single toilet block is clean and well maintained. Facilities for children and disabled visitors. Laundry facilities. Large shop. Restaurant and takeaway. Bar. Heated indoor and outdoor pools. Sauna and jacuzzi. TV room. Bicycle hire. Play area. Fridge hire. Pétanque. Beach volleyball. Miniclub (5-12 yrs). Entertainment and activities (July/Aug). Communal barbecues only. WiFi (charged). Off site: ATM 100 m. Lake 300 m. with sailing, kayaking, swimming and fishing. Léon 800 m. with daily market (15/6-15/9).

**Open:** 4 April - 23 September.

**Directions**

From N10 take exit 12 towards Castets. Take D142 to Léon and at island take first exit to 'Centre Ville'. At T-junction turn left on D652 and after 300 m. turn left at sign for site and lake. After 800 m. site is on the left. GPS: 43.8842, -1.313

**Charges guide**

| Per unit incl. 2 persons and electricity | € 17.00 - € 44.00 |
| extra person | € 5.00 - € 7.00 |

## Les Eglisottes
### Camping l'Eau Vive

6bis Fond de Bournac, F-33230 Les Eglisottes (Gironde) T: 05 57 69 56 09. E: camping-leau-vive@sfr.fr
alanrogers.com/FR33830

This spacious, well maintained campsite with 100 larger than average, level pitches is slightly out of the normal tourist areas, but ideal for a quiet break. It is run by a very friendly Dutch couple who speak excellent English. The campsite borders onto La Dronne river for fishing and is next to a swimming pool with diving board. All pitches have water and 16A electricity. One very clean toilet block has a separate suite for disabled campers. There is a small, very reasonable restaurant and shop on site, and the town of Les Eglisottes is a ten minute walk. Free WiFi.

**Facilities**

One clean and well equipped toilet block with facilities for babies and disabled visitors. Washing machine. Washing line. Motorcaravan services. Shop. Bar with TV. Restaurant and takeaway meals (1/7-30/8). 3 play areas. Children's club. Football. Basketball. Volleyball. Boules. WiFi. Communal barbecue. Mobile homes to rent. Off site: Large swimming pool with diving area (lifeguard July/Aug) 50 m. Tennis 100 m. Goitres 10 km.

**Open:** 1 May - 30 September.

**Directions**

Located 50 km. north east of Bordeaux. From La Roche-Chalais take D674 south for 7.5 km. to Les Eglisottes-et-Chalaures where the site is well signed. GPS: 45.097196, -0.04976

**Charges guide**

| Per unit incl. 2 persons and electricity | € 21.00 |
| extra person | € 3.40 - € 4.90 |

## Les Eyzies-de-Tayac
### Camping la Rivière

3 route du Sorcier, F-24620 Les Eyzies-de-Tayac (Dordogne) T: 05 53 06 97 14. E: la-riviere@wanadoo.fr
alanrogers.com/FR24680

This is a site with some Périgordine character situated beside the Vézère river. The buildings are in the traditional style of the area. It is owned and run by a French family who are friendly and helpful, and visitors to the site speak highly of them. They are proud of the site's ecological credentials. There are 120 pitches of which ten are used for chalets and mobile homes. All have 6/10A electricity connections, 75 also have water and drainage. The pitches are level, easily accessible and offer full shade. The site also provides a six-bedroom hotel. This attractive building also houses the bar, restaurant and shop.

**Facilities**

Three sanitary blocks, two of them new. Facilities for disabled visitors and babies in the new, heated blocks. Washing machine and dryer. Motorcaravan service point. Small shop. Attractive bar/restaurant and outside eating area. Takeaway. Swimming pool and toddler's pool. Play area. Half tennis court. Canoeing. Fishing. Boules. Music evenings and children's shows. WiFi (free). Off site: Fishing 200 m. Bicycle hire and riding 1 km. Golf 20 km.

**Open:** 12 April - 1 November.

**Directions**

From Périgueux take D47 to Les Eyzies. After Manaurie and approaching Les Eyzies, turn right just before the bridge over the river. Then take the next left. Site is signed from D47. GPS: 44.93769, 1.00603

**Charges guide**

| Per unit incl. 2 persons and electricity | € 17.58 - € 26.75 |
| extra person | € 3.90 - € 6.60 |

## Messanges
### Airotel le Vieux Port

Plage Sud, F-40660 Messanges (Landes) T: 01 76 76 70 00. E: contact@levieuxport.com
**alanrogers.com/FR40180**

510

A well established destination appealing particularly to families with teenage children, this lively site has 1,546 pitches (975 for touring) of mixed sizes, most with electricity (6A). The camping area is well shaded by pines and pitches are generally of a good size, attractively grouped around the toilet blocks. There are many tour operators here and well over a third of the site is taken up with mobile homes and chalets. An enormous 7,000 sq.m. aquatic park is now open, and is the largest on any French campsite. This heated complex is exceptional, boasting five outdoor pools (all 25°C), three large water slides plus waves and a heated spa. There is also a heated indoor pool. The area to the north of Bayonne is heavily forested and a number of very large campsites are attractively located close to the superb Atlantic beaches. Le Vieux Port is probably the largest, and certainly one of the most impressive, of these. At the back of the site a path leads across the dunes to a good beach (400 m). Other recent innovations include an outdoor fitness area and a superb riding centre. All in all, this is a lively site with a great deal to offer an active family.

### Facilities

Nine well appointed, recently renovated toilet blocks with facilities for disabled visitors. Motorcaravan services. Good supermarket and various smaller shops in high season. Several restaurants, takeaway and three bars (all open all season). Large pool complex (no Bermuda shorts; open all season) including new covered pool and Polynesian themed bar. Tennis. Multisports pitch. Minigolf. Outdoor fitness area. Fishing. Bicycle hire. Riding centre. Organised activities including frequent discos and karaoke evenings (31/3-14/9). Spa, massages and beauty area. Only communal barbecues are allowed. WiFi over site (charged). Off site: Beach 400 m. Sailing 2 km. Golf 8 km.

**Open:** 23 March - 29 September.

### Directions

Leave RN10 at Magescq exit heading for Soustons. Pass through Soustons following signs for Vieux-Boucau. Bypass this town and site is clearly signed to the left at second roundabout. GPS: 43.79778, -1.40111

### Charges guide

| Per unit incl. 2 persons | |
|---|---|
| and electricity | € 21.55 - € 61.80 |
| extra person | € 4.85 - € 9.10 |
| child (under 13 yrs) | € 3.85 - € 6.25 |
| dog | € 3.10 - € 5.85 |

Camping Cheques accepted.

LE VIEUX PORT
AIROTEL CARAVANING
★★★★★

**Direct access to the beach!**
Heated waterpark, wellness center and animation from the opening!

Winner Alan Rogers Awards 2009

● MESSANGES

Plage sud,
40660 Messanges, Landes

✆ +33 176 76 70 00   💻 www.levieuxport.com

## Limeuil

### Camping la Ferme de Perdigat

F-24510 Limeuil (Dordogne) T: 05 53 63 31 54. E: accueil@perdigat.com
alanrogers.com/FR24750

The delightful French owners, Michel and Noelle Paille, make this a happy place to stay and everyone we spoke to praised it highly. The site nestles beautifully in a very natural environment at the base of tree-lined hills which provide a wonderful scenic background. Flowers, bushes and trees give a superb sense of well being and much care and attention is given to the environment. A superb lake is 100 m. from the site where visitors staying at the farm may fish free of charge. The river is also the same distance away in a different direction. There are 52 touring pitches (all with electricity), and 15 mobile homes to rent.

**Facilities**

The completely refurbished shower block is bright and airy. Laundry facilities. Motorcaravan services. Shop (1/5-30/9). Bar (1/5-30/9) and restaurant with terrace (newly refurbished, 1/5-20/9). Swimming and paddling pools. Games room. WiFi in the bar area. Play area. Private fishing lake and the Vézère river. Canoes and kayaks. Off site: Limeuil listed as one of the most beautiful villages in France. Riding 2 km. Supermarkets 3 km.

**Open:** 23 March - 19 October.

**Directions**

From Le Bugue, take the D703 to La Borie and turn left to Limeuil. Campsite is well signed.
GPS: 44.894765, 0.912509

**Charges guide**

| | |
|---|---|
| Per unit incl. 2 persons and electricity (10A) | € 12.00 - € 18.30 |
| extra person | € 3.00 - € 4.70 |
| child (under 8 yrs) | € 2.00 - € 3.10 |
| dog (max. 2) | free - € 2.00 |

## Messanges

### Camping les Acacias

Quartier Delest, route d'Azur (C3), F-40660 Messanges (Landes) T: 05 58 48 01 78.
E: lesacacias@lesacacias.com alanrogers.com/FR40220

Close to the Atlantic beaches of Les Landes, this small, well designed campsite is quiet and peaceful. Family run and well cared for, it is a site for couples looking for relaxation or families who want a safe environment for young children to play. There are 76 flat touring pitches, all with 6/10A electricity and separated by trees and shrubs. Mobile homes are arranged unobtrusively on two sides of the site. The pitches are easily accessed by tarmac roads, although units longer than 7 m. may have some difficulty. M and Mme Dourthe are constantly seeking to improve this charming campsite.

**Facilities**

One modern, clean toilet block with facilities for disabled visitors. Laundry facilities. Motorcaravan services. Fridge hire. Shop (15/6-15/9). Takeaway (1/7-31/8). Games room. Play area. Children's entertainment. Small library. Boules. Football field. Bicycle hire. Security box hire. Communal barbecues only. WiFi. Off site: Bus service 1 km. Riding 1.5 km. Beach and supermarket 2 km.

**Open:** 25 March - 25 October.

**Directions**

Approaching Messanges from the north, continue through the centre of village on the D652 (site signed). At roundabout turn left onto C3 towards Azur and site is 1.5 km. on left. GPS: 43.79836, -1.37550

**Charges 2013**

| | |
|---|---|
| Per unit incl. 2 persons and electricity | € 14.40 - € 22.50 |
| extra person | € 3.40 - € 4.60 |

## Mézos

### Le Village Tropical Sen-Yan

Le Village Tropical, F-40170 Mézos (Landes) T: 05 58 42 60 05. E: reception@sen-yan.com
alanrogers.com/FR40110

This exotic family site is about 12 km. from the Atlantic coast in the Landes forest area, just outside the village. There are 100 touring pitches set around a similar number of mobile homes. Pitches are marked with hedges and have electricity (6A). The reception, bar and pool area is almost tropical with the luxuriant greenery of its banana trees, palm trees, tropical flowers and its straw sunshades. The covered, heated pool, new water slide, gym with sauna and jacuzzi all add to the attractiveness. A new covered animation area provides entertainment and discos during high season. A stunning new open swimming area (1/7-31/8) is surrounded by white sand.

**Facilities**

Three well maintained and clean toilet blocks with good quality fittings and showers, washbasins in cabins and British style WCs. The newest block is especially suitable for low season visitors with a special section for babies, plus excellent facilities for disabled campers. Shop (from 15/6). Bar, restaurant and snacks (1/7-31/8). Outdoor swimming pools (1/6-15/9). Heated indoor pool (1/5-15/9). Practice golf. Bicycle hire. No charcoal barbecues. WiFi (charged). Archery. Off site: Fishing 500 m. Riding 6 km.

**Open:** 1 May - 15 September.

**Directions**

From N10 take exit 14 (Onesse-Laharie), then D38 Bias/Mimizan road. After 13 km. turn south to Mézos from where site is signed. GPS: 44.07208, -1.15671

**Charges guide**

| | |
|---|---|
| Per unit incl. 2 persons and electricity | € 24.00 - € 34.50 |
| extra person | € 5.00 - € 6.00 |
| dog | free - € 4.00 |
| child (under 7 yrs) | free - € 5.00 |

For latest campsite news, availability and prices visit
**alanrogers.com**

# Mimizan-Plage

## Airotel Club Marina-Landes

Rue Marina, F-40200 Mimizan (Landes) T: 05 58 09 12 66. E: contact@clubmarina.com

**alanrogers.com/FR40080**

Well maintained and clean, with helpful staff, Club Marina-Landes would be a very good choice for a family holiday. Activities include discos, play groups for children, specially trained staff to entertain teenagers and concerts for more mature campers. There are numerous sports opportunities and a superb sandy beach nearby. A nightly curfew ensures that all have a good night's sleep. A new leisure pool is planned. The site has 361 touring pitches (316 with 10A electricity) and 147 mobile homes and chalets for rent. The pitches are on firm grass, most with hedges and they are large (mostly 100 sq.m. or larger). If ever a campsite could be said to have two separate identities, then Club Marina-Landes is surely the one. In early and late season it is quiet, with the pace of life in low gear – come July and until 1 September, all the facilities are open and there is fun for all the family with the chance that family members will only meet together at meal times.

### Facilities

Five toilet blocks (opened as required) are well maintained with showers and many washbasins in cabins. Facilities for babies, children and disabled visitors. Laundry facilities. Motorcaravan services. Fridge hire. Shop (freshly baked bread) and bar (4/5-19/9). Restaurant, snack bar, pizzas and takeaway (4/5-19/9). Covered pool and outdoor pools. Minigolf. Tennis. Bicycle hire. Play area. Entertainment and activities (high season). Gas or electric barbecues only. WiFi (charged). Off site: Beach and fishing 500 m. Bus service and riding 1 km. Golf 8 km. Mimizan 8 km.

**Open:** 4 May - 20 September.

### Directions

Heading west from Mimizan centre, take D626 passing Abbey Museum. Straight on at lights (crossing D87/D67), at next lights turn left. After 2 km. at T-junction turn left. Follow signs to site. GPS: 44.20447, -1.29099

### Charges guide

| | |
|---|---|
| Per unit incl. 3 persons and electricity | € 18.00 - € 52.00 |
| extra person | € 4.00 - € 10.00 |
| child (4-12 yrs) | € 3.00 - € 8.00 |
| dog | € 3.00 - € 5.00 |

**FREE** Alan Rogers Travel Card
Extra benefits and savings - see page 10

## Moliets-Plage
### Le Saint-Martin Camping

Avenue de l'Océan, F-40660 Moliets-Plage (Landes) T: 05 58 48 52 30. E: contact@camping-saint-martin.fr
alanrogers.com/FR40190

A family site aimed mainly at couples and young families, le Saint-Martin is a welcome change from most of the sites in this area in that it has only a relatively small number of mobile homes (127) compared to the number of touring pitches (383). First impressions are of a neat, tidy, well cared for site and the direct access to a wonderful fine sandy beach is an added bonus. The pitches are mainly typically French in style with low hedges separating them, and with some shade. Electricity hook ups are 10/15A and a number of pitches also have water and drainage. Entertainment in high season is low key (with the emphasis on quiet nights) – daytime competitions and a miniclub, plus the occasional evening entertainment, well away from the pitches and with no discos or karaoke. With pleasant chalets and mobile homes to rent, a top-class pool complex and an 18-hole golf course 700 m. away (special rates negotiated), this would be an ideal destination for a golfing weekend or longer stay.

### Facilities

Seven toilet blocks of a high standard and very well maintained, have washbasins in cabins, large showers, baby rooms and facilities for disabled visitors. Motorcaravan service point. Washing machines and dryers. Fridge rental. Supermarket. Bars, restaurants and takeaways. Indoor pool, jacuzzi and sauna (charged July/Aug). Outdoor pool area with jacuzzi and paddling pool (15/6-15/9). Multisport pitch. Play area. Bicycle hire. Beach access. Internet access. Electric barbecues only. Off site: Fishing and beach 300 m. Golf and tennis 700 m.

**Open:** Easter - 1 November.

### Directions

From the N10 take D142 to Lèon, then D652 to Moliets-et-Mar. Follow signs to Moliets-Plage, site is well signed. GPS: 43.85242, -1.38732

### Charges guide

| Per unit incl. 2 persons | |
|---|---|
| and electricity | € 22.70 - € 48.60 |
| extra person | € 6.00 - € 8.50 |
| child (under 13 yrs) | € 4.00 - € 6.00 |
| dog | free - € 5.00 |

Prices are for reserved pitches.

## Monpazier
### Camping le Moulin de David

Gaugeac, F-24540 Monpazier (Dordogne) T: 05 53 22 65 25. E: contact@moulindedavid.com
alanrogers.com/FR24080

Set in a 14 hectare wooded valley, le Moulin de David has 160 pitches split into two sections, 102 are available for touring units – 33 below the central reception complex in a shaded situation, and 69 above on partly terraced ground with varying degrees of shade. All pitches have electricity (10-16A). Spacing is good and there is no crowding. The site has been planted with a variety of shrubs and trees and combined with the small stream that runs through the centre they create a beautiful and tranquil setting. This pleasant and attractive site is one for those who enjoy peace, away from the hustle and bustle of the main Dordogne attractions, yet sufficiently close for them to be accessible.

### Facilities

Three good toilet blocks include facilities for disabled visitors and babies. Laundry room. Good shop. Bar/restaurant with shaded patio, takeaway. Swimming pool and paddling pool, freshwater pool with waterslide. Play area. Boules. Half-court tennis. Trampoline. Library. Events, games and canoe trips. Barbecues for hire. Mobile homes for rent. Bicycle hire. Internet access in reception area and WiFi on the terrace (free).

**Open:** 13 April - 29 September.

### Directions

From Monpazier take the D2 Villeréal road. Take third turning left (after 2 km), signed to Moulin de David and Gaugeac Mairie. Site is 500 m. along this road on the left. GPS: 44.65949, 0.87898

### Charges 2013

| Per unit incl. 2 persons | |
|---|---|
| and electricity | € 18.00 - € 24.00 |
| extra person | € 3.00 - € 5.00 |
| dog | € 3.00 |

For latest campsite news, availability and prices visit
# alanrogers.com

## Montignac
### Camping le Paradis

Saint Léon-sur-Vézère, F-24290 Montignac (Dordogne) T: 05 53 50 72 64. E: le-paradis@perigord.com
**alanrogers.com/FR24060**

Le Paradis is an excellent, very well maintained riverside site, halfway between Les Eyzies and Montignac. The site is landscaped with a variety of mature shrubs and trees. The gardens are beautiful, which gives a wonderful sense of tranquillity. It is very easy to relax on this ecologically friendly site. Systems of reed filters enhance the efficient natural drainage. This is a family run site and you are guaranteed a warm and friendly welcome. There are 200 good sized pitches, with 45 with mobile homes to rent. The 134 touring pitches are level and with easy access, all with 10A electricity, water and drainage. There are some special pitches for motorcaravans. An excellent restaurant offers a good menu, reasonably priced and using fresh local produce where appropriate. The terraced area outside makes for a convivial family atmosphere. There are many sport and leisure activities. Direct access to the Vézère river for canoeing and swimming is possible at one end of the site. Organised games, competitions and evening events are aimed at maintaining a true French flavour. English is spoken. This is a site of real quality, which we thoroughly recommend.

#### Facilities
High quality, well equipped, heated toilet blocks are kept very clean. Well stocked shop (with gas). Good restaurant, takeaway. Good pool complex heated in low season, paddling pool. Play area. Tennis. BMX track. Multisports court. Canoe hire. Fishing. Bicycle hire. Quad bike and horse riding excursions. WiFi throughout. Large units accepted by arrangement. Mobile homes to rent (no smoking) including one for visitors with disabilities (no dogs permitted). Off site: Riding 8 km.

**Open:** 1 April - 20 October.

#### Directions
Site is 12 km. north of Les Eyzies and 3 km. south of St Léon-sur-Vézère, on the east side of the D706. GPS: 45.00207, 1.0711

#### Charges guide
| | |
|---|---|
| Per unit incl. 2 persons and electricity | € 22.50 - € 32.60 |
| extra person | € 5.75 - € 7.90 |
| child (3-12 yrs) | € 4.75 - € 6.80 |

Camping Cheques accepted.

Camping Le Paradis - 24290 St. Leon sur Vézère
tel.: 05 53 50 72 64 - fax: 05 53 50 75 90 - le-paradis@perigord.com - www.le-paradis.fr

## Navarrenx
### Camping Beau Rivage

Allée des Marronniers, F-64190 Navarrenx (Pyrénées-Atlantiques) T: 05 59 66 10 00. E: beaucamping@free.fr
**alanrogers.com/FR64120**

This well cared for site lies just outside the walls of the bastide town of Navarrenx. It is owned and run by an English couple, Richard and Wendy Curtis, who take great pride in their site. Many bushes and trees have been planted and a total of 54 touring pitches are available either on hardstanding with full services or on grass, the latter having more shade. A traffic-free track leads to the town where all essential shops can be found. Richard trained as a pizzaiolo and offers fresh pizzas in the evenings. Within driving distance of the Atlantic Coast and the Pyrenees mountains, this is a good site for touring.

#### Facilities
Two very clean sanitary blocks with good separate facilities for ladies and men include modern facilities for babies and disabled visitors. Laundry facilities. Small shop. Locally produced wines in reception. Homemade pizzas. Small swimming pool (1/5-30/9). Playground for small children. Play field. Max. 2 dogs. Chalets for rent. Caravan storage. WiFi (charged). Off site: Municipal pool adjacent. Shop at end of road. Town is five minutes walk.

**Open:** 25 March - 16 October.

#### Directions
From the north take D936 to Navarrenx. Turn left at first roundabout on D115 into Navarrenx. Turn left at T-junction, go over bridge and follow walls of town all the way around. At next island turn right on D947 and site is signed from here. GPS: 43.32001, -0.761

#### Charges guide
| | |
|---|---|
| Per unit incl. 2 persons and electricity | € 18.50 - € 24.50 |
| extra person | € 4.50 - € 5.50 |

**FREE** Alan Rogers Travel Card
Extra benefits and savings - see page 10

## Nontron

### Camping de Nontron

Saint Martial de Valette, F-24300 Nontron (Dordogne) T: 05 53 56 02 04. E: camping-de-nontron@orange.fr

alanrogers.com/FR24640

Open for almost all the year, this well presented, family run site is ideally situated in the Périgord Vert either as a first stop on route South, or for a much longer stay. There are 64 level, grassy pitches, 60 for touring (10A electricity), two for mobile homes and eight are studios available for rent. All are level with easy access and separated by hedges and trees providing some good shade. In Nontron you can see the famous French pocket knives being made, together with crayons that look like twigs.

**Facilities**

Refurbished and well equipped toilet block with facilities for disabled visitors and babies. Laundry with washing machines and ironing boards. Motorcaravan service point. Shop and takeaway (1/4-1/11). TV and games room. Boules. Play area. Charcoal barbecues only. Free WiFi over part of site. Off site: New sports complex next to site. Riding, karting 10 km. Bicycle hire 20 km. Golf.

**Open:** 3 January - 15 December.

**Directions**

From Angoulême take D939 to Périgueux. Branch left on D4, then D75 to Nontron. After Nontron take D675 towards Brantôme, campsite is 200 m. on left after entering St Martial de Valette. GPS: 45.519967, 0.65875

**Charges guide**

| | |
|---|---|
| Per unit incl. 2 persons and electricity | € 14.90 - € 16.30 |
| extra person | € 3.90 - € 4.30 |

---

## Ondres

Campé●le

### Campéole Ondres Plage

2511 route de la Plage, F-40400 Ondres (Landes) T: 05 59 45 31 48. E: ondres@campeole.com

alanrogers.com/FR40510

Ondres Plage is a recent addition to the Campéole group and is located just 300 m. from an excellent sandy beach. Accommodation here is in mobile homes or fully equipped bungalow style tents. Please note that there are just eight touring pitches at this site, all with 16A electricity. Unusually too, the site is only open to the public until 23 June and from 29 August, and is used as holiday accommodation for EDF staff during the peak season. There is a good swimming pool. Other on-site amenities include tennis and an all-weather sports terrain. This is a good base for exploring the Landes forests and the Basque Country. To the south, Biarritz is within easy reach, and boasts a new, world class maritime museum. Alternatively, the Spanish border town of Irun is worth a trip. Closer to the site, there is an excellent treetop adventure trail, as well as miles of cycle tracks through the forests.

**Facilities**

Motorcaravan services. Swimming pool. Tennis court. All-weather sports terrain. Volleyball. Bouncy castle. Mobile homes and fully equipped tents for rent. Off site: Shops, bars and restaurants in nearby Ondres. Beach and fishing 300 m. Riding 500 m. Golf 10 km.

**Open:** 31 March - 22 June and 29 August - 15 October.

**Directions**

From Ondres follow the road to Ondres-Plage. Site is just before the beach on the left. GPS: 43.574817, -1.481267

**Charges guide**

| | |
|---|---|
| Per unit incl. 2 persons and electricity | € 27.10 |

For latest campsite news, availability and prices visit

# alanrogers.com

## Parentis-en-Born

### Camping l'Arbre d'Or

75 route du Lac, F-40160 Parentis-en-Born (Landes) T: 05 58 78 41 56. E: contact@arbre-dor.com
**alanrogers.com/FR40350**

L'Arbre d'Or is a friendly, family site on the outskirts of Parentis-en-Born. There are 200 pitches here, most with electrical connections (10A). They are separated by small shrubs and have some shade from young trees. Around 90 pitches are occupied by mobile homes and chalets. L'Arbre d'Or lies 400 m. from the large Lac de Parentis where many watersports are available. The nearest coastal beach is at Biscarrosse-Plage, 19 km. distant. The site boasts two swimming pools, one of which is covered in inclement weather, as well as a convivial restaurant and an activity programme.

| Facilities | Directions |
| --- | --- |
| Two well located, clean toilet blocks have preset showers and facilities for disabled visitors. Washing machines. Bar, restaurant and takeaway (15/5-15/9; weekends in low season). Two heated swimming pools, a paddling pool and jacuzzi. Games room. Play area. Multisports court. Bicycle hire. Entertainment and activities in peak season. Communal barbecues. Mobile homes and chalets for rent. WiFi over site (charged). Off site: Lac de Parentis 400 m. | From Bordeaux head south on the A63 and then the N10 as far as Liposthey. Then head west on the D43 to Parentis-en-Born. The site is well signed from here on the Route du Lac. GPS: 44.34622, -1.0929 |

**Charges guide**

Per unit incl. 2 persons
and electricity                                  € 20.90 - € 25.80

**Open:** 1 April - 31 October.

---

## Pauillac

### Camping Municipal les Gabarreys

Route de la Rivière, F-33250 Pauillac (Gironde) T: 05 56 59 10 03. E: camping.les.gabarreys@wanadoo.fr
**alanrogers.com/FR33150**

An attractive, small site with well tended flower beds, les Gabarreys is surrounded by vineyards of the Médoc region. An excellent site, les Gabarreys has 59 pitches, most with hardstanding for caravans or motorcaravans (so pegging out awnings could be a problem), some grass pitches for tents and six mobile homes, most with electric hook-ups (5/10A, some may require long leads). The Maison du Tourisme et du Vin should be your first port of call. The surrounding area is well supplied with wine caves, and being fairly level you could perhaps cycle to some of them.

| Facilities | Directions |
| --- | --- |
| Two immaculate toilet blocks provide open and cubicle washbasins and excellent facilities for disabled visitors. Motorcaravan services. General room with satellite TV, fridge freezer and a small library. New play area. Minigolf (free) and volleyball. New spa and sauna. WiFi (charged). Off site: Fishing and bicycle hire 1 km. Riding 8 km. Beach 35 km. | Pauillac is northwest of Bordeaux. From Bordeaux take D1 to St Laurent, then D206 to Pauillac. At roundabout turn right to Pauillac Guais, then straight ahead at next roundabout and turn right before the Maison du Tourisme. GPS: 45.1852, -0.742397 |

**Charges guide**

Per unit incl. 2 persons
and electricity                                  € 17.50 - € 20.50

**Open:** 30 March - 10 October.

---

## Petit-Palais-et-Cornemps

### Flower Camping le Pressoir

29 Queyrai, F-33570 Petit-Palais-et-Cornemps (Gironde) T: 05 57 69 73 25.
E: contact@campinglepressoir.com  **alanrogers.com/FR33090**

Nestling in the famous wine producing countryside of the Lussac, Pomerol and St Emilion areas north of Bordeaux, le Pressoir is surrounded by fields of vines. The 100 large pitches are arranged on either side of a gravel road leading up a slight hill. Most are shaded by attractive trees, but almost all are sloping. They are over 100 sq.m. and equipped with electricity (10A Europlug). The old barn has been converted into a stylish bar and a really charming, separate restaurant. A quiet, family site, le Pressoir provides a comfortable base for a holiday in this area famous for good food and wine.

| Facilities | Directions |
| --- | --- |
| Fully equipped toilet block with excellent facilities for disabled visitors, and washing machine. Bar and pleasant restaurant with indoor and outdoor seating (open all year). Heated swimming pool (15/4-15/10, no Bermuda shorts). Sauna. Wellness (July/Aug). Playground with timber equipment. Bouncy castle. Trampoline. Kids' club. Pétanque. Mountain bike hire. Free WiFi. Mobile homes and bungalow tents to rent. Bicycle hire. No barbecues, but communal area provided. Off site: Tennis nearby. Fishing 1 km. Riding 5 km. Large aquatic centre 7 km. | From A89 Bordeaux-Périgueux take exit 11 to Saint Médard-de-Guizières. Turn south towards Lussac on D21. From Castillon-la-Bataille on D936 Libourne - Bergerac road, take D17 north towards St Médard then D21 through Petit-Palais. Site signed. GPS: 44.9971, -0.06326 |

**Charges guide**

Per unit incl. 2 persons
and electricity                                  € 16.50 - € 29.00
extra person                                     € 4.00 - € 7.50

**Open:** All year.

---

**FREE** Alan Rogers Travel Card
Extra benefits and savings - see page 10

## Pyla-sur-Mer

### Yelloh! Village Panorama du Pyla

Grande Dune du Pyla, route de Biscarrosse, F-33260 Pyla-sur-Mer (Gironde) T: 04 66 73 97 39.
E: info@yellohvillage-panorama.com  **alanrogers.com/FR33310**

Many campsites set amongst pine trees have a rather untidy look, but Panorama is different. Here the entrance is inviting with well tended flower beds and a pleasant, airy reception. There is a steep climb up to the first of the touring pitches, passing the swimming pool and play area. Some pitches are suitable for caravans and motorcaravans and others suitable for tents. The touring pitches are on terraces amongst the tall pines and have electricity (3-10A). The sea views from some pitches are stunning. Access to the toilet blocks may involve a steep climb (the site is unsuitable for the infirm).

| Facilities | Directions |
|---|---|
| Seven toilet blocks (two open in low season) are clean and have baby rooms and facilities for disabled campers. Fridge hire. Laundry facilities. Motorcaravan services. Restaurant with panoramic sea view. Three heated swimming pools and jacuzzi. 45 m. water slide. Adjacent play area. Tennis. Minigolf. Paragliding. Sub-aqua diving. Gym equipment. Bicycle hire. Entertainment in high season. Library and Internet in reception. WiFi over site (charged). | From N250, just before La Teste, take D259 signed Biscarrosse and Dune de Pyla. At roundabout at end of road turn left (south) on D218 coast road signed Biscarrosse and Dune du Pyla. Site is 4 km. on right. GPS: 44.57265, -1.22053 |

**Open:** 13 April - 1 October.

**Charges guide**

| Per unit incl. 2 persons and electricity | € 17.00 - € 43.00 |
|---|---|
| extra person | € 6.00 - € 8.00 |

## Rouffignac-Saint Cernin

### Camping Bleu Soleil

Domaine Touvent, F-24580 Rouffignac-Saint Cernin (Dordogne) T: 05 53 05 48 30.
E: infos@camping-bleusoleil.com  **alanrogers.com/FR24380**

Camping Bleu Soleil is delightfully and quietly located in the countryside and has magnificent views from all areas of the site. It comprises 70 acres and, at present, has 110 pitches, 84 for touring units and 26 used for wooden chalets and two bungalow tents. Electricity (10A) is available on every pitch. Set in an open, woody, and hilly area, some of the pitches have partial shade from well sited trees and hedges. There is some terracing. The site's restaurant is built in the style of the area. The site is divided by a very quiet minor road. The village of Rouffignac-St Cernin-de-Reilhac, is 1 km. away and is within walking distance. There you will find small bars, restaurants and other amenities.

| Facilities | Directions |
|---|---|
| Three modern unisex sanitary blocks are clean, well maintained and adequate for the number of pitches. En-suite toilet for disabled visitors. Baby room with bath. Enclosed laundry area with two washing machines and dryer. Small bar with TV (from 1/5). Restaurant (from 1/6). 200 sq.m. swimming pool and paddling pool (15/5-15/9). Multisports area. Boules. Small play area and a pen with donkeys and goats. WiFi (free). Off site: Supermarket 2 km. Riding 4 km. Golf 14 kn. Fishing and bicycle hire 15 km. | From Périgueux take N89 east for 17 km. to Thenon, then D31 south (Balou). Continue from Balou for 3 km. to the outskirts of Rouffignac-St Cernin-de-Reilhac and look for site sign on the left. Turn off main road to site. GPS: 45.05497, 0.98691 |

**Open:** 1 April - 30 September.

**Charges guide**

| Per unit incl. 2 persons and electricity (10A) | € 14.50 - € 24.70 |
|---|---|
| extra person | € 3.00 - € 5.60 |

## Saint Antoine-de-Breuilh

### Camping la Rivière Fleurie

180 rue Théophile Cart, F-24230 Saint Antoine-de-Breuilh (Dordogne) T: 05 53 24 82 80.
E: info@la-riviere-fleurie.com  **alanrogers.com/FR24300**

This quiet and pleasant campsite is close to the vineyards of Pomerol and St Emilion, and not far from the towns of St-Foy-la-Grande and Bergerac. There are 66 level, grass pitches of average size, 47 of which are for touring. All have electricity (10A) and 20 are fully serviced. They are separated by shrubs and mature trees provide varying amounts of shade. The site has a tranquil and peaceful ambience, suitable for anyone looking for a quiet and relaxing holiday. You will receive a warm and friendly welcome and there is a convivial, family atmosphere.

| Facilities | Directions |
|---|---|
| Two modern toilet blocks provide all the necessary facilities. Bar, terrace and restaurant/takeaway. Heated swimming pool and paddling pool. TV room. Weekly soirées. Canoe trips. WiFi near reception. Charcoal barbecues are not permitted. Off site: Tennis court adjacent. Fishing 300 m. Riding 3 km. Supermarket 5 km. Bicycle hire 7 km. Golf 10 km. | Leave D936, Bergerac-Bordeaux road at roundabout just west of St Foy-la-Grande (site signed). Follow signs to site, about 3 km. GPS: 44.82905, 0.12238 |

**Open:** 10 April - 20 September.

**Charges guide**

| Per unit incl. 2 persons and electricity | € 20.90 - € 26.90 |
|---|---|
| Camping Cheques accepted. | |

## Saint Astier
### Flower Camping le Pontet

Route D41, F-24110 Saint Astier (Dordogne) T: 05 53 54 14 22. E: camping.lepontet@flowercampings.com
**alanrogers.com/FR24900**

Le Pontet is a good choice for anglers, located on the banks of the small River Isle. Trout, carp, black bass and pike are all regularly caught here. The river is also popular for swimming and canoeing (canoe hire on site), but the site has its own small pool too. There are 131 level, grass pitches with 90 for touring, all with 6A electricity. On-site services include a bar/snack bar and a small shop. Pitches are grassy and of a good size. Most are equipped with electricity.(6A). Since the opening of the A89 motorway (Bordeaux-Clermont-Ferrand) access to this formerly remote region has become more straightforward, making the site a good base for exploring.

**Facilities**

Centrally located toilet blocks are open in style with washbasins and seatless WCs. Showers not controllable. En-suite room for disabled visitors. Bar/snack bar, small shop (15/6-15/9). Small swimming pool, paddling pool (July/Aug). Minigolf. Games room. TV/games room. Play area. Direct river access. Fishing. Canoe hire. WiFi by reception. Off site: Cycle and walking tracks. Supermarket.

**Open:** 1 April - 30 September.

**Directions**

Leave A89 autoroute, exit 14, southwest of Périgueux. Take D6089 west 1 km. At roundabout, turn north on D43, site is on left in 1.3 km. GPS: 45.147353, 0.533121

**Charges guide**

| | |
|---|---|
| Per unit incl. 2 persons and electricity | € 13.90 - € 21.90 |
| extra person | € 2.50 - € 5.00 |

## Saint Crépin-Carlucet
### Camping les Péneyrals

508

Le Poujol, F-24590 Saint Crépin-Carlucet (Dordogne) T: 05 53 28 85 71. E: infos@peneyrals.com
**alanrogers.com/FR24320**

Within easy reach of all the attractions of the Périgord region, M. and Mme. Havel have created a friendly and attractive family campsite at les Péneyrals. There are 250 pitches, 117 of which are for touring. The pitches at the bottom of the hill tend to be quieter as they are further from the main facilities, but are all level and grassy (some on terraces), with electricity (5/10A), and most have some shade. An attractive bar and restaurant with terrace overlook the excellent pool complex and at the bottom of the site is a small fishing lake. The site is set on a wooded hillside, with flowers in abundance (thanks to the dedication of Mme. Havel's mother). Activities are organised over a long season, including archery, various sports tournaments, aquagym, discos and a children's club. On-site entertainment is provided in and around the bar and terrace area every night except Saturdays. The site is used fairly unobtrusively by a UK tour operator (68 pitches) with mobile homes and pre-erected tents. Flights from London arrive at a new airport some 30 km. away which may be popular with visitors using rented accommodation.

**Facilities**

Two modern, unisex toilet blocks provide good quality facilities, including those for babies and disabled visitors. Motorcaravan services. Good value shop, excellent restaurant and takeaway (whole season). Pool complex with two large pools (one heated), paddling pool and four slides with splash pool. Indoor heated pool. Bicycle hire. Minigolf. Tennis (charged). Badminton. Play area. Games room, WiFi throughout (charged), TV room and small library. Fishing. Off site: Amenities in Sarlat 11 km.

**Open:** 4 May - 11 September.

**Directions**

Site is 11 km. north of Sarlat. From D704 Sarlat - Montignac road turn east on D60 towards Salignac-Eyvigues. After 4 km. turn south on D56 towards St Crépin-Carlucet. Site is 500 m. along this road on the right. GPS: 44.95776, 1.2729

**Charges guide**

| | |
|---|---|
| Per unit incl. 2 persons and electricity | € 19.50 - € 36.20 |
| extra person | € 5.00 - € 9.40 |

★ ★ ★ ★ ★ HEATED SWIMMING POOL AND PADDLING POOL, WATER SLIDES, WATER PLAYGROUND, HEATED SANITARY (LOW SEASON), RESTAURANT, BAR, SHOP, TENNIS, FISHING...

All facilities open from 4 May till 11 September

10 km from Sarlat, Dordogne-Périgord

Tel: 0033 55 32 88 571
Fax: 0033 55 32 88 099
WWW.PENEYRALS.COM
Discount in May, June and September

**FREE** Alan Rogers Travel Card
Extra benefits and savings - see page 10

## Saint Avit-de-Vialard

### Castel Camping Caravaning Saint-Avit Loisirs

Le Bugue, F-24260 Saint Avit-de-Vialard (Dordogne) T: 05 53 02 64 00. E: contact@saint-avit-loisirs.com

**alanrogers.com/FR24180**

Although Saint-Avit Loisirs is set amidst rolling countryside, far from the hustle and bustle of the main tourist areas of the Dordogne, the facilities are first class, providing virtually everything you could possibly want without the need to leave the site. This makes it ideal for families with children of all ages. The site is in two sections. One part is dedicated to chalets and mobile homes which are available to rent, whilst the main section of the site contains 199 flat and mainly grassy, good sized pitches, 99 for touring, with electricity (6/10A). With a choice of sun or shade, they are arranged in cul-de-sacs off a main access road and are easily accessible. Environmental friendliness is high on the agenda for this site and each visitor is provided with a bag with instructions as to what should be placed in it before disposal. Two tour operators are in evidence but their tents and mobile homes are so positioned not to detract in any way from the attractiveness of the surroundings. The café, shop and bar open onto a large terrace with a pergola and hanging baskets, which overlooks the excellent pool complex. In high season a variety of activities and entertainment are organised – tournaments, aqua gym, bingo and even weekly films in English. An impressive new activities area has been created away from the pitches and includes a golf driving range and putting green. Although the site is lit, a torch may be useful in some areas.

**Facilities**

Three modern unisex toilet blocks provide high quality facilities, but could become overstretched (particularly laundry and dishwashing) in high season. Shop, bar, good quality restaurant, cafeteria. Outdoor swimming pool, children's pool, water slide, crazy river, heated indoor pool with jacuzzi. Fitness room. Soundproofed disco. Minigolf. Boules. BMX track. Tennis. Quad bikes. Play area. Bicycle hire. Canoe trips and other sporting activities organised. Additional charge for some activities. Walks and cycle routes from site. Off site: Boulangerie, supermarket, Tuesday market, Birdland at Le Bugue 6 km. Sarlat 20 km. Canoeing, golf, riding, fishing nearby.

**Open:** 2 April - 18 September.

**Directions**

Site is 6 km. north of Le Bugue. From D710 Le Bugue-Périgueux road, turn west on narrow and bumpy C201 towards St Avit-de-Vialard. Follow road through St Avit, bearing right and site is 1.5 km. GPS: 44.95161, 0.85042

**Charges guide**

| | |
|---|---|
| Per unit incl. 2 persons and electricity | € 18.60 - € 42.70 |
| extra person | € 3.60 - € 10.70 |
| child (under 4 yrs) | free |
| dog | € 2.00 - € 5.10 |

---

## Saint Cyprien

### Domaine le Cro Magnon

Le Raisse, Allas-les-Mines, F-24220 Saint Cyprien (Dordogne) T: 05 53 29 13 70.
E: contact@domaine-cro-magnon.com  **alanrogers.com/FR24560**

Le Cro Magnon is pleasantly situated in the heart of the Dordogne valley in the Périgord Noir. The 160 spacious, mostly shady pitches are divided in two different types: tent pitches without electricity and serviced pitches (6A electricity hook up, water and waste water drainage). The site also offers various accommodation for rent. The swimming complex includes two pools (one outdoor, one indoor), one heated, water slides, a jacuzzi, sauna and small fitness room with equipment. Near the entrance of the site are a snack bar, pizzeria, bar, a well stocked shop and the reception. From a viewpoint on the site there are beautiful views over the Dordogne valley. The site is ideally situated for exploring the countryside by bike, foot or car (there was no evidence of public transport). There are many waymarked paths and cycle tracks from the site for those who enjoy walking, bicycles can be hired. The village of Saint Cyprien is about 4 km. away and is well worth a visit as are many of the other attractions of the Dordogne region.

**Facilities**

Two toilet blocks provide the usual facilities including those for disabled visitors. Washing machines. Shop. Bar with TV. Snack bar and takeaway. Swimming pools with slides, jacuzzi, sauna and gym. Multisport court. Boules. Play area. Off site: Canoeing, walking and cycling. Fishing and golf 5 km.

**Open:** 13 June - 12 September.

**Directions**

From the A20 (Limoges-Brive) take exit 55 for Souillac and Sarlat. In Sarlat take D57 to Vézac, then D703 to St Cyprien. In St Cyprien follow D703, then D50 (left) to Berbiguières and follow signs for site. GPS: 44.83627, 1.06262

**Charges guide**

| | |
|---|---|
| Per unit incl. 2 persons and electricity | € 14.10 - € 34.70 |
| extra person | € 2.70 - € 7.40 |
| child (under 4 yrs) | free |
| dog | € 1.60 - € 3.60 |

---

For latest campsite news, availability and prices visit
# alanrogers.com

5 stars + 5 red tents Michelin = 53 ha of fun ! Great aquatic resort with 4 swimming pools, including 1 inside exotic heated pool, Jacuzzi, aquatoon, crazy river, toboggan...

On site, multiple shops and activities (sport field, tennis, quad bikes, bungee jumping, driving range, putting green...). Relax in our various accommodations, just happiness! Seminaries, groups, contact us.

**Saint Avit Loisirs le Bugue***** - 24260 Saint Avit de Vialard - France**
**Tél 05 53 02 64 00 - Fax 05 53 02 64 39**
**contact@saint-avit-loisirs.com - www.saint-avit-loisirs.com**

On an estate covering 22 hectares dominating the Dordogne valley, 800 meters from the river and 20 km from Sarlat, the Domaine le Cro Magnon is the ideal location for visiting Perigord's 1001 treasures...

At the heart of a beautiful natural setting, at Cro Magnon you can choose from 160 demarcated pitches and a wide choice of accommodation: Chalets, Cottages

**Domaine Le Cro Magnon**** - 24220 Allas les Mines - France**
**Tél 05 53 29 13 70 - Fax 05 53 29 15 79**
**contact@domaine-cro-magnon.com - www.domaine-cro-magnon.com**

## Saint Cybranet
### Camping Bel Ombrage

F-24250 Saint Cybranet (Dordogne) T: 05 53 28 34 14. E: belombrage@wanadoo.fr
**alanrogers.com/FR24140**

Bel Ombrage is a quiet, well maintained site located in a pretty location by the little River Céou, with a pebble beach that is safe and clean for bathing. The site has a good pool complex, but otherwise there are few on-site facilities. The 180 well shaded, good sized and flat grass pitches are marked by trees and bushes and all have electricity. The quiet and tranquil setting makes the site particularly popular with couples. Bel Ombrage is very close to Domme and Castelnaud and would make an ideal and inexpensive base for visiting the southern Dordogne area. It is a short walk to the village of St Cybranet, with bar, restaurant and a small well stocked supermarket, and a short drive takes you to the beautifully restored village of Daglan.

**Facilities**

Two modern toilet blocks are kept spotlessly clean, with facilities for disabled visitors and babies. Laundry facilities. Bread van. Large swimming pool with sun terrace, children's pool. Paddling pool. Play area. Games room. Fishing. Excursions can be booked at reception. WiFi throughout (free). Off site: Pizzeria next door. Tennis and canoeing nearby. Riding and bicycle hire 3 km. Golf 6 km. More shops at Cénac.

**Open:** 1 June - 5 September.

**Directions**

Site is 14 km. south of Sarlat, on east side of D57 Castelnaud-la-Chapelle-St Cybranet road, 1 km. north of junction with D50. GPS: 44.79128, 1.16214

**Charges guide**

| | |
|---|---|
| Per unit incl. 2 persons and electricity | € 22.40 |
| extra person | € 5.60 |
| child (under 7 yrs) | € 3.60 |
| dog | free |

Bel Ombrage camping-caravaning

24250 St. Cybranet • Tel: 0033 (0)553 28 34 14 • Fax: 0033 (0)553 59 64 64
E-mail: belombrage@wanadoo.fr • www.belombrage.com

## Saint Emilion
### Yelloh! Village Saint Emilion

Domaine de la Barbanne, 2 les Combes - D122, F-33330 Saint Emilion (Gironde) T: 05 57 24 75 80.
E: info@camping-saint-emilion.com **alanrogers.com/FR33080**

Yelloh! Village St Emilion (formerly La Barbanne) is a pleasant site in the heart of the Bordeaux wine region, only 2.5 km. from the famous town of St Emilion. It became part of the Yelloh! group in 2010. With 172 pitches, 125 for touring, the owners have created a carefully maintained, well equipped site. The large, level and grassy pitches have dividing hedges and electricity (long leads necessary). The original parts of the site bordering the lake have mature trees, good shade and pleasant surroundings, whilst in the newer area the trees have yet to provide full shade and it can be hot in summer. Twelve pitches for motorcaravans are on tarmac surrounded by grass.

**Facilities**

Two modern, fully equipped toilet blocks include facilities for children and for campers with disabilities. Motorcaravan services. Well stocked shop. Bar, terrace, takeaway, restaurant. Breakfast service. Two swimming pools, one heated with water slide. Enclosed play area with seats for parents. Children's club. Tennis. Boules. Volleyball. Fishing. Minigolf. Evening entertainment. WiFi (charged). Bicycle hire. Max. 1 dog. Off site: St Emilion and shops 2.5 km. Riding 8 km.

**Open:** 26 April - 29 September.

**Directions**

Site is 2.5 km. north of St Emilion. Caravans and motorcaravans are forbidden in the village of St Emilion and they must approach the site from Libourne on D243 or from Castillon leave D936 and take D130/D243. GPS: 44.91679, -0.14148

**Charges 2013**

| | |
|---|---|
| Per unit incl. 2 persons and electricity | € 18.00 - € 39.00 |
| extra person | € 7.00 - € 8.00 |
| child (3-12 yrs) | free - € 6.00 |
| dog | € 5.00 |

For latest campsite news, availability and prices visit
# alanrogers.com

## Saint Jean-de-Luz

### Camping Atlantica

Quartier Acotz, F-64500 Saint Jean-de-Luz (Pyrénées-Atlantiques) T: 05 59 47 72 44.
E: info@campingatlantica.com **alanrogers.com/FR64250**

This is a friendly, family run site with 200 shady and well kept grass pitches set amongst many shrubs, flowers and hedges. There are 99 pitches for touring, 69 have 6A electricity and 41 have water and drainage. The excellent swimming pool area is attractively landscaped with plenty of sunbeds. With a bar, restaurant and takeaway open June to September, the beach 500 m. and the cosmopolitan town of St Jean-de-Luz only 3 km. away, this site is suitable for families and couples of all ages. If excessively wet, motorcaravans are advised to call ahead to check availability. The three bright and very clean sanitary blocks are well maintained with large showers and piped music. A comprehensive fitness room includes a sauna and during July and August a trained attendant is available for advice.

| Facilities | Directions |
|---|---|
| Three immaculate toilet blocks include facilities for babies and campers with disabilities. Excellent laundry. Motorcaravan services. Shop, bar, restaurant and takeaway, heated outdoor swimming pool and fitness room (all open all season). Games room. Multisports court. Modern, fenced children's play area. Family entertainment (July/Aug). WiFi throughout (charged). Off site: Bus to major town 400 m. Large supermarket 1 km. Golf 4 km. | Leave A63, exit 3, taking N10 toward Bayonne. Take the second left turn signed Acotz-Campings-Plages. At T-junction turn right and follow signs. Campsite is on the right. GPS: 43.41569, -1.61646 |

**Open:** 1 April - 30 September.

**Charges guide**

| Per unit incl. 2 persons | |
|---|---|
| and electricity | € 18.20 - € 36.20 |
| extra person | € 3.30 - € 7.60 |
| child (under 7 yrs) | € 2.20 - € 4.20 |
| dog | free - € 2.50 |

# CAMPING ATLANTICA★★★★

Quartier Acotz - 64500 Saint-Jean-de-Luz
Tel: 0033 559 47 72 44 - Fax: 0033 559 54 72 27
info@campingatlantica.com - www.campingatlantica.com

On 500 m distance from the beach in a green and floral environment for a quiet and pleasant stay in a pleasant family ambiance. Heated water park, relaxing area with spa and sauna, mini golf, sports terrain. All facilities present for pleasant stay. Mobile homes for rent. Dogs not allowed in accommodation.
Campsite open from 1st April till 30th September.

## Saint Jean-de-Luz

### Camping Tamaris Plage

Quartier Acotz, 720 route des Plages, F-64500 Saint Jean-de-Luz (Pyrénées-Atlantiques)
T: 05 59 26 55 90. E: tamaris1@wanadoo.fr **alanrogers.com/FR64080**

This small, pleasant and popular site is well kept and open all year. It is situated outside the town and just across the road from a sandy beach. The 30 touring pitches, all with 7/10A electricity, are of a good size and separated by hedges, on slightly sloping ground with some shade. The site becomes full for July and August with families on long stays, so reservation then is essential. Mobile homes for rent occupy a further 40 pitches. A leisure centre and club provide a heated pool and various other free facilities for adults and children. A gym, Turkish bath, massage and other relaxing amenities are available at an extra charge.

| Facilities | Directions |
|---|---|
| The single heated toilet block of good quality and unusual design should be an ample provision. Facilities for disabled guests. Washing and drying machine. Wellness health club with free facilities: swimming pool, TV/playroom and club for children (4-11 yrs), and some on payment: gym, Turkish bath and other spa facilities, sunbathing area, jacuzzi, adult TV lounge. WiFi. Off site: Beach, fishing, surfing (with instruction) 30 m. Ghéthary with supermarket 2 km. St Jean-de-Luz 4 km. Bicycle hire, boat launching and golf 5 km. Riding 7 km. | Proceed south on N10 and 1.5 km. after Ghéthary take first road on right (before access to the motorway and Carrefour centre commercial) and follow site signs. GPS: 43.41795, -1.623817 |

**Open:** All year.

**Charges guide**

| Per unit incl. 2 persons | |
|---|---|
| and electricity | € 18.00 - € 27.00 |
| extra person (over 2 yrs) | € 6.00 - € 8.00 |
| dog | € 6.00 |

**FREE** Alan Rogers Travel Card
**Extra benefits and savings** - see page 10

## Saint Jean-de-Luz
### Camping International Erromardie

235 avenue de la Source, F-64500 Saint Jean-de-Luz (Pyrénées-Atlantiques) T: 05 59 26 07 74.
E: info@chadotel.com **alanrogers.com/FR64170**

There are not many sites right by the sea in this region. Erromardie, a new member of the Chadotel group, is a good one, with only a small access road to cross to reach a beach of coarse sand and fine shingle. The site is mainly flat and grassy, with several different parts separated by hedges, but not much shade. There are 215 pitches, mainly adjoining access roads and backing onto hedges, including 70 for tourers with electricity (10A), of which 20 also have water and waste water drainage. Some pitches have ocean views and others have views of the Pyrenees.

**Facilities**

The large sanitary buildings are of good quality, with individual cabins and free hot water. Baby changing area. Facilities for disabled visitors. Laundry room. Motorcaravan service point. Shop, bar, restaurant and takeaway (May-Sept). Basic outdoor heated swimming pool (15/5-10/9). Water play area. Playground. Games room. Boules. Fishing. Mobile homes for hire. WiFi throughout (charged). Off site: Beach 50 m. Golf 1 km. Boat ramp 2 km. Biarritz and Spain 15 km.

**Open:** March - November.

**Directions**

Take exit 3 from the A63 (E05, E70) St Jean-de-Luz Nord towards St Jean-de-Luz/Guéthary/Ascain onto ave de Lahanchipia, then left onto ave André Ithurralde (D810), first right ave Claude Farrère and follow site signs. GPS: 43.406247, -1.637286

**Charges guide**

| | |
|---|---|
| Per unit incl. 2 persons and electricity | € 20.50 - € 33.50 |
| extra person | € 6.00 |
| child (2-13 yrs) | € 4.00 |
| dog | € 3.50 |

---

## Saint Martin-de-Seignanx
### Camping Caravaning Lou P'tit Poun

510

110 avenue du Quartier Neuf, F-40390 Saint Martin-de-Seignanx (Landes) T: 05 59 56 55 79.
E: contact@louptitpoun.com **alanrogers.com/FR40140**

The manicured grounds surrounding Lou P'tit Poun give it a well kept appearance, a theme carried out throughout this very pleasing site which will celebrate its 25th anniversary in 2014. It is only after arriving at the car park that you feel confident it is not a private estate. Beyond this point an abundance of shrubs and trees is revealed. Behind a central sloping flower bed lies the open plan reception area. The avenues around the site are wide and the 168 pitches (98 for touring) are spacious. All have 10A electricity, many also have water and drainage and some are separated by low hedges. The jovial owners not only make their guests welcome, but extend their enthusiasm to organising weekly entertainment (held at the café/restaurant) for young and old during high season. A Sites et Paysages member.

**Facilities**

Two unisex sanitary blocks, maintained to a high standard and kept clean, include washbasins in cabins, a baby bath and provision for disabled visitors. Laundry facilities with washing machine and dryer. Motorcaravan service point. Small shop (1/7-31/8). Café/restaurant (1/7-31/8). Swimming pool (1/6-15/9). Play area. Games room, TV. Half-court tennis. WiFi (charged). Off site: Bayonne 6 km. Fishing and riding 7 km. Golf 10 km. Sandy beaches of Basque coast ten minute drive. Trips to the Pyrenees.

**Open:** 2 June - 12 September.

**Directions**

Leave A63 at exit 6 and join D817 towards Pau. Site is signed at Leclerc supermarket. Continue for 3.5 km. and site is clearly signed on right. GPS: 43.52406, -1.41196

**Charges 2013**

| | |
|---|---|
| Per unit incl. 2 persons and electricity | € 23.20 - € 34.70 |

## Saint Julien-en-Born

### Yelloh! Village Lous Seurrots

606 avenue de l'Ocean, Contis Plage, F-40170 Saint Julien-en-Born (Landes) T: 05 58 42 85 82.
E: info@yellohvillage-lous-seurrots.com **alanrogers.com/FR40070**

Lous Seurrots is only a short 400 m. walk from the beach and parts of the site have views across the estuary. There are 602 pitches, mainly in pine woods on sandy undulating ground. They are numbered but many are only roughly marked out, most have good shade and all 277 touring pitches have 6/8A electricity (adaptors required). The site's pool complex is in a superb setting of palm trees and flower beds and the sunbathing areas have wonderful views out to the estuary and the sea. Lous Seurrots is a family site with the emphasis on peace and tranquillity with some entertainment in peak season.

**Facilities**

Three modern toilet blocks with baby rooms and facilities for disabled visitors. Washing machines. Motorcaravan services. Shop and bar (1/5-19/9). Restaurant (19/4-19/9) plus takeaway. Swimming pool complex (1/5-19/9) and a jacuzzi with keep fit classes (July/Aug). Tennis. Archery. Minigolf. Canoeing. Bicycle hire. Fishing. Miniclub. Evening entertainment twice weekly in high season. Electric barbecues only. WiFi (charged). Off site: Beach 400 m.

**Open:** 31 March - 18 September.

**Directions**

Turn off D652 on D41 (15 km. south of Mimizan) to Contis-Plage and site is on left as you reach it.
GPS: 44.08881, -1.31634

**Charges guide**

| Per unit incl. 2 persons and electricity | € 15.00 - € 41.00 |
| extra person | € 5.00 - € 7.00 |
| child (3-7 yrs) | free - € 6.00 |

## Saint Pardoux-la-Rivière

### Kawan Village Château le Verdoyer

Champs Romain, F-24470 Saint Pardoux-la-Rivière (Dordogne) T: 05 53 56 94 64. E: chateau@verdoyer.fr
**alanrogers.com/FR24010**

This 26-hectare estate has three lakes, two for fishing and one with a sandy beach and safe swimming area. There are 135 good sized touring pitches, level, terraced and hedged. With a choice of wooded area or open field, all have electricity (5/10A) and most share a water supply between four pitches. There is a swimming pool complex and high season activities are organised for children (5-13 yrs) but there is no disco. This site is well adapted for those with disabilities, with two fully adapted chalets, wheelchair access to all facilities and even a lift into the pool. Château le Verdoyer has been developed in the park of a restored château and is owned by a Dutch family. We particularly like this site for its beautiful buildings and lovely surroundings. It is situated in the lesser known area of the Dordogne sometimes referred to as the Périgord Vert, with its green forests and small lakes. The courtyard area between reception and the bar hosts evening activities, and provides a pleasant place to enjoy drinks and relax.

**Facilities**

Well appointed toilet blocks include facilities for disabled visitors and baby baths. Serviced launderette. Motorcaravan services. Fridge rental. Shop with gas (from 1/5). Bar, snacks, takeaway and restaurant (from 1/5). Bistro (July/Aug). Two pools, slide, paddling pool. Play areas. Tennis. Minigolf. Bicycle hire. Fishing. Small library. WiFi (charged). Computer in reception for Internet access. Off site: Riding 5 km. Golf 33 km. 'Circuit des Orchidées'. Vélo-rail at Bussière Galant. Market (Wed) in Piegut.

**Open:** 28 April - 30 September.

**Directions**

Site is 2 km. from the Limoges (N21)-Chalus (D6bis-D85)-Nontron road, 20 km. south of Chalus and well signed from main road. Site on D96 4 km. north of village of Champs Romain. GPS: 45.55035, 0.7947

**Charges 2013**

| Per unit incl. 2 persons and electricity | € 21.00 - € 38.50 |
| extra person | € 5.00 - € 6.50 |
| child (6-11 yrs) | € 4.00 - € 5.00 |

Camping Cheques accepted.

## Saint Pée-sur-Nivelle

### Camping Goyetchea

F-64310 Saint Pée-sur-Nivelle (Pyrénées-Atlantiques) T: 05 59 54 19 59. E: info@camping-goyetchea.com
alanrogers.com/FR64300

Camping Goyetchea is located at the heart of Basque country, close to the area's celebrated Atlantic beaches and the classic seaside town of Biarritz. There are 111 pitches with 6A electrical connections. Pitches vary in size (80-120 sq.m) and most have shade from tall trees. There are 26 mobile homes and two Romany-style caravans available for rent. Facilities include a good sized swimming pool with children's pool. This is a green and pleasant site away from the busy coastal areas of Saint Jean-de-Luz and Biarritz, both a short drive away, and a good base for hiking and cycling in the Basque countryside.

| Facilities | Directions |
|---|---|
| Two main toilet blocks are very clean and have preset showers, washbasins in cabins and a baby bath and changing mat. One has facilities for disabled visitors. Washing machines, ironing boards and hairdryers. Snack bar, pizzeria (July/Aug). Swimming pool. Children's pool. Play area. TV room. Library. Board games. Volleyball. Pétanque. Sports tournaments. WiFi. Accommodation for hire (28/4-22/9). Off site: Supermarket 800 m. St Pée-sur-Nivelle 2 km. Beach, golf and bicycle hire 10 km. **Open:** 1 June - 22 September. | Take N10 from Bordeaux and continue on the A63 towards Biarritz leaving at exit 4 (St Pée-sur-Nivelle). Continue following signs to St Pée-sur-Nivelle via D810 and D655. Then take D855 for 6 km. and follow signs to site. GPS: 43.36344, -1.56752 |

**Charges guide**

| Per unit incl. 2 persons and electricity | € 15.00 - € 26.00 |
|---|---|
| extra person | € 3.50 - € 5.00 |

---

## Salignac-Eyvigues

### Flower Camping le Temps de Vivre

Malmont, F-24590 Salignac-Eyvigues (Dordogne) T: 05 53 28 93 21. E: contact@temps-de-vivre.com
alanrogers.com/FR24460

Le Temps de Vivre is situated in the centre of the Périgord Noir, in the countryside and lies about 250 m. above sea level. The area of the campsite covers about 6.5 hectares in total, with 1.5 acres in use at present. It is a small, friendly, family run site with 50 pitches, 30 of which are for touring and 20 for mobile homes available for rent. The pitches are wide and terraces separate some of them. All have electricity connections available (10A) and you will find a variety of trees and bushes often as a natural separation. This is a delightful and peaceful rural site.

| Facilities | Directions |
|---|---|
| One modern unisex sanitary block is very clean and well maintained. En-suite toilet for disabled visitors. Baby room. Covered laundry area. Small shop in reception area. Small bar (15/5-15/9), restaurant and takeaway (1/7-31/8). Two swimming pools (one for children). Boules. Play area. Pottery and painting workshops for young children (weekly in high season). Themed meals (high season). Free WiFi in reception area. No electric barbecues. Off site: Shops and restaurants in the nearby village of Salignac-Eyvigues. **Open:** 21 April - 23 September. | From Brive-La-Gaillarde heading south on the A20, continue for 30 km. to exit 55 signed Souillac. Take D62/D15 northwest for 12 km. until Salignac-Eyvigues. As you drive through the town centre look for blue sign for site. Follow the sign off the main road for 2 km. GPS: 44.96374, 1.32813 |

**Charges guide**

| Per unit incl. 2 persons and electricity | € 15.50 - € 26.90 |
|---|---|
| extra person | € 3.00 - € 5.00 |

---

## Salles

### Camping des Bastides

Terre Rouge, F-47150 Salles (Lot-et-Garonne) T: 05 53 40 83 09. E: info@campingdesbastides.com
alanrogers.com/FR47130

Attractive and well maintained, this six and a half-hectare site is hilly and terraced with good views from the top of the site. The new French owners, Gaelle and Christian, are warm and welcoming. Although the terrain is hilly, most of the 90 medium sized touring pitches are fairly level and moderately shaded (all with 6A electricity). Tight turns with narrow gravel paths and overhanging trees may cause some difficulties for larger units. A range of accommodation including Mongolian tents is available to rent.

| Facilities | Directions |
|---|---|
| Two modern, clean and well maintained sanitary blocks can be heated. Facilities for disabled visitors. Children's facilities with baby bath and child-size facilities. Private en-suite facilities for hire. Shop (with gas). Bar/reception and snack restaurant. Pool complex with swimming pool, pool with slides, paddling pools and a spa. Boules. Play area with bouncy castle. Small indoor play area with TV and books. WiFi (charged). Entertainment (high season). **Open:** 1 May - 30 September. | From Fumel, take D710 north towards Cuzorn. Before reaching Cuzorn, turn northwest on D162 and site is 6 km. on the right hand side (well signed). GPS: 44.5525, 0.8815 |

**Charges guide**

| Per unit incl. 2 persons and electricity | € 17.00 - € 28.50 |
|---|---|
| extra person | € 4.00 - € 5.00 |

For latest campsite news, availability and prices visit
# alanrogers.com

## Sanguinet

### Campéole le Lac Sanguinet

526 rue de Pinton, F-40460 Sanguinet (Landes) T: 05 58 82 70 80. E: lac-sanguinet@campeole.com
**alanrogers.com/FR40440**

Le Lac Sanguinet is a member of the Campéole group, and is located just 100 m. from the large lake of the same name. There are 400 pitches here, of which 290 have electrical connections (10/16A). Around 70 pitches are occupied by mobile homes, chalets and fully equipped bungalow tents, all available for rent, including some models specially adapted for the disabled. An attractive swimming pool was added for the 2008 season and other amenities include volleyball and two children's playgrounds. A marquee is used for activities and entertainment during the peak season. The Lac de Sanguinet is one of Europe's largest lakes (6,800 hectares!) and is renowned for the clarity of its waters. It's understandably popular for fishing but also for water sports. A sailing and windsurfing centre is adjacent to the site. This is a region for superlatives – Europe's highest sand dune, the Dune de Pyla is close, and from the top, there are wonderful views of the Arcachon basin and surrounding forest.

#### Facilities

Four sanitary blocks have hot showers, washbasins in cabins and facilities for disabled visitors. Motorcaravan services. Laundry facilities. Snack bar and pizzas (July/Aug). Small shop. Heated swimming pool. Games room. Bicycle hire. Bouncy castle. Play areas. Activities and entertainment programme. Mobile homes, equipped tents and chalets for rent. Charcoal barbecues in a reserved area only. WiFi (charged). Off site: Lac de Sanguinet 100 m. Sailing centre. Walking and cycle tracks through the forest. Fishing. Dune du Pyla. Bordeaux 60 km.

**Open:** 1 May - 16 September.

#### Directions

Approaching from Bordeaux, head south on the A63 and then join the A660 towards Arcachon. Leave this motorway at the first exit and follow signs to Sanguinet (D216). Upon arrival in Sanguinet follow signs to 'Le Lac' and from here the site is well indicated. GPS: 44.4816, -1.0938

#### Charges guide

| | |
|---|---|
| Per unit incl. 2 persons and electricity | € 17.90 - € 30.60 |
| extra person | € 4.60 - € 9.10 |

## Sarlat-la-Canéda

### Camping les Périères

Rue Jean Gabin, F-24203 Sarlat-la-Canéda (Dordogne) T: 05 53 59 05 84. E: les-perieres@wanadoo.fr
**alanrogers.com/FR24030**

Les Périères is a pleasant small site set on an attractive hillside within walking distance of the beautiful medieval town of Sarlat. The 100 pitches are arranged on wide terraces around the semi-circle of a fairly steep valley, overlooking a central leisure area that includes indoor and outdoor swimming pools and two tennis courts. The pitches are of a very good size, all equipped with 6A electricity, individual water and drainage points and many have dappled shade from the numerous walnut trees on the site (the walnuts can be bought in the campsite shop).

#### Facilities

The toilet blocks are beginning to show their age but are clean and can be heated. Facilities for disabled visitors, baby bathroom, washing machines and dryers. Motorcaravan services. Small shop. Pleasant bar. Small snack bar/takeaway (July/Aug). Outdoor swimming pool (no shorts), paddling pool, indoor spa pool and sauna (all season). Tennis, football, fitness track. Stone cottages to rent. WiFi (free). No electric barbecues. Off site: Sarlat 10 mins. walk. Bicycle hire 1 km. Fishing 5 km.

**Open:** Easter/1 April - 30 September.

#### Directions

Site is on the east side of Sarlat, on the D47 to Ste Nathalène (negotiating Sarlat town centre is best done outside peak hours). GPS: 44.8937, 1.22748

#### Charges guide

| | |
|---|---|
| Per unit incl. 2 persons | € 21.00 - € 28.00 |
| incl. electricity | € 24.80 - € 32.00 |
| extra person | € 6.50 |
| child (under 7 yrs) | € 4.50 |

## Sanguinet

### Camping les Grands Pins

1039 avenue de Losa, F-40460 Sanguinet (Landes) T: 05 58 78 61 74. E: info@campinglesgrandspins.com

**alanrogers.com/FR40250**

Approached by a road alongside the lake, this Airotel group site is surrounded by tall trees. Of the 345 pitches, the 80 sand/gravel pitches are of average size, mostly level with varying degrees of shade. Low hedges and young trees divide those available for tourers and most are set away from the mobile homes and chalets. An impressive central pool complex includes a covered heated indoor pool, an outdoor pool, water slide and flume, children's pool and jacuzzi. There are plenty of walks, cycle rides and the lake to enjoy. The poolside bar, restaurant and shops are open in July and August when the site becomes busier, offering watersports, minigolf, a children's club, boat trips and organised activities. Volleyball, tennis and boules are available all season. Fishing is also available. The charming small village of Sanguinet is 2 km. away with supermarket and shops, bank, restaurants and archaeological museum.

**Facilities**

Four toilet blocks include washbasins in cabins, showers and British style toilets (not all open in low seasons). Baby bath and provision for disabled visitors. Laundry facilities. Motorcaravan service point. Shop, bar, restaurant and takeaway (1/7-31/8). Indoor pool (all season). Outdoor pool complex with jacuzzi (1/4-15/9). Play area. Games room and TV in bar. Tennis, volleyball, boules. Sports equipment available to hire. Bicycle hire. Children's club. WiFi (charged). Dogs are not accepted in July/Aug. Barbecues allowed in dedicated areas provided. Off site: Fishing 200 m. Boat launching 1 km. Golf and riding 15 km. Beach and windsurfing 18 km.

**Open:** 6 April - 22 September.

**Directions**

Enter Sanguinet from the north on the D46. At one way system turn right. Do not continue on one way system but go straight ahead toward lake (signed) on Rue de Lac. Site is 2 km. on left.
GPS: 44.48396, -1.089716

**Charges guide**

| Per unit incl. 2 persons | |
| --- | --- |
| and electricity | € 18.00 - € 41.00 |
| extra person | € 5.50 - € 9.00 |
| child (3-7 yrs) | € 4.50 - € 6.50 |
| dog | € 3.00 |

---

## Sarlat-la-Canéda

### Castel Camping le Moulin du Roch

Route des Eyzies, Allas - D47, F-24200 Sarlat-la-Canéda (Dordogne) T: 05 53 59 20 27.
E: moulin.du.roch@wanadoo.fr  **alanrogers.com/FR24040**

The site has 196 large pitches, of which 124 are for touring units. They are mostly flat (some slope slightly) and grassy and all have electricity (6A). Pitches on the upper levels have plenty of shade, whilst those on the lower level near the amenities and the fishing lake are more open. Entertainment and activities are organised from June to September, with something for everyone from quizzes and sports tournaments to canoeing and riding for the more adventurous. An excellent multi-lingual children's club runs in July and August. Walking and mountain biking routes lead from the site through surrounding woodland. Le Moulin du Roch is set on natural sloping woodland in the grounds of a former water mill and the Dutreux family have worked hard to ensure that it is an attractive and well run family campsite, fully deserving of its place in the Castels and Camping chain. Only 10 km. from the charming medieval town of Sarlat and 52 km. from Périgueux – the capital town of the Périgord region – this campsite is well situated for exploring the natural, historical, cultural and gastronomic riches of the Dordogne.

**Facilities**

Well maintained, very clean toilet blocks. Washing machines, dryers. Good shop. Bar with WiFi and terrace, Takeaway. Superb restaurant. Attractive swimming pool, paddling pool and sun terrace (all open all season) Fishing lake. Tennis. Boules. Playground. Evening entertainment in high season. Pets are not accepted. Off site: Sarlat 10 km. with supermarkets, banks, etc. Bicycle hire and riding 10 km. Golf 15 km.

**Open:** 8 May - 14 September.

**Directions**

Site is 10 km. west of Sarlat-la-Canéda, on the south side of the D47 Sarlat-Les Eyzies road.
GPS: 44.90867, 1.1148

**Charges guide**

| Per unit incl. 2 persons | |
| --- | --- |
| and electricity | € 19.50 - € 37.00 |
| incl. full services | € 24.50 - € 42.00 |
| extra person | € 5.00 - € 9.50 |
| child (3-7 yrs) | free - € 4.50 |
| Camping Cheques accepted. | |

For latest campsite news, availability and prices visit
# alanrogers.com

# LES GRANDS PINS
## camping ★★★★

AT THE LAKESIDE OF LAC DE SANGUINET – LES LANDES

✉ www.campinglesgrandspins.com

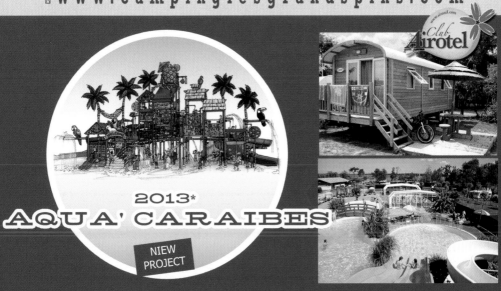

2013*

AQUA' CARAIBES

NIEW PROJECT

Club Airotel

Situated at the lakeside. Aquatic Parc.
The best place to enjoy the Les Landes Sun!
Chalets and mobile homes for rent

Camping Caravaning les Grands Pins
Avenue de Losa (route du lac)  40460 SANGUINET
Tél : 00 33 (0)5 58 78 61 74   Fax : 00 33 (0)5 58 78 69 15
info@campinglesgrandspins.com  www.campingaquitaine.com

## Sarlat-la-Canéda
### Camping les Tailladis

Marcillac-Saint Quentin, F-24200 Sarlat-la-Canéda (Dordogne) T: 05 53 59 10 95. E: tailladis@wanadoo.fr

**alanrogers.com/FR24480**

Les Tailladis is a well situated, mature campsite of some 17 hectares of woodland, owned by the same Dutch and French family for over 47 years. It is 12 km. from Sarlat, Eyzies and Montignac-Lascauax, and 35 km. from Souillac. Four hectares provide 78 medium to large pitches which are grassy, terraced and partially shaded, with electricity (10A), and water points close by. There is also a small stream and pond. The access road and campsite roads/tracks are narrow and winding, which may cause difficulties for some larger units. The hosts are welcoming and enthusiastic and you will be greeted with a drink and warm, friendly service.

**Facilities**

One heated sanitary block is well sited for all pitches. En-suite toilet for disabled visitors. Baby bath and changing area. Laundry room. Large shop (fresh bread and milk to order). Restaurant, bar. Swimming pool and paddling pool. Play area with trampoline. Library. Activities during high season. Internet (charged). Fishing. Off site: Riding 3 km. Bicycle hire 12 km. Golf 25 km. Boat launching 25 km. Medieval town of Sarlat 12 km.

**Open:** 1 March - 30 November.

**Directions**

From Sarlat-la-Canéda, take D704 north. After 10 km. look for signs on left for Marcella-St Quentin. Take this road heading northwest, and site is less than 3 km. after Marcella-St Quentin on left hand side. GPS: 44.97450, 1.18832

**Charges guide**

| Per unit incl. 2 persons and electricity (6A) | € 14.60 - € 22.00 |
|---|---|

---

## Sarlat-la-Canéda
### Camping les Grottes de Roffy

Sainte Nathalène, F-24200 Sarlat-la-Canéda (Dordogne) T: 05 53 59 15 61. E: contact@roffy.fr

**alanrogers.com/FR24130**

About 5 km. east of Sarlat, les Grottes de Roffy is a pleasantly laid out, family site. There are 162 clearly marked pitches, some very large, set on very well kept grass terraces. They have easy access and good views across an attractive valley. Some have plentiful shade, although others are more open, and all have 6A electricity. Those with very large units are advised to check availability in advance. The reception, bar, restaurant and shop are housed in converted farm buildings surrounding a semi-courtyard. The site shop is well stocked with a variety of goods and a tempting épicerie. A good heated outdoor pool complex is open all season and is popular with visitors.

**Facilities**

Two toilet blocks with modern facilities are more than adequate. Well stocked shop. Bar and gastronomic restaurant. Takeaway. Good swimming pool complex comprising two deep pools (one heated), a fountain, paddling pool and heated jacuzzi. Tennis. Games room. Room for teenagers. Play area. Bicycle hire. Entertainment and activities for all ages. Internet access. Free WiFi in courtyard area.

**Open:** 18 April - 21 September.

**Directions**

Take D47 east from Sarlat to Ste Nathalène. Just before Ste Nathalène the site is signed on the right hand side of the road. Turn here and the site is 800 m. along the lane. GPS: 44.90404, 1.2821

**Charges guide**

| Per pitch incl. 1-6 persons and electricity | € 9.30 - € 21.40 |
|---|---|
| with full services | € 11.30 - € 23.40 |

---

## Sarlat-la-Canéda
### Palombière

Sainte Nathalène, F-24200 Sarlat-la-Canéda (Dordogne) T: 05 53 59 42 34. E: contact@lapalombiere.fr

**alanrogers.com/FR24570**

This site is set in a gorgeous, rural part of France amongst the beauty of the Périgord countryside with its rolling green hills and ancient buildings. The restored and preserved buildings at Palombière add to the pleasure of this delightful site. It is evident that much investment has gone into making this holiday destination a place to remember. There are 200 pitches of which 68 are for touring caravans and tents. All have 10A electricity and some are fully serviced. Most are level and shaded from the sun, with some terracing because of the different levels. The remaining pitches are used for chalets and mobile homes.

**Facilities**

Three modern sanitary blocks include facilities for babies and disabled visitors. Washing machines and dryers. Shop. Bar. Restaurant, snack bar and takeaway. Heated swimming pool complex. Gym. Playgrounds. Library. Sports field. Tennis. Minigolf. Boules. Trampoline. Satellite TV. Games room. Bicycle hire. Internet. Free WiFi.

**Open:** 26 April - 15 September.

**Directions**

Take the D47 east from Sarlat to Sainte Nathalène. Site is signed from village and is reached by taking a left turn just beyond it. GPS: 44.90819, 1.29252

**Charges guide**

| Per unit incl. 2 persons and electricity | € 14.70 - € 29.70 |
|---|---|
| extra person | € 4.60 - € 8.20 |

---

For latest campsite news, availability and prices visit
# alanrogers.com

## Sarlat-la-Canéda
### Domaine de Soleil Plage

Caudon par Montfort, Vitrac, F-24200 Sarlat-la-Canéda (Dordogne) T: 05 53 28 33 33. E: info@soleilplage.fr
**alanrogers.com/FR24090**

This site is in one of the most attractive sections of the Dordogne valley, with a riverside location. There are 218 pitches, in three sections, with 119 for touring units. Additionally, there are 52 mobile homes and cottages and 27 chalets for rent. The site offers river swimming from a sizeable sandy bank or there is a very impressive heated pool complex. All pitches are bound by hedges and are of adequate size, 79 with 16A electricity, 45 also have water and a drain. Most pitches have some shade. If you like a holiday with lots going on, you will enjoy this site. Various activities are organised during high season including walks and sports tournaments, and daily canoe hire is available from the site. Once a week in July and August there is a 'soirée' (charged for) usually involving a barbecue or paella, with a band and lots of free wine – worth catching! The site is busy and reservation is advisable. English is spoken. You pay more for a riverside pitch, but these have fine river views. There is some tour operator presence.

### Facilities

Toilet facilities are in three modern unisex blocks. One has been completely renovated to a high standard with heating and family shower rooms. Washing machines and dryer. Motorcaravan service point. Well stocked shop, pleasant bar with TV and attractive, newly refurbished restaurant with local menus and a pleasant terrace (all 7/5-14/9). Picnics available to order. Very impressive heated main pool, paddling pool, spa pool and two slides. Tennis. Minigolf. Three play areas. Fishing. Canoe and kayak hire. Bicycle hire. Currency exchange. Small library. WiFi throughout (charged). Activities and social events (high season). Off site: Golf 1 km. Riding 5 km. Many attractions of the Dordogne are within easy reach.

**Open:** 13 April - 29 September.

### Directions

Site is 6 km. south of Sarlat. From A20 take exit 55 (Souillac) towards Sarlat. Follow the D703 to Carsac and on to Montfort. After Montfort castle site is signed on left. Continue for 2 km. down to the river and site. GPS: 44.825, 1.25388

### Charges guide

| Per unit incl. 2 persons | |
|---|---|
| and electricity | € 21.00 - € 36.60 |
| incl. full services | € 24.50 - € 52.00 |
| extra person | € 5.00 - € 7.70 |
| child (2-8 yrs) | € 3.00 - € 4.60 |
| dog | € 2.50 - € 3.50 |

Camping Cheques accepted.

Take advantage of our prices in low season to enjoy the heated pool & WIFI on all the campsite & New heated toilet block & the beautiful scenery from your chalet or your pitch along the river

*Right on the Dordogne riverside*
*(Sand beach, swimming, fishing, canoeing)*
*An exceptional site, 6 km from Sarlat mediaeval town. In the heart of Périgord beautiful landscapes & castles*

Many quality facilities for couples, families or groups: Mini-mart (fresh bread & croissants), restaurant périgourdin, pizzeria, take-away, bar.
New heated toilet block
Numerous activities: heated pool complex, tennis, mini-golf, multi-sport pitch, hiking, cycling, golf (1km), riding (5km), numerous visits (caves, castles, vines, farms...)

Domaine de Soleil Plage*****
Caudon par Montfort, VITRAC, 24200 SARLAT
www.soleilplage.fr - info@soleilplage.fr
Tel: +33 5 53 28 33 33 - GPS: 44° 49′ 30N - 1° 15′ 14E

## Sarlat-la-Canéda

### Camping la Sagne

Lieu-dit Lassagne, Vitrac, F-24200 Sarlat (Dordogne) T: 05 53 28 18 36. E: info@camping-la-sagne.com

alanrogers.com/FR24940

Camping la Sagne is a family run site and was significantly rebuilt for the 2012 season. The rebuilding programme includes a new reception, bar and snack bar complex and a covered swimming pool and paddling pool with jacuzzi. There are 100 large, level pitches with 68 for touring, all with 16A electricity but long leads are required. Trees and hedges separating the pitches have been planted in the new area, which has little shade as yet, while pitches in the older section are separated by hedges and mature trees providing good shade. The site is close to the Dordogne river and access is available via a track down through the trees. Bathing and fishing are possible in the river and permits can be purchased. There is a programme of entertainment in the high season and all the facilities are open all season.

**Facilities**

The old toilet block has been refurbished. New block has a family bathroom, child size toilet, baby bath and facilities for disabled visitors. Washer/dryers. Small shop. Bar with TV, snack bar and takeaway. Games room. Covered, heated swimming pool, paddling pool and jacuzzi. Playground. River fishing and bathing. WiFi over site (charged). Accommodation to rent. Off site: Golf 800 m. Sarlat with range of shops, bars and restaurants 8 km. Riding 5 km. Bicycle hire 8 km. A good centre for touring the many old market towns with their châteaux and museums. Many marked walks and cycle routes.

**Open:** 6 April - 29 September.

**Directions**

Site is 6 km. south of Sarlat. Leave autoroute A20, exit 55 (Souillac) towards Sarlat. Take D703 to Montfort, turn left following site signs. Site entrance on right in 1 km. GPS: 44.825452, 1.242346

**Charges guide**

| Per unit incl. 2 persons | |
|---|---|
| and electricity | € 15.20 - € 30.40 |
| extra person | € 4.50 - € 6.50 |
| child (2-13 yrs) | € 3.00 - € 4.00 |
| dog | € 3.00 |

CAMPING · CARAVANING · RENTAL

*La* *Sagne* ★★★

PÉRIGORD · 100% NATURE · DORDOGNE

On the banks of the Dordogne

Camping LA SAGNE, 24200 VITRAC - FRANCE

Tél. +33 5 53 28 18 36 - www.camping-la-sagne.com - info@camping-la-sagne.com    at 8km from Sarlat

## Sarlat-la-Canéda

### Camping le Montant

Saint André-d'Allas, F-24200 Sarlat-la-Canéda (Dordogne) T: 05 53 59 18 50. E: lemontant@wanadoo.fr

alanrogers.com/FR24610

Camping le Montant is located on a hillside overlooking beautiful countryside only 2 km. from Sarlat. Run by a pleasant family, there is a friendly welcome. There are 131 pitches, of which 92 are large touring pitches, the remainder being used for a variety of high quality furnished accommodation for rent. The touring pitches, all with 6/10A electricity, are divided into two areas, each with its own sanitary block. One part of the site is shaded with hedges, the other area is more open with flat terraced pitches looking out over the wooded hills. Good amenities include an outdoor pool with slides, a heated indoor pool and large jacuzzi, and a bar/restaurant with terrace built in traditional style and surrounded by flowers.

**Facilities**

Both toilet blocks are very well equipped especially a newer one with its baby room and large laundry. Bar, restaurant and takeaway (all season). Swimming pool complex with outdoor pool (from 9/5), slides, heated indoor pool and large indoor jacuzzi. New playground. Tennis. Multisports area. Minigolf. Boules. Bicycle hire. Activities organised for children, teenagers and adults day and evening (July/Aug). WiFi (free). Off site: Sarlat 2 km.

**Open:** 1 May - 20 September.

**Directions**

Site is 2 km. south of Sarlat off the D57 Sarlat - Baynac road. If approaching from Sarlat, site is signed to the right. Follow this road for 1 km. GPS: 44.865344, 1.187704

**Charges guide**

| Per unit incl. 2 persons | |
|---|---|
| and electricity | € 19.60 - € 29.80 |
| extra person | € 4.80 - € 7.50 |

For latest campsite news, availability and prices visit

# alanrogers.com

## Sarlat-la-Canéda
### Camping les Terrasses du Périgord

Pech-d'Orance, F-24200 Sarlat-la-Canéda (Dordogne) T: 05 53 59 02 25.
E: terrasses-du-perigord@wanadoo.fr **alanrogers.com/FR24670**

Set on a hilltop on the edge of Sarlat, this site has panoramic views across the Périgord. There are 90 pitches, of which 75 are for touring units, with the remaining 15 for chalets and mobile homes for rent. The site is sloping on different levels but the pitches are generally level. All are shady, marked and separated by trees. Electricity is 6/10/16A. For those with larger units, it is essential to phone in advance for pitch availability, as not all are suitable. A warm and friendly welcome is given by the French owners.

**Facilities**

One modern sanitary block divided into two provides all facilities including those for disabled visitors and babies. Washing machine and dryer. Motorcaravan services. Shop. Bar with snack bar and takeaway. Wine tastings. Swimming pool and toddler's pool. Play area with cable slide. Minigolf. Bicycle hire. Gas and electric barbecues only. Evening entertainment. Off site: Caves. Châteaux. Fishing and canoeing 2 km. Riding 8 km.

**Open:** 23 April - 18 September.

**Directions**

From Sarlat, take D47 to Proissans. Continue on D56 to Proissans and site is 500 m. on the left. In Sarlat, follow the signs for hospital as it is nearby. GPS: 44.9058, 1.23598

**Charges guide**

| Per unit incl. 2 persons | |
|---|---|
| and electricity | € 16.80 - € 22.00 |
| extra person | € 4.20 - € 5.40 |
| No credit cards. | |

## Sarlat-la-Canéda
### Camping Domaine des Mathevies

Les Mathevies, Sainte Nathalène, F-24200 Sarlat-la-Canéda (Dordogne) T: 05 53 59 20 86.
E: mathevies@mac.com **alanrogers.com/FR24740**

This gem of a small, family run site is situated in the rural heart of the Périgord, and the delightful owners will give you a warm and friendly welcome. There are only 40 slightly sloping, spacious, grass pitches, 30 for touring, and all have 10A electricity. They are separated by hedging and flowering shrubs, and trees give varying amounts of shade. A shaded terrace is next to the beautiful, original Perigordine building and the barn has been lovingly converted into a bar/restaurant, a superb children's playroom and the toilet facilities. The play area makes this a paradise for toddlers.

**Facilities**

Excellent, clean toilet block with all necessary facilities including a good room for young children and disabled campers. Washing machine and dryer. Bar. Restaurant. Swimming and paddling pools. Tennis court. Library. Satellite TV. Playground. Pétanque. Crèche (under 5 yrs). Boules. Bicycle hire. WiFi over part of site (free). Special interest groups catered for. Off site: Shops, restaurant, bars and Sat. market (bus) in Sarlat. Riding 2 km.

**Open:** 22 April - 23 September.

**Directions**

Leave A20 exit 55, head west through Souillac to Roufillac. Take D61 north then D47B to Sainte Nathalène. Site well signed from there. GPS: 44.918056, 1.277778

**Charges guide**

| Per unit incl. 2 persons | |
|---|---|
| and electricity | € 21.00 - € 29.00 |
| extra person | € 5.00 - € 7.50 |
| child (0-5 yrs) | free - € 5.50 |

## Sauveterre-la-Lemance
### Camping Moulin du Périé

F-47500 Sauveterre-la-Lemance (Lot-et-Garonne) T: 05 53 40 67 26. E: moulinduperie@wanadoo.fr
**alanrogers.com/FR47010**

Set in a quiet area and surrounded by woodlands, this peaceful little site is well away from much of the tourist bustle. It has 95 reasonably sized, grassy touring pitches, all with 6A electricity, divided by mixed trees and bushes with most having good shade. All are extremely well kept, as indeed is the entire site. The attractive front courtyard is complemented by an equally pleasant terrace at the rear. Two small, clean swimming pools overlook a shallow, spring water lake, ideal for inflatable boats and paddling, and bordering the lake, a large grass field is popular for games.

**Facilities**

Two clean, modern and well maintained toilet blocks include facilities for disabled visitors. Motorcaravan services. Fridge, barbecue. Basic shop. Bar/reception, restaurant and takeaway. Two small swimming pools (no Bermuda-style shorts). Boules. Outdoor chess. Play area. Small indoor play area. Bicycle hire. Organised activities in high season include canoeing, riding, wine tasting visits, sightseeing trips, barbecues, gastronomic meals. Winter caravan storage. Internet access (bring your own cable). Off site: Fishing 1 km. Riding 7 km. Small shop in village.

**Open:** 12 May - 18 September.

**Directions**

From D710, Fumel-Périgueux, turn southeast into Sauveterre-la-Lemance. Turn left (northeast) at far end on C201 signed Château Sauveterre and Loubejec (site also signed). Site is 3 km. on right. GPS: 44.59016, 1.04761

**Charges guide**

| Per unit incl. 2 persons | |
|---|---|
| and electricity | € 18.15 - € 27.65 |
| extra person | € 4.50 - € 7.00 |
| Camping Cheques accepted. | |

## Soulac-sur-Mer

### Yelloh! Village Soulac-sur-Mer

8 allée Michel Montaigne, F-33780 Soulac-sur-Mer (Gironde) T: 05 56 09 77 63. E: contact@lelilhan.com
alanrogers.com/FR33330

This is a well established woodland site, popular with families. Now part of the Yelloh! Village group, it has benefited from an extensive programme of investment and development. There are around 50 large touring pitches (all with 10A electricity), the remainder used for mobile homes and chalets to rent. Most pitches are heavily shaded and on natural woodland floor terrain. A special area is kept for younger campers away from the quieter family areas. There is an attractive and well laid out pool complex, together with a small shop selling bread and basic provisions, a bar and a restaurant.

**Facilities**

Three unisex toilet blocks provide a family bathroom with double shower unit, facilities for babies, washbasins in cubicles, and a suite for disabled campers. Laundry facilities. Swimming pool complex, new balnéo, sauna and jacuzzi (15/6-15/9). Shop, bar, restaurant and pizzeria, takeaway (15/6-15/9). Entertainment and children's club (high season). Playground. Minigolf. Tennis. Archery. Riding. Bicycle hire. Internet access. WiFi.

**Open:** 1 April - 15 September.

**Directions**

Soulac-sur-Mer is on the Atlantic coast just south of the tip of the Gironde peninsula. Site is signed off the D101 – turn east on a minor road 3 km. south of Soulac town, and site is on left after a short distance. GPS: 45.48576, -1.1179

**Charges guide**

| | |
|---|---|
| Per unit incl. 2 persons and electricity | € 15.00 - € 39.00 |

No credit cards.

---

## Soustons

### Camping le Framissima Nature

63, avenue du Port d'Albret, F-40140 Soustons (Landes) T: 05 58 77 70 00. E: resa.soustons@fram.fr
alanrogers.com/FR40760

Framissima Nature is a new site located in the heart of the vast Landes pine forest. It is close to Soustons and its huge lake, and around six kilometres from the Atlantic beaches. There are 249 pitches, all occupied by chalet style mobile homes and other rentable accommodation. There are no touring pitches. The site does have an impressive pool complex with a wave pool and wet play area. There is little natural shade, but this is provided in the bar areas. Clubs for children are well organised, with different ages catered for. Cars must be left in a separate parking area at all times.

**Facilities**

Bar. Restaurant. Takeaway. Swimming pool complex (including covered pool). Play area. Football. Volleyball. Basketball. Tennis. Multisports terrain. Gym. Activity and entertainment programme for all ages. Cinema. Mobile homes and chalets for hire. Free WiFi over part of site. Please note that there are no touring pitches on this site. Off site: Supermarket 500 m. Shops in Soustons.

**Open:** 14 April - 1 October.

**Directions**

The site is located on the eastern side of the Etang de Soustons. Heading south on N10, leave at the Magesq exit and head for Soustons on D116. From there follow signs for the site. GPS: 43.75579, -1.35384

**Charges guide**

Contact the site for details.

---

## Thiviers

### Camping le Repaire

F-24800 Thiviers (Dordogne) T: 05 53 52 69 75. E: info@campinglerepaire.com
alanrogers.com/FR24210

Set in quiet countryside in the heart of the Périgord Vert, next to a small fishing lake, le Repaire is a beautiful, spacious and peaceful municipal site, well situated for visiting towns such as Périgueux and Brantôme. There are 110 good sized, slightly sloping, grassy pitches (90 for touring), all with electricity (10A). They are in small groups, separated by shrubs and a variety of trees providing shade to some pitches. A few shadier pitches are available at the edge of the adjoining woodland. The interesting town of Thiviers can be reached in 20 minutes along a footpath and is just 2 km. by road.

**Facilities**

Two clean and functional toilet blocks provide washbasins in cabins, cubicles for disabled visitors, washing machines and drying facilities. One unit is shut in low season. No chemical disposal point. Reception area (no shop but bread to order). Terrace bar and snack/takeaway service (July/Aug). Swimming pool (unheated) and paddling pool (15/6-15/9). Small fishing lake. Play area. Tennis. Boules. Pétanque. Exercise track. Barbecue area. Free WiFi in reception area. Off site: Tennis 300 m. Bicycle hire 1 km.

**Open:** 27 April - 30 September.

**Directions**

Leave N21 at Thiviers, approx 60 km. south west of Limoges. At roundabout turn east, D707, signed Lanouaille. Site is on right in 2 km. GPS: 45.413116, 0.932022

**Charges guide**

| | |
|---|---|
| Per unit incl. 2 persons and electricity | € 17.00 |
| extra person | € 3.50 - € 4.00 |
| child (0-12 yrs) | € 2.50 - € 3.00 |

No credit cards.

# Urrugne
## Sunêlia Col d'Ibardin

220 route d'Olhette, F-64122 Urrugne (Pyrénées-Atlantiques) T: 05 59 54 31 21. E: info@col-ibardin.com
**alanrogers.com/FR64110**

This family owned site at the foot of the Basque Pyrenees is highly recommended and deserves praise. It is well run with emphasis on personal attention, the friendly family and their staff ensuring that all are made welcome, and is attractively set in the middle of an oak wood with a mountain stream cascading through it. Behind the forecourt, with its brightly coloured shrubs and modern reception area, various roadways lead to the 203 pitches. These are individual, spacious and enjoy the benefit of the shade (if preferred a more open aspect can be found). There are electricity hook-ups (6/10A) and adequate water points. A very attractive chalet 'village' has been added. From this site you can enjoy the mountain scenery, be on the beach in 7-10 km. or cross the border into Spain in about 14 km.

### Facilities

Two toilet blocks, one rebuilt to a high specification, are kept very clean. WC for disabled visitors. Laundry facilities. Motorcaravan service point. Shop for basics and bread orders (1/6-15/9). Restaurant, takeaway service and bar (1/6-15/9). Heated swimming pool and paddling pool (with water games). Playground and club (adult supervision). Tennis. Boules. Video games. Multisports area. WiFi (charged). Not suitable for American-style motorhomes. Off site: Supermarket and shopping centre 5 km. Fishing, boat launching, sailing, bicycle hire and golf 7 km. Riding 20 km.

**Open:** 1 April - 30 September.

### Directions

Leave A63 at St Jean-de-Luz sud, exit no. 2 and join RN10 in direction of Urrugne. Turn left at roundabout (Col d'Ibardin) on D4. Site on right after 5 km. Do not turn off to the Col itself, carry on towards Ascain. GPS: 43.33376, -1.68458

### Charges guide

| Per unit incl. 2 persons | |
|---|---|
| and electricity | € 17.50 - € 38.50 |
| extra person | € 3.50 - € 6.50 |
| child (2-7 yrs) | € 2.50 - € 4.00 |
| dog | € 2.80 |

**BASQUE COUNTRY** Located between St Jean de Luz & Hendaye, lovely campsite surrounded by nature. Pitches and accommodations for rent.

TÉL. (00 33) 559 54 31 21 • FAX (00 33) 559 54 62 28 • 64122 URRUGNE • WWW.COL-IBARDIN.COM • INFO@COL-IBARDIN.COM

---

# Urrugne
## Camping Larrouleta

210 route de Socoa, F-64122 Urrugne (Pyrénées-Atlantiques) T: 05 59 47 37 84. E: info@larrouleta.com
**alanrogers.com/FR64180**

Camping Larrouleta is an all year site located at the heart of the Basque country. The site has been developed around a 7.5 hectare lake which has a sandy beach and is ideal for fishing. On-site amenities include a swimming pool which is covered in low season. There is also a bar/restaurant which specialises in local cuisine, and where occasional Basque folk evenings are held in high season. The 327 touring pitches are of a good size (90 sq.m) and are generally shaded by poplars. Most have electrical connections (5A). A number of 'grand confort' pitches are available (large pitches with electricity, water and drainage – supplement charged).

### Facilities

Toilet block (can be heated) with hot showers, washbasins in cabins and facilities for disabled visitors. Washing machine. Shop (July/Aug). Bar. Restaurant (15/6-15/9). Swimming pool (covered in low season). Lake. Fishing. Tennis. Play area. Entertainment and activity programme. WiFi (charged). Off site: Nearest beach, sailing, golf and bicycle hire, all 3 km. Col d'Ibardin (Pyrenees) 7 km.

**Open:** All year.

### Directions

Take exit 2 from A63 motorway (St Jean-de-Luz Sud) and follow signs to Port Fort, crossing N10. From here follow signs to the site. GPS: 43.37024, -1.686161

### Charges guide

| Per unit incl. 2 persons | |
|---|---|
| and electricity | € 19.00 - € 32.50 |

**FREE** Alan Rogers Travel Card
Extra benefits and savings - see page 10

## Vendays-Montalivet
### Campéole Médoc Plage

**Campé●le**

Avenue de l'Europe, F-33930 Vendays-Montalivet (Gironde) T: 05 56 09 33 45. E: montalivet@campeole.com

**alanrogers.com/FR33840**

This is a large site with 361 touring pitches and a further 212 pitches occupied by mobile homes, chalets and Trigano tents, all of which are available for rent. The site has a woodland setting and is 800 m. from the vast, sandy beach, which can be accessed via a footpath from the site. On-site amenities here include a swimming pool, a snack bar and a shop. All amenities are open in July and August, but may be closed in the low season. Cycling is very popular and a number of trails lead from the site through the surrounding forest.

**Facilities**

Four toilet blocks (two new for 2012) have British style WCs, washbasins and showers in cubicles. Facilities for children and disabled visitors. Laundry. Motorcaravan service point. Shop. Bar. Snack bar/takeaway (July/Aug). Heated swimming pool with slides. Beach volleyball. Boules. All-weather sports pitch. Play area. Children's club and entertainment programme (July/Aug). WiFi over part of site (charged). Mobile homes and chalets for rent.

**Open:** 6 April - 16 September.

**Directions**

From the north, use toll ferry across the Gironde then head south on D1215, then D102 to Vendays-Montalivet. 8 km. beyond village, turn left at traffic lights, site is on left after 800 m.
GPS: 45.369989, -1.144606

**Charges guide**

| | |
|---|---|
| Per unit incl. 2 persons and electricity | € 17.10 - € 27.90 |

---

## Vensac
### Camping les Acacias du Médoc

44 route de Saint Vivien, F-33590 Vensac (Gironde) T: 05 56 09 58 81. E: contact@les-acacias-du-medoc.fr

**alanrogers.com/FR33170**

Les Acacias is a medium sized, family run site in a lovely, rural location on the edge of the pretty little village of Vensac. Angelique, Rodolph and their staff offer a warm welcome in the chalet-style reception. The mixed woodland setting, with lots of flowering shrubs, makes a welcome change from the ubiquitous pines on the coast. There are 175 pitches (122 for touring) with 6A electrical connections. The no-frills, heated swimming and paddling pools and jacuzzi are open all season, but the attractive bar and shop are only open in high season.

**Facilities**

Maintenance and cleaning of the attractive, recently refurbished toilet block is of a high standard. Facilities for disabled visitors. Mother and baby room. Washing machines and dryers. Small shop (1/7-30/8). Bar, café and takeaway (1/7-30/8). Swimming and paddling pools (1/6-24/9). Minigolf (free). Play area. Fitness equipment. Volleyball. Trampoline. Bouncy castle. Bicycle hire. Communal barbecue area. Mobile homes to rent. Off site: Bicycle hire in St Vivien 3 km. Beach 12 km.

**Open:** Easter - 30 September.

**Directions**

From the north, take ferry from Royan to Le Verdon then N215 south and turn off to Vensac (20 km).
GPS: 45.40887, -1.03274

**Charges guide**

| | |
|---|---|
| Per unit incl. 2 persons and electricity | € 15.00 - € 27.50 |
| extra person | € 3.50 - € 5.00 |
| child (4-10 yrs) | € 2.00 - € 3.50 |
| dog | € 3.00 |

---

## Veyrines-de-Domme
### Camping les Pastourels

Le Brouillet - D53, F-24250 Veyrines-de-Domme (Dordogne) T: 05 53 29 42 17. E: les.pastourels@orange.fr

**alanrogers.com/FR24970**

Les Pastourels is a very spacious site enjoying an excellent location at the heart of the Périgord Noir, with views stretching across towards the Château de Milandes. The region's capital, Sarlat, can be reached in around 15 minutes. There are just 48 very large touring pitches (and 19 mobile homes) here, all with 6/10A electricity and six are fully serviced. Some pitches are laid out informally in woodland, others are on grass, separated by hedges. The estate is mostly covered by forest (with the characteristic walnut trees found in this area) and pasture. A number of footpaths converge at the site, including the long-distance GR64.

**Facilities**

The modern toilet block includes facilities for babies and disabled visitors. Small shop for basics. Snack bar/pizzeria and takeaway (mid June-mid Sept). Outdoor swimming pool and paddling pool. Playground. Sports and play area. Bicycle hire. Family activities in July/Aug. WiFi near reception. Off site: Fishing 1.5 km. Riding 3 km. Golf 5 km. Castelnaud 3 km. Beynac 4 km.

**Open:** 13 April - 15 September.

**Directions**

From Sarlat head southwest towards Bergerac (D57). At Castelnaud-la-Chapelle turn right (D53) and follow signs to Château de Milandes and the site. GPS: 44.815504, 1.10014

**Charges guide**

| | |
|---|---|
| Per unit incl. 2 persons and electricity | € 19.00 - € 23.00 |
| extra person | € 5.00 |

---

For latest campsite news, availability and prices visit

# alanrogers.com

## Vielle-Saint-Girons
### Sunêlia le Col-Vert

Lac de Léon, 1548 route de l'Etang, F-40560 Vielle-Saint-Girons (Landes) T: 08 90 71 00 01.
E: contact@colvert.com **alanrogers.com/FR40050**

This large, well maintained campsite is well laid out on the shores of Lac de Léon and offers 185 mobile homes for rent and 380 touring pitches. The pitches range from simple ones to those with water and a drain, and there are eight with private, well designed, modern sanitary facilities. In low season it is a quiet site and those pitches beside the lake offer a wonderful backdrop to relaxing pastimes. During the main season it is a lively place for children of all ages. A pool complex offers a main pool for swimming, a pool for children with a water canon and fountains, plenty of sunbeds and a heated indoor pool.

#### Facilities

Four toilet blocks, one heated. One block with fun facilities for children based on Disney characters. Facilities for disabled guests. Laundry facilities. Motorcaravan services. Shops, bar/restaurant, takeaway (13/4-8/9). Swimming pool complex with three pools (all season). Spa, fitness centre and sauna. Games room. Sports areas. Boules. Tennis. Bicycle hire. Minigolf. Fishing. Riding. Sailing school (15/6-15/9). Communal barbecues. WiFi (charged). Off site: Atlantic beaches 5 km. Golf 10 km.

**Open:** 1 April - 22 September.

#### Directions

Site is off D652 Mimizan-Léon road, 4 km. south of crossroads with D42 at St Girons. Site and lake road are signed at Vielle. GPS: 43.90285, -1.3125

#### Charges 2013

| | |
|---|---|
| Per unit incl. 2 persons and electricity | € 17.40 - € 44.60 |
| extra person | € 2.20 - € 7.10 |
| child (3-12 yrs) | € 1.70 - € 6.10 |
| dog | € 1.20 - € 4.50 |

## Vielle-Saint-Girons
### Camping Club International Eurosol

Route de la Plage, F-40560 Vielle-Saint-Girons (Landes) T: 05 58 47 90 14. E: contact@camping-eurosol.com
**alanrogers.com/FR40060**

Eurosol is an attractive, friendly and well maintained site extending over 15 hectares of undulating ground amongst mature pine trees giving good shade. Of the 356 touring pitches, 231 have electricity (10A) with 120 fully serviced. A wide range of mobile homes and chalets are available for rent too. This is very much a family site with multi-lingual entertainers. Many games and tournaments are organised and a beach volleyball competition is held regularly in front of the bar. The adjacent boules terrain is floodlit. An excellent sandy beach 700 metres from the site has supervised bathing in high season and is ideal for surfing. The landscaped swimming pool complex with three large pools, one of which is covered and heated, and a large children's paddling pool. There is a convivial restaurant and takeaway food service. A large supermarket is well stocked with fresh bread daily and international newspapers. A number of cycle trails lead from the site through the vast forests of Les Landes, and a riding centre is located just 100 m. from Eurosol. To the south, the Basque country and Biarritz are within easy access.

#### Facilities

Four main toilet blocks and two smaller blocks are clean and comfortable with facilities for babies and disabled visitors. Motorcaravan services. Fridge rental. Well stocked shop and bar. Restaurant, takeaway (1/6-8/9). Stage for live shows (July/Aug). Outdoor swimming pool and paddling pool. Heated covered pool (low season). Tennis. Multisports court. Bicycle hire. WiFi (charged). No charcoal barbecues. Off site: Surf school 500 m. Beach 700 m.

**Open:** 18 May - 14 September.

#### Directions

Turn off D652 at Saint Girons on D42 towards St Girons-Plage. Site is on left before coming to beach (4.5 km). GPS: 43.95166, -1.35212

#### Charges guide

| | |
|---|---|
| Per unit incl. 2 persons and electricity | € 19.00 - € 37.00 |
| extra person (over 5 yrs) | € 6.00 |
| dog | € 4.00 |

**FREE** Alan Rogers Travel Card
Extra benefits and savings - see page 10

## Vielle-Saint-Girons

### Campéole les Tourterelles

F-40560 Vielle-Saint-Girons (Landes) T: 05 58 47 93 12. E: tourterelles@campeole.com

alanrogers.com/FR40450

Campé●le

Les Tourterelles is a large site extending over 20 hectares of forest and is a member of the Campéole group. The site has direct access to the beach, using two footpaths, one of which is decked. The beach is vast and very popular with surfers. A lifeguard is in attendance during the high season. There are 822 pitches at les Tourterelles, of which around 300 are occupied by mobile homes, chalets and fully equipped bungalow tents, all available for rent, and including some units specially adapted for disabled visitors. Pitches are well shaded by pines and most have electrical connections. Leisure facilities here include a multisports pitch, bicycle hire and several children's play areas. There are many appealing tracks through the surrounding forests and the site organises occasional accompanied walks (high season). Various other activities are on offer including beach volleyball and surfing lessons. A daily children's club is in operation as well as regular evening entertainment, including concerts and discos.

**Facilities**

Toilet blocks have hot showers, washbasins in cabins and facilities for disabled visitors. Motorcaravan service. Laundry facilities. Shop (1/5-30/9). Bar. Takeaway. Direct beach access. Volleyball. Beach volleyball. Bicycle hire. Bouncy castle. Play areas. Games room. Activity and entertainment programme. Mobile homes, chalets and equipped tents for rent. Only communal barbecues are permitted. WiFi (charged). Off site: St Girons Plage (attractive resort with all services) 200 m. Fishing. Walking and cycle tracks through the forest. Basque country.

**Open:** 1 May - 30 September.

**Directions**

Approaching from Bordeaux, take A63 towards Bayonne. Leave at Castets-Vielle-St-Girons exit and continue to Vielle-St-Girons. At traffic lights follow signs to St Girons-Plage (and site). At St Girons-Plage turn right at roundabout and site is a further 50 m. GPS: 43.9397, -1.3258

**Charges guide**

| Per unit incl. 2 persons | |
| --- | --- |
| and electricity | € 17.90 - € 31.70 |
| extra person | € 4.60 - € 9.50 |
| child (2-6 yrs) | free - € 5.60 |

AQUITAINE

Campé●le
CAMPSITES AND RENTALS

**Les Tourterelles** ★★★

Three stars site with direct access to the Ocean, surfing spot, swimming pool, quality touring pitches, new accommodations.

40560 Vielle Saint Girons - Tel.: +33-558-4793-12 - www.campeole.co.uk / tourterelles@campeole.com

## Vieux-Mareuil

### Camping de l'Etang Bleu

F-24340 Vieux-Mareuil (Dordogne) T: 05 53 60 92 70. E: letangbleu@orange.fr

alanrogers.com/FR24330

The English owners at this site, Marc and Jo Finch, are warm and friendly and work hard to maintain high standards. Set in 42 acres, there are only 98 pitches, with three used for mobile homes for rent. All are generously sized and level, enjoying a mixture of sun and shade. Electricity is available (10A). The site's best features are the lake where anglers can fish for carp, the bistro which offers great food, reasonably priced, and the sparkling clean swimming pool. This site is spacious tranquil and relaxing. Entertainment is limited but there are sporting facilities together with themed nights based around the bistro.

**Facilities**

Modern well maintained toilet block provides facilities for babies and disabled visitors. Laundry. Bar with terrace (all season). Bistro. Takeaway. Small shop. Swimming pool, sun terrace. Playground, paddling pool. Boules. Badminton. Entertainment, sporting activities, excursions in high season. WiFi (charged). Off site: Restaurant adjacent to campsite, small supermarket, post office etc. in Mareuil 7 km. Riding and bicycle hire 5 km. Golf 40 km.

**Open:** Easter/1 April - 21 October.

**Directions**

Site is between Angoulême and Périgueux. Leave D939 in Vieux Mareuil, take D93, and follow narrow road. Just after leaving village site signed on right, just past Auberge de l'Etang Bleu. Turn right, follow signs to site. GPS: 45.44614, 0.50859

**Charges guide**

| Per unit incl. 2 persons | |
| --- | --- |
| and electricity | € 17.25 - € 23.00 |
| extra person | € 3.75 - € 5.50 |

For latest campsite news, availability and prices visit

**alanrogers.com**

## Villefranche-de-Queyran
### Camping Moulin de Campech

F-47160 Villefranche-de-Queyran (Lot-et-Garonne) T: 05 53 88 72 43. E: camping@moulindecampech.co.uk
**alanrogers.com/FR47050**

This well shaded, pretty site is run by Sue and George Thomas along with Sue's parents, Dot and Bob Dunn. At the entrance to the site, a trout lake with graceful weeping willows feeds under the restored mill house, which is home to the owners as well as housing the bar and restaurant. Children will need supervision around the lake and at the pool which is on an elevated area above the mill house. The 46 large sized pitches are mostly divided by hedges, with electricity (6A, long leads may be necessary in places, but can be borrowed free of charge).

**Facilities**

The single, rather dated toilet block has modern fittings. Washing machine and dryer. Shop and bar (1/4-30/9). Restaurant (1/5-20/9). Terraced heated swimming pool (1/5-30/9). Open grassy games area. Board games and English library. Boules. Barbecue and quiz nights in high season. Fishing (discounted rate for campers, no permit required). Torch useful. WiFi over part of site (charged). Off site: Watersports, bicycle hire, golf and riding 10 km.

**Open:** 1 April - 7 October.

**Directions**

Take A10 south to Bordeaux. Join A62 for Toulouse and take exit 6 for Damazan. Follow D8 to Mont de Marsan, at Cap du Bosc turn right onto D11 for Casteljaloux. Site is signed, 5 km. on right. GPS: 44.27179, 0.19093

**Charges 2013**

| | |
|---|---|
| Per unit incl. 2 persons and electricity | € 18.00 - € 28.50 |
| extra person | € 3.50 - € 6.25 |

---

## Villeréal
### Yelloh! Village le Chateau de Fonrives

Rives, F-47210 Villeréal (Lot-et-Garonne) T: 05 53 36 63 38. E: chateau.de.fonrives@wanadoo.fr
**alanrogers.com/FR47030**

Le Château de Fonrives is situated in Lot-et-Garonne. The site is set in pretty part-farmed, part-wooded countryside. It is a mixture of hazelnut woodland with a lake and château (mostly 17th century). An attractive tree-lined avenue leads to the barns adjacent to the château, which have been converted to house the site's amenities. There are 301 pitches, 138 of which are for touring units, with electricity. They are of a generous size and are well defined by neatly trimmed hedges and small shrubs. Pitches near the woodland receive moderate shade, but elsewhere there is light shade from hedges and young trees.

**Facilities**

Three well positioned, modern sanitary blocks with facilities for disabled visitors. Laundry facilities. Shop. Restaurant, snacks and takeaway. Bar with disco area and terrace. Covered swimming pool, outdoor pool, water slides, paddling pool. Jacuzzi. Gym. Sauna. Trim trail. Bouncy castle. Play area. Library. Minigolf, tennis, bicycle hire (all charged). Activities organised in season. Hairdresser (July/Aug). WiFi in bar area (charged). Off site: Riding 8 km.

**Open:** 13 April - 29 September.

**Directions**

Site is 2 km. northwest of Villeréal, on west side of the D14/D207 Bergerac-Villaréal road. Pass through Rives, site is signed on left. GPS: 44.65723, 0.72847

**Charges guide**

| | |
|---|---|
| Per unit incl. 2 persons and electricity | € 18.00 - € 46.00 |
| extra person | € 7.00 - € 8.00 |
| child (under 3 yrs) | free |

---

## Villeréal
### Camping de Bergougne

D250, Rives, F-47210 Villeréal (Lot-et-Garonne) T: 05 53 36 01 30. E: info@camping-de-bergougne.com
**alanrogers.com/FR47160**

Camping de Bergougne is a small site located close to the 13th-century bastide of Villeréal in the Haut-Agenais. This restful site is a good choice for either relaxing at the poolside or exploring the surrounding country. There are 60 pitches, 48 for touring, with the remainder for mobile homes and tent-bungalows which are available for hire. The touring pitches are mainly in the shade and all have electricity. One toilet block is situated near the reception area and is converted from an original farm building – be careful, head room is limited!

**Facilities**

Two toilet blocks, one close to reception has limited head room. The second is newly built and of a high standard with facilities for babies and visitors with disabilities. Bar, restaurant, snack bar and takeaway (1/6-15/9). New swimming and paddling pools. Play area. Games room. Library. Pony riding. Fishing. WiFi in bar area (free). Tourist information. Communal barbecue. Off site: Shops and bicycle hire in Villaréal 2 km. Golf 15 km. Within 30 mins. of the Lot Valley and the Valley of the Dordogne.

**Open:** 1 May - 30 September.

**Directions**

Site is northwest of Villeréal. From Villeréal take the northbound D207 and at Rives, follow local signs to site. GPS: 44.652503, 0.723488

**Charges guide**

| | |
|---|---|
| Per unit incl. 2 persons and electricity | € 13.20 - € 19.60 |
| extra person | € 2.70 - € 3.90 |

**FREE** Alan Rogers Travel Card
Extra benefits and savings - see page 10

Rolling fields of yellow sunflowers, the Armagnac vineyards and crumbling, ancient stone buildings amidst the sleepy villages make this colourful region popular with those who enjoy good food, good wine and a taste of the good life.

**DÉPARTEMENTS: 09 ARIÈGE, 12 AVEYRON, 31 HAUTE-GARONNE, 32 GERS, 46 LOT, 65 HAUTES-PYRÉNÉES, 81 TARN, 82 TARN-ET GARONNE.**

**MAJOR CITY: TOULOUSE**

Extending from the Dordogne in the north, to the Spanish border in the south, Midi-Pyrénées is the largest region in France at over 45,000 km². It incorporates parts of historic provinces, including Languedoc and Gascony, whose heritage and traditions lend much to its identity.

It is blessed by radiant sunshine and a fascinating range of scenery. South of the cultivated fields and cliffside villages beside the Lot river, lie the stony lands of the Quercy Causse and the rocky gorges of the Aveyron and Tarn rivers. Centered around Millau, there are tortuous gorges and valleys, spectacular rivers, underground caves and grottoes, and forested mountains. Further south, high chalk plateaux, majestic peaks, tiny hidden valleys and small fortified sleepy villages seem to have changed little since the Middle Ages.

The vibrant university city of Toulouse with its pink brick buildings is the regional capital; it has a wealth of attractions from a Roman amphitheatre to an aerospace museum. Do not miss the historic city of Albi with its magnificent fortified cathedral, and dramatic Rocamadour, clinging to the side of the Alzou canyon.

### Places of interest

*Albi*: birthplace and Museum of Toulouse-Lautrec, imposing Ste Cécile cathedral with 15th-century fresco of The Last Judgement.

*Auch*: capital of ancient Gascony, boasts a fine statue of d'Artágnan.

*Collonges-la-Rouge*: picturesque village of Medieval- and Renaissance-style mansions and manors.

*Foix*: 11th-/12th-century towers on a rocky peak above town; 14th-century cathedral.

*Lourdes*: famous pilgrimage site where Ste Bernadette is said to have spoken to the Virgin Mary in a grotto, and known for the miracles said to have been performed there.

*Martel*: home of the Haute Quercy heritage railway with steam trains in July and August.

### Cuisine of the region

Food is rich and strongly seasoned, making generous use of garlic and goose fat, and there are some excellent regional wines. Seafood such as oysters, saltwater fish, and piballes from the Adour river are popular.

*Cassoulet*: stew of duck, sausages and beans.

*Confit de Canard (d'oie)*: preserved duck meat.

*Croustade aux pommes:* caramelised apple tart sometimes containing Agen prunes.

*Magret de canard*: duck breast fillets

*Ouillat (Ouliat)*: Pyrénées soup with onions, tomatoes, goose fat and garlic.

*Piperade Basque*: an omelette of tomatoes, peppers and local pimentos.

www.tourisme-midi-pyrenees.com
information@crtmp.com
(0)5 61 13 55 48

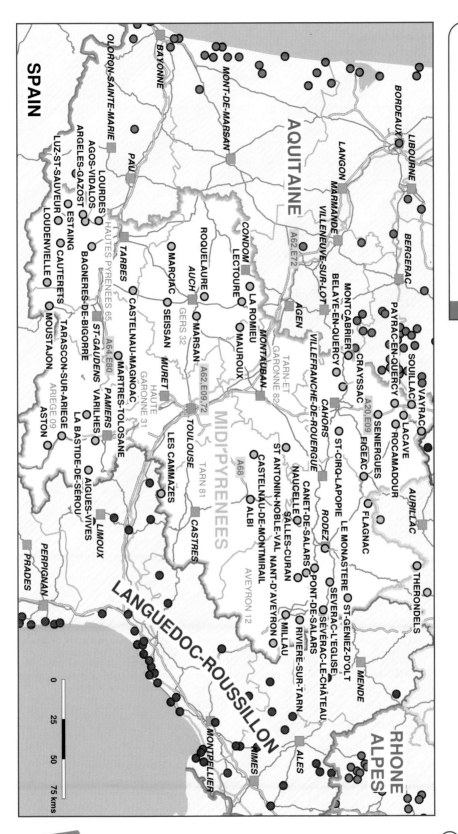

SPAIN

AQUITAINE

MIDI-PYRENEES

LANGUEDOC-ROUSSILLON

RHONE ALPES

BORDEAUX
LIBOURNE
BERGERAC
BAYONNE
MONT-DE-MARSAN
OLORON-SAINTE-MARIE
LANGON
MARMANDE
VILLENEUVE-SUR-LOT
AGEN
PAU
TARBES
LOURDES
AGOS-VIDALOS
ARGELES-GAZOST
ESTAING
LUZ-ST-SAUVEUR
CAUTERETS
LOUDENVIELLE
MOUSTAJON
TARASCON-SUR-ARIEGE
BAGNERES-DE-BIGORRE
ST-GAUDENS
VARILHES
LA BASTIDE-DE-SEROU
AIGUES-VIVES
ASTON
PERPIGNAN
PRADES
LIMOUX
LES CAMMAZES
CASTRES
TOULOUSE
MURET
MARTRES-TOLOSANE
CASTELNAU-MAGNOAC
PAMIERS
SEISSAN
MARSAN
AUCH
MARCIAC
ROQUELAURE
LECTOURE
CONDOM
LA ROMIEU
MAUROUX
MONTAUBAN
ALBI
CASTELNAU-DE-MONTMIRAIL
ST ANTONIN-NOBLE-VAL
NANT-D'AVEYRON
NAUCELLE
SALLES-CURAN
CANET-DE-SALARS
PONT-DE-SALARS
RIVIERE-SUR-TARN
MILLAU
SEVERAC-LE-CHATEAU
SEVERAC-L'EGLISE
ST-GENIEZ-D'OLT
MENDE
RODEZ
CAHORS
VILLEFRANCHE-DE-ROUERGUE
ST-CIRQ-LAPOPIE
LE MONASTERE
BELAYE-EN-QUERCY
MONTCABRIER
CRAYSSAC
PAYRAC-EN-QUERCY
SOUILLAC
LACAVE
ROCAMADOUR
VAYRAC
SENIERGUES
FIGEAC
FLAGNAC
AURILLAC
THERONDELS
MONTPELLIER
NIMES
ALES

HAUTES PYRENEES 65
GERS 32
ARIEGE 09
HAUTE GARONNE 31
TARN-ET GARONNE 82
TARN 81
AVEYRON 12

A62 E72
A64 E80
A62 E09,72
A68
A20 E09

0  25  50  75 kms

**FREE** Alan Rogers Travel Card
Extra benefits and savings - see page 10

## Agos-Vidalos

### Camping Soleil du Pibeste

16 avenue du Lavedan, F-65400 Agos-Vidalos (Hautes-Pyrénées) T: 05 62 97 53 23.
E: info@campingpibeste.com  **alanrogers.com/FR65090**

The Dusserm family, the owners, are very proud of their regional culture and heritage and will ensure you are made welcome. The reception includes an area for local foods, maps and good tourist information. This site offers a diverse range of activities including tai chi, qi gong, massage, archery, walking, climbing and canoeing. Choral and creative activities are also offered. There are 38 touring pitches all with 3-15A electricity. Mobile homes and chalets are available to rent. Mountain view from the terrace.

**Facilities**

Two heated toilet blocks. Baby room. Facilities for disabled visitors (key). Cleaning can be variable. Washing machine, dryer. Motorcaravan services. Bar, snack bar, restaurant and pizzeria (June-Sept). Shop. Bread to order. Swimming pool (June-Sept). New play areas. Multisports pitch. Tennis. Badminton. Bowling. Basketball. Four free activities weekly (July/Aug). Entertainment, children's activities and craft workshops (July/Aug). Massage (charged). Library. WiFi (charged). Off site: Fishing 800 m.

**Open:** 1 May - 30 September.

**Directions**

Agos Vidalos is on the N21, which becomes the D821, 5 km. south of Lourdes. Leave expressway at second exit, signed Agos Vidalos and continue on D921B to site, a short distance on the right. GPS: 43.03557, -0.07093

**Charges guide**

| | |
|---|---|
| Per unit incl. 2 persons and electricity | € 23.00 - € 36.00 |
| extra person | € 8.00 |

## Aigues-Vives

### Domaine de la Serre

Chemin de la Serre 5, F-09600 Aigues-Vives (Ariège) T: 05 61 03 06 16. E: contact@camping-la-serre.com
**alanrogers.com/FR09170**

A beautiful site set in ten hectares of gentle hillside run by Robert and Francoise, a hardworking and very friendly French couple. There are 66 spacious pitches, 46 are touring, all with electricity (5/10A). Most are on well drained grass with shade and privacy, some are on hardstanding and there is additional hardstanding for motorcaravans in wet weather. There is a small, friendly bar and the site takes pride in not having a disco or karaoke, but preferring to enjoy and respect nature - there are superb views towards the Pyrenees. A range of chalets are available for hire. Member of Campings La Via Natura.

**Facilities**

Two main modern sanitary blocks and one small block. Good facilities for disabled visitors. Facilities for children and babies. Family shower rooms. Laundry facilities. Motorcaravan service point. Bar (July/Aug). Swimming pool. Tennis. Volleyball. Pétanque. Mountain bike track. Play area. Observation telescope. Small film theatre. Farming museum. Bicycle hire. Free WiFi over part of site. Off site: Local market, shops, restaurant and bars 3 km.

**Open:** 1 April - 30 September.

**Directions**

From Foix take D117 (15 km) south at Lavelanet turn left onto D625 (7.5 km) to Aigues-Vives, site clearly signed on left just after town. GPS: 42.997617, 1.87201

**Charges guide**

| | |
|---|---|
| Per unit incl. 2 persons and electricity | € 19.00 - € 25.00 |
| extra person | € 5.00 |

Credit cards are not accepted.

## Albi

### Albirondack Park Camping Lodge & Spa

31 allée de la Piscine, F-81000 Albi (Tarn) T: 05 63 60 37 06. E: albirondack@orange.fr
**alanrogers.com/FR81230**

Albirondack Park is ideal for campers seeking something out of the ordinary. This site has a selection of rental accomodation, including Airstream caravans and chalets raised to tree top height. The 54 touring pitches are well shaded and all have 10A electicity. Some of the pitches, which are separated by low wooden barriers giving no privacy, vary in size (60-100 sq.m) so can be a little awkward for large units. The outdoor heated swimming pool, sauna and steam rooms are open all year, as is the restaurant (open to non-residents). The site is relatively quiet and a traffic-free path leads to the town.

**Facilities**

One well equipped, modern toilet block has British style WCs, ensuite showers and washbasins in cabins. Facilities for disabled visitors. Laundry facilities. Motorcaravan service point. Restaurant. Bar. Takeaway. Daily bread. Heated swimming pool. Paddling pool. Sauna and steam room. Jacuzzi. TV room. Play area (July/Aug). WiFi (charged). Off site: Supermarket and shopping centre 600 m. Walks into Albi. River cruises. Fishing, riding and bicycle hire 3 km. Golf 5 km.

**Open:** 1 April - 15 November and 15-31 December.

**Directions**

Approaching Albi from the east on the Route de Millau (D999) follow signs for Camping. GPS: 43.9337, 2.1663

**Charges guide**

| | |
|---|---|
| Per unit incl. 2 persons, electricity, water and waste water | € 20.70 - € 33.70 |
| extra person | € 5.00 - € 7.00 |
| child (2-7 yrs) | € 2.60 - € 4.50 |
| dog | € 5.00 |

For latest campsite news, availability and prices visit
# alanrogers.com

## Argelès-Gazost
### Sunêlia les Trois Vallées

Avenue des Pyrénées, F-65400 Argelès-Gazost (Hautes-Pyrénées) T: 05 62 90 35 47.
E: 3-valles@wanadoo.fr **alanrogers.com/FR65020**

The attractive outdoor pools, jacuzzi, water chutes and heated indoor pool with opening roof are features of this large and lively site. It has 200 level grassy touring pitches, with some mountain views, and 283 mobile homes. All have electricity (3-6A). Reception staff are helpful and friendly. Visitors can gather in the new, imaginatively designed centre to eat, drink, chat, use the WiFi, watch events on the overhead TVs, and in season enjoy the daily programme of professional entertainers. All visitors can enjoy an impressive programme of activities. The pilgrimage town of Lourdes is nearby.

**Facilities**

The toilet blocks are a little dated and could be busy at peak times. Facilities for disabled visitors. Bar/disco. Café, takeaway, restaurant (15/6-15/9). Bread. Swimming pool complex (from 15/5), heated indoor pool (all year), paddling pool, spa bath, jacuzzi and two water slides. TV room. Playground. Volleyball, football, boules, archery. Entertainment and activities in high season. Meeting and eating area with retractable roof and walls. WiFi (charged in high season). Off site: Supermarket across the road. Bicycle hire 50 m. Fishing 500 m.

**Open:** 1 April - 2 November.

**Directions**

Argelès-Gazost is 13 km. south of Lourdes. Take D821 towards Argelès-Gazost, then onto La Voie Rapide and turn right at the first roundabout, after 300 m. right at the new roundabout and you are at the site. GPS: 43.01216, -0.09711

**Charges guide**

| | |
|---|---|
| Per unit incl. 2 persons and electricity | € 13.50 - € 34.00 |
| extra person | € 5.00 - € 10.00 |

## Argelès-Gazost
### Kawan Village du Lavedan

Lau-Balagnas, 44 route des Vallees, F-65400 Argelès-Gazost (Hautes-Pyrénées) T: 05 62 97 18 84.
E: contact@lavedan.com **alanrogers.com/FR65080**

Camping du Lavedan is an old, established, family owned site set in the Argelès-Gazost valley south of Lourdes, where a warm welcome and an impressive mountain view await you. There are 60 level touring pitches, all with electricity (2-10A) and most have shade from trees. They are set away from the 48 mobile homes, of which 12 are for rent. Landscaping has been carefully considered. The large, well designed restaurant and bar area is the scene of some lively evening entertainment in the summer.

**Facilities**

Recent well maintained toilet block. Baby room. Facilities for disabled visitors. Laundry facilities. No shop, bread delivery (1/5-15/9). Restaurant with terrace, pizzeria and snacks (1/5-15/9). Bar, TV (all year). Swimming pool (with cover), paddling pool. Play area. Boules. WiFi (charged). Off site: Trout fishing and bicycle hire 1 km. Supermarket 2 km. Riding 5 km. Golf 15 km. La Voie Verte, a 17 km. traffic-free cycle path from Lourdes south to Soulom.

**Open:** All year.

**Directions**

From Lourdes take the N21 (Voie rapide) south. This becomes the N821/N821A. Take exit 3 (Argelès - Gazost). Take D921 then D921B to Lau-Balagnas. Site is on right at southern edge of town. GPS: 42.98822, -0.089

**Charges guide**

| | |
|---|---|
| Per unit incl. 2 persons | € 15.00 - € 24.00 |
| electricity (10A max) | € 1.00 |

Camping Cheques accepted.

## Aston
### Camping le Pas de l'Ours

F-09310 Aston (Ariège) T: 05 61 64 90 33. E: contact@lepasdelours.fr
**alanrogers.com/FR09110**

In the small town of Aston, which is located in the heart of the scenic Vallées d'Ax in the Haute-Ariège region, you will find the secluded campsite of le Pas de l'Ours. With panoramic views of the mountains, this charming site has a total of 57 pitches, although only 30 of these are for tourers, as the rest are taken up by chalets to rent. Six of the smaller touring pitches are reserved for tents and have no electricity, but the other 24 grassy and mainly level pitches are well kept and attractively laid out, separated by shrubs and bushes and have 6A electricity (French sockets). A Sites et Paysages member.

**Facilities**

Two modern sanitary blocks are well equipped and include pre-set showers. Large en-suite room for disabled visitors. Motorcaravan service point. Bakers van calls every morning in July/Aug. Communal covered purpose built barbecue area with picnic tables. Small play area. Tennis court. Off site: Heated outdoor swimming pool in village adjacent to site (on payment). Shops, restaurant and bars 2 km. Skiing 16 km. Riding 20 km. Golf 30 km.

**Open:** 1 June - 14 September (chalets all year).

**Directions**

From N20 between Ax-les-Thermes and Tarascon take exit to Les Cabannes on D522a signed Verdun and Aston. After 1.8 km. turn left on D520 to Château Verdun and Aston. Site is well signed. GPS: 42.772283, 1.67155

**Charges guide**

| | |
|---|---|
| Per unit incl. 2 persons and electricity | € 17.00 - € 23.00 |
| extra person | € 3.00 - € 5.00 |

**FREE** Alan Rogers Travel Card
Extra benefits and savings - see page 10

## Bagnères-de-Bigorre

### Camping le Monlôo

route de la plaine, F-65200 Bagnères-de-Bigorre (Hautes-Pyrénées) T: 05 62 95 19 65.
E: campingmonloo@yahoo.com **alanrogers.com/FR65160**

A relatively small site of 110 touring pitches, le Monlôo is set in a wide valley in the Pyrenees. The immediate surroundings of farmland, with crops growing and cows at pasture, give way to some magnificent views of the mountains towering away from the front of the site, whilst the back is right at the foot of some smaller foothills. This area is a paradise for walkers and cyclists and just travelling a short distance opens up new horizons with some large waterfalls not far away. The friendly family take their job seriously and will even show you a selection of available pitches from the comfort of their electric car. Shade is available on many pitches, with some tall dividing hedges. Electricity (10A) is available. Although the site lacks modern day entertainments, the visitors we met were all very content with having a good pitch, ample electricity and good facilities. There is a distinct air of friendliness here.

**Facilities**

Ample toilet facilities are provided in three blocks. Facilities for disabled visitors. Washing machines. Motorcaravan services. Bread to order. Open-air heated pool with slide. Simple play area. Gas or electric barbecues are permitted. WiFi throughout (charged). Off site: Spa town of Bagnères-de-Bigorre 2 km.

**Open:** All year (except November).

**Directions**

From the A64 take exit 14 signed Bagnères-de-Bigorre. Enter town and take D8 road to the right for Ordizan. Site is just a few hundred metres along this road, well signed. GPS: 43.08180, 0.15139

**Charges guide**

| Per unit incl. 3 persons | |
| --- | --- |
| and electricity | € 19.00 - € 24.50 |
| extra person | € 3.50 - € 5.00 |
| child (under 8 yrs) | € 2.00 - € 3.50 |
| dog | € 1.50 |

# Camping le Monlôo **** Mail: campingmonloo@yahoo.com
Tel: 0033(0)5.62.95.19.65

*Le Monlôo is situated in the touristique city of Bagnères de Bigorre at a high of 550m.*
*We offer you great service and the comfort of a 4 star campsite*

**65200 Bagnères de Bigorre - Hautes Pyrénées - France - www.lemonloo.com**

## Bélaye-en-Quercy

### Camping la Tuque

Lieu dit La Tuque, F-46140 Bélaye (Lot) T: 05 65 21 34 34. E: info@campinglatuque.fr
**alanrogers.com/FR46130**

The Quercy region of southwest France is renowned for its sunny climate and attractive terrain, ranging from the dry Causse landscape to the lusher Lot valley and vineyards of Cahors. La Tuque extends over 22 acres, close to the pretty village of Bélaye. The 75 touring pitches are large (some to 120 sq.m) and well shaded. Unusually, except for loading and unloading, cars are not allowed in the camping area, and large parking areas are provided at the entrance. This is a good centre for an active holiday – walking, mountain biking, canoeing and rock climbing are all possible and the site also has a large swimming pool and three water slides, as well as a separate children's pool.

**Facilities**

Small shop with daily delivery of fresh bread. Restaurant, bar and snack bar with freshly baked pizzas (22/6-31/8). Swimming pool with water slides and paddling pool. Tennis court. Minigolf. Library. Playground. Games room. Laundry carried out by site staff. Fridge hire. Mobile homes, Safari Lodge and tents for rent. WiFi in bar area (charged). Off site: Walking and cycling. Fishing 5 km. Prayssac with shops and cafés 10 km. Riding 15 km.

**Open:** 27 April - 7 September.

**Directions**

Leave the A20 autoroute at exit 57 (Cahors) and take the D811 (D911) towards Puy l'Evêque. In Prayssac, take the D67 towards Bélaye/Boulvé. From Belaye take the D6, following signs to la Tuque. Site is well signed from here. GPS: 44.44407, 1.17244

**Charges guide**

| Per unit incl. 2 persons | |
| --- | --- |
| and electricity | € 18.50 - € 27.10 |
| extra person | € 4.00 - € 6.30 |

No credit cards.

For latest campsite news, availability and prices visit
# alanrogers.com

## Canet-de-Salars
### Castels Camping le Caussanel

Lac de Pareloup, F-12290 Canet-de-Salars (Aveyron) T: 05 65 46 85 19. E: info@lecaussanel.com
**alanrogers.com/FR12170**

This site has 228 large, fairly level, grassy pitches, 108 for touring. Most have 6A electricity but very long leads may be necessary, and 45 are fully serviced. The pitches are defined by lines and offer little privacy but many have wonderful views over the lake. Most pitches have little shade, a few having good shade. The site has swimming pools with toboggan and slides and a large paddling pool for children with small slides. The adjacent 1200 ha. lake offers a large area for swimming and all the usual watersports.

| Facilities | Directions |
|---|---|
| Modern toilet blocks have all the necessary facilities. Shop. Bar. Restaurant, takeaway (reduced opening in low season). Swimming pool complex. Play area. Boules. Tennis. Table tennis. Football. Activities (July/Aug). Fishing. Bicycle hire (July/Aug). Motorboat launching. Watersports (July/Aug). Swimming in lake. Max. 2 dogs (1 in rentals). WiFi (charged). Off site: Paths by lake. Walks and cycle rides. Shops, banks, restaurants 8 km. Riding 13 km. Golf 30 km. Canoeing, rafting, paragliding and windsurfing.<br><br>**Open:** 6 May - 7 September. | From D911 Rodez-Millau road, just east of Pont de Salars, turn south on D993 signed Salles-Curan. In 6 km. at crossroads turn right on D538 signed le Caussanel. Very shortly turn left and continue to site. GPS: 44.21462, 2.76658 |

**Charges guide**

| | |
|---|---|
| Per unit incl. 2 persons and electricity | € 17.90 - € 33.80 |
| extra person | € 3.90 - € 7.30 |
| Camping Cheques accepted. | |

## Castelnau-de-Montmiral
### Camping du Chêne Vert

F-81140 Castelnau-de-Montmiral (Tarn) T: 05 63 33 16 10. E: campingduchenevert@wanadoo.fr
**alanrogers.com/FR81170**

Camping du Chêne Vert is surrounded by the vineyards of the Gaillac region and is located on the circuit of the Bastides Albigeoises. The site can be found just 3 km. from one of France's most beautiful villages, Castelnau-de-Montmiral. Some pitches are large and grassy. Most have 10A electrical connections. A number of chalets and fully equipped tents are available to rent. On site amenities include a well stocked shop, a bar and a swimming pool. During high season, pizzas and crêpes are available, and a weekly themed meal is organised. A local wine producer visits the site on a regular basis with the opportunity to taste and purchase his produce.

| Facilities | Directions |
|---|---|
| Bar/restaurant. Takeaway. Shop. Swimming pool. TV room. Games room. Volleyball. Play area. Activities and entertainment. Tourist information. WiFi. Chalets and equipped tents for rent. Off site: Hiking and cycle tracks. Riding. Golf. Albi 30 km.<br><br>**Open:** 1 June - 30 September. | Castelnau-de-Montmiral is north of Gaillac. Leave A68 motorway at exit 9 (Gaillac) and head north from Gaillac on D964 to Castelnau-de-Montmiral. The site is well signed. GPS: 43.97664, 1.79052 |

**Charges guide**

| | |
|---|---|
| Per unit incl. 2 persons and electricity | € 15.70 - € 19.00 |
| extra person | € 3.50 - € 4.70 |

## Cauterets
### Camping Cabaliros

93 avenue du Mamelon Vert, F-65110 Cauterets (Hautes-Pyrénées) T: 05 62 92 55 36.
E: info@camping-cabaliros.com **alanrogers.com/FR65110**

This is a delightful site, with friendly family owners who will give you a warm welcome to this magnificent mountain area. The open, grassy site has stupendous panoramic views. A separate field has 36 pitches for small tents and another 60 touring pitches with electricity (6A Europlug). These are large and grassy and some shade is provided by mature trees. A communal room is used by visitors for free WiFi, to make music, play games, watch television, read books and enjoy themselves. The site is within walking distance of Cauterets, with its shops and restaurants.

| Facilities | Directions |
|---|---|
| Sanitary block near site entrance with WCs, hot showers and washbasins in cubicles. Facilities for disabled visitors. Laundry facilities. Motorcaravan services. Large library (some English) and excellent meeting room with television. Play area for over 7s. Fishing. WiFi. Off site: Restaurant (July/Aug) 50 m. Supermarket 1 km. Shops, bars, restaurants and swimming pools 2 km. Route des Cascades 4 km. Pont d'Espagne 9 km. Riding 10 km.<br><br>**Open:** End May - 30 September. | From Argelès-Gazost take D921B followed by the D920A to Cauterets. Site is on right 200 m. after Carrefour supermarket, just before Cauterets. GPS: 42.90347, -0.10714 |

**Charges guide**

| | |
|---|---|
| Per unit incl. 2 persons and electricity (6A) | € 16.20 - € 18.00 |
| tent incl. 2 persons and car | € 12.70 - € 14.10 |
| extra person | € 4.55 - € 5.00 |

**FREE** Alan Rogers Travel Card
Extra benefits and savings - see page 10

## Crayssac

### Campéole les Reflets du Quercy

Mas de Bastide, F-46150 Crayssac (Lot) T: 05 65 30 00 27. E: reflets-du-quercy@campeole.com

**alanrogers.com/FR46170**

Set in the west of the Lot department, this site is set on a wooded hill about 16 km. from the large town of Cahors. It is owned by the Campéole group and is classed as a holiday village. It is very lively here during July and August but otherwise very quiet. There are 150 uneven, stony pitches with shade, just 35 of which are for touring, most with 6A electricity (rock pegs are essential). At the rear of the site is a large area of independently owned mobile homes and residents here also have access to the campsite facilities. The site has a good 25 m. swimming pool overlooked by the terrace of the bar and snack bar. There are several play areas and sport facilities on site and in July and August there is an extensive programme of events for all the family, but probably more appealing to families with active teenagers. There are many ancient market towns and villages to explore and the local produce is worth sampling.

| Facilities | Directions |
|---|---|
| One adequate toilet block with facilities for disabled visitors. Baby room with bath. Laundry facilities. Motorcaravan service point (charged). Shop, bar and snack bar (July/Aug). Swimming and paddling pools. TV and games room, bouncy castle (all July/Aug). Boules. Tennis. Multisport court. Play area. Entertainment (July/Aug). WiFi (charged). Off site: Shop, bar and restaurant at Mercuès 4 km. Canoeing and fishing on the River Lot. Riding 7 km. Bicycle hire 15 km. Water park (Souillac). Shops 16 km. Walks and cycle routes. | At Cahors leave RN20, take D811 northwest signed Fumel, through Mercuès. After a further 4.5 km. turn left D23, signed Crayssac. Just before Crayssac turn right, site signed, entrance in 1.5 km. GPS: 44.50993, 1.32269 |

**Open:** 9 April - 25 September.

**Charges guide**

| Per unit incl. 2 persons | |
|---|---|
| and electricity | € 15.10 - € 24.50 |
| extra person | € 4.00 - € 6.10 |
| child (2-6 yrs) | free - € 4.00 |
| dog | € 2.00 - € 2.60 |

## Figeac

### Kawan Village  Le Domaine du Surgié

Domaine du Surgié, F-46100 Figeac (Lot) T: 05 61 64 88 54. E: contact@marc-montmija.com

**alanrogers.com/FR46320**

Very conveniently placed, this rural site is only 2 km. from the centre of the interesting old town of Figeac. There are 163 pitches, of which 103 are for touring, the remaining 60 for mobile homes and gîtes, all of which are for rent. The grass pitches are level, with a mixture of shade and sun and all have 10A electricity. Access is easy for large outfits. The site is split into different areas with the aquatic centre next to the camping area. There are many organised activities on site and in the surrounding area making it an ideal choice for an active family including teenagers.

| Facilities | Directions |
|---|---|
| Three modern toilet blocks include facilities for babies and disabled visitors. Laundry. Shop, bar, restaurant and takeaway. Swimming pool complex adjacent (15/5-15/9, open to the public). Sports competitions and party nights with themed dining. Children's clubs. Canoeing. Fishing. Minigolf. Boules. Bicycle hire. WiFi near reception (charged). Off site: Riding 2 km. Figeac with shops, bars, restaurants and museums 2 km. | From the west, enter Figeac on the D802 and then turn right across river, signed Base de Loisirs. Shortly turn left at small roundabout and then, at traffic lights, branch left uphill to site. Well signed from the centre of Figeac. GPS: 44.60989, 2.05015 |

**Open:** 1 April - 30 September.

**Charges guide**

| Per unit incl. 2 persons | |
|---|---|
| and electricity | € 14.00 - € 22.00 |
| extra person | € 4.00 - € 6.80 |

Camping Cheques accepted.

For latest campsite news, availability and prices visit

# alanrogers.com

## Estaing
### Camping Pyrénées Natura

Route du Lac, F-65400 Estaing (Hautes-Pyrénées) T: 05 62 97 45 44. E: info@camping-pyrenees-natura.com
**alanrogers.com/FR65060**

Pyrénées Natura, at an altitude of 1,000 m. on the edge of the national park is the perfect site for lovers of nature. The 66 pitches (47 for tourers), all with electricity (3-10A), are in a landscaped area with 75 varieties of trees and shrubs – but they do not spoil the fantastic views. A traditional-style building houses the reception, bar and indoor games/reading room. There is a small, well stocked shop in the former watermill. Prices are very reasonable and homemade bread can be purchased. Children will love the animals, including the unusual hens, the guinea pigs, goat and donkey. On the river there is a small beach belonging to the site for supervised water play. The owners, the Papin family, will do all they can to make your stay a pleasant one. Their aim is that you return home feeling at peace with the world and having learnt something about the area and its flora and fauna, especially the birds which soar above the site. This site belongs to the prestigious Via Natura group of 11 campsites in France, committed to eco-tourism principles.

### Facilities

First class toilet blocks. Facilities for disabled visitors and babies. Washing machine and airers (no lines allowed). Motorcaravan services. Bar, small shop and takeaway (1/5-15/9). Lounge, library, TV, upstairs games/reading room. Bird watching is a speciality of the site and equipment is available. Sauna (free 13.00-17.00), solarium and jacuzzi. Music room. Play area for the very young. Small beach beside river. Boules. Giant chess. Weekly evening meal in May, June and Sept. Internet. Walks organised. WiFi over site (free in Bar).

**Open:** 29 March - 20 October.

### Directions

At Argelès-Gazost, take D918 towards Aucun. After 8 km. turn left on D13 to Bun, cross the river, then right on D103 to site (5.5 km). Narrow road, few passing places. GPS: 42.94152, -0.17726

### Charges 2013

| | |
|---|---|
| Per unit incl. 2 persons and electricity | € 19.00 - € 44.50 |
| extra person | € 5.85 - € 42.00 |
| child (under 8 yrs) | € 3.80 |
| dog | € 3.00 |

# CAMPING PYRENEES NATURA★★★★
In the heart of the mountains, *Camping Pyrénées Natura* invites you to relax and unwind. For all nature lovers!

Tel +33 (0)5 62 97 45 44 • www.camping-pyrenees-natura.com • info@camping-pyrenees-natura.com

## Flagnac
### Flower Camping le Port de Lacombe

F-12300 Flagnac (Aveyron) T: 05 65 64 10 08. E: accueil@campingleportdelacombe.fr
**alanrogers.com/FR12290**

Le Port de Lacombe is well kept, situated on the banks of the Lot river, a location ideal for walking, cycling, fishing and canoeing. The 97 grass touring pitches (with 10A electricity) are level and range in size from 100-130 sq.m. A large natural swimming pool is fed by the river and provides a separate paddling area and a large slide. Using the D42, one can wind through the valley and climb to over 2,000 feet to the Plateau de la Viadene. The scenery is panoramic and picturesque. Running past the site, the Lot river provides a relaxing environment to laze away your holiday, should you wish to do so.

### Facilities

Two separate sanitary blocks, each with the usual facilities including provision for disabled visitors. Washing machine. Shop and bar (all season) with restaurant and takeaway (both 15/6-15/9). TV in function room. Play area. Swimming pool fed from the river. Paddling pool (15/6-15/9). Bicycle hire. Fishing in river. Entertainment (July/Aug). WiFi throughout (charged).

**Open:** 1 April - 30 September.

### Directions

Driving south from Brive-la-Gaillarde, take N140 to Decazeville, turning north on D963 to Flagnac. Site is well signed on the left. From Rodez take N140 to Decazeville, then as above. GPS: 44.60915, 2.23597

### Charges guide

| | |
|---|---|
| Per unit incl. 2 persons and electricity | € 16.00 - € 26.90 |
| extra person | € 2.50 - € 5.50 |

## La Bastide-de-Sérou

511

### Camping l'Arize

Lieu-dit Bourtol, F-09240 La Bastide-de-Sérou (Ariège) T: 05 61 65 81 51. E: mail@camping-arize.com

alanrogers.com/FR09020

The site sits in a delightful, tranquil valley among the foothills of the Pyrénées and is just east of the interesting village of La Bastide-de-Sérou beside the River Arize (good trout fishing). The river is fenced for the safety of children on the site, but may be accessed just outside the gate. The 71 large touring pitches are neatly laid out on level grass within the spacious site. All have 6/10A electricity and are mostly separated into bays by hedges and young trees. Full services are available to some pitches with access to a small toilet block. You will receive a warm welcome from Dominique and Brigitte.

**Facilities**

Toilet block includes facilities for babies and disabled visitors. Laundry room. Motorcaravan services. Shop. Small swimming pool and sunbathing area. Entertainment in high season. Weekly barbecues. Fishing. Bicycle hire. WiFi (charged). Off site: Restaurant at the national stud for the famous Merens horses 200 m (will deliver takeaway meals to your pitch). Restaurants and shops within a few minutes drive. Golf 5 km.

**Open:** 9 March - 10 November.

**Directions**

Site is southeast of the village La Bastide-de-Sérou. Take the D15 towards Nescus and site is on right after 1 km. GPS: 43.00182, 1.44538

**Charges guide**

| Per unit incl. 2 persons | |
|---|---|
| and electricity | € 17.40 - € 29.60 |
| extra person | € 4.20 - € 6.30 |
| child (7-13 yrs) | € 3.80 - € 4.90 |

## Lacave

### Camping la Rivière

Le Bougayrou, F-46200 Lacave (Lot) T: 05 65 37 02 04. E: contact@campinglariviere.com

alanrogers.com/FR46370

Camping la Rivière is situated on the banks of the Dordogne with direct access to the river and a sand and pebble beach. It is a natural rural site and in a pleasant location. The A20 motorway and the town of Souillac are just 15 km. away. The welcome from the owners is warm and friendly and they place much importance on customer service and a family atmosphere is of conviviality. There are 110 pitches of which 15 are for mobile homes (all for rent). The remaining 93 pitches are for touring units, and all have electricity (10A). Of good size, all are level and on grass and divided by trees and shrubs which provide a good amount of shade. There is a lagoon shaped swimming pool together with a paddling pool. Thoughtfully, there are two separate games areas, one for the toddlers and one for the rest. There is a children's club for 5-11 year olds and teen evenings for 11-15 year olds. The site has its own snack bar but within 4 km. there is a choice of numerous gastronomic restaurants. The closest one, which has an excellent reputation, is just 300 m. away. Many interesting places to visit are within a short distance.

**Facilities**

Three toilet blocks include facilities for disabled visitors and babies. Laundry. Shop, bar, snack bar and takeaway (all June-Aug). Two swimming pools including a children's pool. Two games areas. Minigolf. Barbecue and picnic areas. Excursions. Disco and karaoke evenings. Free WiFi in bar/reception. Off site: The Caves of Padirac. Sarlat and numerous theme parks. Rocamadour. Museums. Off road cycling. Canoeing. Fishing. Kayaking. Climbing. Riding. Golf. Bicycle hire 3 km. Lacave 3 km. St Sozy 4 km.

**Open:** 13 April - 21 September.

**Directions**

From Souillac take D803 (direction Martel). After 5 km. turn right onto D15 to St Sozy. Cross river at St Sozy. Take first right signed Lacave. Site is signed on right in 4 km. GPS: 44.86171, 1.559372

**Charges 2013**

| Per unit incl. 2 persons | |
|---|---|
| and electricity | € 17.60 - € 26.40 |
| extra person | € 4.40 - € 5.70 |
| child (under 10 yrs) | € 2.50 - € 3.70 |
| dog | free - € 1.80 |

For latest campsite news, availability and prices visit

# alanrogers.com

# La Romieu

## Le Camp de Florence

Route Astaffort, F-32480 La Romieu (Gers) T: 05 62 28 15 58. E: info@lecampdeflorence.com

**alanrogers.com/FR32010**

Camp de Florence is an attractive and very well equipped site on the edge of an historic village in pleasantly undulating Gers countryside. The 197 large, part terraced pitches (100 for tourers) all have electricity (10A), 20 with hardstanding and 16 fully serviced. They are arranged around a large field with rural views, giving a feeling of spaciousness. The 13th-century village of La Romieu is on the Santiago de Compostela pilgrim route. The Pyrénées are a two hour drive, the Atlantic coast a similar distance. The site has been developed by the friendly Mijnsbergen family who are Dutch (although Susan is English). They have sympathetically converted the old farmhouse buildings to provide facilities for the site. The collegiate church, visible from the site, is well worth a visit (the views are magnificent from the top of the tower), as is the local arboretum, the biggest collection of trees in the Midi-Pyrénées.

### Facilities

Three toilet blocks (one completely rebuilt for 2009), provide all the necessary facilities. Washing machines and dryers. Motorcaravan services. Restaurant (1/5-30/9, also open to the public). Takeaway. Bread. Swimming pool area with water slide. Jacuzzi, protected children's pool (open to public in afternoons). New playgrounds, games and animal park. Bouncy castle, trampoline. Outdoor fitness machines. Games room. Tennis. Pétanque. Bicycle hire. Discos, picnics, musical evenings. WiFi (charged). Max. 2 dogs. Off site: Shop 500 m. in village. Fishing 5 km. Riding 10 km. Walking tours. Walibi theme park nearby.

**Open:** 1 April - 10 October.

### Directions

Site signed from D931 Agen-Condom road. Small units turn left at Ligardes (signed), follow D36 for 1 km, turn right at La Romieu (signed). Otherwise continue to outskirts of Condom and take D41 left to La Romieu, through village to site. GPS: 43.98299, 0.50183

### Charges 2013

| Per unit incl. 2 persons | |
|---|---|
| and electricity | € 17.00 - € 37.00 |
| extra person | € 3.60 - € 7.60 |
| child (4-9 yrs) | free - € 5.40 |
| dog (max. 2) | € 1.50 - € 2.30 |

Special prices for groups, rallies, etc.

Camping Cheques accepted.

Le Camp de Florence - 32480 La Romieu

**Sun * Comfort * Nature * Water**

The Gers - A region waiting to be discovered, an unspoilt landscape of rolling hills, sunflowers and historic fortified villages and castles. Peace, tranquillity, the home of Armagnac, Fois Gras and Magret de Canard. A 4* site with spacious pitches, panoramic views and luxury mobile homes for hire.

Tel: 0033 562 28 15 58 - Fax: 0033 562 28 20 04
E-mail: info@lecampdeflorence.com - www.lecampdeflorence.com

**FREE** Alan Rogers Travel Card
Extra benefits and savings - see page 10

## Le Monastère

### Campéole Domaine de Combelles

F-12000 Le Monastère (Aveyron) T: 05 65 78 29 53. E: combelles@campeole.com

alanrogers.com/FR12400

Domaine de Combelles is a well equipped parc résidentiel which can be found at the heart of the Aveyron, quite close to the village of Le Monastère. Please note that there are no touring pitches here, but a range of attractive chalets and mobile homes are available for rent. This site is also unusual in that it incorporates an excellent riding centre, with opportunities for beginners as well as seasoned riders. Vehicle circulation is not allowed within the site – a large car park is available at the site entrance. This is a spacious site and most facilities are located some distance from the accommodation units, ensuring their tranquillity. On-site amenities include a bar and snack bar, and leisure facilities include a swimming pool and tennis court. Most leisure facilities (including tennis) are free of charge. Bicycle hire and riding are available for a small charge. There are plenty of activities and a lively entertainment programme in the peak season, including a children's club as well as discos and karaoke. The surrounding country is ideal for walking and cycling and the site managers will be pleased to recommend possible routes.

**Facilities**

Bar/restaurant. Swimming pool. Riding centre. Bicycle hire. Volleyball. Bouncy castle. Play area. Activities and entertainment programme. Mobile homes and chalets and permanently erected tents for rent (there are no touring pitches). Off site: Le Monastère (attractive village with shops and restaurants). Walking and cycle tracks. Fishing. Rodez (cathedral city) 5 km. Tarn gorges.

**Open:** 1 May - 31 October.

**Directions**

From Albi head north on N88 towards Rodez via Luc la Primaube and Flavin. From here follow signs to the site which is well indicated. GPS: 44.3301, 2.5901

**Charges guide**

Contact the site for details.

## Lectoure

### Yelloh! Village le Lac des Trois Vallées

F-32700 Lectoure (Gers) T: 05 62 68 83 33. E: contact@lacdes3vallees.fr

alanrogers.com/FR32060

This is a very large 140 hectare site with many facilities. It is a large holiday complex and good for families with young children or teenagers. The large lake provides the opportunity for canoeing and swimming. There is a large safe paddling area and a separate fishing lake. The impressive heated pool complex complete with gymnasium and jacuzzi also has paved areas for sunbathing and a large paddling pool. Of the 600 pitches, over 200 are well situated for touring on shaded or open ground, all with electricity (10A). A fireworks festival is held here in September.

**Facilities**

Eight modern sanitary blocks each with baby bathing facilities. Provision for disabled visitors. Laundry facilities. Motorcaravan services. Supermarket. Restaurants and bars. Lakeside snack bar and drinks kiosk. Heated swimming pool complex. Lake complex with water slides. Multisports pitch. BMX/skateboard area. Fishing. Tennis. Minigolf. Video games room. Disco. Children's club. WiFi (charged). Off site: Golf 10 km. Riding 20 km. Walking and mountain bike trails. Quad bikes. Hot air balloon rides.

**Open:** 1 June - 9 September (with all facilities).

**Directions**

Take N21 south from Lectoure for 2 km. Site is well signed and is a further 2 km. after turning left off the N21. GPS: 43.91250, 0.64852

**Charges guide**

| | |
|---|---|
| Per unit incl. 2 persons and electricity | € 19.00 - € 44.00 |
| extra person | € 5.00 - € 8.00 |
| child (3-7 yrs) | free - € 8.00 |
| dog | € 4.00 |

For latest campsite news, availability and prices visit

# alanrogers.com

## Les Cammazes
### Camping de la Rigole

Route de Barrage, F-81540 Les Cammazes (Tarn) T: 05 63 73 28 99. E: campings.occitanie@orange.fr
**alanrogers.com/FR81100**

La Rigole is located high in the hills above Lac des Cammazes. Although the site slopes, of the 65 pitches, the 34 for touring are on small terraces and many have quite deep shade. All have electricity (8-13A). There is a small bar and snack bar. One evening each week in main season a regional meal is organised. Small children are well catered for with play areas for tiny tots and under 7s. There is a delightful children's farm with animals. The site is totally unsuitable for American RVs and large units.

**Facilities**

Fairly modern toilet block. Baby room. Facilities for disabled campers (although the slopes might be difficult). Washing machines, dryer. Small shop. Bar. Takeaway. Swimming pool and children's pool. All open in high season. Badminton. Volleyball. Boules. WiFi (free). Off site: Lac des Cammazes with its dam 400 m. Fishing 400 m. Riding 1.5 km. Lac de St Ferréol with large sandy beach 5 km.

**Open:** 15 April - 15 September.

**Directions**

Les Cammazes is 25 km. northeast of Castelnaudary, 10 km. southeast of Revel. From Revel take D629 to Cammazes, continue through village, after 1 km. turn left towards Barrage (site signed), site entrance 200 m. on right. GPS: 43.407867, 2.0866

**Charges guide**

| Per unit incl. 2 persons | |
|---|---|
| and electricity | € 18.00 - € 24.00 |
| extra person | € 4.10 - € 5.30 |

---

## Loudenvielle
### Flower Camping Pène Blanche

9 chemin de la Mainette, F-65510 Loudenvielle (Hautes-Pyrénées) T: 05 62 99 68 85.
E: info@peneblanche.com **alanrogers.com/FR65140**

La Pène Blanche is spacious and well kept, in an idyllic location close to Lake Loudenvielle and surrounded by high mountains. There are 120 small pitches, which are not separated; 80 are for touring (40 with 5/10A electricity). The area is ideal for walking, hiking and biking in the mountains. An outdoor swimming pool is just 200 m. away and nearby is the Balnea centre with its spa waters. The resorts of Val Louron and Peyragudes are within easy reach for skiing. For the very brave there is paragliding and hang-gliding or you can relax in the park to watch them gracefully coming in to land.

**Facilities**

Two toilet blocks, one traditional, one modern and heated including facilities for disabled visitors. Laundry facilities. Play area. WiFi (part site, free). Off site: Restaurant, snack bar, bar and local shops all within 100 m. Cinema 200 m. Motorcaravan services 300 m. Within walking distance is the Balnea Centre with its spa water baths and adjacent swimming pool with waterslide. Bicycle hire 1 km. Tennis. Minigolf. Hiking. Mountain biking. Paragliding. Hang-gliding. Skiing.

**Open:** 20 December - 31 October.

**Directions**

From A64 (Tarbes-Toulouse) exit 16 take D929 and follow signs to Arreau, then D618 to D25 signed Loudenvielle. GPS: 42.796107, 0.406679

**Charges guide**

| Per unit incl. 2 persons | |
|---|---|
| and electricity | € 16.00 - € 23.50 |
| extra person | € 3.90 - € 5.50 |
| child (2-7 yrs) | € 2.90 - € 4.50 |
| dog | € 1.80 - € 2.50 |
| No credit cards. | |

---

## Lourdes
### Camping le Moulin du Monge

Avenue Jean Moulin no 28, F-65100 Lourdes (Hautes-Pyrénées) T: 05 62 94 28 15.
E: camping.moulin.monge@wanadoo.fr **alanrogers.com/FR65100**

A well organised, family run site with a friendly welcome, Moulin du Monge is in an ideal location for visiting Lourdes, only 3 km. away. There will be some traffic noise from the nearby N21 and railway line. This attractive garden-like site has 55 pitches, all with electricity (2-6A) in three grassy areas, mostly shaded by trees and easy to access. The swimming pool is slightly apart from most of the pitches. There is a separate adjacent pool for children. There are ten mobile homes available to rent.

**Facilities**

The heated toilet blocks have all necessary facilities, including washing machine and dryer. Facilities for disabled visitors. Baby room. Motorcaravan services. Shop (15/6-20/9). Heated swimming pool, sliding cover (20/5-20/9). Paddling pool. Sauna. Games/TV room. WiFi. Barbecue, terrace. Boules. Playground, trampolines. Off site: Good transport links to the city with its famous grotto and all shops and services. Bicycle hire 500 m. Fishing 3 km. Golf 4 km. Riding 15 km. Golf 16 km.

**Open:** 1 April - 10 October.

**Directions**

Site is just off the N21 on northern outskirts of Lourdes. From north, on N21 (2 km. south of Adé) be prepared to take slip lane in centre of road. Turn left into Ave. Jean Moulin. Site shortly on left. GPS: 43.115516, -0.031583

**Charges guide**

| Per unit incl. 2 persons | |
|---|---|
| and electricity | € 17.30 - € 20.35 |
| extra person | € 5.45 |
| child (0-7 yrs) | € 3.60 |

**FREE** Alan Rogers Travel Card
Extra benefits and savings - see page 10

## Luz-Saint-Sauveur
### Camping Pyrenevasion

Route de Luz-Ardiden, Sazos, F-65120 Luz-Saint-Sauveur (Hautes-Pyrénées) T: 05 62 92 91 54.
E: camping-pyrenevasion@wanadoo.fr **alanrogers.com/FR65130**

In the heart of the Pyrenees, Camping Pyrenevasion has panoramic views of the mountains and the town of Luz-St-Sauveur in the valley below. This welcoming, family run site has 60 well laid out touring pitches, all with electricity (3-10A), on level, grassy hillside terraces partially shaded by young trees. There are 12 modern chalets for rent (all year), ideal for the nearby skiing, and in summer guided walks are arranged, with one free weekly walk. The heated outdoor pool has a separate paddling pool and jacuzzi. A member of Sites et Paysages.

**Facilities**

Heated sanitary block with showers, WCs, washbasins (cubicles and open area). Facilities for disabled visitors, steep access. Baby bath. Washing machine and dryer. Motorcaravan services. Bread to order. Bar. Takeaway (1/6-20/9). Heated swimming and paddling pools (15/5-1/10). Small play area. Sports area. WiFi (charged). Off site: Fishing 200 m. Shops, restaurant and bar 2 km. Riding and skiing 10 km. Golf 30 km.

**Open:** All year excl. 21 October - 19 November.

**Directions**

From the north take the D921 to Luz-St-Sauveur. Follow signs from Luz-St-Sauveur to Luz-Ardiden (D12). Site is on right as you enter the village of Sazos. GPS: 42.88283, -0.02241

**Charges guide**

| Per unit incl. 2 persons | |
|---|---|
| and electricity | € 14.50 - € 33.50 |
| extra person | € 5.50 |

## Marciac
### Camping du Lac

F-32230 Marciac (Gers) T: 05 62 08 21 19. E: info@camping-marciac.com
**alanrogers.com/FR32020**

Summer wine and cheese tastings from local producers are a feature of this site, set in the beautiful Gers region, and close to the ancient fortified town of Marciac. Rob and Louise Robinson, the English owners since 2002, offer a quiet, relaxing stay. The well shaded site has 95 pitches, including 16 used for mobile homes and chalets for rent. There are 80 spacious touring pitches, 60 with electrical connections (6/10A, Europlug) and water. There are five with hardstanding for motorcaravans, and an attractive natural terrace has 20 pitches without electricity for tents.

**Facilities**

The centrally situated sanitary block uses solar energy to help to heat water. Washbasins in cubicles. Facilities for disabled visitors (two separate bathrooms with shower, WC and washbasin). Washing machine. Motorcaravan service point. Shop, bar, takeaway. Bread to order. Swimming pool (15/4-30/9). Small library and communal room. Play area. WiFi (charged). Off site: Fishing, watersports, sailing and riding 300 m. Shops, restaurant and bars 1 km. Golf 7 km.

**Open:** 20 March - 12 October.

**Directions**

The site is 800 m. from Marciac. From the town square take the D3 towards Plaisance. With the lake on your left, turn right and site is 300 m. on the left. GPS: 43.5323, 0.1667

**Charges guide**

| Per unit incl. 2 persons | |
|---|---|
| and electricity (6A) | € 14.00 - € 24.00 |
| extra person | € 2.50 - € 5.00 |
| child (4-16 yrs) | € 1.50 - € 3.50 |

## Marsan
### Flower Camping Aramis

Quartier Gaubette, F-32270 Marsan (Gers) T: 05 62 65 60 11. E: piraux.sylvie@wanadoo.fr
**alanrogers.com/FR32170**

Aramis is a pretty, family campsite located 10 km. east of Auch, former capital of Gascony when it was the land of Musketeers! There are 63 large pitches here, mostly well shaded and with electrical connections. A number of mobile homes and chalets are available for rent. Leisure facilities include a swimming pool and tennis court. A new covered pool and water slide has recently been added. A number of activities take place around the site's convivial bar, particularly during peak season. These include Gascon evenings, evening markets and large scale barbecues.

**Facilities**

Toilet blocks with hot showers and facilities for disabled visitors. Hot water to washing up area. Launderette. Shop, bar, restaurant and takeaway food (all July/Aug). Fresh bread and pastries can be ordered. Swimming pool. Children's pool. Tennis. Play area. Entertainment and activity programme. Mobile homes for rent. Off site: Auch 10 km. Walking and cycle tracks. Riding. Golf.

**Open:** 1 April - 30 September.

**Directions**

Camping Aramis can be found 10 km. east of Auch. From there, head east on N124 to Marsan and then follow signs to the site. GPS: 43.658577, 0.733429

**Charges guide**

| Per unit incl. 2 persons | |
|---|---|
| and electricity | € 15.50 - € 23.00 |
| extra person | € 2.50 - € 5.00 |

For latest campsite news, availability and prices visit
**alanrogers.com**

## Martres-Tolosane
### Camping le Moulin

Lieu-dit le Moulin, F-31220 Martres-Tolosane (Haute-Garonne) T: 05 61 98 86 40.
E: info@campinglemoulin.com **alanrogers.com/FR31000**

With attractive, shaded pitches and many activities, this family run campsite has 12 hectares of woods and fields beside the River Garonne. It is close to Martres-Tolosane, an interesting medieval village. Some of the 60 level and grassy pitches are super-size and all have electricity (6-10A). There are 17 chalets to rent. Summer brings opportunities for guided canoeing, archery and walking. A large sports field is available all season, with tennis, volleyball, basketball, boules and birdwatching on site. Some road noise. Large grounds for dog walking. A member of Sites et Paysages.

| Facilities | Directions |
| --- | --- |
| Large sanitary block with separate ladies' and gents WCs. Communal area with showers and washbasins in cubicles. Separate area for disabled visitors. Baby bath. Laundry facilities. Motorcaravan services. Outdoor bar with WiFi. Restaurant (1/7-20/8). Snack bar and takeaway (1/6-15/9). Daily bakers van (except Monday). Heated swimming and paddling pools (1/6-15/9). Fishing. Tennis. Canoeing. Archery. BMX track. Playground. Games room. Entertainment and children's club (high season). Massage by arrangement (charged). Off site: Martres-Tolosane 1.5 km. Walking trails. Cycle routes. Riding 4 km. | From the A64 motorway (Toulouse-Tarbes) take exit 21 (Boussens) or exit 22 (Martres-Tolosane) and follow signs to Martres-Tolosane. Site is well signed from village. GPS: 43.19048, 1.01788 |

**Open:** 1 April - 30 September.

**Charges guide**

| Per unit incl. 2 persons | |
| --- | --- |
| and electricity | € 18.90 - € 27.90 |
| extra person | € 4.50 - € 6.00 |
| child (under 7 yrs) | € 2.50 - € 3.00 |
| dog | € 2.00 - € 2.50 |

Less 20% outside July/Aug.

## Millau

Camp**é**ole

### Campéole le Millau Plage

Route de Millau-Plage, F-12100 Millau (Aveyron) T: 05 65 61 43 69. E: millauplage@campeole.com
**alanrogers.com/FR12390**

Millau Plage is a recent addition to the Campéole group and is located on the banks of the Tarn river, just 1.5 km. outside the interesting town of Millau, and with good access to the Tarn gorges. A wide variety of trees provide ample shade for the 220 pitches, most with electricity (5A). Around 40 pitches are occupied by mobile homes for rent. There is a pleasant pool next to the restaurant and bar area. Millau is an historic town with shops, bars and restaurants, and is a very popular place for hang-gliding and watersports. Outings could include a visit to view Norman Foster's impressive Millau Viaduct, a drive up the gorges of the valley of the Tarn, or to Le Chaos de Montpellier le Vieux, a rocky labyrinth that can be explored on foot, by Petit Train or on a Via Ferrata.

| Facilities | Directions |
| --- | --- |
| Four toilet blocks along the middle of the site provide easy access from all pitches. Motorcaravan services. Small shop, bar with TV and snack type restaurant with takeaway (all July/Aug). Swimming pool. Children's club in high season. Fishing and river swimming. Activity and entertainment programme. WiFi on part of site (charged). Off site: Bicycle hire 800 m. Riding 2 km. Millau 1.5 km. Lake beach 25 km. Hang-gliding, mountain-biking, canoeing, canyoning, rafting, bungee-jumping and via ferrata or simply walking in the impressive Massif Central. | From north leave A75 (Clermont-Ferrand/Béziers) at exit 44.1 and follow Aguessac (D29) then Paulhe and join D187 towards Millau. Site on right in 4 km. From south leave D909 (Millau) at exit 47. Follow signs for Campings at each roundabout, turn right across river and take third exit at next roundabout. Site is on left in 1.5 km. GPS: 44.11552, 3.08692 |

**Open:** 1 May - 1 October.

**Charges guide**

| Per unit incl. 2 persons | |
| --- | --- |
| and electricity | € 15.10 - € 28.10 |
| extra person | € 4.00 - € 6.40 |

AVEYRON

Camp**é**ole
CAMPSITES AND RENTALS

**Millau Plage**★★★

Three stars site. Heated swimming pool and paddling pool, multi-sports court, extreme sports, many types of leisure and relaxation activities at the doors of the Gorges du Tarn. Pitches and accommodations of high quality at the foot of the Parc régional des Grands Causses.

12120 Millau · Tél.: +33-565-6143-69 / www.campeole.co.uk / millauplage@campeole.com

## Millau
### Camping Caravaning les Rivages

860 avenue de l'Aigoual, F-12100 Millau (Aveyron) T: 05 65 61 01 07. E: info@campinglesrivages.com
**alanrogers.com/FR12020**

Les Rivages is a large, well established site on the outskirts of the town. It is well situated, being close to the high limestone Causses and the dramatic gorges of the Tarn and Dourbie. Smaller pitches, used for small units, abut a pleasant riverside space suitable for sunbathing, fishing and picnics. Most of the 314 pitches are large, and well shaded. A newer part of the site has less shade but larger pitches. All pitches have electricity (6A), and 55 have water and drainage. The site offers a very wide range of sporting activities, close to 30 in all. The gates are shut 23.00-08.00, with a night-watchman.

**Facilities**

Four well kept modern toilet blocks have all necessary facilities. Special block for children. Small shop (1/6-15/9). Terrace, restaurant and bar overlooking swimming pool, children's pool (from 10/5). Play area. Entertainment, largely for children, child-minding, miniclub. Sports centre. Boules. River activities, walking, birdwatching, fishing. WiFi by reception. Off site: Rafting and canoeing arranged. Bicycle hire 1 km. Riding 10 km. Abseiling, paragliding, caving, canyoning and white-water activities all nearby.

**Open:** 15 April - 30 September.

**Directions**

From Millau, cross the Tarn bridge and take D991 road east towards Nant. Site is 400 m. from the roundabout on the right, on the banks of the Dourbie river. GPS: 44.10300, 3.095827

**Charges guide**

| | |
|---|---|
| Per unit incl. 2 persons and electricity | € 18.00 - € 30.00 |
| extra person | € 3.50 - € 6.50 |
| child (2-7 yrs) | € 2.00 - € 5.00 |

---

## Montcabrier
### Camping Moulin de Laborde

F-46700 Montcabrier (Lot) T: 05 65 24 62 06. E: moulindelaborde@wanadoo.fr
**alanrogers.com/FR46040**

Based around a converted 17th-century watermill, Moulin de Laborde has been created by the van Bommel family to provide a tranquil and uncommercial campsite for the whole family to enjoy. Bordered by woods, hills and a small river, there are 90 flat and grassy pitches, all of at least 100 sq.m. with electricity (6A). A variety of pretty shrubs and trees divide the pitches and provide a moderate amount of shade. A gate at the back of the site leads walkers onto a Grande Randonée footpath which passes through the village of Montcabrier, 1 km. away.

**Facilities**

Well designed, clean toilet block, unit for disabled visitors. Washing machine, dryer. Basic shop. Small bar, restaurant, takeaway. Swimming pool, sunbathing area, paddling pool. Play area. Small lake, free rafts and rowing boats. Fishing. Volleyball. Covered recreation area. Rock climbing. Archery. Dogs are not accepted. WiFi (free). Off site: Tennis nearby and canoeing on the Lot. Riding 15 km. The Château of Bonaquil 6 km. Golf 4 km.

**Open:** 1 May - 8 September.

**Directions**

Site is on the north side of the D673 Fumel-Gourdon road 1 km. northeast of the turn to village of Montcabrier. GPS: 44.5475, 1.083883

**Charges guide**

| | |
|---|---|
| Per unit incl. 2 persons and electricity (6A) | € 21.36 - € 26.70 |
| extra person | € 5.52 - € 6.90 |
| No credit cards. | |

---

## Moustajon
### Camping Pradelongue

CD125, Moustajon, F-31110 Luchon (Haute-Garonne) T: 05 61 79 86 44.
E: camping.pradelongue@wanadoo.fr **alanrogers.com/FR31060**

Located within walking distance of Bagneres-de-Luchon this green and pleasant site provides an ideal base for touring. Of the 135 pitches, 121 are for touring with the remainder being occupied by mobile homes for rent. The pitches are level and separated by hedges and small trees. Shade is provided by large mature trees. All have electricity (3-10A) and 18 also have water and waste water drainage. This very well maintained site, situated in the Luchon valley, is surrounded by the Pyrenean mountains. Guided walks are organised and opportunities for paragliding, fishing, climbing and rafting are nearby.

**Facilities**

Three toilet and shower blocks, one heated, some en-suite cabins. Facilities for disabled visitors. Washing machines. Motorcaravan services. Heated swimming pool (1/6-30/9). Paddling pool. Football pitch. Play areas. Boules. Volleyball. Basketball. Trampoline. Adult exercise equipment. Games room. Two TV rooms. Small library. WiFi. Mobile homes to rent. Off site: Supermarket 50 m. Luchon 2 km with casino and ski lift. Minigolf. Paragliding.

**Open:** 1 April - 30 September.

**Directions**

From Bagneres de Luchon take D125c (north) for 1.5 km. Site is well signed on right. GPS: 42.808143, 0.597253

**Charges guide**

| | |
|---|---|
| Per unit incl. 2 persons and electricity | € 15.70 - € 22.55 |
| extra person | € 4.40 - € 6.10 |
| child (under 7 yrs) | € 1.60 - € 2.30 |

For latest campsite news, availability and prices visit
# alanrogers.com

## Nant-d'Aveyron
### RCN Val de Cantobre

Domain de Vellas, F-12230 Nant-d'Aveyron (Aveyron) T: 05 65 58 43 00. E: cantobre@rcn.fr
**alanrogers.com/FR12010**

Imaginatively and tastefully developed by the Dupond family over the past 30 years, this very pleasant terraced site is now owned by the RCN group. Most of the 215 pitches (96 for touring with 6A electricity, and most with water) are peaceful, generous in size and blessed with views of the valley. The terrace design provides some peace and privacy, especially on the upper levels. Rock pegs are advised. An activity programme is supervised by qualified instructors in July and August and a new pleasure pool has been added. The magnificent carved features in the bar create a delightful ambience, complemented by a recently built terrace. Passive recreationists appreciate the scenery, especially Cantobre, a medieval village that clings to a cliff in view of the site. Nature lovers will be delighted to see black vultures wheeling in the Tarn gorge alongside more humble rural residents. Butterflies in profusion, orchids, huge edible snails, glow worms, families of beavers and the natterjack toad all live here.

**Facilities**

The fully equipped toilet blocks are well appointed. Fridge hire. Small shop including many regional specialities, attractive bar, restaurant, pizzeria and takeaway (all season). There are some fairly steep up and down walking from furthest pitches to some facilities. Swimming pools (all season). Minigolf. Play area. Activity programme. Bicycle hire. All-weather multisports pitch. Torch useful. WiFi over site (charged). Off site: Fishing 4 km. Riding 15 km.

**Open:** 29 March - 28 September.

**Directions**

Site is 4 km. north of Nant, on D991 road to Millau. From Millau direction take D991 signed Gorge du Dourbie. Site is on left, just past turn to Cantobre. GPS: 44.04467, 3.30228

**Charges guide**

| | |
|---|---|
| Per unit incl. 2 persons, electricity and water | € 19.90 - € 43.90 |
| dog | € 6.00 |
| extra person (4 yrs and over) | € 2.50 - € 4.90 |

Camping Cheques accepted.

# RCN Val de Cantobre
## Camping - Mobile homes - Chalets

2013

A lovely, terraced campsite situated on a medieval farm in the gorgeous green Dourbie Valley.

www.rcn.fr - 0033 565 584 300 - cantobre@rcn.fr

## Naucelle
### Flower Camping du Lac de Bonnefon

L'Etang de Bonnefon, F-12800 Naucelle (Aveyron) T: 05 65 69 33 20.
E: camping-du-lac-de-bonnefon@wanadoo.fr **alanrogers.com/FR12250**

This small, family run site, popular with French campers, lies in a picturesque region waiting to be discovered, with rolling hills, deep river valleys, lakes and many old fortified villages. This site is more suitable for those seeking a quieter holiday with less in the way of entertainment (some evenings in July and August). There are 112 good sized, grassy, slightly sloping pitches with 69 for touring (all with access to 10A electricity). Some are separated by laurel hedging with others more open, and maturing trees provide some shade. The enthusiastic and friendly owners have recently extended the site and refurbished the facilities to a high standard.

**Facilities**

Two main toilet blocks include some washbasins in cabins and good facilities for disabled visitors. No shop but bread to order. Bar with TV. Snack bar and restaurant (July/Aug). Swimming and paddling pools (1/5-30/9). Playground. Archery. Good lake fishing but no bathing. Activities for all the family in July/Aug. Bicycle hire. WiFi on part of site. Off site: Riding 800 m. Village of Naucelle with a few shops and heated pool complex 1 km.

**Open:** 1 April - 15 October (accommodation all year).

**Directions**

Site is just off the N88 halfway between Rodez and Albi. From Naucelle Gare take D997 towards Naucelle. In just over 1 km. turn left on D58 and follow signs to site in just under 1 km. GPS: 44.18805, 2.34827

**Charges guide**

| | |
|---|---|
| Per unit incl. 2 persons and electricity | € 15.50 - € 23.90 |
| extra person | € 3.50 - € 5.00 |

## Payrac-en-Quercy

### Flower Camping les Pins

F-46350 Payrac-en-Quercy (Lot) T: 05 65 37 96 32. E: info@les-pins-camping.com

alanrogers.com/FR46030

Set amongst 3.5 hectares of beautiful pine forest, Camping les Pins is well situated for exploring the historical and natural splendours of the Dordogne region, as well as being a convenient overnight stop when heading north or south. There are 137 clearly marked, level pitches (100 sq.m), of which 49 are for touring units. The pitches are well marked and separated by small shrubs or hedges. Many have shade from the abundant pine trees and all have 10A electricity connections. There is a bar and a good value restaurant with a terrace overlooking the pool area. The site has recently become very popular and is extremely busy in the high season.

**Facilities**

Three toilet blocks (heated Apr/May), well maintained and include washbasins in cabins and good baby bath facilities. Laundry facilities (with plenty of drying lines). Motorcaravan service point. Shop with basics. Bar with TV. Restaurant and takeaway. Heated swimming pool, three slides and smaller paddling pool. Wellness centre with jacuzzi and sauna. Tennis. Small library. WiFi in bar area (free). Some entertainment in season, including weekly family discos. Walking routes starting from site. Off site: Fishing 7 km. Riding 10 km.

**Open:** 20 April - 8 September.

**Directions**

Site entrance is 16 km. from Souillac on western side of the N20 just south of the village of Payrac-en-Quercy. GPS: 44.78946, 1.47204

**Charges guide**

| Per unit incl. 2 persons | |
|---|---|
| and electricity | € 18.00 - € 33.40 |
| extra person | € 4.50 - € 6.90 |
| child (under 7 yrs) | € 2.00 - € 4.80 |
| dog | € 2.00 - € 3.00 |

Special low season prices.

## Pont-de-Salars

### Flower Camping les Terrasses du Lac

Route du Vibal, F-12290 Pont-de-Salars (Aveyron) T: 05 65 46 88 18. E: campinglesterrasses@orange.fr

alanrogers.com/FR12050

A terraced site, it provides 180 good sized, level pitches, 110 for touring, with or without shade, all with electricity. Some pitches have good views over the lake which has direct access from the site at two places – one for pedestrians and swimmers, the other for cars and trailers for launching small boats. This site is well placed for excursions into the Gorges du Tarn, Caves du Roquefort and nearby historic towns and villages. Although there are good facilities for disabled visitors, the terracing on the site may prove difficult. At an altitude of some 700 m. on the plateau of Le Lévézou, this outlying site enjoys attractive views over Lac de Pont-de-Salars.

**Facilities**

Four toilet blocks with adequate facilities including those for disabled visitors. Washing machine. Motorcaravan services. Fridge hire. Shop. Bar/restaurant with a lively French ambience serving full meals (high season), snacks (at other times) and takeaway (all 1/7-31/8). Heated swimming pool, paddling pool (1/6-30/9). Solarium. Play area. Pétanque. Billiards. Games/TV rooms. Activities in high season. Fishing. Gas and charcoal barbecues permitted. WiFi. Accommodation for rent. Off site: Tennis and bicycle hire 3 km. Riding 5 km. Golf 20 km.

**Open:** 1 April - 30 September.

**Directions**

Using D911 Millau-Rodez road, turn north at Pont-de-Salars towards lake on D523. Follow site signs. Ignore first site and continue, following lake until les Terrasses du Lac on right (about 5 km). GPS: 44.30498, 2.73556

**Charges guide**

| Per unit incl. 2 persons | |
|---|---|
| and electricity | € 16.50 - € 27.90 |
| extra person | € 3.50 - € 5.50 |
| child (2-7 yrs) | € 2.50 - € 4.00 |
| dog | € 1.50 - € 2.00 |

For latest campsite news, availability and prices visit
**alanrogers.com**

## Rivière-sur-Tarn
### Flower Camping Caravaning de Peyrelade

Route des Gorges du Tarn, F-12640 Rivière-sur-Tarn (Aveyron) T: 05 65 62 62 54.
E: campingpeyrelade@orange.fr **alanrogers.com/FR12000**

The 137 touring pitches (100-150 sq.m) are terraced, level and shady with 6A electricity hook-ups (long leads may be required for the riverside pitches). There are also 53 mobile homes for hire. The site is ideally placed for visiting the Tarn, Jonte and Dourbie gorges, and centres for rafting and canoeing are a short drive up the river. Other nearby attractions include the Caves of Aven Armand, the Chaos de Montpellier, Roquefort and the pleasant town of Millau. Many of the roads along and between the Gorges are breathtaking for passengers, but worrying for drivers who may not like looking down!

**Facilities**

Two well equipped toilet blocks. Young children are catered for, also visitors with disabilities. Washing machines, dryer. Bar, restaurant, pizzeria, takeaway (all from 1/6). A new aquapark with a 100 sq.m. children's pool, 120 sq.m. swimming pool and whirlpool (no shorts). Good playground. Games room. Miniclub. Fishing. WiFi in bar area. Only charcoal barbecues allowed. Off site: Bicycle hire 100 m. Riding 3 km. Nearby leisure centre can be booked at reception at reduced charges. Millau with hypermarket, shops and night markets.

**Open:** 15 May - 15 September.

**Directions**

Take autoroute A75 to exit 44-1 Aguessac then onto D907 (follow Gorges du Tarn signs). Site is 2 km. past Rivière-sur-Tarn, on the right. The access road is quite steep. GPS: 44.19047, 3.15638

**Charges guide**

| Per unit incl. 2 persons | |
|---|---|
| and electricity | € 19.00 - € 34.00 |
| extra person | € 3.50 - € 8.00 |
| child (under 7 yrs) | € 2.00 - € 5.00 |
| dog | € 2.00 |

## Rivière-sur-Tarn
### Kawan Village les Peupliers

Route des Gorges du Tarn, F-12640 Rivière-sur-Tarn (Aveyron) T: 05 65 59 85 17.
E: lespeupliers12640@orange.fr **alanrogers.com/FR12160**

Les Peupliers is a friendly, family site on the banks of the Tarn river. Most of the 100 good sized touring pitches have shade, all have electricity (6A), water and a waste water point and are divided by low hedges. It is possible to swim in the river and there is a landing place for canoes. The site has its own canoes (to rent). In a lovely, sunny situation on the site is a swimming pool with a paddling pool, sun beds and a new slide, all protected by a beautifully clipped hedge and with a super view to the surrounding hills and the Château du Peyrelade perched above the village. Some English is spoken.

**Facilities**

Large, light and airy toilet facilities, baby facilities with baths, showers and WCs, facilities for disabled visitors. Washing machines. Shop (1/5-30/9). Bar, TV. Internet. Snack bar, takeaway (1/5-30/9). Swimming pool (heated 1/5-30/9). Games, competitions July/Aug. Fishing. Play area. Weekly dances July/Aug. Canoe hire. WiFi in bar area (free). Off site: Village with shops and restaurant 300 m. Riding 500 m. Bicycle hire 2 km. Golf 25 km. Rock climbing, canyoning, cycling and walking.

**Open:** 1 April - 30 September.

**Directions**

Heading south from Clermont-Ferrand to Millau on the A75 autoroute take exit 44-1 signed Aguessac/Gorges du Tarn. In Aguessac turn left and follow signs to Riviere-sur-Tarn (5 km). Site is clearly signed down a short road to the right. GPS: 44.18577, 3.13068

**Charges guide**

| Per unit incl. 2 persons | |
|---|---|
| and electricity | € 20.00 - € 32.00 |
| extra person | € 5.00 - € 7.00 |
| child (2-7 yrs) | € 2.00 - € 4.00 |

Camping Cheques accepted.

**FREE** Alan Rogers Travel Card
**Extra benefits and savings** - see page 10

## Rocamadour
### Camping Padimadour

La Châtaigneraie, F-46500 Rocamadour (Lot) T: 05 65 33 72 11. E: info@padimadour.fr

alanrogers.com/FR46410

Camping Padimadour is a small friendly, family run campsite in beautiful Quercy countryside, not far from the ancient town of Rocamadour in the Vallée de la Dordogne. There are 50 very large, grassy and slightly sloping pitches with 25 for touring, all with 10A electricity and most with water. There is some shade from maturing trees. The site is undergoing extensive refurbishment and has a superb new toilet block, small bar/snack bar and a games room. Many other improvements are in the pipeline. The site is aimed at couples and families with pre-teen children and there is low key family entertainment in July/August. This region is popular for all manner of adventure sports – including rock climbing, potholing, canyoning and mountain biking. The nearby town of Gramat is a noted riding centre. For those seeking a more relaxed holiday, a visit to Rocamadour is a must. This unique town is an important pilgrimage destination, thanks to the wooden Black Madonna, said to have been carved by St Amator (St Amadour) and housed in the beautiful church of Notre Dame.

**Facilities**

Superb new toilet block including facilities for disabled visitors. Laundry facilities. Small shop for essentials. Snack bar, takeaway (July/Aug). Bar (Jun-Sept). Swimming pool (June-Sept). Play area. Trampolines. Activity and family entertainment (July/Aug). WiFi (charged). Off site: Cycling and walking tracks. Riding. Fishing. Rock climbing. Alvignac with shop and restaurant 2 km. Rocamadour 5 km. Padirac, Gouffre de Padirac 8 km.

**Open:** 9 April - 30 October.

**Directions**

From D840 (Figeac to Brive-la-Gaillarde road) turn east 7 km. north west of Gramat, site signed. Follow small lane to site in just under 2 km. GPS: 44.817742, 1.686267

**Charges guide**

| Per unit incl. 2 persons | |
|---|---|
| and electricity | € 16.80 - € 20.70 |
| extra person | € 4.20 - € 5.50 |
| child (3-12 yrs) | € 2.30 - € 3.50 |

## Roquelaure
### Yelloh! Village le Talouch

F-32810 Roquelaure (Gers) T: 05 62 65 52 43. E: info@camping-talouch.com

alanrogers.com/FR32080

Although enjoying a quiet and rural location, this neat and tidy site is only a short drive from the town of Auch with its famous legendary son, d'Artagnan. The entrance is fronted by a parking area with reception to the right and the bar and restaurant facing. Beyond this point lies the top half of the touring area with generous pitches of at least 120 sq.m. located between mature trees and divided by hedges, some with chalets. There are 100 pitches for touring, with electricity (4,6 or 10A). The rear half of the site has unshaded pitches in a more open aspect.

**Facilities**

Two toilet blocks with open style washbasins and controllable showers. Baby unit. One toilet for disabled visitors. Coin operated washing machine. Small shop (1/4-30/9). Bar, restaurant and takeaway. Two swimming pools, one heated and covered. Sauna and spa. Bicycle hire. GPS hire with pre-programmed walking routes. Play areas. Tennis. Sports area. Entertainment in high season. Small library. Internet and WiFi (charged) in reception. Charcoal barbecues only. Off site: Fishing and riding 8 km.

**Open:** 6 April - 24 September.

**Directions**

Situated some 11 km. north of Auch on the D149, and 64 km. east of Toulouse the site is well signed. From the north approach via the A62 motorway, leaving at Layrac and heading towards Auch on the N21. GPS: 43.71283, 0.5645

**Charges guide**

| Per unit incl. 2 persons | |
|---|---|
| and electricity | € 17.00 - € 38.00 |
| extra person | € 6.00 - € 8.00 |

For latest campsite news, availability and prices visit
## alanrogers.com

## Saint Antonin-Noble-Val
### Flower Camping les Gorges de l'Aveyron

Marsac bas, F-82140 Saint Antonin-Noble-Val (Tarn-et-Garonne) T: 05 63 30 69 76.
E: info@camping-gorges-aveyron.com **alanrogers.com/FR82040**

This is a friendly, family site which is undergoing a process of renovation by its new owners, Stéphane and Johanna Batlo. The site has an attractive wooded location, sloping down to the River Aveyron and facing the Roc d'Anglars. Reception and the two toilet blocks are housed in traditional, converted farm buildings. There are 80 pitches of which 49 are for touring units and these all have electrical connections (3-10A). The pitches are grassy and well shaded and may become very soft in times of poor weather. Some pitches are available close to the river but we would suggest that these are unsuitable for younger children as the river is unfenced. The current owners have built a swimming pool and a modern toilet block. This is a very quiet site in low season and some amenities, notably the snack bar and shop are only available in the peak season. The nearby artisan town of St Antonin-Noble-Val dates back to the eighth century, and is just 1.5 km. from the site. It is accessible on foot via a quiet, shaded road. The town, with its medieval streets, is well worth a visit. It has a good range of shops and restaurants.

| Facilities | Directions |
|---|---|
| Two toilet blocks with washing machines and dryers. Small shop, bar, snack bar and takeaway (June-Sept). Direct access to river. Fishing. Canoeing. Play area. Entertainment and activities in high season. WiFi. Mobile homes for rent. Off site: St Antonin-Noble-Val with a wide choice of shops, restaurants and bars 1.5 km. Bicycle hire 1.5 km. Riding 2 km. Cordes-sur-Ciel 35 km. Many walking paths and cycle trails.<br><br>**Open:** 7 April - 30 September. | From the north, take exit 59 from the A20 autoroute joining the D926 and follow signs to St Antonin. Site can be found on the D115, 1.5 km. east of the town. GPS: 44.1519, 1.7715 |

**Charges guide**

| | |
|---|---|
| Per unit incl. 2 persons and electricity | € 14.40 - € 26.20 |
| extra person | € 3.20 - € 4.50 |
| child (under 7 yrs) | € 1.60 - € 2.50 |

Camping Cheques accepted.

GORGES DE L'AVEYRON
LES GORGES DE L'AVEYRON
★★★
Open from 7/04 to 30/09 - 80 PITCHES
Pitches - Mobile homes and tents

*flower* camping
*friendly camping by nature.*

JOHANNA AND STÉPHANE BATLO
Lieu dit Marsac Bas - 82140 St-Antonin-Noble-Val
Tel: 00 33 (0)3 25 04 13 20
E-mail: info@camping-gorges-aveyron.com
www.camping-gorges-aveyron.com

## Saint Cirq-Lapopie
### Camping de la Plage

F-46330 Saint Cirq-Lapopie (Lot) T: 05 65 30 29 51. E: camping-laplage@wanadoo.fr
**alanrogers.com/FR46070**

You are assured of a warm welcome at Camping de la Plage from the English speaking owners. It is situated beside the River Lot and is within walking distance of the beautiful historic village of Saint Cirq-Lapopie. It provides a good base for those who want an active holiday with organised activities available either on site or in the immediate area. There are 120 good sized, level stony/grass pitches, 90 of which are for touring. Forty are fully serviced (6/10A electricity) and have hardstandings. They are separated by hedges and shrubs, and mature trees give good shade. Cars are parked away from the pitches.

| Facilities | Directions |
|---|---|
| Two sanitary blocks are clean and well maintained. Facilities for disabled visitors. Laundry facilities. Shop. Motorcaravan services (charged). Bar. Restaurant and takeaway (1/5-30/9). Play area. Children's room for activities. Canoeing, kayaking and swimming from beach (lifeguard July/Aug). Fishing. Bicycle hire. Free WiFi over part of site. Off site: Walking, rock climbing, caving, canyoning and shops all nearby. Riding 9 km.<br><br>**Open:** 20 April - 30 September. | From Cahors take D653 east to Vers, then D662 for 17 km. to Tour de Faure. Cross river and site entrance is on right by bar/restaurant. Do not approach via Saint Cirq-Lapopie (very steep, winding and narrow roads). GPS: 44.46926, 1.68135 |

**Charges guide**

| | |
|---|---|
| Per unit incl. 2 persons and electricity | € 20.00 - € 27.00 |
| extra person | € 5.00 - € 7.00 |

**FREE** Alan Rogers Travel Card
Extra benefits and savings - see page 10

## Saint Cirq-Lapopie

### Camping la Truffière

Lieudit Pradines, F-46330 Saint Cirq-Lapopie (Lot) T: 05 65 30 20 22. E: contact@camping-truffiere.com
**alanrogers.com/FR46150**

This site is set in four hectares of mature oak woodland within the Parc Naturel Régional des Causses de Quercy with stunning natural scenery and only 2.5 km. from the cliff top village of St Cirq-Lapopie. La Truffière is well suited to those seeking a peaceful countryside holiday and it is a superb area for hiking. The 90 slightly sloping, terraced pitches are of varying sizes and on a mixture of grass and gravel. All have 6A electricity (long leads may be needed) and most have shade from mature trees. Access is good for large outfits but advanced booking is recommended.

**Facilities**

Two clean, modern toilet blocks (one heated) include facilities for disabled visitors. Motorcaravan services. Fridge hire. Small shop. Bar/restaurant (1/6-31/8), terrace overlooking pool and playing field. Takeaway (1/6-15/9). Swimming pool, paddling pool, sun terrace (1/5-15/9). Playing field. Adventure style play area. Trampolines. Boules. Gas and electric barbecues only on pitches (3 communal areas). WiFi near bar. Off site: Small shop in village 4 km. Fishing and bathing (in the River Lot) and riding 3 km. Bicycle hire 15 km. Supermarkets 25 km.

**Open:** 13 April - 30 September.

**Directions**

From D911 Cahors-Rodez road, at Concots, turn north on D26 (signed St Cirq-Lapopie). Shortly keep left, D42. Site 6 km. on right. Approaching from north on D42 via St Cirq-Lapopie not recommended due to extremely tight turns in village.
GPS: 44.44855, 1.67455

**Charges guide**

| | |
|---|---|
| Per unit incl. 2 persons and electricity | € 21.00 |
| extra person | € 5.50 |

Camping Cheques accepted.

## Saint Geniez-d'Olt

**Campéole**

### Campéole la Boissière

Route de la Cascade, F-12130 Saint Geniez-d'Olt (Aveyron) T: 05 65 70 40 43. E: boissiere@campeole.com
**alanrogers.com/FR12090**

With trout in the river and carp in the lakes, la Boissière is a fisherman's paradise. The site is a member of the Campéole group and is situated on the banks of the River Lot, surrounded by wooded hills. Walking, swimming, canoeing or cycling are alternative pursuits here. Mature trees provide plenty of shade on the generous, partly hedged, grassy pitches, all of which have electricity connections (6A) and frequently placed water points. Reception is housed in an old, converted farmhouse. The nearby old town of Saint Geniez-d'Olt should satisfy all shopping needs and day or longer fishing licences can be obtained there (the helpful site staff will advise). There is direct access through the site to the river, which is suitable for swimming and canoeing. La Boissière has 154 pitches, of which around 70 are used for mobile homes, chalets and fully equipped tents (available for rent). There is much of interest in the area and the Tarn gorges and Grandes Causses are both within easy access.

**Facilities**

Two modern, clean toilet blocks with washbasins in cubicles and preset showers. Baby changing facilities. Basic facilities for visitors with disabilities (no rails). Shop with basic provisions (July/Aug). Bar with terrace. Large, heated swimming pool and paddling pool. Multisport terrain. Bouncy castle and playground. Entertainment in July/Aug. Mobile homes, chalets and tents for rent. Free WiFi and Internet access. Off site: St Geniez-d'Olt 700 m. Bicycle and canoe hire nearby.

**Open:** 29 March - 30 September.

**Directions**

From Saint Geniez-d'Olt follow the D988 eastwards towards Banassac. After 500 m. follow signs on right to la Boissière campsite. GPS: 44.4686, 2.9825

**Charges 2013**

| | |
|---|---|
| Per unit incl. 2 persons and electricity | € 15.70 - € 25.90 |
| extra person | € 4.20 - € 6.50 |
| child (2-6 yrs) | free - € 4.20 |
| dog | € 2.00 - € 2.70 |

MIDI-PYRÉNÉES

**Campéole**
CAMPSITES AND RENTALS

**La Boissière** ★★★★

In the heart of a superb natural area, swimming pool, access to the river Lot. Amenities, pitches and accommodations of high quality.

12130 St Geniez d'Olt - Tel.: +33-565-7040-43 - www.campeole.co.uk / boissiere@campeole.com

For latest campsite news, availability and prices visit
**alanrogers.com**

## Saint Geniez-d'Olt
### Kawan Village Marmotel

F-12130 Saint Geniez-d'Olt (Aveyron) T: 05 65 70 46 51. E: info@marmotel.com

**alanrogers.com/FR12150**

The road into Marmotel passes various industrial buildings and is a little off-putting – persevere, as they are soon left behind. The campsite itself is a mixture of old and new with a total of 90 touring pitches available and a similar number of mobile homes for rent. The old part provides many pitches with lots of shade and separated by hedges. The new area is sunny until the trees grow. These 40 pitches each have a private sanitary unit (extra charge), with shower, WC, washbasin and dishwashing. New and very well designed, they are reasonably priced for such luxury. All the pitches have electricity (10A).

**Facilities**

Good sanitary facilities include baby baths and facilities for disabled visitors. Washing machines. Bar/restaurant with terrace and hill views. Takeaway. Heated swimming pool and paddling pools. Small play area. Multisports area. Entertainment (July/Aug) including disco below bar, cinema, karaoke, dances, miniclub. Bicycle hire. Fishing. Canoeing. WiFi on part of site. Off site: Large supermarket 500 m. Riding 10 km. Bicycle tours and canoe trips.

**Open:** 28 April - 22 September.

**Directions**

Head south on autoroute 75, take exit 41 and follow signs for St Geniez-d'Olt. Site is at western end of village. Site is signed onto D19 to Prades d'Aubrac, then 500 m. on left. GPS: 44.46165, 2.96318

**Charges guide**

| | |
|---|---|
| Per unit incl. 1 or 2 persons and electricity | € 18.00 - € 31.60 |

No credit cards.
Camping Cheques accepted.

## Salles-Curan
### Kawan Village les Genêts

Lac de Pareloup, F-12410 Salles-Curan (Aveyron) T: 05 65 46 35 34. E: contact@camping-les-genets.fr

**alanrogers.com/FR12080**

This family run site is on the shores of Lac de Pareloup and offers both family holiday and watersports facilities. The 163 pitches include 80 grassy, mostly individual pitches for touring units. These are in two areas, one on each side of the entrance lane, and are divided by hedges, shrubs and trees. All have electricity (6A) and many also have water and waste water drain. The site slopes gently down to the beach and lake with facilities for all watersports including water skiing. Entertainment and activities are organised in high season, and there is much to see and do in this very attractive corner of Aveyron.

**Facilities**

Two sanitary units, one refurbished, with suite for disabled guests. Baby room. Laundry. Well stocked shop. Bar, restaurant, snacks (17/6-8/9). Swimming pool, spa pool (unsupervised). Play area. Minigolf. Boules. Bicycle hire. Pedaloes, windsurfers, kayaks. Fishing licences available. WiFi throughout. Off site: Riding 6 km. Canyoning. Walking routes. Millau for shopping and spectacular bridge over the Tarn river. Roquefort cheesemakers.

**Open:** 13 May - 15 September.

**Directions**

From Salles-Curan take D577 for 4 km. and turn right into a narrow lane immediately after a sharp right bend. Site signed. GPS: 44.18933, 2.76693

**Charges guide**

| | |
|---|---|
| Per unit incl. 2 persons and electricity | € 18.00 - € 41.00 |
| extra person | € 4.00 - € 8.00 |

Camping Cheques accepted.

## Seissan
### Domaine Lacs de Gascogne

Rue du Lac, F-32260 Seissan (Gers) T: 05 62 66 27 94. E: info@domainelacsdegascogne.eu

**alanrogers.com/FR32180**

This is a spacious site located at Seissan in the Pyrenean foothills. Its impressive drive sweeps around the largest of three lakes into the spacious and relaxing Domaine. The 50 large, grassy touring pitches mostly have shade and fine lake views. Electricity is 16A (some long leads required). Comfortable chalets and mobile homes (25) can be rented. The bar and restaurant are open all season and the food is very good. The lakes are perfect for fishing, kayaking, and evening beach campfires. Across the lakes is ideal for wilder camping, this area also has five teepees to rent.

**Facilities**

Excellent sanitary facilities in a new block. Second older block across the lake. Baby changing mats and facilities for disabled visitors. Restaurant. Breakfast service. Lounge. TV room. Swimming pool. Health pool. Sauna. Gym. Fishing (carp). Kayaks. Rope raft across lake. Play area. Play room. Tennis. Football. Basketball. Bicycle hire. Entertainment and activities. Mobile home, chalet, teepee and bed and breakfast accommodation. Off site: Riding 5 km. Golf 6 km. Supermarket 7 km. Auch 19 km.

**Open:** 1 April - 1 November.

**Directions**

Head south from Auch on N21 and, at Beaulieu, join the southbound D929. Continue on this road as far as Seissan and then follow signs to the site. GPS: 43.49535, 0.57826

**Charges guide**

| | |
|---|---|
| Per unit incl. 2 persons and electricity | € 12.50 - € 17.50 |
| extra person | € 6.00 |

**FREE** Alan Rogers Travel Card
Extra benefits and savings - see page 10

## Séniergues

### Domaine de la Faurie

F-46240 Séniergues (Lot) T: 05 65 21 14 36. E: contact@camping-lafaurie.com

**alanrogers.com/FR46190**

A stunning array of tended shrubs and thoughtful flower plantings is spread throughout this very pretty 27-hectare site which is located on a hilltop with wide open views of the surrounding hills and valleys. Although hidden away, it is an excellent base for exploring the Lot and Dordogne regions. The site is separated into two distinct areas, an open, lightly shaded front section and a much more densely shaded area with tall pine trees all around the pitches. The pitches are large and most are at least 100 sq.m. The friendly French owners will tell you that they consider the site their personal garden.

**Facilities**

The two sanitary blocks are clean and well maintained. Facilities for disabled visitors. Washing machine. Motorcaravan service point. Excellent gift shop selling regional and local produce (bread available). Bar, restaurant and takeaway. Swimming pool and paddling pool. TV and games rooms. Boules. Bicycle hire. Play area. Small library. Weekly soirées in high season. Max. 1 dog. Off site: Fishing 3 km. Golf 8 km. Riding 15 km.

**Open:** 7 April - 30 September.

**Directions**

From the A20 exit on N56, turn right towards St Germain-du-Bel-Air. Continue for 5 km. and the site is on the right. GPS: 44.69197, 1.53461

**Charges guide**

| Per unit incl. 2 persons | |
|---|---|
| and electricity | € 19.50 - € 28.00 |
| extra person | € 4.50 - € 6.90 |

Camping Cheques accepted.

## Sévérac-l'Eglise

### Flower Camping la Grange de Monteillac

F-12310 Sévérac-l'Eglise (Aveyron) T: 05 65 70 21 00. E: info@la-grange-de-monteillac.com

**alanrogers.com/FR12070**

La Grange de Monteillac is a modern, well equipped site in the beautiful, well preserved small village of Sévérac-l'Église. A spacious 4.5 hectare site, it provides 104 individual pitches, 61 for touring (eight extra large), on gently sloping grass, separated by flowering shrubs and trees offering some shade. All pitches have electricity (6/10A, long leads may be required). There are 43 chalets, mobile homes and tents for rent in separate areas. The friendly owners will advise about the many interesting activities in the region. An evening stroll around this delightful village is highly recommended.

**Facilities**

Modern toilet block with good facilities for babies and disabled visitors. Washing machine, dryer. Shop (10/5-15/9). Two swimming pools (1/5-15/9). Poolside restaurant/snack bar serving pizzas, grills etc. Takeaway (July/Aug). Music or groups feature in the bar (July/Aug). Playground. Bicycle hire. Archery. Floodlit boules court. Organised activities. Children's and teen's clubs. Jacuzzi. WiFi. Off site: Fishing 1 km. Shops in village 3 km. Riding 9 km. Golf 25 km. Canoeing, rafting and canyoning.

**Open:** 27 April - 15 September.

**Directions**

Site is on the edge of Sévérac-l'Église village, just off N88 Rodez-Sévérac Le Château road. From A75 use exit 42. At Sévérac-l'Église turn south onto D28, site is signed. Site entrance is very shortly on left. GPS: 44.3652, 2.85142

**Charges guide**

| Per unit incl. 2 persons | |
|---|---|
| and electricity | € 16.90 - € 34.90 |
| extra person | € 3.00 - € 6.50 |

## Sévérac-le-Château

### Camping les Calquières

17 avenue Jean Moulin, F-12150 Sévérac-le-Château (Aveyron) T: 05 65 47 64 82.
E: contact@camping-calquieres.com  **alanrogers.com/FR12190**

This site is ideally situated, 3 km. from the free A75 autoroute, making an excellent short stay for those en route to the south and a good base for those wishing to visit the Cévennes National Park with its beautiful and rugged scenery. This quiet, neat, family run site nestles below the old village, close to the lower part of the town, all within easy walking distance. There are spectacular views from the Château, floodlit at night. There are 97 good sized, level, grassy pitches, all with electricity (6A) and mostly separated by hedges with maturing trees providing some shade.

**Facilities**

Two good toilet blocks include facilities for disabled visitors. Washing machine. Shop, bar/restaurant, snack bar and takeaway (all 15/6-30/9). Covered and heated swimming pool with sliding roof. TV room. Games room. Trampoline. Play area. Entertainment for children. WiFi on part of site. Off site: Tennis. Fishing 800 m. Riding 1 km. Sévérac le Château 1 km. small range of shops, restaurants and bank. Cévennes National Park. Gorge du Tarn. Valley du Lot. Caves.

**Open:** 1 April - 15 October.

**Directions**

From A75 exit 42 take N9 (Sévérac le Château). Shortly hard right (N88), at crossroads straight on (Centre Ville). Left at station roundabout, follow road beside railway through town. Left at site sign, then left again. Site on right. GPS: 44.31841, 3.06412

**Charges guide**

| Per unit incl. 2 persons | |
|---|---|
| and electricity | € 18.00 - € 24.90 |
| extra person | € 3.00 - € 5.00 |

For latest campsite news, availability and prices visit

# alanrogers.com

## Souillac
### Castel Camping le Domaine de la Paille Basse
F-46200 Souillac-sur-Dordogne (Lot) T: 05 65 37 85 48. E: info@lapaillebasse.com
**alanrogers.com/FR46010**

Set in a rural location some 8 km. from Souillac, this family owned site is easily accessible from the A20 and well placed to take advantage of excursions into the Dordogne. It is part of a large Domaine of 80 hectares, all available to campers for walks and recreation. The site is quite high up and there are excellent views. The 262 pitches are in two main areas – one is level in cleared woodland with good shade, and the other on grass with limited shade. Numbered and marked, the pitches are a minimum 100 sq.m. and often considerably more. All have electricity (10A) with 80 fully serviced.

**Facilities**

Three main toilet blocks all have modern equipment and are kept very clean. Laundry. Small shop with a large selection of wine. Restaurant, bar (open until 2am in high season), terrace, pizza takeaway. Crêperie. Main swimming pool, a smaller one, paddling pool (unheated), water slides. Sun terrace. Soundproofed disco. TV (with satellite). Cinema below the pool area. Tennis. Play area. Library. WiFi in office/bar area (charged). Mini farm. Entertainment for all (July/Aug). Off site: Golf 4 km.

**Open:** 15 May - 15 September.

**Directions**

From Souillac take D15 and then D62 roads leading northwest (Salignac-Eyvignes) and after 6 km. turn right at site sign. Follow steep and narrow approach road for 2 km. GPS: 44.94728, 1.43924

**Charges guide**

| | |
|---|---|
| Per person | € 5.40 - € 7.50 |
| child (under 7 yrs) | € 3.80 - € 5.50 |
| pitch | € 7.80 - € 10.80 |
| incl. water and drainage | € 9.80 - € 13.00 |

Camping Cheques accepted.

## Souillac
### Flower Camping les Ondines
Rue des Ondines, F-46200 Souillac (Lot) T: 05 65 37 86 44. E: info@camping-lesondines.com
**alanrogers.com/FR46390**

Souillac is a picturesque town lying between the Dordogne and Lot. It is just a five minute walk from les Ondines to the town's attractive pedestrianised centre where there are many cafés, restaurants and shops, as well as an abbey and, unusually, a robotic toy museum! There are 242 pitches here. These are grassy and well sized (mostly with electricity). A number of mobile homes and fully equipped tents are available for rent. In peak season, various activities are organised, including a children's club. The site lies on the banks of the Dordogne and canoe rental is available in the town.

**Facilities**

Two traditional toilet blocks with basic but clean facilities, including those for visitors with disabilities. Washing machine. Access to municipal swimming pool (free July/Aug). Pétanque. Volleyball. Play area. Activities and entertainment. Mobile homes and tents for rent. Off site: Swimming pool 300 m. Cafés, shops, restaurants and takeaway in Souillac. Walking and cycle tracks. Riding. Canoeing. Supermarket Quercyland water park.

**Open:** 1 May - 30 September.

**Directions**

From the north, leave the A20 motorway at exit 55 and head for Souilllac. Drive through the town and, 500 m. beyond the traffic lights, turn right following signs to Les Ondines and Quercyland. Follow signs to the site. GPS: 44.888871, 1.474196

**Charges guide**

| | |
|---|---|
| Per unit incl. 2 persons and electricity | € 11.00 - € 16.00 |
| extra person | € 3.00 - € 4.90 |

## Tarascon-sur-Ariege
### Yelloh! Village le Pré Lombard
F-09400 Tarascon-sur-Ariege (Ariège) T: 05 61 05 61 94. E: leprelombard@wanadoo.fr
**alanrogers.com/FR09060**

This busy, good value site is located beside the attractive River Ariège and near the town. There are 180 level, grassy, pitches with shade provided by a variety of trees (electricity 10A). At the rear of the site are 70 site-owned chalets and mobile homes. A gate in the fence provides access to the riverbank for fishing. A wellness chalet offers massage in high season. Open for a long season, it is an excellent choice for early or late breaks, or as a stopover en-route to the winter sun destinations in Spain. This region of Ariège is in the foothills of the Pyrenees and 85 km. from Andorra.

**Facilities**

Five toilet blocks of varying ages, facilities for disabled visitors. Laundry. Motorcaravan services. Shop. Bar and takeaway. Restaurant. Heated swimming pool (all 28/4-15/9). Play areas. Video games machines. Boules. Multisport court. Fishing. Satellite TV. Entertainment (high season), nightclub, children's club, sports tournaments. Activity programmes. Free WiFi. Off site: Supermarket 300 m. Town 600 m. Fishing nearby. Riding 5 km.

**Open:** 15 March - 15 October.

**Directions**

Site is 600 m. south of town, adjacent to the river. From north, turn off main N20 into town, site signed. From south (Andorra) site signed at roundabout on town approach. GPS: 42.83985, 1.612

**Charges guide**

| | |
|---|---|
| Per unit incl. 2 persons and electricity | € 17.00 - € 35.00 |
| extra person | € 6.00 - € 8.00 |

**FREE** Alan Rogers Travel Card
Extra benefits and savings - see page 10

## Therondels
### Flower Camping la Source

Presqu'île de Laussac, F-12600 Thérondels (Aveyron) T: 05 65 66 27 10. E: info@camping-la-source.com
**alanrogers.com/FR12210**

This extremely spacious, steeply terraced site borders the long and narrow Lac de Sarrans with its steep wooded sides. The site is run by a very friendly family and is better suited for the younger family wanting to 'get away from it all'. All the facilities are first class, although the layout of the site means that pitches may be some distance and a steep climb away. The owners prefer to provide tractor assistance for caravans. There are 101 medium to large, slightly sloping, grassy pitches with 62 for touring, all with 6/10A electricity, water and drainage. Rock pegs are essential. The site is not suitable for very large units, or for those with walking difficulties.

**Facilities**

Two large, well appointed and clean toilet blocks with all the necessary facilities including those for babies and campers with disabilities. Bar with TV (all season). Shop, restaurant and takeaway (30/6-31/8). Heated swimming pool with toboggan and paddling pool (all season). Play area. TV room. Activities in high season for all the family. Lake fishing. Barbecues permitted. WiFi (charged). Off site: Boat ramp 500 m. Golf 6 km. Riding and bicycle hire 15 km.

**Open:** 17 May - 9 September.

**Directions**

Leave the A75 at exit 28 or 29 (St Flour). Go through town and take D921 towards Rodez. After 12 km. turn right on D990 to Pierrefort and 3 km. after village turn left on D34, signed Laussac. Follow narrow twisting lanes down to site (about 9 km). GPS: 44.853716, 2.77105

**Charges guide**

| Per unit incl. 2 persons | |
| --- | --- |
| and electricity | € 17.00 - € 29.00 |
| extra person | € 3.00 - € 5.50 |
| child (0-7 yrs) | free - € 4.50 |
| dog | free - € 2.00 |

## Vayrac
### Camping les Granges

F-46110 Vayrac (Lot) T: 05 65 32 46 58. E: info@les-granges.com
**alanrogers.com/FR46310**

Situated just over 3 km. outside Vayrac in a very rural position, this site nestles quietly beside the river in a tranquil and peaceful area. Pitches along the river frontage are popular, but children will need to be supervised as the river is unfenced. There is access to the river at one end of the site, ideal for those wishing to discover the pleasures of the River Dordogne. There are 150 level grassy pitches, shaded by a variety of mature trees, with 116 for touring. Most have 10A electricity. In July/August there is some family entertainment, but only in French.

**Facilities**

Two modern toilet blocks include facilities for disabled visitors. Washing machine and ironing board. Small shop, bar, snack bar and takeaway (July/Aug). Swimming pool and paddling pool (May-Sept). Play area. Family entertainment (12/7-16/8). Fishing and river beach. Max. 1 dog. Electric barbecues are not permitted. Off site: Bicycle hire 1 km. Shops, bars and restaurant in Vayrac 3 km. Golf and riding 10 km.

**Open:** 1 May - 18 September.

**Directions**

From Brive, take the D20 towards Figeac. In Vayrac turn right just before the church at sign for Campings and Stade. Site is signed from here in 3 km. GPS: 44.93462, 1.67981

**Charges guide**

| Per unit incl. 2 persons | |
| --- | --- |
| and electricity | € 16.72 - € 19.60 |
| extra person | € 4.08 - € 5.10 |
| child (2-10 yrs) | € 2.32 - € 2.90 |
| dog (max. 1) | € 1.28 - € 1.60 |

For latest campsite news, availability and prices visit
## alanrogers.com

# Digital iPad editions

**FREE** Alan Rogers bookstore app
- digital editions of all 2013 guides

**alanrogers.com/digital**

Languedoc and Roussillon form part of the Massif Central. With its huge sandy beaches, the mountainous Languedoc region is renowned for its long sunshine records, and the pretty coastal villages of the Roussillon are at their most beautiful at sunset, erupting in a riot of colour.

**DÉPARTEMENTS: 11 AUDE, 30 GARD, 34 HÉRAULT, 48 LOZÈRE, 66 PYRÉNÉES-ORIENTALES**

**MAJOR CITIES: MONTPELLIER, PERPIGNAN, CARCASSONNE**

Stretching from the Rhône Valley in the east to the Spanish border in the south west, Languedoc-Roussillon is a mixture of rugged mountains, fertile coastal plains and a long sandy coastline dotted with modern resorts. Yet, away from the brash developments there is plenty of opportunity to discover reminders of the region's dramatic history – the Roman remains at Nîmes, the walled city of Carcassonne and the many Cathar castles perched on rocky hilltops.

Today, the plains are given over to agriculture and wine; fruit and vegetables in the Roussillon in particular, while Languedoc is responsible for around one third of France's total wine production, with appellations such as Corbières, Minervois and the sparkling Blanquette de Limoux.

Above all, the uncrowded expanses of sand and long hours of sunshine draw holidaymakers, both to the old coastal villages of Collioure and Banyus, and to the vibrant resorts of La Grande Motte and Cap d'Agde, which are a popular alternative to the Côte d'Azur.

### Places of interest

*Aigues-Mortes*: medieval city.

*Béziers*: wine capital of the region, St Nazaire cathedral, Canal du Midi.

*Carcassonne*: largest medieval walled city in Europe.

*Collioure*: picturesque coastal village popular with artists.

*Limoux*: medieval town, Notre Dame de Marseilla Basilica, St Martin church.

*Montpellier*: universities, Roman sites; Gothic cathedral.

*Nîmes*: Roman remains, Pont du Gard.

*Perpignan*: Kings Palace; Catalan characteristics, old fortress.

*Sigean*: 700-acre African safari park.

### Cuisine of the region

Cooking draws heavily on local produce: garlic, olive oil, tomato sauces and herbs from the 'garrigue'; apricots, peaches and cherries in jams and puddings.

*Aïgo Bouido*: garlic soup.

*Boles de picoulat*: small balls of diced beef and pork, garlic and eggs.

*Bourride*: a fish stew with garlic mayonnaise.

*Boutifare*: a sausage-shaped pudding of bacon and herbs.

*Cargolade*: snails, stewed in wine.

*Cassoulet*: hearty stew of haricot beans, sausage or pork and preserved goose.

*Touron*: a pastry of almonds, pistachio nuts and fruit.

www.sunfrance.com
contact.crtlr@sunfrance.com
(0) 4 67 20 02 20

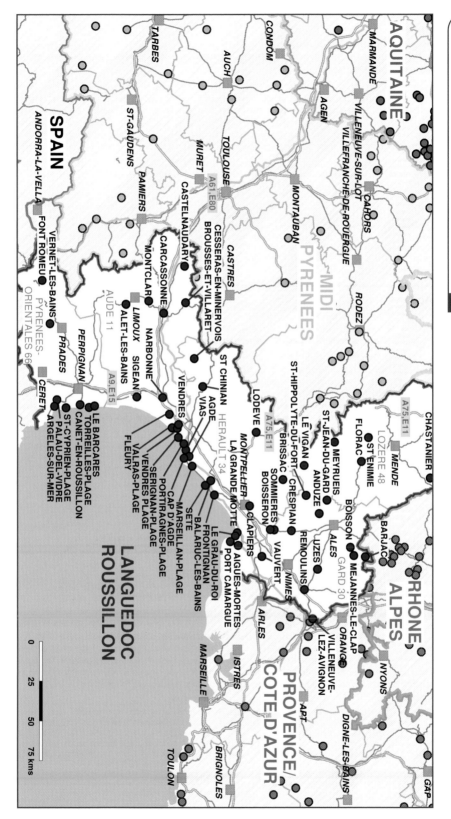

**FREE** Alan Rogers Travel Card
Extra benefits and savings - see page 10

## Agde
### Flower Camping le Neptune

46 boulevard du Saint Christ, F-34300 Agde (Hérault) T: 04 67 94 23 94. E: info@campingleneptune.com
**alanrogers.com/FR34130**

Camping le Neptune is a rare find in this area. This small, family run site with only 165 pitches makes a delightful change. The pitches are mostly separated by flowering bushes, with some shade, most with 6/10A electricity. There are 20 mobile homes to rent. The Fray family are welcoming and even though this is a busy area, this site is an oasis of calm, suited to couples and young families. Situated alongside the splendid Hérault river, one can cycle or walk into the village of Le Grau d'Agde or on into the historic centre of Agde itself. The site's swimming pool is in a sunny position and is overlooked by the bar.

**Facilities**

Two toilet blocks provide preset showers, washbasins in cabins, three cold showers for hot weather. Facilities for disabled visitors. Laundry. Small shop, bar (15/5-15/9). Snacks and takeaway (20/6-21/8). Heated swimming pool (15/4-30/9, bracelets required). Field for sports. WiFi (charged). Boat mooring facility on the River Hérault across the road. Only one dog allowed. Barbecues are not permitted. Max. 1 dog. Off site: Beach, riding, Canal du Midi and lock 2 km. Golf 5 km. Fishing in Hérault.

**Open:** 1 April - 30 September.

**Directions**

From A9 exit 34 follow signs for Agde then Cap d'Agde. Exit for Grau d'Agde. At roundabout (with statue) turn left (Grau d'Agde), and left again at 2nd roundabout. Continue to 5th roundabout turning left and under bridge. GPS: 43.29803, 3.45628

**Charges guide**

Per unit incl. 2 persons
and electricity                    € 19.90 - € 35.20
Camping Cheques accepted.

## Agde
### Kawan Village les Champs Blancs

Route de Rochelongue, F-34300 Agde (Hérault) T: 04 67 94 23 42.
E: contact@campingleschampsblancs.com  **alanrogers.com/FR34190**

Les Champs Blancs is set amongst tall trees, 2 km. from Agde and 2 km. from the sea at Rochelongue in a shady environment. There are over 300 pitches, with 117 level, sandy pitches for touring units. Bordered with bushes and plenty of trees, all pitches have 10A electricity and unusually, 60 have private sanitary cabins. Mobile homes occupy separate areas. The area nearest the road is bordered by trees to deaden possible road noise. The pool area has been augmented by a super irregular pool, with toboggans, cascade, jacuzzi, bridges and palms but retaining the original pool and paddling pool.

**Facilities**

Modern, fully equipped toilet blocks include 60 en-suite private cabins containing WC, shower and washbasin. Unit for disabled visitors. Washing machines and dryers. Motorcaravan services. Good shop (15/5-30/9, bread only in low season). Bar (from 1/6). Restaurant/takeaway (20/6-15/9). Swimming complex (from 8/4 depending on weather). Good play area. Minigolf. Tennis. Multisports court. WiFi throughout (charged). Off site: Riding 1 km.

**Open:** 8 April - 30 September.

**Directions**

From A9 exit 34, follow N312 for Agde, joins N112 Béziers-Sète road. Cross bridge over river, take first turn (Rochelongue), turn right at roundabout, next left, then next left (Agde). Site on left before another bridge back over N112. GPS: 43.29702, 3.47547

**Charges guide**

Per unit incl. 2 persons
and electricity                    € 16.00 - € 45.00
Camping Cheques accepted.

## Agde
### Camping les Romarins

Route du Grau, F-34300 Agde (Hérault) T: 04 67 94 18 59. E: contact@romarins.com
**alanrogers.com/FR34420**

A small family campsite beside the River Hérault, les Romarins is only 1 km. from a wide sandy beach and 800 metres from the village. With 120 level pitches separated by shrubs, 80 are available for touring units, the rest are taken by mobile homes and chalets (40 to let). Electricity (6A) is available on all pitches, some of which have more shade than others. A pleasant walk beside the river and past the fish quay, takes you to the shops, restaurants and beach of Le Grau. You walk the other way for the town of Agde, famous for its black cathedral and round lock by which boats gain access to the Canal du Midi.

**Facilities**

Two modern toilet blocks are fully equipped. Good facilities for babies and disabled visitors. Motorcaravan services (charged). Bar with snacks. Bread can be ordered. Heated pool. Large playing field and play area at the back of the site (closed at night). Bicycle hire. Multisports court. Outdoor gym equipment. Sports activities and evening entertainment in season. WiFi (charged). Off site: Shops and restaurants 700 m. Beach 900 m. Riding 2 km.

**Open:** 2 April - 1 October.

**Directions**

From A9 exit 34, follow N112 towards Agde. Cross river and take exit for Grau d'Agde. Turn left at two roundabouts, then straight over next two roundabouts towards river. Left at roundabout beside river, along riverside (one way). Site is third on left opposite fish quay. GPS: 43.29446, 3.45005

**Charges guide**

Per unit incl. 2 persons
and electricity                    € 18.00 - € 29.30

For latest campsite news, availability and prices visit
**alanrogers.com**

## Agde
### Village Center les 7 Fonts
Route de Sète, F-34300 Agde (Hérault) T: 04 99 57 21 21. E: contact@village-center.com
**alanrogers.com/FR34590**

If you are seeking a less hectic option, 7 Fonts has a rural feel to it, albeit that it is situated on the edge of the town of Agde, close to the Canal du Midi. A long time ago it was a vineyard but the traditional three storied house with its courtyard (now reception) is the only evidence remaining. The site is now owned by the Village Center Group. It is split into two parts separated by a small road. There are around 300 grass pitches, partially separated by shrubs and with good shade from tall trees. At least half are taken by mobile homes, some of which are for rent.

**Facilities**

Two traditional style toilet blocks. Facilities for disabled visitors. Small shop. Bar, simple restaurant and takeaway. Swimming pool complex with water slides and spa bath (1/5-15/9). Hairdressing and beauty salon (1/7-31/8). Bicycle hire. Activity and entertainment programme (1/7-31/8). Mobile homes and equipped tents to rent. Free shuttle bus for beach (high season). WiFi around reception (charged). Off site: Riding, golf, beach and fishing all 4 km.

**Open:** 27 May - 18 September.

**Directions**

From autoroute take exit 34 (Agde, Bessan). Follow N312 (Agde, Vias) then pick up N112 (Agde, Sète). Pass turnings for Agde until road divides, bearing left for Agde and centre commercial. Site is signed some 250 m. up this road. Turn right immediately after small garden centre. Carefully cross junction to site (narrow entrance). GPS: 43.31157, 3.49844

**Charges guide**

| | |
|---|---|
| Per unit incl. 2 persons | € 14.00 - € 34.00 |
| extra person | € 3.00 - € 8.00 |

Camping Cheques accepted.

## Aigues-Mortes
### Yelloh! Village la Petite Camargue
B.P. 21, D62, F-30220 Aigues-Mortes (Gard) T: 04 66 53 98 98. E: info@yellohvillage-petite-camargue.com
**alanrogers.com/FR30020**

La Petite Camargue sets a very high standard and is a well organised site with much to offer. With the fascinating Camargue on its doorstep, the medieval walled city of Aigues Mortes, and the Mediterranean beaches close by, it makes an ideal holiday centre. A large site (532 pitches) on 40 hectares, it has a swimming pool complex and other sporting amenities, including a riding school. There are 144 good sized touring pitches (6/10A electricity) on level, sandy grass, laid out in shady avenues with colourful, flowering shrubs. They are located among more than 300 mobile homes and 145 tour operator pitches.

**Facilities**

Three toilet blocks provide many combined showers and washbasins. Laundry facilities. Motorcaravan service point. Shops, bar/restaurant with pizzeria and takeaway. Hairdresser and beauty centre. Swimming pool with jacuzzi. Aquagym. Scuba diving. Play area, and children's club. Mini animal park. Tennis. Multisports court. Bicycle hire. Diving school. Free shuttle bus to beach (July/Aug). Disco/nightclub (over 16 years). Free WiFi in bar.

**Open:** 23 April - 19 September.

**Directions**

From A9, exit 26 (Gallargues), towards Le Grau-du-Roi, site 18 km. Continue past Aigues-Mortes on D62, site is 2 km. on the right, just before large roundabout for La Grand-Motte and Le Grau-du-Roi junction. GPS: 43.56307, 4.15888

**Charges guide**

| | |
|---|---|
| Per unit incl. 2 persons and electricity | € 17.00 - € 44.00 |
| extra person | € 5.00 - € 9.00 |

## Alet-les-Bains
### Camping Val d'Aleth
F-11580 Alet-les-Bains (Aude) T: 04 68 69 90 40. E: camping@valdaleth.com
**alanrogers.com/FR11110**

In the gateway to the upper Aude valley, open all year round, this popular small site is run by Christopher and Christine Cranmer, who offer a warm welcome. The mellow, medieval walls of Alet-les-Bains form one boundary of the site, while on the other and popular with anglers, is the River Aude (fenced for safety). Beyond this is the D118 and a railway which produces noise at times. The 37 mainly small, numbered pitches, around half of which are on hardstandings, all have electricity hook-ups (4-10A) and are separated by hedges and mature trees which give shade.

**Facilities**

Modern toilet blocks, fully equipped and heated in winter. Facilities for disabled visitors. Washing machine and dryer. Reception with small shop, drinks, wine, beer, use of freezer. Small play area. Mountain bike hire. Internet. Off site: White-water sports. Bus and train services to Carcassonne and Quillan. Limoux 10 km. 2nd weekend in June Fete de l'Eau (with jazz, food and wine).

**Open:** All year.

**Directions**

From Carcassonne take D118 south for 32 km. Ignore first sign to Alet (to avoid narrow stone bridge) and after crossing the river, turn into town. Site is 800 m. on the left (signed). GPS: 42.99482, 2.25605

**Charges guide**

| | |
|---|---|
| Per unit incl. 2 persons and electricity | € 17.75 - € 20.00 |
| extra person | € 3.75 - € 3.95 |

**FREE** Alan Rogers Travel Card
Extra benefits and savings - see page 10

## Anduze
### Camping Cévennes-Provence

Corbés-Thoiras, F-30140 Anduze (Gard) T: 04 66 61 73 10. E: marais@camping-cevennes-provence.com
**alanrogers.com/FR30200**

You are sure of a very warm welcome at this spacious, family owned site. New arrivals are taken on a tour so that they can select a good pitch. There are 242 touring pitches on the various levels, 200 with electricity (10A). Some are on the level land close to the river and others are scattered on high terraces having privacy and fine views across the Cévennes countryside. The river is very popular for swimming and in a separate section one can enjoy the rough and tumble of small rapids. There are few on-site activities. However, the family is happy to advise visitors who wish to explore off site, perhaps negotiating a discount on their behalf. There is a special area, away from the main site, where teenagers can safely let off steam. This is easily accomplished in the 30 hectares of this natural and unusual site. The site lighting is turned off at 22.30, to encourage early nights. Young children can enjoy one of the best play areas we have seen. Cleanliness of the whole site, including the toilet blocks (one new one for 2012), is paramount (there are ten blocks so that no-one has to walk too far up and down hill).

**Facilities**

ten excellent, modern, clean toilet blocks (one heated). Good facilities for disabled visitors. Shop (1/4-1/10). Restaurant, takeaway, bar (13/4-15/9). Good play area. Minigolf. Volleyball. River bathing and fishing. Many off site activities arranged at reception. Internet point. Free WiFi near reception. Charcoal barbecues are not permitted. Communal barbecue. Bicycle hire. Off site: Riding 4 km. Golf 10 km. Adventure and discovery park on opposite bank of river offering many sports facilities.

**Open:** 20 March - 1 October.

**Directions**

Only viable access. From D907 Anduze, take D284 alongside the river. Site signed on right 3 km. from town. Take care on the approach – narrow lane for 100 m, then a narrow bridge, visibility good. GPS: 44.07763, 3.96484

**Charges 2013**

| Per unit incl. 2 persons | |
|---|---|
| and electricity | € 18.40 - € 28.90 |
| extra person | € 3.90 - € 7.70 |
| child (2-12 yrs) | € 2.50 - € 5.50 |

## Anduze
### Domaine de Gaujac

Boisset-et-Gaujac, F-30140 Anduze (Gard) T: 04 66 61 67 57. E: contact@domaine-de-gaujac.com
**alanrogers.com/FR30000**

The 293 level, well shaded pitches include 175 for touring, with electricity (4-10A), and 22 are fully serviced. Access to some areas can be difficult for larger units due to narrow winding access roads, trees and hedges. Larger units should ask for lower numbered pitches (1-148) where access is a little easier. In high season this region is dry and hot, thus grass quickly wears off many pitches leaving just a sandy base. There are 12 special hardstanding pitches for motorcaravans near the entrance. The site has a new covered entertainment area and courtyard terrace. Only gas and electric barbecues.

**Facilities**

Toilet blocks (one heated) include facilities for disabled visitors. Washing machines and dryer. Motorcaravan services. Shop (2/6-27/8). Newsagent. Bar, restaurant and takeaway/crêperie (5/5-15/9). New heated swimming, paddling pool (all season with lifeguard 5/7-15/8) and jacuzzi. Playground, sports field. Tennis. Minigolf. Communal barbecue (charcoal), on pitches only gas or electric. Free WiFi in bar area. Off site: Fishing 100 m. Riding, golf 8 km. Bicycle hire 10 km. River beach 70 m.

**Open:** 1 April - 20 September.

**Directions**

From Alès take N110 (Montpellier). At St Christol-les-Alès fork right on D910 (Anduze) and in Bagard, at roundabout, turn left on D246 to Boisset et Gaujac. Follow signs to site (5 km). GPS: 44.03580, 4.02425

**Charges guide**

| Per unit incl. 2 persons | |
|---|---|
| and electricity | € 20.50 - € 31.50 |

Credit cards accepted in high season only.
Camping Cheques accepted.

For latest campsite news, availability and prices visit
**alanrogers.com**

## Anduze
### Camping Castel Rose

610 chemin de Recoulin, F-30140 Anduze (Gard) T: 04 66 61 80 15. E: castelrose@wanadoo.fr
**alanrogers.com/FR30360**

Spacious and wooded, le Castel Rose campsite stretches for more than a kilometre along the banks of one of France's most beautiful rivers, the Gardon d'Anduze. The site's long, private river beach is protected from the currents of the river by an artificial breakwater. The 218 touring pitches, all with 10A electricity, are level and marked out with mature trees. The site is set away from the busy main road and at night all you will hear is the sound of the water. The pretty town of Anduze is a 15 minute walk from the site where you can admire and buy its world famous pottery. Local attractions include the 'bambouseraie', a bamboo plantation which is unique in Europe and the steam train of the Cevennes, not forgetting the impressive regional arts and crafts, produce, markets and museums.

### Facilities

Five toilet blocks with open style washbasins, private cabins and spacious shower cubicles. Baby bath and children's toilets. Washing machines and dryers. Bar and restaurant with terrace. Spa, sauna and steam room. Games room. Children's club (July/Aug). Fishing, swimming, and canoeing in the river. Play area. Boules. Multisports area. Free WiFi over part of site.
Off site: Anduze with small shops, cafés, crafts. Nearby supermarkets. Steam train. Bamboo forest of La Bambouseraie. Riding 2 km.

**Open:** 1 April - 30 September.

### Directions

From Alès take N110 (D6110) towards Sommières, then D910a to Anduze. From village centre follow signs for St Jean-du-Gard and then campsite. There is a railway viaduct over road and shortly after a sign on right: 'Chemin de Recoulin'. Turn sharp right here, down towards the river. GPS: 44.0643, 3.97694

### Charges guide

| | |
|---|---|
| Per unit incl. 2 persons and electricity | € 11.00 - € 28.00 |
| extra person | € 4.30 - € 8.00 |
| child (under 7 yrs) | free - € 5.00 |

No credit cards.

## Argelès-sur-Mer
### Camping le Littoral

Route du Littoral, F-66700 Argelès-sur-Mer (Pyrénées-Orientales) T: 04 68 81 17 74.
E: infos@camping-le-littoral.fr **alanrogers.com/FR66060**

Sites with access to the beach are difficult to find and, even though le Littoral is not directly beside the beach, it is only 800 metres away by footpath. It offers much accommodation in mobile homes as well as 20 good sized, level touring pitches with shade and 6A electricity. An attractive pool area is open from May to September. Argelès is a very popular holiday resort with good sandy beaches. The border with Spain is only 30 km. away. The site is situated on the north side of Argelès, between the coast road and the beach, so access is good, although there could be some road noise in high season. The site has been taken over by a new group, Camp'Atlantic and is looking smart with a new reception and tarmac roadways. However, there are now fewer touring pitches and the emphasis is on mobile homes with over 127 to let and 105 privately owned. The site is well looked after and the pool area is very welcoming.

### Facilities

Large modern toilet block, fully equipped and with some washbasins in cabins. Baby bath. Some facilities for disabled visitors. Washing machines. Shop, bar, restaurant and takeaway (all season). Heated swimming pool (May-Sept). Entertainment in high season. Play area. Bicycle hire. WiFi throughout (charged). Path to beach. Only gas barbecues permitted. Off site: Tourist train in high season. Aquatic park, adventure park, karting, riding and minigolf all within walking distance.

**Open:** 13 April - 22 September.

### Directions

From A9 take exit 42 (Perpignan-Sud) and follow N114 for Argelès. At exit 10 follow directions for Taxo d'Avall then Plage Nord. Site is clearly signed off coast road in the St Cyprien direction. GPS: 42.580606, 3.032854

### Charges guide

| | |
|---|---|
| Per unit incl. 2 persons and electricity | € 21.00 - € 39.00 |
| extra person | € 5.00 - € 9.00 |
| child (0-10 yrs) | free - € 6.00 |
| dog | € 5.00 |

**FREE** Alan Rogers Travel Card
Extra benefits and savings - see page 10

## Argelès-sur-Mer
### Camping Club la Sirène
Route de Taxo à la Mer, F-66702 Argelès-sur-Mer (Pyrénées-Orientales) T: 04 68 81 04 61.
E: contact@camping-lasirene.fr **alanrogers.com/FR66560**

From the moment you step into the hotel-like reception area you realise that this large site offers the holiday maker everything they could want, including a super pool complex, in a well managed and convenient location close to Argelès-sur-Mer and the beaches. There are 740 pitches over the 17-hectare site, and 520 mobile homes and chalets. They are modern in design, all less than five years old, and laid out in pretty avenues with flowering shrubs and shade from tall trees. There are now just ten touring pitches, with 16A electricity and water, and some 200 taken by tour operators. All the shops and amenities are near reception making the accommodation areas quite peaceful and relaxing. There is an amazing variety of activities on offer, and in the main season visitors have the option of using the free bus service to the beach where the site has its own club, Club Eméraude.

**Facilities**

Two well equipped toilet blocks with facilities for babies and disabled visitors (key access). Laundry. Traditional restaurant and fast food bar, bar and takeaway, large shop and bazaar, large aqua park, paddling pools, slides, jacuzzi. Games room. Two play areas. Multisports field. Tennis courts. Archery. Minigolf. Football. Theatre, evening entertainment, discos. Riding. Bicycle hire. Watersports. WiFi in bar area. Gas and electric barbecues only. Off site: Resort of Argelès-sur-Mer with beaches with the site's private Eméraude Beach Club 2 km.

**Open:** 20 April - 28 September.

**Directions**

Leave A9 motorway at exit 42, take D114, towards Argelès. Leave D114, exit 10 and follow signs for Plage Nord. Site signed after first roundabout and is on right 2 km. after last roundabout.
GPS: 42.57093, 3.02906

**Charges guide**

| Per unit incl. 1-3 persons | |
|---|---|
| and electricity | € 26.00 - € 43.00 |
| extra person | € 6.00 - € 9.00 |
| child (under 5 yrs) | € 4.00 - € 6.00 |

---

## Argelès-sur-Mer
### Camping l'Hippocampe
Route de Taxo à la Mer, F-66702 Argelès-sur-Mer (Pyrénées-Orientales) T: 04 68 81 04 61.
E: contact@camping-lasirene.fr **alanrogers.com/FR66570**

A sister site to la Sirène opposite, this site has some 32 touring pitches and around 130 mobile home and chalet pitches, and is aimed at families with young children, and adults looking for a quieter site. Some of the mobile homes and chalets are privately owned along with some 40 odd site-owned ones to rent, all modern, well maintained with hedging and space around them to provide privacy, and various trees providing shade. The pool on site is dedicated to smaller children. Entertainment, shops, bars and the full range of activities are offered by la Sirène, just across the road.

**Facilities**

Large central toilet block is fully equipped with controllable showers, baby bath and changing mats. Washing machine. Swimming pool complex with small slides and jacuzzi (lifeguard). Shop. Small bar. Play area. Multisports court. Gas and electric barbecues only. All other facilities are at la Sirène. Riding. Bicycle hire. Free WiFi. Transport to beach in main season. Off site: Beach within 2 km.

**Open:** 20 April - 28 September.

**Directions**

Leave A9 at 42 on D114, Argelès road. Leave D114 exit 10, following signs for Plage Nord. Site signed after the first roundabout, and is on the left 2 km. after last roundabout. GPS: 42.5705, 3.03065

**Charges guide**

| Per unit incl. 1-3 persons | |
|---|---|
| and electricity | € 26.00 - € 43.00 |
| extra person | € 6.00 - € 9.00 |

---

## Argelès-sur-Mer
### Camping le Bois du Valmarie
Le Racou, F-66700 Argelès-sur-Mer (Pyrénées-Orientales) T: 04 68 81 09 92. E: contact@camping-lasirene.fr
**alanrogers.com/FR66590**

Pitches here are exclusively for mobile home and chalet accommodation. Le Bois du Valmarie is a member of the same group of sites as la Sirène (FR66560) and l'Hippocampe (FR66570) and run to the same high standards. The site has 181 pitches, the majority of which are available for booking via tour operators or the site itself and is located south of the port, beside Racou beach. The site's location involves some up and down walking, but its range of amenities includes a wonderful, heated swimming pool complex with sea views. The sea is just 50 m. from the site entrance with a sandy beach.

**Facilities**

One smart and fully equipped toilet block. Supermarket, restaurant, bar, takeaway, swimming pool with waterslides and separate children's pool. Beach shop. Play area. Mobile homes for rent. Gas barbecues only. WiFi in reception (charged). Off site: Argelès town centre 3 km.

**Open:** 20 April - 28 September.

**Directions**

Leave autoroute at Perpignan Sud exit and join the N114 southbound towards Argelès. Take exit 13 and follow signs to Le Racou. Site is well signed from here. GPS: 42.53784, 3.05445

**Charges 2013**

Contact site.

---

For latest campsite news, availability and prices visit
**alanrogers.com**

## Argelès-sur-Mer
### Camping le Soleil

Route du Littoral, F-66702 Argelès-sur-Mer (Pyrénées-Orientales) T: 04 68 81 14 48.
E: camping.lesoleil@wanadoo.fr **alanrogers.com/FR66040**

Le Soleil is an attractive site with direct access to the sandy beach, but also with an impressive heated pool complex. It is a busy, popular, family owned site which over the years has developed into a small village. It has over 800 pitches of ample size, of which 132 are used by tour operators, and a further 430 for touring units, on sandy/grassy ground and with a mixture of tall trees and shrubs providing light shade. All have electricity (6A) and 24 are fully serviced. Caravans sometimes need to take care on the narrow access roads. The site has a wide range of amenities, including an impressive pool complex.

| Facilities | Directions |
|---|---|
| Six toilet blocks (one heated in low season) with external access to individual units. Some family cabins with washbasins, showers. Washing machines. Supermarket, general shop, press, tabac. Restaurant. Takeaway. Bar with disco (July/Aug), beach bar. Heated swimming pool complex and entertainment area. Adventure playground. TV room. Internet. WiFi. Tennis. Diving and riding in high season (charged). Dogs are not accepted. | Site is at north end of the beach, 1 km. from Argelès-Plage village. GPS: 42.57552, 3.04232 |

**Charges guide**

| Per unit incl. 2 persons and electricity | € 22.00 - € 46.10 |
|---|---|
| extra person (over 8 yrs) | € 5.00 - € 11.20 |

**Open:** 14 May - 17 September.

## Argelès-sur-Mer
### Castel Camping les Criques de Porteils

RD 114, Corniche de Collioure, F-66701 Argelès-sur-Mer (Pyrénées-Orientales) T: 04 68 81 12 73.
E: contactcdp@lescriques.com **alanrogers.com/FR66150**

This is an amazing site situated on the cliff top with views across the sea to Argelès, set against a backdrop of mountains and close to Collioure, the artists' paradise. What more could you ask for? Much work has been carried out to improve the facilities and pitches have been redesigned for easier access. There are around 250 of varying sizes and shapes due to the nature of the terrain, level in places, up and down in others. All have 10A electricity available and either a sea view or views towards the mountains. There are eight small coves accessed by steep steps (gated). There is a new bar and restaurant and some unusual artistic workshops for children. Some road and train noise may be experienced.

| Facilities | Directions |
|---|---|
| Two renovated toilet blocks (one can be heated) are colourful, fully equipped with super children's room, and all small equipment. Laundry room with Internet point. Motorcaravan service point. Shop. New bar and terraced restaurant with takeaway. Swimming pool. TV/games room. Play area. Golf practice. Tennis. Volleyball. Boules. Fishing. Duck pond and small animal area. Only gas barbecues are allowed. WiFi over site. | Exit A9 at Perpignan Sud or Le Boulou. At Argelès pick up signs for Collioure par la Corniche. Watch for site signs coming into a bend as you come down a hill by hotel. GPS: 42.53508, 3.06854 |

**Charges guide**

| Per unit incl. 2 persons and electricity | € 27.00 - € 48.00 |
|---|---|
| extra person | € 6.00 - € 11.00 |

**Open:** 31 March - 20 October.

## Argelès-sur-Mer
### Chadotel Camping les Jardins Catalans

Taxo d'Avall, chemin de Taxo à la Mer, F-66410 Argelès-sur-Mer (Pyrénées-Orientales) T: 04 68 81 11 68.
E: info@chadotel.com **alanrogers.com/FR66410**

This site does not accept touring units. Situated in one of France's most popular holiday areas adjoining the sea, yet with a superb mountain backdrop, this attractive, quiet chalet park has been continually developed and improved, but has other busy parks next to it. In total there are 169 chalets and cottages with 60 available to hire. They are less than seven years old and all clean and well maintained, on large plots with hedging and trees to provide lots of privacy. An attractive pool area with toboggan and paddling pool is overlooked by the bar. All facilities are open 1 April to mid September.

| Facilities | Directions |
|---|---|
| Small bar and restaurant with takeaway service (1/6-10/9). Swimming pool. Clean modern laundry. Gym. Play area. Bicycle hire. WiFi throughout (charged). Off site: Beach less than 1 km. (tourist train in season). Luna Park outdoor pleasure park 1 km. Riding 2 km. Karting. Bowling. | Leave A9 motorway at exit 42 and take right hand fork for Argelès on D114. Leave D114 at exit 10, follow signs for Plage Nord and site cannot be missed on the left. GPS: 42.5715478, 3.02796721 |

**Charges guide**

| per unit incl. 2 persons and electricity | € 15.00 - € 32.50 |
|---|---|
| extra person | € 5.90 |

**Open:** March - November.

For latest campsite news, availability and prices visit
## alanrogers.com

## Balaruc-les-Bains
### Camping le Mas du Padre

4 chemin du Mas du Padre, F-34540 Balaruc-les-Bains (Hérault) T: 04 67 48 53 41.
E: contact@mas-du-padre.com  **alanrogers.com/FR34100**

Mas du Padre is a pleasant little site run by the Durand family and it makes a good base from which to explore the Sète area or 'take the waters' at Balaruc-les-Bains. Madame Durand speaks excellent English. On a hillside, just 2.5 km. from Balaruc-les-Bains and near the Etang de Thau, this small site is unusually situated in a residential area that has developed around it over the years. The secluded pitches are of varying sizes and are marked by hedges, mature trees and shrubs. Some are on a very gentle slope and hard ground. There are 94 touring pitches with 6/10A electricity and 22 mobile homes to let.

**Facilities**

Fully equipped toilet blocks include baby changing area, facilities for disabled campers, washing machines. Reception sells basics. Swimming pool (1/5-30/9). Half-court tennis. Boules. Playground. Sports programme, tournaments, aquarobics, entertainment for children, weekly dance when a temporary bar is organised (all in high season). WiFi (free). Torch useful. Off site: Lake beach, bicycle hire and riding 2 km. Sea beach 10 km.

**Open:** 31 March - 21 October.

**Directions**

From A9, exit Sète, follow N800 to Balaruc-le-Vieux, first roundabout (D2), second roundabout both following Balaruc-les-Bains/Sète. After 50 m. right for Balaruc-les-Bains, immediately left across road, double back down it (50 m). Immediately right, follow Chemin du Mas du Padre. GPS: 43.45219, 3.69241

**Charges guide**

| | |
|---|---|
| Per unit incl. 2 persons and electricity | € 15.25 - € 38.15 |

---

## Boisseron
### Flower Camping Domaine de Gajan

Rue de Pie Bouquet, F-34160 Boisseron (Hérault) T: 04 66 80 94 30. E: info@campingdomainedegajan.com
**alanrogers.com/FR34910**

Domaine de Gajan lies midway between the Cevennes hills and the Mediterranean, with good access to the Camargue. Pitches here are of a good size, flat and well shaded by trees. Most have electrical connections (16A). A range of fully equipped mobile homes and chalets are available for rent, and four wooden safari tents on stilts fit well into the rural environment overlooking the countryside. On-site amenities include a bar/snack bar overlooking the large, welcoming swimming pool. The site becomes livelier in July and August with a full programme of activities and entertainment.

**Facilities**

Large, central, fully equipped toilet block has facilities for babies and for disabled visitors. Washing machines and dryer. Bar/snack bar. Takeaway. Swimming pool. Aquagym. Spa and wellness centre. Bicycle hire. Sports field. Play area. Tourist information. Free WiFi in bar/terrace area. Mobile homes and chalets for rent. Off site: Small shop in Boisseron 800 m. Fishing 1 km. Supermarket 2 km. Cycling and walking routes.

**Open:** 1 April - 1 October.

**Directions**

Leave A9 autoroute at exit 27 (Lunel) and take D34 (Boisseron, Sommières). After Saturargues and Saint-Sériès, turn right (roundabout) towards Boisseron and Sommières. Continue to Boisseron and, on approach to village centre, turn right following sign to site. GPS: 43.76667, 4.07472

**Charges guide**

| | |
|---|---|
| Per unit incl. 2 persons and electricity | € 17.50 - € 29.00 |

---

## Boisson
### Castel Camping le Château de Boisson

Boisson, F-30500 Allègre-les-Fumades (Gard) T: 04 66 24 85 61. E: reception@chateaudeboisson.com
**alanrogers.com/FR30070**

Château de Boisson is a quiet family site within easy reach of the Cévennes, Ardèche and Provence. The site is hilly and the 178 pitches, with 102 for touring are on two levels. They are separated by neat hedges and a variety of trees providing some shade. All have 6/10A electricity. Twenty-eight are fully serviced and seven have personal bathrooms. Rock pegs are essential. The large attractive swimming pools, one indoor (heated all season) with paddling pool and toboggan are near the château in a sunny location at the top of the site. Gas and electric barbecues only. Dogs not accepted in July/August.

**Facilities**

Two excellent, very clean toilet blocks with all necessary facilities including those for disabled visitors. Small shop (7/4-15/9). Good restaurant, bar, snacks (all season). Play area. Pools – indoor (all season), outdoor (1/5-22/9). Bridge tournaments in low season. Painting classes. Tennis. Boules. WiFi throughout (charged). Off site: Fishing 2 km. Riding 4 km. Allègre les Fumades (thermal baths and Casino) 5 km. Alès 16 km. Golf 30 km.

**Open:** 7 April - 22 September.

**Directions**

From Alès take D16 northeast through Salindres and Auzon. After Auzon turn right across river, then left, signed Barjac and site. Shortly turn right to site entrance. Only route for tourers. Do not drive through village of Boissons. GPS: 44.20967, 4.25625

**Charges guide**

| | |
|---|---|
| Per unit incl. 2 persons and electricity | € 20.40 - € 56.00 |
| extra person | € 3.00 - € 9.00 |

**FREE** Alan Rogers Travel Card
Extra benefits and savings - see page 10

## Brissac

### Domaine d'Anglas

F-34190 Brissac (Hérault) T: 04 67 73 70 18. E: contact@camping-anglas.com

alanrogers.com/FR34600

In the upper Hérault valley to the south of the Cévennes mountains, Camping d'Anglas is a delightful small site. The top part of the site is on quite stony ground with pitches divided by vines and mixed trees that provide a degree of shade. The lower part is more open, with some mature trees and pitches are not clearly divided but it makes a wonderful spot to camp. With 100 pitches in total, there are 78 for touring units. A stream runs through the site, dry when we visited, but it is quite possibly a torrent in winter time. Wooden bridges allow access to the toilet blocks on the other side.

### Facilities

Two toilet blocks provide all necessary facilities. Baby bath. Facilities for disabled visitors but some up and down walking on site. Washing machine. Shop for bread and basics. Communal barbecue. Play field. Wine evening. WiFi (free). Off site: Register at reception for canoeing, climbing, karting, mountain biking, walks and adventure tours through the woods and on Thursday (1/7-31/8) Saturday (30/4-30/6) evenings tour the owner's vineyard.

**Open:** 27 April - 9 September.

### Directions

From Montpellier follow the D986 north towards Ganges. After 40 km, just before entering the village of St Bauzille de Putois turn right signed Brissac. Cross the Hérault river over a narrow bridge and pick up site signs. GPS: 43.876056, 3.716083

### Charges guide

| Per unit incl. 2 persons | |
|---|---|
| and electricity | € 13.20 - € 33.90 |
| extra person | € 3.70 - € 6.20 |

## Canet-en-Roussillon

### Kawan Village Caravaning Ma Prairie

1 avenue des Coteaux, F-66140 Canet-en-Roussillon (Pyrénées-Orientales) T: 04 68 73 26 17. E: ma.prairie@wanadoo.fr  alanrogers.com/FR66020

Ma Prairie is an excellent site and its place in this guide goes back over 30 years. Then it was simply a field surrounded by vineyards. The trees planted then have now matured and more continue to be planted, along with colourful shrubs providing a comfortable, park-like setting with 208 touring pitches, all with 10A electricity and 15 with water and drainage. There are also 50 mobile homes available to rent and ten privately owned. It is a peaceful haven some 3 km. back from the sea but within walking distance of Canet village itself. The Gil family still provide a warm welcome and reception boasts an impressive international collection of hats, helmets and uniform caps. The restaurant and bar is across the road and overlooks a modern, attractive pool complex and wonderful old palm tree. Today there is Internet access, some mobile homes and modern housing has crept up but there are still vineyards close and the wine sold in reception is from the family vineyard.

### Facilities

Fully equipped toilet blocks, baby bath. Washing machines and dryers. No shop but bread can be ordered. Covered snack bar/takeaway. Air-conditioned bar and restaurant. Large adult pool, splendid children's pool. Multisports court. TV. Amusement machines. Busy daily activity and entertainment programme (high season; 6-12 yrs). WiFi over site (charged). Internet access in reception. Communal barbecue, no charcoal barbecues. Tourist train stops at site (April-June and Sept). Off site: Supermarket 400 m. Riding 600 m. Sandy beach 3 km. Golf 6 km.

**Open:** 24 April - 15 September.

### Directions

Leave autoroute A9 at Perpignan North towards Barcarès. Site access is from the D11 Perpignan road (exit 5), close to the junction with D617 in Canet-Village. Go under bridge, right at roundabout then left to site. GPS: 42.70135, 2.99968

### Charges 2013

| Per unit incl. 2 persons | |
|---|---|
| and electricity | € 19.00 - € 50.00 |
| extra person | € 5.00 - € 9.00 |

Camping Cheques accepted.

For latest campsite news, availability and prices visit

# alanrogers.com

# Canet-en-Roussillon
## Yelloh! Village le Brasilia

B.P. 204, F-66141 Canet-en-Roussillon (Pyrénées-Orientales) T: 04 68 80 23 82. E: info@lebrasilia.fr

**alanrogers.com/FR66070**

Situated across the yacht harbour from the upmarket resort of Canet-Plage, le Brasilia is an impressive, well managed family site directly beside the beach. It is pretty, neat and well kept with an amazingly wide range of facilities – indeed, it is camping at its best. There are 447 neatly hedged touring pitches, all with electricity (6-10A) and 315 with water and drainage. They vary in size from 80 to 120 sq.m. and some of the longer pitches are suitable for two families together. With a range of shade from pines and flowering shrubs, less on pitches near the beach, there are neat access roads (sometimes narrow for large units). There are also 179 pitches with mobile homes and chalets to rent (the new ones have their own gardens). The sandy beach here is busy, with a beach club (you can hire windsurfing boards) and a naturist section is to the west of the site. A completely new pool complex is planned with pools catering for all ages and hydrotherapy facilities for adults, all overlooked by its own snack bar and restaurant. The village area of the site offers shops, a busy restaurant and bar, entertainment (including a nightclub) and clubs for children of all ages. In fact, you do not need to stir from the site which is almost a resort in itself. It does have a nice, lively atmosphere but is orderly and well run. If you would like to visit Canet-Plage, a free tourist train runs in summer and a small ferry crosses the harbour. A member of Yelloh! Village and Leading Campings group.

### Facilities

Nine modern sanitary blocks are very well equipped and maintained, with British style WCs (some Turkish) and washbasins in cabins. Good facilities for children and for disabled campers. Laundry room. Motorcaravan services. Range of shops. Gas supplies. Bars and restaurant. New pool complex (heated). Play areas. Sports field. Tennis. Sporting activities. Library, games and video room. Hairdresser. Internet café and WiFi. Daily entertainment programme. Bicycle hire. Fishing. ATM. Exchange facilities. Post office. Weather forecasts. Only gas or electric barbecues are allowed. Off site: Boat launching and sailing 500 m. Riding 5 km. Golf 12 km.

**Open:** 13 April - 5 October.

### Directions

From A9 exit 41 (Perpignan Centre, Rivesaltes) follow signs for Le Barcarès and Canet on D83 for 10 km. then for Canet (D81). At first Canet roundabout, turn fully back on yourself (Sainte-Marie) and watch for Brasilia sign almost immediately on right. GPS: 42.70467, 3.03483

### Charges guide

| | |
|---|---|
| Per unit incl. 2 persons and electricity (6A) | € 23.00 - € 57.00 |
| extra person | € 6.00 - € 9.00 |
| child (3-6 yrs) | free - € 8.50 |
| dog (max. 2) | € 5.00 |

LE BRASILIA
CAMPING-VILLAGE
CANET-EN-ROUSSILLON - FRANCE
★★★★★
FONDÉ EN 1964

Your peninsula, your secret

Le Brasilia has chosen as its home port a beautiful, peaceful beach located at the far end of Canet-en-Roussillon. There, between the river and the port, in the hollow of a deep pine forest with its Mediterranean scents, Le Brasilia will reveal to you all the little secrets of well-being and the good life. The delightful Seychellois atmosphere of the 'Archipel' water park will immediately transport you to the Tropics. Our village is a garden of nature where you can get away from it all, and yet so much closer to your dream holidays.

Comfortable pitches, rental of cottages and bungalows, pool heated out of season, tropical water park, cardio-fitness training room, multi-sports pitches, entertainment, shops, disco, bar restaurant, cabaret, children's clubs, and so much more. All our shops and services are open throughout the whole time that the site is open.

2, avenue des Anneaux du Roussillon - 66140 Canet-en-Roussillon - France
Tél. : +33 (0)4 68 80 23 82 - Fax : +33 (0)4 68 73 32 97
info@lebrasilia.fr - www.brasilia.fr

*The Leading Campings of Europe*

yelloh!
VILLAGE

**FREE** Alan Rogers Travel Card
Extra benefits and savings - see page 10

## Canet-en-Roussillon
### Camping Mar Estang

Route de Saint Cyprien, F-66140 Canet-en-Roussillon (Pyrénées-Orientales) T: 04 68 80 35 53.
E: contactme@marestang.com **alanrogers.com/FR66090**

Le Mar Estang is a large, impressive, 'all singing, all dancing' site with something for everyone. Situated on the edge of Canet, between the Etang (part of the Réserve Naturelle de Canet/St Nazaire) and the sea, there is access to the sandy beach from the site by two tunnels under the road. If you don't fancy the beach, the site has not one but two attractive pool complexes linked by a bridge. They are amazing, providing slides, toboggans, jacuzzi, paddling pool and a heated pool, all with lifeguards. You can swim seriously, learn to swim or scuba dive or just enjoy the fun pools. Who needs the beach! There are 600 pitches in total, some 300 for touring units, with 6A electricity, and some degree of shade, on sandy ground. The rest are used by tour operators or have site-owned mobile homes to rent. A very wide range of activities and entertainment is organised all season, with children's clubs in high season and a beach club for watersports. Children and teenagers would have a great time here and parents would enjoy Canet-Plage with its esplanade, shops and restaurants. It is quite a smart resort watched over by Mount Canigou with its snowy peak.

### Facilities

Nine well equipped sanitary blocks are well placed around the site. Facilities for babies. Laundry. Motorcaravan service point. Shops, bars, restaurant and takeaway all open when site is open. Swimming pools with lifeguards, jacuzzi and solarium. Fitness club. Children's clubs. Artistic workshops (pottery, crafts etc). Daily sports and entertainment programme. Day trips. Evening entertainment with cabaret. Disco. Communal barbecue. Sailing club. Beach club. Tennis. Bicycle hire. Play areas. WiFi. Direct access to beach. Off site: Riding nearby. Rafting, canoeing and quad bike treks by arrangement. Canet 500 m. with tourist train in high season. Perpignan 10 km. Collioure, Port Vendres and the Spanish border.

**Open:** 21 April - 15 September.

### Directions

Take exit 41 from A9 autoroute and follow signs for Canet. On outskirts of town follow signs for Saint Cyprien/Plage Sud. Site is very clearly signed on southern edge of Canet Plage. GPS: 42.6757, 3.03135

### Charges guide

| | |
|---|---|
| Per unit incl. 2 persons and electricity | € 20.00 - € 44.00 |
| extra person | € 7.00 - € 13.00 |
| child (0-5 yrs) | free - € 7.00 |
| dog | free - € 4.00 |

## Brousses-et-Villaret
### Camping le Martinet Rouge

F-11390 Brousses-et-Villaret (Aude) T: 04 68 26 51 98. E: campinglemartinetrouge@orange.fr
**alanrogers.com/FR11040**

Le Martinet Rouge provides a peaceful retreat in the Aude countryside to the north of Carcassonne. The owners, Isobelle and John, are very proud of the improvements they have made to the site and provide a warm welcome, speaking English. An unusual feature of the site are the massive granite boulders (outcrops of smooth rock from the last ice age) beloved by all children! The site offers 53 pitches for touring units, all with electricity (6/10A), in two contrasting areas, the original one is well secluded with irregularly shaped, fairly level, large pitches amongst a variety of trees and shrubs, while the other is on a landscaped gentle hill with mature trees overlooking the pool.

### Facilities

Two small, original sanitary blocks have been refurbished and are used in high season. Two modern blocks with facilities for disabled visitors and babies, can be heated in low season. Washing machine and dryer. Shop for basics (no others locally). Bar, terrace, TV (1/7-15/9). Snack bar (1/7-31/8). Swimming pool and water slide (15/6-15/9). Barbecue area. Fitness room. Croquet. Half court tennis. Multisports court. Play area for most ages. WiFi over site (charged). Off site: Fishing possible accessed from site (license from village). Visit the paper mill in the village. Tennis and riding nearby.

**Open:** March - end September.

### Directions

Site is south of Brousses-et-Villaret, 20 km. northwest of Carcassonne. Best approached via D118, Carcassonne-Mazamet road. Turn onto D103 15 km. north of Carcassonne to Brousses-et-Villaret. Western outskirts of village turn south to site (signed) in 50 m. GPS: 43.33932, 2.25201

### Charges guide

| | |
|---|---|
| Per unit incl. 2 persons and electricity | € 18.50 - € 29.00 |
| extra person | € 7.00 - € 7.50 |

For latest campsite news, availability and prices visit
# alanrogers.com

# Mar Estang

★★★★

Route de St Cyprien
66140 Canet Plage
www.marestang.com
contactme@marestang.com
TEL: +33(0)4 68 80 35 53
FAX: +33(0)4 68 73 32 94

# LES CRIQUES DE PORTEILS

★★★★★

RD 114 - Corniche de Collioure
66701 Argelès-sur-Mer
www.lescriques.com
contactcdp@lescriques.com
TEL: +33(0)4 68 81 12 73
FAX: +33(0)4 68 95 85 76

LES CASTELS
★★★★
Hôtellerie de Plein Air

## Cap d'Agde
### Yelloh! Village Mer et Soleil

Chemin de Notre Dame à Saint Martin, Rochelongue, F-34300 Cap d'Agde (Hérault) T: 04 67 94 21 14.
E: contact@camping-mer-soleil.com **alanrogers.com/FR34290**

Close to Cap d'Agde, this is a popular, well equipped site with many facilities. The pool area is very attractive with large palm trees, a whirlpool and slides as well as a gym and wellness centre. An upstairs restaurant overlooks this area and the entertainment stage next to it. All ages are catered for and evening entertainment in July and August includes live shows. There are 467 pitches, around half taken by mobile homes and chalets (some to let, some privately owned). The touring pitches are hedged and have good shade from tall trees, all with 6A electricity. A smart new reception has been built, and a state-of-the-art balnéo can be found at the front of the site offering a wide range of treatments. It is open for public use with a 10% reduction offered to campers. The design inside is very impressive with a central grass area and fountain. The hydro pools are under a church-like roof and the massage rooms, sauna and hammam are off to the sides providing a very calm and relaxed atmosphere. From the back of the site, a 1 km. long path leads to the white sandy beach at Rochelongue.

**Facilities**

One large toilet block plus two smaller ones are fully equipped. Attractive units for children with small toilets, etc. Units for disabled visitors. Washing machine. Shop. Bar, snacks and restaurant. Heated swimming pools. Gym. State-of-the-art balnéo with hydro pools, massage rooms, sauna and Turkish bath. Play area. Tennis. Archery. Sporting activities and evening entertainment. Miniclub for kids and teens. Library. Hairdresser. Doctor. Video games. Television room. Bakery. WiFi over site (charged). Off site: Pool complex opposite site. Beach and riding 1 km.

**Open:** 14 April - 6 October.

**Directions**

From A9 exit 34, follow N312 for Agde. It joins the N112 Béziers-Sète road. Cross bridge over Hérault river and turn right for Rochelongue. Take the second exit at next roundabout and site is a little further on the right. GPS: 43.286183, 3.478

**Charges guide**

| | |
|---|---|
| Per unit incl. 2 persons and electricity | € 17.00 - € 41.00 |
| extra person | € 4.00 - € 8.00 |
| child (3-7 yrs) | free - € 7.00 |

1 WEEK PAID = 1 WEEK FREE*
from 13/04 till 29/06 & from 31/08 till 05/10
(* see general terms of sale)

★★★★

Yelloh Village & Spa Club ★★★★
Chemin de Notre Dame à Saint-Martin
F-34300 CAP D'AGDE
Tel: +33(0)4 67 94 21 14 - Fax: +33(0)4 67 94 81 94
www.camping-mer-soleil.com
contact@camping-mer-soleil.com

## Carcassonne
### Camping la Cité

Route de Saint Hilaire, F-11000 Carcassonne (Aude) T: 04 68 10 01 00. E: camping@carcassonne.fr
**alanrogers.com/FR11100**

A visit to the medieval city of Carcassonne is a must and Camping la Cité is within walking distance along a shaded footpath beside a stream. The majority of pitches are very large, separated by bushes and with good shade. There are also some undefined places under trees for small tents. In total there are 200, with 143 for touring, 95 having 10A electricity and the rest used for mobile homes and chalets to hire. Because of its situation it is very popular and you need to arrive early in the high season. A swimming pool, snack bar and small shop make this a very comfortable and useful site.

**Facilities**

Three traditional, fully equipped toilet blocks, with (few) mainly Turkish toilets. Laundry. Motorcaravan service point. Fridge hire. Shop, bar and snack bar/takeaway meals (limited opening outside July/Aug). TV and games room. Multisport pitch. Swimming and paddling pools (15/6-15/9). Play area. Communal barbecue (only gas or electric on pitches). Chalets and mobile homes to rent. WiFi (charged). Off site: Golf and bicycle hire 2 km.

**Open:** 2 April - 15 October.

**Directions**

From A61 autoroute take exit 24 onto the N113 following signs for la Cité. Site is well signed from all roads into the city. Avoid 12.00-14.00 outside July/Aug. Reception is closed with queues blocking the entrance! GPS: 43.200315, 2.353767

**Charges guide**

| | |
|---|---|
| Per unit incl. 2 persons and electricity | € 20.10 - € 29.00 |
| extra person | € 4.50 - € 7.40 |

For latest campsite news, availability and prices visit
# alanrogers.com

## Castelnaudary
### Yelloh! Village le Bout du Monde

Ferme de Rhodes, Verdun-en-Lauragais, F-11400 Castelnaudary (Aude) T: 04 68 94 95 96.
E: info@yellohvillage-leboutdumonde.com **alanrogers.com/FR11230**

Le Bout du Monde is a really special place at the heart of the Montagne Noire, on the edge of the Haut Languedoc regional park. Here you can experience life as it used to be. Children help with the animals on the farm, roam the woods, swim in the natural pool and learn to make bread and pottery. Grown ups have a chance to unwind in wonderful natural surroundings. This small site is a member of the Yelloh! Village group and at present there are 26 large grass pitches with water and 8A electricity, most hedged. The toilet blocks are in keeping with the ethos; one is in a converted pigeon house, the other, under a turf roof, has a bees' nest behind glass – both however have modern fittings!

**Facilities**

Two fully equipped toilet bocks. Washing machine. Small shop, wine bar for simple food. Auberge (specialising in local cuisine, open all year). Takeaway. Swimming pool and natural swimming pool. Entertainment and activity programme. Archery. Sports field. Fishing lake. Children's farm. Electric barbecues only. Mobile homes for rent. WiFi. No charcoal barbecues. Off site: Riding 7 km. GR7 long distance footpath. Haut Languedoc Regional Park. Sailing. Canoeing. Accrobranche aerial assault course.

**Open:** 6 April - 30 September.

**Directions**

From A61 take Castelnaudary exit and proceed to Castelnaudary. Here, take D103 towards Saissac. After passing through St Papoul, turn left to join D803 to Verdun-en-Lauragais. Join northbound D903 (narrow uphill road) and site is well signed with distinctive goat logo. GPS: 43.37671, 2.07463

**Charges guide**

| | |
|---|---|
| Per unit incl. 2 persons and electricity | € 17.00 - € 33.00 |

## Chastanier
### Camping les Sous Bois du Lac

Bessettes, F-48300 Chastanier (Lozère) T: 04 66 69 52 43. E: joel.feminier@wanadoo.fr
**alanrogers.com/FR48180**

Started by the Feminier family in 1992, this spacious rural site of 14 hectares borders a small fishing river and is close to the large Lac de Naussac where sailing and watersports are available. There are 139 good sized, level, grassy/stony pitches separated by shrubs and mature trees. There are 79 for touring units, about half with shade, and most have 6/10A electricity (long leads may be needed). There is a varied entertainment programme for all ages and a good bar/restaurant. Rock pegs are advised.

**Facilities**

Two main toilet blocks have a mixture of British and Turkish style WCs and preset showers. Facilities for babies and for disabled campers. Washing machine. Motorcaravan service point. Shop. Large restaurant and bar, takeaway food (July/Aug). Swimming pool with paddling area. Children's playground. Entertainment for children and adults. River for fishing. Tourist information. WiFi (charged). Accommodation to rent. Off site: 30 km. cycle route.

**Open:** 1 May - 1 November.

**Directions**

Leave N88 (Le Puy - Mende) just southwest of Langogne. Turn north on D26 towards Lac de Naussac (500 m) then turn left onto D34 towards Chastanier and follow signs to site on right (7.5 km). GPS: 44.7381, 3.76918

**Charges guide**

| | |
|---|---|
| Per unit incl. 2 persons and electricity | € 15.48 - € 17.20 |

Camping Cheques accepted.

## Clapiers
### Camping le Plein Air des Chênes

Route de Castelnau, F-34830 Clapiers (Hérault) T: 04 67 02 02 53. E: pleinairdeschenes@sandaya.fr
**alanrogers.com/FR34230**

Le Plein Air des Chênes is situated just outside the village of Clapiers, about 5 km. from the interesting city of Montpellier, yet merely 20 km. from a choice of Mediterranean beaches. However, the site itself has much to offer, with an amazing pool complex with toboggans, cascades, pools and a wonderful children's pool area, not to mention an Auberge (open all year). In the main season, there is plenty of entertainment, but it is also a good base from which explore the countryside. There are 73 touring pitches with 10A electricity (some large with individual toilet cabin), all in a shaded terraced setting.

**Facilities**

Two well equipped modern toilet blocks have washbasins in cabins and facilities for babies (code) and disabled visitors. Washing machines. Fridge hire. Good restaurant open to the public. Bar, pool side bar, café/takeaway (1/6-15/9). Swimming pools (1/6-15/9; limited public access). Aqua bicycles. Multisports court. Play area. Miniclub. Evening entertainment in main season. WiFi over site (charged). Off site: Clapiers 800 m.

**Open:** All year.

**Directions**

Site is north of Montpellier, 8 km. from A9. Exit 28 on N113 towards Montpellier passing Vendargues. Follow signs for Millau on D65, then Clapiers and follow site signs. GPS: 43.65135, 3.89607

**Charges guide**

| | |
|---|---|
| Per unit incl. 2 persons and electricity | € 25.00 - € 48.00 |
| extra person | € 4.00 - € 9.00 |

**FREE** Alan Rogers Travel Card
**Extra benefits and savings** - see page 10

## Crespian
### Kawan Village le Mas de Reilhe
Chemin du Mas de Reilhe, F-30260 Crespian (Gard) T: 04 66 77 82 12. E: info@camping-mas-de-reilhe.fr
alanrogers.com/FR30080

This is a pleasant family site in the heart of the Gard region with a favourable climate. There are 95 pitches, 70 for tourers, 57 have electricity (6/10A), 25 also have water and waste water and some of the upper ones may require long leads. The large lower pitches are separated by tall poplar trees and hedges, close to the main facilities but may experience some road noise. The large terraced pitches on the hillside are scattered under mature pine trees, some with good views, more suited to tents and trailer tents but with their own modern sanitary facilities. The heated swimming pool is in a sunny position and overlooked by the attractive bar/restaurant. There are no shops in the village, the nearest being in the medieval city of Sommières 10 km. away (and well worth a visit). From here you can explore the Cévennes gorges, enjoy the Mediterranean beaches, visit the Petite Camargue or Nîmes with its Roman remains, and other old Roman cities. The entertainment in July and August is mainly for children with just the occasional competition and musical evening for adults.

**Facilities**

Excellent, clean toilet blocks with facilities for campers with disabilities. Washing machine. Reception. Limited shop (bread to order). Bar, takeaway, restaurant (1/5-16/9). Heated swimming pool (27/4-16/9). Small play area on grass. Pétanque. Internet access. WiFi over site (charged). Only gas or electric barbecues on pitches. Bicycle hire. Motorcaravan services. Off site: Tennis 500 m. Fishing 3 km. Riding 5 km. Golf 25 km. Sea and gorges 30 km.

**Open:** 14 April - 16 September.

**Directions**

From the A9 take exit 25, Nimes-ouest signed Alès, then D999 towards Le Vigan (about 23 km). Turn north on the D6110, site shortly on right at southern edge of Crespian. GPS: 43.87931, 4.09637

**Charges guide**

| | |
|---|---|
| Per unit incl. 2 persons and electricity | € 20.00 - € 26.00 |
| extra person | € 5.00 - € 6.00 |

Camping Cheques accepted.

Camping Le Mas de Reilhe****

SPECIAL OFFERS IN LOW SEASON

www.camping-mas-de-reilhe.fr
info@camping-mas-de-reilhe.fr

Le Mas de Reilhe

Camping Le Mas de Reilhe
30260 CRESPIAN
Tel : 33 (0)4 66 77 82 12

## Florac
### Camping le Pont du Tarn
Route de Pont de Montvert (RN106), F-48400 Florac (Lozère) T: 04 66 45 18 26.
E: contact@camping-florac.com alanrogers.com/FR48100

Le Pont du Tarn, just outside Florac and close to the River Tarn, is an excellent base for touring this beautiful Cévennes region of France. There are 181 pitches with 28 occupied by mobile homes and chalets (available for rent). The pitches are large, level, grassy and well shaded. All have electricity (10A) and 36 are fully serviced. Access to this site and on-site is good for large outfits. Leisure amenities include a swimming pool, a paddling pool, minigolf and a sports area. A children's club is also operated in peak season. Only gas and electric barbecues are allowed on site (a communal one is provided).

**Facilities**

The clean toilet facilities are housed in an older-style, heated building, with a second similar block, and include good sized preset showers. Facilities for disabled visitors and babies. Shop. Bar/restaurant/takeaway (10/5-30/8). Swimming pool, paddling pool (8/5-30/9). Sports area. Minigolf. Play area. Motorcaravan services. River beach. Entertainment and activities (high season). WiFi (free). Off site: Shops and restaurants in Florac 2.5 km. Bicycle hire 3 km. Tennis. Walking and cycle trails. Riding 12 km.

**Open:** 1 April - 1 November.

**Directions**

Florac is 56 km northwest of Alès on N106. Bypass Florac and at roundabout turn right onto D998, signed Pont de Montvert, site shortly on left. GPS: 44.33569, 3.589729

**Charges guide**

| | |
|---|---|
| Per unit incl. 2 persons and electricity | € 15.70 - € 22.20 |
| extra person | € 3.20 - € 4.00 |
| child (under 13 yrs) | € 2.50 - € 3.00 |

For latest campsite news, availability and prices visit
**alanrogers.com**

## Font-Romeu
### Huttopia Font-Romeu

Route de Mont-Louis, F-66120 Font-Romeu (Pyrénées-Orientales) T: 04 68 30 09 32.
E: font-romeu@huttopia.com **alanrogers.com/FR66250**

This is a large, open site of some seven hectares, with 125 touring pitches (100 with 10A electricity), nestling on the side of the mountain at the entrance to Font-Romeu. This part of the Pyrenees offers some staggering views and the famous Mont Louis is close by. An ideal base for climbing, hiking and cycling, it would also provide a good stopover for a night or so whilst travelling between Spain and France, or to and from Andorra. The terraced pitches are easily accessed, with those dedicated to caravans and motorcaravans at the top of the site, whilst tents go on the lower slopes.

#### Facilities
Two clean toilet blocks are traditional in style with modern fittings. Toilet for children and good facilities for disabled visitors. Shop (as site). Bar, restaurant and takeaway service (all July/Aug). Outdoor heated swimming pool (20/6-16/9). Washing machines and dryers at each block. Large games hall. Only electric barbecues are permitted. Max. 1 dog. Off site: Bicycle hire 0.3 km. Golf and riding 2 km. Opportunities for walking and climbing are close by as are, fishing, cycling and tennis. Beach 8 km.

**Open:** 20 June - 16 September.

#### Directions
Font-Romeu is on the D118, some 12 km. after it branches off the N116 heading west, just after Mont Louis. This is an interesting road with magnificent views and well worth the climb. The site is just before the town, on the left and accessed off the car park. GPS: 42.51171, 2.04972

#### Charges 2013
| | |
|---|---|
| Per unit with 2 persons and electricity | € 21.00 - € 37.70 |
| extra person | € 5.40 - € 7.20 |

---

## La Grande Motte
### Camping le Garden

44 place des Tamaris, F-34280 La Grande Motte (Hérault) T: 04 67 56 50 09. E: campinglegarden@orange.fr
**alanrogers.com/FR34020**

Le Garden is a well cared for and pretty site, situated amongst tall pines and flowering shrubs, some 400 m. back from a fine sandy beach. The pitches are of a good size (100 sq.m) on sandy grass. There are 116 mobile homes to rent and 86 touring pitches, most with 10A electricity, water and drainage. An attractive pool is overlooked by the restaurant. The site also has a small 'centre commercial' with a range of shops and a bar next door, which is open to the public. Le Garden is a very comfortable and quiet site (possible road noise during the day) within pleasant walking distance of the town centre and port. La Grande Motte is a product of the sixties tourist boom when much building went on and, at the time the apartment blocks seemed very futuristic. It has now matured into a smart, upmarket seaside resort with plenty of green space. There is much to see in the area, being on the edge of the Petite Camargue.

#### Facilities
Three well situated toilet blocks, smartly refurbished in Mediterranean colours, include washbasins in cabins and baby bath. Laundry facilities. Unit for disabled visitors. Shops to one side of the site with groceries, cigarettes, newspapers and boutique (1/3-30/9). Bar, restaurant and takeaway (15/5-30/9). Swimming pool and paddling pool (15/5-30/9). Play area. TV room. Internet access and WiFi. Gas and electric barbecues only. Off site: Beach 400 m. Tennis, riding and bicycle hire 500 m. Golf 2 km.

**Open:** 1 April - 15 October.

#### Directions
Entering La Grande Motte from D62, keep right following signs for 'campings' and petite Motte. Turn right at lights by the Office de Tourism, and right again by Bar Le Garden and site is immediately on right. GPS: 43.56322, 4.07278

#### Charges 2013
| | |
|---|---|
| Per unit incl. 1-3 persons, electricity, water and drainage | € 44.00 |
| extra person | € 9.80 |

Bracelet required for pool € 10.

CAMPING ★★★★
**LE GARDEN**
LA GRANDE MOTTE

Avenue de la Petite Motte
34280 La Grande Motte
France
Tél. : 00 33 (0)4 67 56 50 09
Fax : 00 33 (0)4 67 56 25 69
**www.legarden.fr**

# Frontignan
## Camping les Tamaris

140 avenue d'Ingril, F-34110 Frontignan-Plage (Hérault) T: 04 67 43 44 77. E: les-tamaris@wanadoo.fr
**alanrogers.com/FR34440**

This is a super site, unusually situated on a strip of land that separates the sea from the étang, or inland lake, and therefore Frontignan Ville from Frontignan Plage. The design of the site is unusual which adds to its attractiveness. The pitches are laid out in hexagons divided by tall hedging and colourful shrubs. In total, there are 250 pitches with 100 taken by mobile homes which are let by the site. All are 'grand confort' with 10A electricity, water and waste water and on level sandy grass. Direct access to the sandy beach is possible via three gates.

### Facilities

Three modern toilet blocks with some en-suite showers and washbasins. Excellent facilities for children. Unit for disabled visitors. Motorcaravan service point. Shop, bar, restaurant, takeaway, swimming pool (all season). Hairdresser. Gym. Play area. Miniclub. Archery. Bicycle hire. Internet access in reception and WiFi throughout (free). Entertainment for all ages. Off site: Riding 150 m. Sailing 1 km. Boat launching 2.5 km. Golf 15 km.

**Open:** 3 April - 22 September.

### Directions

From north on A9 take exit 32 and follow N112 towards Sète and Frontignan. After 16 km. ignore sign for Frontignan town and continue to Frontignan-Plage following site signs along the road between the sea and étang. GPS: 43.44970, 3.80603

### Charges guide

| | |
|---|---|
| Per unit incl. 2 persons and all services | € 25.00 - € 48.00 |

No credit cards.

# Le Barcarès
## Camping Club le Floride et l'Embouchure

Route de Saint Laurent, F-66423 Le Barcarès (Pyrénées-Orientales) T: 04 68 86 11 75.
E: campingfloride@aol.com  **alanrogers.com/FR66290**

Essentially a family run enterprise, le Floride et l'Embouchure is really two sites in one – l'Embouchure the smaller one with direct access to the beach and le Floride on the opposite side of the road into Le Barcarès village. There are a number of pitches with their own individual sanitary facility and in total the site offers 632 reasonably sized pitches, 280 for touring, all with 10A electricity. A good range of chalets and mobile homes are available for rent. This is a friendly, family-centred site, very popular with Dutch visitors. It is relatively inexpensive, especially outside the July/August peak period.

### Facilities

Four fully equipped toilet blocks on le Floride and two on l'Embouchure where 50 pitches near the beach have individual facilities. Facilities for babies and disabled visitors. Family shower room. Motorcaravan service point. Shop, bar, restaurant and takeaway (all 15/6-5/9). Pool complex (all season). Play area. Multisports court. Gym. Tennis. Entertainment and sports programmes (mid June-mid Sept). Bicycle hire. Charcoal barbecues are not permitted. Max. 1 dog. WiFi over site (charged). Off site: Beach 100 m. Fishing 1 km. Riding 1.5 km.

**Open:** 1 April - 30 September.

### Directions

From A9 take exit 41 (Perpignan Nord) and follow signs for Canet and Le Barcarès via D83. At exit 9 follow D81 (Canet) then next left into Le Barcarès Village. Site is 1 km. on the left and right sides of the road. GPS: 42.77855, 3.0301

### Charges guide

| | |
|---|---|
| Per unit incl. 2 persons and electricity | € 14.00 - € 41.70 |
| incl. individual sanitary facility | € 18.00 - € 52.50 |
| extra person | € 2.90 - € 6.70 |

# Le Barcarès
## Yelloh! Village le Pré Catalan

Route de Saint Laurent, F-66420 Le Barcarès (Pyrénées-Orientales) T: 04 68 86 12 60.
E: info@yellohvillage-pre-catalan.com  **alanrogers.com/FR66300**

The green foliage from the mixed trees and flowering shrubs makes this 4.5 hectare site very attractive and an avenue of palms is particularly spectacular. There has been a camping site here since 1960 but the present owners, the Galidie family, took over in 1982 and the site is now run to a very high standard by their son, François, and his English wife, Jenny. With 250 pitches in total, 140 are taken by mobile homes and chalets, and some are used by tour operators. These are mixed amongst the 80 touring pitches which are on level, sandy ground, clearly divided by hedging and all with 10A electricity.

### Facilities

Good modern facilities include small showers for children. Laundry. Small shop. Bar, restaurant and takeaway (all season). Heated swimming pool complex including fun pools, whirlpool and paddling pool. Play area. Tennis. Archery. Library. Activities for children with miniclub and evening entertainment (July/Aug). No charcoal barbecues. Free WiFi. Off site: Beach 900 m. River fishing 1 km.

**Open:** 27 April - 23 September.

### Directions

From A9 exit 41 (Perpignan Nord), follow signs for Le Barcarès and Canet (D83). At exit 9 take D81 (Canet), then first left to Le Barcarès (D90). Site is in 500 m. next to Le California. GPS: 42.78106, 3.02282

### Charges guide

| | |
|---|---|
| Per unit incl. 2 persons and electricity | € 17.00 - € 40.00 |
| extra person | € 5.00 - € 8.00 |

For latest campsite news, availability and prices visit
# alanrogers.com

## Le Barcarès
### Camping Club Village l'Europe

Route de Saint Laurent, F-66420 Le Barcarès (Pyrénées-Orientales) T: 04 68 86 15 36.
E: reception@europe-camping.com **alanrogers.com/FR66670**

Le Barcarès is a popular resort with a busy market and a fishing port. It has a good number of campsites but l'Europe is a little different in that it is open all year and each pitch has its own private sanitary facilities. There is a gate at the back of the site for the sandy beach which is a walk of some 600 m. However, the site has its own pool complex overlooked by the bar/restaurant and stage where nightly shows are performed in high season. In total, there are 339 pitches of a good size (100 for touring units) and with some shade from mixed trees and shrubs. The partly hedged pitches are level on sandy grass. The fact that the site is open all year round and that Perpignan airport is nearby has proved popular with visitors looking to buy their own mobile home. There are 75 mobile homes or chalets to rent and 145 privately owned. A new concept financed by the local authority has resulted in a tarmac path, the Voie Verte de l'Agly which follows the Agly river running past the site. It is 15 km. long from Le Barcarès to Rivesaltes and is used for cycling, jogging, walking or roller skating (but no cars). It is popular with those who wish to keep fit.

**Facilities**

Individual sanitary facilities on every pitch including dishwashing sink. Laundry. Shop (15/4-30/9). Bar, restaurant and takeaway (high season, on demand at other times). Outdoor pool (15/4-30/9). Wellness. Play area. Tennis. Evening shows and children's club (high season). Only gas and electric barbecues allowed. WiFi at reception. Off site: Nearest beach 600 m. Supermarket. Fishing. Watersports. Le Barcarès resort with many shops, cafés, restaurants and market.

**Open:** All year.

**Directions**

From A9 take exit 41 (Perpignan Nord) and follow signs for Canet and Le Barcarès via the D83. At exit 9 follow the D81 (Canet), then next left for Le Barcarès. Site is almost immediately on the right. GPS: 42.774931, 3.021004

**Charges guide**

| | |
|---|---|
| Per unit incl. 2 persons and electricity | € 23.50 - € 49.00 |
| extra person | € 4.00 - € 8.00 |

## Le Grau-du-Roi
### Yelloh! Village Secrets de Camargue

Route de l'Espiguette, F-30240 Le Grau-du-Roi (Gard) T: 04 66 80 08 00.
E: info@yellohvillage-secrets-de-camargue.com **alanrogers.com/FR30380**

Les Secrets de Camargue is part of the same group as la Petite Camargue and les Petits Camarguais, and is of the same high standard. Les Secrets, however, is rather special for two reasons: firstly, it is reserved for over 18s and for families with children under three years old; secondly, it is environmentally aware and the identity of the Camargue area is maintained by careful planting and the use of thatch and timber. This can be clearly seen in the pool area, which appears to blend seamlessly into the sand dunes beyond. In total there are 176 pitches with 28 for touring units (with 10A electricity) on level sandy grass.

**Facilities**

Fully equipped sanitary block includes excellent provision for babies, and facilities for disabled visitors. Small shop (2/4-19/9). Bar/restaurant. Heated swimming pool. Aquagym. Bicycle hire. Small play area (under 3s). Activities and entertainment. Mobile homes and chalets for rent. Off site: Large shop at les Petites Camargues 400 m. Free use of facilities at nearby Camping les Petits Camarguais. Riding 800 m. Nearest beach 1.5 km.

**Open:** 20 April - 2 October.

**Directions**

Leave the A9 at exit for Gallargues and head for Aigues-Mortes on the D979. Continue to Le Grau-du-Roi and then follow signs to Port Camargue on the D62, continuing to join the D255. Site is well signed from this point. GPS: 43.48736, 4.14202

**Charges guide**

| | |
|---|---|
| Per unit incl. 2 persons | € 17.00 - € 45.00 |
| extra person | € 5.00 - € 9.00 |

**FREE** Alan Rogers Travel Card
Extra benefits and savings - see page 10

## Le Grau-du-Roi

### Yelloh! Village les Petits Camarguais

Route de l'Espiguette, F-30240 Le Grau-du-Roi (Gard) T: 04 66 51 16 16. E: info@les-petits-camarguais.fr

**alanrogers.com/FR30390**

Les Petits Camarguais is sister site to FR30020 and FR30380 and is also a member of the Yelloh! Village group. There are 219 pitches here, all for mobile homes or chalets, with a good range of facilities including an impressive and attractive swimming pool complex with slides, whirlpools and an island, which is very popular. The facilities are all of a high quality and there are lots of organised activities for children during the day, and entertainment for adults during the evenings. In high season there is a free shuttle to the nearest beach (1.8 km. distant). The beach is L'Espiguette, reputedly the largest French Mediterranean beach, including a naturist area. The accommodation is well spaced out in avenues among flowering shrubs and trees.

**Facilities**

Two high quality toilet blocks provide extra provision. Laundry. Shop. Bar. Restaurant. Takeaway. Heated swimming pool complex. Aquagym (high season). Miniclub. Play area. Multisports court. Activity and entertainment programme. Dogs are not accepted. Bicycle hire. Free WiFi in reception area. Mobile homes and chalets for rent. Off site: Nearest beach 1.8 km. (free shuttle in peak season). Riding 1 km.

**Open:** 6 April - 16 September.

**Directions**

Leave the A9 autoroute at the Gallargues exit and head for Aigues-Mortes on the D979. Continue to Le Grau-du-Roi and then follow signs to Port Camargue on the D62, continuing to join the D255b, then follow signs to Phare l'Espiguette and pick up site signs. GPS: 43.50847, 4.14554

**Charges guide**

Contact site.

## Le Vigan

### Camping le Val de l'Arre

Route du Pont de la Croix, F-30120 Le Vigan (Gard) T: 04 67 81 02 77. E: valdelarre@wanadoo.fr

**alanrogers.com/FR30230**

Camping Val de l'Arre is situated along the Arre river, a tributary of the Herault river and in the centre of the Cévennes National Park. The site is well managed by the very friendly Triaire family, who speak English, Dutch, Spanish and French. There are 170 grassy, level pitches, 135 for touring, many have some shade and most have electricity (10A). There is a pleasant swimming pool with an outdoor bar. A pebble beach at the river bank provides opportunities for play and fishing enthusiasts will also certainly appreciate the river. Only gas and electric barbecues on site. There are numerous possibilities for outdoor activities such as white water rafting, canoeing and mountain biking. Qualified guides may take you on mountain expeditions on foot or by bicycle. Les Grottes des Demoiselles nearby are some of France's foremost caves. There is also the opportunity to taste the great wines of the Hérault region.

**Facilities**

Three clean and well appointed toilet blocks are well spaced around the site with controllable showers. Facilities for babies and visitors with disabilities. Washing machines. Shop, open air bar with snacks and restaurant (all 1/6-31/8). Swimming and paddling pools (1/6-15/9). Boules. Play area. Motorcaravan services. Guided walks organised. WiFi throughout (charged). Off site: Bicycle hire 2.5 km. Riding 8 km. Many opportunities for walkers, cyclists and mountain bikers.

**Open:** 1 April - 10 September.

**Directions**

Leave A75 at exit 48, follow D7, then D999 east to Le Vigan (43 km). Drive through town, signed Nîmes, at roundabout turn right D110B, site signed. Cross river, turn left to site 800 m. GPS: 43.992067, 3.6374

**Charges guide**

| | |
|---|---|
| Per unit incl. 2 persons and electricity | € 17.00 - € 24.50 |
| extra person | € 4.00 - € 6.50 |
| child (2-6 yrs) | € 3.00 - € 4.00 |
| dog | € 2.50 |

## Marseillan-Plage
### Camping la Créole

74 avenue des Campings, F-34340 Marseillan-Plage (Hérault) T: 04 67 21 92 69.
E: campinglacreole@wanadoo.fr **alanrogers.com/FR34220**

This is a surprisingly tranquil, well cared for small campsite in the middle of this bustling resort that will appeal to those seeking a rather less frenetic ambience typical of many sites in this area. Essentially a family orientated site, it offers around 118 good sized, level, sandy pitches, all with 6A electricity and mostly with shade from trees and shrubs. There are also 17 mobile homes available to rent. It benefits from direct access to an extensive sandy beach (secure gated access) and the fact that there is no swimming pool actually contributes to the tranquillity (deckchairs in high season). It may even be seen as an advantage for families with younger children. The beach will be the main attraction here no doubt, and the town's extensive range of bars, restaurants and shops are all within a couple of minutes walk. It is well situated for visiting Sète, a miniature Venice, or Pézenas with an interesting history and lots of art and craft shops. Cap d'Agde, a modern resort with its large marina and super water park for children is popular. If you take a trip on the Canal du Midi you may get to see the oyster beds in the Etang de Thau, the inland saltwater lake. There are many vineyards to visit and it is the home area of Muscat wine.

| Facilities | Directions |
|---|---|
| Toilet facilities are in a traditional building, modernised inside to provide perfectly adequate, if not particularly luxurious, facilities including some washbasins in private cabins, a baby room and dog shower. Motorcaravan service point. Fitness and sports area. In high season beach games, dances, sangria evenings etc, are organised, along with a bar/snack bar. Communal barbecues only. WiFi over site (charged). Off site: Local market Tuesday. Bicycle hire outside site. Riding 1 km. | From A9 exit 34 take N312 towards Agde, then N112 towards Sète keeping a look-out for signs to Marseillan-Plage off this road. Site is well signed in Marseillan-Plage. GPS: 43.3206, 3.5501 |

**Open:** 1 April - 15 October.

**Charges 2013**

| Per unit incl. 2 persons and electricity | € 16.30 - € 33.50 |
|---|---|

CAMPING ★★★
# LA CREOLE
Direct access to the beach
Located in the Heart of
Marseillan-Plage
Low prices in low season
Open from 1/04 to 15/10

74 avenue des campings
34340 Marseillan-Plage
Tel : +33 (0)4 67 21 92 69
Fax : +33 (0)4 67 26 58 16

campinglacreole@wanadoo.fr
www.campinglacreole.com

## Meyrueis
### Camping Caravaning le Champ d'Ayres

Route de la Brèze, F-48150 Meyrueis (Lozère) T: 04 66 45 60 51. E: campinglechampdayres@wanadoo.fr
**alanrogers.com/FR48000**

You can be sure of a warm welcome at this traditional, family run site, set in the heart of the Cévennes and its magnificent gorges. Champ d'Ayres is neat, tidy and well kept and is run with young families in mind. The 85 slightly sloping grass pitches, 62 for touring, are mostly hedged with well trimmed bushes and many have some shade. All have electricity (6/10A) but some may require long leads. The area is surrounded by mountains and gorges and some of the narrow and winding roads are not for the faint hearted or those with large and underpowered units.

| Facilities | Directions |
|---|---|
| The toilet block is kept very clean and has all the necessary facilities. A new block is planned. Baby room. Facilities for disabled visitors. Laundry facilities. Shop, small bar and takeaway (all 1/5-15/9). New heated swimming and paddling pools (12/5-22/9). Play area. Games room. Boules. Activities arranged (July/Aug). WiFi over site (free). Off site: The small, pretty town of Meyrueis (500 m) has many good shops and restaurants. | Leave A75 at exit 44-1, east on D29 through Aquessac, D907 to Le Rozier then D996 to Meyrueis. In Meyrueis (narrow roads) cross river and follow signs for Ayres. Site is 500 m. east of the town. GPS: 44.18077, 3.43507 |

**Open:** 6 April - 22 September.

**Charges guide**

| Per unit incl. 2 persons | € 13.00 - € 25.00 |
|---|---|
| extra person | € 3.50 - € 5.00 |

**FREE** Alan Rogers Travel Card
Extra benefits and savings - see page 10

## Meyrueis

### Kawan Village de Capelan

Route de Millau, F-48150 Meyrueis (Lozère) T: 04 66 45 60 50. E: info@campingcapelan.com
**alanrogers.com/FR48020**

The Lozère is one of France's least populated regions but offers some truly spectacular, rugged scenery, wonderful flora and fauna and old towns and villages. Le Capelan, which is only 1 km. from the pretty market town of Meyrueis, has 116 level, grassy pitches strung out alongside the unfenced River Jonte. Of these, 72 are for touring, most with some shade and all with electrical connections (6/10A). There is direct river access from the site with a 3 km. stretch available for trout fishing. Although there are special facilities, the site is not ideal for disabled visitors. English and Dutch are spoken. Meyrueis is accessible from the campsite via a riverside walk, marking the start of the Gorges de la Jonte, with the better known Gorges du Tarn running a little to the north.

**Facilities**

Well maintained toilet blocks, facilities for disabled visitors (but not ideal for those with walking difficulties). Three bathrooms for rent. Small shop. Bar (both from 1/6). Takeaway (from 1/7). Swimming, paddling pools, sunbathing terrace (from 1/6), access via 60 steps. Multisports terrain. Satellite TV. Play area. Leisure activities including supervised rock climbing. Fishing. Internet access and free WiFi. Communal barbecue area, only gas and electric barbecues. Off site: Town centre with many shops, bars and restaurants 1 km. Bicycle hire 1 km.

**Open:** 6 May - 15 September.

**Directions**

Exit A75 at 44-1, take D29 to Aguessac, D907 to le Rozier, then D996 towards Meyrueis. The site is on the right 1 km. before town. It is well signed. GPS: 44.18583, 3.41988

**Charges guide**

| Per unit incl. 2 persons | |
|---|---|
| and electricity | € 18.00 - € 28.50 |
| extra person | € 3.70 - € 5.80 |
| child (under 7 yrs) | € 2.10 - € 3.60 |

Camping Cheques accepted.

## Montclar

### Yelloh! Village Domaine d'Arnauteille

F-11250 Montclar (Aude) T: 04 68 26 84 53. E: info@yellohvillage-domaine-arnauteille.com
**alanrogers.com/FR11060**

Enjoying some beautiful and varied views, this site is ideal for exploring the little known Aude département and for visiting the walled city of Carcassonne. The site is set in farmland on hilly ground with the original pitches on gently sloping, lightly wooded land. Newer ones are on open ground, of good size, with water, drainage and electricity (5/10A), semi-terraced and partly hedged. The most recent have views of Montclar village. Of the 198 pitches, 138 are for touring. The facilities are quite spread out with the swimming pool complex, in the style of a Roman amphitheatre, set in a hollow basin surrounded by fine views. Access, although much improved, could be difficult for large, twin-axle caravans.

**Facilities**

Three toilet blocks, two with a Roman theme, are fully equipped with some en-suite provision. Laundry, facilities for disabled visitors, children and babies. Motorcaravan services. Small shop, bar, restaurant in converted stable block and takeaway (all 15/5-15/9). Swimming pool (25 m. open 1/5-30/9), two toboggans, paddling pool, river with water massage and sunbathing terrace. Multisports court. Boules. Play area. Riding (1/7-31/8). Day trips. Library, games room, TV. WiFi (charged). Gas barbecues only. Off site: Fishing 3 km. Bicycle hire 8 km.

**Open:** 9 April - 25 September.

**Directions**

D118 from Carcassonne, pass Rouffiac d'Aude. Before the end of dual carriageway, turn right to Montclar up narrow road (passing places) for 2.5 km. Site signed very sharp left up hill before village. GPS: 43.12714, 2.25953

**Charges guide**

| Per unit incl. 2 persons | |
|---|---|
| and electricity | € 15.00 - € 44.00 |
| extra person | € 4.00 - € 8.00 |
| child (3-7 yrs) | free - € 7.00 |

For latest campsite news, availability and prices visit
**alanrogers.com**

## Narbonne
### Yelloh! Village les Mimosas

**512**

Chaussée de Mandirac, F-11100 Narbonne (Aude) T: 04 68 49 03 72. E: info@lesmimosas.com
**alanrogers.com/FR11070**

Six kilometres inland from the beaches of Narbonne and Gruissan, this site benefits from a less hectic situation than others by the sea. The site is lively with plenty to amuse and entertain the younger generation whilst offering facilities for the whole family. A free club card is available in July/August for use at the children's club, gym, sauna, tennis, minigolf, billiards etc. There are 266 pitches, 150 for touring, many in a circular layout, and of a very good size, most with 6A electricity. There are a few 'grand confort' pitches with reasonable shade, mostly from two metre high hedges. There are also a number of mobile homes and chalets to rent. This could be a very useful site offering many possibilities to meet a variety of needs, on-site entertainment (including an evening on Cathar history), and easy access to popular beaches. Nearby Gruissan is a fascinating village with its wooden houses on stilts, beaches, ruined castle, port and salt beds. Narbonne has Roman remains and inland Cathar castles are to be found perched on rugged hilltops.

### Facilities

Sanitary buildings refurbished to a high standard include a baby room. Washing machines. Shop and Auberge restaurant (open all season). Takeaway. Bar (low season only at w/e). Small lounge, amusements (July/Aug). Heated pool with slides and islands (open 1/4), plus the original pool and children's pool (high season). Play area. Minigolf. Mountain bike hire. Tennis. Sauna and new gym. Children's activities, sports, entertainment (high season). Bicycle hire. Multisports ground. WiFi over site (charged). Off site: Lagoon with boating and fishing via footpath 200 m. Riding and windsurfing/sailing school 300 m. Gruissan's beach 10 minutes.

**Open:** 28 March - 1 November.

### Directions

From A9 exit 38 (Narbonne Sud) take last exit on roundabout, back over the autoroute (site signed from here). Follow signs for La Nautique and then Mandirac and site (6 km. from autoroute). Also signed from Narbonne centre.
GPS: 43.13662, 3.02562

### Charges guide

| | |
|---|---|
| Per unit incl. 2 persons and electricity | € 16.00 - € 41.00 |
| extra person | € 5.00 - € 8.00 |
| child (3-6 yrs) | free - € 7.00 |
| dog | € 4.00 |

VILLAGE-CAMPING
Les Mimosas

Un Air de Vacances.

**Discover the secret of successful holidays.**

Nestling in the heart of lush greenery in the regional nature park, between the beaches of Gruissan and the Bages lagoon, Les Mimosas ensures a pleasant holiday experience.
The 2000 m² water complex with 3 swimming pools, 4 waterslides, Jacuzzi, sauna, mini-golf, fitness centre, 2 playgrounds, restaurant, bar, grocery shop and the proposed animation from April to September offering long hours of fun and relaxation for all ages. Without forgetting the large choice of rentals and shady places.

Les Mimosas
VILLAGE-CAMPING
NARBONNE ★ ★ ★ ★ MÉDITERRANÉE

**INFORMATIE-RESERVERING**
Narbonne - France
Tel. +33 (0)4 68 49 03 72
www.lesmimosas.com

yelloh! VILLAGE

## Narbonne
### Camping la Nautique

Chemin de la Nautique, F-11100 Narbonne (Aude) T: 04 68 90 48 19. E: info@campinglanautique.com
**alanrogers.com/FR11080**

Owned and run by a very welcoming Dutch family, this well established site has pitches each with an individual sanitary unit. It is an extremely spacious site situated on the Etang de Bages, where flat water combined with strong winds make it one of the best windsurfing areas in France. La Nautique has 390 huge, level pitches, 270 for touring, all with 10A electricity and water. Six or seven overnight pitches with electricity are in a separate area. A range of mobile homes are available to hire. The flowering shrubs and trees give a pleasant feel. Each pitch is separated by hedges making some quite private and providing shade. Entertainment is organised for adults and children from Easter to September (increasing in high season), plus windsurfing, sailing, rafting, walking, pedaloes and canoeing (some activities are charged for). The unspoilt surrounding countryside is excellent for walking and cycling (reception has a booklet with routes), and locally there is horse riding and fishing. This site caters for families with children including teenagers and is fenced off from the water for their protection.

### Facilities

Each pitch has its own fully equipped sanitary unit. Specially equipped facilities for disabled visitors. Laundry. Shop. Bar/restaurant, terrace, TV. Takeaway. All 1/5-30/9. Snack bar 1/7-31/8. Outdoor, heated swimming pool, water slide, paddling pool (1/5-30/9). Play areas. Tennis. Minigolf. Pétanque. Bicycle hire. Miniclub (high season). Games room. WiFi (charged). Only electric barbecues are permitted. Torch useful. Off site: Narbonne is only 4 km. Large sandy beaches at Gruissan (12 km) and Narbonne Plage (20 km). Walking and cycling. Kite surfing.

**Open:** 1 March - 31 October.

### Directions

From A9 take exit 38 (Narbonne Sud). Go round roundabout to last exit and follow signs for la Nautique and site, then further site signs to site on right in 2.5 km. GPS: 43.14696, 3.00439

### Charges guide

| | |
|---|---|
| Per unit incl. 2 persons, electricity, water and sanitary unit | € 19.50 - € 43.00 |
| extra person | € 5.00 - € 8.00 |
| child (2-12 yrs) | € 7.00 |
| dog | € 2.50 - € 4.00 |

## Narbonne
### Campéole la Côte des Roses

Route de Gruissan, F-11100 Narbonne-Plage (Aude) T: 04 68 49 83 65. E: cote-des-roses@campeole.com
**alanrogers.com/FR11130**

This is a large site between Gruisson and Narbonne Plage, on the edge of a vast sandy beach which has been taken over by the Campéole group. There are over 800 pitches with 90 Bengali tents, and a large number of mobile homes and chalets were being sited when visited. A new reception was being completed and further upgrading is due. Shade comes from the sort of trees and shrubs which grow near the beach, and pitches are of a reasonable size but sandy, with 6A electricity available. A shop, bar and snack bar provide pizzas and other snacks, and there are musical evenings in July and August.

### Facilities

The colourful renovated toilet blocks are fully equipped and were clean when we visited. Some en-suite showers and basins. Attractive provision for children and babies and facilities for disabled visitors. Washing machine. Shop, bar, restaurant. Play area. Communal barbecue. Motorcaravan service point. WiFi. Off site: Beach 400 m. Sailing, jet skis, go-karting 1 km.

**Open:** 27 April - 9 September.

### Directions

Exit A9 at Nabonne Est. Follow D168 to roundabout by Narbonne Plage and take D332 direction Gruisson and watch for site on right. GPS: 43.143677, 3.144708

### Charges guide

| | |
|---|---|
| Per unit incl. 2 persons and electricity | € 17.90 - € 31.00 |

## Palau-del-Vidre
### Kawan Village le Haras

1 ter avenue Joliot Curie, Domaine Sant Galdric, F-66690 Palau-del-Vidre (Pyrénées-Orientales)

T: 04 68 22 14 50. E: haras8@wanadoo.fr  **alanrogers.com/FR66050**

Situated in the mature grounds of an old hunting lodge, later developed into an arboretum, le Haras is a rather special site. The 131 pitches are in bays of four arranged amidst an amazing variety of trees and shrubs that provide colour and shade for 97 touring units and some 34 mobile homes (18 to rent). All the touring pitches have 10A electricity, 29 are fully serviced. Some of the access roads are narrow. Under the same family management as Ma Prairie at Canet Village (FR66020), this is a comfortable site popular with British visitors. Rail noise is possible, although the line is screened by large trees.

### Facilities

Fully equipped toilet blocks. Facilities for disabled visitors. Washing machines. Motorcaravan service point. Fridge hire. Bar, restaurant and takeaway (all 15/4-30/9). Swimming and paddling pools (1/5-15/9). Play area. Archery (10/7-25/8). Only gas or electric barbecues are allowed. Internet access (charged) and WiFi (free). Max. 1 dog. No charcoal barbecues. Off site: Three bakers in the village, two butchers and a general stores. Fishing 500 m. Riding 2 km. Bicycle hire 6 km. Golf 7 km. Beaches 10 minutes drive.

**Open:** 1 April - 30 September.

### Directions

From A9, exit 43 (Le Boulou) follow D618 towards Argelès for 13 km. From the bypass at St André, turn left for Palau-del-Vidre (D11). Bear right through village, on D11 towards Elne. Site is end of village, before railway bridge. GPS: 42.57639, 2.96444

### Charges guide

| Per unit incl. two persons | |
|---|---|
| and electricity (5A) | € 19.00 - € 31.00 |
| extra person | € 3.50 - € 6.50 |
| child (under 7 yrs) | free - € 3.80 |
| dog | € 3.00 - € 4.00 |

Camping Cheques accepted.

---

## Port Camargue
### Camping Abri de Camargue

320 route du Phare de l'Espiguette, Port Camargue, F-30240 Le Grau-du-Roi (Gard) T: 04 66 51 54 83.

E: contact@abridecamargue.fr  **alanrogers.com/FR30030**

Situated 1 km. from the Mediterranean and 1.5 km. from the town of Le Grau-du-Roi, this pleasant, family oriented site has an attractive pool area. Overlooked by the bar with its outdoor tables on a pleasant sheltered terrace, the larger outdoor pool has surrounds for sunbathing. The smaller indoor pool is heated. With 277 level pitches, there are 48 for touring units, mainly of 100 sq.m (there are also smaller ones). Electricity (6A) and water are available on most, and the pitches are well maintained and shaded, with trees and flowering shrubs, quite luxuriant in parts. Recent additions include an air-conditioned cinema and a new sports area.

### Facilities

Well appointed toilet blocks and facilities for disabled visitors. Motorcaravan services. Shop. Bar with TV. Restaurant and takeaway. Heated indoor pool, outdoor pool and paddling pool. New sports area. Outdoor fitness room. Cinema (air conditioned). High quality play area. Entertainment programme and children's club (high season). Pétanque. Music room for young visitors in high season. WiFi over site (charged). Site access card (deposit € 15). Off site: Tennis 800 m. Beach at Port Camargue 900 m. Riding, bicycle hire 1 km. Fishing 2 km.

**Open:** 1 April - 30 September.

### Directions

Site is 45 km. southwest of Nîmes. From A9 exit 26, Gallargues to Le Grau-du-Roi. From bypass follow signs Port Camargue and Campings. Then follow Rive gauche signs towards Phare l'Espiguette. Site is opposite Toboggan Park. GPS: 43.5225, 4.1491

### Charges guide

| Per unit incl. 2 persons | |
|---|---|
| and electricity | € 28.00 - € 57.00 |
| with 3-5 persons | € 39.00 - € 67.00 |
| dog | € 7.00 |

**FREE** Alan Rogers Travel Card
Extra benefits and savings - see page 10

## Portiragnes-Plage

### Camping Caravaning les Mimosas

Port Cassafières, F-34420 Portiragnes-Plage (Hérault) T: 04 67 90 92 92.

E: les.mimosas.portiragnes@wanadoo.fr **alanrogers.com/FR34170**

Les Mimosas is quite a large site with 400 pitches – 200 for touring units, the remainder for mobile homes – in a rural situation. The level, grassy pitches are of average size, separated and numbered, all with 6A electricity (long leads may be required), some have good shade others have less. The pool area, a real feature of the site, includes a most impressive wave pool, various toboggans, the 'Space Hole' water slide, a large swimming pool and a super paddling pool (nine pools in all) with lots of free sun beds. This is a friendly, family run site with families in mind, with something new for each year. Les Mimosas has a less hectic situation than sites closer to the beach. However, it is possible to walk to a lovely sandy beach (1.2 km). There is lots going on and many day trips and excursions are arranged all season, from canoeing to visiting castles. Portiragnes-Plage is about 2 km. away and can be reached by cycle tracks. The Canal du Midi runs along the edge of the site (no access), providing another easy cycle route.

### Facilities

Good, modern toilet blocks include baby rooms, children's toilets, facilities for disabled visitors (whole site wheelchair friendly). En-suite facilities on payment. Washing machines and dryers. Motorcaravan services. Fridge hire. Large well stocked shop, bar, restaurant, takeaway, swimming pool complex (all open as site), lifeguards all season. Good play area. Miniclub (4-8 yrs). Boules. Gym with instructor and sauna. Multisports court. Bicycle hire. Games/TV room. Variety of evening entertainment. Internet access and WiFi (charged). Communal barbecue (only gas and electric permitted on pitches). Off site: Fishing and riding 1 km. Portiragnes-Plage with beach bars and restaurants 2 km. Golf 10 km.

**Open:** 18 May - 4 September.

### Directions

From A9 exit 35 (Béziers Est) take N112 south towards Sérignan (1 km). Large roundabout follow signs for Cap d'Agde, watch carefully for D37, Portiragnes (1-2 km), follow signs for Portiragnes-Plage. Site well signed before Portiragnes-Plage (5 km). GPS: 43.29153, 3.37348

### Charges guide

| | |
|---|---|
| Per unit incl. 2 persons and electricity | € 20.00 - € 42.00 |
| extra person | € 5.00 - € 10.00 |
| child (under 4 yrs) | free - € 4.00 |
| dog | € 2.00 - € 5.50 |
| private sanitary unit | € 8.50 - € 10.00 |

Special offers for May and June.

## Portiragnes-Plage
### Camping les Sablons

Avenue des Muriers, F-34420 Portiragnes-Plage (Hérault) T: 04 67 90 90 55. E: contact@les-sablons.com
**alanrogers.com/FR34400**

Les Sablons is an impressive and popular site with lots going on, a village in itself. Most of the facilities are arranged around the entrance with shops, a restaurant, a bar and a large pool complex with no less than five slides and three heated pools. There is also direct access to a white sandy beach at the back of the site, close to a small lake. There is good shade on the majority of the site, although some of the newer touring pitches have less shade but are nearer the gate to the beach. On level sandy grass, all have 6A electricity. Of the 800 pitches, around half are taken by a range of mobile homes and chalets (many for hire, and a few for use by tour operators). A new entertainment office enables you to book a wide range of sporting, cultural and musical activities as well as excursions. Children's clubs and evening entertainment are organised. In fact, this is a real holiday venue aiming to keep all the family happy. Some visitors simply stay on the site for their entire holiday – it certainly has everything. The site is very convenient for Béziers airport.

#### Facilities

Well equipped, modernised toilet blocks include large showers, some with washbasins. Baby baths and facilities for disabled visitors. Supermarket, bakery and newsagent. Restaurant, bar and takeaway. Swimming pool complex. Entertainment and activity programme with sports, music and cultural activities. Children's club. Beach club. Tennis. Archery. Play areas. Electronic games. ATM. Internet access. WiFi throughout (charged). Off site: Village and bicycle hire 100 m. Beach and riding 200 m. Canal du Midi 1 km. Parc Adventure (high wire adventure) 1.5 km.

**Open:** 1 April - 30 September.

#### Directions

From A9 exit 35 (Béziers Est) follow signs for Vias and Agde (N112). After large roundabout pass exit to Cers then take exit for Portiragnes (D37). Follow for 5 km. and pass over Canal du Midi towards Portiragnes-Plage. Site is on left after roundabout. GPS: 43.28003, 3.36396

#### Charges guide

| | |
|---|---|
| Per unit incl. 2 persons and electricity | € 20.00 - € 50.00 |
| extra person | € 6.00 - € 10.00 |
| child (under 13 yrs, acc. to age) | free - € 10.00 |
| dog | € 4.00 |

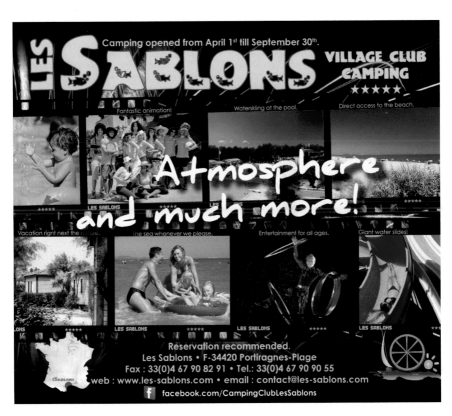

**FREE** Alan Rogers Travel Card
Extra benefits and savings - see page 10

## Remoulins

### Camping la Soubeyranne

1110 route de Beaucaire, F-30210 Remoulins (Gard) T: 04 66 37 03 21. E: soubeyranne@franceloc.fr

**alanrogers.com/FR30140**

Owned by the group FranceLoc, this site is well positioned for visiting the Pont du Gard, Nîmes and Uzès, famed for their Roman connections. The 200 pitches offer extremely generous amounts of shade and keeping the 6 hectares watered involves over 5 km. of hose pipe. The 79 touring pitches are large, level, numbered and separated, and all have 6A electricity connections. An entertainment programme (July/August) is aimed mainly at young children (teenagers may find the site rather quiet).

**Facilities**

One unisex toilet block is basic but clean and has more than adequate facilities and includes washbasins in cubicles. Motorcaravan service point. Fridges for hire. Small shop selling basics. Restaurant, bar and takeaway (all 4/4-27/9); menu not extensive but adequate and moderately priced. Heated swimming pool complex (4/4-27/9) with 20x10 m. pool and smaller toddlers' pool (unsupervised). Play area including inflatable castle. Minigolf. Boules. Tennis. Bicycle hire. Off site: Fishing 1 km.

**Open:** 4 April - 27 September.

**Directions**

From Uzès take D981 to Remoulins, turn right at lights over river bridge, left at roundabout, then left (signed D986 Beaucaire). Site is 1.5 km. further on left. GPS: 43.942282, 4.559669

**Charges guide**

| | |
|---|---|
| Per unit incl. 2 persons and electricity | € 19.70 - € 31.20 |
| extra person | € 4.70 - € 7.00 |

---

## Sainte Enimie

### Camping Couderc

Route de Millau, F-48210 Sainte Enimie (Lozère) T: 04 66 48 50 53. E: contact@campingcouderc.fr

**alanrogers.com/FR48080**

A spacious rural site, Couderc stretches for 1 km. along the clear shallow River Tarn, with access possible at each end of the site. The beautiful Gorges du Tarn and the high plateaux are well worth exploring. Come in May and June to see the wonderful flowers and butterflies with vultures soaring overhead. There are 130 good sized, level, grassy/stony pitches here, separated by vines and mature trees. With 123 for touring units, most have welcome shade and 10A electricity (long leads may be needed). Rock pegs are advised. The local roads are winding and narrow, but access on the site is good.

**Facilities**

Four toilet blocks with adequate facilities including those for children. Facilities for disabled visitors. Bar/TV room. Breakfast (all season). Basic shop, bread to order. Swimming and paddling pools. Play area. Canoe hire and trips run from site. Boules. River fishing. Only electric barbecues on pitches. WiFi. Off site: Ste Enimie with shops, restaurants, bars and a bank 1.5 km. Grottos, canyoning, rock climbing, caving. Gorges of the Tarn.

**Open:** 1 April - 30 September.

**Directions**

Leave A75 at exit 40 for La Canourgue. Take the D998 to Ste Enimie (28 km) following signs for Millau, Gorges du Tarn. Take the D907 to site on left in 1.5 km. Approach from south not recommended for large outfits. GPS: 44.353606, 3.401347

**Charges guide**

| | |
|---|---|
| Per unit incl. 2 persons and electricity | € 16.00 - € 25.00 |
| extra person | € 3.00 - € 5.00 |

---

## Saint Cyprien-Plage

### Camping Cala Gogo

Avenue Armand Lanoux, les Capellans, F-66750 Saint Cyprien-Plage (Pyrénées-Orientales)
T: 04 68 21 07 12. E: camping.calagogo@wanadoo.fr **alanrogers.com/FR66030**

This is an excellent, well organised site and it is agreeably situated by a superb sandy beach with a beach bar and boat launching. There are 649 pitches in total with 378 average sized, level, pitches for touring, regularly laid out, with electrical connections (6/10A) and some shade. Twenty fully serviced pitches have been added. The site has a most impressive pool complex, part heated and attractively laid out with palm trees and sunbathing areas. The large bar complex overlooking the pool area becomes very busy in season and dancing or entertainment is arranged on some evenings.

**Facilities**

Fully equipped toilet blocks with some Turkish style WCs are of a high standard. Motorcaravan service point. Good supermarket and small shopping mall. Sophisticated restaurant with excellent cuisine. Self-service restaurant with simple menu. Takeaway. Bar. Small beach bar (high season). Fridge hire. Disco. TV. Three swimming pools (heated) plus one for children. Play area. Tennis. Fishing. Diving club. Free WiFi over part of site. Bicycle hire. Torches useful. Only gas or electric barbecues allowed.

**Open:** 4 May - 21 September.

**Directions**

Using D81 (southward) avoid St Cyprien-Plage and continue towards Argelès. Turn right at roundabout signed St Cyprien Sud and Aquapark and pick up site signs. GPS: 42.59939, 3.03761

**Charges guide**

| | |
|---|---|
| Per unit incl. 2 persons and electricity | € 20.00 - € 42.40 |
| extra person | € 5.00 - € 10.80 |

For latest campsite news, availability and prices visit
# alanrogers.com

## Saint Hippolyte-du-Fort

### Camping de Graniers

Route de Monoblet, Graniers, F-30170 Saint Hippolyte-du-Fort (Gard) T: 04 66 25 19 24.
E: contact@camping-graniers.com **alanrogers.com/FR30430**

Les Graniers is a friendly site with new owners, located on the fringe of the Cevennes National Park. Pitches are well shaded by tall trees, and of a good size. Most have electrical connections. A number of mobile homes, chalets and fully equipped bungalow style tents are available for rent. Unusually, les Graniers also offers two Mongolian-style yurts for rent. On-site leisure facilities include a swimming pool, volleyball and a snack bar. There are many footpaths and cycling routes close to the site, and a day trip to the seaside is possible, around one hour's drive away at Le Grau-du-Roi.

#### Facilities

Fully equipped toilet block. Swimming pool (15/5-30/9). Bar/snack bar. Takeaway. Games room. Play area. Volleyball. Fishing. Bicycle hire. Entertainment and activity programme. Accommodation for rent. Off site: Walking and cycling. St Hippolyte-du-Fort 3 km. Anduze 10 km. Riding 10 km. Beach 60 km.

**Open:** 13 March - 17 October.

#### Directions

The site is located to the northeast of St Hippolyte-du-Fort. Approaching from Anduze, head south on D907 and D982 to St Hippolyte, follow signs in village to les Graniers. GPS: 43.980104, 3.884885

#### Charges guide

| | |
|---|---|
| Per unit incl. 2 persons and electricity | € 23.50 |
| extra person | € 4.00 |

## Saint Jean-du-Gard

### Camping Mas de la Cam

Route de Saint André de Valborgne, F-30270 Saint Jean-du-Gard (Gard) T: 04 66 85 12 02.
E: camping@masdelacam.fr **alanrogers.com/FR30180**

Camping Mas de la Cam is a superb, high quality, family run touring site; you are assured of a warm welcome here (English and Dutch spoken). It is a very pleasant and spacious site with well trimmed grass and hedges and a profusion of flowers and shrubs. Lying alongside the small Gardon river, the banks have been left free of pitches giving neat grass for sunbathing and some trees for shade, whilst children can amuse themselves in the water (no good for canoes). The 200 medium to large pitches, all for touring, are on low level terraces, with varying amounts of shade and have electricity (6/10A). In the low season bridge drives, painting courses and boules are organised. In the high season there is some family entertainment and a musical evening once a week. Nearby, one can walk in the footsteps of Robert Louis Stevenson (Travels with a Donkey), ride on a steam train, explore deep underground caverns, or visit a giant bamboo forest. Entrance is via a narrow unfenced bridge, so not ideal for large outfits.

#### Facilities

Three high quality, very clean toilet blocks with baby bath and facilities for visitors with disabilities. Washing machines. Bar/restaurant, terrace. Small shop. Large swimming pool (heated) and paddling pools. Excellent play and sports areas, multisports court for football, volleyball and basketball. Boules. Club, used in low season for bridge, in high season as games room. Fishing. WiFi. Off site: St Jean-du-Gard with shops and Tues. market 3 km. (bus twice a day). Riding 5 km. Bicycle hire 15 km. Many narrow lanes, old towns and villages. Steam train from St Jean-du-Gard to Anduze.

**Open:** 26 April - 20 September.

#### Directions

Site is 3 km. northwest of St Jean-du-Gard in direction of St André-de-Valborgne on D907, site signed, fork left, descend across a narrow unfenced bridge to site. Site entrance not accessible from north. GPS: 44.11235, 3.8541

#### Charges guide

| | |
|---|---|
| Per unit incl. 2 persons and electricity | € 19.00 - € 37.00 |
| extra person | € 3.90 - € 8.20 |
| child (under 7 yrs acc to age) | free - € 4.50 |
| dog | € 2.20 - € 4.00 |

camping mas de la cam
F-30270 St Jean du Gard
Cévennes
www.masdelacam.fr

## Sérignan-Plage
### Yelloh! Village le Sérignan-Plage

Le Sérignan Plage, F-34410 Sérignan-Plage (Hérault) T: 04 67 32 35 33. E: info@leserignanplage.com

**alanrogers.com/FR34070**

With direct access onto a superb 600 m. sandy beach (including a naturist section) and with three swimming pools, this is a must for a Mediterranean holiday. It is a busy, friendly, family orientated site with a very comprehensive range of amenities. Having recently acquired an adjacent site complete with a small lake, there are now over 1,100 pitches with 278 available for touring units. These vary in size and in terms of shade. They are mainly on sandy soil and all have 6A electricity. The collection of spa pools (balnéo) built in Romanesque style with colourful terracing and columns, overlooked by a very smart restaurant, Le Villa, is still the 'pièce de résistance' and available to use in the afternoons (used by the adjacent naturist site in the mornings). The enthusiastic owners, Jean-Guy and Catherine, continually surprise us with their unique style and new developments – when we visited, a most dramatic play area featuring Hansel and Gretel style wooden play houses had been added. There are over 300 mobile homes and chalets to let, plus some 400 privately owned units. The heart of the site developed in the local Catalonian style is some distance from reception and is a busy and informal area with shops, another good restaurant, the Au Pas d'Oc, an indoor pool and a super roof-top bar. There is a range of sporting activities, children's clubs and evening entertainment, indeed something for all the family.

### Facilities

Seven modern blocks with good facilities including showers with washbasin and WC. Facilities for disabled visitors. Baby bathroom. Launderette. Motorcaravan services. Supermarket, bakery, newsagent and other shops (all season). ATM. Restaurants, bar and takeaway. Hairdresser. Balnéo spa (afternoons). Gym. Heated indoor pool. Outdoor pools (all season). Tennis courts. Multisports courts. Play areas. Trampolines. Children's clubs. Evening entertainment. Sporting activities. Bicycle hire. Bus to Sérignan village (July/Aug). Beach (lifeguards 15/6-15/9). WiFi (charged). Gas barbecues only. Off site: Fishing 1 km. Riding 1.5 km. Golf 15 km. Sailing and windsurfing school on beach. Local markets.

**Open:** 26 April - 2 October.

### Directions

From A9 exit A75 (Béziers Centre) and exit 64 towards Sérignan, D64 (9 km). Before Sérignan, turn left, Sérignan-Plage (4 km). At small sign (blue) turn right. At T-junction turn left over small road bridge and after left hand bend. Site is 100 m. GPS: 43.26308, 3.31976

### Charges guide

| Per unit incl. 2 persons | |
|---|---|
| and electricity | € 15.00 - € 52.00 |
| extra person | € 5.00 - € 8.50 |
| child (3-7 yrs) | free - € 8.50 |

## Saint Jean-du-Gard
### Camping les Sources

Route de Mialet, F-30270 Saint Jean-du-Gard (Gard) T: 04 66 85 38 03. E: camping-des-sources@orange.fr

**alanrogers.com/FR30150**

This is a small, family run site situated in the foothills of the beautiful Cévennes. There are 92 average to good sized, slightly sloping pitches on small terraces with 72 for touring units, all with electricity (6/10A). A number of attractive mobile homes and chalets are also available for rent. They are separated by a variety of flowering shrubs and trees offering good shade. Near the entrance is the attractive reception, bar, restaurant and terrace overlooking the swimming pools and children's play area. The emphasis here is on a quiet family holiday with little organised activity.

### Facilities

Two well appointed, modern toilet blocks with washbasins in cabins. Facilities for babies and visitors with disabilities. Washing machine. Motorcaravan service point. Bar/restaurant with takeaway, good menu and small shop (all season). Small swimming and paddling pools (from late May). Games/TV room. Play area. Gas and electric barbecues. Occasional children's activities and family evening meals. WiFi (free). Off site: St Jean-du-Gard 1.5 km. Bus service to Nîmes and Alès a few times daily. Fishing and bathing 1.5 km. Riding 12 km. Bicycle hire 14 km. Golf 20 km.

**Open:** 1 April - 30 September.

### Directions

From Alès take D910A to Anduze, then D907 to St Jean-du-Gard. Take ring road (autre directions) towards Florac. Turn right at traffic lights on D98. Right onto D50 (site signed). Very shortly, on sharp right-hand bend, fork right to site. Access impossible from the north. GPS: 44.11322, 3.89052

### Charges guide

| Per unit incl. 2 persons | |
|---|---|
| and electricity | € 17.50 - € 25.00 |
| extra person | € 3.50 - € 4.50 |
| child (0-8 yrs) | € 2.50 - € 3.50 |
| dog | € 2.50 |

For latest campsite news, availability and prices visit

**alanrogers.com**

Imagine – hot sunshine, blue sea, vineyards, olive and eucalyptus trees, alongside a sandy beach – what a setting for a campsite – not just any campsite either! With three pool areas, one with four toboggans surrounded by sun bathing areas, an indoor pool for baby swimmers plus a magnificent landscaped, Romanesque spa-complex with half Olympic size pool and a superb range of hydro-massage baths to let you unwind and re-charge after the stresses of work. And that's not all – two attractive restaurants, including the atmospheric "Villa" in its romantic Roman setting beside the spa, three bars, a mini-club and entertainment for all ages, all add up to a fantastic opportunity to enjoy a genuinely unique holiday experience.

Le Sérignan Plage

The Mediterranean
The place for your holidays

34410 Sérignan Tél : +33 (0)4 67 32 35 33 Fax : +33 (0)4 67 32 68 39
info@leserignanplage.com www.leserignanplage.com

yelloh! VILLAGE

## Saint Chinian

### Camping les Terrasses

555 route de Saint Pons, F-34360 Saint Chinian (Hérault) T: 06 12 90 14 55.
E: contact@campinglesterrasses.net **alanrogers.com/FR34950**

Les Terrasses is a small, friendly site located next to the wine-growing area of St Chinian in the Hérault hinterland, set back from the busy Mediterranean coastline. There are 54 terraced, grass pitches, all with 10A electricity, views across the vineyards to the hills of the garrigue. On-site facilities include a good little swimming pool with decking for sunbathing, or for a more rustic setting, the river (800 m) has natural pools for a cooling dip. The site was orignally a municipal, but is now being run by the enthusiastic Cathy Dubost, who makes you very welcome and does a great deal for motorcaravans.

**Facilities**

The traditional, fully equipped sanitary block has facilities for babies and disabled visitors. Washing machine and freezer. Motorcaravan service point. Bar. Fresh bread to order. Swimming pool. Small play area. Tennis. Communal barbecues only. WiFi. Off site: Local market (Thursday and Sundays). Supermarket 800 m. Bars and restaurants 1.5 km. Hiking. Bicycle hire 1 km. Tennis. Riding 3 km.

**Open:** 1 April - 30 September.

**Directions**

From Béziers take D612 towards Saint Chinian, continue through town following signs for St Pons to pick up municipal camping signs just outside town. GPS: 43.421243, 2.934374

**Charges guide**

| Per unit incl. 2 persons | |
|---|---|
| and electricity | € 15.00 - € 19.00 |
| dog | free |

## Sérignan-Plage

### Yelloh! Village Aloha

F-34410 Sérignan-Plage (Hérault) T: 04 67 39 71 30. E: info@alohacamping.com
**alanrogers.com/FR34390**

An impressive and well run site beside the beach at Sérignan-Plage, Aloha offers a wide range of good quality facilities, all open when the site is open. There are 465 pitches with 170 mobile homes for hire in attractively landscaped settings. The 295 pitches for touring units are of a good size, regularly laid out on level, sandy grass. Easily accessed from tarmac roads, all have 10A electricity. Half are on one side of the small beach road with the swimming pools and other facilities, the other half are somewhat quieter with more grass but less shade across the road.

**Facilities**

Seven toilet blocks, including three large ones, offer all modern facilities and are well equipped for children. Laundry. Motorcaravan service point. Supermarket including fresh produce market. Bakery. Newsagent. Bazaar. Hairdresser. Bar, restaurant, snack bar, pizzeria and takeaway. Large heated pool and fun pools. Paddling pool. Playground. Tennis. Multisports facility. Bicycle hire. Miniclub. Activity programme. Internet access and WiFi. ATM. Off site: Minigolf and trampolines 500 m.

**Open:** 25 April - 13 September.

**Directions**

From A9 exit 35 (Béziers Est) follow signs for Sérignan then Sérignan-Plage (D37, 10 km). Once at Sérignan-Plage continue straight. Follow the sign for Aloha to right after the pink building. GPS: 43.273333, 3.348333

**Charges guide**

| Per unit incl. 2 persons | |
|---|---|
| and electricity | € 15.00 - € 46.00 |
| extra person | € 5.00 - € 8.00 |

## Sète

### Village Center le Castellas

RN 112, F-34200 Sète (Hérault) T: 04 99 57 21 21. E: contact@village-center.com
**alanrogers.com/FR34240**

One would expect a campsite beside a beachside main road and a railway to be noisy, whereas once within the confines of this site it is surprisingly peaceful offering everything one could want. It is situated across the road from 14 km. of superb sandy beach, with the Etang du Thau behind, yet within a short drive of Sète, Marseillan-Plage and Agde. It is a very large site with over 800 mobile homes and chalets to rent. There are also 200 sandy and hedged pitches for touring units, most with 6A electricity and some have been purpose-built for motorcaravans. Pitches are accessed by hard roads with a variety of shade.

**Facilities**

The toilet facilities include en-suite showers and basins. Laundry. Provision for disabled visitors. Fridge hire. Large supermarket, range of smaller shops and café open to public as well. Restaurant, bars, snack bars. Swimming pool with lifeguards (heated April-June). Toboggans. Games room. Multisport court. Sports field. Archery. Play area, bouncy castles. Outdoor fitness area. WiFi (charged). ATM. Wide range of entertainment. Miniclub and teenage club (July/Aug). Sea fishing. Watersports.

**Open:** 3 April - 26 September.

**Directions**

Site is beside RN112 which links Marseillan-Plage and Sète. This road can get very busy indeed in main season but it is being re-routed behind the site. GPS: 43.34192, 3.58449

**Charges guide**

| Per unit incl. 2 persons | |
|---|---|
| and electricity (6A) | € 18.00 - € 40.00 |
| extra person (over 5 yrs) | € 4.00 - € 8.00 |
| Camping Cheques accepted. | |

For latest campsite news, availability and prices visit
# alanrogers.com

## Sigean
### Village Center Ensoya

54 avenue de Perpignan, F-11130 Sigean (Aude) T: 08 25 00 20 30. E: contact@village-center.com
**alanrogers.com/FR11350**

Camping Ensoya, a former municipal site, is now part of the Village Center group. It it situated on the edge of Sigean, a 14th-century Languedoc border town, now best known for its famous African animal reserve, echoed in the site's range of safari tents for rent. There are 232 pitches in total, (up to 150 sq.m), some taken by mobile homes and tents, leaving 189 for tourers. Most have electricity. Pitches are on level grass with new hedging and mature trees providing some shade. The site has use of the town's municipal pool adjacent, and there are shops and restaurants in the town.

**Facilities**

The central toilet block was being renovated at the time of our visit. When finished it will provide facilities for disabled visitors. Small play area. Children's activity programme. Safari tents and mobile homes for rent. WiFi in reception area (charged). Off site: Municipal swimming pool adjacent. Shops and restaurants at Sigean 300 m. Sigean Wildlife Park 5 km. Beaches 7 km. Walking and cycling tracks. Watersports on Etang de Bages. Terra Vinea.

**Open:** 15 June - 9 September.

**Directions**

Approaching from the north (Narbonne), leave A9 autoroute at exit 39 (Sigean) and head east to Sigean on D6139. Site is on south side of town. GPS: 43.024785, 2.977123

**Charges guide**

| Per unit incl. 2 persons and electricity | € 16.00 - € 24.00 |
| extra person | € 3.00 - € 5.00 |

Camping Cheques accepted.

## Sommières
### Castel Camping Domaine de Massereau

Les Hauteurs de Sommières, route d'Aubais, F-30250 Sommières (Gard) T: 04 66 53 11 20.
E: camping@massereau.com **alanrogers.com/FR30290**

Two brothers, one a wine producer and one a hotelier, opened Domaine de Massereau in August 2006. It is set within a 50-hectare vineyard dating back to 1804, and the idea was to promote their wine, so tours are arranged and they now produce their own olive oil as well. There are 120 pitches, 75 available for touring units (45 with 16A electricity, water and drainage). Pitch sizes range from 150-250 sq.m. but the positioning of trees on some of the pitches could limit the usable space. The area is lightly wooded and most pitches are now hedged with flowering shrubs. The other pitches are used for chalets and mobile homes to rent. The site is a member of the Castels Group and good English is spoken. Amenities include an attractive pool area with water slide and heated pool, a trim trail, mountain bike path and large grass play area including a trampoline. The camping area is accessed via a narrow bridge (3 m. wide) passing over a section of the 25 km. of cycle routes on which visitors can explore the surrounding area.

**Facilities**

The modern toilet block incorporates excellent facilities for children and disabled visitors. Laundry area. Motorcaravan service point. Well stocked shop and newspapers. Restaurant, bar, pizzeria and outdoor grill, takeaway, (all open 7/4-30/9). Heated swimming pool with slide. Paddling pool. Sauna, steam bath and jacuzzi. Play area. Trampoline. Minigolf. Bicycle hire. Fitness trail. Pétanque. Short tennis. TV room. Barbecue hire. Fridge hire. Tent hire (2 person). Gas. WiFi (charged). Charcoal barbecues are not allowed. Off site: Fishing and riding 3 km.

**Open:** 1 April - 15 November.

**Directions**

From the north, there is a width and weight restriction in Sommières. To avoid this remain on N110, then take N2110 into Sommières, crossing river over a narrow bridge controlled by traffic lights, and turn right onto the D12. Site is on left in 1 km. GPS: 43.765786, 4.097426

**Charges guide**

| Per unit incl. 2 persons and electricity | € 21.40 - € 41.90 |
| extra person | € 3.50 - € 10.00 |

**FREE** Alan Rogers Travel Card
Extra benefits and savings - see page 10

## Torreilles-Plage
### Sunêlia les Tropiques

Boulevard de la plage, F-66440 Torreilles-Plage (Pyrénées-Orientales) T: 04 68 28 05 09.
E: contact@campinglestropiques.com **alanrogers.com/FR66190**

Les Tropiques is a very attractive site with a large pool complex, only 400 metres from a sandy beach. It will provide families with children of all ages with an ideal seaside holiday. There are 450 pitches with 78 for touring units, all with 10A electricity. Pleasant pine and palm trees with other Mediterranean vegetation give shade and provide a pleasant environment. Activities are provided for all including a large range of sports, activities, cabarets and shows.

**Facilities**

Modern, fully equipped sanitary facilities, provision for disabled visitors. Launderette. Shop (13/4-29/9). Bar and Restaurant (15/5-15/9). Takeaway and pizzeria (1/7-31/8). Heated pool and water slides. Paddling pool. Wellness centre. Outdoor fitness equipment. TV/billiards room. Tennis (floodlit). Multisports area. Pétanque. Archery (1/7-31/8). Play area. Disco (every evening). Miniclub (6-12 yrs and 13-17 yrs; July/Aug). Bicycle hire. WiFi over site (charged). Off site: Minigolf 300 m. Riding 400 m.

**Open:** 13 April - 29 September.

**Directions**

From A9 exit Perpignan Nord, follow D83 towards Le Barcarès for 9 km. Take D81 south towards Canet for 3 km. turn left at roundabout for Torreilles-Plage. Site is the last but one. GPS: 42.7675, 3.02972

**Charges 2013**

| Per unit incl. 2 persons and electricity | € 18.00 - € 51.00 |
| extra person | € 3.85 - € 9.60 |

---

## Torreilles-Plage
### Chadotel Camping le Trivoly

Route des Plages, F-66440 Torreilles-Plage (Pyrénées-Orientales) T: 04 68 28 20 28. E: info@chadotel.com
**alanrogers.com/FR66240**

The popularity of Torreilles derives mainly from its huge sandy beach and for some off-site nightlife, shopping, etc. but for smarter resorts one really needs to visit Le Barcarès or Canet a few kilometres distance in either direction. Le Trivoly (a member of the French Chadotel Group) is about 800 m. gentle stroll from the beach, in a fairly tranquil setting. In total there are 273 pitches, of which 60 are used for touring units. These are of a good size, well shaded and hedged with electricity (6A). The remainder are either used by tour operators or for site mobile homes to rent.

**Facilities**

Four toilet blocks, although not new, provide modern facilities, including washbasins in (rather small) cabins, and were all clean and well cared for when we visited. Small shop (June-mid Sept). Snack bar/restaurant and takeaway (June-mid Sept). Heated pool (1/5-15/9) with water slide and paddling pool. Terraced restaurant. Play area. Tennis. Minigolf. Bicycle hire. Entertainment programme in high season. WiFi (charged). Off site: Centre Commercial 500 m. Beach 800 m. Riding 1 km.

**Open:** 3 April - 25 September.

**Directions**

From A9 exit 42 (Perpignan-Nord) towards Le Barcarès for 9 km, then turn south on D81 towards Canet. After 3 km. turn left at roundabout, signed Torreilles-Plage. Site is on left, in 500 m. GPS: 42.765808, 3.02681

**Charges guide**

| Per unit incl. 2 persons and electricity | € 19.60 - € 32.00 |
| extra person | € 5.80 |

---

## Uzès
### Camping du Mas de Rey

Arpaillargues, F-30700 Uzès (Gard) T: 04 66 22 18 27. E: info@campingmasderey.com
**alanrogers.com/FR30110**

A warm welcome from the English-speaking Maire family is guaranteed at this small, attractive, 70 pitch site. Most of the 60 large (150 sq.m) touring pitches are separated by bushes, many are shaded and all have 10A electricity. A good site for couples and families with young children. Due to the wonderful climate, grass can at times be hard to find. The reception, bar, restaurant and shop are in the same large, airy building. The owners are always willing to give advice on the numerous things to see and do in the area. Only gas and electric barbecues allowed on site; there is a communal charcoal barbecue.

**Facilities**

Two well maintained excellent, very clean toilet blocks, both quite new with solar heating, facilities for disabled visitors, baby room and en-suite family cubicles. Laundry facilities. Shop (Jul/Aug), bread to order (all season). Takeaway (1/5-30/9) and terrace restaurant with French meals (1/7-31/8). New heated swimming pool and paddling pool (1/5-15/10, closed lunchtimes). New chalets. WiFi throughout (free). Charcoal barbecues are not permitted. Off site: Golf 4 km. River bathing 12 km.

**Open:** 1 April - 15 October.

**Directions**

Leave A9 autoroute, exit 23, signed Pont du Gard. Take N86 then D981 to Uzès (18 km). Take D982 west, signed Arpaillargues, Moussac. Site signed on left, 3 km. GPS: 43.99843, 4.38424

**Charges guide**

| Per unit incl. 2 persons and electricity | € 20.80 - € 36.50 |

Credit cards accepted in July/Aug. only.

For latest campsite news, availability and prices visit
**alanrogers.com**

## Valras-Plage
### Camping Blue Bayou

Vendres-Plage Ouest, F-34350 Valras-Plage (Hérault) T: 04 67 37 41 97. E: infobluebayou@orange.fr

**alanrogers.com/FR34370**

A pleasant site, Blue Bayou is situated at the far end of Vendres-Plage near Le Grau Vendres (the port of Vendres). It is therefore in a much quieter location than many other sites, away from the more hectic, built-up areas of Vendres and Valras-Plage. The beach is 300 m. across sand dunes and there are open views from the site creating a feeling of spaciousness. There are 281 pitches, all with 10A electricity, with 41 privately owned mobile homes and 120 to let, including some chalets. The touring pitches are large, some with their own sanitary arrangements. Light shade is provided by a mixture of trees. The new restaurant and bar area is very attractive, overlooking two swimming pools, one with a toboggan, joined by a bridge where lifeguards station themselves. The owners and their family are very proud of their site and you are made to feel very welcome. The site would make a good choice for couples and families, perhaps best visited outside the height of the season when it becomes very busy. In July and August a tourist train runs to link Valras and Vendres.

| Facilities | Directions |
|---|---|
| Individual toilet units for 56 touring pitches. Two separate blocks were renovated for 2011. Baby bath and facilities for children. Facilities for disabled visitors. Laundry. Shop (15/6-15/9). Bar and restaurant (1/5-20/9), takeaway (1/7-31/8). Swimming pool (heated). Multisports court. Play area. Miniclub and entertainment (high season). WiFi throughout (charged). Bouncy castle (Tuesdays and Thursdays). Electric barbecues only. Off site: Fishing, boat launching and riding 1 km. Bicycle hire 3 km. Golf 25 km. | From A9 exit 36 (Béziers Ouest) follow directions for Valras-Plage and Vendres-Plage over four roundabouts. At fifth roundabout (Port Conchylicole) follow sign for Vendres-Plage Ouest and site is 500 m. on the left past the Ranch and tourist office. The entrance is quite tight. GPS: 43.227408, 3.243536 |

**Open:** 6 April - 28 September.

**Charges 2013**

| Per unit incl. 2 persons and electricity | € 22.00 - € 48.00 |
|---|---|

Camping Cheques accepted.

# Blue Bayou ★★★★★

300 meters from one of the most beautiful Mediterranean find-sand beaches, Blue Bayou welcomes you with its heated swimming pool area and with its various hosting arrangements in comfortable Mobile Homes, Chalets or its Camping area for tents and caravans.

We offer 40 pitches with private sanitary
New main sanitary block for the whole family!

*Tennis, beach ball, biking, swimming for sportive holidays!*
*Entertainment, shows or thematic dinners for unforgettable holidays!*

**Open: 06/04/2013 - 28/09/2013**

**Vendres Plage Ouest - F-34350 Valras-Plage - France**
**Tel: 0033 (0)4 67 37 41 97 - Fax: 0033 (0)4 67 37 53 00**

infobluebayou@orange.fr
**www.bluebayou.eu**

## Valras-Plage
### Camping Caravaning Domaine de la Yole

B.P. 23, F-34350 Valras-Plage (Hérault) T: 04 67 37 33 87. E: info@campinglayole.com

**alanrogers.com/FR34090**

A busy, happy holiday village with over 1,100 pitches could seem a little daunting. There are 590 pitches for touring with the remainder occupied by mobile homes available to rent. Pitches are of a good size, all are level, hedged and have electricity (5A), water and waste water points and, very importantly for this area, they all have shade. The extensive pool area is impressive, more like an aqua park with its six pools and water slides. These are heated in low season and there are plenty of sunbathing areas. The central shopping and entertainment area form the heart of the site and provide everything you need. The beach, a long stretch of beautiful sand, is 500 m. and there is trampolining, paragliding and jet skis to enjoy.

| Facilities | Directions |
|---|---|
| Well maintained toilet blocks include baby rooms. Facilities for families and/or disabled visitors. Washing machines, dryers. Motorcaravan service points. Fridge hire. Shops. Good restaurant, amphitheatre for daily entertainment (in season). Large pool complex. Tennis courts. Multisports court. Play areas. High wire adventure park. Bicycle hire. Miniclub. Youth club. Boules. Internet access and WiFi. | From A9 autoroute take Béziers Ouest exit for Valras-Plage (13-14 km) and follow Casino signs. Site is on the left, just after sign for Vendres-Plage. GPS: 43.23708, 3.26234 |

**Open:** 25 April - 19 September.

**Charges guide**

| Per unit incl. 2 persons and all services | € 20.00 - € 57.40 |
|---|---|
| extra person | € 5.90 - € 8.50 |

## Vauvert
### Flower Camping Mas de Mourgues
Gallician, F-30600 Vauvert (Gard) T: 04 66 73 30 88. E: info@masdemourgues.com
**alanrogers.com/FR30040**

Sandra and Cyril are proud of their campsite on the edge of the Petite Camargue region, a unique area of France. It can be hot here, the Mistral can blow and you may have some road noise, but the situation between Nîmes and Arles is ideal for exploring the Camargue and visiting towns such as Aigues Mortes. There are 71 pitches with 46 for touring units on level grass (10A electricity), nine mobile homes/bungalow tents to rent and a further 16 privately owned. Originally a vineyard on stony ground (strong pegs needed), some of the vines are now used to mark the pitches, although many other varieties of trees and shrubs have been planted.

**Facilities**

Two small toilet blocks provide for all needs. Facilities for disabled visitors. Washing machine. Motorcaravan service point (charged). Chips and panini to takeaway (high season). Breakfast served. Reception keeps essentials and bottled water. Bread to order. Play area. Games for children once a week (July/Aug). Internet access and WiFi (charged). Communal barbecue. Mobile homes and tents to rent. Off site: Fishing 2 km. (licence not required).

**Open:** 15 March - 31 October.

**Directions**

Leave A9 autoroute at exit 26 (Gallargues) and follow signs for Vauvert. At Vauvert take N572 towards Arles and St Gilles. Site is on left after 4 km. at crossroads for Gallician. GPS: 43.6575, 4.2943

**Charges guide**

| Per unit incl. 2 persons | |
|---|---|
| and electricity | € 15.00 - € 24.50 |
| extra person | € 3.00 - € 4.50 |

## Vendres
### Camping Club les Vagues
F-34350 Valras-Plage (Hérault) T: 04 67 37 33 12. E: lesvagues34@free.fr
**alanrogers.com/FR34120**

Camping les Vagues is a member of the Sandaya group and can be found at the popular seaside resort of Valras-Plage, 500 m. from a fine sandy beach. Les Vagues has an excellent swimming pool complex extending over 2,000 sq.m. and an impressive range of amenities, including a buffet-style restaurant (with carvery), a multisport pitch and a minigolf course. Pitches are well shaded and most have 6/10A electrical connections. A wide range of mobile homes and chalets are available for rent. This is a lively site in peak season with frequent evening entertainment and activities for all ages.

**Facilities**

Four modern toilet blocks provide large showers, washbasins mainly in cabins, baby baths and provision for disabled visitors. Laundry facilities. Shop, bar, restaurant and snack bar. Swimming pool complex. All open all season. Children's pool. Play area. Minigolf. Games room. Multisports court. Entertainment and miniclub (July/Aug). Gas or electric barbecues. Tourist train (July/Aug). WiFi (charged). Mobile homes and chalets for rent. Off site: Sandy beach and shops in Valras-Plage 500 m.

**Open:** 1 April - 30 September.

**Directions**

Les Vagues is on the southern side of Valras-Plage. Approaching from A9 autoroute, leave at the Vendres exit and head south on the D64. Having passed Vendres and shortly before reaching Valras, watch for site signs at roundabout and turn right. GPS: 43.231023, 3.25356

**Charges guide**

| Per unit incl. 2 persons | |
|---|---|
| and electricity | € 20.00 - € 54.00 |
| extra person | € 2.00 - € 9.00 |

## Vendres-Plage
### Campéole les Mûriers

Campé●le

37E route départemental, F-34350 Vendres-Plage (Hérault) T: 04 67 37 25 79. E: muriers@campeole.com
**alanrogers.com/FR34620**

Les Mûriers is a member of the Campéole group and is located among a group of sites situated on the route to le Grau de Vendres, the port of Vendres at the mouth of the River Aude. A marina has been developed there recently and there is also access to a lovely sandy beach, an 800 m. walk across the flat dunes. You need to look carefully for the Campéole reception as there is a large reception for a separate mobile home site under the same name. There are 105 bungalow tents available to rent, quite distinctive and fully equipped. They are arranged in a circular layout on grass pitches with hedging served by two toilet blocks. Please note that there are no pitches for tourers here.

**Facilities**

Two fully equipped toilet blocks. Washing machine. Bar/restaurant (28/6-30/8), takeaway, shop, heated swimming pool (all 15/6-15/9). Entertainment and miniclub (5-12 yrs, 28/6-28/8). Play area. Volleyball/basketball court. WiFi (charged). No barbecues. Off site: Beach and sailing 800 m. Fishing and boat launching 1 km.

**Open:** 12 June - 10 September.

**Directions**

From A9 take exit 36 (Béziers Ouest), towards Valras-Plage and Vendres-Plage. Continue over 4 roundabouts. At 5th (Port Conchylicole) follow signs for Vendres-Plage Ouest. Continue for 800 m. and site is on right. GPS: 43.223433, 3.23945

**Charges guide**

Contact site.

For latest campsite news, availability and prices visit
# alanrogers.com

## Vernet-les-Bains
### Hotel de Plein Air l'Eau Vive

Chemin de Saint-Saturnin, F-66820 Vernet-les-Bains (Pyrénées-Orientales) T: 04 68 05 54 14.
E: contact@leauvive-camping.com  **alanrogers.com/FR66130**

Enjoying dramatic views of the Pic du Canigou (3,000 m), this rather special and peaceful, natural site is only 1.5 km. from the centre of Vernet-les-Bains in the Pyrenees. The 70 tourist pitches are on grass, with electricity (4/10A) and 45 fully serviced, are on a slight slope, part hedged and some terraced, with a separate tent field. Most pitches have some shade and there are 11 chalets and mobile homes to rent. The 'pièce de résistance' is the unique natural pool, 'le plan d'eau biologique'. It is fed from the nearby bubbling stream with a special filtration system. No chlorine or chemicals are used and it has the appropriate certificates. It is really quite impressive, and it's warm as well!

**Facilities**

Fully equipped toilet facilities and provision for babies and disabled visitors. Washing machine. Bread, main season. Bar/restaurant/takeaway with terrace (15/6-31/8). Natural swimming pool. New play area with trampoline, basketball and table tennis. WiFi (free) on the terrace. Off site: Fishing 200 m. Swimming pool, thermal centre in village 1 km. Rafting, canoeing, hydrospeed trips. Bicycle hire 2 km.

**Open:** 15 May - 30 September.

**Directions**

Following N116 towards Andorra, at Ville Franche, turn south, D116, for Vernet-les-Bains. After 5 km. keep right avoiding town. Turn right over bridge towards Sahorre. Immediately turn right (ave de Saturnin) for 1 km. GPS: 42.55506, 2.37779

**Charges guide**

| | |
|---|---|
| Per unit incl. 2 persons and electricity | € 19.50 - € 26.50 |

Credit cards accepted 1/6-31/8 only.

## Vias
### Camping International le Napoléon

1171 avenue de la Méditerranée, F-34450 Vias-Plage (Hérault) T: 04 67 01 07 80
**alanrogers.com/FR34030**

Le Napoléon is a smaller, family run site situated in the village of Vias-Plage bordering the Mediterranean. The Graziani family celebrated their 40th anniversary at Napoléon in 2009. Vias-Plage is hectic to say the least in season, but once through the security barrier and entrance to le Napoléon, the contrast is marked – tranquillity, yet still only 150 m. from the beach and other attractions. It has a Californian-style pool, amphitheatre for entertainment and other new facilities, but thoughtful planning and design ensure that the camping area is quiet. With good shade from many tall trees, there are 239 fairly small, hedged and level pitches, 92 for touring units, all with 10A electricity.

**Facilities**

Fully equipped sanitary blocks are of a reasonable standard. Baby bath. Facilities for disabled visitors. Laundry. Motorcaravan services. Supermarket and bakery. Bar. Restaurant/pizzeria. Swimming pool complex with lively piped music. Gym/fitness room. Bicycle hire. Tennis, archery, boules. TV. Children's club. Amphitheatre, wide range of free entertainment until midnight. Disco outside site (Easter-Sept). Internet and WiFi (charged).

**Open:** 6 April - 30 September.

**Directions**

From autoroute A9 take exit Agde-Pézenas, direction Béziers. Continue for 5 km. direction Vias-Vias-Plage. Site is on the right near the beach; watch carefully for turning between restaurant and shops. GPS: 43.29197, 3.41535

**Charges guide**

| | |
|---|---|
| Per unit incl. 2 persons and electricity | € 20.00 - € 45.00 |
| extra person (over 4 yrs) | € 6.00 - € 9.00 |

## Vias
### Yelloh! Village le Club Farret

Chemin des Rosses, F-34450 Vias-Plage (Hérault) T: 04 67 21 64 45. E: farret@wanadoo.fr
**alanrogers.com/FR34110**

An excellent site for families, well maintained and attractively landscaped with flowering shrubs, giving a truly Mediterranean feel. Staff are helpful and everywhere is neat and tidy. It is a large, busy site but well organised with a relaxed atmosphere. There are 772 good sized, level, grassy pitches, with 346 for touring (6A electricity) with some shade from many trees. The large heated pool has lots of sunbathing space and a special area with sand and a paddling pool has been created for youngsters and their parents. The safe beach is alongside the site so some pitches have sea views.

**Facilities**

Very clean toilet blocks have facilities for children and disabled visitors. Washing machines. Dog shower. Supermarket. Hairdresser. Bars with pizzas, snacks, takeaway. Restaurant. Crêperie with minigolf. Heated swimming pool complex with lifeguard all season. Spa and wellness centre. Gym. Play areas. Miniclub. Tennis. Archery. Multisports court. Bicycle hire. WiFi (charged).

**Open:** 29 March - 29 September.

**Directions**

Site is south of Vias at Vias-Plage. From N112 (Béziers-Agde) take D137 signed Vias-Plage. Site is signed on the left. GPS: 43.17.27, 3.25.07

**Charges guide**

| | |
|---|---|
| Per unit incl. 2 persons and electricity | € 19.00 - € 50.00 |
| extra person | € 6.00 - € 8.00 |

## Vias

### Sunêlia Domaine de la Dragonnière

RD 612, F-34450 Vias-sur-Mer (Hérault) T: 04 67 01 03 10. E: contact@dragonniere.com
**alanrogers.com/FR34450**

La Dragonnière makes up for being set back from the sea by offering an amazing selection of swimming pools and a wide range of sporting activities and entertainment. It is a busy holiday village, between the popular resorts of Vias and Portiragnes, and very well organised. In total, there are 880 pitches split into two areas, most occupied by a range of smart mobile homes and chalets, but there are still around 50 grass touring pitches, with some shade. All have electricity (10A) as well as water and drainage. La Dragonnière lies 5 km. from the nearest beach and a free shuttle operates in peak season.

**Facilities**

One fully equipped toilet block includes facilities for babies and disabled visitors. Laundry. Supermarket. Stalls selling local produce. Bar and restaurant complex, with good range of meals (9/4-18/9) takeaway service (18/6-11/9). Two heated swimming pool complexes. Play area. Sauna and gym (9/4-18/9). Sports competitions, children's club and evening entertainment in high season. Multisports pitch. Activities in low season. Bicycle hire. WiFi (charged).

**Open:** 9 April - 18 September.

**Directions**

Take Béziers Est exit from A9 autoroute. Follow directions to Villeneuve, Sérignan and Valras-Plage. After 800 m. at large roundabout, follow signs to Vias aéroport on N112. After a further 7 km, site is on the right. GPS: 43.313, 3.36517

**Charges guide**

| Per unit incl. 3 persons and all services | € 20.00 - € 51.00 |
|---|---|
| extra person | € 7.00 - € 9.00 |

## Vias

### Camping les Salisses

Route de la Mer, F-34450 Vias-Plage (Hérault) T: 04 67 21 64 07. E: info@salisses.com
**alanrogers.com/FR34520**

A traditional-style French campsite, les Salisses is well run and managed with an impressive range of swimming pools and other facilities. The 400 plus level pitches of average size are separated by flowering shrubs and trees that provide shade – all rather pretty. There are just over 100 places for touring units with 8A electricity, the rest being taken by a range of mobile homes, some to let. Vias-Plage is a busy, somewhat hectic resort and les Salisses has its own section of beach with a bar.

**Facilities**

Four fully equipped toilet blocks. Facilities for disabled visitors. Laundry. Shop (16/6-19/9). Bar and restaurant (16/6-19/9). Takeaway pizzeria (1/7-31/8). One indoor pool (heated for low season; used by naturists in high season). Two other pool complexes. Play area. Sports field (rugby posts). Multisports court. Tennis. Minigolf. Bicycle hire. Wide range of entertainment and activities. WiFi (free). Communal barbecue areas.

**Open:** 16 April - 19 September.

**Directions**

From the A9 take exit 34, then the N312 towards Vias and Agde. Join the N112 to avoid Vias town to pick up sign for Vias-Plage. Site is first on the right. GPS: 43.29657, 3.4164

**Charges guide**

| Per unit incl. 2 persons and electricity | € 26.00 - € 40.00 |
|---|---|

Camping Cheques accepted.

## Vias

### Camping l'Air Marin

F-34450 Vias-Plage (Hérault) T: 04 67 21 64 90. E: info@camping-air-marin.fr
**alanrogers.com/FR34530**

A shaded haven, l'Air Marin is set back beside the Canal du Midi, away from the busy hectic centre of Vias-Plage. It is a good site for families, regularly laid out with a degree of individuality and some distinctive sculptures, including decoratively tiled water points. The facilities are to one side and form the core of the site, attractively arranged overlooking the pool complex. Flowering shrubs separate the 150 pitches for chalets and mobile homes to let, while the 150 level grass places for touring units are more open among tall trees and occasional shrubs. All have 6A electricity. The site opens quite early in the season compared with some in the area, with all facilities also said to be open all season.

**Facilities**

Two fully equipped toilet blocks provide good facilities including for babies and children. En-suite unit for disabled visitors. Laundry facilities. Shop. Restaurant, bar and takeaway café. Attractive pool complex with sliding cover for heated pool, larger outdoor pool and paddling pool. Gym. Play area. Tennis (30/6-30/8). Multisports court. Playing field. Activities and entertainment organised in high season. WiFi. Off site: Beach 1 km. Golf 8 km.

**Open:** 15 April - 15 September.

**Directions**

From A9 autoroute exit 34, follow N312 towards Agde for 9 km. Pick up N112 (Béziers) and take next left for Vias-Plage. At tourist centre follow signs for Campings Est alongside the Canal du Midi to pick up site signs. GPS: 43.30135, 3.42304

**Charges guide**

| Per unit incl. 2 persons and electricity | € 40.00 |
|---|---|

No credit cards.

For latest campsite news, availability and prices visit
**alanrogers.com**

## Villeneuve-lez-Avignon

### Campéole Ile des Papes

Campé●le

1497 route départementale 780, F-30400 Villeneuve-lez-Avignon (Gard) T: 04 90 15 15 90.
E: ile-des-papes@campeole.com **alanrogers.com/FR30120**

Camping Ile des Papes is a large, open and very well equipped site. Avignon and its palace and museums are 8 km. away. The site has an extensive swimming pool area and a fishing lake with beautiful mature gardens. The railway is quite near but noise is not too intrusive. The 381 pitches, 176 for touring (all with 10A electricity), are of a good size on level grass, but with little shade. Games and competitions for all ages are organised in high season. This site is very popular with groups and is especially busy at weekends and in high season. In July and August a minibus is available for transport to Avignon, the airport and the railway station; the local bus can take you directly to Avignon. A good base to explore the famous Routes des Vins and the old villages and ancient towns of the Provençal region. There are many walks and cycle routes close by.

### Facilities

Good quality toilet blocks (may be stretched when busy) include baby rooms and facilities for campers with disabilities. Washing machines. Motorcaravan services. Well stocked shop. Bar and restaurant (1/4-20/10 limited hours in low season). Large swimming pool complex and pool for children, all unheated, (15/4-31/10). Play area. Lake for fishing. Archery, tennis, minigolf and basketball (all free). Bicycle hire. Only gas and electric barbecues allowed. Communal barbecue. Off site: Riding 3 km. Boat launching 5 km. Parachuting, paintball, jetski. Villeneuve-lez-Avignon with shops, bars, restaurants. Avignon 6 km. Golf 6 km.

**Open:** 26 March - 5 November.

### Directions

Leave the A9 at exit 22 (Roquemaure) and take D976 to Roquemaure, turn south D980 towards Villeneuve. Near railway bridge turn hard left, D780 (site signed). Cross river, immediately turn right to site. GPS: 43.97660, 4.79440

### Charges guide

| Per unit incl. 2 persons | |
|---|---|
| and electricity | € 19.10 - € 29.00 |
| extra person | € 4.50 - € 4.90 |
| child (under 7 years) | free - € 3.90 |
| dog | € 2.00 - € 2.90 |

Various special offers.
Camping Cheques accepted.

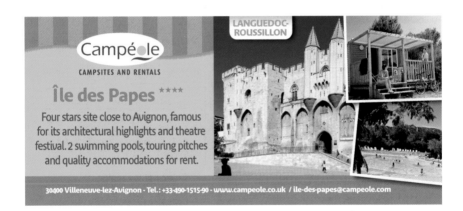

**FREE** Alan Rogers Travel Card
Extra benefits and savings - see page 10

The sleepy villages, sunny vineyards and pretty lavender fields of Provence sit in stark contrast to the cosmopolitan towns and thronging beaches of the Côte d'Azur, one of France's most popular destinations.

**DÉPARTEMENTS: 04 ALPES-DE-HAUTE-PROVENCE, 05 HAUTES-ALPES, 06 ALPES-MARITIME, 13 BOUCHES-DU-RHÔNE, 83 VAR, 84 VAUCLUSE**

**MAJOR CITIES: NICE, CANNES, MONTE CARLO (MONACO), MARSEILLES**

Provence is characterised by bleached landscapes, olive groves and herb-scented garrigue. The colours and amazing intensity of light have encouraged artists and writers to settle in the sleepy villages, their ancient dwellings topped by distinctive terracotta tiles, and their narrow streets fragrant with the perfume of wild herbs and lavender. Roman monuments can be seen at Orange, and Vaison-la-Romaine, and the spectacular Palais des Papes at Avignon is a 'must see'. The extinct volcanic cone of Mont Ventoux provides dramatic views and is one of the most gruelling stages in the Tour de France.

In contrast, the glittering Côte d'Azur is a beautiful stretch of coast studded with sophisticated towns such as Monte Carlo, Nice and Cannes, and of course the glamorous resort of St Tropez. With its vast expanses of golden sand and long hours of sunshine, this is a paradise for sun worshippers. The quaint harbours and fishing villages have become chic destinations full of luxury yachts, harbour-side cafés and crowded summertime beaches. Inland, St Paul-de-Vence with its shops and galleries set on narrow, winding streets, and Grasse, perfume capital of the world, are popular destinations for visitors.

### Places of interest

*Aix-en-Provence*: old town, cathedral of St. Sauveur, Cézanne museum.

*Antibes:* old city with 17th-century ramparts, 12th-century castle.

*Camargue*: wetland and nature reserve with white horses, flamingoes and bulls.

*Cannes:* popular for conventions and festivals, la Croisette, old city.

*Marseille*: bustling port city with boat trips to the Château d'If prison on a nearby island.

*Menton:* warmest of coastal cities, year round resort.

*Orange*: Roman city, gateway to the Midi, Colline St Europe.

### Cuisine of the region

*Aigo Bouido*: garlic and sage soup with bread (or eggs and cheese).

*Aïoli (aïlloli)*: a mayonnaise sauce with garlic and olive oil.

*Bagna Cauda*: raw vegetables in a fondue of hot olive oil, garlic and anchovies.

*Bouillabaisse*: fish soup served with rouille sauce, saffron and aioli.

*Pissaladière*: Provençal bread dough with onions, anchovies, olives.

*Porquetta*: stuffed suckling pig.

*Salade niçoise*: salad of anchovies, tuna, tomatoes, peppers, eggs and olives.

*Socca*: a crêpe made with chick pea flour and cooked in a wood-fired oven.

**www.guideriviera.com**
**info@guideriviera.com**
**(0)4 93 37 78 78**

**www.discover-southoffrance.com**
**information@cft-paca.fr**
**(0)4 91 56 47 00**

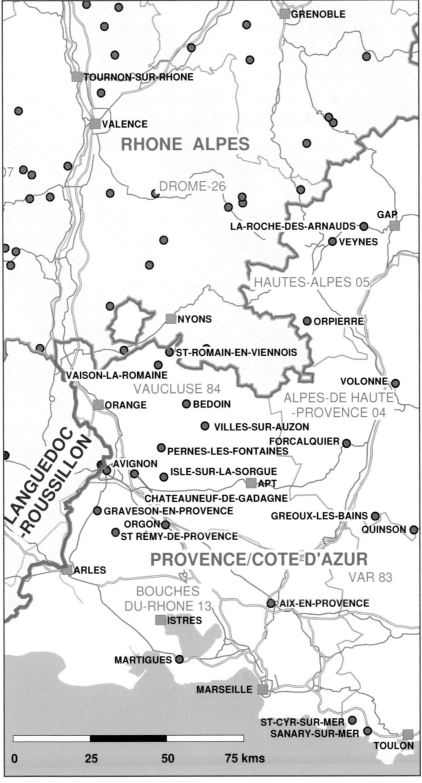

**GRENOBLE**

**TOURNON-SUR-RHONE**

**VALENCE**

## RHONE ALPES

DROME-26

GAP

LA-ROCHE-DES-ARNAUDS

**VEYNES**

HAUTES-ALPES 05

**NYONS**   **ORPIERRE**

**ST-ROMAIN-EN-VIENNOIS**

**VAISON-LA-ROMAINE**

VOLONNE

VAUCLUSE 84

**ORANGE**   **BEDOIN**

ALPES-DE HAUTE
-PROVENCE 04

**VILLES-SUR-AUZON**

FORCALQUIER

**PERNES-LES-FONTAINES**

**AVIGNON**

**ISLE-SUR-LA-SORGUE**

**APT**

**CHATEAUNEUF-DE-GADAGNE**

**GRAVESON-EN-PROVENCE**   **GREOUX-LES-BAINS**

**ORGON**   QUINSON

**ST RÉMY-DE-PROVENCE**

## PROVENCE/COTE D'AZUR

VAR 83

**ARLES**

BOUCHES
DU-RHONE 13   **AIX-EN-PROVENCE**

**ISTRES**

**MARTIGUES**

**MARSEILLE**

**ST-CYR-SUR-MER**
**SANARY-SUR-MER**

**TOULON**

LANGUEDOC-ROUSSILLON

0    25    50    75 kms

Provence/Côte d'Azur – west

**FREE** Alan Rogers Travel Card
Extra benefits and savings - see page 10

BRIANCON
VALLOUISE
LES-VIGNEAUX

HAUTES-ALPES 05

ITALY

GUILLESTRE
CHÂTEAUROUX-LES-ALPES
ST-APOLLINAIRE

ST-VINCENT-LES-FORTS
MONTCLAR

ALPES-DE HAUTE
-PROVENCE 04

VILLARS-COLMARS

PROVENCE/COTE D'AZUR

DIGNE-LES-BAINS

PUGET-THENIERS

MOUSTIERS-STE-MARIE
CASTELLANE
CHASTEUIL

CONTES
MONTE-CARLO
NICE

MONTAGNAC-MONTPEZAT
VENCE
LE BAR-SUR-LOUP
GRASSE
LA COLLE-SUR-LOUP
VILLENEUVE-LOUBET
VILLENEUVE-
LOUBET PLAGE

QUINSON
REGUSSE
VILLECROZE-LES-GROTTES
PUGET-SUR ARGENS
DRAGUIGNAN
A8,E80
ANTIBES
MANDELIEU LA NAPOULE

LE MUY
ROQUEBRUNE-SUR ARGENS
SAINT RAPHAEL
AGAY

BRIGNOLES
VAR 83
FREJUS
ST AYGULF
LES ISSAMBRES

GRIMAUD
COGOLIN
GASSIN RAMATUELLE
LA MOLE
CAVALAIRE-SUR-MER
BORMES-LES-MIMOSAS
TOULON
LE LAVANDOU
HYERES
CARQUEIRANNE

Provence/Côte d'Azur – east

For latest campsite news, availability and prices visit

**alanrogers.com**

## Agay
### Camping Caravaning Esterel
Avenue des Golfs, Agay, F-83530 Saint Raphaël (Var) T: 04 94 82 03 28. E: contact@esterel-caravaning.fr
**alanrogers.com/FR83020**

Esterel is a quality, award-winning caravan site east of St Raphaël, set among the hills beyond Agay. The site is 3.5 km. from the sandy beach at Agay where parking is perhaps a little easier than at most places on this coast, but a shuttle runs from the site to and from the beach several times daily in July and August (€1). It has 164 touring pitches for caravans but not tents; all have 10A electricity and a water tap, 18 special ones have their own en-suite washroom adjoining whilst others also have a washing machine, a dishwasher, a jacuzzi, 16A electricity and free WiFi. Pitches are on shallow terraces, attractively landscaped with good shade and a variety of flowers, giving a feeling of spaciousness.

**Facilities**

Excellent refurbished, heated toilet blocks. Individual toilet units on 18 pitches. Facilities for disabled visitors. Laundry room. Motorcaravan services. Shop. Gift shop. Takeaway. Bar/restaurant. Five swimming pools (two heated). Spa with sauna, etc. Disco. Archery. Minigolf. Tennis. Pony rides. Pétanque. Squash. Playground. Nursery. Bicycle hire. Internet access. Organised events in season. No barbecues. WiFi throughout. Baby club. Off site: Golf nearby. Fishing and beach 3 km.

**Open:** 23 March - 28 September.

**Directions**

From A8, exit Fréjus, follow signs for Valescure, then for Agay, site is on left. The road from Agay is the easiest to follow but it is possible to approach from St Raphaël via Valescure. Look carefully for site sign, which is difficult to see. GPS: 43.453775, 6.832817

**Charges 2013**

| Per unit incl. 2 persons | |
|---|---|
| and electricity | € 18.00 - € 99.00 |
| extra person | € 9.00 - € 11.00 |

## Aix-en-Provence
### Camping Chantecler
41 avenue du Val Saint André, F-13100 Aix-en-Provence (Bouches du Rhône) T: 04 42 26 12 98.
E: info@campingchantecler.com  **alanrogers.com/FR13120**

Aix is a busy, attractive town with a delightful pedestrian-friendly centre just waiting to be explored. There is much to visit in the area and Marseilles is within easy reach using the frequent train service. Chantcler is a pleasant campsite which is particularly well situated on the southeast edge of the town, close to the motorway and only minutes from the city centre and the main station on a good bus service. The site provides 271 pitches (over 200 for touring units) arranged in mature woodland with good facilities. Whilst this is a popular site which can get very busy in July and August, it is well run by an enthusiastic management. The town has something to offer everyone, from excellent, modern shopping to numerous museums and cultural sites, and endless restaurants and bars. Cézanne's studio is nearby and the Office du Tourisme arranges a variety of excursions on a weekly basis to the surrounding area, ranging from bird sanctuaries in the Camargue to Marseille and the Luberon.

**Facilities**

At the height of the season four sanitary blocks provide ample WCs, washbasins and hot showers around the site. Motorcaravan service point. Bar and restaurant (1/5-15/9). Swimming pool (1/5-30/9). Tennis. Boules. Internet access. WiFi throughout (charged). Charcoal barbecues not permitted. Twin-axle units are not accepted. Mobile homes to rent. Off site: Bus service 200 m. Riding 2 km. Aix-en-Provence 2 km. Golf 5 km.

**Open:** All year.

**Directions**

Leave the A8 at exit 31 (Aix-Sud) and at roundabout turn right. At second set of lights turn left and within 300 m. at roundabout turn right to the site in 200 m. GPS: 43.51636, 5.47495

**Charges guide**

| Per unit incl. 2 persons | |
|---|---|
| and electricity | € 23.75 - € 25.10 |
| extra person | € 6.30 - € 6.70 |
| child (under 7 yrs) | € 3.75 - € 3.85 |

**FREE** Alan Rogers Travel Card
Extra benefits and savings - see page 10

## Agay/Saint Raphaël

### Campéole du Dramont

986 boulevard 36ème Division Texas, F-83530 Agay/Saint Raphaël (Var) T: 04 94 82 07 68.
E: dramont@campeole.com  alanrogers.com/FR83700

Le Dramont stretches over a shady hillside, sloping gently down to a pebble beach (direct access), close to the attractive resort of Agay. This site is popular with scuba divers, and is an ideal base for exploring the turquoise waters. There is an international diving school on site and other amenities here include a beauty salon (July and August) and a sports field. Le Dramont has 400 pitches, of which 188 are occupied by mobile homes, chalets and fully equipped tents, for rent. Pitches are well shaded and generally of a good size. Some are near the main road so there may be some road noise.

**Facilities**

Three sanitary blocks include seatless toilets, modern preset showers and washbasins. Facilities for children. Wet room for disabled visitors. Rather dated laundry facilities. Shop. Snack bar. Beauty salon. Takeaway. Games room. Playground. Diving school. Boat launching (charged). Multisport pitch. Activities and entertainment. Direct beach access. Mobile homes, chalets and tents for rent. WiFi (charged). Off site: Fishing. Golf. Rock climbing.

**Open:** 20 March - 9 October.

**Directions**

From Saint Raphaël, take the RN98 (Cannes). The site is 7 km beyond Saint Raphaël (between Boulouris and Agay). GPS: 43.417864, 6.848195

**Charges guide**

| Per unit incl. 2 persons | |
|---|---|
| and electricity | € 21.10 - € 43.00 |
| extra person | € 5.50 - € 9.30 |
| child (2-6 yrs) | € 3.20 - € 3.90 |

## Antibes

### Camping le Sequoia

Avenue du Pylone, F-06600 Antibes (Alpes-Maritimes) T: 04 93 74 44 75. E: sequoia-antibes@orange.fr
alanrogers.com/FR06170

Camping le Sequoia is a family run, family oriented site with carefully maintained facilities and a beautiful pool. The owner, who is justifiably proud of her oasis of calm greenery in this very busy tourist area, lives on site. It is only 800 metres from the new SNCF station at Biot with a very frequent train service that serves the entire coast from Monaco, Nice and Cannes to Antibes. A small, quiet site, there are just 20 touring pitches and 24 mobile homes for rent. Beaches are 800 m. distant and the theme parks of Marineland and Aquasplash are a short walk along the N7.

**Facilities**

One unisex toilet block provides WCs, showers and washbasins. Facilities for disabled campers. Washing machine. Shop, bar and restaurant (15/6-30/8). Swimming pool (6/4-23/9). Play area. Boules. Mobile homes to rent. WiFi (charged). Off site: Beach 800 m. Antibes. Marineland, Aquasplash and much more.

**Open:** Mid April - 22 September.

**Directions**

East of Antibes continue on the N7, drive past the SNCF station Gare de Biot and at next roundabout turn to Biot. After 100 m. turn left into Avenue Mozart, then right into Avenue du Pylone and follow signs to site. GPS: 43.61221, 7.11543

**Charges guide**

| Per unit incl. 2 persons | |
|---|---|
| and electricity | € 20.70 - € 29.65 |
| extra person | € 4.00 - € 5.60 |
| Credit cards accepted for over € 30. | |

## Avignon

### Camping du Pont d'Avignon

10 chemin de la Barthelasse, Ile de la Barthelasse, F-84000 Avignon (Vaucluse) T: 04 90 80 63 50.
E: info@camping-avignon.com  alanrogers.com/FR84090

This site is very close to the large town, yet it is in a quiet location and only a short walk or free ferry ride from the centre. The well shaded and neat layout of the pitches and the very good access will ensure a pleasant stay. There are 300 level pitches, some on grass and some with gravel, 214 with 10A electricity. A good play area, tennis courts and volleyball pitch are in the centre of the site separating the two halves. Nearly all the pitches are separated by hedges. The restaurant, bar and terrace overlook the attractive pool. During the season there are musical and themed evenings in the restaurant.

**Facilities**

Well maintained and clean toilet blocks, facilities for disabled visitors. Washing machines, dryer. Motorcaravan services. Well stocked shop. Bar/restaurant and takeaway. Swimming pool, paddling pool (15/5-25/9). Play area with climbing frame. Tennis. Bicycle hire. Internet access. WiFi near reception. Off site: Bicycle hire 2 km. Riding 3 km. Golf 10 km. Avignon with famous bridge and Pope's Palace. Ferry to town centre. Excellent shopping in town.

**Open:** 3 March - 24 November.

**Directions**

Site is on an island in River Rhône. Well signed from roads into Avignon, ring road has complex junctions. Accessed from Pont Daladier towards Villeneuve les Avignon. Just after crossing first section of river fork right to site in 500 m. GPS: 43.95661, 4.80215

**Charges guide**

| Per unit incl. 2 persons | |
|---|---|
| and electricity | € 17.40 - € 28.30 |
| extra person | € 3.40 - € 5.00 |

For latest campsite news, availability and prices visit

# alanrogers.com

## Bormes-les-Mimosas

### Camp du Domaine

B.P. 207 La Favière, F-83230 Bormes-les-Mimosas (Var) T: 04 94 71 03 12. E: mail@campdudomaine.com

**alanrogers.com/FR83120**

Camp du Domaine, 3 km. south of Le Lavandou, is a large, attractive beachside site with 1,200 pitches set in 45 hectares of pinewood, although surprisingly it does not give the impression of being so big. The pitches are large and most are reasonably level, 800 with 10A electricity. The most popular pitches are beside the beach, but the ones furthest away are generally larger and have more shade. Amongst the trees, many are more suitable for tents. The price for all the pitches is the same – smaller but near the beach or larger with shade. The beach is the attraction and everyone tries to get close. American motorhomes are not accepted. Despite its size, the site does not feel too busy, except perhaps around the supermarket. This is mainly because many pitches are hidden in the trees, the access roads are quite wide and it all covers quite a large area (some of the beach pitches are 600 m. from the entrance). Its popularity makes early reservation necessary over a long season (about mid June to mid Sept) as regular clients book from season to season. A good range of languages are spoken. A member of Leading Campings Group.

### Facilities

Ten modern, well used but clean toilet blocks. Mostly Turkish WCs. Facilities for disabled visitors (but steep steps). Baby room. Washing machines. Fridge hire. Well stocked supermarket, bars, pizzeria (all open all season). No swimming pool. Excellent play area. Boats, pedaloes for hire. Wide range of watersports. Games, competitions (July/Aug). Children's club. Tennis. Multisports courts. Only gas and electric barbecues are allowed. Dogs are not accepted 10/7-21/8. WiFi throughout (charged). Off site: Bicycle hire 500 m. Riding and golf 15 km.

**Open:** 30 March - 31 October.

### Directions

From Bormes-les-Mimosas, head east on D559 to Le Lavandou. At roundabout, turn off D559 towards the sea on road signed Favière. After 2 km. turn left at site signs. GPS: 43.11779, 6.35176

### Charges guide

| | |
|---|---|
| Per unit incl. 2 persons and electricity | € 29.00 - € 45.00 |
| extra person | € 6.00 - € 10.00 |
| child (under 7 yrs) | free - € 4.90 |
| dog (not 10/7-21/8) | free |

Camp du Domaine
Var • Provence • Côte d'Azur

An excellent site with direct access to one of the best beaches at the Côte d'Azur offering a dream holiday in the sun.

Discover more and book at:
**www.campdudomaine.com**

join us

Camp du Domaine BP 207 La Favière 83230 Bormes-Les-Mimosas FRANCE
Tél. +33 (0)4 94 71 03 12 • Fax +33 (0)4 94 15 18 67 • mail@compdudomaine.com
GPS N : 43° 7' 4" E : 6° 21' 73"

**CAMPING AND CARAVANNING • BUNGALOWS • MOBILE HOMES**
Entertainment • Bar-Restaurants • Supermarket • WIFI • Wellness

**FREE** Alan Rogers Travel Card
Extra benefits and savings - see page 10

## Carqueiranne
### Campéole les Arbousiers

Campé●le

Chemin des Arbousiers, le Canebas, F-83320 Carqueiranne (Var) T: 04 94 58 56 56.
E: arbousiers@campeole.com **alanrogers.com/FR83670**

Les Arbousiers is a small site located on a hilltop overlooking the beautiful Gulf of Giens. There are 77 pitches occupied by mobile homes, chalets and fully equipped bungalow tents; a further 23 pitches are for small tents only. Access to pitches by car is authorised for arrivals and departures only, and vehicles are parked in a large car park close to reception. With all the activities taking place at the bar/restaurant area, this ensures a tranquil ambiance within the site. The pool area has plenty of relaxation space and will attract people looking for a peaceful vacation.

**Facilities**

Two modern, clean sanitary blocks. Laundry facilities. Bar/restaurant with takeaway (1/6-1/9). Swimming pool and children's pool with beach area. Boules pitch. Volleyball. Play area. Activity and entertainment programme. Mobile homes, chalets and tents for rent. WiFi (charged). Off site: Beach 3 km. Riding and bicycle hire 5 km. Golf 6 km. Sailing 10 km. Hyères old town 10 km. Close to parc naturel for bird watching and walks.
**Open:** 1 April - 30 September.

**Directions**

From the A57 motorway (Aix-en-Provence-Toulon), take exit 2 and follow signs for Carqueiranne and Le Pradet. Upon reaching Carqueiranne, follow signs to Le Canebas and Fort de la Bayarde and the campsite. GPS: 43.093081, 6.058429

**Charges guide**

| Per unit incl. 2 persons | |
| --- | --- |
| and electricity | € 17.90 - € 27.60 |
| extra person | € 4.60 - € 7.90 |

## Castellane
### RCN les Collines de Castellane

Route de Grasse, F-04120 Castellane (Alpes-de-Haute-Provence) T: 04 92 83 68 96. E: collines@rcn.fr
**alanrogers.com/FR04040**

RCN, a Dutch company, runs a chain of nine good campsites in the Netherlands. They also operate seven sites in France, all with Dutch managers who speak good French and English. Les Collines de Castellane is pleasantly situated in the mountainous landscape of the Alpes-de-Haute-Provence. There are 160 touring pitches spread over a series of flat terraces and most have shade provided by trees. Access roads are very steep and it is quite a long way down to the bottom of the site. At the top of the site, near the entrance, is a combined reception and small restaurant area.

**Facilities**

Tiled, modern toilet facilities include individual cabins and facilities for disabled visitors and babies. Laundry facilities. Shop. Library. Small restaurant (including takeaway) with terrace. Heated swimming pool with slides and paddling pool. Tennis court. Boules. Play areas. Organised activities (May-Sept). WiFi room (charged). Off site: Castellane 6 km. with shops, bars and restaurants. Riding 6 km. Beach and golf 10 km.
**Open:** 20 April - 21 September.

**Directions**

Take the N85 (Route Napoléon) from Digné-les-Bains towards Castellane and Grasse. Site is 6 km. south of Castellane, on the right hand side of the road. GPS: 43.82412, 6.56962

**Charges guide**

| Per unit incl. 2 persons, | |
| --- | --- |
| electricity and water | € 18.90 - € 39.90 |
| extra person | € 2.50 - € 4.90 |

Camping Cheques accepted.

## Castellane
### Camping International

Route Napoléon RD4085, F-04120 Castellane (Alpes-de-Haute-Provence) T: 04 92 83 66 67.
E: info@camping-international.fr **alanrogers.com/FR04100**

Camping International has very friendly, English speaking owners and is a reasonably priced, less commercialised site situated in some of the most dramatic scenery in France. The 274 pitches, 130 good sized ones for touring, are clearly marked, separated by trees and small hedges, some are on a slight slope and all have electricity and water. Access is good for larger units. The bar/restaurant overlooks the swimming pool with its sunbathing area set in a sunny location with fantastic views.

**Facilities**

Nine toilet blocks, some of the smaller blocks are of an older design. One newer block has modern facilities, including those for disabled visitors. Laundry facilities. Motorcaravan services. Shop. Restaurant/takeaway (May-Sept). Swimming pool (1/5-30/9). Club/TV room. Play area. Boules. Children's entertainment, occasional evening entertainment (July/Aug). Internet access. WiFi throughout (charged). Bicycle hire. Off site: Riding 1 km. Fishing 2 km. Castellane 1.5 km. with river, canyon and rapids, ideal for canoeing, rafting and canyoning etc.
**Open:** 31 March - 1 October.

**Directions**

Site is 1 km. north of Castellane on the N85 Route Napoléon. GPS: 43.85866, 6.49803

**Charges 2013**

| Per unit incl. 2 persons | |
| --- | --- |
| and electricity | € 19.00 - € 32.00 |
| extra person | € 3.00 - € 5.00 |
| dog | € 2.00 |

Camping Cheques accepted.

For latest campsite news, availability and prices visit
# alanrogers.com

## Castellane
### Castel Camping le Domaine du Verdon

513

Camp du Verdon, F-04120 Castellane (Alpes-de-Haute-Provence) T: 04 92 83 61 29.
E: contact@camp-du-verdon.com **alanrogers.com/FR04020**

Close to the Route des Alpes and the Gorges du Verdon. Du Verdon is a large level site, part meadow, part wooded, with 500 partly shaded, rather stony pitches (390 for tourists). Numbered and separated by bushes, they vary in size, have 6A electricity, and 125 also have water and waste water. They are mostly separate from the mobile homes (60) and pitches used by tour operators (110). Some overlook the unfenced River Verdon, so watch the children. This is a very popular holiday area, the gorge, canoeing and rafting being the main attractions, ideal for active families. Two heated swimming pools and numerous on-site activities during high season help to keep non-canoeists here. One can walk to Castellane without using the main road where there are numerous shops, cafés and restaurants. Dances and discos in July and August suit all age groups. The latest finishing time is around 23.00, after which time patrols make sure that the site is quiet. The site is popular and very busy in July and August.

### Facilities

Refurbished toilet blocks include facilities for disabled visitors. Washing machines. Motorcaravan services. Babysitting service. Restaurant, terrace, log fire for cooler evenings. New supermarket. Pizzeria/crêperie. Takeaway. Heated swimming pools, paddling pool with mushroom fountain (all open all season). Fitness equipment. Organised entertainment (July/Aug). Play areas. Minigolf. Archery. Organised walks. Bicycle hire. Riding. Small fishing lake. Room for games and TV. Internet access and WiFi (free). Off site: Bus stop outside main entrance (only one bus each day). Castellane and the Verdon Gorge 1 km. Riding 2 km. Boat launching 4.5 km. Golf 20 km. Watersports.

**Open:** 15 May - 15 September.

### Directions

From Castellane take D952 westwards towards Gorges du Verdon and Moustiers. Site is 1 km. on left. GPS: 43.83921, 6.49396

### Charges guide

| | |
|---|---|
| Per unit (low season 2 or high season 3 persons) and electricity | € 26.00 - € 44.00 |
| extra person (over 4 yrs) | € 8.00 - € 13.00 |
| dog | € 3.00 |

**FREE** Alan Rogers Travel Card
**Extra benefits and savings** - see page 10

## Cavalaire-sur-Mer

### Camping Cros de Mouton

F-83240 Cavalaire-sur-Mer (Var) T: 04 94 64 10 87. E: campingcrosdemouton@wanadoo.fr

**alanrogers.com/FR83220**

Cros de Mouton is an attractive and reasonably priced campsite in a popular area. High on a steep hillside, about 2 km. from Cavalaire and its popular beaches, the site is a calm oasis away from the coast. There are stunning views of the bay but, due to the nature of the terrain, some of the site roads are very steep – the higher pitches with the best views are especially so. There are 199 large, terraced pitches (electricity 10A) under cork trees with 126 available for touring. Half of these are more suitable for tents with parking close by. A range of languages is spoken by the welcoming and helpful owners. The terrace of the restaurant and the pool area share the wonderful view of Cavalaire and the bay. Olivier and Arnaud are happy to take your caravan up with their 4 x 4 Jeep if you are worried, and they will help you set up if necessary – all part of the service.

### Facilities

Clean, well maintained toilet blocks have all the usual facilities including those for disabled customers (although site is perhaps a little steep in places for wheelchairs). Washing machine. Shop (1/4-15/10). Bar/restaurant with reasonably priced meals and takeaway (1/4-30/9). Swimming and paddling pools with many sunbeds on the terrace and small bar for snacks and cold drinks. Small play area. Games room. Bicycle hire. No charcoal barbecues on pitches. WiFi. Off site: Beach 1.8 km. Riding 3 km. Golf 15 km.

**Open:** 15 March - 11 November.

### Directions

Take the D559 to Cavalaire (not Cavalière 4 km. away). Site is 1.5 km. north of Cavalaire-sur-Mer, very well signed from the approach to the town. GPS: 43.18247, 6.5161

### Charges guide

| | |
|---|---|
| Per unit incl. 2 persons and electricity | € 25.10 - € 31.40 |
| extra person | € 6.80 - € 8.90 |
| child (under 7 yrs) | € 4.30 - € 4.80 |
| dog | free - € 2.00 |

Camping Cheques accepted.

For latest campsite news, availability and prices visit
**alanrogers.com**

## Chasteuil/Castellane
### Camping des Gorges du Verdon

Clos d'Arémus, F-04120 Chasteuil/Castellane (Alpes-de-Haute-Provence) T: 04 92 83 63 64.
E: aremus@camping-gorgesduverdon.com **alanrogers.com/FR04250**

Located at an altitude of 660 metres, between pinewoods and the River Verdon, Camping des Gorges du Verdon is a family site with large, shaded or semi-shaded pitches and a range of chalets and mobile homes. The site is bisected by the D952, has an inviting swimming pool, and offers direct access to the Verdon (with its own river beach). The main sight here is, of course, the stunning canyon of the Gorges du Verdon, a grandiose area of vertiginous cliffs towering above the emerald river below. There are some superb walks and this is also an ideal location for white-water rafting or canoeing.

**Facilities**

Two sanitary blocks with a mixture of French and English style toilets and controllable showers. Special toilets for children. Facilities for disabled visitors. Bar/restaurant. Shop. Swimming pool. River beach. Volleyball. Games room. Fishing. Play areas. Nursery rooms. Activities and entertainment. Mobile homes and chalets for rent. WiFi around most of site. Off site: Walking and cycle tracks. Rafting and canoeing. Restaurants in Castellane.

**Open:** 1 May - 15 September.

**Directions**

Site is west of Castellane. Leave the village on the D952 headed towards the Gorges du Verdon and the site is 9 km. GPS: 43.82343, 6.43095

**Charges guide**

| | |
|---|---|
| Per unit incl. 2 persons and electricity | € 19.90 - € 31.90 |
| extra person | € 4.50 - € 5.90 |
| child (under 4 yrs) | € 1.50 - € 2.50 |

## Châteauneuf-de-Gadagne
### Camping Fontisson

1125 route d'Avignon, F-84470 Châteauneuf-de-Gadagne (Vaucluse) T: 04 90 22 59 77.
E: info@campingfontisson.com **alanrogers.com/FR84210**

Camping Fontisson is west of Avignon close to the pretty Provençal village of Châteauneuf-de-Gadagne. The site is well located for visiting the Luberon and close to the fascinating city of Avignon and its Palais des Papes. There are 55 pitches here, 25 of which are occupied by mobile homes, chalets and equipped tents (available for rent). Pitches are large and generally well shaded and all have 10A electrical connections. On-site amenities include a swimming pool and a recently refurbished toilet block, as well as a tennis court and minigolf.

**Facilities**

Bar and snack bar (July/Aug). Bread and milk service. Outdoor swimming pool (mid May - Sept). Tennis. Multisports field. Boules. Play area. Entertainment and activity programme. WiFi throughout (charged). Off site: Châteauneuf-de-Gadagne with shops, cafés and restaurants. Riding and fishing 2 km. Golf 5 km. Bicycle hire 10 km. L'Isle-sur-la-Sorgue 15 km. Avignon 15 km.

**Open:** 1 April - 12 October.

**Directions**

Leave the A7 motorway at exit 23 (Avignon North). Head south on the D6 bypassing St Saturnin-lès-Avignon until you arrive at Châteauneuf-de-Gadagne. Site signed from here. GPS: 43.92883, 4.93347

**Charges guide**

| | |
|---|---|
| Per unit incl. 2 persons and electricity | € 15.30 - € 26.20 |
| extra person | € 3.50 - € 6.60 |

## Châteauroux-les-Alpes
### Camping les Cariamas

Fontmolines, F-05380 Châteauroux-les-Alpes (Hautes-Alpes) T: 04 92 43 22 63. E: cariamas@hotmail.fr
**alanrogers.com/FR05070**

Set 1,000 metres up in the stunning scenery of the Alps, les Cariamas is at the gateway to the Ecrin National Park and within easy reach of the Serre-Ponçon lake and the Rabioux-Durance river. Of the 150 pitches, 120 are for touring and all have electrical connections (6-10A), are pleasantly shaded and many offer countryside views. These pitches are close to some of the mobile homes and chalets available for rent but they are large enough for this not to be a problem. Fully equipped tents are also available to rent. It would be an idea to check the availability of the amenities prior to arrival, especially in low season. Part of the site is close to a main road so there may be some noise during peak times.

**Facilities**

Sanitary facilities include washbasins in cabins and hot showers. No facilities for disabled visitors. Laundry. Small shop and takeaway (from 1/5). Communal barbecue area. Swimming pool (1/5-30/9). Play area. Mountain bike hire. Fishing. WiFi (free). Off site: Bar and shop in the nearby village. Large supermarkets in Embrun 3 km. Bus service from village to Gap via several small villages. Riding 15 km. Canoeing, climbing, hiking, mountain biking and rafting. Tennis. Skiing.

**Open:** 1 April - 31 October (mobile homes all year).

**Directions**

From Gap follow signs to Embrun Briançon. Take turning for Châteauroux-les-Alpes at first roundabout after Embrun. Shortly (800 m) before the village turn right and follow signs to site. Access to the site is via a 700 m. narrow lane with some passing places. GPS: 44.60293, 6.52180

**Charges guide**

| | |
|---|---|
| Per unit incl. 2 persons and electricity | € 20.75 |
| extra person | € 5.50 |
| child (under 6 yrs) | € 2.75 |

**FREE** Alan Rogers Travel Card
Extra benefits and savings - see page 10

447

## Cogolin
### Camping l'Argentière

Chemin de l'Argentiere (D48), F-83310 Cogolin (Var) T: 04 94 54 63 63. E: campinglargentiere@wanadoo.fr
**alanrogers.com/FR83310**

This little jewel of a site is in a pleasant setting and the intervening wooded area seems to give it sufficient screening to make the campsite itself quite peaceful. It is only 5 km. from the beach at Cogolin or St Tropez, so its position is handy for one of the showplaces of the Riviera, but away from the hustle and bustle of the beach resorts. There are 150 good sized touring pitches (out of 238 with the others used for mobile homes to rent). All have electricity although long leads may be necessary.

**Facilities**

Two of three toilet blocks are near the touring pitches and are well kept and clean. Washbasins have warm water (some in cabins). Washing machines (near site entrance). Water has to be taken from the sanitary block. Shop (15/6-30/9). Bar (15/4-30/9). Restaurant (15/6-15/9) and takeaway (15/6-15/9). Large swimming pool (15/5-30/9). Play equipment. Bicycle hire. Barbecues on a communal area only. WiFi around bar area. Off site: Shops nearby. Riding 2 km. Fishing 4 km. Beach 5 km. Golf 6 km.

**Open:** 1 April - 30 September.

**Directions**

From the A8 (Aix-en-Provence-Cannes) take exit 36 (Le Muy), then, D25 to Ste Maxime and the coast road N98 (St Tropez). After Grimaud keep following signs for Cogolin. When near that village follow D48 (St Maur-en-Collobrière), then signs to site in the suburb of L'Argentière. GPS: 43.256083, 6.5124

**Charges guide**

| | |
|---|---|
| Per unit incl. 2 persons and electricity | € 20.00 - € 41.00 |
| extra person | € 3.00 - € 6.00 |

No credit cards.

## Contes
### La Ferme de Riola

5309 route des Clos, F-06390 Contes (Alpes-Maritimes) T: 04 93 79 03 02. E: la.riola@free.fr
**alanrogers.com/FR06220**

La Ferme de Riola is a very small site with just 35 pitches for touring and six gîtes, attractively dispersed amongst olive trees around the four-hectare terrain. Areas for tents are spread all around the site, mostly situated on the terraces amongst olive trees. Pitches are large and generally well shaded. All are equipped with electrical connections. Leisure facilities include a swimming pool, a volleyball court and a children's playground. This is a working farm and fresh produce including olives, olive oil and fresh eggs is available at the site's small shop.

**Facilities**

Two sanitary blocks have preset pushbutton showers and include a family shower room, baby room and facilities in one block for disabled visitors. Small shop. Swimming pool (April-Sept). Volleyball. Games room. Play area. WiFi around reception area. Off site: Sclos de Contes 1 km. Fishing 5 km. Contes 6 km. Riding 12 km. Nice 18 km.

**Open:** 1 April - 30 October.

**Directions**

Head north from Nice on D2204 (Col de Nice). Continue towards Sospel, then join D215 and D115 to Sclos de Contes. GPS: 43.81612, 7.34324

**Charges guide**

| | |
|---|---|
| Per unit incl. 2 persons and electricity | € 21.00 |
| extra person | € 9.00 |

No credit cards.

## Forcalquier
### Camping le Moulin de Ventre

Niozelles, F-04300 Forcalquier (Alpes-de-Haute-Provence) T: 04 92 78 63 31. E: moulindeventre@aol.com
**alanrogers.com/FR04030**

This is a friendly, family run site in the heart of Haute-Provence, near Forcalquier, a bustling, small, French market town. Attractively located beside a small lake and 28 acres of wooded, hilly land, which is available for walking. Herbs of Provence can be found growing wild and flowers, birds and butterflies abound – a nature lovers' delight. The 124 level, grassy pitches for tourists are separated by a variety of trees and small shrubs, 114 of them having electricity (6A; long leads may be needed). Some pitches are particularly attractive, bordering a small river which runs through the site. A Sites et Paysages member.

**Facilities**

Refurbished toilet block. Facilities for disabled visitors. Baby bath. Laundry facilities. Fridge hire. Bread. Bar/restaurant and takeaway. Themed evenings (high season). Pizzeria. Swimming pools (15/5-30/9). New playground. Bouncy castle. Fishing. boules. Some activities organised in high season. No discos. Only electric or gas barbecues. Internet access. WiFi (free). Off site: Shops, local market, doctor, tennis 2 km. Supermarket, chemist, riding, bicycle hire 5 km.

**Open:** 9 April - 30 September.

**Directions**

From A51 motorway take exit 19 (Brillanne). Turn right on N96 then turn left on N100 westwards (signed Forcalquier) for 3 km. Site is signed on left, just after a bridge 3 km. southeast of Niozelles. GPS: 43.93364, 5.86815

**Charges guide**

| | |
|---|---|
| Per unit incl. 2 persons and electricity | € 20.00 - € 29.00 |
| extra person (over 4 yrs) | € 4.20 - € 6.00 |

No credit cards.

For latest campsite news, availability and prices visit
# alanrogers.com

## Forcalquier

### Camping Indigo Forcalquier

Route de Sigonce, F-04300 Forcalquier (Alpes-de-Haute-Provence) T: 04 92 75 27 94.
E: forcalquier@camping-indigo.com **alanrogers.com/FR04120**

Although Camping Indigo is an urban site, there are extensive views over the surrounding countryside where there are some excellent walks. The pitches are on grass and are of a good size, all with electricity, six fully serviced. The site is secure, with an electronic barrier (card deposit required) and there is no entry between 22.30 and 07.00. Local guides lead tours of the historic town and area. This is an excellent base for visiting Forcalquier, a 15th-century fortified hill town, and the Monday market (the best in Haute-Provence). Since Camping Indigo acquired this site, an extensive modernisation programme has been put into effect. You can be sure of a friendly welcome from the managers at reception where good English is spoken and a wealth of information is available for activities and places to visit in the area. Their policy is that tourists should not feel they have to stay at the campsite to be entertained but should instead venture out and explore the many and varied attractions within the region. The walk up to the citadel is worth the effort for the stunning panoramic view. The splendid bar/restaurant with its terraced outdoor seating area is an ideal place to relax after an exhausting day out, or one could cool off with a refreshing dip in the adjacent pool.

**Facilities**

Two refurbished toilet blocks with washbasins in cubicles and excellent facilities for disabled visitors. Bar (all season). Snack bar and takeaway (July and August). Play area. Heated swimming and paddling pools (all season). Range of activities in high season, often involving local people, including, food tasting and storytelling. Max. 1 dog. WiFi (free). Off site: All shops, banks etc. in town centre 200 m. Riding 5 km. Fishing 15 km. Golf 20 km.

**Open:** 18 April - 30 September.

**Directions**

From town centre, follow D16 signed to Montlaux and Sigonce. Site is 500 m. on the right. Well signed from town. GPS: 43.96206, 5.78743

**Charges 2013**

| | |
|---|---|
| Per unit incl. 2 persons and electricity | € 19.90 - € 27.80 |
| extra person | € 5.00 - € 6.20 |
| child (2-7 yrs) | free - € 4.40 |
| dog | € 2.00 - € 4.00 |

 **FREE** Alan Rogers Travel Card
Extra benefits and savings - see page 10

# Fréjus

## Camping Resort la Baume-la Palmeraie

3775 rue des Combattants d'Afrique du Nord, F-83618 Fréjus (Var) T: 04 94 19 88 88.
E: reception@labaume-lapalmeraie.com **alanrogers.com/FR83060**

La Baume is a large, busy site about 5.5 km. from the long sandy beach of Fréjus-Plage, although with its fine and varied selection of swimming pools many people do not bother to make the trip. The pools, with their palm trees, are remarkable for their size and variety (water slides, etc) – the very large feature pool being a highlight. There is also an aquatic play area and two indoor pools with a slide and a spa area. The site has nearly 250 adequately sized, fully serviced pitches with some separators and most have shade. Although tents are accepted, the site concentrates mainly on caravanning. It becomes full in season. Adjoining la Baume is its sister site, la Palmeraie, providing self-catering accommodation, its own landscaped pool and some entertainment to supplement that at la Baume. There are 500 large pitches with mains sewerage for mobile homes. La Baume's convenient location has its downside as there is traffic noise on some pitches from the nearby autoroute – somewhat obtrusive at first but we soon failed to notice it. It is a popular site with tour operators.

**Facilities**

Five toilet blocks. Supermarket, several shops. Two bars, terrace overlooking pools, TV. Restaurant, takeaway. Six swimming pools (heated all season, two covered, plus steam room and jacuzzi), seven slides. Fitness centre. Tennis. Archery (July/Aug). Skateboard park. Organised events, daytime and evening entertainment, some in English. Amphitheatre. Discos all season. Children's club (all season, 4-11 yrs). 2 play areas renovated. WiFi (charged). Off site: Bus to Fréjus passes gate. Riding 2 km. Fishing 8 km. Golf and beach 5 km.

**Open:** 30 March - 28 September (with full services).

**Directions**

From west, A8, exit Fréjus, take N7 southwest (Fréjus). After 4 km, turn left on D4 and site is 3 km. From east, A8, exit 38 Fréjus and follow signs for Cais. Site is signed. GPS: 43.45998, 6.72048

**Charges guide**

| | |
|---|---|
| Per unit incl. 2 persons, electricity, water and drainage | € 19.00 - € 49.00 |
| extra person | € 5.00 - € 14.00 |
| child (under 7 yrs) | free - € 7.00 |
| dog | € 5.00 |

Min. stay for motorcaravans 2 nights.
Large units should book.

---

# Fréjus

## Yelloh! Village Domaine du Colombier

Route de Bagnols-en-Forêt, 1052 rue des Combattants d'AFN, F-83600 Fréjus (Var) T: 04 66 73 97 39.
E: info@domaine-du-colombier.com **alanrogers.com/FR83230**

Domaine du Colombier is located between Cannes and St Tropez, alongside a main road 2 km. from the centre of Fréjus and 4 km. from the sandy beaches of Fréjus-Saint Raphaël. There are 52 touring pitches, ranging in size from 80-150 sq.m. and all with 16A electricity. Over recent years there has been much ongoing investment in high quality facilities. An attractive pool complex includes a heated pool (600 sq.m), a large paddling pool, water slides and jacuzzis and is surrounded by sun loungers, a fitness area and a grill restaurant. Plenty of activities and excursions are arranged all season and the site caters principally for families.

**Facilities**

Three well maintained, fully equipped toilet blocks (two heated and with baby rooms). Facilities for disabled visitors. Laundry. Well stocked shop. Bar/restaurant, takeaway. Soundproofed nightclub. Large heated swimming pool with paddling pool, slides and jacuzzis (all season). Fitness facilities. Three play areas and four sports areas. Picnic area with communal barbecue. Internet access and WiFi over site. Fridge, safe and barbecue hire. Off site: Bus stop 50 m.

**Open:** 28 March - 12 October.

**Directions**

From A8 exit 37, follow signs for Fréjus, turning left at second lights (D4) and site is 1 km. on right. From A8 exit 38 east (Nice) straight on at three roundabouts, then right at fourth and fifth. Site is 300 m. on right. GPS: 43.44583, 6.72727

**Charges guide**

| | |
|---|---|
| Per unit incl. 2 persons and electricity | € 15.00 - € 49.00 |
| extra person | € 5.00 - € 9.00 |
| child (3-7 yrs) | free - € 7.00 |
| dog | € 4.00 |

For latest campsite news, availability and prices visit
**alanrogers.com**

# La Baume
### CAMPING RESORT
★ ★ ★ ★ ★

# La Palmeraie
### RESIDENCE DE TOURISME
★ ★

*Le Sud grandeur Nature*

Bastidons for rent
1or 2 bedrooms - 4/6 persons
or 3 bedrooms - 6/8 persons
Mobil-homes 4/6 persons
Mobil-homes 2/4 persons
3 rooms - air conditioning
Appartment 6 or 10 persons

From April to September :
On going entertainment
Cabaret - Show
Disco - Children's club
5 kilometers from
the sandy beaches
of Fréjus
and Saint Raphaël.

Heated sanitary blocks,
marked-out pitches,
6 swimming pools including
2 covered and heated,
1 heated aquatic park
6 water-slides and jacuzzi.

3775, Rue des Combattants d'Afrique du Nord   83618 FREJUS Cedex
Tel: +33 (0)4 94 19 88 88   -   Fax: +33 (0)44 94 19 83 50
E-mail : reception@labaume-lapalmeraie.com

# www.labaume-lapalmeraie.com

## Fréjus

### Camping Caravaning les Pins Parasols

3360 rue des Combattants d'Afrique du Nord, F-83600 Fréjus (Var) T: 04 94 40 88 43.
E: lespinsparasols@wanadoo.fr **alanrogers.com/FR83010**

Les Pins Parasols with its 189 pitches is a comfortably sized site, which is quite easy to walk around. It is family owned and run. Although on very slightly undulating ground, virtually all the pitches (all have electricity 6A) are levelled or terraced and separated by hedges or bushes with pine trees for shade. There are 48 pitches equipped with their own fully enclosed sanitary unit, with WC, washbasin, hot shower and dishwashing sink. These pitches cost more but may well be of interest to those seeking a little bit of extra comfort. The nearest beach is Fréjus-Plage with its new marina, adjoining St Raphaël.

### Facilities

Good quality toilet blocks (one heated) providing facilities for disabled visitors. Small shop with reasonable stock, restaurant, takeaway (15/4-20/9). Heated swimming pool with attractive rock backdrop, separate long slide with landing pool and small paddling pool. Half-court tennis. General room, TV. Volleyball. Basketball. Play area. Internet in reception and WiFi (charged). Off site: Bicycle hire and riding 2 km. Bus from the gate into Fréjus 5 km. Beach and fishing 6 km. Golf 10 km.

**Open:** 7 April - 29 September.

### Directions

From A8 take exit 38 for Fréjus Est. Turn right immediately on leaving pay booths on a small road which leads across to D4, then right again and under 1 km. to site. GPS: 43.46290, 6.72570

### Charges guide

| | |
|---|---|
| Per unit incl. 2 persons and electricity | € 18.40 - € 28.45 |
| pitch with sanitary unit | € 23.15 - € 35.48 |
| extra person | € 4.60 - € 6.58 |
| child (under 7 yrs) | € 3.05 - € 3.97 |
| dog | € 1.90 - € 2.85 |

## Fréjus

### La Pierre Verte Camping Village

1880, Route Départementale 4, F-83600 Fréjus (Var) T: 04 94 40 88 30. E: info@campinglapierreverte.com
**alanrogers.com/FR83360**

This attractive, terraced site, set on a hillside under umbrella pines, has been gradually and thoughtfully developed. The genuine, friendly welcome means many families return year upon year. The site is divided into terraces, each with its own toilet block. The 200 generous pitches for touring units enjoy good shade from trees and have 6/10A electricity. There are 200 mobile homes in separate areas. For those seeking to 'get away from it all' in an area of outstanding natural beauty, there can be few more tranquil sites, but the many beaches, watersports and excursions the Gulf of Saint Tropez has to offer can also be enjoyed. Height restrictions could be an issue for larger units. For those staying on site, there are two large, (one heated) swimming pools with large sunbathing areas and exciting water slides. Not far away, some exhilarating hang-gliding and parascending can be enjoyed.

### Facilities

Five toilet blocks with WCs and washbasins in cubicles are extremely clean and accessible from all levels. Baby bath. Laundry facilities. Supermarket. Bar with takeaway service. One heated (15x15 m) and one unheated swimming pool (25x15 m) and paddling pool. Play area. Boules. Games room. Fridge hire. Entertainment and activities in high season. Bicycle hire. WiFi throughout (charged). Electric barbecues only. Off site: Riding 1 km. Shops 2 km. Shopping centre Fréjus 8 km. Fishing 8 km.

**Open:** 13 April - 5 October.

### Directions

From the A8 (Aix-en-Provence-Nice) take exit 38 onto D4 towards Bagnols-en-Forêt. Site is along this road past a military camp, clearly marked at the roundabout. GPS: 43.48389, 6.72058

### Charges 2013

| | |
|---|---|
| Per unit incl. 2 persons and electricity | € 22.00 - € 40.00 |
| extra person | € 7.00 - € 9.00 |
| child (2-6 yrs) | € 4.00 - € 6.00 |

## Gassin

### Camping Parc Saint James-Gassin

Route de Bourrian, F-83580 Gassin (Var) T: 04 94 55 20 20. E: gassin@camping-parcsaintjames.com

**alanrogers.com/FR83620**

A member of the Parc Saint James Group, this attractive campsite was formerly known as Parc Montana and is very well positioned close to Saint Tropez. The majority of the pitches are occupied by privately owned mobile homes and chalets plus 127 bungalows for hire, but there are also 30 touring pitches on the lower part of the site. The 30-hectare estate clings to the hillside with fragrant woodland providing good shade to the mainly terraced pitches. There is a good range of activities here, many concentrated around the large swimming pool complex. There are plans to include another heated fun pool area with flumes and jacuzzi. In high season, the activity and entertainment programme is popular and includes soirées on the site's attractive bar terrace. The site lies close to many places of interest – Saint Tropez is close at hand, as well as Ramatuelle with its famous beach of Pampelone. The site is also well located for Port Grimaud, Sainte Maxime and Gassin itself with its restaurants and superb views over the gulf.

**Facilities**

Five toilet blocks provide adequate facilities, though rather dated. Facility for disabled visitors in one block. Laundry. Small supermarket, bar and takeaway (Apr-Sep). Restaurant (July-Aug). Heated outdoor swimming pools and separate children's pool (13/4-15/9). Play area. Tennis. Multisports area. Games room. Children's club. Evening entertainment. Disco. Mobile homes and chalets for rent. WiFi throughout (charged). Off site: St Tropez, Port Grimaud and Cogolin. Nearest beaches 5 km. Riding. Fishing. Walking trails.

**Open:** 12 January - 24 November.

**Directions**

From A8 autoroute take Le Muy exit and follow signs to St Tropez and La Croix-Valmer. Pass Sainte Maxime and continue on the N98. At large roundabout take signs to Gassin. Cross first roundabout and turn left at next traffic lights. Site is also signed as Parc Montana in places. GPS: 43.24035, 6.57345

**Charges guide**

| | |
|---|---|
| Per unit incl. 2 persons and electricity | € 19.00 - € 40.00 |
| extra person | € 3.00 - € 6.00 |
| child (4-10 yrs) | € 2.00 - € 5.00 |
| dog | € 5.00 |

Digital iPad editions

alan rogers

Available on the App Store

**FREE** Alan Rogers bookstore app - digital editions of all 2013 guides

**alanrogers.com/digital**

La Pierre Verte

Camping Village ★★★★

www.campinglapierreverte.com

E-mail : info@campinglapierreverte.com

8 km from the sandy beaches of Fréjus

1880, Route Départementale 4 83600 FREJUS FRANCE Tél: 0033 4 94 40 88 30 Fax: 00 33 4 94 40 75 41

**FREE** Alan Rogers Travel Card

**Extra benefits and savings** - see page 10

# PARC SAINT-JAMES
## VILLAGES CLUB

Parc Saint-James is a small group of 4* campsites, all located in the South of France on the Côte d'Azur.

These three 'village-club' style campsites offer a warm welcome, a decent range of facilities with a real family atmosphere and a great location for beach-based holidays.

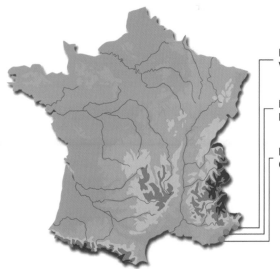

Parc Saint-James 'Le Sourire'
Villeneuve Loubet

Parc Saint-James 'Oasis Village'
Puget sur Argens

Parc Saint-James 'Gassin'
Gassin

# Parc Saint-James

**In Their Own Words...**

### Come and discover the Côte d'Azur South of France

Enjoy the pleasure of spending your holidays outdoors in village-clubs where everything has been designed for your leisure and well being.

A superb environment, a warm welcome, a friendly setting where your family can get together in a privileged world and experience true moments of happiness.

### Active holidays

Parc Saint-James offers the opportunity to enjoy many activities such as volleyball, tennis, badminton and fitness. Camping Parc Saint-James Le Sourire, is a hub of sports activities. Guests can also enjoy horse riding, windsurfing, rowing, diving and climbing.

### ...or relaxing holidays

Parc Saint-James campsites village club is for you! You'll find a swimming pool, sun deck and shady trees. Each campsite works hard to ensure you don't need to lift a finger – just relax and we'll take care of you. Enjoy our bars and TV lounges.

### Your evening

Parc Saint-James ensures you are always close to some activity and entertainment. A short distance from Fréjus and Saint-Raphaël, our location in the Gulf of St. Tropez allows you to party through the night. And the Parc Saint-James campsites organise evenings exclusively for residents, with a different daily themed programme (musical groups and/or shows) and at Oasis, from 11pm, a disco party.

### Children's kingdom

At Parc Saint-James campsites, children are heroes! Children from 4 to 10 years can enjoy our mini-club and a whole range of fun activities: treasure hunts, contests, make-up, crafts and sports. They will also enjoy our playground with slides and swings or go paddling safely under the eye of a lifeguard. Older children can do battle with friends in our arcades or play ping-pong, soccer and volleyball.

www.camping-parcsaintjames.com

## Graveson-en-Provence
### Camping les Micocouliers

445 route de Cassoulen, F-13690 Graveson-en-Provence (Bouches du Rhône) T: 04 90 95 81 49.
E: micocou@orange.fr **alanrogers.com/FR13060**

M. and Mme. Riehl started work on les Micocouliers in 1997 and they have developed a comfortable site. On the outskirts of the town, the site is only some 10 km. from Saint Rémy and Avignon. Purpose built, terracotta houses in a raised position provide all the facilities at present. The 115 pitches radiate out from here with the pool and entrance to one side. The pitches are on level grass, separated by small bushes, and shade is developing well. Electricity connections are possible (4-13A). There are also a few mobile homes. The popular swimming pool is a welcome addition.

**Facilities**

Several unisex units provide toilets and facilities for disabled visitors (by key), showers and washbasins in cabins, and dishwashing and laundry facilities. A new block has just been added. Small shop (July/Aug). Bread to order. Swimming pool (12x8 m; 1/6-15/9). Paddling pool (1/7-31/8). Play area. Gas and electric barbecues permitted. WiFi in some areas (charged). Off site: Riding and bicycle hire 1 km. Golf and fishing 5 km. Beach 60 km. at Ste Marie-de-la-Mer.

**Open:** 15 March - 15 October.

**Directions**

Site is southeast of Graveson. From the N570 at new roundabout take D5 towards St Rémy and Maillane and site is 500 m. on the left. GPS: 43.84397, 4.78131

**Charges guide**

| | |
|---|---|
| Per unit incl. 2 persons and electricity | € 19.80 - € 29.00 |
| extra person | € 5.30 - € 7.30 |

Camping Cheques accepted.

## Gréoux-les-Bains
### Yelloh! Village Verdon Parc

Domaine de la Paludette, F-04800 Gréoux-les-Bains (Alpes-de-Haute-Provence) T: 04 66 73 97 39.
E: info@yellohvillage-verdon-parc.com **alanrogers.com/FR04110**

Friendly and family run, this very spacious site borders the River le Verdon and is close to the attractive spa town of Gréoux-les-Bains. The 280 medium to very large, stony or gravel pitches (150 for touring units) are in two sections. The main part of the campsite has large pitches laid out in rows separated by poplar trees. Along the river bank the larger, more natural pitches are scattered amongst the trees and are of irregular shape and size. These have very pleasant views across the river to the town beyond. Electrical connections (10A) and water taps are reasonably close to most pitches.

**Facilities**

Several toilet blocks (one heated in low season) are clean and of a high standard. Facilities for disabled visitors. Laundry room. Motorcaravan services. Small shop. Bar. Restaurant and takeaway (Apr-Sept). TV. Internet point. Play area. Miniclub (high season). Organised sports. Evening entertainment. Dogs are not accepted 30/6-25/8. Gas and electric barbeques only. Off site: Gréoux-les-Bains 1 km. Riding and bicycle hire 1 km. Small lakeside beach 8 km. Local markets.

**Open:** 21 March - 29 October.

**Directions**

Leave A51 at Manosque and take D907 southeast (Gréoux-les-Bains). Turn right on D4, then left on D82 to Gréoux-les-Bains. Follow main road through town to roundabout with fountain. Take second right, (D8 St Pierre) and descend for 1 km. Cross river and immediately left to site. GPS: 43.75198, 5.89403

**Charges guide**

| | |
|---|---|
| Per unit incl. 2 persons and electricity | € 17.00 - € 34.00 |
| extra person | € 4.00 - € 6.00 |

## Grimaud
### Camping les Mures

RD 559, F-83310 Grimaud (Var) T: 04 94 56 16 97. E: info@camping-des-mures.com
**alanrogers.com/FR83390**

Les Mures is a friendly, family site situated northeast of the busy holiday centre of Port Grimaud and has been run by the Grau family for four generations. The site extends over 11 hectares of undulating ground with 600 of its 669 pitches reserved for touring (200 pitches are beside the sea). This high proportion of touring pitches is relatively unusual for this area. All have 6A electricity and the pitches are generally of a good size, well shaded by mature trees. Although there is no pool, the site lies right beside a lovely sandy beach with views across the bay to Saint Tropez.

**Facilities**

Six toilet blocks, all reasonably clean when visited. Four units for disabled visitors including a special block near the beach. Laundry facilities. Shop, bar, restaurant and takeaway. Play area. Sports pitch. Bicycle hire in high season. Internet access. Electric and non-flaming gas barbecues only. Mobile homes and chalets for rent. Off site: Fishing and golf 1 km. Bicycle hire 3 km.

**Open:** 23 March - 5 October.

**Directions**

From the A8 (Aix-en-Provence-Cannes) take exit 36 (Le Muy) and D25 to St Maxime, then the RD559 towards St Tropez. Site is 4.5 km. on the right of this road. GPS: 43.284017, 6.5918

**Charges guide**

| | |
|---|---|
| Per unit incl. 2 persons and electricity | € 29.50 - € 50.50 |
| extra person | € 5.00 - € 9.00 |

For latest campsite news, availability and prices visit
**alanrogers.com**

## Grimaud
### Club Holiday Marina

Le Ginestel, RN98/RD559, F-83310 Grimaud (Var) T: 04 94 56 08 43. E: info@holiday-marina.com
**alanrogers.com/FR83400**

Owned and operated by an English family, this site is an established favourite with British families. It is located in the busy holiday area of the Gulf of St Tropez. The site has a large and well kept pool area and its own adjacent moorings for small boats. There are 230 good sized pitches of which 49 are for touring units. Each of these has its own bathroom with a good shower, washbasin and WC and outdoor sink. The Grand Luxe plus pitches have a small mobile home instead of the sanitary unit, with kitchen, bathroom, bedroom and terrace and are suitable for extra large motorcaravans. On level, rather sandy ground, with variable shade, all have 16A electricity. Cars are parked separately to reduce noise.

**Facilities**

Private toilet blocks include washbasin, shower and WC, heated in low seasons. Laundry. Two restaurants (15/6-31/8). Snacks and takeaway. Bar and games room. TV room. Heated swimming and paddling pools (1/4-31/9). Miniclub. Evening entertainment in season. Fishing in adjacent canal. Mobile homes for hire. WiFi (charged). Off site: Beach and port within walking distance (busy road to cross) with shops and restaurants and some of the boats are available to hire. Golf 4 km. St Tropez.

**Open:** 1 March - 31 October.

**Directions**

From the A8 (Aix-en-Provence-Cannes) take exit 36 (Le Muy) and D25 to St Maxime. Follow N98 coast road (St Tropez) and site is 10 km. after very busy roundabout at Grimaud. GPS: 43.26978, 6.57311

**Charges guide**

| Per unit incl. 2 persons | |
|---|---|
| and electricity | € 21.00 - € 79.00 |
| family (2 adults, up to 3 childen) | € 21.00 - € 95.00 |
| extra person | € 5.00 - € 16.00 |

## Grimaud
### Domaine des Naïades

Quartier Cros d'Entassi, Saint Pons-les-Mûres, F-83310 Grimaud (Var) T: 04 94 55 67 80.
E: info@lesnaiades.com **alanrogers.com/FR83640**

Les Naïades is a well equipped site with an enviable setting close to the modern resort of Port Grimaud and the Gulf of St Tropez. The 454 pitches (219 are used for mobile homes for rent) are of a good size and well shaded, most have 10A electricity. The site boasts an Olympic sized pool and two water slides, as well as a separate pool for children. The restaurant specialises in Mediterranean cuisine and local wines. Les Naïades becomes lively in high season with activities and entertainment, as well as a miniclub for children. Port Grimaud is a stylish resort, built in the 1960s in the marshy delta of the Giscle.

**Facilities**

Four basic but adequate toilet blocks. Facilities for disabled visitors, but access can be difficult. Laundry facilities. Supermarket. Bar. Restaurant. Swimming pool with water slides. Play area. Motorcaravan services. Mobile homes for rent. Off site: Port Grimaud. St Tropez. Fishing. Watersports. Walking and cycle routes.

**Open:** 31 March - 21 October.

**Directions**

The site is slightly to the north of Port Grimaud. From D98 head north to N98, Pons-les-Mûres and site is clearly signed. GPS: 43.285278, 6.579722

**Charges guide**

| Per unit incl. 2-3 persons | |
|---|---|
| and electricity | € 29.00 - € 55.00 |
| extra person (over 7 yrs) | € 5.00 - € 8.00 |

## Guillestre
### Camping la Rochette

Route des Campings, F-05600 Guillestre (Hautes-Alpes) T: 04 92 45 02 15. E: guillestre@aol.com
**alanrogers.com/FR05110**

At a height of 800 metres, this attractive municipal site looks fresh and well kept. Located in a beautiful mountainous region, it is run under contract by a very welcoming young couple who are fully responsible for the day to day running of the site. English and Dutch are spoken. There are 190 grassy pitches separated by trees that give welcome shade with 185 for touring, all with 4-10A electricity. The excellent, clean facilities are immaculately kept. Although there are few amenities on site, most can be found in the town only 10 minutes walk away. The Monday market is well worth a visit.

**Facilities**

Three well appointed toilet blocks are clean and modern. Facilities for disabled visitors. Small shop, snack bar/takeaway (July/Aug). Heated, outdoor swimming pool (July/Aug). Play area. Boules. Bicycle hire. Only gas and electric barbecues are permitted. Internet access and WiFi (charged). Off site: Municipal heated swimming pool and tennis adjacent. Guillestre, restaurant, bars, shops and supermarket 800 m. Bicycle hire 1 km. Riding 3 km. Lake, river 3 km. Climbing, rafting, canoeing, canyoning.

**Open:** 15 May - 30 September.

**Directions**

Between Briançon and Gap on the RN94, at roundabout signed Guillestre, turn towards the village. Site is signed with the entrance in 900 m. GPS: 44.65854, 6.63816

**Charges guide**

| Per unit incl. 2 persons | |
|---|---|
| and electricity | € 15.50 - € 18.80 |
| extra person | € 3.00 - € 4.00 |
| child (under 10 yrs) | € 2.00 - € 2.60 |

**FREE** Alan Rogers Travel Card
Extra benefits and savings - see page 10

## Hyères
### Campéole Eurosurf

Campé**o**le

Plage de La Captel, F-83400 Hyères (Var) T: 04 94 58 00 20. E: eurosurf@campeole.com
**alanrogers.com/FR83690**

Facing towards the shimmering island of Porquerolles, Campéole Eurosurf has an enviable setting with direct access to a fine sandy beach. This is a large site with 402 pitches, of which just 13 are available for touring units. The remainder are occupied by mobile homes, chalets and fully equipped tents, available for rent. Pitches are mainly on sand, in the open and back onto the main road from which there is very likely to be road noise. Some of the overhanging branches from trees are very low so care should be taken when driving through the site to the pitches.

**Facilities**

The toilet blocks have showers and washbasins (some with cold water only). Facilities for disabled visitors. Baby room. Laundry facilities. Bar/restaurant. Snack bar. Shop. Takeaway. Games room. Playground. Diving school. Boat launching (charged). Sports area. Entertainment and activities. Internet point. WiFi in reception area (charged). Direct beach access. Mobile homes, chalets and tents for rent. Off site: Sentier des Douaniers coastal walk. Fishing. Etang des Pesquiers (bird sanctuary). Windsurfing. Riding.
**Open:** 14 March - 4 November.

**Directions**

Take the A57 motorway as far as Hyères. Then follow signs to Giens/Les Iles. The site is on the left hand side of the road, 1 km. after the village of La Capte. GPS: 43.0561, 6.1475

**Charges guide**

| Per unit incl. 2 persons | |
|---|---|
| and electricity | € 21.10 - € 43.00 |
| extra person | € 5.50 - € 9.30 |
| child (2-6 yrs) | € 3.00 - € 4.70 |

---

## Isle-sur-la Sorgue
### Camping Caravaning la Sorguette

871 Route d'Apt, F-84800 Isle-sur-la Sorgue (Vaucluse) T: 04 90 38 05 71. E: sorguette@wanadoo.fr
**alanrogers.com/FR84050**

This popular, well organised site is well placed, 1.5 km. from Isle-sur-la Sorgue. Arranged in groups of four, the 164 medium sized level pitches (124 for touring) all have 6/10A electricity. Each group is separated by tall hedges and most have a little shade during the day. In high season a few competitions are organised (boules or volleyball), plus some children's entertainment, but this is quite low key. Running alongside the site, the River Sorgue is only six kilometres from its source in the mountains. It is still very clear and used for canoeing, swimming and fishing.

**Facilities**

Well maintained toilet blocks. Washing machines. Units for disabled visitors. Baby room. Motorcaravan services. Fridge hire. Shop, bar, snacks (1/7-25/8). Entertainment in July/Aug. Play area, volleyball, half-court tennis, basketball. Canoe, bicycle hire. Internet point. Indian teepees, yurts; Mongolian circular tents and Inuit-style tents with kitchens. 40 mobile homes. WiFi throughout (charged). No twin-axle caravans. Off site: Indoor/outdoor swimming pools 2 km. Fishing and riding 5 km. Canoeing.
**Open:** 15 March - 15 October.

**Directions**

Site is 1.5 km. east of Isle-sur-la Sorgue on the D901 towards Apt. It is well signed from the town. GPS: 43.91488, 5.07758

**Charges guide**

| Per unit incl. 2 persons | |
|---|---|
| and electricity | € 21.50 - € 26.30 |
| extra person | € 6.05 - € 7.55 |
| child (1-11 yrs) | € 3.00 - € 3.80 |
| dog | € 2.50 - € 3.40 |

---

## La Colle-sur-Loup
### Camping les Pinèdes

Route du Pont de Pierre, F-06480 La Colle-sur-Loup (Alpes-Maritimes) T: 04 93 32 98 94.
E: info@lespinedes.com  **alanrogers.com/FR06100**

Les Pinèdes is 7 km. inland from the busy coast, at the centre of all the attractions of the Côte d'Azur, yet far enough away to be a peaceful retreat at the end of a busy day. Run by the third generation of family owners, the site is terraced on a wooded hillside where olives and vines used to grow. All the level pitches have electricity (6-10A), most also with water and they are separated by low bushes. Twelve new pitches at the top of the site and also a small children's pool have recently been completed. In May the evenings are alive with fireflies. A Sites et Paysages member.

**Facilities**

Two excellent new toilet blocks. One block has facilities for disabled visitors. Baby room. Shop, bakery. Bar, restaurant, takeaway. Swimming pool. New children's play area. Field for volleyball, basketball, football, archery, boules. Fitness area. Riding. Entertainment (July/Aug). Weekly walks in the hills June-Sept. New mobile homes to rent. WiFi. Twin-axle caravans not accepted. Off site: River fishing 50 m. Village 1 km. St Paul-de-Vence is nearby.
**Open:** 15 March - 30 September.

**Directions**

From A8 take D2 towards Vence. At Colle-sur-Loup roundabout take D6 signed Grasse, site on right in 3 km. at large sign after the restaurant entrance. GPS: 43.6817, 7.08335

**Charges 2013**

| Per unit incl. 2 persons | |
|---|---|
| and electricity | € 25.10 - € 40.60 |
| extra person | € 4.40 - € 6.00 |

---

For latest campsite news, availability and prices visit
# alanrogers.com

## La Mole
### Camping Pachacaïd

Route du Canadel, F-83310 La Mole (Var) T: 04 94 55 70 80. E: pacha@pachacaid.com
**alanrogers.com/FR83720**

Pachacaïd is a very popular holiday village on the edge of the Massif des Maures. Please note that there are no touring pitches here. The site is located 17 km. from Saint Tropez and 8 km. from Rayol Canadel with its famous creeks and beaches. At the heart of Pachacaïd is its amazing Niagara water park with seven massive water slides, a huge Californian-style swimming pool and numerous jacuzzis and other water features. Other on-site amenities are of a high standard, such as the Pacha Café restaurant and well stocked shop. The site extends over a 50 hectare pine forest, with mobile homes available for rent.

**Facilities**

Shop, bar, restaurant, café (all 30/4-18/9). Niagara water park (swimming pools and large water slides, 30/4-18/9). Water aerobics. Archery. Football. Volleyball. Play area. Entertainment and activities. Bicycle hire. Caravans for rent. Riding, bicycle and kayak activities organised. WiFi (charged). Off site: Riding 5 km. Beach 8 km. Golf 10 km. St Tropez 15 km. Azur Park (Gassin) 15 km.

**Open:** 6 April - 29 September.

**Directions**

From the A8, use the Le Luc exit and follow signs to St Tropez. On reaching Grimaud, take westbound N98 (Toulon) and continue beyond Cogolin and pass an aerodrome. Turn left following signs to site (before reaching La Mole). GPS: 43.190181, 6.470887

**Charges guide**

Contact the site for details.

---

## La Roche-des-Arnauds
### Camping le Parc des Sérigons

F-05400 La Roche-des-Arnauds (Hautes-Alpes) T: 04 92 57 81 77. E: contact@camping-serigons.com
**alanrogers.com/FR05160**

Set in woodlands and surrounded by wooded mountain scenery, this site gives the feeling of being with nature. The pitches are large and all numbered but are randomly situated amongst the trees with no obvious boundaries. Of the 94 touring pitches, 80 have electricity (5-10A). Mobile homes, chalets, bungalow tents and pre-erected furnished tents are available to rent. Located alongside the D994, just 15 km. from Gap and 1 km. from the small village of La Roche-des-Arnauds, the site is well placed to explore the various attractions the region has to offer.

**Facilities**

Three sanitary blocks include showers and some washbasins in cabins, one with facilities for disabled visitors. Washing machines. Motorcaravan service point. Outdoor swimming pool (unheated, 11/6-9/9). Shop (1/7-31/8). Bar, restaurant and takeaway (11/6-9/9). TV in bar. Tennis. Boules. Play areas. WiFi around bar area. Torch useful. Off site: La Roche-des-Arnauds 1 km. Veynes 10 km with markets. Lake for watersports 12 km.

**Open:** 1 April - 31 October.

**Directions**

From Gap follow D994 signed towards Orange, Valance and Veynes. Pass through small village of La Roche-des-Arnauds and site is signed on the right 1 km. beyond village. GPS: 44.56416, 5.9175

**Charges guide**

| Per unit incl. 2 persons | |
|---|---|
| and electricity | € 11.80 - € 22.60 |
| extra person | € 2.40 - € 4.70 |
| child (3-7 yrs) | € 1.70 - € 3.30 |

---

## Le Bar-sur-Loup
### Camping Caravaning les Gorges du Loup

965 chemin des Vergers, F-06620 Le Bar-sur-Loup (Alpes-Maritimes) T: 04 93 42 45 06.
E: info@lesgorgesduloup.com **alanrogers.com/FR06090**

Les Gorges du Loup is situated on a steep hillside above Grasse. The one kilometre lane which leads to the site is narrow with passing places. The 70 pitches are on level terraces, all with electricity and many have stupendous views. Some pitches are only suitable for tents and the site roads are quite steep. A quiet family site, there is no organised entertainment. Grasse is surrounded by fields of lavender, mimosa and jasmine and has been famous for the manufacture of perfume since the 16th century. The friendly and enthusiastic owners provide 4x4 assistance and there is a new parking area at the entrance.

**Facilities**

Clean toilet blocks with washbasins and hot showers. Laundry facilities. Reception, small shop, bread. Small bar/restaurant with terrace, takeaway (all 19/5-14/9). Swimming pool, small slide, diving board, but no pool for small children. Boules. Skittles. TV room, board games, library. WiFi (charged). Children's climbing frame, slide. Only gas barbecues permitted. Fridge hire. Chalets, mobile homes for hire. Off site: Bar-sur-Loup with its few shops, restaurants is only a 500 m. walk. Fishing 1 km. Golf, riding and bicycle hire 5 km. Beach 15 km.

**Open:** 6 April - 21 September.

**Directions**

From Grasse, D2085 Nice road. D3 briefly to Châteauneuf Pré du Lac. D2210 to Pont-de-Loup, Vence. Site signed on right. Pass village of Bar-sur-Loup on left, after sharp right turn, follow narrow access road 750 m (passing places). GPS: 43.7017, 6.9948

**Charges guide**

| Per unit incl. 2 persons | |
|---|---|
| and electricity | € 18.70 - € 30.00 |
| extra person | € 5.00 |

No credit cards.

**FREE** Alan Rogers Travel Card
Extra benefits and savings - see page 10

## Le Lavandou
### Camping Saint Pons

Avenue Maréchal Juin, F-83190 Le Lavandou (Var) T: 04 94 71 03 93. E: info@campingstpons.com

**alanrogers.com/FR83680**

Camping Saint Pons enjoys an attractive setting within walking distance of the delightful family resort of Le Lavandou. This is a relatively small, quiet and uncomplicated site extending over two hectares, with many flowering shrubs and bushes. There are 155 pitches here, well shaded and of a fair size. Most have electrical connections. A number of mobile homes are available for rent. There is no shop on site but there is a supermarket just 500 m. away. The Littoral cycle track runs close to the site and provides an appealing way of exploring the coast and a number of pretty Provençal villages. Saint Pons is a relaxed site with little by way of on-site entertainment which will be welcomed by many in this otherwise busy area. Le Lavandou is also one of the Riviera's more restrained resorts, named apparently after the river where local women came to do their washing because the water was so soft. The village boasts no fewer than 12 beaches, some wide and sandy, and others tiny, rocky coves. All can be reached by a small tourist train that runs along the coast. Boat trips are possible to the Ile du Levant, home to Heliopolis, Europe's first naturist resort, and also to the island of Porquerolles and as far afield as St Tropez.

**Facilities**

Two clean sanitary blocks with controllable pushbutton showers. Wet room for disabled visitors. Laundry facilities. Play area. Boules. Mobile homes for rent. Dogs are not accepted 5/7-26/8. Good English is spoken. Off site: Bar and restaurant next door. Le Lavandou 500 m. Nearest beach 800 m. Cycle tracks. Golf. Boat trips. Fishing.

**Open:** 1 May - 1 October.

**Directions**

From Hyères (A570) head east on D98 to Bormes-les-Mimosas, then southeast (D559) to Le Lavandou. Follow site signs. GPS: 43.136047, 6.354416

**Charges guide**

| | |
|---|---|
| Per unit incl. 2 persons and electricity | € 18.00 - € 32.90 |
| extra person | € 4.30 - € 6.20 |
| child (under 7 yrs) | € 3.10 - € 4.40 |

Camping *** SAINT-PONS — Camping*** Saint-Pons

Avenue Maréchal Juin - 83980 LE LAVANDOU
Tél : +33 (0)4 94 71 03 93 - Fax : +31 (0)4 94 71 09 46
info@campingstpons.com - www.campingstpons.com

## Le Muy
### RCN Domaine de la Noguière

1617 route de Fréjus, F-83490 Le Muy (Var) T: 04 94 45 13 78. E: noguiere@rcn.fr

**alanrogers.com/FR83090**

Domaine de la Noguière is located close to the town of Le Muy and is owned by RCN, a Dutch company with a chain of campsites in the Netherlands. Run by an enthusiastic young couple, this is a friendly and informal campsite. Set in 15 hectares, with delightful views of the beautiful Provençal scenery, it has 146 touring pitches, mainly level and with sizes to suit all units up to 120 sq.m. Reception has a small shop adjacent selling fresh bread daily, while the bar/restaurant serves local specialities. There is a good swimming pool complex with toboggan slides and a snack bar nearby. This site is ideally situated close to the Gorges du Verdon, yet only 16 km. from the Mediterranean beaches.

**Facilities**

Two modern sanitary buildings have been added with family showers and children's rooms. Toilets provide access for disabled visitors. Laundry facilities. Shop. Bar/restaurant with takeaway. Swimming pool complex with slides and snack bar (12/4-27/10). Meeting room with library and TV. Tennis. Boules. Games field. Play area. WiFi. Gas/electric barbecues only. Off site: Riding 5 km. Bicycle hire, golf, beach and sailing 15 km.

**Open:** 17 March - 27 October.

**Directions**

From A8 autoroute exit 36 Le Muy, take DN7 Le Muy. At roundabout in town, take direction Route de Fréjus. Site is 2 km. from centre of village. GPS: 43.46832, 6.59202

**Charges guide**

| | |
|---|---|
| Per unit incl. 2 persons, electricity and water | € 20.70 - € 45.65 |
| incl. up to 4 persons | € 25.90 - € 55.85 |
| Camping Cheques accepted. | |

For latest campsite news, availability and prices visit
# alanrogers.com

## Le Muy
### Parc Camping les Cigales

4 chemin du Jas de la Paro, F-83490 Le Muy (Var) T: 04 94 45 12 08. E: contact@camping-les-cigales-sud.fr
**alanrogers.com/FR83160**

Parc les Cigales is a pleasant site benefiting from the shady environment of cork umbrella pines, further enhanced by olives, palm trees and colourful shrubs. The terrain is typical of the area with rough, sloped and stony, dry ground but the pitches are of a good size, terraced where necessary and nestling amongst trees. There are 356 pitches in total, 200 for tourers with 10A electricity and 119 mobile homes and chalets to rent. The restaurant/bar area overlooks the pool complex including a children's pool with sloping beach effect. Convenient for the autoroute, this is a spacious family site away from the coast.

**Facilities**

Four sanitary blocks of varying size include facilities for disabled visitors. Laundry facilities. Shop, bar, restaurant and takeaway (1/4-30/9). Heated pool complex (19/3-15/10). An aqua park is planned. Adventure play area. Survival courses. Multisports area. Trampoline. Riding. Canoeing. Hang-gliding. Evening entertainment in season, disco twice weekly, daytime activities for children and senior citizens. Free WiFi around the restaurant area. No charcoal barbecues. Off site: Le Muy with shops, supermarket, markets and fishing 2 km. Golf 10 km.

**Open:** 15 March - 15 October.

**Directions**

From A8, Le Muy exit, site is signed (west of Le Muy on N7, 2 km). After the toll booth, at the first roundabout turn left. Site is well signed.
GPS: 43.46222, 6.54361

**Charges guide**

| Per unit incl. 2 persons | |
|---|---|
| and electricity | € 24.60 - € 40.35 |
| extra person | € 3.40 - € 10.20 |
| child (under 7 yrs) | € 2.25 - € 5.65 |
| dog | free - € 2.50 |

## Les Vigneaux
### Campéole le Courounba

Le Pont du Rif, D994, F-05120 Les Vigneaux (Hautes-Alpes) T: 04 92 23 02 09. E: courounba@campeole.com
**alanrogers.com/FR05140**

Le Courounba is a member of the Campéole group, located at the entrance to the magnificent Parc National des Ecrins. Pitches are shady and spacious, dispersed around 12 hectares of woodland. Many of the 160 touring pitches have superb views of the surrounding mountain scenery. Ninety mobile homes for rent (including specially adapted units for the disabled). There is also a good sized swimming pool with a water slide and other on-site amenities include two tennis courts and volleyball pitch. Adjacent to the site is a friendly bar/restaurant and a small, basic shop during high season only. There is dramatic mountain scenery all around. The Mont Brison is the highest limestone rock face in France and the Mont Pelvoux, at 3943 metres has an all year snow cap. Le Courounba is on the banks of the River Gyronde, popular for fishing. A little further afield, Briançon is a superb town, fortified by Vauban and worth a visit.

**Facilities**

Four modern sanitary blocks include washbasins and showers. Facilities for children and disabled visitors. Motorcaravan services. Washing machine. Heated swimming pool and water slide (all July/Aug). Volleyball. Tennis. Bouncy castle. Play area. Entertainment and activities in high season. Mobile homes for rent. WiFi (charged). Multisports court. Electric barbecues only on pitches. Off site: Adjacent bar/restaurant and basic shop. Fishing 100 m. Hiking and cycling. Riding, bicycle hire 5 km. White water sport. Rock climbing and bouldering.

**Open:** 22 May - 26 September.

**Directions**

The site is close to the village of Les Vigneaux, south of Briançon. From Briançon, head south on N94 as far as Prelles and then join the D4 to Les Vigneaux. The site is well indicated from here.
GPS: 44.82483, 6.52566

**Charges guide**

| Per unit incl. 2 persons | |
|---|---|
| and electricity | € 17.10 - € 26.00 |
| extra person | € 4.50 - € 6.50 |
| child (2-6 yrs) | free - € 4.50 |

## Les Issambres

### Camping Au Paradis des Campeurs

La Gaillarde-Plage, F-83380 Les Issambres (Var) T: 04 94 96 93 55
alanrogers.com/FR83080

Family owned and run, this popular site has 180 pitches, all with 6A electricity and 132 with water and drainage. The original pitches vary in size and shape but all are satisfactory and most have some shade. The newer pitches are all large and have rather less shade although trees and bushes are maturing nicely. There is no entertainment which gives peaceful nights. The gates are surveyed by CCTV (especially the beach gate) and a security man patrols all day. With direct access to a sandy beach (via an underpass) and being so well maintained, the site has become deservedly popular so it is essential to book for June, July and August.

**Facilities**

Excellent, refurbished, well maintained toilet blocks. Facilities for babies and children with shower at suitable height. En-suite for disabled visitors. Washing machines and dryer. Motorcaravan services. Shop, restaurant and takeaway service (all season). TV room. Internet and WiFi. Excellent play areas with top quality safety bases, catering for the under and over 5s. Boules. Car wash area. Mobile homes for rent. Off site: Bicycle hire 2.5 km. Riding 3 km. Golf 6 km.

**Open:** 1 April - 3 October.

**Directions**

Site is signed from N98 coast road at La Gaillarde, 2 km. south of St Aygulf. GPS: 43.36593, 6.71230

**Charges guide**

| | |
|---|---|
| Per unit incl. 2 persons and electricity | € 19.00 - € 29.00 |
| incl. water and drainage | € 21.00 - € 33.00 |
| extra person | € 6.00 |
| child (under 5 yrs) | € 3.00 |

## Les Vigneaux

### Campéole les Vaudois

Campé●le

La Ruinette, F-05120 Les Vigneaux (Hautes-Alpes) T: 04 92 23 02 09. E: vaudois@campeole.com
alanrogers.com/FR05150

Les Vaudois is located at the edge of the Parc National des Ecrins. The site stands on the banks of the River Gyronde and at the foot of Mont Brison, France's highest limestone rock face. There are very few amenities on site but guests are able to use the facilities at the sister site, le Courounba, around 2 km. away. Amenities there include a swimming pool (with water slide) and a bar/restaurant. There are 108 touring pitches at les Vaudois, most equipped with electricity (6A). The site is ideal for groups and clubs seeking adventure sports and is well located for a wide range of activities, including white-water rafting, rock climbing and mountain biking. The Parc National des Ecrins is a vast area, one of only nine French national parks, established back in 1913 as the Parc National Bérarde. There are over 700 km. of marked footpaths in the park and a great wealth of wildlife.

**Facilities**

At le Courounba: Laundry facilities. Shop (fresh bread daily in high season). Bar/restaurant/snack bar (high season). Heated swimming pool with slides and paddling pool (lifeguard; no Bermuda shorts July/Aug). Children's entertainment programme (high season). TV/games room. Play area. Tennis. Volleyball. Tourist information. Gas and electric barbecues only. Off site: Bicycle hire and fishing 4 km. Riding 5 km. Cycle and walking tracks. Tennis. Canoeing. White-water sports on the Gyronde.

**Open:** 29 June - 1 September.

**Directions**

From Briançon, take N94 towards Prelles and St Martin de Queyrières, and then follow signs for l'Argentière. Take the D104A to La Batie des Vigneaux and then continue to Les Vigneaux and the campsite. GPS: 44.8213, 6.5355

**Charges guide**

| | |
|---|---|
| Per unit incl. 2 persons and electricity | € 15.10 - € 18.90 |

Advantage all the way

alan rogers Travel Card

Got yours yet?

Extra benefits and savings - see page 10

For latest campsite news, availability and prices visit

**alanrogers.com**

# Mandelieu-la-Napoule

## Camping Caravaning les Cigales

505 avenue de la Mer, F-06210 Mandelieu-la-Napoule (Alpes-Maritimes) T: 04 93 49 23 53.
E: campingcigales@wanadoo.fr **alanrogers.com/FR06080**

It is hard to imagine that such a quiet, peaceful site could be in the middle of such a busy town and so near Cannes. The entrance (quite easily missed) has large electronic gates that ensure that the site is very secure. There are only 115 pitches (42 mobile homes) so this is quite a small, personal site. There are three pitch sizes, from small ones for tents to pitches for larger units and all have electricity (6A), some fully serviced. All are level with much needed shade in summer, although the sun will get through in winter when it is needed. The site is alongside the Canal de Siagne and for a fee, small boats can be launched at La Napoule, then moored outside the campsite's side gate. Les Cigales is open all year so it is useful for the Monte Carlo Rally, the Cannes Film Festival and the Mimosa Festival, all held out of the main season. English is spoken.

### Facilities

Well appointed, clean, heated toilet blocks. Excellent facilities for babies and disabled visitors. Laundry area. Motorcaravan services. Restaurant and takeaway (May-Oct). Attractive swimming pool, heated according to the weather conditions, and large sunbathing area (April-Oct). Play area. River fishing. WiFi (free). Only gas barbecues allowed. Max 1 dog per pitch. Off site: Beach 800 m. The town is an easy walk. Two golf courses within 1 km. Railway station 1 km. for trains to Cannes, Nice, Antibes, Monte Carlo. Hypermarket 2 km. Bus stop 30 m.

**Open:** All year.

### Directions

From A8, exit 40, bear right. Remain in right-hand lane, continue right (Plages-Ports, Creche-Campings). Casino supermarket on right. Continue under motorway to T-junction. Turn left, site is 60 m. on left opposite Chinese restaurant. Other approaches have a 3.3 m. height restriction. GPS: 43.5391, 6.94275

### Charges 2013

| | |
|---|---|
| Per unit incl. 2 persons and electricity | € 38.20 - € 58.20 |
| extra person | € 4.00 - € 8.60 |
| dog | € 1.50 |

# Mandelieu-la-Napoule

## Camping de l'Argentière

264 avenue du Bon Puits, F-06210 Mandelieu-la-Napoule (Alpes-Maritimes) T: 04 93 49 95 04.
E: contact@campingdelargentiere.com **alanrogers.com/FR06240**

This well situated site, currently under dynamic new ownership, is open all year and is located in the stylish resort of Mandelieu-la-Napoule, with easy access to Cannes and Nice. There are 62 well shaded pitches with 25 for touring units, most with electricity. Mobile homes for rent are placed on the remaining 37 pitches. Many trees and shrubs have been planted around the site, including eucalyptus and mimosa. The nearest beach (La Napoule) is 800 m. Several municipal tennis courts are adjacent, and the Mandelieu golf club is also very close. The new owners are working hard to update and have completed a new toilet block incorporating the latest equipment.

### Facilities

New toilet block with good facilities. Laundry. Small shop. Bar. Restaurant. Play area. Library. Gym. Tourist information. WiFi (charged). Mobile homes for rent. Off site: Bus and train services nearby. Nearest beach 800 m. Shops and restaurants. Tennis. Golf. Fishing. Cannes.

**Open:** All year.

### Directions

Leave A8 motorway at exit 40 and follow signs to Mandelieu Centre. Join the N7 towards Cannes, and, at the roundabout follow signs to the campsite. GPS: 43.5254, 6.9334

### Charges guide

| | |
|---|---|
| Per unit incl. 2 persons and electricity | € 23.00 - € 29.00 |
| extra person | € 4.00 - € 4.50 |

**FREE** Alan Rogers Travel Card
Extra benefits and savings - see page 10

## Martigues
### Flower Camping le Marius

Route de la Saulce, la Couronne, F-13500 Martigues (Bouches du Rhône) T: 04 42 80 70 29.
E: contact@camping-marius.com **alanrogers.com/FR13140**

East of the Camargue and south of the Etang de Berre, this is the protected and wild coastline between Marseille and Martigues. Camping Marius is tucked away beside a calanque (or inlet) on this rocky coast. A private gate leads to steps up and then down through pine trees to the beach (200 m) across the rocky cliffs. The site is a colourful oasis, regularly laid out with shade from shrubs and trees. It provides 108 pitches, of which 62 are occupied by mobile homes for rent and 21 are seasonal pitches, leaving 25 for touring units (with electricity). Although rather small each pitch has its own sink and water supply.

**Facilities**

A good modern toilet block is supplemented by a smaller one. Baby bath. Facilities for disabled visitors. Very small shop. Bar and restaurant. Play area. Bicycles and canoes can be borrowed. Activities and entertainment (until 2/10). Direct access via steep steps and some rough walking to beach 200 m. Chalets for rent. Max. 1 dog accepted. Gas barbecues only. WiFi (free). Off site: Snack bar 200 m. Beach 200 m (steps). La Couronne with shops and restaurants and railway station. Riding 5 km.

**Open:** 1 April - 31 October.

**Directions**

Approach Martigues from the north on the D5 and cross the Canal de Caronte, continuing south on the D5, then D49 to La Couronne. At roundabout on outskirts of La Couronne, turn left for Sausset-les-Pins and Saint Croix. On A55 from Marseille take exit for Carry-le-Rouet. GPS: 43.335, 5.0673

**Charges guide**

| | |
|---|---|
| Per unit incl. 2 persons and electricity (6A) | € 22.00 - € 31.00 |
| extra person | € 4.00 - € 7.00 |

## Montagnac-Montpezat
### Village Center Côteau de la Marine

Route de Baudinaud, F-04500 Montagnac-Montpezat (Alpes-de-Haute-Provence) T: 04 99 57 21 21.
E: contact@village-center.com **alanrogers.com/FR04200**

Located to the west of the Lac de Sainte Croix and the Gorges du Verdon, Côteau de la Marine is a well equipped site with a fine setting. The site is a member of the Village Center group and has direct access to the River Verdon and its own small harbour. There are 49 touring pitches (60-120 sq.m), mostly with electrical connections (10A). These are situated at the bottom end of the site overlooking the river but it is quite a steep climb up to the main site facilities. There is plenty of activity in high season, with a club for children and various competitions and tournaments.

**Facilities**

Two toilet blocks include controllable pushbutton showers and washbasins. Facilities for disabled visitors. Laundry. Small supermarket. Restaurant/snack bar and takeaway. Bar. Swimming and paddling pools. Play area. Sports field. Activity and entertainment programme. Direct river access. WiFi (charged). Mobile homes, chalets and tents for rent. Off site: Watersports centre adjacent. Montagnac-Montpezat 5 km. Riez with supermarket, shops, bars and restaurants 10 km.

**Open:** 8 April - 2 October.

**Directions**

Approaching from the north (Gap), leave the A51 at exit 19 (La Brillane) and follow signs to Oraison. From here, head south on D4 and then D15 to Valensole. Then head southeast on D6 to Riez and then follow signs to Montagnac-Montpezat. Site is clearly signed from here. GPS: 43.74768, 6.09845

**Charges guide**

| | |
|---|---|
| Per unit incl. 2 persons and electricity | € 16.00 - € 29.00 |

Camping Cheques accepted.

## Montclar
### Yelloh! Village l'Etoile des Neiges

F-04140 Montclar (Alpes-de-Haute-Provence) T: 04 66 73 97 39. E: info@yellohvillage-etoile-des-neiges.com
**alanrogers.com/FR04080**

This attractive, family run site near the mountain village and ski resort of St Jean Montclar is open most of the year. Being at an altitude of 1,300 m. the nights can get quite cold in summer. The 130 shady, terraced pitches, with 70 for touring, are separated by small shrubs and alpine trees. All pitches are close to electricity and water points. The bar and restaurant overlooks the two outdoor swimming pools. A new indoor complex with pool, gym, jacuzzi, sauna and steam room makes a splendid addition.

**Facilities**

Central toilet block (heated in winter) and facilities for disabled visitors. Two washing machines. Motorcaravan services. Bar/restaurant. Two outdoor swimming pools and new indoor complex with heated pool, gym, jacuzzi, sauna and steam room (all 15/5-9/9). Tennis. Boules. Play areas. Multisport pitch. Rafting, walking (July/Aug). WiFi. Off site: Shops, bicycle hire and riding in village a few minutes walk. Fishing 1.5 km. Beach 7 km.

**Open:** All year excl. 26/3-29/4 and 16/9-19/12.

**Directions**

Site is 35 km. south of Gap via D900B. Beyond Serre Ponçon, turn right, D900 (Selonnet, St Jean Montclar). Entering St Jean Montclar turn left, pass shops, fork right down lane to site in 250 m. Roads are steep and icy in winter. GPS: 44.40921, 6.34826

**Charges guide**

| | |
|---|---|
| Per unit incl. 2 persons and electricity (6A) | € 25.00 - € 33.00 |
| extra person | € 7.00 |

For latest campsite news, availability and prices visit
## alanrogers.com

## Moustiers-Sainte-Marie
### Camping Manaysse

Rue Fréderic Mistral, F-04360 Moustiers-Sainte-Marie (Alpes-de-Haute-Provence) T: 04 92 74 66 71.
E: manaysse@orange.fr **alanrogers.com/FR04190**

Manaysse is a little gem of a family campsite on the outskirts of the famous hillside village of Moustiers-Sainte-Marie (900 m) and is ideal for exploring the magnificent Gorges du Verdon region. There are 97 terraced pitches on grass and gravel, with 93 for touring (electricity 6/10A). Some of the pitches are on a slight slope, however those at the top of the site have a beautiful view of Moustiers-Sainte-Marie. There are both shady and sunny pitches available. Large units should approach with care as there is a short, steep incline up to reception.

**Facilities**

Simple but clean toilet blocks. Facilities for disabled visitors. Washing machines. Bread is delivered. Small play area. Boules. Minigolf. No charcoal barbecues. Torches may be useful. WiFi (charged). Off site: Fishing 600 m. Moustiers 900 m. Bicycle hire 2 km. Lake, beach, water sports 4 km. Riding 12 km. Magnificent region waiting to be explored.

**Open:** 1 April - 2 November.

**Directions**

Moustiers is between Riez and Gorges du Verdon on the D952. From Riez turn north at first roundabout in Moustiers, site signed, entrance in 200 m. GPS: 43.84486, 6.21566

**Charges guide**

| | |
|---|---|
| Per unit incl. 2 persons and electricity (6/10A) | € 13.40 - € 14.40 |
| extra person | € 3.70 |

No credit cards.

---

## Orgon
### Camping la Vallée Heureuse

Impasse Lavau, F-13660 Orgon (Bouches du Rhône) T: 04 90 44 17 13.
E: information@camping-lavalleeheureuse.com **alanrogers.com/FR13310**

Camping la Vallée Heureuse lies hidden in a valley of outstanding natural beauty, surrounded by cliffs and steep, wooded hills. The site is very popular with hikers and climbers. It is also close to the parks of the Cévennes, the Carmargue and the Luberon making it an ideal centre for touring this very interesting region, as well as the coast a little further south. The site is terraced with 180 stony, grassy pitches, some quite large (good for large outfits) and many with shade and 16A electricity. The swimming pool with sunbathing area, is ideal for unwinding at the end of a day exploring the region.

**Facilities**

Modern toilet block with all necessary facilities. Small shop. Bar (from May). Restaurant (July/Aug). Swimming and paddling pools (from May). Solarium. Play area. Minigolf. Boules. Fishing. Bicycle hire. TV room. Internet point. WiFi (free). Entertainment programme and children's club. Off site: Restaurant and snacks 1 km. Lake swimming and fishing close by. Rock climbing walls. Golf 10 km. Cavaillon 3 km. St Rémy 15 km.

**Open:** 1 April - 15 September.

**Directions**

Leave A7 autoroute at exit 25 signed St Rémy-de-Provence. Shortly, at roundabout, take D26 to Orgon and then the N7. Site signed on the right south of the village. Go through industrial area to unspoilt countryside beyond. GPS: 43.781891, 5.040225

**Charges guide**

| | |
|---|---|
| Per unit incl. 2 persons and electricity | € 19.32 - € 24.00 |
| extra person | € 5.00 - € 6.50 |

---

## Pernes les Fontaines
### Camping les Fontaines

125 chemin de la Chapelette, route de Sudre, F-84210 Pernes-les-Fontaines (Vaucluse) T: 04 90 46 82 55.
E: contact@campingfontaines.com **alanrogers.com/FR84190**

Camping les Fontaines is a small, family run site set in two and a half hectares, with magnificent views of Mont Ventoux and the mountains of the Vaucluse. There are 90 pitches in total, with 60 for tourers. Good shade on most of the level pitches is provided by mature trees and shrubs, electricity (6A) and water are nearby. On-site amenities include a 200 sq.m. lagoon-style pool, an excellent restaurant and cocktail bar with a wide choice of smoothies. The whole site enjoys WiFi coverage at no extra charge. A warm welcome awaits the holidaymaker from the owners, Pierine and Pascal.

**Facilities**

Modern, clean sanitary block. Small nursery for babies and children and good facilities for disabled visitors. Laundry. Motorcaravan service point. Bar, restaurant with decked terrace overlooking the pool, takeaway food (all May-Sept). Lagoon-style pool with large 'beach' area. Small shop in reception selling basics and fresh bread daily. Play area. Free WiFi over site. Off site: Bicycle hire, riding 2 km. Golf, fishing 10 km.

**Open:** 1 April - 20 October.

**Directions**

From autoroute A7 take exit 23 Avignon Nord, towards Carpentras. Then D16 Entraigues. Follow signs for Pernes-les-Fontaines. Site is signed from roundabout in town. GPS: 44.006351, 5.038771

**Charges guide**

| | |
|---|---|
| Per unit incl. 2 persons and electricity | € 19.90 - € 31.70 |
| extra person | € 5.50 - € 7.70 |

Camping Cheques accepted.

---

**FREE** Alan Rogers Travel Card
Extra benefits and savings - see page 10

## Orpierre
### Camping des Princes d'Orange

F-05700 Orpierre (Hautes-Alpes) T: 04 92 66 22 53. E: campingorpierre@wanadoo.fr

**alanrogers.com/FR05000**

This attractive, terraced site, set on a hillside above the village has been thoughtfully developed. Muriel, the owner, speaks excellent English and the genuine, friendly welcome means many families return year upon year, bringing in turn new generations. Divided into five terraces, each with its own toilet block, some of its 100 generously sized pitches (96 for touring) enjoy good shade from trees and have electricity connections (10A). In high season, one terrace is reserved as a one-star camping area for young people. Orpierre has an enchanting maze of medieval streets and houses, almost like a trip back through the centuries. Whether you choose to drive, climb, walk or cycle, there is plenty of wonderful scenery to discover in the immediate vicinity, whilst not far away, some exhilarating hang-gliding and parascending can be enjoyed. It is renowned as a world class rock climbing venue, with over 600 climbing routes in the surrounding mountains. For those seeking to 'get away from it all' in an area of outstanding natural beauty, there can be few more tranquil sites. There can be no doubt that you will be made most welcome and will enjoy the quiet splendours the region has to offer.

**Facilities**

Six well equipped toilet blocks. Baby bath. Laundry facilities. Bread. Bar (1/4-31/10). Heated swimming pool, paddling pool (15/6-15/9). Play area. Boules. Games room. Fridge hire. Only gas barbecues are permitted. Free WiFi around reception area. Off site: Orpierre with a few shops and bicycle hire 500 m. Fishing 7 km. Shopping centre Laragne 12 km. Riding 19 km. Hang-gliding. Parascending. Rock climbing. Walking. Mountain biking.

**Open:** 1 April - 31 October.

**Directions**

Turn off N75 road at Eyguians onto the D30. Site is signed on left at crossroads in the centre of Orpierre village. GPS: 44.31121, 5.69677

**Charges 2013**

| | |
|---|---|
| Per unit incl. 2 persons and electricity | € 23.00 - € 30.00 |

No credit cards.

Camping Cheques accepted.

05700 Orpierre
Tel: 0033 492 662 253
Fax: 0033 492 663 108
campingorpierre@wanadoo.fr
www.campingorpierre.com

## Puget-sur-Argens
### Camping Club la Bastiane

1056 chemin de Suvières, F-83480 Puget-sur-Argens (Var) T: 04 94 55 55 94. E: info@labastiane.com

**alanrogers.com/FR83040**

La Bastiane is an attractive, well established site which celebrated its 40th anniversary in 2012. It has good amenities and is well located for exploring the Côte d'Azur and with easy access to nearby beaches. There are 180 pitches here of which 47 are reserved for touring. They are generally of a good size and are all supplied with electrical connections (10A). The terrain is somewhat undulating but most of the pitches are on level terraces. There is a good swimming pool and a range of amenities including a shop, bar and restaurant with a well priced menu.

**Facilities**

Three toilet blocks, clean and very well maintained. Facilities for disabled visitors. Laundry facilities. Shop, bar, restaurant and takeaway. Heated swimming pool. Tennis. Multisport terrain. Children's club. Play area. Games/TV room. Bicycle hire. Evening entertainment in peak season. Excursions. Only electric barbecues. WiFi throughout (charged). Max. 1 dog. Mobile homes and chalets for rent. Off site: Riding 500 m. Fishing 3 km. Beach 7 km.

**Open:** 11 April - 20 October.

**Directions**

Leave A8 at exit 37 (Puget), take right turn at first roundabout (signed Roquebrune), join N7. Turn right, first traffic lights (200 m), then left at roundabout. Site signed from here, on the right 2.5 km. from the motorway. GPS: 43.46966, 6.67845

**Charges guide**

| | |
|---|---|
| Per unit incl. 2 persons and electricity | € 18.00 - € 44.00 |

For latest campsite news, availability and prices visit
# alanrogers.com

## Quinson
### Village Center les Prés du Verdon

F-04500 Quinson (Alpes-de-Haute-Provence) T: 04 99 57 21 21. E: contact@village-center.com

**alanrogers.com/FR04230**

This family site is attractively located close to the River Verdon, and it is a good base for exploring the famous gorges. The site boasts a fine pool complex with a large main pool and separate paddling pool. There are 70 touring pitches here (from 70 to 110 sq. m), some well shaded and others rather sunnier. Most are equipped with electrical connections. A further 131 pitches are used for mobile homes and bungalow tents, most of which are available for rent. This is a great region for an active holiday. Popular activities include rafting, canoeing on the Verdon river and canyoning.

**Facilities**

Two toilet blocks have controllable pushbutton showers and washbasins. Wet room for disabled visitors. Baby room. Swimming pool with paddling pool. Play area. TV room. Children's club. Volleyball. Entertainment and activity programme. Off site: Tennis just beyond site entrance. River, lake, fishing and canoeing all 100 m. Supermarket 200 m. Climbing 500 m. Friday morning market in Quinson during summer.

**Open:** 6 April - 30 September.

**Directions**

Approaching on A51 motorway, head for Digne les Bains and leave at exit 17 (St Paul-les-Durance and Gréoux Les Bains). After Gréoux, follow signs to Quinson and Musée de la Préhistoire. The site is then clearly signed. GPS: 43.69713, 6.04162

**Charges guide**

| Per unit incl. 2 persons | |
|---|---|
| and electricity | € 14.00 - € 18.00 |
| extra person | € 3.00 - € 5.00 |

Camping Cheques accepted.

## Ramatuelle
### Yelloh! Village les Tournels

Route de Camarat, F-83350 Ramatuelle (Var) T: 04 94 55 90 90. E: info@yellohvillage-les-tournels.com

**alanrogers.com/FR83210**

Les Tournels is a large site set on a hillside and pitches have panoramic views of the Gulf of Saint Tropez and Pampelonne beach. The hillside is covered in parasol pines and old olive trees. The pitches are reasonably level and shady, of variable size, most with electricity. The swimming pool, play area, shop and bar may be some distance away. The site has a superb new spa centre with gym, sauna and jacuzzi, with an excellent pool alongside, all reserved for over 18s, and a new restaurant with a large terrace.

**Facilities**

Well equipped toilet blocks, some heated, baby baths, children's WCs, facilities for disabled visitors. Laundry facilities. Bar and restaurant (1/4-30/10). Takeaway. Bar and disco well away from most pitches. Large heated swimming pool (1/4-30/10). Fitness centre and pool. Play area. Boules. Archery. Miniclub (over 5 yrs). Electric and gas barbecues permitted. Off site: Shopping centre with shuttle bus service 500 m. Beach 1.5 km. Golf 6 km.

**Open:** 1 April - 7 January.

**Directions**

From A8 exit 36 take D25 to Ste Maxime, then D98 towards St Tropez. Take D93 to Ramatuelle. Site is clearly marked after 9 km. GPS: 43.20596, 6.65083

**Charges guide**

| Per unit incl. 2 persons | |
|---|---|
| and electricity and water | € 17.00 - € 62.00 |
| extra person | € 7.00 - € 8.00 |
| child (3-6 yrs) | free - € 7.00 |

## Ramatuelle
### Campéole la Croix du Sud

Campé●le

Route des Plages, CD93, F-83350 Ramatuelle (Var) T: 04 94 55 51 23. E: croix-du-sud@campeole.com

**alanrogers.com/FR83710**

La Croix du Sud is perched on a little hill and pleasantly shaded by parasol pines and eucalyptus trees. The nearby fine sandy beach of Pampelonne is maybe the most celebrated in France, and famed for its association with St Tropez (although it is actually closer to Ramatuelle!). There are 120 pitches here, of which just 13 are available for touring units. Pitches are well shaded and mostly equipped with 6A electricity. Other pitches are occupied by mobile homes, chalets and tents, available for rent. The beach (Pampelonne) is 1.6 km. away and can be accessed by cycle track with just one road to cross.

**Facilities**

Sanitary facilities include a baby room but there is no provision for disabled visitors. Shop, restaurant, bar/snack bar (all 1/5-30/9). Takeaway pizza (all season). Swimming pool (1/5-30/9). Children's pool. Games room. Playground. Sports field. Activity and entertainment programme. Bicycle hire. WiFi over part of site (charged). Mobile homes, chalets and tents for rent. Gas barbecues only. Off site: Nearest beach 2.5 km. Fishing 5 km. Golf. Walking and mountain biking. St Tropez. Ramatuelle.

**Open:** 1 April - 14 October.

**Directions**

From the A8 (La Provençale) motorway take the exit to Le Luc. Take the D558 (La Garde-Freinet and Saint Tropez), then D93 (Ramatuelle). In Ramatuelle, follow the signs to Les Plages and Pampelonne, at the second roundabout go straight on for 1.5 km. then left to site. GPS: 43.21422, 6.64096

**Charges guide**

| Per unit incl. 2 persons | |
|---|---|
| and electricity | € 21.10 - € 44.50 |
| extra person | € 5.50 - € 9.30 |

**FREE** Alan Rogers Travel Card
Extra benefits and savings - see page 10

## Régusse
### Camping les Lacs du Verdon

Domaine de Roquelande, F-83630 Régusse (Var) T: 04 94 70 17 95. E: info@lacs-verdon.com

**alanrogers.com/FR83140**

In beautiful countryside and within easy reach of the Grand Canyon du Verdon and its nearby lakes, this site is only 90 minutes from Cannes. It is now part of the Homair Vacances chain and is currently run by Christophe Laurent and his team who are immensely proud of their site and the high standard they have achieved. The 30 acre wooded park is divided in two by a minor road. The 480 very stony but level pitches (rock pegs advised) are marked and separated by stones and trees. Of these, 107 are available for touring units, many of an irregular shape, but all of average size with 16A electricity (long leads may be necessary). The site is very attractive, clean and well cared for and is most suitable for families.

**Facilities**

Modernised toilet blocks have mainly British style WCs and some washbasins in cubicles. Laundry facilities. Small supermarket. Bar. Restaurant and pizzeria. Heated pool complex. Artificial grass tennis courts. Minigolf. Outdoor exercise equipment. Boules. Bicycle hire. Playground. TV and teenage games room. Entertainment. Discos, dances and theme nights. Electric barbecues only. WiFi (charged). Off site: Régusse 2.5 km. Aups 7 km. Beach 15 km.

**Open:** 29 April - 23 September.

**Directions**

Leave A8 motorway at St Maximin and take D560 northeast (Barjols). At Barjols turn left on D71 (Montmeyan), turn right on D30 (Régusse) and follow site signs. GPS: 43.6602, 6.1511

**Charges guide**

| Per unit incl. 1 or 2 persons | |
|---|---|
| and electricity | € 15.00 - € 26.00 |
| extra person | € 3.00 - € 5.50 |
| child (3-6 yrs) | free - € 4.50 |

---

## Saint Apollinaire
### Campéole le Clos du Lac

Campéⓞle

Route des Lacs, F-05160 Saint Apollinaire (Hautes-Alpes) T: 04 92 44 27 43. E: clos-du-lac@campeole.com

**alanrogers.com/FR05130**

Le Clos du Lac can be found close to the little mountain village of St Apollinaire on the southern fringe of the immense Ecrins National Park. The site is at an altitude of 1450 m. and has 68 pitches including 50 for touring units (most with 7A electricity), and 18 mobile homes. Many of the pitches have fine views all around. There is a small lake nearby, for 'no kill' fly fishing, and also for swimming. A special astronomy week is held in August to watch the night sky. The nearby Boscodon forest has been officially acknowledged as the least polluted place in France. Access to the site is via a 2.2 km. steep, single track and therefore not suitable for large units. The Lac de Serre Ponçon is popular for water sports and the site is well located for exploring this mountainous landscape. Montagne aux Marmottes animal park is nearby, as is the Cathedral of Notre Dame du Réal at Embrun. Le Clos du Lac is a good base for walking and mountain biking and the site's friendly managers will be pleased to recommend possible itineraries.

**Facilities**

A new, modern sanitary block provides preset showers and open style washbasins. Good facilities for babies and disabled visitors. Laundry facilities. Shop (July/Aug). New wellness centre includes jacuzzi, sauna and showers. Play area. Tourist information. Mobile homes for rent. No barbecues on pitches, communal area provided. WiFi on part of site. Off site: St Apollinaire (shops and restaurants). Canoe hire. Fishing. Minigolf. Watersports. Hiking and mountain biking. Bicycle hire. National Park of Les Ecrins.

**Open:** 21 May - 24 September.

**Directions**

St Apollinaire is on the north side of Lac de Serre Ponçon. From Gap head west on N94 (Embrun). At Chorges join the D9 to St Apollinaire from where the site is well indicated. GPS: 44.5647, 6.3652

**Charges guide**

| Per unit incl. 2 persons | |
|---|---|
| and electricity | € 15.10 - € 19.30 |
| extra person | € 3.80 - € 5.40 |
| child (2-6 yrs) | free - € 2.50 |
| dog | € 1.80 - € 2.00 |

## Roquebrune-sur-Argens
### Camping Caravaning Leï Suves

Quartier du Blavet, F-83520 Roquebrune-sur-Argens (Var) T: 04 94 45 43 95.
E: camping.lei.suves@wanadoo.fr **alanrogers.com/FR83030**

This quiet, pretty site is a few kilometres inland from the coast, 2 km. north of the N7. Close to the unusual Roquebrune rock, it is within easy reach of Saint Tropez, Sainte Maxime, Saint Raphaël and Cannes. The site entrance is appealing – wide and spacious, with a large bank of well-tended flowers. Mainly on a gently sloping hillside, the 310 pitches are terraced with shade provided by the many cork trees which give the site its name. All pitches have electricity and access to water. A brand new, well appointed toilet block was opened in 2012. There is a pleasant pool and a new children's pool beside the bar/restaurant and entertainment area. It is possible to walk in the surrounding woods. There are 150 mobile homes available to rent.

### Facilities

Modern, well kept toilet blocks include facilities for disabled visitors, washing machines and dryers. Shop (2/4-30/9). Good sized swimming pool, paddling pool. Bar, terrace, snack bar, takeaway (all 30/3-15/10). Outdoor stage near the bar for evening entertainment in high season. Excellent play area. Table tennis, tennis, sports area. WiFi over whole site. Only gas barbecues are permitted. Off site: Bus stop at site entrance. Riding 1 km. Fishing 3 km. Bicycle hire 5 km. Golf 7 km. Beach at St Aygulf 15 km.

**Open:** 30 March - 15 October.

### Directions

Leave autoroute at Le Muy and take the N7 towards St Raphaël. Turn left at roundabout onto D7 heading north signed La Bouverie (site also signed). Site on right in 2 km. GPS: 43.47793, 6.63881

### Charges 2013

| Per unit incl. 2 persons | |
|---|---|
| and electricity | € 26.50 - € 48.00 |
| incl. 3 persons | € 28.50 - € 51.50 |
| child (under 7 yrs) | € 4.20 - € 7.10 |
| dog | € 2.00 - € 3.50 |

## Roquebrune-sur-Argens

### Camping Domaine de la Bergerie

Vallée du Fournel, route du Col-du-Bougnon, F-83520 Roquebrune-sur-Argens (Var) T: 04 98 11 45 45.
E: info@domainelabergerie.com  **alanrogers.com/FR83170**

This excellent site near the Côte d'Azur will take you away from all the bustle of the Mediterranean to total relaxation amongst the cork, oak, pine and mimosa in its woodland setting. The 60 hectare site is well spread out with semi-landscaped areas for mobile homes and 200 separated pitches for touring caravans and tents. All pitches average over 80 sq.m. and have electricity, with those in one area also having water and drainage. The restaurant/bar, a converted farm building, is surrounded by shady patios, whilst inside it oozes character with high beams and archways leading to intimate corners. Activities are organised daily and, in the evening, shows, cabarets, discos, cinema, karaoke and dancing at the amphitheatre prove popular (possibly until midnight). A superb new pool complex supplements the original pool, with further outdoor pools with slides and a river feature, a jacuzzi, sauna, Turkish bath, massage, reflexology and gym.

**Facilities**

Four new toilet blocks are kept clean and include washbasins in cubicles, facilities for babies and disabled visitors. Supermarket. Bar/restaurant. Takeaway. Pool complex with indoor pool (1/4-15/10) and fitness centre (body building, sauna, gym, etc). Tennis. Archery. Roller skating. Minigolf. English speaking children's club. Mini-farm for children. Fishing. WiFi throughout (charged). Only gas barbecues permitted. Off site: Riding and golf 2 km. Bicycle hire 7 km. Beach, St Aygulf and Ste Maxime 7 km. Water skiing and rock climbing nearby.

**Open:** 28 April - 30 September
(mobile homes 1 March - 15 November).

**Directions**

Leave A8 at Le Muy exit on D7 towards Roquebrune. At Roquebrune proceed for a further 9 km. then at roundabout turn right on D8 signed St Aygulf. Continue for 2 km. to site on the right. GPS: 43.3988, 6.675417

**Charges guide**

| | |
|---|---|
| Per unit incl. 2 persons | € 20.50 - € 48.00 |
| incl. electricity, water and drainage | € 24.50 - € 54.00 |
| extra person | € 5.80 - € 11.50 |
| child (under 7 yrs) | € 4.30 - € 8.00 |

For latest campsite news, availability and prices visit
**alanrogers.com**

# Roquebrune-sur-Argens

## Camping les Pêcheurs

F-83520 Roquebrune-sur-Argens (Var) T: 04 94 45 71 25. E: info@camping-les-pecheurs.com

alanrogers.com/FR83200

Les Pêcheurs will appeal to families who appreciate natural surroundings with many activities, cultural and sporting. Interspersed with mobile homes, the 110 good sized touring pitches (10A electricity) are separated by trees or flowering bushes. The Provençal-style buildings are delightful, especially the bar, restaurant and games room with its terrace down to the river and the site's own canoe station (locked gate). Across the road is a lake with a sandy beach and restaurant. Enlarged spa facilities include a swimming pool, a large jacuzzi, massage, a steam pool and a sauna. Developed over three generations by the Simoncini family, this peaceful, friendly site is set in more than four hectares of mature, well shaded countryside at the foot of the Roquebrune Rock. Activities include climbing the Rock with a guide, trips to Monte Carlo, Ventimigua (Italy) and the Gorges du Verdon, etc. The medieval village of Roquebrune is within walking distance.

### Facilities

Modern, refurbished, well designed toilet blocks, baby baths, facilities for disabled visitors. Washing machines. Shop. Bar and restaurant (all open all season). Heated outdoor swimming pool (09.00-19.00, all season, lifeguard in high season, swim shorts not permitted), separate paddling pool, ice cream bar. Games room. Separate adults only pool and spa facilities. Playing field. Fishing. Minigolf. Miniclub (July/Aug). Activities for children and adults (high season), visits to local wine caves. Only electric barbecues allowed. WiFi throughout (charged). Security bracelets for all guests. Off site: Bicycle hire 1 km. Riding and golf 5 km.

**Open:** 1 April - 30 September.

### Directions

From A8 take Le Muy exit, follow N7 towards Fréjus for 13 km. bypassing Le Muy. After crossing A8, turn right at roundabout towards Roquebrune-sur-Argens. Site is on left after 1 km. just before bridge over river. GPS: 43.450783, 6.6335

### Charges guide

| | |
|---|---|
| Per unit incl. 2 persons and electricity | € 23.00 - € 46.50 |
| extra person | € 4.00 - € 8.80 |
| child (acc. to age) | free - € 6.75 |
| dog (max. 1) | € 3.20 |

Village camping ☆☆☆☆

LES PECHEURS

Un jardin en Provence

10 km away from the beaches of Fréjus Saint Raphaël, calm and landscaped.

www.camping-les-pecheurs.com

Wellness : spa, spa aqua trainer, sauna, restaurant, canoeing, family atmosphere. Rental of Mobile homes and Cabanes des pêcheurs.

83520
Roquebrune sur Argens
Tél : + 33 (0)4 94 45 71 25

Provence
Côte d'Azur

**FREE** Alan Rogers Travel Card
Extra benefits and savings - see page 10

## Saint Aygulf
### Caravaning l'Etoile d'Argens

Chemin des Etangs, F-83370 Saint Aygulf (Var) T: 04 94 81 01 41. E: info@etoiledargens.com

**alanrogers.com/FR83070**

First impressions of l'Etoile d'Argens are of space, cleanliness and calm. This is a site run with families in mind and many of the activities are free, making it an excellent choice for a good value holiday. There are 450 level, fully serviced grass pitches (all with 10/16A electricity). Separated by hedges, they range in size from 100-250 sq.m. and mainly have good shade. The pool and bar area is attractively landscaped with olive and palm trees on beautifully kept grass. There are two heated pools (one for adults, one for children), both of which are designed very much with families in mind. Reception staff are very friendly and English is spoken. The exceptionally large pitches could easily take two caravans and cars or one family could have a very spacious plot with a garden like atmosphere. The river runs alongside the site with a free boat service to the beach (15/6-15/9). This is an ideal family site for the summer but is also good in low season for a quiet stay in a superb location with excellent pitches. There are 88 mobile homes for rent. For a large site, l'Etoile d'Argens is unusually calm and peaceful, even in July.

### Facilities

Over 20, well kept, small toilet blocks. Supermarket and gas supplies. Bar, restaurant, pizzeria, takeaway. Two adult pools (heated 1/4-30/6), paddling pool, jacuzzi, solarium. Floodlit tennis with coaching. Minigolf. Aerobics. Archery (July/Aug). Football and swimming lessons. Boules. Good play area. Children's entertainment (July/Aug). Activity programme with games, dances and escorted walking trips to the surrounding hills within 3 km. Off site: Golf and riding 2 km. Beach 3.5 km.

**Open:** 1 April - 30 September (with all services).

### Directions

From A8 exit 36, take the N7 towards Le Muy, Fréjus. After 8 km. at roundabout take D7 signed Roquebrune, St Aygulf. In 9.5 km. (after roundabout) turn left signed Fréjus. Site is signed. Ignore width and height limit signs as site is before the limit (500 m). GPS: 43.41593, 6.705566

### Charges guide

| | |
|---|---|
| Per tent pitch (100 sq.m) incl. electricity and 2 persons | € 14.00 - € 38.00 |
| comfort pitch (130 sq.m) incl. 3 persons with water and drainage | € 20.00 - € 63.00 |
| luxury pitch (180 sq.m) incl. 4 persons | € 36.00 - € 78.00 |
| extra person | € 6.00 - € 10.00 |
| child (under 7 yrs) | € 5.00 - € 8.00 |

## Saint Aygulf
### Camping Résidence du Campeur

189 les grandes Chateaux de Villepey, RD 7, F-83370 Saint Aygulf (Var) T: 04 94 81 01 59.
E: accueilcampeur@sandaya.fr **alanrogers.com/FR83050**

This excellent site near the Côte d'Azur will take you away from all the bustle of the Mediterranean coast. Spread out over ten hectares, this is a well equipped holiday destination with pitches arranged along avenues. The 177 touring pitches average 100 sq.m. in size and all have electricity connections and, unusually, private sanitary facilities. There are 235 accommodation units for rent, the majority of which were installed after significant investment by the owners, Sandaya, in 2012. A pleasant pool complex is available for those who wish to stay on site instead of going swimming from the Mediterranean beaches. The nearest beach and Saint Aygulf are 2.5 km. away.

### Facilities

Private toilet blocks include a washbasin, shower and WC. Laundry area with washing machines. Very well stocked supermarket. Bar/restaurant with evening entertainment. Takeaway (all open all season). Large swimming pool complex with four water slides (high season). Two tennis courts. Minigolf. Boules. Fishing. Bicycle hire. Play area. Games/TV room. WiFi over site (charged). Only gas or electric barbecues are permitted. Off site: Riding 1.5 km. Golf 2 km. Beach and St Aygulf 2.5 km. Water skiing nearby.

**Open:** 31 March - 14 October.

### Directions

Leave A8 at Le Muy exit 36 on N555 towards Draguignan then onto the N7 towards Fréjus. Turn right on D7 signed St Aygulf and site is on the right 2.5 km. before the town. GPS: 43.40905, 6.70893

### Charges guide

| | |
|---|---|
| Per unit incl. 2 persons and electricity | € 25.00 - € 60.00 |
| extra person | € 3.50 - € 7.00 |
| child (3-7 yrs) | € 1.00 - € 5.00 |
| dog | € 5.00 |

For latest campsite news, availability and prices visit
# alanrogers.com

# L'ETOILE D'ARGENS

★★★★

## Côte d'Azur

Camping & Caravaning

+33 4 94 81 01 41  **www.etoiledargens.com**

Chemin des Etangs - F-83370 Fréjus-St Aygulf   info@etoiledargens.com

## Saint Cyr-sur-Mer
### Camping Clos Sainte-Thérèse
Route de Bandol, F-83270 Saint Cyr-sur-Mer (Var) T: 04 94 32 12 21. E: camping@clos-therese.com
**alanrogers.com/FR83300**

This is a very attractive, family run campsite set in hilly terrain four kilometres from the beaches of Saint Cyr. The terraced pitches are level, some with sea views, the helpful owners offering a tractor service if required. With good shade from pines, olives, almonds and evergreen oaks, there are 88 pitches for touring units, all with electricity and 35 for chalets or mobile homes. Five pitches are fully serviced. The landscaped pool complex is pretty and well kept, with a small slide, jacuzzi and a separate paddling pool. This is a friendly, small site, ideal for couples or families with younger children.

### Facilities
Clean, well maintained toilet facilities. Shop (1/4-30/9). Bar, restaurant and takeaway (15/6-15/9). Swimming pools (one heated) and paddling pool (1/4-30/9). Games room. TV room and library. Boules. Play area. Activities in high season. WiFi (charged). Off site: Golf course 500 m. Riding 2 km. Beach 2.5 km. Bicycle hire and fishing 3 km.

**Open:** 1 April - 30 September.

### Directions
From A50 exit 10 take D559 to Saint Cyr. Continue towards Bandol and site is 3 km. on the left. GPS: 43.159783, 5.729004

### Charges guide
| | |
|---|---|
| Per unit incl. 2 persons and electricity | € 21.20 - € 31.10 |
| extra person | € 3.90 - € 6.40 |

---

## Saint Raphaël
### Castel Camping Douce Quiétude
3435 boulevard Jacques Baudino, F-83700 Saint Raphaël (Var) T: 04 94 44 30 00.
E: info@douce-quietude.com **alanrogers.com/FR83250**

Douce Quiétude is 5 km. from the beaches at Saint Raphaël and Agay but is quietly situated at the foot of the Estérel massif. There are 400 pitches, only 70 of these are for touring. Set in pleasant pine woodland or shaded, green areas, the pitches are of a comfortable size, separated by bushes and trees with 10A electricity, water, drainage and telephone/TV points provided. This mature site offers a wide range of services and facilities complete with a pool complex. It can be busy in the main season yet is relaxed and spacious. Security is good, with the wearing of identity bracelets mandatory throughout your stay. This area is a golfers' paradise, with many beautiful courses close by. You can book to play these courses at reception, as well as arranging lessons and equipment hire. The owner is ever present on site and constantly striving to improve the facilities. You can relax and enjoy your stay, reassured by the state-of-the-art watering system installed to combat the fire risk present during the summer months. The management has embraced green issues in relation to the everyday running of the site, and many changes have been made. This is an excellent site with professional staff and is meticulously maintained.

### Facilities
Modern toilet blocks include facilities for babies and disabled visitors. Launderette. Bar, restaurant, takeaway, pizzeria (3/4-3/9). Shop. Three swimming pools (two heated). Water slide, jacuzzi. Play area. Children's club, activities for teenagers (all July/Aug). Sports area. Games room. Tennis. Minigolf. Archery. Fitness centre, sauna. Evening entertainment, shows, karaoke, discos (July/Aug). Mountain bike hire. Gas barbecues only. Off site: Golf and riding 2 km. Windsurf hire and sea fishing 5 km.

**Open:** 3 April - 2 October.

### Directions
From A8 exit 38 (Fréjus/St Raphaël) take D100, signed Valescure then Agay. Follow site signs. Access via N98 coast road turning north at Agay on D100. Pass Esterel Camping, then site signed. GPS: 43.44727, 6.80600

### Charges guide
| | |
|---|---|
| Per unit incl. 2 persons and electricity | € 20.00 - € 58.00 |
| extra person | € 6.10 - € 10.60 |
| child (3-13 yrs) | € 5.10 - € 8.60 |

Camping Cheques accepted.

For latest campsite news, availability and prices visit
**alanrogers.com**

## Saint Rémy-de-Provence
### Camping Monplaisir

Chemin de Monplaisir, F-13210 Saint Rémy-de-Provence (Bouches du Rhône) T: 04 90 92 22 70.
E: reception@camping-monplaisir.fr **alanrogers.com/FR13040**

Only a kilometre from the centre of Saint Rémy, in the foothills of the Alpilles mountains, this is one of the most pleasant and well run sites we have come across. Saint Rémy is a very popular town with tourists and the site is frequently fully booked. Everything about it is of a high standard and quality. The good impression created by the reception and shop continues through the rest of the site. In all there are 130 level grass touring pitches with nine taken by smart mobile homes, with 10A electricity throughout. Flowering shrubs and greenery abounds, roads are tarmac and all is neat and tidy. There are six toilet blocks strategically placed for all areas. All are heated and one is larger, but all are unisex. The recreation area with a swimming pool (18x10 m), jacuzzi and paddling pool is overlooked by the bar. Open in July and August, it provides light meals and snacks and some entertainment.

**Facilities**

Six very modern, unisex toilet blocks are all heated in low season and have some washbasins in cabins. Family rooms and en-suite facilities for disabled visitors in two. Washing machines. Two motorcaravan service points. Refurbished shop selling essentials and local produce. Bar with snacks (July/Aug). Swimming pool (1/5-26/10). Play area. Boules. WiFi throughout. Gas and electric barbecues only. Mobile homes and chalets for hire. Off site: Saint Rémy 1 km. Bicycle hire 1 km. Fishing 2 km. Riding 5 km. Les Baux 5 km. Golf 10 km. Beach 60 km.

**Open:** 11 March - 26 October.

**Directions**

From St Rémy town centre follow signs for Arles and Nîmes. At roundabout on western side of town take D5 signed Maillane and immediately left by left. GPS: 43.79695, 4.82372

**Charges guide**

| Per unit incl. 2 persons | |
|---|---|
| and electricity (6A) | € 19.60 - € 31.80 |
| extra person | € 5.00 - € 8.00 |
| child (2-7 yrs) | € 3.00 - € 6.00 |
| dog | € 2.00 |

CAMPING MONPLAISIR

- Overflowing swimming and paddling pool
- Snack bar in high season, Laundry
- 140 pitches, 2.8 ha of comfort, quietness and garden area
- Boules, children's games, table tennis, grocery
- Mobile homes to let

CHEMIN MONPLAISIR - F-13210 ST. RÉMY DE PROVENCE - FRANCE
TEL : +33 (0)4 90 92 22 70 - FAX : +33 (0)4 90 92 18 5
www.camping-monplaisir.fr
reception@camping-monplaisir.fr

## Saint Rémy-de-Provence
### Camping Mas de Nicolas

Avenue Plaisance du Touch, F-13210 Saint Rémy-de-Provence (Bouches du Rhône) T: 04 90 92 27 05.
E: camping-masdenicolas@nerim.fr **alanrogers.com/FR13050**

The site has a very spacious feel to it, due mainly to the central area of gently sloping grass, dotted with shrubs, that is kept clear of pitches and used for leisure and sunbathing. The 130 pitches are separated by hedges and flowering shrubs, 34 for mobile homes, the remainder for touring units. The pitches all have 6A electricity, water and drainage, and access roads are wide. Some pitches are an irregular shape and some are sloping, but many have views and they are mostly organised into groups of two and four. There is a pool area with Balnéotherapie et Remise en form, or as we would call it, a spa and gym.

**Facilities**

Good, modern toilet blocks including baby bathroom can be heated. Plans to refurbish one block. Washing machines. Small bar. Occasional paella evenings. Swimming pool. Sauna, steam room, spa bath, gym. Play area. Bicycle hire. WiFi throughout (free). Gas barbecues permitted. Off site: Adjacent municipal gym, tennis, volleyball courts. Riding 1 km. Fishing 2 km. Golf 15 km. Saint Rémy has a wide selection of restaurants, and a Wednesday market.

**Open:** 15 March - 30 October.

**Directions**

St Rémy-de-Provence is located where the D571 from Avignon connects with the D99 Tarascon-Cavaillon road. Site is signed from the village centre on the north side. Leave the A7 at Cavaillon or Avignon-Sud. GPS: 43.79622, 4.83879

**Charges guide**

| Per unit incl. 2 persons | |
|---|---|
| and electricity | € 15.80 - € 25.00 |
| extra person | € 5.00 - € 8.00 |
| child (under 10 yrs) | € 2.50 - € 6.00 |

**FREE** Alan Rogers Travel Card
Extra benefits and savings - see page 10

## Saint Romain-en-Viennois

### Camping le Soleil de Provence

Route de Nyons, F-84110 Saint Romain-en-Viennois (Vaucluse) T: 04 90 46 46 00.
E: info@camping-soleil-de-provence.fr **alanrogers.com/FR84100**

The site has been developed to a high standard. The 162 average sized pitches, 150 for touring are separated by hedges and a variety of young trees offering only a little shade (10A electricity). The excellent pool, surrounded by a sunbathing terrace, and overlooked by the bar, is an unusual shape with an island in the centre. Although there is no paddling pool one end of the pool is very shallow. There is some organised entertainment in July and August but the emphasis is on a quiet and peaceful environment and is an ideal site for relaxing and unwinding.

**Facilities**

Modern well appointed, heated toilet blocks, facilities for disabled visitors, baby room. Washing machine, dryer. Motorcaravan services. Small shop for bread, open on demand. Bar, snack bar. New aqua park with waterslides and paddling pool. Small play area. Volleyball, table tennis, boules. Off site: Tennis 1 km. Rafting, hiking, cycling, mountain biking 4 km. Bicycle hire 5 km. Fishing 15 km.

**Open:** 15 March - 31 October.

**Directions**

Site is 4 km. north of Vaison-la-Romaine on D938 road to Nyons. Turn right (St Romain-en-Viennois) Site signed, first left to site. GPS: 44.26902, 5.10597

**Charges guide**

| | |
|---|---|
| Per person | € 3.50 - € 7.50 |
| pitch incl. electricity (10A) | € 7.00 - € 10.00 |
| car | € 3.00 - € 6.00 |

No credit cards.

## Saint Vincent-les-Forts

Campé●le

### Campéole le Lac

Le Fein, F-04340 Saint Vincent-les-Forts (Alpes-de-Haute-Provence) T: 04 92 85 51 57.
E: lac@campeole.com **alanrogers.com/FR04210**

Le Lac is a member of the Campéole group and enjoys a fine location in the mountains of Haute-Provence. The site can be found at an altitude of 800 m. on the banks of the large Lac de Serre Ponçon and many of the site's 300 pitches (210 for touring units) have fine views of the lake and the surrounding mountains. All are of a good size with electricity hook ups and ample water points. The access road down to the site (3 km) is fairly steep and winding but it is certainly worth the effort. The waters of the lake have an alluring blue-green hue and shelve gradually from the site's beach. There is also an ecological swimming pool, using natural water, consistent with this stunning natural setting. Other on-site amenities include a shop, restaurant and various sports facilities. A number of pitches have lakeside locations and are popular with fishermen. Water sports are popular and a hire service is offered, including canoes, electric boats and wakeboards. This is a great area for hiking and mountain biking, with a number of excellent routes passing close to the campsite. Reception staff have full details.

**Facilities**

Several toilet blocks have all the usual facilities. Wet room for disabled visitors. Laundry areas. Bar and restaurant (1/6-15/9). Shop and takeaway (1/7-31/8). Eco swimming pool (with lifeguard). Fishing. Volleyball. Tennis. Play area. Canoes and boat hire. Activity and entertainment programme. Mobile homes, chalets and equipped tents for rent. Free WiFi in reception area. Off site: Hiking and cycle tracks. Montagne aux Marmottes (animal park). Riding 10 km. Serre Ponçon dam. Popular area for paragliding and white-water sports.

**Open:** 20 May - 25 September.

**Directions**

The site is close to the village of St Vincent-les-Forts. From Gap, head south on N85, then join D900b following signs to Barcelonnette. Continue on, along the Durance Valley passing the Barrage de Serre Ponçon and on towards St Vincent-les-Forts. The site is signed from here. GPS: 44.45682, 6.36529

**Charges guide**

| | |
|---|---|
| Per unit incl. 2 persons and electricity | € 17.10 - € 26.60 |
| extra person | € 4.50 - € 6.80 |
| child (2-6 yrs) | free - € 4.30 |

For latest campsite news, availability and prices visit
# alanrogers.com

## Sanary-sur-Mer
### Campasun Parc Mogador

167 chemin de Beaucours, F-83110 Sanary-sur-Mer (Var) T: 04 94 74 53 16. E: mogador@campasun.com
**alanrogers.com/FR83320**

This site in the Mediterranean countryside is very much geared for family holidays with children. Some 20 minutes on foot from the beach, the site has a very large and well kept pool area and a stage for entertainment. Somewhat smaller than other sites of this type, there are 122 good sized pitches (61 for touring units). The ground is mainly level, if rather stony and sandy. Variable shade is available and all pitches have 10A electricity. There are plans to enlarge some of the smaller, 80 sq.m. pitches. The attractive pool, is surrounded by ample paved sunbathing areas.

**Facilities**

Two large, super deluxe toilet blocks (toilets automatically cleaned and disinfected), one including washbasins and showers in cabins. Laundry. Motorcaravan services. Restaurant (1/4-5/11), also snacks, pizzas and takeaway. Swimming and paddling pools (heated 1/4-20/9). Solarium. Boules. Bicycle hire. Miniclub and evening entertainment in season. WiFi (charged). No barbecues. No dogs July/Aug. Off site: Beach 800 m. Riding 10 km.

**Open:** 24 March - 10 November.

**Directions**

Take Bandol exit 12 from A50 and head for Six Fours on the N559. Arriving at Sanary-sur-Mer turn left towards Beaucours and site is on left after 100 m. GPS: 43.12377, 5.78767

**Charges guide**

| | |
|---|---|
| Per unit incl. 2 persons and electricity | € 22.50 - € 47.00 |
| extra person | € 5.70 - € 8.90 |
| child (1-7 yrs) | € 4.60 - € 8.00 |

---

## Vaison-la Romaine
### Camping du Théatre Romain

Chemin du Brusquet, F-84110 Vaison-la-Romaine (Vaucluse) T: 04 90 28 78 66.
E: info@camping-theatre.com  **alanrogers.com/FR84290**

This family friendly site is ideally situated within easy walking distance of the delightful town of Vaison and its excellent tourist office, shops, restaurants and museums. There are 66 level pitches and these all have electricity (5/10A), water and drainage, and are of a good size (100 sq.m). Most pitches are part grass and part gravel and are generally separated by hedges and mature trees, giving partial shade. The site also has nine mobile homes for rent. This is a quiet site with no organised entertainment, perfect for a relaxing holiday and a good base for exploring the surrounding Provençal countryside.

**Facilities**

Two heated sanitary blocks include facilities for babies and disabled visitors. Launderette. Fresh bread delivered daily. Pizza van twice a week. Hot and cold drinks machine. Swimming pool (10/5-30/9). Play area. Snooker. Pétanque. WiFi in some areas (free). Off site: Bicycle hire 1 km. Riding 5 km. Shops, supermarkets and restaurants in Vaison-la Romaine. Local markets. Wine tasting.

**Open:** 15 March - 5 November.

**Directions**

From the north, take A7 and exit at Bollène. Follow signs to Vaison-la Romaine. Continue on D975 through the town and follow signs to site. GPS: 44.244959, 5.078508

**Charges guide**

| | |
|---|---|
| Per unit incl. 2 persons and electricity | € 17.00 - € 26.50 |
| extra person | € 5.00 - € 7.00 |

---

## Vaison-la-Romaine
### Camping de l'Ayguette

Faucon (D86), F-84110 Vaison-la-Romaine (Vaucluse) T: 04 90 46 40 35. E: info@ayguette.com
**alanrogers.com/FR84060**

Set in 4 hectares of the beautiful region of north Provence, surrounded by vineyards and wooded hills, the 99 slightly sloping, stony pitches, 85 for touring, are widely spaced out on terraces amongst pine and oak trees giving plenty of dappled shade, only a few suitable for large units. All have 10A electricity (long leads necessary) but some are a considerable distance from the amenities, not ideal for those with walking difficulties. Rock pegs are essential. The reception building houses a bar, snack bar, small shop and terrace. Close by is an attractive swimming pool (heated all season) and sunbathing area.

**Facilities**

Two well equipped toilet blocks, one heated. Room for disabled visitors or families with young children. Washing machines. Outdoor heated swimming pool. Snack bar. takeaway (1/7-25/8). Bar, small shop, bread to order. Table tennis, volleyball, badminton. Multisports ground. Playground. Occasional entertainment, some activities for children. Internet access. WiFi (free). Gas and electric barbecues only. Off site: Faucon with bar and restaurant 1 km. Vaison-la-Romaine 5 km. Fishing, river bathing and bicycle hire 5 km. Riding 7 km. Mont Ventoux 35 km.

**Open:** 30 March - 28 September.

**Directions**

From Nyons, follow signs for Vaison la Romaine. At the roundabout after Mirabel-aux-Baronnies, turn left through Puyméras-Faucon and then follow site signs. GPS: 44.26220, 5.129133

**Charges 2013**

| | |
|---|---|
| Per unit incl. 2 persons and electricity | € 17.50 - € 30.40 |
| extra person | € 4.00 - € 5.00 |
| child (2-12 yrs) | € 2.50 - € 3.50 |
| dog | € 1.80 - € 2.00 |

---

**FREE** Alan Rogers Travel Card
Extra benefits and savings - see page 10

## Vallouise

### Camping Indigo Vallouise

Chemin des Chambonnettes, F-05290 Vallouise (Hautes-Alpes) T: 04 92 23 30 26.
E: vallouise@camping-indigo.com **alanrogers.com/FR05440**

This former municipal site is a recent addition to the Indigo group of campsites and is located close to the pretty village of Vallouise, deep in the Hautes-Alpes. The site extends over 6.5 hectares and enjoys some magnificent views of the surrounding mountain scenery. There are 130 touring pitches here, bordered by two streams. Most have 10A electricity. A number of fully equipped safari-style tents are available for rent. The site lies at the foot of the vast Ecrins National Park and is an ideal base for many adventure sports, including paragliding, rock climbing and mountain biking. The GR54 long-distance footpath passes through Vallouise, and there are many other excellent paths close at hand, including routes to the hamlet of Puy Aillaud or to Le Monetier, passing the Lac de l'Eychauda. Vallouise is a very pleasant mountain village lying at the spur of two valleys. The village has some good restaurants and a beautiful 15th-century church, as well as the Maison du Parc des Ecrins and a useful tourist office.

**Facilities**

Two toilet blocks, one new and one refurbished. Shop. Snack bar (July-Aug). Play area. Tourist information. Fully equipped tents for rent. Heated outdoor pool. WiFi (free). Off site: Fishing 100 m. Bicycle hire 200 m. Shops and restaurants in Vallouise. Mountain sports. Hiking and mountain biking.

**Open:** 27 June - 16 September.

**Directions**

Vallouise can be found west of Briançon. From Grenoble, head south on N85 (Vizille), then D1091 to Briançon, passing through Bourg d'Oisans. From Briançon, head south on N94, then D4 and D994 to Vallouise. Site signed. GPS: 44.844153, 6.490084

**Charges 2013**

| | |
|---|---|
| Per unit incl. 2 persons and electricity | € 20.20 - € 30.50 |
| extra person | € 4.90 - € 5.90 |

No credit cards.

## Vence

### Camping Caravaning Domaine de la Bergerie

1330 chemin de la Sine, F-06140 Vence (Alpes-Maritimes) T: 04 93 58 09 36.
E: info@camping-domainedelabergerie.com **alanrogers.com/FR06030**

La Bergerie is a quiet, family owned site that celebrated its 60th anniversary in 2012. It is situated in the hills 3 km. from Vence and 10 km. from the sea at Cagnes-sur-Mer. An extensive, natural, lightly wooded site, it is in a secluded position at about 300 m. above sea level. Most of the pitches are shaded and all are of a good size. There are 450 pitches, 245 with electricity (2/5A), including 65 also with water and drainage. Some areas are a little distance from the toilet blocks. With the aim of keeping this a quiet and tranquil place to stay, there are no organised activities and definitely no groups accepted.

**Facilities**

Refurbished toilet blocks include provision for disabled visitors (pitches near the block are reserved for disabled visitors). Shop. Small bar/restaurant, takeaway (all 1/5-30/9). Large swimming pool and smaller pool (1/5-30/9). Play area. Tennis. 12 shaded boules pitches (lit at night). No charcoal barbecues. Two mobile homes and new camping pods to rent. Off site: Beach at Cagnes-sur-Mer 10 km. Riding and fishing 10 km. Golf 18 km. Grasse, famous perfume centre 25 km.

**Open:** 25 March - 15 October.

**Directions**

From A8 exit 48 take Cagnes-sur-Mer road towards Vence (do not follow sat nav instructions to turn off this road before you reach Vence). At first roundabout in Vence follow signs for Centre Ville and site is well signed from here. GPS: 43.71174, 7.0905

**Charges guide**

| | |
|---|---|
| Per unit incl. 2 persons and electricity (2A) | € 20.00 - € 33.50 |

Camping Cheques accepted.

For latest campsite news, availability and prices visit
**alanrogers.com**

## Veynes

### Camping les Rives du Lac

Plan d'eau Les Iscles, F-05400 Veynes (Hautes-Alpes) T: 04 92 57 20 90. E: contact@camping-lac.com
**alanrogers.com/FR05200**

Les Rives du Lac lies within the Buech region of the Hautes-Alpes department, close to the small resort town of Veynes. This is a good base for outdoor activities, such as hiking, riding, paragliding, mountain biking, rock climbing or potholing. The site is located on the banks of the 5.5 ha. lake, Les Iscles, which offers good opportunities for water based activities. The lake is shallow and lifeguards are on duty during July and August. There are 110 semi-shaded touring pitches here, all of which have electrical connections (10A). Fifteen Alpine chalets and mobile homes are also available for rent.

**Facilities**

Modern sanitary facilities are of a high standard. Laundry. Facilities for disabled visitors (key access). Baby room. Laundry. Bar/snack bar/pizzeria. Takeaway. Covered swimming pool and paddling pool. Direct lake access. Fishing. Games room. Play area. Minigolf. Sports field. Bicycle hire. Activities and entertainment. Mobile homes and chalets for rent. WiFi over part of site. Max. 2 dogs. Off site: Shop within 2 km. Riding 300 m.

**Open:** 28 April - 29 September.

**Directions**

Approaching from Gap or Grenoble, follow directions for Valence at large roundabout. Approx. 1 km. after Veynes, follow signs to site. GPS: 44.51889, 5.7988

**Charges guide**

| Per unit incl. 2 persons | |
|---|---|
| and electricity | € 16.50 - € 26.50 |
| extra person | € 4.50 - € 7.00 |
| child (2-9 yrs) | € 2.50 - € 5.00 |

---

## Villars-Colmars

### Camping Caravaning le Haut-Verdon

RD 908, F-04370 Villars-Colmars (Alpes-de-Haute-Provence) T: 04 92 83 40 09.
E: campinglehautverdon@wanadoo.fr **alanrogers.com/FR04060**

For those seeking a quiet, family site set in most spectacular scenery, Camping le Haut-Verdon is ideal. It is on the banks of the Verdon, an excellent trout river, which flows through the spectacular gorge. The river can be fast flowing. Surrounded by the majestic peaks of the Alpes-de-Haute-Provence, it is on the doorstep of the Mercantour National Park. Set amongst the pines, the 109 pitches are mostly on the large size but are rather stony. With 73 for touring units, all have electricity but some require long leads.

**Facilities**

Refurbished, heated toilet block. Washing machines. Freezer for ice packs. Room for tent campers for inclement weather. Motorcaravan services. Small shop. Bar/restaurant, takeaway. Heated swimming, paddling pools (from 1/6). Small play area. Giant chess. Boules. Skittle alley. Tennis. Trim trail in the woods. TV room. Organised games and competitions. Fishing. Barbecue areas (portable ones banned). Free WiFi in bar area. Off site: Colmars is nearby with a small supermarket, restaurants and bars. Riding adjacent. Bicycle hire 3 km.

**Open:** 1 May - 30 September.

**Directions**

Follow D955 north from St André-les-Alpes towards Colmar. After 11 km. road number changes to D908. Site on right at southern edge of Villars-Colmars. Caravans not advised to use the D908 from Annot or Col d'Allos from Barcelonnette. GPS: 44.1601, 6.60625

**Charges guide**

| Per unit incl. 2 persons | |
|---|---|
| and electricity (6A) | € 16.00 - € 28.00 |
| extra person | € 3.00 - € 5.00 |
| child (2-7 yrs) | € 2.00 - € 3.00 |

---

## Villecroze-les-Grottes

### Camping Club le Ruou

Les Esparrus 309, RD 560, F-83690 Villecroze-les-Grottes (Var) T: 04 94 70 67 70. E: info@leruou.com
**alanrogers.com/FR83410**

This is a family oriented site in the Provençal countryside, very much geared for family holidays with children. Some 45 minutes by car from the coast at Fréjus, the site has a large and well kept pool area and a mobile stage for entertainment. There are 134 good sized pitches (50 for touring units). On mainly terraced, rather stony ground with good shade, all have 6/10A electricity. Some of the pitches for caravans are along a steep path but there is a 4x4 available to assist. There may be some road noise.

**Facilities**

One new super deluxe toilet block includes washbasins in cabins. Facilities for babies and disabled visitors. Laundry facilities. Snacks and takeaway (June-Sept). Bar and entertainment room with TV. Area for shows, cabarets, etc. with mobile stage. Two swimming pools. Boules. Outdoor exercise equipment. Play area. Miniclub for children and evening entertainment in season. No charcoal barbecues. WiFi (charged). Off site: Fishing, riding and bicycle hire 5 km. Golf 25 km. Beach 35 km.

**Open:** 1 April - 30 October.

**Directions**

Villecroze-les-Grottes is northwest of Fréjus. From A8 (Toulon-Mandelieu-la-Napoule) take exit 13 onto N7 (Le Muy). At Les Arcs turn left on D555 (Draguignan), then D557 (Villecroze). About 4 km. before village take D560. Site on left. GPS: 43.55345, 6.297983

**Charges guide**

| Per unit incl. 2 persons | |
|---|---|
| and electricity | € 18.20 - € 38.50 |
| extra person | € 3.50 - € 7.00 |
| Camping Cheques accepted. | |

## Villeneuve-Loubet

### Parc Saint James le Sourire

Route de Grasse, F-06270 Villeneuve-Loubet (Alpes-Maritimes) T: 04 93 20 96 11.
E: info@camping-parcsaintjames.com **alanrogers.com/FR06190**

Le Sourire is a member of the Parc Saint James group. There are 411 pitches here and many are occupied by mobile homes and chalets. There are, however, 241 touring pitches dispersed throughout the wooded terrain, some of which are on soft sandy soil. The site is close to the impressive La Vanade sports complex which has a massive range of activities including no fewer than 55 tennis courts, a riding centre and a 9-hole golf course. There is a good range of activities on site too, including a large swimming pool with a regular programme of aqua gym, water polo and other activities. Some pitches are close to the main road so you may experience some road noise.

| Facilities | Directions |
|---|---|
| Sanitary facilities (with key access) include preset pushbutton showers. Baby room planned. Laundry. Shop (June-Aug). Bar (July/Aug). Restaurant and takeaway (May-Aug). Swimming pool and separate children's pool (May-Aug). Play area. TV room. Gym. Games room. Sports competitions. Entertainment in high season. Off site: Cannes and Nice. Nearest beaches 4 km. Marineland water park. Leisure park at La Vanade.<br><br>**Open:** 13 April - 28 September. | Take the Villeneuve-Loubet exit from the A8 autoroute and follow signs to Grasse joining the D2085. The site can be found on the left, 2 km. from Villeneuve Loubet. GPS: 43.6603, 7.10429 |

**Charges 2013**

| Per unit incl. 2 persons | |
|---|---|
| and electricity | € 17.00 - € 31.00 |
| extra person | € 3.00 - € 5.00 |
| child (4-10 yrs) | € 2.00 - € 4.00 |

## Villeneuve-Loubet-Plage

### Camping la Vieille Ferme

296 boulevard des Groules, F-06270 Villeneuve-Loubet-Plage (Alpes-Maritimes) T: 04 93 33 41 44.
E: info@vieilleferme.com **alanrogers.com/FR06050**

In a popular resort area and open all year, la Vieille Ferme is a family owned site with good facilities. It has 119 level, gravel based touring pitches, all fully serviced and the majority separated by hedges. Some are only small, simple pitches for little tents. There is also a fully serviced pitch on tarmac for motorcaravans. There are special winter rates for long stays with quite a few long stay units on site. The entrance to the site is very colourful with well tended flower beds. English is spoken at reception and the whole place has a very friendly feel to it.

| Facilities | Directions |
|---|---|
| Modern, heated, well kept toilet blocks, children's toilets, baby room, facilities for disabled visitors. Motorcaravan services. Washing machines, dryer. Shop (Easter-Sept). Machine with drinks, sweets, ices in TV room. Gas, bread, milk to order. Swimming pool, children's pool, heated and covered for winter use (closed mid Nov-mid Dec). Jacuzzi. Internet. WiFi (charged). Boules. Games and competitions in July/Aug. Off site: Beach and fishing 1 km. Golf and bicycle hire 2 km. Riding 6 km. Marineland water park.<br><br>**Open:** All year. | From west, A8, exit 44 Antibes, D35, 3.5 km. Left towards Nice, N7. After 3.5 km. turn left for site between Marineland and Parc de Vaugrenier. Site is 150 m. on right. Avoid N98 Route du Bord de Mer. GPS: 43.62002, 7.12586 |

**Charges guide**

| Per unit incl. 2 persons | |
|---|---|
| and electricity (6A) | € 25.50 - € 42.00 |
| extra person | € 5.00 - € 7.00 |

## Villes-sur-Auzon

### Camping les Verguettes

Route de Carpentras, F-84570 Villes-sur-Auzon (Vaucluse) T: 04 90 61 88 18.
E: info@provence-camping.com **alanrogers.com/FR84110**

Friendly and family run by a new owner, this small campsite is surrounded by fields and vineyards and should appeal to those seeking a more relaxed holiday. It lies at the foot of Mont Ventoux and is close to the Nesque Gorge (1 km). It is probably not the ideal site for active youngsters. The 78 compact pitches are attractively laid out and arranged in groups of five. There are 70 for touring units, separated by a variety of trees and shrubs, and with 10A electricity connections (long leads may be necessary). Near the swimming pool is the bar with terrace – a pleasant place to relax after a day sightseeing.

| Facilities | Directions |
|---|---|
| Two toilet blocks, the buildings are old but have been refurbished to a high standard, one is heated in low season. Motorcaravan services. Bar. Swimming pool (1/5-30/9). Tennis. Minigolf. Boules. Small games/TV room. Internet point. WiFi in some areas (charged). Off site: Bicycle hire 500 m. Fishing 2 km. Riding 5 km. Golf 20 km. Mont Ventoux, Nesque Gorge 1 km.<br><br>**Open:** 7 April - 30 September. | Leave A7, exit 22 just south of Orange, take D950 to Carpentras. Take D942 east (Sault and Mazan). Site is 10 km. on right just after a roundabout on entering village of Villes-sur-Auzon. GPS: 44.05685, 5.22820 |

**Charges guide**

| Per unit incl. 2 persons | |
|---|---|
| and electricity | € 19.00 - € 29.00 |
| extra person | € 5.00 - € 6.30 |

For latest campsite news, availability and prices visit
**alanrogers.com**

## Volonne
### Sunêlia l'Hippocampe

Route de Napoléon, F-04290 Volonne (Alpes-de-Haute-Provence) T: 04 92 33 50 00.
E: camping@l-hippocampe.com **alanrogers.com/FR04010**

L'Hippocampe is a friendly family run, all action, lakeside site, with families in mind, situated in a beautiful area of France. The perfumes of thyme, lavender and wild herbs are everywhere and the higher hills of Haute-Provence are not too far away. There are 447 level, numbered pitches (177 for touring units), medium to very large (130 sq.m) in size. All have electricity (10A) and 140 have water and drainage, most are separated by bushes and cherry trees. Some of the best pitches border the lake. The restaurant, bar, takeaway and shop have all been completely renewed. Games, aerobics, competitions, entertainment and shows, plus a daily club for younger family members are organised in July/August. A soundproofed underground disco is set well away from the pitches and is very popular with teenage customers. Staff tour the site at night ensuring a good night's sleep. The site is, however, much quieter in low season and, with its good discounts, is the time for those who do not want or need entertaining. The Gorges du Verdon is a sight not to be missed and rafting, paragliding or canoe trips can be booked from the site's own tourist information office. Being on the lower slopes of the hills of Haute-Provence, the surrounding area is good for both walking and mountain biking. All in all, this is a very good site for an active or restful holiday and is suitable for outfits of all sizes. English is spoken.

### Facilities

Toilet blocks vary from old to modern, all with good clean facilities that include washbasins in cabins. Washing machines. Motorcaravan service point. Bread available (from 7/5). Shop, bar, restaurant and pizzeria (7/5-11/9). Large, heated pool complex (27/4-30/9) with five waterslides, (second pool 1/6-30/9) with five waterslides, (second pool 1/6-30/9). Tennis. Fishing. Canoeing. Boules. Bicycle hire. Sports facilities (some with free instruction). No charcoal barbecues. WiFi (charged). Off site: Volonne 600 m (market on Fridays). Riding 12 km.

**Open:** 16 April - 30 September.

### Directions

Approaching from the north turn off N85 across river bridge to Volonne, then right to site. From the south right on D4, 1 km. before Château Arnoux. GPS: 44.10462, 6.01688

### Charges guide

| Per unit incl. 2 persons | |
|---|---|
| and electricity | € 16.00 - € 33.00 |
| with full services | € 16.00 - € 43.00 |
| extra person (over 4 yrs) | € 3.00 - € 7.00 |

Camping Cheques accepted.

The island of Corsica is both dramatic and beautiful. The scenery is spectacular with bays of white sand lapped by the clear blue waters of the Mediterranean. At certain times of the year the entire island is ablaze with exotic flowers, aided by Corsica's excellent sunshine record.

**DÉPARTEMENTS: 2A CORSE-DU-SUD; 2B HAUTE-CORSE**

**MAJOR CITIES: AJACCIO AND BASTIA**

The 'scented isle' of Corsica is a mountainous region of France with over 1,000 km. of largely unspoilt coastline, with soaring cliffs, sandy beaches and hidden coves. The island has a complex and bloody history, having been disputed by the Greeks and Romans, invaded by the Byzantines and Moors, and ruled by the Genoese. This legacy has shaped the island with its hilltop villages featuring rustic, unadorned churches and a few Romanesque examples too.

The diverse landscape of glacial lakes, mountain streams, thick pine and chestnut forests and fragrant maquis makes it a paradise for walkers who can choose from the many paths that criss-cross the island, or tackle the famous GR20. The highest mountains lie to the west, while the gentler ranges, weathered to strange and often bizarre shapes, lie to the south and a continuous barrier forms the island's backbone.

**Places of interest**

*Ajaccio*: a dazzling white city full of Napoleonic memorabilia; Musée Fesch.

*Bastia*: historic citadel towering over the headland. The old town has preserved its streets in the form of steps connected by vaulted passages, converging on the Vieux port (the old port). The new port is the real commercial port of the island.

**Cuisine of the region**

*Brocchui*: sheeps' milk cheese is used much in cooking in both its soft form (savoury or sweet) or more mature and ripened.

*Capone*: local eels, cut up and grilled on a spit over a charcoal fire.

*Dziminu*: fish soup, like bouillabaise but much hotter. Made with peppers and pimentos.

*Figatelli*: a sausage made of dried and spiced pork with liver. A popular snack between meals.

*Pibronata*: a highly spiced local sauce.

*Prizzutu*: a peppered smoked ham; resembles the Italian prosciutto, but with chestnut flavour added.

www.visit-corsica.com
info@visit-corsica.com
(0)4 95 51 00 00

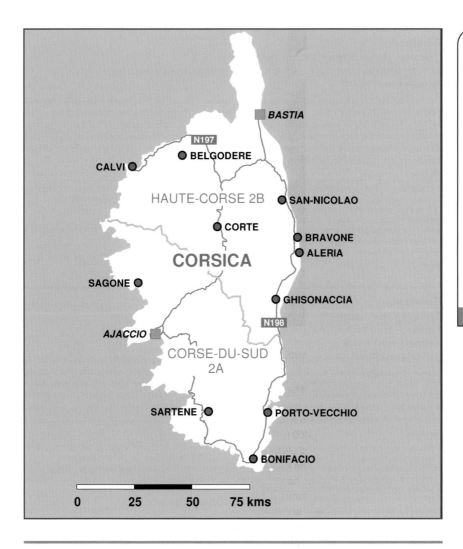

## Belgodère

Campé●le

### Campéole le Belgodère

Hameau Lozari, RN1197, F-20226 Belgodère (Haute-Corse) T: 04 95 60 20 20. E: belgodere@campeole.com

**alanrogers.com/FR20190**

This small uncomplicated site is set out primarily with many French Bengali tents and some mobile homes. Both types of accommodation are permanently on site. Camping pitches are located around the perimeter, they are of grass and sand, and vary from 40-80 sq.m; most have 6A electricity. There is some shade for the tent pitches, and very limited space for larger units (we suggest you contact the site ahead of time). The site slopes upward from the reception area, where there is a basic restaurant/bar with a menu of the day, also there is a small shop. A big comfortable room with a large TV, and an area dedicated to the children's club are located below the snack bar.

### Facilities

One dated but clean toilet block with baby changing and facilities for disabled visitors. Shop stocks basics (limited opening hours). Bar, snack bar with fresh bread daily (July/Aug) and simple restaurant. TV/games room. Book exchange and games to borrow. Play area. Volleyball. WiFi in reception (charged). Dogs accepted. Off site: Beach 400 m. Golf, riding, ATM and shops in Ile Rousse 7 km. Excursions to towns of Rousse, Calvi and Belgodère.

**Open:** 2 May - 26 September.

### Directions

Site is in the north of the island. On the N197 Calvi/Bastia road, look for the D363 turn to Palasca near the N197 31 km. marker. The site is at this point on the N197 but not very well signed. GPS: 42.637778, 9.019722

### Charges guide

| Per unit incl. 2 persons | |
|---|---|
| and electricity | € 17.90 - € 27.60 |
| extra person | € 4.60 - € 7.90 |
| child (2-6 yrs) | free - € 4.70 |

**FREE** Alan Rogers Travel Card
Extra benefits and savings - see page 10

## Bonifacio
### Camping U-Farniente de Pertamina Village

RN 198, F-20169 Bonifacio (Corse-du-Sud) T: 04 95 73 05 47. E: pertamina@wanadoo.fr

alanrogers.com/FR20000

This is a well run site with plenty to offer for a family holiday. The 120 pitches, many in delightful settings, have electricity (3A), are partially terraced and are hedged with trees and bushes, providing shade. They are fairly flat and vary in size, many being well over 100 sq.m. A central feature of the site is the large attractive swimming pool, surrounded by terraces. The bar, restaurant, pizzeria/grill and crêperie are on a series of terraces above the pool and patios. This site will suit campers who like a large pool complex and do not mind a drive to the beach.

**Facilities**

Two toilet blocks include washbasins in semi-private cubicles, British and Turkish style WCs, washing machines plus drying and ironing facilities. Motorcaravan service point at entrance (public usage). Shop. Takeaway. Bar, restaurant, pizzeria/grill serving set meals and à la carte menu at reasonable prices. Swimming pool. Tennis. Play area. TV room. Excellent gym. Off site: Bonifacio 4 km.

**Open:** Easter - 15 October.

**Directions**

Site is on the RN198 road, 4 km. north of Bonifacio to the east. Well signed as Pertamina Village. GPS: 41.41790, 9.17990

**Charges guide**

| | |
|---|---|
| Per unit incl. 2 persons and electricity | € 23.00 - € 36.00 |
| extra person | € 6.50 - € 10.00 |

Camping Cheques accepted.

## Bonifacio
### Camping Rondinara

Suartone, F-20169 Bonifacio (Corse-du-Sud) T: 04 95 70 43 15. E: reception@rondinara.fr

alanrogers.com/FR20240

The views from every pitch in this site are stunning, either coastal or the rolling hills and cliffs inland. The great outdoors describes this campsite which is away from any tourist over-development and is at one with nature. The natural and informal pitches sit on the hillside above a superb bay with sheltered water, fine silver sand and safe swimming. Most pitches have shade from foliage. Large boulders make natural divisions and some pitches need long leads for the 6A electricity. The beach is a 400 m. walk down a rough track through the maquis.

**Facilities**

Three excellent, modern toilet blocks are very clean and offer hot water throughout, hot showers and single sex British style toilets. Motorcaravan service point. Shop. Pizza restaurant. Bar. Swimming pool. Play area. Games room. Electronic games. Entertainment and family activities. Torches are essential here. Off site: Beach, boat launching and fishing 400 m. Golf, riding and sailing 15 km.

**Open:** 15 May - 30 September.

**Directions**

Site is midway between Bonifacio and Porto-Vecchio off the RN198. Take the D158 to Baie de la Rondinara for 7 km. (site is well signed). The road is rough and narrow but large units will have no trouble negotiating it. GPS: 41.47323, 9.26316

**Charges guide**

| | |
|---|---|
| Per unit incl. 2 persons and electricity | € 22.10 - € 27.00 |
| extra person | € 5.90 - € 7.70 |

## Calvi
### Paduella

Route de Bastia, F-20260 Calvi (Haute-Corse) T: 04 95 65 06 16. E: camping.paduella@wanadoo.fr

alanrogers.com/FR20170

Camping Paduella is a beautifully maintained, simple site which has been run by the friendly Peretti family for 40 years. As it is a popular site, it is best to book ahead for high season. There is a wide choice of pleasant pitches (137 in total), some shaded under pines, others grassed and hedged with less shade. All are well maintained on level terraces with good access and 4/16A electricity. The surroundings are pleasant and the site is peaceful. The main reception area with its small shop, pizzeria and bar are at the front of the site. There is a fairly busy road and light railway to cross to get to the lovely, white sand beach (300 m) but most of the walk is through the shaded beach parkland.

**Facilities**

Two centrally located modern sanitary blocks (British style WCs). Well equipped showers with facilities for diasbled visitors. Baby bathroom. Laundry with washing machines, ironing board. Small shop with basic supplies and fresh bread. Pizzeria and bar. Internet access. WiFi (charged). Play area. Sports ground. Fridge hire can be arranged. Off site: Supermarket and ATM 200 m. Adventure activities 200 m. Riding and bicycle hire 700 m. Marina 1 km.

**Open:** 10 May - 5 October.

**Directions**

From the north, site is just before the town of Calvi. It is directly off the RN197 on the left and is well signed. GPS: 42.5521, 8.7641

**Charges guide**

| | |
|---|---|
| Per unit incl. 2 persons and electricity | € 23.05 - € 27.65 |
| extra person | € 6.50 - € 8.00 |

No credit cards. Cash only.

For latest campsite news, availability and prices visit
**alanrogers.com**

## Calvi
### Camping la Pinède

Route de la Pinède, F-20260 Calvi (Haute-Corse) T: 04 95 65 17 80. E: info@camping-calvi.com
**alanrogers.com/FR20180**

Camping la Pinède is a well ordered, family site of 185 touring pitches, all with 4-16A electricity. The pitches are marked and level (although the pine roots are a nuisance in places). There is access for large units in some areas. Water points are spread around the site and everything is kept tidy and clean. Under the mature pines it can be quite dark but there are plenty of alternatives in the light. The site is divided into areas of accommodation – pitches for tour operators, mobile homes and tourers. Unusually, all facilities are in separate buildings.

**Facilities**

Three well maintained and well placed concrete sanitary buildings offer hot showers, facilities for disabled campers and unisex toilets and showers. Washing machines. Motorcaravan service point. Shop (June-Sept). Bar. Restaurant (May-Sept). Swimming pool (no lifeguard). Play area. Tennis. Minigolf (charged). WiFi (charged). Overnight parking for late arrivals. Off site: Beach and fishing 200 m. Riding 500 m. Boat launching and bicycle hire 2 km.

**Open:** 1 April - 31 October.

**Directions**

Site is north of Calvi off the RN197, just south of the D251 road to the airport. Look for signs off the roundabout here and take care along a narrow road with leaning fir trees. GPS: 42.55320, 8.7686

**Charges guide**

| | |
|---|---|
| Per unit incl. 2 persons | |
| and electricity | € 21.50 - € 30.50 |
| extra person | € 6.50 - € 9.50 |
| child (0-7 yrs) | € 3.50 |
| dog | € 2.00 |
| Camping Cheques accepted. | |

## Corte
### Camping Restonica

Faubourg Saint Antoine, F-20250 Corte (Haute-Corse) T: 04 95 46 11 59. E: vero.camp@worldonline.fr
**alanrogers.com/FR20110**

Tucked away alongside the pretty Restonica river and near the Pont Neuf leading into the stunning mountainside old city of Corte, Camping Restonica is ideally placed for tourists wanting to visit Corte or travel on the popular inland mountain railway (the station is only a few hundred metres from the site). This is a small, simple site catering for those who want to enjoy the many delights of Corte. The entrance is steep but manageable, there are flat pitches for campers and caravans in the middle of the site, and many beautiful terraced pitches for tents dotted along the river bank under shady trees. The river is great for paddling or a shallow swim.

**Facilities**

Single, central toilet block is unisex and somewhat dated, although very clean. Toilet for disabled visitors but site not really suitable. Washing machine. Bread to order. Bar and snack bar. River fishing. WiFi throughout (charged). No barbecues. No pets. Off site: Sightseeing. Famous train journeys across Corsica. Museum. Only university in Corsica (politically significant).

**Open:** 15 April - 30 September.

**Directions**

Site is south of Corte town and the rivers Tavignano and Restonica. Approaching the town, turn left at first roundabout onto ave du 9 Septembre. Site is 300 m. on the right. It is signed from the roundabout and at the top of the steep, narrow access road. GPS: 42.3015, 9.152

**Charges guide**

| | |
|---|---|
| Per unit incl. 2 persons | |
| and electricity | € 19.40 - € 24.20 |
| extra person | € 7.60 |
| child (0-7 yrs) | € 3.80 |

**FREE** Alan Rogers Travel Card
**Extra benefits and savings** - see page 10

## Ghisonaccia
### Camping Arinella Bianca

Route de la Mer, F-20240 Ghisonaccia (Haute-Corse) T: 04 95 56 04 78. E: arinella@arinellabianca.com

**alanrogers.com/FR20010**

Arinella is a lively, family oriented site on Corsica's east coast. The 381 good sized, level, grassy pitches (141 for touring units with 10A electricity) are amply shaded by a variety of trees and shrubs. Some pitches overlook the attractive lakes, which have fountains and are lit at night. The site has direct access to a huge long beach of soft sand. The brilliantly designed resort-style pools and paddling pool, overlooked by an attractive large restaurant, terraced bar and very professional entertainment area, form the hub of Arinella Bianca. The extremely active children's club with an information point, boutique and supermarket complete the facilities. When we visited the site was buzzing with activity at night and appeared to delight everyone by incorporating excellent family entertainment. This excellent site includes a wellness centre and offers a vast range of services and plenty of sport and leisure facilities to choose from. This site is a tribute to its owner's design and development skills as it appears to be in entirely natural glades where, in fact, these have been created from former marshland.

**Facilities**

Four open plan sanitary blocks provide solar heated showers, washbasins in cabins, mainly British style WCs. Laundry. Motorcaravan services. Shop, bar and restaurant with terrace. Wellness centre. Amphitheatre. Snack bar. Swimming pool (all season, heated). Multisports centre. Windsurfing. Canoeing. Fishing. Tennis. Riding. Bicycle hire. Canyoning can be organised. Miniclub. Play area. Disco. Superb entertainment programme in the main season. Communal barbecue area. WiFi (charged). Only 1 dog per pitch. Off site: Sailing 300 m. Boat launching 2 km. Excursions. Subaqua diving.

**Open:** 13 April - 5 October.

**Directions**

Site is 4 km. east of Ghisonaccia. From N198 in Ghisonaccia look for sign 'La Plage, Li Mare'. Turn east on D144 at roundabout just south of town. Continue for 3.5 km. to further roundabout where site is signed to right. Site is 500 m. GPS: 41.9984, 9.442

**Charges guide**

| Per unit incl. 2 persons and electricity | € 30.00 - € 50.00 |
|---|---|

Camping Cheques accepted.

**★★★★★**
**20240 Ghisonaccia – Corsica - tel: 0033 (0)4.95.56.04.78 - fax: 0033 (0)4.95.56.12.54**

Welcome to Arinella Bianca, a Corsican campsite between sea and mountain, directly at the beach and with a family atmosphere. Animations, Mini Club, fishing, watersports, hiking and a beautiful spa.

**web: www.arinellabianca.com - email: arinella@arinellabianca.com**

## Porto-Vecchio
### Camping la Vetta

Route de Bastia, la Trinité, F-20137 Porto-Vecchio (Corse-du-Sud) T: 04 95 70 09 86.
E: info@campinglavetta.com **alanrogers.com/FR20060**

The French/English owners Marieline and Nick Long have created a peaceful country park setting for their campsite to the north of La Trinité village. The 8.5 hectares of well maintained campsite are part sloping, part terraced, with an informal pitch allocation system. It seems to stretch endlessly. The abundance of tree varieties including many cork oaks give shade to 111 pitches which all have 10A electricity. The site has a pleasant lagoon-style pool with a bar, snacks and ice cream.

**Facilities**

Clean, traditional style toilet facilities have plenty of hot water. Laundry facilities. Bread and milk, lunchtime snacks and bar (all July/Aug). Swimming pool, paddling pool and water play area (all season). Snooker table. Play area. TV. Occasional Corsican evenings (high season). WiFi. Off site: Beach, fishing, watersports and boat launching 1.5 km. Good restaurant 1.5 km. Supermarket 2 km. Riding 4 km. Bicycle hire 5 km. Golf 7 km.

**Open:** 1 June - 1 October.

**Directions**

Site is in La Trinité village, off the RN198 (east side), north of Porto-Vecchio. GPS: 41.6316, 9.2929

**Charges guide**

| Per unit incl. 2 persons and electricity | € 22.00 - € 27.00 |
|---|---|
| extra person | € 6.50 - € 8.00 |
| child (under 7 yrs) | € 3.00 - € 4.00 |

For latest campsite news, availability and prices visit
**alanrogers.com**

## Sagone
### Camping le Sagone

Route de Vico, F-20118 Sagone (Corse-du-Sud) T: 04 95 28 04 15. E: sagone.camping@wanadoo.fr
**alanrogers.com/FR20230**

Situated outside the bustling seaside resort of Sagone, surrounded by protective hills, this campsite which used to be a fruit farm is in an ideal location for exploring Corsica's wild and rocky west coast or its mountainous interior. The large site borders a pleasant river and has 276 marked, shaded pitches, 250 with 6A electricity. The restaurant/bar overlooks the pool and they are the focal point of this well managed site. The site provides an amazing array of sports and specialises in sports activities for groups in the low season.

| Facilities | Directions |
|---|---|
| Clean, fully equipped toilet blocks with washbasins in cubicles. Facilities for disabled visitors. Baby baths. Washing machines, dryers. Motorcaravan services. Large supermarket (all year). Restaurant, pizzeria, bar. Swimming pools (June-Sept). Superb sports facilities. Fully equipped gym. Tennis. Play area. Barbecues are not permitted. Satellite TV. WiFi in restaurant. Car wash. Putting and senior golf practice area. Off site: Riding 500 m. Mountain biking, windsurfing, diving, fishing and bicycle hire nearby. **Open:** 1 February - 1 December. | From Ajaccio take the RD81 in direction of Cergése and Calvilby (by coast road). In Sagone take RD70 in direction of Vico, Sagone can be found on left after 1.5 km. next to supermarket. GPS: 42.1304, 8.7055 |

**Charges guide**

| Per unit incl. 2 persons and electricity | € 22.00 - € 36.50 |
|---|---|
| extra person | € 5.00 - € 8.40 |

Camping Cheques accepted.

## San Nicolao
### Camping Merendella

Moriani-Plage, F-20230 San Nicolao (Haute-Corse) T: 04 95 38 53 47. E: merendel@orange.fr
**alanrogers.com/FR20030**

This attractive site has the advantage of direct access to a very pleasant, 300 m. sandy beach. It is peacefully situated on level grass and sand with many trees and shrubs providing shade and colour. There are 196 pitches, all large and well spaced with electricity (10A, long leads may be required). The choice of placement is impressive with some hedged for privacy under the cool shade of mature trees. Many have direct beach access with beautiful sea views and the sound of the waves. An excellent bar, snack bar/pizzeria and restaurant are all available on the beach, providing great views and a wonderful atmosphere, particularly when dining in the evening.

| Facilities | Directions |
|---|---|
| Modern toilet blocks plus two smaller cabin units near the beach. Washbasins in private cubicles. Mostly British style WCs. Facilities for disabled visitors. Laundry facilities. Motorcaravan services. Shop. Bar/restaurant, pizzeria on the beach. Solar heated swimming pool with sliding cover (uncovered high season). TV room. Games room. Late arrival area. Diving centre. Play area. Torches essential. WiFi (charged). Communal barbecue area. No dogs. **Open:** 1 April - 10 October. | Site is to seaward side of the RN198, 800 m. south of Moriani Plage. GPS: 42.3656, 9.5296 |

**Charges guide**

| Per unit incl. 2 persons and electricity | € 30.10 - € 35.00 |
|---|---|
| extra person | € 7.45 - € 8.85 |
| child (2-12 yrs) | € 4.80 - € 5.55 |

## Sartène
### Campéole l'Avena

Campé●le

Tizzano, F-20100 Sartène (Corse-du-Sud) T: 04 95 77 02 18. E: avena@campeole.com
**alanrogers.com/FR20290**

Campéole l'Avena is a young site which is in the process of being improved. It sits in a valley with a beach 400 m. away along a sandy track. There are 211 flat pitches with 90 for tourers, all with 16A electricity. Some are closely placed and there are differing levels of shade. The small snack bar and shop provide an adequate service, but remember the closest village is 15 km. away. Reception is smart and air conditioned. A play area was supplemented with a bouncy castle when we visited.

| Facilities | Directions |
|---|---|
| Single, dated unisex sanitary block, which was struggling when we visited. Hot showers. No provision for children or disabled visitors. Washing machines. Shop/snack bar (high season). WiFi (charged). Communal barbecue. Off site: Beach, watersports and fishing 400 m. Riding 1 km. Archaeological sites. Walking. Diving. **Open:** 28 May - 25 September. | Site is on the west coast of Corsica. From the RN196 take the D48 towards Tizzano, site is off to the left down a rough track and is well signed. GPS: 41.5343, 8.8633 |

**Charges guide**

| Per unit incl. 2 persons and electricity | € 17.90 - € 27.60 |
|---|---|
| extra person | € 4.60 - € 7.90 |
| child (2-6 yrs) | free - € 4.70 |

**FREE** Alan Rogers Travel Card
Extra benefits and savings - see page 10

Naturism is something of a way of life, and today many more people than one might think enjoy the freedom and sense of equality found in naturist campsites. Being in harmony with nature, whether by the sea or in a woodland setting, can be a unique and liberating experience.

**Some are dedicated naturists who practise their way of life wherever they may be, and who, in the UK, may well belong to clubs of like-minded people. For others, especially those who have enjoyed sunbathing on one of the many designated naturist areas on European beaches and feel comfortable with it, the logical next step is to try a holiday in a naturist village or campsite.**

This growing number of 'holiday naturists' clearly enjoy the relaxed atmosphere prevailing on naturist sites. If they are not members of British Naturism, they can pick up a naturist card on the first site they visit. The rules are simple: respect for the environment and for other visitors. You are encouraged to strip off but, in reality, it is up to you, except in and around the swimming pool where there is always a 'no clothes' rule. Clothes do tend to label people and without them there is a relaxed informality and sense of equality often missing in today's 'designer society'.

We feature some 27 naturist campsites in this guide and have been impressed by the friendly welcome and cultural aspects of their entertainment and range of activities – classical music beside the pool, walking trails to discover local wildlife or book-binding classes, for example. Most campsites make an effort to provide good entertainment and to make your holiday memorable; on the naturist sites in particular, this is usually achieved quite elegantly without the frenzy that sometimes pervades more commercially-minded sites.

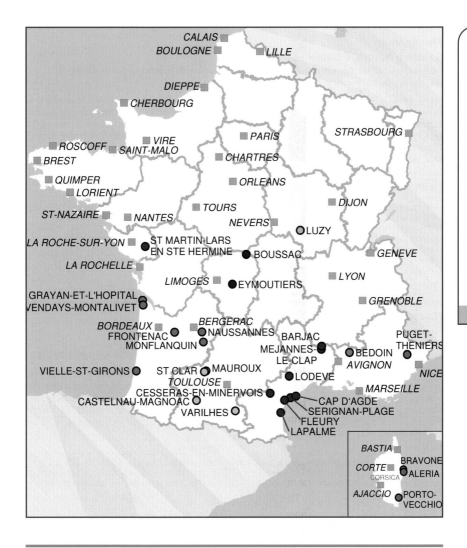

## Grayan et l'Hôpital
### Espace Naturiste Euronat

F-33590 Grayan-et-l'Hôpital (Gironde) T: 05 56 09 33 33. E: info@euronat.fr
**alanrogers.com/FR33160**

Euronat is a well established naturist resort with extensive facilities, direct access to 1.5 km. of sandy beach and a thalassotherapy centre. With a total of 3,000 pitches, those for touring (around 1,200) are in two areas separated from the chalets and mobile homes. A variety of good sized, fairly flat and sandy pitches, include some suitable for large motorcaravans. All pitches have 5/10A electricity and some also have water and drainage. The recently enhanced centre is superb with two supermarkets, an organic supermarket, cash point, butcher, fish shop, bakery, restaurants including fish, brasserie, pizzeria/crêperie, and a takeaway with a selection of hot and cold dishes and desserts.

### Facilities

Sanitary blocks are well maintained with some heated. Facilities for disabled campers. Launderette. Motorcaravan services. Shops, restaurants. Swimming pool, flumes, children's pool. Swimming lessons. Activities and workshops, archery, pony club, riding, tennis, pétanque, fishing. Bicycle hire. Children's activities and day care. TV rooms, video/games centre. Library. Multi-purpose hall for sport and entertainment. Supervised beach. Communal barbecues only. Torch may be useful. WiFi (charged).

**Open:** 23 March - 3 November.

### Directions

From Bordeaux ring road take exit 7, then D1215 to Lesparre and Vensac, then follow (large) signed route. GPS: 45.41627, -1.13178

### Charges guide

| | |
|---|---|
| Per unit incl. 2 persons and services | € 17.00 - € 46.00 |
| tent incl. 2 persons | € 11.00 - € 32.00 |

Camping Cheques accepted.

**FREE** Alan Rogers Travel Card
Extra benefits and savings - see page 10

## Monflanquin

### Camping Naturiste Domaine Laborde

Paulhiac, F-47150 Monflanquin (Lot-et-Garonne) T: 05 53 63 14 88. E: domainelaborde@wanadoo.fr

**alanrogers.com/FR47140**

Ideally situated on the border of Lot-et-Garonne and Dordogne, Domain Laborde is a naturist site of outstanding quality, with sweeping views from many of the higher pitches. This hilly site has 150 well maintained pitches, all for touring; many are shaded, some partially shaded and all are surrounded by woodland. Electricity (3-15A) is available (long leads may be required). There are also 40 chalets for rent. The site has something for everyone and even in low season it is very popular. If you are new to naturist sites, then this is a must. The ambience is good and you will make new friends. A Sites et Paysages member.

**Facilities**

The three clean sanitary blocks and a new wash block (one with underfloor heating). Washing machines and dryer. Shop with fresh bread and milk daily. Bar with TV. Snack bar serving pizzas. Restaurant (15/4-15/9). Two large swimming pools with slides, whirlpool, sauna, children's pool and indoor heated pool. Massage. Hammam. Trampoline. Two play areas. Boules. Giant chess. Communal barbecue (no charcoal on pitches). Activities for children (high season). Free WiFi in cybercafé.

**Open:** 1 April - 30 September.

**Directions**

From Monflanquin take D272 towards Monpazier. 10 km. along the road look for the signs to site. It is very well signed at regular intervals and will read 'Domaine Laborde'. GPS: 44.613889, 0.835556

**Charges guide**

| | |
|---|---|
| Per unit incl. 2 persons and electricity | € 23.00 - € 31.50 |
| extra person | € 5.00 - € 6.50 |

## Naussannes

### Centre Naturiste le Couderc

Le Couderc, F-24440 Naussannes (Dordogne) T: 05 53 22 40 40. E: info@lecouderc.com

**alanrogers.com/FR24190**

This is a very spacious site set in 33 hectares of open countryside with large pitches naturally laid out around sloping meadows. There is a feeling of calm and tranquillity and the family owners ensure that visitors enjoy their stay. There are 180 pitches of which 158 are for touring, all with 6A electricity. The site is on different levels with undulating slopes but the generous pitches are level and easily accessible. Generally open, but mature trees all around offer some shade. A varied programme of events, for all the family, are run throughout most of the season.

**Facilities**

Five clean, modern toilet blocks with facilities for children and disabled visitors. Outdoor showers. Washing machines and dryer. Restaurant and bar. Takeaway. Terrace. Shop. Heated swimming pools. Jacuzzi. Sauna. Bicycle hire. Two ponds, one for fishing the other with cable slide. Children's club with sculpture and circus lessons. Play area. Some entertainment. WiFi (charged). Walking tracks. Caravan storage. Torches essential.

**Open:** 1 April - 1 October.

**Directions**

From Bergerac take N21. Turn left on D25 to Issigeac. Continue towards Naussannes for 8 km. Turn left at signpost indicating Naussannes 2 km. Le Couderc is 350 m. on the right. GPS: 44.75602, 0.70212

**Charges guide**

| | |
|---|---|
| Per unit incl. 2 persons and electricity | € 23.46 - € 36.26 |
| extra person | € 4.60 - € 7.80 |

## Vendays-Montalivet

### Centre Naturiste Helio-Marin de Montalivet

46 avenue de l'Europe, F-33930 Vendays-Montalivet (Gironde) T: 05 56 73 73 73.
E: infos@chm-montalivet.com **alanrogers.com/FR33370**

This is a very large naturist village with everything that you could need during your holiday without leaving the site. It has direct access to the sea with its own beautiful, golden sandy beaches with coastguard surveillance in high season. Watersports are numerous with lessons if you require. The main emphasis here is to keep the family entertained. There are 3,072 pitches, of which 622 are for touring. Pitches are level, on grass or sand, and mature trees provide shade in some areas. A circus school, dancing classes and skateboarding are just some of the activities organised here.

**Facilities**

Numerous sanitary blocks with facilities for children and disabled visitors. Launderette. Motorcaravan service point. Shops, restaurants and bars. Two swimming pool complexes with slides and toboggan. Children's clubs. Evening entertainment. Playgrounds. Sports grounds. TV rooms and cinema. Large library. Wellness centre offering numerous treatments and massage as well as saunas and jacuzzis. Bicycle hire. Fishing. WiFi (charged).

**Open:** 30 March - 28 September.

**Directions**

From Royan, take the ferry to Verdon-sur-Mer and continue on N215 for 34 km. Turn right on D102 to Montalivet. Nearing the sea turn left for Hourtins and site is 1 km. on the right. GPS: 45.36348, -1.14575

**Charges guide**

| | |
|---|---|
| Per unit incl. 2 persons and electricity | € 18.50 - € 35.80 |
| extra person | € 4.20 - € 7.60 |
| Camping Cheques accepted. | |

For latest campsite news, availability and prices visit
**alanrogers.com**

## Vielle-Saint-Girons

### Domaine Naturiste Arnaoutchot

5008 route de Pichelebe, F-40560 Vielle-Saint-Girons (Landes) T: 05 58 49 11 11. E: contact@arna.com

**alanrogers.com/FR40120**

'Arna' is a large naturist site with extensive facilities and direct access to the beach. Even with 500 pitches, its layout in the form of a number of sections, each with its own character, makes it quite relaxing and very natural. These sections amongst the trees and bushes of the Landes provide a variety of reasonably sized pitches, most with electricity (3/6A), although the hilly terrain means that only a limited number are flat enough for motorcaravans. The centrally located amenities are extensive and of excellent quality. We suggest that new visitors telephone before arrival as the site can require them to be proposed by a family who have stayed at the campsite for at least three years. English, Dutch and German are spoken at reception. A member of France 4 Naturisme.

**Facilities**

Heated sanitary facilities include the usual naturist site type of blocks with communal hot showers and also a number of tiny blocks. Motorcaravan services. Supermarket, bar/restaurant, pizzeria and tapita (fish) bar (8/5-23/9). Heated indoor swimming pool with solarium, whirlpool and slide. Outdoor pool, sunbathing area. New paddling pool. Spa, sauna, steam room and massage. TV, games rooms. Cinema. Library. Internet point. Bicycle hire. Fishing. Torches useful. Charcoal barbecues are not permitted. American-style motorhomes not accepted. Off site: Riding and golf 5 km.

**Open:** 1 April - 29 September.

**Directions**

Site is signed off the D652 road at Vielle-Saint-Girons. Follow D328 for 3-4 km. GPS: 43.9075, -1.361683

**Charges guide**

| Per unit incl. 2 persons | |
|---|---|
| and electricity | € 16.40 - € 46.05 |
| extra person (over 3 yrs) | € 2.50 - € 8.00 |
| dog | € 1.70 - € 3.70 |

Deposit on arrival for accommodation € 50.

Camping Cheques accepted.

## Luzy

### Centre de Vacance Naturiste Domaine de la Gagère

F-58170 Luzy (Nièvre) T: 03 86 30 48 11. E: info@la-gagere.com

**alanrogers.com/FR58060**

At this secluded and attractive campsite, you will receive a really good welcome from the enthusiastic owners, Thom and Betty. The site is spacious and well equipped with 100 good sized, level, grassy pitches, some shaded, some open, all are available for tourers. Many are arranged in groups around three sides of rectangles, between hedges. Electricity (4-10A) is supplied to 90 pitches, six of which are fully serviced, but some require leads of up to 40 m. There are plenty of water points. In high season there are organised activities and entertainment and a children's club meets twice per week. The site lies near the southern end of the Morvan Regional Natural Park, surrounded by wooded hills, but within easy reach of attractions such as the European community sponsored Museum of Celtic History and Kagyu Ling, the largest Buddhist temple in Europe.

**Facilities**

Three modern unisex toilet blocks, one heated, with British style WCs, washbasins and preset showers. Facilities for disabled visitors. Baby changing. Motorcaravan services. Laundry facilities. Shop (15/5-15/9). Bar (all season). Restaurant with snack bar and takeaway (1/5-15/9). Satellite TV. Two heated swimming pools (one all season, the other 15/5-15/9). Sauna and health suite. Play areas. Boules. Bicycle hire. Only gas and electric barbecues permitted (available for hire). WiFi throughout (charged) Off site: Luzy 10 km. Fishing 10 km. Riding 20 km. Golf 27 km.

**Open:** 1 April - 1 October.

**Directions**

Leave Autun on N81, southwest towards Bourbon-Lancy. In 27 km. turn left (signed Gagère) down narrow lane. Site is 3 km. GPS: 46.81692, 4.05636

**Charges guide**

| Per unit incl. 2 persons | |
|---|---|
| and electricity | € 30.75 - € 34.00 |
| extra person | € 7.00 |
| child (3-12 yrs) | € 4.00 |

Admin fee for stays of 3 nights or less (€ 5).

**FREE** Alan Rogers Travel Card
Extra benefits and savings - see page 10

## Aléria
### Riva Bella Nature Resort & Spa
B.P. 21, F-20270 Aléria (Haute-Corse) T: 04 95 38 81 10. E: rivabella.corsica@gmail.com
**alanrogers.com/FR20040**

This is a relaxed, informal, spacious site alongside an extremely long and beautiful beach. Riva Bella is naturist from 16 May to 19 September only. It offers a variety of pitches situated in beautiful countryside and seaside. The site is divided into several areas with 200 pitches (133 for touring with 6A electricity), some of which are alongside the sandy beach with little shade. Others are in a shady, wooded glade on the hillside. The huge fish-laden lakes are a fine feature of this site and a superb balnéotherapy centre offers the very latest beauty and relaxation treatments (men and women) based on marine techniques. The charming owner, Marie Claire Pasqual, is justifiably proud of the site and the fairly unobtrusive rules are designed to ensure that everyone is able to relax. Cars are parked away from the pitches. The restaurant offers a sophisticated menu and the excellent beach restaurant/bar has superb sea views.

**Facilities**

High standard toilet facilities. Provision for disabled visitors, children and babies. Laundry. Large shop (15/5-15/10). Fridge hire. Two restaurants with sea and lake views with reasonable prices. Beach restaurant/bar. Watersports, sailing school, pedaloes, fishing. Balnéo centre. Sauna. Aerobics. Giant chess. Archery. Fishing. Mountain bike hire. Half-court tennis. Walking with llamas. Internet. WiFi (charged). Professional evening entertainment programme. Off site: Tours of the island. Walking. Riding 4 km. Scuba diving 10 km. Paragliding.

**Open:** All year (naturist 16/5-19/9).

**Directions**

Site is 12 km. north of Aleria on N198 (Bastia) road. Watch for large signs and unmade road to site and follow for 4 km. GPS: 42.16151, 9.55269

**Charges guide**

| | |
|---|---|
| Per unit incl. 2 persons | |
| and electricity | € 23.30 - € 40.80 |
| extra person | € 5.00 - € 9.50 |
| child (3-8 yrs) | € 2.00 - € 6.50 |
| dog | € 2.00 - € 4.00 |

Special offers and half-board arrangements available.

# Domaine Naturiste Riva Bella
RIVA BELLA
THALASSO & SPA RESORT
**For all: Village-Camping-Thalasso. Camping 4\* - Tourism Residence 3\***
Yearly opening dates: NON NATURIST: from 20-09 untill 15-05. Closed from 20-12 untill 20-01

BP21 - 20270 Aleria
Corsica
Tel: +33 (0)495 38 81 10
riva-bella@orange.fr
www.rivabella-inf.com

## Bravone
### Camping Bagheera Naturisme
Route 198, F-20230 Bravone (Haute-Corse) T: 04 95 38 80 30. E: bagheera@bagheera.fr
**alanrogers.com/FR20080**

An extremely long private road leads you to this naturist site which is alongside a 3 km. beach of fine sand and has been run by the same family for 30 years. There are 250 informal pitches which are separated from the bungalows. Well shaded under huge eucalyptus trees, all have 10A electricity (long leads may be necessary). Some beach-side pitches have sea views, the others are further back but all are within 200 m. of the sea. All pitches are on sandy grass and are kept clean and neat. The main restaurant and beach bar/restaurant have superb panoramic views of the sea and extensive menus.

**Facilities**

Five very comfortable sanitary blocks can be heated and offer hot water throughout. Baby rooms. Washing machines. Excellent restaurant (Corsican menu, children's menu). Bar. Comprehensive beach restaurant and bar. Pizzeria. Shop. All amenities 1/6-30/9. Play area. Fitness circuit. Gym. Massage. Sauna. Pedaloes. Pétanque. Windsurfing. Subaqua diving. Beach umbrella rental. Refrigerated lockers for hire. Tennis. Bicycle hire. Fishing (lake or sea). Entertainment programme all season. TV. WiFi (charged). Off site: Commercial centre 6 km. Riding.

**Open:** All year.

**Directions**

Site is between Bastia and Aleria near Bravone, 7 km. north of Aleria on the RN198. It is well signed off the RN198. Follow site road 4 km. east to beach. GPS: 42.2206, 9.5380

**Charges guide**

| | |
|---|---|
| Per unit incl. 2 persons | |
| and electricity | € 20.00 - € 32.50 |
| extra person | € 4.65 - € 9.90 |
| child (acc. to age) | free - € 4.70 |
| dog | € 2.00 - € 4.10 |

For latest campsite news, availability and prices visit
**alanrogers.com**

## Porto-Vecchio
### Village Naturiste la Chiappa

Route de Palombaggia, F-20137 Porto-Vecchio (Corse-du-Sud) T: 04 95 70 00 31. E: chiappa@wanadoo.fr
**alanrogers.com/FR20050**

This is a large naturist campsite on the Chiappa peninsula with 200 pitches, some with good sea views, for tourers and tents, plus 250 bungalows. The pitches are informally marked and are a variety of shapes and sizes, some with difficult slopes and access, especially for large units (75-125 sq.m). Cars are parked separately. Very long electricity leads are necessary here for most pitches (10A electricity). The beaches are between long rocky outcrops and it is generally safe to swim, or alternatively enjoy the swimming pool by the main beach. Two beach restaurants and bars enjoy good views and there is an animation programme in high season plus extensive watersports. The touring areas are a considerable distance from the amenities and an off-road bicycle would make life easier. The bungalows have the prime places, as do the seasonal pitches.

### Facilities

The sanitary facilities were clean when we visited. Washing machines. Well stocked shop. Two bars and restaurants with snacks. Bistro. Swimming pool. Play area. Riding. Tennis. Minigolf. Fishing. Diving, windsurfing and sailing schools. Keep fit, yoga, sauna (extra cost). Pottery. Riding. Satellite TV. WiFi. Torches essential. Off site: Excursions.

**Open:** 14 May - 8 October.

### Directions

From Bastia, N198 heading south, take Porto-Vecchio bypass (signed Bonofaccio). At southern end, take first left signed Pont de la Chiappa, unclassified road. After 8 km. site signed. Turn left and follow rough track for 2 km. to site. GPS: 41.59387, 9.35713

### Charges guide

| | |
|---|---|
| Per unit incl. 2 persons and electricity | € 27.00 - € 37.00 |
| per person | € 8.00 - € 10.00 |
| child (5-13 yrs) | € 4.00 - € 5.00 |
| dog | € 5.00 |

Special offers available.

- F-20137 Porto Vecchio (Corse)
- (+33) 04 95 70 00 31 • chiappa@wanadoo.fr
www.chiappa.com

A forest right behind the sea

A road invaded by the scents of rock-roses and wild flowers, leads to an almost unimaginable eucalyptus forest. A pond hidden under the reeds of the awaited blue between the sand and the infinite seal
At Bagheera, it is so immense, that everything, including the welcoming structure, the accommodations, the catering, the supplying and the leisure activities, blends into the site, the dream of any naturist.
All this made in the hope of sharing, one day, a clean planet.

www.bagheera.fr - bagheera@bagheera.fr

**Bagheera**

Corsica, the sea and.. some guests.

Village de vacances et camping naturiste
20230 Bravone - Corse - France
Tél. +33 (04) 95 38 80 30
Fax +33 (04) 95 38 83 47

**FREE** Alan Rogers Travel Card
Extra benefits and savings - see page 10

## Puget-Theniers
### Domaine Naturiste Club Origan

F-06260 Puget-Theniers (Alpes-Maritimes) T: 04 93 05 06 00. E: origan@orange.fr
**alanrogers.com/FR06070**

Origan is a naturist site set in the mountains behind Nice at a height of 500 m. The access road is single track and winding with few passing places, so arrival is not recommended until late afternoon. The site's terrain is fairly wild and the roads are stony, so it is unsuitable for caravans longer than six metres due to the steep slopes, although the site will assist with a 4x4 vehicle if requested. The 100 touring pitches, in three areas, are irregular sizes and shapes with good views. Electricity connection (6A) is possible on most pitches (by long cable). A member of France 4 Naturisme.

| Facilities | Directions |
|---|---|
| Sanitary facilities are clean and of a standard and type associated with most good naturist sites – mostly open plan hot showers. Laundry facilities. Shop (1/6-30/8). Bar/restaurant. Takeaway. Heated swimming pools (1/6-30/8). Jacuzzi and sauna. Tennis. Fishing. Organised activities for all (high season). Gas and electric barbecues only. Torches advised. WiFi around reception. | Heading west on the N202, just past the town of Puget-Theniers, turn right at campsite sign at level crossing; site is 2 km. GPS: 43.957633, 6.860883 |

**Open:** 15 April - 30 September.

**Charges guide**

| | |
|---|---|
| Per unit incl. 2 persons and electricity | € 18.00 - € 34.00 |
| extra person | € 4.00 - € 9.00 |

## Barjac
### Camping Naturiste de la Sablière

Domaine de la Sablière, Saint Privat-de-Champclos, F-30430 Barjac (Gard) T: 04 66 24 51 16.
E: contact@villagesabliere.com **alanrogers.com/FR30100**

Spectacularly situated in the Cèze Gorges, this well equipped, spacious naturist site, tucked away within its wild and dramatic terrain offers a wide variety of facilities, all within a really peaceful, wooded setting. There are 497 pitches, 240 for touring. Many are large and most have electricity (6/10A). Long leads and rock pegs may possibly be needed. Nudity is only obligatory around the pool complex. There are long and steep walks between many pitches and the facilities. Cars can be used in low season and there is a shuttle service in July and August. Large outfits not advised. Only gas and electric barbecues on site.

| Facilities | Directions |
|---|---|
| Six open-plan unisex sanitary blocks. Naturist style baths and facilities for visitors with disabilities. Laundry. Good supermarket. Bar (1/4-22/9). Excellent open-air, covered restaurant and takeaway (1/4-22/9). Small café/crêperie. Swimming pool complex. Fitness room. TV room. Disco. Tennis. Minigolf. Play areas. River bathing. Fitness trail. Archery. Full entertainment programme. Only gas and electric barbecues allowed. Free WiFi at reception. Off site: Walking and cycling. Bicycle hire 8 km. Barjac with Fri market 8 km. Riding 10 km. Golf 12 km. | From Alès take D16 then D979 northeast towards Barjac. 5 km. beyond St Jean-de-Maruéjols turn right D266 signed St Privat and site. Site is 5 km. along winding lane. GPS: 44.26685, 4.35202 |

**Open:** 2 April - 2 October.

**Charges guide**

| | |
|---|---|
| Per unit incl. 2 persons and electricity (10A) | € 19.80 - € 35.30 |
| extra person | € 4.40 - € 8.00 |

Camping Cheques accepted.

## Cap d'Agde
### Centre Hélio-Marin René Oltra

1 rue des Néréides, B.P. 884, F-34307 Cap d'Agde (Hérault) T: 04 67 01 06 36. E: infos@chm-reneoltra.fr
**alanrogers.com/FR34270**

A large, naturist site situated within the Cap d'Agde Village Naturiste and alongside a wonderful sandy beach. Regularly laid out in sheltered avenues covering 35 hectares, it is well organised with 2,546 level sandy pitches and 1,038 privately-owned mobile homes. The remainder is divided between touring pitches (5A electricity) and site-owned mobile homes and chalets, some very smart and almost on the beach. A wide range of sports facilities are available including children's clubs for 6-10 yrs, 11-13 yrs and for teenagers over 14 yrs. Bread, fresh fruit and vegetable stalls and several shops are at the Centre Naturiste; there is a smart new beach bar, which is very popular.

| Facilities | Directions |
|---|---|
| Over 25 toilet blocks of varying sizes. Mainly open style showers typical of naturist sites. Laundry. Motorcaravan service point. Two bars, snack bar (1/5-30/9). Bread and fruit stalls (15/4-30/9). Children's clubs. Entertainment programme, cabarets, dancing. Open-air cinema. Beauty centre. Outdoor fitness equipment. Multisports court. Football. Volleyball. Archery. Tennis. Play area. Communal barbecue. WiFi (charged). | Follow signs for Cap d'Agde Tourist office then pick up signs for 'Naturisme'. GPS: 43.29723, 3.52782 |

**Open:** 15 March - 15 October.

**Charges guide**

| | |
|---|---|
| Per unit incl. 2 persons and electricity (5A) | € 20.00 - € 39.00 |
| extra person | € 8.00 - € 16.00 |
| child | free - € 6.00 |
| dog | € 3.40 |

For latest campsite news, availability and prices visit
**alanrogers.com**

## Cesseras-en-Minervois
### Camping Naturiste le Mas de Lignières

Montcélèbre, F-34210 Cesseras-en-Minervois (Hérault) T: 04 68 91 24 86. E: lemas1@wanadoo.fr
**alanrogers.com/FR34050**

A naturist site hidden in the hills of the Minervois, only 3 km. from the medieval town of Minerve. There are marvellous views to the Pyrenees, the Corbières and the coast at Narbonne. Jeanne continues to run the site and keep alive the memory of Gilles, offering a warm welcome to all. The site now has just 20 very large pitches (electricity 6/10A), and six caravan holiday homes. Mainly on level grass, they are separated by mature hedges which give considerable privacy. There is natural shade and a variety of flora and fauna including four types of orchid.

| Facilities | Directions |
|---|---|
| Clean toilet block has open washbasins and showers, facilities for disabled visitors. Washing machine. Bread (15/6-15/9). Swimming pool, sliding cover for use when cold. Paddling pool. Room for general use with TV, library, separate provision for young visitors. Playground. Tennis. Boules. Torch useful. WiFi (charged). Only gas barbecues are permitted. Off site: Sailing, riding and canoeing at nearby Lac de Jouarres. Canal du Midi. | From A61 take exit for Lézignan-Corbières, D611 to Homps, then D910 to Olonzac. Through village following signs to Minerve (D10). Continue. 4 km. Turn left to Cesseras (D168). At Cesseras follow signs Fauzan for 4 km. (site signed) on right, narrow, winding road. GPS: 43.34092, 2.70648 |

**Open:** 27 April - 30 September.

**Charges guide**

Per unit incl. 2 persons
and electricity      € 24.50 - € 28.80

---

## Fleury
### Domaine Naturiste la Grande Cosse

Saint Pierre-la-Mer, F-11560 Fleury (Aude) T: 04 68 33 61 87. E: contact@grandecosse.com
**alanrogers.com/FR11190**

Any slight difficulty in finding this secluded naturist site is compensated for the moment you arrive. The abundance of flowers, shrubs and the generally peaceful ambience makes this a delightful place for a relaxing naturist holiday, and the extensive facilities mean you only need to leave the site for sightseeing rather than for necessities. In total there are 480 pitches, of which about 146 are for mobile homes, and the mainly large touring pitches, all with 8A electrical connections, are informally and very attractively arranged in a variety of different areas.

| Facilities | Directions |
|---|---|
| Five sanitary blocks, one heated, are opened progressively as required. Fully equipped modern facilities, including a choice of private or communal showers, and some washbasins in cabins. Laundry facilities. Motorcaravan service point. Gas. Well stocked shop, bar, restaurant and takeaway (all season). Three heated swimming pools, two for adults and a smaller one for children (all season). Play area. Tennis. Archery. Playing field. Bicycle hire. Internet and WiFi (charged). Communal barbecues. | From A9 take exit 36 to Vendres. Pass through town, continue to Lespignan, then Fleury. At roundabout turn left (Cabanes-de-Fleury). Follow for 4 km. to pick up site sign to left. Continue for 2 km. and site signed to right. GPS: 43.20582, 3.21099 |

**Open:** 9 April - 9 October.

**Charges guide**

Per unit incl. 2 persons
and electricity      € 18.00 - € 41.00
Camping Cheques accepted.

---

## Lodève
### Domaine Naturiste de Lambeyran

Hameau de Lambeyran, F-34700 Lodève (Hérault) T: 04 67 44 13 99. E: lambeyran@wanadoo.fr
**alanrogers.com/FR34540**

A wooded valley covering 348 hectares allows Domaine de Lambeyran a place in the Guinness Book of Records for having the largest area available for naturists in the world. It is a wonderful natural area with amazing views across to Lodève and the spectacular surrounding countryside. Naturists can enjoy the marked trails around the valley or the large, heated pool whilst choosing from 160 huge pitches, 100 with electricity (4/6A) and many quite private. Where necessary the pitches have been levelled with local stone which has also been used to create short stairways in the terrain.

| Facilities | Directions |
|---|---|
| Three toilet blocks are fully equipped, including baby baths, but no facilities for disabled visitors. Washing machine. Small shop, bar and snack bar (all 7/6-31/8). Large, solar-heated swimming pool (from 20/5). Some play equipment for children and indoor area for older children. Dancing, films and organised trips such as canoeing down the Orb Gorges. Communal barbecue area. Dogs are only allowed in one area. | From A75 (Béziers, Clermont-Ferrand) take exit for Lodève and follow signs for town centre. Cross town following signs for Lunas (D35). Ignore right turn for Les Plans and take next right and continue up hill for 3 km. to site. GPS: 43.73648, 3.26483 |

**Open:** 10 May - 20 September.

**Charges guide**

Per unit incl. 2 persons
and electricity      € 21.10 - € 29.60
extra person      € 4.60 - € 6.70

---

## Méjannes-le-Clap

### Camping Naturiste la Genèse

Route de la Genèse, F-30430 Méjannes-le-Clap (Gard) T: 04 66 24 51 82. E: info@lagenese.com
**alanrogers.com/FR30400**

La Genèse is a well equipped naturist site close to the banks of the River Cèze on the northern edge of the Cévennes national park. This is a large site with 480 well shaded pitches, 160 are for touring. These are divided into 'sauvage' (without electricity) and 'prairie' (with electricity 6A and closer to the main facilities). A wide variety of activities are on offer here, including art and craft workshops, bridge evenings and a cinema. Sports amenities include a large swimming pool with aquagym sessions in high season, separate children's pool, tennis, archery and river bathing. Electric or communal barbecues only.

**Facilities**

Five clean and well maintained toilet blocks, one refurbished. Facilities for disabled campers. Shop (1/5-31/8). Bar, restaurant, takeaway. Swimming pool and children's pool. Sauna. Archery. Games room. Art and craft workshops. Cinema. Canoe hire. Play area. Activity and entertainment programme. Direct access to river, fishing. Mobile homes and chalets for rent. Motorcaravan services. WiFi (charged). Off site: Bicycle hire and riding 7 km. Cycle and walking tracks in the Cévennes national park. Amenities in Méjannes-le-Clap. Orange 50 km.

**Open:** 30 March - 28 September.

**Directions**

From Pont St Esprit, take D901 west to Barjac, then D979 to Rochegude. Shortly beyond Rochegude, take D167 to Méjannes-le-Clap and follow signs to site (6 km). GPS: 44.26772, 4.37013

**Charges 2013**

| | |
|---|---|
| Per unit incl. 2 persons and electricity | € 21.00 - € 30.00 |
| extra person | € 4.50 - € 6.80 |
| child (4-17 yrs) | € 3.40 - € 4.50 |
| dog | free - € 4.20 |

Camping Cheques accepted.

## Sérignan-Plage

### Camping le Sérignan-Plage Nature

Route de l'Orpellière, F-34410 Sérignan-Plage (Hérault) T: 04 67 32 09 61. E: info@leserignannature.com
**alanrogers.com/FR34080**

Sérignan-Plage Nature benefits from the same 600 m. of white, sandy beach as its sister site next door. Being a naturist site, it actually abuts the naturist section of the beach with direct access to it. It also has the use of the Sérignan-Plage balnéotherapy pool in the mornings, an excellent facility with spa and jacuzzi pools in a Romanesque-style setting. The site has 286 good sized pitches on level sandy grass of which 99 are available for touring (6A electricity). There is plenty of shade except on the pitches beside the beach. Eighty three mobile homes and chalets are available to rent. A friendly bar and shop serve the site although visitors may use the facilities at le Sérignan-Plage.

**Facilities**

Two toilet blocks of differing designs (one refurbished to a very modern design) offer modern facilities with some washbasins in cabins. All clean and well maintained. Washing machines. Supermarket, fruit and vegetables, newsagent/souvenir shop and ice cream kiosk. Small bar/café. Evening entertainment. Play area, miniclub and disco for children. Facilities and pools at Sérignan-Plage. Only gas barbecues are permitted. WiFi throughout (charged). Off site: Bicycle hire 200 m. Fishing 500 m. Riding 800 km. Golf 2 km.

**Open:** 26 April - 6 October.

**Directions**

From A9 exit 35 (Béziers Est) towards Sérignan, D64 (9 km). Before Sérignan, take road to Sérignan-Plage. At small sign (blue) turn right for 500 m. At T-junction turn left over bridge, site is 75 m. just after left-hand bend (the second naturist site). GPS: 43.263409, 3.320148

**Charges guide**

| | |
|---|---|
| Per unit incl. 2 persons and electricity | € 17.00 - € 53.00 |
| extra person | € 6.00 - € 10.00 |
| child (1-7 yrs) | free - € 10.00 |

Camping Cheques accepted.

For latest campsite news, availability and prices visit
# alanrogers.com

## Boussac
### Creuse Nature Naturisme
Route de Bétête (D15), F-23600 Boussac (Creuse) T: 05 55 65 18 01. E: creuse.nature@wanadoo.fr
**alanrogers.com/FR23030**

You are sure of a warm welcome by the Dutch owners of this very spacious, naturally laid out and well maintained naturist site. It is set in the beautiful but lesser known Limousin region in the centre of France. There are 100 large grassy/stony pitches, 80 of which are for touring with 10A electricity. Some are slightly sloping and there are varying degrees of shade. They are laid out in an open, wooded, parkland setting around the perimeter of the site or beside the small fishing lake. An attractive central feature is the swimming pool, sauna, bar and restaurant complex.

**Facilities**

Four modern, clean toilet blocks with the usual facilities (open-plan, so little privacy). Facilities for disabled visitors. Laundry facilities. Small shop (baker calls). Indoor (heated) and outdoor pools. Paddling pool. Bar and restaurant. Archery (high season). Boules. Bicycle hire. Lake fishing. Internet access with free WiFi. Gas barbecues only on pitches. Accommodation for hire.

**Open:** 1 April - 31 October.

**Directions**

Boussac is 35 km. west of Montluçon between the A20 and A71 autoroutes. In Boussac site is well signed. Take D15 west for 3 km. Site is on right. GPS: 46.34902, 2.18691

**Charges guide**

| Per unit incl. 2 persons | |
|---|---|
| and electricity | € 21.50 - € 29.50 |
| extra person | € 4.00 - € 7.00 |

## Eymoutiers
### Camping Naturiste Domaine des Monts de Bussy
Bussy Varache, F-87120 Eymoutiers (Haute-Vienne) T: 05 55 69 68 20. E: montsdebussy@wanadoo.fr
**alanrogers.com/FR87050**

Domaine des Monts de Bussy is a naturist site in the Millevaches natural park in the Limousin. The site is located alongside a footpath leading to the River Vienne and extends over ten hectares, with some fine views over the surrounding country. Pitches are large, grassy and many are equipped with electricity. A number of fully equipped mobile homes are available for rent. On-site amenities include a swimming pool, a children's play area and a convivial bar. Canoe trips on the Vienne are popular and the site also has a rock climbing centre.

**Facilities**

Two toilet blocks with one controllable shower in a cubicle and two outdoor open showers. No facilities for children or disabled visitors. Washing machines (€ 3 incl. powder). Bar. Swimming pool (May-Oct). Playground. Rock climbing. Picnic areas. Naturist walks. Mobile homes for rent. Off site: Beach 300 m. Eymoutiers 3 km. Fishing, riding and bicycle hire 3 km. Golf 16 km. Walking and cycling trails.

**Open:** 16 April - 31 October.

**Directions**

Take exit 35 from the A20 and follow D979 towards Eymoutiers (for 40 km). Just before Eymoutiers, turn left and take D129A towards Bussy. Follow D129A for 2 km, and drive through Bussy, then 300 m. beyond the village take small road on right to site. GPS: 45.750583, 1.692077

**Charges guide**

| Per unit incl. 2 persons | |
|---|---|
| and electricity | € 21.00 - € 27.00 |
| extra person | € 4.00 - € 6.00 |

## Castelnau-Magnoac
### Domaine Naturiste l'Eglantière
Aries-Espenan, F-65230 Castelnau-Magnoac (Hautes-Pyrénées) T: 05 62 39 88 00. E: info@leglantiere.com
**alanrogers.com/FR65010**

A delightful site with an air of calm and repose, l'Eglantière is set within 50 hectares of organic farmland and woodland for walking. The fast-flowing River Gers runs through the site, bringing opportunities for watersports and fishing. Pitches are large and naturally shaped, most have electricity (16A, long leads). Many are separated by wild flowers, grasses and trees, ensuring shade and privacy. There is a separate wild area for tents. The clubhouse bar, restaurant and terrace overlook the attractive swimming pool area where nudity is compulsory. The owners are welcoming and keen to promote the area.

**Facilities**

Two toilet blocks in typically naturist style, providing undercover, open plan, facilities. Small block has individual cubicles. Shop (June-Aug). Clubhouse, bar. Takeaway food. Heated swimming pool. Soundproofed disco and activities area, playroom for younger children. Play area. Children's entertainment (in season). Volleyball. Archery. Badminton. Pétanque. River activities. Canoe, mountain bike hire. Trekking. Cross-country cycling. Torches useful. WiFi. Off site: Restaurants in the nearby village.

**Open:** Easter - October.

**Directions**

From Auch take D929 south towards Lannemezan. After Castelnau-Magnoac go past aerodrome then onto D9 towards Monleon-Magnoac. Take first left towards Ariès-Espénan and follow site signs. GPS: 43.26466, 0.52119

**Charges guide**

| Per unit incl. 2 persons | |
|---|---|
| and electricity | € 17.90 - € 40.40 |
| extra person | € 4.00 - € 7.20 |
| Camping Cheques accepted. | |

**FREE** Alan Rogers Travel Card
Extra benefits and savings - see page 10

## Mauroux

### Camping Naturiste les Roches

Le Néry, F-32380 Mauroux (Gers) T: 05 62 66 30 18. E: campinglesroches@wanadoo.fr
alanrogers.com/FR32190

A pleasant and friendly site in beautiful wooded countryside, where visitors can relax. The 36 large, shady pitches, some are 200 sq.m, have electricity (6A). The cool, traditional reception buildings include a bar, games room and seasonal restaurant. The site is calm with woodland walks and the swimming pool (20x8 m) is away from the pitches. Nudity is expected unless the weather prevents it. Activities are easy going: boules, lake fishing, archery and volleyball. The owners can arrange trips to local wine, garlic and foie gras producers. St Clar is a lovely village 4km away and well worth a visit.

**Facilities**

All necessary facilities, including those for visitors with disabilities. Washing machine and dryer. Restaurant (1/6-15/9) and bread in high season. Bar and takeaway. Swimming pool. Sauna (€7.50 including drink at bar). Lake for fishing. Various indoor games. Communal barbecue only. Small playground. Saturday communal meal. Sunday boules tournament. Internet point. No motorcaravan services. Some lighting switched off after 23.00. Torches needed. Off site: Village of St Clar for most amenities 4 km. Bicycle hire and riding 15km. Golf 16 km. Local producers.

**Open:** 1 May - 15 September.

**Directions**

From Lectoure take the D7 to St Clar. At St Clar turn left onto D13 then after 1 km. turn right onto D167 to Gaudonville. Site is then well signed and along a fairly narrow bumpy roadway.
GPS: 43.898035, 0.811234

**Charges guide**

| Per unit incl. 2 persons | |
|---|---|
| and electricity (6A) | € 9.20 - € 13.00 |
| extra person | € 3.10 - € 4.75 |
| child (0-10 yrs) | free - € 3.25 |

No credit cards.

## Varilhes

### Naturiste Camping Millefleurs

Le Tuilier Gudas, F-09120 Varilhes (Ariège) T: 05 61 60 77 56. E: simone.groot@orange.fr
alanrogers.com/FR09090

Millefleurs is a beautifully quiet site in a secluded location for naturists. It is peaceful with some 70 acres of woods and meadows providing naturist walks in total privacy. The site has 40 large, flat, mostly terraced pitches (34 with 6/10A electricity), long leads if pitching off the terraces. There are also very secluded pitches in wooded areas with shade, or you can pitch a tent in the meadows if you prefer. There are few of the normal commercial camping leisure facilities here, and the site is definitely aimed at the more mature naturist camper, but would provide a good introduction to the novice.

**Facilities**

An excellent toilet block with facilities for disabled campers. Bread available to order in high season. Guests dine together in the the farmhouse two nights a week or just meet friends for a drink. Refrigerator with drinks. Pétanque. Guide book for walks and cycle rides. Torches useful. Pick ups from airports and stations arranged. There is no mobile phone reception, but a telephone is available. Off site: The coast is 1.5 hours away. Tuesday market at Varilhes. Bicycle hire 10 km. Fishing 20 km. Golf and riding 30 km.

**Open:** 1 April - 1 November.

**Directions**

From Varilhes, 8 km. south of Pamiers on D624 (parallel to N20). Take D13 for Dalou and Gudas cross railway and N20. The site is 2 km. past Gudas, on right. GPS: 42.9927, 1.6788

**Charges guide**

| Per unit incl. 2 persons | |
|---|---|
| and electricity | € 21.00 - € 24.00 |
| extra person | € 5.75 - € 6.75 |
| child (4-12 yrs) | € 2.50 - € 3.00 |
| dog | € 2.25 |

No credit cards.

For latest campsite news, availability and prices visit
**alanrogers.com**

## Bédoin
### Domaine Naturiste de Bélézy

Domaine de Bélézy, F-84410 Bedoin (Vaucluse) T: 04 90 65 60 18. E: info@belezy.com
**alanrogers.com/FR84020**

At the foot of Mont Ventoux, surrounded by beautiful scenery, Bélézy is an excellent naturist site with many amenities and activities and the ambience is relaxed and comfortable. The 320 pitches, 248 for touring (12A electricity, long leads required) are set amongst many varieties of trees and shrubs giving space and privacy. The attractive bar/restaurant and terrace overlook the swimming pool area and have superb views over the large recreational area and hills beyond. The site has an ecological theme with a small farm, a fish pond and a vegetable garden especially for the children. Only gas and electric barbecues are permitted. Pets are not accepted.

| Facilities | Directions |
|---|---|
| Four toilet blocks with very good facilities for campers with disabilities – newer ones are excellent, some have hot showers in the open air. A superb children's section. Shop. Bar. Excellent restaurant/takeaway (all 31/3-30/9). Swimming pools. Sauna. Tennis. Adventure play area. Activities all season. Archery. Guided walks. Children's club. Hydrotherapy centre (31/3-30/9). Only gas barbecues are allowed. WiFi throughout (charged). Off site: Bédoin with shops and restaurants 1.5 km. Discover the riches of Provence with its many interesting old market towns and villages. Superb area for walking and cycling with the challenge of Mont Ventoux. | From A7 autoroute (exit 22) or RN7, south of Orange, take D950 southeast to Carpentras, then D974 northeast to Bédoin. In Bédoin turn right at roundabout, site is in 2 km. and signed. GPS: 44.13352, 5.18745 |

**Charges guide**

| Per unit incl. 2 persons | |
|---|---|
| and electricity | € 15.00 - € 40.20 |
| extra person | € 6.00 - € 9.40 |
| child (3-8 yrs) | free - € 9.30 |

**Open:** 31 March - 5 October.

## Saint Martin-Lars-Sainte Hermine
### Camping Naturiste le Colombier

Le Colombier, F-85210 Saint Martin-Lars-Sainte Hermine (Vendée) T: 02 51 27 83 84.
E: lecolombier.nat@wanadoo.fr **alanrogers.com/FR85140**

A countryside site for naturists near La Roche sur Yon, just right for those seeking a peaceful holiday. It provides around 160 pitches in seven very natural fields on different levels linked by informal tracks. There are level, terraced areas for caravans and a feeling of spaciousness with pitches around the edges of fields, unmarked and with electricity (6/10A, some may require long leads). The bar/restaurant is in a converted barn. The site's 125 acres provide many walks throughout the attractive, wooded valley and around the lake. English is spoken by the Dutch owner and staff.

| Facilities | Directions |
|---|---|
| Fully equipped toilet blocks are good, providing some showers in cubicles. Laundry. Facilities for disabled visitors. Small shop. Bar/restaurant with à la carte and full menu (order before 12.00). Heated swimming pool (15/4-30/9). Sauna. Jacuzzi. Turkish steam bath. Masseuse visits. Fishing. Volleyball, boules and table tennis. Playground. Pony rides. One day a week children can make their own bread. Free WiFi. Off site: Charming towns such as Lucon, Bazoges and Fontenay-le-Comte. | From N148, La Roche-sur-Yon-Niort road, at St Hermine, turn onto D8 eastward for 4 km. Turn left on D10 to St Martin-Lars. Site is signed. GPS: 46.59795, -0.96936 |

**Charges guide**

| Per unit incl. 2 persons | |
|---|---|
| and electricity | € 22.30 - € 26.30 |
| extra person | € 6.00 - € 7.00 |
| child (3-16 yrs acc to age) | € 3.90 - € 5.30 |
| dog | € 4.00 |

**Open:** 1 April - 30 September.

**FREE** Alan Rogers Travel Card
Extra benefits and savings - see page 10

# Accommodation

Over recent years many of the campsites featured in this guide have added large numbers of high quality mobile homes and chalets. Many site owners believe that some former caravanners and motorcaravanners have been enticed by the extra comfort they can now provide, and that maybe this is the ideal solution to combine the freedom of camping with all the comforts of home.

Quality is consistently high and, although the exact size and inventory may vary from site to site, if you choose any of the sites detailed here, you can be sure that you're staying in some of the best quality and best value mobile homes available.

Home comforts are provided and typically these include a fridge with freezer compartment, gas hob, proper shower – often a microwave and radio/cassette hi-fi too, but do check for details. All mobile homes and chalets come fully equipped with a good range of kitchen utensils, pots and pans, crockery, cutlery and outdoor furniture. Some even have an attractive wooden sundeck or paved terrace – a perfect spot for outdoors eating or relaxing with a book and watching the world go by.

Regardless of model, colourful soft furnishings are the norm and a generally breezy décor helps to provide a real holiday feel.

Although some sites may have a large number of different accommodation types, we have restricted our choice to one or two of the most popular accommodation units (either mobile homes or chalets) for each of the sites listed.

The mobile homes here will be of modern design, and recent innovations, for example, often include pitched roofs which substantially improve their appearance.

Design will invariably include clever use of space and fittings/furniture to provide for comfortable holidays – usually light and airy, with big windows and patio-style doors, fully equipped kitchen areas, a shower room with shower, washbasin and WC, cleverly designed bedrooms and a comfortable lounge/dining area (often incorporating a sofa bed).

In general, modern campsite chalets incorporate all the best features of mobile homes in a more traditional structure, sometimes with the advantage of an upper mezzanine floor for an additional bedroom.

Our selected campsites offer a massive range of different types of mobile home and chalet, and it would be impractical to inspect every single accommodation unit. Our selection criteria, therefore, primarily takes account of the quality standards of the campsite itself.

However, there are a couple of important ground rules:

- Featured mobile homes must be no more than 5 years old

- chalets no more than 10 years old

- All listed accommodation must, of course, fully conform with all applicable local, national and European safety legislation.

For each campsite we have given details of the type, or types, of accommodation available to rent, but these details are necessarily quite brief. Sometimes internal layouts can differ quite substantially, particularly with regard to sleeping arrangements, where these include the flexible provision for 'extra persons' on sofa beds located in the living area. These arrangements may vary from accommodation to accommodation, and if you're planning a holiday which includes more people than are catered for by the main bedrooms you should check exactly how the extra sleeping arrangements are to be provided!

## Charges

An indication of the tariff for each type of accommodation featured is also included, indicating the variance between the low and high season tariffs. However, given that many campsites have a large and often complex range of pricing options, incorporating special deals and various discounts, the charges we mention should be taken to be just an indication. We strongly recommend therefore that you confirm the actual cost when making a booking.

We also strongly recommend that you check with the campsite, when booking, what (if anything) will be provided by way of bed linen, blankets, pillows etc. Again, in our experience, this can vary widely from site to site.

On every campsite a fully refundable deposit (usually between 150 and 300 euros) is payable on arrival. There may also be an optional cleaning service for which a further charge is made. Other options may include sheet hire (typically 30 euros per unit) or baby pack hire (cot and high chair).

# Low Cost Flights

### An Inexpensive Way To Arrive At Your Campsite

Many campsites are conveniently served by a wide choice of low cost airlines. Cheap flights can be very easy to find and travellers increasingly find the regional airports often used to be smaller, quieter and generally a calmer, more pleasurable experience.

Low cost flights can make campsites in more distant regions a much more attractive option: quicker to reach, inexpensive flights, and simply more convenient.

Many campsites are seeing increased visitors using the low cost flights and are adapting their services to suit this clientele. An airport shuttle service is not uncommon, meaning you can take advantage of that cheap flight knowing you will be met at the other end and whisked to your campsite. No taxi queues or multiple drop-offs.

Obviously, these low cost flights are impractical when taking all your own camping gear but they do make a holiday in campsite owned accommodation much more straightforward. The low cost airline option makes mobile home holidays especially attractive: pack a suitcase and use bed linen and towels provided (which you will generally need to pre-book).

### Pricing Tips

- Low cost airlines promote cheap flights but only a small percentage of seats are priced at the cheapest price. Book early for the best prices (and of course you also get a better choice of campsite or mobile home)
- Child seats are usually the same costs as adults
- Full payment is required at the time of booking
- Changes and amendments can be costly with low cost airlines
- Peak dates can be expensive compared to other carriers

### Car Hire

For maximum flexibility you will probably hire a car from a car rental agency. Car hire provides convenience but also will allow you access to off-site shops, beaches and tourist sights.

## FR29180 Camping les Embruns
▶ see report page 56

2 rue du Philosophe Alain, le Pouldu Plages, F-29360 Clohars-Carnoët (Brittany)

| AR1 – ARMOR + VERANDA – Mobile Home | AR2 – ATLANTIQUE + VERANDA – Mobile Home |
|---|---|
| Sleeping: 2 bedrooms, sleeps 4: 1 double, 2 singles, pillows and blankets provided | Sleeping: 3 bedrooms, sleeps 6: 1 double, 2 singles, bunk bed, pillows and blankets provided |
| Living: heating, shower, WC | Living: heating, shower, WC |
| Eating: fitted kitchen with hobs, oven, microwave, grill, coffee maker, fridge, freezer | Eating: fitted kitchen with hobs, oven, microwave, grill, coffee maker, fridge, freezer |
| Outside: table & chairs, parasol, 2 sun loungers | Outside: table & chairs, parasol, 2 sun loungers |
| Pets: accepted (with supplement) | Pets: accepted (with supplement) |

Other (AR1 and AR2): bed linen, cot, highchair to hire

| Open: 13 April - 21 September | | |
|---|---|---|
| Weekly Charge | AR1 | AR2 |
| Low Season (from) | € 350 | € 400 |
| High Season (from) | € 690 | € 860 |

## FR29010 Castel Camping le Ty-Nadan
▶ see report page 59

Route d'Arzano, F-29310 Locunolé (Brittany)

| AR1 – IRM – Mobile Home | AR2 – CHALET – Chalet |
|---|---|
| Sleeping: 2 bedrooms, sleeps 6: 1 double, 2 singles, sofa bed, pillows and blankets provided | Sleeping: 2 bedrooms, sleeps 6: 1 double, 2 singles, bunk bed, sofa bed, pillows and blankets provided |
| Living: heating, shower, WC, separate WC | Living: heating, shower, WC |
| Eating: fitted kitchen with hobs, microwave, grill, coffee maker, fridge | Eating: fitted kitchen with hobs, oven, microwave, coffee maker, fridge |
| Outside: table & chairs, parasol, 2 sun loungers | Outside: table & chairs, parasol, 2 sun loungers, barbecue |
| Pets: accepted (with supplement) | Pets: accepted (with supplement) |

Other (AR1 and AR2): bed linen, cot, highchair to hire

| Open: 20 April - 2 September | | |
|---|---|---|
| Weekly Charge | AR1 | AR2 |
| Low Season (from) | € 366 | € 492 |
| High Season (from) | € 952 | € 1211 |

## FR29090 Camping le Raguénès-Plage
▶ see report page 60

19 rue des Iles, F-29920 Névez (Brittany)

| AR1 – VARIANTE – Mobile Home | AR2 – OHARA COTTAGE – Mobile Home |
|---|---|
| Sleeping: 2 bedrooms, sleeps 5: 1 double, 2 singles, sofa bed, pillows and blankets provided | Sleeping: 2 bedrooms, sleeps 4: 1 double, 2 singles, sofa bed, pillows and blankets provided |
| Living: heating, air conditioning, shower, seperate WC | Living: heating, air conditioning, shower, seperate WC |
| Eating: fitted kitchen with hobs, oven, microwave, coffee maker, fridge, freezer | Eating: fitted kitchen with hobs, microwave, coffee maker, fridge, freezer |
| Outside: table & chairs, parasol, 2 sun loungers, barbecue | Outside: table & chairs, parasol, 2 sun loungers, barbecue |
| Pets: accepted (with supplement) | Pets: accepted (with supplement) |

Other (AR1 and AR2): bed linen to hire

| Open: 29 March - 29 September | | |
|---|---|---|
| Weekly Charge | AR1 | AR2 |
| Low Season (from) | € 320 | € 340 |
| High Season (from) | € 720 | € 750 |

## FR29050 Castel Camping l'Orangerie de Lanniron

see report page 67

Château de Lanniron, F-29000 Quimper (Brittany)

### AR1 – ZEN – Mobile Home

**Sleeping:** 3 bedrooms, sleeps 6: 1 double, 3 singles, bunk bed, pillows and blankets provided

**Living:** heating, air conditioning, shower, separate WC

**Eating:** fitted kitchen with hobs, microwave, coffee maker, fridge, freezer

**Outside:** table & chairs, parasol, 2 sun loungers, barbecue

**Pets:** not accepted

### AR2 – CONFORT – Mobile Home

**Sleeping:** 2 bedrooms, sleeps 5: 1 double, 2 singles, sofa bed, pillows and blankets provided

**Living:** heating, shower, separate WC

**Eating:** fitted kitchen with hobs, microwave, coffee maker, fridge, freezer

**Outside:** table & chairs, parasol, 2 sun loungers, barbecue

**Pets:** not accepted

**Other** (AR1 and AR2): bed linen, cot, highchair to hire

| **Open:** 28 March - 15 November | | |
|---|---|---|
| Weekly Charge | AR1 | AR2 |
| Low Season (from) | € 518 | € 420 |
| High Season (from) | € 1085 | € 966 |

## FR27070 Camping de l'Ile des Trois Rois

see report page 80

1 rue Gilles Nicolle, F-27700 Andelys (Normandy)

### AR1 – MOBILE HOME 4 PERS – Mobile Home

**Sleeping:** 2 bedrooms, sleeps 4: 1 double, 2 singles

**Living:** heating, shower, WC

**Eating:** fitted kitchen with hobs, fridge

**Outside:** table & chairs, barbecue

**Pets:** not accepted

### AR2 – MOBILE HOME 6 PERS – Mobile Home

**Sleeping:** 3 bedrooms, sleeps 6: 1 double, 4 singles

**Living:** heating, shower, WC, separate WC

**Eating:** fitted kitchen with hobs, fridge

**Outside:** table & chairs, barbecue

**Pets:** not accepted

| **Open:** 15 March - 14 November | | |
|---|---|---|
| Weekly Charge | AR1 | AR2 |
| Low Season (from) | € 340 | € 400 |
| High Season (from) | € 540 | € 640 |

## FR80060 Camping le Val de Trie

see report page 109

Rue des Sources, Bouillancourt-sous-Miannay, F-80870 Moyenneville (Picardy)

### AR1 – MOREVA – Mobile Home

**Sleeping:** 2 bedrooms, sleeps 6: 2 doubles, 2 singles, sofa bed, pillows and blankets provided

**Living:** heating, shower, WC, separate WC

**Eating:** fitted kitchen with hobs, microwave, coffee maker, fridge, freezer

**Outside:** table & chairs, parasol, barbecue

**Pets:** not accepted

### AR2 – GRAND CONFORT – Chalet

**Sleeping:** 3 bedrooms, sleeps 6: 1 double, 4 singles, bunk bed, pillows and blankets provided

**Living:** heating, shower, WC, separate WC

**Eating:** fitted kitchen with hobs, microwave, dishwasher, coffee maker, fridge, freezer

**Outside:** table & chairs, parasol, barbecue

**Pets:** not accepted

**Other** (AR1 and AR2): bed linen, cot, highchair to hire

| **Open:** 29 March - 15 October | | |
|---|---|---|
| Weekly Charge | AR1 | AR2 |
| Low Season (from) | € 326 | € 492 |
| High Season (from) | € 623 | € 854 |

## FR80070 Kawan Village la Ferme des Aulnes

▶ see report page 110

1 rue du Marais, Fresne-sur-Authie, F-80120 Nampont-Saint Martin (Picardy)

| AR1 – CONFORT – Mobile Home | AR2 – PRIVILEGE – Mobile Home |
|---|---|
| Sleeping: 2 bedrooms, sleeps 5: 1 double, 3 singles, sofa bed, pillows and blankets provided | Sleeping: 3 bedrooms, sleeps 6: 1 double, 4 singles, bunk bed, pillows and blankets provided |
| Living: heating, TV, shower, separate WC | Living: heating, TV, shower, separate WC |
| Eating: fitted kitchen with hobs, microwave, coffee maker, fridge, freezer | Eating: fitted kitchen with hobs, oven, microwave, grill, dishwasher, coffee maker, fridge, freezer |
| Outside: table & chairs, parasol, barbecue | Outside: table & chairs, parasol, barbecue |
| Pets: accepted (with supplement) | Pets: accepted (with supplement) |

Other (AR1 and AR2): bed linen, cot, highchair to hire

**Open:** 30 March - 3 November

| Weekly Charge | AR1 | AR2 |
|---|---|---|
| Low Season (from) | € 490 | € 590 |
| High Season (from) | € 690 | € 790 |

## FR80150 Camping Airotel Le Walric

▶ see report page 112

Route d'Eu, F-80230 Saint Valery-sur-Somme (Picardy)

| AR1 – 4 COUCHAGES – Mobile Home | AR2 – 6 COUCHAGES – Mobile Home |
|---|---|
| Sleeping: 2 bedrooms, sleeps 4: 1 double, 2 singles, pillows and blankets provided | Sleeping: 3 bedrooms, sleeps 6: 1 double, 4 singles, pillows and blankets provided |
| Living: heating, TV, shower, WC, separate WC | Living: heating, TV, shower, WC, separate WC |
| Eating: fitted kitchen with hobs, microwave, coffee maker, fridge, freezer | Eating: fitted kitchen with hobs, microwave, coffee maker, fridge, freezer |
| Outside: table & chairs, parasol, barbecue | Outside: table & chairs, parasol, barbecue |
| Pets: accepted (with supplement) | Pets: accepted (with supplement) |

Other (AR1 and AR2): cot, highchair to hire

**Open:** 1 April - 1 November

| Weekly Charge | AR1 | AR2 |
|---|---|---|
| Low Season (from) | € 315 | € 415 |
| High Season (from) | € 655 | € 755 |

## FR41070 Kawan Village la Grande Tortue

▶ see report page 145

3 route de Pontlevoy, F-41120 Candé-sur-Beuvron (Val de Loire)

| AR1 – IRM SUPER MERCURE – Mobile Home | AR2 – LOUISIANE ZEN – Mobile Home |
|---|---|
| Sleeping: 2 bedrooms, sleeps 5: 1 double, 2 singles, bunk bed, pillows and blankets provided | Sleeping: 3 bedrooms, sleeps 6: 1 double, 4 singles, pillows and blankets provided |
| Living: heating, shower, separate WC | Living: heating, shower, separate WC |
| Eating: fitted kitchen with hobs, microwave, coffee maker, fridge | Eating: fitted kitchen with hobs, microwave, coffee maker, fridge |
| Outside: table & chairs, 2 sun loungers | Outside: table & chairs, 2 sun loungers |
| Pets: accepted (with supplement) | Pets: accepted (with supplement) |

Other (AR1 and AR2): bed linen, cot, highchair to hire

**Open:** 13 April - 22 September

| Weekly Charge | AR1 | AR2 |
|---|---|---|
| Low Season (from) | € 345 | € 549 |
| High Season (from) | € 742 | € 798 |

## FR44220 Le Domaine de Léveno

see report page 162

Route de Sandun, F-44350 Guérande (Pays de la Loire)

| AR1 – COTTAGE CONFORT – Mobile Home | AR2 – COTTAGE CONFORT – Mobile Home |
|---|---|
| Sleeping: 2 bedrooms, sleeps 6: 1 double, 2 singles, sofa bed, pillows and blankets provided | Sleeping: 3 bedrooms, sleeps 6: 1 double, 4 singles, pillows and blankets provided |
| Living: heating, shower, separate WC | Living: shower, separate WC |
| Eating: fitted kitchen with hobs, fridge | Eating: fitted kitchen with hobs, fridge |
| Outside: table & chairs, parasol | Outside: table & chairs, parasol |
| Pets: accepted (with supplement) | Pets: accepted (with supplement) |

Other (AR1 and AR2): bed linen, cot, highchair to hire

| Open: 7 April - 29 September | | |
|---|---|---|
| Weekly Charge | AR1 | AR2 |
| Low Season (from) | € 315 | € 350 |
| High Season (from) | € 875 | € 903 |

## FR44210 Castel Camping de l'Océan

see report page 168

15 route de la Maison Rouge, F-44490 Le Croisic (Pays de la Loire)

| AR1 – COTTAGE OCEAN ESPACE – Mobile Home | AR2 – COTTAGE OCEAN ESPACE FAMILLE – Mobile Home |
|---|---|
| Sleeping: 2 bedrooms, sleeps 6: 2 doubles, 2 singles, bunk bed, sofa bed, pillows and blankets provided | Sleeping: 3 bedrooms, sleeps 6: 1 double, 4 singles, bunk bed, pillows and blankets provided |
| Living: heating, shower, WC, separate WC | Living: heating, TV, shower, WC, separate WC |
| Eating: fitted kitchen with hobs, microwave, coffee maker, fridge | Eating: fitted kitchen with hobs, oven, microwave, grill, coffee maker, fridge |
| Outside: table & chairs, parasol | Outside: table & chairs, parasol, 2 sun loungers, barbecue |
| Pets: accepted (with supplement) | Pets: accepted (with supplement) |

Other (AR1 and AR2): bed linen, cot, highchair to hire

| Open: 5 April - 30 September | | |
|---|---|---|
| Weekly Charge | AR1 | AR2 |
| Low Season (from) | € 511 | € 637 |
| High Season (from) | € 973 | € 1281 |

## FR44090 Kawan Village du Deffay

see report page 172

B.P. 18 Le Deffay, Sainte Reine-de-Bretagne, F-44160 Pontchâteau (Pays de la Loire)

| AR1 – MOBILE HOME 6 – Mobile Home | AR2 – CHALET 4/6 – Chalet |
|---|---|
| Sleeping: 3 bedrooms, sleeps 6: 1 double, 4 singles, bunk bed, pillows and blankets provided | Sleeping: 2 bedrooms, sleeps 6: 1 double, 4 singles, bunk bed, sofa bed, pillows and blankets provided |
| Living: heating, TV, shower, WC, separate WC | Living: heating, shower, WC |
| Eating: fitted kitchen with hobs, microwave, dishwasher, coffee maker, fridge, freezer | Eating: fitted kitchen with hobs, oven, microwave, grill, dishwasher, coffee maker, fridge, freezer |
| Outside: table & chairs, parasol, 2 sun loungers, barbecue | Outside: table & chairs, parasol, 2 sun loungers, barbecue |
| Pets: not accepted | Pets: not accepted |

Other (AR1 and AR2): bed linen, cot, highchair to hire

| Open: 1 April - 31 October | | |
|---|---|---|
| Weekly Charge | AR1 | AR2 |
| Low Season (from) | € 304 | € 254 |
| High Season (from) | € 796 | € 726 |

## FR44180 Camping de la Boutinardière

see report page 174

Rue de la Plage de la Boutinardière 23, F-44210 Pornic (Pays de la Loire)

| **AR1 – MOBILE HOME 5 Persons – Cottage** | **AR2 – MOBILE HOME 6 Persons – Mobile Home** |
| --- | --- |
| Sleeping: 2 bedrooms, sleeps 5: 1 double, 2 singles, sofa bed, pillows and blankets provided | Sleeping: 3 bedrooms, sleeps 6: 1 double, 4 singles, pillows and blankets provided |
| Living: heating, TV, shower, WC, separate WC | Living: heating, TV, shower, WC, separate WC |
| Eating: fitted kitchen with hobs, microwave, coffee maker, fridge | Eating: fitted kitchen with hobs, microwave, coffee maker, fridge |
| Outside: table & chairs, parasol | Outside: table & chairs, parasol |
| Pets: accepted (with supplement) | Pets: accepted (with supplement) |

Other (AR1 and AR2): bed linen, cot, highchair to hire

**Open:** 2 April - 1 October

| Weekly Charge | AR1 | AR2 |
| --- | --- | --- |
| Low Season (from) | € 260 | € 360 |
| High Season (from) | € 950 | € 1000 |

## FR17280 Camping la Grainetière

see report page 215

Route de Saint Martin, Chemin des Essarts, F-17630 La Flotte-en-Ré (Poitou-Charentes)

| **AR1 – ROULOTTE – Gipsy wagon/Roulotte** | **AR2 – LUXE – Mobile Home** |
| --- | --- |
| Sleeping: 2 bedrooms, sleeps 4: 1 double, 2 singles, bunk bed, pillows and blankets provided | Sleeping: 2 bedrooms, sleeps 5: 1 double, 2 singles, sofa bed, pillows and blankets provided |
| Living: heating, TV, shower, WC, separate WC | Living: heating, TV, shower, WC, separate WC |
| Eating: fitted kitchen with hobs, microwave, coffee maker, fridge, freezer | Eating: fitted kitchen with hobs, oven, microwave, coffee maker, fridge, freezer |
| Outside: table & chairs, parasol | Outside: table & chairs, parasol |
| Pets: accepted (with supplement) | Pets: accepted (with supplement) |

Other (AR1 and AR2): bed linen, cot, highchair to hire

**Open:** 1 April - 30 September

| Weekly Charge | AR1 | AR2 |
| --- | --- | --- |
| Low Season (from) | € 275 | € 275 |
| High Season (from) | € 830 | € 840 |

## FR17010 Camping Bois Soleil

see report page 228

2 avenue de Suzac, F-17110 Saint Georges-de-Didonne (Poitou-Charentes)

| **AR1 – COTTAGE 3 CHB MER – Mobile Home** | **AR2 – COTTAGE BOIS – Mobile Home** |
| --- | --- |
| Sleeping: 3 bedrooms, sleeps 8: 2 doubles, 4 singles, sofa bed, pillows and blankets provided | Sleeping: 2 bedrooms, sleeps 4: 1 double, 2 singles, pillows and blankets provided |
| Living: heating, TV, air conditioning, shower, WC, separate WC | Living: heating, air conditioning, shower, WC, separate WC |
| Eating: fitted kitchen with hobs, microwave, dishwasher, coffee maker, fridge, freezer | Eating: fitted kitchen with hobs, microwave, coffee maker, fridge, freezer |
| Outside: table & chairs, parasol, 1 sun lounger | Outside: table & chairs, parasol |
| Pets: not accepted | Pets: not accepted |

Other (AR1 and AR2): bed linen, cot, highchair to hire

**Open:** 30 March - 4 October

| Weekly Charge | AR1 | AR2 |
| --- | --- | --- |
| Low Season (from) | € 500 | € 310 |
| High Season (from) | € 1250 | € 1050 |

**Mobile homes & chalets**

## FR71070 Castel Camping Château de l'Epervière

▶ see report page 238

Rue du Château, F-71240 Gigny-sur-Saône (Burgundy)

| AR1 – LOUISIANE Pacifique 3XL – Mobile Home | AR2 – CHATEAU GITE – Gîte |
|---|---|
| Sleeping: 3 bedrooms, sleeps 6: 1 double, 4 singles, pillows and blankets provided | Sleeping: 2 bedrooms, sleeps 5: 1 double, 3 singles, bunk bed, pillows and blankets provided |
| Living: heating, TV, shower, separate WC | Living: heating, TV, shower, WC |
| Eating: fitted kitchen with hobs, microwave, dishwasher, coffee maker, fridge, freezer | Eating: fitted kitchen with hobs, oven, microwave, dishwasher, coffee maker, fridge, freezer |
| Outside: table & chairs, parasol, 2 sun loungers | Outside: table & chairs, parasol |
| Pets: not accepted | Pets: not accepted |

Other (AR1 and AR2): bed linen, cot, highchair to hire

| Open: 1 April - 30 September | | |
|---|---|---|
| Weekly Charge | AR1 | AR2 |
| Low Season (from) | € 419 | € 429 |
| High Season (from) | € 869 | € 889 |

## FR07660 Castel Domaine de Sévenier

▶ see report page 289

Sévenier, F-07150 Lagorce (Rhône Alpes)

| AR1 – CHENE BLANC – Chalet | AR2 – CHENE VERT – Chalet |
|---|---|
| Sleeping: 2 bedrooms, sleeps 4: 1 double, 2 singles, bunk bed, sofa bed, pillows and blankets provided | Sleeping: 3 bedrooms, sleeps 6: 1 double, 4 singles, sofa bed, pillows and blankets provided |
| Living: heating, air conditioning, shower, separate WC | Living: heating, air conditioning, shower, separate WC |
| Eating: fitted kitchen with hobs, microwave, dishwasher, coffee maker, fridge, freezer | Eating: fitted kitchen with hobs, microwave, dishwasher, coffee maker, fridge, freezer |
| Outside: table & chairs, 1 sun lounger | Outside: table & chairs, 1 sun lounger |
| Pets: accepted (with supplement) | Pets: accepted (with supplement) |

Other (AR1 and AR2): bed linen, cot, highchair to hire

| Open: 22 March - 11 November | | |
|---|---|---|
| Weekly Charge | AR1 | AR2 |
| Low Season (from) | € 483 | € 679 |
| High Season (from) | € 1169 | € 1666 |

## FR24320 Camping les Péneyrals

▶ see report page 351

Le Poujol, F-24590 Saint Crépin-Carlucet (Aquitaine)

| AR1 – MERCURE – Mobile Home | AR2 – EQUINOXE – Chalet |
|---|---|
| Sleeping: 2 bedrooms, sleeps 5: 1 double, 2 singles, sofa bed, pillows and blankets provided | Sleeping: 3 bedrooms, sleeps 7: 1 double, 4 singles, sofa bed, pillows and blankets provided |
| Living: heating, shower, separate WC | Living: heating, TV, shower, separate WC |
| Eating: fitted kitchen with hobs, microwave, coffee maker, fridge | Eating: fitted kitchen with hobs, microwave, coffee maker, fridge |
| Outside: table & chairs, parasol, 2 sun loungers, barbecue | Outside: table & chairs, parasol, 2 sun loungers, barbecue |
| Pets: accepted (with supplement) | Pets: accepted (with supplement) |

Other (AR1 and AR2): bed linen to hire

| Open: 4 May - 11 September | | |
|---|---|---|
| Weekly Charge | AR1 | AR2 |
| Low Season (from) | € 310 | € 500 |
| High Season (from) | € 890 | € 1100 |

## FR24090 Domaine de Soleil Plage

▶ see report page 363

Caudon par Montfort, Vitrac, F-24200 Sarlat-la-Canéda (Aquitaine)

**AR1 – CHALET PRESTIGE – Chalet**

Sleeping: 3 bedrooms, sleeps 6: 1 double, 4 singles, sofa bed, pillows and blankets provided

Living: heating, TV, shower, WC, separate WC

Eating: fitted kitchen with hobs, microwave, grill, dishwasher, coffee maker, fridge, freezer

Outside: table & chairs, parasol, 2 sun loungers, barbecue

Pets: accepted (with supplement)

**AR2 – CHALET RÈVE (Renovated) – Chalet**

Sleeping: 2 bedrooms, sleeps 5: 1 double, 3 singles, bunk bed, sofa bed, pillows and blankets provided

Living: heating, TV, shower, separate WC

Eating: fitted kitchen with hobs, microwave, dishwasher, coffee maker, fridge, freezer

Outside: table & chairs, parasol, 2 sun loungers, barbecue

Pets: accepted (with supplement)

Other (AR1 and AR2): bed linen, cot, highchair to hire

**Open:** 13 April - 29 September

| Weekly Charge | AR1 | AR2 |
| --- | --- | --- |
| Low Season (from) | € 470 | € 350 |
| High Season (from) | € 1260 | € 995 |

## FR33110 Airotel Camping de la Côte d'Argent

▶ see report page 336

F-33990 Hourtin-Plage (Aquitaine)

**AR1 – SAVANNAH – Mobile Home**

Sleeping: 2 bedrooms, sleeps 5: 1 double, 2 singles, sofa bed, pillows and blankets provided

Living: shower, WC

Eating: fitted kitchen with hobs, microwave, coffee maker, fridge, freezer

Outside: table & chairs, parasol

Pets: not accepted

**AR2 – SUPER FAMILY – Mobile Home**

Sleeping: 3 bedrooms, sleeps 6: 1 double, 4 singles, pillows and blankets provided

Living: shower, WC

Eating: fitted kitchen with hobs, microwave, coffee maker, fridge, freezer

Outside: table & chairs, parasol, 2 sun loungers

Pets: not accepted

**Open:** 17 May - 15 September

| Weekly Charge | AR1 | AR2 |
| --- | --- | --- |
| Low Season (from) | € 252 | € 284 |
| High Season (from) | € 1071 | € 1169 |

## FR40100 Camping Resort la Rive

▶ see report page 324

Route de Bordeaux, F-40600 Biscarrosse (Aquitaine)

**AR1 – SAVANNAH – Mobile Home**

Sleeping: 2 bedrooms, sleeps 6: 1 double, 2 singles, sofa bed, pillows and blankets provided

Living: heating, TV, shower, WC, separate WC

Eating: fitted kitchen with hobs, microwave, fridge, freezer

Outside: table & chairs, parasol, 2 sun loungers

Pets: not accepted

**AR2 – COTTAGE 3 – Mobile Home**

Sleeping: 3 bedrooms, sleeps 6: 1 double, 4 singles, pillows and blankets provided

Living: heating, TV, shower, WC, separate WC

Eating: fitted kitchen with hobs, microwave, fridge, freezer

Outside: table & chairs, parasol

Pets: not accepted

Other (AR1 and AR2): bed linen, cot, highchair to hire

**Open:** 6 April - 8 September

| Weekly Charge | AR1 | AR2 |
| --- | --- | --- |
| Low Season (from) | € 597 | € 604 |
| High Season (from) | € 1241 | € 1255 |

## FR40180 Airotel le Vieux Port

▶ see report page 343

Plage Sud, F-40660 Messanges (Aquitaine)

| AR1 – BUNGALOW ECO – Bungalow | AR2 – SOLARIUM – Mobile Home |
|---|---|
| Sleeping: 2 bedrooms, sleeps 4: 1 double, 2 singles, bunk bed, pillows and blankets provided | Sleeping: 2 bedrooms, sleeps 6: 1 double, 2 singles, sofa bed, pillows and blankets provided |
| Living: heating, TV | Living: heating, TV, air conditioning, shower, WC, separate WC |
| Eating: fitted kitchen with hobs, microwave, coffee maker, fridge | Eating: fitted kitchen with hobs, microwave, dishwasher, coffee maker, fridge, freezer |
| Outside: table & chairs, parasol, 2 sun loungers | Outside: table & chairs, parasol, 2 sun loungers |
| Pets: not accepted | Pets: not accepted |

Other (AR1 and AR2): bed linen, cot, highchair to hire

New 2012   New 2012

**Open:** 23 March - 29 September

| Weekly Charge | AR1 | AR2 |
|---|---|---|
| Low Season (from) | € 162 | € 416 |
| High Season (from) | € 735 | € 1855 |

## FR40190 Le Saint-Martin Camping

▶ see report page 346

Avenue de l'Océan, F-40660 Moliets-Plage (Aquitaine)

| AR1 – DUO – Chalet | AR2 – ZEPHYR – Chalet |
|---|---|
| Sleeping: 1 bedroom, sleeps 3: 2 singles, pillows and blankets provided | Sleeping: 2 bedrooms, sleeps 5: 1 double, 2 singles, sofa bed, pillows and blankets provided |
| Living: heating, shower, separate WC | Living: heating, shower, separate WC |
| Eating: fitted kitchen with hobs, microwave, coffee maker, fridge, freezer | Eating: fitted kitchen with hobs, microwave, coffee maker, fridge, freezer |
| Outside: table & chairs | Outside: table & chairs |
| Pets: accepted (with supplement) | Pets: accepted (with supplement) |

Other (AR1 and AR2): cot to hire

**Open:** 8 April - All Saints

| Weekly Charge | AR1 | AR2 |
|---|---|---|
| Low Season (from) | € 220 | € 430 |
| High Season (from) | € 620 | € 1320 |

## FR40140 Camping Caravaning Lou P'tit Poun

▶ see report page 356

110 avenue du Quartier Neuf, F-40390 Saint Martin-de-Seignanx (Aquitaine)

| AR1 – FABRE REVE – Chalet |
|---|
| Sleeping: 2 bedrooms, sleeps 5: 1 double, 3 singles, pillows and blankets provided |
| Living: shower, WC |
| Eating: fitted kitchen with fridge |
| Outside: table & chairs, parasol, 2 sun loungers |
| Pets: not accepted |

Other (AR1 and AR2): bed linen, cot, highchair to hire

**Open:** 1 June - 14 September

| Weekly Charge | AR1 |
|---|---|
| Low Season (from) | € 476 |
| High Season (from) | € 805 |

## FR40250 Camping les Grands Pins

▶ see report page 360

1039 avenue de Losa, F-40460 Sanguinet (Aquitaine)

| **AR1** – OHARA OCEANE<br>– Mobile Home | **AR2** – ROULOTTE 4 PLACES<br>– Gipsy wagon/Roulotte |
|---|---|
| Sleeping: 3 bedrooms, sleeps 6: 1 double, 4 singles, pillows and blankets provided | Sleeping: 2 bedrooms, sleeps 4: 1 double, 2 singles, bunk bed, pillows and blankets provided |
| Living: heating, shower, separate WC | Living: heating, shower, separate WC |
| Eating: fitted kitchen with hobs, microwave, coffee maker, fridge, freezer | Eating: fitted kitchen with hobs, microwave, coffee maker, fridge, freezer |
| Outside: table & chairs, parasol, 1 sun lounger | Outside: table & chairs, parasol |
| Pets: not accepted | Pets: not accepted |

| **Open:** 1 April - 29 September | | |
|---|---|---|
| Weekly Charge | AR1 | AR2 |
| Low Season (from) | € 672 | € 560 |
| High Season (from) | € 1183 | € 1036 |

## FR09020 Camping l'Arize

▶ see report page 380

Lieu-dit Bourtol, F-09240 La Bastide-de-Sérou (Midi-Pyrénées)

| **AR1** – LOUISIANE FLORES CONFORT PLUS<br>– Mobile Home | **AR2** – CHALET 3 BEDROOMS<br>– Chalet |
|---|---|
| Sleeping: 2 bedrooms, sleeps 7: 1 double, 2 singles, bunk bed, sofa bed, pillows and blankets provided | Sleeping: 3 bedrooms, sleeps 8: 1 double, 3 singles, bunk bed, sofa bed, pillows and blankets provided |
| Living: heating, shower, separate WC | Living: heating, shower, separate WC |
| Eating: fitted kitchen with hobs, microwave, grill, fridge, freezer | Eating: fitted kitchen with hobs, microwave, grill, fridge, freezer |
| Outside: table & chairs, parasol, barbecue | Outside: table & chairs, parasol, barbecue |
| Pets: accepted (with supplement) | Pets: accepted (with supplement) |

| **Open:** All year | | |
|---|---|---|
| Weekly Charge | AR1 | AR2 |
| Low Season (from) | € 385 | € 483 |
| High Season (from) | € 798 | € 903 |

## FR32010 Le Camp de Florence

▶ see report page 381

Route Astaffort, F-32480 La Romieu (Midi-Pyrénées)

| **AR1** – LOUISIANE ZEN – Mobile Home | **AR2** – IRM DELUXE – Mobile Home |
|---|---|
| Sleeping: 3 bedrooms, sleeps 6: 1 double, 2 singles, bunk bed, pillows and blankets provided | Sleeping: 2 bedrooms, sleeps 6: 1 double, 2 singles, sofa bed, pillows and blankets provided |
| Living: heating, shower, separate WC | Living: heating, shower, separate WC |
| Eating: fitted kitchen with hobs, microwave, coffee maker, fridge, freezer | Eating: fitted kitchen with hobs, microwave, coffee maker, fridge, freezer |
| Outside: table & chairs, 2 sun loungers | Outside: table & chairs, 2 sun loungers |
| Pets: accepted (with supplement) | Pets: accepted (with supplement) |

Other (AR1 and AR2): bed linen, cot, highchair to hire

| **Open:** 1 April - 10 October | | |
|---|---|---|
| Weekly Charge | AR1 | AR2 |
| Low Season (from) | € 413 | € 364 |
| High Season (from) | € 784 | € 714 |

## **FR11070** Yelloh! Village les Mimosas

▶ see report page 421

Chaussée de Mandirac, F-11100 Narbonne (Languedoc-Roussillon)

| **AR1 – PLANCHA – Mobile Home** | **AR2 – FLORS – Mobile Home** |
|---|---|
| Sleeping: 2 bedrooms, sleeps 4: 1 double, 2 singles, pillows and blankets provided | Sleeping: 3 bedrooms, sleeps 6: 1 double, 4 singles, pillows and blankets provided |
| Living: heating, shower, WC | Living: heating, air conditioning, shower, WC |
| Eating: fitted kitchen with hobs, microwave, coffee maker, fridge, freezer | Eating: fitted kitchen with hobs, microwave, coffee maker, fridge, freezer |
| Outside: table & chairs, 2 sun loungers, barbecue | Outside: table & chairs, 2 sun loungers |
| Pets: not accepted | Pets: not accepted |

Other (AR1 and AR2): bed linen, cot, highchair to hire

| **Open: 25 March - 1 November** | | |
|---|---|---|
| Weekly Charge | AR1 | AR2 |
| Low Season (from) | € 301 | € 364 |
| High Season (from) | € 798 | € 1029 |

## **FR34070** Yelloh! Village le Sérignan-Plage

▶ see report page 428

Le Sérignan Plage, F-34410 Sérignan-Plage (Languedoc-Roussillon)

| **AR1 – CHALET ROBINSON – Chalet** | **AR2 – COTTAGE CABANE – Mobile Home** |
|---|---|
| Sleeping: 2 bedrooms, sleeps 5: 1 double, 2 singles, bunk bed, pillows and blankets provided | Sleeping: 3 bedrooms, sleeps 6: 1 double, 2 singles, bunk bed, pillows and blankets provided |
| Living: heating, air conditioning, shower, separate WC | Living: heating, TV, air conditioning, shower, separate WC |
| Eating: fitted kitchen with hobs, microwave, dishwasher, coffee maker, fridge, freezer | Eating: fitted kitchen with hobs, microwave, dishwasher, coffee maker, fridge, freezer |
| Outside: table & chairs, parasol, 2 sun loungers | Outside: table & chairs, 2 sun loungers |
| Pets: not accepted | Pets: not accepted |

Other (AR1 and AR2): bed linen, cot, highchair to hire

| **Open: 26 April - 2 October** | | |
|---|---|---|
| Weekly Charge | AR1 | AR2 |
| Low Season (from) | € 378 | € 455 |
| High Season (from) | € 1645 | € 2044 |

## **FR66070** Yelloh! Village le Brasilia

▶ see report page 409

B.P. 204, F-66141 Canet-en-Roussillon (Languedoc-Roussillon)

| **AR1 – OKAVANGO – Mobile Home** | **AR2 – PINÈDE – Bungalow** |
|---|---|
| Sleeping: 2 bedrooms, sleeps 6: 1 double, 2 singles, bunk bed, pillows and blankets provided | Sleeping: 2 bedrooms, sleeps 4: 1 double, 2 singles, bunk bed, pillows and blankets provided |
| Living: heating, TV, shower, WC | Living: heating, TV, shower, WC |
| Eating: fitted kitchen with hobs, microwave, grill, coffee maker, fridge, freezer | Eating: fitted kitchen with hobs, microwave, grill, coffee maker, fridge, freezer |
| Outside: table & chairs, parasol, 2 sun loungers | Outside: table & chairs, 2 sun loungers |
| Pets: not accepted | Pets: not accepted |

Other (AR1 and AR2): bed linen, cot, highchair to hire

| **Open: 13 April - 5 October** | | |
|---|---|---|
| Weekly Charge | AR1 | AR2 |
| Low Season (from) | € 301 | € 301 |
| High Season (from) | € 1155 | € 1155 |

## FR04020 Castel Camping le Domaine du Verdon

▶ see report page 445

Camp du Verdon, F-04120 Castellane (Provence)

| AR1 – WATIPI – Mobile Home | AR2 – TITOM – Mobile Home |
|---|---|
| Sleeping: 2 bedrooms, sleeps 4: 1 double, 2 singles, pillows and blankets provided | Sleeping: 2 bedrooms, sleeps 4: 1 double, 2 singles, bunk bed, pillows and blankets provided |
| Living: shower, WC | Living: shower, WC |
| Eating: fitted kitchen with hobs, fridge | Eating: fitted kitchen with hobs, fridge |
| Outside: table & chairs, 2 sun loungers | Outside: table & chairs, 2 sun loungers |
| Pets: accepted | Pets: accepted |

Other (AR1 and AR2): bed linen, cot, highchair to hire

**Open:** 15 May - 15 September

| Weekly Charge | AR1 | AR2 |
|---|---|---|
| Low Season (from) | € 336 | € 378 |
| High Season (from) | € 742 | € 791 |

## FR83060 Camping Resort la Baume-la Palmeraie

▶ see report page 450

3775 rue des Combattants d'Afrique du Nord, F-83618 Fréjus (Provence)

| AR1 – BASTIDON – Bungalow | AR2 – CYCA – Mobile Home |
|---|---|
| Sleeping: 3 bedrooms, sleeps 8: 1 double, 4 singles, sofa bed | Sleeping: 3 bedrooms, sleeps 6: 1 double, 4 singles, sofa bed |
| Living: TV, shower, WC | Living: TV, air conditioning, shower, WC |
| Eating: fitted kitchen with hobs, microwave, fridge, freezer | Eating: fitted kitchen with hobs, microwave, dishwasher, fridge, freezer |
| Outside: table & chairs, 4 sun loungers | Outside: table & chairs, 2 sun loungers |
| Pets: accepted | Pets: accepted |

Other (AR1 and AR2): bed linen, cot, highchair to hire

**Open:** 31 March - 28 September

| Weekly Charge | AR1 | AR2 |
|---|---|---|
| Low Season (from) | € 490 | € 455 |
| High Season (from) | € 1525 | € 1490 |

## FR83030 Camping Caravaning Leï Suves

▶ see report page 469

Quartier du Blavet, F-83520 Roquebrune-sur-Argens (Provence)

| AR1 – TYPE D – Mobile Home | AR2 – LUXE – Mobile Home |
|---|---|
| Sleeping: 2 bedrooms, sleeps 6: 1 double, 2 singles, sofa bed | Sleeping: 2 bedrooms, sleeps 5: 1 double, 2 singles, sofa bed |
| Living: shower, WC | Living: shower, WC |
| Eating: fitted kitchen with hobs, oven, fridge | Eating: fitted kitchen with hobs, oven, fridge |
| Outside: table & chairs | Outside: table & chairs, barbecue |
| Pets: not accepted | Pets: not accepted |

**Open:** 30 March - 15 October

| Weekly Charge | AR1 | AR2 |
|---|---|---|
| Low Season (from) | € 480 | € 520 |
| High Season (from) | € 960 | € 1000 |

## Open All Year

The following sites are understood to accept caravanners and campers all year round. It is always wise to phone the site to check as the facilities available, for example, may be reduced.

| Brittany | | | | Burgundy | | |
|---|---|---|---|---|---|---|
| FR56150 | Haras | 76 | | FR21090 | Arquebuse | 234 |
| | | | | FR58030 | Bezolle | 243 |
| Normandy | | | | Auvergne | | |
| FR76090 | Etennemare (Mun) | 96 | | FR63210 | Haute Sioule | 269 |

| Nord-Pas de Calais | | | | Rhône Alpes | | |
|---|---|---|---|---|---|---|
| FR62120 | Eté Indien | 103 | | FR74230 | Giffre | 307 |
| | | | | FR69010 | Lyon | 283 |

| Paris-Ile de France | | | | Aquitaine | | |
|---|---|---|---|---|---|---|
| FR91010 | Beau Village de Paris | 121 | | FR33410 | Bordeaux Lac | 329 |
| FR75020 | Indigo Paris | 118 | | FR47110 | Cabri | 334 |
| FR77140 | Paris/Ile-de-France | 116 | | FR64040 | Gaves | 340 |
| | | | | FR64180 | Larrouleta | 367 |
| Lorraine | | | | FR33090 | Pressoir | 349 |
| FR88400 | Gadémont Plage | 131 | | FR64080 | Tamaris Plage | 355 |
| FR88040 | Lac de Bouzey | 134 | | | | |
| FR88090 | Lac de la Moselotte | 134 | | Midi-Pyrénées | | |
| | | | | FR65080 | Lavedan | 375 |

| Alsace | | | | Languedoc-Roussillon | | |
|---|---|---|---|---|---|---|
| FR68140 | Bouleaux | 140 | | FR34230 | Chênes | 413 |
| | | | | FR66670 | Europe (Le Barcarès) | 417 |
| Pays de la Loire | | | | FR11110 | Val d'Aleth | 401 |
| FR44490 | Bois de Beaumard | 173 | | | | |
| FR44430 | Pindière | 163 | | Provence/Côte d'Azur | | |
| | | | | FR06240 | Argentière | 463 |
| Vendée | | | | FR13120 | Chantecler | 441 |
| FR85385 | Bellevue (Vendée) | 194 | | FR06080 | Cigales | 463 |
| | | | | FR06050 | Vieille Ferme | 480 |

| Poitou-Charentes | | | | Corsica | | |
|---|---|---|---|---|---|---|
| FR86040 | Futuriste | 227 | | FR20080 | Bagheera (Naturiste) | 492 |
| FR16130 | Paradis | 218 | | FR20040 | Riva Bella (Naturiste) | 492 |

# Dogs

Many British campers and caravanners prefer to take their pets with them on holiday. However, pet travel rules changed on 1 January 2012 when the UK brought its procedures into line with the European Union. From this date all pets can enter or re-enter the UK from any country in the world without quarantine provided they meet the rules of the scheme, which will be different depending on the country or territory the pet is coming from. Please refer to the following website for full details: www.defra.gov.uk/wildlife-pets/pets/travel

For the benefit of those who want to take their dogs to France, we list here the sites which have indicated to us that they do not accept dogs or have certain restrictions. If you are planning to take your dog we do advise you to phone the site first to check – there may be limits on numbers, breeds, or times of the year when they are excluded.

**Never** – sites that do not accept dogs at any time:

| Normandy | | |
|---|---|---|
| FR14090 | Brévedent | 92 |

| Alsace | | |
|---|---|---|
| FR68080 | ClairVacances | 141 |
| FR67040 | Ferme des Tuileries | 138 |

| Vendée | | |
|---|---|---|
| FR85210 | Ecureuils | 184 |
| FR85020 | Jard | 188 |

| Poitou-Charentes | | |
|---|---|---|
| FR16020 | Gorges du Chambon | 220 |

| Rhône Alpes | | |
|---|---|---|
| FR26090 | Truffières | 287 |

| Aquitaine | | |
|---|---|---|
| FR24040 | Moulin du Roch | 360 |
| FR40040 | Paillotte | 320 |
| FR64060 | Pavillon Royal | 321 |

| Midi-Pyrénées | | |
|---|---|---|
| FR46040 | Moulin de Laborde | 386 |

| Languedoc-Roussillon | | |
|---|---|---|
| FR30390 | Petits Camarguais | 418 |
| FR66040 | Soleil | 406 |

| Corsica | | |
|---|---|---|
| FR20030 | Merendella | 487 |
| FR20110 | Restonica | 485 |

**Sometimes** – sites that accept dogs but with certain restrictions:

| Brittany | | |
|---|---|---|
| FR29430 | Escale Saint-Gilles | 40 |
| FR29470 | Deux Fontaines | 61 |
| FR22320 | Cap Horn | 65 |
| FR22130 | Port l'Epine | 77 |

| Normandy | | |
|---|---|---|
| FR50060 | Grand Large (Les Pieux) | 89 |

| Paris-Ile de France | | |
|---|---|---|
| FR75020 | Indigo Paris | 118 |
| FR78040 | Rambouillet | 119 |
| FR78060 | Versailles | 121 |

| Champagne-Ardenne | | |
|---|---|---|
| FR10020 | Lac Forêt d'Orient | 126 |

| Val de Loire | | |
|---|---|---|
| FR37140 | Rillé | 154 |
| FR28140 | Senonches | 155 |

| Pays de la Loire | | |
|---|---|---|
| FR72040 | Molières | 178 |

| Vendée | | |
|---|---|---|
| FR85930 | Forges | 181 |
| FR85480 | Chaponnet | 182 |
| FR85310 | Trévillière | 183 |
| FR85770 | Ferme du Latois | 183 |
| FR85270 | Oceano d'Or | 184 |
| FR85450 | Roses | 189 |
| FR85000 | Petit Rocher | 190 |
| FR85440 | Brunelles | 190 |
| FR85720 | Noirmoutier | 191 |

# Travelling - in Europe

When taking your car (and caravan, tent or trailer tent) or motorcaravan to the continent you do need to plan in advance and to find out as much as possible about driving in the countries you plan to visit. Whilst European harmonisation has eliminated many of the differences between one country and another, it is well worth reading the short notes we provide in the introduction to each country in this guide in addition to this more general summary.

Of course, the main difference from driving in the UK is that in mainland Europe you will need to drive on the right. Without taking extra time and care, especially at busy junctions and conversely when roads are empty, it is easy to forget to drive on the right. Remember that traffic approaching from the right usually has priority unless otherwise indicated by road markings and signs. Harmonisation also means that most (but not all) common road signs are the same in all countries.

## Your vehicle

Book your vehicle in for a good service well before your intended departure date. This will lessen the chance of an expensive breakdown. Make sure your brakes are working efficiently and that your tyres have plenty of tread (3 mm. is recommended, particularly if you are undertaking a long journey).

Also make sure that your caravan or trailer is roadworthy and that its tyres are in good order and correctly inflated. Plan your packing and be careful not to overload your vehicle, caravan or trailer – this is unsafe and may well invalidate your insurance cover (it must not be more fully loaded than the kerb weight of the insured vehicle).

### CHECK ALL THE FOLLOWING:

- GB sticker. If you do not display a sticker, you may risk an on-the-spot fine as this identifier is compulsory in all countries. Euro-plates are an acceptable alternative within the EU (but not outside). Remember to attach another sticker (or Euro-plate) to caravans and trailers. Only GB stickers (not England, Scotland, Wales or N. Ireland) stickers are valid in the EU.

- Headlights. As you will be driving on the right you must adjust your headlights so that the dipped beam does not dazzle oncoming drivers. Converter kits are readily available for most vehicles, although if your car is fitted with high intensity headlights, you should check with your motor dealer. Check that any planned extra loading does not affect the beam height.

- Seatbelts. Rules for the fitting and wearing of seatbelts throughout Europe are similar to those in the UK, but it is worth checking before you go. Rules for carrying children in the front of vehicles vary from country to country. It is best to plan not to do this if possible.

- Door/wing mirrors. To help with driving on the right, if your vehicle is not fitted with a mirror on the left hand side, we recommend you have one fitted.

- Fuel. Leaded and Lead Replacement petrol is increasingly difficult to find in Northern Europe.

## Compulsory additional equipment

The driving laws of the countries of Europe still vary in what you are required to carry in your vehicle, although the consequences of not carrying a required piece of equipment are almost always an on-the-spot fine.

To meet these requirements you should make sure that you carry the following:

- FIRE EXTINGUISHER
- BASIC TOOL KIT
- FIRST AID KIT
- SPARE BULBS

- TWO WARNING TRIANGLES – two are required in some countries at all times, and are compulsory in most countries when towing.

- HIGH VISIBILITY VEST – now compulsory in France, Spain, Italy and Austria (and likely to become compulsory throughout the EU) in case you need to walk on a motorway.

- BREATHALYSERS – now compulsory in France. Only breathalysers that are NF-approved will meet the legal requirement. French law states that one breathalyser must be produced, but it is recommended you carry two in case you use or break one.

## Insurance and Motoring Documents

### Vehicle insurance

Contact your insurer well before you depart to check that your car insurance policy covers driving outside the UK. Most do, but many policies only provide minimum cover (so if you have an accident your insurance may only cover the cost of damage to the other person's property, with no cover for fire and theft).

To maintain the same level of cover abroad as you enjoy at home you need to tell your vehicle insurer. Some will automatically cover you abroad with no extra cost and no extra paperwork. Some will say you need a Green Card (which is neither green nor on card) but won't charge for it. Some will charge extra for the Green Card. Ideally you should contact your vehicle insurer 3-4 weeks before you set off, and confirm your conversation with them in writing.

### Breakdown insurance

Arrange breakdown cover for your trip in good time so that if your vehicle breaks down or is involved in an accident it (and your caravan or trailer) can be repaired or returned to this country. This cover can usually be arranged as part of your travel insurance policy (see below).

### Documents you must take with you

You may be asked to show your documents at any time so make sure that they are in order, up-to-date and easily accessible while you travel.

These are what you need to take:

- Passports (you may also need a visa in some countries if you hold either a UK passport not issued in the UK or a passport that was issued outside the EU).

- Motor Insurance Certificate, including Green Card (or Continental Cover clause)

- DVLA Vehicle Registration Document plus, if not your own vehicle, the owner's written authority to drive.

- A full valid Driving Licence (not provisional). The new photo style licence is now mandatory in most European countries.

Personal Holiday insurance

Even though you are just travelling within Europe you must take out travel insurance. Few EU countries pay the full cost of medical treatment even under reciprocal health service arrangements. The first part of a holiday insurance policy covers people. It will include the cost of doctor, ambulance and hospital treatment if needed. If needed the better companies will even pay for English language speaking doctors and nurses and will bring a sick or injured holidaymaker home by air ambulance.

An important part of the insurance, often ignored, is cancellation (and curtailment) cover. Few things are as heartbreaking as having to cancel a holiday because a member of the family falls ill. Cancellation insurance can't take away the disappointment, but it makes sure you don't suffer financially as well. For this reason you should arrange your holiday insurance at least eight weeks before you set off.

Whichever insurance you choose we would advise reading very carefully the policies sold by the High Street travel trade. Whilst they may be good, they may not cover the specific needs of campers, caravanners and motorcaravanners.

Telephone 01580 214000 for a quote for our Camping Travel Insurance with cover arranged through leading leisure insurance providers.
Alternatively visit our website at: alanrogers.com/insurance

## European Health Insurance Card (EHIC)

Make sure you apply for your EHIC before travelling in Europe. Eligible travellers from the UK are entitled to receive free or reduced-cost medical care in many European countries on production of an EHIC. This free card is available by completing a form in the booklet 'Health Advice for Travellers' from local Post Offices. One should be completed for each family member. Alternatively visit www.ehic.org.uk and apply on-line. Please allow time to send your application off and have the EHIC returned to you.

The EHIC is valid in all European Community countries plus Iceland, Liechtenstein, Switzerland and Norway. If you or any of your dependants are suddenly taken ill or have an accident during a visit to any of these countries, free or reduced-cost emergency treatment is available – in most cases on production of a valid EHIC.

Only state-provided emergency treatment is covered, and you will receive treatment on the same terms as nationals of the country you are visiting. Private treatment is generally not covered, and state-provided treatment may not cover all of the things that you would expect to receive free of charge from the NHS.

Remember an EHIC does not cover you for all the medical costs that you can incur or for repatriation - it is not an alternative to travel insurance. You will still need appropriate insurance to ensure you are fully covered for all eventualities.

## Travelling with children

Most countries in Europe are enforcing strict guidelines when you are travelling with children who are not your own. A minor (under the age of 18) must be accompanied by a parent or legal guardian or must carry a letter of authorisation from a parent or guardian. The letter should name the adult responsible for the minor during his or her stay. Similarly, a minor travelling with just one of his/her parents, must have a letter of authority to leave their home country from the parent staying behind. Full information is available at www.fco.gov.uk

# FREE

## The Alan Rogers
# Travel Card

Advantage all the way

**NEW**

alan rogers

Travel Card

Across the Alan Rogers guides you'll find a network of thousands of quality inspected and selected campsites. We also work with numerous organisations, including ferry operators and tourist attractions, all of whom can bring you benefits and save you money.

Our brand **NEW** Travel Card binds all this together, along with exclusive extra content in our cardholders' area at **alanrogers.com/travelcard**

# Advantage all the way

Carry the Alan Rogers Travel Card on your travels and save money all the way.
Enjoy exclusive offers on many partner sites - as well as hotels, apartments and campsite accommodation. We've even teamed up with Camping Cheque, the low season discount scheme, so you can load your card with Cheques before you travel. So register today - hundreds of campsites already have special offers just for you.

Holiday **discounts**, **free** kids' meals, **free** cycle hire, **discounted** meals, **free** sports activities, **free** gifts on arrival, **free** wine with meals, **free** wifi, **free** tennis, **free** spa day, **free** access to local attractions.

Check out all the offers at **alanrogers.com/travelcard** and present your card on arrival.

## Benefits that add up

- Offers and benefits on many Alan Rogers campsites across Europe

---

- Save up to 60% in low season on over 600 campsites

---

- Savings on rented accommodation and hotels at over 400 locations

---

- Free cardholders' magazine

---

- Exclusive cardholders' area on our website – exchange opinions with other members

---

- Discounted ferries

---

- Savings on Alan Rogers guides

---

- Travel insurance deals

## Register today - and start saving

### Step 1
Register at www.**alanrogers.com/travelcard** (you can now access exclusive content on the website).

---

### Step 2
You'll receive your activated card, along with a Welcome email containing useful links and information.

---

### Step 3
Start using your card to save money or to redeem benefits during your holiday.

Register now at
**alanrogers.com/travelcard**

# Been to any good campsites lately?
## We have

You'll find them here...

The UK's market leading independent
guides to the best campsites

Also available on iPad alanrogers.com/digital

... also here...

101 great campsites, ideal for your specific
hobby, pastime or passion

**Also available on iPad alanrogers.com/digital**

# Want independent campsite reviews at your fingertips?

You'll find them here...

Over 3,000 in-depth campsite reviews at
**www.alanrogers.com**

...and even here...

# Getting the most from off peak touring

**£13.95/night**
**single tariff**
**2 people**

There are many reasons to avoid high season, if you can. Queues are shorter, there's less traffic, a calmer atmosphere and prices are cheaper. And it's usually still nice and sunny!

And when you use Camping Cheques you'll find great quality facilities that are actually open and a welcoming conviviality.

## Did you know?

Camping Cheques can be used right into mid-July and from late August on many sites. Over 90 campsites in France alone accept Camping Cheques from 20th August.

## Save up to 60% with Camping Cheques

Camping Cheque is a fixed price scheme allowing you to go as you please, staying on over 600 campsites across Europe, always paying the same rate and saving you up to 60% on regular pitch fees. One Cheque gives you one night for 2 people + unit on a standard pitch, with electricity. It's as simple as that.

Special offers mean you can stay extra nights free (eg 7 nights for 6 Cheques) or even a month free for a month paid! Especially popular in Spain during the winter, these longer-term offers can effectively halve the nightly rate. See Site Directory for details.

**Check out our amazing Ferry Deals!**

## Why should I use Camping Cheques?

- It's a proven system, recognised by all 600+ participating campsites
  - so no nasty surprises.

- It's flexible, allowing you to travel between campsites, and also countries, on
  a whim - so no need to pre-book. (It's low season, so campsites are rarely full,
  though advance bookings can be made).

- Stay as long as you like, where you like - so you travel in complete freedom.

- Camping Cheques are valid 2 years - so no pressure to use them up.
  (If you have a couple left over after your trip, simply keep them for the following
  year, or use them up in the UK).

## Tell me more... (but keep it brief!)

Camping Cheques was started in 1999 and has since grown in popularity each
year (nearly 2 million were used last year). That should speak for itself. There
are 'copycat' schemes, but none has the same range of quality campsites that
save you up to 60%.

Ask for your **FREE** continental road map,
which explains how Camping Cheque works

## 01580 214002

**FREE**

downloadable Site Directory
**alanrogers.com/directory**

## campingcheque.co.uk

Start 2013
in real style...

# Is there *any* better way to pitch up in France?

Whether you're camping or caravanning, book your next trip with Brittany Ferries and enjoy the widest choice of routes from Portsmouth, Poole and Plymouth, straight to the finest regions of France.

Not only will you save on driving by arriving closer, but our comfortable cabins, top-class facilities and award-winning services mean you'll begin your next adventure refreshed, relaxed and ready to go.

Book early for the best choice of travel dates and sailings – there's no better way to pitch up in France.

**Book early for just £25 deposit. Call 0871 244 0514 or visit brittanyferries.com**
Calls cost 10p per minute plus network extras. Reserve your sailings for a deposit of £25 with balance payable 46 days before departure.

# Digital iPad
# editions

**FREE** Alan Rogers bookstore app
- digital editions of all 2013 guides

**alanrogers.com/digital**

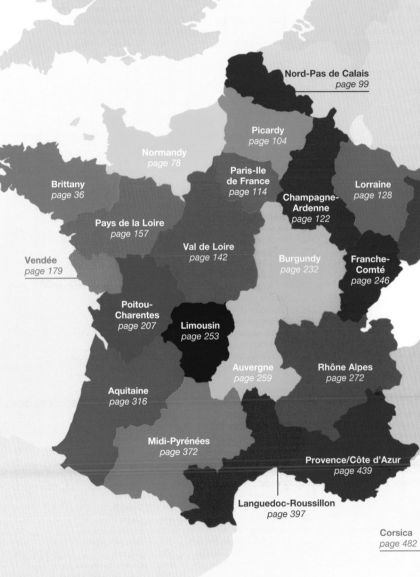

Regions of France

Nord-Pas de Calais
*page 99*

Picardy
*page 104*

Normandy
*page 78*

Brittany
*page 36*

Paris-Ile
de France
*page 114*

Lorraine
*page 128*

Champagne-
Ardenne
*page 122*

Alsace
*page 136*

Pays de la Loire
*page 157*

Val de Loire
*page 142*

Burgundy
*page 232*

Franche-
Comté
*page 246*

Vendée
*page 179*

Poitou-
Charentes
*page 207*

Limousin
*page 253*

Auvergne
*page 259*

Rhône Alpes
*page 272*

Aquitaine
*page 316*

Midi-Pyrénées
*page 372*

Provence/Côte d'Azur
*page 439*

Languedoc-Roussillon
*page 397*

Corsica
*page 482*

# Town & Village Index

# Town & Village Index continued

## Town & Village Index continued

# Index by Campsite Region & Name